FUNDAMENTALS OF
Psychology

FUNDAMENTALS OF
Psychology

Michael W. Eysenck

Psychology Press
Taylor & Francis Group
an informa business

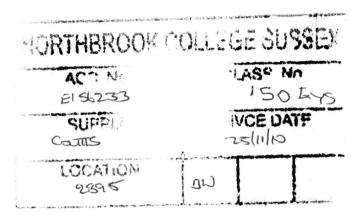
First published 2009 by Psychology Press,
an imprint of Taylor & Francis
27 Church Road, Hove, East Sussex, BN3 2FA

Simultaneously published in the USA and Canada
by Psychology Press
270 Madison Ave, New York, NY 10016

*Psychology Press is an imprint of the Taylor & Francis Group,
an informa business*

British Library Cataloguing in Publication Data
A catalogue record for this book is available from the British Library

Library of Congress Cataloging-in-Publication Data
Eysenck, Michael W.
    Fundamentals of psychology / Michael W. Eysenck.
      p. cm.
    Includes bibliographical references and index.
     ISBN 978–1–84169–371–2 (hbk)—ISBN 978–1–84169–372–9 (pbk.)
    1. Psychology. I. Title.
    BF121.E945 2009
    150—dc22
                                           2008000676

ISBN: 978–1–84169–371–2 (hbk)
ISBN: 978–1–84169–372–9 (pbk)

Cartoons by Sean Longcroft
Consultant for case studies and boxes: Evie Bentley

Cover design by Sandra Heath
Typeset in Sabon by Newgen Imaging Systems (P) Ltd
Printed and bound in Slovenia

It is the mark of an instructed mind to rest satisfied with the degree of precision which the nature of the subject permits and not to seek exactness when only an approximation of the truth is possible. (Aristotle)

To Maria with love

Contents

About the author

Michael W. Eysenck is one of the best-known psychologists in Europe. He is Professor of Psychology in the psychology department at Royal Holloway University of London, where he was Head of Department between 1987 and 2005. He is especially interested in cognitive psychology (about which he has written several books) and most of his research focuses on the role of cognitive factors in anxiety within normal and clinical populations. He has published 36 books. His previous textbooks published by Psychology Press include *Psychology for AS Level (4th ed.)* (2008), *Psychology for A2 Level* (2001), *A2 Psychology: Key Topics (2nd ed.)* (2006), *Psychology: An International Perspective* (2004), *Psychology: A Student's Handbook (5th ed.)* (with Mark Keane) (2005), *Simply Psychology (3rd ed.)* (2007), *Fundamentals of Cognition* (2006), *Psychology: A Student's Handbook* (2000), *Perspectives on Psychology* (1994), and *Individual Differences: Normal and Abnormal* (1994). He has also written two research books for Psychology Press based on his research on anxiety: *Anxiety: The Cognitive Perspective* (1992) and *Anxiety and Cognition: A Unified Theory* (1997), as well as the popular title *Happiness: Facts and Myths* (1990). He is also a keen supporter of Crystal Palace football club and lives in hope that one day they will return to the Premiership.

Chapter 1

Contents

Introduction

1

WHAT IS PSYCHOLOGY?

What is psychology? As is clear from media coverage, psychology is amazingly wide-ranging. Here are just a few examples. Some psychologists are involved in treating mental disorders and use many techniques not dreamt of by Sigmund Freud. There are also forensic psychologists such as Cracker (Eddie Fitzgerald) of UK television fame who engage in offender profiling and tracking down criminals. Other psychologists study the human brain using scanners, with their research producing the brightly colored pictures of patterns of activation in the brain found in magazines. Still other psychologists (known as health psychologists) are hard at work trying to persuade us to adopt healthier lifestyles with less smoking and drinking and more physical exercise.

What is the common element to the varied activities of psychologists? Probably the most frequent definition of psychology is that it is the scientific study of behavior. However, this definition is too limited, because most psychologists are trying to understand *why* people behave in certain ways. To achieve that understanding, we must consider internal processes and motives. Thus, we arrive at the following definition:

> *Psychology is a science in which behavioral and other evidence (including individuals' reports of their thoughts and feelings) is used to understand the internal processes leading people (and members of other species) to behave as they do.*

As you read this book, you may be bewildered (hopefully not too bewildered!) by the numerous approaches psychologists have adopted in their attempts to understand human behavior. These approaches exist because our behavior is jointly determined by several factors including the following:

- The specific stimuli presented to us
- Our recent experiences (e.g., being stuck in a traffic jam)
- Our genetic endowment
- Our physiological system
- Our cognitive system (our perceptions, thoughts, and memories)
- The social environment
- The cultural environment
- Our previous life experiences (including those of childhood)
- Our personal characteristics (including intelligence, personality, and mental health)

The notion that there are various levels of explanation can be illustrated by taking a concrete example. Suppose one man attacks another man very aggressively by punching him repeatedly on the head and body. How can we understand this behavior? It may depend in part on the genes the man has inherited from his parents. It may also depend on the attacker's childhood experiences, for example, the presence of violence within the family. It may also depend on a recent stressful experience such as being caught in heavy traffic. The attacker's clinical history may also be relevant—he may have a history of psychopathic or antisocial behavior. His behavior may depend on his thoughts and feelings (e.g., he may have misinterpreted the other person's behavior as threatening). His behavior may depend on social factors. For example, the man behaving aggressively may believe the other man has insulted members of his family. His behavior may depend on the physiological state of the man behaving aggressively—his internal bodily state may be highly aroused and agitated. Finally, the attacker's behavior may depend on cultural factors, in that expressing aggression by punching is regarded as more acceptable (or less unacceptable) in some cultures than in others.

The crucial point of the above example is that there is no *single* "correct" interpretation of the aggressive man's behavior. Indeed, it is probable that several of the factors discussed above contributed to his behavior, and the same is true of the great majority of the behavior we observe in everyday life. Thus, the scope of psychology needs to be very broad if we are to understand human behavior.

Some of the main approaches within psychology are as follows: biological psychology; cognitive psychology; individual differences; developmental psychology; and social psychology. Below we consider *how* each approach developed, and *why* that approach is important. Note that these approaches are all related to each other. For example, personality is discussed within the individual differences approach. However, individual differences in personality depend in part on genetic factors (biological approach), on cognitive processes (cognitive approach), on childhood experiences (developmental approach), and on interactional processes (social psychology). Thus, the various approaches are not as separate as might be assumed.

BIOLOGICAL PSYCHOLOGY

It is difficult to imagine the enormous impact that *The Origin of Species* by Charles Darwin (1809–1882) had on the way people think about themselves. Before its publication in 1859, most people assumed that human beings were radically different from (and far superior to) all other species. The notion that human beings had evolved from other species indicated that this view of the importance of the human species needed reassessment. However, not surprisingly, many people found it very difficult to accept that human beings should be regarded simply as members of the animal kingdom. Indeed, the millions of people who believe in intelligent design (i.e., humans were created by an intelligent designer) still do not accept Darwin's approach.

MR. BERGH TO THE RESCUE.

THE DEFRAUDED GORILLA. "That *Man* wants to claim my Pedigree. He says he is one of my Descendants."

MR. BERGH. "Now, Mr. DARWIN, how could you insult him so?"

A cartoon about evolution, circa 1871. Charles Darwin is rebuked for slighting a gorilla by claiming man may be descended from apes.

Darwin was a biologist rather than a psychologist. However, his views on evolution had several major implications for psychology. First, psychologists began to realize that it was worth considering human behavior from the biological perspective. Second, Darwin emphasized the importance of heredity, and the notion that offspring tend to resemble their parents. This suggested to psychologists that the role of heredity in influencing human behavior should be explored. Third, Darwin focused on variations among the members of a species with evolution favoring some members rather than others (i.e., survival of the fittest). This led to an interest in the role of heredity in explaining individual differences in intelligence and personality.

Why is this approach to psychology of importance? First, everyone (apart from identical or monozygotic twins) has their own unique set of genes, and genes influence our intelligence, personality, and behavior. Second, our motivational systems (e.g., hunger; sex) developed originally as a result of the biological imperative to survive and to pass on our genes to successive generations. Third, the processes studied by biological psychologists are involved in nearly all human behavior.

COGNITIVE PSYCHOLOGY

The study of human cognition with its focus on thinking and other mental processes originated with Plato and Aristotle. It remained the dominant area within psychology for 2000 years. However, it was relatively ignored during the first half of the twentieth century. The reason was that psychology (especially in the United States) was dominated by **behaviorism**, an approach with an emphasis on observable behavior rather than internal processes. According to the behaviorists, it is more scientific and "objective" to measure human behavior than it is to rely on people's possibly entirely mistaken reports of their internal thoughts and feelings, and so these reports should be ignored. The absurdity of carrying this approach to its logical conclusion is captured in the following joke. Two behaviorists are talking to each other after having had sex. One says to the other, "Your behavior tells me that you enjoyed that. Did I enjoy it?"

In the mid-1950s, the cognitive revolution began. Several major cognitive psychologists (e.g., Donald Broadbent, Jerome Bruner, George Miller, Herb Simon) started to explore human cognition in detail. They focused on the internal processes and structures involved in cognition, including perception, attention, learning, memory, language, thinking, and reasoning. They (and other cognitive psychologists) were interested in observable responses mainly to the extent that they provide information about these underlying processes and structures.

Plato and Aristotle, shown here in a painting by Raphael, were the originators of study concerning human cognitive processes.

For many years, cognitive psychologists focused mainly on the cognitive processes exhibited by volunteer participants taking part in artificial experiments under laboratory conditions. In recent years, cognitive psychologists have become interested in the role played by cognitive processes in accounting for people's behavior in the real world. However, we must be careful not to exaggerate the changes within cognitive psychology. After all, people use the same cognitive system whether performing a task in the laboratory or coping with everyday life.

Let's consider an example of the approach taken by cognitive psychologists. Patients with social phobia (excessive fear of social situations) interpret their own social behavior as much more inadequate than it appears to other people (Rapee & Lim, 1992). Cognitive psychologists regard social phobics' misinterpretation of their own behavior as shedding important light on the internal processes maintaining their disorder. More specifically, this misinterpretation helps to explain why social phobics shun most social occasions and experience considerable distress in demanding social situations.

Why is the cognitive approach to psychology so important? First, the understanding of human cognition developed by cognitive psychologists has had a great impact on social, developmental, and abnormal psychology. For example, we can only understand the behavior of children or of patients with mental disorders by taking account of the ways in which they perceive and interpret themselves and the world around them. Second, the insights obtained by cognitive psychologists have had real-life application in the design of computer and other systems in order to make them relatively easy to use. Third, cognitive psychology has had very beneficial effects on the treatment of depression and the anxiety disorders. More specifically, cognitive therapy uses insights from cognitive psychologists to change the maladaptive cognitive processes and structures of depressed and anxious patients.

Key Term
Behaviorism: an American school of psychology with an emphasis on measuring and predicting observable behavior.

INDIVIDUAL DIFFERENCES

The systematic study of individual differences started with the work of Sir Francis Galton (1822–1911), a cousin of Charles Darwin. The publication of Galton's book *Hereditary Genius* in 1869 was a landmark in the study of individual differences. Researchers on individual differences have focused mainly on intelligence and personality, although obviously people differ from each other in almost limitless ways. One of the key issues is to try to understand the factors responsible for individual differences in intelligence and

Sir Francis Galton, 1822–1911.

The experiences we have during childhood have a great impact on our adult lives.

personality. As mentioned earlier, both are influenced by genetic factors, by developmental factors, by cognitive factors, and by social factors.

Why is this approach to psychology important? First, individual differences in intelligence and personality influence most forms of behavior. Second, if our educational system is to be effective, we need to take account of the particular skills and abilities possessed by individual children. Third, it is desirable in many real-life situations to use information about individuals' intelligence and personality (e.g., in personnel selection).

DEVELOPMENTAL PSYCHOLOGY

It was only when Sigmund Freud's psychoanalytic theories became widely known in the early part of the twentieth century that serious attention was paid to developmental psychology. Thereafter, the greatest impetus to developmental psychology came from the Swiss psychologist, Jean Piaget (1896–1980). He spent several decades studying the childhood development of thinking and intelligence and produced a more comprehensive theory of cognitive development than anyone else.

Developmental psychology is concerned mainly with changes occurring during the course of childhood, and with the impact of childhood experiences on adult behavior. There are two main areas within developmental psychology. First, there is cognitive development, involving the child developing increasingly complex skills (e.g., reading; writing; numerical skills). Second, there is social development. Children acquire social skills and interact more effectively with other people as they grow up.

Why is this approach to psychology of importance? First, we can obtain some understanding of the behavior of adults by considering their childhood experiences. Second, if we could understand factors facilitating cognitive development, this would help to improve the educational system. Third, if we understood more clearly the factors underlying social development, this knowledge could be used to ensure that nearly all children develop good social skills. This would in turn lead to a reduction in juvenile delinquency and crime.

SOCIAL PSYCHOLOGY

Surprisingly, social psychology was one of the last areas of psychology to be fully accepted. Indeed, it was only after the Second World War that serious research in social psychology began. Social psychology covers a very wide range of topics. Some social psychologists are interested in processes within individuals (e.g., their attitudes and beliefs). Other social psychologists focus on networks of friendships and relationships characterizing the social interactions of everyday life. Still other social psychologists consider broader issues concerned with intergroup relations including issues such as prejudice and discrimination.

There is an important difference between social psychology in the United States and social psychology in Europe. Many (or even most) American social psychologists are mainly interested in the ways in which individuals make sense of their social environment and behave with respect to it. European social psychologists share those interests, but also focus on the functioning of groups (e.g., social; work). European social psychologists are more inclined than American ones to believe that an individual's sense of self depends importantly on the kinds of involvement he/she has with groups that are perceived as important.

Research in social psychology takes many forms. Experiments are often carried out either in the laboratory or in the field. In addition, there are surveys, in which questionnaires and/or interviews are used to obtain detailed information about social issues. There are also field studies, in which the researchers observe the social behavior of groups (e.g., adolescent gangs; members of an organization in a meeting). Finally, there are case studies, in which an individual or a group is studied in great detail. Case studies are especially valuable in the investigation of rare phenomena (e.g., coping with natural disasters; weird cults).

Why is this approach to psychology of importance? First, it takes full account of the fact that we are social animals who spend much of our time with other people. Even when we are on our own, we use social knowledge to make sense of our lives, and we reflect on social events we have experienced. Second, social psychologists have discovered that our perceptions of ourselves and of other people are often inaccurate or distorted. It is desirable that we develop an understanding of the limitations of our social perceptions. Third, our behavior is often influenced by other people to a much greater extent than we realize. Once again, it is desirable that we become more fully aware of the powerful impact of social influence on our everyday behavior.

Social psychology looks at our relationships with other people and society.

IS PSYCHOLOGY A SCIENCE?

Interesting questions often don't have a single, simple answer, and that is certainly true of the question, "Is psychology a science?" Most psychologists would answer that question, "Yes." However, some psychologists (including the author) are skeptical that *all* of the enormously diverse research in psychology can reasonably be regarded as scientific. We can make some progress by seeing the extent to which psychology possesses the main criteria of science (considered shortly).

Note that there is no necessary relationship between being scientific and being useful—psychological approaches and research that are not scientific can nevertheless be extremely useful. Here are two examples. First, there is the important phenomenon of groupthink, in which groups often make irrational decisions because of considerable pressures on the members of the group to reach a unanimous decision (see Chapter 19). Most of the research on groupthink has involved the careful study of documentation concerning famous (or notorious) political decisions rather than the carrying out of experiments, and so can be regarded as unscientific. Second, Sigmund Freud developed a form of therapy for mental disorders known as psychoanalysis on the basis of individual case studies, and his approach is generally thought to be unscientific (see Chapter 22). However, psychoanalysis and the general psychodynamic approach that developed out of psychoanalysis have been found to be moderately effective (see Jarvis, 2004, for a review) and are thus very useful.

1. *Controlled experiments* In most sciences (except astronomy and a few others), it is typical for experiments to involve observing the effects of some specific manipulation (e.g., mixing two chemicals together). As applied to psychology, the use of controlled experiments is based on the **experimental method**. This involves observing the effects of some manipulation of the environment on participants' behavior. For example, we can see whether reward enhances learning by comparing speed of learning in one group receiving reward (environmental manipulation) with that in another group not receiving reward.

   The fact that hundreds of thousands of experiments in psychology have been carried out using the experimental method may suggest that psychology comfortably satisfies the criterion of controlled experiments. Sadly, that is not really the case. The experimental method often works extremely well when we are interested in studying the effects of the *immediate situation* on behavior. However, our behavior is also determined by numerous factors in addition to the immediate situation, most of which can't be manipulated. These factors include recent events (e.g., row with partner), our physical health, our personality, childhood events (e.g., parents divorcing), genetic factors, cultural expectations, and so on.

2. *Objectivity* It is sometimes argued that science requires the collection of data in an objective way. However, some philosophers of science doubt whether that is possible.

A Skinner box (or operant conditioning chamber) is an enclosed environment in which the behavior of an animal can be studied. The animal is given a stimulus and its response is noted. This rat is in a box with a lever. Such levers can perform numerous functions, both positive ones, such as releasing food, or negative ones, such as giving an electric shock.

Thus, it may be more realistic to claim that scientists should be as objective as possible in their research. Popper (1969, 1972) pointed out that scientific observations are theory-driven rather than objective. The famous demonstration he used in his lectures involved telling his audience, "Observe!" Their obvious and immediate retort was, "Observe what?" This demonstration makes the point that no one observes without some idea of what they are looking for. Thus, what you observe depends in part on what you expect to see.

Let's consider a concrete example of how difficult it is to be totally objective. Some of the most famous experiments in psychology were carried out by Skinner. He put rats into a box containing a lever. They received a food pellet when they pressed the lever, and there was a mechanism that recorded every time the lever was pressed. That sounds completely objective. However, there are grounds for arguing that it isn't. Weak lever presses didn't activate the mechanism and so weren't recorded. In addition, the mechanism was activated by a strong lever press regardless of whether it was produced by the rat's left paw, its right paw, its nose, or its tail. Skinner claimed that it didn't matter how the animal pressed the lever, but that is an assumption rather than an objective fact.

3. *Replicability*   It is important in science that we can repeat or replicate the findings from any given experiment. This is the criterion of **replicability**. If we obtained different findings every time we carried out an experiment, the situation would be chaotic and we couldn't make any real progress.

Experiments in psychology vary considerably in terms of replicability. At one extreme, everyone (or virtually everyone) experiences the phenomenon of **apparent motion**. This is an illusion in which we perceive motion when a series of still images is presented very rapidly. We experience apparent motion every time we go to the movies—films are presented at a rate of 24 frames per second but we perceive smooth and coherent motion. At the other extreme, there are findings in social psychology. Our social behavior is heavily influenced by cultural factors, and this greatly reduces replicability. Smith and Bond (1998) reviewed the literature, and concluded that only one research finding in social psychology has been convincingly replicated around the world (discussed in more detail shortly).

Psychologists have generally focused on the findings from individual experiments. However, there is an alternative approach. In essence, what we can do is combine the findings from numerous similar studies into one very large analysis; this is known as **meta-analysis**. It is claimed that meta-analyses have the great advantage of providing a coherent overall picture of the research findings in any given area. For that reason, there has been a huge increase in the number of meta-analyses carried out.

As we will see at many points in this book, meta-analyses have proved valuable in making sense of complex research findings. However, there are various potential problems with meta-analyses. Sharpe (1997) identified three such problems:

(i) The "Apples and Oranges" problem: Studies that are not very similar to each other may nevertheless be included within a single meta-analysis.

(ii) The "File Drawer" problem: It is generally more difficult for researchers to publish studies with nonsignificant findings. Since meta-analyses often ignore unpublished findings that remain in file drawers, the studies included may not be representative of all the studies on a given topic.

(iii) The "Garbage in—Garbage out" problem: Many psychologists carrying out meta-analyses include all the relevant studies they can find. However, this means that very poor and inadequate studies are often included along with good quality ones.

Key Terms

Replicability:
the ability to repeat or replicate findings obtained from an experiment.

Apparent motion:
the illusion of movement created by the rapid presentation of still images.

Meta-analysis:
an analysis in which all of the findings from many studies relating to a given hypothesis are combined for statistical testing to obtain an overall picture.

Note that the above three problems are identified as *potential* problems. Psychologists have become increasingly sophisticated in the ways they carry out meta-analyses, as a result of which there are now fewer problems than in the past. The "Apples and Oranges" and "Garbage in—Garbage out" problems can be greatly reduced by establishing clear criteria that have to be met by any studies included in the meta-analysis. There are techniques for estimating the magnitude of any "File Drawer" problem, and it can be reduced by asking leading researchers in the area of the meta-analysis to supply their unpublished data.

What conclusions can we draw? Our behavior is typically influenced by numerous factors, most of which can't be controlled and some of which can't even be identified. In view of this complexity, it can be claimed that psychology has made reasonable progress in meeting the criterion of replicability. Meta-analyses have facilitated the task of deciding what general trends exist in research in any given area.

4. *Testing theoretical predictions*   Scientific experiments are typically carried out to test the predictions of some theory. That makes very good sense. There is essentially an infinite number of experiments that could be carried out, and scientific theories assist in the task of identifying which experiments are worthwhile.

How does psychology match up to this criterion? There are thousands of theories in psychology, and most experiments are designed to test one or more of these theories. However, numerous experiments lack any real theoretical purpose. For example, hundreds (or even thousands) of brain-imaging experiments were motivated by curiosity rather than by theory. The researchers concerned wondered which parts of the brain would be activated when people performed a given task, but had no theoretical predictions.

5. *Falsifiability*   According to Popper (1969), the hallmark of science is **falsifiability**. This is the notion that scientific theories can potentially be disproved by negative evidence. Why did Popper focus on being able to prove a theory false rather than on proving it to be correct? The reason is that it is impossible to prove conclusively that a theory is correct! Suppose that a theory has been supported by the findings from hundreds of experiments, and there are no findings inconsistent with it. It is still possible that it may be disproved in the future, perhaps in some culture in which the theory has not been tested so far.

We can see the power of Popper's views by considering the fate of turkeys. As the philosopher Bertrand Russell pointed out, a scientist turkey might form the hypothesis, "Every day I am fed," because for all of his life that has been the case. However, this hypothesis provides no certainty that the turkey will be fed tomorrow, and if tomorrow is Christmas Eve it is likely to prove false.

How well does psychology meet the criterion of falsifiability? The picture is very mixed. At one extreme, many of Freud's theoretical ideas are unfalsifiable. For example, he argued that the mind is divided up into the ego (conscious mind), the id (basic motivational forces), and the superego (the conscience). It is difficult (or even impossible!) to think of any findings that could disprove this position. At the other extreme, there are numerous theories that are not only falsifiable but have actually been falsified. For example, several theorists have claimed that we possess the fundamental attribution error. This involves exaggerating the extent to which other people's behavior is determined by their personality and minimizing the role of situational factors. Several studies (especially those in non-Western cultures) have failed to obtained any evidence for the fundamental attribution error (see Chapter 17).

In sum, many theories in psychology are falsifiable and many are not. Bear in mind that falsifying a theory *doesn't* necessarily mean that researchers immediately abandon it. Even in physics, Newton's theory of gravity was falsified well over a hundred years before it was replaced by Einstein's theories! What is typically the case is that a theory is only abandoned when someone puts forward a better and more comprehensive theory. Even then, the advocates of the discredited theory may be too proud to accept that they were wrong.

6. *Use of a paradigm*   According to Kuhn (1962, 1977), the most essential ingredient in science is a paradigm. A **paradigm** is a general theoretical orientation accepted by the

Key Terms

Falsifiability:
the notion that all scientific theories can in principle be disproved by certain findings.

Paradigm:
according to Popper, a general theoretical orientation commanding wide support.

Before Copernicus showed that the planets, including the earth, revolved around the sun, all astronomical theories had been based on the paradigm that the earth was the center of the universe. The complete change in science post-Copernicus is an example of a paradigm shift.

great majority of researchers in a given field of study. Kuhn argued that there are three distinct stages in the development of a science:

(i) There is pre-science, in which there is no paradigm and a wide range of opinion about the best theoretical approach to adopt.

(ii) There is normal science, in which there is a generally accepted paradigm. Most scientists are very attached to the paradigm they are using, and so the current paradigm is likely to be adhered to well after its "sell by" date.

(iii) There is revolutionary science, in which problems with the current paradigm become so great that it is eventually overthrown and replaced by a different paradigm. This is known as paradigm shift.

According to Kuhn (1962), psychology has failed to develop a paradigm and so remains at the pre-science stage. In support of this argument is the fact that psychology is an unusually fragmented discipline. It has connections with several other disciplines including biology, physiology, biochemistry, neurology, and sociology. This fragmentation and diversity make it unlikely that agreement can be reached on a common paradigm or general theoretical orientation.

CONCLUSIONS

We have seen that some research in psychology (but by no means all) meets most of the six criteria discussed above. Where does that leave us? In my opinion, it leaves us in a position resembling that of the psychologist in the old story. A psychologist is walking along a deserted path late at night with a friend when a thief snatches his wallet and throws it into a bush 15 yards (14 meters) off the path. The psychologist goes to the nearest light and starts looking for his wallet there. When his friend points out that he is looking in the wrong place, the psychologist replies, "But I can see what I'm doing here!"

In similar fashion, many psychologists carry out very respectable scientific research in the laboratory using the experimental method. However, this research focuses on aspects of the immediate situation that influence behavior and tends to ignore all the other important factors involved. As a result, researchers adopting this approach are in danger of being like the psychologist looking under the light. What they are doing is easy but unfortunately of limited value. In contrast, researchers who focus on all the other factors influencing behavior other than the immediate situation are looking in the right place (i.e., in the bush). However, they are in danger of not being very scientific because they are studying factors that don't lend themselves to the scientific method.

The ideas expressed above are somewhat oversimplified. However, it is certainly true that the challenge for psychology is to study important issues while remaining scientific. As we will see throughout this book, the good news is that psychologists are increasingly meeting that challenge. They are making use of more-and-more sophisticated experimental approaches, they have access to new technology (e.g., brain scanners), and they are increasingly prepared to address some of the most complex and important issues in psychology.

PSYCHOLOGY AROUND THE WORLD

Most research in psychology is carried out in the Western world, especially the United States. According to Rosenzweig (1992), 64% of the world's 56,000 researchers in psychology at the start of the 1990s were Americans. Smith and Bond (1998) considered several textbooks in social and organizational psychology. They concluded as follows: "The universe of social and organizational behaviors that is being sampled is almost entirely restricted to studies done within less than a dozen of the more than 200 countries in the world, constituting little more than 10 per cent of the world's population."

In spite of what has just been said, American psychologists don't carry all before them. Haggbloom et al. (2002) identified the 100 most eminent psychologists of the twentieth century. Just under 20% of them were non-American, nearly all European. For interest's sake, the 50 most eminent psychologists in order are shown in the box below.

Rank	Name	Rank	Name	Rank	Name
1.	B.F. Skinner	18.	Kurt Lewin	35.	R.B. Zajonc
2.	Jean Piaget	19.	Donald Hebb	36.	Endel Tulving
3.	Sigmund Freud	20.	George Miller	37.	Herbert Simon
4.	Albert Bandura	21.	Clark Hull	38.	Noam Chomsky
5.	Leon Festinger	22.	Jerome Kagan	39.	Edward Jones
6.	Carl Rogers	23.	Carl Jung	40.	Charles Osgood
7.	Stanley Schachter	24.	Ivan Pavlov	41.	Solomon Asch
8.	Neal Miller	25.	Walter Mischel	42.	Gordon Bower
9.	Edward Thorndike	26.	Harry Harlow	43.	Harold Kelley
10.	A.H. Maslow	27.	J.P. Guilford	44.	Roger Sperry
11.	Gordon Allport	28.	Jerome Bruner	45.	Edward Tolman
12.	Erik Erikson	29.	Ernest Hilgard	46.	Stanley Milgram
13.	H.J. Eysenck	30.	Lawrence Kohlberg	47.	Arthur Jensen
14.	William James	31.	Martin Seligman	48.	Lee Cronbach
15.	David McClelland	32.	Ulric Neiser	49.	John Bowlby
16.	Raymond Cattell	33.	Donald Campbell	50.	Wolfgang Kohler
17.	John Watson	34.	Roger Brown		

CROSS-CULTURAL PSYCHOLOGY

Similarities and differences across cultures are studied within **cross-cultural psychology**. What exactly is a culture? According to Fiske (2002, p. 85), "A culture is a socially transmitted or socially constructed constellation consisting of such things as practices, competencies, ideas, schemas, symbols, values, norms, institutions, goals, constitutive rules, artefacts [man-made objects], and modifications of the physical environment."

How important is cross-cultural psychology? If human behavior is similar across all cultures, the findings obtained from American and European research may suffice to develop adequate psychological theories. In fact, there are major differences across cultures, and so many theories based only on Western research have limited applicability. Note, however, that we would expect basic psychological processes (e.g., apparent motion; limited capacity of attention) to be very similar in every culture. In contrast, most social behavior is likely to be influenced by the cultural context. Smith and Bond (1998) considered cross-cultural attempts to replicate several phenomena in social psychology found in American research. They concluded as follows: "The only topic on which there is much evidence for consistently successful replication are the studies on obedience" (Smith & Bond, 1998, p. 31). As you will see in Chapter 19, Milgram (1974) found that most people are remarkably willing to administer potentially lethal electric shocks to another person.

Most studies in cross-cultural psychology have involved comparisons between different countries. However, a country is generally *not* the same as a culture. For example, it is generally assumed that the American culture is one based on individual independence and responsibility. Vandello and Cohen (1999) found that was the case in the Mountain West and the Great Plains. In the Deep South, however, the culture was based more on interdependence and sharing of responsibility within the family or other group.

Key Term

Cross-cultural psychology: an approach to psychology focusing on the similarities and differences across cultures.

There is a tendency for one culture to judge another as being "undeveloped" or "primitive".

Are you still doubtful whether cultural differences are sufficiently great to be worth bothering about? Perhaps you will be convinced by this quotation from Westen (1996, p. 679) even though it is somewhat over the top:

By twentieth century Western standards, nearly every human who has ever lived outside the contemporary West is lazy, passive, and lacking in industriousness. In contrast, by the standards of most cultures in human history, most Westerners are self-centered and frenetic.

Individualism vs. collectivism

One starting point for cross-cultural psychology is to assign cultures to various categories that capture important differences among them. Many psychologists argue there is a crucial difference between cultures emphasizing **individualism** and those emphasizing **collectivism**. Oyserman, Coon, and Kemmelmeier (2002, p. 5) defined these terms as follows: "[We may] conceptualize individualism as a worldview that centralizes the personal—personal goals, personal uniqueness, and personal control—and peripheralizes the social . . . the core element of collectivism is the assumption that groups bind and mutually obligate individuals."

Oyserman et al. (2002) considered the components of individualism and collectivism as assessed by 27 questionnaires. They identified six components of individualism and eight components of collectivism:

Individualism	Collectivism
1. Independent (free; control over one's life).	1. Related (considering close others as part of the self).
2. Goals (striving for one's own goals and achievements).	2. Belong (enjoying belonging to groups).
3. Compete (personal competition and success).	3. Duty (being willing to make sacrifices as a group member).
4. Unique (focus on one's unique characteristics).	4. Harmony (concern for group harmony).
5. Private self-know (keeping one's thoughts private from others).	5. Advice (turning to close others for help with decisions).
6. Direct communicate (stating clearly what one wants and needs).	6. Context (self alters across situations).
	7. Hierarchy (emphasis on status issues).
	8. Group (preference for working in groups).

The first theoretical account of individualism and collectivism was proposed by Hofstede (1980, 1983). He argued that individualism and collectivism are opposites. Individualistic cultures are those with an emphasis on *independence* and individual responsibility whereas collectivistic ones emphasize *interdependence* and group membership.

Findings

Hofstede (1980, 1983) surveyed work-related values among IBM employees from 53 countries. The countries scoring highest on individualism were the United States (rank 1), Australia (rank 2), Great Britain (rank 3), and Canada and The Netherlands (joint rank 4). Hofstede assumed (mistakenly as it happens) that countries scoring lowest on individualism were the highest on collectivism. Those scoring lowest on individualism were Guatemala (rank 53), Ecuador (rank 52), Panama (rank 51), and Venezuela (rank 50).

Key Terms

Individualism: characteristic of cultures emphasizing independence, personal responsibility, and personal uniqueness.

Collectivism: characteristic of cultures emphasizing interdependence, sharing of responsibility, and group membership.

Several countries in the Far East (e.g., Indonesia, South Korea, Taiwan, and Thailand) also scored low on individualism.

One of Hofstede's key findings was that individualism correlated +.82 with modernity as measured by national wealth. This suggests that wealthier countries are generally individualistic. The most likely explanation is that affluent individuals have less need to be reliant on other people.

There is increasing evidence that individualism and collectivism are *not* opposites of each other as was assumed by Hofstede. Triandis et al. (1993) obtained several measures of individualism and collectivism across several cultures. Their key finding was that individualism and collectivism were essentially independent or uncorrelated with each other.

Gelfand, Triandis, and Chan (1996) presented American students with concepts relating to individualism (e.g., choosing own goals; broad-minded), to collectivism (e.g., family security; reciprocate favors), and to authoritarianism (e.g., submissiveness; punish deviates). There were two key findings. First, individualism and collectivism were unrelated to each other. Second, authoritarianism was the opposite of individualism. In general terms, individualists want to control their own lives, whereas authoritarians want to control other people's lives.

It has often been assumed that what is true at the level of a culture is also true at the level of individuals within that culture. However, that is not strictly correct. Triandis et al. (2001) studied several cultures. Only about 60% of those living in individualistic cultures have individualistic beliefs, and only about 60% of those in collectivistic cultures have collectivistic beliefs. Thus, there is only a moderate tendency for matching between individuals and the culture in which they live.

Evaluation

- There is an important distinction between individualism and collectivism.

- The distinction between individualism and collectivism has been more influential than any other distinction in cross-cultural research.

- Hofstede's research was limited in that his sample consisted mainly of male workers from IBM's marketing and serving division.

- Individualism and collectivism are essentially unrelated to each other rather than being opposites as was originally assumed.

- The concepts of individualism and collectivism are both very broad and involve several components. As Fiske (2002, p. 83) pointed out, "IND [individualism] amalgamates Thomas Paine, Vincent van Gogh, Mahatma Gandhi, Michael Jordan, Hugh Hefner, and Adolf Hitler into one category!"

- The heavy reliance on questionnaires to assess individualism and collectivism is adequate only if people have access to *all* relevant information about themselves and their culture. This is most unlikely to be the case.

Cultural influences: Fixed or flexible?

It is generally assumed that the culture to which we belong has a fixed and constant impact on us. As Hong, Morris, Chiu, and Benet-Martinez (2000, p. 709) pointed out, "Cultural knowledge is [typically] conceptualized to be like a contact lens that affects the individual's perceptions of visual stimuli all of the time." Is it really true that cultural influences are constant across different situations? According to Hong et al., the answer is, "No." Cultural influences have more influence on us when we are in situations that make culture-relevant information readily accessible than in situations that do not. For

Feelings of patriotism are likely to be more intense when we watch our country play football than at other times. This demonstrates that cultural influences are flexible in nature, and the extent to which they impact on our emotions and behavior is often contextually determined.

example, you may identify more with your own culture when you hear the national anthem being played than at other times.

The clearest evidence that cultural influences are flexible and changeable has been obtained in studies on bicultural individuals who have internalized two different cultures. Such individuals often report frame switching, in which they switch from one cultural outlook to the other. For example, Padilla (1994, p. 30) quotes the following experience of a Mexican-American individual: "At home with my parents and grandparents the only acceptable language was Spanish . . . Everything was really Mexican . . . But at school, I felt really different because everyone was American, including me. Then I would go home in the afternoon and be Mexican again."

Hong, Chiu, and Kung (1997) studied Westernized Chinese students in Hong Kong. Participants were shown pictures strongly related to either the American culture (e.g., the American flag; Marilyn Monroe; the Capitol Building) or to the Chinese culture (e.g., a Chinese dragon; a Chinese opera singer; the Great Wall). After that, they were shown a realistic picture of a fish swimming in front of a group of other fish. Participants exposed to symbols of American culture favored an internal or individualistic interpretation of the fish's behavior (the one fish is leading the other fish). In contrast, those exposed to symbols of Chinese culture favored an external or collectivistic interpretation (the one fish is being chased by the other fish).

In sum, the extent to which we are affected by cultural influences depends very much on the situation in which we find ourselves (see Lehman, Chiu, & Schaller, 2004, for a review). That is an important insight, and one that is likely to become the focus of much future research.

HOW USEFUL IS PSYCHOLOGY?

Most people think psychology is an interesting subject (which it is!). We are all interested in trying to understand ourselves and other people, and that is the central goal of psychology. However, there is more controversy concerning the usefulness of psychology. Skeptics argue that psychology tells us what we already know (the science of the bleeding obvious), that findings obtained in the laboratory don't generalize to everyday life, and that most psychological research is trivial (e.g., rats running through mazes). There are many ways of refuting such arguments. However, I will concentrate on two issues. First, the argument that psychology is no better than (or even the same as) common sense will be discussed. Second, the major contributions that have been made in the areas of clinical psychology and health psychology will be considered.

"Look before you leap" vs. "He who hesitates is lost."

"PSYCHOLOGY IS JUST COMMON SENSE"

An unusual feature of psychology is that everyone is to some extent a psychologist. We all observe the behavior of other people and of ourselves, and everyone has access to their own thoughts and feelings. One of the main tasks of psychologists is to predict behavior, and the prediction of behavior is important in everyday life. The better we can anticipate how people will react in any given situation, the more contented and rewarding our social interactions and relationships are likely to be.

The fact that everyone is a psychologist has led many people to underestimate the achievements of scientific psychology. If the findings of scientific psychology are in line with common sense, it can be argued that they tell us nothing we didn't already know. On the other hand, if the findings don't accord with common sense, then people often respond, "I don't believe it!"

There are various problems with the view that psychology is no better than common sense. It is misleading to assume that common sense forms a coherent set of assumptions about behavior. This can be seen if we regard proverbs as providers of commonsensical views. A girl parted from her lover may be saddened if she thinks of the proverb, "Out of sight, out of mind." However, she may cheer herself up if she tells herself that, "Absence makes the heart grow fonder." Another pair of proverbs expressing opposite meanings is the following: "Look before you leap" versus "He who hesitates is lost." As common sense involves such an inconsistent view of human behavior, it can't be used as the basis for explaining that behavior.

There is another reason for not trusting commonsensical views. People's views about issues in psychology often reflect their own experience rather than any objective reality. For example, Furnham (1982) carried out a study in the UK on people's beliefs about the factors causing poverty. Conservative party voters (who tend to be wealthier than those voting for other parties) argued that poverty is a result of problems within poor individuals (e.g., lack of effort; lack of thrift). In contrast, Labour party voters (who tend to be less well-off) argued that poverty is a result of problems within society (e.g., prejudice and discrimination; low wages in some industries).

The notion that psychology is just common sense can also be disproved by considering psychological studies in which the findings were very unexpected. A famous example is the work of Stanley Milgram (1974; discussed in Chapter 19). The experimenter divided his participants into pairs to play the roles of teacher and learner in a simple learning task. The "teacher" was told to give electric shocks to the "learner" every time the wrong answer was given, and to increase the shock intensity each time. The situation was rigged so that the learner was always a confederate of the experimenter. This confederate was a middle-aged man who allegedly had a heart condition. At 180 volts, the learner yelled, "I can't stand the pain!," and by 270 volts his response had become an agonized scream. If the teacher showed reluctance to give the shocks, the experimenter (a professor of psychology) urged him/her to continue.

Do you think you would be willing to give the maximum (and potentially fatal) 450-volt shock in such an experiment? What percentage of people do you think would be willing to do it? Milgram (1974) found that everyone denied they personally would do any such thing. Psychiatrists at a leading medical school predicted that only one person in a thousand would go to the 450-volt stage. In fact, about 60% of Milgram's participants gave the maximum shock, which is 600 times as many as the expert psychiatrists had predicted! Thus, people are much more conformist and obedient to authority than they realize. There is a strong tendency to go along with the decisions of someone (e.g., a professor of psychology) who seems to be a competent authority figure.

The fact that Milgram's findings are very different from those predicted by common sense doesn't say anything about all the other hundreds of thousands of findings in psychology. Accordingly, let's extend this discussion to include a quiz covering a wide range of topics in psychology (many taken from Furnham, 1988). For each item, decide whether you think it is true or false.

Psychology quiz

1. In making decisions, committees tend to be more conservative than individuals. TRUE/FALSE
2. In small amounts, alcohol is a stimulant. TRUE/FALSE
3. Flashbulb memories (i.e., vivid memories of dramatic world events like 9/11) are exceptionally accurate and long-lived. TRUE/FALSE
4. There is some truth in many national and ethnic stereotypes. TRUE/FALSE
5. A schizophrenic is someone with a split personality. TRUE/FALSE
6. To change people's behavior towards members of ethnic minority groups, we must first change their attitudes. TRUE/FALSE

7. A person who is fatigued invariably does poorer work than someone who is fully rested.	TRUE/FALSE
8. Intelligence plays a smaller role in human happiness than does emotion.	TRUE/FALSE
9. Very intelligent children tend to be less strong physically than children of average intelligence.	TRUE/FALSE
10. Physically attractive adults have better social skills and physical health than unattractive ones.	TRUE/FALSE
11. Human progress is a result of increased native intelligence from age to age.	TRUE/FALSE
12. Most people feel sympathy for the victims of serious accidents or natural disasters and don't hold them responsible for the harm they have suffered.	TRUE/FALSE
13. Patients with amnesia have very poor long-term memory but can still acquire many skills such as learning to play the piano.	TRUE/FALSE
14. People's behavior in most situations depends much more on their personality than on the situation itself.	TRUE/FALSE
15. Eyewitness testimony about an event often reflects not only what he/she actually saw but information they obtained later.	TRUE/FALSE

The correct answer to most of the questions is "False". The exceptions (where the correct answer is "True") are questions 4, 8, 10, 13, and 15. How did you get on? I tried to select questions so that the correct answer differs from common sense, but I may or may not have been successful. If you scored 12 or more, then I suspect you have already spent some time studying psychology. If not, you must be a very keen student of human behavior! If you scored fewer than 12, then perhaps you will agree that there may be more to psychology than meets the eye.

Some of the topics forming the items in the quiz are discussed in various chapters of this book. For example, Chapter 8 deals with items 3, 13, and 15, Chapter 11 deals with item 11, Chapter 12 deals with item 14, Chapter 18 with item 10, Chapter 19 with item 1, Chapter 20 with items 4 and 6, and Chapter 21 with item 5.

CLINICAL PSYCHOLOGY

Mental disorders cause untold human misery to millions of people around the world. The most common mental disorders are depression or mood disorders and anxiety, and so we will focus on them. Between 5% and 8% of the European population suffers from depression during any given year (Andlin-Sobocki, Olesen, Wittchen, & Jönsson, 2005), and the figure is 12% for anxiety disorders (Andlin-Sobocki & Wittchen, 2005). Apart from the costs in human misery, there are very large financial costs as well. It has been estimated that the total annual cost of mental disorders is 240 billion euros (about £200 billion, or $370) when account is taken of lost workdays and productivity loss (Andlin-Sobocki, Jönsson, Wittchen, & Olesen, 2005). All of the figures given are only estimates, but they show clearly the extremely damaging effects of mental disorders.

What has psychology contributed to the treatment of mental disorders? Many different forms of psychological therapy have emerged since Sigmund Freud developed psychoanalysis approximately 100 years ago. However, the evidence indicates that overall there are only small differences in the effectiveness of different forms of therapy (e.g., Wampold et al., 1997). Matt and Navarro (1997) combined data from 28 meta-analyses on the effects of therapy. They found that 75% of patients receiving therapy improved more than the average untreated control patient, which indicates that all forms of therapy are at least moderately effective. Approximately 85 million people in Europe suffer from anxiety and/or depression in any given year, and the great majority receive little in the way of effective therapy. Nevertheless clinical psychology has contributed substantially to improving mental health. There is enormous scope for it to contribute much more if the resources were available to train more clinical psychologists.

HEALTH PSYCHOLOGY

Ünal, Critchley, Fidan, and Capewell (2005) estimated that the number of people in England and Wales dying from heart disease was 68,230 fewer in 2000 than in 1981. This reduction produced a gain of about 925,415 life years. There are two main ways in which we might explain this reduction in mortality from heart disease. First, and most obviously, there have been substantial advances in medicine. These advances include the development of more precise and effective surgical interventions, increased use of aspirin to prevent heart attacks, treatment for hypertension, and the use of statins (drugs that reduce cholesterol). Second, there are changes in lifestyle. Some of these changes are clearly beneficial (e.g., reduction in smoking), but others have adverse effects (e.g., increased obesity; decreased physical activity).

Here is a question based on the above information. What percentage of the reduced mortality from heart disease is attributable to medical advances and what percentage to lifestyle changes? The answer may surprise you—Ünal et al. (2005) concluded that 79% of the gain in life years (731,270 in total) was a result of lifestyle changes and only 21% (194,145 life years) was a result of medical interventions! Lifestyle changes had a massively positive effect overall even though some changes (e.g., reduced physical activity; increased obesity) had a negative effect on mortality from heart disease.

What is the relevance of all this to psychology? Lifestyle changes involve changing behavior, and the experts in devising ways of changing behavior are . . . psychologists. More specifically, many health psychologists focus on interventions designed to produce beneficial lifestyle changes. The lifestyle change having by far the greatest impact on reduced mortality from heart disease was a reduction in the number of people smoking. Indeed, almost 45% of the total gain in life years from lifestyle changes and medical interventions was attributable to a reduction in smoking.

Health psychology, such as basic counseling and social skills training, can be used as part of multi-component packages to help change behavior, and thus make the lifestyle changes necessary for successful smoking cessation, for example.

Viswesvaran and Schmidt (1992) carried out a meta-analysis of 633 smoking cessation studies. The annual success rate achieved by health psychologists was 30% with multi-component packages (e.g., basic counseling; information on the health effects of smoking; social skills training; nicotine patches) compared to 6% for smokers receiving no treatment. Since there are still about 10 million smokers in the UK, there is scope for health psychologists to reduce mortality from heart disease considerably in the future.

We have only focused on mortality from heart disease. However, smoking increases mortality from a very wide range of diseases. On average, smokers lose about 10 years of their lives as a direct consequence of smoking. Imagine if all 10 million smokers in the UK received multi-component smoking cessation packages from health psychologists. In principle, this could produce a gain of 24 *million* life years!!!

Chapter Summary

What is psychology?

- Psychology is the science devoted to understanding human (and social) behavior.
- Biological psychology is an approach that emphasizes the importance of internal processes and structures such as attention, perception, learning, memory, language, thinking, and reasoning.
- Cognitive psychology is an approach that focuses on understanding the internal processes and structures that influence behavior in nearly every situation.
- The individual differences approach emphasizes the ways in which any individual's behavior is influenced by his/her intelligence and personality.
- Developmental psychology is an approach concerned with the changes occurring during childhood and with the impact of childhood experiences on adult behavior.
- Social psychology is an approach that emphasizes the fact that we are social animals who spend much of our time with other people and being influenced by them.

Is psychology a science?

- Most science involves carrying out controlled experiments, collecting objective data, replicating findings, testing theoretical predictions, falsifiability of predictions, and use of a paradigm.
- Much research in psychology fulfills most of the criteria for a science. However, the most scientific research in psychology sometimes addresses relatively minor issues.

Psychology around the world

- There is an important distinction between individualistic and collectivistic cultures.
- Individualism and collectivism are very broad concepts, and are *not* opposites as has often been assumed.

How useful is psychology?

- Psychology is *not* just common sense. Common sense doesn't provide a coherent account of human behavior and nonpsychologists' predictions about human behavior are frequently disconfirmed.
- Mental disorders are extremely expensive in human and financial terms. Clinical psychologists have been increasingly successful in alleviating human misery (and saving very large sums of money) in recent years.
- A substantial proportion of recent increases in longevity in Western countries is a result of lifestyle changes rather than improvements in medical interventions. Health psychologists have an increasingly important role to play in persuading people to adopt healthier lifestyles that will extend their lives.

Further Reading

- Furnham, A. (1988). *Lay theories: Everyday understanding of problems in the social sciences*. Oxford, UK: Pergamon. Adrian Furnham has asssembled a formidable amount of evidence on the limitations of commonsensical views of psychology.
- Oyserman, D., Coon, H.M., & Kemmelmeier, M. (2002). Rethinking individualism and collectivism: Evaluation of theoretical assumptions and meta-analyses. *Psychological Bulletin, 128*, 3–72. This reference is very useful if you want to gain more understanding of cross-cultural differences.
- Smith, P.B., & Bond, M.H. (1998). *Social psychology across cultures* (2nd ed.). London: Prentice Hall. The major findings from cross-cultural research are discussed in a well-informed and critical way.

Chapter 2

Contents

Historical and conceptual issues

This chapter is divided into two major sections. The first such section is concerned with the history of psychology. It focuses on the major approaches to psychology that have been developed over the past century or so. The second section is devoted to major conceptual issues and debates in psychology. We will reserve discussion of those issues and debates until later in the chapter.

In Chapter 1, we saw how psychology is related to several other disciplines. For example, psychology has been influenced by physiology, genetics, biology, medicine, and anthropology. These influences help to explain the complexity and the richness of contemporary psychology, and shed light on the ways in which psychology has developed over the past century or so. However, the development of psychology has also been powerfully influenced by a relatively small number of theoretical approaches or "schools" of psychology.

The following five approaches are considered in this chapter: psychodynamic approach; behaviorism; humanism; cognitive psychology; and evolutionary psychology. They are considered in that order because it corresponds to the historical order in which the approaches were developed. The psychodynamic approach was developed by Sigmund Freud in Vienna at the start of the twentieth century. It was based mainly on a form of clinical therapy known as psychoanalysis. However, Freud extended the psychodynamic approach to account for childhood development and the development of personality. The behaviorist approach was developed by John Watson and other American psychologists from about 1912 onwards. This approach had its origins in animal research, and was mainly concerned with understanding the processes of learning under highly controlled conditions.

Humanism is sometimes known as the "third force" in psychology, with the psychodynamic and behaviorist approaches being the other two forces. It was developed by psychologists such as Carl Rogers and Abraham Maslow in the United States in the 1950s, and had its origins in philosophy. The humanist approach shared with the psychodynamic approach a major focus on therapy. The cognitive approach was developed mainly in the United States and the United Kingdom. This approach became increasingly influential from about the middle of the 1950s onwards. Cognitive psychology had some of its origins in the behaviorist approach, with its emphasis on controlled observation of behavior. However, the cognitive approach is much broader, since it considers a wide range of cognitive processes (e.g., attention; perception; reasoning; memory) as well as learning.

Finally, there is evolutionary psychology, which has been popularized by Steven Pinker (e.g., 1997). According to this approach, the process of evolution has served to shape our minds and behavior. As a result, much of human behavior is adaptive. That means it is well suited to the environment in which we find ourselves. This approach has proved controversial. In the eyes of many psychologists, it exaggerates the importance of

Sigmund Freud, 1856–1939.

genetic factors in influencing our behavior and de-emphasizes the role played by social and cultural factors.

PSYCHODYNAMIC APPROACH

Sigmund Freud (1856–1939) is the most influential figure in the entire history of psychology. He was Austrian, and trained in medicine before going on to specialize in neurology. His fame rests largely on his position as the founder of psychoanalysis. Note that psychoanalysis consists of two somewhat separate strands: (1) a complex set of theories about human emotional development; and (2) a form of treatment based in part on those theoretical ideas. Over the years, psychoanalysis was developed and extended by many others including his daughter Anna Freud, Karen Horney, and Erik Erikson. This entire approach is often described as "psychodynamic," and is discussed very well by Jarvis (2004).

Some of Freud's main contributions are discussed elsewhere in the book. His theory of psychosexual development (an approach to personality) is dealt with in Chapter 12, and his therapeutic approach is considered in Chapter 22. At a very general level, Freud assumed that the mind is divided into three parts. First, there is the id. This contains the sexual and aggressive instincts, and is located in the unconscious mind. Second, there is the ego. This is the conscious, rational mind, and it develops during the first 2 years of life. It works on the reality principle, taking account of what is going on in the environment. Third, there is the superego. This develops at about the age of 5 when the child adopts many of the values of the same-sexed parent (a process of identification). It is partly conscious and partly unconscious. It consists of the conscience and the ego-ideal. The conscience is formed as a result of the child being punished, and it makes the child feel guilty after behaving badly. The ego-ideal is formed through the use of reward. It makes the child feel proud after behaving well.

According to Freud, there are frequent conflicts among the id, ego, and superego. Most commonly, conflicts involve the id and the superego. The id wants to satisfy its basic motivational urges but the superego or conscience is opposed to that, and the ego tries to resolve the conflict. The ego protects itself by using various defense mechanisms (strategies designed to reduce anxiety). The main defense mechanism is repression, which involves forcing threatening thoughts and feelings into the unconscious. Other defense mechanisms are denial (refusing to accept the reality of a threatening event) and displacement (moving impulses away from a highly threatening object towards a less threatening one). Someone who has been made angry by their boss might show displacement by going home and kicking their cat.

Freud assumed that the mind exists at three levels: the conscious; the preconscious; and the unconscious. The conscious consists of those thoughts that are currently the focus of attention. The preconscious consists of information and ideas that could be retrieved easily from memory and brought into consciousness. The unconscious consists of information that is either very difficult or almost impossible to bring into conscious awareness.

Psychoanalysis as a form of therapy can be regarded as the first "talking cure." Freud argued that individuals experiencing traumatic events in childhood (e.g., sexual abuse) tend to repress their memories for those events by forcing them into the unconscious. Crucial to the success of therapy is allowing patients to gain access to their repressed feelings and thoughts, with the goal being to provide them with insight into the true nature of their problems. The retrieval of repressed memories can be facilitated by free association or by dream analysis. In free association, patients are asked to respond rapidly to various words presented to them with the first ideas that come into their minds. Freud regarded dream analysis as important because he argued that people's deep-seated feelings and concerns influence their dreams. People's reports of their dreams are typically fairly innocuous, but psychoanalysis can reveal the hidden meanings contained in them.

After Freud's death, neo-Freudians such as Anna Freud and Karen Horney developed ego analysis, which is based on the notion that therapy should focus on strengthening the ego so that it can achieve more gratification. Ego analysis makes use of free association and other techniques associated with psychoanalysis. However, it differs from psychoanalysis in that it focuses much more on the patient's *current* social and interpersonal problems than on their childhood experiences. It also differs in that ego analysts regard society as being a positive force in most people's lives, whereas Freud emphasized the ways in which society inhibits individuals.

Another neo-Freudian approach to therapy is based on Melanie Klein's object relations theory (discussed by Segal, 1964). The main focus is on early relationships and the effects that these relations have on later life. In essence, the therapist seeks to identify consistent relationship problems experienced by the client, and to find ways to improve matters.

Psychoanalyst Sigmund Freud and his daughter and fellow psychoanalyst Anna Freud arrive in Paris in 1938, after fleeing the Nazi occupation of their home country, Austria. They went on to London, where Sigmund died the next year. Anna did major work in the field of child psychology until her death in 1982.

Evaluation

+ Freud hugely expanded the scope of psychology. Before Freud, psychology was rather narrow, focusing on topics such as simple learning and associations of ideas. In contrast, Freud argued that psychology is relevant to virtually all human behavior, and history has proved him right.

+ Some of Freud's very general ideas have survived extremely well and are still generally accepted. For example, Freud argued that childhood experiences influence adult behavior and personality, that unconscious processes and motives influence our behavior, and that many of the behavioral symptoms of patients with anxiety disorders can be understood as attempts to reduce their anxiety level.

+ Freud developed the first systematic form of therapy for mental disorders based on psychological principles. Remarkably, psychoanalysis was as good as (or better than) most competing forms of therapy for more than 50 years after it was put forward.

+ Freud's theory of psychosexual development was the first systematic theory of personality.

+ As Williams (1987) pointed out, "Psychoanalysis has been society's most influential theory of human behavior . . . it profoundly altered Western ideas about human nature and changed the way we viewed ourselves and our experience."

− Many of Freud's theoretical ideas are unscientific in that they lack falsifiability, i.e., the possibility of disproof. For example, we can't devise an experiment to prove (or disprove) the notion that the mind is divided into the id, ego, and superego.

− Most of Freud's evidence for his ideas was obtained from clients during therapy. This evidence was probably contaminated—what patients said was influenced by what Freud had said previously and his known views. In addition, Freud may well have used his theoretical preconceptions to produce distorted interpretations of what patients said.

− When Freud's specific ideas can be tested, they have generally been found to be wrong. For example, there is very little evidence supporting the existence of an Oedipus complex (young boys' sexual desire for their mother and consequent fear of their father). Another example is that Freud exaggerated the differences between males and females ("anatomy is destiny"), and has often been criticized for being sexist.

Freud's work was largely with middle-class women in Vienna in the 1890s and 1900s. How relevant do you think his ideas are to other cultures, particularly given the social changes during the twentieth century?

BEHAVIORISM

John Watson, 1878–1958.

The behaviorist approach to psychology started in the United States in the early years of the twentieth century. The central figure in this approach was John Watson (1878–1958). According to Watson (1913):

> *Psychology as the behaviorist views it is a purely objective, experimental branch of natural science. Its theoretical goal is the prediction and control of behavior. Introspection forms no essential part of its method.*

Note that Watson believed that a major goal of psychology is to control behavior. This helps to explain the emphasis the behaviorists placed on the study of learning rather than on other aspects of psychological functioning. If you want to change someone's behavior, you need to provide the relevant learning experience.

Watson and the other early behaviorists were greatly influenced by the work of Ivan Pavlov (1849–1936) on classical conditioning in dogs (see Chapter 7). Dogs salivate when food is put in their mouths, and Pavlov found they could be trained to salivate to a neutral stimulus such as a tone. This tone was presented just before food on several occasions, so that the tone signaled the imminent arrival of food to the dog. Finally, Pavlov presented the tone on its own without any food, and found that this led to the dog salivating. This form of learning is known as classical conditioning.

Russian psychologist Ivan Pavlov, a dog, and his staff, photographed circa 1925–1936.

Why was Watson so impressed by Pavlov's work? First, Pavlov focused on observable stimuli and responses, and so his research seemed to be scientific. For example, the amount of learning could be assessed by the quantity of salivation produced by the tone. Second, Pavlov's work suggested that learning involves the formation of an association between a stimulus (e.g., a tone) and a response (e.g., salivation). Watson assumed that most (or all) learning was of this type.

Burrhus Fred Skinner (1904–1990) was the most influential behaviorist. His main assumption was that nearly all behavior is under the control of reward or reinforcement. Responses followed by reward will increase in frequency, whereas those not followed by reward will decrease in frequency. This is known as operant conditioning (see Chapter 7). The responses studied by Skinner were very simple (e.g., lever pressing; pecking), and it is unlikely that operant conditioning explains more complex forms of learning.

Skinner seems to have favored the notion of equipotentiality, according to which virtually any response can be conditioned in any stimulus situation. This notion is simply incorrect. For example, Breland and Breland (1961) tried to train a pig to perform the (apparently) simple task of inserting a wooden token into a piggy bank for reward. However, the pig turned the token up with its snout, tossed it in the air, and so on. Thus, the pig behaved in ways that came "naturally" to it rather than those required to receive reward.

The behaviorists believed strongly (but wrongly!) that behavior is determined almost entirely by environmental factors and by learning. They argued that genetic factors are relatively unimportant: "There is no such thing as an inheritance of capacity, talent, temperament, mental constitution and characteristics. These things depend on training that goes on mainly in the cradle" (Watson, 1924).

The behaviorists' emphasis on *external* stimuli and responses was accompanied by a virtual ignoring of *internal* physiological (and other) processes. For example, Skinner (1980) argued that, "A science of behavior has its own facts . . . No physiological fact has told us anything about behavior that we did not know already." Even more dubiously, the behaviorists did not regard the brain as being of central importance. According to Murphy and Kovach (1972), "Though the brain remains a connecting station, it is for the

B.F. Skinner, 1904–1990.

behaviorist no more intelligible to say that we think with the brain than to say that we walk with the spinal cord."

Behaviorism has influenced the development of psychology in two important ways. First, the behaviorists spelled out more systematically than had been done before exactly how psychology could achieve scientific status. In particular, they claimed that the careful observation of behavior in controlled settings is of fundamental importance to psychology, a claim that still seems valid one century later.

Second, behaviorism has had a powerful influence on the treatment of mental disorders through the development of behavior therapy (see Chapter 21). This form of therapy is based on the assumptions that abnormal behavior develops through conditioning, and that conditioning principles can be used to achieve recovery. How effective is behavior therapy compared to other psychological forms of treatment? Matt and Navarro (1997) considered 63 meta-analyses in which different types of therapy had been compared in what we might call a meta-meta-analysis. Behavior therapy and cognitive therapy seemed to be slightly more effective than psychodynamic or client-centered therapy. However, this probably exaggerated the value of behavior and cognitive therapy. Clients treated by behavior or cognitive therapy often had less serious symptoms, and behavior and cognitive therapists tended to use less stringent measures of recovery than did psychodynamic and client-centered therapists.

Evaluation

- ⊕ The behaviorists' general approach to psychology based on controlled experiments and observations of behavior has proved of lasting value.

- ⊕ Behavior therapy is an effective form of treatment for several mental disorders.

- ⊖ Skinner argued that we learn mainly by performing responses that are rewarded. In fact, however, much of our learning occurs through observing the behavior of other people (Bandura, 1977; see Chapter 7).

- ⊖ The most general problem with behaviorism is that it understated the impact of internal factors (e.g., past knowledge; goals) on behavior. According to Skinner, our behavior is controlled by *current* rewards and punishments. If that were true, then we would be like weather vanes, being blown about by changes in the rewards and/or punishments in the environment (Bandura, 1977). In fact, of course, much of our behavior is relatively consistent because we are controlled in part by various long-term goals (e.g., obtaining a psychology degree).

- ⊖ The behaviorists assumed that reward or reinforcement has a major impact on learning. However, they often blurred the distinction between learning and performance. If someone offered you a money reward every time you said, "The earth is flat," you might be persuaded to say it hundreds of times. Although the reward would have influenced your performance or behavior, it is most unlikely that it would have influenced your learning to the extent that you started to believe that the earth is actually flat. However, you would have learned a simple way of accumulating a lot of money!

HUMANISTIC APPROACH

The humanistic approach to psychology was developed mainly by Carl Rogers and Abraham Maslow in the United States during the 1950s. Humanistic psychology "is concerned with topics that are meaningful to human beings, focusing especially upon subjective experience and the unique, unpredictable events in individual human lives" (Cartwright, 1979, pp. 5–6). Humanistic psychologists focus on issues such as personal responsibility, free will, and the

Abraham Maslow (left) and Carl Rogers (right), two of the main developers of the humanistic approach to psychology.

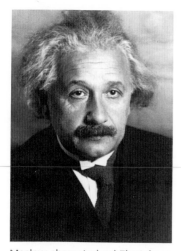

Maslow characterized Einstein as a famous individual who demonstrated "self-actualization"— including characteristics such as self-acceptance, resistance to cultural influences, empathy, and creativeness.

individual's striving towards personal growth and fulfillment. Of particular importance, humanistic psychologists favor a reliance on **phenomenology**, which involves reporting pure experience with no attempt at interpretation by the person doing the reporting. According to Rogers (1951, p. 133), "This kind of personal, phenomenological type of study . . . is far more valuable than the traditional 'hard-head' empirical approach. This kind of study, often scorned by psychologists as being 'merely self-reports,' actually gives the deepest insight into what the experience has meant."

As the above quotation suggests, humanistic psychologists did not subscribe to the scientific approach to psychology. Their anti-scientific approach was expressed forcefully by Maslow (1968, p. 13): "The uniqueness of the individual does not fit into what we know of science. Then so much the worse for that conception of science."

One of the main achievements of the humanistic approach is Maslow's hierarchical theory of motivation (discussed fully in Chapter 3). Maslow argued that previous theories of motivation were limited, because they focused only on basic motives such as sex, hunger, and thirst. He argued that most humans are also motivated by several other needs. Of particular importance is the need for self-actualization, which involves fulfilling one's potential in the broadest sense. Maslow (1954) identified Abraham Lincoln and Albert Einstein as two famous people who were self-actualized.

Another major achievement of the humanistic approach was Rogers' client-centered therapy, which was later called person-centered therapy. This form of therapy was based on the notion that the concept of "self" is of fundamental importance to an understanding of human behavior. Rogers (1967, p. 108) had this to say when discussing what mattered to his clients:

> *Below the level of the problem situation about which the individual is complaining— behind the trouble with studies or wife or employer . . .—lies one central search. It seems to me that at the bottom each person is asking "Who am I, really? How can I get in touch with this real self, underlying all my surface behavior? How can I become myself?"*

Rogers (1975) developed these ideas. He argued that the main goals of therapy should be to allow clients to develop a sense of personal agency and to become self-actualized by thinking about themselves in an honest and accepting way. These goals can be achieved provided the therapist consistently displays three qualities:

1. *Unconditional positive regard*: The therapist is always supportive.
2. *Genuineness*: The therapist is spontaneous and open.
3. *Empathy*: The therapist has a good understanding of the client's feelings and concerns.

There are two other important features of Rogers' approach to therapy. First, he was one of the first therapists to make available detailed information about what happened in treatment sessions (e.g., use of tape recordings). That made it easy for other therapists to identify key aspects of client-centered therapy. Second, most therapists modify the therapy they provide to take account of the specific disorder from which the client is suffering. In contrast, Rogers did not believe in the value of categorizing mental disorders. He believed that a single approach based on unconditional positive regard, genuineness, and empathy was nearly always appropriate.

Key Term

Phenomenology: an approach in which the focus is on the individual's direct reports of experience.

Evaluation

+ Humanistic psychology focused on issues of major concern to people (e.g., development of the self).

+ Major ingredients of client-centered (or person-centered) therapy such as therapist empathy, genuineness, and warmth or acceptance (related to unconditional positive regard) are predictive of therapeutic success (Orlinsky, Grave, & Parks, 1994).

+ A meta-analysis of studies on client-centered therapy indicated that the average client showed more improvement than 80% of individuals not receiving treatment (Greenberg, Elliott, & Lietaer, 1994). This suggests that client-centered therapy is moderately effective.

− The emphasis on phenomenology means that humanistic psychologists haven't systematically explored unconscious processes and structures.

− Client-centered therapy is reasonably effective when treating less severe disorders, but is of little value in treating severe mental disorders (Rudolph, Langer, & Tausch, 1980).

− The refusal by humanistic psychologists to adopt a scientific approach to psychology has limited the value of humanistic psychology, and has meant that its current impact is modest.

COGNITIVE APPROACH

As we saw in Chapter 1, cognitive psychology developed in the 1950s under the influence of key figures such as Donald Broadbent, Herb Simon, and George Miller. One of the main reasons why the cognitive approach started to become influential at that time was a growing dissatisfaction with the behaviorist approach. Suppose that we want to understand cognitive abilities such as our mastery of language or the processes involved in problem solving. It is difficult to do that from the behaviorist perspective with its emphasis on observable behavior. What is needed is a focus on internal processes, which is what cognitive psychologists do. They study the main *internal* psychological processes involved in making sense of the environment and deciding what actions might be appropriate. These processes include attention, perception, learning, memory, language, problem solving, reasoning, and thinking. These processes are discussed in detail in Chapters 6–10 of this book and also by Eysenck (2006).

Research in cognitive psychology during the 1950s, 1960s, and much of the 1970s consisted almost entirely of laboratory experiments in which healthy participants (typically undergraduate students) performed various tasks under well-controlled or "scientific" conditions. Such research remains important to this day. It has contributed enormously to our understanding of human cognition and has had a massive influence on the cognitive neuropsychological and cognitive neuroscience approaches that followed (discussed below).

The cognitive approach expanded in the 1970s with the development of cognitive neuropsychology. There is an apparent paradox with cognitive neuropsychology because it involves studying brain-damaged patients in order to shed light on cognitive processes in intact individuals. It is based on the assumption that, "Complex systems often reveal their inner workings more clearly when they are malfunctioning than when they are running smoothly" (McCloskey, 2001, p. 594). As an example, McCloskey described how he only began to understand

Cognitive psychology developed in the 1950s, largely taking the form of laboratory-based experiments performed under well-controlled conditions.

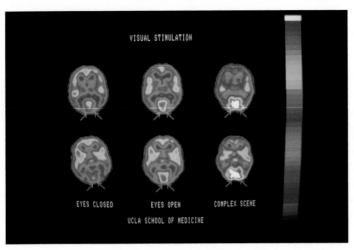

VISUAL STIMULATION

EYES CLOSED   EYES OPEN   COMPLEX SCENE

UCLA SCHOOL OF MEDICINE

An example of a PET scan. Cognitive neuroscience makes use of brain imaging such as this to study activation levels in different parts of the brain, and so increase our understanding of cognitive processes.

how his laser printer worked when it started misprinting things. Thus, we may develop an understanding of cognitive processing in intact individuals by focusing on the particular problems in cognition experienced by brain-damaged patients. For example, it has been found that some brain-damaged patients have very poor long-term memory but intact short-term memory, whereas others have poor short-term memory but intact long-term memory (Eysenck, 2006). This strongly suggests that there are separate short-term and long-term memory systems located in separate parts of the brain.

Since the early 1990s, there has been a phenomenal increase in **cognitive neuroscience**. This is a branch of cognitive psychology in which brain imaging is used in conjunction with behavioral measures in order to increase our understanding of the cognitive processes involved in performing a given task. You have almost certainly seen brightly colored pictures of the brain in action—such pictures are produced by using brain imaging to identify the activation levels in different parts of the brain when a task is performed.

The cognitive neuroscience approach can be very effective. For example, there has been controversy concerning the processes involved in visual imagery (imagining an object or scene with your eyes closed). The major possibilities are that visual imagery involves the same processes as visual perception or that it involves more abstract thinking based on our knowledge of objects and situations. Brain-imaging studies have shown that the same brain areas are generally activated during visual imagery and visual perception, including those brain areas involved in the early stages of visual perception (see Kosslyn & Thompson, 2003, for a meta-analysis).

As mentioned in Chapter 1, cognitive psychology has been very influential in the development of cognitive therapy (see Chapter 22). Cognitive therapy is based on the assumption that anxious and depressed patients have dysfunctional thoughts and beliefs about themselves and about the world. For example, Newmark, Frerking, Cook, and Newmark (1973) found that the statement, "One must be perfectly competent, adequate, and achieving to consider oneself worthwhile," was agreed to by 80% of anxious patients compared with 25% of nonpatients.

There are various forms of cognitive therapy, and it is often combined with behavior therapy to produce cognitive-behavior therapy. In essence, however, cognitive therapy is designed to replace dysfunctional thoughts and beliefs with more accurate and positive ones. This can be done by having patients challenge their dysfunctional thoughts. For example, snake phobics who greatly exaggerate the threateningness of snakes generally have more realistic beliefs about snakes after they have been persuaded to spend time in close proximity to them.

Evaluation

+ Cognitive psychology has proved extremely effective in enhancing our understanding of human cognition. The development of cognitive neuropsychology and cognitive neuroscience has contributed greatly to this effectiveness.

+ Cognitive psychology has benefited from extensive use of the experimental method. This has led to well-controlled experiments producing numerous replicable findings.

+ As mentioned in Chapter 1, cognitive psychology has become increasingly influential in several other areas of psychology, including social psychology, developmental psychology, and abnormal psychology. Some of the fruits of that influence will be discussed in various chapters of this book.

Key Term

Cognitive neuroscience: an approach within cognitive psychology that involves combining brain-imaging data with behavioral measures to understand human cognition.

+ Cognitive therapy is generally effective and compares well against other forms of therapy (e.g., Matt & Navarro's, 1997, meta-analysis; see Chapter 22).

– Laboratory research on cognitive processes may lack **ecological validity**, which is the extent to which the findings of laboratory studies apply to everyday life. In the real world, people typically try to have an impact on the environment. In contrast, the stimuli presented to participants in most cognitive experiments are determined by the experimenter's plan and are uninfluenced by the participants' behavior.

– Measures of the speed and accuracy of task performance provide only *indirect* evidence about the internal processes.

– Discovering that brain areas x and y are activated when people perform a given task does not directly tell us what cognitive processes occurred in those areas.

– Many cognitive psychologists fail to take account of individual differences, and thus seem to assume that everyone's cognitive system is similar and is used in similar ways. However, there is increasing recognition that individual differences are important and need to be considered.

EVOLUTIONARY PSYCHOLOGY

As we saw in Chapter 1, Darwin's theory of natural selection assumes that evolution selectively favors some members of any given species over others. This is known as survival of the fittest, meaning that those individuals whose characteristics equip them best to cope with the environment will be most likely to reproduce. In recent decades, Darwin's influence has manifested itself in evolutionary psychology, an approach that focuses on the effects of natural selection on the development of the human mind. In the words of one of the leading evolutionary psychologists, Steven Pinker (1997, p. 42):

Charles Darwin, 1809–1882.

Natural selection . . . acts by designing the generator of behavior: the package of information processing and goal-pursuing mechanisms called the mind. Our minds are designed to generate behavior that would have been adaptive, on average, in our ancestral environment.

Many of the key assumptions made by evolutionary psychologists are contained in the figure on the following page. **Inclusive fitness** is the notion that natural selection favors organisms that maximize replication of their genes directly by reproduction or indirectly by helping those with whom they share genes (e.g., immediate family). **Kin selection** is the notion that organisms are selected to favor their own offspring and other genetically related family members. **Differential parental investment** is the notion that females typically have a greater parental investment than males. Why is that the case? When a child is born, the mother typically devotes years of her life to looking after it. In contrast, the "costs" incurred by the father are often much less.

The other theoretical assumptions shown in the figure on the following page follow more or less directly from the assumptions just discussed. For example, it is assumed that cuckoldry (discovering their partner has had sex with someone else) causes more jealousy in males than in females. The explanation is as follows. Men can only justify their parental investment in a child provided it was actually fathered by them. If their partner is unfaithful, they cannot be sure that any child is actually theirs. In contrast, women always know for certain whether any given child is theirs regardless of whether their partner is faithful or not.

Key Terms

Ecological validity:
the extent to which the findings of laboratory studies are applicable to everyday settings and generalize to other locations, times, and measures.

Inclusive fitness:
the notion that natural selection favors individuals who maximize replication of their genes either directly via reproduction or indirectly by helping others who are genetically related to them.

Kin selection:
the notion that natural selection favors individuals assisting those genetically related to them.

Differential parental investment:
the notion that females have greater parental investment than males, as a result of which they are more selective in their choice of mates.

The theoretical approach adopted by evolutionary psychologists, with the most general assumptions at the top and the most specific assumptions at the bottom. From Kenrick (2001). Copyright © American Psychological Association. Reproduced with permission.

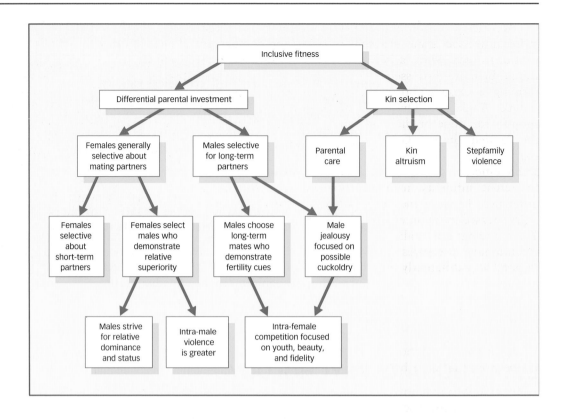

It would be easy to assume that evolutionary psychologists believe that humans are *always* well-adapted to their environment. In fact, that assumption is false, because it can take thousands of generations for natural selection to produce substantial genetic changes. As Buss (1999, p. 29) pointed out, "We carry around a Stone-Aged brain in a modern environment. A strong desire for fat, adaptive in a past environment of scarce food resources, now leads to clogged arteries and heart attacks."

According to evolutionary psychologists, a central goal of our lives is to ensure the survival of our genes. However, this is by no means necessarily a *conscious* goal. What evolutionary psychologists actually believe was expressed by Pinker (1997, p. 44): "Our goals are subgoals of the ultimate goal of the genes, replicating themselves . . . As far as *we* are concerned, our goals . . . are not about genes at all, but about health and lovers and children and friends." Thus, the success most of us have in spreading our genes often occurs as a by-product of our goals in life rather than in a direct way.

Evidence that the sexual attitudes and behavior of men and women differ approximately as predicted by evolutionary psychology is discussed in Chapter 3. The prediction that we should be more willing to behave altruistically (unselfishly) towards close relatives than towards distant relatives or strangers was tested by Burnstein, Crandall, and Kitayama (1994; see also Chapter 18). They presented participants with scenarios in which individuals had problems, and asked whether they would be willing to help. As predicted, participants were much more willing to help close relatives than other people. This was especially the case with a serious emergency (a house was burning rapidly, and only one of the three people in the house could be saved).

Since Burnstein et al. (1994) used hypothetical situations, it is possible that the participants responded in socially desirable ways rather than in the way they would in real life. However, Essock-Vitale and McGuire (1985) obtained similar findings based on real-life data. Female participants described occasions on which they had received or given help. They were five or six times more likely to have helped their close kin (e.g., children) than less close kin (e.g., nephews or nieces).

The ability to wrestle with a mammoth went down well with the ladies.

According to evolutionary psychology, men should be more distressed than women if their partner enjoyed passionate sex with another person, whereas women should be more distressed by the thought of their partner forming a close emotional bond with another person. Buunk, Angleitner, Oubaid, and Buss (1996) obtained support for these predictions among men and women in the United States, Germany, and The Netherlands. However, this study focused on *hypothetical* rather than *actual* infidelity. Harris (2002) examined people's reactions to actual infidelity in their partners, and found no differences between men and women. Members of both sexes focused more on emotional than on sexual infidelity. These findings are totally inconsistent with the notion that evolutionary pressures have led men and women to respond very differently to sexual and emotional infidelity.

Parental care and altruism

"Bringing up baby" involves heavy costs to many animal parents: in mammals this includes biological investment in egg production, growth and development of the fetus in the womb, milk production after birth, time and effort spent in care and defense, etc. In birds there is a similar amount of investment in nest building, egg production, incubation, feeding, etc. These behaviors could be argued to be of no benefit to the parents directly, and so could come under the heading of altruism. This altruism is even more marked if the parents are assisted by other family members, i.e., others who share the same genes. Mumme (1992) observed a type of Florida jay whose older broods acted as helpers with younger offspring, with the result that the younger brood had a greatly increased survival rate.

Evaluation

+ Evolutionary psychology focuses on determinants of behavior (e.g., natural selection) that have been ignored by other approaches to psychology.

+ Evolutionary psychology has produced several original insights on topics such as altruism and mate selection.

− Any type of behavior can be explained by claiming it is adaptive in an evolutionary sense if it is desirable (e.g., parenting) or maladaptive because of evolutionary time lag if undesirable (e.g., male violence). There is a danger of evolutionary psychologists providing unconvincing explanations of human behavior, many of which cannot be tested empirically.

− Evolutionary psychology often seems to focus too much on evolutionary processes and not enough on the relevance of such processes for human behavior.

− Numerous social and cultural factors are not considered fully by evolutionary psychologists. As a consequence, evolutionary psychologists tend to minimize the importance of cross-cultural differences.

ETHICAL ISSUES IN PSYCHOLOGY

Scientists often confront important and difficult ethical issues in the course of their work. For example, was it morally defensible for physicists to develop the atomic bomb during the 1940s? Should scientists participate in the development of chemical weapons that could potentially kill millions of people? All of these ethical questions are difficult to answer because there are good arguments for and against each program of research.

There are probably more ethical issues associated with research in psychology than in any other scientific discipline. There are various reasons why this is the case. First, all psychological experiments involve the study of living creatures (whether human or the members of some other species), and the rights of these participants to be treated in a caring and respectful way can be infringed by an unprincipled or careless experimenter.

Second, the findings of psychological research may reveal unpleasant or unacceptable facts about human nature, or about certain groups within society. No matter how morally upright the experimenter may be, there is always the danger that extreme political organizations will use research findings to further their political aims.

Third, these political aims may include social control. There is a danger that the techniques discovered in psychological research might be exploited by dictators or others seeking to exert unjustifiable influence on society or to inflame people's prejudices.

MILGRAM

We will start by considering two famous (or perhaps infamous) studies in psychology. First, there is Milgram's (1963, 1974) research on obedience to authority (see Chapter 19). He asked his participants to adopt the role of a teacher and to administer very strong (and potentially lethal) electric shocks to the learner, who was said to suffer from a heart condition. Approximately two-thirds of people agreed to administer these very strong shocks. In fact, the learner did not receive any shocks, but the teacher was unaware of that. At one point, the learner yelled, "I can't stand the pain," and later his response was an agonized scream.

The effects of this experiment on the teachers were dramatic, as Milgram (1974) pointed out. For example, as one observer reported, "I observed a mature and initially poised businessman enter the laboratory smiling and confident. Within 20 minutes he was reduced to a twitching, stuttering wreck, who was rapidly approaching a point of nervous collapse. He constantly pulled on his earlobe, and twisted his hands. At one point, he pushed his fist into his forehead and muttered: 'Oh God, let's stop it.' And yet he . . . obeyed to the end." Another participant was a housewife called Mrs. Elinor Rosenblum: "Every time I pressed the button, I died. Did you see me shaking? I was just dying here to think that I was administering shocks to the poor man."

You are probably thinking that Milgram's research was completely unethical, and such research certainly wouldn't be permitted in most countries today. However, Milgram had some arguments on his side. All of the participants were fully debriefed at the end of the experiment—the true purpose of the experiment was explained and they were told that the learner had not received any shocks. As many as 84% of the participants said they were pleased to have taken part, with only 1% expressing negative feelings. Approximately 80% of participants said that more experiments of this kind should be carried out, and 74% said that they felt they had learned something of personal importance.

ZIMBARDO

Zimbardo's (1973) Stanford Prison Experiment is another well-known study raising major ethical issues. In this study, a mock prison was set up with mock guards and mock prisoners. Some of the "guards" behaved very aggressively, and the overall level of violence in the prison increased over the days. After only 1 day in the prison, one of the prisoners became emotionally disturbed and starting screaming and crying uncontrollably. He had to be released. On the fourth day, two more prisoners showed symptoms of severe emotional disturbance and had to be released. Another prisoner developed a stress-induced rash all over his body, and also had to be released.

Savin (1973) referred to the mock prison as a "hell." He argued that, "Professors who, in pursuit of their own academic interests and professional advancement, deceive, humiliate, and otherwise mistreat their students, are subverting the atmosphere of mutual trust and intellectual honesty without which . . . neither education nor free inquiry can flourish."

Zimbardo (1973) answered his critics. He pointed out that day-long debriefing sessions were held to discuss the moral conflicts involved in the study and to reassure participants. All the participants had signed an "informed consent" form that made it clear there would be an invasion of privacy, loss of some civil rights, and harassment. Questionnaires were sent to participants of the Stanford Prison Experiment at regular intervals after the study. The replies indicated that there was a large reduction in negative feelings about the experiment as time went by.

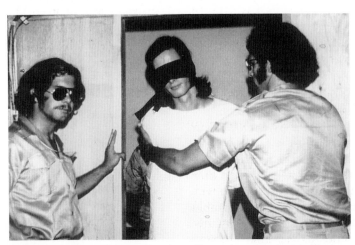

Zimbardo tried to minimize the after-effects of participation in his Stanford prison experiment by asking the participants to sign an informed consent form before the experiment began. Even so, some of the mock guards became very aggressive during the experiment, and four of the mock prisoners had to be released early.

RESOLVING ETHICAL ISSUES

What can be done to resolve the ethical issues that arise from the fact that participants in experiments often have a power deficiency relative to the experimenter? Kimmel (1996) compared the ethical codes or guidelines produced by 11 different countries. Most of them focus on three basic principles:

1. Protection of individuals from physical harm
2. Protection of individuals from psychological harm
3. Confidentiality of the data obtained from individual participants.

There is general agreement that full informed consent (i.e., participants are told in detail what will happen in the experiment and agree to it) and avoidance of deception are important in ensuring that the first two principles are achieved. However, it is sometimes difficult to do this. Small children and patients with certain mental disorders may be unable to provide informed consent, in which case it is usual for a close relative to do so. The notion that deception should always be avoided in psychological research is too stringent, because it ignores the fact that many forms of deception are entirely harmless. For example, some memory researchers are interested in incidental learning, which involves people's ability to remember information they weren't asked to remember. This can only be done by deceiving participants as to the true purpose of the experiment until the memory test has been presented. Deception is justifiable if it is essential, not potentially damaging, and the research is important scientifically.

Another important factor in ethical research is that participants are explicitly told that they can withdraw from the experiment at any time without providing a reason. Finally, there should be a debriefing at the end of the experiment, with participants being given fairly detailed information about the nature of the research.

SOCIALLY SENSITIVE RESEARCH

So far we have focused mainly on the wellbeing of those who participate in experiments. However, much research raises issues of relevance to society as a whole. This is especially so with socially sensitive research, which was defined by Sieber and Stanley (1988, p. 49) as, "studies in which there are potential social consequences or implications either directly for the participants in research or the class of individuals represented by the research." Socially sensitive research can produce risks for many people other than those directly involved as participants. For example, McCosker et al. (2001) carried out a study in which women who had been abused were interviewed. Transcribers who had the task of typing up what had been said in the interviews often became distressed. As a result, arrangements were made for them to have immediate access to crisis counseling if required.

> **Application of findings**
>
> The research carried out by psychologists such as John Bowlby and Sir Cyril Burt, among others, had a profound effect on social policy. These studies examined the role of the mother in childcare, and the development of IQ, and resulted in policies such as encouraging mothers to stay at home rather than going out to work, and the introduction of the 11-plus examination. The studies posed ethical dilemmas for the researchers because their findings could be used to manipulate human behavior and life choices, as well as adding to the knowledge-base of science.

Sieber and Stanley (1988) argued that important ethical concerns can arise with respect to four major aspects of socially sensitive research:

1. *Deciding on the research question or hypothesis to be tested*   Problems may arise if the issues studied are private or stressful (e.g., sexuality), are associated with stigmatization or fear (e.g., focusing on illegal behavior), or are regarded as relevant by extreme political groups (Lee, 1993). An example is research on homosexuality. Morin (1977) found in a review of studies on gays and lesbians published between 1967 and 1974 that 70% of these studies addressed issues such as whether homosexuals are mentally ill, ways in which homosexuality can be identified, and the causes of homosexuality. Focusing on such issues suggests that being homosexual was regarded almost like a disease that need to be "cured."

2. *The conduct of research and the treatment of participants*   This has been covered already.
3. *The institutional context*   If the institutional context is perceived to be prestigious, it may make participants feel powerless and thus affect their behavior. Milgram (1974) found there was much more obedience to authority when his research took place at Yale University rather than in a run-down office building.
4. *Interpretation and application of research findings*   An infamous example is the research of Goddard (1913). He gave intelligence tests to immigrants arriving in New York, claiming that 87% of Russians were "feeble-minded," as were 79% of Italians. He reached this ludicrous conclusion by ignoring the obvious fact that most of these immigrants had a very limited command of the English language. In spite of the woeful inadequacy of this research, it influenced the American government to reduce the level of immigration from southern and eastern Europe.

Striking a balance

We have seen the potential dangers of socially sensitive research. However, such research (while it may generate uncomfortable evidence) can produce valuable knowledge that can be used for the benefit of society as a whole. It is important to strike a balance. The American Psychological Association did this in its *Ethical Principles in the Conduct of Research with Human Participants* (1982, p. 74):

> On one side is an obligation to research participants who may not wish to see derogatory information . . . published about their valued groups. On the other side is an obligation to publish findings one believes relevant to scientific progress, an objective that in the investigator's views will contribute to the eventual understanding and amelioration of social and personal problems.

BIASES IN PSYCHOLOGY

Psychologists have frequently been accused of bias in their theoretical ideas and in their research. Thankfully, there is probably substantially less bias in psychology than used to be the case. However, it is worth considering in some detail three types of bias still to be found within psychology: gender bias; cultural bias; racial bias.

GENDER BIAS

The greatest difficulty in considering gender bias is to distinguish genuine gender differences from culturally created ones. For example, there is a common view that women are more emotional than men. This is not simply bias, because women *on average* are more emotional than men. For example, females score significantly higher than males on measures of negative affectivity (a personality dimension relating to negative emotions such as anxiety and depression) (e.g., Denollet, 2005).

Hare-Mustin and Marcek (1988) argued that there are two kinds of gender bias: **alpha bias** and **beta bias**. According to them (p. 457), "Alpha bias is the tendency to exaggerate differences; beta bias is the tendency to minimize or ignore differences." We can see these biases in the work/family literature (Febbraro, 2003). The argument that women experience much greater work/family stress than men, and so male-dominated structures need to be transformed as a result, is an example of alpha bias. Beta bias is involved when it is claimed that multiple roles (e.g., parent, spouse, worker) increase the wellbeing of women in the same way as men.

Within Western cultures, alpha bias is more common than beta bias. For example, Freud argued that girls suffer from "penis envy" when they discover that they lack a penis. He also claimed that children's superego or conscience develops when they identify with the same-sexed parent. Girls don't identify with their mother as strongly as boys identify with their father, and so allegedly girls develop weaker superegos than boys. The evidence doesn't support Freud. Hoffman (1975) found that (if anything) girls were better than boys at resisting the temptation to do what they had been told not to do.

Evolutionary psychology has often been criticized for its alpha bias. According to evolutionary psychologists, evolutionary processes explain why women typically have much more parental involvement than men in their offspring, and why men are more likely to commit adultery. There is some validity in these views, but it is also important to take account of major cultural changes. For example, Schmitt (2005) found that men scored higher than women on a questionnaire concerned with a preference for promiscuity and avoidance of emotional investment in all 48 countries studied. However, the gender difference was much smaller in those countries in which women had access to money and power.

There is some evidence for alpha bias in the diagnosis of mental disorders. Ford and Widiger (1989; see Chapter 21) argued that histrionic personality disorder (involving excessive emotionality) is regarded as a distortion of stereotypical feminine traits, whereas antisocial personality disorder (involving hostility and aggression) is a distortion of stereotypical masculine traits. Therapists were given case studies of patients with these personality disorders. Therapists were much more likely to diagnose histrionic personality disorder when the patient was allegedly female rather than male, and to diagnose antisocial personality disorder when the patient was male rather than female.

There is evidence of beta bias in experimental research, that is, a tendency to reduce or minimize gender differences. Male and female participants are used in most studies. However, there is typically no attempt to analyze the data to see whether there are significant sex differences, presumably because it is assumed that none would be found. Some sex differences probably occur simply because male experimenters treat their female participants differently from their male ones. Rosenthal (1966) reported that male experimenters were more pleasant, friendly, honest, and encouraging with female than with male participants. This led him to conclude: "Male and female subjects may, psychologically, simply not be in the same experiment at all."

Finally, we consider methodological gender bias: the design of a study biases the chances of the researcher obtaining some particular finding. Methodological gender bias is most likely to be found when the direction of gender differences depends on the precise measures of behavior that are taken. For example, Bjorkqvist, Lagerspetz, and Kaukianen (1992) found boys displayed much more physical aggression than girls, but girls showed more indirect aggression (e.g., gossiping). Armed with that knowledge, you could design a study apparently showing that boys are more aggressive than girls or vice versa!

What can be done? Bem (1993) used the concept of an "enculturated lens" to suggest that the view of gender we receive from our culture distorts how we see men and women. Bem (1993, p. 2) suggested that we should make those lenses:

visible rather than invisible, to enable us to look at the culture's gender lenses rather than through them, for it is only when Americans apprehend the more subtle and systemic ways in which the culture reproduces male power that they will finally comprehend the unfinished business of the feminists' agenda.

In sum, researchers' growing awareness of alpha bias, beta bias, and methodological gender is contributing to a reduction in these biases. It is worth remembering that, even when there are gender differences in behavior, there is still nearly always a substantial overlap in the behavior shown by males and females.

CULTURAL BIAS

We discussed cross-cultural differences in Chapter 1. In that chapter, we focused on the major distinction between collectivistic cultures in which one's key responsibility is to the group, and individualistic cultures in which people have a strong sense of personal responsibility for their own lives. Here we focus on the various approaches taken by psychologists who are interested in cultural differences.

Berry (1969) distinguished between emic constructs and etic constructs. **Emic constructs** are specific to a given culture, and so vary across cultures. In contrast, **etic constructs**

Key Terms

Emic constructs:
these are constructs that are meaningful within any given culture but vary considerably across cultures.

Etic constructs:
these are constructs that are meaningful within most or all cultures.

refer to universal factors common to all cultures. For example, the notion of the "family" is an etic construct, whereas the "nuclear family" (just parents and children) is an emic construct. According to Berry, it is common in the history of psychology for what are actually emic constructs to be mistaken for etic constructs.

The study of intelligence can be used to illustrate the above point. In the past, many psychologists argued that the same abilities of problem solving, reasoning, memory, and so on define intelligence in every culture. However, much of the evidence refutes that argument. For example, Cole, Gay, Glick, and Sharp (1971) asked adult members of the Kpelle tribe in Africa to sort familiar objects into groups. In most Western societies, people would sort the objects into categories (e.g., foods, tools). What the Kpelle tribespeople did was to sort them into functional groups (e.g., a knife with an orange, because an orange can be cut with a knife). Thus, what is regarded as intelligent behavior can differ from one culture to another. By the way, the Kpelle tribespeople showed that they could sort the objects into categories when asked to do so—they didn't do this spontaneously because they thought it was a stupid way of sorting.

An **imposed etic** is a technique or theory rooted in a researcher's own culture that is used to study other cultures. Much cross-cultural research on intelligence and personality has been based on the use of imposed etics. We have already seen an example in the field of intelligence (study by Cole et al., 1971) and here is one from the field of personality. Western research led to the identification of the Big Five personality factors (conscientiousness; agreeableness; extraversion; neuroticism; and openness; see Chapter 12). Kuo-shu, Yang, and Bond (1990) asked Taiwanese students to describe several people they knew using adjectives relating to the Big Five personality factors and adjectives taken from Chinese newspapers. Five factors emerged from an analysis of data using the adjectives from Chinese newspapers: social orientation, expressiveness, competence, self-control, and optimism. There was some agreement between the two sets of factors (e.g., agreeableness correlated +.66 with social orientation), but the overall similarity was fairly low. This suggests that personality structure in Taiwanese culture differs from that in Western cultures.

There may be profound cultural differences in ways of regarding personality. The entire Western notion of semi-permanent personality characteristics determining behavior seems to be less applicable in collectivistic cultures in which it is assumed that individuals will change to fit in with group expectations. For example, it has been found that East Asians regard personality traits as much more flexible and changeable than do people from Western cultures (Norenzayan, Choi, & Nisbett, 1999).

Berry (1969) proposed an appropriate method for cross-cultural research based on a **derived etic**. Emic studies in each of several cultures are conducted by local researchers using local techniques, and the findings are then compared. We can see this approach in action in the area of diagnosing mental disorders. DSM-IV (APA, 1994), which is American-based, focuses mainly on mental disorders common in the Western world (see Chapter 21). However, there is a short appendix in DSM-IV on culture-bound syndromes that have been found in other parts of the world. This appendix is very incomplete, because it leaves out many disorders totally ignored by DSM-IV. Here are a few examples:

- *pa-feng* (fear of wind) found in China
- *amafufunyana* (violent behavior caused by spirit possession) found in South Africa
- *brain fag* (problems in concentrating and thinking produced by excessive study—one to avoid!) found in West Africa.

In sum, there are grounds for optimism concerning cultural bias. There has been a dramatic rise in the amount of cross-cultural research, and such research is increasingly sensitive to the substantial differences from one culture to another. For example, this increased sensitivity can be seen in research on intelligence, personality, and categories of mental disorder. However, as was pointed out in Chapter 1, a full understanding of cultural differences will involve moving beyond simple categorizations of cultures (e.g., into individualistic and collectivistic).

Key Terms

Imposed etic:
this involves applying techniques and/or theories based on one culture to other cultures without considering differences among cultures; see **derived etic**.

Derived etic:
this involves researchers in various cultures developing techniques that are appropriate within their culture and then comparing the findings; see **imposed etic**.

RACIAL BIAS

Racial bias is a particularly unpleasant form of cultural bias. Howitt and Owusu-Bempah (1990) studied racial bias by considering every issue of the *British Journal of Social and Clinical Psychology* between 1962 and 1980. They were dismayed at the way in which Western personality tests such as the 16PF were used inappropriately in non-Western cultures. They pointed out that, "There were no studies which attempted to explore, for example, the Ghanaian or Chinese personality structures in their own terms rather than through Western eyes" (Howitt & Owusu-Bempah, 1990, p. 399). Since 1990, however, several researchers have systematically tried to do precisely that (see Chapter 12 and a review by Triandis & Suh, 2002).

Owusu-Bempah and Howitt (1994) claimed to have found evidence of racism in the American textbook by Atkinson, Atkinson, Smith, and Bem (1993). They pointed out that Atkinson et al. tended to categorize Western cultures together, and to do the same for non-Western ones. Owusu-Bempah and Howitt's (1994, p. 163) central point was that Atkinson et al. (1993) evaluated other cultures in relation to the technological and cultural achievements of the United States and Europe: "Cultures that fall short of this arbitrary Euro-centric standard are frequently described as 'primitive,' 'undeveloped,' or, at best, 'developing.' Religion, morality, community spirit, etc., are ignored in this racist ideological league table."

Controversy concerning racial differences has been especially heated with respect to intelligence. The starting point for controversy is that the mean difference in IQ between white and black people in the United States (and other countries) is about 15 points (favoring white people). This is only an average figure, and about 20% of black people have a higher IQ than that of the average white person. Most psychologists have assumed that the difference between white and black people is due entirely to the environmental deprivation suffered by black people, an assumption supported by much evidence (e.g., Brooks-Gunn, Klebanov, & Duncan, 1996; Mackintosh, 1986). However, some psychologists (e.g., H.J. Eysenck, 1981; Jensen, 1969) have argued that genetic factors might be involved.

This controversial issue is of very little scientific interest in that it is unlikely to tell us anything about the processes involved in human intelligence. It is based on the incorrect assumption that white and black people form separate biological groups; indeed, the concept of "race" itself has no precise scientific definition. Furthermore, it is impossible to carry out definitive research. Even H.J. Eysenck (1981, p. 79) admitted, "Can we . . . argue that genetic studies . . . give direct support to the hereditarian position? The answer must, I think, be in the negative . . . none of the studies carried out on white people alone, such as twin studies, are feasible." Finally, research on racial differences in intelligence poses major ethical issues. Extreme groups such as the British National Party have used the findings to promote racial disharmony, which is totally unacceptable.

What many psychologists (including the author) regard as a particularly offensive example of racial bias is the research of Rushton (e.g., 1990) on racial differences. He compared three racial groups he described as mongoloids (Asians), caucasoids (white people), and negroids (black people). His central argument was that mongoloids are more

Racial bias has unfortunately long been evident in some areas of psychological research. To apply a standard Western personality test to a Ghanaian community, for example, is inappropriate, given its cultural specificity. To glean meaningful results would require exploring the Ghanaian personality structures on their own terms, not from a Western perspective.

advanced than caucasoids in evolutionary terms, and caucasoids are more advanced than negroids. He claimed that evolutionary development has led to **neoteny**, which is an increase in the duration of childhood. One aspect of neoteny is an extended period of brain development, which is useful because it allows the brain to shape itself to some extent to fit the environment. The "evidence" he provided is shown in the table in the box below.

Rushton's controversial relative ranking of the mongoloid, caucasoid, and negroid races on several measures. Based on Rushton (1990).	Mongoloids	Caucasoids	Negroids
Brain weight and intelligence			
Cranial capacity	1448 cc	1408 cc	1334 cc
Brain weight at autopsy	1351 g	1336 g	1286 g
IQ test scores	107	100	85
Maturation rate			
Age of walking	Late	Medium	Early
Age of first intercourse	Late	Medium	Early
Lifespan	Long	Medium	Short
Personality and temperament			
Aggressiveness	Low	Medium	High
Cautiousness	High	Medium	Low
Dominance	Low	Medium	High
Impulsivity	Low	Medium	High
Sociability	Low	Medium	High
Reproductive effort			
Size of genitalia	Small	Medium	Large
Permissive attitudes	Low	Medium	High
Sexually transmitted diseases	Low	Medium	High
Social organization			
Law abidingness	High	Medium	Low
Marital stability	High	Medium	Low
Mental health	High	Medium	Low

Many of the "facts" contained in the table (e.g., alleged race differences in age of walking and in mental health) are open to dispute. However, the greatest criticism is that the so-called evidence can be explained in simple, uncontroversial ways. Many of the differences (even if genuine) can be explained on the basis of the greater affluence of mongoloids and caucasoids than negroids. For example, it would not be surprising if poverty and deprivation led to a short lifespan, aggressiveness, low levels of law abidance, and impaired mental health. Banyard (1999, p. 85) attacked Rushton's (1990) article as being "academically shallow but openly racist," which is fair comment.

Some recent research has focused on reducing racial bias in people taking part in experiments. Plant, Peruche, and Butz (2005) used a computerized situation in which white participants pretended they were police officers deciding rapidly whether to shoot at suspects who were black or white. There was a greater tendency to shoot at black suspects. However, extensive practice in which race was unrelated to the presence or absence of a gun eliminated that racial bias. Thus, at least some aspects of racial bias can be altered fairly easily.

In sum, there is much less racial bias in psychological research now than was the case in years gone by. That is wholly desirable. Racial bias poses very serious ethical issues, and can be exceptionally dangerous when racially biased research is used by political extremists for their own ends.

FREE WILL VS. DETERMINISM

The issue of free will versus determinism has occupied philosophers and psychologists for centuries. According to those who believe in determinism, people's actions are totally

Key Term
Neoteny: an extended period or duration of childhood resulting from evolution.

determined by the external and internal forces operating on them. An example of an *external* force would be the influence of parents when rewarding certain behaviors. An example of an *internal* force could be hormones influencing the way in which someone behaves.

Those who believe in free will argue that matters are more complicated. Most of them accept that external and internal forces exist. However, they argue that people have free will because each individual nevertheless has some ability to choose his/her own behavior. Note that the typical positions adopted by advocates of determinism and of free will are not that far apart—determinists argue that behavior is totally controlled by external and internal forces, whereas those favoring free will argue that behavior is mostly controlled by external and internal forces but with the addition of free will.

The distinction between free will and determinism can be seen if we consider the following question: "Could an individual's behavior in a given situation have been different if he/she had willed it?" Believers in free will answer that question "Yes." In contrast, advocates of determinism respond "No." Some of the main arguments for and against these positions are discussed next.

DETERMINISM

Determinists argue that a proper science of human behavior is only possible if psychologists adopt a deterministic account, according to which everything that happens has a definite cause. Free will, by definition, doesn't have a definite cause. If free will is taken into account, it becomes impossible to predict human behavior with any precision. In Chapter 1, we saw that an important aspect of the scientific approach to psychology is that it involves carrying out controlled experiments in which we manipulate certain variables (e.g., difficulty of the learning material) to observe their effects on behavior (e.g., speed of learning). It is simply not possible to manipulate free will in that way.

According to some determinists, it is often possible with other sciences to make very accurate predictions from a deterministic position (e.g., forecasting planetary motion). If determinism is regarded as not applicable to psychology, then psychology is either a very different science from physics, chemistry, and so on, or it is not really a science at all.

Chemistry can be said to be an example of a deterministic science, in that certain results can be accurately predicted. Mixing chemical "a" and chemical "b" will produce chemical "c," for example.

Hard vs. soft determinism

We can distinguish between hard determinism and soft determinism. **Hard determinism** as it applies to psychology is based on two key assumptions. First, no action or behavior is free if it must occur. Second, every human action has antecedent causes that ensure that that *particular* action is performed rather than any other. The conclusion from these assumptions is that all human actions are determined and none of them is free. Those who believe in hard determinism include B.F. Skinner and Sigmund Freud.

Hard determinism has been applied extensively in other sciences (especially physics). It seemed appropriate in the eighteenth and nineteenth centuries when most physicists believed they would eventually be able to make very precise and accurate predictions about everything relevant to physics. However, what happened in the twentieth century suggested that they were unduly optimistic. According to chaos theory (Hilborn, 1999), very small changes in initial conditions can produce major changes later on. For example, theoretically the flap of a butterfly wing in one part of the world could ultimately change the whole weather system in a different part of the world. Such a chain of events doesn't lend itself to prediction, and so we can't show that an approach based on hard determinism is appropriate.

Many (probably most) psychologists favor an alternative position labeled **soft determinism** by William James. According to this position, it is accepted that all human actions have a cause. However, it is assumed that there is a valid distinction between behavior highly constrained by the situation (that appears involuntary) and behavior only modestly constrained by the situation (that appears voluntary). For example, a child may apologize for swearing because he/she will be punished if an apology isn't forthcoming (highly constrained behavior) or because he/she is genuinely upset at causing offence (modestly constrained behavior). The underlying causes are more obvious when behavior is highly constrained by situational forces.

Evidence consistent with the views of William James was reported by Westcott (1988). Canadian students indicated how free they felt in various situations. They experienced the greatest feeling of freedom in situations involving an absence of responsibility or release from unpleasant stimulation (e.g., a nagging headache). In contrast, they felt least free in situations in which they recognized that there were limits on their behavior (e.g., when they had to curtail their desires to fit their abilities).

There are various limitations with soft determinism. First, there is excessive reliance on our subjective beliefs—the fact that some actions feel voluntary whereas others feel involuntary doesn't necessarily mean they are really different. Second, it can be argued that soft determinists want to have their cake and eat it—actions are free if they are voluntary, but those actions are still caused. This could be regarded as a confusing blend of free will and determinism.

Behaviorist and Freudian approaches

Determinism is espoused by more approaches in psychology than is free will. The behaviorists believed strongly in determinism. Skinner argued that virtually all of our behavior is determined by environmental factors. He claimed that we repeat behavior that is rewarded, and we don't repeat behavior that isn't rewarded. Other behaviorists argued that we can predict how someone will respond given knowledge of the current stimulus situation and that individual's previous conditioning history.

Skinner (1971) developed his ideas about hard determinism most fully in his book, *Beyond Freedom and Dignity*. He argued that common beliefs about free will and personal moral responsibility (which he called "dignity") were wrong and should be abandoned. According to Skinner, the way to change human behavior is by structuring the environment so that people are rewarded for behaving in desirable ways (i.e., operant conditioning) rather than by focusing on meaningless notions like freedom and dignity.

Bandura (1977, p. 27) pointed out a serious limitation with Skinner's approach: "If actions were determined solely by external rewards and punishments, people would behave like weather vanes, constantly shifting in radically different directions to conform to the whims of others." In fact, we often behave in line with long-term goals.

What is missing from Skinner's approach? Skinner focused excessively on the notion that the external environment determines behavior. However, our behavior also determines the external environment—if you don't like a television program you are watching, you switch to another channel or turn the television off. In addition, our personality helps to determine the environment in which we find ourselves and it also influences our behavior. Thus, there are multiple determinants of behavior, but Skinner largely ignored most of them.

Freud was a strong believer in hard determinism, claiming that none of our behavior "just happens" or is a result of free will. He even argued that trivial phenomena, such as missing an appointment or calling someone by the wrong name, had definite causes within the individual's motivational system. Of particular importance is what is known as the **Freudian slip**—a motivated but involuntary error in which someone says or does something revealing their true desires. Motley et al. (1983) obtained evidence of Freudian slips. Male participants had to say out loud pairs of words such as *tool–kits*, some of which could be turned into sexually explicit words. When the experimenter was an attractive female, participants tended to make Freudian slips—for example, saying *cool–tits* instead of *tool–kits*.

Freud's emphasis on determinism and rejection of free will may well owe something to the fact that he focused on individuals suffering from mental disorders (especially anxiety disorders). Such individuals are presumably highly motivated to change their

Key Term

Freudian slip:
an error in speech or action that is motivated by unconscious desires.

behavior and eliminate the disorders but are often unable to do so—this seems somewhat difficult to explain if they possess free will.

Testability

Determinism (whether soft or not) cannot really be submitted to a proper test. If it could be, then the issue of free will versus determinism would have been settled, and so would no longer exist as an issue! If all behavior is determined by internal and external forces, then in principle it should be possible to predict behavior accurately from a knowledge of these causal factors. In fact, we usually only have very limited knowledge of the internal and external forces influencing an individual's behavior. Thus, it remains only an article of faith that human behavior can eventually be predicted accurately.

Free will

Most people feel that they possess free will, in the sense that they can freely choose what to do from various options. Most people also have feelings of personal responsibility, because they feel in at least partial control of their behavior. Free will fits with society's view that people should accept responsibility for their actions and should expect to be punished (e.g., sent to prison) if they break the law.

Humanistic approach

Humanistic psychologists such as Carl Rogers and Abraham Maslow believed in free will. They argued that people exercise choice in their behavior, and they denied that people's behavior is at the mercy of outside forces. Rogers' client-centered therapy is based on the assumption that the client has free will. The therapist is called a "facilitator" precisely because his/her role is to make it easier for the client to exercise free will so as to maximize the rewardingness of the client's life. Humanistic psychologists argue that regarding human behavior as being determined by external forces is "de-humanizing" and incorrect.

Rogers claimed that we are motivated to minimize the discrepancy between our self-concept and our ideal self (the self-concept we would most like to possess). If we have free will and our behavior isn't determined by external forces, it might be expected that we would have little difficulty in doing this. The fact that there are millions of people with mental disorders who have a substantial discrepancy between the two suggests that free will either doesn't exist or is often very ineffective in producing highly desired changes.

Causality

Believers in free will have to confront various problems. First, it is hard to define precisely what is meant by free will. Second, determinism is based on the assumption that all behavior has one or more causes, and it could be argued that free will implies that behavior is random and has no cause. However, very few people would want to argue for such an extreme position. Anyone whose behavior seemed to be random would probably be classified as mentally ill or very stupid. If free will doesn't imply that behavior has no cause, then we need to know how free will helps to cause behavior. Third, most sciences are based on the assumption of determinism. It is possible that determinism applies to the natural world but doesn't apply to humans. If so, then there are enormous implications for psychology that have hardly been addressed.

Evaluation and summary

- It is not clear that it makes much sense to talk about "free will," because this assumes there is an agent (i.e., the will) that may or may not operate in an unrestrained way. As

---

Determinism vs. Free will

Determinism	Free will
Behaviorism	Humanistic approach
Freudian psychodynamics	

Do you think the cognitive psychologists fit into one or other of these lists? Can you explain your answer?

the philosopher John Locke (1632–1704) pointed out, "We may as properly say that the singing faculty sings and the dancing faculty dances as that the will chooses."

- The issue is philosophical rather than scientific, as it is impossible to design an experiment to decide whether or not free will influences human behavior. As William James (1890, p. 323) put it, "The fact is that the question of free will is insoluble on strictly psychological grounds." Thus, we can never know whether an individual's behavior in a given situation could have been different if he/she had so willed it.

- There is more common ground between advocates of determinism and free will than is generally realized. Most psychologists accept that heredity, past experience, and the present environment all influence our behavior. Although some of these factors (e.g., the environment) are external to the individual, others are internal. Most of these internal factors (such as character or personality) are the results of causal sequences stretching back into the past. The dispute then narrows to the issue of whether a solitary internal factor (variously called free will or self) is somehow immune from the influence of the past.

- There is little real incompatibility between determinism and free will at all. According to determinists, it is possible in principle to show that an individual's actions are caused by a sequence of physical activities in the brain. If free will (e.g., conscious thinking and decision making) forms part of that sequence, it is possible to believe in free will and human responsibility at the same time as holding to a deterministic position. This would not be the case if free will is regarded as an intruder forcing its way into the sequence of physical activities in the brain. However, there are no good grounds for adopting this position. Thus, the entire controversy between determinism and free will may be somewhat artificial.

REDUCTIONISM

Key Term

Reductionism:
the notion that psychology can ultimately be reduced to more basic sciences such as physiology or biochemistry.

According to Reber (1993), **reductionism** "is the philosophical point of view that complex phenomena are best understood by a componential analysis which breaks the phenomena down into their fundamental, elementary aspects." Within the context of psychology, the term "reductionism" refers to several somewhat different theoretical approaches. First (and most importantly), there is the belief that the phenomena of psychology can potentially be explained within the framework of more basic sciences or disciplines (e.g., physiology; biochemistry) (physiological reductionism). Second, there is the assumption that complex forms of behavior can be explained with reference to relatively simple forms of behavior such as stimulus–response associations (experimental reductionism). Third, there is the notion that the complexities of human cognition can be compared to computer functioning (machine reductionism). Fourth, there is the assumption that human behavior can be understood with reference to other, less complex, species (animal reductionism). We will consider each of these types of reductionism in turn.

Reductionism: the analysis of complex things into simple constituents.

PHYSIOLOGICAL REDUCTIONISM

According to physiological reductionism, we need to consider psychology in the light of other scientific disciplines. Scientific disciplines can be regarded as being organized in a hierarchical way, with the more general sciences at the top and the more specific and precise ones at the bottom. Some reductionists argue that sciences towards the top of the hierarchy will eventually be replaced by those towards the bottom. Here is an example of such a hierarchy:

- Sociology: The science of groups and societies.
- Psychology: The science designed to understand human and animal behavior.
- Physiology: The science of the functional working of the healthy body.
- Biochemistry: The science of the chemistry of the living organism.

Physiological and psychological explanations
Neurology and biochemistry underlie all behavior. What happens when a person sees a sunset? The physiological explanation would be that light reflected from the landscape forms an image on the retina, which is converted into a neural signal and transmitted to the brain, and so on. No one disputes that this is true, and the process is absolutely essential, but does it give a full and adequate explanation of what is going on? A psychological explanation would probably include the personal and social relevance of the experience, which many would argue are of equal value.

Of particular importance, all psychological processes are accompanied by physiological processes. Understanding those physiological processes (especially those associated with brain activity) might assist us in understanding human behavior. At the very least, psychological theories need to be consistent or compatible with relevant findings from physiology (and biochemistry).

There are various problems with physiological reductionism. First, much human behavior does not seem to lend itself to an explanation in terms of basic physiological processes. For example, if you wanted to predict how various people were going to vote in a forthcoming election, you wouldn't engage in a detailed physiological examination of their brains! Second, psychology typically describes the *processes* involved in performing some activity, whereas physiology focuses more on the *structures* involved (Valentine, 1992). Thus, psychologists are interested in *what* and *how* questions, whereas physiologists are interested in *where* questions. Third, there are no cases in which psychological phenomena have been fully understood on the basis of findings from disciplines such as physiology or biochemistry. What has happened is that findings from disciplines such as physiology have often added to our understanding. Examples include research on sexual motivation and hunger (see Chapter 3).

EXPERIMENTAL REDUCTIONISM

According to experimental reductionism, complex psychological phenomena can be reduced to simple constituent parts. The behaviorists were reductionists in this sense. They argued that many complex forms of behavior (e.g., use of language; problem solving) can be explained by assuming that they involve the use of numerous stimulus–response units and by assigning key importance to rewards or reinforcements. It is generally accepted that our behavior is influenced by rewards, but few now believe that that influence is as great as was believed by the behaviorists.

Experimental reductionism has often not fared well. It has been found consistently that simple explanations of behavior in virtually all areas of psychology have proved inadequate, and have had to be replaced by more complex ones. For example, Skinner (1957) tried to explain the complexities of language acquisition by arguing that children produce words and sentences that are rewarded or reinforced. As we will see in Chapter 10, the processes involved in language are so complex that Skinner's reductionist approach falls well short of providing a satisfactory explanation.

Experimental reductionism has proved most successful when it comes to designing experiments. As we saw in Chapter 1, use of the experimental method consists of designing well-controlled experiments. This typically involves ignoring much of the complexity of everyday life in order to expose participants to very limited situations under laboratory conditions. The advantages and disadvantages of experimental reductionism can be seen clearly if we consider two forms of validity. First, there is **internal validity**, which refers to the validity of an experiment within the context in which

Key Term
Internal validity: the validity of an experiment in terms of the context in which it is carried out, including the extent to which its findings can be replicated; also the extent to which research findings are genuine and can be regarded as being caused by the **independent variable**; see **external validity**.

it is carried out. Well-controlled experiments that produce findings that other researchers can replicate or repeat possess high internal validity. Second, there is **external validity**, which refers to the applicability of the findings from an experiment to other, everyday situations. In essence, well-controlled experiments based on experimental reductionism generally have high internal validity, but this is often achieved at the expense of external validity.

MACHINE REDUCTIONISM

Humans often try to understand the unknown in terms of the known. One way of doing that is by trying analogies or comparisons between what is known and what is not known. For example, numerous theorists have tried to understand the functioning of the brain or mind (especially its memory system) by comparing it to a wide variety of objects (this is machine reductionism). As Roediger (1980) noted, the brain has been conceptualized as a switchboard, a gramophone, a tape recorder, a library, a conveyor belt, and an underground or subway map. In recent decades, however, cognitive psychologists have most often drawn an analogy between the human brain and computers. This has two large and obvious advantages over previous analogies. First, computers are very flexible and versatile, and can be programmed in progressively more sophisticated ways to approximate more closely human information processing. Second, computers are capable of very complex functioning. For example, a chess program called Deep Blue managed to beat the then world chess champion Garry Kasparov in May 1997.

The ever more sophisticated and human-like cognitive capabilities of computers are exemplified by the computer program Deep Junior that in 2003 played a 6-game match against Garry Kasparov that resulted in a 3–3 tie with the ex-world chess champion.

Newell and Simon (1972) provided a successful example of machine reductionism with their approach to understanding problem solving (see Chapter 9). They started by asking people to think aloud while they solved various problems. Newell and Simon used the information so acquired to devise a computer program called General Problem Solver that solves problems in ways resembling those used by humans. However, there are some differences. General Problem Solver is better than humans at remembering past moves on a problem, but it is worse than humans at forward planning.

In spite of the successes of the computer analogy to human thinking, there are some serious limitations of this approach. First, computer programs often function in ways very different from those of people. The chess program Deep Blue plays chess outstandingly well. However, it does so by considering several million moves every second, which is radically different from the thought processes of human grandmasters.

Second, the claim that the functioning of some computer programs closely resembles that of neurons in the brain is hotly disputed (see Eysenck & Keane, 2005). More specifically, the brain contains huge numbers of interconnected neurons, and it is argued that the basic processing units within connectionist networks (a type of computer program) resemble biological neurons. However, the number of such processing units is typically a tiny fraction of the number of neurons in the human brain. In addition, each neuron in the human brain is connected to only about 3% of neurons in the surrounding square millimeter of cortex (Churchland & Sejnowski, 1991), which is substantially less than the massive interconnectivity often found within connectionist networks.

Third, human cognitive functioning involves an interplay between a cognitive system (the Pure Cognitive System) and a biological system (the Regulatory System)

Cognitive science

The precision of detail needed to mimic human thought processes using computers is demonstrated by a story that may or may not be an account of a real experiment. A group of cognitive scientists wanted to see if a computer-controlled robot could be programmed to mimic a human being building a pile of wooden bricks. However, the first few attempts failed because someone forgot to include the effects of gravity in the computer program, and the robot tried to begin the pile at the top! No human being would make such a mistake; we all understand about gravity from a very early age, but remembering to include every single item of such knowledge in a computer program is a huge task.

Key Term

External validity:
the validity of an experiment outside the research situation itself; the extent to which its findings are applicable to everyday life and generalize across populations, locations, measures, and times; see **internal validity**.

(Norman, 1980). Much of the activity of the Pure Cognitive System is determined by the various needs of the Regulatory System, including the need for survival, for food and water, and for protection of oneself and one's family. Computer programs focus on the Pure Cognitive System and virtually ignore the key role played by the Regulatory System.

Fourth, it is difficult to imagine computers having consciousness or experiencing emotion, and I am not aware of any computer programs showing either of these characteristics. This pessimistic conclusion has been challenged by some experts. Sloman (1997) argued that it should be possible to design a machine that could fall in love. According to him, what we would need to do is the following: "Read what poets and novelists and playwrights say about love, and ask yourself: what kinds of information processing mechanisms are presupposed." For example, if X is in love with Y, we would expect X to find it hard to think of anything except Y. Personally, I will be amazed if anyone ever succeeds in devising a machine that can fall in love.

CONCLUSIONS

There are many forms of reductionism, including physiological reductionism, experimental reductionism, and machine reductionism. All of these forms of reductionism have proved useful, but they all suffer from important limitations. Physiological findings can enhance our understanding of psychological phenomena, but cannot replace the need for psychological explanations. Experimental reductionism permits the designing and carrying out of well-controlled experiments, but often fails to ensure that the findings obtained generalize to everyday life. Machine reductionism based on the computer analogy has provided useful insights into human thinking, but it is limited in part because motivational and emotional factors are generally ignored.

Chapter Summary

Psychodynamic approach

- Psychoanalysis consists of various theories about human emotional development but is also a form of therapy.
- According to Freud, the mind is divided into three parts (id, ego, and superego) that are often in conflict with each other.
- Psychoanalysis as a form of therapy is designed to allow patients to achieve insight into the true nature of their problems. Many of these problems stem from traumatic events in childhood.
- Many of Freud's general ideas are still generally accepted. However, most of his more specific ideas are either untestable or have been disproved.

Behaviorism

- The behaviorists claimed that most behavior could be explained in terms of environmental rather than genetic factors.
- According to Skinner, learning and behavior are under the control of reward or reinforcement.
- The behaviorists had a lasting influence on psychology through their emphasis on careful observation of behavior in controlled settings and the development of behavior therapy.
- The behaviorists greatly underestimated the impact of internal factors (e.g., past knowledge; goals; heredity) on behavior.

Humanistic approach

- Humanistic psychologists favored the use of phenomenology (reporting of pure experience) and were skeptical of the scientific approach.
- Maslow argued that the need for self-actualization (fulfilling one's entire potential) is of central importance to many people.

- Rogers developed client-centered therapy, which required the therapist to display unconditional positive regard, genuineness, and empathy.
- Humanistic psychologists focused on issues of major concern to people, and client-centered therapy is moderately effective in treating less severe disorders.
- Client-centered therapy is ineffective in treating severe disorders, and the unscientific nature of humanistic psychology has seen its influence wane considerably.

Cognitive approach

- Cognitive psychologists carry out well-controlled laboratory experiments to understand processes such as attention, perception, learning, language, and problem solving.
- Two major determinants of cognitive psychology are cognitive neuropsychology (studying cognition in brain-damaged patients) and cognitive neuroscience (using brain imaging to identify the brain areas associated with specific cognitive processes).
- Cognitive psychology (in conjunction with cognitive neuropsychology and cognitive neuroscience) has proved very effective at enhancing our understanding of human cognition. It led to the development of cognitive therapy, which is an effective form of treatment for anxiety disorders and depression.
- The behavioral and brain-imaging data collected by cognitive researchers provide only indirect measures of underlying cognitive processes. The use of laboratory experiments raises issues concerning ecological validity.

Evolutionary psychology

- According to evolutionary psychologists, natural selection favors individuals who maximize replication of their genes. This is achieved in part by helping those with whom we share our genes.
- Evolutionary psychologists also assume that the greater parental investment of females than of males has led to various gender differences (e.g., in sexual attitudes and behavior).
- As predicted by the theory, most people are more willing to help close relatives than other people. Predicted differences in sexual attitudes and behavior between males and females have also been reported (see Chapter 3).
- It is difficult to test most of the hypotheses of evolutionary psychologists, and they underestimate the importance of social and cultural factors.

Ethical issues in psychology

- Milgram's research on obedience to authority and Zimbardo's Stanford prison experiment are now regarded as unethical, in part because of the stress and discomfort experienced by the participants.
- Full informed consent, avoidance of deception, and the participant's right to withdraw at any point are all very important features of ethical research.
- Ethical issues are posed by socially sensitive research that can have damaging consequences for people not directly involved in the experiment.
- What is ethically acceptable depends in part on the likely scientific value of the proposed research.

Biases in psychology

- Gender bias can involve exaggerating gender differences (alpha bias) or minimizing them (beta bias). Alpha bias is found in the work of Freud and evolutionary psychologists.
- There is also methodological gender bias—the design of an experiment can bias the nature of the gender differences likely to be found.
- Much cultural bias occurs because researchers mistakenly believe that emic constructs (culture-specific) are actually etic ones (universal).
- Cross-cultural research on intelligence and personality has often involved the use of imposed etics (use of culture-specific tests).

- The claim that black people are genetically less intelligent than white ones is an example of racial bias. The issue is of little or no scientific interest, and raises serious ethical issues.
- Rushton claims that mongoloids are more evolutionarily developed than caucasoids, who in turn are more developed than negroids. This claim is unsupported by evidence and is racist.

Free will vs. determinism

- Determinists (e.g., Freud; Skinner) argue that behavior is totally controlled by external and internal factors, whereas advocates of free will claim that behavior is also controlled by free will.
- Soft determinists claim that there is a valid distinction between behavior highly constrained by the situation and behavior only modestly constrained by the situation.
- Determinism seems more consistent than free will with the scientific approach, but it cannot be submitted to a proper test.
- It is difficult to define "free will" precisely. If free will means that we can freely choose our own behavior, it is hard to see why millions of people (e.g., those with mental disorders) feel unable to control their behavior.
- If free will forms part of the sequence of physical activities in the brain causing an individual's actions, then it would be possible to believe in free will and in determinism at the same time.

Reductionism

- According to physiological reductionism, more general sciences such as sociology and psychology will eventually be replaced by more specific sciences such as physiology and biochemistry.
- Physiological findings have often enhanced our understanding of psychological phenomena, but that does not eliminate the need for psychological explanations.
- According to experimental reductionism, complex psychological phenomena can be reduced to simple constituent parts by producing simple explanations or by carrying out simple experiments.
- Simple explanations of complex phenomena (e.g., by the behaviorists) are generally oversimplified. Simple, well-controlled experiments often have good internal validity but poor external validity.
- According to machine reductionism, human functioning can be understood with reference to machines (especially computers).
- Computers can function in flexible, complex ways. However, their functioning is often very different to that of humans, they lack consciousness, and they are generally uninfluenced by motivational and emotional factors.

Further Reading

- Glassman, W.E. (1995). *Approaches to psychology* (2nd ed.). Buckingham, UK: Open University Press. This book provides a good overview of historically important theoretical approaches in psychology.
- Jarvis, M. (2000). *Theoretical approaches in psychology*. London: Routledge. This is a very readable introduction to theoretical approaches that have been influential in the history of psychology.
- Valentine, E.R. (1992). *Conceptual issues in psychology* (2nd ed.). London: Routledge. Liz Valentine provides a balanced approach to some of the key conceptual and philosophical issues within psychology.

INTRODUCTION TO
Biological Psychology

B iological psychology (often shortened to biopsychology) has been defined as "the study of behavior and experience in terms of genetics, evolution, and physiology, especially the physiology of the nervous system" (Kalat, 1998, p. 1). More generally, biological psychology involves using a biological approach to study psychology and to obtain an understanding of human (and animal) behavior.

Within the field of biological psychology, Pinel (1997) identified five main approaches. First, there is physiological psychology. The key aspect of this approach is that there is direct manipulation of the nervous system of nonhuman animals to observe the effects of such manipulation on the neural mechanisms of behavior. This direct manipulation can take various forms, including surgery, electrical stimulation, or the use of chemicals. For obvious ethical reasons, most of the interventions discussed above simply can't be used with human participants. There is some controversy concerning the relevance of research on nonhuman species for an understanding of human functioning. We can generally only be confident that findings from nonhuman animals are applicable to humans when there is clear supporting evidence from human research.

Second, there is psychopharmacology, which is concerned with the effects of various drugs on neural activity and on behavior. The emphasis in much psychopharmacological research is on the development of drugs having beneficial effects and minimal adverse side effects. However, some pharmacologists study the effects of drugs in order to shed light on the detailed chemical processes occurring in the brain.

Third, there is psychophysiology, which involves studying the relationship between physiological activity on the one hand and psychological processes on the other hand. Most psychophysiological research is carried out on humans. Psychophysiologists make use of a wide range of measures, including heart rate, electrical conductance of the skin, pupil dilation, and the electroencephalogram (EEG; based on recordings of electrical brain activity measured at the surface of the scalp). In recent years, several brain-imaging techniques have been developed (see the "Introduction to cognitive psychology," Part II).

Fourth, there is neuropsychology, which is mainly concerned with assessing the effects of brain damage in humans on their psychological functioning and behavior. Neuropsychologists often try to determine which part or parts of the brain have been damaged, using a variety of techniques including magnetic resonance imaging (MRI; see the Introduction to cognitive psychology). There are various similarities between neuropsychology and cognitive neuropsychology (see the Introduction to cognitive psychology). Other neuropsychologists study neurologically intact individuals with a view to understanding brain mechanisms of behavior. For example, Annett (e.g., 1999) has carried out much research on differences in cognition between people who are left-handed and those who are right-handed.

Fifth, there is comparative psychology, in which similarities and differences in behavior across various species are considered. Comparative psychologists also compare

Austrian botanist Gregor J. Mendel (1822–1884) photographed circa 1880.

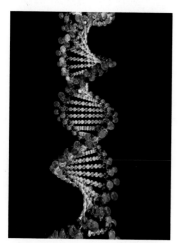

Computer artwork of part of a strand of DNA. The DNA molecule carries genetic information in all cellular organisms. It consists of two strands wound around each other in a double helix.

different species with respect to their evolutionary history and the current adaptiveness of their behavior, although their underlying interest is often in trying to use information about other species to try to explain human behavior.

GENETICS AND BEHAVIOR

One of the most influential of current approaches is evolutionary psychology (see Chapter 2), which stems from Darwin's theory of natural selection. Evolutionary psychologists argue that evolutionary pressures have influenced the human mind and behavior. Darwin (1859) argued that offspring tend to resemble their parents more than other members of the same species through inheritance. However, he couldn't answer the question, "How are characteristics passed on from one generation to the next?" By one of those quirks of history, Darwin actually had in his possession a manuscript (unread or unappreciated) containing the answer to that question (namely, through genetic inheritance)! The manuscript had been sent to him by an obscure monk called Gregor Mendel (1822–1884), whose work is discussed below.

Mendel studied inheritance in pea plants. He started by cross-breeding the offspring of pea plants that produced only green seeds with the offspring of pea plants producing only yellow seeds. All of the first-generation offspring had green seeds. However, when the first-generation offspring were bred with each other, about three-quarters of the second-generation offspring had green seeds and one-quarter had yellow seeds. The characteristic or trait found in all the first-generation offspring and three-quarters of the second-generation offspring is called a dominant trait, and depends on a dominant gene. The trait found in one-quarter of the second-generation offspring is called a recessive trait, and depends on a recessive gene. In humans, for example, brown eyes are dominant and blue eyes are recessive.

How did Mendel explain his findings? He argued that there are two kinds of factors (e.g., green-seed factor and yellow-seed factor) for simple traits that can occur only in one of two forms. Such inherited factors are now called genes. Each organism possesses two inherited factors or genes for each simple trait. In the case of pea plants, they can have two yellow-seed genes, two green-seed genes, or one gene of each type.

Mendel then assumed that offspring receive one gene at random from each of their "parents." When the two genes are identical (e.g., both yellow-seed genes), then the offspring will have the trait associated with those genes. When the two seeds differ (e.g., one yellow-seed gene and one green-seed gene), then the offspring will have the trait associated with the dominant gene. Mendel's findings suggest that there is an important distinction between the **genotype** (underlying genetic potential) and the **phenotype** (observable traits or characteristics). As we have seen, Mendel found that one-quarter of the offspring resulting from breeding with green seeds had yellow seeds. This represents an important difference between the phenotype (observed yellow seeds) and the genotype (one green-seed gene and one yellow-seed gene).

Genetic transmission in humans is often far more complicated than what happens with pea plants. Most human traits (e.g., intelligence) are controlled by a large number of different genes rather than being controlled by a single gene. In addition, many genes don't function in a dominant or recessive way. Some genes are additive (with all genes contributing towards the offspring's phenotype), whereas others have interactive effects on each other. Other genes have **partial penetrance**, meaning that they influence an individual's life only in certain circumstances. For example, genes increasing the risk of alcoholism will not influence someone living in a culture in which alcohol is not available.

What is the nature of genes? In essence, chromosomes are strands of deoxyribonucleic acid (DNA) bearing the genes. Chromosomes appear in matched pairs, with humans having 23 pairs of chromosomes in each of their body cells. Each strand of DNA consists of a sequence of four nucleotide bases (adenine, thymine, guanine, and cytosine) arranged in a particular order, and these strands essentially form the genetic code. The two strands of DNA forming each chromosome are coiled around each other in a double helix (spiral) pattern. These strands are bonded together, with guanine on one strand binding with cytosine on the other strand, and adenine binding with thymine.

BEHAVIORAL GENETICS

Our knowledge of genetic transmission allows us to understand the extent of genetic similarity (or degree of relatedness) between the members of a family. We know that children share 50% of their genes with each of their parents, that siblings also share 50% of their genetic material with each of their parents, that the figure is 25% for grandparents and grandchildren, and that it is 12.5% for first cousins. Monozygotic (identical) twins have the same genetic make-up, whereas dizygotic (fraternal) twins share only 50% of their genetic make-up. This is because identical twins come from the same zygote (fertilized egg cell) which splits post-fertilization, whereas fraternal twins come from two different eggs.

NERVOUS SYSTEM

The nervous system contains all the nerve cells in the body. As we will see, the various parts of the nervous system are specialized for different functions. The nervous system itself is made up of between 15 and 20 billion neurons (cells specialized to conduct electrical impulses). The nervous system itself is divided into two main sub-systems:

- *Central nervous system.* This consists of the brain and the spinal cord; it is protected by bone and by fluid circulating around it.
- *Peripheral nervous system.* This consists of all the other nerve cells in the body. It is divided into the somatic nervous system, which is concerned with voluntary movements of skeletal muscles (those attached to our bones), and the autonomic nervous system, which is concerned with involuntary movements of nonskeletal muscles (e.g., those of the heart).

CENTRAL NERVOUS SYSTEM

We will focus our coverage of the central nervous system on the brain. In order to understand the brain, we must learn about its structure and about the functions of the various parts. It has proved easier to study structure than function. Only fairly recently have technological advances allowed us to identify the functions of different brain areas by observing the brain in action (see the Introduction to cognitive psychology).

In view of the importance of the brain, it is not surprising that it is the most protected part of the body. Both the brain and the spinal cord are encased in bone and covered by protective membranes. In addition, there is the blood–brain barrier. This is a protective mechanism permitting blood to flow freely to the brain, but ensuring that most substances in the bloodstream do not reach the brain tissue.

The brain is divided into three main regions (see the figure on the following page): hindbrain, midbrain, and forebrain. These terms refer to their location in the embryo's nervous system, and do not indicate clearly the relative position of the different brain regions in adults. The hindbrain is at the back of the brain, and consists of the medulla, the pons, and the cerebellum. The medulla is involved in the control of various crucial functions such as breathing, vomiting, salivation, and the regulation of the cardiovascular system. The pons and medulla together contain the reticular formation, which is involved in controlling levels of arousal and is also of relevance to consciousness. The cerebellum is involved in the control of balance and of movement.

The midbrain is relatively smaller in mammals (including humans) than it is in reptiles, birds, and fish. It is

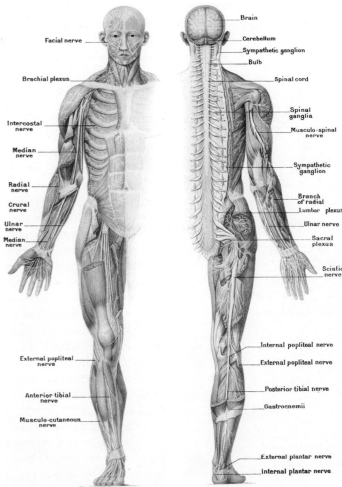

The nervous system within a human male figure. The brain and spinal cord constitute the central nervous system. The CNS integrates all nervous activities. There are 31 pairs of nerves that branch off the spinal cord into a network; they carry nerve impulses from the CNS to various structures of the body and back from these structures to the CNS. Nerves outside the CNS are part of the peripheral nervous system.

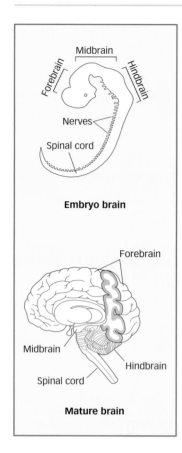

Embryo brain

Forebrain

Midbrain

Hindbrain

Spinal cord

Mature brain

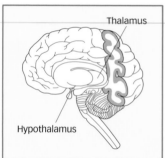

Thalamus

Hypothalamus

divided into the tectum or roof and the tegmentum, which is the middle part of the midbrain. The tectum consists of the superior colliculus and the inferior colliculus, both of which are used as routes for sensory information.

The forebrain is easily the largest and most important division of the human brain. About 90% of the human cerebral cortex is neocortex (literally new cortex), which consists of six layers. The cerebral cortex plays a crucial role in thinking, the use of language, perception, and numerous other cognitive abilities (see the cognitive section in this book). It is a continuous sheet resembling a crunched-up blanket stuffed into a box (David Carey, personal communication). Parts of the forebrain lie underneath the cerebral cortex. Two series of interconnected structures in this part of the brain are the limbic system and the basal ganglia motor system. The limbic system consists of various structures including the amygdala, the septum, the hippocampus, the hypothalamus, the cingulate cortex, the fornix, and the mammillary body. The main functions of the limbic system are to regulate several kinds of motivated behavior, including eating, aggression, avoidance behavior, and sexual behavior, and emotions such as anger and anxiety (see Chapter 4). The basal ganglia consist of the striatum, globus pallidus, and the amygdala (which is often regarded as part of this system as well as of the limbic system). The basal ganglia assist in the production of voluntary motor responses.

The thalamus and the hypothalamus are both important structures. The hypothalamus is much smaller than the thalamus. It is situated below the thalamus (see the figure on the left). The hypothalamus is involved in the control of several functions such as body temperature, hunger, and thirst. It is also involved in the control of sexual behavior. Finally, the hypothalamus plays an important role in the control of the endocrine (hormonal) system. For example, the hypothalamus is directly connected to the anterior pituitary gland, which has been described as the body's "master gland."

What about the thalamus? It acts as a relay station passing signals on to higher brain centers. For example, the medial geniculate nucleus receives signals from the inner ear and sends them to the primary auditory cortex. In similar fashion, the lateral geniculate nucleus receives information from the eye and sends it to the primary visual cortex, and the ventral posterior nucleus receives somatosensory (bodily sensation) information and sends it to the primary somatosensory cortex. In addition, there are projections in the opposite direction, proceeding for example from the primary visual cortex down to the thalamus.

PERIPHERAL NERVOUS SYSTEM

The peripheral nervous system consists of all the nerve cells in the body not contained within the central nervous system. It consists of two parts: the somatic nervous system and the autonomic nervous system (see the figure on the following page for a summary of their functions). The somatic nervous system is concerned with interactions with the external environment, whereas the autonomic nervous system is concerned with the body's internal environment. Most of the nerves of the peripheral nervous system project from the spinal cord. Some spinal nerves are involved in receiving signals from (and sending them to) skeletal muscles within the somatic nervous system, whereas others receive signals from (and send them to) the internal organs within the autonomic nervous system. In addition, there are connections between the central nervous system and the peripheral nervous system via 12 pairs of cranial nerves.

The somatic nervous system consists of afferent nerves that carry signals from the eyes, ears, skeletal muscles, and the skin to the central nervous system, and efferent nerves that carry signals from the central nervous system to the skeletal muscles, skin, and so on.

The autonomic nervous system is concerned with regulating the functioning of the internal environment, including the heart, stomach, lungs, intestines, and various glands (e.g., pancreas, salivary glands, and adrenal medulla). It is called the autonomic nervous system because many of the activities it controls are autonomous or self-regulating (e.g., digestion). These activities do not require conscious effort on our part, and continue even when we are asleep. As is the case with the somatic nervous system, the autonomic nervous system consists of afferent nerves and efferent nerves. The afferent nerves carry sensory signals from the internal organs to the central nervous system, whereas the efferent nerves carry motor signals from the central nervous system to the internal organs.

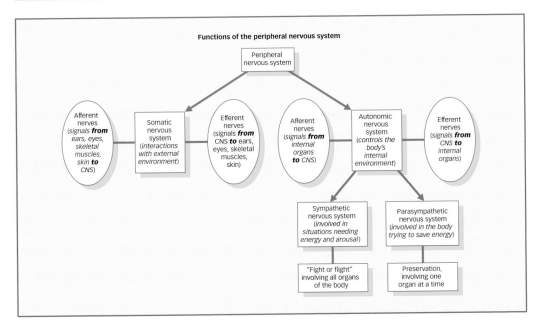

The autonomic nervous system is divided into the sympathetic nervous system and the parasympathetic nervous system. Nearly all the internal organs of the body receive signals from both sympathetic and parasympathetic nerves. In general terms, the effects of activation of the sympathetic and parasympathetic nervous systems are opposite. The sympathetic nervous system is called into play in situations needing energy and arousal (e.g., fight or flight). For example, the body's initial response to a stressor involves the sympathetic adrenal medullary system (see Chapter 4). What happens is that epinephrine and norepinephrine (adrenaline and noradrenaline) are secreted, which causes increased arousal of the sympathetic nervous system. The sympathetic nervous system produces increased heart rate, reduced activity within the stomach, pupil dilation (expansion), and relaxation of the bronchi of the lungs. In contrast, the parasympathetic nervous system is involved when the body is trying to save energy. The parasympathetic nervous system produces decreased heart rate, increased activity within the stomach, pupil contraction, and constriction of the bronchi of the lungs. In general terms, the sympathetic nervous system tends to act as a whole, whereas the parasympathetic nervous system often affects only one organ at a time.

The sympathetic and parasympathetic nervous systems often operate in opposition to each other. However, there are some exceptions (Atkinson et al., 1993). For example, the sympathetic nervous system is very active in states of fear or excitement, and yet parasympathetic activity can cause people who are fearful or excited to have an involuntary discharge of their bladder or bowels. Another example is sex in the male. Parasympathetic activity is required to obtain an erection, whereas sympathetic activity is needed for ejaculation.

ORGANIZATION OF THE BIOLOGICAL PSYCHOLOGY SECTION

There are three chapters in this section of the book. In Chapter 3, we discuss various approaches to motivation. Human motivation is complex, and depends on cognitive factors as well as on biological ones. However, biological factors are clearly of considerable importance in hunger and sexual motivation, and these factors are considered in detail. In Chapter 4, we discuss emotion, stress, and coping. There is substantial evidence that cognitive factors are important in determining the emotions we experience, how stressed we feel, and how we cope with stress. However, it is impossible to understand emotion or stress thoroughly without considering the biological (especially physiological) processes involved. In Chapter 5, states of awareness are analyzed, focusing on consciousness, sleep, and dreaming. Different physiological processes are associated with these various states of awareness, and are discussed in detail in this chapter.

Contents

Human motivation

The study of motivation is of major importance to developing a full understanding of human behavior. Motivation helps to determine how well we do academically, the kind of job we have, how successfully we perform that job, and how we choose to spend our leisure time. Motivation is very relevant to the following:

- *Direction of behavior*: The goal or goals being pursued.
- *Intensity of behavior*: The amount of effort, concentration, and so on invested in behavior.
- *Persistence of behavior*: The extent to which a goal is pursued until it is reached.

All of the above ingredients are to be found in Colman's (2001, p. 464) definition of "motivation": "A driving force or forces responsible for the initiation, persistence, direction, and vigor of goal-directed behavior." For example, if someone is very hungry, we would expect their behavior to be directed towards the goals of finding and eating food. In addition, we would expect them to put in much effort to find food, and we would expect them to keep looking for food until they found some.

It is difficult to achieve a good understanding of human motivation. There are two main reasons for this. First, human beings are motivated by a bewildering range of goals, and these goals vary between the very short-term (e.g., have an Indian meal) and the life-long (e.g., become the most successful psychologist in the world). Most of us are motivated to eat and drink, to find an attractive sexual partner, to have a high level of self-esteem, to be liked by other people, to earn money, and to enjoy life. Some of us are motivated to become a great athlete, to write books, to sail around the world, or to become a celebrity.

Second, motivation typically involves processes operating at several different levels. For example, consider hunger drive and eating behavior. Eating behavior depends in part on basic physiological processes. However, it also depends on various psychological factors, such as the habit of eating at certain times (e.g., around mid-day) and the desire to lose weight.

In this chapter, we start by considering a very general approach to motivation, namely, Maslow's (1954) hierarchical theory. After that, we focus on a few of the main forms of motivation. First, we discuss the factors underlying hunger and eating behavior. Second, we consider processes associated with sex motivation and sexual behavior. Third, we turn the spotlight on work motivation, identifying some of the factors influencing success at work.

MASLOW'S HIERARCHICAL THEORY

Need theories provide a comprehensive approach to motivation. Most need theories make two key assumptions:

1. Humans have a wide range of needs that motivate them.
2. The particular needs of greatest importance to a given individual vary over time.

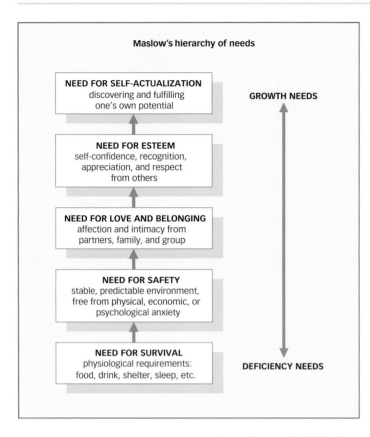

Maslow's hierarchy of needs

NEED FOR SELF-ACTUALIZATION
discovering and fulfilling
one's own potential

GROWTH NEEDS

NEED FOR ESTEEM
self-confidence, recognition,
appreciation, and respect
from others

NEED FOR LOVE AND BELONGING
affection and intimacy from
partners, family, and group

NEED FOR SAFETY
stable, predictable environment,
free from physical, economic, or
psychological anxiety

NEED FOR SURVIVAL
physiological requirements:
food, drink, shelter, sleep, etc.

DEFICIENCY NEEDS

The best-known need theory is Maslow's (1954, 1970) hierarchical theory. According to this theory, we have a hierarchy of needs (see the figure on the left). Physiological needs or requirements (e.g., those for food, drink, air, and sleep) are at the bottom level of the hierarchy. Safety needs are at the next level; they include the need for security, freedom from fear, for protection, and for structure and order. In the middle of the hierarchy are needs for affection and intimacy. Maslow argued that there are two types of love: D-love and B-love. D-love is based on deficiency. It is selfish in that it involves taking rather than giving. However, we need to experience D-love before moving on to B-love, which is a "love for the being of another person." B-love is unselfish, and is based on a growth need rather than on deficiency.

The next level moving up the hierarchy is the need for esteem. There are two aspects to this: (1) the need for admiration and respect; and (2) the need to regard oneself as competent and successful. Finally, the need for **self-actualization** (fulfilling one's potential) is at the top of the hierarchy.

Maslow regarded all the needs towards the bottom of the hierarchy as deficiency needs, because they are designed to reduce inadequacies or deficiencies. Needs towards the top of the hierarchy (e.g., self-actualization) represent growth needs and are designed to promote personal growth. The key notion of self-actualization was described as follows by Maslow (1954): "A musician must make music, an artist must paint, a poet must write, if he [sic] is to be ultimately at peace with himself. What a man can be, he must be. This need we may call self-actualization." Self-actualized individuals (examples are Abraham Lincoln and Albert Einstein) typically possess various characteristics. These include: an acceptance of themselves; spontaneity; the need for privacy; resistance to cultural influences; empathy; profound interpersonal relationships; a democratic character structure; creativeness; and a philosophical sense of humour.

How can we assess self-actualization? Maslow (1962) focused on peak experiences. **Peak experiences** involve experiencing the world totally for what it is with accompanying feelings of euphoria, wonder, and awe. According to Maslow (1968, p. 111), "All peak experiences may be fruitfully understood as completions-of-the-act . . . or complete

Key Terms

Self-actualization:
the need to discover and
fulfill one's own potential.

Peak experiences:
heightened experiences
associated with feelings of joy
and wonder.

Self-concept

Self-actualization

Ideal self

orgasm, or as total discharge, culmination, climax, consummation, emptying or finishing." Peak experiences occur most often during sexual intercourse or when listening to music, and sometimes when doing both at the same time. Maslow found that self-actualized individuals had more peak experiences than other people. Self-actualization can also be assessed by self-report questionnaires (e.g., the Index of Self-Actualization).

Maslow believed that most people work upwards through the hierarchy. However, he accepted that some individuals have to satisfy their need for self-esteem before they can satisfy their needs for love. Maslow also accepted that we are often motivated by various needs at the same time. For example, sex is often motivated by the need for sexual release, but can also "be motivated by a need to win or express affection, a sense of conquest or mastery, or a desire to feel masculine or feminine" (Burger, 1993, p. 337).

FINDINGS

Maslow assumed that human growth is associated with maturity. It follows from that assumption that younger adults should focus more than older ones on needs low in the hierarchy and less on the "higher" needs. Support for this prediction was reported by Reiss and Havercamp (2005). "Lower" motives (e.g., eating; exercise) were stronger in younger than in older adults, whereas the higher motives (e.g., honor; idealism) were stronger in older than younger adults.

Aronoff (1967) tested the prediction that higher needs will only emerge when lower ones are satisfied. He compared fishermen and cane cutters in the British West Indies. Fishermen worked on their own, generally earning more than cane cutters working in groups. Cane cutting was a more secure job, because the rewards fluctuated much less than for fishermen, and because cane cutters were paid even when unwell. According to Maslow's theory, those choosing the more challenging and responsible job of fisherman should be mainly those whose security and esteem needs were met. This prediction was confirmed by Aronoff.

In apparent contrast to the findings of Aronoff (1967) are those of Sumerlin and Norman (1992). They compared self-actualization scores in homeless men and college students. Since homeless men were much less likely than college students to be satisfying their basic needs, it was predicted that college students would have much higher self-actualization scores. In fact, however, the two groups didn't differ in self-actualization.

Sumerlin and Bundrick (2000) explored self-actualization among homeless men. As predicted by Maslow's theory, they found that those men who had the highest self-actualization scores also tended to be the happiest.

According to Maslow, individuals high up the hierarchy of needs should have more peak experiences than those lower down the hierarchy. Supporting evidence was reported by Mathes, Zevon, Roter, and Joerger (1982), who devised a Peak Scale to assess individual differences in the tendency to have peak experiences. As predicted, high scorers on the Peak Scale were more likely than low scorers to emphasize higher-level values (e.g., beauty; truth; justice) in their everyday lives. They were also less likely to focus on lower-level deficiency values (e.g., taking from others rather than giving).

There may be important cultural differences in peak experiences. Privette, Hwang, and Bundrick (1997) found that Americans reported more peak experiences than Taiwanese. This may be because collectivistic cultures (such as the Taiwanese) emphasize group processes, whereas peak experiences typically have a very personal feel about them.

Maslow was wrong to suggest that all peak experiences are positive. There is much evidence (e.g., Wilson & Spencer, 1990) that some peak experiences are negative and occur in threatening situations.

Aronoff (1967) found that most West Indian fishermen had their security and esteem needs met, and this enabled them to handle an income and lifestyle that was less predictable than cane cutting.

Motivation and tourism

Cameron and Gatewood (2003) suggest that the motivation for the increasing popularity of heritage-site tourism is spiritual, which fits in with Maslow's concept of self-actualization. Surveys show that actual historical knowledge is not an important factor, and suggest that people's imaginations, feelings, empathy, and memories are more important motivators in making these visits. Typical statements that bring agreement include:

- I like to use my mind to go back in time while visiting historic sites and museums.
- I am sometimes able to connect deeply with the objects displayed in exhibits.
- I enjoy reflecting on a site or museum after visiting it.
- I enjoy imagining the day-to-day life of people who lived in the past.
- Some sites and museums provoke an almost "spiritual" response in me.

⊕ Maslow's approach to motivation is unusually comprehensive in scope.

⊕ Maslow emphasized the more positive aspects of human motivation, whereas many previous theorists (e.g., Freud) had devoted most of their attention to the negative side of human nature.

⊕ Individuals whose lower needs are satisfied are often more likely to focus on higher needs than those whose lower needs aren't satisfied. However, some evidence (e.g., Sumerlin & Norman, 1992) doesn't support the prediction.

⊖ As Hanley and Abell (2002, p. 37) pointed out, Maslow's model "is based heavily on Western and individualistic ideals of personal growth that de-emphasize the importance of relatedness in self-actualization." They argued that relatedness to other people is crucial at all levels of psychological development, especially in collectivistic cultures.

⊖ Maslow was too optimistic in his assumption that everyone has the potential to become self-actualized. The fact that the average British person spends 25 hours a week slumped in front of a television set suggests there are many people whose motivation for personal growth is not enormous!

⊖ Maslow didn't emphasize enough the importance of the environment in facilitating the development of self-actualization. In fact, individuals who become self-actualized usually owe much to environmental factors such as schooling, supportive parents, and interesting opportunities for training.

HUNGER MOTIVATION

It may seem as if it is easy to understand hunger and eating behavior. We start eating when our stomach and other parts of the body signal that the level of nutrients [nourishing substances] is too low, and we stop eating when our stomach is full. In fact, that is only a small part of what actually happens. For example, the fact that we generally eat *before* we experience much hunger suggests that basic physiological responses may not be all that important. Of particular significance, we often eat simply because it is the normal time for lunch or dinner. As Bolles (1990) pointed out, our wristwatch is one of the most important determinants of whether we feel hungry and start eating.

De Castro and de Castro (1989) found that social factors are important influences on eating behavior. Participants kept a diary record of all the food they ate and the number of other people present when they were eating. There were two key findings. First, the more people who were present, the more food the participants consumed. Second, the amount of food eaten was influenced by the time since the last meal for participants eating on their own, but not for those eating with other people. Thus, social factors were more important than the body's energy needs in determining how much food was eaten. Hetherington et al. (2006) shed light on why eating in the presence of others leads to more eating. They found that eating with friends increased energy intake by 18% compared to eating alone, and that eating alone while watching television increased energy intake by 14%. What happens is that people tend to eat more when they are *distracted* from attending to the food they are eating.

Standardized eating times are the norm, with work and social schedules being planned around them.

BASIC PROCESSES

There are more factors determining when, what, and how much we eat than you can shake a stick at. Here we will consider only the most important ones. The body needs to turn food into energy, and glucose is a sugar playing a key role in energy utilization. Glucose is the main source of energy used by the brain, and the body can also make use of glucose as an energy source. It would be very dangerous if no glucose were readily available at any time. This danger is avoided because there is a storage system in the liver for excess glucose. More specifically, glucose molecules are combined to form a carbohydrate known as **glycogen**. When the need arises, the liver simply converts glycogen back into glucose molecules and releases them into circulation.

How is glucose turned into glycogen, and glycogen into glucose? A protein hormone in the pancreas known as insulin assists in the breakdown of glucose into glycogen. Another protein hormone in the pancreas (glucagon) assists in the breakdown of glycogen into glucose.

So far we haven't considered long-term energy storage. This is provided in the form of fat cells, which form part of what is known as adipose tissue. Some fat is present in the food we eat, but fat is also manufactured in the body from various nutrients including glucose. As overweight people know to their cost, when we eat more than is needed for current energy demands, some of the surplus is stored away in fat cells.

Our discussion so far has minimized the fundamental importance of the protein hormone insulin in energy utilization. We have already seen that insulin is involved in converting glucose into glycogen. In addition, insulin is needed for the body to make use of glucose. If insulin is not available, our bodies are reliant on fatty acids to provide energy.

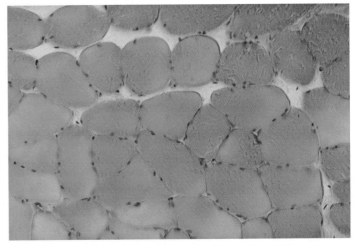

Magnification of the adipocytes (fat cells) that make up adipose connective tissue. Adipose connective tissue forms a thick layer under the skin, which insulates the body and acts as a reserve energy store.

What roles do glucose, insulin, and adipose or fat tissue play in weight regulation? According to Woods, Seeley, Porte, and Schwartz (1998), weight regulation depends crucially on maintaining a relatively constant amount of adipose or fat tissue in the body. To achieve this, information about levels of adipose tissue must be transmitted to the brain and other regions having a direct influence on eating behavior and satiety. Two hormones (insulin and leptin) are heavily involved. **Leptin** is a protein hormone secreted by fat cells and is associated with reduced levels of eating.

According to the theory, insulin and leptin are both secreted in large amounts when the fat stores are larger than usual. However, they are secreted in small amounts when the fat stores are smaller than usual. Large amounts of insulin and leptin inhibit eating behavior, and so help to maintain a moderate body weight.

Findings

According to the theory, individuals with large fat stores should generally have higher levels of leptin and insulin. Considine et al. (1996) found that leptin levels were *four* times higher in obese people than in those of normal weight, and Venner, Lyon, and Doyle-Baker (2006) reviewed similar findings in obese children. Why don't such high levels of leptin lead obese people to reduce their food intake? Many obese individuals are relatively insensitive to leptin, which doesn't reduce their hunger in the way that it does with individuals of normal weight.

As predicted, insulin and leptin both act to reduce food intake. For example, Woods, Camacho-Hubner, Savage, and Clark (1996) found that the more insulin was injected into animals' brains, the greater the reduction in their food intake and body weight. In similar fashion, Campfield et al. (1995) found there was a decrease in hunger when the levels of leptin injected into the hypothalamus were high. Some of the most dramatic findings were reported by Farooqi et al. (2002). They studied three obese children who had suffered from leptin deficiency since birth. When given leptin therapy, these children showed very large reductions in weight. Their food intake when allowed to decide how much to eat at a given meal was reduced by up to 84%.

Key Terms
Glycogen: a carbohydrate produced by combining glucose molecules to create an energy store.
Leptin: a protein secreted by fat cells that decreases feeding behavior.

How does leptin reduce hunger? Leptin and insulin both activate receptors in the hypothalamus, which plays an important role in eating behavior (see below). When leptin activates receptors in the hypothalamus, this inhibits the release of neuropeptide Y. **Neuropeptide Y** is a neurotransmitter stimulating hunger and eating behavior. Injections of neuropeptide Y into the hypothalamus cause satiated rats to start eating again immediately (Wickens, 2000). Repeated injections of neuropeptide Y into the paraventricular nucleus of the hypothalamus produce obesity within several days (Stanley, Kyrkouli, Lampert, & Leibowitz, 1986). The overall situation is complex: neuropeptide Y *increases* eating behavior, but this increase is prevented by leptin. As a result, leptin leads to a *reduction* in eating behavior and to a loss of body weight.

Evaluation

- ⊕ Overweight individuals typically have higher levels of leptin and insulin than those who are not.

- ⊕ Regulation of body weight in most people seems to depend on levels of insulin and leptin.

- ⊖ Obese individuals are often insensitive to the effects of leptin, but we generally don't know why that is the case.

- ⊖ It isn't known in detail how the system described in the theory interacts with other physiological processes underlying satiety.

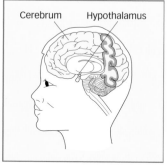

Cerebrum   Hypothalamus

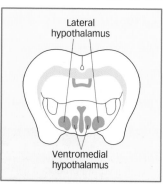

Lateral hypothalamus

Ventromedial hypothalamus

Key Term

Neuropeptide Y:
a neurotransmitter that increases feeding behavior.

BRAIN SYSTEMS

At one time, it was believed that *two* brain systems influence eating behavior. First, there was a brain system responsible for initiating food intake (the feeding center). This feeding center was allegedly based in the lateral [side] hypothalamus at the base of the brain (Anand & Brobeck, 1951). Second, there was a brain system responsible for cessation of feeding. It was known as the satiety center (meaning that it signaled that enough had been eaten), and was allegedly based in the ventromedial [bottom middle] hypothalamus (Hetherington & Ranson, 1940).

Perhaps predictably, matters are actually less simple than described in the previous paragraph. In this section, we will show that the traditional view of feeding and satiety centers based in different parts of the hypothalamus cannot account for several important findings. Note that much research has involved various species of mammals other than humans. It is generally assumed that the basic processes involved in eating behavior and weight regulation are very similar across nearly all mammals. However, this assumption may be only partially true.

Feeding center

If the feeding center is located in the lateral hypothalamus, then a lesion [deliberate cut] in that area should lead to a refusal to eat. Precisely that result was obtained by Anand and Brobeck (1951). Rats with lesions of the lateral hypothalamus stopped eating and rapidly lost weight. Teitelbaum and Stellar (1954) also found that lesions of the lateral hypothalamus in rats caused substantial reductions in eating. However, some of the rats began to eat again about a week after the operation, suggesting that other areas of the brain can be involved. These other brain areas include the frontal cortex and parts of the amygdala in the base of the brain (Rosenzweig, Leiman, & Breedlove, 1999).

More evidence that the lateral hypothalamus may be less crucial than originally thought was reported by Keesey and Boyle (1973) in a study on rats having lesions in that area. The lesioned rats maintained a lower body weight than healthy rats. However, both groups of rats responded in similar ways to manipulations of their diet. For example, lesioned and healthy rats both showed a substantial increase in body weight when only very rich food (eggnog) was available.

What are the effects of damage to the lateral hypothalamus on hunger in humans? Lesions or tumors of the lateral hypothalamus have variable effects on humans. However, such lesions often lead to considerable weight loss (White & Hain, 1959).

The lateral hypothalamus has a broader range of functions than simply acting as a feeding center. Pinel (2006) reviewed the research evidence, and concluded that, "LH [lateral hypothalamus] lesions produce a wide range of severe motor disturbances and a general lack of responsiveness to sensory input (of which food and drink are but two examples)."

Satiety center

If the satiety center is located in the ventromedial hypothalamus, then damage to this area should cause substantial weight gain. As predicted, rats with lesions in the ventromedial hypothalamus became obese (Hetherington & Ranson, 1940). Humans with a tumor in this part of the hypothalamus sometimes put on weight at the rate of over 10 kilos a month (Al-Rashid, 1971). However, their weight eventually reaches a plateau at a high level.

In spite of the above findings, we should reject the hypothesis that the satiety center is located in the ventromedial hypothalamus. First, rats with lesions in that area become obese, but strangely they don't seem very hungry in some ways. For example, lesioned rats given bitter-tasting food don't eat very much (Sclafini, Springer, & Kluge, 1976). Indeed, their body weight sometimes becomes *lower* than that of healthy rats exposed to the same bitter food.

Second, Hoebel and Teitelbaum (1966) found that lesions in the ventromedial hypothalamus produced complex effects. There was an initial dynamic phase (lasting 4–12 weeks), during which rats ate two or three times the normal amount of food. After that, there was a static phase. During that phase, the rats showed no further increase in body weight—they regulated their food consumption to maintain the weight reached at the end of the dynamic phase.

Third, it is not *only* damage to the ventromedial hypothalamus that produces larger increases in feeding. For example, Ahlskog, Randall, and Hoebel (1975) found large increases in body weight following damage to the ventral noradrenergic bundle running through the hypothalamus. Rats with damage to the paraventricular nucleus of the hypothalamus also put on substantial amounts of weight (Leibowitz, Hammer, & Chang, 1981).

Fourth, the pattern of feeding shown by rats with lesions in and around the ventromedial hypothalamus is not precisely as predicted. We would expect such rats to eat much larger meals than healthy ones because they have lost their satiety center. In fact, lesioned rats differ from non-lesioned ones in having *more* meals rather than *larger* ones (Hoebel & Hernandez, 1993).

What is the role of the ventromedial hypothalamus? According to Pinel (2006), the original notion that animals with lesions to the ventromedial hypothalamus become obese because they overeat is wrong. It is more accurate to say that such animals overeat because they become obese. King, Smith, and Frohman (1984) found that damage to the ventromedial hypothalamus produced a long-lasting increase in blood insulin levels leading to increased production of body fat. Since many of the calories ingested by lesioned animals are simply converted into fat, they have to eat large amounts of food to provide themselves with enough energy.

Hunger and cannabis

The brain produces naturally occurring cannabis-type compounds, called cannabinoids, and these compounds bind with brain receptors to give us normal hunger pangs. When cannabis is smoked or ingested the plant cannabinoids have a similar effect, giving rise to the strong hunger pangs sometimes called "the munchies." Scientists in France, the USA, and Britain have been working to produce drugs that block these receptors, thus suppressing hunger, and the British drug is currently being trialed as a possible treatment for obesity.

+ The lateral hypothalamus plays a role in initiating eating behavior and the ventromedial hypothalamus has some involvement in the cessation of eating.

− Initiation and cessation of eating both involve brain areas outside of the hypothalamus.

− Lesions in the lateral hypothalamus reduce responsiveness to most sensory input including food and drink, and so that area is not simply a hunger center.

− Animals with lesions in the ventromedial hypothalamus are "finicky, lazy and show exaggerated reactions to palatability [pleasantness of taste] . . . these findings do not square very well with the theory that the ventromedial hypothalamus is the brain's satiety center" (Wickens, 2000, p. 118).

− Lesions to the ventromedial hypothalamus lead to increased blood insulin levels and production of body fat, and so this area can't accurately be described as a satiety center.

DIETARY VARIETY

You have probably had the experience of working your way through a three- or four-course meal. When you have finished, you may feel surprised how easy it was to eat much more food than usual. What is going on here? We typically consume more food when a meal contains plenty of variety in taste. This helps to explain why the courses served up in large meals generally contain a mixture of savory (salty or spicy) and sweet dishes.

Evidence that dietary variety is important was provided by Rolls, van Duijvenvoorde, and Rolls (1984). Human participants were provided with a meal consisting of four courses. In the dietary variety condition, one course consisted of sausages, one of bread and butter, one of chocolate dessert, and one of bananas. In the other condition, participants were given four courses consisting of only one of these foods presented four times. Those participants exposed to dietary variety consumed 44% more food and 60% more calories than those receiving the same food throughout.

Lack of dietary variety can influence long-term eating patterns as well as short-term ones. For example, Cabanac and Rabe (1976) persuaded participants to consume only a vanilla-flavored diet for 3 weeks. There was an average weight loss of 3.12 kilos (7 pounds) over the three-week period.

A number of studies have concluded that increased dietary variety leads to increased consumption of food. The availability of a wide variety of high-calorie foods may have contributed to the increase in obesity in Western societies.

Sensory-specific satiety

Why does dietary variety lead to greater food consumption? According to Rolls (1981), the main reason is **sensory-specific satiety**: the pleasantness of any given taste or flavor decreases progressively with continuous exposure to it. The effects are specific because there is generally no reduction in the perceived pleasantness of other tastes or flavors. Sensory-specific satiety encourages us to consume a varied diet, which helps to ensure that we have the full range of nutrients we need.

Evidence for sensory-specific satiety was obtained by Rolls et al. (1984). They classified sausages, bread and butter, potato chips, and cheese and crackers as savory foods, and chocolate whipped dessert, yogurt, bananas, and oranges as sweet foods. When *one* of the sweet foods was eaten, this decreased the pleasantness ratings of *all* the sweet foods, but had no effect on the pleasantness ratings of savory foods. In similar fashion, eating one of the savory foods reduced the pleasantness ratings of the other savory foods but not of the sweet ones.

Sensory-specific satiety was originally studied in connection with taste. However, it applies to other aspects of food as well. For example, Rolls and Rolls (1997) found sensory-specific satiety with respect to the smells of different foods. Rolls, Rowe, and Rolls (1982) asked participants to eat chocolate sweets of a given color. The rated pleasantness of chocolate sweets of that color decreased more than that of chocolate sweets of a different color even though the taste was the same. Thus, sensory-specific satiety extends to food color.

OBESITY

Obesity is defined as a body mass index (BMI) of more than 30. **Body mass index** is defined as weight in kilos divided by height in meters squared. Individuals with a BMI lying between 20 and 25 are of normal weight, and those with BMIs between 25 and 30 are overweight. Finally, those with BMIs over 30 are obese. BMI is limited in some ways. For example, professional footballers with highly developed muscles sometimes have a BMI that categorizes them as overweight!

There is an epidemic of obesity in the Western world. For example, in the United States, 22% of adults are obese and 54% are overweight (Hill & Peters, 1998). In the United Kingdom in 2003, 22% of men were obese and 43% overweight, and 23% of women were obese and 33% overweight (Zaninotto et al., 2006).

Most people assume that obesity poses extremely serious health risks. It is certainly true that obesity is associated with several health problems (e.g., high blood pressure; heart attacks; various cancers) (Wickelgren, 1998). However, we are talking about an *association*, which doesn't prove that obesity is the causal factor. For example, most obese individuals take less exercise than other people, and their lack of physical fitness may be important. Wickelgren discussed an American study in which it was found that unfit men of normal weight had twice the mortality of physically fit men who were obese or nearly so. Being obese and being physically unfit both contribute to physical ill-health and reduced longevity.

What causes obesity?

Genetic factors play a part in determining who does (and who doesn't) become obese. Maes et al. (1997) analyzed data from over 30 twin studies. Monozygotic or identical twins were much more similar to each other in weight and body mass than were dizygotic or fraternal twins, with genetic factors accounting for much of the variation in BMI across individuals. Plomin, DeFries, and McClearn (1997) found that 60–70% of identical twins were very similar in weight, compared to only 30–40% of fraternal twins. The much greater genetic similarity of identical twins than fraternal twins (100% vs. 50%, respectively) accounts for their much greater similarity in weight. In a study specifically on obesity, Bulik, Sullivan, and Kendler (2003) studied 2163 female twins. The key finding was that the heritability of obesity was 0.86, meaning that 86% of individual differences in obesity are attributable to genetic factors.

The notion that genetic factors are of prime importance in determining weight suggests that family environment should have little or no effect. Stunkard et al. (1986) considered the weight of adults adopted as infants. Their body weight wasn't correlated with that of their adoptive parents. However, it was highly correlated with the body weight of their biological parents, suggesting that genetic factors are more important than environmental ones.

Dramatic environmental changes can also have powerful effects on weight. The inhabitants of the island of Nauru used to have a very low standard of living. However, their island has rich supplies of seabird excrement, which has for many years been used by fertilizer companies as a source of phosphates. The Nauru islanders now have one of the highest standards of living in the world, and buy a wide range of expensive imported foods. As a result, large numbers of them became obese within a single generation (Gibbs, 1996).

Key Terms
Obesity: the condition of being substantially overweight, defined as having a **body mass index** exceeding 30.
Body mass index (BMI): an individual's weight in kilos divided by his/her height in meters squared; the normal range is between 20 and 25.

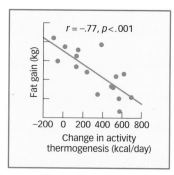

Fat gain following 8 weeks of overfeeding as a function of increases or decreases in non-exercise changes in thermogenesis (kcal/day). From Levine et al. (1999). Copyright © 1999 AAAS. Reproduced with permission.

Reduced amounts of exercise in Western countries help to account for the steep increase in obesity. Over the past 25 years or so, the average daily calorie intake in several Western countries has actually *decreased* (Hill & Peters, 1998). This hasn't led to a reduction in obesity because most people walk less and use cars more than ever. Exercise uses up energy (and therefore calories), and anyone will put on weight if the calories he/she consumes are greater than those used in energy expenditure.

A somewhat neglected factor is nonexercise activity thermogenesis, which is heat generated by activities such as fidgeting and the maintenance of posture. Levine, Eberhardt, and Jensen (1999) carried out a study in which volunteers were fed 1000 calories per day more than were needed for weight maintenance. Those individuals who had the lowest levels of nonexercise activity thermogenesis showed the greatest weight gain (see the figure on the left).

Finally, obese individuals typically have problems with **adipocytes**, which are body cells that store fat. There are two major kinds of problems. First, while most people have about 2.5 billion adipocytes, many obese individuals have a much larger number. Second, the fat cells in many obese individuals are enlarged rather than unduly numerous.

In sum, several factors are involved in obesity. Genetic factors are very important, but environmental factors (e.g., increased access to rich and fatty foods) also play a role. In addition, reductions in the amount of exercise taken by most people can lead to weight increases. Finally, most obese individuals store fat more readily than nonobese ones.

SEX AND SEXUAL BEHAVIOR

Human sex drive involves several biological factors (e.g., sex hormones). However, that is only part of the story. As Westen (1996, p. 387) remarked, "The primary sexual organ in humans is arguably not the genitals but the brain." In this section of the chapter, we initially consider biological influences on sexual behavior. After that, we focus on relevant psychological factors.

Key Terms

Adipocytes:
body cells that store fat; overweight individuals often have many more of these cells than those of normal weight.

Gametes:
sexual reproductive cells consisting of sperm in males and of eggs in females.

SEXUAL REPRODUCTION

Why does sexual reproduction exist? That may seem like an odd question, and you may well think that the answer is obvious. However, as Grier and Burk (1992, p. 319) pointed out there are several disadvantages associated with sex:

> *Sexual behavior involves the expenditure of large amounts of time and energy, and its conspicuousness often increases the risk of predation [being preyed upon] . . . Worst of all, from an evolutionary standpoint, sexual reproduction is a particularly ineffective method of passing on one's particular alleles [genes].*

What are the evolutionary advantages of sexual reproduction? The most important one is that sexual reproduction produces genetic diversity. As can be seen in large human families, two parents typically produce offspring differing significantly in height, shape, intelligence, and personality. This occurs in part because the precise genetic make-up of each child is different except in the case of monozygotic or identical twins. Environmental conditions often change in unpredictable ways, and genetic diversity maximizes the chances of the members of any given species coping with such changes.

Of fundamental importance to reproduction are **gametes**. These are sexual reproductive cells (eggs in females and sperm in males) that fuse together during fertilization. If any individual's genes are to be passed on directly to the next generation his/her gametes need to survive long enough for them to be involved in sexual reproduction. One strategy for achieving this is to produce a few large gametes designed to survive in an unfriendly environment. This strategy is used by females with their

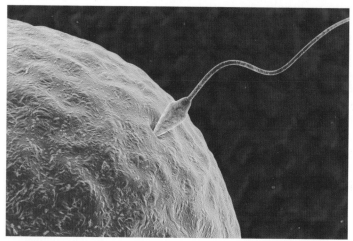

Fertilization of a human egg by a sperm. An example of anisogamy, where the gametes of the two sexes are dissimilar.

eggs. Another strategy is to produce large numbers of very mobile gametes so that one or more of them may fertilize the female's egg before this is done by another individual. This strategy is used by males with their sperm.

Human females produce relatively few eggs, whereas males produce extremely large numbers of sperm. Indeed, there are enough sperm in a typical male ejaculation to fertilize 500 million females! Thus, each female gamete is much more valuable than each male gamete or sperm. Females can usually maximize their reproductive success by providing food and care for a relatively small number of offspring. In contrast, males can often maximize their reproductive success by fertilizing several females rather than by caring for their offspring (see Chapter 2).

Human females have a menstrual cycle lasting about 28 days, with ovulation (release of an egg from the ovaries) occurring in the middle of each cycle. Sexual intercourse has to occur around the time of ovulation to maximize the chances of conception. Most evidence suggests that women don't have more sex around the time of ovulation than at other points in the menstrual cycle. However, as Wallen (2001, p. 354) pointed out, what is true of sexual behavior isn't necessarily true of sexual desire:

Ovulation in humans is hidden but in many other species there is a visual manifestation of ovulation. For example, in the female chacma baboon (above) a swelling and reddening of the rump occurs around the time of ovulation. This indicates to the males that the female is sexually receptive.

The specific patterns of sexual behavior engaged in by women reflect an interaction between their level of sexual desire, which is affected by their hormonal state, the level of their partner's sexual desire, and the woman's or the couple's desire to avoid, or achieve, pregnancy.

There is considerable evidence that women's sexual desire peaks around the time of ovulation. For example, Stanislaw and Rice (1988) asked married women to keep a daily record of their sexual desire over a 2-year period. The women expressed sexual desire much more frequently around the time of ovulation, with a steady increase in the days beforehand and a steady decrease afterwards. Pillsworth, Haselton, and Buss (2004) replicated that finding among women in long-term committed relationships who were not taking oral contraceptives. However, there was no peak in sexual desire around the time of ovulation for women not in a committed relationship.

Hormones and attractiveness

A small study in Texas (Davis, 2001) showed physiological and psychological changes when a woman is most fertile, but these changes relate to her attractiveness or sexiness. The female curvy shape becomes accentuated around ovulation as the breasts are more symmetrical and the waist shrinks by a centimeter or so. Figure-hugging clothing is chosen, which also reveals more skin, and more make-up is worn. The participants' diaries also showed increased thoughts about love and sex, decreased stress levels, more positive moods, and fewer headaches. Presumably all these effects are down to the balance of sex hormones at ovulation.

Orgasm

The experience of orgasm represents the peak of sexual pleasure during sexual intercourse. William Masters and Virginia Johnson (1966) directly observed and measured the sexual behavior of 700 people having intercourse to clarify the role of orgasm within the sexual response cycle. They identified four phases in this cycle:

1. *Excitement phase*: There is increased muscle tension, filling of blood vessels in the genitals, and sometimes flushing of the skin.
2. *Plateau phase*: This involves the highest level of arousal with maximum heart rate, muscle tension, and blood pressure.
3. *Orgasm phase*: During this phase, males release sperm and females experience vaginal contractions.
4. *Resolution phrase*: This phase involves a gradual return to normal psychological and physiological functioning.

Vance and Wagner (1976) found that the subjective experiences associated with orgasm were very similar in males and females. Indeed, psychologists and gynecologists couldn't distinguish between men's and women's descriptions of their orgasms. Here are two descriptions obtained by Vance and Wagner:

The feeling of orgasm in my opinion is a feeling of utmost relief of any type of tension. It is the most fulfilling experience I have ever had of enjoyment. The feeling is exuberant and the most enjoyable feeling I have ever experienced.

An orgasm feels like heaven in the heat of hell; a tremendous build-up of pleasure that makes the tremendous work of releasing that pleasure worthwhile.

One of those descriptions was written by a man and the other by a woman. Can you work out which is which? In fact, the first one was written by a woman and the second by a man.

Hormonal factors

There are two major classes of sex hormones: **androgens** and **estrogens**. The most common androgen is testosterone, and the most common estrogen is estradiol. Males have higher levels of androgens than estrogens, whereas the opposite is the case for females. This gender difference has led some people to describe androgens as "male hormones" and estrogens as "female hormones." This is misleading because males and females produce both types of hormones. However, the level of androgens is 10 times higher in men than in women, and the level of estrogens is 10 times higher in women than in men.

How important are sex hormones in influencing human sexual behavior? They are of some importance, but less so than in many other species. For example, estrogen levels in females are 10 times higher around the time of ovulation than at the start of the menstrual cycle. However, this large increase is associated with only small effects on sexual behavior and fairly modest effects on sexual desire. Evidence that estrogen levels can have a fairly large effect on women's sexual interest was reported by Sherwin (1991). Different groups of post-menopausal women were given varying amounts of estrogen. Those receiving the largest doses showed the greatest increases in sexual interest during the course of treatment. The effects of estrogen on male sexuality tend to be very small and inconsistent (see Bancroft, 2005, for a review).

There is strong evidence that androgens (especially testosterone) can influence male and female sexual desire. Bancroft (2005) discussed studies on hypogonadal men who do not produce sex hormones. Testosterone replacement therapy typically restores sexual desire and arousability, whereas withdrawal of testosterone leads to a reduction in sexual desire. However, most healthy men have sufficiently high testosterone levels that additional testosterone has little or no effect on their level of sexual desire.

Female sex drive may be determined more by androgens such as testosterone than by estrogens such as estradiol. Shifren et al. (2000) studied surgically menopausal women with low sexual desire and sexual satisfaction who were given estrogen. Those who also received a large dose of the androgen testosterone showed the greatest increase in sexual functioning. Segraves and Woodard (2006) reviewed the evidence on the treatment of

Key Terms

Androgens:
sex hormones found in greater amounts in males than in females.

Estrogens:
sex hormones found in greater amounts in females than in males.

Case Study: *Testosterone Replacement Therapy*

Additional evidence that sex hormones are important to male sexuality comes from studies of testosterone replacement therapy. For example, consider the case of a 38-year-old World War I veteran whose testes had been destroyed by a shell fragment. Testosterone replacement therapy had a dramatic effect on him: "Testosterone had resurrected a broken man to a manhood he had believed lost forever" (de Knuif, 1945, p. 100).

hypoactive sexual desire disorder [unusually low levels of sexual interest] in women. They concluded that, "The major evidence of efficacy concerns the use of testosterone therapy" (Segraves & Woodard, 2006, p. 408). Finally, Morris, Udry, Khan-Dawood, and Dawood (1987) found that frequency of intercourse in married women was associated much more with their testosterone levels than with their estradiol levels. In spite of these findings, it should be noted that the evidence generally indicates that there are substantial differences among women in terms of their responsiveness to testosterone (Bancroft, 2005).

In sum, sex hormones play some role in determining sexual desire and sexual behavior in men and women. However, psychological factors (e.g., availability of a sexually attractive member of the opposite sex) are generally far more important. The one major exception may be that women with high levels of testosterone experience higher levels of sexual desire and have more frequent sexual intercourse than other women.

EVOLUTIONARY PSYCHOLOGY

One of the most ambitious theoretical approaches to human sexuality is provided by evolutionary psychology (see Chapter 2). According to evolutionary psychologists, much of human behavior and cognition depends on evolutionary processes of natural selection. Evolutionary psychology has provided explanations for many of the differences in sexual attitudes and behavior between men and women. Of crucial importance is the notion that having sex can have much greater long-term consequences for a woman than for a man. In the words of Buss (1999, p. 102):

> A man in evolutionary history could walk away from a casual coupling having lost only a few hours or even a few minutes. A woman in evolutionary history risked getting pregnant as a result, and therefore could have incurred the cost of that decision for years.

The evolutionary approach could help to explain a striking difference between American male and female students reported by Clark and Hatfield (1989). Attractive male and female students approached students of the opposite sex, and said: "Hi, I've been noticing you around town lately, and I find you very attractive. Would you have sex with me?" This offer was received much more enthusiastically by male students. None of the female students accepted the invitation, whereas 75% of the male students did. Some of the men who refused offered their apologies (e.g., "My fiancée is in town at the moment").

According to evolutionary psychology, the fact that women typically have a much greater parental investment in their offspring than do men has important implications for their sexual behavior. More specifically, men in all cultures should be less attracted to monogamy and heavy emotional investment in relationships. This hypothesis was tested by Schmitt (2005) in a study in which the Sociosexual Orientation Inventory was administered to people in 48 countries. High scores on this questionnaire indicate a preference for promiscuity and avoidance of emotional investment. As predicted, men in every country had significantly higher sociosexual scores than women. However, the differences between men and women in sociosexual scores were less in countries in which there was reasonable equality of the sexes in terms of, for example, career opportunities. Women in such countries have access to money and to power, which may make their sexual attitudes and behavior more like those of men. Another possibility is that women in countries with reasonable equality are more likely than other women to have access to modern contraception and safe abortion.

GENDER DIFFERENCES IN SEXUALITY

Peplau (2003) argued that there are four important gender differences in sexuality: sexual desire; importance of committed relationships; sexuality and aggression; and sexual plasticity. We will consider all four briefly.

Key Study

Buss (1989): Cross-cultural support for the evolutionary account of mate choice

According to evolutionary psychology, people should select a mate who maximizes their chances of having offspring that will survive and procreate. Buss obtained findings from 37 cultures around the world which he claimed provided support for that prediction. Men in all 37 cultures said they would prefer a mate younger than they were, whereas women in 36 cultures (Spain was the exception) preferred men older than themselves. This can be explained by assuming that younger women are more likely to be able to have children, and older men are more likely to have the resources to be able to provide adequately for children. As expected, women rated good financial prospects in a potential mate as more important than did men.

There are two limitations with Buss's (1989) study. First, he only assessed preferences, and there can be a large gap between preferences and people's actual behavior. Second, there were large differences across cultures. In general, there were much smaller sex differences in mate preferences in more developed countries.

Discussion points
1. Does this research provide strong support for the evolutionary approach?
2. Why do you think that sex differences in mate preference vary between Western and non-Western cultures?

KEY STUDY EVALUATION
The findings of Buss (1989) are of key importance, but they are less clear cut than they seem for two main reasons. First, they do not actually show that sex differences in mate preference are consistent across cultures. In fact, there were much smaller sex differences in more developed cultures than in less developed ones on most measures, including preferred age differences, importance of financial prospects, and the value of chastity in a mate. Second, the sociobiological approach is more concerned with behavior than with the preferences assessed by Buss. In fact, the actual average age difference between husband and wife across cultures was 2.99 years, which is similar to the preferred age differences for males (2.66 years) and for females (3.42 years). However, it is by no means clear that there would be this level of agreement between preferences and behavior for the other measures obtained by Buss.

First, men are generally more interested in sex than women. For example, Oliver and Hyde (1993) found that men masturbate much more often than women. In addition, as Peplau (2003) pointed out, when heterosexual couples disagree about the frequency with which they have sex, it is typically the man who wants to have sex more often than the woman does.

Second, men are less concerned than women to express their sexuality within a committed relationship. As we saw earlier, Schmitt (2005) found that men in 48 different countries were more interested than women in promiscuity and in uninvolved sex. Oliver and Hyde (1993) found that men were much more accepting than women of casual premarital sex and extramarital sex.

Third, there is a much closer link between sexuality and aggression in men than in women. For example, men in heterosexual relationships are typically more assertive than women in initiating sexual interactions. Andersen, Cyranowski, and Espindle (1999) studied people's sexual self-concepts. Only men's sexual self-concepts were characterized by a dimension of aggression (e.g., being aggressive; being powerful).

Fourth, men have less sexual or erotic plasticity than women. According to Baumeister (2000, p. 348), "The female sex drive is more malleable [flexible] than the male, indicating

Women are promiscuous, naturally

"So many men, so little time!" The actress Mae West jested about it, but scientists—male ones anyway—are convinced they have proved it. Women—far from being naturally monogamous—are, like men, naturally promiscuous. Biologists believe that women are genetically programmed to have sex with several different men in order to increase their chances of healthy children.

This theory helps to explain the high incidence of mistaken paternity. One study suggested that as many as one in seven people may not be the biological child of the man he or she thinks is the father but other studies suggest the true figure is much lower.

Two recent reports have added to a growing body of evidence that females from across the animal kingdom—including birds, bees, fish, scorpions, crabs, reptiles, and mammals—are promiscuous. Promiscuity is suggested by the "good gene" theory, as shown in the great weed warbler. The female warbler may nest with a male with a small song repertoire but she will seek "extra-pair copulation" with males with big song repertoires, which tend to live longer. This way she gets the best offspring (from mate 2) and they are looked after (by mate 1).

"We don't all get the exact partner we want, we make some kind of compromise. That's true of humans as well. A woman might find a man who is good at providing food and looking after children, but she doesn't necessarily want him to be the father of her kids," says Tim Birkhead, professor of evolutionary psychology.

The only comfort that men can take from the animal world is that females have an incentive not to have all their offspring from adulterous liaisons.

"If they are totally unfaithful to their social partner, they might just be abandoned," said Birkhead.

Adapted from A. Brown (2000). "Women are promiscuous, naturally." The *Observer*, 3 September.

higher average erotic plasticity. More precisely, female sexual responses and sexual behaviors are influenced by cultural, social, and situational factors to a greater extent than male." Evidence in line with this hypothesis was reported by Barry and Schlegel (1984). They reviewed findings on adolescent sexual behavior in 186 cultures, and found that females showed greater cross-cultural variation than males on all their measures of sexual behavior. According to the erotic plasticity hypothesis, genetic factors should influence male sexuality more than female sexuality. Evidence relevant to this prediction was reported by Dunne et al. (1997). They studied age at first intercourse among people growing up after the "sexual revolution" of the 1960s. Genetic factors accounted for 72% of individual differences among males in age at first intercourse compared to only 40% in females.

In sum, as Peplau (2003, p. 39) concluded, "The size of gender differences [in sexuality] tends to be large . . . These differences are pervasive, encompassing thoughts, feelings, fantasies, and behavior."

Women's sexual orientations

Veniegas and Conley (2000) evaluated the available scientific evidence on factors influencing female homosexual behavior. They point out that only gay male brains have been studied. Only one pair of female twins raised apart has been studied for sexual orientation, and no genetic markers for lesbian behavior have been found. The public belief that exposure in utero to abnormal hormone levels leads, in females, to lesbian behavior is challenged by empirical research, which shows the great majority to be heterosexual in behavior and also in their fantasies. Levels of hormones and body shape and type are also unrelated to sexual orientation. This seems to mean that we know quite a lot about what does not affect sexuality, but not much about what does!

WORK MOTIVATION AND PERFORMANCE

A high level of motivation is essential for success in academic courses and in a career. In this section, we consider the relationship between work motivation and performance. Any given individual's level of work motivation depends on several factors. For example, his/her personality makes a difference. Workers' motivation also depends on whether they feel fairly treated, on the amount of support and encouragement provided by their employers, and so on. According to Bandura, the individual's belief in his/her ability to perform a given task also important (see Chapter 12).

In order to succeed in an academic course a high level of motivation is needed!

However, what most determines our level of performance on a task or at work is the goals we set ourselves. Accordingly we will focus on goal-setting theory, which has probably been the most influential approach to work motivation. According to Mitchell and Daniels (2003, p. 231), "It [goal-setting theory] is quite easily the single most dominant theory in the field, with over a thousand articles and reviews published on the topic in a little over 30 years."

GOAL-SETTING THEORY AND BEYOND

Goal-setting theory was originally put forward by Edwin Locke (1968) and subsequently modified (e.g., Locke & Latham, 1990, 2002, 2006). It has probably been the most influential approach to work motivation. What are the key assumptions of goal-setting theory? First, it is assumed that conscious goals have a major impact on people's motivation and behavior. A goal is "the object or aim of an action, for example, to attain a specific standard of proficiency, usually within a specified time limit" (Locke & Latham, 2002, p. 705). Ideally, the goal should be "specific, measurable, attainable, relevant, and have a time-frame (SMART)" (Latham, 2003, p. 309). We can generally discover what an individual's goal is by direct questioning.

Second, it is assumed that there is a straightforward relationship between goal difficulty and performance. According to Locke (1968, p. 162), "the harder the goal the higher the level of performance." The reason is that individuals try harder and show more persistence when they have set themselves difficult goals.

Third, Locke (1968) argued that task performance also depends on goal commitment, which is the determination to reach the goal. According to the theory, high performance occurs only when goal difficulty *and* goal commitment are both high. Goal commitment is especially important when goals are difficult, because such goals require high levels of effort and are associated with smaller chances of success than easy goals. Expressed differently, the beneficial effects on performance of setting high goals are greater when goal commitment is high than when it is low. These assumptions lead to the predictions shown in the figure on the following page.

Findings

In an early test of goal-setting theory, Latham and Yukl (1975) studied workers whose job involved cutting and transporting wood. The workers were divided into three kinds of groups:

1. Groups simply instructed to "do your best" (do-your-best groups).
2. Groups assigned to a specific hard goal in terms of cubic feet of wood per week (assigned groups).
3. Groups in which everyone participated in setting a hard production goal (participative groups).

Latham and Yukl (1975) found that the do-your-best groups set the easiest goals, and so were predicted to have the poorest work performance. In contrast, the participative groups set the hardest goals, and so were predicted to perform the best. In line with the predictions, the do-your-best groups averaged 46 cubic feet, the assigned groups averaged 53 cubic feet, and the participative groups averaged 56 cubic feet. These differences may not seem large. However, the work performance of the participative groups was almost 22% higher than that of the do-your-best groups and any company would be delighted to increase the productivity of its workers by 22%! For example, assigning truck drivers a hard goal involving increasing their daily trips of logs to the mill produced savings of 2.7 million dollars (over £1.4 million) in 18 weeks (Latham & Saari, 1982).

Latham and Brown (2006) investigated the academic performance of students doing an MBA (Master's in Business Administration). Some of the students set themselves vague general goals (e.g., performing well at the end of the program), whereas others set themselves hard, specific goals (e.g., learn to network; master key course subject matter). Those who set themselves hard, specific goals performed better and had higher satisfaction with their course than did those setting themselves general goals.

Klein et al. (1999) carried out a meta-analysis of studies on the effects of goal setting and goal commitment to task performance. The pattern of the findings was as predicted from goal-setting theory (see figure on the right). Higher levels of goal commitment were associated with higher levels of performance, especially when goal difficulty was high. Various factors influenced the level of goal commitment. Two of the key factors were attractiveness of goal attainment and expectancy of goal attainment provided that the individual applied reasonable effort. Other factors producing high levels of goal commitment were having high ability, being personally involved in the setting of the goal, and receiving performance feedback.

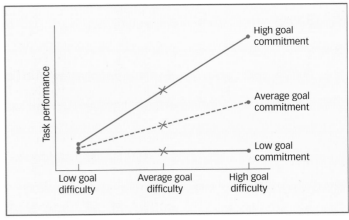

The effects of goal difficulty and goal commitment on task performance according to Locke's goal-setting theory. From Klein, Wesson, Hollenbeck, and Alge (1999). Copyright © American Psychological Association. Reproduced with permission.

There is considerable support for the theory, as was emphasized by Locke and Latham (2006, p. 265): "Support for goal-setting effects has been found on more than 88 different tasks, involving more than 40,000 male and female participants in Asia, Australia, Europe, and North America . . . Goal effects have been found in both laboratory and field settings, using both correlational and experimental designs." In spite of this success, there are various limitations with goal-setting theory. Two of the most important ones are discussed below.

First, most of the research on the theory has involved situations in which a single, specific task is performed over a short period of time in the absence of distractions. In contrast, as Yearta, Maitlis, and Briner (1995, p. 239) pointed out, "Employees in organizations are often trying to achieve multiple goals simultaneously, in the midst of many other distractions, and over an extended period of time . . . 54 per cent of organizations surveyed set performance requirements over a six- to 12-month period." Do these differences matter? They probably do. Yearta et al. studied scientists and professional staff working at the research center of a large multi-national company. Within that organization, work performance was *negatively* related to goal difficulty, which is diametrically opposite to the prediction from goal-setting theory.

Second, the theory focuses on factors (e.g., goal setting; goal commitment) that influence motivation and performance. However, that is nothing like the whole story. There are clearly individual differences in the difficulty level of the goals that people set themselves and in their commitment to those goals. We all know some people who are consistently well-motivated, committing themselves to difficult goals, whereas other people are very poorly motivated. Any complete theory would include an analysis of relevant individual-difference variables. As yet, there has been relatively little progress in this area. However, Locke and Latham (2006) argued that goal commitment is influenced by individual differences in self-efficacy (expectations concerning one's ability to perform a task successfully).

> **Motivation and children's behavior**
>
> A study in Beijing has shown that high motivation links to a reduction in noncompliant behavior. In this study 216 preschool children were videotaped as they played with a familiar toy. A novel toy was available, but the children had to wait before being allowed to play with it. The most compliant, and perhaps the most motivated, children were the girls. According to Alderfer (1969), this could mean that the boys found the wait more frustrating, and redirected their focus elsewhere in a noncompliant way.

We have discussed two major limitations with goal-setting theory. In what follows, we consider ways of addressing these limitations.

Implementation intentions

As we have seen, the complex issue of how people can move from goal setting to goal attainment in a world full of complications and distractions is de-emphasized within goal-setting theory. Gollwitzer has focused on precisely this issue. His key concept is that of **implementation intentions**, which "specify the when, where, and how of responses leading to goal attainment" (Gollwitzer, 1999, p. 494). Suppose a student called Natalie has set herself the goal of spending 4 hours on a given Saturday revising for a forthcoming exam. However, there are obstacles in the way. Natalie normally chats for several hours a day with her flatmates, and she also likes to watch television. Thus, there is a real danger that Natalie will be distracted from her studies, and so finish up doing much less revision than she intended.

How can Natalie ensure her revision gets done? According to Gollwitzer's (1999) theory, this is where implementation intentions come in. Two possible implementation intentions are as follows: (1) "When one of my flatmates knocks on the door, I will tell her that I'll see her in the pub at 8 o'clock"; (2) "If I discover there's something interesting on television, I'll ask my flatmates to video it so I can watch it later." According to Gollwitzer, most goals are much more likely to be attained if individuals form implementation intentions.

Evidence supporting the importance of implementation intentions was reported by Gollwitzer and Brandstätter (1997). Participants were given the goal of writing a report on how they spent Christmas Eve within the following 2 days. Half the participants formed implementation intentions by indicating when and where they intended to write the report. The goal of writing the report very shortly after Christmas was achieved by 75% of those who formed implementation intentions but by only 33% of those who didn't.

Implementation intentions have been found to increase the chances of people achieving health-related goals. For example, Orbell, Hodgkins, and Sheeran (1997) studied women who reported strong goal intentions to perform a breast self-examination during the next month. Of those women told to form implementation intentions, 100% performed the breast self-examination compared to only 53% of women not forming such intentions. In similar fashion, Armitage (2004) found that people were more successful in reducing their fat intake over a 1-month period if they had formed an implementation intention (e.g., "I will eat only low-fat food for lunch every day starting tomorrow").

Why are implementation intentions so effective in enhancing the chances of people achieving their goals? According to Gollwitzer (1999), forming an implementation intention is like creating an "instant habit." Our habits (e.g., always going for lunch at 1 o'clock; always having a Coke in the Student Union) are reliably triggered by relevant cues providing information about *when* and/or *where* certain actions occur. In a similar way, implementation intentions specify where and when we are going to initiate behavior to attain our goal.

Individual differences: Core self-evaluations

Which kinds of people are highly motivated and generally commit themselves to hard goals? Various answers have been proposed. For example, it seems reasonable that individuals high in conscientiousness (one of the Big Five personality factors—see Chapter 12) should be highly motivated. Barrick and Mount (1993) found that sales representatives high in conscientiousness set themselves harder goals (and were more committed to them) than those low in conscientiousness. As predicted, conscientiousness was positively associated with work performance.

Judge, Locke, and Durham (1997) adopted an alternative approach to individual differences in motivation based on core self-evaluations (the basic evaluations individuals make about themselves). They argued that four personality traits are of direct relevance to core self-evaluations. First, there is self-esteem, which reflects the overall value one places on oneself as a person. Second, there is emotional stability (low neuroticism), which indicates the tendency to be confident and secure. Third, there is internal locus of control, with internals believing they can control numerous factors in their lives. Fourth, there is generalized self-efficacy, which is the ability to perform effectively and to be successful.

Judge et al. (2002) found that all four traits correlated moderately highly with each other, suggesting they were assessing the same underlying construct (i.e., core self-evaluations). As a result, Judge, Erez, Bono, and Thoresen (2003) developed a measure of core self-evaluations called the Core Self-Evaluations Scale. This scale correlated highly with all four personality traits.

Key Term

Implementation intentions: intentions specifying in detail how an individual is going to achieve some goal.

Judge and Bono (2001) carried out meta-analyses to assess the ability of the four personality traits underlying core self-evaluations to predict job performance. All of the correlations were significantly positive: self-esteem correlated +.26 with job performance, generalized self-efficacy correlated +.23, internal locus of control correlated +.22, and emotional stability correlated +.19.

Erez and Judge (2001) found that the core self-evaluations factor correlated +.35 with task performance in a laboratory study. In a second study, they considered the job performance of insurance agents. Core self-evaluations correlated +.44 with supervisory ratings of job performance and +.35 with sales volume. Of particular relevance here, core self-evaluations correlated +.42 with goal setting and +.59 with goal commitment. When they combined goal setting and goal commitment into a single measure of goal-setting motivation, Erez and Judge (2001) found that core self-evaluations influenced goal-setting motivation, which influenced activity level (e.g., phone calls to prospective clients; number of interviews with clients), which influenced productivity (i.e., sales volume) and rated performance (see the figure below). Thus, the beneficial effects of high core self-evaluations on performance occur mainly because they lead individuals to adopt hard goals and to be committed to them.

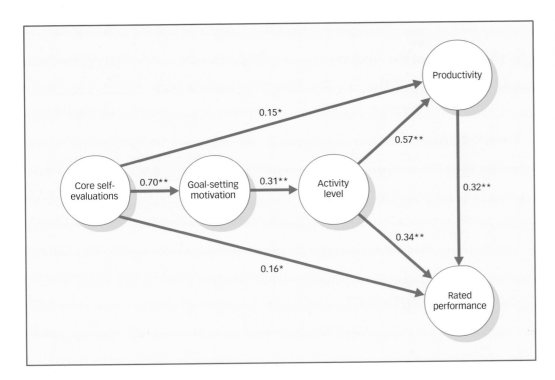

The estimated relationships of core self-evaluations to goal-setting motivation, activity level, productivity, and rated performance. The numbers indicate the strengths of each relationship. From Erez and Judge (2001). Copyright © American Psychological Association. Reproduced with permission.

Overall Evaluation

⊕ Goal setting and goal commitment both partially determine the level of work performance as predicted by goal-setting theory.

⊕ Highly motivated workers set themselves higher goals and are more committed to them than are other workers.

⊕ Goal-setting theory could be made more comprehensive by including implementation intentions and core self-evaluations within its scope.

⊖ Goal-setting theory in its present form is less applicable within work organizations than in the laboratory. This is partly because it doesn't emphasize enough the processes (e.g., implementation intentions) intervening between goal setting and goal achievement.

- An individual's goals and his/her commitment to them are seen as corresponding to his/her conscious intentions. However, people's motivational forces are not always accessible to conscious awareness.

- Goal-setting theory focuses too much on cognitive factors associated with motivation and not enough on emotional factors. For example, some people are very motivated because they fear failure or because they anticipate experiencing pride or joy if they succeed.

Chapter Summary

Maslow's hierarchical theory

- According to Maslow, we have a hierarchy of needs with deficiency needs at the bottom and growth needs at the top.
- At the very top of the hierarchy of needs is self-actualization. Self-actualized individuals realize their potential, accept themselves, are creative, and have many peak experiences.
- There is evidence that those whose lower needs are satisfied are more likely to focus on higher needs as predicted by the theory.
- Maslow's approach to self-actualization has an excessive focus on individual growth and de-emphasizes the importance of relatedness.

Hunger motivation

- Weight regulation involves maintaining a relatively constant amount of fat tissue in the body. Two hormones (leptin and insulin) are secreted in large amounts when the fat stores are larger than usual; these hormones inhibit eating behavior.
- It used to be argued that there is a feeding center in the lateral hypothalamus. In fact, this area has broader functions. It is responsible for sensory input of many kinds including food and drink.
- It used to be argued that there is a satiety center located in the ventromedial hypothalamus. Animals with lesions in that area become obese. However, this is because they need to eat large amounts of food to provide themselves with enough energy rather than because it is a satiety center.
- Obesity depends to a large (!) extent on genetic factors. Easy access to fatty foods, lack of exercise, and little nonexercise activity thermogenesis are other contributory factors.

Sex and sexual behavior

- The most important evolutionary advantage of sexual reproduction is that it produces genetic diversity.
- The sexual response cycle consists of successive excitement, plateau, orgasm, and resolution phases.
- Sexual desire in humans is only modestly influenced by sex hormones such as testosterone and estradiol. Female sex drive may be influenced more by "male hormones" than by "female hormones."
- According to evolutionary psychologists, the fact that women typically have a much greater parental investment in their offspring than men means that women are less interested in casual sex and in promiscuity. This has been found in virtually every culture.
- There are several gender differences in sexuality. On average men have more sex desire than women, men are less concerned about having committed relationships, men associate aggression more closely with sexuality than do women, and men have less erotic or sexual plasticity than women.

Work motivation and performance
- According to goal-setting theory, performance depends on the difficulty of the goals we set ourselves and our commitment to those goals.
- There is considerable support for the theory, especially when a single task is performed over a short period of time in the absence of distraction.
- One of the omissions from goal-setting theory is the notion of implementation intentions. These consist of detailed strategies for achieving goals and resemble "instant habits."
- Individuals who set themselves difficult goals and commit themselves to those goals are often high in core self-evaluations. Such individuals have high self-esteem and high emotional stability.
- Goal-setting theory focuses too much on cognitive factors associated with motivation and not enough on emotional factors.

Further Reading

- Kalat, J.W. (2004). *Biological psychology* (8th ed.). Pacific Grove, CA: Brooks/Cole. Reasonably detailed accounts of most of the topics discussed in this chapter are contained in this well-written textbook.
- Latham, G.P., & Pinder, C. (2005). Work motivation theory and research at the dawn of the twenty-first century. *Annual Review of Psychology*, 56, 485–516. This article contains a good review of theories of work motivation including goal-setting theory.
- Locke, E.A., & Latham, G.P. (2006). New directions in goal-setting theory. *Current Directions in Psychological Science*, 15, 265–268. This article provides a short and readable account of goal-setting theory.
- Pinel, J.P.J. (2006). *Biopsychology* (6th ed.). Boston: Allyn & Bacon. This textbook provides reader-friendly accounts of key topics in motivation.
- Reeve, J. (2005). *Understanding motivation and emotion* (4th ed.). Hoboken, NJ: Wiley. Most of the main topics in motivation are dealt with at length in this textbook.
- Rosenzweig, M.R., Breedlove, S.M., & Leiman, A.L. (2004). *Biological psychology: An introduction to behavioral, cognitive, and clinical neuroscience* (4th ed.). Sunderland, MA: Sinauer Associates. There are readable and fairly comprehensive accounts of biological approaches to motivation in this textbook.
- Wade, C. (2005). *Psychology* (8th ed.). New York: Prentice Hall. Chapter 12 in this introductory textbook is devoted to motivation, including a discussion on hunger and sexual motivation.

Chapter 4

Contents

Emotion, stress, and coping

Most (or even all!) of the really important events in our lives are associated with high levels of emotion. When we embark on a new relationship we feel excited, when we pass major examinations we feel elated, when we fail to achieve something we had set our heart on we feel depressed, and when someone close to us dies we experience overpowering grief. Thus, emotions play a central role in our lives. We start this chapter with a discussion of research and theory on emotion. After that, the focus shifts to stress. Among the issues considered are an assessment of the effects of stress on our physical health and ways of coping with stress.

PSYCHOLOGY OF EMOTION

What is emotion? According to Watson and Clark (1994, p. 89):

> [Emotions] *we can define as distinct, integrated psychophysiological response systems ... An emotion contains three differentiable response systems: (1) a prototypic form of expression (typically facial), (2) a pattern of consistent autonomic changes, and (3) a distinct subjective feeling state.*

We will apply the above definition to fear. When someone is fearful, they typically have a particular expression on their face. The eyebrows are raised and close together, the eyes are opened wider than usual, the lips are pulled back, and there is tension in the lower lip. So far as the second component of emotion is concerned, fear is associated with a substantial increase in autonomic nervous system activity (e.g., sweating; faster heart rate). Finally, fearful individuals describe their subjective feeling state as "nervous," "frightened," and "scared to death."

HOW MANY EMOTIONS ARE THERE?

The question, "How many emotions are there?" sounds easy. Alas, there is little agreement on the answer, in part because the question is ambiguous. When answering the question, we can focus either on the number and nature of *basic* emotions or we can also include *complex* emotions derived from the basic ones. In either case, the boundary between one emotion and another is often fuzzy. Indeed, we sometimes find it hard to decide which emotion we are experiencing!

In what follows, we consider only the basic emotions. In doing so, we focus on three main kinds of evidence: (1) facial expressions; (2) self-reports; and (3) brain systems.

Facial expressions

We all display many facial expressions, and it seems reasonable to assume that each of our basic emotions has its own distinctive expression. Ekman, Friesen, and Ellsworth

Facial expressions associated with emotion are generally recognized across cultures, suggesting that the expressive aspect of emotion is innate.

(1972) reviewed the literature on facial expressions and emotion. They concluded that observers can reliably detect six emotions in faces: happiness; surprise; anger; sadness; fear; and disgust combined with contempt.

Nearly all the studies reviewed by Ekman et al. (1972) were carried out in Western societies and are thus limited in scope. Accordingly, Ekman et al. (1987) carried out cross-cultural research on facial expressions in 10 different countries (Estonia, Germany, Greece, Hong Kong, Italy, Japan, Scotland, Sumatra, Turkey, and the United States). The findings were very similar across all cultures, suggesting that the six emotions identified by Ekman et al. (1972) are universal.

Much research on facial expressions is rather narrow and artificial. Individuals typically follow instructions about which muscles to contract to produce the facial expressions characteristic of various emotions. When they have succeeded, photographs are taken and presented to observers. Apart from its artificiality, this type of research is limited because it ignores two of the three main components of emotion (i.e., autonomic changes; subjective feeling state). Levenson, Ekman, and Friesen (1990) addressed the above issues. Participants moved their facial muscles to produce certain expressions while their autonomic activity was measured. They also described the emotions they experienced. Voluntarily producing various facial expressions generated real emotions in which all three emotion components (expression; autonomic changes; subjective feeling state) were present. Of most importance, participants mostly reported experiencing the predicted emotional states associated with the various facial expressions.

The greatest limitation with Ekman's approach is that there are no good reasons for assuming that *all* emotions are associated with a readily identifiable facial expression. As a result, Ekman has omitted some important emotions. For example, Sabini and Silver (2004) argued persuasively that jealousy and love should be regarded as emotions. As they pointed out, "The short answer to why love and jealousy are missing from [Ekman's] list is that they do not have unique facial expressions; there is no facial expression that all and only jealous people have, or that all and only people experiencing love have" (Sabini & Silver, 2004, p. 700).

Self-report approach

We can address the issue of the number of emotions by using self-report inventories. These inventories typically consist of numerous adjectives (e.g., sad, lonely, happy, nervous, irritable), and participants indicate those indicating their feelings "at this moment." The Positive and Negative Affect Schedule (PANAS-X; Watson & Clark, 1994) measures 11 different emotions or moods (fear, sadness, hostility, guilt, shyness, fatigue, surprise, joviality, self-assurance, attentiveness, and serenity). However, as we will see, that doesn't necessarily mean there are 11 basic emotions. Many of the scales correlated highly with other scales, suggesting that they are measuring similar emotional states.

A two-level hierarchical model of emotion. Based on Watson and Clark (1992).

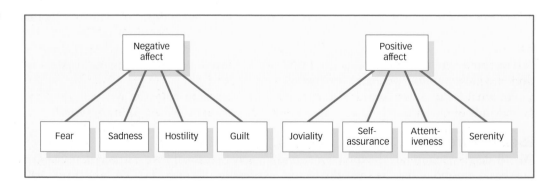

Watson and Tellegen (1985) and Watson and Clark (1992) argued that the evidence was consistent with a hierarchical model (see the figure on the left). In this model, there are several correlated (but distinguishable) emotional states at the lower level. At the upper level, there are two broad and independent factors called Negative Affect and Positive Affect. All emotional or mood states can be related to the two-dimensional structure formed by Negative and Positive Affect. You probably find it difficult to think of positive and negative affect as being *independent* of each other rather than as *opposites*. Russell (e.g., Barrett & Russell, 1998) proposed a two-dimensional model of emotion more in line with our intuitions. According to this model, there are two independent dimensions: (1) pleasure–misery; and (2) arousal–sleep. The first dimension concerns the type of emotional experience (i.e., pleasurable or displeasurable) and the second dimension concerns its intensity. This model seems rather different from the one put forward by Watson and Tellegen (1985) but is actually remarkably similar (see the figure on the right). Detailed analyses of findings using emotion questionnaires indicate that these two models are alternative descriptions of the same two-dimensional space (Russell & Barrett, 1999).

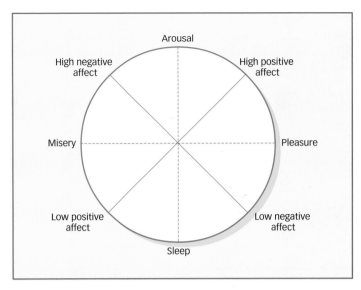

The two-dimensional framework for emotion showing the two dimensions of pleasure–misery and arousal–sleep (Barrett & Russell, 1998) and the two dimensions of Positive Affect and Negative Affect (Watson & Tellegen, 1985). Based on Barrett and Russell (1998).

Brain systems

Panksepp (2000, p. 143) argued that the brain is of special importance in distinguishing among emotions. He proposed that our main emotions are based on various circuits involving the limbic area and the midbrain. He identified seven basic emotional systems centered on the brain:

- Seeking/expectancy
- Rage/anger
- Fear/anxiety
- Lust/sexuality
- Care/nurturance
- Panic/separation
- Play/joy.

We can compare this list with the one proposed by Ekman et al. (1972; discussed above) on the basis of facial expressions. The good news is that three of the emotions identified by Ekman et al., namely, anger, fear, and happiness, are very similar to emotions identified by Panksepp (2000). The bad news is that there is otherwise practically no overlap! Ekman et al. also identified surprise, sadness, and disgust, which are simply missing from Panksepp's list.

HOW USEFUL ARE EMOTIONS?

It is popularly believed that negative emotions such as anxiety and depression are useless and undesirable. That belief is understandable for various reasons. First, no one wants to become anxious or depressed. Second, emotions often disrupt our current activities and behavior. Third, as Keltner and Gross (1999, pp. 467–468) pointed out, emotions "generally lack the logic, rationality, and principled orderliness of reason and other cognitive processes."

Case Study: *Phineas Gage*

The link between brain damage and emotions was famously demonstrated in the case of Phineas Gage, who was working on the construction of a railway. On September 13, 1848, he had a terrible accident, in which an explosion caused a large iron rod to enter his skull close to his left eyebrow and to exit through the top of his head. The force of the explosion was such that the iron rod landed 30 meters away! Gage survived this accident, and eventually showed good physical recovery. However, the accident changed his personality, making him much more aggressive and irritable than before, and unable to make long-term plans. After his death, Gage's skull was kept in a museum at Harvard Medical School, and was re-examined by Damasio, Grabowski, Frank, Galaburda, and Damasio (1994) using neuroimaging techniques involving computer simulation. They concluded the brain damage Gage suffered was in both frontal lobes, especially the left orbitofrontal cortex.

Danger causes anxiety, which produces an epinephrine (adrenaline) rush. This is adaptive as it enables the person to react quickly to avoid the danger.

In spite of the above arguments, the dominant view nowadays is that emotions are useful and serve valuable functions. For example, anxiety is associated with selective attention to threat-related stimuli, and rapid detection of danger can be extremely valuable in threatening environments (Eysenck, 1992). In addition, the increased physiological activity associated with fear and anxiety is useful because it prepares the individual for fight or flight. Lee, Wadsworth, and Hotop (2006) found another advantage. Individuals rated as highly anxious by their teachers at the age of 13 were much less likely than those rated as nonanxious to die in accidental circumstances before the age of 25 (0.1% vs. 0.7%, respectively). Anxious individuals are more cautious and so more inclined to avoid taking risks than their less anxious counterparts.

According to Watson and Andrews (2002), depression is caused by an important loss, and serves two valuable functions. First, it increases the focus on accurate analysis and solution of major problems facing the individual. Second, the obvious distress and unhappiness displayed by depressed individuals may help to persuade other people to help them. As predicted, recovery from depression is speeded up when depressed individuals have strong social support (e.g., Brugha et al., 1997). This approach minimizes the downside of depression. It is associated with very low levels of energy and motivation, which is hardly the ideal state for engaging in complex social problem solving! In addition, depressed people who make their partner's life a misery often find themselves losing their partner rather than receiving the help they seek.

Oatley and Johnson-Laird (1987) focused on the positive functions of emotions in their influential theory. They identified five basic emotions, and argued that each one occurs at a key point with respect to a current goal or plan:

1. *Happiness*: Progress has been made on a current goal.
2. *Anxiety*: The goal of self-preservation is threatened.
3. *Sadness*: The current goal can't be achieved.
4. *Anger*: The current goal is frustrated or blocked.
5. *Disgust*: A gustatory [taste] goal is violated.

An unconscious subjective emotional response

Murphy and Zajonc (1996) have found that subliminal viewing of smiling faces produces a measurable rise in positive frame of mind—a 4 millisecond presentation is too short-lived to reach the conscious mind, and yet it makes the viewer happier. This positive emotion then influences the viewer's response to other things, i.e., their mood.

According to Oatley and Johnson-Laird (1987), emotions serve the crucial function of influencing individuals to pursue whatever goal has the greatest survival or other value in the current situation. For example, happiness encourages the individual to continue with the current goal. In contrast, sadness leads people to abandon their current (unachievable) goal and to conserve energy so they can subsequently pursue a more realistic goal. Anxiety motivates individuals to deal with threats to the achievement of some important goal.

You may still not be convinced that all emotions are useful, especially if you consider that negative ones can be disruptive and unpleasant. Levenson (1999, p. 496) made an interesting attempt to bridge the gap between the emotions-are-useful and the emotions-are-disruptive positions: "Viewed from the perspective of what we were trying to accomplish prior to the emotion taking hold, the subsequent emotional behaviour may appear chaotic and *disorganized*. But, viewed from the perspective of the survival of the organism, the emotional behavior represents an elegant, adaptive, and highly *organized* state of affairs."

THEORIES OF EMOTION

There is a bewildering variety of theories of emotion. They differ considerably because of the different aims of the theorists concerned. Some theorists have viewed emotion mainly from a physiological perspective, whereas others emphasize the cognitive processes associated with emotion. Still other theorists have provided an overall account of the relationships among the cognitive, physiological, and behavioral systems.

The first major theory of emotion was put forward independently by William James in the United States and Carl Lange in Denmark in the mid-1880s. This could explain why the theory is generally known as the James–Lange theory. According to this theory, three successive stages are involved in producing emotion:

1. There is an emotional stimulus (e.g., a car comes rapidly towards you as you cross the road).
2. This produces bodily changes (e.g., arousal in the autonomic nervous system).
3. Feedback from the bodily changes leads to the experience of emotion (e.g., fear or anxiety).

Common sense might suggest that (2) and (3) are in the wrong order. For example, James gave this example of the predicted sequence according to the theory: "I see a bear, I run away, I feel afraid" (see the figure below). It seems more likely that the sequence would be as follows: "I see a bear, I feel afraid, I run away."

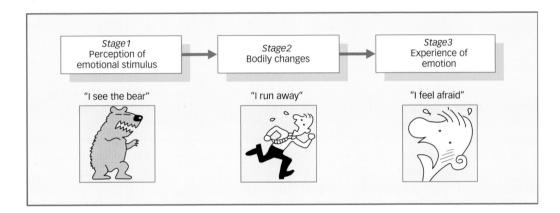

There is some mileage in the James–Lange theory. For example, consider patients with panic disorder experiencing a panic attack. The key reason they experience extremely high levels of anxiety is because they catastrophically misinterpret their own bodily symptoms (e.g., interpreting a fast heart rate as indicating an imminent heart attack) (Clark, 1986). However, the theory assumes mistakenly that each emotion is associated with its own specific pattern of physiological activity. In addition, evidence from patients with damage to the spinal cord is not favorable to the theory. These patients have greatly restricted awareness of their own physiological symptoms, and so should have a large reduction in their emotional experience. However, Bermond, Nieuwenhuyse, Fasotti, and Schwerman (1991) found that most of their patients with spinal damage reported *increased* intensity of emotions. Cobos, Sánchez, Pérez, and Vila (2004) found that patients with spinal cord injuries reported that their current emotional experiences across several emotions were at least as great as prior to injury. Thus, strong feedback from bodily changes is *not* essential for emotion to be experienced.

AROUSAL-INTERPRETATION THEORY

Schachter and Singer (1962) started the modern era in emotion research with its emphasis on cognitive factors. According to their arousal-interpretation theory, the experience of emotion depends on two factors both of which must be present:

1. High physiological arousal.
2. An emotional interpretation of that arousal.

They argued that very similar states of physiological arousal are associated with every emotion. We experience fear, anger, or whatever, because of the specific way in which the arousal is interpreted.

The theory predicts that no emotion will be experienced if *either* high physiological arousal *or* an emotional interpretation is missing. Marañon (1924) obtained findings supporting that prediction. Participants were injected with epinephrine (adrenaline), a drug whose effects resemble those of a naturally occurring state of arousal. When asked how they felt, 71% simply reported their physical symptoms with no emotional experience. Most of the remaining participants reported "as if" emotions, that is, emotions lacking their normal intensity. Participants perceived their state of arousal as having been produced by the drug, and so they didn't interpret it as indicating an emotional state.

Schachter and Singer (1962) carried out an expanded version of Marañon's (1924) study—see the Key Study below.

Findings difficult to account for on the theory were reported by Mezzacappa, Katkin, and Palmer (1999). Participants watched film clips known to produce anger, fear, or amusement. Those given epinephrine (but misinformed about its effects) expressed increased fear to the fear films, but didn't report increased anger to the anger films or amusement to the amusement

Key Study

Schachter and Singer (1962): Suproxin

All participants were told the study was designed to test the effects of the vitamin compound "Suproxin" on vision. In fact, they were injected with epinephrine (adrenaline) (to produce arousal) or a salt-based solution having no effect on arousal. Some of those given epinephrine were correctly informed about the drug's effects. Others were misinformed or uninformed (being told that the injection would have no side-effects). After the injection, participants were put in a situation designed to produce either euphoria (joy) or anger. This was done by putting them in the same room as someone who acted joyfully or angrily.

Which groups were the most emotional? Theoretically, it should have been those groups given epinephrine who wouldn't have interpreted the arousal created as having been produced by the drug. Thus, the misinformed and uninformed groups given epinephrine should have been the most emotional. The findings broadly supported the predictions, but many effects were rather small or nonsignificant.

Discussion points

1. How does the approach adopted by Schachter and Singer differ from those of previous theorists?
2. What are the weaknesses with this research and this theoretical approach?

KEY STUDY EVALUATION

For such a classic study, it is surprising how inadequately it was carried out. Here are just a few of the problems. First, physiological arousal was assessed only by means of pulse rate, which is a poor single measure to use. Second, the judges who rated emotion knew which condition the participants were in, and this may have biased their ratings. Third, the judges didn't use a standardized coding system for recording the participants' behavior.

One of the reasons why the study by Schachter and Singer (1962) didn't produce convincing findings may have been because those given the salt-based solution became physiologically aroused by being put into an emotional situation. If so, they would have had the high arousal *and* emotional interpretation, which together produce a strong emotional state. Schachter and Wheeler (1962) argued that the way to stop people becoming aroused was to give them a depressant drug to reduce arousal. The participants were given a depressant, or epinephrine, or a substance having no effects, and were told in each case that the drug had no side-effects. They then watched a slapstick film called *The Good Humour Man*. As predicted, those given epinephrine (and thus aroused) found the film the funniest, whereas those given the depressant (and thus de-aroused) found it least funny.

films. People interpret high levels of unexpected arousal as signaling a negative state of affairs, whereas the theory claims that epinephrine should enhance *any* emotional state.

Evaluation

⊕ Emotional experience depends on arousal and on emotional interpretation.

⊕ The arousal-interpretation theory was very influential in its emphasis on the role of cognitive factors in emotion.

⊖ The theory has little to say about how the interpretive process works and leads to the experience of a given emotion (this deficiency was addressed by appraisal theory, discussed below).

⊖ High levels of unexpected arousal are interpreted negatively regardless of the situation.

⊖ Different emotions are associated with different patterns of physiological arousal (e.g., Levenson et al., 1990), whereas the theory predicts the same arousal pattern for every emotion.

⊖ Schachter and Singer (1962) focused on very artificial situations in which high levels of arousal were difficult to interpret. The relevance of such situations to typical everyday situations is unclear.

APPRAISAL THEORY

According to Lazarus (1982, 1991) emotional experience is crucially dependent on **cognitive appraisal**, which is the interpretation of the current situation. Cognitive appraisal can be subdivided into three more specific forms of appraisal:

* *Primary appraisal*: The situation is perceived as being positive, stressful, or irrelevant to wellbeing.
* *Secondary appraisal*: Account is taken of the resources available to the individual to cope with the situation.
* *Re-appraisal*: The stimulus situation and coping strategies are monitored, with the primary and secondary appraisal being modified if necessary.

This approach was developed by Smith and Lazarus (1993) to account for our experience of different emotions. They argued that there are six appraisal components, two involving primary appraisal and four involving secondary appraisal (see the figure below):

* *Primary*: Motivational relevance—related to personal commitments?
* *Primary*: Motivational congruence—consistent with the individual's goals?
* *Secondary*: Accountability—who deserves the credit or blame?
* *Secondary*: Problem-focused coping potential—how can the situation be resolved?
* *Secondary*: Emotion-focused coping potential—can the situation be handled psychologically?
* *Secondary*: Future expectancy—how likely is it the situation will change?

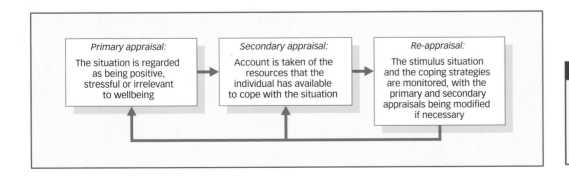

Key Term

Cognitive appraisal: assessment of a situation to decide whether it is stressful and whether the individual has the resources to cope with it.

Different emotional states can be distinguished on the basis of which appraisal components are involved. For example, anger, guilt, anxiety, and sadness all possess the primary appraisal components of motivational relevance and motivational incongruence (these emotions only occur when goals are blocked). However, they differ in terms of secondary appraisal components. Guilt involves self-accountability, anxiety involves low or uncertain emotion-focused coping potential, and sadness involves low future expectancy for change.

Smith and Lazarus (1993) used scenarios in which participants identified with the central character. In one scenario, the central character has performed poorly in an important course, and he appraises the situation. Other-accountability was produced by having him put the blame on the unhelpful teaching assistants. Self-accountability was produced by having him accept he made many mistakes (e.g., doing work at the last minute). Low emotion-focused coping potential was produced by thinking there was a great danger he would finish with a poor academic record. Low future expectancy for change was produced by having him think it was impossible to succeed with his chosen academic path. The appraisal mechanisms generally had the predicted effects on participants' reported emotional states, indicating that there are fairly close links between appraisal and experienced emotion.

Kuppens, van Mechelen, Smits, and de Boeck (2003) found that the relationship between cognitive appraisal and specific emotional experience is more *flexible* than is assumed in appraisal theory. They studied four appraisals (goal obstacle; other accountability; unfairness; and control) relevant to the experience of anger. Participants described recently experienced unpleasant situations in which one of the four appraisals was present or absent. The key finding was that none of the four appraisals was either necessary or sufficient for anger to be experienced. Thus, for example, we can feel angry without the appraisal of unfairness or the presence of a goal obstacle.

The main limitation with earlier versions of appraisal theory is that little was said about the *processes* involved in appraisal. Smith and Kirby (2001) addressed this issue (see the figure below). They distinguished between two types of appraisal:

1. *Reasoning*: This involves a controlled and deliberate thinking process that takes time and requires attentional resources;
2. *Associative processing*: This involves rapid activation of relevant information stored in memory and occurs rapidly and automatically.

Mechanisms involved in the appraisal process. From Smith and Kirby (2001), Toward delivering on the promise of apprais theory. In K.R. Scherer, A. Schoor, & T. Johnson (Eds.), *Appraisal processes in emotion: Theory, methods, research.* Reprinted by permission of Oxford University Press, Inc.

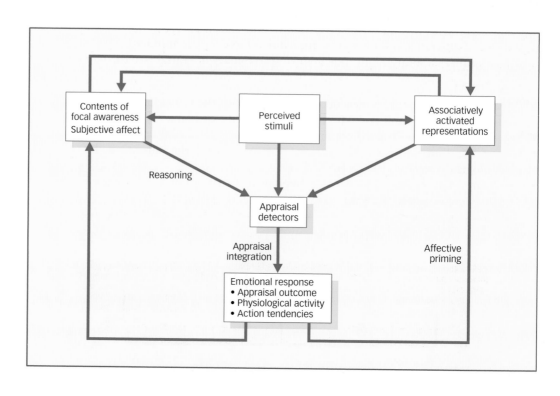

Appraisal detectors monitor appraisal information from the reasoning and associative processes. This appraisal information determines the individual's emotional experience. This newer approach draws a clear distinction between appraisal processes of which the individual is aware and those of which he/she is not aware.

Evaluation

⊕ Lazarus's appraisal theory sheds light on the cognitive processes influencing the emotions we experience in different situations.

⊕ The theory also helps to explain why people vary in their emotional experience in any given situation.

⊖ The notion of appraisal is broad and vague. For example, Lazarus (1991, p. 169) referred to two kinds of appraisal processes: "one that operates automatically without awareness or volitional [deliberate] control, and another that is conscious, deliberate, and volitional." However, Smith and Kirby (2001) have made a start on increasing the precision with which appraisal processes are described.

⊖ Smith and Lazarus (1993) argued that the exact emotions we experience depend crucially on the various appraisal components. However, as Parkinson (2001) pointed out, the appraisal components only predicted emotion ratings to a fairly modest extent in the Smith and Lazarus study.

⊖ The relationship between different types of cognitive appraisal and the experience of a given emotion is more flexible and variable than assumed by the theory.

⊖ The focus is too much on an individual thinking about his/her personal reactions to the current situation. What is relatively ignored is the *social context* in which emotion is typically experienced.

MULTI-LEVEL APPROACH

Many people report complex reactions to certain potentially threatening stimuli or situations. For example, some people are scared to fly in airplanes even though they know flying is very safe. In similar fashion, spider phobics become very frightened in the presence of a spider in spite of knowing that most spiders are harmless. Such reports suggest that the emotion system is complex, with emotional processing at one level sometimes combined with a lack of such processing at another level. Precisely this assumption was included by Power and Dalgleish (1997) in their Schematic Propositional Associative and Analogical Representational Systems (SPAARS) approach.

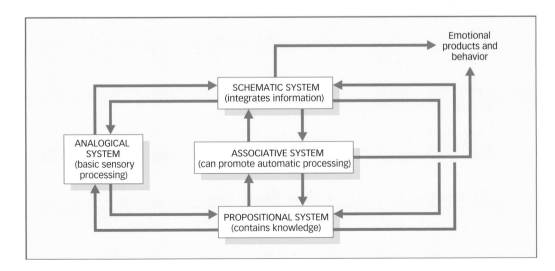

The Schematic Propositional Associative and Analogical Representational Systems (SPAARS) approach put forward by Power and Dalgleish (1997).

Emotion: Is it a physiological or a cognitive experience?

Some kinds of emotional experience are more physiological, others are more cognitive.

- *A physiological experience.* A jet screams over your head, you duck and experience a tightness in your chest. Past experience and individual differences will determine the emotion you might report feeling—fear, surprise, elation. For each of us it will be different, but the basis will be arousal. Such responses are more related to emotion as an adaptive response.
- *A cognitive experience.* You hear that you have passed an exam and feel ecstatic, which may lead to physiological sensations.

This might explain why emotion can sometimes occur with arousal and sometimes without it. It also fits in with LeDoux's suggestion that there are two pathways in the brain, one more physiological and the other more related to higher-order processing.

The SPAARS approach is shown in the figure on the previous page. Its main components are as follows:

- *Analogical system*: This is involved in basic sensory processing of environmental stimuli.
- *Propositional system*: This is an essentially emotion-free system containing information about the world and the self.
- *Schematic system*: In this system, facts from the propositional system are combined with information about the individual's current goals to produce a model of the situation. This produces an emotional response if the current goals are being thwarted.
- *Associative system*: "If the same event is repeatedly presented in the same way at the schematic level, then an associative representation will be formed such that, on future encounters of the same event, the relevant emotion will be *automatically* elicited" (Dalgleish, 1998, p. 492).

We can use the SPAARS approach to shed light on the reactions of people who are scared of flying or who have a spider phobia. Such people exhibit an automatic fear reaction via the associative system but realize that airplanes and spiders are not threatening via the propositional and schematic systems. Evidence that emotional processing can be automatic and below the level of conscious awareness was reported by Ohman and Soares (1994). They presented snake and spider phobics with pictures of snakes, spiders, flowers, and mushrooms, shown so rapidly they couldn't be identified consciously. In spite of that, the spider phobics reacted emotionally to the spider pictures, as did the snake phobics to the snake pictures. There were greater physiological responses to the phobia-relevant pictures, and the participants felt more negative when exposed to those pictures.

Evidence for the existence of two systems for fear has been obtained by LeDoux (1992, 1996). He emphasizes the role of the amygdala which forms part of the limbic system. According to LeDoux, sensory information about emotional stimuli is relayed from the thalamus simultaneously to the amygdala and to the cortex. There are two different emotion circuits for fear (both supported by much evidence):

1. A slow-acting thalamus–cortex–amygdala circuit involving detailed analysis of sensory information and resembling the system within SPAARS involving the propositional and schematic systems.
2. A fast-acting thalamus–amygdala circuit based on simple stimulus features (e.g., intensity). This circuit bypasses the cortex and resembles the associative system within SPAARS.

Evaluation

+ Multi-level theories such as SPAARS explain emotional conflict.
+ Emotional reactions can be produced automatically at the associative level without involving conscious processing.
− SPAARS de-emphasizes the role of physiological processes in emotion.
− SPAARS provides a framework within which to understand emotion rather than a detailed theory generating several testable hypotheses.

Amygdalotomies

As a result of work such as that of Kluver and Bucy (1939), "psychosurgeons" in the United States carried out numerous operations on criminals serving jail sentences. Many of these operations were amygdalotomies, in which parts of the amygdala were destroyed. This was done by putting fine wire electrodes into the amygdala through a small hole drilled in the skull, and then passing strong electric currents through the electrodes. These amygdalotomies reduced fear and anger in those operated on, but they often had very unfortunate side-effects. For example, Thomas R was a 34-year-old engineer who suffered delusions and could not work after surgery. He was found on one occasion walking about with his head covered by bags, rags, and newspapers. He justified his behavior by saying he was frightened other bits of his brain might be destroyed. Thankfully, amygdalotomy is very rarely carried out nowadays.

STRESS

It has often been said that ours is the "age of stress." It is probably true that more people than ever *report* being highly stressed. However, it isn't clear that most people are more stressed than used to be the case. Our ancestors had to contend with major epidemics, poor life expectancy, poverty, and an almost complete absence of holidays. Taking all that into account, my hunch is that stress levels nowadays are much the same as in the past.

What is stress? According to Colman (2001, p. 711), stress is "the psychological and physical strain or tension generated by physical, emotional, social, economic, or occupational circumstances, events, or experiences that are difficult to manage or endure." Thus, for example, driving is stressful to a learner driver because he/she has limited ability to meet the demands of handling a car in traffic. Driving is not stressful to experienced drivers, because they are confident their driving ability will allow them to cope with most driving situations.

What are the effects of being exposed to stress? There are four major kinds of effects: physiological; emotional; cognitive; and behavioral (see the figure below). We start by considering physiological or bodily effects. Stress involves an immediate shock response followed by a countershock response. The first (shock) response depends mainly on the sympathetic adrenal medullary system (SAM), whereas the second or countershock response involves the hypothalamic–pituitary–adrenocortical axis (HPA). These two response systems (discussed below) are shown in the figure on the following page.

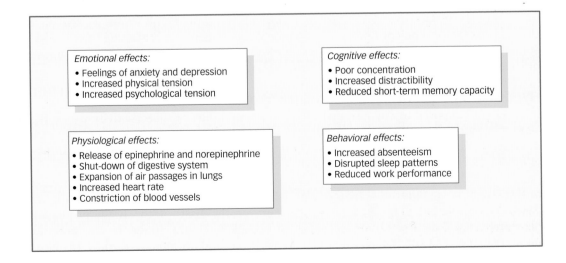

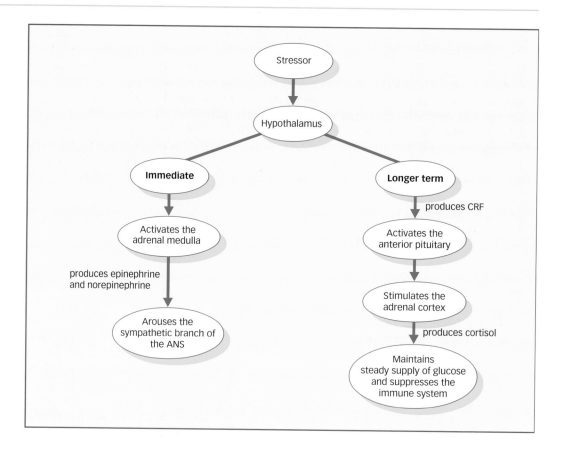

Sympathetic adrenal medullary system

The initial shock response involves the sympathetic adrenal medullary system (SAM). Activity in the sympathetic branch of the autonomic nervous system (ANS) stimulates the adrenal medulla, which forms part of the adrenal glands. The adrenal medulla secretes the hormones epinephrine and norepinephrine (outside of the US widely referred to as adrenaline and noradrenaline, respectively). These hormones lead to increased arousal of the sympathetic nervous system and reduced activity in the parasympathetic nervous system (see the "Introduction to biological psychology" section).

Heightened activity of the sympathetic nervous system prepares us for "fight or flight." There is an increase in energy, increased alertness, increased blood flow to the muscles, increased heart and respiration rate, reduced activity in the digestive system, and increased release of clotting factors into the bloodstream to reduce blood loss in the event of injury. Epinephrine and norepinephrine increase the output of the heart, which can cause an increase in blood pressure.

SAM activity forms an important part of the stress response, because it prepares us for fight or flight. However, SAM activity is not only associated with stress. We also have elevated levels of epinephrine and norepinephrine when concentrating on a task. Sometimes we perceive heightened activity in SAM as indicating we are stressed, but at other times we interpret such activity as excitement.

Hypothalamic–pituitary–adrenocortical axis

If someone is exposed to any given stressor for several hours or more, activity within the SAM system increasingly uses up bodily resources. As a result, there is a countershock designed to minimize any damage. This countershock response involves the hypothalamic–pituitary–adrenocortical axis (HPA), the details of which are discussed below.

The glands of the endocrine system are distributed throughout the body, with most of the system being controlled by the hypothalamus (see the "Introduction to biological psychology" section). This is a small structure at the base of the brain producing hormones (e.g., corticotropin-releasing factor or CRF) that stimulate the anterior pituitary gland. The anterior pituitary gland releases several hormones, of which the most important is adrenocorticotropic hormone (ACTH). ACTH stimulates the adrenal cortex, which forms part of the adrenal glands. The adrenal cortex produces glucocorticoids, which are hormones having effects on glucose metabolism. The key glucocorticoid with respect to stress is cortisol, which is sometimes called the "stress hormone." This is because excess amounts are found in the urine of individuals experiencing stress.

What kinds of stress produce increased levels of cortisol? This issue was addressed by Dickerson and Kemeny (2004) in a meta-analysis of 208 laboratory stress studies using motivated performance tasks. Tasks that were uncontrollable and associated with social-evaluative threat produced the highest levels of cortisol, the greatest ACTH changes, and the longest recovery time. Stroud, Salovey, and Epel (2002) reported interesting sex differences in stress response. Male and female participants were exposed to achievement stressors (complex tasks) and to social rejection (being excluded from a conversation). Only male participants showed a significant increase in cortisol after exposure to achievement stressors, and only female participants had increased cortisol after social rejection. These sex differences are consistent with stereotyped notions about men being more concerned than women about achievement and women being more concerned about social acceptance.

Cortisol is important for coping with long-term stress, because it permits maintenance of a steady supply of fuel. The secretion of cortisol and other glucocorticoids has various effects. First, the glucocorticoids help to conserve glucose for neural tissues. Second, they elevate or stabilize blood glucose concentrations. Third, they mobilize protein reserves. Fourth, they conserve salts and water.

Activity of the hypothalamic–pituitary–adrenocortical axis is very useful in allowing us to cope with stress. The HPA reduces many of the effects of the first or shock response to stress. We can see this by considering individuals without adrenal glands who can't

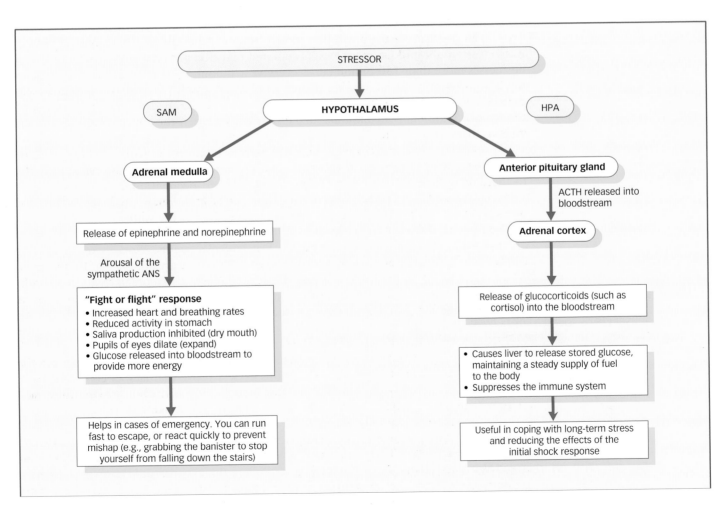

produce the normal amounts of glucocorticoids. When exposed to a stressor, they have to be given additional quantities of glucorticoids to survive (Tyrell & Baxter, 1981).

The beneficial effects of HPA activity are achieved at considerable cost. As Westen (1996, p. 427) pointed out, "The blood still has elevated levels of glucose (for energy) and some hormones (including epinephrine and the pituitary hormone ACTH), and the body continues to use its resources at an accelerating rate. Essentially, the organism remains on red alert." Among the disadvantages of continuing HPA activity is that the anti-inflammatory action of glucocorticoids slows wound healing. More generally, glucocorticoids suppress the immune system, which protects the body against intruders such as viruses and bacteria. When immune responses are low, we are more likely to develop a disease (e.g., Kiecolt-Glaser et al., 1984).

The SAM and HPA have been discussed as if they form different systems. This is approximately correct, but the two systems don't operate in complete independence of each other (see the figure on the previous page). As Evans (1998, p. 60) pointed out, "At the level of the central nervous system, the crucially important SAM and HPA systems can be considered as one complex: they are as it were the lower limbs of one body."

STRESS AND ILLNESS

A key topic within stress research is the relationship between stress and disease. Stress has been linked with numerous physical illnesses, including headaches, infectious disease (e.g., influenza), cardiovascular disease, diabetes, asthma, and rheumatoid arthritis (Curtis, 2000). It has also been linked with various mental disorders including the anxiety disorders and depression. In a short while, we will discuss the broad issue of the relationship between stressful experiences and physical disease or mental disorder. After that, we focus on individual differences in susceptibility to stress. Finally, we consider the mechanisms causing stress to have adverse effects on our health. First of all, however, we consider the negative effects of occupational stress on health.

Millions of adults attribute their highly stressed state mainly to the demands of their work. This is unsurprising given that most of them spend almost 2000 hours a year at work. Cartwright and Cooper (1997) estimated that occupational stress costs American businesses more than 150 billion euros every year (about $220 billion). What is it about the work environment that makes people stressed? Karasek (1979) argued persuasively that lack of perceived control is of key importance. He claimed that workers can cope successfully with highly demanding jobs if they perceive that they have control over their work activities.

Spector, Dwyer, and Jex (1988) assessed perceived control in workers. Low levels of control were associated with frustration, anxiety, headaches, stomach upsets, and visits to the doctor. Ganster, Fox, and Dwyer (2001) studied occupational stress in a 5-year study on nurses. High perceived control at the start of the study predicted less use of medical services and better mental health over the course of the study.

Marmot et al. (1997) and Bosma, Stanfeld, and Marmot (1998) reported dramatic findings from a 5-year study on over 9000 British civil servants. Workers on the lowest employment grades were *four* times more likely to die of a heart attack than those on the most senior grade. They were also more likely to suffer from cancer, strokes, and gastrointestinal disorders. These differences seemed to occur because those in the lower positions had much less control over their work than those in the higher positions. However, all the findings were based on associations or correlations between control and various diseases, and this doesn't prove that lack of control actually caused the diseases. Individuals who are mentally and physically robust may be more likely to rise to senior job positions *and* to be resistant to the effects of stress, but it is unlikely that this accounts for all the findings.

There is a final point on occupational stress. Several work factors other than perceived control influence workers' psychological wellbeing. For example, Warr

---

Workplace stress in a sawmill

Frankenhaeuser (1975) found a link between perceived lack of control at work and high levels of stress. Some sawmill workers were given jobs where they fed logs into the mill machines, continually, all day. This repetitive and monotonous task also isolated them as it was extremely noisy, and the machine speeds dictated how fast the workers fed in the logs. The workers felt isolated, with a minimum of control. And, compared to the other mill workers who had more control and were not similarly isolated, these workers suffered far more from headaches, digestive disorders such as ulcers, and high blood pressure.

(1996) identified the following important factors: availability of money; opportunity for skills' use; work demands; variety; physical security; opportunity for interpersonal contact; environmental clarity; and valued social position. Thus, workers with high levels of control in their work may still suffer from occupational stress if their work is very demanding, poorly paid, and dangerous!

LIFE EVENTS AND HASSLES

We can draw a distinction between life events and hassles. **Life events** are often major negative events or occurrences (e.g., death of a loved one) that cause high levels of stress, although some life events are relatively minor. In contrast, **hassles** are the minor challenges and interruptions (e.g., arguing with a friend; malfunctioning computer) of everyday life. On average, people experience at least one hassle on about 40% of the days in each week (Almeida, 2005).

Holmes and Rahe (1967) developed the Social Readjustment Rating Scale to assess life events. Participants indicate which out of 43 life events have happened to them over a period of time (usually 6 or 12 months). These life events are assigned a value according to their likely impact. Here are a few life events taken from this scale with their associated life change units in brackets:

death of a spouse (100)
divorce (73)
marital separation (65)
jail (63)
death of a close family member (63)
change in eating habits (15)
holiday (13)
minor violation of the law (11).

Changes can be stressful, even the usually pleasant ones associated with going on holiday.

Why are holidays (which are supposed to be fun!) treated as stressful life events? According to Holmes and Rahe, any change (whether desirable or undesirable) can be stressful.

There is reasonable evidence that life events are associated with various diseases. Rahe, Mahan, and Arthur (1970) used the Social Readjustment Rating Scale to divide naval personnel into high-risk and low-risk groups on the basis of their life events over the previous 6 months. Members of the high-risk group were twice as likely to develop illnesses during their first month at sea. In general, people experiencing events totaling more than 300 life change units over a period of 1 year are more at risk for many physical and mental illnesses (see Martin, 1989, for a review). These illnesses include heart attacks, diabetes, TB, asthma, anxiety, and depression. However, the correlations between number of life change units and susceptibility to any particular illness are rather low, indicating a weak relationship between life events and illness.

There are individual and group differences in the reactions to life events. Miller and Rahe (1997) compared the reactions of men and women to several life events. Women experienced more stress than men following the death of a close family member, a major injury or illness, loss of a job, reduced income, or moving home.

There are some limitations with most of the evidence. First, and most important, it is generally not clear whether life events have caused stress or some stress-related illness or whether stress caused the life events. For example, divorce can cause stress, but someone who is already stressed may be more likely to behave in ways that lead to divorce. Van Os, Park, and Jones (2001) studied life events in individuals low and high in the personality dimension of neuroticism (involving anxiety, depression, and susceptibility to stress). Neuroticism assessed at the age of 16 predicted the number of stressful life events experienced 27 years later. Thus, individuals with a susceptibility to stress have an increased likelihood of experiencing stressful life events.

Second, the impact of any given life event varies considerably depending on the individual's particular circumstances. For example, marital separation is likely to be less

| Key Terms |

Life events:
predominantly negative occurrences (and often of major consequence) that typically produce increased stress levels.

Hassles:
the irritating challenges of everyday life that can increase stress levels.

stressful for someone who has already established an intimate relationship with someone else. Third, it has too often been assumed that *any* major life event can help to produce almost *any* type of illness. However, there are more specific effects. For example, anxious patients are more likely than depressed patients to have experienced danger events (involving future threats) than depressed patients. In contrast, depressed patients are more likely to have experienced loss events (involving past losses such as death of a loved one) (Finlay-Jones & Brown, 1981).

Hassles

What are the main categories into which our daily hassles and stressors fall? Almeida (2005) found that 37% involved danger (e.g., potential for future loss), 30% involved some kind of loss (e.g., of money), and 27% were frustrations or events outside the individual's control. People reported more psychological distress and physical symptoms on days when they encountered hassles than on stress-free days. However, college-educated adults had less psychological distress and fewer physical symptoms than less-educated ones in spite of experiencing more daily stressors. Presumably college-educated people have more effective coping strategies at their disposal.

Stone, Reed, and Neale (1987) considered the hassles and desirable events experienced by participants during the 10 days before they developed a respiratory illness. They had experienced more hassles and fewer desirable events during that period than had control participants who didn't develop a respiratory illness.

VULNERABILITY TO STRESS

What kinds of people are most vulnerable to the adverse effects of stress? We consider two of the best-known attempted answers in turn. First, we consider the **Type A personality**. Individuals with this personality type possess "extremes of competitive achievement striving, hostility, aggressiveness, and a sense of time urgency" (Matthews, 1988, p. 373). Second, we focus on **negative affectivity**, a personality dimension characterized at the high end by frequent unpleasant emotional states (e.g., anxiety; depression). The dimension of negative affectivity is essentially the same as neuroticism (discussed in Chapter 12).

Type A personality

Meyer Friedman and Ray Rosenman (1959) distinguished between individuals with Type A personality and those with Type B personality. Type A individuals are hard-driving, competitive, and aggressive individuals, whereas Type B individuals are more relaxed and laid-back. These personality types were identified by using the Structured Interview, during the course of which the interviewer deliberately interrupts the person being interviewed. Account is taken of the individual's answers to the questions as well as his/her behavior (e.g., speed of talking; impatience or irritability when interrupted).

Friedman and Rosenman (1959) predicted that Type A individuals would be more stressed and thus more at risk of coronary heart disease than Type Bs. These predictions were tested in the Western Collaborative Group Study (Rosenman et al., 1975). Of nearly 3200 men having no symptoms at the start of the study, Type As were nearly twice as likely as Type Bs to have developed coronary heart disease over the following 8.5 years. The findings remained basically unchanged when account was taken of other factors (e.g., blood pressure; smoking) known to be associated with heart disease.

There have been numerous studies of Type A and heart disease since the pioneering study by Rosenman et al. (1975). The findings have been rather inconsistent. Miller et al. (1991) found that positive findings were more common when the Structured Interview was used rather

> **Key Terms**
>
> **Type A personality:**
> a personality type characterized by impatience, competitiveness, time pressure, and hostility.
>
> **Negative affectivity:**
> a personality dimension involving a tendency to experience negative emotional states such as anxiety and depression.

The stock exchange is the ideal environment for individuals with a Type A behavior pattern.

than self-report measures. This is probably because only the Structured Interview provides information about people's actual behavior in a stressful situation.

There have been various attempts to identify the most important aspect of the Type A personality. Matthews, Glass, Rosenman, and Bortner (1977) re-analyzed the data from the Western Collaborative Group Study, finding that the hostility component of Type A was most closely associated with heart disease. Ganster, Schaubroeck, Sime, and Mayes (1991) put participants in stressful situations. Only the hostility component of Type A was associated with high levels of physiological reactivity (e.g., blood pressure; heart rate).

Negative affectivity and Type D personality

Individuals high in negative affectivity generally report being much more stressed and distressed than those low in negative affectivity (see Watson & Clark, 1984, for a review). However, Watson and Pennebaker (1989) found that it is very important to distinguish between *complaints* about poor health and *actual* physical disease. Individuals high in negative affectivity report suffering more than those low in negative affectivity from colds, coughing, sore throats, dizziness, stomach pains, irritable bowel syndrome, and so on. They also report more chest pain and angina pectoris (sudden intense pains in the chest) than other people. However, high negative affectivity is scarcely associated with physical illness more objectively considered. For example, a meta-analysis of studies on heart disease found only a very small correlation (+.14) between anxiety (closely related to negative affectivity) and heart disease (Booth-Kewley & Friedman, 1987). Shekelle et al. (1981) found that measures of negative affectivity were not associated with overall mortality among middle-aged men. Thus, individuals high in negative affectivity exaggerate the extent to which the stresses of life are impairing their physical health.

Denollet (2005) argued that individuals highest in susceptibility to stress are those having the Type D personality. The **Type D personality** consists of a combination of high

---

Case Study: *Don't Let It Get You Down*

"Comfort always, cure rarely" is an old medical motto. And it may be nearer the truth than modern medicine would like to admit. Perhaps if patients were less depressed and more optimistic they might be more likely to recover from stressful operations.

In one study of 100 patients about to undergo bone marrow transplants for leukemia it was found that 13 of the patients were severely depressed. Of these patients 12 had died within a year of the operation (92%) whereas only 61% of the not-depressed died within 2 years of the study.

Other research has looked at the effects of pessimism and found this to be the biggest single predictor of death from a heart attack. For example, 122 men were evaluated for pessimism or optimism at the time they had a heart attack. Eight years later their state of mind was found to correlate with death more highly than any of the other standard risk factors such as damage to the heart, raised blood pressure, or high cholesterol levels. Of the 25 men who were most pessimistic 21 had died, whereas only 6 of the most optimistic 25 had died.

Peterson, Seligman, and Vaillant (1988) studied optimists and pessimists. They suggested that pessimists tended to explain setbacks in their lives as the result of things within their personality that were unchangeable. In contrast, optimists tended to explain setbacks as the result of things arising from situations within their control, but which were not their own fault. Peterson et al. rated a number of Harvard undergraduates for pessimism and optimism on the basis of essays they wrote `about their wartime experiences. After an interval of more than 20 years, the pessimists (aged 45) were more likely to be suffering from some chronic disease. However, smaller effects of personality on disease have been reported in other research.

Adapted from Goleman (1991).

Key Term

Type D personality: a personality type characterized by high **negative affectivity** and social inhibition.

negative affectivity plus high social inhibition (inhibited behavior in social situations to avoid disapproval). Denollet reported findings from people aged between 40 and 70. Type D personality was much more common among hypertension patients (54%) and coronary patients (27%) than it was among people from the general population (19%). Type D individuals are also at much greater risk than non-Type D ones for post-traumatic stress, reduced longevity, and development of cancer (see Denollet, 2005, for a review). The size of many of the effects is impressive. In one study, for example, 27% of cardiac patients with Type D personality died over a 10-year period compared to only 7% of the others (Denollet et al., 1996).

Overall Evaluation

+ Type A individuals report high levels of stress, as do those high in negative affectivity or with Type D personality.

+ Type A individuals are generally slightly more likely than Type Bs to develop coronary heart disease.

+ Type D individuals are more susceptible than others to various diseases, especially heart disease. The evidence suggests that the Type D personality may be the personality type most associated with stress-related diseases.

− Negative affectivity is only slightly associated with actual physical illness.

− Some evidence suggests that the hostility component of Type A personality is most associated with coronary heart disease, but this has not been clearly established.

MECHANISMS: HOW DOES STRESS CAUSE ILLNESS?

At the most general level, there are two main ways in which stress might cause illness:

1. *Indirect route*: Stressed individuals tend to adopt an unhealthy lifestyle (e.g., smoking or drinking too much).
2. *Direct route*: Stress reduces the body's ability to fight illness.

Indirect route

Lifestyle has a major impact on illness and longevity. For example, Belloc and Breslow (1972) asked residents of Alameda County in California to indicate which of the following seven health behaviors they practiced regularly:

Stress can lead to an unhealthy lifestyle.

- Not smoking
- Having breakfast each day
- Having no more than one or two alcoholic drinks per day
- Taking regular exercise
- Sleeping 7 to 8 hours per night
- Not eating between meals
- Being no more than 10% overweight.

Adults practicing most of the above health behaviors reported they were healthier than those practicing few or none. More striking findings were reported in a follow-up study 9.5 years later. Breslow and Enstrom (1980) found that individuals practicing all seven health behaviors had only 23% of the mortality of those practicing fewer than three. My personal score is five which is modestly encouraging! Schoenborn (1993) carried out a follow-up 17 years after the first survey. The strongest predictors of longevity were not smoking, taking physical exercise, and regular breakfast eating.

Stressed individuals tend to smoke more, to drink more alcohol, to take less exercise, and to sleep less than non-stressed individuals (Cohen & Williamson, 1991). For example, adolescents experiencing high levels of stress are more likely to start smoking than those whose lives are less stressful (Wills, 1985). Adults experiencing much stress in their lives are more likely to resume smoking after having given up (Carey et al., 1993). Stress also influences alcohol consumption. There is much support for tension reduction theory (Ogden, 1996). According to this theory, tension in the form of anxiety or depression leads to increased alcohol consumption to reduce the level of tension.

Direct route

It is often believed that stress causes illness fairly directly by impairing the functioning of the **immune system**. This system is located in various parts of the body including the bone marrow, lymph nodes, tonsils, spleen, appendix, and small intestines. Cells in the immune system have receptors for various chemical substances (hormones and neurotransmitters) involved in the stress response, so stress certainly might influence immune system functioning.

The immune system is very complex, and so it is difficult to decide how well it is functioning. As Evans, Clow, and Hucklebridge (1997, p. 303) pointed out, we should "think of the immune system as striving to maintain a state of delicate balance." There is an important distinction between natural immunity and specific immunity (Segerstrom & Miller, 2004). Cells involved in natural immunity (e.g., natural killer cells) are all-purpose cells that can attack various **antigens** (foreign bodies) such as viruses relatively rapidly. In contrast, cells involved in specific immunity (e.g., T-helper cells; B cells) are much more specific in their effects and take longer to work.

Long-term or chronic stress often impairs the functioning of the immune system. For example, Schliefer et al. (1983) studied husbands whose wives had breast cancer. The husbands' immune system seemed to function less well after their wives had died than before. Segerstrom and Miller (2004) analyzed the findings from six studies in which the death of a spouse was the stressor. Overall, losing a spouse was associated with a highly significant reduction in effectiveness of natural killer cells within the immune system.

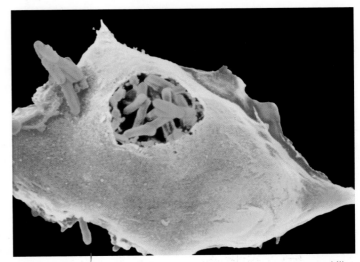

Like some monster in a movie, some cells of the immune system kill "invaders" by engulfing them. In the photograph a macrophage cell is engulfing *M. tuberculosis* bacteria.

So far we have seen that long-term stress often has adverse effects on immune system functioning. However, stress does *not* invariably impair immune system functioning. Indeed, short-term stress sometimes produces an improvement in some aspects of immune system functioning. Zeier, Brauchli, and Joller-Jemelka (1996) studied air traffic controllers on a work shift. During this shift, they showed an increase in **antibodies** (protein molecules that mark invaders out for destruction), suggesting some enhancement of immune system functioning. In similar fashion, Delahanty et al. (1996) found increased natural killer cell activity during two short stressful tasks (e.g., immersing hand in very cold water) performed under laboratory conditions.

Segerstrom and Miller (2004) pointed out that it wouldn't make any sense in evolutionary terms if humans were designed so that even short-term stress impaired the functioning of the immune system. An adaptive response would be for short-term stress to be associated with enhanced functioning of at least some aspects of the immune system. Segerstrom and Miller (2004) carried out various meta-analyses to clarify the precise effects of stress on immune system functioning. Their key findings were as follows:

- Short-lived stressors (e.g., public speaking) produce increased natural immunity (e.g., increased availability of natural killer cells) but don't alter specific immunity.

Key Terms

Immune system: a system of cells in the body involved in fighting disease.

Antigens: foreign bodies such as viruses.

Antibodies: protein molecules that attach themselves to invaders, marking them out for subsequent destruction.

- Stressful event sequences involving loss of a spouse produces a reduction in natural immunity (e.g., reduced effectiveness of natural killer cells).
- Stressful event sequences involving disasters produce small increases in natural and specific immunity.
- Life events are associated with significant reductions in natural and specific immunity in individuals over 55 years or age, but aren't associated with changes in the immunity system in those under 55.

In sum, the precise effects of stress depend much more than is generally thought on the specific nature and duration of the stressor.

Evaluation

+ Stress produces various changes in the immune system, and increases the likelihood of developing certain physical diseases.

+ We now have a fairly clear picture of the effects of different kinds of stressor on the immune system.

− Stress typically has fairly modest effects on the functioning of the immune system. Indeed, its functioning typically remains within the normal range (Bachen, Cohen, & Marsland, 1997).

− We know that stress affects the immune system and also increases the probability of certain illnesses. However, we still don't know the extent to which the effects of stress on susceptibility to disease depend on changes within the immune system.

COPING WITH STRESS

We have considered stress in some detail. How do we manage to handle and resolve it in our everyday lives? Much research has been devoted to **coping**, defined as "the thoughts and behaviours used to manage the internal and external demands of situations that are appraised as stressful" (Folkman & Moskowitz, 2004, p. 745). Thus, coping can involve behavioral or cognitive strategies (or both). As the definition implies, most research on coping has focused on how people cope with events that have occurred or are occurring in the present. However, coping can also involve preparing to deal with possible future stressors. Aspinwall and Taylor (1997) identify various forms of proactive coping (e.g., increasing one's financial and social resources).

Most of the coping strategies that have been identified (and which are discussed shortly) focus on what the individual can do through his/her own efforts. However, there is often value in relying on the help provided by other people. We can distinguish between structural social support and functional social support. The former is an individual's basic network of social relationships whereas the latter is concerned with the *quality* of social support. According to Schaefer, Coyne, and Lazarus (1981), functional social support is positively related to health and to wellbeing. In contrast, structural social support is unrelated to wellbeing. There can even be negative effects, because it is very time-consuming and demanding to maintain a large social network.

Brown and Harris (1978) showed the importance of functional social support in a study on women who had experienced a very stressful life event in the previous 9 months. Of these women, 37% of those without an intimate friend became depressed, against only 10% of those who had a very close friend.

There are important implications of social support for physical health as well as mental health. House, Landis, and Umbesson (1988) reviewed several large studies, and reported that individuals with high levels of social support had much lower mortality rates than those with poor social support. How does social support influence mortality? Uchino, Cacioppo, and Kiecolt-Glaser (1996) reported across numerous studies that blood pressure was lower in individuals with good social support. Individuals with good social support also tended to have stronger functioning of the immune system (e.g., greater natural killer cell responses).

Two points need to be borne in mind. First, social support doesn't always improve matters. For example, Bolger, Foster, Vinokur, and Ng (1996) found that high levels of social support for patients suffering from breast cancer didn't reduce their distress or the progression of the disease. Second, most studies report an association or correlation between social support and some measure of wellbeing. Perhaps part of what is happening is that individuals who enjoy good mental and physical health find it easier to develop strong friendships and relationships than those who do not. Thus, we can't always be confident that social support has causal effects on wellbeing.

GENDER DIFFERENCES

How do men and women react differently to stress? A major difference was identified by Schachter (1959). Some participants were told they were going to receive mild electric shocks whereas the others were told they would receive painful electric shocks. They had the choice of waiting alone or with another participant while the equipment was set up. Those expecting a painful electric shock were far more likely to choose to wait with another participant. Of key importance, the wish to affiliate or be close to others when under stress was much stronger in women than in men. Indeed, Schachter found so little evidence of affiliative behavior in stressed men that he used only females in all his subsequent research! Luckow, Reifman, and McIntosh (1998) reviewed 26 studies on gender differences in seeking and using social support. Women sought social support more than men in 25 of these studies.

Women are more likely than men to "tend and befriend" in times of anxiety and stress and will often seek the social support of others.

Taylor et al. (2000) developed a theory based in part on findings such as those just discussed. They argued that men are much more likely to respond to stressful situations with a "fight-or-flight" response, whereas women generally respond with a "tend-and-befriend" response. Thus, women respond to stressors by protecting and looking after their children (the tend response) and by actively seeking social support from others (the befriend response). Taylor et al. emphasized the role of **oxytocin**, a hormone secreted by men and women as part of the stress response. Oxytocin makes people less anxious and more sociable, and so is associated with the tend-and-befriend response. Of crucial importance, its effects are reduced by male sex hormones but increased by the female hormone estrogen.

Findings

David and Lyons-Ruth (2005) found that female infants show more evidence of the tend-and-befriend response than male ones. When their mother's behavior became more frightening, female infants were more likely than male infants to approach her. Turton and Campbell (2005) identified the four factors of fight, flight, tend, and befriend in a factor analysis of stress responses. As predicted by Taylor et al.'s (2000) theory, females were more likely than males to report using tend-and-befriend responses in stressful situations. There is also support for the notion that males are more likely than females to respond to stressful situations with the fight-or-flight response. Eagly and Steffen (1986) carried out a meta-analysis and found that males are on average somewhat more physically aggressive than females.

Uvnäs-Moberg (1996) found that oxytocin in breastfeeding women was associated with calm and self-reported sociability. Taylor, Klein, Greendale, and Seeman (1999) found that higher levels of oxytocin in women were associated with smaller cortisol stress responses and with faster recovery of the HPA after exposure to a stressful situation.

Key Term
Oxytocin: a hormone produced in response to stress that reduces anxiety and increases sociability.

Evaluation

- ➕ The theory identifies some of the major behavioral responses to stress (i.e., fight, flight, tend, and befriend).

- ➕ The theory identifies important gender differences in coping with stress.

- ➕ The theory may help us to understand why women live on average 5–7 years longer than men.

- ➖ As Taylor et al. (2000, p. 422) admitted, "We have suggested that oxytocin and endogenous opioids may play important roles in female responses to stress, and it remains to be seen if these are as significant players as we have suggested."

- ➖ Neuroendocrine responses vary from stressor to stressor (Sapolsky, 1992), but the theory doesn't account for such variations.

- ➖ Any individual's behavioral response to a stressful situation depends on his/her personality, past experience, and the precise nature of the stressor as well as on gender.

COPING STRATEGIES: TRADITIONAL

One of the most common ways of studying coping strategies is by means of self-report questionnaires. These questionnaires differ in many ways, but traditionally there was reasonable agreement that there are only a few major coping strategies. The Multidimensional Coping Inventory (Endler & Parker, 1990) is fairly representative, and we will consider it in some detail. It assesses three major coping strategies:

1. *Task-oriented strategy*: This involves obtaining information about the stressful situation and alternative courses of action and their probable outcome. It also involves deciding on priorities and dealing directly with the stressful situation.
2. *Emotion-oriented strategy*: This can involve efforts to maintain hope and to control one's emotions. It can also involve venting feelings of anger and frustration, or deciding that nothing can be done to change things.
3. *Avoidance-oriented strategy*: This involves denying or minimizing the seriousness of the situation. It also involves conscious suppression of stressful thoughts and their replacement by self-protective thoughts.

Individuals high in the personality dimension of trait anxiety experience much stress and anxiety. They tend to use the emotion-oriented and avoidance-oriented strategies rather than the task-oriented strategy (Endler & Parker, 1990). In contrast, individuals low in trait anxiety tend to use the task-oriented strategy.

Which coping strategy do you think is the most effective? As Lazarus (1993, p. 238) pointed out, "Of the two functions of coping, problem-focused [task-oriented] and emotion-focused, there is a strong tendency in western values to venerate the former and distrust the latter . . . taking action against problems rather than re-appraising the relational meaning seems more desirable." There is support for this point of view. Folkman et al. (1986) asked people to report the coping strategies they had used to handle stressful events. They also asked them to rate the extent to which the outcome had been satisfactory. Planned problem solving tended to be associated with satisfactory outcomes, whereas confrontational coping (e.g., expressing anger) and distancing (trying to forget about the problem) were associated with unsatisfactory outcomes.

Problem-solving coping sometimes produces negative as well as positive outcomes. For example, Wu, Forkman, McPhee, and Lo (1993) found that doctors who accepted responsibility for their own mistakes made constructive changes to their work habits, which was a positive outcome. In addition, however, they experienced more distress (a negative outcome) at the same time.

Carver et al. (1993) found that avoidance-oriented coping was relatively ineffective in a study on women with breast cancer. Women who used avoidant coping strategies

Avoidance-oriented strategy

such as denial or simply refusing to try to cope had higher levels of distress than those who accepted the diagnosis and retained a sense of humor. Epping-Jordan, Compas, and Howell (1994) studied young men and women suffering from cancer. The disease had progressed further over a 1-year period among those who used avoidant coping (e.g., "I try not to think about it") than among those who did not.

In spite of the evidence discussed so far, we should not conclude that any given type of coping is *always* effective or ineffective. In reality, the effectiveness of any coping strategy depends on the individual, the context, and the nature of the stressful situation. The task- or problem-oriented coping strategy is generally effective but not when there is little or nothing the individual can do to improve matters. For example, Collins, Baum, and Singer (1983) considered people living close to Three Mile Island shortly after a major nuclear incident. Those using problem-oriented coping were more distressed than those using emotion-oriented coping.

Avoidance-oriented coping is also effective in some circumstances. For example, Cohen and Lazarus (1973) considered the coping strategies used by patients during hospitalization after surgery. Patients using denial showed an improved rate of healing (and had fewer minor complications) than those who did not.

Many stressful situations change over time, and so the best coping strategy may also change. For example, Folkman and Lazarus (1985) found students faced with a stressful examination sought information and social support before the examination. Afterwards, while waiting to hear the results, they typically made use of avoidance coping (e.g., forgetting all about the examination). In a different context, the avoidance-oriented strategy of denial is dangerous when an individual has just suffered a heart attack, but is useful during the subsequent period of hospitalization (Levine et al., 1987). Denial becomes dangerous again if it continues for a long period of time after discharge from hospital (Levine et al., 1987).

Evaluation

+ Coping strategies are important in determining the effects of stressful events on an individual's mental and physical state.

+ There is reasonable agreement on the major coping strategies (e.g., task-oriented; avoidance-oriented).

− The coping strategies used by individuals in their actual behavior may not be the same as the coping strategies they claim to use on self-report questionnaires.

− Questionnaires often focus on individuals' preferred coping strategies in a very *general* way. Such a broad assessment may not allow us to predict how individuals will respond to a *specific* stressor.

− As Lazarus (1993, p. 242) pointed out, "Coping process measures would be far more meaningful and useful if we knew more about the persons whose coping thoughts and actions are being studied." For example, responding to possible failure on a future examination by using an avoidance-oriented coping strategy makes sense *only* if the individual is not motivated to achieve success.

COPING STRATEGIES: CORE FAMILIES

Skinner, Edge, Altman, and Sherwood (2003) identified some additional limitations with approaches to coping strategies such as that of Endler and Parker (1990). First, task- or problem-oriented coping and emotion-focused coping are not really mutually exclusive: "Most ways of coping can serve both functions and thus could fit into both categories. For example, making a plan not only guides problem solving but also calms emotion" (Skinner et al., 2003, p. 227). Second, several forms of coping don't fit neatly into the traditional approach based on two or three major types of coping strategy. Examples include observation, aggression, rumination [contemplation], and accommodation [active attempts to adjust to the situation].

What is the way forward? Skinner et al. (2003) used comprehensive information from 100 different assessments of coping to identify the most important coping strategies. Their analyses suggested that there are several families of coping. Each family is a broad category and contains within it several specific forms of categories. According to Skinner et al. (2003), nine families of coping are of special importance:

1. *Problem solving*: This includes various activities, including instrumental action; direct action; decision making; and planning.
2. *Support seeking*: This includes comfort seeking; help seeking; and spiritual support.
3. *Escape*: This includes avoidance; disengagement; and denial.
4. *Distraction*: This includes acceptance and engaging in alternative pleasurable activities (e.g., exercise; reading).
5. *Positive cognitive restructuring*: This includes positive thinking and self-encouragement.
6. *Rumination*: This includes intrusive thoughts; negative thinking; self-blame; and worry.
7. *Helplessness*: This includes inaction; passivity; giving up; and pessimism.
8. *Social withdrawal*: This includes social isolation; avoiding others; and emotional withdrawal.
9. *Emotional regulation*: This includes emotional expression; emotional control; and relaxation.

This approach to coping represents one of the most thorough attempts to identify all of the major coping strategies used when people are stressed. It is more realistic than previous approaches based on assuming that there are only two or three coping responses. What remains to be done is to investigate in detail the effectiveness of these nine coping strategies across different kinds of stressful situations.

Chapter Summary

Psychology of emotion
- Six emotions can be reliably identified from facial expressions across cultures. Self-report measures of emotion produce two main independent dimensions (positive affectivity vs. negative affectivity or pleasure–misery vs. arousal–sleep). Seven basic emotional systems (expectancy; anger; anxiety; sexuality; nurturance; separation; and joy) have been identified in the brain.
- Most (or all) emotions serve useful functions. According to Oatley and Johnson-Laird, emotions influence individuals to pursue whatever goal has the greatest survival or other value in the current situation.

Theories of emotion
- According to the James–Lange theory, our emotional experience is determined by perceiving our own bodily changes. However, most patients with spinal cord damage having greatly restricted awareness of their own physiological activity nevertheless report intense emotional experiences.
- According to Schachter and Singer, the experience of emotion requires high physiological arousal *and* an emotional interpretation of that arousal. This theory makes the erroneous assumption that all emotions are associated with the same arousal pattern.
- According to Lazarus, emotional experience is crucially dependent on cognitive appraisal of the current situation. It is difficult to assess cognitive appraisals, many of which occur below the level of conscious awareness.
- According to the SPAARS approach, emotions can be produced either fairly automatically via the associative system or in a more controlled way via the propositional and schematic systems.

Stress
- Stress involves an immediate shock response involving the sympathetic adrenal medullary system followed by a countershock response involving the hypothalamic–

pituitary–adrenocortical axis. The countershock response reduces many of the effects of the shock response but at the cost of impairing immune functioning.

- The key factor in work stress is lack of perceived control. Those in lower positions within a work organization have less control than those in higher positions and suffer more from various illnesses.
- Life events and daily hassles both increase the chances of a wide range of mental and physical health problems.
- Type A individuals high in hostility are at increased risk of cardiovascular disease. Those with Type D personality are vulnerable to a range of diseases.
- Long-lived stressors affect health via impaired immune system functioning and via lifestyle changes. However, short-lived stressors enhance immunity.

Coping with stress

- Social support (especially provided by an intimate friend) reduces the adverse effects of stress on physical health.
- According to Taylor et al., men respond to stress with a fight-or-fight response, whereas women respond with a tend-and-befriend response that may be due in part to oxytocin.
- Many theorists have argued there are a few main coping strategies (e.g., task-oriented; emotion-oriented; avoidance-oriented). The effectiveness of any coping strategy depends on the individual and the situation.
- Coping strategies are generally assessed by self-report questionnaires and may not reflect people's actual behavior.
- Skinner et al. have developed a new approach to coping strategies based on the entire literature in the area. They identified nine families of coping to provide a comprehensive account.

Further Reading

- Belaise, C., with contributions by S. Acharya, R.A. Askew, E. Caffo, D.G. Cruess, & K.V. Oxington (2005). *Psychology of stress*. Hauppauge, NY: Nova Biomedical Books. Most of the main issues in stress research are discussed in this book.
- Folkman, S., & Moskowitz, J.T. (2004). Coping: Pitfalls and promise. *Annual Review of Psychology, 55*, 745–774. The authors provide an overview of coping research with an emphasis on relatively recent developments.
- Niedenthal, P.M., Krauth-Gruber, S., & Ric, F. (2006). *Psychology of emotion: Interpersonal, experiential, and cognitive approaches*. Hove, UK: Psychology Press. This book provides an unusually comprehensive account of theory and research on emotion, and relates contemporary thinking to its historical context.
- Reeve, J. (2005). *Understanding motivation and emotion* (4th ed.). Hoboken, NJ: Wiley. Much of this introductory textbook is devoted to mainstream research and theory on emotion.
- Segerstrom, S.C., & Miller, G.E. (2004). Psychological stress and the human immune system: A meta-analytic study of 30 years of inquiry. *Psychological Bulletin, 130*, 601–630. The authors provide an excellent analysis of what is known about the effects of psychological stress on the workings of the immune system and on disease.
- Skinner, E.A., Edge, K., Altman, J., & Sherwood, H. (2003). Searching for the structure of coping: A review and critique of category systems for classifying ways of coping. *Psychological Bulletin, 129*, 216–269. Previous approaches to categorizing coping strategies are criticized effectively, and an alternative approach is discussed in detail.
- Strongman, K.T. (2003). *Psychology of emotion: From everyday life to theory*. Hoboken, NJ: Wiley. Strongman provides accessible accounts of the leading theories of emotion in the context of our day-by-day experiences.
- Wade, C. (2005). *Psychology* (8th ed.). New York: Prentice Hall. Chapter 11 of this introductory textbook is devoted to emotion from the physiological, psychological, and cultural perspectives.

Chapter 5

Contents

States of awareness

5

Every day of our lives we experience various states of awareness. Some of the main states of awareness form the basis of this chapter. For example, there is clearly an important difference between the waking and sleeping states, and within the sleeping state we need to distinguish between dreaming and nondreaming. In this chapter, we consider the sleeping state. This includes a discussion of dreaming, and of the various theories accounting for our dreams. Before discussing sleep and dreaming, however, we focus on the key issue of consciousness. Our coverage deals with the functions of consciousness, whether it is possible to have more than one consciousness, and theoretical attempts to understand the underlying differences between conscious and nonconscious states and processes. Before embarking on a discussion of consciousness, however, we briefly discuss a few states of awareness, including some not considered later in the chapter.

TRANSIENT HYPOFRONTALITY HYPOTHESIS

Dietrich (2003) discussed several states of consciousness, including hypnosis, dreaming, and meditation. In spite of the fact that there are obvious differences among these states of consciousness, Dietrich argued in his transient hypofrontality hypothesis that they all share one crucial feature—there is a relatively short-lived reduction in activation within the prefrontal area of the brain. Why is this important? In essence, the prefrontal cortex (especially the dorsolateral prefrontal cortex) plays a significant role in several complex functions including attentional control, willed action, self-reflection, and cognitive flexibility. As is discussed in the next section, several different areas of the brain in addition to the prefrontal cortex are typically activated when an individual is in a state of alert consciousness. However, as Dietrich (2003, p. 232) pointed out, "The prefrontal cortex enables the top layers of consciousness by contributing the highest-order cognitive functions to the conscious experience."

Two main lines of evidence support Dietrich's (2003) transient hypofrontality hypothesis. First, there is research focusing on the cognitive functions impaired or absent in various altered states of consciousness. According to the hypothesis, functions involving the prefrontal cortex should be the ones most adversely affected. Second, there is research designed to assess brain activation when individuals are in various states of consciousness. The obvious prediction is that states of consciousness such as dreaming and daydreaming should be associated with reduced activation within the prefrontal cortex.

The evidence on hypnosis is broadly supportive of the theory. The main distinguishing feature of the hypnotic state is that individuals show a lack of willed action. Gruzelier (2000) attributed this to frontal inhibition (impairments in the inhibition function of the prefrontal cortex). Inhibition is important on the Stroop task. On this task, participants see a series of color words, each presented in a color that differs from its associated word (e.g., RED is presented in green; BLUE is presented in yellow). The task involves naming the colors as rapidly as possible while inhibiting the color words. Hypnotized individuals perform poorly on this task (e.g., Kallio et al., 2001). Studies using event-related potentials indicate that hypnotized individuals have decreased prefrontal activation compared to nonhypnotized ones (e.g., Nordby et al., 1999).

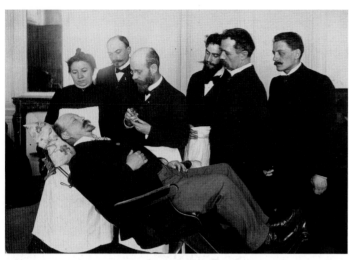

This late nineteenth century photograph shows a group of doctors observing a colleague putting his patient into a hypnotic trance. Once hypnotized, individuals generally show a lack of willed action, and a decrease in prefrontal activation.

The evidence on dreaming is strongly supportive of the theory (see discussion later in the chapter). Dreaming is associated with an absence of self-reflection, distortions of time, reduced motivational control, and unfocused attention (Dietrich, 2003), all of which are associated with impaired functioning of the prefrontal cortex. Most (but not all) dreaming occurs during rapid eye movement (REM) sleep in which most of the brain is active with the exception of the prefrontal cortex. As Braun et al. (1997, p. 1190) pointed out, "REM may constitute a state of generalized brain activity with the specific exclusion of executive systems."

The evidence on meditation partially supports the hypothesis, but there are some complicating factors. On the positive side, meditators report a sense of timelessness, an absence of planning, little emotional experience, and a lack of self-reflection (Dietrich, 2003), all of which are indicative of reduced prefrontal functioning. In addition, meditation is often associated with increased alpha activity in the EEG across the brain that is consistent with reduced brain activation (Cahn & Polich, 2006). However, meditation is typically experienced as a state in which there is sustained concentration and good attentional control, both of which are suggestive of good prefrontal functioning. In addition, brain-imaging techniques typically indicate that meditation is associated with *increased* activation in dorsolateral prefrontal cortex. The meditative state is often described as involving "relaxed alertness"—it may be a state in which *some* aspects of prefrontal functioning (especially attentional control) are functioning well even though most are not.

In sum, it is a reasonable generalization that most altered states of consciousness involved reduced activation in the prefrontal cortex. However, that generalization applies better to hypnosis and to dreaming than it does to meditation. The transient hypofrontal hypothesis does not directly explain how states of consciousness differ from each other. However, part of what is happening would seem to be that the precise prefrontal functions that are impaired vary from one state to another.

CONSCIOUSNESS

This section of the chapter is concerned with consciousness. What exactly do we mean by the term "consciousness"? According to Colman (2001, p. 160), consciousness is, "the normal mental condition of the waking state of humans, characterized by the experience of perceptions, thoughts, feelings, awareness of the external world, and often in humans . . . self-awareness."

Understanding consciousness is often regarded as one of psychology's great unsolved mysteries. However, that view is becoming increasingly out of date. There has been a dramatic increase in the amount of research devoted to consciousness, and researchers are starting to grapple successfully with important issues.

FUNCTIONS OF CONSCIOUSNESS

Why do humans have consciousness? Humphrey (1983) argued that the main function of consciousness is social. Humans have lived in social groups for tens of thousands of years. In such groups, you need to predict, understand, and manipulate the behavior of other people. This is much easier to do if you possess the ability to imagine yourself in their position. Humans developed conscious awareness of themselves, and this helped them to understand others. In the words of Humphrey (2002, p. 75), "Imagine that a new form of sense organ evolves, an 'inner eye,' whose field of view is not the outside world but the brain itself."

It is argued that another reason we have consciousness is to control our actions. Much of the time we find ourselves consciously thinking of doing something and then doing it. For example, "I think I'll go to the pub" is followed by us finding ourselves in the familiar surroundings of our local pub. As Wegner (2003, p. 65) pointed out, "It certainly doesn't take a rocket scientist to draw the obvious conclusion . . . consciousness is an active force, an engine of will."

I imagine you agree with what was said in the previous paragraph, because it fits with our everyday experience. However, there has been a systematic onslaught on that position in recent years. This onslaught is considered below.

Conscious intentions?

Wegner (2002) argued that we have only the *illusion* of conscious or free will. According to him, our actions are actually caused by unconscious processes. However, we *infer* that our thoughts cause our actions. Inferences can be wrong, and so it follows that we should often make mistakes (e.g., assuming we didn't cause something to happen even though we did). Support for this position comes from the unlikely source of the spiritualist movement that swept through nineteenth century Europe. Advocates of spiritualism believed that spirits of the dead could convey messages and even move tables. For example, several people would sit around a table with their hands resting on the top and pressing down on it. After a while, the table would start to vibrate and eventually would move about and spell out answers to questions. The sitters firmly believed that they had not caused movements of the table but that spirits were responsible. Unfortunately for the spiritualists, the scientist Michael Faraday showed convincingly that the sitters were causing the table to move.

Late nineteenth century European spiritualists would indulge in activities such as séances, where inanimate objects and tables seemed to inexplicably move of their own accord. Michael Faraday demonstrated, however, that the sitters themselves were unwittingly causing the objects to move.

The spiritualists made much use of ouija boards (the odd name comes from the French and German words for "yes"). Several people sit around a table with their forefingers on an upturned glass in the center of a ring of letters. Eventually the glass moves and spells out words. Everyone denies they moved the glass, and so it is assumed that spirits of the dead are communicating to the living.

Wegner and Wheatley (1999) used an updated version of the ouija board using a 20 cm square board mounted onto a computer mouse. Two participants placed their fingers on the board. When they moved the board, this caused a cursor to move over a screen showing numerous pictures of small objects. Every 30 seconds or so, the participants were told to stop the cursor and to indicate the extent to which they had consciously intended the cursor to stop where it did.

Both participants wore headphones. One participant was genuine but the other was a confederate working for the experimenter. This confederate received instructions through the headphones to make certain movements. On crucial trials, the confederate was told to stop on a given object (e.g., a cat) and the genuine participant heard the word "cat" 30 seconds before, 5 seconds before, 1 second before, or 1 second after the confederate stopped the cursor. Genuine participants believed they had caused the cursor to stop where it did when they heard the name of the object on which it stopped 1 or 5 seconds beforehand. Thus, they mistakenly believed their conscious intention had caused the action when it hadn't.

How can we explain Wegner and Wheatley's (1999) findings? According to Wegner (2003, p. 67), we infer that our conscious thoughts have caused our action based on the principles of priority, consistency, and exclusivity:

> *When a thought appears in consciousness just before an action (priority), is consistent with the action (consistency), and is not accompanied by conspicuous alternative causes of the action (exclusivity), we experience conscious will and ascribe authorship to ourselves for the action.*

Pronin, Wegner, and McCarthy (2006) carried out an interesting study on voodoo curses in American college students. Some participants encountered another person (the "victim") who was offensive. After the encounter, they stuck pins into a voodoo doll representing the victim in his presence. When the victim subsequently reported a headache, participants tended to believe that their practice of voodoo had helped to cause his symptoms. They had this belief because their negative thoughts and actions about the victim occurred shortly before his symptoms developed.

The above findings are not really the kiss of death for the notion that conscious intentions play an important role in determining our actions. For example, Wegner and Wheatley (1999) used a very elaborate and artificial set-up to show that we are sometimes mistaken when we decide we caused an action. To draw a comparison, no one would argue that visual perception is hopelessly fallible simply because we make mistakes when identifying objects in a thick fog.

Libet et al. (1983) used a very different approach in an attempt to show that conscious intentions are less important than we imagine. Participants were asked to bend their wrist and fingers at a time of their choosing. The moment at which they became consciously aware of the intention to perform the movement and the moment at which the hand muscles were activated were both recorded. Libet et al. (1983) also recorded the readiness potential in the brain—this is thought to reflect pre-planning of a bodily movement. The readiness potential occurred 350 ms *before* participants were consciously aware of the intention to bend the wrist and fingers. Thus, it seemed as if the brain "decided" to make a movement before there was any conscious awareness of the decision.

Libet et al.'s (1983) study is somewhat limited. The readiness potential isn't a direct measure of preparation for bodily movement. Trevena and Miller (2002) repeated Libet et al.'s (1983) experiment measuring lateralized readiness potential, which is a more direct measure. This lateralized readiness potential typically occurred (on about 80% of trials) before participants were consciously aware of the decision to move their hand. Thus, voluntary initiation of hand movement (as reflected in brain activity) generally preceded conscious awareness that the decision had been made. However, this time difference was much less than in Libet et al.'s (1983) research, and so the findings are not really clear-cut.

In sum, our assumption that our actions are closely related to our immediately preceding conscious thoughts may need revision. Sometimes people think their conscious intentions are responsible for their actions when that doesn't seem to be the case (e.g., Libet et al., 1983; Pronin et al., 2006; Trevena & Miller, 2002; Wegner & Wheatley, 1999). However, this is such a complex issue that we need much more research before coming to any definitive conclusions.

IN TWO MINDS?

Nearly everyone agrees that we possess a single, unitary consciousness. Suppose, however, we consider individuals in whom the connections between the two halves of the brain have been severed. In these **split-brain patients**, the corpus callosum (the major connection between the two halves or hemispheres of the brain) was cut surgically to contain severe epileptic seizures within one hemisphere. Do split-brain patients have two minds, each with its own distinctive consciousness?

Different answers to the above question have been offered by experts. On one side of the argument is Roger Sperry (1913–1994), who won the Nobel Prize for his influential

---

Conscious awareness of pain

If you have ever stepped on a sharp object, or mistakenly picked up a very hot plate, you will know that first of all you leap off the nail or drop the plate. Only then does the pain kick in, after we are "safe." This is so because the nerves (known as the reflex arc) organizing the reception of and response to the threat are fast, and those transmitting pain are slow. It's obvious that it is more important to retreat from the harmful stimulus and that feeling the pain and learning from it can wait a second.

Key Term

Split-brain patients: individuals in whom the corpus callosum connecting the two halves of the brain has been severed.

research on split-brain patients. He claimed that these patients have two consciousnesses:

> *Each hemisphere seemed to have its own separate and private sensations . . . the minor hemisphere [the right one] constitutes a second conscious entity that is characteristically human and runs along in parallel with the more dominant stream of consciousness in the major hemisphere [the left one] (Sperry, 1968, p. 723).*

On the other side of the argument are Gazzaniga, Ivry, and Mangun (2002). According to them, split-brain patients have only a single conscious system based in the left hemisphere. They called this system the interpreter, defining it as, "A left-brain system that seeks explanation for internal and external events in order to produce appropriate response behavior" (Gazzaniga et al., 2002, p. G-5). Cooney and Gazzaniga (2003) argued that brain-damaged patients use the interpreter to produce an understanding of what is happening even when it has access to only very limited information. As a result, brain-damaged patients' understanding is often incorrect.

Findings

The first split-brain patient studied by Sperry and his colleagues was W.J., a charming and socially dominant Second World War veteran. Discovering that each of his brain hemispheres could process information independently of the other was a major scientific contribution. According to Gazzaniga (who studied him), "W.J. lives happily in Downey, California, with no sense of the enormity of the findings or for that matter any awareness that he had changed."

It is easy to imagine that split-brain patients struggle to cope effectively with the world around them. In fact, this is *not* the case. They move their eyes around to make sure that all the important information from the environment reaches both hemispheres. It was only when Sperry conducted experiments in which visual stimuli were presented so rapidly that no eye movements could be made that split-brain patients showed severely impaired performance.

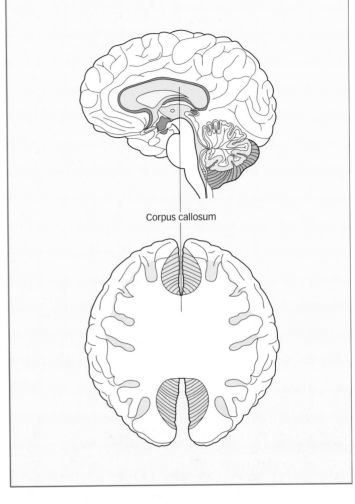

Corpus callosum

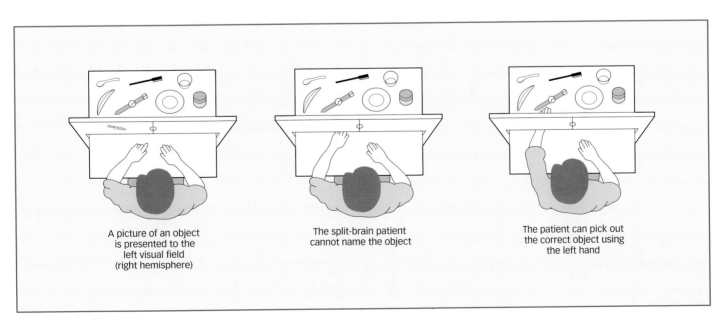

A picture of an object is presented to the left visual field (right hemisphere)

The split-brain patient cannot name the object

The patient can pick out the correct object using the left hand

Each hemisphere in split-brain patients has its own strengths. The right hemisphere is better than the left hemisphere on tasks that require taking account of the shapes of objects. For example, only the right hemisphere can recognize the faces of familiar people (Uddin, Rayman, & Zaidel, 2005). In contrast, the left hemisphere is better than the right hemisphere on tasks requiring speech. In Sperry's research, patients generally responded fluently when tasks were presented to the left hemisphere. When tasks were presented to the right hemisphere, "The subjects often gave no response. If urged to reply, they said that there might have been some weak and ill-defined event, or else they confabulated [invented] experiences" (Trevarthen, 2004, p. 875). Note, however, that the right hemisphere showed some ability to understand simple language.

The fact that the right hemisphere of most split-brain patients lacks speech makes it difficult to know whether it possesses its own consciousness. However, Paul S. is a split-brain patient with reasonably good language abilities in his right hemisphere. The left hand is connected to the right hemisphere, and Paul S. showed limited evidence of consciousness in his right hemisphere by responding accurately to questions using his left hand. For example, he could spell out his own name, that of his girlfriend, his hobbies, and his current mood.

Paul S. showed some interesting differences between his hemispheres. His right hemisphere said he wanted to be a racing driver whereas his left hemisphere wanted him to be a draughtsman!

In one study (Gazzaniga, 1992), Paul S. was presented with a chicken claw to his left hemisphere and a snow scene to his right hemisphere. When asked to select relevant pictures from an array, he chose a picture of a chicken with his right hand (connected to the left hemisphere) and a picture of a shovel with his left hand (connected to the right hemisphere). These findings *don't* indicate that Paul S. had a separate consciousness in each hemisphere. When asked to explain his choices, Paul said, "Oh, that's simple. The chicken claw goes with the chicken, and you need a shovel to clean out the chicken shed" (Gazzaniga, 1992, p. 124). As Gazzaniga pointed out, Paul's left hemisphere was interpreting behavior initiated by the right hemisphere, and there was no clear evidence that the right hemisphere was contributing much to the interpretation.

Findings indicating that Paul S.'s left hemisphere often overruled his right hemisphere led Gazzaniga et al. (2002) to argue that he (and other split-brain patients) has very limited right-hemisphere consciousness. For example, the right hemispheres of split-brain patients can understand words such as "pin" and "finger," but they find it very difficult to decide which of six words best describes the causal relationship between them ("bleed"). According to Gazzaniga et al. (2002, p. 680), "[The right hemisphere] deals mainly with raw experience in an unembellished [basic] way. The left hemisphere, though, is constantly . . . labeling experiences, making inferences as to cause, and carrying out a host of other cognitive activities. The right hemisphere is simply monitoring the world." The evidence suggests that the left hemisphere contains an interpreter that provides coherent interpretations of experienced events.

Wolford, Miller, and Gazzaniga (2000) reported findings consistent with the notion that there is an interpreter in the left hemisphere but not in the right one. Split-brain patients predicted whether a light would appear in the top or the bottom of a computer screen on numerous trials. The right hemisphere adopted the simple strategy of choosing the more probable alternative on nearly every trial. In contrast, the left hemisphere adopted the more complex strategy of interpreting the structure of the task, and so distributed its responses according to the probability that each was appropriate.

More promising evidence that dual consciousness may exist in some split-brain patients was reported by Baynes and Gazzaniga (2000). They discussed the case of V.J., whose writing is controlled by the right hemisphere whereas her speech is controlled by the left hemisphere. According to Baynes and Gazzaniga (2000, p. 1362), "She [V.J.] is the first split . . . who is frequently dismayed by the independent performance of her right and left hands. She is discomfited by the fluent writing of her left hand [controlled by the right hemisphere] to unseen stimuli and distressed by the inability of her right hand to write out words she can read out loud and spell." Perhaps V.J. has somewhat separate consciousnesses in each hemisphere.

SCRAPER-SKY

A left-handed drawing by a split-brain patient attempting to draw a skyscraper. He saw the word "scraper" in the left visual field and the word "sky" in the right visual field. He managed to draw sky and scraper, but neither hemisphere could combine the two words to make the emergent concept "skyscraper."

Evaluation

⊕ The left hemisphere in split-brain patients plays the dominant role in consciousness, and is the location of an interpreter or self-supervisory system.

⊕ The evidence generally suggests that the right hemisphere can engage in various low-level processing activities (e.g., identifying shapes) but lacks its own consciousness.

⊖ The fact that the right hemisphere in most split-brain patients has a limited ability to communicate makes it difficult to decide the extent to which it may have its own consciousness.

⊖ The emphasis has been on the independent functioning of the two hemispheres in split-brain patients, but most of the time their two hemispheres function effectively together.

THEORETICAL APPROACHES

Several theorists (e.g., Baars, 1997; Baars & Franklin, 2003; Dehaene & Naccache, 2001) have put forward similar theories of consciousness. These theories are known as global workspace theories because it is assumed that consciousness is associated with a global workspace in the brain. Here are the main assumptions built into these theories:

1. Most information processing occurs in parallel (more than one process at a time) below the level of conscious awareness.
2. Conscious awareness depends very much on focal attention. Baars (1997) invited us to consider sentences such as, "We look in order to see" or "We listen in order to hear." According to Baars (1997, p. 364), "The distinction is between selecting an experience and being conscious of the selected event. In everyday language, the first word of each pair ["look"; "listen"] involves attention; the second word ["see"; "hear"] involves consciousness." Thus, attention resembles choosing a television channel and consciousness resembles the picture on the screen.
3. Consciousness involves integrating and combining information from various specific nonconscious processes distributed throughout the brain. It is involved in planning novel strategies and ensuring their successful execution.
4. The specific brain areas associated with consciousness depend in part on the content of the conscious experience and the specific processes involved. However, Dehaene and Naccache (2001) argued that the prefrontal cortex and the anterior cingulate are typically activated during conscious experience.

Findings

The most general theoretical prediction is that brain activation is more *coordinated* or *integrated* (and sometimes more widespread) during conscious processing than during processing below the conscious level. One way of testing this prediction is to present all participants with the same stimuli and the same task. Brain-imaging data are then analyzed separately for those who were consciously aware of some aspect of the experimental situation and for those who weren't. For example, Rodriguez et al. (1999) presented pictures that were easily perceived as faces when presented upright (face-perception condition) but which were seen as meaningless black-and-white shapes when presented upside-down (control condition). The key

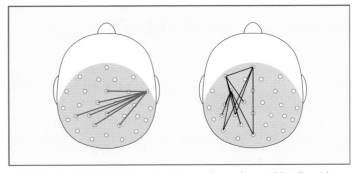

Phase synchrony (black lines) and phase desynchrony (blue lines) in EEG 180–360 ms after stimulus presentation in the no-face-perception (left side) and face-perception (right side) conditions. From Rodriguez et al. (1999). Copyright © 1999 by the Nature Publishing Group. Reproduced with permission.

findings related to brain activity at the time after picture presentation (180–360 ms) at which faces were perceived in the upright condition. As predicted, there was much more coordinated or synchronized activity across the brain on the face-perception condition than in the control condition (see the figure on the previous page).

An alternative approach involves presenting the same stimuli so they can (one condition) or can't (second condition) be perceived consciously. One way of preventing a stimulus being perceived consciously is to follow it almost immediately with a second stimulus that acts as a mask and inhibits processing of the first stimulus. Dehaene et al. (2001) presented words either masked or unmasked. When the words were masked and so not consciously perceived, brain activation was mostly restricted to the visual cortex. When the same words were unmasked, there was a much larger increase in activation in the visual cortex, and there was also widespread parietal and prefrontal activation. Baars (2002) reviewed 13 studies in which conscious and nonconscious conditions were compared. He concluded, "Conscious perception . . . enables access to widespread brain sources, whereas unconscious input processing is limited to sensory regions."

The prefrontal cortex and anterior cingulate are typically involved in conscious awareness (see Dehaene & Naccache, 2001, for a review). For example, Lumer, Friston, and Rees (1998) carried out a study on binocular rivalry. What happens in **binocular rivalry** is that two visual stimuli are presented (one to each eye), but the observer consciously perceives only one of them. The stimulus that is consciously perceived changes over time. Lumer et al. presented a red drifting grating to one eye and a green face to the other, and observers indicated which stimulus they were consciously perceiving. As predicted, the prefrontal cortex and anterior cingulate were among the brain areas showing increased activation immediately prior to a switch in conscious perception from one stimulus to the other.

Evaluation

+ The notion that conscious awareness is associated with integrated or coordinated widespread brain activity has received much support.

+ Activation of the prefrontal cortex and anterior cingulate is typically associated with conscious awareness.

− We now have a reasonable knowledge of brain processes associated with conscious awareness. However, we are still a long way away from knowing *why* physical processes in the brain give rise to conscious experience.

− The theory has little to say about the nature and content of our conscious experiences.

SLEEP

Sleep is an important part of our lives. It is probably the most time-consuming form of human behavior (apart from breathing!). Sleep generally occupies about one-third of our time, but the proportion decreases as we get older. First of all, we consider some of the basic facts about sleep. After that, we address the complex issue of the precise functions served by sleep—*why* do we need to sleep?

SLEEP–WAKE CYCLE

There is a 24-hour sleep–wake cycle, meaning that each day is typically divided into one period awake and one period asleep. The term **circadian rhythm** describes any biological rhythms that last about 24 hours. Why is the sleep–wake cycle 24 hours long? Perhaps it is strongly influenced by external events such as the light–dark cycle, and the fact that each dawn follows almost exactly 24 hours after the previous one. Another possibility is

Case Study: *Sleep Problems on a Space Station*

Back in 1997 Jerry Linenger lived on space station Mir for 5 months. He had real sleep problems because the station lights, which were meant to mimic a 24-hour light–dark cycle, were so dim. The best light cues came in through the windows, and the sun's light was very, very bright. But as Mir orbited the earth every 90 or so minutes this produced 15 day–night (i.e., light–dark) cycles every 24 hours. Jerry says he tried to cope, but couldn't, and that he'd see his Russian colleagues suddenly nod off and float around the cabin. Monk (2001) monitored Jerry during his time in space and reported findings that after 90 days the astronaut's quality of sleep deteriorated very rapidly. Monk thinks the brain's endogenous pacemaker had become disrupted by the abnormal light rhythm.

Case Study: *The Sleep–Wake Cycle*

Michel Siffre was studied for 7 months in 1972 when he volunteered to live underground in caves out of any contact with daylight and without any other clues about what time of day it was, that is, no watch or clocks or TV. He was safe and well fed, and the caves were warm and dry. He was always monitored via computers and video cameras, he had a 24-hour phone-link to the surface, and was well catered for in mind and body with books and exercise equipment. In this isolated environment he quickly settled into a regular cycle of sleeping and waking. The surprise was that his cycle was of almost 25 hours, not 24! It was a very regular 24.9-hour rhythm, so that each "day" he was waking up nearly an hour later. The effect of this was that by the end of his months underground he had "lost" a considerable number of days and thought he had been underground for much less time than had actually passed (Bentley, 2000).

that the sleep–wake cycle is based on **endogenous mechanisms**, that is, ones that are internal and biological.

One way of exploring the sleep–wake cycle is to study individuals having no contact with daylight. For example, Michel Siffre spent 7 months in a dark cave. He developed a regular 25-hour sleep–wake cycle, which misled him into thinking he had been underground for several days less than was actually the case. Similar findings have been reported in studies on people spending weeks or months in a bunker or isolation suite (Wever, 1979). Such findings suggest there is an endogenous pacemaker having a period of about 25 hours.

The above findings are rather odd, because it isn't clear *why* we would have an endogenous rhythm differing in length from the 24-hour day we typically experience. In fact, there is an important limitation in the studies, because the participants controlled their own lighting conditions (free-running paradigm). Czeisler et al. (1999) also made use of a forced desynchrony paradigm in which artificial 20- or 28-hour days were imposed on participants, because they couldn't control the lighting conditions. There was a 25-hour circadian rhythm in temperature with the free-running paradigm. However, the temperature circadian rhythm averaged 24 hours and 10 minutes with both the 20- and 28-hour days. Thus, the endogenous circadian pacemaker has a period of 24 hours, but can be lengthened in artificial environments.

The free-running paradigm led to overestimation of the duration of the circadian pacemaker because participants could turn the lights on whenever they wanted. This is important because light is a **zeitgeber** (literally,

Key Terms

Endogenous mechanisms: mechanisms that are internal and biological and are relatively uninfluenced by external factors.

Zeitgeber: external events (e.g., light) that partially determine biological rhythms.

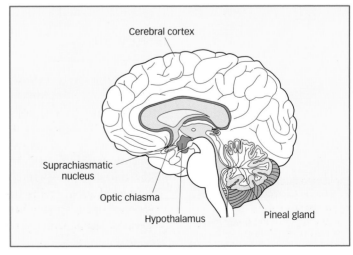

Cerebral cortex

Suprachiasmatic nucleus

Optic chiasma

Hypothalamus

Pineal gland

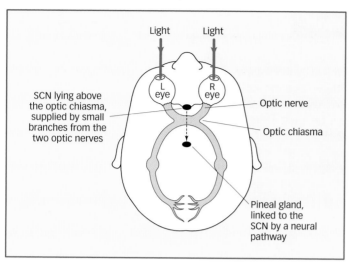

The visual pathway in the brain showing the connection to the suprachiasmatic nucleus (SCN) and onward to the pineal gland.

"time giver") that partially controls biological rhythms. You probably wake up earlier in the summer than in the winter because you respond to the light outside. Czeisler et al. (1999) found that there was an advance in the circadian temperature rhythm when participants were exposed to bright light in the early morning. In contrast, there was a delay in the circadian temperature rhythm when bright light was presented in the late evening.

Much is known of the physiological systems involved in the sleep–wake cycle. The suprachiasmatic nucleus (SCN), which is located within the hypothalamus at the base of the brain, is of special importance (see the figure on the left). The SCN (there are actually two nuclei very close together) is responsive to light and forms the main circadian clock. This was shown convincingly by Ralph, Foster, Davis, and Menaker (1990). They transplanted the SCNs from the fetuses of hamsters belonging to a strain having a 20-hour sleep–wake cycle into adult hamsters belonging to a strain with a 25-hour sleep–wake cycle. These adult hamsters rapidly adopted a 20-hour sleep–wake cycle.

Meijer et al. (1998) took recordings of SCN activity in freely moving animals living in conditions in which lighting remained constant. There was much activity during the part of the animals' circadian rhythm that normally falls in the light and much lower activity during the part of the rhythm typically falling in the night.

Activity in the SCN leads to the release of the hormone **melatonin** from the pineal gland, with more melatonin being released when light levels are low. Melatonin influences the brainstem mechanisms involved in sleep regulation and so helps to control the timing of sleep and waking periods. The involvement of melatonin in the sleep–wake cycle was shown by Schochat, Luboshitzky, and Lavie (1997)—see the Key Study below. There is further evidence. People flying across several time zones often take melatonin, because it makes them feel sleepy 2 hours afterwards (Haimov & Lavie, 1996).

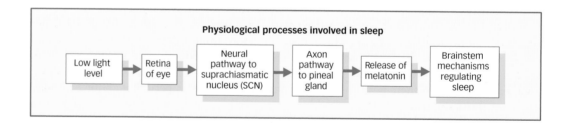

Physiological processes involved in sleep

Low light level → Retina of eye → Neural pathway to suprachiasmatic nucleus (SCN) → Axon pathway to pineal gland → Release of melatonin → Brainstem mechanisms regulating sleep

Key Study

Schochat et al. (1997): Melatonin and the sleep–wake cycle

Convincing evidence of the involvement of melatonin in the sleep–wake cycle was reported by Schochat, Luboshitzky, and Lavie (1997). They used the ultra-short sleep–wake paradigm, with six male participants spending 29 hours between 7 a.m. one day and noon the following day in the sleep laboratory. Throughout that time the participants spent 7 minutes in every 20 lying down in bed in a completely darkened room trying to sleep. This method allowed the experimenters to measure sleep propensity (the tendency to sleep) at different times of day. The period of greatest sleep propensity is known as the "sleep gate," and starts in the late evening.

Surprisingly, the period of lowest sleep propensity (the "wake maintenance zone") occurs in the early evening shortly before the sleep gate.

Shochat et al. (1997) measured the levels of melatonin by taking blood samples up to three times an hour during the 29-hour session. The key finding was as follows: "We demonstrated a close and precise temporal relationship between the circadian rhythms of sleep propensity and melatonin; the noctural [night] onset of melatonin secretion consistently precedes the noctural sleep gate by 100–120 min" (p. R367). This close relationship between increased melatonin levels and increased sleep propensity doesn't prove they are causally related. However, Shochat et al. (1997) discussed other studies strengthening the argument that melatonin is important in determining sleep propensity. For example, individuals suffering from insomnia find it much easier to get to sleep when given melatonin about 2 hours before bedtime (Rosenzweig, Breedlove, & Leiman, 2002).

Discussion points
1. What are some of the good features of the study carried out by Shochat et al.?
2. What are the limitations of their approach?

KEY STUDY EVALUATION
Schochat et al.'s results were important in demonstrating that melatonin plays a role in sleep–wake cycles. However, it could be argued that trying to sleep in a laboratory situation is a task that does not have a great deal of ecological validity. The demand characteristics of the experiment and evaluation apprehension may have affected the participants, possibly even at a hormonal level. The sample used by Schochat et al. was also very small, consisting of only six male volunteers, and was not really representative. However, the study, like many others, provides a strong basis for future work.

STAGES OF SLEEP
It is now time to consider what happens during sleep. There are various ways of understanding sleep. However, the electroencephalograph or EEG has proved of particular value. Scalp electrodes are used to obtain a continuous measure of brainwave activity recorded as a trace. Other useful physiological measures include eye-movement data from an electro-oculogram or EOG and muscle movements from an electromyogram or EMG.

There are two main aspects to EEG activity: frequency and amplitude. Frequency is the number of oscillations of EEG activity per second, and amplitude is half the distance between the high and low points of an oscillation. Frequency is used more often than amplitude to describe EEG activity.

Research using the EEG has revealed five different stages of sleep:

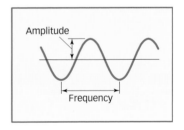

- *Stage 1*: This is a state of drowsiness. It involves high-amplitude alpha waves in the EEG, slow eye rolling, and reductions in heart rate, muscle tension, and temperature.
- *Stage 2*: The EEG waves become slower and larger, but with short bursts of high-frequency sleep spindles. There is little EOG activity.
- *Stage 3*: This is a deeper stage of sleep than either of the first two stages. The EOG and EMG records are similar to Stage 2, but there are many long, slow delta waves with some sleep spindles.
- *Stage 4*: This is a deeper stage of sleep than any of the first three stages. There is a majority of the long, slow delta waves present in smaller amounts in the previous stage, and very little activity in the EOG or EMG.
- *Stage 5*: This is rapid eye movement sleep or **REM sleep**. There are rapid eye movements, a very low level of EMG activity, and small-amplitude fast EEG waves. REM sleep is sometimes called paradoxical sleep, because it is more difficult to awaken someone from REM sleep than from any of the other stages even though the EEG indicates the brain is very active.

Key Term

REM sleep:
a stage of sleep involving rapid eye movements and associated with dreaming.

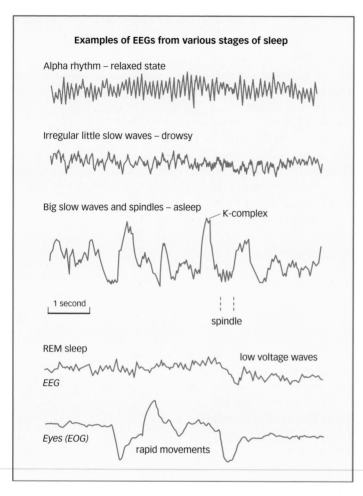

Examples of EEGs from various stages of sleep

Alpha rhythm – relaxed state

Irregular little slow waves – drowsy

Big slow waves and spindles – asleep

K-complex

1 second

spindle

REM sleep

low voltage waves

EEG

Eyes (EOG)

rapid movements

After the sleeper has worked through the first four stages of progressively deeper sleep, he/she reverses the process. Stage 4 is followed by Stage 3, and then by Stage 2. However, Stage 2 is followed by REM sleep (Stage 5). After REM sleep, the sleeper starts another sleep cycle, working his/her way through Stages 2, 3, and 4, followed by Stage 3, Stage 2, and then REM sleep again. A complete sleep cycle lasts about 90 minutes. Most sleepers complete about five sleep cycles during a normal night's sleep. The proportion of the cycle devoted to REM sleep *increases* from one cycle to the next, whereas the time spent in Stage 4 sleep *decreases*.

REM is the most interesting stage of sleep. It is associated with dreaming, with people in REM sleep who are woken up generally reporting that they have just been dreaming. However, dreaming, doesn't only occur in REM sleep. Foulkes and Vogel (1965) found that up to 50% of awakenings from non-REM sleep produced dream reports. However, dreams during REM sleep tend to be vivid and detailed, whereas non-REM dreams contain much less detail and are more "thought-like" (Solms, 2000a). More evidence against a very close association between REM sleep and dreaming was reported by Solms (1997). Damage to the REM-generating parts of the brain stem doesn't stop people from dreaming.

SLEEP DEPRIVATION

We spend about one-third of our lives asleep, making almost 200,000 hours of sleep in the course of an average lifetime! Presumably we wouldn't spend so much of our lives asleep unless sleep served one or more important functions. However, it has proved difficult to identify those functions. One way of trying to work out *why* we sleep is to deprive people of sleep. The problems and impairments experienced by sleep-deprived individuals may be those that sleep is designed to prevent.

People often cope surprisingly well when deprived of sleep for long periods. For example, consider Randy Gardner, a 17-year-old student who remained awake for 264 hours and 12 minutes (11 days) in 1964 (see Horne, 1988). It was difficult to keep him awake from the third night onwards. However, the psychologist William Dement found that playing basketball always did the trick: "We almost had to drag him out to the backyard, but once he was there and got moving, he was much better." Towards the end of the 11-day period, he suffered from disorganized speech, blurred vision, and some paranoia. For example, he thought other people regarded him as stupid because of his impaired functioning.

Randy Gardner was relatively unaffected by sleep deprivation. For example, on the last night of his period of sleep deprivation, he went to an amusement arcade with the psychologist William Dement. They competed several times in a basketball game, and Randy Gardner won every time! At a large press conference at the end of his ordeal, Randy Gardner spoke coherently without slurring his words. Afterwards, he slept for 15 hours. However, over several nights after that he only recovered 25% of the sleep he had missed. In spite of that, he recovered almost 70% of Stage 4 deep sleep and 50% of REM sleep, with very small recovery percentages for the other stages of sleep. These findings suggest that Stage 4 and REM sleep are of special importance.

The effects of sleep deprivation on 10 people were shown on British television in early 2004 in a programme called "Shattered." Ten people were sleep deprived for up to 1 week, with the person staying awake the longest winning £97,000 (approx $188,000). The winner was Clare. She endured 178 hours of sleep deprivation and helped to keep herself awake by tensing her feet until they hurt. One of the contestants thought he was the Prime Minister of Australia, one thought she was in an underground station, and two were certain someone had stolen their clothes.

Hüber-Weidman (1976) reviewed numerous studies on sleep deprivation. After 1 night of sleep deprivation, most people report feeling somewhat uncomfortable. After 2 nights of sleep deprivation, there is a much greater urge to sleep (especially between 3 and 5 a.m.). After 3 nights, performance on complex tasks is much affected, particularly if they are boring. After 4 nights, people become very irritable and confused. They have micro-sleep periods, each lasting about 3 seconds and involving a brief loss of awareness. After 5 nights, some people experience delusions. After 6 nights, there is evidence of "sleep deprivation psychosis" involving a lost sense of personal identity and increased difficulty in coping with other people.

Van Dongen, Maislin, Mullington, and Dinges (2003) studied the effects of restricting sleep to 4 or 6 hours per day for 14 days or to 0 hours for 3 days on a range of cognitive tasks. They found that, "even relatively moderate sleep restriction can seriously impair waking neurobehavioral functions [i.e., on cognitive tasks] in healthy adults" (p. 117). This occurred even though sleepiness ratings suggested that participants had little awareness of the adverse effects on them of sleep deprivation.

Lugaressi et al. (1986) studied a 52-year-old man who hardly slept at all because of damage to parts of his brain (e.g., the thalamus) involved in sleep regulation. Not surprisingly, he became absolutely exhausted and couldn't function effectively. Some individuals (including the man studied by Lugaressi et al., 1986) inherit a defect in the gene for the prion protein, leading to degeneration of the thalamus and to **fatal familial insomnia**. The typical age of onset is about 35 or 40 years. However, it ranged between 20 and 60 in an Austrian family with fatal familial insomnia in five consecutive generations (Almer et al., 1999). Individuals with fatal familial insomnia typically die within 2 years of the onset of the insomnia (Almer et al., 1999; Medori et al., 1992).

In sum, there is remarkably little evidence that sleep deprivation for up to 1 week has major long-term consequences. There are emotional changes (e.g., irritability; tension) and intellectual changes (e.g., some confusion; performance impairment), but these changes are rapidly reversed by 1 long night's sleep. Even very prolonged sleep deprivation as in fatal familial insomnia can continue for several months or even a year or two before it leads to death.

Overview of sleep-deprivation studies	
Nights without sleep	*Effects*
1	People do not feel comfortable, but can tolerate 1 night's sleep loss
2	People feel a much greater urge to sleep, especially when the body-temperature rhythm is lowest at 3–5 a.m.
3	Cognitive tasks are much more difficult, especially giving attention to boring ones. This is worst in the very early hours.
4	Micro-sleep periods start to occur, lasting about 3 seconds, during which the person stares blankly into space and temporarily loses awareness. They become irritable and confused.
5	As well as what is described above, the person may start to experience delusions, though cognitive ability (for example problem solving) is all right.
6	The person starts to lose their sense of identity, to be depersonalized. This is known as sleep-deprivation psychosis.

Source: Bentley (2000), p. 47.

THEORIES OF SLEEP

Evidence relevant to the issue of the functions served by sleep can be obtained by considering sleep amounts across different species. There are surprisingly large variations. For example, bats and opossums sleep for 18–20 hours per day, whereas elephants and giraffes sleep only 3–4 hours a day.

Siegel (2005) reviewed the evidence about sleep in numerous species of mammal. He concluded that the large variations in sleeping time across species indicate that the functions of sleep differ in complex ways from one species to another. Most theories of sleep can be assigned to two broad classes or categories: (1) recovery or restoration theories; and (2) adaptive or evolutionary theories. Pinel (1997, p. 301) gave a brief indication of the essence of each type of theory: "Recuperation [recovery] theories view sleep as a nightly repairman [sic] who fixes damage caused by wakefulness, while circadian [adaptive] theories regard sleep as a strict parent who demands inactivity because it keeps us out of trouble."

We will discuss both types of theories shortly. Before doing so, however, it is worth emphasizing that the two theories are complementary rather than in direct conflict.

Key Term
Fatal familial insomnia: an inherited disorder in which the ability to sleep disappears in middle age and is followed by death several months later.

The amount of sleep varies quite drastically across different species. Bats and possums sleep for 18–20 hours per day, whereas elephants and giraffes sleep for just 3–4.

Recovery/restoration theories focus mainly on the issue of *why* we need to sleep. In contrast, adaptive-evolutionary theories concentrate on the issues of *when* we sleep and *how long* we sleep each day. Combining the insights of the two theories provides promising answers to the main questions concerning the functions of sleep in humans and other species.

RECOVERY OR RESTORATION THEORIES

It is reasonable to assume that sleep serves the functions of saving energy and permitting the restoration of tissue. These notions are central to recovery or restoration theories (e.g., Horne, 1988, 2001; Oswald, 1980). According to Oswald's recovery theory, slow-wave sleep (Stages 1–4) is useful for recovery processes in the body. For example, there is a substantial release of growth hormone from the pituitary gland during slow-wave sleep (Takahashi, 1979). Horne (2001) argued that sleep is important for the recovery of brain function, especially that of the prefrontal cortex. The prefrontal cortex is involved in decision making and effective responding to unexpected events, both of which are impaired by sleep deprivation (Harrison & Horne, 2000). For example, serious disasters or near-disasters at four nuclear power stations (Chernobyl, Three Mile Island, Rancho Seco in Sacramento, and Davis-Beese in Ohio) all occurred very early in the morning.

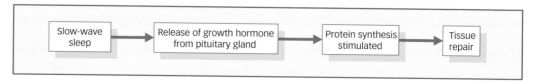

Findings

Allison and Cicchetti (1976) considered the amount of time spent in slow-wave sleep and in REM sleep across 39 species of mammals. Body weight was the best predictor of short-wave sleep, with smaller mammals having more such sleep. Metabolic rate, which is highly correlated (negatively) with body weight, was also very predictive of short-wave sleep. Different factors predicted the amount of REM sleep. Vulnerability to danger (e.g., danger of being preyed on) was the best predictor of REM sleep—those most vulnerable had the least REM sleep. That makes sense given that it is most difficult to waken an animal when in the REM stage.

So far as recovery theories are concerned, Allison and Cicchetti's (1976) key finding was the association between metabolic rate and the duration of slow-wave sleep. This association may occur because small mammals are in particular need of the energy conservation function of sleep because of their high metabolic rate. Another interpretation is that large mammals (especially herbivores who live on grass or other plants) need to spend most of their time searching for food and so can't afford the luxury of long periods asleep.

Oswald (1980) claimed that important recovery processes occur in the brain during REM sleep. In support, newborn infants (who experience enormous brain growth) spend a very high percentage of their time asleep devoted to REM sleep (Green, 1994). More generally, growth processes of all kinds are much more important in newborn infants and young children. Their greater need for the release of growth hormone during sleep may help to explain why neonates sleep for about 16 hours a day, reducing to 12 hours a day by the age of 2.

If an important function of sleep is recovery, then individuals who are extremely active during the day (or who are sleep deprived) would presumably need more sleep than other people. This might be especially the case for the most important stages of sleep (Stage 4 slow-wave sleep and REM sleep). There is support for these predictions. Shapiro et al. (1981) studied runners who had taken part in an ultra-marathon covering 57 miles. These runners slept about 90 minutes longer than usual on the 2 nights afterwards. In addition, they showed an especially large increase in the amount of time devoted to Stage 4 sleep. Earlier we discussed the case of Randy Gardner who stayed awake for 11 days. He slept for 15 hours after his extremely long period of sleep deprivation, and an unusually high proportion of his sleep time was devoted to REM and Stage 4 sleep.

A major difference between recovery and adaptive theories is that only the former claim that sleep is essential. The finding (discussed earlier) that individuals suffering from fatal familial insomnia typically die within 2 years of the start of the insomnia (e.g., Almer et al., 1999) provides some support for recovery theories.

What about Horne's (2001) assumption that sleep permits recovery of brain function, especially that of the prefrontal cortex? Maquet (2000) found that there was a considerable amount of brain shutdown during slow-wave sleep (especially Stage 4), and this shutdown was very pronounced in the prefrontal cortex. Muzur, Pace-Schott, and Hobson (2002) reviewed evidence indicating that there is deactivation of the dorsolateral prefrontal cortex in sleep, which impairs its functions such as self-consciousness and analytical thought. Brain-imaging studies indicate that sleep deprivation has especially great effects on the prefrontal cortex (Drummond et al., 2000). Nilsson et al. (2005) found that only 1 night's sleep deprivation produced significant impairment on a task requiring executive functions dependent on activity in the prefrontal cortex.

Although studies show that people need extra sleep following extreme exertion, there is no evidence that people who take little or no exercise reduce their sleeping time.

Evaluation

+ Recovery theories provide plausible reasons why sleep is important and essential.

+ The fact that sleep is found in virtually all species (except perhaps some whales and dolphins—see Siegel, 2005) is consistent with the notion that it is essential.

+ The fact that total sleep deprivation in fatal familial insomnia leads to death within 2 years supports the view that sleep is essential.

+ The finding that sleep deprivation and excessive activity both lead to unusually long periods of sleep and enhanced proportions of Stage 4 and REM sleep supports recovery theories.

+ There is increasing evidence that sleep permits recovery of the executive functions of the prefrontal cortex, whereas sleep deprivation has adverse effects on those functions and on the prefrontal cortex.

- It has proved difficult to specify in detail the physiological processes restored by sleep.

- Evidence about relative amounts of sleep time in different species of mammals is open to various interpretations and doesn't strongly support recovery theories.

ADAPTIVE OR EVOLUTIONARY THEORIES

According to various theorists (e.g., Kavanau, 2005; Meddis, 1979), sleep is adaptive behavior favored by evolution. For example, the sleep behavior shown by many species may depend on the need to adapt to environmental threats and dangers. Sleep can serve the function of keeping animals fairly immobile and safe from predators during periods of time when they can't engage in feeding and other kinds of behavior. In the case of those species dependent on vision, it is adaptive to sleep during the hours of darkness. In addition, sleep fulfills the useful function of conserving energy.

It seems to follow that species in danger from predators should sleep more of the time than those species that are predators. In fact, however, predators tend to sleep more than those preyed on (Allison & Cicchetti, 1976). This might seem inconsistent with adaptive theories of sleep. However, species in danger from predators might well benefit from remaining vigilant most of the time and sleeping relatively little. This seems like an example of having your cake and eating it, in that any pattern of findings can be explained by the adaptive or evolutionary approach! However, the basic assumption that the pattern of sleep shown by each species has been influenced by evolutionary pressures seems reasonable although difficult to prove.

Kavanau (2005) has recently put forward an interesting evolutionary approach to understanding sleep. He pointed out that visual perception in many species (including humans) requires very large amounts of brain processing. Indeed, a substantial proportion of the human brain is devoted to visual processing. According to Kavanau, sleep frees the brain from effortful visual processing and thus allows memory processing to proceed more efficiently.

Herbivores, such as these springbok, need to graze most of the time and be on their guard against predators, so sleep relatively little.

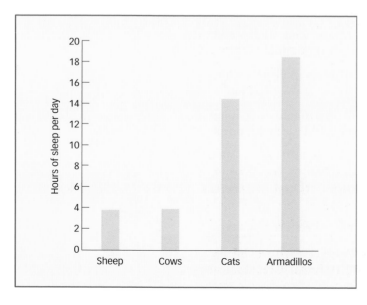

Findings

Support for the notion that the pattern of sleep is often dictated by the environmental threats faced by animals was reported by Pilleri (1979). Dolphins living in the river Indus are in constant danger from debris floating down the river. As a result, these dolphins sleep for only a few seconds at a time to protect themselves from the debris. More generally, as we have seen, species vulnerable to attack by other species sleep less than those under little or no threat (Allison & Cicchetti, 1976).

Sleep patterns within most species are adaptive. Several species of mammal that are unlikely to be attacked and that eat food rich in nutrition sleep most of the time. For example, cats sleep 14.5 hours a day, and armadillos sleep 18.5 hours a day. In contrast, herbivores (plant eaters) need to graze most of the time and be on their guard against predators, and so sleep relatively little. For example, sheep sleep on average 3.8 hours per day, and cows 3.9 hours a day.

What evidence indicates that sleep is useful in conserving energy as predicted by adaptive theories? The body temperature of most mammals is slightly lower during sleep, suggesting sleep is helpful for energy conservation. Stronger evidence was reported by Berger and Phillips (1995). Animals responded to food shortages by increasing the amount of time they spent asleep or by decreasing their body temperature more than usual in the sleeping conservation. However, sleep in humans is of little value in energy conservation. As Horne (2001, p. 302) pointed out, "The energy saved by being asleep throughout the night rather than sitting relaxed but awake is trivial— the energy equivalent to a slice of bread."

Kavanau's (2005) assumption that sleep is useful because it frees us from the high processing demands of visual perception fits many findings. First, sleep is found mainly in species that engage in detailed visual processing. Species that are genetically blind (e.g., cave fishes) don't sleep (see Kavanau, 2005). Evidence supporting this theory comes from the study of box jellyfish (*Chironex fleckeri*), which are found in tropical Australia and can kill humans within minutes. It had been thought that jellyfish didn't sleep but recent research discussed by Kavanau (2006) indicates that box jellyfish often sleep 15 hours a day. Box jellyfish have 24 eyes of four different types, and it is likely that the typical demands of visual processing on their simple nervous system explain their need for so much sleep. However, the situation is very different in box jellyfish that live in captivity and are hand fed. These jellyfish do not need to engage in complex visual processing (e.g., to locate prey and avoid predators) nor do they need to remember where food is to be found. As a result of the limited demands on their visual and memory systems, captive box jellyfish hardly sleep at all.

Second, most species that sleep have to block their vision in order to sleep. Third, there are many species of birds and marine mammals in which the brain instantly falls asleep when they close their eyelids and instantly awakens when they open their eyelids.

Sleep is generally regarded as less essential within adaptive theories than within recovery theories. Modest support for adaptive theories comes from individuals leading healthy lives in spite of regularly sleeping for very short periods of time each day (e.g., Meddis, Pearson, & Langford, 1973). For example, Miss M was a cheerful 70-year-old nurse who typically slept for only 1 hour per day. She generally sat on her bed reading or writing until about 2 in the morning, after which she would sleep for about 1 hour. When she was studied under laboratory conditions, she slept an average of 67 minutes per night.

Evaluation

⊕ Adaptive theories provide reasonably plausible explanations of why species vary in their sleeping patterns.

⊕ Adaptive theories have identified factors (e.g., vulnerability to attack; feeding patterns; importance of vision) helping to determine differences in amount and timing of sleep across species.

⊕ The notion that sleep serves to conserve energy is supported by the evidence from numerous species.

⊕ There is support for Kavanau's (2005, 2006) theory that an important evolutionary function of sleep is to eliminate visual processing and permit long-term storage of information.

⊖ Most adaptive theories provide no obvious explanation for the existence of fatal familial insomnia, in which prolonged sleep deprivation causes death.

⊖ Some of the claimed benefits of sleep (e.g., energy conservation; preventing effortful visual processing) could be obtained by simply resting with the eyes closed (Gamundi et al., 2005).

DREAMING

What is dreaming? According to Solms (2000a, p. 849), it is "the subjective experience of a complex hallucinatory episode during sleep." There are several important differences between dreaming and waking consciousness. As was discussed earlier, many of these differences seem to reflect reduced activation in the prefrontal cortex during dreaming. First, we typically feel we have little or no control over our dreams. In contrast, we nearly always have a sense (perhaps mistaken!) of conscious control in our waking lives. However, people occasionally have lucid dreams, in which they know they are dreaming and can sometimes control the dream content. For example, LaBerge, Greenleaf, and Kedzierski (1983) studied a woman who could create lucid sex dreams producing orgasms.

Sleepwalking

Dreams don't always occur in REM sleep. REM dreaming is accompanied by paralysis, probably to protect the sleeper from acting out their dreams and injuring themselves. People also dream in non-REM (NREM) sleep, but less often, and they are not in a paralyzed state. It is possible to act out NREM dreams, which can lead to sleepwalking.

Sleepwalking is more common than one might guess. Thirty percent of all children between the ages of 5 and 12 have walked in their sleep at least once, and persistent sleepwalking occurs in 1–6% of youngsters. Boys walk in their sleep more often than girls, and the tendency to wander during deep sleep is sometimes inherited from one of the parents.

The typical sleepwalking episode begins about 2 hours after the person goes to sleep, when they suddenly "wake" and abruptly sit up in bed. Although their eyes are wide open, they appear glassy and staring. When asked, sleepwalkers respond with mumbled and slurred single-word speech. The person may perform common acts such as dressing and undressing, opening and closing doors, or turning lights on and off. Sleepwalkers seem to see where they are going since they avoid most objects in their way, but they are unaware of their surroundings. Unfortunately, this means that they cannot tell the difference between their bedroom door and the front door, or the toilet and the wastebasket. The sleepwalker is usually impossible to awaken and does not remember the episode in the morning. The episode typically lasts 5 to 15 minutes and may occur more than once in the same night.

Although sleepwalkers avoid bumping into walls and tripping over furniture, they lack judgment. A sleepwalking child might do something like going to the garage and getting in the car, ready to go to school at 4 o'clock in the morning. Sometimes their lack of judgment can be dangerous. One sleepwalking child climbed a tree and another was found by the police walking down the street in the middle of the night. Therefore, sleepwalkers are in danger of hurting themselves and must be protected from self-injury.

Most children outgrow sleepwalking by the time they are teenagers, but for a small number of individuals the pattern continues into adulthood.

Christian Murphy escaped with cuts and bruises when he fell from his first-floor bedroom window while sleepwalking. His mother's Mercedes that was parked below broke his fall. Once he had landed he got up, still sleepwalking, and set off down the road.

Second, dreams often contain elements that would seem illogical or nonsensical in our waking consciousness. For example, dreams sometimes include impossible events or actions (e.g., someone floating above the ground), and they can also include various hallucinations and delusions.

Third, we are often totally absorbed by our dream imagery, reflecting what Empson (1989) described as "the single-mindedness of dreams." In contrast, when we are awake, we can usually stand back from our conscious thoughts and avoid being dominated by them.

Most dreams take place during REM (rapid eye movement) sleep. However, the common view that dreaming *only* occurs during REM sleep and that REM sleep is always associated with dreaming is profoundly mistaken. Nielsen (1999) reviewed studies in this area. On average, individuals woken up during REM sleep recalled dream-like material on only 82% of occasions compared to 42.5% during non-REM sleep. What was recalled from REM sleep was typically more vivid, more emotionally loaded, and of less relevance to waking life than recall from non-REM sleep.

According to Dietrich's (2003) transient hypofrontality hypothesis (discussed earlier), a key characteristic of dreaming is that it is associated with low levels of prefrontal activation. Muzur, Pace-Schott, and Hobson (2002, p. 475) reviewed the evidence on dreaming and sleep, and came to the following conclusion: "As a consequence of deactivation of the dorsolateral prefrontal cortex (DLPFC) during sleep, executive functions such as self-consciousness and analytical thought are severely impaired in NREM sleep and are weak in REM sleep."

We spend on average over 2 hours a night dreaming. It doesn't seem that we dream that much, because we forget more than 95% of our dreams. What are these forgotten dreams about? Researchers have answered this question by using sleep laboratories, in which sleepers are woken up mainly during REM sleep. The dreams typically forgotten tend to be more ordinary and less bizarre than those we remember in everyday life (Empson, 1989). This means that the dreams we remember spontaneously are not typical of our dreams in general. It would thus *not* be appropriate to base a theory of dreaming purely on the 5% of dreams we normally remember.

There is another potential problem. As Coenen (2000, p. 923) pointed out, "A dream is what someone describes upon awakening and researchers infer a one-to-one relationship between the dream and the way it is reported. It is therefore impossible to exclude such confounding factors as poor memory, overestimation, suppression or the effects of psycho-emotional factors on recall."

This patient's brain activity during the various cycles of sleep is being measured as part of a sleep research program. The electrical activity of the brain is measured by placing electrodes on the patient's scalp to produce an electroencephalogram (or EEG).

FREUD'S WISH FULFILLMENT THEORY

According to Sigmund Freud (1900, p. 377), dreams are like "a firework that has been hours in the preparation, and then blazes up in a moment." However, his central claim was that "wish fulfillment is the meaning of each and every dream" (Freud, 1900, p. 106). Why is wish fulfillment the main goal of dreams? According to Freud, our minds when asleep aren't influenced by the external environment or by the constraints it imposes on our behavior. Instead, we are influenced by internal factors (e.g., basic sexual and other motivational forces). We imagine acting in accordance with these motivational forces when dreaming, and this preserves sleep.

Dreamers' wish fulfillments are often regarded as unacceptable by the dreamer, leading Freud to describe dreams as "the insanity of the night." How do dreamers deal with the unacceptable nature of their dreams? According to Freud, the actual dream and its meaning (the **latent content**) are distorted into a more acceptable form (the **manifest content**) by the time dreamers are consciously aware of their dream. Dream-work is involved in transforming and "cleaning up" the original unconscious wishes into the manifest content of the reported dream. Here are some of the mechanisms used in dream-work:

1. *Displacement*: An element in the dream is substituted by something else (e.g., having sex is represented by riding a horse).
2. *Regression*: Thoughts are transformed into perceptions (e.g., the sizes of individuals in a dream reflect their significance to the dreamer).
3. *Condensation*: Several dream elements are combined in a single image (e.g., failure and sadness are represented as a descending escalator).

How can we identify the original latent content of a dream on the basis of its manifest content? This involves some of the techniques of psychoanalysis. For example, the dreamer provides associations to the various aspects of the manifest content, and these associations form the basis for working out the underlying themes. This might reveal that licking a lollipop is a symbol for oral sex or a cigar is a symbol for a penis. However, as Freud himself admitted, "Sometimes a cigar is only a cigar."

Findings

Freud (1900) provided some examples apparently showing that dreams involve wish fulfillment. For example, he reported that his 19-month-old daughter Anna called out in

Key Terms
Latent content: in Freud's theory, the underlying meaning of a dream that is difficult to recollect consciously; see **manifest content**.
Manifest content: in Freud's theory, the remembered, "cleaned up" meaning of a dream; see **latent content**.

her sleep, "Anna Freud, strawberry, wild strawberry, scrambled eggs, mash," after not having eaten anything all day (Freud, 1900, p. 104). In similar fashion, Wood (1962) found that people who had been kept socially isolated throughout the day were more likely than controls to dream about being with other people.

If dreams represent wish fulfillments, most of them should be associated with positive emotional states. In fact, that is not the case. Hall and van de Castle (1966) found in a study of 1000 dreams that seven times as many involved misfortune (e.g., mishaps; danger) as good fortune. Zadra (1996) examined recurrent dreams in children and adults. About 85% of these dreams contained negative or unpleasant emotions, and only 10% contained exclusively pleasant emotions. Even Freud (1955, p. 32) admitted that, "It is impossible to classify as wish fulfillments the dreams . . . which occur in traumatic neurosis [suffered by combatants in the First World War], or the dreams during psychoanalysis which bring to memory the traumas of childhood."

> **Politics and dream content**
>
> The Association for the Study of Dreams (2001) found that political views could influence dream content. People with right-wing views report having more violent and scary dreams than people with left-wing views. If this is true, it could support the Freudian view that dreams have a hidden content or message.

Freud based his theory on dreams spontaneously remembered by dreamers. However, such dreams account for only about 5% of all dreams. In fact, most dreams are concerned with the trivial matters of everyday life and lack the dramatic emotional quality that Freud attributed to them.

Freud's theory is also wrong in other respects. First, it is untrue that dreams are infrequent and very short-lasting. In fact, they are much more frequent and long-lasting than Freud assumed (Empson, 1989). Second, Freud argued that dreams preserve sleep. However, Solms and Turnbull (2002) found that only 49% of patients who had lost the ability to dream reported disrupted sleep. Third, Freud claimed that reported dreams (the manifest content) involve substantial distortions from the underlying dream (the latent content). However, various studies have indicated that the differences are much smaller than would be predicted on Freud's theory (see Domhoff, 2001, for a review).

Solms (2000b) has carried out research more supportive of Freud. He has found that dreaming is eliminated in patients with damage to the "seeking system" connecting the midbrain to the limbic system and the frontal lobes. This system "instigates goal-seeking behaviors and an organism's appetitive interactions with the world" (Panksepp, 1985, p. 273). Solms claimed that this system is associated with the sexual instinct emphasized by Freud in his dream theory.

Evaluation

⊕ Freud put forward the first systematic theory of dream function. He explained why dreams often seem rather incoherent (transformation of the latent content into the manifest content).

⊕ As Freud argued, dreams tell us something about the thoughts and feelings of the dreamer, but less than he imagined.

⊕ Brain areas of crucial importance in dreaming are of relevance in sexual and other motivation.

⊖ Freud emphasized that dreams involve repressed unacceptable desires. However, that seems much less relevant in today's permissive society than in nineteenth century Vienna. In addition, most dreams not recalled spontaneously are concerned with rather ordinary and trivial events.

⊖ It is difficult to regard most dreams (e.g., nightmares) as wish fulfilling even in a distorted way.

⊖ The assumptions that dreams are infrequent and brief, that they preserve sleep, and that reported dreams are very distorted from the original dreams are all incorrect.

ACTIVATION–SYNTHESIS THEORY

Hobson and McCarley (1977) were impressed by the fact that parts of the brain are as active during rapid eye movement (REM) sleep as during normal waking. This led them to put forward the activation–synthesis theory of dreaming. According to this theory, the state of activation during REM sleep depends mainly on the pontine brain stem, which is also responsible for triggering dreaming. Activity in the pontine brain stem produces high levels of activation in several parts of the brain, including those involved in perception, action, and emotional reactions. Of key importance, this activation is essentially *random*.

The forebrain then makes "the best of a bad job in producing even partially coherent dream imagery from the relatively noisy signals sent up to it from the brain stem" (Hobson & McCarley, 1977, p. 1347). How does the brain make coherent sense of random activity? According to Hobson (1988), "The brain is so inexorably bent upon the quest for meaning that it attributes and even creates meaning when there is little or none in the data it is asked to process."

In sum, the activation–synthesis theory makes three main assumptions:

1. A high level of activation in pontine brainstem mechanisms is needed for dreaming to occur.
2. Activation in pontine brainstem mechanisms produces REM sleep as well as dreaming. It was originally assumed that all dreams occur during REM sleep but it is now accepted that dreaming can occur in non-REM sleep as well (Hobson et al., 2000).
3. The forebrain tries to impose meaning on the more-or-less random activation from the brain stem to produce partially coherent dreams.

Findings

Some of the evidence supports activation–synthesis theory. For example, Hobson, Pace-Schott, and Stickgold (2000) reviewed studies showing activation of the pontine brain stem and parts of the forebrain during REM sleep. It follows from the theory that brainstem lesions should eliminate REM sleep, and this has been found in studies on patients with lesions in the brain stem (Solms, 2000a).

According to the theory, lesions of the pontine brain stem should also eliminate dreaming. However, this is typically *not* the case. Solms (2000a) concluded that there was clear evidence of cessation of dreaming in only one out of 26 patients with severe damage to the pontine brain stem.

According to the theory, brain-damaged patients who dream rarely or never shouldn't have REM sleep. Solms (2000a) showed convincingly that this is not the case. He reviewed 111 cases of nondreamers, all but one of whom had preserved REM sleep. Thus, the presence of REM sleep doesn't guarantee that dreaming will occur.

According to the theory, most dreams should be rather incoherent and even bizarre. *Some* dreams are certainly bizarre, but that is not true of the great majority. For example, Hall (1966) examined 815 reports of dreams occurring at home or in the laboratory. Only about 10% contained at least one "unusual element." However, it is true that people when dreaming are much less likely to realize that events are outlandish or absurd than when they are awake (Kahn & Hobson, 2005).

Why did Hobson and McCarley (1977) claim that dreams are bizarre and incoherent? According to Vogel (2000, p. 1014), this view "is based mostly upon reported dreams that are spontaneously recalled in the morning. These dreams are likely the most dramatic, bizarre dreams and are not representative of dream life in general. The collection of large dream samples from throughout the night from ordinary people . . . has shown that dreams are mundane, organized, everydayish stories."

Evaluation

- The theory is based on detailed information about brain activity during sleep and dreaming.
- Dreams are often triggered by activation of the pontine brain stem, but such stimulation is not essential (Solms, 2000a).

⊕ Random activity in the brain and inefficiently functioning attentional processes may make some dreams difficult to understand.

⊖ The original idea that dreaming occurs only during REM sleep has had to be abandoned. As Solms (2000a, p. 843) pointed out, "REM is controlled by cholinergic brainstem mechanisms whereas dreaming seems to be controlled by dopaminergic forebrain mechanisms."

⊖ The theory exaggerates the importance of the pontine brain stem (see Solms, 2000a) and minimizes the reduction in prefrontal activity found during dreaming (Muzur, Pace-Schott, & Hobson, 2002).

⊖ Most dreams are reasonably coherent rather than bizarre as predicted by the theory.

Chapter Summary

Consciousness
- It has been argued that humans developed consciousness to understand other people and to control our actions.
- According to Wegner, we have only the illusion of conscious or free will. We use the evidence available to us to *infer* that our thoughts caused our actions. However, Wegner only showed that we are occasionally mistaken when deciding what caused one of our actions.
- It has sometimes been claimed that split-brain patients have two consciousnesses. It is more likely that they have a single conscious system (the interpreter) based in the left hemisphere.
- According to global workspace theories, there is a close connection between focal attention and consciousness. In addition, consciousness is associated with the combining and integrating of information from nonconscious processes throughout the brain.
- Many different brain areas can be associated with conscious awareness. However, two areas that are typically involved are the prefrontal cortex and the anterior cingulate.

Sleep
- In the free-running paradigm (in which individuals can control their own lighting conditions), individuals often exhibit a 25-hour sleep–wake cycle. However, there is evidence for a 24-hour cycle when a forced desychrony paradigm is used.
- Activity in the suprachiasmatic nucleus leads to the release of the hormone melatonin, which is followed 2 hours later by sleepiness.
- There are five major stages of sleep defined physiologically. Rapid eye movement (REM) sleep is the stage most associated with dreaming.
- Individuals generally cope surprisingly well with prolonged sleep deprivation. However, lengthy sleep deprivation often leads to impaired performance, irritability, and delusions.
- Individuals with fatal familial insomnia hardly sleep at all and typically die within 2 years of the onset of the insomnia.
- Recovery or restoration theories claim that sleep saves energy and restores tissue. In contrast, adaptive or evolutionary theories argue that sleep serves the function of keeping humans and other species out of trouble or that it reduces the demands of constant visual processing. The two types of theories can be regarded as complementary rather than in conflict with each other.

Dreaming
- Most dreams occur during REM sleep, but many dreams occur during non-REM sleep. About 95% of dreams are forgotten.

- According to Freud, dreams involve wish fulfillment. They are short-lasting and infrequent, they preserve sleep, and reported dreams are distorted versions of the original dream.
- Freud explained why dreams can be incoherent. As he predicted, brain areas associated with sexual motivation tend to be activated during dreaming.
- Most dreams involve unpleasant emotions, and it is implausible to claim that such dreams involve wish fulfillment. Most of the other assumptions made by Freud are incorrect.
- According to activation–synthesis theory, dreaming involves the forebrain trying to make sense of essentially random activation coming from the pontine brain stem and responsible for REM sleep.
- Dreams are often (but not always) triggered by activation of the pontine brain stem.
- The role of the pontine brain stem is exaggerated in activation–synthesis theory, and most dreams are more coherent than predicted by that theory. In addition, the importance of the reduction in prefrontal activation found during dreaming is minimized.

Further Reading

- Blackmore, S. (2003). *Consciousness: An introduction*. London: Hodder & Stoughton. This interesting book is written in a lively and entertaining way and provides the ideal introduction to the topic of consciousness.
- Blackmore, S. (2005). *Conversations in consciousness*. Oxford, UK: Oxford University Press. This is an interesting book based on the author's interviews with leading experts.
- Breedlove, S.M., Rosenweig, M.R., & Watson, N.V. (2007). *Biological psychology: An introduction to behavioral, cognitive, and clinical neuroscience* (5th ed.). Sunderland, MA: Sinauer Associates. The biological approach to sleep is covered in detail in this textbook.
- Domhoff, G.W. (2001). Why did empirical dream researchers reject Freud? A critique of historical claims by Mark Solms. *Dreaming, 14*, 3–17. Domhoff pinpoints with clarity the major limitations with Freud's theory of dreaming.
- Hobson, J.A., Pace-Schott, E.F., & Stickgold, R. (2000). Dreaming and the brain: Toward a cognitive neuroscience of conscious states. *Behavioral and Brain Sciences, 23*, 793–842. This long article provides a revised version of one of the most influential theories of dreaming.
- Roser, M., & Gazzaniga, M.S. (2004). Automatic brains—interpretive minds. *Current Directions in Psychological Science, 13*, 56–59. This article summarizes contemporary views on consciousness, including the relevance of split-brain research.
- Siegel, J.M. (2005). Clues to the functions of mammalian sleep. *Nature, 437*, 1264–1271. This article provides an up-to-date review of evidence relating to the possible functions of sleep.
- Solms, M. (2000a). Dreaming and REM sleep are controlled by different brain mechanisms. *Behavioral and Brain Sciences, 23*, 843–850. Some of the main brain areas associated with dreams are identified clearly in this article by an expert in the field.
- Wegner, D.M. (2002). *The illusion of conscious will*. Cambridge, MA: MIT Press. This controversial book is based on the assumption that we are mistaken when we believe our actions are determined by our conscious intentions.

INTRODUCTION TO
Cognitive
Psychology

FOUR MAJOR APPROACHES

O ne of the most dramatic changes within cognitive psychology in recent decades has been the huge increase in the number of weapons available to cognitive psychologists. Forty years ago, most cognitive psychologists carried out laboratory studies on healthy individuals. Nowadays, in contrast, many cognitive psychologists study brain-damaged individuals, others construct elaborate computer-based models of human cognition, and still others use numerous brain-imaging techniques.

Four major approaches to human cognition have now been developed:

- *Experimental cognitive psychology*: This is the traditional approach and involves carrying out experiments on healthy individuals, typically under laboratory conditions.
- *Cognitive neuropsychology*: This approach involves studying patterns of cognitive impairment shown by brain-damaged patients to provide valuable information about normal human cognition.
- *Computational cognitive science*: This approach involves developing computational models to further our understanding of human cognition.
- *Cognitive neuroscience*: This approach (which has become of major importance within the last 15 years) involves using numerous brain-imaging techniques to study aspects of brain functioning and structure relevant to human cognition. Note that the term "cognitive neuroscience" is often used in a broader sense to indicate an approach to understanding human cognition based on considering evidence about brain functioning as well as about behavior, and about how brain functioning influences behavior. What is common to both definitions is the importance attached to the use of brain-imaging techniques.

There is no need for researchers to select only one of these approaches at the expense of the other three. Indeed, cognitive psychologists increasingly use two (or even three) of these approaches in their research.

EXPERIMENTAL COGNITIVE PSYCHOLOGY

Experiments carried out on healthy individuals under laboratory conditions tend to be tightly controlled and "scientific." Experimental cognitive psychology was for many years the engine room of progress in cognitive psychology. Indeed, all three of the newer approaches to cognitive psychology have benefited from it. For example, consider the case of cognitive neuropsychology. It was only when cognitive psychologists had developed reasonable accounts of normal human cognition that the performance of brain-damaged patients began to be understood properly. Before that, it was hard to decide which patterns of cognitive impairment were theoretically important. Cognitive neuropsychologists often carry out studies on individual patients, and use the data from such patients to test theoretical predictions coming from experimental cognitive psychology. Such studies would be of little interest in the absence of an appropriate pre-existing theory.

Problems about the artificiality of laboratory research have often been expressed by claiming that such research lacks external validity or ecological validity (see Chapter 2). Ecological validity has two aspects: (1) representativeness; and (2) generalizability. Representativeness refers to the naturalness of the experimental situation, stimuli, and task. Generalizability refers to the extent to which the findings of a study are applicable to the real world. Generalizability is more important than representativeness. As a result, we need to reassure ourselves that experimental studies possess generalizability (many don't!).

COGNITIVE NEUROPSYCHOLOGY

Cognitive neuropsychology is concerned with the cognitive performance of brain-damaged patients, using the information gained to understand normal cognition. We consider two of the main assumptions of cognitive neuropsychology (see Coltheart, 2001). First, the cognitive system is based on modularity, meaning that it consists of numerous independent processors or modules. For example, the modules or processors involved in understanding speech differ somewhat from those involved in speaking. As a result, some brain-damaged patients are good at language comprehension but poor at speaking, whereas others have the opposite pattern.

Second, cognitive neuropsychologists assume it is important to search for dissociations. A dissociation occurs when a brain-damaged patient performs at the same level as healthy individuals on one task but is severely impaired on a second task. For example, amnesic patients perform well on tasks involving short-term memory but have very poor performance on most long-term memory tasks (see Chapter 8). This suggests that short-term memory and long-term memory involve separate modules. However, it might be that brain damage reduces the ability to perform difficult (but not easy) tasks, and that long-term memory tasks are more difficult than short-term memory ones. Suppose, however, that we found other patients with very poor performance on most short-term memory tasks but intact long-term memory. We would then have a **double dissociation**: some patients performing at the same level as healthy individuals on task X but being impaired on task Y, with others showing the opposite pattern. This double dissociation provides strong evidence that there are separate short-term and long-term memory systems. Double dissociations have also provided support for the notion that there are two main routes in reading (Chapter 10).

There are various limitations with the cognitive neuropsychological approach. First, the organization of the human brain is far less neat and tidy than implied by cognitive neuropsychologists with their emphasis on modularity. As Banich (1997, p. 52) pointed out, "The brain is composed of about 50 billion *interconnected* neurons. Therefore, even complex cognitive functions for which a modular description seems apt rely on a number of interconnected brain regions or systems."

Second, cognitive neuropsychology is generally more comfortable dealing with relatively *specific* aspects of cognitive functioning, perhaps because more general aspects do not lend themselves readily to a modular account. For example, consider research on language. Much of it has been on the reading and spelling of individual words by brain-damaged patients, with little emphasis on broader issues concerned with the comprehension of texts or speech.

Third, it would be ideal to find patients in whom brain damage had affected only *one* module. However, brain damage is typically much more extensive than that. When several different processing modules or processors are damaged, it is generally difficult to interpret the findings.

COMPUTATIONAL COGNITIVE SCIENCE

The computational models developed by computational cognitive scientists can show us how a given theory may be specified in detail. This is a definite advantage over many previous theories in cognitive psychology, which were expressed so vaguely that it was

Key Term

Double dissociation:
the finding that some individuals (often brain-damaged) do well on task A and poorly on task B, whereas others show the opposite pattern.

unclear exactly what predictions followed from them. What that means is that theoretical inadequacies are easier to spot, and this can prompt the development of more adequate theories.

In recent years, connectionist networks have become very popular. **Connectionist networks** typically consist of elementary or neuron-like units or nodes connected together. They have different structures or layers (e.g., a layer of input links, intermediate layers, and a layer of output links). Within such networks, memories are distributed over the network rather than being in a single location.

Connectionist networks are popular because the numerous elementary units within a connectionist network superficially resemble the neurons in the brain. Another reason is that connectionist networks can to some extent program themselves and so "learn" to produce specific outputs when certain inputs are given to them. In spite of these promising features, connectionist networks fail to resemble the human brain (see Chapter 2). They typically use thousands or tens of thousands of connected units to model a task that might be performed by tens of millions of neurons in the brain.

COGNITIVE NEUROSCIENCE

Technological advances mean we now have numerous new and exciting ways of obtaining detailed information about the brain's functioning and structure. We can work out *where* and *when* in the brain specific cognitive processes occur. Such information allows us to determine the order in which different parts of the brain become active when someone is performing a task. It also allows us to find out whether two tasks involve the same parts of the brain in the same way, or whether there are important differences.

Before discussing the techniques that have been developed, it is important to consider the brain in some detail. The cerebral cortex is divided into four main divisions or lobes (see the figure below). There are four lobes in each hemisphere: frontal; parietal; temporal; and occipital. The frontal lobes are divided from the parietal lobes by the central sulcus (*sulcus* means furrow or groove), and the parieto-occipital sulcus and the pre-occipital notch divide the occipital lobe from the parietal and frontal lobes.

For future reference, it is useful to know the meaning of various terms used to describe more precisely the brain area activated during the performance of some task. Some of the main terms are as follows:

- *dorsal*: superior or on top
- *ventral*: inferior or at the bottom
- *lateral*: situated at the side
- *medial*: situated in the middle.

Brief information concerning techniques for studying brain activity is contained in the box overleaf (fuller descriptions are given in Eysenck and Keane, 2005). Which technique is the best? There is no simple answer. Each technique has its own strengths and limitations, and so researchers focus on matching the technique to the issue they are addressing. The techniques vary in the precision with which they identify the brain areas active when a task is performed (spatial resolution) and the time course of such activation (temporal resolution). Thus, they differ in their ability to provide precise information concerning *where* and *when* brain activity occurs. The spatial and temporal resolutions of some of the main techniques are shown in the figure overleaf. High spatial and temporal resolutions are advantageous if a very detailed account of brain functioning is required. In contrast, low temporal resolution can be more useful if a general overview of brain activity during an entire task is needed.

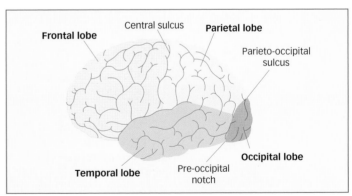

The four lobes, or divisions, of the cerebral cortex in the left hemisphere.

Key Term

Connectionist networks: they consist of elementary units or nodes that are strongly interconnected; each network has various layers.

Major techniques used to study the brain

Single-unit recording: This technique involves inserting a micro-electrode one 10,000th of a millimeter in diameter into the brain to study activity in single neurons. This is a very sensitive technique.

Event-related potentials (ERPs): The same stimulus is presented repeatedly, and the pattern of electrical brain activity recorded by several scalp electrodes is averaged to produce a single waveform. This technique allows us to work out the timing of various cognitive processes.

Positron emission tomography (PET): This technique involves the detection of positrons, which are the atomic particles emitted from some radioactive substances. PET has reasonable spatial resolution but poor temporal resolution, and it only provides an indirect measure of neural activity.

Functional magnetic resonance imaging (fMRI): This technique involves the detection of magnetic changes in the brain. fMRI has superior spatial and temporal resolution to PET, but provides only an indirect measure of neural activity.

Magneto-encephalography (MEG): This technique measures the magnetic fields produced by electrical brain activity. It provides fairly detailed information at the millisecond level about the time course of cognitive processes, and its spatial resolution is reasonably good.

Transcranial magnetic stimulation (TMS): This is a technique in which a coil (or pair of coils) is placed close to the participant's head and a large, very brief pulse of current is run through it. This produces a short-lived magnetic field, inhibiting processing in the brain area affected. This technique has (jokingly!) been compared to hitting someone's brain with a hammer (Johannes Zanker, personal communication).

The spatial and temporal ranges of some techniques used to study brain functioning. Adapted from Churchland and Sejnowski (1991).

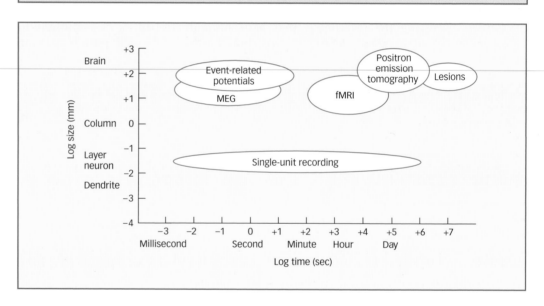

Do brain-imaging techniques answer all our prayers? There are three reasons for skepticism. First, most brain-imaging techniques indicate only that there are *associations* between patterns of brain activation and behavior (e.g., performance on a reasoning task is associated with activation of the prefrontal cortex at the front of the brain). Such associations are essentially correlational. As Walsh and Rushworth (1999, p. 126) pointed out, "Mapping techniques record brain activity which is correlated with some behavioral event. But the correlations do not show that an area is necessary for a particular function." For example, suppose a given brain area x is activated when we solve a complex problem. We cannot be certain that important processes associated with problem solution occur in brain area x. It is possible that anxiety associated with thoughts of possible failure on the problem causes activation of that brain area, or the activation might reflect high motivation to solve the problem.

Second, numerous brain-imaging studies have lacked any clear theoretical basis. Far too often, researchers have merely found that some parts of the brain are activated during performance of a given task whereas others parts are not. Such findings are of no particular interest if not predicted on the basis of some theory. The good news is that there is a clear trend towards more and more brain-imaging studies being theoretically based.

Third, consider the colored maps you must have seen claiming to show which areas of the brain were activated when a given task was performed. In fact, all the colored areas are those where the amount of brain activity exceeded some threshold level determined by the experimenter. The problem is that the number of brain areas identified as active during performance of a task can vary wildly depending on the threshold level that is set (Savoy, 2001). To make matters worse, there are generally no very convincing arguments as to the appropriate setting of the threshold level.

Much progress has been made in addressing the limitations identified above, with researchers starting to move away from purely correlational data. For example, we can show that activity in a given area of the brain is necessary to perform a task effectively by using transcranial magnetic stimulation (TMS) (discussed in the box opposite). In essence, TMS involves applying pulses of current to some area of the brain, thus causing a "temporary lesion." Suppose you believed that brain area x was involved in performing a task. If TMS applied to that particular brain area led to impairment of task performance, we could conclude that that brain area is necessary for good task performance. On the other hand, if TMS applied to that brain area had *no* effect on task performance, we would conclude that that brain area is not needed to perform the task effectively.

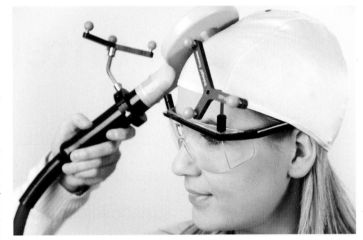

A patient undergoing image-guided transcranial magnetic stimulation (TMS).

What about the criticism that brain-imaging studies contribute nothing to our theoretical understanding? That is less true now we have a reasonably clear idea of the kinds of processing associated with most brain areas. For example, we know that the early stages of visual perception involve Areas 17 and 18, both of which are in the occipital area of the cortex. Kosslyn (e.g., 1994) has argued that visual imagery involves the same processes as visual perception. We can thus predict that Areas 17 and 18 should be activated when people are engaged in visual imagery. To cut a long story short, visual imagery is often (but not always) associated with much activation in those brain areas (see Kosslyn and Thompson, 2003, for a review).

ORGANIZATION OF CHAPTERS 6–10

Everyone agrees that understanding fully how the brain works is one of the crucial scientific challenges of the twenty-first century. What is really exciting is that scientists finally have access to the technology and approaches needed to meet that challenge successfully. As a result, there has probably been more progress in understanding human cognition in the past decade than ever before, and the omens are favorable for the future.

Our current understanding of the major areas in cognitive psychology is discussed over the next five chapters. We start in Chapter 6 with a discussion of the processes involved in attention. We also consider some of the factors determining how well (or how badly!) we cope with trying to do two tasks at the same time. Finally, key processes involved in visual perception are discussed, including the crucial issue of how we manage to identify the objects in the world around us. Chapter 7 deals with learning, starting with traditional approaches based on conditioning and then moving on to more cognitive approaches involved in accounting for complex learning (e.g., acquisition of expertise). Chapter 8 deals with human memory, including short-term and long-term memory, and the processes involved in the storage and subsequent retrieval of information. Chapter 9 addresses the key area of thinking. The focus is on problem solving and decision making, with full consideration being given to the issue of whether our thinking is generally rational and logical. Finally, in Chapter 10, we consider the surprisingly complex processes involved in the comprehension and production of language.

Chapter 6

Contents

Visual perception and attention

Visual perception is of enormous importance to us in our everyday lives. It allows us to move around freely, to see other people, to read magazines and books, and to watch movies and television. It is very important for visual perception to be accurate—if we misperceive how close cars are to us as we cross the road, the consequences may be fatal. It is no coincidence that far more of the human cortex is devoted to vision than to any other sensory modality.

Visual perception seems so simple and effortless that we are in danger of taking it for granted. In fact, however, it is very complex. Supporting evidence comes from the efforts of researchers in artificial intelligence, who have tried to program computers to "perceive" the environment. As yet, no computer can match more than a fraction of the skills of visual perception possessed by nearly every adult human.

There are an enormous number of different aspects of visual perception, and we can only discuss a few of the most important ones here. First, we consider object recognition—how do we know we are looking at a cat or a tree? Second, we consider the theoretical assumption that we have two rather different visual systems. Strong evidence in support of this assumption has come from the study of visual illusions, and we focus mainly on that evidence. Third, we consider the assumption that visual perception is by its very nature conscious. In fact, there is reasonably convincing evidence that many perceptual processes occur below the level of conscious awareness, and that unconscious perception is a reality. Fourth, we consider the relationship between visual perception and attention. Our belief that we can see clearly the entire visual scene in front of us is incorrect. We only have a detailed awareness of those aspects of the visual scene to which we have paid attention, and rarely notice changes to unattended aspects.

Only visual perception is covered in this chapter. However, some aspects of auditory perception are discussed elsewhere in this book. For humans, a crucial use to which we put our auditory system is speech perception, and that is one of the main topics dealt with in Chapter 10.

The most obvious characteristic of attention is that it is *selective*—for example, we choose to attend to certain people or objects in the environment and more or less ignore everything else. It has been argued that visual attention is like a spotlight or a zoom lens focusing on a given area within the visual field. The strengths and limitations of these notions are considered. After that, there is coverage of auditory attention.

Finally, we consider an issue of great relevance in today's 24/7 world—how we cope with trying to do several things at the same time (often known as multitasking). As we will see, we are not as good at multitasking as we like to think.

OBJECT RECOGNITION

Something we all do tens of thousands of times every day is to identify or recognize objects in the world. At this very moment, you are aware that you are looking at a book (perhaps with your eyes glazed over!). If you raise your eyes, then perhaps you can see a wall, windows, and so on in front of you. I imagine you would agree with me that it seems incredibly easy to recognize common objects. In fact, there are powerful reasons for arguing that the processes involved in object recognition are actually far more complex than seems to be the case:

1. Many objects in the environment overlap with each other, so you have to decide where one object ends and the next one begins.
2. We can all recognize an object such as a chair without any apparent difficulty. However, chairs (and many other objects) vary enormously in their visual properties (e.g., color; size; shape), and it is not immediately clear how we assign such different stimuli to the same category.
3. We recognize objects accurately over a wide range of viewing distances and orientations. For example, most plates are round but we can still identify a plate when it is seen from an angle and so appears elliptical.

In sum, there is much more to object recognition than might initially be supposed (than meets the eye?). We turn now to some of the key processes involved.

PERCEPTUAL ORGANIZATION

A fundamental issue in visual perception is perceptual segregation, that is, our ability to work out accurately which parts of the visual information presented to us belong together and thus form objects. The Gestaltists (e.g., Koffka, Köhler, Wertheimer) studied perceptual segregation (and the perceptual organization to which it gives rise) in the early twentieth century. Their primary principle of perceptual organization was the law of Prägnanz: "Of several geometrically possible organizations that one will actually occur which possesses the best, simplest and most stable shape" (Koffka, 1935, p. 138).

The Gestaltists proposed several other laws, but most of them are simply specific examples of the law of Prägnanz (see the figure on the left). The fact that three horizontal arrays of dots rather than vertical groups are seen in part (a) indicates that visual elements tend to be grouped together if they are close to each other (the law of proximity). Part (b) of the figure illustrates the law of similarity, which states that elements will be grouped together perceptually if they are similar. Vertical columns rather than horizontal rows are seen because the elements in the vertical columns are the same, whereas those in the horizontal rows are not. We see two crossing lines in part (c) of the figure because according to the law of good continuation we group together those elements requiring the fewest changes or interruptions in straight or smoothly curving lines. Finally, part (d) illustrates the law of closure, according to which missing parts of a figure are filled in to complete the figure. Thus, a circle is seen even though it is incomplete.

The Gestaltists emphasized the importance of **figure–ground segregation**: one object or part of the visual field is identified as the figure (central object) with the rest of the visual field forming the ground. The laws of perceptual organization permit this segregation into figure and ground to happen. According to the Gestaltists, the figure is seen as having a distinct form or shape, whereas the ground lacks form. In addition, the figure is perceived as being in front of the ground, and the contour separating the figure from the ground is seen as belonging to the figure.

You can check the Gestaltists' claims about figure and ground by looking at reversible figures such as the faces–goblet figure (see the figure on the left). When the goblet is the figure, it seems to be in front of a dark background, whereas the faces are in front of a white background when forming the figure.

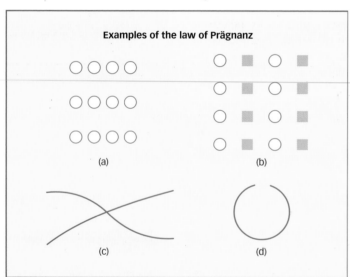

Examples of the law of Prägnanz

(a)

(b)

(c)

(d)

The faces–goblet ambiguous figure is an example of figure and ground—which is figure and which is ground?

What are the limitations of the Gestaltist approach? First, the Gestaltists mostly studied *artificial* figures, and so their findings may not apply to more realistic stimuli. However, some reassurance was provided by Elder and Goldberg (2002). They presented pictures of natural objects, and found that observers used proximity as a cue when deciding which contours belonged to which objects. They also found that the cue of good continuation was used. Second, the Gestaltists' various laws provide a description of what happens but fail to explain *why* and *how* perceptual organization occurs. Third, the Gestaltists didn't focus enough on the complexities involved when different laws of grouping are in *conflict*. For example, consider a display such as the one used by Quinlan and Wilton (1998; see the figure above). How do you think most observers grouped the stimuli? About 50% grouped the stimuli by proximity and the remaining 50% by similarity. Alas, the Gestaltists didn't indicate how we can explain such individual differences!

Display involving a conflict between proximity and similarity.

OBJECT RECOGNITION: DOES VIEWPOINT MATTER?

Form a visual image of a bicycle. I expect your visual image involves a side view in which both bicycle wheels can be seen clearly. We can use this example to raise a controversial issue. Suppose some people saw a picture of a bicycle shown in the typical view as in your visual image, whereas other people were presented with a picture of the same bicycle viewed end on or from above. Both groups of people are instructed to identify the object as rapidly as possible. Would the group given the typical view of a bicycle perform this task faster than the other group?

The assumption that object recognition is faster and easier when objects are seen from certain angles is made by **viewpoint-dependent theories**. In contrast, the notion that object recognition is equally rapid and easy regardless of the angle from which an object is viewed is made by **viewpoint-invariant theories**. Tarr and Bülthoff (1995, 1998) put forward a viewpoint-dependent theory. According to them, we have observed most common objects from several different angles or perspectives. As a result, we have several stored views of such objects in long-term memory. Object recognition is easier when the view we have of an object corresponds closely to one of those stored views.

In contrast, Biederman's (1987) recognition-by-components theory is an example of the viewpoint-invariant approach. According to him, objects consist of basic shapes or components known as "geons" (geometric ions). Examples of geons are blocks, cylinders, spheres, arcs, and wedges. According to Biederman (1987), there are about 36 different geons, which can be arranged in almost endless different ways. For example, a cup can be described by an arc connected to the side of a cylinder, and a pail can be described by the same two geons but with the arc connected to the top of the cylinder. Object recognition depends primarily on the identification of geons. Since an object's geons can be identified from numerous viewpoints, object recognition should not depend on viewpoint provided that all of an object's geons are visible.

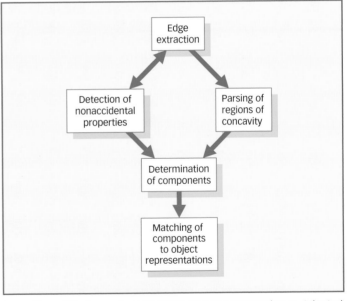

An outline of Biederman's recognition-by-components theory. Adapted from Biederman (1987).

Findings

It is easy in principle to compare the two theories. We simply present the same object from several viewpoints and record the time taken to identify it from each viewpoint. According to viewpoint-dependent theorists, the times should vary across viewpoints, whereas the times shouldn't

Key Terms

Viewpoint-dependent theories:
theories of object recognition based on the assumption that objects can be recognized more easily from some angles than from others; see **viewpoint-invariant theories**.

Viewpoint-invariant theories:
theories of object recognition based on the assumption that objects can be recognized equally easily from all angles; see **viewpoint-dependent theories**.

vary according to viewpoint-invariant theorists. In reality, the findings are somewhat inconsistent.

Biederman and Gerhardstein (1993) argued from their viewpoint-invariant theory that object naming should be facilitated as much by two different views of an object as by two identical views provided the same geon-based description could be constructed from both views. Their findings supported the prediction even when there was an angular difference of 135° between the two views. However, these findings are the exception rather than the rule.

Tarr and Bülthoff (1995) gave participants extensive practice at recognizing novel objects from certain specified viewpoints. What they found in each of several experiments was very consistent: "Response times and error rates for naming a familiar object in an unfamiliar viewpoint increased with rotation distance between the unfamiliar viewpoint and the nearest familiar viewpoint" (Tarr & Bülthoff, 1995, p. 1500). Thus, as predicted by viewpoint-dependent theories, it was easier to recognize objects presented from viewpoints that matched stored views.

The available evidence indicates that object recognition is sometimes viewpoint-dependent and sometimes viewpoint-invariant. Viewpoint-dependent mechanisms are most likely to be used when the task involves complex discriminations (e.g., between different makes of car), whereas viewpoint-invariant mechanisms are used when the task is easy (e.g., discriminating between trees and flowers). Supporting evidence was reported by Vanrie, Béatsie, Wagemans, Sunaert, and van Hecke (2002). Participants were presented with pairs of three-dimensional block figures in different orientations and had to decide whether they represented the same figure. There were two conditions differing in difficulty level. As predicted, object recognition was viewpoint-invariant in the simpler condition, but it was viewpoint-dependent in the harder condition.

Foster and Gilson (2002) proposed an alternative theoretical approach. According to them, viewpoint-dependent and viewpoint-invariant information is often combined. Participants had to decide whether two images of three-dimensional objects showed the same object or two different objects. The key finding was that participants used *both* kinds of information. This suggests we use *all* available information rather than confining ourselves to only some of it.

Evaluation

- It has been established that object recognition is sometimes viewpoint-dependent and sometimes viewpoint-invariant.

- There is an increasing understanding of the conditions in which object recognition is viewpoint-independent or viewpoint-invariant. For example, object recognition is much more likely to be viewpoint-invariant when the task is very easy than when it is complex and involves fine discriminations.

- It is not altogether clear whether viewpoint-invariant and viewpoint-dependent information is generally combined during object recognition.

- The theories put forward by Biederman (1987) and by Tarr and Bülthoff (1995) only address some of the key issues concerning object recognition. A more detailed approach to the processes underlying object recognition is discussed below.

FIVE PROCESSING STAGES

There has been much research on brain-damaged patients experiencing problems in object recognition. What is striking about this research is the enormous variety of problems they report. This suggests that there are several different stages of processing involved in object recognition, any one of which can be damaged. At each stage, more detailed information about visual objects is processed. Riddoch and Humphreys (2001) have provided a hierarchical model of object recognition (see the figure on the right) based on five stages or processes:

1. *Edge grouping by collinearity* (collinear means having a common line): This is an early stage of processing during which an object's edges are worked out.
2. *Feature binding into shapes*: During this stage, object features that have been extracted are combined to form shapes.
3. *View normalization*: During this stage, processing occurs to allow a viewpoint-invariant representation to be worked out.
4. *Structural description*: During this stage, individuals gain access to stored knowledge about the structural descriptions of objects (i.e., their overall form and shape).
5. *Semantic system*: The final stage in object recognition involves gaining access to stored knowledge of semantic information relating to an object.

What predictions follow from this model? The most obvious one is that there should be patients having problems in object recognition at each of the stages of processing identified in the model. As we will see, there is reasonable support for this prediction.

Findings

Many patients have problems with edge grouping (stage 1). Milner et al. (1991) studied a patient, DF (discussed later in the chapter), who recognized only a few real objects and who couldn't recognize any objects shown in line drawings. She also had poor performance when making judgments about simple patterns grouped on the basis of various properties (e.g., proximity).

The most-studied patient having particular problems with feature binding (stage 2) is HJA. According to G.W. Humphreys (e.g., 1999), this patient suffers from **integrative agnosia**, a condition in which there are problems combining or integrating features of an object during recognition. Giersch, Humphreys, Boucart, and Kovacs (2000) presented HJA with an array of three geometric shapes that were spatially separated or superimposed or occluded (covered) (see the figure on the right). Then a second visual array was presented, which was either the original array or a distractor array in which the positions of the shapes had been re-arranged.

HJA performed reasonably well with separated shapes but not with superimposed or occluded shapes. Thus, he had poor ability for shape segregation.

Patients having problems with view normalization (stage 3) would find it hard to recognize that two objects are the same when viewed from different angles. Such findings were reported by Warrington and Taylor (1978). Patients were presented with pairs of photographs, one of which was a conventional or typical view and the other of which was an unusual view. For example, the usual view of a flat-iron was photographed from above, whereas the unusual view showed only the base of the iron and part of the handle. The task was to decide whether the same object was shown in both photographs. The patients performed poorly on this task, finding it hard to identify an object shown

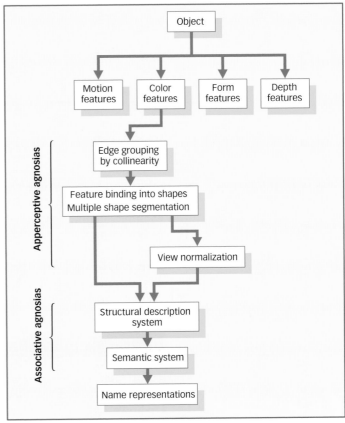

A hierarchical model of object recognition and naming, specifying different component processes which, when impaired, can produce varieties of apperceptive and associative agnosia. From Riddoch and Humphreys (2001).

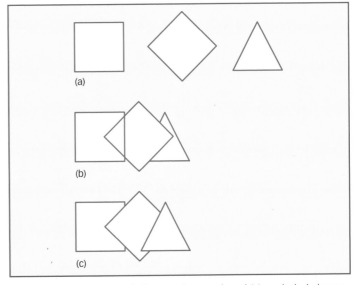

Examples of (a) separated, (b) superimposed, and (c) occluded shapes used by Giersch et al. (2000). From Riddoch and Humphreys (2001).

Key Term

Integrative agnosia: a condition in which the patient experiences great difficulty in integrating features of an object when engaged in object recognition.

from an unusual angle even when they had already identified it from the accompanying usual view.

We turn now to patients having problems with structural descriptions (stage 4). Fery and Morais (2003) studied such a patient (DJ). In spite of his problems, several processes relating to object recognition were essentially intact. For example, he was correct on 93% of trials on a difficult animal-decision task requiring a decision as to which one out of various drawings was an animal. However, DJ recognized only 16% of common objects presented visually, indicating that he couldn't easily access information stored in memory about the structural descriptions of objects on the basis of visual information.

Finally, we turn to patients who find it difficult to gain access to relevant stored information about objects. Some of these patients suffer from **category-specific deficits**, meaning they have problems with certain semantic categories but not others. For example, many such patients have greater problems in identifying pictures of living than of nonliving things (see Martin & Caramazza, 2003). It is likely that the problems with object recognition experienced by patients with category-specific disorders center on accessing certain kinds of semantic knowledge about objects rather than on any of the earlier stages of processing.

Evaluation

● Riddoch and Humphreys' (2001) model of object recognition provides a useful framework within which to consider the various problems with object recognition shown by brain-damaged patients.

● There is evidence supporting each of the separate stages of edge grouping, feature binding, view normalization, structural descriptions, and access to semantic knowledge.

● It is assumed that each stage of processing uses the output from the previous one, but precisely *how* this happens remains unclear.

● It is assumed that processing in object recognition proceeds in an orderly way through five successive stages. In fact, the stored knowledge about structural descriptions and semantic information about objects associated with stages 4 and 5 often influences processing at earlier stages.

The Müller–Lyer illusion

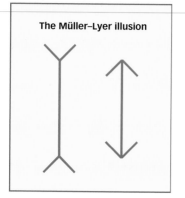

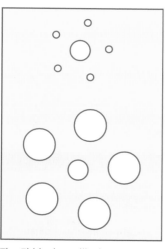

The Ebbinghaus illusion.

VISUAL ILLUSIONS: TWO SYSTEMS

When we look at the world around us, we are usually confident that what we see corresponds precisely to what is actually there. Indeed, the human species would probably have become extinct a very long time ago if we perceived the environment inaccurately. For example, if we thought the edge of a precipice was further away than was actually the case or that the jump from a wall to the ground was 3 feet (1 meter) when it was actually 9 feet (3 meters), then our lives would be in danger. In spite of these apparently persuasive arguments in favor of accurate visual perception, psychologists have found that we are subject to numerous visual illusions, a few of which are discussed below.

First, there is the Müller–Lyer illusion (see the figure on the left). Your task is to compare the lengths of the two vertical lines. Nearly everyone says that the vertical line on the left looks longer than the one on the right. In fact, however, they are the same length, as can be confirmed by using a ruler! Second, there is the Ebbinghaus illusion (see the figure on the left). In this illusion, the central circle surrounded by smaller circles looks larger than a central circle of the same size surrounded by larger circles. In fact, the two central circles are the same size. Third, there is the Ponzo illusion (see the figure on the right). In this illusion, the rectangle labeled A seems larger than the rectangle labeled B in spite of the fact that they are the same length.

WHAT CAUSES VISUAL ILLUSIONS?

The existence of the Müller–Lyer, Ebbinghaus, and Ponzo illusions (plus many others) leaves us with an intriguing paradox. How has the human species been so successful given that our visual perceptual processes are apparently very prone to error? Consider your answer before reading on.

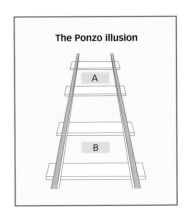

The Ponzo illusion

One plausible answer is that most visual illusions involve very artificial figures, and so can be dismissed as tricks played by psychologists with nothing better to do. There is some truth in this argument, but it doesn't account for all visual illusions. For example, you can show the Müller–Lyer illusion by following the lead of DeLucia and Hochberg (1991). They observed the typical Müller–Lyer effect when three 2-foot high fins were placed on the floor in an arrangement like that shown in the figure on the right. Place three open books in a line so that the ones on the left and the right are open to the right and the one in the middle is open to the left (see the figure below). The spine of the book in the middle should be the same distance from the spines of each of the other two books. However, the distance between the spine of the middle book and the spine of the book on the right will look longer.

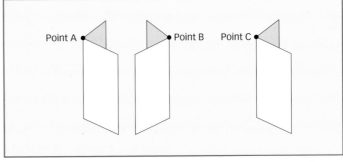

In DeLucia and Hochberg's study, three fins that were 2 feet high were positioned on the floor and participants asked to say whether point A was closer to point B than B was to C. The Müller–Lyer illusion persists even though depth is obvious in this three-dimensional situation, a fact that does not fit Gregory's misapplied size-constancy theory.

Two visual systems

The most successful explanation of the paradox that visual perception can be error-prone in the laboratory in spite of being very accurate in everyday life was proposed by Milner and Goodale (1995, 1998). Their starting point was the startling assumption that we basically have *two* visual perceptual systems! In crude terms, one system allows us to move safely around our environment without knocking into objects or falling over precipices, whereas the other system is used to recognize objects and to perceive visual illusions. These two systems generally operate together but can function fairly independently. One of these systems (the vision-

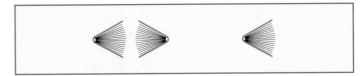

The spine of the middle book is closer to the spine of which other book? Now check your answer with a ruler.

for-perception system) is used to make sense of the visual illusions, whereas the other system (the vision-for-action system) is used to move around the environment rapidly and safely.

We will now consider the two visual systems in more detail. The vision-for-perception system is what we immediately think of when considering visual perception. It is the system used to decide that the animal in front of us is a cat or a buffalo or to admire the paintings of Cézanne. More generally, this is the system allowing us to construct an internal model of the world. In contrast, the vision-for-action system is used for visually guided action. It is the system we use when running to return the ball when playing tennis or some other sport. We are not consciously aware that two systems are involved in visual perception and action, but our conscious experience is a fallible guide to what is actually happening.

Much evidence supports the perception–action approach of Milner and Goodale (1995, 1998). If there are two visual systems, they should involve different parts of the brain. Progress has been made in identifying the parts of the brain associated with each visual system (see the figure on the following page). Both visual systems start in V1, which is concerned with early visual processing. After that, however, the visual system involved in object recognition (based on a ventral pathway) projects to the inferotemporal cortex, whereas the visual stream involved in the guidance of action (based on a dorsal pathway) projects to the posterior parietal cortex.

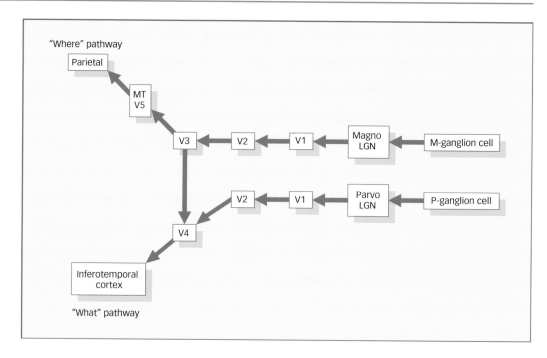

A very simplified illustration of the pathways and brain areas involved in vision. There is much more interconnectivity within the brain (V1 onwards) than is shown, and there are additional unshown brain areas involved in vision. Adapted from Goldstein (1996).

How can we test this theory with visual illusions? Suppose we carried out studies on the visual illusions so that participants would use the vision-for-action system rather than the vision-for-perception system. We could do this by using three-dimensional versions of the illusions and instructing participants to reach for a key object (e.g., one of the central circles in the Ebbinghaus illusion). Milner and Goodale (1995, 1998) argued that this system should generally *not* be deceived by the visual illusions. If illusions present when the vision-for-perception system is used disappear when the vision-for-action system is used, this would provide strong support for the theoretical approach.

The relevant evidence mostly provides general support for the theory (see Glover, 2004, for a review). For example, Aglioti, Goodale, and DeSouza (1995) constructed a three-dimensional version of the Ebbinghaus illusion, and obtained the usual illusion effect when observers reported on the apparent size of the central disk. However, when observers reached to pick up one of the central disks (and so used the vision-for-action system), the maximum grip aperture of their reaching hand was almost entirely determined by the actual size of the disk. Thus, the illusion disappeared under these conditions.

Haart, Carey, and Milne (1999) used a three-dimensional version of the Müller–Lyer illusion (see the figure on p. 139). The usual illusion effect was found when observers had to indicate the apparent length of each vertical shaft. However, there was no illusion effect at all when they used the vision-for-action system to grasp one of the figures lengthwise using their index finger and thumb.

According to Milner and Goodale's perception–action model, we are generally not deceived by visual illusions when we respond to them with our vision-for-action system. However, matters are more complex than that. Glover (2004) reviewed the evidence. He discovered that people's *initial* hand movements towards illusion figures are often influenced by the illusion even though their hand movements thereafter become progressively more accurate as they approach it. Glover accounted for such findings by arguing that the production of human action involves two systems: a planning system and a control system. The planning system is involved in deciding how to grasp an object and is used mainly before a hand movement starts. In contrast, the control system is used in ensuring that movements are accurate and in making adjustments if required. It operates during the carrying out of a movement. According to this model, the planning system is affected by visual illusions but the control system is not.

Cognitive neuropsychology

The notion that there are two somewhat separate visual systems (one specialized for perception and one for action) can also be investigated by studying brain-damaged patients. We would expect to find some patients (those with damage to the dorsal stream) having reasonably intact vision for perception but severely impaired vision for action. There should be other patients (those with damage to the ventral stream) who show the opposite pattern.

We start by considering patients with **optic ataxia**, a condition in which reasonable visual perception is accompanied by problems with visually guided reaching. Perenin and Vighetto (1988) found that patients with optic ataxia had great difficulty in rotating their hands appropriately when given the task of reaching towards and into a large oriented slot in front of them. As expected, such patients typically have damage in parts of the posterior parietal lobe forming part of the dorsal pathway.

Glover (2004) reviewed evidence indicating that most patients with optic ataxia don't actually have problems with *all* aspects of reaching for objects. According to Glover, optic ataxia primarily involves deficits in the control system rather than in the planning system. For example, Jakobson et al. (1991) studied VK, a patient with optic ataxia who had difficulty in grasping objects. Close inspection of her grip aperture at different points in grasping indicated that her initial planning was essentially intact.

What about patients with deficient vision for perception but intact vision for action? Some patients with visual agnosia fit this pattern. **Visual agnosia** is a condition involving severe problems with object recognition. DF is the most studied patient having visual agnosia coupled with fairly good spatial perception. Dijkerman, Milner, and Carey (1998) assessed DF's performance on various tasks when presented with several differently colored objects. DF showed good vision for action in that she reached out and touched the objects as accurately as healthy individuals. However, she had poor vision for perception. She couldn't copy the objects in their correct spatial positions, and couldn't distinguish accurately between the colored objects.

According to Milner and Goodale's perception–action model, DF's brain damage should be in the ventral stream underlying object recognition rather than in the ventral

> **Key Terms**
>
> **Optic ataxia:**
> a condition involving brain damage in which the patient has difficulty in making visually guided movements in spite of having reasonably intact visual perception.
>
> **Visual agnosia:**
> a condition in which there are great problems in recognizing objects presented visually even though visual information reaches the visual cortex.

Case Study: *The Man Who Mistook His Wife for a Hat*

Mr. P was "a musician of distinction, well-known for many years as a singer, and then at the local School of Music, as a teacher. It was here, in relation to his students, that certain strange problems were first observed. Sometimes a student would present himself, and Mr. P would not recognize him; or specifically, would not recognize his face. The moment the student spoke, he would be recognized by his voice. Such incidents multiplied, causing embarrassment, perplexity, fear—and, sometimes, comedy."

"At first these odd mistakes were laughed off as jokes, not least by Mr. P himself . . . His musical powers were as dazzling as ever; he did not feel ill . . . The notion of there being 'something the matter' did not emerge until some three years later, when diabetes developed. Well aware that diabetes could affect his eyes, Mr. P consulted an ophthalmologist, who took a careful history, and examined his eyes closely. 'There's nothing the matter with your eyes,' the doctor concluded. 'But there is trouble with the visual parts of your brain. You don't need my help, you must see a neurologist.' "

And so Mr. P went to see Oliver Sacks who found him quite normal except for the fact that, when they talked, Mr. P faced him with his *ears* rather than his eyes. Another episode alerted Sacks to the problem. He asked Mr. P to put his shoe back on.

" 'Ach,' he said, 'I had forgotten the shoe,' adding *sotto voce*, 'The shoe? The shoe?' He seemed baffled.

He continued to look downwards, though not at the shoe, with an intense but misplaced concentration. Finally his gaze settled on his foot: 'That is my shoe, yes?'

Did he mis-hear? Did he mis-see?

'My eyes,' he explained, and put his hand to his foot. '*This* is my shoe, no'

'No that is not. That is your foot. *There* is your shoe.'

'Ah! I thought it was my foot.'

Was he joking? Was he mad? Was he blind?"

Oliver Sacks helped Mr. P put on his shoe and gave him some further tests. His eyesight was fine, for example he had no difficulty seeing a pin on the floor. But when he was shown a picture of the Sahara desert and asked to describe it, he invented guesthouses, terraces, and tables with parasols. Sacks must have looked aghast but Mr. P seemed to think he had done rather well and decided it was time to end the examination. He reached out for his hat, and took hold of his wife's head, and tried to lift it off. He apparently had mistaken his wife's head for his hat.

The condition Mr. P suffered from is called visual agnosia and results from brain damage of some kind.

Adapted from Sacks (1985).

stream underlying vision for action. James et al. (2003) carried out a brain-imaging study on DF and obtained findings consistent with prediction.

Evaluation

+ There is much evidence from healthy individuals supporting the notion of two visual systems: vision-for-perception and vision-for-action.

+ Milner and Goodale's perception–action model provides an explanation of why there is often no illusion effect when people grasp three-dimensional visual illusions.

+ Patients with optic ataxia and visual agnosia support the model in general terms by showing that one visual system can be reasonably intact even though the other visual system is severely damaged.

− The vision-for-action system is more complicated than implied by the perception–action model. It consists of a planning system and a control system, with the former being deceived by visual illusions.

− The two visual systems interact in complex ways that are poorly understood.

UNCONSCIOUS PERCEPTION

Most people assume that visual perception is a conscious process in that we are consciously aware of the object or objects at which we are looking. If that is the case, then there is no such thing as **unconscious perception**, in which perception occurs in the absence of conscious awareness. Before we proceed, ask yourself whether you think that unconscious perception exists.

SUBLIMINAL PERCEPTION

The case for unconscious perception apparently received strong support from the notorious "research" carried out in 1957 by James Vicary, who was a struggling market researcher. He claimed to have flashed the words EAT POPCORN and DRINK COCA-COLA for 1/300th of a second (well below the threshold of conscious awareness) numerous times during showings of a movie called *Picnic* at a cinema in Fort Lee, New Jersey. A grand total of 45,699 people allegedly received these messages over a 6-week period. The power of unconscious perception was apparently shown in the finding that there was an increase of 18% in the cinema sales of Coca-Cola and a 58% increase in popcorn sales. Alas, Vicary admitted in 1962 that the study was a fabrication. Trappery (1996) combined data from 23 studies and found that stimuli presented below the conscious threshold had little or no effect on consumer behavior.

The finding that stimuli below the level of conscious awareness (**subliminal stimuli**) don't influence buying behavior doesn't mean that such stimuli have *no* effect. How can we decide whether an observer is consciously aware of a given visual stimulus? Merikle, Smilek, and Eastwood (2001) argued that there is an important distinction between two criteria or thresholds:

1. *Subjective threshold*: This is defined by an individual's failure to report conscious awareness of a stimulus, and is the most obvious measure to use.
2. *Objective threshold*: This is defined by an individual's inability to make an accurate forced-choice decision about a stimulus (e.g., guess at above-chance level whether it is a word).

The objective threshold is more stringent than the subjective threshold. As a result, observers often show "awareness" of a stimulus assessed by the objective threshold even

Key Terms

Unconscious perception: perception occurring below the level of conscious awareness.

Subliminal stimuli: these are stimuli presented below the level of conscious awareness.

when it doesn't exceed the subjective threshold. What should we do in these circumstances? The objective threshold may seem unduly stringent, but many psychologists argue that it is more valid than reliance on people's possibly inaccurate or distorted reports of their conscious experience. What is indisputable is that evidence for subliminal perception based on the objective threshold is more convincing than evidence based on the subjective threshold.

Findings

Dehaene et al. (1998) carried out an experiment using the objective threshold in which they initially showed that observers couldn't distinguish between trials on which a masked digit (subliminal stimulus) was or was not presented very briefly. After that, observers were presented on each trial with a masked digit followed by a clearly visible target digit—their task was to decide whether this target digit was larger or smaller than 5. The masked digit was either *congruent* with the target digit (both numbers on the same side of 5) or *incongruent*. Performance was slower on incongruent trials than on congruent ones, showing that information from the masked digit had been processed.

Snodgrass, Bernat, and Shevrin (2004) combined the data from nine published studies to assess the strength of the evidence for unconscious perception at the objective threshold. They obtained highly significant evidence of above-chance performance on measures designed to assess unconscious perception. In a further analysis, they found no significant evidence of above-chance performance on measures of conscious perception. Thus, they reported strong evidence for the existence of subliminal perception.

An alternative approach is to show that the effects of subliminal perception are very *different* from those of typical conscious perception rather than merely being weaker. This approach was adopted by Debner and Jacoby (1994). They assumed that information perceived with awareness permits us to control our actions, whereas information perceived without awareness does not. They tested these assumptions by presenting observers with a word for either 50 ms (subliminal stimulus) or 150 ms (consciously perceived stimulus) followed by a mask. Immediately after that, the first three letters of the word were presented again, and observers were instructed to think of the first word coming to mind starting with those letters *except* for the word that had just been masked (exclusion condition). There was also a control condition in which each word stem was preceded by an unrelated word.

When the masked word was presented for 150 ms, the participants followed instructions to avoid using that word on the word-stem completion task (see figure on the right). They perceived the masked word consciously, and so deliberately avoided using it. In contrast, when the masked word was presented for only 50 ms, it was often used to complete the word (see figure on the right). Limited processing of the masked word below the conscious level automatically triggered activation of its representation in memory and made it accessible on the word-stem completion task.

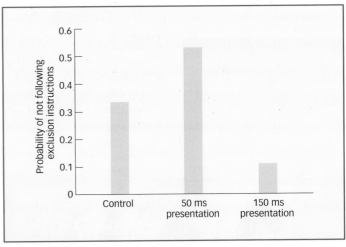

Probability of not following exclusion instructions in control (no relevant preceding word), 50 ms word presentation, and 150 ms word presentation conditions. Based on data in Debner and Jacoby (1994).

BLINDSIGHT

An army doctor by the name of Riddoch treated numerous British soldiers in the First World War who had received head injuries in battle. Those with damage to the primary visual cortex (involved in the early stages of visual processing) often had a loss of conscious perception in some parts of the visual field. What fascinated Riddoch (1917) was that some of these patients could still detect motion in those parts of the visual field in which they claimed to be blind! Brain-damaged patients having some visual perception in the absence of any conscious awareness are said to have **blindsight**, which neatly captures the apparently paradoxical nature of their condition.

Key Term
Blindsight: the ability of some brain-damaged patients to respond appropriately to visual stimuli in the absence of conscious visual perception.

What perceptual abilities do blindsight patients show in the parts of the visual field for which they have no conscious perceptual experience? According to Farah (2001, p. 162), "Detection and localization of light, and detection of motion are invariably preserved to some degree. In addition, many patients can discriminate orientation, shape, direction of movement, and flicker. Color vision mechanisms also appear to be preserved in some cases."

The phenomenon of blindsight becomes less paradoxical if we consider its assessment in more detail. The experimenter typically obtains two measures: (1) patients' subjective reports that they cannot see some stimulus presented to their blind region, and (2) patients' performance on a forced-choice test in which they have to guess (e.g., stimulus present or absent?) or point at the stimulus they cannot see. These measures are very different. In addition, performance on the forced-choice test (although significantly above chance level) is nevertheless way below the performance of normally sighted individuals.

Evidence that blindsight does not depend on conscious visual experience was reported by Rafal et al. (1990). Blindsight patients performed at chance level when given the task of detecting a light presented to the blind area of the visual field. However, their speed of reaction to a light presented to the intact part of the visual field was slowed down when a light was presented to the blind area at the same time. Thus, a light that didn't produce any conscious awareness nevertheless received enough processing to disrupt visual performance on another task.

Evaluation

+ Numerous studies on healthy individuals and blindsight patients have obtained evidence for the existence of subliminal perception.

+ Some of the most convincing evidence for subliminal perception comes from studies on healthy individuals either using the objective criterion or showing that the effects of conscious and unconscious perception can be very different.

− It is difficult to be certain that any given individual has no conscious visual experience of a rapidly presented stimulus.

− The reports of blindsight patients sometimes suggest there is residual conscious experience. According to Weiskrantz, Barbur, and Sahraie (1995), this visual experience is characterized by "a contentless kind of awareness, a feeling of something happening, albeit not normal seeing."

Key Term

Inattentional blindness: failure to detect an unexpected object appearing in a visual display; see **change blindness**.

Frame showing a woman in a gorilla suit in the middle of a game of passing the ball. From Simons and Chabris (1999). Copyright © Daniel J. Simons. Figure provided by Daniel Simons.

CHANGE BLINDNESS

Suppose you watch a film in which students are passing a ball to each other. At some point a woman in a gorilla suit walks right into camera shot, looks at the camera, thumps her chest, and then walks off. Altogether she is on the screen for 9 seconds. Are you very confident that you would spot the woman dressed up as a gorilla almost immediately? Of course you are! In fact, Simons and Chabris (1999) carried out an experiment along the lines just described (see the photo on the left). What percentage of their participants failed to spot the gorilla? Think about your answer before reading on.

It seems reasonable to assume that under 5% (or even under 1%) of people would fail to notice a gorilla taking 9 seconds to stroll across a scene. In fact, however, 50% of observers didn't notice the woman's presence! This phenomenon is known as **inattentional blindness**, defined as the failure to notice an unexpected object appearing in a visual display. We will consider possible explanations for this finding shortly.

In another experiment, Levin and Simons (1997) showed participants various videos involving two people having a conversation in a restaurant. In one video, the plates on their table change from red to white, and in another a scarf worn by one of them disappears. A third video showed a man sitting in his office and then walking into the hall to answer the phone. When the view switches from the office to the hall, the first person has been replaced by another man wearing different clothes. Levin and Simons (1997) found that no participants detected any of the changes. This phenomenon is known as **change blindness**, defined as a failure to detect that an object has moved or disappeared.

Levin, Drivdahl, Momen, and Beck (2002) obtained convincing evidence that we greatly underestimate our proneness to change blindness. They showed participants the videos used by Levin and Simons (1997) and asked them to indicate whether they thought they would have noticed the changes if they had not been forewarned about them. The percentages claiming they would have noticed the changes were as follows: 78% for the disappearing scarf; 59% for the changed man; and 46% for the change in color of the plates. Levin et al. (2002) used the term **change blindness blindness** to describe the wildly optimist belief in our ability to detect visual changes.

Our woefully mistaken belief that we perceive and remember nearly everything about us is good news for those who make movies and for conjurors. So far as movies are concerned, change blindness means that we rarely spot visual changes when the same scene has been shot more than once with parts of each shot being combined in the finished version of the movie. I will take the risk of appearing nerdy by providing two examples. In *Grease*, while John Travolta is singing "Greased Lightning," his socks change color several times between black and white. In the movie *Diamonds Are Forever*, James Bond tilts his car on two wheels to drive through a narrow alleyway. As he enters the alleyway, the car is balanced on its *right* wheels, but when it emerges on the other side it is miraculously on its *left* wheels!

How do conjurors and magicians capitalize on the phenomenon of change blindness blindness? In essence, most tricks involve **misdirection**, in which the conjuror or magician directs spectators' attention away from some action crucial to the success of the trick. Jakobsen (2004) discussed various ways of misdirecting an audience, of which we consider two. First, if magicians make a larger and a smaller movement at the same time, spectators will attend to the larger movement. As a result, conjurors can prepare the trick with the smaller movement. Second, spectators will typically look wherever the magician is looking. That means magicians can direct spectators' attention away from the crucial action they want to perform.

FACTORS INFLUENCING CHANGE BLINDNESS AND INATTENTIONAL BLINDNESS

The extent to which observers show change blindness and inattentional blindness depends on several factors. One factor is whether or not observers are aware beforehand that something is going to change. Observers are much more likely to show change blindness or inattentional blindness when they not informed of any possible change (see Simons and Rensink, 2005, for a review). For example, nearly 100% of observers would probably have detected the gorilla in the study by Simons and Chabris (1999) if they had been instructed beforehand to look out for something unexpected. Indeed, observers who watched the film a second time were very surprised they had missed the gorilla on first viewing!

A second factor determining whether change blindness or inattentional blindness occurs is the *similarity* between an unexpected object and other objects in the visual display. You will remember the surprising finding of Simons and Chabris (1999) that 50% of observers failed to detect a woman dressed in black as a gorilla. In that experiment, observers counted the number of passes made by members of the team dressed in white. The dissimilarity in color between the unexpected stimulus (gorilla) and the task-relevant stimuli (members of attended team) probably played a part in producing so much inattentional blindness. This was confirmed by Simons and Chabris (1999) in another

Key Terms

Change blindness: failure to detect changes in the visual environment.

Change blindness blindness: people's mistaken belief that they would notice visual changes that are in fact very rarely detected.

Misdirection: the various techniques used by magicians to make spectators focus on some irrelevant aspect of the situation while they perform the crucial part of a trick.

experiment in which observers counted the passes of the team dressed in white or the team in black. The gorilla's presence was detected by 83% of observers when the attended team was dressed in black compared to only 42% when it was dressed in white.

A third factor influencing change blindness is whether the object that changes has been attended to prior to the change occurring. Hollingworth and Henderson (2002) pointed out that there is an important distinction between two kinds of change to an object:

1. Type change, in which an object is replaced by an object from a different category (e.g., a plate is replaced by a bowl).
2. Token change, in which an object is replaced by an object from the same category (e.g., one plate is replaced by a different plate).

Token changes are smaller and less obvious than type changes, and so we would predict there would be more change blindness with token changes.

(a) Percent correct change detection as a function of form of change (type vs. token) and time of fixation (before vs. after change); also false alarm rate when there was no change. (b) Mean percent correct change detection as a function of the number of fixations between target fixation and change of target and form of change (type vs. token). From Hollingworth and Henderson (2002). Copyright © 2002 by the American Psychological Association. Reprinted with permission.

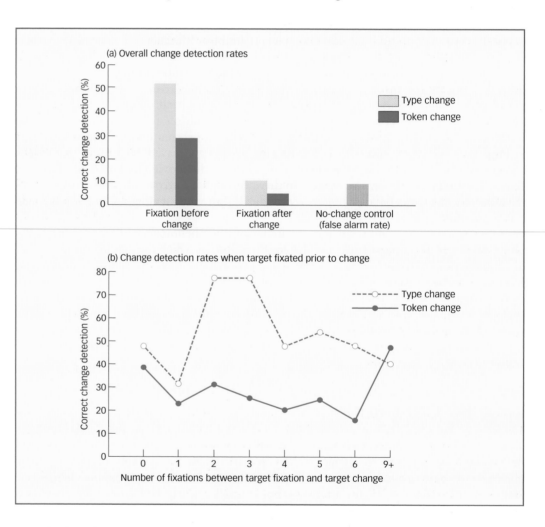

The key findings of Hollingworth and Henderson (2002) are shown in the figure above. Changes in objects were much more likely to be detected when the changed object had received attention (been fixated) beforehand. In addition, change detection was much better when there was a type change rather than a token change.

WHAT CAUSES CHANGE BLINDNESS?

Hollingworth and Henderson (2002) provided an explanation for change blindness. According to them, we form fairly detailed (but not very detailed) visual representations of objects that are the focus of attention. These representations are fitted into a mental map providing a spatial layout of the overall visual scene. Information about these visual representations and about the overall spatial layout is stored in long-term memory. Information about nonattended objects is typically not stored in long-term memory, and so we have very limited ability to detect changes in nonattended objects.

If reasonably detailed information about visual scenes is stored in long-term memory, it follows that observers should retain some memory of objects they fixated and attended to several minutes earlier. This prediction was tested by Hollingworth and Henderson (2002). Between 5 and 30 minutes after viewing various scenes, observers were presented with two scenes:

1. The original scene with a target object marked with a green arrow.
2. A distractor scene identical to the original scene except that there was a different object in the location of the target object.

The observers decided which was the original object. Overall, 93% of type changes were detected as well as 81% of token changes.

So far we have seen that people have a remarkably impressive ability to detect certain kinds of changes to a visual scene even when 30 minutes intervene between seeing the original scene and the changed one. However, Hollingworth and Henderson (2002) argued that the information stored in long-term memory about visual scenes is not very detailed. Henderson and Hollingworth (2003) presented observers with complex real-world scenes in which half of each scene was hidden by vertical gray bars. The entire scene changed whenever the observer's gaze crossed either of two invisible vertical lines so that the previously visible parts of the scene were hidden and the hidden parts became visible. Even though the observers knew the precise nature of the changes that might occur, they detected only 2.7% of them.

In sum, our belief that we have a clear and detailed representation of our visual environment is exaggerated but not entirely incorrect. What we actually have is a fairly clear and detailed representation of those parts of the visual environment to which we have recently paid attention. Change blindness is especially likely to be found when the changed part of the visual scene hasn't previously been the focus of attention.

VISUAL ATTENTION

What is attention? According to Colman (2001, p. 62), attention is "sustained concentration on a specific stimulus, sensation, idea, thought, or activity." Try focusing your attention on the world around you. As James (1890) pointed out, you probably found yourself attending to one object at a time or at one part of the visual space around you. Several psychologists (e.g., Posner, 1980) have argued that visual attention is like a spotlight: it illuminates a small part of the visual field, little can be seen outside its beam, and it can be re-directed flexibly to focus on any object of interest. Other psychologists (e.g., Eriksen & St. James, 1986) developed the notion of an attentional beam by comparing focused attention to a zoom lens. The basic idea is that we can increase or decrease the area of focal attention at will in the same way that a zoom lens can be moved in or out to alter the visual area it covers. This makes sense. For example, when driving a car it is typically desirable to attend to as much of the visual field as possible to anticipate danger. In contrast, when we come upon an unexpected phrase when reading, we narrow our attention to that phrase and try to make sense of it.

Focused attention is more like a zoom lens than a spotlight. Consider a study by Müller et al. (2003). On each trial, participants were presented with four squares arranged as in the figure on the right. They were then cued

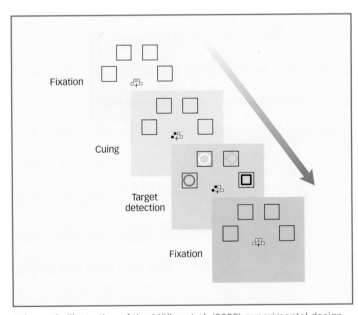

Schematic illustration of the Müller et al. (2003) experimental design. Cues were presented for 4, 7, or 10 seconds and indicated the possible locations of the target (white circle). Either one, two (as in this example), or four locations were cued, determining the size of the attended region. From Müller 2003. Copyright © 2003 Society for Neuroscience. Reproduced with permission.

to focus their attention on one given square, on two given squares, or on all four squares. After that, four objects were presented (one in each square), and participants decided whether a target (blue circle) was among them. When a target was present, it was always in one of the cued squares. For reasons that will become apparent shortly, Müller et al. (2003) made use of brain imaging to obtain information about brain activation in the various conditions.

There were two key findings. First, as predicted by zoom-lens theory, targets were detected fastest when the attended region was small (i.e., only one square) and slowest when it was large (i.e., all four squares). Second, brain imaging revealed that activation in early visual areas was most widespread when the attended region was large and was most limited in scope when the attended region was small. This finding provides support for the notion that the attentional beam can be wide or narrow.

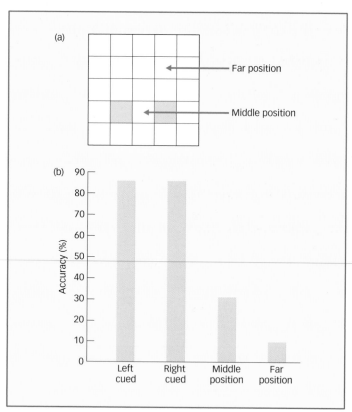

(a) One cue arrangement with the shaded squares being cued. On 80% of trials the targets were presented to the cued squares; on 20% of trials the targets were presented to the middle and far positions. Adapted from Awh and Pashler (2000). (b) Target detection as a function of whether target was cued (left or right) or not (middle and far positions). Data from Awh and Pashler (2000).

Are you convinced by now that visual attention can accurately be described as resembling a spotlight or a zoom lens? If so, you are mistaken! In fact, visual attention is more *flexible* than implied by the analogy with a spotlight or zoom lens. For example, we can exhibit **split attention**, in which we direct attention to two regions of space *not* adjacent to each other. Awh and Pashler (2000) presented participants with a 5 × 5 visual display containing 23 letters and 2 digits. They had to report the identity of the two digits. Just before the display was presented, participants received two cues indicating the probable locations of the two digits. However, these cues were invalid or misleading on 20% of trials. The crucial condition was one in which the cues were invalid, with one of the digits being presented in between the cued locations.

How did participants perform on the digit presented between the two cued locations? According to the spotlight and zoom-lens theories, focal attention should have included the two cued locations and the space in between. In that case, performance should have been high for the digit because it received full attention. In contrast, if split attention is possible, performance should have been poor because only the cued locations would have received full attention. In fact, performance was much lower for digits presented between cued locations than for digits presented to cued locations (see the figure on the left). Thus, split attention is possible and the spotlight/zoom-lens approach is inadequate. The existence of split attention suggests that attention can be shaped like a doughnut in which there is nothing in the middle.

ATTENTION TO LOCATIONS OR TO OBJECTS?

Spotlight and zoom-lens theories of visual attention have proved reasonably successful in spite of their problems in accounting for split attention. Such theories assume that visual attention is directed to a given location or area within the visual field. In fact, however, visual attention can be directed to objects rather than to particular regions. Neisser and Becklen (1975) superimposed two moving scenes on top of each other. Participants found it easy to attend to one scene while ignoring the other, even though the two scenes were in the same location. These findings suggest that objects within the visual environment can be the main focus of attention.

O'Craven, Downing, and Kanwisher (1999) carried out a study resembling that of Neisser and Becklen (1975). They also found that visual attention could be directed to objects rather than to a particular location. Participants were presented with two stimuli (a face and a house) that overlapped transparently at the same location with one of the objects moving slightly. They were told to attend either to the direction of motion of the moving stimulus or to the position of the stationary stimulus. Suppose attention was location-based in this study. In that case, participants would always have attended to both stimuli, because they were both in the same location. In contrast, suppose attention was object-based. In that case, processing of the attended stimulus would have been more thorough than that of the unattended one.

O'Craven et al. (1999) tested the above competing predictions by assessing brain activation in areas selectively involved in processing faces or houses. There was more activity in the face-specific brain area when the face stimulus was attended and more activity in the house-specific brain area when the house stimulus was attended. Thus, visual attention seemed to be object-based rather than location-based in this experiment.

Is attention focused on the object or the location?

WHAT HAPPENS TO UNATTENDED STIMULI?

We turn now to the fate of unattended visual stimuli. Unattended visual stimuli receive less processing than attended ones. Martinez et al. (1999) compared event-related potentials (ERPs) to attended and unattended visual displays. The attended displays produced a greater first positive wave (P1) 70–75 ms after stimulus presentation and a greater first negative wave (N1) 130–140 ms after stimulus presentation. These findings indicate that attended stimuli are processed more thoroughly than unattended ones. However, ERPs 50–55 ms after stimulus presentation showed no difference between attended and unattended displays, so attentional processes don't influence the very early stages of processing.

Further evidence that unattended visual stimuli receive less processing than attended ones was reported by Wojciulik, Kanwisher, and Driver (1998). Participants were presented with displays containing two faces and two houses. They attended to the faces or to the houses with the other type of stimulus being unattended. There was significantly more activity in a part of the brain involved in face processing when the faces needed to be attended to than when they did not. This indicates that the faces received less processing when unattended.

DISORDERS OF ATTENTION

We can discover much about attentional processes by studying brain-damaged patients suffering from various attentional disorders. We will consider two of the main ones: neglect and extinction. **Neglect** (or unilateral neglect) is typically found after brain damage in the right parietal lobe (towards the back of the brain) and is often caused by a stroke. Neglect patients with right-hemisphere damage don't notice (or fail to respond to) objects presented to the left side of the visual field. This occurs because of the nature of the visual system—information from the left side of the visual field proceeds to the right hemisphere of the brain. Driver and Vuilleumier (2001, p. 40) described some of the problems of neglect patients, who "often behave as if half of their world no longer exists. In daily life, they may be oblivious to objects and people on the neglected side of the room, may eat from only one side of their plate . . . and make-up or shave only one side of their face."

Extinction is a phenomenon often found in neglect patients although the two disorders are distinct. The two disorders often co-exist because they involve damage to anatomically close brain areas (Karnath, Himmelbach, & Küker, 2003). In extinction, a *single* stimulus on either side of the visual field can be judged as well as by healthy individuals. However, when *two* stimuli are presented together, the one further toward the neglected side of the visual field tends to go undetected. Some patients only show extinction when the objects presented simultaneously are the same. Extinction is a serious condition because we are typically confronted by multiple stimuli at the same time in everyday life.

Key Terms

Neglect:
a disorder of visual attention in which stimuli (or parts of stimuli) presented to the side opposite the brain damage are not detected; the condition resembles **extinction** but is more severe.

Extinction:
a disorder of visual attention in which a stimulus presented to the side opposite the brain damage is not detected when another stimulus is presented at the same time.

Explaining extinction

Most experts argue that *competition* among stimuli is of crucial importance in understanding extinction. For example, Marzi et al. (2001, p. 1354) argued that, "The presence of extinction only during bilateral [on both sides] stimulation is strongly suggestive of a competitive mechanism, whereby the presence of a more salient [prominent] stimulus presented on the same side of space as that of the brain lesion (ipsilesional side) captures attention and hampers the perception of a less salient stimulus on the opposite (contralesional) side."

Rees et al. (2000) assessed the processing of extinguished stimuli using brain imaging. Extinguished stimuli produced moderate levels of activation in the primary visual cortex and nearby areas. These findings suggest that stimuli of which the patient was unaware were nevertheless processed reasonably thoroughly.

Explaining neglect

Neglect can be understood in part in the context of a theoretical approach put forward by Corbetta and Shulman (2002). According to this approach, there are two major attentional systems. One attentional system is voluntary or goal-directed, whereas the other system is involuntary or stimulus-driven. According to Corbetta and Shulman, the goal-directed or top-down system is involved in the selection of sensory information and responses. It is influenced by expectation, knowledge, and current goals. In contrast, the stimulus-driven or bottom-up system is involved in the detection of salient or conspicuous unattended visual stimuli (e.g., the lights on a speeding ambulance turning on and off). This system has a circuit-breaking function, meaning that visual attention is redirected from its current focus. In practice, these two systems generally influence and interact with each other to determine what is attended.

How can we relate this theory to neglect? Corbetta and Shulman (2002) argued that neglect patients typically have damage to the stimulus-driven attentional system. This is supported by the finding that many neglect patients have damage to the right temporo-parietal junction (Vallar & Perani, 1987), an important part of the stimulus-driven system.

Bartolomeo and Chokron (2002) agreed that neglect is the result of an impaired stimulus-driven system, and argued that the goal-directed system is reasonably intact in neglect patients. It follows that the attentional performance of neglect patients should be much better than usual when they can use the goal-directed or top-down attentional system. Smania et al. (1998) compared the time taken to detect stimuli when the side of the visual field was predictable (thus permitting use of the goal-directed system) and when it was determined at random (thus not permitting use of that system). Neglect patients responded faster in the attended field *and* the unattended (neglect) field when the side to which stimuli would be presented was predictable.

Duncan et al. (1999) presented arrays of letters briefly, and asked neglect patients to recall all the letters or only the ones in a prespecified color. It was assumed that the goal-directed or top-down attentional system could only be used effectively when target letters were identified by color. As expected, recall of letters presented to the left (neglect) side was much worse than of letters presented to the right side when all letters had to be reported. However, neglect patients resembled healthy controls in showing comparable recall of letters presented to each side of the visual field when only letters in a certain color were reported. Thus, neglect patients showed reasonably good top-down attentional control.

How do we distinguish and follow one conversation out of many in situations like this?

AUDITORY ATTENTION

One of the important issues in auditory attention is to explain our ability to follow just one conversation when several people are talking at once. Colin Cherry (1953) referred to this issue as the "cocktail party" problem, and carried out research on it—see the Key Study below.

Key Study

Cherry (1953): The cocktail party problem

Cherry found that we make use of physical differences between the various auditory messages to select the one of interest. These physical differences include differences in the sex of the speaker, in voice intensity, and in the speaker's location. When Cherry presented two messages in the same voice at once (thus removing these physical differences), listeners found it very hard to separate out the two messages purely on the basis of meaning.

Cherry (1953) also carried out studies using the **shadowing task**, in which one auditory message had to be shadowed (repeated back aloud) while a secondary auditory message was presented to the other ear. Very little information seemed to be processed from the secondary or unattended message. Listeners rarely noticed when that message was spoken in a foreign language or in reversed speech. In contrast, physical changes (e.g., the insertion of a pure tone) were usually detected, and listeners noticed the speaker's sex. The conclusion that unattended auditory information receives minimal processing is supported by the finding that there is very little memory for words on the unattended message presented 35 times (Moray, 1959).

Discussion points
1. Are you surprised by any of Cherry's findings?
2. Why do you think that Broadbent found Cherry's findings of great interest?

KEY STUDY EVALUATION
The research by Colin Cherry is a very good example of how a psychologist, noticing a real-life situation, is able to devise a hypothesis and carry out research in order to explain a phenomenon, in this case the "cocktail party" effect. Cherry tested his ideas in a laboratory using a shadowing technique and found that participants were really only able to give information about the physical qualities of the nonattended message (whether the message was read by a male or a female, or if a tone was used instead of speech). Cherry's research could be criticized for having moved the real-life phenomenon into an artificial laboratory setting. However, this work opened avenues for other researchers, beginning with Broadbent, to elaborate theories about focused auditory attention.

Broadbent (1958) discussed findings from the **dichotic listening task**. What usually happens is that three digits are presented one after the other to one ear, while at the same time three different digits are presented to the other ear. After the three pairs of digits have been presented, participants recall them in whatever order they prefer. Recall is typically ear by ear rather than pair by pair. If 496 were presented to one ear and 852 to the other ear, recall would be 496852 rather than 489562.

CLASSIC THEORIES

Broadbent (1958) proposed the first detailed theory of auditory attention. The key assumptions in his filter theory were as follows (see the figure on the following page):

- Two stimuli or messages presented at the same time gain access in parallel (at the same time) to a **sensory buffer**, which contains information briefly before it is attended to or disappears from the processing system.

Key Terms

Shadowing task:
a task in which there are two auditory messages, one of which has to be repeated back aloud or shadowed.

Dichotic listening task:
a task in which pairs of items are presented one to each ear, followed by recall of all items.

Sensory buffer:
a mechanism that maintains information for a short period of time before it is processed.

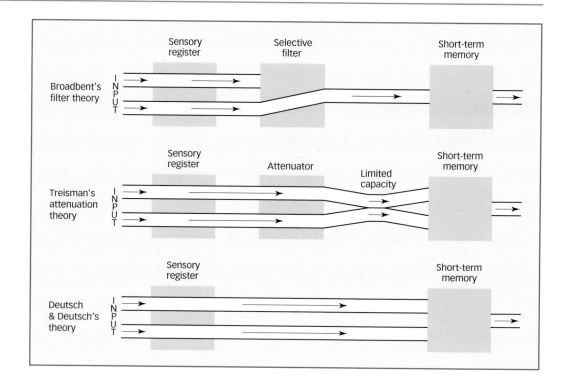

- One input is then allowed through a filter on the basis of its physical characteristics, with the other input remaining in the buffer.
- It takes approximately 500 ms to switch attention, and so there is rarely time to switch attention to information in the sensory buffer before it is lost.
- The filter prevents overloading of the limited-capacity mechanism beyond the filter; this mechanism processes the input thoroughly.
- There is no identification or recognition of an object (involving processing of its meaning) without attention.

   This theory handles Cherry's basic findings, with unattended messages being rejected by the filter and thus receiving very little processing. It also accounts for performance on Broadbent's original dichotic listening task. This is based on the assumption that the filter selects one input on the basis of the most obvious physical characteristic distinguishing the two inputs (i.e., the ear of arrival).
   Treisman (1964) proposed a modified version of Broadbent's filter theory. In her attenuation theory, the processing of unattended stimuli is only attenuated or reduced. In Broadbent's theory, it was proposed that there is a bottleneck early in processing. In Treisman's theory, the location of the bottleneck is more flexible (see the figure above). It is as if people possess a "leaky" filter, making selective attention less efficient than assumed by Broadbent (1958).
   According to Treisman (1964), stimulus processing proceeds systematically, starting with analyses based on physical cues, and then moving on to analyses based on meaning. If there is insufficient processing capacity to allow full stimulus analysis, then some later analyses are omitted with "unattended" stimuli. This theory neatly predicts Cherry's (1953) finding that physical characteristics of unattended inputs (e.g., sex of the speaker) are noticed rather than their meaning.
   The third and final of the classic theories was put forward by Deutsch and Deutsch (1963). They claimed that all stimuli are analyzed fully, with the most important or relevant stimulus determining the response. This theory differs from filter and attenuation theories in placing the bottleneck closer to the response end of the processing system (see the figure above). Deutsch and Deutsch's assumption that all stimuli are analyzed

completely, but that most of the analyzed information is lost almost immediately, seems implausible.

In sum, all three theories explain why it is that we attend (and respond) to just one auditory input when two or more such inputs are presented at the same time. The key difference among the theories is in terms of the predicted amount of processing of unattended stimuli:

1. Processing is typically limited to physical features (Broadbent).
2. Processing is flexible and sometimes includes semantic features (Treisman).
3. Processing of unattended stimuli is thorough (Deutch & Deutsch).

Below we consider these theories in the light of the evidence. Before we do so, there is one final point that needs to be made. All three theories were initially applied only to studies on auditory attention. However, processing bottlenecks can occur in visual attention as well as auditory attention, and so the theories are also of relevance to studies on visual attention.

Findings

Deutsch and Deutsch's (1963) theory has proved the least successful of the classic theories. Treisman and Riley (1969) asked participants to shadow one of two auditory messages presented at the same time. Whenever they detected a target word in either message, they were to stop shadowing and tap. According to Deutsch and Deutsch, there is complete processing of all stimuli, and so it would be expected that there would be no difference in detection rates between the two messages. In fact, many more target words were detected on the shadowed message than on the nonshadowed one, presumably because listeners were attending to the shadowed message.

Neurophysiological studies provide substantial evidence against Deutsch and Deutsch's theory (see Lachter, Forster, & Ruthruff, 2004, for a review). For example, Coch, Sanders, and Neville (2005) used a dichotic listening task in which participants attended to one of two auditory messages. Their task was to detect probe targets presented on the attended or the unattended message. Event-related potentials (ERPs) were recorded. ERPs about 100 ms after probe presentation were greater when the probe was presented on the attended message than on the unattended one, suggesting that there was more processing of attended than of unattended probes. This is inconsistent with Deutsch and Deutsch's assumption that *all* inputs are processed thoroughly.

The battleground between Broadbent's filter theory and Treisman's attenuation theory has focused mainly on the fate of unattended stimuli. Treisman's theory allows for more processing (including semantic processing) of unattended stimuli than does Broadbent's theory. There is much evidence that apparently unattended stimuli are sometimes processed fairly thoroughly, thus supporting Treisman's approach. Underwood (1974) asked listeners to detect digits presented on the shadowed (attended) or nonshadowed (unattended) message. Those who had not done the task before detected only 8% of the digits on the nonshadowed message. In contrast, an experienced researcher in the area detected 67% of the nonshadowed digits. Von Wright, Anderson, and Stenman (1975) gave listeners two auditorily presented lists of words, telling them to shadow one list and ignore the other. When a word previously associated with electric shock was presented on the non-attended list, there was sometimes a physiological response (galvanic skin response). There was the same effect when a word very similar in sound or meaning to the shocked word was presented. Thus, sound and meaning information on the unattended message was sometimes processed. Since physiological responses were observed on only relatively few trials, thorough processing of unattended information occurred only some of the time.

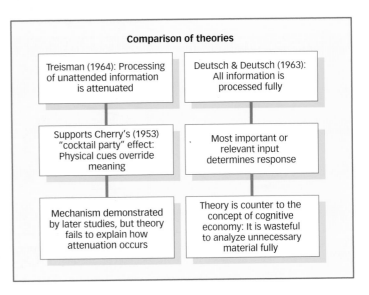

Comparison of theories

Treisman (1964): Processing of unattended information is attenuated

Deutsch & Deutsch (1963): All information is processed fully

Supports Cherry's (1953) "cocktail party" effect: Physical cues override meaning

Most important or relevant input determines response

Mechanism demonstrated by later studies, but theory fails to explain how attenuation occurs

Theory is counter to the concept of cognitive economy: It is wasteful to analyze unnecessary material fully

Conway, Cowan, and Bunting (2001) found that many listeners detected their own name when it was presented on the unattended auditory input. This finding suggests that important unattended semantic information can get through the "leaky" filter.

There is a simple way of modifying Broadbent's theory to account for the above findings. Remember that Broadbent argued that there is a sensory buffer or immediate memory that briefly holds information in a relatively unprocessed state. We now know that there are separate sensory buffers for the auditory modality (echoic memory: Neisser, 1967) and the visual modality (iconic memory: Sperling, 1960). If we could switch our attention rapidly to the information in the appropriate sensory buffer, we would be able to process "unattended" stimuli thoroughly. Broadbent (1958) was pessimistic about the possibility of doing that because he argued that it takes 500 ms (half a second) to shift attention. In fact, as Lachter et al. (2004) pointed out, Broadbent greatly exaggerated the time needed, since involuntary shifts of attention can occur in as little as 50 ms (Tsal, 1983). The crucial point is that shifting attention to information in a sensory buffer can be almost as effective as shifting attention to the actual object. You may have had the experience of being asked a question while doing something else, and immediately replying, "What did you say?" Before you have finished your sentence, you realize that you do know what the person said. This "playback" facility depends on echoic memory.

We now have *two* contrasting explanations for the occasional semantic processing of "unattended" stimuli. According to Treisman, this depends on a leaky filter. According to Broadbent's modified theory, it depends on what Lachter et al. (2004) called "slippage," meaning that attention is shifted to allegedly "unattended" stimuli, and so they aren't really unattended at all. Close inspection of the evidence suggests that slippage may well be more important than leakage. For example, remember that Von Wright et al. (1975) found heightened physiological responses (galvanic skin responses) to shock-associated words presented on the "unattended" message. Dawson and Schell (1983) replicated that finding. However, they then identified trials on which there was evidence that listeners had shifted attention to the "unattended" message (e.g., failures of shadowing on the "attended" message). Most of the enhanced physiological responses occurred on trials on which it seemed likely that listeners had shifted attention.

As discussed above, Conway et al. (2001) found that listeners sometimes detected their own name presented on the "unattended" input. However, when they divided listeners into those with low and high memory span, it was predominantly those with low memory span who showed this effect. Since individuals with low memory span are more distractible than those with high memory span (Barrett, Tugade, & Engle, 2004), they would have been more likely than those with high memory span to attend to stimuli on the "unattended" channel.

Lachter et al. (2004) argued that what was needed was to devise a situation in which slippage was almost impossible. This can be done by not giving participants sufficient time to switch attention to "unattended" information in a sensory buffer. They used a lexical-decision task in which participants decided whether a string of letters formed a word. This letter string was immediately preceded by a prime word either the same as or unrelated to the target word presented for lexical decision. This prime word was presented for 55 ms, 110 ms, or 165 ms, and was attended or unattended. The extent of any priming effect was assessed by seeing how much faster the lexical decision was when the prime word was the same as the target word rather than being unrelated.

What predictions can we make? According to the modified version of Broadbent's theory, participants would need to shift attention to the "unattended" prime to show a priming effect. Since attentional shifting takes at least 50 ms, there should be no priming effect when the prime word in the unattended location was presented for 55 ms. However, a priming effect should be detectable when it was presented for 110 ms or 165 ms. That is precisely what happened (see the figure on the left). There was no evidence

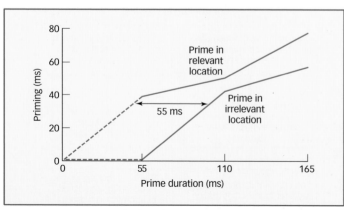

Priming in ms as a function of prime duration and whether the prime was presented to the attended (relevant) location or the unattended (irrelevant) location.

that the "unattended" prime word was processed when stringent steps were taken to eliminate slippage but not to prevent leakage. This suggests that slippage is needed if unattended stimuli are to be processed.

Evaluation

⊕ Broadbent's filter theory is of great historical importance. It was the first theory incorporating the notion of an information-processing system with several interrelated processes.

⊕ Treisman's attenuation theory is more flexible than filter theory. The notion of a "leaky" filter accurately predicts that there will sometimes be fairly thorough processing of unattended stimuli.

⊕ A modified version of Broadbent's theory in which it is assumed that attention can be shifted rapidly can account for most of the findings. This modified theory explains the findings of Lachter et al. (2004).

⊖ Detailed consideration of the evidence suggests that thorough processing of unattended stimuli may depend less on leakage than was assumed by Treisman.

⊖ Deutsch and Deutsch's late-selection theory seems implausible and has attracted little clear support.

⊖ As Styles (1997, p. 28) pointed out, "Finding out *where* selection takes place may not help us to understand *why* or *how* this happens."

MULTITASKING

Most people find that their lives are becoming busier and busier as time goes by. Indeed, life is so busy that we often try to do two things at the same time. For example, we may buy bus or train tickets while holding a conversation on a mobile phone or we access our emails while chatting with someone. The term **multitasking** refers to the performance of more than one task at a time, and our focus in this section is on the effectiveness (or otherwise!) of our attempts to multitask.

The fact that most of us often engage in multitasking suggests we believe ourselves capable of performing two tasks successfully at the same time. Indeed, the main reason we multitask is because we think it will save us precious time compared to the traditional approach of doing one thing at a time. If that isn't the case, then we are simply wasting our time and incurring higher stress levels!

It is commonly believed that women are better than men at multitasking, perhaps because women spend more of their time than men trying to do two things at once.

Skilled touch typists can hold a conversation and attend to other stimuli with very little effect on their typing speed or accuracy.

There are surprisingly few studies in which the multitasking abilities of men and women have been compared directly. However, Rubinstein, Meyer, and Evans (2001) found no evidence of any gender differences in multitasking performance in several experiments.

It is also commonly believed that less intelligent people are worse at multitasking than more intelligent ones. This notion was given vivid expression by American President Lyndon Johnson. He claimed that Gerald Ford (a slow-witted Congressman who later became President) "can't fart and chew gum at the same time." We don't know whether this claim was true, but intelligence *is* related to the ability to perform two tasks together. For example, Engle, Tuholski, Laughlin, and Conway (1999) asked participants to

Key Term

Multitasking:
performing two or more tasks at the same time by switching rapidly between them.

perform either one or two tasks at the same time. Intelligence was a good predictor of dual-task performance but was unrelated to single-task performance.

THINKING AND DRIVING

When we consider multitasking in everyday life, an issue of considerable practical importance is whether the ability to drive a car is impaired when the driver uses a mobile phone. There has been much controversy on this issue. More than a dozen countries (including the UK) have passed laws restricting the use of mobile phones while driving, but millions of irate motorists complain that such legislation infringes civil liberties. We turn to a consideration of the evidence.

Redelmeier and Tibshirani (1997) studied the mobile-phone records of 699 drivers who had been involved in a car accident. One quarter of them had used their mobile phone within the 10-minute period preceding the accident, and the figure was similar for those using handheld and hands-free phones. They concluded that use of a mobile phone produced a four-fold increase in the likelihood of having a car accident.

David Strayer and William Johnston (2001) carried out an experiment in which participants braked as rapidly as possible when they detected a red light. This task was carried out on its own or at the same time as the participants held a conversation using a handheld or hands-free mobile phone. Participants missed significantly more red lights when using a mobile phone (7% vs. 3%, respectively), with performance being very similar in the handheld and hands-free conditions. In addition, the time taken to respond to the red light was about 50 ms longer in the mobile phone conditions. That may sound trivial. However, consider a motorist driving at 70 mph (110 kph). The additional 50 ms taken to brake would mean that the motorist's car would travel an extra 5 feet (1.5 meters) before stopping. That might mean the difference between stopping just behind the car in front or smashing into the back of it.

> ### Switch off your mobile!
>
> Believe it or not, some students feel that cognitive psychology has little relevance to everyday life. However, research on divided attention is of direct relevance to a practical issue that has been much debated in recent years, namely whether motorists should be allowed to use mobile phones while driving. As someone who has nearly been hit by two mobile-using motorists who were driving on the wrong side of the road, I have my own personal views on the matter. What about the scientific evidence? Strayer and Johnston (2001) found that the chances of missing a red light more than doubled when the participants were engaged in conversation on a handheld mobile phone, and the effects were almost as great when using a hands-free mobile phone. In addition, using a mobile phone greatly reduced the speed of responding to those traffic signals that were detected. These various adverse effects were greater when the participants were talking than when they were listening, but both effects were significant.
>
> The above findings led Strayer and Johnston (2001, p. 462) to conclude that, "[Mobile]-phone use disrupts performance by diverting attention to an engaging cognitive context other than the one immediately associated with driving." That conclusion strongly suggests that the use of mobile phones while driving should be restricted or banned, as is already the case in more than a dozen countries.

Strayer, Drews, and Johnston (2003) explored in more detail the negative effects of using a mobile phone. They found that drivers using a handheld mobile phone missed or had poor recall of billboard signs along the route. The eye movements of these drivers showed that they often did not look at such signs, even when the information was presented in the center of the visual field. Thus, use of mobile phones leads drivers to withdraw at least some of their attention from the visual scene in front of them.

DOES PRACTICE MAKE PERFECT?

The findings discussed above suggest that the Roman sage Publilius Syrus may have been correct when he said that, "To do two things at once is to do neither." However, common sense suggests that multitasking is most successful when the two tasks being performed together are well-practiced and so involve relatively automatic skills. In other words, "Practice makes perfect." For example, skilled drivers can drive while listening to the radio, air-traffic controllers can monitor the positions of numerous air-planes at the same time, and a one-man band can play several instruments at once.

Evidence supporting commonsensical views on the value of practice was reported by Spelke, Hirst, and Neisser (1976). Two students (Diane and John) received 5 hours training a week for 3 months on various tasks. Their first task was to read short stories for comprehension while writing down words to dictation. Initially they found it very hard to combine these tasks, with their reading speed and handwriting both suffering considerably. After 6 weeks of training, however, Diane and John could read as rapidly and with as much comprehension when taking dictation as when only reading, and the quality of their handwriting had also improved.

Spelke et al. (1976) were still not satisfied with the students' performance. For example, Diane and John could recall only 35 out of the thousands of words they had written down at dictation. Even when 20 successive dictated words formed a sentence or came from the same category (e.g., four-footed animals), the students were unaware of that. With further training, however, they could write down the names of the categories to which the dictated words belonged while maintaining normal reading speed and comprehension.

In spite of findings such as those of Spelke et al. (1976), several experts (e.g., Pashler, Johnston, & Ruthruff, 2001) argue that we will always find evidence of interference or disruption in dual-task performance if we use sufficiently sensitive techniques. One such technique involves presenting people with two stimuli (e.g., two lights) each of which is associated with a different response (e.g., pressing different buttons). Their task is to respond to each stimulus as rapidly as possible. When the second stimulus is presented very shortly after the first, there is typically a marked slowing of the response to the second stimulus. This interference effect is known as the **psychological refractory period (PRP) effect**, and it has been obtained in numerous studies (see Pashler et al., 2001, for a review). This effect does *not* occur simply because people aren't used to responding to two immediately successive stimuli. Pashler (1993) discussed one of his studies in which the PRP effect was still observable after more than 10,000 practice trials.

Schumacher et al. (2001) challenged the notion that a PRP effect will always be found. They used two tasks: (1) say "one," "two," "three" to low-, medium-, and high-pitched tones; (2) respond with different fingers to four stimuli (0 - - -; - 0 - -; - - 0 -; and - - - 0) having a disk (0) in different locations. These two tasks were performed on over 2000 trials, at the end of which 5 of the 11 participants performed them virtually as well together as singly (see the figure on the right). In contrast, four participants had high levels of dual-task interference (150 ms or more) even after extensive practice (see the figure on the right). According to Schumacher et al. (2001, p. 107), "Participants may use a variety of task-scheduling strategies (e.g., a cautious one with minimal temporal overlap in processing for the two tasks, or a daring strategy with a great deal of processing overlap) during the course of practice, and so exhibit various amounts of dual-task interference."

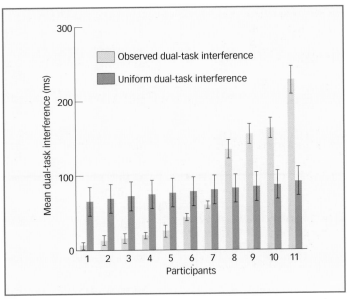

Observed (light bars) and expected uniform (dark bars) amounts of dual-task interference in ms at the end of practice rank-ordered from smallest to largest for 11 participants. From Schumacher et al. (2001). Copyright © 2001 Blackwell Publishing. Reprinted with permission.

In sum, two tasks can rarely be performed at the same time with no disruption or interference. When dual-task performance is very successful (e.g., Schumacher et al., 2001; Spelke et al., 1976), this is nearly always as a result of using easy tasks and extensive practice. We turn now to a consideration of *how* practice has this beneficial effect.

PRACTICE AND AUTOMATICITY

It has often been argued (e.g., Shiffrin & Schneider, 1977) that practice leads to improved dual-task performance because it allows some processing activities to become automatic and so not reliant on attention. Here are some of the main criteria for automatic processes:

- They are fast
- They don't require attention, and so don't reduce the capacity to perform other tasks at the same time
- They are unavailable to consciousness
- They are unavoidable, meaning they always occur when an appropriate stimulus is presented.

Key Study

Schneider and Shiffrin: Automatic processing

Classic studies on automatic processing were reported by Shiffrin and Schneider (1977) and Schneider and Shiffrin (1977). They used a task in which participants memorized up to four letters (the memory set) and were then shown a visual display containing up to four letters. Their task was to decide rapidly whether one of the letters in the visual display was the same as any of the letters in the memory set. The crucial manipulation was the type of mapping used:

1. *Consistent mapping*: Only consonants were used as members of the memory set, and only numbers were used as distractors in the visual display (or vice versa).
2. *Varied mapping*: A mixture of numbers and consonants formed the memory set and provided distractors in the visual display.

What do you think happened in terms of performance speed? You probably guessed that consistent mapping led to faster performance than varied mapping, but the actual difference may be greater than you thought (see the figure below). The numbers of items in the memory set and in the visual display greatly affected decision speed in the varied mapping conditions but not in the consistent mapping conditions. According to Shiffrin and Schneider (1977), participants performed well with consistent mapping because they used automatic processes operating at the same time. These automatic processes have developed as a result of many years of practice in distinguishing between letters and numbers. In contrast, performance with varied mapping required controlled processes, which are of limited capacity and require attention. As a result, participants had to compare each item in the memory set with each item in the visual display one at a time until a match was found or every comparison had been made.

You may be thinking that automatic processes are more useful than controlled ones. However, automatic processes suffer from the serious limitation that they are rigid and inflexible. As a result, performance based on automatic processes suffers when there is a change in what is required. Shiffrin and Schneider (1977) showed this in an experiment on consistent mapping when the consonants B to L formed one set and the consonants Q to Z formed the other set. As before, items from only one set were always used in the formation of the memory set and the distractors in the visual

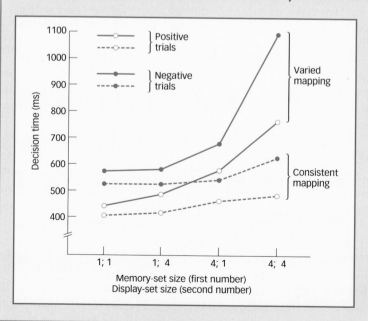

Response times on a decision task as a function of memory-set size, display-set size, and consistent versus varied mapping. Data from Shiffrin and Schneider (1977).

display were all selected from the other set. The initial 2100 trials with one consistent mapping were followed by a further 2100 trials with the reverse consistent mapping. Thus, the items in the memory set were now always drawn from the consonants Q to Z if they had previously been drawn from the set B to L. This reversal of the mapping conditions greatly disrupted performance—it took nearly 1000 trials before performance recovered to its level at the very start of the experiment!

What conclusions can we draw from the above findings? "Automatic processes function rapidly and in parallel but suffer from inflexibility; controlled processes are flexible and versatile but operate relatively slowly and in a serial fashion" (Eysenck, 1982, p. 22). Thus, automatic and controlled processes both possess advantages and disadvantages.

Discussion points

1. How useful is this research by Shiffrin and Schneider (see next for some pointers)?
2. Think of some examples of automatic and controlled processes in your everyday life.

KEY STUDY EVALUATION

Schneider and Shiffrin's work on controlled and automatic processing is another good example of a theory being tested and supported by the use of experiments. Interestingly, some advertising has made use of similar combinations of letters and numbers to good effect, for example the film *SE7EN* (Seven), which demonstrates how difficult it can be to override the automatic process of reading. The research by Schneider and Shiffrin supplies confirmation of what may seem obvious, that some processes become automatic with time, but it does not specify how or what is actually occurring.

SIMILARITY

As a general rule of thumb, tasks that are similar to each other are more difficult to perform reasonably well together than dissimilar ones. For example, you can probably study while listening to music, but might find it very difficult to rub your stomach with one hand while patting your head with the other.

There are various ways in which two tasks can be similar. First, they can be similar in terms of stimulus modality (e.g., both involving visual or auditory presentation). Treisman and Davies (1973) found that two monitoring tasks interfered with each other much more when the stimuli on both tasks were in the same modality (visual or auditory) than when they were in different modalities. Second, they can be similar in terms of central processing (e.g., both involving spatial processing). Third, tasks can be similar in terms of responses (e.g., both requiring manual responses). Think back to the study by Schumacher et al. (2001) in which they found that two tasks could be performed at the same time without interference. The two tasks differed in stimulus modality (visual vs. auditory) and in type of response (manual vs. vocal).

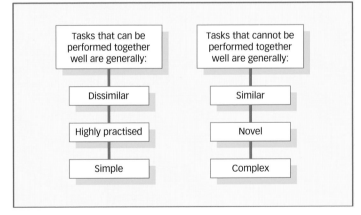

Direct evidence that response similarity is important was reported by Van Selst, Ruthruff, and Johnston (1999). They initially used two tasks, one of which required a vocal response and the other a manual response. After extended practice, the interference or PRP effect in responding to the second stimulus was only 50 ms. However, the interference effect was much larger when the experiment was repeated with both tasks requiring manual responses.

It is often hard to decide just how similar or dissimilar two tasks are. For example, how similar are piano playing and poetry writing or driving a car and listening to the radio?

TASK DIFFICULTY

Our ability to perform two tasks at the same time depends on their difficulty level. For example, Sullivan (1976) asked participants to repeat back (shadow) an auditory message and to detect words on a nonshadowed message at the same time. The key manipulation involved varying the complexity of the shadowed message. When the shadowing task was difficult, fewer targets were detected on the nonshadowed message than when the shadowing task was easy.

Greenwald (2003) argued that the easiest tasks are those in which there is a very direct and obvious relationship between stimulus and response. Saying "A" or "B" in response to hearing those letter names is an example of such a task. Another example is moving a joystick switch to the left to an arrow pointing left and moving it to the right to an arrow pointing right. Participants performed these two tasks as well together as on their own.

THEORETICAL PERSPECTIVES

Many theories have been put forward to account for how well (or poorly) we manage to perform two tasks at the same time. Here we consider two of the main theoretical approaches: central capacity theories and multiple-resource theories.

Central capacity theories

We can account for many dual-task findings by assuming there is some central capacity having limited capacity (perhaps resembling the central executive component of working memory—see Chapter 8). The extent to which two tasks can be performed together depends on the demands each task makes on those resources. If the combined demands of the two tasks don't exceed the total resources of the central capacity, then the two tasks won't interfere with each other. However, if the resources are insufficient, then performance disruption will occur.

Key Study

Bourke et al. (1996): Support for central capacity

Predictions of central capacity theory were tested by Bourke, Duncan, and Nimmo-Smith (1996) using four different tasks. These tasks were performed in all possible pairings with one task being identified as more important than the other. According to the theory, the task making most demands on the central capacity should interfere most with all three of the other tasks. In contrast, the task making fewest demands on central capacity should interfere least with all the other tasks. Here are the four tasks in order from most to least demanding:

1. *Random generation*: Generating letters at random.
2. *Prototype learning*: Working out the features of two patterns or prototypes from seeing various examples.
3. *Manual task*: Screwing a nut down to the bottom of a bolt and back up to the top, and then down to the bottom of a second bolt and back up, and so on.
4. *Tone task*: Detecting the occurrence of a target tone.

What did Bourke et al. (1996) find? The main findings were as predicted (see the figure on the following page). The most demanding task (random generation) consistently interfered most with the prototype, manual, and tone tasks, and did so whether it was the primary or secondary task. The least demanding task (tone task) consistently interfered least with each of the other three tasks.

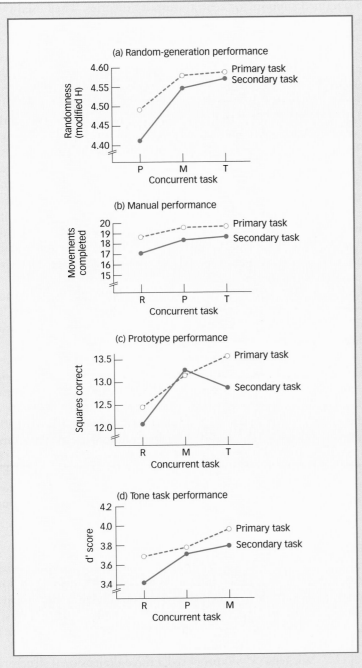

(a) Random-generation performance

(b) Manual performance

(c) Prototype performance

(d) Tone task performance

Performance on random generation (R), prototype learning (P), manual (M), and tone (T) tasks as a function of concurrent task. Adapted from Bourke et al. (1996).

Discussion points

1. Is it surprising that these very different tasks interfered with each other?
2. Why do you think that the random generation task interfered the most with other tasks, whereas the tone task interfered the least?

KEY STUDY EVALUATION

As we have seen, the four tasks used by Bourke et al. are very different from each other. If performance depended only on very specific processes, then there would presumably have been little or no interference between tasks. The fact that there was considerable interference is strong evidence for a general central processing capacity. It may have occurred to you that participants with special expertise might have found it easier to combine some of the tasks; for example, a mechanic might be very good at handling nuts and bolts. However, the participants were recent university students, and lacked special expertise for any of the tasks.

Just et al. (2001) also obtained support for central capacity theories. They used two tasks performed together or on their own. One task was auditory sentence comprehension (e.g., deciding whether "The pyramids were burial places and they are one of the seven wonders of the ancient world" was true or false). The other task involved mentally rotating three-dimensional figures to decide whether they were the same. These tasks were selected so they would involve very different processes in different parts of the brain.

What did Just et al. (2001) find? First, performance of both tasks was significantly impaired under dual-task conditions compared to single-task conditions. Second, the two tasks mainly activated different parts of the brain (the temporal lobe for the language task and the parietal lobe for the mental rotation task). Third, and most importantly, Just et al. compared the amount of activation associated with each task under single- and dual-task conditions. Brain activation in regions associated with the language task decreased by 53% under dual-task conditions compared to single-task conditions. In similar fashion, brain activation in regions involved in the mental rotation task decreased by 29% under dual-task conditions. The need to distribute a limited central capacity (probably attention) across two tasks meant the amount each task could receive was reduced compared to the single-task condition.

Central capacity theories possess various limitations. First, dual-task performance doesn't *only* depend on some central capacity. The finding that dual-task performance is worse when both tasks involve the same type of response than when they don't (e.g., van Selst et al., 1999) is not directly a result of limitations with some central capacity.

Second, it is possible to "explain" dual-task interference by arguing that the resources of some central capacity have been exceeded, and the absence of interference by assuming the two tasks didn't exceed those resources. However, unless we can measure central processing capacity, we may simply be re-describing the findings rather than providing a proper explanation. In that connection, the use of brain-imaging data to clarify the involvement of attentional processes in single- and dual-task conditions is an important step forward.

Third, it is very hard to assess the total demands on central capacity imposed by performing two tasks at the same time. Each task imposes its own demands. However, there are also additional demands from coordinating processing on two tasks at the same time, preventing interference between competing responses, and so on.

Multiple-resource model

Wickens (e.g., 1984) argued that the processing system consists of independent processing mechanisms in the form of multiple resources each having limited capacity. If so, then it is clear why the degree of similarity between two tasks is so important: similar tasks compete for the same specific limited resources, and thus produce interference. In contrast, dissimilar tasks involve different resources, and so don't interfere with each other.

Wickens (1984) proposed a three-dimensional structure of human processing resources (see the figure on the left). According to his model, there are three successive stages of processing (encoding, central processing, and responding). Encoding involves the perceptual processing of stimuli, and typically makes use of the visual or auditory modality. Encoding and central processing can involve spatial or verbal codes. Finally, responding involves manual or vocal responses. There are two key assumptions in this model:

1. There are several pools of resources based on the distinctions among stages of processing, modalities, codes, and responses.
2. If two tasks make use of different pools of resources, then people should be able to perform both tasks without disruption.

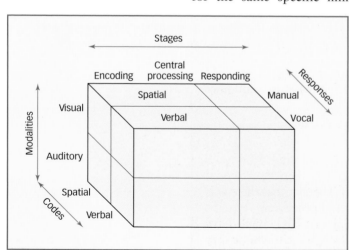

A proposed three-dimensional structure of human processing resources. From Wickens (1984). Copyright © 1984 Elsevier. Reproduced with permission.

There is much support for this multiple-resource model and its prediction that several kinds of task similarity influence dual-task performance. For example, there is more interference when two tasks share the same modality (e.g., Treisman & Davies, 1973) or when they share the same type of response (e.g., van Selst et al., 1999). However, the model has some limitations. First, it focuses only on visual and auditory inputs or stimuli, but tasks can be presented in other modalities (e.g., touch). Second, there is often some disruption to performance even when two tasks make use of the same modality (e.g., Treisman & Davies, 1973). Third, the model assumes that several tasks could be performed together without interference provided each task used different pools of resources. However, Just et al. (2001) found that two very different tasks (auditory sentence comprehension and mental rotation) couldn't be performed together without interference. Their brain-imaging data suggested there was a limitation on the capacity of some general capacity available for processing, but such a capacity is not included in Wickens' model. Wickens' model can be compared to leaving the Prince of Denmark out of the play *Hamlet*.

Chapter Summary

Object recognition

- The Gestaltists identified several laws of perceptual organization including the law of proximity, the law of similarity, the law of good continuation, and the law of closure. These laws are descriptive rather than explanatory.
- According to viewpoint-dependent theories, object recognition is easier when objects are seen from familiar angles. According to viewpoint-invariant theories, objects are equally well recognized from all angles. Object recognition is much more likely to be viewpoint-invariant when the task is very easy than when it is complex.
- Riddoch and Humphreys (2001) put forward a five-stage model of object recognition, with successive stages concerned with edge grouping, feature binding, view normalization, structural description, and the semantic system.
- Brain-damaged patients have been found with problems of object recognition at each of the five stages identified by Riddoch and Humphreys, thus providing support for their theory. However, they de-emphasize interactions among the different stages.

Visual illusions: Two systems

- Visual perception is typically very accurate, but most people are deceived by a large number of visual illusions.
- According to Milner and Goodale, we have two visual systems. The vision-for-perception system is used for object recognition and is based on a ventral pathway. The vision-for-action system is used for visually guided action and is based on a dorsal pathway.
- There is evidence that the vision-for-perception system is more affected by visual illusions than is the vision-for-action system.
- Patients with optic ataxia have problems mainly with the vision-for-action system, whereas those with visual agnosia have problems centered on the vision-for-perception system.
- The vision-for-action system consists of planning and control systems, only the latter of which is unaffected by visual illusions.

Unconscious perception

- We can assess conscious awareness of visual stimuli by using a relatively lenient subjective threshold or a more stringent objective threshold.
- Several studies on healthy individuals have produced evidence of subliminal perception even when the objective threshold is used. In addition, there is evidence that the effects of subliminal perception can differ substantially from those of conscious perception.

- Brain-damaged patients with blindsight show various perceptual abilities in parts of the visual field for which they report no conscious perceptual experience. For example, they nearly all show some ability to detect light and motion, and some can discriminate shape, direction or movement, and object orientation.
- It is difficult to be certain that any given individual totally lacks conscious experience of a visual stimulus. For example, some blindsight patients describe a "contentless kind of awareness."

Change blindness

- Most people believe that they perceive and remember most of the information in visual scenes. However, this belief is mistaken, as is revealed by the phenomena of change blindness and inattentional blindness.
- Change blindness and inattentional blindness occur most often when observers are not warned of possible changes to the visual environment, when an unexpected object is similar to other objects, and when the object that is changed has not been attended to prior to the change occurring.
- We form fairly detailed visual representations of objects that are the focus of attention. These representations are fitted into a mental map providing a spatial layout of the overall visual scene, which is stored in long-term memory. We tend to assume that the information in long-term memory is more detailed than is actually the case.

Visual attention

- Much of the evidence indicates that visual attention is more like a zoom lens than a spotlight. However, the existence of split attention means that visual attention is not always directed to a given region in visual space.
- Visual attention is flexible. It can be directed either to a given location or to a given object.
- Unattended visual stimuli are generally processed to a moderate extent but less than attended ones.
- Extinction occurs because of competition among stimuli. Neglect patients have a reasonably intact goal-directed system but a severely impaired stimulus-driven system. They show a reasonable ability to detect stimuli in the neglected field when they can use the goal-directed system to predict where target stimuli are likely to be presented.

Auditory attention

- Early research on selective auditory attention suggested that there is very limited processing of unattended stimuli.
- Subsequent research indicated that there is sometimes extensive processing of unattended stimuli.
- There has been controversy as to the location of a bottleneck in processing. Most of the evidence is inconsistent with late-selection theories.
- There has also been controversy as to whether thorough processing of "unattended" stimuli is a result of spillage (Broadbent) or of leakage (Treisman).
- The evidence is not conclusive, but recent findings suggest that spillage may be more important than leakage.

Multitasking

- Mobile-phone use impairs driving performance. It leads to an increase in brake response time and a decreased ability to respond to other drivers.
- When people perform two tasks at the same time, there is nearly always some evidence of interference or disruption. This is seen in the psychological refractory period effect that is still observable even after 10,000 trials.
- Practice typically has a substantial effect on dual-task performance, leading to a marked reduction in interference.

- Practice often results in the development of automatic responses that occur rapidly but suffer from inflexibility.
- Dual-task performance is worse when the two tasks are either difficult or similar to each other.
- According to central capacity theories, dual-task performance depends on the demands that each task imposes on some central capacity. Such theories can account for the effects of practice on dual-task performance, but de-emphasize the role of more specific processing resources.
- According to the multiple-resource model, the processing system consists of independent processing mechanisms having limited capacity. These processing mechanisms are based on distinctions among stages of processing, modalities, codes, and responses. This model can account for many similarity effects but de-emphasizes more general processing resources (e.g., central capacity).

Further Reading

- Bruce, V., Green, P.R., & Georgeson, M.A. (2003). *Visual perception: Physiology, psychology and ecology* (4th ed.). Hove, UK: Psychology Press. Chapter 9 of this outstanding book is devoted to object recognition. In addition, there is full coverage of research on the existence of two visual systems.
- Driver, J. (2001). A selective review of selective attention research from the past century. *British Journal of Psychology*, *92*, 53–78. This article provides a useful historical overview of research on visual attention.
- Eysenck, M.W. (2006). *Fundamentals of cognition*. Hove, UK: Psychology Press. The topics discussed in this chapter are considered at greater length in this textbook.
- Merikle, P.M., Smilek, D., & Eastwood, J.D. (2001). Perception without awareness: Perspectives from cognitive psychology. *Cognition, 79*, 115–134. There is good coverage of research on subliminal perception in this article.
- Morgan, M. (2003). *The space between our ears: How the brain represents visual space.* London: Weidenfeld & Nicolson. Many key issues in visual perception are discussed in this entertaining book.
- Pashler, H., Johnson, J.C., & Ruthroff, E. (2001). Attention and performance. *Annual Review of Psychology*, *52*, 629–651. This article discusses in detail dual-task performance, practice effects, and the development of automatic processes.
- Sekuler, R., & Blake, R. (2005). *Perception* (5th ed.). New York: McGraw-Hill. There is good introductory coverage of numerous topics in perception in this American textbook.
- Simons, D.J., & Rensink, R.A. (2005). Change blindness: Past, present, and future. *Trends in Cognitive Sciences, 9*, 16–20. The key findings on change blindness are discussed succinctly in this article by two of the leading researchers in the area.

Chapter 7

Contents

Conditioning and learning

7

Compared to most other species, we are extremely good at learning. Learning is of the utmost importance to us in our everyday lives. Adults are much better equipped than children to deal with the complexities of life because they have spent many years acquiring knowledge and skills. Not surprisingly, the study of learning was *the* major focus of research when psychology emerged as a scientific discipline around the start of the twentieth century. This can be seen in the work of Pavlov and the early behaviorists such as John Watson and Fred Skinner (see Chapter 2).

The behaviorists focused mostly on simple forms of learning such as learning to salivate when a bell sounds or learning to press a lever for food reward. Such forms of learning (known as conditioning) involve a person's or an animal's behavior becoming dependent on certain environmental stimuli. We deal initially with the conditioning approach to learning. However, that approach can't account for most human learning. Accordingly, we then move on to consider other forms of learning. First, we discuss observational learning, which involves learning successful ways of behaving by observing the behavior of others. Second, we discuss implicit learning. This is learning apparently occurring in the absence of conscious awareness of what has been learned. Third, we discuss ways in which prolonged practice can lead to the development of expertise.

CLASSICAL CONDITIONING

Imagine you have gone to see your dentist. As you lie down on the reclining chair, you start to feel frightened. Why are you frightened *before* the dentist has caused you any pain? The sights and sounds of the dentist's surgery lead you to expect that you are shortly going to be in pain. Thus, you have formed an *association* between the neutral stimuli of the surgery and the painful stimuli involved in drilling. Such associations are of crucial importance in **classical conditioning**. In essence, the fear created by the drilling is now triggered by the neutral stimuli of the surgery.

Textbook writers nearly always focus on unpleasant everyday examples of classical conditioning (I've just been guilty of that myself!). However, there are also pleasant examples. Most middle-aged people have especially positive feelings for the music that was popular when they were in their teens and early twenties. Associations are formed between the music and various exciting kinds of stimuli encountered during adolescence.

Classical conditioning may be relevant to the development of some phobias, which involve an extreme fear of certain objects (e.g., snakes; spiders). It has been argued that phobias develop when neutral stimuli become associated with stimuli causing fear, leading to the neutral stimuli triggering a fear response (see Chapter 21). Some forms of behavior therapy used in the treatment of mental disorder make use of classical conditioning (see Chapter 22).

BASIC FINDINGS

The best-known example of classical conditioning comes from the work of Ivan Pavlov (1849–1936). Dogs (and other animals) salivate when food is put in their mouths. In technical terms, what we have here is an unlearned or **unconditioned reflex** involving a

Key Terms

Classical conditioning: a basic form of learning in which simple responses (e.g., salivation) are associated with a new or conditioned stimulus.

Unconditioned reflex: the new association between a stimulus and response formed in classical conditioning.

Learned assciations

Imagine something nice, something delicious, your favorite food. Is it strawberries, chocolate, a barbecue, a curry? Think about it and visualize it, and you will find your mouth is watering! There is no such food nearby, you cannot really see, smell, or taste it, but you have learned that you love this food and this learned association has made you salivate. This will not happen if you are presented with a food you have never seen before, as you have not learned an association to it. If your most disliked sort of food were actually presented to you, your mouth would not water either. A different association would have been learned, and possibly a different response too.

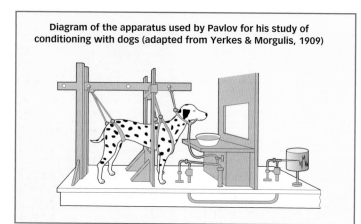

Diagram of the apparatus used by Pavlov for his study of conditioning with dogs (adapted from Yerkes & Morgulis, 1909)

connection between the **unconditioned stimulus** of the food in the mouth and the **unconditioned response** of salivation. Pavlov discovered he could train dogs to salivate to other stimuli (see the figure on the left). In some studies, he presented a tone (a neutral stimulus which became the **conditioned stimulus**) just before food several times, so that the tone signaled the imminent arrival of food. Finally, he presented the same tone (the test stimulus) on its own without any food following, and found the dog salivated to the tone. The dog had acquired a conditioned reflex, in which the conditioned stimulus (the tone) was associated with the unconditioned stimulus (sight of food), and the learned or **conditioned response** was salivation. Note that it is essential for the food to follow very shortly after the tone for a **conditioned reflex** to be formed.

Similar findings have been obtained in numerous studies on humans. In eyeblink conditioning, for example, a tone (conditioned stimulus) is presented shortly before a puff of air (unconditioned stimulus) is administered to the eye. After a series of trials, participants react to the tone with an eyeblink (the conditioned response).

Pavlov discovered several features of classical conditioning in his research on dogs. For example, the conditioned response of salivation was greatest when the tone presented on its own was the same as the tone that had previously been presented just before food. A smaller amount of salivation was obtained when a different tone was used. **Generalization** refers to the fact that the strength of the conditioned response (e.g., salivation) depends on the similarity between the test stimulus and the previous training stimulus. Another phenomenon is **discrimination**. Suppose a given tone is paired several times with the sight of food. The dog will learn to salivate to the tone. Then another tone is presented on its own. It produces a smaller amount of salivation than the first tone through generalization. Next the first tone is paired with food several more times, but the second tone is never paired with food. Salivation to the first tone increases, whereas that to the second tone decreases. Thus, the dog has learned to discriminate between the two tones.

Another key feature of classical conditioning is extinction. When Pavlov presented the tone on its own several times after conditioning had occurred, there was less and less salivation. Thus, the repeated presentation of the conditioning stimulus in the absence of the

Key Terms

Unconditioned stimulus:
a stimulus that produces an **unconditioned response** in the absence of learning.

Unconditioned response:
an unlearned response to an **unconditioned stimulus**.

Conditioned stimulus:
a stimulus that becomes associated through learning with the **unconditioned stimulus**.

Conditioned response:
a response which is produced by the **conditioned stimulus** after a learning process in which the conditioned stimulus has been paired several times with the **unconditioned stimulus**.

Conditioned reflex:
the new association between a stimulus and response formed in **classical conditioning**.

Generalization:
the tendency of a **conditioned response** to occur (but in a weaker form) to stimuli similar to the **conditioned stimulus**.

Discrimination:
the strength of the **conditioned response** to one **conditioned stimulus** is strengthened at the same time as that to a second conditioned stimulus is weakened.

unconditioned stimulus removes the conditioned response (this is **extinction**). Extinction does *not* mean that the dog or other animal has lost the relevant conditioned reflex. Animals brought back into the experimental situation after extinction has occurred produce some salivation in response to the tone (this is **spontaneous recovery**). It shows that the salivary response to the tone was inhibited rather than lost during extinction.

WHAT IS GOING ON?

At first glance, it seems that two factors are of special importance in classical conditioning. First, the conditioned and unconditioned stimuli need to be presented very close together in time. Second, there is a process of stimulus substitution, with the conditioned stimulus simply acting as a *substitute* for the unconditioned stimulus. For example, the sight of the dentist's surgery evokes the fear originally associated with the dentist's drilling.

In fact, the above account is incorrect. So far as the first factor is concerned, it is true that conditioning is greatest when the conditioned stimulus is presented about half a second before the unconditioned stimulus. However, there is little or no conditioning if the order of the stimuli alters so that the unconditioned stimulus is presented shortly before the conditioned stimulus.

Kamin (1969) showed that classical conditioning does *not* always occur when a conditioned stimulus is followed closely by an unconditioned stimulus. The animals in the experimental group received light (conditioned stimulus 1) paired with electric shock, and learned to react with fear and avoidance when the light came on. The animals in the contrast group had no training. Then both groups received a series of trials with a light–tone combination followed by shock. Finally, both groups received only the tone (conditioned stimulus 2). The contrast group responded with fear to the tone on its own, but the experimental group did not.

How can we explain Kamin's (1969) findings? The experimental animals learned that light (conditioned stimulus 1) predicted shock, and so ignored the fact that the tone (conditioned stimulus 2) also predicted shock. The phenomenon of a conditioned stimulus failing to produce a conditioned response because another conditioned stimulus already predicts the arrival of the unconditioned stimulus is known as **blocking**. The contrast animals did learn that the tone predicted shock, because they had not previously learned something different.

What about the notion that the conditioned stimulus acts as a substitute for the unconditioned stimulus? Let us go back to Pavlov's research. When food is presented to a dog, it typically engages in chewing and swallowing as well as salivating (unconditioned response). However, the conditioned stimulus (e.g., tone) produces salivation but *not* chewing and swallowing. In addition, the tone often produces conditioned responses (e.g., tail wagging; looking at the place where food is usually presented) that don't occur in response to the food itself (Jenkins, Barrera, Ireland, & Woodside, 1978). The clear differences between the conditioned and unconditioned responses indicate that the unconditioned stimulus is *not* simply a substitute for the unconditioned stimulus.

Rescorla and Wagner (1972) put forward a very influential theoretical approach to classical conditioning. Their central assumption was that associative learning occurs between a conditioned stimulus and an unconditioned stimulus when the conditioned

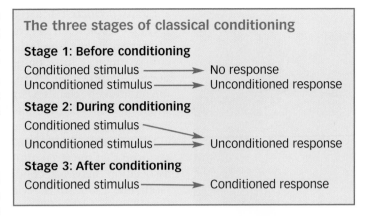

The three stages of classical conditioning

Stage 1: Before conditioning
Conditioned stimulus ⟶ No response
Unconditioned stimulus ⟶ Unconditioned response

Stage 2: During conditioning
Conditioned stimulus ⟶
Unconditioned stimulus ⟶ Unconditioned response

Stage 3: After conditioning
Conditioned stimulus ⟶ Conditioned response

Key Terms

Extinction:
the elimination of a response when it is not followed by reward (**operant conditioning**) or by the unconditioned stimulus (**classical conditioning**).

Spontaneous recovery:
the re-emergence of responses over time in **classical conditioning** following experimental extinction.

Blocking:
the failure of a conditioned stimulus to produce a conditioned response because another conditioned stimulus already predicts the presentation of the unconditioned stimulus.

Many caterpillars are poisonous and can be deadly; therefore potential predators must quickly learn not to eat them. If too many are eaten before the predators learn to avoid them, then the brightly colored signaling strategy is not working.

stimulus *predicts* the arrival of the unconditioned stimulus. This assumption allowed them to account for several phenomena. First, if the conditioned stimulus is presented *after* the unconditioned stimulus, it can't predict the arrival of the unconditioned stimulus and so there is little or no conditioning. Second, a second conditioned stimulus that doesn't improve an animal's or a human's ability to predict the arrival of the unconditioned stimulus is redundant and so blocking occurs. Third, dogs in the Pavlov situation respond to a tone by wagging their tails and looking at the place where food is generally presented because they expect food to be presented.

Most of the limitations of the Rescorla–Wagner model occur because it is incorrectly assumed that the strength of conditioned responses accurately reflects the strength of the association between conditioned and unconditioned stimuli (see Miller, Barnet, & Grahame, 1995, for a review). For example, the existence of blocking is taken to mean that the second conditioned stimulus hasn't formed an association with the conditioned stimulus. This is not the case. For example, the blocked conditioned stimulus produces the conditioned response when presented on its own outside the experimental context (Balaz, Gutsin, Cachiero, & Miller, 1982). Another example concerns experimental extinction, which is attributed to unlearning of the association between the conditioned and unconditioned stimuli. The existence of spontaneous recovery means that the association has *not* been unlearned.

ECOLOGICAL PERSPECTIVE

Can we produce conditioned responses equally well with almost any combination of conditioned and unconditioned stimuli? According to psychologists favoring the ecological perspective (e.g., Hollis, 1997), the answer is, "No!" They argue that animals and humans have inherited behavioral tendencies helping them to survive in their natural environment. These behavioral tendencies are often modified through learning to equip animals and humans to cope successfully with their environment. From this perspective, certain forms of learning are more useful than others, and tend to be acquired more easily.

It is essential for the members of all species to avoid poisonous foods, and so the ecological perspective is especially relevant to food-aversion learning. Garcia and Koelling (1966) studied such learning using three conditioned stimuli at the same time: saccharin-flavored water; light; and sound. Some rats had these stimuli paired with the unconditioned stimulus of X-rays, which caused nausea. Other rats had these stimuli paired with a different unconditioned stimulus (electric shock). After that, Garcia and Koelling presented each conditioned stimulus on its own. Rats that had experienced nausea showed an aversion to the flavored water but not to the light or sound cues. In contrast, the rats exposed to electric shock avoided the light and sound stimuli but not the flavored water. Thus, the animals learned to associate being sick with taste, and they learned to associate shock with light and sound stimuli.

What do these findings mean? They indicate there is a biological readiness to associate some stimuli together but not others. For example, there is obvious survival value in learning rapidly to develop a taste aversion to any food followed by illness. This is an example of the phenomenon known as **preparedness**.

IS AWARENESS NECESSARY?

Do we need to be consciously aware of the relationship between the conditioned stimulus and the unconditioned stimulus for conditioning to occur? Lovibond and Shanks (2002) reviewed the relevant evidence. They found that it was relatively rare for studies to report conditioning in the absence of awareness. In those studies, the measures of awareness that were used may well have underestimated conscious knowledge. They also found that the correspondence between conscious awareness and conditioned responses was often fairly weak, indicating that conscious awareness is not *essential* for conditioning to occur. Lovibond and Shanks concluded that the evidence is most consistent with the view that the learning occurring in conditioning experiments has two rather separate consequences: (1) conscious awareness of the relationship between the conditioned and unconditioned stimuli; and (2) production of conditioned responses (see the figure on the following page).

Key Term

Preparedness:
the notion that each species finds some forms of learning more "natural" and easier than others.

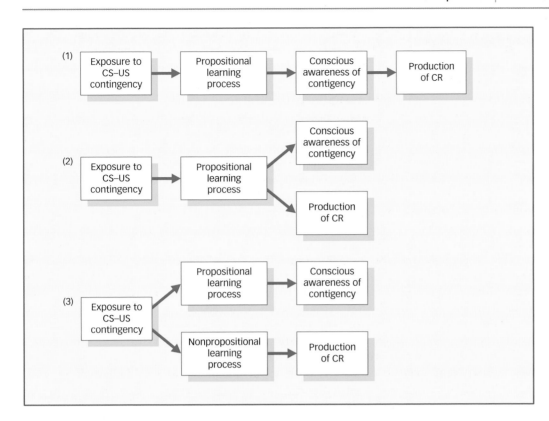

Three models of conditioning and awareness.
CS = conditioned stimulus; US = unconditioned stimulus; CR = conditioned response.
From Lovibond and Shanks (2002). Copyright © 2002 by the American Psychological Association. Reprinted with permission.

OPERANT CONDITIONING

In everyday life, people often behave in certain ways when a reward or reinforcement is offered. For example, young people deliver the morning papers because they are paid for doing so, and students work hard at their studies to be rewarded with good marks and improved career prospects. In contrast, we avoid engaging in behavior (e.g., stealing; cheating on exams) likely to be followed by punishment. These are all examples of **operant conditioning**, a form of learning in which behavior is controlled by rewards (also called positive reinforcers) and by unpleasant or aversive stimuli. Much of operant conditioning is based on the **law of effect**: The probability of a given response occurring increases if followed by a reward or positive reinforcer such as food or praise, whereas the probability of a given response decreases if followed by negative consequences.

According to Burrhus Fred Skinner (1904–1990), operant conditioning is of enormous importance. He believed that what we learn and how we behave in everyday life are both very heavily influenced by the conditioning experiences we have had throughout our lives. Operant conditioning has several practical applications. First, it is used extensively in the training of circus animals. Second, operant conditioning is used in the treatment of individuals with mental disorders (Chapter 22). For example, there are token economies in which patients (e.g., schizophrenics) who behave in desirable ways receive tokens that can be exchanged for various rewards. Third, there is biofeedback, which is used in the treatment of conditions such as high blood pressure and migraine.

"Well, I simply trained them to give me fish by pressing this over and over again."

Key Terms

Operant conditioning:
a form of learning in which behavior is controlled by its consequences (i.e., rewards or positive reinforcers and unpleasant or aversive stimuli).

Law of effect:
the probability of a response being produced is increased if it is followed by reward but is decreased if it is followed by punishment.

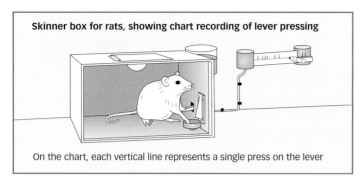

Skinner box for rats, showing chart recording of lever pressing

On the chart, each vertical line represents a single press on the lever

What happens in biofeedback is that the individual receives a signal whenever a given physiological measure (e.g., heart rate) moves in the desired direction.

BASIC FINDINGS

The best-known example of operant conditioning is provided by the work of Skinner. He placed a hungry rat in a small box (often called a Skinner box; see figure on the left) containing a lever. When the rat pressed the lever, a food pellet appeared. The rat slowly learned that food could be obtained by lever pressing, and so pressed the lever increasingly often. This is a clear example of the law of effect. Skinner found that the effects of a reward or positive reinforcer were greater if it followed shortly after the response had been produced than if it were delayed.

After operant conditioning has occurred, the experimenter can then decrease the probability of the conditioned response (e.g., lever pressing) occurring by removing the positive reinforcer (this is extinction). As with classical conditioning, there is usually some spontaneous recovery after extinction has occurred.

There are two main types of positive reinforcers or rewards: primary reinforcers and secondary reinforcers. **Primary reinforcers** are stimuli needed for survival (e.g., food; water; sleep; air). **Secondary reinforcers** are rewarding because we have learned to associate them with primary reinforcers. Secondary reinforcers include money, praise, and attention.

Key Study

Skinner (1938): Schedules of reinforcement

It seems reasonable to assume that we keep doing things that are rewarding and stop doing things that aren't rewarding. However, Skinner (1938) found some complexities in operant conditioning. So far we have considered continuous reinforcement, in which the reinforcer or reward is given after every response. However, it is rare in everyday life for our actions to be continuously rewarded. Skinner considered what happened with partial reinforcement, in which only some responses are rewarded. He identified four main schedules of partial reinforcement:

- **Fixed ratio schedule:** Every nth (e.g., fifth; tenth) response is rewarded. Workers who receive extra money for achieving certain targets are on this schedule.

Although these gamblers have no idea when or if they will receive a payout, they continue to play. This is an example of the most successful reinforcement schedule—variable ratio reinforcement.

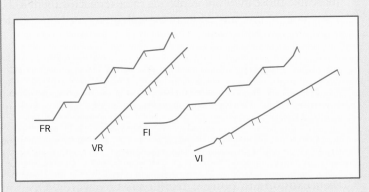

Typical pattern of responding over time on the four main schedules of partial reinforcement: FR (fixed ratio); VR (variable ratio); FI (fixed interval); and VI (variable interval). From Atkinson et al. (1996). Copyright © by Harcourt Brace. Reproduced with permission.

- **Variable ratio schedule:** On average, every nth response is rewarded. However, the actual gap between two rewards may be very small or fairly large. This schedule is found in fishing and gambling.
- **Fixed interval schedule:** The first response produced after a given interval of time (e.g., 60 seconds) is rewarded. Workers who are paid regularly every week are basically on this schedule—they receive reward after a given interval of time, but don't need to produce a specific response.
- **Variable interval schedule:** On average, the first response produced after a given interval of time (e.g., 60 seconds) is rewarded. However, the actual interval is mostly shorter or longer than this. As Gross (1996) noted, self-employed workers whose customers make payments are rewarded at variable intervals, but they don't need to produce a specific response.

The patterns of responding produced by these various schedules are shown in the figure above. It might be thought that continuous reinforcement (with reward available after every response) would lead to better conditioning than partial reinforcement. In fact, the opposite is the case. Continuous reinforcement leads to the *lowest* rate of responding, with the variable schedules (especially variable ratio) leading to very fast rates. This helps to explain why compulsive gamblers often find it difficult to stop their addictive behavior.

What about extinction? Those schedules of reinforcement associated with the best conditioning also show the most resistance to extinction. Thus, rats trained on the variable ratio schedule will keep responding in the absence of reward longer than rats on any other schedule. In contrast, rats trained with continuous reinforcement stop responding the soonest. One reason why continuous reinforcement leads to rapid extinction is that there is a very obvious shift from reward being provided on every trial to reward not being provided at all. Animals trained on the variable schedules are used to reward being provided infrequently and irregularly, and so it takes much longer for them to realize they are no longer going to be rewarded for responding.

Discussion points
1. Can you think of some examples of situations in everyday life involving the various schedules of reinforcement?
2. What are the limitations of Skinner's operant conditioning approach?

Key Terms

Variable ratio schedule: on average every nth response is rewarded, but there is some variation around that figure.

Fixed interval schedule: a situation in which the first response produced after a given interval of time is rewarded or reinforced.

Variable interval schedule: a situation in which the first response produced after a given interval of time is rewarded but with some variation around that time interval.

Shaping: a form of operant conditioning in which behavior is changed slowly in the desired direction by requiring responses to become more and more like the wanted response for reward to be given.

In operant conditioning, the animal (or human) has to make the required response before it can be reinforced. How can we condition an animal to produce a complex response it wouldn't produce naturally? The answer is by **shaping**, in which the animal's behavior moves slowly towards the desired response through successive approximations. Suppose we wanted to teach pigeons to play table tennis. To begin with, they would be rewarded for making any contact with the table-tennis ball. Over time, their actions would need to become more and

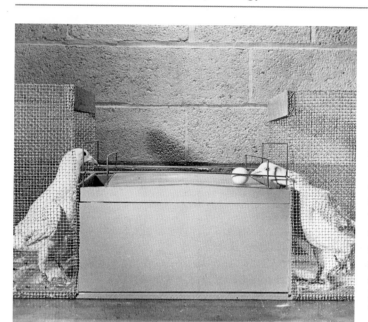

Skinner taught pigeons to play a basic form of table tennis by rewarding them every time they made contact with a table-tennis ball.

Key Terms

Positive punishment:
a form of operant conditioning in which the probability of a response is reduced by following it with an unpleasant or aversive stimulus; sometimes known simply as punishment.

Negative punishment:
a form of operant conditioning in which the probability of a response being produced is reduced by following it with the removal of a positive reinforcer or reward.

Case Study: *Punishment*

Using punishment alone to affect behavior is regarded by most psychologists today as a technique that is morally and ethically dubious. When this belief is added to research that has shown how punishment on its own has at best only short-lived effects, it is surprising that punishments are still used in so many situations, from family life to warring nations.

Many cultures, such as our own, still use punishment to deal with criminal offenders. Fines or prison sentences are serious punishers in their own right, but research suggests that they would be more effective if linked to some kind of reward for not re-offending. Figures from the UK Central Statistical Office (1996) show that punishment alone does not have much success. In England and Wales between 1987 and 1990, three in every five males sent to prison became re-offenders, and in 1991 75% of young male offenders had been reconvicted within 2 years, 12% within 3 months of their release from prison.

more like those involved in playing table tennis for them to be rewarded. In this way, Skinner actually persuaded pigeons to play a basic form of table tennis!

PUNISHMENT: POSITIVE AND NEGATIVE

So far we have considered mainly the effects of positive reinforcers or rewards on performance. However, operant conditioning can also involve unpleasant or aversive stimuli such as electric shocks or failure feedback. Humans and other species learn to behave in ways that reduce their exposure to aversive stimuli just as they learn to increase their exposure to positive reinforcers or rewards. Operant conditioning in which a response is followed by an aversive stimulus is known as **positive punishment** (sometimes simply called punishment). If the aversive stimulus occurs shortly after the response, it has the effect of reducing the likelihood that the response will be produced subsequently. There is also **negative punishment** in which a positive reinforcer or reward is removed following the production of a particular response. For example, a child who refuses to eat properly and starts throwing food on the floor may have the food removed from him/her. The typical effect of negative punishment is to reduce the probability that the punished response will be produced thereafter.

Baron (1977) reviewed the effects of positive punishment on children's aggressive behavior. He identified the following requirements for punishment to reduce aggressive behavior:

1. There should be a very short time interval between the aggressive action and the punishment.
2. Punishment should be relatively strong.
3. Punishment should be applied consistently and predictably.
4. The person giving the punishment shouldn't be seen as an aggressive model.
5. The person receiving punishment should understand clearly why he/she is being punished.

Positive punishment sometimes has various unwanted effects. Gershoff (2002) carried out several meta-analyses to identify the main effects on children of being physically punished by parents. Punishment typically produced immediate compliance to the parent's wishes. However, it was associated with aggressive and antisocial behavior in childhood and adulthood, impaired mental health (e.g., depression), and a tendency to abuse their own children or spouse in adulthood.

Negative punishment is used in the time-out technique. For example, a child who behaves aggressively is prevented from continuing with such behavior by being sent to his/her room. Negative punishment is involved, because the child is removed from pleasurable activities. The time-out technique often improves children's behavior while avoiding the negative effects associated with positive punishment (Rortvedt & Miltenberger, 1994). This is especially the case if parents are firm and relatively unemotional.

AVOIDANCE LEARNING

Nearly all drivers stop at red traffic lights because of the possibility of aversive stimuli in the form of an accident or trouble with the police if they don't. This is a situation in which no aversive stimulus is presented if suitable action is taken, and is an example of **avoidance learning**. Many aversive stimuli strengthen any responses stopping the aversive stimuli being presented; they are known as *negative reinforcers.*

Avoidance learning can be very effective, as was shown by Solomon and Wynne (1953). Dogs were placed in a two-compartment apparatus. A change in the lighting served as a warning that a strong electric shock was about to be presented. The dogs could avoid being shocked by jumping into the other compartment. Most dogs received a few shocks early in the experiment. After that, however, they generally avoided shocks for the remaining 50 or more trials.

Mowrer (1947) proposed two-process learning theory to account for avoidance learning. According to this theory, the first process involves classical conditioning. The pairing of neutral (e.g., walls of the compartment) and aversive stimuli (electric shock) produces conditioned fear. The second process involves operant conditioning. The avoidance response of jumping into the other compartment is rewarded or reinforced by fear reduction.

Two-process theory provides a plausible account of avoidance learning. However, there are problems with the notion that the avoidance response occurs to reduce fear. Dogs in the Solomon and Wynne (1953) study typically responded to the warning signal in about 1.5 seconds, which is probably too little time for the fear response to have developed. After the avoidance response started being produced regularly, the dogs didn't behave as if they were anxious. Thus, it is difficult to argue that their avoidance behavior was motivated *only* by fear reduction.

THEORETICAL PERSPECTIVES

What is learned in operant conditioning? According to Skinner, reinforcement or reward strengthens the association between the discriminative stimulus (e.g., the inside of the Skinner box) and the reinforced response (e.g., lever press). In contrast, Tolman (1959) proposed a more cognitive theory according to which animals learn much more than is implied by Skinner's views. Tolman argued that operant conditioning involves the learning of means–end relationships. A **means–end relationship** is the knowledge that the production of a given response in a given situation will have a specific effect. For example, it might be the knowledge that pressing a lever in the Skinner box will lead to the presentation of a food pellet.

There is much evidence that animals *do* learn means–end relationships. For example, Dickinson and Dawson (1987) trained rats to press a lever to receive sugar water, whereas others were trained to press a lever for dry food pellets. Some of the rats were then deprived of food, whereas others were deprived of water. Finally, all of them were tested under extinction conditions in which no reward was provided. The key findings involved the rats who were thirsty. Those who had been reinforced previously with sugar water produced far more lever presses in extinction than did those who had been reinforced with dry food pellets. The rats used their knowledge of the expected reinforcer to decide how worthwhile it was to press the lever. Thirsty rats wanted something to drink. As a result, the expectation of dry food pellets didn't encourage them to engage in much lever pressing.

Evidence that animals acquire detailed knowledge about the reinforcer to which they have been exposed was reported by Pecoraro, Timberlake, and Tinsley (1999). Rats became accustomed to a certain amount of reinforcement but then started receiving less reinforcement. This produced a **negative contrast effect** involving a marked decrease in response rate. Indeed, these rats had a slower response rate than rats that had received the smaller reinforcement throughout.

Limitations on operant conditioning?

Skinner assumed that virtually any response can be conditioned in any stimulus situation. This is known as **equipotentiality**. Skinner's assumption is false. For example, Breland

In Gaffan et al.'s 1983 study, the rats avoided revisiting the same arm of a T-maze where they had previously found food. The ecological perspective would predict this behavior.

and Breland (1961) tried to train a pig to insert a wooden token into a piggy bank for reward. The pig picked up the token, but then repeatedly dropped it on the floor. In the words of Breland and Breland, the pig would "root it [turn it up with its snout], drop it again, root it along the way, pick it up, toss it in the air, drop it, root it some more, and so on." They argued that their findings showed evidence of instinctive drift, meaning that what animals learn tends to resemble their instinctive behavior.

Additional evidence that instinctive behavior plays a much larger role in operant conditioning than Skinner believed was provided by Moore (1973). He took films of pigeons pecking at keys for either food or water reward. Students were then asked to decide what the reward was by looking at the films of the pigeons' pecking behavior. They were correct 87% of the time. Birds pecking for food usually struck the key with an open beak, and made sharp, vigorous pecks. When pecking for water, on the other hand, the pigeons had their bills closed and there was a more sustained contact with the key.

Ecological perspective

The evidence discussed above suggests it may be useful to consider operant conditioning from the ecological perspective. According to this perspective, animals should find it easier to learn forms of behavior enabling them to cope with their natural environment. Supporting evidence was reported by Gaffan, Hansel, and Smith (1983). Rats in a T-shaped maze had to decide whether to turn left or right. Suppose a rat turns left and finds food at the end of that arm of the maze. According to conditioning principles, the rat has been rewarded for turning left, and so should turn left on the following trial. However, in the rat's natural environment it is generally not sensible to return to a place from which all the food has just been removed. Gaffan et al. found that rats early in training tended to avoid the arm of the T-shaped maze in which they had previously found food, as predicted from the ecological perspective.

Overall Evaluation

+ Operant conditioning is often very effective. The behavior of humans and other species can be controlled by clever use of reinforcement (e.g., the training of circus animals).

+ Operant conditioning has been used successfully in the treatment of various mental disorders (see Chapter 22).

− In real life, we don't learn things mainly by performing responses that are rewarded. Instead, we learn an enormous amount simply by *observing* the behavior of other people (Bandura, 1977, see next section). Operant conditioning only accounts for some relatively simple forms of learning.

− Skinner exaggerated the importance of *external* or environmental factors as influences on behavior and minimized the role of *internal* factors (e.g., goals). As Bandura (1977, p. 27) pointed out, "If actions were determined solely by external rewards and punishments, people would behave like weather vanes, constantly shifting in radically different directions to conform to the whims of others."

− Operant conditioning often has more effect on performance than on learning. Suppose someone offered you $1 every time you said, "The earth is flat." You might (especially if burdened by debt!) say that sentence hundreds of times, so that the reinforcement or reward would have influenced your performance or behavior. However, it wouldn't affect your knowledge or learning so that you really believed that the earth is flat.

− Skinner's notion of equipotentiality is incorrect, as is his assumption that operant conditioning is uninfluenced by instinctive behavior. The ecological approach provides an appealing alternative perspective.

OBSERVATIONAL LEARNING

Skinner and other advocates of operant conditioning argued that most human learning requires us to produce responses that are then rewarded or punished. In contrast, Bandura (1977, 1986, 1999) emphasized the importance of **observational learning**. This is learning occurring as a result of observing the behavior of some other person or model. (The relevance of Bandura's approach to the understanding of personality is discussed in Chapter 12 and the effects of observational learning on aggression are considered in Chapter 15).

According to Bandura (1999, p. 170):

> *Humans have evolved an advanced capacity for observational learning that enables them to expand their knowledge and competencies rapidly through the information conveyed by the rich variety of models. Virtually all behavioral, cognitive, and affective learning from direct experience can be achieved vicariously [second-hand] by observing people's actions and the consequences for them.*

Why is observational learning so important to humans? One key reason is because it is typically much more efficient than learning (e.g., operant conditioning) that involves actually experiencing a given situation. In the course of a single day, you can readily observe the behavior of numerous people in hundreds of situations. In contrast, it would be very difficult (or impossible) to put yourself in all of those situations in a short period of time. It can also be safer to observe the fate of others who engage in dangerous actions than to perform the same actions yourself!

Findings

In a classic study, Bandura (1965) explored the issue of the relationship between observational learning and performance—see the Key Study below.

Key Study

Bandura (1965): Observational learning and the Bobo doll

Young children watched a film in which an adult model behaved aggressively towards an inflatable Bobo doll (it has a weight in the bottom that makes it bob back up when it is knocked down). In one condition, a second adult appeared towards the end of the

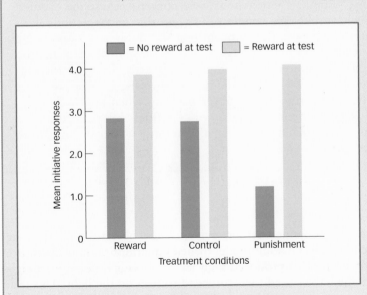

Imitation of aggressive behavior by children as a function of the way an aggressive adult was treated (reward, control, punishment) and whether the children were or were not rewarded at the test for imitating the adult's aggressive behavior. Data from Bandura (1965).

Key Term

Observational learning: learning occurring as a consequence of watching the behavior of another person (often called a model).

Adult "models" and children attack the Bobo doll.

film and gave the model some sweets and a soft drink for having put up a "championship performance" (reward condition). In a second condition, the second adult scolded and spanked the model for behaving aggressively (punishment condition). In a third condition, the model didn't receive reward or punishment (control condition).

Bandura (1965) then observed the behavior of the children in the presence of the Bobo doll. Children in the reward and control conditions imitated more of the aggressive actions of the model than did the children in the punishment condition (see the figure above). It could be argued that children in the punishment condition had not achieved much observational learning. However, when children in that condition were offered some fruit juice and toys for showing what they had learned from the adult model, they exhibited as much observational learning as the children in the other two conditions.

Discussion points
1. What are some of the limitations of this famous research by Bandura?
2. How important do you think observational learning is with respect to producing aggressive behavior?

KEY STUDY EVALUATION
In his classic Bobo doll study, Bandura controlled the behavior of his adult models. They used novel actions such as hitting the doll with a hammer, or throwing it in the air and saying "Pow! Boom!" These actions were chosen because the children would be unlikely to behave like this spontaneously, so that if the actions were produced, the researchers could be fairly confident that the children were imitating the adult model. Bandura's (1965) study is more limited than generally acknowledged. He found that children readily imitated aggressive behavior towards a doll. However, children are much less likely to imitate aggressive behavior towards another child. In addition, the Bobo doll bounces back up when knocked down, which gives it novelty value. Children unfamiliar with the Bobo doll were five times more likely to imitate aggressive behavior against it than those who had played with it before (Cumberbatch, 1990).

Meltzoff (1988) apparently obtained strong evidence for observational learning. Infants of 14 months watched while an adult model turned on a table-mounted pressure-sensitive light using her forehead. This produced high levels of observational learning— 1 week later, two-thirds of the babies used their forehead to turn on the light. This is an impressive finding given that babies rapidly discover how to use their hands to change the environment.

In an important study, Gergely, Bekkering, and Kiraly (2002) showed that the findings from Meltzoff's (1988) study are less conclusive than they seem (see the figure on the right). In that study, the model's hands were on the table, and so the infants could see she had deliberately preferred to use her forehead rather than her hands to turn the light on. Gergely et al. included a second condition in which the adult model pretended to be cold and so had her hands under the table wrapped in a blanket. This apparently small change had a dramatic effect on the results. When the model's hands were free, 69% of the infants (who were 14 months old) copied her behavior by using their forehead to put on the light. In contrast, when the model's hands were *not* free, only 21% of the babies copied her behavior.

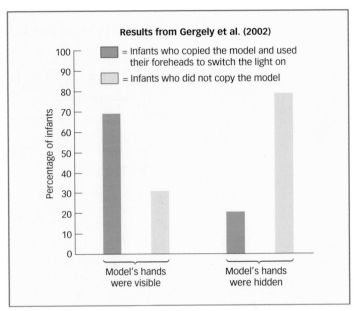

Observational learning in infants is strongly influenced by the context.

What can we conclude from Gergely et al.'s (2002) study? First, the findings indicate that observational learning is more complex than suggested by Bandura. According to Bandura, children who observe a model performing an action that is successful or rewarded should imitate that action. However, that simply didn't happen in the condition in which the model's hands were under the blanket.

Second, the findings suggest that even infants are capable of fairly complex processing. The infants had already learned from experience that hands are very useful for touching objects and altering the environment. As a result, observational learning only influenced their behavior when they believed the model had *deliberately* preferred to use her forehead rather than her hands to turn on the light. According to Gergely et al. (2002, p. 755), "Imitation by 14-month-olds goes beyond emulation [imitation]. We conclude that the early imitation of goal-directed actions is a selective, inferential process that involves evaluation of the rationality of the means in relation to the constraints of the situation."

Third, it needs to be borne in mind that the infants in Gergely et al.'s (2002) study were only 14 months of age. If their tendency to imitate (or not to imitate) a model depends on complex thought processes, then this will be even more true of older children. Thus, we must consider cognitive processes at all ages to understand things as apparently simple as observational learning and imitation.

Similar findings were reported by Schwier et al. (2006). Twelve-month-olds observed an adult make a toy animal perform a particular action to reach a goal. In one condition, there was a barrier in the way that forced the adult to make that action. In the other condition, there was no barrier and the adult freely chose to make that action. The infants imitated the adult's action much more often when the adult had freely chosen it than when she was forced to use it. The take-home message is that even infants show some ability to consider the actor's *intention* as well as his/her behavior, and use that information to decide how closely to imitate the actor's behavior (see Fenstermacher and Saudino, 2006, for a review).

Is observational learning as effective as learning based on actually performing the behavior in question? Evidence that it is was reported by Blandin and Proteau (2000). Participants performed a four-segment timing task under one of three conditions: (1) prior observational learning; (2) prior physical practice; and (3) no prior experience. Observational learning and prior physical practice led to comparable levels of performance that were significantly higher than those shown by controls. In addition, participants in the observational learning condition developed error correction mechanisms at least as effective as those developed by participants in the physical practice condition.

+ Observational learning occurs very often in children and in adults.

+ Observational learning can have powerful effects on subsequent behavior comparable in size to learning based on actual performance (e.g., Blandin & Proteau, 2000).

− The findings of Gergely et al. (2002) and Schwier et al. (2006) indicate that observational learning doesn't always lead to simple, mindless imitation of a rewarded model. Instead, even infants take account of factors such as the actor's intention and situational constraints on the model's behavior.

− There is only modest evidence for observational learning in children's acquisition of language. They initially produce much shorter utterances than adults, and rapidly move on to producing novel utterances (see Chapter 13). Neither of these aspects of children's language seems to involve observational learning.

− As Fenstermacher and Saudino (2006) pointed out, there are substantial (and largely unexplained) individual differences in imitative behavior following observational learning. For example, Fouts and Click (1979) found that extraverted children imitated modeled behavior more than introverted ones, possibly because the extraverted children pay more attention to social stimuli.

IMPLICIT LEARNING

Do you think you could learn something without being aware of what you had learned? It sounds improbable. For example, suppose you went to a lecture on social psychology yesterday. No matter how boring the lecture was, I imagine you learned some useful new information about social psychology. You can probably bring to mind some of that information and you have a strong conscious awareness of having learned certain things. In that context, the notion of learning without conscious awareness seems very suspect. Moreover, if we *did* acquire information without any conscious awareness, it might seem somewhat pointless and wasteful—if we don't realize we have learned something, then it appears unlikely we are going to be able to make much use of it.

In the terms used by psychologists, we have started to discuss **implicit learning**, which is, "Learning without conscious awareness of having learned" (French & Cleeremans, 2002, p. xvii). Implicit learning can be contrasted with **explicit learning**, which involves conscious awareness of what has been learned. We have just dismissed the notion of implicit learning, but (as so often in psychology) there is another side to the story. Consider the following fuller definition of implicit learning offered by Cleeremans and Jiménez (2002, p. 20): "Implicit learning is the process through which we become sensitive to certain regularities in the environment (1) in the absence of intention to learn about these regularities; (2) in the absence of awareness that one is learning; and (3) in such a way that the resulting knowledge is difficult to express." You can probably think of skills you possess that are hard to express in words. For example, it is notoriously difficult to express what we know about riding a bicycle. Indeed, the verbal descriptions most people give of how to steer a bicycle around a corner are inaccurate and would lead anyone following them to fall off pretty quickly! Another example is that most of us speak reasonably grammatically even though we have little or no conscious access to the grammatical rules in the English language.

One of the tasks most used to study implicit learning is artificial grammar learning. In a typical study (e.g., Reber, 1967), participants are initially asked to memorize meaningless letters strings (e.g., PVPXVPS; TSXXTVV). After that, they are told that the memorized letter strings all follow the rules of an artificial grammar, but they aren't told the nature of these rules. Next, the participants classify *novel* strings as grammatical or ungrammatical. Finally, they are asked to describe the rules of the grammar.

What is typically found from studies on artificial grammar learning? First, the classification task is performed significantly above chance level, thus indicating that some learning has occurred. Second, the participants cannot describe the grammatical rules when asked to do so. This combination of learning plus an inability to express what has been learned seems superficially to fit Cleereman and Jiménez's definition of implicit learning very neatly. Alas, as we will see, there has been much controversy about the proper interpretation of findings from the artificial grammar task.

ROLE OF CONSCIOUSNESS

At the heart of the controversy over implicit learning is the issue of the importance of conscious awareness in human learning and behavior. Cleereman and Jiménez (2002) identified two extreme positions on this issue. One extreme is the notion of a "Commander Data" type of consciousness based on Star Trek's character Data. He is an android [robot resembling a human being] who can describe his internal states in enormous detail. Commander Data theorists assume that consciousness has great power and that any knowledge expressed through behavior is available to it. The opposite extreme is the notion of a zombie consciousness in which we have no conscious awareness of the knowledge influencing our behavior. According to Cleeremans and Jiménez (2002), neither extreme position is plausible. What is most likely is that consciousness is sometimes (but by no means always) of relevance to learning and to human cognition.

EXPERIMENTAL APPROACHES

There are three main experimental approaches to implicit learning, all of which are discussed below:

1. Studies designed to see whether healthy individuals can learn fairly complex material in the absence of conscious awareness of what they have learned.
2. Studies on brain-damaged patients with amnesia, in which the focus is on whether their implicit learning is essentially intact even though their explicit learning is severely impaired. If so, it would suggest that different processes underlie implicit and explicit learning.
3. Brain-imaging studies: If implicit and explicit learning are different forms of learning, then different brain areas should be active during implicit and explicit learning.

Be warned that the findings from all three approaches are nothing like clear-cut!

Complex normal learning

How do we know when learning is implicit? A key problem is that the failure of participants when questioned to indicate conscious awareness of what they have learned (e.g., on an artificial grammar learning task) does *not* necessarily prove that their learning

---

Implicit learning

How do you know which faucet to turn on when you want hot water? How do you know where a light switch is at home—just putting out your hand without actually thinking about it? According to Howard (2006) this sort of knowledge is gained by implicit learning, and it "happens when people are just going about their daily business, when they are focused on living, not on memorizing or on learning per se."

One of her studies has research participants taking a computer-based test in which they predict as quickly as they can where the next in a sequence of moving dots will appear on the screen. Some of these occur in a predictable pattern or location, and some are random.

What the participants are not told is that some of the events occur in a predictable location or pattern, whereas others are completely random. Most participants are not consciously aware that some dots appear predictably, and yet they begin to respond faster and more accurately to the predictable events than to the random ones. This means that they have learned this without knowing it, which is implicit learning. We do this all the time in everyday life, enabling us to adapt to new situations and people.

was implicit. Shanks and St. John (1994) argued that two criteria need to be met to show the existence of implicit learning:

1. *Information criterion*: The information participants are asked to provide on the awareness test must be the information responsible for the improved level of performance.
2. *Sensitivity criterion*: "We must be able to show that our test of awareness is sensitive to all of the relevant knowledge" (Shanks & St. John, 1994, p. 374). People may be consciously aware of more task-relevant knowledge than appears on an insensitive awareness test, and this may lead us to underestimate their consciously accessible knowledge.

Shanks and St. John (1994) also discussed what they called the "retrospective problem." Participants may be consciously aware of what they are learning at the time, but have simply forgotten by the end of the experiment when questioned about their conscious awareness.

The serial reaction time task has been used in many studies (e.g., Nissen & Bullemer, 1987) on implicit learning. There are typically dozens or hundreds of trials on this task. On each trial, a stimulus appears at one out of several locations on a computer screen, and the participant responds as rapidly as possible with the response key corresponding to its location. There is a complex repeating sequence over trials in the various stimulus locations, but participants are not told this. Towards the end of the experiment, there is a block of trials conforming to a *novel* sequence. Participants typically respond more rapidly to stimuli in the repeating sequence than to those in the novel sequence, indicating they have learned information about the repeating sequence. However, when questioned at the end of the experiment, participants usually show *no* conscious awareness that there was a repeating sequence.

Evidence that participants have *some* conscious awareness of what they have learned on the serial reaction time task was reported by Wilkinson and Shanks (2004). Participants received either 1500 (15 blocks) or 4500 (45 blocks) trials on the task and showed clear evidence of sequence learning. They were then told there had been a repeating sequence, following which they were presented on each of 12 trials with part of the sequence under one of two conditions. In the *inclusion* condition, they guessed the next location in the sequence. In the *exclusion* condition, they were told to *avoid* guessing the next location in the sequence. If sequence knowledge is totally implicit, then performance shouldn't differ between the inclusion and exclusion conditions. If it is partly explicit, then guesses in the inclusion condition should correspond more often to the actual sequence than those in the exclusion condition. The findings indicated that some explicit knowledge was acquired on the serial reaction time task (see the figure below).

Mean number of completions (guessed locations) corresponding to the trained sequence (own) or the untrained sequence (other) in inclusion and exclusion conditions as a function of number of trials (15 vs. 45 blocks). From Wilkinson and Shanks (2004). Copyright © American Psychological Association. Reprinted with permission.

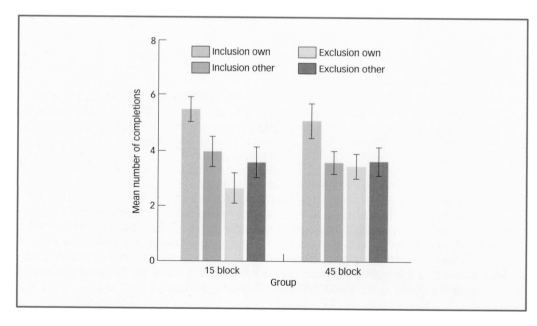

What about the artificial grammar learning task described earlier? Alas, people's ability to discriminate above chance between grammatical and ungrammatical letter strings does *not* prove they have acquired knowledge of the underlying grammatical rules. Indeed, Channon et al. (2002) found that participants' decisions on the grammaticality of letter strings didn't depend at all on knowledge of grammatical rules. Instead, they classified letter strings as grammatical when they shared letter pairs (bigrams) with the letter strings memorized initially and as ungrammatical when they did not. Thus, participants' above-chance performance when classifying letter strings may well depend on conscious awareness of two-letter fragments relevant to the grammatical rules even though they have no direct knowledge (explicit or implicit) of the rules themselves.

Evaluation

(+) Many of the findings provide some (albeit controversial) evidence of implicit learning.

(+) Evidence that explicit learning plays some role in explaining performance improvement with practice does *not* mean that no implicit learning has occurred. Indeed, implicit learning may often precede explicit learning, with explicit knowledge being based on previous implicit learning (Sun, Slusarz, & Terry, 2005).

(−) Research on the artificial grammar learning and serial reaction time tasks is mostly inconclusive because it is not clear that the information and sensitivity criteria have been satisfied.

Learning in amnesics

Amnesic patients (who have severe problems with long-term memory because of brain damage) have impaired explicit memory (involving conscious recollection) but not implicit memory (not involving conscious recollection; see Chapter 8). If amnesic patients have impaired explicit learning but intact implicit learning, that would provide ammunition for those claiming that implicit learning is very different from explicit learning. Why are implicit learning and implicit memory discussed in separate chapters? One reason is because remarkably little research has considered both within a single study. Another reason is that studies of implicit learning have typically used fairly complex novel stimuli, whereas studies of implicit memory have used simple and familiar ones.

Knowlton, Ramus, and Squire (1992) carried out an early study on implicit learning in amnesic patients using the artificial grammar learning task. Amnesic patients had impaired explicit learning on this task but their implicit learning was comparable to that of healthy controls. Different findings were obtained by Channon et al. (2002) in a study mentioned earlier in which they used complex versions of the artificial grammar learning task. Amnesic patients and healthy controls failed to learn the underlying abstract rules of grammar, but did learn about fragments (e.g., letter pairs). The key finding was that amnesic patients learned fewer fragments than the normal controls, suggesting that they had poorer implicit learning.

Findings apparently contradicting those of Channon et al. (2002) were reported by Meulemans and Van der Linden (2003). They used an artificial grammar learning task in which the test of implicit learning was such that fragment knowledge couldn't influence the accuracy of grammaticality judgments. They also used a test of explicit learning on which participants wrote down 10 letter strings they considered to be grammatical. The amnesic patients did much worse than controls on explicit learning, but they performed at a comparable level to controls on implicit learning. Similar findings on the serial reaction time task were reported by Nissen, Willingham, and Hartman (1989).

Evaluation

⊕ Most findings suggest that amnesic patients have intact implicit learning but impaired explicit learning. This pattern is consistent with the notion that different mechanisms underlie explicit and implicit learning.

⊖ In spite of several positive findings, the implicit learning performance of amnesic patients is sometimes worse than that of normal controls (e.g., Channon et al., 2002).

⊖ We don't always know *what* information is being used by amnesics to perform implicit learning tasks. When we lack this information, it is hard to assess whether implicit or explicit learning is involved.

Brain-imaging research

If separate cognitive systems underlie explicit and implicit learning, different brain regions should be activated for these two types of learning. More specifically, since conscious awareness is associated with brain areas within the prefrontal cortex such as the anterior cingulate and the dorsolateral prefrontal cortex (see Chapter 5), these areas should be much more active during explicit learning than implicit learning.

As you may have guessed, the evidence is somewhat inconsistent. Positive findings were reported by Grafton, Hazeltine, and Ivry (1995) on a task involving learning motor sequences. Explicit learning was associated with more activation in the anterior cingulate and areas in the parietal cortex involved in voluntary attention than was implicit learning. Aizenstein et al. (2004) also obtained positive findings using a version of the serial reaction time task. The explicit task involved learning a sequence of shapes. At the same time, the colors of the shapes used in the explicit task formed a sequence that was used on the implicit learning task. Some brain regions were activated during both explicit and implicit learning. However, there was greater prefrontal activation with explicit than with implicit learning, which is precisely in line with prediction.

Negative findings were reported by Schenden, Searl, Melrose, and Stern (2003) in a study on implicit and explicit sequence learning. Both forms of learning activated the same brain areas. Schenden et al. (2003, p. 1020) concluded that, "Both implicit and explicit learning of higher order sequences involve the MTL [medial temporal lobe] structures implicated in memory functions."

Evaluation

⊕ There is some evidence that explicit and implicit learning are associated with activation in different brain areas.

⊕ There is suggestive evidence that brain areas known to be involved in conscious awareness and attention are more activated during explicit learning than during implicit learning.

⊖ At present, the available evidence is sufficiently inconsistent and sparse that no very firm conclusions are possible.

SUMMARY AND CONCLUSIONS

Much of the available behavioral evidence from healthy individuals and from amnesic patients suggests that implicit learning exists and is separate from explicit learning, and the same is true to a lesser extent of brain-imaging evidence from healthy controls. The main counter-argument is that very few studies satisfy the information and sensitivity criteria and avoid the retrospective problem, and so we can't be confident about the validity of the findings. Those skeptical of the existence of implicit learning emphasize the fact that evidence of explicit learning has been found in many studies allegedly focusing on implicit learning. However, finding that *some* explicit learning is involved in performance of a given task doesn't necessarily mean that *no* implicit learning was involved. It seems likely that performance of many tasks depends on a combination of explicit and implicit learning (Sun et al., 2005).

HOW DO YOU BECOME AN EXPERT?

Anyone wanting a successful career soon discovers that a very considerable amount of learning is required. More specifically, it is essential for them to develop **expertise**, which can be defined as "highly skilled, competent performance in one or more task domains [areas]" (Sternberg & Ben-Zeev, 2001, p. 365).

What makes an expert? Most people (including many psychologists) argue that a high level of intelligence is of key importance in the achievement of real expertise. Just think for a moment whether you agree. If you do, you may be surprised to discover that there is evidence suggesting some real experts have only average levels of intelligence. For example, Ceci and Liker (1986) studied individuals with great expertise about harness racing. Harness racing (which is popular in the United States) involves horses pulling a sulky (a light two-wheeled cart) holding one person (the driver). Ceci and Liker identified 14 experts and 16 nonexperts. However, the term "nonexperts" is a relative one in this context, because they knew a vast amount about harness racing and attended horse races nearly every day. The IQs of the experts ranged from 81 to 128, and those of the non-experts from 80 to 130. Four of the experts had IQs in the low 80s, which is well below the population mean of 100.

The experts and nonexperts were given information about 50 unnamed horses and an unnamed standard horse. Fourteen pieces of information were provided in each case (e.g., each horse's lifetime speed; race driver's ability; track size). The participants worked out the probable odds for 50 comparisons with each horse in turn being compared against the standard horse. The experts' performance was outstanding, and superior to that of the nonexperts. They took account of complex interactions among up to seven variables at the same time. Thus, the significance of any one piece of information was interpreted in the context of several other pieces of information about the same horse. It would require complicated statistical formulae to express these interactions mathematically.

The key finding was that the experts' high level of performance didn't depend at all on a high IQ—the correlation between their performance and IQ scores was $-.07$. Thus, experts with very low IQs were successful at combining information in extremely complex ways. Ceci and Liker (1986) concluded that IQ is unrelated to many forms of intelligent behavior. However, all the experts had devoted thousands of hours to developing their expertise, and Ceci and Liker may have exaggerated the complexity of the knowledge they possessed.

Dramatic findings have also been obtained from individuals patronizingly known as **idiot savants** (knowledgeable idiots) (see Howe, 1998, for a review). Idiots savants generally have mental retardation and low IQs, but they possess some special expertise. For example, they can work out in a few seconds the day of the week corresponding to any specified date in the past or the future, or they perform complex multiplications at high speed, or they know the value of pi to thousands of places of decimals.

In spite of impressive findings like those just described, we need to be aware of their limitations. The expertise (harness racing; exceptional memory; calculating power) is very narrow and specific, and intelligence or IQ is much more likely to be important when we consider broad and general expertise. This was shown in a review article by Gottfredson (1997) on IQ and long-term career success (see Chapter 11). The correlation between intelligence and work performance was only $+.23$ with low-complexity jobs (e.g., shrimp picker; corn-husking machine operator). However, with high-complexity jobs (e.g., biologist; city circulation manager), the correlation between intelligence and job performance rose to $+.58$, indicating that intelligence is an important determinant of

Key Terms
Expertise: the specific knowledge an expert has about a given domain (e.g., that an engineer may have about bridges).
Idiot savants: individuals who have limited outstanding expertise in spite of being mentally retarded.

success in such jobs. Mackintosh (1998) reviewed evidence showing that the average IQ is about 120–130 (top 15% of the population) for those in very complex occupations (e.g., accountants; lawyers; doctors; even academics!). Thus, high intelligence is of real importance for obtaining (and succeeding in) occupations of high complexity requiring high levels of general expertise.

CHESS PLAYING

In this section we focus on chess-playing expertise. According to Gobet, deVoogt, and Retschitzki (2004), there are several reasons why it is useful to study chess players. First, we can assess very precisely chess players' level of skill. Second, expert chess players develop specific cognitive skills (e.g., pattern recognition; selective search) that are useful in many other areas of expertise. Third, information about chess experts' remarkable memory for chess positions generalizes very well to many other types of expertise.

Everyone accepts that huge amounts of practice are essential in the development of the chess-playing skills of a grandmaster. However, working out *exactly* what expert chess players know that nonexpert players don't is hard to do. A breakthrough came with the influential research of De Groot (1965). He found that expert players were much better than nonexpert ones at remembering chess positions. He gave his participants brief presentations (between 2 and 15 seconds) of board positions from actual games. After removing the board, De Groot asked them to reconstruct the position. Chess masters recalled the positions very accurately (91% correct) whereas less expert players made many errors (only 41% correct). These findings were *not* obtained because chess masters have generally better memories—they were no better than nonexperts at recalling *random* chess positions.

Chunks or templates?

How do chess players use their knowledge to memorize chess positions? According to Chase and Simon (1973), they break chess positions down into about seven chunks or units corresponding to information previously stored in long-term memory. In contrast, Gobet and Waters (2003) argued that the low-level chunks used frequently by chess players develop into more complex (and more flexible) structures known as templates. A **template** is a schematic structure more general than actual board positions. It consists of a *core* (very similar to the information stored in chunks) plus *slots* (containing variable information about pieces and locations).

According to template theory (Gobet & Waters, 2003), chess positions are typically stored in three templates, with each template storing information relating to about 10 pieces. It is assumed that outstanding chess players owe their excellence mostly to their superior template-based knowledge of chess and their ability to form larger templates. This knowledge can be accessed rapidly, thus allowing them to narrow down with great speed the possible moves they need to consider. Finally, it is predicted that expert chess players will have better recall of random chess positions than nonexperts, because some patterns relating to stored templates occur by chance even in random positions.

Most findings support template theory. Gobet and Clarkson (2004) found that the superior recall of chess-board positions by expert players was a result of the larger size of their templates—the maximum template size was about 13–15 for masters compared to only six for beginners. The number of templates didn't vary as a function of playing strength and averaged out at about two, close to the predicted figure of three.

According to template theory, individual differences in chess-playing ability are a result more of differences in template-based knowledge than of the ability to search successfully through possible moves. Relevant evidence was reported by Burns (2004). He used information about expert chess players' performance in normal competitive games and in blitz chess, in which the entire game has to be completed in 5 minutes (less than 5% of the time available in normal chess). The key assumption was that any player's performance in blitz chess must depend mainly on his/her template-based knowledge because there is so little time to engage in relatively slow search processes. Thus,

Key Term
Template:
as applied to chess, an abstract, schematic structure consisting of a mixture of fixed and variable information about chess pieces.

template-based knowledge is readily available to players in both blitz and normal chess, whereas search processes are much more available in normal chess than in blitz chess. If template theory is correct, then players performing best in normal chess should also perform best in blitz chess—the reason is that the key to successful chess (i.e., template-based knowledge) is available in both forms of chess.

What did Burns (2004) find? Performance in blitz chess correlated highly with performance in normal chess. In three samples, the correlation varied between +.78 and +.90, indicating that template theory is correct in emphasizing the importance of template-based knowledge. However, we must *not* draw the conclusion that search processes are irrelevant—the same players playing chess under normal conditions and under blitz conditions made superior moves in the former condition that provided time for much slow searching.

Gobet and Waters (2003) tested the prediction that experts will recall random chess positions better than nonexperts. Their findings supported template theory (see the figure below): the number of pieces recalled was significantly higher for the most expert players than for the least expert ones.

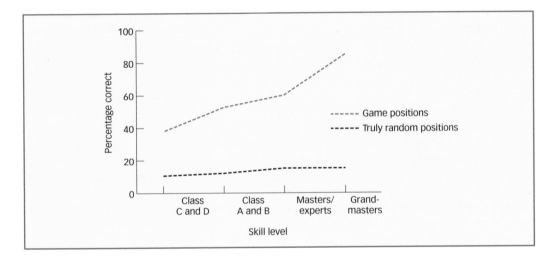

Percentage of pieces correctly recalled by class C and D players (weak club standard), class A and B players (moderate or strong club players), masters/experts, and grandmasters. Adapted from Gobet and Waters (2003).

Evaluation

+ Outstanding chess players possess much more template-based knowledge of chess positions than nonexperts; this knowledge allows them to assess chess positions very rapidly.

+ Template theory provides an explanation for the effective performance of experts playing blitz chess and their superior ability to recall random chess positions.

− Charness (1981) found that experts and grandmasters think about five moves ahead whereas class D players (who have a low level of skill) think only an average of 2.3 moves ahead. This difference cannot be readily accounted for in terms of template knowledge.

− Hatano and Inagaki (1986) distinguished between **routine expertise** (involved when a player can solve familiar chess problems rapidly and efficiently) and **adaptive expertise** (involved when a player has to develop a strategy when confronted by a novel board position). Template theory provides a convincing account of what is involved in routine expertise, but doesn't shed much light on adaptive expertise.

Key Terms

Routine expertise: using acquired knowledge to develop strategies for dealing with novel problems; see **adaptive expertise**.

Adaptive expertise: using acquired knowledge to solve familiar problems efficiently; see **routine expertise**.

DELIBERATE PRACTICE

We all know that prolonged and carefully organized practice is essential in the development of *any* kind of expertise. However, what we really need is a theory spelling out the details of what is involved in effective practice. Precisely that was done by Ericsson and Lehmann (1996), who emphasized that a wide range of expertise can be developed through deliberate practice. **Deliberate practice** has four aspects:

1. The task is at an appropriate level of difficulty (not too easy or too hard).
2. The learner is given informative feedback about his/her performance.
3. The learner has adequate chances to repeat the task.
4. The learner has the opportunity to correct his/her errors.

What exactly happens as a result of prolonged deliberate practice? According to Ericsson and Kintsch (1995), experts can get round the limited capacity of working memory. They proposed the notion of **long-term working memory**: Experts learn how to store relevant information in long-term memory so it can be accessed readily through retrieval cues held in working memory. This doesn't mean that experts have greater working memory capacity than the rest of us. Rather, they are more efficient at combining the resources of long-term memory and working memory.

Where the approach adopted by Ericsson and Lehmann (1996) becomes controversial is in the additional assumption that deliberate practice is *all* that is needed to develop expert performance. Thus, innate talent or ability is said to have practically no influence on expert performance.

Findings

Evidence supporting the theory was reported by Ericsson, Krampe, and Tesch-Römer (1993) who studied violinists in a German music academy. The key difference between 18-year-old students having varying levels of expertise on the violin was the amount of deliberate practice they had had over the years. The most expert violinists had spent on average nearly 7500 hours engaged in deliberate practice compared to the mere (!) 5300 hours clocked up by the good violinists.

A potential problem with the study by Ericsson et al. (1993) is that their evidence was correlational and so doesn't prove that deliberate practice *caused* the higher level of performance. Perhaps those musicians with the greatest innate talent and/or musical success chose to spend more time practicing than those with less talent. However, some evidence goes against that interpretation. Sloboda, Davidson, Howe, and Moore (1996) compared highly successful young musicians with less successful ones. The two groups didn't differ in the amount of practice time they required to achieve a given level of performance.

Is it really true that innate ability or IQ is irrelevant to the development of expertise? This issue was addressed by Hulin, Henry, and Noon (1990), who combined the data from numerous studies. There were two key findings:

1. The correlation or association between IQ and performance *decreased* steadily over time as expertise developed.
2. The correlation between IQ and performance was only very slightly positive among individuals with over 5 years of professional experience.

Not surprisingly, Hulin et al. (1990) concluded that innate ability (intelligence as assessed by IQ) is of little importance at high levels of expertise. However, many of the studies included in their analyses were concerned with fairly narrow types of learning, and so their conclusions may not apply to more general forms of learning.

One of the few studies to consider *both* the amount of deliberate practice and innate ability was reported by Horgan and Morgan (1990). Improvement in chess-playing performance was determined mainly by deliberate practice, motivation, and the degree of parental support. However, individual differences in nonverbal intelligence were also of importance, accounting for 12% of the variation in chess-playing performance.

Key Terms

Deliberate practice: systematic practice in which the learner is given informative feedback about his/her performance and has the opportunity to correct his/her errors.

Long-term working memory: this is used by experts to store relevant information in long-term memory and to access it through retrieval cues in **working memory**.

Case Study: *Practice Makes Perfect*

David Garret, once a child prodigy violinist, is now an adult virtuoso with a full concert and recording schedule. How did he get where he is? He started playing violin aged 4 and a year later was being taken from his home in Germany to Holland each weekend to study music. From 7 through 10 years old he was making a 6-hour journey every Thursday evening to practice and learn in northern Germany, with the return journey on Sunday nights, and at 10 he was playing with the Hamburg Philharmonic Orchestra. He was practicing 7 to 8 hours a day. Would his amazing performances be achievable by anyone who put in the same number of hours for the same number of years? What do you think?

Evaluation

⊕ Prolonged practice is clearly essential for the development of expertise.

⊕ The most effective form of practice is deliberate practice, and Ericsson and Lehmann (1996) have identified its key features.

⊖ Deliberate practice is typically necessary but *not* sufficient for the development of expertise, especially broadly based expertise. As Sternberg and Ben-Zeev (2001, p. 302) argued, "Is one to believe that anyone could become a Mozart if only he or she put in the time? . . . Or that becoming Einstein is just a matter of deliberate practice?"

⊖ The most important kind of expertise developed by most people consists of work-related skills. Work expertise (based on work performance) correlates +.58 with intelligence for high-complexity jobs (Gottfredson, 1997). Thus, work-related expertise is not determined entirely by deliberate practice.

Chapter Summary

Classical conditioning
- The repeated presentation of a conditioned stimulus shortly before an unconditioned stimulus produces classical conditioning.
- The repeated presentation of the conditioned stimulus on its own after classical conditioning has occurred produces experimental extinction.
- According to the Rescorla–Wagner model, the key feature of classical conditioning is that the conditioned stimulus *predicts* the arrival of the unconditioned stimulus. This accounts for the phenomenon of blocking and makes it clear why the conditioned stimulus must precede the unconditioned stimulus for conditioning to occur.
- According to the ecological perspective, associations are learned more readily between certain conditioned and unconditioned stimuli than others. Research on food-aversion learning supports this approach.

Operant conditioning
- Operant conditioning is produced by following a given response with reward. Extinction occurs when that response is no longer followed by reward.

- The pattern of responding in operant conditioning depends on the precise schedule of reinforcement used. The variable ratio schedule generally produces the fastest rate of responding, and continuous reinforcement the slowest rate.
- Effective operant conditioning can also be produced by positive punishment, negative punishment, and avoidance learning.
- Animals exposed to operant conditioning seem to learn means–end relationships, or what leads to what.
- Skinner assumed that virtually any response can be conditioned in any stimulus situation. This notion of equipotentiality is incorrect. What actually happens is more accurately predicted by the ecological approach.
- Skinner exaggerated the importance of external or environmental factors as influences on behavior and minimized the role of internal factors (e.g., goals).

Observational learning
- As Bandura argued, observational learning is an important method for acquiring new ways of behaving.
- There is evidence suggesting that observational learning is as effective as learning based on actually performing the behavior to be learned.
- The processes involved in observational learning can be much more complex than simply imitating someone else's behavior, including an assessment of the model's intentions.

Implicit learning
- Findings on healthy participants from the artificial grammar learning and serial reaction time tasks have apparently provided evidence for implicit learning. However, most studies fail to satisfy the information and sensitivity criteria.
- Amnesic patients have shown evidence of intact implicit learning but impaired explicit learning. However, we often don't know what information is being used by amnesic patients during implicit learning.
- There is some evidence that explicit learning and implicit learning involve different brain areas, with the prefrontal cortex being more activated during explicit learning. However, the findings are generally inconsistent.
- Most of the evidence is consistent with the notion that there is implicit learning as well as explicit learning on many tasks, with implicit learning often preceding explicit learning.

How do you become an expert?
- Idiot savants have very low IQs but nevertheless possess high levels of expertise on certain specific tasks. However, high intelligence is almost essential for developing the expertise needed to succeed in high-complexity jobs.
- Much of the expert knowledge possessed by top-level chess players is in the form of templates (schematic structures). Chess positions are typically stored in three templates with each template containing information relating to about 10 pieces.
- Grandmasters possess more template-based knowledge than lower-level players. In addition, they are superior strategically (e.g., thinking more moves ahead).
- According to Ericsson and Lehmann (1996), prolonged deliberate practice is all that is needed to develop expert performance. In fact, it is much more likely that deliberate practice is necessary but not sufficient.

Further Reading

- Eysenck, M.W. (2006). *Fundamentals of cognition*. Hove, UK: Psychology Press. Implicit learning (Chapter 13) and expertise (Chapter 25) are discussed in more detail in this textbook.
- French, R.M., & Cleeremans, A. (2002). *Implicit learning and consciousness: An empirical, philosophical and computational consensus in the making.*

Hove, UK: Psychology Press. This edited book contains useful contributions by several of the leading researchers on implicit learning.

- Gray, P. (2006). *Psychology* (5th ed.). New York: Worth. There are very clear accounts of classical and operant conditioning in this textbook.
- Robertson, S.I. (2001). *Problem solving*. Hove, UK: Psychology Press. Chapters 8 and 9 of this book contain good coverage of theory and research on expertise.
- Shanks, D.R. (2004). Implicit learning. In K. Lamberts and R. Goldstone (Eds.), *Handbook of cognition*. London: Sage. David Shanks puts forward a powerful case for being skeptical about the existence of implicit learning in this chapter.
- Staddon, J.E.F., & Cerutti, D.T. (2003). Operant conditioning. *Annual Review of Psychology*, *54*, 115–144. This article provides a reasonably up-to-date account of the modern complexities of research and theory on operant conditioning.

Chapter 8

Contents

Human memory

Imagine for a moment what it would be like to have no memory. You wouldn't recognize anyone or anything as familiar. You wouldn't be able to talk, read, or write, because you would have no knowledge of language. You would have a very limited personality, because you would know nothing about the events of your own life, and would therefore have no sense of self. The devastating effects associated with the progressive destruction of the human memory system can be seen in patients suffering from Alzheimer's disease.

There are numerous topics in the area of human memory, and only a few of the most important ones are covered here. We start with the fundamental distinction between short-term and long-term memory that has been influential throughout most of the history of research on human memory. We then move on to a more detailed consideration of current thinking on short-term memory, increasingly regarded as a complex working memory system involving processing and temporary storage of information. Next we address the issue of the number and nature of long-term memory systems that we possess. The other side of remembering is, of course, forgetting, which we discuss after having dealt thoroughly with short-term and long-term memory. Finally, we consider aspects of memory in everyday life. More specifically, we discuss autobiographical memory (the story of our lives) and eyewitness testimony (can we believe what eyewitnesses to a crime say they have seen and heard?). Some of the processes and structures involved in remembering stories and other texts are discussed in Chapter 9.

THE LONG AND THE SHORT OF MEMORY

What does human memory look like? Does it consist of a *single* memory system or does it consist of two or more memory systems? There are no easy answers to these questions. However, we start by arguing that there is an important distinction between the information stored away in our brains for periods of time running into months or years (long-term memory) and information held very briefly in memory (short-term memory).

Short-term memory has been assessed in various ways (see Cowan, 2000, for a review). For example, there is **digit span**: people listen to a random series of digits and then try to repeat them back immediately in the correct order. Other span measures are letter span and word span. The maximum number of units (e.g., digits) recalled without error is usually "seven plus or minus two" (Miller, 1956). However, two qualifications need to be put on that finding. First, Miller (1956) argued that the capacity of short-term memory should be assessed in terms of the number of **chunks** (integrated pieces or units of information). For example, "IBM" is *one* chunk for those familiar with the company name International Business Machines but *three* chunks for everyone else. The capacity of short-term memory as assessed by span measures has often been reported as being about seven chunks. However, Simon (1974) found that the span in chunks was less with larger chunks (e.g., eight-word phrases) than with smaller chunks (e.g., one-syllable words).

Second, Cowan (2000) argued that the capacity of short-term memory is only four chunks. According to him, estimates of short-term memory capacity are often inflated because participants' performance depends on rehearsal (i.e., saying the items under one's breath) and on long-term memory as well as on "pure" short-term memory capacity. When these additional factors are eliminated, the capacity of short-term memory is only four chunks. More generally, however, short-term memory capacity (whether four or seven chunks) is hugely less than the essentially unlimited capacity of long-term memory.

Key Terms

Digit span:
the number of random digits that can be repeated back correctly in order after hearing them once; it is used as a measure of short-term memory capacity.

Chunks:
stored units formed from integrating smaller pieces of information.

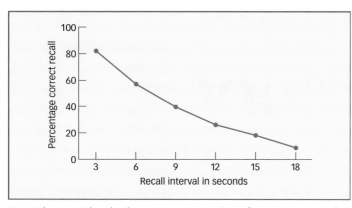

Forgetting over time in short-term memory. Data from Peterson and Peterson (1959).

Another (very obvious) difference between short-term and long-term memory is in the length of time for which information is remembered. Much information (e.g., our own names; the names of our parents and friends) remains in long-term memory for a lifetime, whereas information in short-term memory is lost rapidly. Peterson and Peterson (1959) studied the duration of short-term memory by using the task of remembering a three-letter stimulus while counting backwards by threes. The ability to remember the three letters in the correct order reduced to only about 50% after 6 seconds and forgetting was almost complete after 18 seconds (see the figure on the left).

What is the most convincing evidence that short-term and long-term memory are distinct? Surprisingly, the strongest evidence comes from brain-damaged patients! Suppose there was only *one* memory system dealing with short-term and long-term memory. If that one and only memory system were damaged, performance would be impaired on *all* memory tasks regardless of whether they involved short-term or long-term memory. In contrast, suppose there are separate short-term and long-term memory systems located in different parts of the brain. It follows that some brain-damaged patients should have impaired long-term memory but intact short-term memory, whereas others should have impaired short-term memory but intact long-term memory. If such findings were obtained, they would form a **double dissociation** (i.e., some patients perform normally on task A but poorly on task B, whereas others perform normally on task B but poorly on task A).

The findings from brain-damaged patients provide evidence for a double dissociation. Patients with **amnesia** have severe problems with long-term memory but have essentially intact short-term memory as assessed by span measures. Indeed, Spiers, Maguire, and Burgess (2001) in a review of 147 amnesic patients concluded that *none* had a significant problem with short-term memory. There are also a few patients having severely impaired short-term memory but intact long-term memory. For example, consider K.F., who suffered brain damage after a motorcycle accident. He had no problems with long-term learning and recall, but his digit span was greatly impaired (Shallice & Warrington, 1970).

Key Terms

Double dissociation: the finding that some individuals (often brain-damaged) do well on task A and poorly on task B, whereas others show the opposite pattern.

Amnesia: a condition caused by brain damage in which there is substantial impairment of long-term memory; the condition includes both **anterograde amnesia** and **retrograde amnesia**.

MULTI-STORE MODEL

How are short-term and long-term memory related? An influential answer was provided by Atkinson and Shiffrin (1968) in their multi-store model (see the figure below). They assumed that stimulation from the environment is initially received by the sensory stores. These stores are modality-specific, meaning there is a separate one for each sensory modality (e.g., vision; hearing). Information is held briefly in the sensory stores, with some fraction being attended to and processed further within the short-term store. The short-term store itself has very limited capacity. Some information processed in the short-term store is transferred to the long-term store, which has unlimited capacity. Long-term storage of information often depends on rehearsal, with a direct relationship between the amount of rehearsal in the short-term store and the strength of the stored memory trace.

According to Atkinson and Shiffrin (1968), short-term memory is involved *before* long-term memory. However, an increasingly popular view is that short-term memory is only involved *after* long-term memory. According to Ruchkin, Grafman, Cameron, and Berndt (2003, p. 711), "Short-term memory corresponds to activated long-term memory and information is stored in the same systems that initially processed the information." For once, a theoretical controversy can be resolved without discussing experimental findings in detail. The information processed in short-term memory *must* already have made contact with information in long-term memory (Logie, 1999). For example, our ability to engage in verbal rehearsal of

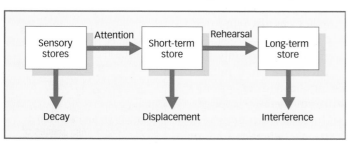

The multi-store model of memory.

visually presented words depends on prior contact with stored information concerning pronunciation. In similar fashion, we can only rehearse "IBM" as a single chunk in short-term memory by using relevant information stored in long-term memory. Thus, access to long-term memory occurs *before* information is processed in short-term memory.

There is another reason why Atkinson and Shiffrin's (1968) assumption that information is processed in short-term memory before reaching long-term memory should be rejected (Marc Brysbaert, personal communication). Atkinson and Shiffrin assumed that information in short-term memory represents "the contents of consciousness," implying that *only* information processed consciously can be stored in long-term memory. However, there is reasonable (if not conclusive) evidence for the existence of learning without conscious awareness of what has been learned (this is known as implicit learning—see Chapter 7). It would seem that implicit learning would be impossible within Atkinson and Shiffrin's (1968) model.

Evaluation

- The assumption within the model that there are separate short-term and long-term stores has been influential and is approximately correct.

- As we will see, it is a gross oversimplification to argue that there is a *single* short-term memory store (see section on working memory).

- It is a gross oversimplification to argue that there is a *single* long-term memory store (see section on types of long-term memory). It seems very doubtful that knowledge that Russell Crowe is a film star, that 2 +2 = 4, that we had muesli for breakfast, and information about how to ride a bicycle are all stored in the same long-term memory store.

- It doesn't make sense to argue that processing in the short-term store occurs before contact has been made with long-term memory.

- In contradiction of the assumptions of the multi-store model, learning can probably occur without conscious awareness of what has been learned.

WORKING MEMORY

What is the point of short-term memory in everyday life? Textbook writers sometimes argue that it allows us to remember a telephone number for the few seconds taken to dial it. However, even that function is rapidly becoming obsolete now most people have mobile phones that store all the phone numbers needed on a regular basis.

In 1974, two British psychologists, Alan Baddeley and Graham Hitch, came up with a convincing answer to the above question. They argued that we use short-term memory much of the time when engaged in the performance of complex tasks. You have to carry out various processes to complete the task, but you also have to briefly store information about the outcome of early processes in short-term memory as you move on to later processes. For example, suppose you were given the addition problem 13 + 18 + 24. You would probably add 13 and 18 and keep the answer (i.e., 31) in short-term memory. You would then add 24 to 31 and produce the correct answer of 55. Baddeley and Hitch (1974) used the term **working memory** to refer to a system combining processing and short-term memory functions. According to Baddeley and Logie (1999, p. 28), "Working memory comprises multiple specialized components of cognition that allow humans to comprehend and mentally represent their immediate environment, to retain information about their immediate past experience, to support the acquisition of new knowledge, to solve problems, and to formulate, relate, and act on current goals."

As we saw earlier, Atkinson and Shiffrin (1968) emphasized the importance of verbal rehearsal in short-term memory. Baddeley (e.g., 1986, 2001) accepted that verbal

Key Term

Working memory:
a system having the functions of cognitive processing and the temporary storage of information.

rehearsal is important. However, he argued that other kinds of information can also be stored in short-term memory. For example, suppose you are driving along focusing on steering the car, avoiding pedestrians, and keeping a safe distance behind the car in front. In addition, you may be holding some visual and spatial information in short-term memory (e.g., speed limit on the road; width of the road; the distance of the car behind you) to assist you in driving.

In what follows, we will mainly consider the theoretical approach to working memory put forward by Baddeley and his colleagues. However, other theorists have proposed different approaches to working memory. These other approaches are discussed in a book edited by Miyake and Shah (1999).

WORKING MEMORY MODEL

Baddeley's basic working memory model consisted of three components:

- *Central executive*: This is a limited-capacity processing system resembling attention. It is modality-free, meaning it can process information from any sensory modality (e.g., visual; auditory).
- *Phonological loop*: This is a temporary storage system holding verbal information in a phonological (speech-based) form; it is used for verbal rehearsal.
- *Visuospatial sketchpad*: This is a temporary memory system holding spatial and/or visual information.

The working memory system is hierarchical (see the figure below). The phonological loop and the visuospatial sketchpad are both "slave" systems at the base of the hierarchy. They are slave systems in the sense that they are used by the central executive or attention-like system for various purposes. This figure also shows the episodic buffer, which was only added to the working memory model 25 years after it was first put forward. The episodic buffer is a limited-capacity storage system that integrates information from the phonological loop and the visuospatial sketchpad. Since relatively little is as yet known about the episodic buffer, we won't be discussing it further.

The major components of Baddeley's working memory system. Figure adapted from Baddeley (2001).

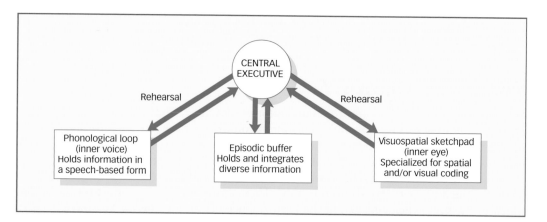

All three components of the basic working memory system have limited capacity. However, each component can function relatively independently of the others. These assumptions permit us to make two crucial predictions concerning whether two tasks can be performed successfully at the same time:

1. If two tasks require the *same* component of working memory, they can't be performed successfully together, because that component's limited capacity will be exceeded.
2. If two tasks require *different* components, it should be possible to perform them as well together as separately.

At this point, let's consider a concrete example of how this works in practice. Robbins et al. (1996) wondered which components of working memory are involved in playing chess. Weaker and stronger players selected continuation moves from various chess positions while performing one of the following secondary tasks at the same time:

- *Random number generation*: This task requires participants to try to produce a random series of digits; it involves the central executive.
- *Pressing keys on a keypad in a clockwise pattern*: This task involves the visuospatial sketchpad.
- *Rapid repetition of the word "see-saw"*: This task involves the phonological loop.
- *Repetitive tapping*: This very simple task places minimal demands on working memory.

Before we discuss the findings, ask yourself which components of working memory you think are involved in playing chess. Chess is a mentally demanding game, and so probably involves the central executive. It also requires considering the layout of the pieces on the board, and so presumably involves the visuospatial sketchpad. The findings were in line with these predictions (see the figure below). The quality of the chess moves selected was reduced by random number generation and by pressing keys in a clockwise fashion, secondary tasks using the central executive and the visuospatial sketchpad, respectively. In contrast, rapid word repetition didn't reduce the quality of chess moves, and so the phonological loop is *not* involved in selecting chess moves. The effects of the various secondary tasks on the quality of the chess moves selected were similar for weaker and stronger players, meaning that both groups used the working memory system similarly when choosing moves. There is more coverage of dual-task performance in Chapter 6.

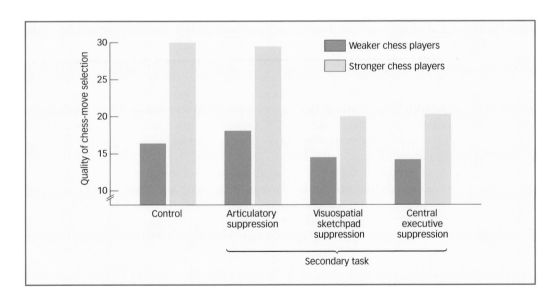

Effects of secondary tasks on quality of chess-move selection in stronger and weaker players. Adapted from Robbins et al. (1996).

Phonological loop

Why do we need a phonological loop? According to Baddeley, Gathercole, and Papagno (1998), it is very useful when we are learning new words. Supporting evidence was provided by Papagno, Valentine, and Baddeley (1991). They found that the learning of foreign vocabulary was greatly slowed down when participants performed another task using the resources of the phonological loop at the same time.

Most early research on the phonological loop focused on the notion that verbal rehearsal (i.e., saying words over and over to oneself) is of central importance. Evidence for this comes from the **phonological similarity effect**. When a short list of visually presented words has to be recalled immediately in the correct order, recall performance is worse when the words are phonologically similar (i.e., having similar sounds). For example, FEE, HE, KNEE, LEE, ME, and SHE form a list of phonologically similar words, whereas BAY, HOE, IT, ODD, SHY, and UP form a list of phonologically

Key Term

Phonological similarity effect:
the finding that immediate recall of word lists in the correct order is impaired when the words sound similar to each other.

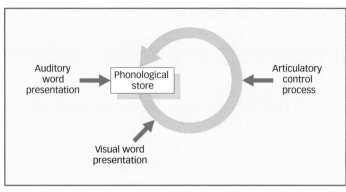

Phonological loop system as envisaged by Baddeley (1990).

dissimilar words. Larsen, Baddeley, and Andrade (2000) used those lists, and found ordered recall was 25% worse with the phonologically similar list. This phonological similarity effect occurs because participants use speech-based rehearsal processes within the phonological loop.

According to Baddeley (1986, 1990), the phonological loop has two main components (see the figure on the left). There is a phonological or speech-based store and an articulatory control process. The phonological store is directly concerned with speech *perception*, whereas the articulatory process is linked to speech *production*. Supporting evidence comes from studies on brain-damaged patients. Some patients have very poor short-term memory for words presented auditorily but have normal speech production (Vallar & Baddeley, 1984). These patients have a damaged phonological store but an intact articulatory control process. Other patients have the opposite pattern of an intact phonological store but a damaged articulatory process preventing verbal rehearsal (Vallar, Di Betta, & Silveri, 1997).

Visuospatial sketchpad

The visuospatial sketchpad is used for the temporary storage and manipulation of visual patterns and spatial movement. It is used in many situations in everyday life (e.g., finding the route when walking; playing computer games). Logie et al. (1989) studied performance on a complex computer game called Space Fortress, which involves maneuvering a space ship around a computer screen. Performance on Space Fortress was initially severely impaired when participants also performed a secondary visuospatial task. However, the adverse effects were greatly reduced after 20 hours of training. Thus, participants made more use of the visuospatial sketchpad early in practice than later on.

A key issue is whether there is a *single* system combining visual and spatial processing or whether there are *separate* visual and spatial systems. Klauer and Zhao (2004) explored this issue. They used two main tasks: one was a spatial task (memory for dot locations) and the other was a visual task (memory for Chinese ideographs). There were also three secondary task conditions: (1) a movement discrimination task (spatial interference); (2) a color discrimination task (visual interference); and (3) a control condition (no secondary task).

What would we predict if there are separate spatial and visual processes? First, the spatial interference task should disrupt performance more on the spatial main task than on the visual main task. Second, the visual interference task should disrupt performance more on the visual main task than on the spatial main task. Both predictions were confirmed (see the figure on the left).

Central executive

The central executive, which resembles an attentional system, is the most important and versatile component of the working memory system. Alas, it is also the least well understood. The central executive is used to perform several functions, but it has proved difficult to establish the number (and nature) of these functions. However, Miyake et al. (2000) and Friedman and Miyake (2004) have provided evidence for three major functions of the central executive:

1. *Inhibition + resistance to distractor interference*: This function is used to prevent task-irrelevant stimuli (and responses) from interfering with performance on a current task.

Amount of interference on a spatial task (dots) and a visual task (ideographs) as a function of secondary task (spatial: movement discrimination vs. visual: color discrimination). From Klauer and Zhao (2004). Copyright © American Psychological Association. Reprinted with permission.

2. *Shifting*: This function is used to shift attention from one task to another. For example, if you were presented with a list of two-digit numbers and had to alternate between adding 3 and subtracting 3 from the numbers (i.e., add 3 to the first number, subtract 3 from the second number, and so on), this would involve the shifting function.

3. *Updating and monitoring*: This function is used when information being held in working memory has to be updated by new information. For example, it would be used if you had to keep track of the last four letters presented in a sequence such as T H G B S K R W F.

Which brain areas are used for central executive functions? According to a review by Collette and Van der Linden (2002), the prefrontal cortex is activated during the performance of most central executive tasks, but other areas including parietal cortex are also sometimes activated. It is unsurprising that the prefrontal cortex should be activated, since it is involved in numerous complex cognitive processes.

TYPES OF LONG-TERM MEMORY

It was argued earlier that the assumption within the multi-store model that there is a single long-term store is highly dubious. Some of the most convincing evidence that there are various long-term memory systems has come from amnesic patients who have serious problems with long-term memory. Before we discuss the relevant experimental evidence, we will have a closer look at amnesia.

AMNESIA

When considering the memory problems of amnesic patients, it is important to distinguish between anterograde and retrograde amnesia. **Anterograde amnesia** involves poor long-term memory for information learned *after* the onset of the amnesia—the findings discussed earlier in the chapter relate to anterograde amnesia. In contrast, **retrograde amnesia** involves poor long-term memory for information learned *before* the onset of amnesia. The extent of retrograde amnesia varies considerably from patient to patient. However, there is generally a *temporal gradient*, with forgetting being greater for memories acquired closer to the onset of the amnesia than those acquired longer ago.

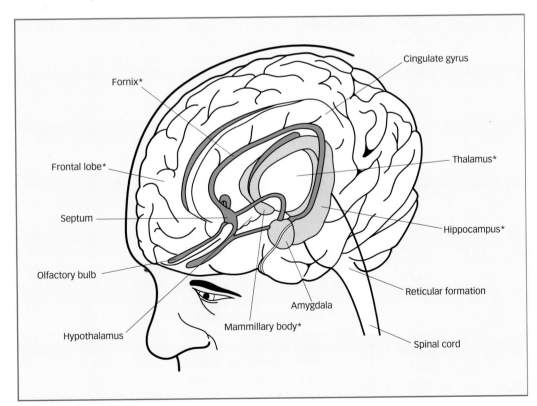

Diagram of the limbic system and related structures. Areas indicated with an asterisk are known to be associated with memory function. From Parkin (2001).

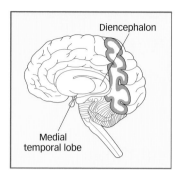

Amnesic patients vary in the precise brain areas damaged. However, the key structures are in a sub-cortical brain region (the diencephalon) and a cortical region (the medial temporal lobe) (see the figures on the left and on the previous page).

The devastating effects of amnesia can be seen in the case of Clive Wearing, one of the most extreme cases of amnesia ever recorded (see France, 2005, for a detailed discussion). He was a successful 46-year-old musician and Renaissance music scholar. On Tuesday March 26, 1985, he suddenly developed a high temperature. This was as a result of encephalitis (infection of the brain) caused by herpes simplex, the cold-sore virus. As a result of the encephalitis, Clive Wearing can remember practically nothing of his daily activities and can't even remember the names of his children from his first marriage.

When Clive Wearing began to have a vague awareness that there was something terribly wrong with him, he wept almost nonstop for a month. One of his favorite questions was, "What's it like to have one long night lasting . . . how long? It's like being dead."

EXPLICIT VS. IMPLICIT MEMORY

It is perhaps natural to assume that patients with amnesia would have problems with *all* aspects of long-term memory, but that assumption is completely wrong. We can obtain some inkling of what is actually going on by considering a hackneyed anecdote from Edouard Claparède (1873–1940) reported by him in 1911. He studied a female patient (living in what Claparède described, with a total absence of political correctness, as a lunatic asylum!) who suffered from amnesia resulting from chronic alcoholism. She couldn't recognize doctors and nurses she saw virtually every day for several years, and she didn't know what day it was or her own age. One day, Claparède hid a pin in his hand before shaking hands with this patient. The following day she was very sensibly reluctant to shake hands with him but felt very embarrassed because she couldn't explain her reluctance.

What does this anecdote tell us? First, the patient had no conscious recollection of what had happened the previous day. Second, in spite of that, her *behavior* indicated very clearly that she *did* possess some long-term memory of what had happened. Thus, long-term memory can depend less on conscious recollection than we imagine.

Similar findings to those of Claparède (1911) have been obtained in much more recent studies on amnesic patients (see Parkin, 1996, for a review). For example, patients given a series of piano-playing lessons may have no conscious recollection of having received any previous lessons. However, their piano-playing ability typically improves as rapidly as that of normal controls—thus, their behavior shows that their long-term memory is very good in some ways. Such findings indicate the necessity of distinguishing between explicit and implicit memory: "Explicit memory is revealed when performance on a task requires conscious recollection of previous experiences . . . Implicit memory is revealed when performance on a task is facilitated in the absence of conscious recollection" (Graf & Schacter, 1985, p. 501). Thus, amnesic patients have impaired explicit memory but intact implicit memory.

Key Terms

Episodic memory:
a form of long-term memory concerned with personal experiences or episodes that happened in a given place at a specific time; see **semantic memory**.

Semantic memory:
a form of long-term memory consisting of general knowledge about the world, language, and so on; see **episodic memory**.

Declarative memory:
a form of long-term memory concerned with knowing that something is the case; it includes **episodic memory** and **semantic memory**.

EPISODIC AND SEMANTIC MEMORY

Tulving (1972) distinguished between two long-term memory systems he called episodic memory and semantic memory. **Episodic memory** involves conscious recollection of events or episodes from one's past, generally involving some memory for the relevant time and place. For example, you might remember meeting a friend at a café last Wednesday. In contrast, **semantic memory** is concerned with our general knowledge (e.g., "Paris is the capital of France"). Episodic and semantic memory are both forms of **declarative memory**, which is concerned with knowing that something is the case. They also involve explicit memory.

Do amnesic patients with anterograde amnesia always have impaired episodic and semantic memory for memories

acquired after the onset of amnesia? The most definitive answer was provided by Spiers et al. (2001) in their extensive review of 147 cases of amnesia. There was impaired episodic memory in *all* 147 cases, and many (but by no means all) also had poor ability to form new semantic memories. This evidence suggests that episodic memory is more vulnerable to impairment than semantic memory.

Stronger evidence that episodic and semantic may form separate memory systems was reported by Vargha-Khadem et al. (1997). Beth and Jon had suffered brain damage at an early age before they had had the chance to develop semantic memories. Both children had very poor episodic memory for the day's activities, television programs, and telephone conversations. In spite of this, Beth and Jon attended ordinary schools, and their levels of speech and language development, literacy, and factual knowledge (e.g., vocabulary) were within the normal range. Thus, they had very poor episodic memory but virtually intact semantic memory.

If episodic and semantic memory are really separate from each other, *why* do so many amnesics have great problems with both of them? Vargha-Khadem et al. (1997) argued that the brain areas of central importance to episodic memory and semantic memory are very close. Episodic memory depends mainly on the hippocampus, whereas semantic memory depends on its underlying cortices [outer layers]. Thus, brain damage sufficient to impair episodic memory will typically also impair semantic memory.

Finally, we turn to retrograde amnesia (impaired memory for learning occurring before the onset of amnesia). Tulving (2002, p. 13) discussed the case of a patient (KC) whose "retrograde amnesia is highly asymmetrical: he cannot recollect any personally experienced events ... whereas his semantic knowledge acquired before the critical accident is still reasonably intact. His knowledge of mathematics, history, geography, and other 'school subjects,' as well as his general knowledge of the world is not greatly different from others' at his educational level." The opposite pattern was reported by Yasuda, Watanabe, and Ono (1997). A female amnesic patient had very poor ability to remember public events, cultural items, historical figures, and some items of vocabulary from the time prior to the onset of the amnesia. However, she was reasonably good at remembering personal experiences from episodic memory dating back to the pre-amnesia period.

FORGETTING

Our ability to remember information and the events of our own lives is of tremendous importance. In the absence of memory, we would be in a similar position to a newborn infant, with everything seeming to be completely novel and surprising. It is useful to consider the factors leading to forgetting so we can minimize the amount of information we forget.

Most people believe their memory is worse than average, which if you think about it can't be true! Evidence that our memories can be poor for important information comes from the study of passwords. Brown, Bracken, Zoccoli, and Douglas (2004) found that 31% of their sample of American students admitted to having forgotten one or more passwords. As Brown et al. (2004, p. 650) pointed out, "We are faced with a continuing dilemma in personal password construction between security and convenience: fool the password hacker and you are likely to fool yourself." They found that 45% of students avoided this dilemma by using their own name in password construction—not the way to have a secure, unguessable password!

In spite of our generally pessimistic views of our own memory ability, most people feel they remember dramatic events (e.g., September 11) in much detail and with great accuracy over long periods of time. The term **flashbulb memories** is used to describe such memories. Brown and Kulik (1977) argued that flashbulb memories are more accurate

Key Term
Flashbulb memories: vivid and detailed memories of dramatic events (e.g., September 11).

What were you doing when you heard about the World Trade Center attacks on September 11 2001? Why do so many people have a vivid memory for this and other extremely emotional and important events?

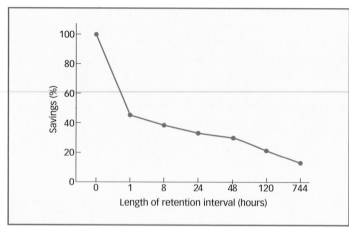

Forgetting over time as indexed by reduced savings. Data from Ebbinghaus (1885/1913).

Case Study: *What Happened to Susan?*

Zimbardo reports the case of Susan, an 8-year-old who vanished when playing with her friend. Twenty years later, when looking into her own daughter's eyes, this friend started to remember what had happened. She recalled her own father sexually assaulting Susan before killing her. He then threatened his own daughter with the same fate if she revealed what she had seen. As a result of the recovered memory there was a police investigation and the man concerned was convicted and imprisoned. This could be an example of a recovered repressed memory, and the memory would certainly fulfill Freud's concept of very threatening material. However, there is no way of testing whether this memory was truly repressed, or whether it was suppressed until the friend was adult enough to feel safe in remembering it.

and long-lasting than other memories because they activate a special neural mechanism that "prints" the details of dramatic events permanently in the memory system.

Alas, our flashbulb memories are often far less accurate than was predicted by Brown and Kulik (1977) or than we imagine. Pezdek (2003) asked American students the following question: "On September 11, did you see the videotape on television of the first plane striking the first tower?" Seventy-three percent of the students said "Yes," which is incorrect (only videotape of the *second* tower being hit was shown on September 11). Talarico and Rubin (2003) found (surprisingly) that students' memories for the events of September 11 changed as much as their memories for everyday events. However, the students *claimed* that their flashbulb memories were much more vivid than their everyday memories.

Why do we mistakenly think our flashbulb memories are vivid and long-lasting? Winningham, Hyman, and Dinnel (2000) provided an important part of the answer. They studied memory for the unexpected acquittal of O.J. Simpson (a retired American football star) who had been accused of murdering his ex-wife and her friend. They found that people's memories changed considerably in the first few days after hearing about the acquittal but became consistent after that. This version of a dramatic event that is constructed over the first few days afterwards may indeed be long-lasting and vivid. However, it is *not* what we memorized at the time of learning about the event.

The central issue in forgetting research was identified by the German psychologist Hermann Ebbinghaus (1885/1913). He carried out extensive studies with himself as the only participant (not a practice to be recommended or copied!). His basic approach involved learning a list of nonsense syllables having little or no meaning. He then re-learned the list and assessed forgetting by the savings method (the reduction in the number of trials during re-learning compared to original learning). As can be seen in the figure on the left, forgetting increased over time (this is known as the forgetting curve). Explaining *why* this happens is the goal of much forgetting research.

ARE TRAUMATIC MEMORIES REPRESSED?

The bearded Austrian psychologist Sigmund Freud (1856–1939) put forward one of the most influential theories of forgetting. According to him, very threatening or traumatic memories are often stored in the unconscious and can't gain access to conscious awareness—this phenomenon is known as **repression**. However, Freud sometimes used the concept of repression to refer merely to the inhibition of the capacity for emotional experience (Madison, 1956), with traumatic memories being consciously accessed but drained of their emotional significance.

The whole issue of repression is the subject of current debate. Much of the relevant evidence is based on adult patients claiming to have recovered repressed memories of sexual and/or physical abuse suffered in childhood. There is controversy as to whether these recovered memories are genuine or false.

Andrews et al. (1999) reported evidence supporting the view that many recovered memories are genuine. They obtained detailed information from over 200 patients, and found 41% had supporting evidence for their claims (e.g., someone else had also reported being abused by the alleged perpetrator). In addition, 22% of the patients claimed the trigger for the first recovered memory occurred before therapy started. This is important, because it is often assumed that direct pressure from the therapist influences patients' false memories. For example, Lief and Fetkewicz (1995) studied 40 patients who had admitted their "memories" of childhood abuse were false. In 80% of these cases, the therapist had made direct suggestions that the patient had been the victim of childhood abuse.

Evidence casting some doubt on recovered memories was reported by Clancy, Schacter, McNally, and Pitman (2000). They used a memory task known to produce false memories: people are given lists of words all related in meaning, and then falsely "recognize" other words related in meaning to those presented. They compared women with recovered memories of childhood abuse with women who believed they had been sexually abused but couldn't recall the abuse, women who had always remembered being abused, and control women. Women reporting recovered memories showed higher levels of false recognition than any of the other groups (see the figure above). As Clancy et al. (2000, p. 30) concluded, "The results are consistent with the hypothesis that women who report recovered memories of sexual abuse are more prone than others to develop certain types of illusory memories."

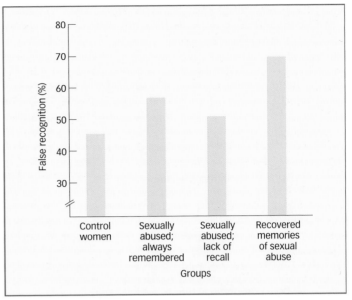

False recognition of a word related to those presented in four groups of women (controls; sexually abused, always remembered; sexually abused, lack of recall; and women with recovered memories of sexual abuse). Data from Clancy et al. (2000).

Evaluation

+ There is strong evidence that repressed memories of childhood abuse exist.

− Some recovered memories have been shown to be false (e.g., Lief & Fetkewicz, 1995).

− Repression theory is very limited, because most forgetting doesn't relate to traumatic events.

INTERFERENCE THEORY

If any of your female acquaintances are married, you may have found yourself remembering their maiden name rather than their married name. Thus, what used to be their name interferes with or disrupts your ability to recall their current name. The notion that interference is important in forgetting can be traced back at least to the nineteenth century and to a German psychologist called Hugo Münsterberg (1863–1916). Men had pocket watches in those days, and Münsterberg kept his watch in one particular pocket. When he started to keep it in a different pocket (for reasons lost in the mists of time), he found he was often fumbling around in confusion when asked for the time.

The above anecdote shows the key features of what became known as interference theory. Münsterberg had learned an association between the stimulus, "What's the time, Hugo?," and the response of removing the watch from his pocket. Subsequently the stimulus remained the same, but a different response was now associated with it. This is an example of **proactive interference**, in which previous learning disrupts later learning

After reorganizing the contents of kitchen cupboards, you may find yourself looking for something in its old location, even weeks after everything has been moved. This is an example of interference—memory for the old location is interfering with memory for the new one.

Methods of testing for proactive and retroactive interference

Proactive interference

Group	Learn	Learn	Test
Experimental	A–B (e.g. Cat–Tree)	A–C (e.g. Cat–Dirt)	A–C (e.g. Cat–Dirt)
Control	–	A–C (e.g. Cat–Dirt)	A–C (e.g. Cat–Dirt)

Retroactive interference

Group	Learn	Learn	Test
Experimental	A–B (e.g. Cat–Tree)	A–C (e.g. Cat–Dirt)	A–B (e.g. Cat–Tree)
Control	A–B (e.g. Cat–Tree)	–	A–B (e.g. Cat–Tree)

Note: for both proactive and retroactive interference, the experimental group exhibits interference. On the test, only the first word is supplied, and the subjects must provide the second word.

and memory (see the box on the left). There is also **retroactive interference**, in which later learning disrupts memory for earlier learning (see the box on the left). Proactive and retroactive interference are both greatest when two different responses are associated with the same stimulus (e.g., Münsterberg with his watch), intermediate when two similar stimuli are involved, and least with two very different stimuli (Underwood & Postman, 1960).

Numerous laboratory studies have produced large proactive and retroactive interference effects. Many of these studies involved paired-associate learning (e.g., learn "Cat–Tree" and then respond "Tree" when "Cat" is presented on its own). These findings with artificial tasks don't necessarily mean that interference is important in everyday life. However, Isurin and McDonald (2001) argued that retroactive interference explains why people forget some of their first language when acquiring a second language. Bilingual participants fluent in two languages were first presented with various pictures and the corresponding words in Russian or Hebrew. Some were then presented with the same pictures and the corresponding words in the other language. Finally, they were tested for recall of the words in the first language. There was substantial retroactive interference—recall of the first-language words became progressively worse the more learning trials there were with the second-language words.

It has generally been assumed that individuals who find their memory performance disrupted by interference *passively* allow themselves to suffer from interference. However, doesn't it seem likely that you would adopt some *active* strategy to minimize any interference effects? Kane and Engle (2000) explored this issue. They found that intelligent individuals with high attentional capacity were better able to resist proactive interference than less intelligent ones with low attentional capacity.

Evaluation

+ Much forgetting inside and outside the laboratory is a result of proactive and retroactive interference.
+ As predicted, the amount of interference (proactive or retroactive) is greatest when the same stimulus is paired with two different responses.
- Interference theory tells us little about the internal processes involved in forgetting.
- Interference theory accounts for much forgetting, but doesn't directly explain the precise nature of the forgetting curve.

Key Term

Retroactive interference: disruption of memory by learning of other material during the retention interval; see **proactive interference**.

Encoding specificity principle: the notion that retrieval depends on the overlap between the information available at retrieval and the information within the memory trace.

CUE-DEPENDENT FORGETTING

Tulving (e.g., 1979) argued that successful retrieval depends on two kinds of information: (1) the information stored in the memory trace; and (2) the information available at the time of retrieval. We are most likely to remember something when the information available at the time of retrieval *matches* the information in the memory trace. This is known as the **encoding specificity principle**. Tulving also assumed that the memory trace generally contains contextual information (e.g., the learner's mood state; details of the room in which learning occurs) in addition to information about the to-be-remembered material.

What does Tulving's approach tell us about forgetting? In essence, memory performance will be worse (and so forgetting will be greater) when the contextual information present at the time of retrieval *differs* from that stored in memory. This effect (illustrated by **mood-state-dependent memory**) was shown amusingly in the film *City Lights*. Charlie Chaplin saves a drunken millionaire from attempted suicide and is befriended in return. When the millionaire sees Charlie again, he is sober and fails to recognize him. However, when the millionaire becomes drunk again, he treats Charlie like a long-lost friend, and takes him home with him. The next morning, when the millionaire is sober again, he forgets that Charlie is his invited guest, and gets his butler to throw him out.

The film *City Lights* illustrates the concept of mood-state-dependent memory.

Kenealy (1997) obtained good evidence for mood-state-dependent memory. She put people into a happy or sad mood before asking them to look at a map and learn instructions concerning a given route. The next day they were again put into a happy or sad mood, and told to recall as much information as possible. There was much more forgetting when the mood at learning and at test was different than when it was the same (see the figure on the right).

We all know that recognition memory is better than recall. For example, we may be unable to recall the name of an acquaintance, but if someone mentions their name we recognize it instantly. Why is recognition memory generally better than recall? According to Tulving, the match between the information in the memory trace and that available on the memory test is typically greater on a recognition test (the whole item is presented). Intriguingly, however, Tulving's theory predicts that recall *can* be better than recognition memory provided that the information in the recall cue matches the stored information better than the information in the recognition cue.

The above prediction was tested by Muter (1978). Participants were presented with names of people (e.g., DOYLE) and told to circle those they "recognized as a person who was famous before 1950." They were then given recall cues in the following form (e.g., author of the Sherlock Holmes stories: Sir Arthur Conan _____). You may well have found the recall item easier than the recognition one because so much more information was supplied. What Muter (1978) discovered was that participants recognized only 29% of the names but recalled 42% of them.

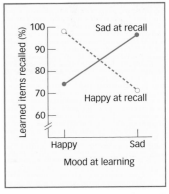

Free recall as a function of mood state (happy or sad) at learning and at recall. Based on data in Kenealy (1997).

Evaluation

+ What we remember or forget depends in part on the extent to which information in the memory trace matches that available at the time of retrieval.

+ There is reasonable evidence for mood-state-dependent memory.

+ There is evidence (e.g., Muter, 1978) for the surprising prediction that recall can be better than recognition memory.

− Retrieval is often more complex than simply comparing the information in the memory trace with that available on the memory test. For example, you might use a complex strategy to remember what you did 6 days ago.

− Tulving (1979) assumed that context influenced recall and recognition in the same way. In fact, however, it generally influences recall much more than recognition (Godden & Baddeley, 1975, 1980).

Key Terms

Mood-state-dependent memory: the finding that memory is better when the mood state at retrieval is the same as that at learning than it is when the two mood states differ.

Consolidation: a process mostly completed within several hours, but which can last for years, which fixes information in **long-term memory**.

CONSOLIDATION IS THE ANSWER!

The most adequate answer to the question of why the forgetting curve exists is provided by consolidation theory. According to this theory, **consolidation** is a long-lasting process fixing information in long-term memory. The theory's crucial assumption is that recently formed memories in an early stage of consolidation are especially vulnerable to interference and forgetting. More specifically, "New memories are clear but fragile and old ones are faded but robust" (Wixted, 2004, p. 265). The initial phase of consolidation lasts for several hours and is centered on the hippocampus.

Support for consolidation theory comes from patients with retrograde amnesia, in which there is impaired memory for events occurring before the onset of the amnesia. Many of these patients have damage to the hippocampus, and so memories formed just before the accident should be most impaired. This pattern has been found in numerous patients with retrograde amnesia (Manns, Hopkins, & Squire, 2003).

The assumption that memories are most vulnerable during the early stages of consolidation has been tested in studies on interference. We saw earlier that retroactive interference can cause forgetting. According to consolidation theory, people should be most susceptible to retroactive interference *early* in the retention interval. There is much experimental support for this prediction (see Wixted, 2004, for a review).

Evaluation

+ Consolidation provides a plausible explanation of *why* the rate of forgetting decreases over time.

+ Consolidation theory successfully predicts that retrograde interference effects will be greater shortly after learning has occurred than they will be later on.

− Consolidation provides a rather general account, and doesn't explain why retroactive interference is greatest when two different responses are associated with the same stimulus.

− Consolidation theory has little or nothing to say about the mechanisms underlying cue-dependent forgetting.

Key Term

Ecological validity:
the extent to which the findings of laboratory studies are applicable to everyday settings and generalize to other locations, times, and measures.

Everyday memory research studies: Two contrasting examples of research into everyday memory

Green (1995) measured cognitive performances such as vigilance, reaction speed, and memory and then asked participants to complete a questionnaire. The memory and other deficits his tests showed up were in those who were on diets—and equivalent to deficits expected after drinking two units of alcohol. Further research confirmed his findings, but only for people dieting to lose weight, not those on diets for medical reasons. And people trying but not succeeding in losing weight had the greatest memory deficits. Green suggests that the cause of these deficits is psychological, a combination of anxiety/stress and the use of mental processing capacity in thinking about food, diet, and weight.

Chan, Ho, and Cheung (1998) investigated memory in women who had at least 6 years of music lessons before the age of 12, and in women with no musical training. None of her participants were professional musicians. She found no difference in visual memory between her two groups, but the women with the music lessons background did much better in memory tests involving words—possibly because their brains had the extra sound-processing experience. She suggests there might be an application of these findings in therapy for patients with language impairments.

EVERYDAY MEMORY

As you have read this chapter, you may have wondered whether memory in everyday life works in the same way as memory studied in the laboratory. The key issue here is that of **ecological validity**, which concerns the extent to which laboratory findings generalize (or are applicable) to real life. It is important not to exaggerate the seriousness of this issue. Laboratory studies provide clear and replicable findings under controlled conditions and have contributed much to our understanding of human memory. You might imagine that the way to increase our understanding of everyday memory would be to carry out studies in naturalistic conditions even if such studies lacked experimental control. However, what has actually proved very successful is to carry out laboratory tasks involving memory phenomena of importance in the real world. Two examples of this approach are discussed in the box on the left.

AUTOBIOGRAPHICAL MEMORY

Of all the hundreds of thousands (or even millions) of memories we possess, those relating to our own past, to the experiences we have had, and to the people who have really mattered to us have special importance and significance. This is the territory of autobiographical memory.

If you have read any autobiographies, you probably wondered whether the authors provided an unduly positive view of themselves and their accomplishments. Wilson and Ross (2003, p. 137) reviewed the evidence on autobiographical memories and concluded that, "People's constructions of themselves through time serve the function of creating a coherent—and largely favorable—view of their present selves and circumstances." For example, Karney and Frye (2002) found that spouses often recalled their past contentment as lower than their present level of satisfaction. However, this apparent improvement over time was generally illusory, because spouses mostly underestimated their past contentment.

What do elderly people remember?

Suppose we ask 70-year-olds to recall personal memories triggered by cue words. From which parts of their lives would most of the memories come? Is it really true that they mostly recall distant childhood memories? The short answer is, "No." As can be seen in the figure below, there are three key features when we look at the periods of their life from which 70-year-olds recall more and fewer memories:

- **Infantile amnesia** (also known as childhood amnesia): This is shown by the almost total lack of memories from the first 3 years of life.
- A **reminiscence bump**, consisting of a surprisingly large number of memories coming from the years of adolescence and early adulthood (especially 15 to 25).
- A *retention function* for memories up to 20 years old, with the older memories being less likely to be recalled than more recent ones. This merely reflects the normal course of forgetting and so won't be discussed further.

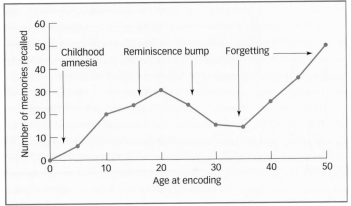

Idealized representation of the age at which autobiographical memories were formed in elderly people recalling the past. From Conway & Pleydell-Pearce (2000). Copyright © American Psychological Association. Reprinted with permission.

How can we explain infantile amnesia (a phenomenon found in adolescents and young adults as well as the elderly)? According to Freud's (1915/1957) famous (or notorious) account, it occurs through repression (discussed in the forgetting section), with threat-related experiences in early childhood being consigned to the unconscious. Alas, there is practically no support for this theoretical position, and it doesn't explain why *pleasant* early memories can't be recalled.

Howe and Courage (1997) argued that infants can only form autobiographical memories after they have developed a sense of self (they called it "cognitive self") towards the end of the second year of life. The finding that the cognitive self appears shortly before the onset of autobiographical memory fits the theory. Howe, Courage, and Edison (2003) found in infants aged between 15 and 23 months that those showing evidence of a cognitive self had better memory for personal events than infants who did not. When they studied a group of infants from 15 to 23 months, they found that no child showed good performance on a memory test for personal events before achieving self-recognition.

The social-cultural-developmental theory (Fivush & Nelson, 2004) emphasizes other factors involved in infantile amnesia. According to this theory, language and culture both play central roles in the early development of autobiographical memory. Language is important because we use language to communicate our memories, and experiences occurring before children develop language are hard for them to express in language later on. Support for this theory comes from Simcock and Hayne (2002). They asked young children of 3 and 4 to describe their memories for complex play activities that had occurred 12 months earlier. The children *only* used words they had known at the time of the event even though they had acquired hundreds of new words subsequently. Harley and Reese (1999) found there was less infantile amnesia in children whose mothers often discussed the past than in children whose mothers rarely talked about the past.

In sum, it is likely that the onset of autobiographical memory in infants depends on the emergence of the self. Its subsequent expression is heavily influenced by social factors,

Key Terms

Infantile amnesia:
the inability of adults to recall autobiographical memories from early childhood.

Reminiscence bump:
the tendency of older people to recall a disproportionate number of autobiographical memories from the years of adolescence and early adulthood.

cultural factors, and infants' development of language (see Baddeley, Anderson, & Eysenck, 2009).

How can we explain the reminiscence bump? According to Rubin, Rahhal, and Poon (1998), the key factors are novelty and stability. Early adulthood is a time of life in which many important novel events occur. Novel events have the advantage in memory that there is a relative lack of proactive interference (interference from previous similar events). A sense of adult identity develops in early childhood, and this heralds a period of relative stability. If the structure of autobiographical memory established in early adulthood remains fairly stable throughout the rest of one's life, it provides an effective way of cuing memories of early adulthood.

Pillemer, Goldsmith, Panter, and White (1988) showed that novelty is important. When they asked middle-aged people to recall four memories from their first year at college over 20 years previously, 41% of their autobiographical memories came from the first month of the course.

Theoretical views

According to Conway and Pleydell-Pearce (2000), autobiographical memory depends on an autobiographical memory base and the working self. The autobiographical memory base contains personal information at three levels of specificity: lifetime periods (e.g., time at high school; time spent living with someone); general events (e.g., a holiday in the United States); and event-specific knowledge (e.g., a specific occurrence on a holiday). The working self is concerned with the self, what it may become in future, and with the individual's current goals. The goals of the working self influence the memories stored within the autobiographical knowledge base and also help to determine which autobiographical memories we recall. As a result of the role played by the working self, "Autobiographical memories are primarily records of success or failure in goal attainment" (Conway & Pleydell-Pearce, 2000, p. 266).

Convincing evidence that our major goals influence our autobiographical memories was reported by Woike, Gershkovich, Piorkowski, and Polo (1999). They identified two types of personality: (1) agentic personality type, with an emphasis on independence, achievement, and personal power; and (2) communal personality type, with an emphasis on interdependence and similarity to others. Participants wrote about a positive or negative autobiographical memory. When the experience was positive, nearly all the communal participants recalled communal memories (e.g., involving love or friendship) whereas two-thirds of the agentic participants recalled agentic memories (e.g., involving success). With negative experiences, nearly all communal participants recalled communal memories (e.g., involving betrayal of trust) whereas half of the agentic individuals recalled agentic memories (e.g., involving failure).

The goals important to us change somewhat during the course of our lives. According to Erikson (e.g., 1968), we go through several psychosocial stages of development, and the goals and problems at each stage differ. More specifically, we go through the following psychosocial stages:

1. Childhood: wanting to be nurtured; having fun.
2. Identity/identity confusion: relating to peers and friends.
3. Intimacy/isolation: trying to achieve mutual intimacy.
4. Generativity/stagnation: being concerned/unconcerned about others' welfare.
5. Integrity/despair: focus on meaningful/meaningless nature of life.

Conway and Holmes (2004) asked older adults to recall up to three memories from each decade of their lives. The memories recalled were assigned to the psychosocial stages identified above. As predicted, autobiographical memories from each decade tended to reflect the psychosocial goals and problems that would have been dominant at that time (see the figure on the following page).

Evidence for the notion that there are three types of autobiographical knowledge was discussed by Conway and Rubin (1993). Brain-damaged patients with retrograde amnesia (widespread forgetting of events preceding the brain injury) often cannot recall

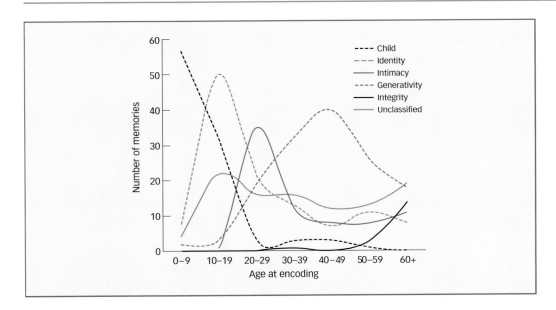

Numbers of memories recalled by older adults classified by psychosocial stage and by the age at which the event occurred. From Conway and Holmes (2004). Copyright © 2004 Blackwell Publishing. Reprinted with permission.

event-specific memories. However, they can recall general events and knowledge of lifetime periods. Other patients can recall only information about lifetime periods. Thus, event-specific knowledge is most vulnerable to loss or disruption, and knowledge of lifetime periods is least vulnerable.

Evaluation

⊕ The notion that autobiographical memory has a hierarchical structure is plausible and in line with the evidence.

⊕ There is support for the notion that the self and its goals are important in autobiographical memory.

⊖ Our understanding of the role of the working self is based mainly on consciously accessible information. However, some aspects of the working self (e.g., some of its goals) may not be consciously accessible.

⊖ As yet, we know little of how the working self interacts with the autobiographical knowledge base to produce recall of specific autobiographical memories.

EYEWITNESS TESTIMONY

You are a juror in a murder case. You are undecided whether the defendant is the murderer because the evidence is unclear. However, one piece of evidence seems very direct and revealing. An eyewitness was present at the time of the murder, and he has identified the defendant as the murderer in an identification line-up. When you see the eyewitness being questioned in court, he seems very confident he has correctly identified the murderer. As a result, you and your fellow jurors decide the defendant is guilty of murder, and he is sentenced to life imprisonment.

Most jurors are strongly influenced by eyewitness testimony, especially when they are very confident they have identified the culprit. Many psychologists are concerned about our tendency to accept without question what eyewitnesses report. The advent of DNA tests means we can often establish whether the person convicted of a crime was actually responsible. In the United States, more than 100 convicted people have been

Eyewitness testimony has been found by psychologists to be extremely unreliable, yet jurors tend to find such testimony highly believable.

shown to be innocent by DNA tests, and more than 75% of them were found guilty on the basis of mistaken eyewitness identification. The 100th innocent person freed after DNA testing was Larry Mayes of Indiana. He was convicted of raping a cashier at a filling station after she identified him in court. Thomas Vanes, the lawyer who prosecuted Mayes, believed at the time of the trial that Mayes was guilty. However, the DNA evidence led him to conclude that, "He [Mayes] was right, and I was wrong."

Findings

Why do you think eyewitness testimony is often inaccurate? The most obvious explanation is that eyewitnesses often fail to pay sufficient attention to the crime and to the criminal(s). After all, they were pursuing their own goals when unexpectedly a crime took place close to them. However, Elizabeth Loftus and John Palmer argued that what happens *after* an eyewitness has observed a crime is also very important. More specifically, they claimed that eyewitness memories are fragile and can surprisingly easily be distorted by subsequent questioning (often referred to as post-event information).

Key Study

Loftus and Palmer (1974): Leading questions

Loftus and Palmer (1974) obtained support for their point of view in a study in which people were shown a film of a multiple-car accident. After viewing the film, participants described what had happened, and then answered specific questions. Some were asked, "About how fast were the cars going when they hit each other?," whereas for others the verb "hit" was substituted for "smashed into." Control participants were not asked about car speed. The estimated speed was affected by the verb used in the question, averaging 41 mph when the verb "smashed" was used versus 34 mph when "hit" was used.

One week later, all participants were asked, "Did you see any broken glass?" There wasn't actually any broken glass in the accident, but 32% of those previously asked about speed using the verb "smashed" said they had seen broken glass. In contrast, only 14% of those asked using the verb "hit" said they had seen broken glass, and the figure was 12% for the control participants. Thus, our memory for events is so fragile that it can be distorted by changing *one* word in *one* question!

Discussion points
1. How confident can we be that such laboratory-based findings resemble what would be found in the real world?
2. What are some of the practical implications of this research?

KEY STUDY EVALUATION
Methodologically, this study was well controlled, although, as is common, students were used as participants and it could be argued that students are not necessarily representative of the general population. However, the experiment lacks ecological validity, in that the participants were not real-life witnesses, and it could be said that the emotional effects of being a real-life witness could affect recall. On the one hand film clips may not contain as much information as you would get in real life, but on the other hand the participants knew that something interesting was being shown to them and therefore they were paying full attention to it. In real life, eyewitnesses are typically taken by surprise and often fail to pay close attention to the event or incident, therefore this research lacks mundane realism. The study has real-life applications, particularly in respect of the credence given to eyewitness testimony in court, and the use of taped interviews in police stations.

How concerned do we need to be about the distorting effects of post-event information? Such distorting effects may be less damaging than might be imagined. There is often much more memory distortion for peripheral or minor details (e.g., presence of broken glass) than there is for central details (e.g., features of the criminal) (Heath & Erickson, 1998).

There has been much research on **weapon focus**. This is a phenomenon in which the eyewitness attends so closely to the criminal's weapon that he/she fails to recall details about the criminal and the environment. For example, Loftus, Loftus, and Messo (1987) asked participants to watch one of two sequences:

1. A person pointing a gun at a cashier and receiving some cash.
2. A person holding a cheque to the cashier and receiving some cash.

Key Term
Weapon focus: the finding that eyewitnesses pay so much attention to a weapon that they tend to ignore other details.

Weapon focus is the phenomenon in which eyewitnesses are so distracted by the weapon used in a crime that they will fail to recall other details of the event.

Eyewitnesses looked more at the gun than they did at the cheque. As a result, memory for details unrelated to the gun/cheque was poorer in the weapon condition.

Pickel (1999) argued that a weapon may attract attention either because it poses a threat or because it is unexpected in the context in which it is seen. Pickel produced four videos involving a man approaching a woman while holding a handgun to evaluate these explanations:

1. Low threat; expected: gun barrel pointed at the ground; setting was a shooting range.
2. Low threat; unexpected: gun barrel pointed at the ground; setting was a baseball field.
3. High threat; expected: gun pointed at the woman who shrank back in fear; setting was a shooting range.
4. High threat; unexpected: gun pointed at the woman who shrank back in fear; setting was a baseball field.

Eyewitnesses' descriptions of the man with the gun were much better when the gun was seen in a setting in which guns are expected (a shooting range) than in a setting in which they are unexpected (a baseball field). However, the level of threat had no influence at all on how much eyewitnesses could remember. Thus, it seems that the weapon focus effect may occur because the presence of a weapon is unexpected rather than because it is threatening.

It seems reasonable to assume that eyewitnesses who are confident they have correctly identified the culprit are more likely to be accurate than those lacking confidence. However, Kassin, Tubb, Hosch, and Memon (2001) found that over 80% of experts in eyewitness testimony agreed that an eyewitness's confidence is *not* a good predictor of his/her identification accuracy. Sporer, Penrod, Read, and Cutler (1995) combined the findings from numerous studies into a meta-analysis. They distinguished between choosers (eyewitnesses making a positive identification) and nonchoosers (those not making a positive identification). There was practically no correlation between confidence and accuracy among nonchoosers, but the average correlation was +.41 among choosers. This indicates that confident choosers were somewhat more likely than nonconfident choosers to make an accurate identification.

Perfect and Hollins (1996) found that participants' confidence didn't predict the accuracy of their memory for a film about a kidnap. They argued that this happens because eyewitnesses don't know whether their ability to remember details of a witnessed event is better or worse than that of other people. However, participants' confidence did predict the accuracy of their performance on general-knowledge questions. Presumably this happened because they knew whether their general knowledge was relatively good or bad compared to other people.

Most eyewitness research is carried out under laboratory conditions. How much confidence can we have that the memory errors made by eyewitnesses in the laboratory would be found in real-world settings? Reassuring evidence was provided by Ihlebaek, Løve, Eilertsen, and Magnussen (2003). They used a staged robbery involving two armed robbers. In the live condition, the eyewitnesses were ordered repeatedly to "Stay down." A video taken during the live condition was presented to eyewitnesses in the video condition. Participants in both conditions exaggerated the duration of the event, and the patterns of memory performance (i.e., what was well and poorly remembered) were similar. However, eyewitnesses in the video condition recalled more information. They estimated the robbers' age, height, and weight more closely, and identified the robbers' weapons more accurately. Thus, the inaccuracies and distortions in eyewitness memory obtained under laboratory conditions *underestimate* eyewitnesses' memory deficiencies for real-life events.

The performance of eyewitnesses when trying to select the suspect from an identification line-up is very fallible. In 300 real line-ups organized by the London Metropolitan Police, Valentine, Pickering, and Darling (2003) found that 40% of witnesses identified the suspect, 20% identified a nonsuspect, and 40% failed to make an identification.

"Well I know he was wearing tights."

What can be done to improve eyewitnesses' identification performance? It has often been argued that warning eyewitnesses that the culprit may not be present in the line-up reduces the chances of mistaken identification. Support for this argument was reported by Steblay (1997), who combined the findings from several studies. Warnings reduced mistaken identification rates in culprit-absent line-ups by 42% while reducing accurate identification rates in culprit-present line-ups by only 2%.

Line-ups are generally simultaneous, meaning the eyewitness is presented with everyone in the line-up at the same time. An alternative is to have sequential line-ups in which the eyewitness sees only one person at a time. Steblay, Dysart, Fulero, and Lindsay (2001) considered 25 relevant studies. Sequential line-ups reduced the chances of mistaken identification when the culprit was absent by almost 50%. However, sequential line-ups also produced a significant reduction in accurate identification rates when the culprit was present. What happens is that eyewitnesses adopt a more *stringent* criterion for identification with sequential than with simultaneous line-ups.

Evaluation

+ Important phenomena have been identified (e.g., distorting effects of post-event information; weapon focus effect; poor relationship between eyewitness confidence and accuracy).

+ Ways of improving the identification performance of eyewitnesses (e.g., warning that the culprit may not be present; sequential rather than simultaneous line-ups) have been discovered.

− Post-event information may not distort memory for important information as much as for trivial information (Heath & Erickson, 1998).

− Research on eyewitness identification has practical value but has been relatively uninfluenced by theoretical ideas.

214

Chapter Summary

The long and the short of memory
- Short-term memory has a capacity of between 4 and 7 chunks of information, and information in short-term memory is held for up to about 18 seconds.
- Some brain-damaged patients have intact short-term memory but impaired long-term memory, and others have the opposite pattern.
- It was assumed incorrectly within the multi-store model that there is only a single short-term store and a single long-term store.
- Baddeley's basic working memory model consists of three components: central executive; phonological loop; and visuospatial sketchpad. The sketchpad seems to consist of fairly separate components specialized for visual and for spatial processing.

Working memory
- Working memory is used when we need to combine processing and short-storage functions.
- The basic working memory model of Baddeley and Hitch consists of a central executive, a phonological loop, and a visuospatial sketchpad.
- The phonological loop has a phonological store and an articulatory control process.
- The visuospatial sketchpad has somewhat separate visual and spatial sub-systems.
- The central executive is attention-like. It is used for various functions, probably including inhibition, shifting, and updating.

Types of long-term memory
- Amnesic patients have problems with explicit memory (involving conscious recollection) but not with implicit memory (not involving conscious recollection).
- All amnesic patients have impaired ability to form new episodic memories. However, impairments of the ability to acquire new semantic memories (general knowledge) are less widespread.

Forgetting
- Numerous adults claim to have recovered repressed memories of sexual and/or physical abuse suffered in childhood. However, there is much controversy concerning the genuineness of these claims.
- Much forgetting is a result of retroactive interference (later learning disrupting memory for earlier learning) and of proactive interference (previous learning disrupting later learning and memory).
- According to the encoding specificity principle, we are most likely to remember something when the information available at the time of retrieval *matches* the information stored in long-term memory. This helps to explain mood-state-dependent memory and the typical superiority of recognition over recall.
- According to consolidation theory, recently formed memories at an early stage of consolidation are especially vulnerable to interference and forgetting. This explains why the rate of forgetting is most rapid shortly after learning.

Everyday memory
- When elderly people recall personal memories to cues, a disproportionate number come from the years of adolescence and early adulthood. This occurs in part because this is a period of life characterized by memorable novel experiences.
- The autobiographical memory base contains personal information about lifetime periods, general events, and event-specific knowledge.
- Our autobiographical memories are influenced by our major goals.
- Many of the inaccuracies of eyewitness testimony are a result of misleading post-event information and others may be because of weapon focus.
- Eyewitnesses' confidence in the accuracy of their memory often fails to predict the actual accuracy.
- Fewer errors are made on identification parades when eyewitnesses are warned that the culprit may not be present, or the line-up is sequential rather than simultaneous.

Further Reading

- Baddeley, A.D., Eysenck, M.W., & Anderson, M.C. (2009). *Memory*. Hove, UK: Psychology Press.
- Emilien, G., Durlach, C., Antoniadis, E., van der Linden, M., & Maloteaux, J.-M. (2004). *Memory: Neuropsychological, imaging, and psychopharmacological perspectives*. Hove, UK: Psychology Press. The first chapter of this book provides a useful overview of memory research.
- Eysenck, M.W. (2006). *Fundamentals of human cognition*. Hove, UK: Psychology Press. The topics discussed in this chapter are dealt with at greater length in this textbook (Chapters 11–16).
- Loftus, E.F. (2004). Memories of things unseen. *Current Directions in Psychological Science, 13*, 145–147. Elizabeth Loftus considers ways in which our memories can be distorted.

Chapter 9

Contents

Thinking: Problem solving and decision making

9

The challenges we face in our everyday lives require us to engage in thinking. In general terms, the more effective our thinking is, the more successfully we are likely to lead our lives. Thinking takes many forms. However, two of the most important forms are problem solving and decision making. In problem solving, we move from recognizing that there is a problem to finding some strategy to produce the required solution. In decision making, we are presented with various options or possibilities and try to select the one with the best consequences for us. These two forms of thinking are the focus of this chapter.

FINDING THE SOLUTION

Life presents us with numerous problems to solve. These problems come in many different shapes and sizes. Some problems are fairly trivial and short (e.g., "How can I get to Cambridge cheaply?"), but others are important and long term (e.g., "How am I going to pass my psychology exam?"). What, if anything, do all attempts at problem solving have in common?

According to Mayer (1990, p. 284), problem solving is "cognitive processing directed at transforming a given situation into a goal situation when no obvious method of solution is available to the problem solver." This definition suggests there are three major aspects to problem solving:

1. It is purposeful in the sense of being goal directed.
2. It requires the use of cognitive processes rather than automatic ones.
3. A problem only exists when someone lacks the relevant knowledge to produce an immediate solution.

Sternberg (2003) argued that there are seven steps in the problem-solving cycle:

1. Problem identification: realizing there is a problem.
2. Problem definition and representation: clarifying the nature of the problem.
3. Strategy formulation: deciding how to tackle the problem.
4. Organization of information: assembling information needed to solve the problem.
5. Resource allocation: deciding which parts of the problem require the greatest allocation of resources.
6. Monitoring: checking progress towards problem solution.
7. Evaluation: assessing whether the proposed solution to the problem is adequate.

Escaping from, or reaching the middle of, a maze is an example of a well-defined problem. It is clear when a solution is reached.

How to retrieve your car keys from a locked car is an ill-defined problem. It can be very hard to identify the best solution.

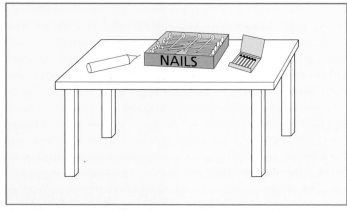

The objects presented to participants in the candle problem.

There are major differences among problems. Some problems are well-defined whereas others are ill-defined. **Well-defined problems** are ones in which all aspects of the problem are clearly specified, including the range of possible moves or strategies and the goal or solution. Mazes are well-defined problems in which reaching the center is the goal. In contrast, **ill-defined problems** are under-specified. Suppose you have locked your keys inside your car, and want to get into it without causing any damage. However, you have very urgent business to attend to elsewhere, and there is no one around to help you. In such circumstances, it may be difficult to identify the best solution to the problem.

Most everyday problems are ill-defined, but psychologists focus mainly on well-defined problems. Why is this? One important reason is that well-defined problems have a best strategy for their solution. As a result, we can clearly identify the errors and deficiencies in the strategies adopted by human problem solvers.

There is another difference between laboratory and everyday problems. Laboratory studies generally focus on knowledge-lean problems in which the information required to solve the problems is contained in the initial problem statement. In contrast, everyday life often presents us with knowledge-rich problems, which can only be solved if we have a considerable amount of relevant specific knowledge.

HOW USEFUL IS PAST EXPERIENCE?

Common sense tells us that our ability to solve a problem is much better if we have relevant past experience with similar problems. Indeed, the crucial reason why adults can solve most problems much faster than children is because of their enormous relevant past experience.

Is past experience *always* useful? The answer is, "No!" For example, Duncker (1945) obtained evidence of **functional fixedness**. This is a phenomenon in which we fail to solve a problem because we assume from past experience that any given object only has a limited number of uses. Duncker gave participants a candle, a box of nails, and several other objects (see the figure below). Their task was to attach the candle to a wall by a table so it didn't drip onto the table. Most participants tried to nail the candle directly to the wall or to glue it to the wall by melting it. Only a few came up with the correct answer, using the inside of the nail-box as a candle holder and then nailing it to the wall.

Duncker (1945) argued that his participants "fixated" on the box's function as a container rather than as a platform. This view was supported by an additional finding. More correct solutions were produced when the nail-box was empty (rather than full) at the start of the experiment. When the nail-box was empty, it looked less like a container.

It is generally assumed that functional fixedness occurs because problem solvers rely too much on their past knowledge and experience. If so, older children might show more functional fixedness than younger children, as was shown by Defeyter and German (2003). Children aged between 5 and 7 removed an object from a transparent tube. This could only be done by using a long stick presented along with several other objects. The main function of this stick (to make light or to make music in different conditions) was demonstrated to some of the children before being given the task.

What did Defeyter and German (2003) find? When the stick's main function had not been shown to the children, there were no differences among them in the time taken to select the stick to free the object from the tube (see the figure on the right). However, when its main function had been shown (and so there was a possibility of functional fixedness), the older children took significantly longer than the youngest ones to use the stick. The key finding was that the youngest children (with their limited past experience and knowledge) showed no evidence of functional fixedness.

Past experience doesn't only create problems of functional fixedness. It can also lead us to persevere with problem-solving strategies that are no longer appropriate. Luchins (1942) and Luchins and Luchins (1959) presented water-jar problems involving three water jars of varying capacity. Participants imagined pouring water from one jar to another to finish up with a specified amount of water in one of the jars (see the figure on the right).

The striking findings obtained by Luchins can be illustrated by considering one of his studies in detail. One problem was as follows: Jar A can hold 28 quarts of water, Jar B 76 quarts, and Jar C 3 quarts. The task is to end up with exactly 25 quarts in one of the jars. The solution is not difficult: Jar A is filled and then Jar C is filled from it, leaving 25 quarts in Jar A. Unsurprisingly, 95% of participants who had previously been given similar problems solved it. Other participants were trained on a series of problems all of which had the same complex three-jar solution. Of these participants, only 36% managed to solve this extremely simple problem! The previous problems had created a mental set or "mechanized state of mind" (Luchins, 1942, p. 15) preventing participants from seeing the obvious.

Positive transfer

So far we have been discussing **negative transfer**, meaning interfering effects of previous experience on a current problem. In the real world, however, the effects of past experience on problem solving are predominantly positive. The term **positive transfer** describes that state of affairs. Positive transfer is of great practical importance (honestly!). For example, nearly everyone involved in education firmly believes that what students learn at school or university facilitates learning later in life. Thus, it is assumed there is substantial positive transfer from the classroom or lecture theater to subsequent forms of learning (e.g., work-related skills).

Positive transfer often involves making use of analogies or similarities between the current problem and one or more problems solved in the past. For example, consider a study by Gick and Holyoak (1980). They used Duncker's (1945) radiation problem in which a patient has a malignant tumor and can only be saved by a special kind of ray. However, a ray strong enough to destroy the tumor will also destroy the healthy tissue, and a ray that won't harm healthy tissue will be too weak to destroy the tumor.

What is the answer to the radiation problem? If you haven't found it yet, here is an analogy to help you. A general wants to capture a fortress but the roads leading to

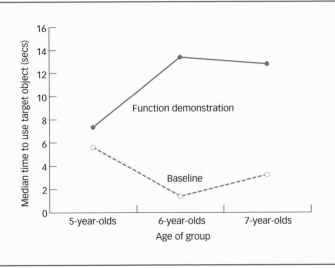

Median time (in seconds) to select the stick as a function of age and of whether its main function had been shown (function demonstration) or not (baseline). From Defeyter and German (2003). Copyright © 2003 Elsevier. Reproduced with permission.

An example of one of the water-jar problems used by Luchins (1942) and Luchins and Luchins (1959); Jar A holds 28 quarts, Jar B holds 76 quarts, and Jar C holds 3 quarts.

Key Terms

Well-defined problems:
problems in which the initial state, goal, and methods available for solving them are clearly laid out.

Ill-defined problems:
problems in which the definition of the problem statement is imprecisely specified; the initial state, goal state, and methods to be used to solve the problem may be unclear.

Functional fixedness:
the inflexible use of the usual function(s) of an object in problem solving.

Negative transfer:
past experience in solving problems disrupts the ability to solve a current problem.

Positive transfer:
past experiencing of solving problems makes it easier to solve a current problem.

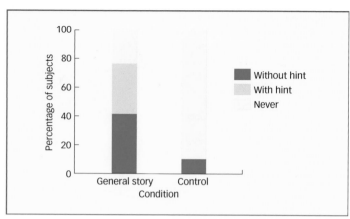

Some of the results from Gick and Holyoak (1980, experiment 4) showing the percentage of participants who solved the radiation problem when they were given an analogy (general-story condition) or were just asked to solve the problem (control condition). Note that just under half of the participants in the general-story condition had to be given a hint to use the story analog before they solved the problem.

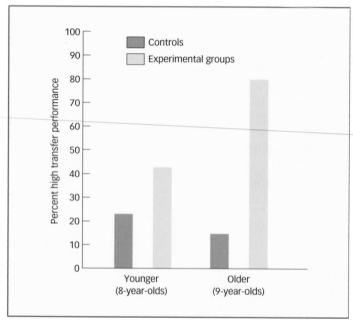

Percentage of children performing at a high level on the transfer test (13 or more out of 15) as a function of age (8 vs. 9) and previous relevant training (control vs. experimental). Based on data from Chen and Klahr (1999).

it are too narrow to allow the entire army to march along any one of them. Accordingly, the general has his army converge at the same time on the fortress by walking along several different roads. Gick and Holyoak (1980) found that 80% of participants solved the radiation problem when told this story was relevant (the solution is to direct low-intensity rays at the tumor from several different directions). Only 40% of participants not informed of the story-relevance solved the problem, and even fewer (10%) of those who weren't exposed to the story managed to solve it (see the figure on the left).

Most laboratory research on positive transfer has focused on the *immediate* application of knowledge and skills from one situation to a rather similar one. This is known as near transfer. In education, however, what matters is positive transfer over long periods of time to situations differing considerably from that of the original learning (far transfer). For example, educationalists hope that what students learn at school and university will enhance their ability to learn useful career skills 10–20 years later.

Chen and Klahr (1999) carried out a study on far transfer. Children aged 7–10 were trained to design and to evaluate experiments in the domain of physical science. Of central importance in the children's learning was the control-of-variables strategy involving the ability to create sound experiments and identify confounded experiments. Chen and Klahr tested for far transfer 7 months after training, including a control group of children who hadn't received training. The test assessed mastery of the control-of-variables strategy in five new domains (e.g., plant growth; biscuit making). There was clear evidence of positive transfer. Children who had received the previous training were much more likely than control children to perform well on the test (see the figure on the left).

De Corte (2003) wondered whether far transfer depends on **metacognition** (the beliefs and knowledge we have about our own cognitive processes and strategies). Students of business economics were given 7 months of training in two metacognitive skills: orienting and self-judging. Orienting involves preparing oneself to solve problems by thinking about possible goals and cognitive activities. Self-judging is a motivational activity designed to allow students to calculate accurately the effort required for successful task completion.

Far transfer was assessed when students subsequently learned statistics. Students who had received metacognitive training performed better than those who had not. Within the group that had received training, academic performance in statistics correlated positively with orienting and self-judging behavior.

DOES INSIGHT EXIST?

Many problems require us to work slowly but surely towards the solution. For example, solving a complicated problem in multiplication involves several processing operations that must be performed in the correct sequence. Do you agree that the overwhelming majority of problems are "grind-out-the-solution" ones? If you do, you are in for a rude shock! There are many problems in which the solution depends on **insight** or an "aha" experience involving a sudden transformation of the problem. Take the mutilated checkerboard (or draughtboard) problem (see the figure on the right). The board is initially completely covered by 32 dominoes occupying two squares each. Then two squares from diagonally opposite corners are removed. Can the remaining 62 squares be filled by 31 dominoes? What nearly everyone does is to start by mentally covering squares with dominoes (Kaplan & Simon, 1990). Alas, this is not a great strategy—there are 758,148 possible permutations of the dominoes!

Since very few people solve this problem unaided, I'll assume you are in that large majority. However, if I tell you something you already know, the chances are much greater that you will rapidly solve the problem. Remember that each domino covers one white and one black square. If that clue doesn't do the trick, think about the colors of the two removed squares—they must have the same color. Thus, the 31 dominoes *cannot* cover the mutilated board.

The take-home message from the above problem is that how we think about a problem (the **problem representation**) is of great importance in problem solving. With many problems, we initially construct one or more problem representations. Eventually we form the correct problem representation, which involves a sudden restructuring of the problem (known as insight).

Bowden, Jung-Beeman, Fleck, and Kounios (2005) identified a part of the brain involved in insight. Participants performed the Remote Associates Test. On this test, three words are presented (e.g., "fence"; "card"; and "master"), and the task is to find a word (e.g., "post") that can go with each of them to form a compound word. Participants pressed a button to indicate whether they solved each problem using insight. In the first experiment, fMRI revealed that the anterior superior temporal gyrus [ridge] in the right hemisphere was activated *only* when solutions involved insight. In the second experiment, Beeman and Bowden recorded event-related potentials (ERPs). There was a burst of high-frequency brain activity one-third of a second before participants indicated they had achieved an insightful solution. This brain activity was centered on the right anterior temporal gyrus. This brain area seems to be especially important to insight because it is involved in processing general semantic (meaning) relationships.

Our subjective experience tells us insight occurs suddenly and unexpectedly. Here is one person's experience of producing an insightful solution on an anagram task: "The solution came to mind suddenly, seemingly out of nowhere. I have no awareness of having done anything to try to get an answer" (Novick & Sherman, 2003). Is what is true of our subjective experience also true of the underlying processes? Novick and Sherman obtained evidence that the answer is, "No." They found initially that expert anagram solvers reported far more "pop-out" or insight-based solutions than nonexperts. Then they presented participants very briefly with letter strings that could or couldn't be rearranged to form words. Even though the time period was too short to permit the anagrams to be solved, experts were much better than nonexperts at deciding which letter strings formed anagrams. Thus, some relevant processing occurs *before* "insight" anagram solutions, even though people have no conscious awareness of such processing.

What produces insight?

Ohlsson (1992) pointed out that we often encounter a block in problem solving because we are using an inappropriate representation of the problem. According to him, insight typically occurs only when we change such a problem representation into the correct one. This can occur in three ways:

1. *Constraint relaxation*: Inhibitions on what is regarded as permissible are removed.
2. *Re-encoding*: Some aspect of the problem representation is reinterpreted.
3. *Elaboration*: New problem information is added to the representation.

Our earlier discussion of the mutilated checkerboard or draughtboard showed how important it can be to change the problem representation via re-encoding. The key to insight in that problem is the realization that each domino covers a black square and a white one. Knoblich, Ohlsson, Haider, and Rhenius (1999) found that insight can involve relaxing constraints. They used mathematical problems involving sticks representing

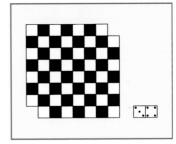

The mutilated checkerboard problem.

Two of the matchstick problems used by Knoblich et al. (1999), and the cumulative solution rates produced for these types of problems in their study.

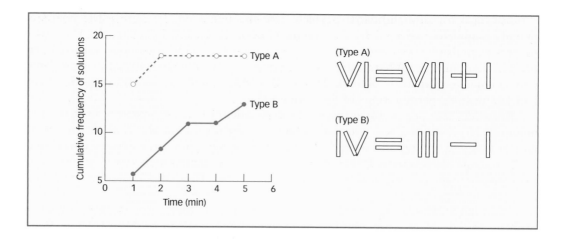

Roman numerals (see the figure above). Each problem that was presented was initially false, and the task was to move *one* stick to turn into a true statement. For example, VI = VII + I (6 = 7 + I) becomes true by turning it into VII = VI + I (7 = 6 + I).

Knoblich et al. (1999) found that problems like the one just discussed were typically solved easily. However, most participants struggled to solve problems such as the following: IV = III − I (4 = 3 − I). The correct answer is IV − III = I (4 − 3 = 1). According to Knoblich et al., our experience of arithmetic tells us that many operations change the *values* (numbers) in an equation (as in our first example). Relatively few operations change the *operators* (i.e., plus, minus, and equal signs) as in our second example. Thus, insight on problems of the second type requires that we relax the normal constraints of arithmetic.

Many people believe that putting a problem to one side for a while or simply "sleeping on it" can be effective in getting around a block in problem solving. Psychologists use the term **incubation** to refer to this phenomenon. Dodds, Ward, and Smith (2004) reviewed 39 studies on incubation, of which 29 produced incubation effects. In general, beneficial effects of incubation were greater among participants of high ability than those of low ability. Wagner et al. (2004) found that sleep can be a useful form of incubation. Participants performed a complex mathematical task and were then re-tested several hours later. Very few of them discovered the short-cut solution to the mathematical problems on initial testing, and what was of interest was to see how many found this solution on re-testing. Of those who slept between training and testing, 59% found that short cut compared to only 25% of those who didn't.

Why does incubation work? Simon (1966) argued that it involves a special kind of forgetting. What tends to be forgotten over time is control information relating to the strategies tried by the problem solver. This forgetting makes it easier to adopt a new approach to the problem after the incubation period. Support for that viewpoint was reported by Smith and Blankenship (1991) using the Remote Associates Test (e.g., find a word ("chair") that links "wheel," "electric," and "high"). In an interference condition, participants were also presented with words emphasizing the differences in meanings of the three words (e.g., "low" is opposite in meaning to "high"). There was a strong incubation effect in this interference condition (but not in a control condition), presumably because information about the interfering words was forgotten during the incubation period.

INFORMATION-PROCESSING APPROACH

One of the greatest landmarks in problem-solving research was the publication in 1972 of Allen Newell and Herb Simon's book entitled *Human problem solving*. It was the first systematic attempt to provide an information-processing account of problem solving. Newell and Simon's central insight was that the strategies we use when tackling complex problems take account of our limited ability to process and store information. They assumed we have strictly limited short-term memory capacity and that complex information processing is typically serial (only one process at a time). These assumptions were incorporated into their General Problem Solver, a computer program designed to solve numerous well-defined problems.

According to Newell and Simon (1972), we cope with our limited processing capacity by making much use of **heuristics** or rules of thumb (e.g., only make moves that leave you closer to the goal). Heuristics have the advantage that they don't require extensive information processing. However, they suffer from the disadvantage that they aren't guaranteed to produce the problem solution. In contrast, there are **algorithms**, which are complex methods or procedures that will definitely lead to problem solution. For example, the rules of multiplication form an algorithm. Algorithms have the advantage that you are guaranteed to solve the problem if they are used correctly. However, they have the disadvantage that we often lack the processing capacity to use them properly.

The most important heuristic identified by Newell and Simon (1972) was **means–ends analysis**:

- Note the difference between the current state of the problem and the goal state.
- Form a sub-goal that will reduce the difference between the current and goal states.
- Select a mental operator that will permit attainment of the sub-goal.

Another important heuristic is hill climbing. **Hill climbing** involves changing the present state within the problem into one that is closer to the goal or problem solution. As Robertson (2001, p. 38) pointed out, "Hill climbing is a metaphor for problem solving in the dark." It is used when the problem solver has no clear understanding of problem structure. It is thus a more primitive heuristic than means–ends analysis.

Newell and Simon (1972) gained an understanding of problem solving by asking people to solve problems while thinking aloud. These verbal reports revealed the general strategy being used on each problem. Newell and Simon then specified the problem-solving strategy in sufficient detail for it to be programmed in their General Problem Solver. In the General Problem Solver, problems are represented as a problem space. The **problem space** consists of the following:

1. The initial state of the problem.
2. The goal state.
3. All the possible mental operators (i.e., moves) that can be applied to any state to change it into a different state.
4. All the intermediate states of the problem.

As we have seen, the process of problem solving involves a sequence of different knowledge states. These knowledge states intervene between the initial state and the goal state, with mental operators providing the shift from one knowledge state to the next. It is much more difficult (or even impossible) to identify the problem space with ill-defined problems than with well-defined ones. This helps to explain why Newell and Simon (1972) focused on well-defined problems.

We can see more clearly what Newell and Simon (1972) had in mind if we consider the Tower of Hanoi problem (see the figure above). In this problem, the initial state of the problem consists of up to five disks piled in decreasing size on the first of three pegs. The goal state involves having all the disks piled in the same arrangement on the last peg. Only one disk can be moved at a time, and a large disk can't be placed on top of a smaller one. These rules restrict the possible mental operators on each move.

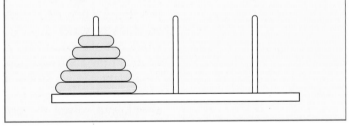

The initial state of the five-disk version of the Tower of Hanoi problem.

Key Terms

Heuristics:
rules of thumb that often (but not invariably) solve any given problem.

Algorithms:
computational procedures providing a specified set of steps to a solution.

Means–ends analysis:
a **heuristic** for solving problems based on noting the difference between a current and a goal state, and creating a sub-goal to overcome this difference.

Hill climbing:
a **heuristic** that involves changing the present state of a problem into one apparently closer to the goal.

Problem space:
an abstract description of all the possible states of affairs that can occur in a problem situation.

Findings

People very often use heuristics such as hill climbing and means–ends analysis when solving well-defined problems. However, they also use other strategies. For example, Simon and Reed (1976) considered performance on the

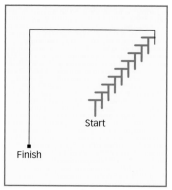

The image used in the study by Sweller and Levine (1982). Adapted from Sweller and Levine (1982).

Key Term

Progress monitoring: this is a **heuristic** used in problem solving in which insufficiently rapid progress towards solution produces criterion failure and the adoption of a different strategy.

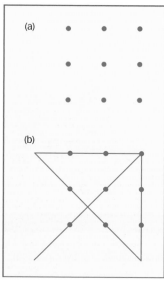

Scheerer's (1963) nine-dot problem requires you to draw four continuous straight lines, connecting all dots without lifting your pen off the paper. Most people find it difficult to solve this because they assume all lines have to stay within the square formed by the dots. In Gestalt terms, participants have "fixated" on the shape, which results in a state of functional fixedness.

missionaries-and-cannibals problems. In this problem, missionaries and cannibals have to be transported across a river in a boat holding only two people. The cannibals must never outnumber the missionaries on either side of the river. This problem can be solved in 11 moves, but participants took 30 moves on average to solve it.

What strategies did problem solvers use? Initially, they adopted a *balancing strategy*, in which they focused on ensuring there were equal numbers of missionaries and cannibals on each side of the river. After that, they shifted to *means–ends analysis*, in which the emphasis was on moving more people to the goal side of the river. Finally, participants used an *anti-looping heuristic* to avoid any moves reversing the immediately preceding move.

Sweller and Levine (1982) decided to find out just how attached we are to means–ends analysis. They used a problem in which use of means–ends analysis would lead problem solvers to make consistently *wrong* moves. In such circumstances, would problem solvers stick with means–ends analysis or would they abandon it? What Sweller and Levine did was to give participants the maze shown in the figure on the left, but most of it was not visible to them. All participants could see the current problem state (i.e., where they were in the problem). Some of them could also see the goal state (goal-information group), whereas the others couldn't (no-goal-information group).

What do you think happened on this apparently simple problem (simple because its solution only involved alternating left and right moves)? Use of means–ends analysis requires knowledge of goal location, so only the goal-information group could have used that heuristic or rule of thumb. However, the problem was cunningly designed so that means–ends analysis wouldn't be useful, because every move involved turning *away* from the goal. Participants in the no-goal-information group solved the problem in only 38 moves on average. In contrast, of those in the goal-information group, only 10% solved the problem in 298 moves! Thus, the participants were remarkably attached to means–ends analysis, continuing to use it even when it greatly impaired problem-solving performance.

Why do we typically engage in only a modest amount of planning when involved in problem solving? According to Newell and Simon (1972), we have limited short-term capacity and so can't plan several moves ahead. Another possibility is that we find planning several moves ahead demanding in time and effort, but we can do it if necessary. Delaney, Ericsson, and Knowles (2004) obtained evidence supporting the latter possibility. They used water-jar problems in which the task was to finish up with specified amounts of water in each of three water jars. Half the participants were instructed to work out the complete solution before making any moves (the planning group). In contrast, the control group was free to use any strategy they wanted.

Delaney et al. (2004) found that the control participants showed little evidence of planning ahead. However, participants in the planning group did plan several moves ahead, and solved the problems in far fewer moves than control participants. Thus, people can plan much more effectively than is usually assumed. However, they often choose not to plan unless required to do so.

Newell and Simon (1972) assumed that problem solvers would shift strategies or heuristics if the ones they were using proved ineffective. This idea was developed by MacGregor, Ormerod, and Chronicle (2001), who argued that problem solvers use a heuristic known as **progress monitoring**. With this heuristic, the rate of progress towards the goal is assessed. Criterion failure occurs if progress is too slow to solve the problem within the maximum number of moves. Criterion failure acts as a "wake-up call" leading problem solvers to change strategy.

MacGregor et al. (2001) obtained evidence for the importance of progress monitoring in a study on the nine-dot problem (see part (a) of the figure on the left). In this problem, you must draw four straight lines connecting all nine dots without taking your pen from the paper (the solution is shown in part (b) of the figure). They used two conditions to vary the likelihood of experiencing criterion failure. As predicted, more participants in the group more likely to experience criterion failure solved the problem than those in the other group (53% vs. 31%). The take-home message is that if the strategy you are using doesn't allow you to solve a problem, the sooner you realize that is the case the better.

Evaluation

+ The Newell and Simon approach works well with several well-defined problems.

+ The approach is generally consistent with our knowledge of human information processing (e.g., limited short-term memory capacity).

− The General Problem Solver is of limited applicability to the ill-defined problems of everyday life.

− The General Problem Solver is better than humans at remembering what has happened on a problem but inferior at planning future moves. It focuses on only a single move whereas people often plan small sequences of moves (e.g., Greeno, 1974).

− Newell and Simon (1972) didn't focus enough on the motivational factors causing us to shift strategies. This gap was filled by MacGregor et al. (2001) with their progress monitoring heuristic.

DECISIONS, DECISIONS

Life is full (sometimes too full!) of decisions. Which movie will I go to see tonight? Would I rather go with Dick or Harry? Which subject will I study at university? Who will I share an apartment with next year? Barry Schwartz, an American expert on decision making, believes we live in a society in which decision making is rapidly becoming more difficult because of an explosion in the choices available to us. He was in a shop called "The Gap," and wanted to buy a pair of jeans. "I told them my size, and they asked if I wanted relaxed fit, easy fit, slim fit, boot cut, button-fly, zipper-fly, acid-washed, or stone-washed. And I said, 'I want the kind that used to be the only kind'."

Evidence that we sometimes simply give up when confronted by too many choices was reported by Iyengar and Lepper (2000). They set up a tasting booth in Draeger's supermarket in Menlo Park, California. On one weekend, this booth offered six kinds of jelly, but it offered 24 kinds of jelly on another weekend. Nearly 30% of shoppers faced by six choices bought some jelly, but the figure slumped to only 3% when there were 24 choices.

The study of decision making is of direct relevance to real life. For example, Carlson and Russo (2001) showed potential jurors a video explaining the importance of not making decisions before seeing all the evidence. After that, they were presented with affidavits [written declarations made under oath], case backgrounds, and opening arguments. After each new piece of evidence was presented, the participants decided whether it benefited the plaintiff or the defendant. Most participants showed "pre-decisional distortion"—they often regarded the new evidence as supporting whichever party (plaintiff or defendant) they favored before it was presented. Pre-decisional distortion may allow jurors to create a coherent account of what they think happened but can obviously be very bad news for innocent defendants!

Worrying evidence that important real-life decisions may be inadequate was reported by Elstein et al. (1999). They presented doctors working in critical care with six realistic case scenarios, asking them to assess the benefits of various treatments and to decide on appropriate treatment. There were two versions of each case scenario differing in the probability of survival, with half of the doctors receiving each one. Amazingly, neither treatment choice nor perceived treatment benefit depended on the probability of survival! The doctors simply followed their typical approach to treatment regardless of the precise circumstances.

How do we decide how good a decision is? That sounds like a strange question, but it has important implications. Most people argue that what really matters is the outcome—did the decision lead to the desired consequences? However, many experts argue that most decisions are like gambling in that they are made under uncertainty. Thus, a decision can be "good" in the sense of being based on sound reasoning, but may nevertheless produce undesirable consequences. Thus, it can make sense for a surgeon to claim, "The operation was a success but unfortunately the patient died."

Too much choice!

Many of us would think that choice is a good thing but Howe, Butt, and Timmons (2004) say that psychology experiments prove otherwise. For example, one experiment had subjects comparing chocolate chip cookies from a jar of 10 cookies with those from a jar of two cookies. Participants rated the cookie from the smaller jar better, more valuable, more desirable to eat in the future, and more attractive as a consumer item than the one from the larger jar. In reality the cookies were identical. Participants felt that more choice had made the sample less desirable.

You'll have to drop her to catch me, so are you feeling lucky, punk?

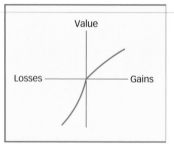

A hypothetical value function. From Kahneman and Tversky (1984). Copyright © American Psychological Association. Reprinted with permission.

Case Study: *Picking Lottery Numbers*

In general, people have a very poor understanding of randomness and probability, as evidenced by the types of numbers commonly selected in national lotteries. Even people who claim to understand that any given number is as likely to come up as any other will be heard to despair: "Oh, I'll never win with that—four numbers in a row!," or "All my numbers are bunched up under 20—I'd better spread them out a bit to get a better pattern." In fact, statistics suggest that you're actually better off picking numbers with a skewed or bunched appearance: you're no more likely to win, but in the unlikely event that you do, you'll be less likely to have to share your prize with anyone else!

LOSSES AND GAINS

All of us strive to achieve gains (e.g., emotional; financial; academic success) while avoiding losses. You would probably argue that we make decisions so as to maximize the chances of making a gain and minimize the chances of making a loss. Suppose someone offered you $200 if a tossed coin came up heads and a loss of $100 if it came up tails. You would jump at the chance (wouldn't you?) given that the bet provides an average expected gain of $50 per toss.

Here are two more decisions. Would you prefer to make a sure gain of $800 or an 85% probability of gaining $1000 and a 15% probability of gaining nothing? Since the expected value of the latter decision is greater than that of the former decision ($850 vs. $800, respectively), you might well choose the latter alternative. Finally, would you prefer to make a sure loss of $800 or an 85% probability of losing $1000 with a 15% probability of not incurring any loss? The average expected loss is $800 for the former choice and $850 for the latter one, so you go with the former choice don't you?

The first problem above was taken from Tversky and Shafir (1992) and the other two problems come from Kahneman and Tversky (1984). In all three cases, most participants did *not* make what appear to be the best choices. Two-thirds of them refused to bet on the toss of a coin, and a majority preferred the choices with the smaller expected gain and the large expected loss! What on earth is going on here? Kahneman and Tversky (1984) accounted for such findings within their prospect theory based on two key theoretical assumptions:

1. People identify a reference point generally representing their current state.
2. People are much more sensitive to potential losses than to potential gains; this is known as **loss aversion**.

Both of the above assumptions are shown in the figure on the left. The reference point is the point at which the line labeled losses and gains intersects the line labeled value. The positive value associated with gains increases relatively slowly as gains become greater. In contrast, the negative value associated with losses increases relatively rapidly as losses become greater.

There is further prediction following from prospect theory. When people make decisions, they attach more weight to low-probability events than they merit according to their actual probability of occurrence. In contrast, high-probability events receive less weight than they deserve. This helps to explain the human tendency for risk seeking with gains (e.g., gambling on remote events such as winning a fortune on the lottery) and for risk avoidance with losses (e.g., buying insurance) (Jonathan Evans, personal communication).

Prospect theory does a good job of explaining the findings discussed earlier. If people are much more sensitive to losses than to gains, they will be unwilling to accept bets involving potential losses even though the potential gains outweigh the potential losses. They will also prefer a sure gain to a risky but potentially greater gain. Finally, please note that prospect theory does *not* predict that people will always avoid risky decisions. If offered the chance of avoiding a loss (even if it means the average expected loss increases from $800 to $850), most people will take that chance because they are so concerned to avoid losses.

Prospect theory can be contrasted with previous theoretical views based on the notion of "rational man" (or "rational person"). According to this approach, we work systematically through the available evidence and make the decision most likely to produce a desirable outcome.

This notion is found in **normative theories**, which focus on how people *should* make decisions rather than on how they actually make them. For example, von Neumann and Morgenstern's (1947) utility theory claimed that people try to maximize *utility*, which is the subjective value we attach to an outcome. When we choose between options, we assess the expected utility or expected value of each one as follows:

Expected utility = (probability of a given outcome) × (utility of the outcome)

As we will see, prospect theory for all its imperfections is clearly superior to normative theories.

Findings

Suppose we give different people precisely the same problem phrased in two different ways. In one version, the potential gains associated with various decisions are emphasized, whereas the potential losses associated with the decisions are emphasized in the other version. Since the problem is exactly the same, common sense would suggest that people would make the same decisions regardless of problem phrasing. According to prospect theory, changing the wording should matter because people are more motivated to avoid losses than to achieve gains. This is known as a **framing effect**, meaning the decision is influenced by irrelevant aspects of the situation.

The Asian disease problem has often been used to study the framing effect. Tversky and Kahneman (1987) told participants there was likely to be an outbreak of an Asian disease in the United States, and it was expected to kill 600 people. Two programs of action had been proposed: Program A would allow 200 people to be saved; Program B would have a 1/3 probability that all 600 people would be saved and a 2/3 probability that none of the 600 would be saved. When the issue was expressed in this form, 72% of participants favored Program A, although the two programs if carried out several times would on average lead to the saving of 200 lives. This is a framing effect based on loss aversion.

Other participants in the study by Tversky and Kahneman (1987) received the same problem negatively framed: Program A would lead to 400 people dying, whereas Program B carried a 1/3 probability that no one would die and a 2/3 probability that 600 would die. With this wording, the findings were very different—78% of participants chose Program B, a framing effect resulting from loss aversion.

Why are people more sensitive to losses than to gains? Interesting evidence was provided by Kermer, Driver-Linn, Wilson, and Gilbert (2006). Participants were initially given $5, and forecasted how they would feel if they won $5 on the toss of a coin or lost $3. They forecast that losing $3 would have more impact on their happiness immediately and 10 minutes later than would gaining $5, which is a clear example of loss aversion. In fact, however, participants who lost felt happier than they had predicted at both time intervals, and the actual impact on happiness of losing $3 was no greater than the actual impact of gaining $5.

Why don't we learn from experience that losses often have less negative emotional impact than we had anticipated? One reason is that people often rationalize or explain away losses in ways that are difficult to predict ahead of time. For example, Kermer et al. (2006)

Full-fat milk?

Using this argument we can offer an explanation as to why food retailers might advertise or label full-fat milk as "94% fat free" in order to draw customer attention away from its high fat content when compared to skimmed milk. Retailers may have decided to reverse the tendency for customers to associate higher fat content in milk with bad dietary habits by stating the high-percentage fat-free quality of milk.

Key Study

Wang (1996): The framing effect

Wang (1996) carried out important research on the framing effect. Wang pointed out that our decision making in everyday life is very often influenced by social and moral considerations. Prospect theory is limited because it fails to consider such considerations. Wang used various versions of the Asian disease problem in his research. Participants chose between definite survival of two-thirds of the patients (the deterministic option) and a 1/3 probability of all patients surviving and a 2/3 probably of none surviving (the probabilistic option). The deterministic option is much better than the probabilistic one, because it leads on average to the survival

Key Terms

Normative theories: as applied to decision making, theories focusing on how people should make decisions.

Framing effect: the influence of irrelevant aspects of a situation (e.g., wording of the problem) on decision making.

of twice as many patients. As predicted, the overwhelming majority of participants chose the deterministic option when the problem was phrased in terms of 600 unknown patients (see the figure below).

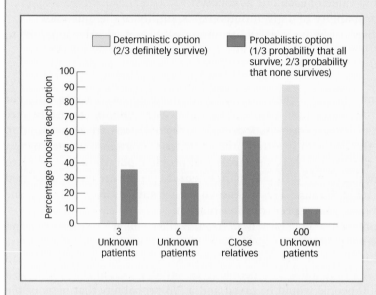

Effects of fairness manipulation on choice of the option with selected or with non-selected survivors. Data from Wang (1996).

More interesting and dramatic findings were obtained by Wang (1996) when the Asian disease problem was phrased in terms of 6 unknown patients, 3 unknown patients, or 6 close relatives. There was a large increase in the percentage of participants choosing the probabilistic option with small group size, especially with close relatives (see the figure above). Why was this? Participants chose the probabilistic option with close relatives because it seemed *fair* to give all of them the same chances of surviving. Thus, social and moral factors (not considered directly by prospect theory) can outweigh the rational approach of simply trying to maximize the numbers of people saved.

More evidence that social factors are important was reported by Wang, Simons, and Brédart (2001). They studied the framing effect using a life-and-death problem involving either 6 billion human lives or 6 billion extraterrestrial lives. There was the usual framing effect when human lives were at stake, but no framing effect at all when only extraterrestrial lives were involved.

Discussion points
1. Think of an experience in your own life where the decision you made was determined by the situation. How might the outcome have been different if the situational variables had been different?
2. Your neighbor's dog has been hit by a vehicle and seems to have broken a leg. Would what you do about this vary depending on how you get on with your neighbor?

KEY STUDY EVALUATION
Wang's (1996) important research was influential in showing that previous research designed to test prospect theory had been too narrowly based. More specifically, Wang showed that we can only understand framing effects fully by taking account of the social and moral context in which we arrive at decisions. However, it is important to note that Wang's research was laboratory-based, and might not apply in the real world. Which option would you choose if you were placed in the horrific position of deciding between definitely saving 4 out of 6 close relatives or probably seeing all 6 die? Note also that there was only a small majority in favor of the probabilistic option with 6 close relatives. This suggests that there are important individual differences involved in making that kind of agonizing choice.

found that participants who had lost $3 focused much more on the fact that they nevertheless finished with a profit of $2 than they had predicted beforehand.

Rottenstreich and Shu (2004, pp. 458–459) argued that decision making can be based on "two separate systems—an affective [emotional] system and a perhaps more cognitive system compatible with prospect theory." Supporting evidence comes in a study by Rottenstreich and Hsee (2001). American participants imagined they might win a $500 coupon that could be used for tuition payments or towards the costs of a holiday in Paris, Venice, or Rome. It was assumed that the prospect of a holiday abroad would create more emotion than using the money for tuition. Different groups of participants were told that the chances were either 1% or 99% of winning the coupon. When there was only a 1% chance, most participants decided they would use the coupon for a holiday. In contrast, most participants given a 99% chance of winning decided they would use the coupon for tuition fees. Thus, the emotional system was dominant when there was a small hope of winning the prize, whereas the cognitive system was dominant when the odds were very favorable.

Another limitation of prospect theory is that it ignores individual differences, in spite of the fact that we all know some people are more willing to take risks than others. Josephs, Larrick, Steele, and Nisbett (1992) used a task in which individuals chose between a sure win of $10 versus a 50% chance of winning $20 on a gamble. Individuals low in self-esteem were 50% more likely than those high in self-esteem to choose the sure gain. Why was this? People with low self-esteem are concerned that negative or threatening events will reduce their fragile self-esteem.

A final limitation with prospect theory is that it ignores cross-cultural differences. Do you think Americans would be more inclined to take risky financial decisions than Asians? I hazard a guess that your answer is, "Yes." In fact, the correct answer is the opposite. Weber and Hsee (2000) discussed several of their studies in which they found Americans *less* inclined than Chinese individuals to make risky financial decisions. The main reason is that Chinese individuals can afford to take greater financial risks because they enjoy more protection from their family and social networks. As predicted, Americans with strong networks were more willing than those with weak networks to make risky financial decisions, and Chinese people with weak networks were risk-averse.

Evaluation

+ Prospect theory provides a more accurate account of human decision making than previous theories.

+ The notion that we attach more weight to losses than to gains provides an explanation for many phenomena (e.g., loss aversion; framing effect).

− The theory doesn't consider the impact of social and emotional factors on decision making (e.g., Rottenstreich & Hsee, 2001; Wang, 1996).

− The theory neglects individual differences in the willingness to take risks (e.g., Josephs et al., 1992).

− The theory ignores cultural differences in risk taking (e.g., Weber & Hsee, 2000).

− As Hardman and Harries (2002, p. 76) pointed out, "There is no apparent rationale for . . . the value function . . . The value function is descriptive of behavior but does not go beyond this." In other words, we aren't given a convincing explanation of *why* people are more sensitive to losses than to gains. As we have seen, part of the answer is that we tend to exaggerate how badly we will feel about losses (Kermer et al., 2006).

WHAT WILL PEOPLE THINK?

As Tetlock (1991, p. 453) pointed out, "Subjects in laboratory studies . . . function in a social vacuum . . . in which they do not need to worry about the interpersonal consequences of their conduct." This is an important point, because our everyday decision making is strongly influenced by the social and cultural context in which we live.

More specifically, as Tetlock (2002) argued, we often behave like intuitive politicians concerned to justify our decisions to other people. In this section, we consider evidence relating to Tetlock's social functionalist approach.

Findings

We can see how social factors influence decision making by focusing on the behavior of New York cab drivers. Camerer, Babcock, Loewenstein, and Thaler (1997) studied how many hours these cab drivers worked each day. From a purely economic perspective, they should work fewer hours when business is slack and longer hours when business is good. In fact, many cab drivers do precisely the opposite. They set themselves a target income for each day, and only stop work when they have reached it. Thus, New York cab drivers work unnecessarily long hours when business is poor and miss out on easy money when business is good. Why do they behave in this apparently illogical way? The answer is that their behavior is "an adaptive response to no-excuses accountability pressures from the home front to bring home the bacon" (Tetlock & Mellers, 2002, p. 98).

We can see the importance people attach to being able to justify their decisions to others in a study by Simonson and Staw (1992). The study focused on the **sunk-cost effect**, which involves a tendency to throw good money after bad in an attempt to recoup one's losses. Participants were told about a beer company selling light beer and non-alcoholic beer. They had to recommend which product should receive an additional $3 million for advertising purposes. When they had done that, they were informed that the president of the company had made the same decision, but this had produced disappointing results. The participants were then told the company had decided to allocate an additional $10 million from the advertising budget to be divided between the two products.

The three key conditions varied in the emphasis given to justifying one's decision to others:

1. High-accountability condition: Participants were told that information about their decision might be shared with other students and instructors. They were also asked to give permission to record an interview about their decision.
2. Medium-accountability condition: Participants were told the information provided to them should be sufficient to make a good decision.
3. Low-accountability condition: Participants were informed that their decisions would be confidential.

Simonson and Staw (1992) assessed the extent of the sunk-cost effect (putting extra money into the product that had already fruitlessly received previous advertising money). The tendency towards a sunk-cost effect was greatest in the high-accountability condition and lowest in the low-accountability condition (see the figure on the left). Participants in the high-accountability condition tried to justify their previously ineffective course of action (i.e., investing in one type of beer) by increasing their commitment to it.

Schwartz, Chapman, Brewer, and Bergus (2004) found that even the decisions of medical experts can be swayed by considerations of accountability. Doctors were presented with the case of a patient with osteoarthritis for whom anti-inflammatory drugs had proved ineffective. In the two-option condition, they chose between referring the patient to an orthopedic specialist to discuss surgery or combining referral with prescribing an untried anti-inflammatory drug. In the three-option condition, there were the same two options plus referral combined with a different untried anti-inflammatory drug. The doctors were *more* likely to select the referral-only option in the

Key Term

Sunk-cost effect: expending additional resources to justify some previous commitment (i.e., throwing good money after bad).

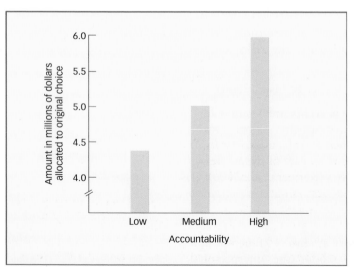

Millions of dollars allocated to original choice (sunk-cost effect) as a function of accountability. Data from Simonson and Staw (1992).

three-option condition, which seems contrary to common sense. This bias was greater when they were made accountable for their decisions. What is going on here? In the three-option condition, it is very difficult to justify selecting one anti-inflammatory drug over the other one. Selecting the remaining option (i.e., referral only) made it easier for the doctors to justify their decision.

Evaluation

+ The assumption within the social functionalist approach that our decisions in everyday life are generally influenced by social and cultural factors is absolutely right.

+ We often experience pressure to justify our decisions to others, and this is the case even with experts (e.g., Schwartz et al., 2004).

− Important factors within prospect theory (e.g., our greater sensitivity to losses than gains) are ignored by the social functionalist approach.

− Tetlock and others favoring the social functionalist approach have often criticized other researchers for conducting experiments not making any real demands on social responsibility. Ironically, much the same can be said of their own research!

COMPLEX DECISION MAKING

So far we have mainly considered decision making applied to fairly simple problems. In real life, however, we sometimes have to make very complex decisions (e.g., Shall I marry John? Shall I move to Australia?). How do we approach such decisions? According to multi-attribute utility theory (Wright, 1984), the decision maker should go through the following stages:

1. Identify dimensions relevant to the decision.
2. Decide how to weight those dimensions.
3. Obtain a total **utility** (i.e., subjective desirability) for each option by summing its weighted dimensional values.
4. Select the option with the highest weighted total.

We can see how this theory might work in practice by considering what happens when someone decides which apartment to rent. First, consideration is paid to the relevant dimensions (e.g., number of rooms; location; rent per week). Second, the relative utility of each dimension is calculated. Third, the various apartments being considered are compared in terms of their total utility, and the individual chooses the one with the highest total utility.

As you have probably guessed, people rarely follow the dictates of this theory in real life. There are various reasons for this. The procedure can be very complex, the set of relevant dimensions can't always be worked out, and the dimensions themselves may not be clearly separate from each other.

BOUNDED RATIONALITY

Herb Simon (1957) drew an important distinction between unbounded rationality and bounded rationality. Within models of unbounded rationality (multi-attribute utility theory is an example), it is assumed that all relevant information is used by the decision maker. As a consequence, people are in a position to make the best possible decision or choice. This approach doesn't bear much relationship to real life. As Klein (2001, p. 103) pointed out, "In the majority of field settings, there is no way to determine if a decision choice is optimal owing to time pressure, uncertainty, ill-defined goals, and so forth."

Simon (1957) argued that we possess bounded rationality rather than unbounded rationality. The essence of **bounded rationality** is that we produce reasonable or workable solutions to problems in spite of our limited processing capacity by using short-cut

Key Terms

Utility:
the subjective desirability of a given outcome in decision making.

Bounded rationality:
the notion that people are as rational as their processing limitations permit.

strategies including heuristics or rules of thumb. More specifically, decision making can be "bounded" by constraints in the environment (e.g., information costs; time costs) or by constraints in the mind (e.g., limited attention; limited memory). What is important is the degree of fit or match between the mind and the environment. According to Simon (1990, p. 7), "Human rational behavior is shaped like a scissors whose blades are the structure of the task environment and the computational capabilities of the actor." If we consider only one blade (i.e., the task environment or the individual's abilities) we will have only a partial understanding of how we make decisions. In similar fashion, we couldn't understand how scissors cut if we focused on only one blade.

How does bounded rationality work in practice? According to Simon (1978), we often use a heuristic or rule of thumb known as satisficing. The essence of **satisficing** (formed by combining satisfactory and sufficing) is that individuals consider various options one at a time and select the first one meeting their minimum requirements. Satisficing does not guarantee the decision is the best one, but it is especially useful when the different options become available at different points in time. For example, you might decide who to marry on the basis of the satisficing heuristic by setting a minimum acceptable level. The first person reaching (or exceeding) that level would be chosen. If you set the level too low, you may spend many years bitterly regretting having used the satisficing heuristic!

Tversky (1972) put forward a theory of decision making resembling Simon's bounded rationality approach. According to his elimination-by-aspects theory, decision makers eliminate options by considering one relevant attribute after another. For example, someone buying a house may initially consider the attribute of location, eliminating all houses not lying within a given area. Next they may consider the attribute of price, eliminating all those properties costing above a certain figure. This process continues until only one option remains. This strategy has the advantage of being fairly undemanding. However, the option selected depends on the order in which the attributes are considered, and so frequently someone using this strategy won't make the best choice.

Dijksterhuis and Nordgren (2006) proposed unconscious thought theory. According to this theory, there is an important distinction between conscious thought (involving attention) and unconscious thought (thinking occurring without attention). Most people assume that complex decision making is better when people use conscious thought, but Dijksterhuis and Nordgren argued precisely the opposite. Conscious thought has the disadvantage of limited processing capacity (because of the involvement of attention). In addition, when we are thinking consciously, we often attribute excessive weight or importance to only a small fraction of the information presented to us. Since unconscious thought does not possess these disadvantages, it can produce superior decision making to conscious thought when the problem is a complex one.

Findings

Payne (1976) addressed the issue of the extent to which decision makers behave as predicted by Simon and by Tversky. Participants decided which apartment to rent on the basis of information about various attributes (e.g., rent; cleanliness; noise level; and distance from campus). The number of apartments to be considered ranged between 2 and 12 and the number of attributes per apartment varied between 4 and 12.

When there were many apartments to consider, participants typically started by using a simple strategy such as satisficing or elimination-by-aspects. Here is one participant's account of using elimination-by-aspects: "I'm going to look at landlord attitude. In H it's fair. In D it's poor. In B it's fair, and in A it's good. In L, the attitude is poor. In K it's poor. In J it's good, and in I it's poor . . . So, that's important to me . . . So, I'm not going to live any place where it's poor" (Payne, 1976, p. 379). When only a few apartments remained to be considered, there was often a switch to a more complex strategy corresponding to the assumptions of multi-attribute utility theory.

An important factor influencing decision-making strategies is time pressure. Payne, Bettman, and Johnson (1988) found that moderate time pressure led decision makers to become slightly more selective in their processing. When the time pressure was severe, however, decision makers speeded up their processing, focused their attention on only a fraction of the available information, and changed their processing strategies.

Key Term
Satisficing: selection of the first choice that meets certain minimum requirements; the word is formed from the two words satisfactory and sufficing.

It seems reasonable to assume (and it was assumed within multi-attribute utility theory) that any given individual's assessment of the utility or preference (desirability × importance) of any given attribute remains constant over time. In fact, our preferences are actually subject to change. Simons, Krawczyk, and Holyoak (2004) asked participants to decide between job offers from two department store chains, "Bonnie's Best" and "Splendor." There were four relevant attributes (salary; holiday package; commuting time; and office accommodation). Each job offer was preferable to the other on two attributes and inferior on two attributes. Participants assessed their preference for each attribute. They were then told that one of the jobs was in a much better location than the other. This often tipped the balance in favor of choosing the job in the better location. The participants then assessed their preference for each attribute again. Preferences for desirable attributes of the chosen job increased and preferences for undesirable attributes of that job decreased. Such preference changes make sense because they increase decision makers' satisfaction with their choice.

We turn now to unconscious thought theory. Some of the most convincing evidence in its support was obtained by Dijksterhuis (2004), who used three conditions in research on decision making. In the control condition, participants made immediate decisions when the various options had been presented. In the conscious thought condition, participants had a few minutes to think about their decision. In the unconscious thought condition, participants were distracted for a few minutes and then made their decision in the virtual absence of conscious thought.

Participants were presented with detailed information about four hypothetical apartments in Amsterdam. Each apartment was described in terms of 15 attributes. The most attractive apartment had 8 positive, 4 negative, and 3 neutral attributes, whereas all the others had 5 positive, 6 negative, and 4 neutral attributes. The task was to select the best apartment. Performance was best in the unconscious thought condition and worst in the control condition (see the figure on the right). The participants were then asked whether their choice was based on a global judgment or on one or two specific attributes. Far more of those in the unconscious thought condition than in the conscious thought condition indicated that they had made a global judgment (55.6% vs. 26.5%, respectively). This suggests that the relatively poor performance in the conscious thought condition occurred because participants focused too much on only a small fraction of the available information.

We have seen that unconscious thought can lead to superior decisions to conscious thought when decision making is complex. However, it is predicted by unconscious thought theory that there should be an interaction between mode of thought and complexity of decision making. Since conscious thought is precise but has limited capacity, it is well suited to simple decision making but becomes increasingly ineffective as decision making becomes more complex. Findings consistent with these prediction were reported by Dijksterhuis, Bos, Nordgren, and van Baaren (2006). Participants read information concerning four hypothetical cars. In the simple condition, each car was described in terms of 4 attributes. In the complex condition, each car was described in terms of 12 attributes. Participants either spent 4 minutes thinking about the cars (conscious thought condition) or they solved

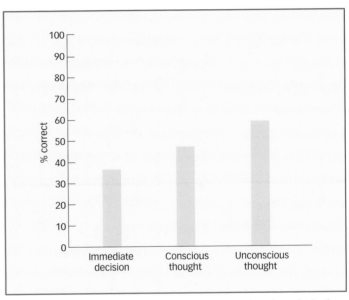

Performance on an apartment-selection task as a function of whether the decision was immediate or delayed and based on conscious or unconscious thought. Data from Dijksterhuis (2004).

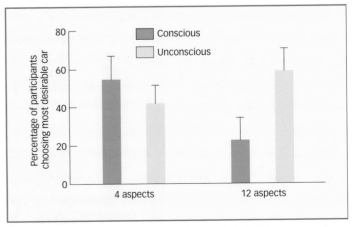

Percentage of participants choosing the most desirable car as a function of decision complexity and mode of thought (conscious vs. unconscious). From Dijksterhuis et al. (2006). Copyright © 2006 AAAS. Reproduced with permission.

anagrams for 4 minutes before choosing a car (unconscious thought condition). The findings are shown in the figure on the previous page). As predicted, more participants in the unconscious thought condition than in the conscious thought condition selected the most desirable car when the decision was complex, with the opposite pattern being found when the decision was simple.

In sum, it is clear that unconscious thought can be superior to conscious thought when people are confronted by a complex problem. However, that is only the case under certain conditions. In Dijksterhuis's experiments, participants in the conscious thought condition had to rely heavily on their memory for the information contained in the problem. It is probable that conscious thought would have proved more effective than unconscious thought if participants had been allowed access to problem information throughout the time preceding their decision.

Evaluation

+ There is much support for the assumptions that humans possess bounded rationality and frequently use the satisficing heuristic.

+ Several factors influencing decision making (e.g., number of choices remaining to be considered; extent of time pressure) have been identified.

+ Some of the strengths and limitations of conscious thought and of unconscious thought have been identified.

− Most theories implicitly assume that attribute preferences don't change over time, but there is evidence (e.g., Simons et al., 2004) that this assumption is incorrect.

− Insufficient attention has been paid to individual differences. For example, Schwartz et al. (2002) found that some individuals are satisficers (content with making reasonable decisions), whereas others are maximizers (perfectionists). Satisficers are happier than maximizers and experience less regret and self-blame.

− Superiority of unconscious thought over conscious thought with complex decision making would probably not be found if people had full access to problem information throughout the decision-making process.

Chapter Summary

Finding the solution
- The phenomenon of functional fixedness and our persistence with problem-solving strategies that are no longer appropriate reveal that past experience isn't always useful for problem solving.
- Beneficial effects of past experience on current problem solving (positive transfer) often involve making use of analogies.
- Positive transfer over long periods of time and to new situations is facilitated by metacognitive training (e.g., orienting; self-judging).
- Insight typically consists of a sudden restructuring of a problem in which an incorrect problem representation is replaced by the correct one. This can involve constraint relaxation, re-encoding, or elaboration.
- Incubation (putting a problem to one side for a while) often leads to effective problem solving, probably because it produces forgetting of incorrect strategies.
- According to Newell and Simon in their General Problem Solver, we have limited processing capacity and so make use of heuristics or rules of thumb (e.g., means–ends analysis) in problem solving.

- Problem solvers engage in progress monitoring, changing their strategy when progress towards a solution is too slow.

Decisions, decisions

- We can assess the quality of decision making by focusing either on the outcome or on the reasoning involved.
- According to prospect theory, people are much more sensitive to potential losses than to potential gains. The theory explains the framing effect, why people are unwilling to accept potential losses even though the potential gains exceed the potential losses, and why they prefer a sure gain to a risky but potentially greater gain.
- Prospect theory is limited because insufficient attention is paid to emotional, social, and moral factors, to individual differences, and to cross-cultural differences.
- Decision making (even among medical experts) is often influenced by the great importance we attach to justifying our decisions to others.
- People possess bounded rationality and often use the satisficing heuristic when engaged in complex decision making.
- Complex decision making is influenced by time pressure, by the number of options to be considered, and by changing attribute preferences.
- Conscious thought has been found to be superior to unconscious thought on simple decision-making tasks, with the opposite being the case with complex tasks.

Further Reading

- Bowden, E.M., Jung-Beeman, M., Fleck, J., & Kounios, J. (2005). New approaches to demystifying insight. *Trends in Cognitive Sciences*, 9, 322–328.
- Eysenck, M.W. (2006). *Fundamentals of cognition*. Hove, UK: Psychology Press. The topics discussed in this chapter are dealt with more fully in Chapters 23 and 24 of this introductory textbook on cognitive psychology.
- Hardman, D., & Macchi, L. (2003). *Thinking: Psychological perspectives on reasoning, judgement and decision making*. Chichester, UK: Wiley. Several chapters in this edited book provide good reviews of decision making.
- Koehler, D.J., & Harvey, N. (2004). *Blackwell handbook of judgement and decision making*. Oxford, UK: Blackwell. This book contains interesting chapters by several well-known experts on decision making.
- Robertson, S.I. (2001). *Problem solving*. Hove, UK: Psychology Press. There is good coverage of many topics in problem solving in this introductory textbook.
- Sternberg, R.J. (2003). *Cognitive psychology* (3rd ed.). Belmont, CA: Wadsworth. This textbook provides a useful introductory account of research on problem solving.

Contents

Language

10

Language is of absolutely central importance to our lives. Our social interactions with other people depend very heavily on language, and language plays a key role in most of our thinking. Imagine trying to study psychology without a good command of language! The main reason why we are much more knowledgeable than people of previous generations is that knowledge (mostly in the form of language) is passed on from one generation to the next.

What is language? According to the *Oxford Dictionary of Psychology* (2001), language is, "a conventional system of communicative sounds and sometimes (though not necessarily) written symbols." The crucial word is "communicative"—the main purpose of language is communication. However, Crystal (1997) identified a total of *eight* language functions, of which communication was one. We also use language for thinking, to record information, to express emotion (e.g., "I love you"), to pretend to be animals (e.g., "Woof! Woof!"), to express identity with a group (e.g., singing in church), and so on.

There are four main language skills: reading; listening to speech; speaking; and writing. It is easy to assume that any given person will have generally strong or weak language skills. This assumption may sometimes (but certainly not always) be correct with respect to an individual's first language. However, it is often incorrect with second language acquisition. After having spent 10 years at school learning French, I can just about read newspapers and easy novels in French and can write French reasonably well. However, I find it agonizingly difficult to understand rapid spoken French, and I have very limited ability to speak French.

In this chapter, we are concerned with three of the four main language skills with writing being omitted. As someone who has written over 7 million words for publication, that isn't because I think writing is unimportant! The reason is that much less is known about the processes involved in writing than any other language skill. We start with a discussion of the basic processes involved in reading, followed by an analysis of what is involved in speech perception. After that, we focus on the comprehension processes used to understand language whether presented in the form of text or spoken words. Finally, we focus on the processes involved in speech production.

READING

Reading is an extremely important skill in most societies, and adults without effective reading skills are at a great disadvantage. It is also important to study reading because most mental activities are related to reading. Indeed, it has sometimes been described as "visually guided thinking."

We focus on basic reading processes mainly at the level of the individual word within sentences. In addition, we consider the processes involved in working out the syntactical or grammatical structure of sentences. Processes involved in the comprehension of texts are discussed later in the chapter.

EYE MOVEMENTS

We can obtain some understanding of basic processes in reading by recording readers' eye movements. Our eyes seem to move smoothly across the page when reading but actually move in rapid jerks (**saccades**). Reading saccades take 20–30 ms to complete and are separated by fixations lasting for 200–250 ms. The length of each saccade is about

Key Term

Saccades:
fast eye movements or jumps that cannot be altered after being initiated.

Reading is a vital skill in most societies and a lack of this skill in adults is a distinct disadvantage.

eight letters or spaces. Information is extracted from the text only during each fixation and not during the intervening saccades.

Readers typically fixate 80% of content words (nouns, verbs, and adjectives) compared to 20% of function words (articles, conjunctions, and pronouns). Words not fixated tend to be common, short, or predictable. In contrast, words fixated for longer than average are generally rare words or words unpredictable in the sentence context. Common words are usually more predictable than rare words, making it important to disentangle the effects of word frequency and word predictability. McDonald and Shillcock (2003) found that many of the apparent effects of word frequency on length of eye fixations were actually a result of word predictability. Finally, there is the **spillover effect**: The fixation time on a word is longer when preceded by a rare or unpredictable word rather than a common or predictable one.

How can we explain these various findings? Perhaps readers fixate a word until they have processed it adequately, after which they immediately fixate the next word until it in turn has been adequately processed. Alas, there are two problems with that viewpoint. First, it takes upwards of 80 ms to execute an eye-movement program. If readers didn't start to plan the next eye movement until they had finished processing the current word, they would waste time waiting for their eyes to move to the next word. Second, it is difficult to see how readers could decide to skip words, because they would know nothing about the next word until they had started fixating it.

Reichle et al. (1998, 2003) provided an answer to the question posed in the previous paragraph in their E-Z Reader model (see the figure on the left). They argued that the next eye movement is programmed after only *part* of the processing of the currently fixated word has occurred. This assumption makes a lot of sense, because it greatly reduces the time between completion of processing on the current word and movement of the eyes to the next word. Any spare time is used to start processing the next word. There is typically less spare time available with rare or unpredictable words than with common or predictable ones, and that accounts for the spillover effects described above. If the processing of the next word is completed rapidly enough (e.g., it is highly predictable in the sentence context), it is skipped.

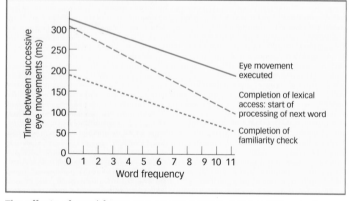

The effects of word frequency on eye movements according to the E-Z Reader model. Adapted from Reichle et al. (1998).

The E-Z Reader model indicates the processes determining *when* we move our eyes in reading and *where* we move them. However, it is limited in that it doesn't tell us much about *what* kinds of processing readers are engaged in during reading.

SOUND IN READING

It is easy to think of reading as being only a visual skill since all the information presented to the reader is visual. However, when reading a really difficult chapter in a book, you have probably found yourself muttering some of the words in the text to yourself. This suggests that **phonology** (the sound of words) may play an important role in reading. According to Frost's (1998) strong phonological model, phonological processing is *always* involved in reading. In fact, as we will see, phonological processing is often (but not always) used in reading.

Phonological processing is more likely to be used when reading is difficult. For example, Jared, Levy, and Rayner (1999) found using a proofreading task that the use of phonology depended on the nature of the words and on participants' reading ability. More specifically, phonological processing was used to access the meaning of low-frequency

Key Terms

Spillover effect: any given word is fixated longer during reading when it is preceded by a rare or unpredictable word rather than a common or predictable word.

Phonology: information about the sounds of words and parts of words.

words but not high-frequency ones. In addition, poor readers were more likely than good readers to use phonological processing to access meaning.

Hanley and McDonnell (1997) reported reasonable evidence that accessing word meaning doesn't have to involve prior phonological processing. They studied a patient (PS) who didn't seem to have access to an internal phonological representation of words, and who couldn't pronounce words accurately. In spite of this, PS understood the meaning of words while reading.

READING ALOUD

Reading aloud familiar words (and even most nonwords) seems about as easy a task as you can imagine. Indeed, I would be very surprised if you had any difficulty at all in reading out the following list of words and nonwords:

CAT   FOG   COMB   PINT   MANTINESS   FASS

However, close inspection of what you have just done reveals some hidden complexities. For example, how do you know the "b" in "comb" is silent, and that "pint" doesn't rhyme with "hint"? Presumably you have specific information stored in long-term memory about how to pronounce these words. However, that can't explain your ability to pronounce nonwords such as "mantiness" and "fass" that you have never seen before. Perhaps nonwords are pronounced by analogy with real words (e.g., "fass" is pronounced to rhyme with "mass"). Alternatively, we may use rules governing the translation of letter strings into sounds to generate pronunciations for nonwords.

Dual-route model

The take-home message from the above paragraph is that reading words aloud can be achieved in more than one way. This insight is at the heart of the dual-route model put forward by Coltheart et al. (2001; see the figure on the right). According to this model, there are three routes between the printed word and speech, all of which start with orthographic analysis (used for identifying and grouping letters in printed words). Why is a model with *three* routes called a *dual*-route model? The reason is that the key distinction is between a lexical look-up route based on a lexicon or mental dictionary (Routes 2 and 3) and a non-lexical route (Route 1). The nonlexical route involves converting spelling (graphemes or basic units of written language) into sound (phonemes or basic units of sound). This is known as grapheme–phoneme conversion. To oversimplify somewhat, people reading aloud will generally rely mainly on the lexical or dictionary look-up route when reading words. However, they will use the non-lexical route when reading nonwords because nonwords don't have dictionary entries. More precisely, words and nonwords activate *both* routes, and what readers say is determined by which route first provides a pronunciation.

How can we test this model? One approach involves identifying brain-damaged patients who are largely reliant on only *one* of the routes. What would happen if a patient had access only to Route 1? The use of rules for converting letters into sounds should permit accurate pronunciation of *regular* words (i.e., words in which the pronunciation is predictable

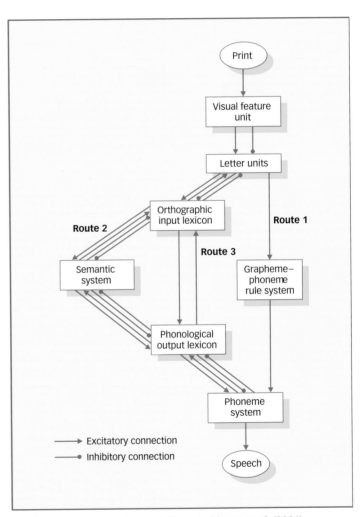

The dual-route cascaded model. From Coltheart et al. (2001). Copyright © American Psychological Association. Reprinted with permission.

Regular words	Irregular words
fantasy	chemistry
meet	hierarchy
passenger	sapphire
Swiss	Worcester

The English language contains a high degree of irregularity, so the same rules of pronunciation cannot be applied to all words with similar spellings.

BOUGH   COUGH   DOUGH

from the letters). Such words (e.g., "fine"; "save") can be read with no special knowledge of the word. The use of grapheme–phoneme conversion rules also allows nonwords to be pronounced accurately. However, such patients should struggle with *irregular* words in which the pronunciation is *not* predictable from the spelling (e.g., "island"; "yacht").

Patients conforming most closely to the above predictions suffer from **surface dyslexia**, a condition in which regular words can be read but irregular ones cannot. McCarthy and Warrington (1986) studied a surface dyslexic (KT) who read 100% of nonwords accurately as well as 81% of regular words. However, he was successful with only 41% of irregular words, with more than 70% of his errors involving treating irregular words as if they were regular.

What would happen if a patient had access only to Route 2, which involves the lexicon or mental dictionary and the semantic system? He/she would be able to pronounce familiar words (whether regular or irregular) and understand them. This is because Route 2 goes through the semantic or meaning system and provides access to information about the sound pattern of words in that system. However, the patient should find it difficult to pronounce unfamiliar words and nonwords, because he/she wouldn't be able to use grapheme–phoneme conversion. Patients with **phonological dyslexia** fit this pattern, because it involves problems with reading unfamiliar words and nonwords. For example, Beauvois and Derouesné (1979) presented a phonological dyslexic (RG) with 40 words and 40 nonwords. RG read 100% of the real words accurately but only 10% of the nonwords.

What would happen if a patient had access only to Route 3, in which the lexicon is used but not the semantic system or grapheme–phoneme conversion? Such a patient would be able to pronounce regular and irregular words accurately. However, he/she wouldn't understand the meanings of regular or irregular words, and would have great problems with nonwords. Some phonological dyslexics fit this pattern. For example, Funnell (1983) found that WB could read about 85% of words but had poor ability to make semantic judgments about these words. These findings support the notion that WB bypassed the semantic system when reading words. As predicted, WB couldn't pronounce any nonwords.

Studies on healthy individuals have also produced findings consistent with the model. Seidenberg et al. (1984) found that irregular words took longer to name than regular ones with low-frequency words but not with high-frequency ones. According to the model, the lexical route operates more slowly with low-frequency words than with high-frequency ones. As a result, the naming of low-frequency irregular words is especially slow because conflicting information about their pronunciation is received from the lexical and nonlexical routes.

Coltheart et al. (2001) developed a computational model to test their theoretical approach. They presented the model with 7981 words, and found that 7898 (99.5%) were read accurately. When the model was presented with 7000 one-syllable nonwords, it read 98.9% of them correctly.

Evaluation

⊕ The dual-route model has been applied successfully to reading in healthy individuals.

⊕ The dual-route model provides a very good account of reading disorders such as surface dyslexia and phonological dyslexia.

⊖ The model is very good at naming words and nonwords accurately. However, it is much less successful at accounting for naming *times* (especially for words).

⊖ Coltheart et al. (2001, p. 236) admitted their model couldn't be applied to several major languages: "The Chinese, Japanese, and Korean writing systems are structurally so different from the English writing system that a model like the [dual-route model] would simply not be applicable: for example, monosyllabic non-words cannot even be written in the Chinese script or in Japanese kanji, so the distinction between a lexical and non-lexical route for reading aloud cannot even arise."

PARSING

It is very important in reading a sentence to identify its syntactical (grammatical) structure; this is known as **parsing**. Grammar is concerned with the way words are combined within a sentence to convey meaning. Much research on parsing has focused on ambiguous sentences. Why is that the case? Parsing typically occurs very rapidly and accurately, and this makes it difficult to study the processes involved. However, observing the problems readers have with ambiguous sentences provides revealing information about parsing processes. Such sentences can also be the source of jokes. For example, Groucho Marx in the film *Animal Crackers* came out with the line: "One morning I shot an elephant in my pyjamas. How he got into my pyjamas, I don't know."

PARSING AND AMBIGUITY: "She bit into the doughnut with relish."

"she bit into the doughnut, with relish"

"She bit into, the doughnut with relish"

| Key Term

Parsing:
an analysis of the syntactical or grammatical structure of sentences.

A central issue concerns *when* semantic (meaning) information is used in parsing. According to one-stage models, *all* sources of information (syntactic and semantic) are used at the same time to construct a syntactic model of sentences. In contrast, the first stage of processing in two-stage models uses *only* syntactic information, with semantic information being used during the second stage. The most influential two-stage approach is the garden-path model (Frazier & Rayner, 1982) and the most influential one-stage approach is the constraint-based theory of MacDonald, Pearlmutter, and Seidenberg (1994).

Two-stage approach

Frazier and Rayner's (1982) garden-path model was given that name because readers can be misled or "led up the garden path" by ambiguous sentences. Its crucial assumption is that semantic factors don't influence the construction of the initial syntactic or grammatical structure. Support for this prediction was reported by Ferreira and Clifton (1986). Eye movements were recorded while participants read sentences such as the following:

- The defendant examined by the lawyer turned out to be unreliable.
- The evidence examined by the lawyer turned out to be unreliable.

If (contrary to the model) readers initially make use of semantic information, they will experience ambiguity for the first sentence but not for the second. The reason is that the defendant could possibly examine something but the evidence could not. In fact, readers experienced ambiguity equally for both sentences. This implies that semantic information did *not* influence the formation of the initial syntactic structure.

Trueswell, Tanenhaus, and Garnsey (1994) argued that the semantic manipulations used by Ferreira and Clifton (1986) were too weak to allow semantic information to influence the early stages of parsing. Accordingly, they used sentences with stronger semantic constraints. With their sentences, semantic information *was* used at an early stage to assist rapid identification of the correct syntactic structure.

One-stage approach

According to MacDonald et al.'s (1994) constraint-based theory, all relevant sources of information (including semantic) are available immediately to the parser. Competing analyses of the current sentence are activated at the same time, with these analyses being ranked according to the strength of their activation. The syntactic structure receiving the most support from the available information is highly activated. Readers become confused when reading ambiguous sentences if the correct syntactic structure is less activated than one or more incorrect structures.

The study by Trueswell et al. (1994; discussed above) suggested that semantic information is used early in parsing and so is in line with the model. Additional support was provided by Boland and Blodgett (2001). Their main focus was on noun/verb homographs (e.g., duck; train)—words that can be used as nouns or verbs. For example, if you read a sentence starting, "She saw her duck and . . . ," you wouldn't know whether "duck" was being used as a noun (" . . . and chickens near the barn") or as a verb (" . . . and stumble near the barn"). According to the theory, readers should initially try to form a syntactic structure in which the homograph is used in its most common meaning. For example, "duck" is a verb more often than a noun, whereas "train" is more often a noun. As predicted, readers had greater problems in parsing when noun/verb homographs were used in their less common meaning.

Boland and Blodgett (2001) pointed out that if meaning is used very early in parsing then readers should take account of information from the preceding context (e.g., the previous sentence). They arranged matters so the prior context was sometimes misleading and sometimes not. Consider the following example in which the context is misleading:

As they walked around, Kate looked at all of Jimmy's pets.
She saw her duck and stumble near the barn.

As predicted, it took longer to read the second sentence when the context was misleading than when it was not. However, context influenced parsing *later* in processing than predicted by the theory.

Overall Evaluation

+ There is reasonable support for both one-stage and two-stage models or theories, suggesting that each approach works well in some circumstances.

+ Semantic information is sometimes used from the outset to clarify the syntactic structure of ambiguous sentences as predicted by constraint-based theory. It seems efficient that readers should use all relevant information in this way.

− Semantic information is sometimes used later in processing than assumed by constraint-based theory (e.g., Boland & Blodgett, 2001).

− It has proved difficult to obtain findings distinguishing clearly between the two approaches. As Harley (2001, p. 264) argued, "Proponents of the garden-path model argue that the effects that are claimed to support constraint-based models arise because the second stage of parsing begins very quickly, and that many experiments that are supposed to be looking at the first stage are in fact looking at the second stage of parsing."

SPEECH PERCEPTION

We can generally understand what other people are saying to us even when they speak in a strange dialect and/or ungrammatically. Indeed, we take our ability to understand others' speech for granted. This is not surprising in view of the enormous experience we have all had in using the English language and in listening to other people.

Can you think of any reasons why speech perception might be much more complex than it appears? Consider the problems you have probably experienced trying to understand foreigners speaking in a language you studied for several years at school. If your experience is anything like mine, what you hear is someone who seems to be talking incredibly rapidly without any pauses for breath. This illustrates two of the problems listeners have to contend with all the time. First, language is typically spoken at the rate of about 10 **phonemes** (basic speech sounds conveying meaning) per second, so we must process spoken language very rapidly. Second, there is the **segmentation problem**, which is the difficulty of separating out or distinguishing words from the pattern of speech sounds. This problem occurs because speech typically consists of a continuously changing pattern of sound with few periods of silence. This makes it difficult to know when one word ends and the next one begins.

We tend to take our ability to understand the speech of others for granted, but speech perception is more complex than it might appear.

How do we cope with the segmentation problem in everyday life? First, we use our knowledge of what is possible in the English language. For example, a stretch of speech lacking a vowel can't form a word. Evidence that we use this knowledge was reported by Norris et al. (1997). Listeners found it very easy to detect the word "apple" in "vuffapple," because "vuff" could conceivably be an English word. In contrast, listeners found it difficult to identify the word "apple" in "fapple" because the [f] couldn't possibly be an English word.

Second, there is stress. In the English language, the initial **syllable** (a rhythmic unit of speech) is stressed in most content words (e.g., nouns; verbs). Suppose that listeners assume when they hear a word that its first syllable will be stressed. If so, they should find it difficult to identify strings of words in which the stress is *not* on the first syllable.

Key Terms

Phonemes:
basic speech sounds that distinguish one word from another and so convey meaning.

Segmentation problem:
the listener's problem of dividing the almost continuous sounds of speech into separate **phonemes** and words.

Syllable:
a rhythmic unit of speech; words consist of one or more syllables.

When such strings of words (e.g., "conduct ascents uphill") were presented very faintly, they were often misheard (Cutler & Butterfield, 1992). Note, however, that stress is mostly used as a cue to identifying word boundaries when the speech signal is faint or impoverished. It is little used when the speech signal is reasonably strong (Mattys, 2004).

Listeners also have to cope with the problem of **co-articulation**. What this means is that how a speaker produces a given phoneme depends in part on the phonemes preceding and following it. Thus, the pronunciation of any phoneme varies, and the listener has to adjust to variations in pronunciation.

It is generally known that deaf people use lip-reading to help them to understand speech. Less well known is that people whose hearing is intact also use lip-reading. Clear evidence was reported by McGurk and MacDonald (1976). They prepared a videotape of someone saying "ha" repeatedly. The sound channel then changed so there was a voice saying "ga" in synchronization with lip movements still indicating "ba." Listeners said they heard "da," which is based on a blending of the visual and auditory information. This combining of visual and auditory information when the sources of information are in conflict is known as the **McGurk effect**.

In what follows, we focus mainly on the processes involved in identifying words and sentences in spoken language. Issues concerning listeners' overall comprehension or understanding of what a speaker is saying are considered later.

CONTEXT EFFECT

We have seen that listeners contend with various problems when working out what a speaker is saying. Not surprisingly, listeners struggling to identify a spoken word often make use of information from the surrounding sentence context. For example, consider a study by Warren and Warren (1970). Listeners heard a sentence in which a small portion of one word had been removed and replaced with a meaningless sound. The sentences used were as follows (the asterisk indicates a deleted portion of a word):

- It was found that the *eel was on the axle.
- It was found that the *eel was on the shoe.
- It was found that the *eel was on the table.
- It was found that the *eel was on the orange.

Listeners' perception of the crucial element in the sentence (i.e., "*eel") was influenced by sentence context. Those listening to the first sentence heard "wheel," those listening to the second sentence heard "heel," and those exposed to the third and fourth sentences heard "meal" and "peel," respectively. The auditory stimulus (i.e., "*eel") was always the same so *all* that differed was the contextual information. This phenomenon is known as the **phonemic restoration effect**.

What causes the phonemic restoration effect? Samuel (1997) identified two major possibilities:

1. Sentence context has a *direct* and immediate effect on speech processing (i.e., the missing phoneme is processed almost as if it were present).
2. Sentence context has an *indirect* effect involving guessing the identity of the missing phoneme after basic speech processing has occurred.

The evidence (e.g., Samuel, 1981, 1987) favors the second possibility. Samuel added noise to the crucial phoneme or replaced the missing phoneme with noise. If listeners processed the missing phoneme as if it were there, they would have heard the crucial phoneme plus noise in both conditions. However, listeners readily distinguished between the conditions, which seems inconsistent with the first possibility.

COHORT MODEL

Two of the most influential theoretical approaches to speech perception are the TRACE model (McClelland & Elman, 1986) and the cohort model originally proposed by Marslen-Wilson and Tyler (1980). We focus on the cohort model because its predictions are better supported than those of the TRACE model.

The four key assumptions of the original cohort model are as follows:

1. Early in the auditory presentation of a word, all the words conforming to the sound sequence to that point become active. This is the "word-initial cohort."
2. Words belonging to this word-initial cohort are subsequently eliminated if they don't match additional information from the word being presented, or if they are inconsistent with the semantic or other context.
3. Various knowledge sources (e.g., lexical; syntactic; semantic) are processed in parallel (at the same time). These knowledge sources interact and combine with each other.
4. Processing of the presented word continues up until the moment at which information from the word itself and contextual information have eliminated all but one of the words in the word-initial cohort. This is the "recognition point."

> ### A word-initial cohort
>
> This idea suggests that our brains process a word in sections, as it is said, gradually identifying it.
>
> | gen- | gener- | generous |
> |------|--------|----------|
> | gendarme | general | |
> | gender | generate | |
> | general | generous | |
> | generate | | |
> | generous | | |
> | gentleman | | |
> | gentian | | |
> | gentile | | |

Findings

Support for this model was reported by Marslen-Wilson and Tyler (1980). Listeners had to detect specified targets (a given word; a member of a given category; or a word rhyming with a given word) presented within spoken sentences. The sentences were normal (providing useful semantic and syntactic context), syntactic (providing useful grammatical information only), or random (unrelated words lacking any useful context). Listeners used the contextual information available to reduce the time taken to detect targets, often identifying them before the entire word had been presented (see figure on the right).

O'Rourke and Holcomb (2002) tested the prediction that a spoken word is identified when the point is reached (the recognition point) at which only *one* word is consistent with the acoustic signal. Listeners heard words and nonwords, and decided whether each one was a word. The words were selected so that some had an early recognition point whereas others had a late recognition point. As predicted, listeners realized that a word had been presented shortly after its recognition point had been reached. As a result, listeners worked out faster that a word had been presented when its recognition point was early.

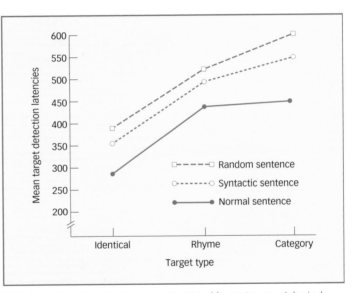

Detection times for word targets presented in sentences. Adapted from Marslen-Wilson and Tyler (1980).

In the original cohort model, it was argued that the processing of the *initial* part of a word was of special importance. Indeed, it was assumed that a spoken word wouldn't be recognized if its initial phoneme was unclear or ambiguous. However, this assumption is too strong. Accordingly, Marslen-Wilson (1990) revised the cohort model so the word-initial cohort can contain words having *similar* initial phonemes to the presented word rather than being limited to words having exactly the same initial phoneme. This revision is an improvement. For example, Allopenna, Magnuson, and Tanenhaus (1998) found a tendency for listeners to activate words rhyming with the auditory input (e.g., "beaker" activated "speaker"). Thus, some words *not* sharing an initial phoneme with the auditory input are nevertheless included in the word cohort.

According to the original version of the cohort model, context influences word recognition very early in processing. In contrast, the effects of context on word recognition are more limited in the revised version and occur only fairly late in processing. Earlier we saw that the effects of sentence context on the phonemic restoration effect occur late in processing (e.g., Samuel, 1981, 1987). However, sentence context sometimes influences the early stages of word processing. Van Petten et al. (1999) used sentence contexts allowing listeners to predict the final word before it was presented. For example, guess what the last word is going to be in this sentence: "Sir Lancelot spared the man's life when he begged for ____ ." The last word was "mercy" when it was *congruent* with the sentence context and "mermaid" when it was *incongruent* with the context. Brain activity to congruent and incongruent words differed 200 ms *before* the recognition point was reached. This suggests that context can influence spoken word processing earlier than expected within the revised version of the cohort model.

Evaluation

+ The cohort model is probably the most adequate theoretical approach to speech perception.

+ The revised version of the model accurately predicts that most contextual effects on spoken word recognition occur relatively late in processing.

+ The assumption in the revised model that membership of the word-initial cohort is flexible is correct.

− The revised model is less precise than the original version. As Massaro (1994, p. 244) pointed out, "These modifications are necessary to bring the model in line with empirical results, but they . . . make it more difficult to test against alternative models."

− The task of identifying a word's starting point from the acoustic signal is complex (remember our earlier discussion of the segmentation problem). However, the cohort model doesn't make it clear how this is accomplished.

DISORDERS OF SPEECH PERCEPTION

Consider the task of repeating a spoken word immediately after hearing it. In spite of the apparent simplicity of this task, many brain-damaged patients who aren't deaf experience difficulties with it. These patients show different patterns of impairment, and this has proved useful in identifying the processes involved in repeating spoken words.

Processing and repetition of spoken words. Adapted from Ellis and Young (1988).

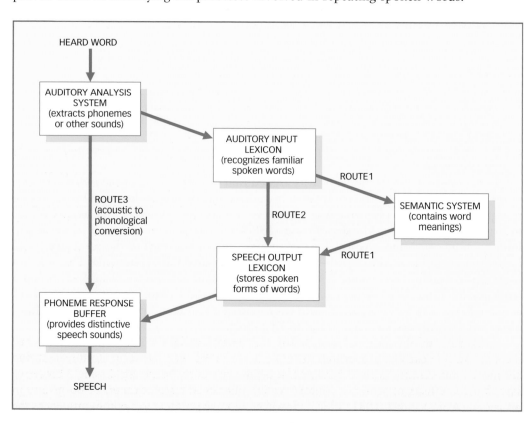

The figure on the previous page provides a framework for making sense of the findings from brain-damaged patients. The most striking feature is the notion that saying a spoken word can be achieved using *three* different routes. This is probably two more than most people would have guessed. Routes 1 and 2 are designed to be used with familiar words, whereas Route 3 is for use with unfamiliar words and nonwords. When Route 1 is used, a heard words activates relevant stored information about it, including its meaning and its spoken form. Route 2 closely resembles Route 1 except that information about the meaning of heard words is *not* accessed. Thus, someone using Route 2 can say familiar words accurately, but doesn't have access to their meaning. Finally, Route 3 involves using rules about the conversion of the acoustic information contained in heard words into the appropriate spoken forms of those words (see the figure on the right).

According to the model shown in the figures on the right, there should be brain-damaged patients who use only one or two routes when repeating heard words. Patients using Routes 1 and 2 but not Route 3 would be able to perceive and to understand spoken familiar words. However, they would be impaired at perceiving and repeating unfamiliar words and nonwords. This pattern is found in patients with **auditory phonological agnosia**. For example, a patient (ORF) repeated words much more accurately than nonwords (85% vs. 39%, respectively) (McCarthy & Warrington, 1984).

Patients who can only use Route 2 would be able to repeat familiar words but would often not understand their meaning. In addition, they should have problems in saying unfamiliar words and nonwords, because nonwords can't be processed through Route 2. Patients with **word meaning deafness** fit this description. Dr. O's ability to repeat words was dramatically better than his ability to repeat nonwords (80% vs. 7%, respectively) (Franklin et al., 1996). In addition, his ability to understand the meaning of words (especially abstract ones) was impaired.

In sum, there is support for the three-route model of the processing and repetition of spoken words. However, there would be more support for the model if patients could be found who use mainly Route 3. As yet, no clear cases have been reported in the literature.

UNDERSTANDING LANGUAGE

The processes involved in understanding or comprehending language are very similar whether we are reading text or listening to speech. As a result, individuals good at understanding written texts are also generally good at understanding spoken language (e.g., Daneman & Carpenter, 1980). However, it is generally easier to understand written text than spoken language. Written text is continuously available and so we can re-read earlier parts of the text if the need arises. In contrast, spoken language is only fleetingly available and we can't listen again to what the speaker said several seconds ago.

How good are we at correctly understanding the information contained in texts and spoken language? Sometimes we aren't as good as we like to think. For example, consider the Moses illusion (Erickson & Mattson, 1981). When asked, "How many animals of each sort did Moses put on the ark," many people reply, "Two." In fact, the correct answer is, "None" (think about it!). Ferreira (2003) argued that people often assume that the subject of a sentence is responsible for some action whereas the object of the sentence is the recipient of the action. That assumption generally works well (e.g., "The mouse ate the cheese"; "The woman visited the man"). However, Ferreira found that the assumption often led to misinterpretations when sentences such as the following were presented auditorily: "The mouse was eaten by the cheese"; "The man was visited by the woman."

INFERENCE DRAWING

What happens when we read texts or listen to speech? The obvious answer is that we focus on the words and the sentences, and try to make sense of them. In terms of our conscious experience, that is certainly what we seem to be doing. In fact, however, language comprehension is more complex. What we read or hear rarely contains *all* the information needed for complete understanding, and so we have to draw inferences to fill

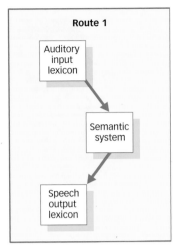

Route 1

Auditory input lexicon → Semantic system → Speech output lexicon

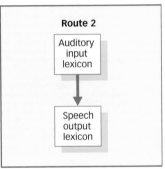

Route 2

Auditory input lexicon → Speech output lexicon

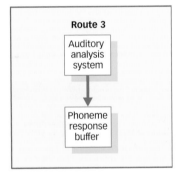

Route 3

Auditory analysis system → Phoneme response buffer

in the gaps in the information provided. For example, consider the following very short story taken from Rumelhart and Ortony (1977):

1. Mary heard the ice-cream van coming.
2. She remembered the pocket money.
3. She rushed into the house.

You probably made various assumptions or inferences while reading the story. For example, Mary wanted to buy some ice-cream; buying ice-cream costs money; Mary had some pocket money in the house; and Mary had only a limited amount of time to get hold of this money before the ice-cream van arrived. None of these assumptions is explicitly stated in the three sentences. It is simply so common for us to draw inferences that we are generally unaware of doing so.

There has been much controversy on the issue of precisely *which* inferences are drawn when readers try to understand a text. The focus of this controversy has been on **elaborative inferences**, which add details to the text but aren't essential for a proper understanding of what we are listening to or reading. Here is an example of an elaborative inference taken from a study by Singer (1994):

> *The tooth was pulled painlessly. The patient liked the new method.*
> *A dentist pulled a tooth (elaborative inference).*

Singer found that readers were relatively slow to draw this elaborative inference, indicating that such inferences are not drawn automatically.

According to the minimalist hypothesis put forward by McKoon and Ratcliff (1992), people generally draw only those inferences that are very important to establish the meaning of what is being read. As a result, elaborative inferences are typically not drawn. In contrast, Graesser, Singer, and Trabasso (1994) argued in their search-after-meaning theory that more inferences are generally drawn than is proposed by the minimalist hypothesis. For convenience, the predictions of the two approaches are shown in the box below.

Key Term

Elaborative inferences: inferences that add details to a text that is being read but that are not essential to understanding.

"Sam had been in pain all night. In the morning the dentist drilled and filled his tooth."

Logical inference: Sam is male.

Bridging inference: The dentist treated Sam's tooth.

Elaborative inference: Sam phoned the dentist early to get an emergency appointment. The treatment cured the pain.

The types of inferences normally drawn, together with the predictions from the search-after-meaning and minimalist perspectives. Adapted from Graesser et al. (1994).

	Type of inference	Answers query	Predicted by search-after-meaning theory	Predicted by minimalists	Normally found
1.	Referential	To what previous word does this apply? (e.g., anaphora)	✓	✓	✓
2.	Case structure role assignment	What is the role (e.g., agent, object) of this noun?	✓	✓	✓
3.	Causal antecedent	What caused this?	✓	✓	✓
4.	Supraordinate goal	What is the main goal?	✓		✓
5.	Thematic	What is the overall theme?	✓		?
6.	Character emotional reaction	How does the character feel?	✓		✓
7.	Causal consequence	What happens next?			✗
8.	Instrument	What was used to do this?			✗
9.	Subordinate goal-action	How was the action achieved?			✗

The findings favor the search-after-meaning theory over the minimalist hypothesis. For example, Suh and Trabasso (1993) used texts in which a character's initial goal was or wasn't satisfied. In one text, Jimmy wants a bicycle and his mother either buys him one immediately or doesn't buy him one. Later on, Jimmy has earned a lot of money and sets off for a department store. In the condition in which Jimmy hasn't satisfied his goal of having a bicycle, readers inferred that his intention was to buy one in the store. However, the minimalist hypothesis doesn't lead to the prediction that such inferences would be drawn.

Evaluation

+ Readers and listeners often draw inferences when reading text or listening to speech, respectively.

+ There is some validity in the minimalist and search-after-meaning theories. According to Graesser, Millis, and Zwaan (1997, p. 183), "The minimalist hypothesis is probably correct when the reader is very quickly reading the text, when the text lacks global coherence, and when the reader has very little background knowledge. The [search-after-meaning] theory is on the mark when the reader is attempting to comprehend the text for enjoyment or mastery at a more leisurely pace."

− Insufficient attention has been paid to individual differences. For example, individuals of greater intellectual ability draw more inferences than those of lesser ability (see Eysenck & Keane, 2005, for a review).

SCHEMAS

Our stored knowledge and experience play an important role in reading and listening because they allow us to fill in the gaps in what we read or hear. Bartlett (1932) argued that our knowledge and experience can have much more dramatic effects. His central claim was that the knowledge we possess can produce systematic *distortions* in what we remember about what we have read. According to Bartlett, this knowledge is in the form of **schemas** (organized packets of knowledge about the world, events, or people). According to Bartlett, remembering is a process of *reconstruction* in which we use schematic knowledge to organize and make sense of the information in a previously read text. Some schemas are in the form of **scripts**, which contain organized information about typical events (e.g., going to a restaurant).

Bartlett (1932) had the ingenious idea of presenting people with stories involving *conflict* between the information contained in the story and their prior schematic knowledge. His participants were mostly students from Cambridge University in the UK and the stories (e.g., "The War of the Ghosts") were often tales from the very different North American Indian folk culture. He argued that the students would read each folk tale from the standpoint of their own cultural background. Bartlett's findings supported his predictions, with most of the recall errors being in the direction of making the story read more like a conventional English story. He used the term **rationalization** for this type of error. He also found other kinds of errors, including flattening (failure to recall unfamiliar details) and sharpening (elaboration of certain details).

Bartlett (1932) made a further prediction. He argued that memory for the precise information contained in the story would be forgotten over time, whereas participants' relevant schematic knowledge would not. As a result, rationalization errors (dependent on participants' knowledge) should increase at longer retention intervals. Bartlett's findings supported this prediction.

Bartlett's (1932) experimental approach was hardly ideal. The instructions he gave his participants were deliberately vague, and he practically never used any statistical tests on his data! More worryingly, many of the recall distortions he obtained were a result of conscious guessing rather than genuine problems in memory. Perhaps the participants were trying to be helpful by guessing when they couldn't remember some aspect of the story. Convincing evidence that this is a problem was produced by Gauld and Stephenson

Key Terms

Schemas:
in Bartlett's theory, organized information about the world, events, or people stored in long-term memory.

Scripts:
organized information or schemas representing typical events.

Rationalization:
in Bartlett's theory, the tendency to recall stories in distorted ways influenced by the reader's cultural expectations and **schemas**.

Key Study

Bartlett (1932): The War of the Ghosts

In one of his studies Bartlett asked his English participants to read a North American Indian folk tale called "The War of the Ghosts," after which they tried to recall the story. Part of the story was as follows:

> One night two young men from Edulac went down the river to hunt seals, and while they were there it became foggy and calm. Then they heard war-cries, and they thought: "Maybe this is a war-party." They escaped to the shore, and hid behind a log. Now canoes came up, and they heard the noise of paddles, and saw one canoe coming up to them. There were five men in the canoe, and they said: "What do you think? We wish to take you along. We are going up the river to make war on the people."
>
> ... one of the young men went but the other returned home...[it turns out that the five men in the boat were ghosts and after accompanying them in a fight, the young man returned to his village to tell his tale]...and said: "Behold I accompanied the ghosts, and we went to fight. Many of our fellows were killed, and many of those who attacked us were killed. They said I was hit, and I did not feel sick."
>
> He told it all and then he became quiet. When the sun rose he fell down. Something black came out of his mouth. His face became contorted...He was dead. (p. 65)

One of the subject's recall of the story (two weeks later):

> There were two ghosts. They were on a river. There was a canoe on the river with five men in it. There occurred a war of ghosts...They started the war and several were wounded and some killed. One ghost was wounded but did not feel sick. He went back to the village in the canoe. The next morning he was sick and something black came out of his mouth, and they cried: "He is dead." (p. 76)

Bartlett found that the participants' recall distorted the content and style of the original story. The story was shortened, and the phrases, and often words, were changed to be similar to the English language and concepts (e.g., "boat" instead of "canoe"). He also found other kinds of errors, including flattening (failure to recall unfamiliar details) and sharpening (elaboration of certain details).

Discussion points
1. Why do you think that Bartlett's research has been so influential?
2. Do you think that the kinds of errors and distortions observed by Bartlett would be found with other kinds of material?

KEY STUDY EVALUATION

Bartlett's research is important because it provided some of the first evidence that what we remember depends in an important way on our prior knowledge, in the form of schemas.

However, Bartlett's studies are open to criticism. He did not give very specific instructions to his participants (Bartlett, 1932, p. 78: "I thought it best, for the purposes of these experiments, to try to influence the subjects' procedure as little as possible.") As a result, some distortions observed by Bartlett were a result of conscious guessing rather than deficient memory. Gauld and Stephenson (1967) found that instructions emphasizing the need for accurate recall eliminated almost half the errors usually obtained.

Another criticism of Bartlett's work was that his approach to research lacked objectivity. Some psychologists believe that well-controlled experiments are the only way to produce objective data. Bartlett's methods were somewhat casual. He simply asked his group of participants to recall the story at various intervals and there were no special conditions for this recall. It is possible that other factors affected their performance, such as the conditions around them at the time they were recalling the story, or it could be that the distortions were simply guesses by participants who were trying to make their recall seem coherent and complete rather than genuine distortions in recall.

On the other hand, one could argue that his research is more ecologically valid than those studies that involve the recall of syllables or lists of words. In recent years there has been an increase in the kind of research conducted by Bartlett, looking more at "everyday memory."

(1967). Clear instructions emphasizing the need for accurate recall (and so reducing deliberate guessing) eliminated many of the errors obtained using Bartlett's vague instructions. However, it should be noted that Bartlett's key findings have been replicated in well-controlled studies (e.g., Sulin & Dooling, 1974).

It is generally assumed that schema- or script-based information can be distinguished from information about individual words or concepts. If so, it seems reasonable to predict that some brain-damaged individuals will have greater problems with the former than the latter. Support for this prediction was reported by Cosentino et al. (2006), who studied patients with fronto-temporal dementia who showed attentional deficits and poor executive functioning. These patients and healthy controls were presented with various scripts. Some of these scripts contained sequencing errors (e.g., dropping fish in a bucket occurring *before* casting the fishing line) whereas others contained semantic or meaning errors (e.g., placing a flower on the hook in a story about fishing). Healthy controls detected as many sequencing errors as semantic ones, but the patients failed to detect almost twice as many sequencing errors as semantic ones. It seems that these patients had relatively intact semantic knowledge of concepts but fairly severe impairment of script-based knowledge.

Do schemas influence the process of *comprehension* when people are reading a text or do they influence the subsequent processes of *retrieval*? Bartlett (1932) argued that schemas influence retrieval, but the evidence indicates that schemas influence comprehension as well as retrieval. For example, Bransford and Johnson (1972) presented a passage of which this is the start:

The procedure is quite simple. First, you arrange items into different groups. Of course one pile may be sufficient depending on how much there is to do. If you have to go somewhere else due to lack of facilities that is the next step; otherwise, you are pretty well set. It is important not to overdo things. That is, it is better to do too few things at once than too many. In the short run this may not seem important but complications can easily arise.

What on earth was that all about? Participants hearing the passage in the absence of a title rated it as incomprehensible and recalled very little of it. In contrast, those supplied beforehand with the title, "Washing clothes," found it easy to understand and recalled twice as much. The title indicated the nature of the underlying schema and helped comprehension of the passage rather than retrieval. We know this because participants receiving the title *after* hearing the passage (but *before* recall) had as poor recall as those never receiving the title.

Evidence that schemas influence retrieval processes was reported by Anderson and Pichert (1978). Participants initially recalled a story from the perspective of a burglar or of someone interested in buying a home. After they had recalled as much as possible, they shifted to the alternative perspective (from burglar to home buyer or vice versa) before recalling the story again. Accessing different schematic knowledge in this way at the time of retrieval led to enhanced recall.

Evaluation

➕ We use schematic knowledge during comprehension (e.g., Bransford & Johnson, 1972) and retrieval (e.g., Anderson & Pichert, 1978).

➕ The use of schematic knowledge creates errors and distortions when there is a conflict between that knowledge and information in the text.

➕ There is evidence from brain-damaged patients supporting a distinction between knowledge of concepts and schema- or script-based knowledge (e.g., Cosentino et al., 2006).

➖ It has proved difficult to establish clearly the characteristics of schemas.

➖ As Harley (2001, p. 331) argued, "The primary accusation against schema . . . approaches is that they are nothing more than re-descriptions of the data."

CONSTRUCTION–INTEGRATION MODEL

The construction–integration model (Kintsch, 1988, 1992, 1998) is the leading theoretical approach to language comprehension (see the figure below). Here are its main assumptions:

1. The sentences in the text are turned into propositions (a **proposition** is a statement making an assertion or denial; it may be true or false).
2. *Construction process*: Readers use their knowledge base to retrieve propositions relevant to the text propositions (e.g., inferences). These propositions and text propositions together form an *elaborated propositional net*. This seems inefficient, because many propositions in this net are of only marginal relevance to the text's theme.
3. *Integration process*: Contextual information provided by the previous parts of the text is used to select from the elaborated propositional net only those propositions most relevant to the theme of the text.
4. *Three* levels of text representation are constructed:
   (i) Surface representation (the test itself); this representation lasts for the shortest time.
   (ii) Propositional representation (propositions formed from the text).
   (iii) Situational representation (a mental model describing the situation referred to in the text). Schemas (packets of knowledge) can be used as the building blocks for the construction of situational representations or models. This representation lasts for the longest time.

Key Term

Proposition:
a statement that makes an assertion or denial and which can be true or false.

The construction–integration model. Adapted from Kintsch (1994).

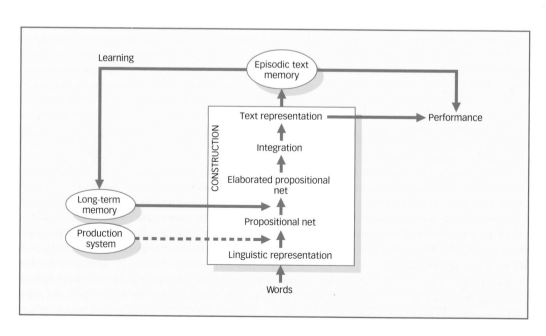

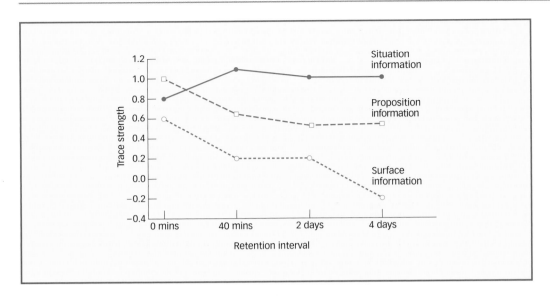

Forgetting functions for situation, proposition, and surface information over a 4-day period. Adapted from Kintsch et al. (1990).

In sum, the initial construction process uses semantic knowledge to form a large number of propositions. Then the integration process uses contextual information from the text to weed out those propositions of little relevance while retaining those most related to the theme of the text.

Findings

A striking assumption of the construction–integration model is that no fewer than *three* representations are formed when we read a text. This assumption was tested by Kintsch et al. (1990). Participants were given brief descriptions of very stereotyped situations (e.g., going to see a movie) and then their recognition memory was tested immediately or at times ranging up to 4 days later.

The forgetting functions for the surface, propositional, and situational representations differed considerably (see the figure above). There was rapid and complete forgetting of the surface representation, whereas information from the situational representation showed no forgetting over 4 days. Propositional information differed from situational information in that there was only partial forgetting. Thus, the findings were as predicted by the model.

Subsequent research has indicated that readers don't *always* construct all three forms of text representation. In a study by Zwaan and van Oostendorp (1993), participants read an edited mystery novel describing the details of a murder scene, including the locations of the body and various clues. Most readers did *not* construct a situational representation when they read normally, something of which a legion of detective story writers since Agatha Christie have taken advantage. However, situational representations were formed (at the cost of a substantial increase in reading time) when the initial instructions emphasized the importance of constructing a spatial representation. Thus, limited processing capacity may often restrict the formation of situational representations.

Kaup and Zwaan (2003) found that there are circumstances in which readers don't even form propositional representations. They pointed out that nearly all previous research involved the use of texts in which all the objects referred to each sentence were present. According to construction–integration theory, propositional representations should contain information in which *all* the objects referred to in each sentence even if they were absent. However, Kaup and Zwaan wondered whether people would bother to construct propositional representations referring to absent objects. Accordingly, they presented stories containing sentences such as, "Sam was relieved that Laura was not wearing her pink dress." Information about absent objects was less accessible than that about present objects only 1.5 seconds after a sentence had been read. This suggests that information about absent objects was generally not included in the propositional representation.

According to the model, it is only late on in language comprehension that contextual information from the text is used. However, Cook and Myers (2004) found that contextual information can be used at a very early stage of processing. For example, suppose you read a short story about the making of a movie. The story contains the contextual information that the budget was so low that everyone had to take on extra jobs. When this information was provided, readers very rapidly understood why it was the actress rather than the director who said, "Action!"

Evaluation

+ There is reasonable support for the notion that text comprehension involves successive stages of construction and integration.

+ There is evidence for the three levels of representation (surface; propositional; and situational) specified in the model.

− The three representations are not always formed. Sometimes the situational representation isn't constructed (Zwaan & van Oostendorp, 1993) and sometimes the propositional representation isn't formed (Kaup & Zwaan, 2003).

− Contextual information can be used much earlier in language comprehension than assumed by the model.

− There may be other levels of representation ignored by Kintsch. For example, Graesser, Millis, and Zwaan (1997) argued there is the *text genre* level, which is concerned with the nature of the text (e.g., narration; description; jokes). How the information is to be interpreted varies greatly as a function of the type or genre of text.

Sports commentators use preformulation extensively. Repeating stock phrases and jargon enables them to speak quickly about the sporting event as it happens.

Key Terms

Preformulation:
this is used in speech production to reduce processing costs by using phrases often used previously.

Underspecification:
a strategy used to reduce processing costs in speech production by producing simplified expressions.

SPEECH PRODUCTION

Speech production seems almost effortless as we chat with friends or acquaintances about the topics of the day. Indeed, we often seem to speak without much preparation or planning, which can cause us to say things we immediately regret saying! Speech production is sufficiently easy that we typically speak at three words a second or almost 200 words a minute. That simply wouldn't be possible if we had to think everything out carefully in advance.

The impression created in the previous paragraph is deliberately misleading. Speech production is actually much more complex than might be imagined. As M. Smith (2000) pointed out, most of us resort to various strategies when talking to reduce the processing demands on us. Here are three of those strategies. First, there is **preformulation**, which involves reducing processing costs by producing phrases used before. About 70% of our speech consists of word combinations we use repeatedly (Altenberg, 1990). Sports commentators (who often need to speak very rapidly) make extensive use of preformulation (e.g., "They're on their way"; "They're off and racing now") (Kuiper, 1996).

Second, there is **underspecification**, which involves using simplified expressions. Smith (2000) illustrated underspecification as follows: "Wash and core six cooking apples. Put them in an oven." In the second sentence, the word "them" underspecifies the phrase, "six cooking apples."

Third, when we have a chat with someone, we often use the strategy of copying phrases and even sentences produced by the other person (Pickering & Garrod, 2004). In addition, we typically make extensive use of the ideas communicated by the other person. Both of these processing strategies reduce the processing burden associated with speech production.

SPEECH PLANNING

How much do we plan what we are going to say before saying it? The answer varies from person to person. You probably know some motormouths who don't seem to plan at all. In fact, nearly all speakers plan what they are about to say to some extent, but there is controversy concerning the extent of such planning.

One possibility is that speech planning extends over an entire **clause**, a part of a sentence containing a subject and a verb. There is support for this view from speech errors (e.g., Garrett, 1982). For example, word-exchange errors involve two words exchanging places. The words exchanged often come from different phrases but belong to the same clause (e.g., "My chair seems empty without my room"). The fact that word-exchange errors rarely involve words from different clauses strengthens the argument that the clause is a key unit in speech planning. Additional evidence was reported by Holmes (1988). Speakers often had hesitations and pauses before the start of a clause, suggesting they were planning the forthcoming clause.

Other evidence suggests that speech planning is at the level of the **phrase**, a group of words expressing a single idea and smaller in scope than a clause. Martin, Miller, and Vu (2004) asked people to produce sentences to describe moving pictures. The sentences either had a simple initial phrase (e.g., "The ball moves above the tree and the finger") or they had a complex initial phrase (e.g., "The ball and the tree move above the finger"). Speakers took longer to initiate speech when using complex initial phrases than when using simpler ones. Thus, participants planned the initial phrase before starting to speak.

What probably happens is that the amount of planning that precedes speech is *flexible*, varying as a function of the speaker's skills and situational demands. We can draw an analogy with diving from the high board in a swimming pool. If time permits, there will be careful planning before the diver launches himself/herself into the dive. However, a skilled diver can dive reasonably well with little or no planning.

Evidence that the diving analogy applies to speech production was reported by Ferreira and Swets (2002). Participants answered mathematical problems varying in difficulty level and spoke their answers. In their first experiment, task difficulty affected the time taken to start speaking but not the time spent speaking. These findings suggest that participants fully planned their responses before speaking. However, the findings differed in a second experiment. In this experiment, participants had to start producing their answers very rapidly for them to count. What happened here was that some planning occurred before participants started to speak, with additional planning occurring while they were speaking. Thus, speakers are flexible. They do only as much planning as is feasible in the time available before they need to start talking.

SPEECH PRODUCTION LEVELS

Most theorists assume that several levels or stages of processing are involved in speech production. So far we have focused on the initial level or stage of processing during which the meaning of what the speaker wants to say is worked out. The main levels or stages were identified by Dell (1986; see the figure overleaf). It is assumed that speakers start with an overall idea of what they want to

> **Key Terms**
>
> **Clause:**
> part of a sentence that contains a subject and a verb.
>
> **Phrase:**
> a group of words expressing a single idea; it is shorter than a clause.

The sentence "I want a biscuit" broken down into spreading-activation levels identified by Dell (1986).

Spreading-activation level	Explanation	Example			
Semantic	Abstract representation of idea(s)				
Syntactic	Outline, including grammar	Subject	Verb	Article	Object
Morphological	Vocabulary in position	I	want	a	biscuit
Phonological	Information about pronunciation	ai	wǒn	ei	biskit

say, and this gradually becomes more detailed and specific through successive stages of processing.

Initial planning of the message to be communicated is considered at the semantic level. At the syntactic level, the grammatical structure of the words in the planned utterance is decided. At the morphological level, the **morphemes** (basic units of meaning or word forms) in the planned sentence are worked out. At the phonological level, the *phonemes* or basic units of sound within the sentence are added.

The figure above implies that the processes involved in speech and word production proceed in an orderly way from the semantic level through the syntactic and morphological levels down to the phonological level. There has been much disagreement concerning the extent to which the processes involved do actually occur in this neat sequential way (discussed later).

There are several theories of speech production. However, we will focus on the spreading-activation theory put forward by Dell (1986) and by Dell and O'Seaghdha (1991). Let's start with the key notion of **spreading activation**. It is assumed that the nodes within a network (many corresponding to words) vary in their activation or energy. When a node or word is activated, activation or energy spreads from it to other related nodes. For example, strong activation of the node corresponding to "tree" may cause some activation of the nodes corresponding to "plant" and to "oak."

A key theoretical assumption is that processing can occur at the same time at all four levels (semantic; syntactic; morphological; and phonological). However, it is typically more advanced at the semantic and syntactic levels than the morphological and phonological ones. Thus, the system operates flexibly. It also operates in parallel, meaning that several processes can all occur together. What is the advantage of having such a speech production system? According to Dell, this flexibility makes it easier for us to produce novel sentences in our speech.

The notion that speech production involves several processes at the same time may sound like a recipe for chaos. However, two kinds of rules help to prevent that from happening:

1. *Categorical rules*: These rules impose constraints on the categories of items produced at each level. As a result, selected items will belong to the appropriate category (e.g., noun or verb at the syntactic level).
2. *Insertion rules*: These rules select the items to be included in the representations at each level according to the following criterion: the most highly activated node or word belonging to the appropriate category (e.g., noun) is selected.

After an item has been selected, its activation level immediately reduces to zero. This ensures it will not be selected repeatedly.

As we will see, much of the support for spreading-activation theory comes from the study of speech errors. Most of this evidence comes from errors personally heard by the researcher concerned (e.g., Stemberger, 1982). You might imagine this would produce distorted data, since some errors are easier to detect than others. However, the types and proportions of speech errors obtained in this way are very similar to those obtained from analyzing tape-recorded conversations (Garnham, Oakhill, & Johnson-Laird, 1982).

Findings

According to the theory, speech errors will occur whenever an incorrect item is more activated than the correct one. Several findings from speech errors support the theory. First, the existence of categorical rules means that errors should typically belong to the appropriate category (e.g., an incorrect noun replacing the correct one). Relevant evidence comes from *semantic substitution errors*, in which the correct word is replaced by a word of similar meaning. For example, someone might say, "Where is my tennis bat?" instead of "Where is my tennis racket?" In 99% of cases, the substituted word is of the same form class as the correct word (e.g., nouns substitute for nouns) (Hotopf, 1980).

Second, the theory assumes that many sounds and words are all activated at the same time. As a result, there will be anticipation errors, in which a sound or word is spoken earlier in the sentence than intended. Anticipation errors are found with *word-exchange errors*, in which two words in a sentence switch places. For example, someone says, "I must let the house out of the cat" instead of "I must let the cat out of the house." *Sound-exchange errors* are another type of anticipation error. They involve two sounds exchanging places (e.g., "barn door" instead of "darn bore").

Third, the theory accounts for the **mixed error effect**. This happens when an incorrect spoken word is semantically *and* phonemically related to the correct word. Dell (1986) quoted the example of someone saying, "Let's stop" instead of, "Let's start." The spoken word and the correct word are generally both more similar in sound (as well as meaning) than would be expected by chance alone (Dell & O'Seaghdha, 1991). According to the theory, activation often occurs at the semantic and phonological levels at the same time, and this helps to produce the mixed error effect.

There is a major issue on which the predictions from spreading-activation theory differ from those of the influential WEAVER++ model (Levelt, Roelofs, & Meyer, 1999). According to this model, the processing involved in speech production is typically neat and tidy. For example, we decide on the meaning of a word we want to use in a spoken sentence before we access phonological (sound) information about the word in question. In other words, the process of deciding on word meaning is complete before the sound of the word is accessed. Support for this view comes from the **tip-of-the-tongue phenomenon**, in which we have a concept or idea in mind but search in vain for the right word to describe it. People in the tip-of-the-tongue state "appear to be in a mild torment, something like the brink of a sneeze" (Brown & McNeill, 1966, p. 325).

It follows from WEAVER++ that we can only access the sound of *one* word at a time. In contrast, it is assumed within spreading-activation theory that processing is flexible, and so phonological or sound processing of two or more words can occur at the same time. Morsella and Miozzo (2002) compared the two theories. Participants were presented with two colored pictures with one superimposed on the other. They had to name the picture in a given color (target picture) while ignoring the picture in a different color (distractor picture). Some distractor pictures were related in sound to the target pictures (e.g., *bell* as a distractor presented with *bed*), but others weren't related in sound (e.g., *hat* as a distractor presented with *bed*). Target pictures were named faster when accompanied by phonologically related distractors rather than by unrelated ones. This means that the sounds of both words were activated at the same time, precisely as predicted by spreading-activation theory.

Key Terms
Mixed error effect: speech errors that are semantically and phonologically related to the intended word.
Tip-of-the-tongue phenomenon: the experience of having a specific concept in mind but being unable to access the correct word to describe it.

According to spreading-activation theory, speech production often involves parallel processing in which irrelevant words are activated as well as relevant ones. That suggests that there should be numerous errors when incorrect words are readily available. This prediction was tested by Glaser (1992), who studied the time taken to name pictures (e.g., a table). Theoretically, there should have been a large increase in errors when each picture was accompanied by a semantically related distractor word (e.g., chair). In fact, there was only a modest increase in the error rate. Thus, there seems to be more limited processing of distractor words than expected on Dell's theory.

Evaluation

- The four levels assumed to be involved in speech production are consistent with the evidence.

- The notion that speech production involves flexible, parallel processing is basically correct.

- The theory makes precise (and accurate) predictions about the kinds of errors occurring most often in speech production.

- The theory focuses on individual words rather than on broader issues relating to message construction.

- The theory predicts the nature and number of errors produced in speech. However, it can't predict the *time* taken to produce spoken words, because there are no theoretical assumptions about the timing of speech processes.

- The theory seems to predict too many errors when irrelevant words are activated at the same time as relevant ones (e.g., Glaser, 1992).

SPEECH DISORDERS

As we have seen in several chapters of this book, we can often learn much about human cognition by studying brain-damaged patients. It has been claimed that some speech-disordered patients speak reasonably grammatically but have great difficulties in accessing content words (e.g., nouns; verbs), whereas other patients have the opposite pattern. If that is the case, it would provide some support for those theories (e.g., spreading-activation theory; WEAVER++) assuming that speech production involves separate stages of syntactic processing and word finding.

Patients suffering from **jargon aphasia** apparently speak fairly grammatically but cannot find content words. They substitute one word for another, and often produce **neologisms** (made-up words). Ellis, Miller, and Sin (1983) studied a jargon aphasic, RD. Here is his description of a picture of a scout camp with the words he seemed to be looking for in brackets: "A b-boy is swi'ing (SWINGING) on the bank with his hand (FEET) in the stringt (STREAM). A table with orstrum (SAUCEPAN?) and . . . I don't know . . . and a three-legged stroe (STOOL) and a strane (PAIL)—table, table . . . near the water." RD, in common with most jargon aphasics, produced more neologisms or invented words when the word he wanted wasn't a common one.

Robson, Pring, Marshall, and Chiat (2003) studied a jargon aphasic, LT, whose speech consisted almost entirely of neologisms. He often produced consonants common in the English language regardless of whether or not they were correct. This finding can be explained on Dell's spreading-activation theory (discussed earlier). In essence, the resting activation level of frequently used consonants is greater than that of rarely used consonants. This increases the probability of producing frequently used consonants correctly and incorrectly.

Key Terms

Jargon aphasia:
a brain-damaged condition in which speech is reasonably correct grammatically, but there are great problems in finding the right words.

Neologisms:
made-up words that are often found in the speech of patients with **jargon aphasia**.

Case Study: *Expressive Language Disorder*

Three percent to 5% of children have expressive language disorder, which develops at about age 4. It produces ongoing difficulties in understanding and using language, for example having for their developmental stage a markedly limited vocabulary, making errors in tense, having difficulty recalling words or producing sentences of appropriate length and complexity. Sufferers from this disorder show problems with educational or occupational achievement, and social difficulties.

A 7-year-old girl with the disorder was described at school as not an independent worker but this was because she did not have the skills needed to work independently. She found following instructions, e.g., in science lessons, difficult, as was the writing of stories, and mathematics. Extra help such as discussing the use of silent (i.e., sub-vocal) speech is a technique that helps some young people with the disorder.

Can you explain how the difficulties of this disorder contributed to this girl's reduced educational achievement?

Patients with **agrammatism** can generally find the right words but can't order them grammatically. They typically produce short sentences containing content words (e.g., nouns; verbs) but lacking function words (e.g., the; in; and) and word endings. In addition, it has often been assumed that patients with agrammatism have problems in understanding syntactically complex sentences. Guasti and Luzzati (2002) found that agrammatic patients had very impaired syntactic processing especially as revealed in their inappropriate use of verbs. They often failed to adjust the form of verbs to take account of person or number. Most of the time they used only the present tense of verbs, and omitted many verbs altogether.

In sum, research on patients with jargon aphasia and agrammatism has provided general support for the notion that there are separate stages of syntactic processing and word finding in speech production. However, the pattern of intact and impaired language abilities in any given patient is typically rather complex. Second, and related to the first point, it is a serious oversimplification to assume that all patients assigned to the same category (e.g., agrammatism) have the same impairments. For example, Berndt, Mitchum, and Haendiges (1996) discussed the findings from several studies on comprehension of active and passive sentences by patients with agrammatism. Some patients performed at chance level on both kinds of sentences, whereas other patients had reasonable comprehension performance on active and passive sentences, especially active ones.

Chapter Summary

Reading
- Readers fixate 80% of content words and 20% of function words, with nonfixated words tending to be common, short, and predictable.
- Reading is more likely to involve phonological processing when reading is difficult.
- There are two main routes to reading words aloud. One is a lexical look-up route based on a mental dictionary and the other is a nonlexical route based on converting spelling into sound via grapheme–phoneme conversion.
- Patients with surface dyslexia mainly use the nonlexical route, whereas those with phonological dyslexia mainly use the lexical route.
- According to two-stage models of parsing, syntactic information is used in the first stage and semantic information is used in the second stage.

Key Term

Agrammatism:
a condition in brain-damaged patients in which speech lacks grammatical structure and many function words and word endings are omitted.

- According to one-stage models of parsing, all relevant information is available immediately to the parser. There is little clear evidence favoring one type of model over the other.

Speech perception
- Listeners have to cope with various problems including the segmentation problem, co-articulation, and the fact that speakers typically produce 10 phonemes per second.
- Listeners use contextual information from the surrounding sentence context when identifying individual words. This is shown in the phonemic restoration effect, in which listeners guess the identity of a missing phoneme.
- According to the cohort model, processing of a spoken word continues until one word is consistent with all of the available information. Contextual information is used mainly at a fairly late stage of processing.
- Saying a spoken word can be achieved using three different routes. Two of the routes are used with familiar words and the other route is used with unfamiliar words and nonwords.
- Support for the three-route model comes from patients with auditory phonological agnosia who repeat words more accurately than nonwords. It also comes from patients with word meaning deafness who don't understand the meaning of words they repeat and who find it harder to repeat nonwords than words.

Understanding language
- Readers draw inferences when reading texts or listening to speech.
- According to the minimalist hypothesis, fewer nonessential inferences are drawn than is assumed within search-after-meaning theory. The evidence generally favors search-after-meaning theory, but the number of inferences drawn depends on the reader's goals.
- Recall of text is systematically distorted when there is a conflict between readers' schematic knowledge and the information in the text.
- Schemas influence processes occurring during comprehension as well as those occurring during retrieval.
- According to the construction–integration model, a construction process is used to retrieve propositions relevant to the text. The integration process then selects those propositions of most relevance to the theme of the text.
- According to the construction–integration model, surface, propositional, and situational representations are formed. In fact, readers often don't construct all three representations.

Speech production
- Speakers use preformulation, underspecification, and copying what someone else has just said to simplify the task of speech production.
- The amount of planning that precedes speech varies as a function of the speaker's skills and the demands of the situation.
- Speech production involves four levels of processing: semantic; syntactic; morphological; and phonological.
- According to Dell's spreading-activation theory, processes at different levels of speech production take place in parallel. The assumption that whichever word is most activated will be produced accounts for many speech errors. However, the theory doesn't consider broader issues relating to message construction.
- Patients with jargon aphasia speak fairly grammatically but can't find content words, whereas those with agrammatism can generally find the correct words but can't order them grammatically. These patterns of impairments are consistent with the notion that there are separate stages of syntactic processing and word finding.

Further Reading

- Butcher, K.R., & Kintsch, W. (2003). Text comprehension and discourse processing. In R.W. Proctor & A.F. Healy (Eds.), *Handbook of psychology: Experimental psychology* (Vol. 4). New York: Wiley. This chapter discusses what is known about language comprehension.
- Eysenck, M.W. (2006). *Fundamentals of cognition*. Hove, UK: Psychology Press. Theory and research on language are discussed in Chapters 17–21 of this introduction to cognitive psychology.
- Harley, T.A. (2008). *The psychology of language: From data to theory* (3rd ed.). Hove, UK: Psychology Press. Several chapters in this excellent textbook provide clear accounts of the topics discussed in this chapter.
- Jay, T.B. (2003). *The psychology of language*. Upper Saddle River, NJ: Prentice Hall. This textbook has good basic coverage of research and theory on language.

INTRODUCTION TO
Individual Differences

Most of psychology is devoted to the search for broad generalizations and laws of behavior that are applicable to nearly everyone. For example, consider most of the research on cognitive psychology (covered in Chapters 6–10). Most cognitive psychologists assume that everyone (apart from brain-damaged patients) makes use of the same attentional and perceptual processes, has a working memory system, forgets information over time, makes certain inferences when reading text, and so on. The situation is similar in social psychology (Chapters 17–20). It is assumed that people tend to be obedient to authority, to conform to the views of other group members, to fall in love with people who are similar to them, to show prejudice in certain circumstances, and so on.

The above approach has proved very successful, and numerous very important generalizations have emerged as a result. However, an approach that focuses on universally applicable generalizations is necessarily limited. What it misses is the extraordinary diversity of human behavior, which is obvious to us nearly all the time in the course of our everyday lives. For example, some people are much better than others at remembering information over long periods of time, some people can control their attention much better than others, some people are more willing than others to obey the orders of authority figures, and some people are bigoted and biased in their views of minority groups whereas others are not.

Individual differences (which form the subject matter of Chapters 11 and 12) have a great influence on our behavior. For example, if you need advice when writing a coursework essay, you probably find it easier to approach some people rather than others, perhaps because they are friendlier or more knowledgeable. In similar fashion, we take full account of individual differences when choosing friends. Thus, we are more likely to become friends with other people who seem similar to us, who are warm and sociable, and who can be trusted with secrets.

Cronbach (1957) argued that there are two scientific disciplines within psychology. One is devoted to the search for general laws, and the other is devoted to the study of individual differences. Cronbach's most important point was that what was needed for psychology to realize its potential were wholehearted attempts to combine these two scientific disciplines. According to him, it should be possible to consider general laws and individual differences within a single approach. It is disappointing (and surprising) that relatively little has been done along the lines suggested by Cronbach over 50 years ago although there are recent very encouraging signs.

Human behavior is extraordinarily diverse, and so approaches that do not take into account individual differences but rely solely on universally applicable generalizations are limited.

ASPECTS OF INDIVIDUAL DIFFERENCES

Which aspects of individual differences are most important? This is not an easy question to answer given that people differ from each other in a bewildering number of ways. Indeed, if you sat down to draw up a list, you could probably identify literally dozens of interesting ways in which the people you know differ from each other. However, academic and occupational psychologists have (rightly or wrongly) focused mainly on individual differences in intelligence and personality, although some research on other aspects of individual differences (e.g., social attitudes) has also been carried out.

There has been much emphasis on individual differences within occupational psychology. It is common for the intelligence and personality of job applicants to be assessed in personnel selection. There are sound reasons for focusing on these aspects of individual differences. For example, highly intelligent individuals on average have superior work performance and career development than those who are less intelligent, and this is especially the case when the job concerned is relatively complex (Gottfredson, 1997). This is one of the many issues discussed in Chapter 11.

You may feel that it is fairly obvious that intelligence predicts the ability to perform complex tasks and jobs. However, individual differences in intelligence are also relevant to many other life outcomes. Individuals who are highly intelligent have a much smaller probability than those who are unintelligent of being divorced within 5 years of marriage (9% vs. 21% based on American data; Gottfredson, 1997). Highly intelligent women have only one-quarter the probability of unintelligent women of having an illegitimate child and one-seventh the probability of finding themselves in prison (Gottfredson, 1997).

Individual differences in personality are also important in predicting individuals' behavior in numerous real-world situations. The personality we have helps to determine how happy we are and how many friends we have. In addition, there are interesting associations between certain types of personality on the one hand and various mental disorders on the other hand. These associations suggest that your personality influences the probability that you will develop any given mental disorder.

When we think of individual differences, we generally focus on personality. We know that Kate is always cheerful and friendly, whereas Nancy is neurotic and emotional. Why are their personalities so different? Did Kate have a happier and more secure childhood than Nancy? Do the differences lie in the genes? Is some kind of mixture or interaction of genetic factors and environmental ones responsible for the personality differences between Kate and Nancy? Tentative answers to these questions are provided in Chapter 12.

Three issues are of central importance to researchers who study individual differences. First, we need to understand the *nature* of individual differences, including the structure of intelligence and personality. More specifically, what are the main components of human intelligence and what are the main dimensions of personality? Second, we need to establish the *origins* of these individual differences. Are some individuals more intelligent or more extraverted because of their genetic make-up, because of their experiences in life, or because of a combination of the two? Third, we need to identify the underlying *mechanisms* (e.g., physiological; cognitive) responsible for individual differences in behavior and personality. The first issue is concerned with description and the second and third issues are concerned with explanation. Not surprisingly, it has proved easier to provide answers at the descriptive level than at the explanatory level.

Chapter 11

Contents

Intelligence

INTRODUCTION

What do we mean by "intelligence"? According to Sternberg (2004, p. 472), it involves "the capacity to learn from experience and adaptation to one's environment." An important implication of that definition is that we need to pay attention to cultural differences—what is needed to adapt successfully in one environment may be very different from what is required in another environment. We can distinguish between individualistic cultures (e.g., the United States; the United Kingdom) with a focus on individuals accepting responsibility for their own behavior, and collectivistic cultures (e.g., many Asian and African cultures) with an emphasis on the group rather than the individual (see Chapter 1). We would expect social considerations to loom larger in definitions of "intelligence" in collectivistic cultures (see Sternberg and Kaufman, 1998) than in individualistic ones. For example, the word for intelligence in Zimbabwe is *ngware*, meaning to be careful and prudent in social relationships. In similar fashion, the Taiwanese Chinese people emphasize interpersonal intelligence, that is, the ability to understand (and to get on well with) other people.

There has been more controversy about intelligence than almost any other area within psychology. Some experts argue that individual differences in intelligence are of great importance in understanding why people vary so much in their behavior. In contrast, others argue that intelligence is an almost valueless concept. Some researchers (e.g., H.J. Eysenck, 1981) believe that individual differences in intelligence are almost entirely a result of heredity, whereas others (e.g., Kamin, 1981) claim that only environmental factors matter. Both of these issues are considered in detail later in the chapter.

EMOTIONAL INTELLIGENCE

Traditionally, most intelligence tests focused mainly on individuals' ability to think and to reason effectively. In recent years, however, there have been various attempts in the United States and Europe to develop tests to assess the more social and interpersonal aspects of intelligence emphasized in many non-Western cultures. Most of these attempts have focused on **emotional intelligence**, which has been defined as "the ability to monitor one's own and others' emotions, to discriminate among them, and to use the information to guide one's thinking and actions" (Salovey & Mayer, 1990, p. 189).

Most early research on emotional intelligence made use of self-report questionnaire measures. For example, Bar-On (1997) developed the Emotional Quotient Inventory to assess five dimensions of emotional intelligence: intrapersonal (e.g., emotional self-awareness); interpersonal (e.g., empathy); stress management (e.g., impulse control); adaptability (e.g., flexibility); and general mood (e.g., happiness). The overall score on the Emotional Quotient Inventory (EQ-i) correlated $-.72$ with neuroticism, $+.56$ with extraversion, and $+.43$ with agreeableness (Geher, 2004). However, EQ-i scores are generally uncorrelated with IQ and have only a small relationship with academic achievement at university (see Geher, 2004). Thus, emotional intelligence as assessed by the Emotional Quotient Inventory mainly involves re-packaging well-established personality dimensions and has little resemblance to intelligence as conventionally defined.

Key Term
Emotional intelligence: the ability to understand one's own emotions as well as those of others.

Davies, Stankov, and Roberts (1998) carried out several studies to work out exactly what is being measured by various questionnaire measures of emotional intelligence and arrived at the same conclusions. They found that measures of emotional intelligence were unrelated to intelligence assessed by IQ tests, so casting doubt on the notion that "emotional intelligence" is a form of intelligence at all. They also found that high levels of emotional intelligence were associated with high levels of extraversion (i.e., sociability) and low levels of neuroticism (i.e., experience of negative emotional states).

In recent years, various ability-based measures of emotional intelligence have been developed. Of particular importance is the Mayer–Salovey–Caruso Emotional Intelligence Test (MSCEIT) (Mayer, Salovey, & Caruso, 2002), which is a development of the Multi-Factor Emotional Intelligence Scale (Mayer, Caruso, & Salovey, 1999). The MSCEIT is based on the notion that *four* main abilities underlie emotional intelligence:

1. *Perceiving emotions*: Identification of emotion in oneself and in others (e.g., identifying facial emotions).
2. *Using emotions*: Facilitating thought and action through experiencing the optimal emotion. For example, being in a positive mood can enhance creative thinking (e.g., Isen, Johnson, Mertz, & Robinson, 1985).
3. *Understanding emotions*: The ability to comprehend the language of emotion and to make sense of complicated relationships among emotions.
4. *Managing emotions*: Regulation of emotion in oneself and in others (e.g., evaluating various courses of action in emotional circumstances).

The MSCEIT provides separate assessments of the four abilities described above. It is assumed that individuals high in emotional intelligence are in tune with social norms, and so the MSCEIT is scored in a consensual way. In other words, high scores indicate that an individual has responded to the items in a similar way to a very large sample of respondents across the world. It is also possible to calculate a score based on similarity between an individual's responses and those of experts (21 emotion researchers). Both methods produce very similar results, with correlations between them often exceeding +.90 (Mayer, Salovey, Caruso, & Sitarenios, 2003; Palmer, Gignac, Manocha, & Stough, 2005). Both scoring methods indicate that females score significantly higher than males (e.g., Palmer et al., 2005). It has sometimes proved difficult to find evidence for the ability of using emotion to facilitate thought with the MSCEIT (Palmer et al., 2005).

The MSCEIT has small or moderate correlations with most intelligence and personality factors (see Mayer, Salovey, & Caruso, 2004, for a review). The ability factor understanding emotions correlates about +.30 with IQ, and total scores on the MSCEIT correlate approximately +.20 with openness to experience and agreeableness and even less with the other Big Five factors.

What has been found using the MSCEIT? First, emotional intelligence as assessed by the MSCEIT predicted deviant behavior in male adolescents even when controlling for the effects of the Big Five personality factors and analytic intelligence (Brackett, Mayer, & Warner, 2004). Second, students with high scores on the MSCEIT were rated more positively for personal qualities than those with low scores (Lopes et al., 2004). Third, heterosexual couples in which both individuals had high MSCEIT scores were much happier than couples in which both had low scores (Brackett et al., 2004). Fourth, employees with higher scores on the MSCEIT were rated by colleagues as easier to

---

Test your own EQ

It's fairly difficult to test any sort of intelligence, but emotional intelligence includes whether a person is basically optimistic or pessimistic in outlook. It is suggested that how we respond to hassles, setbacks, and obstacles is a clue to this aspect of EQ.

Test yourself! Look at these five sample statements and choose either A or B as your response to each.

1. You put on weight on holiday and now can't lose it
   A. I'll never be thin
   B. The latest fad diet isn't right for me
2. You've had a nasty fall playing sport
   A. I'll never be any good at sport
   B. The ground was very slippery
3. You've lost your temper with a friend
   A. We always end up arguing
   B. Something must have upset her/him
4. You are feeling really run-down and exhausted
   A. I never get the chance to relax
   B. I've been unusually busy this month
5. You've forgotten your best friend's birthday
   A. I'm just bad at remembering birthdays
   B. I have had so much on my mind this week

More As: You tend to take setbacks personally—you are naturally pessimistic.
More Bs: You believe that life's obstacles can be overcome—you are naturally optimistic.

deal with, as more interpersonally sensitive, more tolerant of stress, more sociable, and having greater potential for leadership than those with lower scores (Lopes et al., 2004). In addition, higher scorers on the MSCEIT earned more and had more promotions.

On the negative side, findings showing that the MSCEIT has some ability to predict job performance may be less impressive than they appear. One reason is that the MSCEIT in part assesses aspects of ability and personality that aren't new or distinctive but merely duplicate those assessed by previous tests. Another reason is that the measures of job performance sometimes used are inadequate. For example, Janovics and Christiansen (2002) found that the MSCEIT correlated +.22 with job performance assessed by supervisors' ratings even when controlling for general ability and conscientiousness. However, supervisors' ratings are influenced by employees' personality as well as by their job performance, and no attempt was made to control for likely relevant personality factors (e.g., neuroticism; extraversion).

Evaluation

- ➕ Emotional intelligence is of real importance and deserves to be the focus of research.

- ➕ Traditional approaches to intelligence are somewhat narrow, and an emphasis on emotional intelligence serves to broaden intelligence research.

- ➕ The MSCEIT is a reasonably promising measure of emotional intelligence and seems to assess interpersonal sensitivity and related abilities.

- ➖ Most self-report questionnaire measures of emotional intelligence are seriously deficient, and assess mainly well-established personality dimensions.

- ➖ There is little evidence that any measures of emotional intelligence predict job performance or success over and above that predicted by pre-existing ability and personality measures (Matthews, Roberts, & Zeidner, 2004; Zeidner, Matthews, & Roberts, 2004).

- ➖ More research is needed to establish that emotional intelligence is actually an important type of intelligence.

PRACTICAL IMPORTANCE OF INTELLIGENCE

Of what practical usefulness is it to assess individual differences in intelligence? There is convincing evidence that intelligence is very important in everyday life. For example, job performance and academic achievement among students are both moderately well predicted by intelligence or IQ (Mackintosh, 1998). The fact that IQ predicts real-world success indicates that it is assessing something valuable.

Let's consider the impact of intelligence on job performance in more detail. Hunter and Hunter (1984) considered over 32,000 workers performing 515 different jobs. They identified five levels of job complexity: professional-managerial jobs; high-level complexity technical jobs; medium-complexity jobs; semi-skilled jobs; and completely unskilled jobs. The average correlations between intelligence and job performance were as follows: +.58 for professional jobs, +.56 for complex technical jobs, +.51 for medium-complexity jobs, +.40 for semi-skilled jobs, and +.23 for unskilled jobs.

It may seem surprising that something as general and broad as intelligence predicts job performance so well across such a wide range of jobs. For example, it is plausible to assume that a musician needs highly specific musical skills to perform his/her job effectively. However, the evidence indicates that specific ability or aptitude tests typically contribute surprisingly little to predicting job performance over and above that provided by general measures of intelligence (e.g., Ree et al., 1994). The most convincing evidence was reported by Hunter (1983). He studied four very large samples of military personnel undergoing job training programs. In all four samples, intelligence strongly predicted training performance and also strongly predicted specific aptitude or ability scores. There were *no* direct effects of specific abilities on training performance because the apparent effects of specific abilities were caused by their relationship with general intelligence.

Why is there a strong association between intelligence and job performance? We will discuss two possible answers. The first starts with the finding that there is a moderate correlation between intelligence and socioeconomic status (Mackintosh, 1998). As a result, at least some of the apparent effects of intelligence on job performance might actually be due to socioeconomic status and related factors such as school quality or neighborhood. This possibility was apparently disproved by Murray (1998). He used a sample of male full biological siblings in intact families, thus controlling for socioeconomic status, schools, neighborhood, and so on. The siblings with higher intelligence had more prestigious jobs and higher income. When they were in their late 20s, a person with average intelligence earned on average nearly $18,000 (£9000) less per annum than his sibling with an IQ of at least 120, but over $9000 (£4500) more than his sibling with an IQ of 80 or less.

The second answer to the question above was provided by Hunter and Schmidt (e.g., 1996). They argued that the ability to learn rapidly is of crucial importance in most jobs, and learning ability is determined by intelligence. Successful job performance also sometimes requires that workers respond in an innovative or adaptive fashion, and more intelligent workers can respond more adaptively than less intelligent ones. Relevant evidence was provided by Hunter (1986), who combined the data from 14 studies on civilian and military groups (discussed in detail by Gottfredson, 1997). Three findings supported the theory. First, there was a high correlation between intelligence and job knowledge with both types of jobs (see figure on the left). Second, learning in the form of job knowledge was strongly associated with job performance. Third, there was a direct influence of intelligence on job performance that didn't depend on job knowledge. This may reflect the greater ability of intelligent workers to respond adaptively.

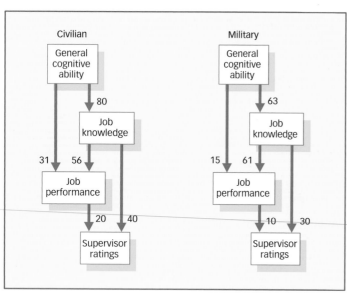

A path analysis of findings from studies on civilian and military groups showing direct and indirect (via job knowledge) effects of intelligence (general cognitive ability) on job performance. The numbers indicate the strength of the relationship between factors. From Hunter (1986) Copyright © 1986 Elsevier. Reproduced with permission.

Health and longevity

Individual differences in intelligence also predict health and longevity (Gottfredson & Deary, 2004). For example, Whalley and Deary (2001) found that individuals at a 15-point disadvantage in IQ relative to other individuals were only 79% as likely to live to age 76. Among the women, the less intelligent ones had a 40% increase in cancer deaths compared to the more intelligent ones, and the comparable figure for men was 27%.

How can we explain the effects of intelligence on health? It is difficult to answer that question because numerous factors could be involved. For example, part of the answer is that more intelligent individuals on average have more money and so can afford better food and living conditions. However, there is another important factor. If you are to maximize your chances of having a long life, you need to interpret your bodily symptoms, take account of information on health issues, adhere to instructions for taking medicine, avoid destructive habits such as smoking, and so on. In other words, you need good **health literacy**. More intelligent individuals have greater health literacy than less intelligent ones (see Gottfredson & Deary, 2004). The problems posed by low levels of health literacy were considered by Williams et al. (1995). Of those with "inadequate" health literacy, 65% didn't understand directions for taking medicine on an empty stomach and 40% couldn't work out from an appointment slip when their next appointment was due.

INTELLIGENCE TESTING

The first proper intelligence test was produced in 1905 by two French psychologists, Alfred Binet and Théodore Simon. It measured comprehension, memory, and various other psychological processes. Among the well-known tests that followed are the Stanford-Binet test produced at Stanford University in the United States, the Wechsler Intelligence Scale for Children, and the British Ability Scales. These (and other) tests are designed to measure several aspects of intelligence. They often contain mathematical items, and many contain vocabulary tests in which individuals are asked to define the meanings of various words. Many tests contain problems based on analogies (e.g., "Hat is to head as shoe is to ____"), and items relating to spatial ability (e.g., "If I start walking northwards, then turn left, and then turn left again, what direction will I be facing?").

The French psychologist, Alfred Binet (1857–1911).

CALCULATING IQ

Suppose you complete an intelligence test containing 150 items, and you obtain a score of 79. Have you done well or badly? The only way to answer that question is by comparing your performance against that of other people. That can only be done effectively by using a **standardized test**, that is, one that has been given to a large, representative sample of the population. When your score has been compared to those of others, it is possible to calculate your IQ or **intelligence quotient**, an overall measure of intellectual ability.

How is IQ calculated? Most intelligence tests are devised so that the IQs from the general population are normally distributed. The normal distribution is a bell-shaped curve in which there are as many scores above the mean as below it (see the figure below). Most of the scores are close to the mean, and there are fewer and fewer scores as we move away from the mean in either direction. The spread of scores in a normal distribution is usually indicated by the **standard deviation**. In a normal distribution, 68% of the scores fall within one standard deviation of the mean or average, 95% fall within two standard deviations, and 99.73% are within three standard deviations. Intelligence tests are designed to produce a mean IQ of 100 and a standard deviation of about 16. Thus, if you have an IQ of 116, your IQ is greater than that of 84% of the population. That is the case because 50% fall below 100, and a further 34% between the mean and one standard deviation above it. Note that intelligence-test designers take steps to ensure that their test has a normal distribution of IQs—it is very difficult to know whether this corresponds to the "true" distribution.

Those with high IQs don't usually perform well on all the tests on an intelligence-test battery, and nor do those with low IQs perform poorly on every test. As a result, tests are generally constructed to obtain measures of various abilities (e.g., numerical; spatial; reasoning; perceptual speed). We can obtain a more accurate assessment of an individual's intellectual ability by considering the profile of his/her performance across these abilities rather than by focusing only on IQ.

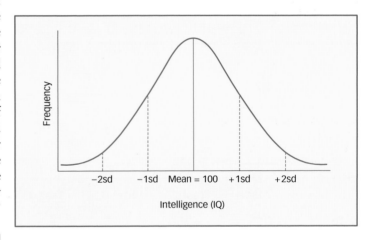

RELIABILITY AND VALIDITY

We have seen that intelligence tests need to be standardized in order to be useful. Two other essential features are reliability and validity. **Reliability** refers to the extent to which a test provides consistent or replicable findings, whereas **validity** refers to the extent to which a test measures what it is supposed to be measuring. The most common way

Key Terms

Standardized test:
a test given to large representative samples so that an individual's scores can be compared to those of the population.

Intelligence quotient:
a measure of general intellectual ability; the mean IQ is 100.

Standard deviation:
a measure of the spread of scores in a bell-shaped or normal distribution. It is the square root of the variance, takes account of every score, and is a sensitive measure of dispersion or variation.

Reliability:
the extent to which a test gives consistent findings on separate occasions.

Validity:
the extent to which a test measures what it claims to be measuring.

to assess reliability is by the test–retest method. A group of people take the same test on two separate occasions, and their two scores are correlated. The higher the correlation (a measure of the relationship between the two scores), the greater is the reliability of the test. The highest possible correlation is +1.00, which would indicate perfect agreement or reliability. In contrast, a correlation of .00 would indicate no reliability. In fact, reliability correlations tend to be about +.85, which indicates high reliability.

What about validity? The most direct approach is to relate IQ to some external criterion or standard. This is known as **concurrent validity** when IQ is correlated with currently available information about a criterion, and as **predictive validity** when the criterion measure is obtained after the intelligence test has been administered. For example, we would expect more intelligent people to achieve greater academic success than less intelligent ones, and to move on to have more successful careers. However, academic and career success obviously also depend on several other factors such as motivation, support of family and friends, the quality of teaching or training provided, and so on. In spite of that, IQ typically correlates about +.50 with academic achievement and with occupational status (see Mackintosh, 1998, for a review). As discussed above, IQ predicts job performance to a greater extent with complex jobs than with relatively simple ones (Hunter & Hunter, 1984).

THEORIES OF INTELLIGENCE

So far we have focused mainly on IQ, which is a very general measure of intelligence. You may well be thinking that many people are much more intelligent in some ways than others, but this information is lost in a general measure such as IQ. The evidence indicates strongly that we need to identify general *and* specific aspects of intelligence. The most common approach that is used is **factor analysis**, which is a statistical technique used to decide on the number and nature of the factors underlying intelligence as measured by a test. The first step in factor analysis is to give a large number of items to a large number of individuals, and to obtain scores from each individual on each item. The correlations between these items are then calculated. If two items correlate highly with each other, this means that those who perform well on one item tend to perform well on the other item. The key assumption is that two items correlating highly with each other are assessing the same factor of intelligence. It is also assumed that two items correlating weakly or not at all with each other are *not* assessing the same factor of intelligence. Thus, the pattern of correlations is used to identify the main aspects of intelligence (or factors as they are known).

We can see what happens in simplified fashion by considering the box on the left. How many factors should we extract from this correlation matrix? The answer is two. Tests 1 and 2 correlate highly with each other, and so are measures of the same factor. Tests 3 and 4 correlate highly with each other (but not with test 1 or test 2), and so they form a different, second factor.

	Test 1	Test 2	Test 3	Test 4
Test 1	–	+.85	+.12	+.10
Test 2	+.85	–	+.08	+.11
Test 3	+.12	+.08	–	+.87
Test 4	+.10	+.11	+.87	–

Key Terms

Concurrent validity:
assessing **validity** by correlating scores on a test with some currently available relevant criterion (e.g., academic achievement in the case of an intelligence test).

Predictive validity:
assessing **validity** by correlating scores on a test with some future criterion (e.g., career success in the case of an intelligence test).

Factor analysis:
a statistical technique applied to intelligence tests to find out the number and nature of the aspects of intelligence they are measuring.

FACTOR THEORIES

The first factor theory of intelligence was put forward by the British psychologist Charles Spearman (1923). In his two-factor theory, there is a general factor of intelligence that he called "g." He argued that there is a general factor because practically all of the tests contained within an intelligence-test battery correlate positively with each other. However, most of these positive correlations are fairly low, so we can't account for all the data in terms of a general factor. Accordingly, Spearman argued that there are specific factors associated with each test.

Thurstone (1938) wasn't convinced of the need to assume that there is a general factor of intelligence. Instead, he identified seven factors that he referred to as primary mental abilities. These primary mental abilities were as follows: inductive reasoning; verbal meaning; numerical ability; spatial ability; perceptual speed; memory; and verbal fluency. There is one major problem with this approach. All seven primary abilities correlate positively with each other. As a result, factor analysis of Thurstone's seven factors produces the general factor ignored by Thurstone (Sternberg, 1985).

Hierarchical approach

Nowadays there is fairly general agreement that intelligence is organized hierarchically. One of the most influential hierarchical theories is that of Carroll (1993), who argued that we should combine the insights of Spearman and of Thurstone. He discussed evidence based on factor analysis of over 460 data sets obtained over a 60-year period from more than 130,000 people. His theory (shown in the figure below) identifies *three* levels in the hierarchy:

- At the top level, there is the general factor of intelligence (often referred to as "g"); this is the main ingredient in IQ.
- At the middle level, there are various fairly general factors, including crystallized intelligence (involving the use of acquired knowledge) and fluid ability (used when coping with novel problems and situations).
- At the bottom level, there are very specific factors associated with only one item or a small number of tests.

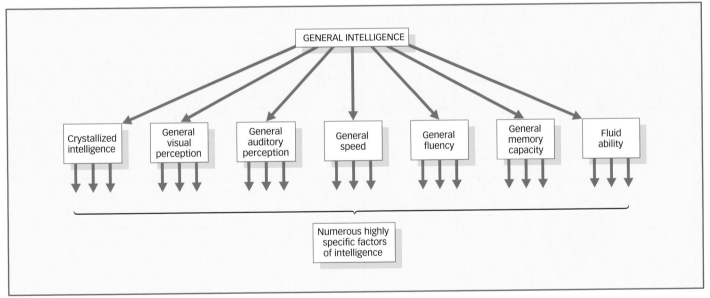

Carroll's (1986) three-level hierarchical model of intelligence.

MULTIPLE INTELLIGENCES

Howard Gardner (1983) argued strongly that most intelligence tests and most theories of intelligence are based on an excessively narrow view of the nature of intelligence. According to Gardner, there are seven separate intelligences and no single general factor. Here are his seven intelligences:

1. *Logical-mathematical intelligence*: This is of special value in handling abstract problems of a logical or mathematical nature.
2. *Spatial intelligence*: This is used when deciding how to go from one place to another, how to arrange suitcases in the trunk of a car, and so on.
3. *Musical intelligence*: This is used both for active musical processes (e.g., playing an instrument; singing) and for more passive processes (e.g., appreciating music).

Gardner's seven intelligences

Logical-mathematical

Spatial

Musical

Bodily kinesthetic

Linguistic

Intrapersonal

Interpersonal

4. *Bodily kinesthetic intelligence*: This is involved in the fine control of bodily movements in activities such as sport and dancing.
5. *Linguistic intelligence*: This is involved in language activities (e.g., reading; writing; speaking).
6. *Intrapersonal intelligence*: This intelligence "depends on core processes that enable people to distinguish among their own feelings" (Gardner, Kornhaber, & Wake, 1996, p. 211).
7. *Interpersonal intelligence*: This intelligence "makes use of core capabilities to recognize and make distinctions among others' feeling, beliefs, and intentions" (Gardner et al., 1996, p. 211).

Gardner (1998) proposed adding naturalistic intelligence to the seven intelligences he had previously identified. Naturalistic intelligence is shown by individuals who can perceive patterns in nature. Charles Darwin is an example of a famous person having outstanding naturalistic intelligence. Gardner also suggested that there might be two additional intelligences: spiritual intelligence and existential intelligence. Spiritual intelligence is based on a concern for cosmic issues, and with the achievement of the spiritual as a state of being. Existential intelligence is based on concerns about ultimate issues of existence.

How did Gardner come up with his original seven intelligences? He argued that we should only identify an intelligence when it satisfies various criteria. First, it should depend on identifiable brain structures. Second, studies of brain-damaged patients should indicate that it can be impaired without disrupting any other intelligence. Third, it should involve the use of distinct cognitive processes. Fourth, there should be exceptional individuals showing a remarkable ability (or deficit) with respect to the intelligence. Fifth, in evolutionary terms the development of the intelligence should have improved humans' adaptation to the environment. Sixth, it should be measurable by appropriate intelligence tests.

In spite of its popularity, there is surprisingly little direct evidence to support Gardner's theory of multiple intelligences. An exception is the work of Gardner (1993), who used the theory to study creativity. He chose seven individuals who showed outstanding creativity during the early part of the twentieth century with respect to one of the seven intelligences. Albert Einstein was the representative of logical-mathematical intelligence. The other outstanding figures were Pablo Picasso (spatial intelligence), Igor Stravinsky (musical intelligence), Martha Graham (bodily kinesthetic intelligence), T.S. Eliot (linguistic intelligence), Sigmund Freud (intrapersonal intelligence), and Mahatma Gandhi (interpersonal intelligence). Nearly all of them were brought up in families forcing them to meet standards of excellence. They all had childlike qualities, showing signs of behaving like a "wonder-filled child." They were all very ambitious, which led them to sacrifice other aspects of their lives and to cause suffering to their families.

Three of the individuals selected by Gardner (1993) to demonstrate his theory of multiple intelligences: Igor Stravinsky (for musical intelligence), Pablo Picasso (for spatial intelligence), and Mahatma Gandhi (for interpersonal intelligence).

This genius-based approach to identifying intelligences may be flawed. As Jensen (in Miele, 2002, p. 58) pointed out sarcastically, the logic of this approach is that we could claim that "Al Capone displayed the highest level of 'Criminal Intelligence,' or that Casanova was 'blessed' with exceptional 'Sexual Intelligence.'" In other words, Gardner's criteria for what constitutes an intelligence are so lenient that almost anything goes. For example, face recognition and the ability to learn foreign languages appear to meet his criteria for an intelligence (Mackintosh, 1998).

Evaluation

- Gardner's approach to intelligence is broader in scope than most others.

- There is some supporting evidence (e.g., from geniuses; from brain-damaged patients) for all seven intelligences originally proposed by Gardner.

- The seven intelligences correlate positively with each other, whereas Gardner (1983) assumed they were independent. That means that Gardner was wrong to disregard the general factor of intelligence. As Jensen (in Miele, 2002, p. 59) pointed out, the evidence indicates that, "A level of g [general factor] beyond the 90th percentile [IQ over 120] is probably necessary for recognized achievement in politics, the military, business, finance, or industry."

- Musical and bodily kinesthetic intelligences are less important than the other intelligences in Western cultures, with many very successful people being tone-deaf and poorly coordinated.

- The criteria for an intelligence are too lenient.

- The theory is descriptive rather than explanatory—it fails to explain *how* each intelligence works.

HEREDITY AND ENVIRONMENT

Why are some children and adults more intelligent than others? At the most general level, only two factors could be responsible: heredity or environment. Heredity consists of a person's genetic endowment, and environment consists of the situations and experiences encountered by people in the course of their lives. The only sensible view is that both heredity and environment contribute to individual differences in intelligence. However, what is much more complex is to decide on their relative importance.

It is perhaps natural to think of heredity and environment as having entirely separate or *independent* effects on intelligence. However, the reality is very different, because our genetic make-up influences the types of environmental experiences we have. We can see how implausible it is to assume that heredity and environment have entirely separate effects by applying that dubious assumption to basketball performance (Dickens & Flynn, 2001):

> *Good coaching, practising, preoccupation with basketball, and all other environmental factors that influence performance must be unrelated to whether genes contribute to someone being tall, slim, and well coordinated. For this to be true, players must be selected at random for the varsity basketball team and get the benefits of professional coaching and intense practice, without regard to build, quickness, and degree of interest.*

In fact, of course, individuals whose genes predispose them to be outstanding at basketball are more likely to put themselves into an environment supporting excellent basketball performance than are those whose genes do not.

We can apply precisely the same logic directly to intelligence. No one believes that the probability that a given individual will choose to read hundreds of books or to go to university has nothing to do with his/her level of genetic ability. In fact, individuals with the highest levels of genetic ability are much more likely to seek out intellectually demanding situations than are those with less genetic ability. In the words of Dickens and Flynn (2001, p. 347), "Higher IQ leads one into better environments causing still higher IQ, and so on." Thus, individual differences in intelligence depend to a fairly large extent on the effects of heredity on environment.

Nicotine as nurture

We are all familiar with the fact that nicotine has an effect on the brain, but most of the media publicity relates to its physical ill effects such as increasing the risks of developing lung cancer and cardiovascular disease. However, there are other, more subtle behavioral effects. Jacobsen's (2007) team at Yale University studied groups of teenagers. One group were smokers; another group had mothers who had smoked when pregnant; a third group were nonsmokers; the fourth group had mothers who did not smoke during pregnancy. The first two groups were the experimental groups (a natural experiment, obviously) and the second two groups were the controls, with the groups being comparable in age, educational attainment, IQ, parental education, and symptoms of inattention. A consistent finding was that the first two groups had changes in their brain structure in the brain connections in the areas which process auditory information. What effect did these changes have? Those groups of teenagers had more difficulty in focusing their auditory attention when there were distractions going on. The adverse effect of nicotine both antenatally and in adolescence is to disrupt the development of anterior cortical white matter in the auditory cortex. This seems to lead to a deficiency in attentional processing so that there is too much "noise" reaching that part of the cortex, thus reducing the efficiency of selecting what is important. This means that not only did indirect exposure to nicotine before birth seem to cause deficits in brain development, but also that in the teenage years when many neural pathways are maturing nicotine can also have an adverse effect. Further research to investigate whether these effects of nurture on nature are permanent is already being done. Overall, the results will not be known for some time.

Overall, the research shows that though brain structure is controlled by genes, and so is an example of nature, environmental factors at key times in life can alter or modify this structure and so such factors are a real example of nurture—and nature and nurture interact.

Plomin (1990) identified three types of interdependence between genetic endowment and environment:

1. *Active covariation*: This occurs when children of differing genetic ability look for situations reinforcing their genetic differences (e.g., children of high genetic ability reading numerous books).
2. *Passive covariation*: This occurs when parents of high genetic ability provide a more stimulating environment than parents of lower genetic ability.
3. *Reactive covariation*: This occurs when an individual's genetically influenced behavior helps to determine how he/she is treated by other people.

When we consider the role of heredity in determining individual differences in intelligence, we are interested in an individual's genetic potential (known as the **genotype**). However, we cannot assess the genotype directly. All we can measure directly are an individual's observable characteristics (the **phenotype**). How psychologists have grappled with this problem is discussed below.

TWIN STUDIES

The most valuable approach to assessing the roles of heredity and environment in determining individual differences in intelligence involves studying twins. Identical or **monozygotic twins** derive from the same fertilized ovum, and so have essentially identical genotypes. In contrast, fraternal or **dizygotic twins** derive from two different fertilized ova. As a result, their genotypes are no more similar than those of two ordinary siblings, that is, they share on average 50% of their genes (see the figure on the right). If heredity influences individual differences in intelligence, then identical twins should be more alike in intelligence than fraternal twins. In contrast, if environmental factors are all-important, then identical twins should be no more alike than fraternal twins.

The degree of similarity in intelligence shown by pairs of twins is usually reported in the form of correlations. A correlation of +1.00 would mean that both twins in a pair have very similar or the same IQs, whereas a correlation of 0.00 would mean that there is no relationship between the IQs of twins. Bouchard and McGue (1981) reviewed 111 studies, and reported that the mean correlation for identical twins was +.86 compared to +.60 for fraternal twins. McCartney, Harris, and Bernieri (1990) reported similar findings from a later analysis of numerous studies: the mean correlation for identical twins was +.81 compared to +.59 for fraternal twins.

On the face of it, the above findings indicate clearly that individual differences in intelligence depend to a fair extent on genetic factors. However, there are complicating factors. For example, there is the prenatal environment. All fraternal twins have separate placentas in the womb, whereas two-thirds of identical twins share a placenta. As a result, the prenatal environment of most identical twins is more similar than that of fraternal twins. Phelps, Davis, and Schwartz (1997) reviewed several studies in which it was found that identical twins

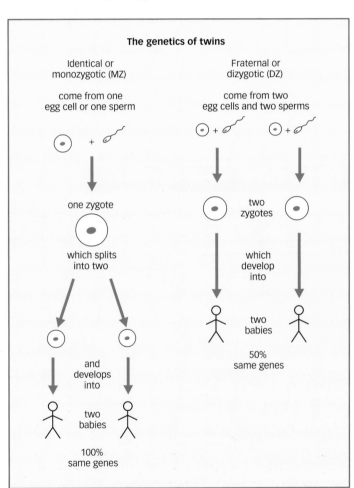

The genetics of twins

Key Terms

Genotype:
an individual's potential in the form of genes.

Phenotype:
an individual's observable characteristics based on his/her genotype plus life experiences.

Monozygotic twins:
identical twins derived from a single fertilized ovum and sharing 100% of their genes.

Dizygotic twins:
fraternal twins derived from two fertilized ova and sharing 50% of their genes.

sharing a single placenta were more similar in intelligence than those having separate placentas. Thus, the greater similarity in IQ between identical twins than fraternal ones may depend in part on the greater similarity of the prenatal environment for most identical twins.

Another potential problem is that identical twins are treated in a more similar way than fraternal twins in terms of parental treatment, playing together, and being taught by the same teachers (Loehlin & Nichols, 1976). However, these differences are relatively small, and parents may treat identical twins more similarly than fraternal twins because they are responding to the greater genetically influenced similarities in the behaviour of identical twins (i.e., reactive covariation).

Identical twins are relatively rare, and identical twins brought up in separate families are obviously even rarer (see the Case Study below). However, they are of particular value in assessing the roles of heredity and environment in determining individual differences in intelligence. Identical twins brought up apart should be very similar to each other in IQ if genetic factors are very important. In contrast, those favoring an environmentalist position would argue that placing twins in different environments should ensure they are not similar in intelligence.

On the face of it, the findings support the hereditarian position. Bouchard et al. (1990) studied more than 40 adult identical twin pairs separated at a mean age of 5 months. In spite of the fact that these twin pairs had been separated in infancy, their IQs correlated +.75. However, there is a real limitation in this and other studies

Case Study: *Separated Twins*

Once upon a time in New York a pair of twin girls were born and, after being put separately into foster care, were adopted by two different couples. Neither the girls, nor the couples, were aware that they were twins separated at birth.

Elyse grew up, didn't marry, went to Paris and worked as an independent movie maker. Paula remained in New York, and made a career in journalism specializing in film. She had a partner and a baby daughter. Paula was not interested in her biological past but Elyse was, and returned to New York to investigate her heritage. And one day, 35 years after their separation, the phone rang in Elyse's rented New York apartment and for the first ever time the identical twin sisters spoke.

Physically the identical twin sisters are, as one would expect, very similar. Other similarities include a tendency to introspection and depression and the same mannerisms, allergies, political views, and taste for obscure, independent movies. As children they sucked their fingers the same way, and had eating disorders in their teens. They both write, and at high school edited their student newspapers. They both went to university to do movie studies. They even wear the same shade of lipstick! These are behavioral and cognitive similarities, and the question is whether they are caused by the identical genes or by upbringing—nature or nurture.

It is a fact that identical twins have identical genotypes. However these two women had rather different childhood environments. Paula had a secure and affluent home, whereas Elyse's mother died when the girl was only 6 years old, and her adopted brother developed schizophrenia.

So while nature was identical, nurture was not. And yet both women have a caring, nurturing approach, and both prefer the same sorts of people though they are clearly not the same person. For example, Elyse seems quieter, more thoughtful, and takes more time before answering, compared to Paula.

A separate but critically important question is why the twins were split up in the first place, and the answer is uncomfortable. The psychiatrist at the adoption agency, together with a prominent psychologist, decided to use the twins and four other similar twin pairs plus one set of triplets as a secret experiment, a study of nature versus nurture on human development. These siblings were deliberately split up, separated at birth and adopted separately by couples who did not know the baby was one of two or three. This was seen as a great research opportunity as fewer than 300 twin pairs who were separated at birth have been identified, and most of these had contact with each other or were brought up by relatives who knew they were twins. By today's standards the ethical issues with this experiment are huge and very disturbing. Once the researchers realized that their actions were likely to be heavily criticized the files on the study were sealed until 2066, continuing the secrecy until the twins, if still alive, will be nearly 100 years old.

What do you feel this case history tells us about the nature–nurture debate?
What would you identify as the most important ethical issues in this experiment?

focusing on identical twins brought up apart. More than half of such twin pairs were brought up in different branches of the same family. As a result, their environments may well have been rather similar, which could explain at least some of the similarity in their IQs.

What conclusions can we draw from the evidence? Psychologists trying to be as precise as possible about the contributions of heredity and environment to intelligence generally assess heritability. The technical definition of **heritability** is the ratio of genetically caused variation to total variation (genetic + environmental variation) within any given population. Thus, heritability tells us something about the role of genetic factors in producing individual differences in intelligence. It is important to note that heritability is a *population* measure, and so varies considerably from one population to another. The more similar the environmental factors experienced by those living in a given culture, the greater will be the effect of genetic factors in determining individual differences in intelligence. For example, Brace (1996) found that the heritability of intelligence was much higher among people living in affluent white American suburbs than among people living in American urban ghettos. This occurred because the great majority of those living in affluent white suburbs enjoy a favorable environment throughout childhood.

There is another important point to be made about the heritability measure. In essence, it combines two kinds of genetic influence. First, there is a *direct* genetic influence on intelligence. Second, there is an *indirect* genetic influence on intelligence in which genetic factors affect the environments in which an individual finds himself/herself and the environment then affects his/her intelligence. For example, individuals of high genetic ability are far more likely to go to university than those of low genetic ability, and the educational environment provided by a university enhances the intelligence of those who go there. These indirect effects in which genetic factors influence the environment, which then influences intelligence, are counted as genetic effects when heritability is calculated—you may feel that is somewhat unfair given that environmental effects are strongly involved.

Mackintosh (1998) reviewed the evidence based on heritability measures. He concluded that between 30% and 75% of individual differences in intelligence in modern industrialized societies are a result of genetic factors. However, large differences in heritability have been found as a function of age. According to Plomin (1988, p. 420), the genetic influence on individual differences in IQ "increases from infancy (20%) to childhood (40%) to adulthood (60%)." It is not known for certain why the heritability of intelligence increases during development. However, adolescents and adults select and control their own environment to a greater extent than children, and this reduces the impact of the environment on intelligence. Thus, the increase in heritability of intelligence during the course of development may reflect what Plomin (1990) called active covariation (discussed earlier).

ADOPTION STUDIES

Adoption studies provide another way of assessing the relative importance of heredity and environment in determining individual differences in intelligence. If heredity is more important than environment, adopted children's IQs will be more similar to those of their biological parents than those of their adoptive parents. The opposite pattern will be found if environment is more important. In fact, the IQs of adopted children typically resemble those of their biological parents more than those of their adoptive parents, suggesting that genetic factors are important.

It is difficult to interpret the findings from most adoption studies. There is the issue of **selective placement**, meaning that adopted children tend to be placed in homes resembling those of their biological parents in social and educational terms. Thus, some of the similarity in IQ between adopted children and their biological parents may occur because they are living in an environment resembling the one their mother would have provided.

Capron and Duyne (1989) carried out an important study on adopted children, in which there was little evidence of selective placement. They used four very different

Key Terms
Heritability: the ratio of genetically caused variation to total variation (a combination of genetic and environmental variation) within a given population.
Selective placement: placing adopted children in homes with similar educational and social backgrounds to those of their biological parents.

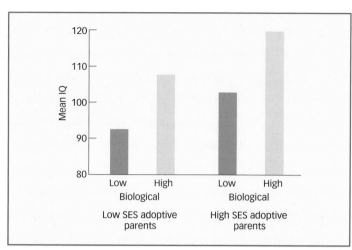

Mean IQs of adopted children as a function of socioeconomic status (SES) of their biological parents (low vs. high) and their adoptive parents (low vs. high). Data from Capron and Duyne (1989).

groups of adopted children. These groups consisted of all four combinations of high and low socioeconomic status biological parents and high and low socioeconomic status adoptive parents.

What do you think happened in the study by Capron and Duyne (1989)? If genetic factors are of more importance, the intelligence of the adopted children should have depended mainly on the socioeconomic status of the biological parents. In contrast, if environmental factors are more important, the adopted children's intelligence should have depended mainly on the socioeconomic status of the adoptive parents. In fact, the effects of the socioeconomic status of the biological and of the adoptive parents were comparable (see the figure on the left). Thus, genetic and environmental factors were equally important in determining the adopted children's intelligence.

ENVIRONMENTAL STUDIES

The evidence from twin and adoption studies indicates clearly that genetic factors are only partly responsible for individual differences in intelligence. That means that environmental factors are also important. We can use data from twin and adoption studies to assess two kinds of environmental influence: shared environment and non-shared environment. **Shared environment** refers to all the common influences within a family that make children resemble each other. **Nonshared environment** refers to all those influences unique to any given child (e.g., experiences with peers; instruction from particular teachers).

Twin and adoption studies suggest that about 20% of individual differences in intelligence are a result of nonshared environment. The impact of shared environment changes over time. Shared environment accounts for 25% of individual differences in intelligence in childhood but very little after adolescence. This happens because adolescents spend much less time than children being exposed to the influence of parents and home.

Some of the strongest evidence that environmental factors can have a substantial effect on intelligence was reported by Flynn (1987, 1994). He obtained evidence

Key Terms

Shared environment:
environmental influences common to the children within a given family.

Nonshared environment:
environmental influences that are unique to a given individual.

Flynn effect:
the rapid rise in average IQ in several Western countries in recent decades.

General criticisms of IQ tests, adoption studies, and twin studies

IQ tests	Adoption studies	Twin studies
Debatable whether IQ is an adequate measurement of intelligence	Selective placement makes it hard to determine the effects of heredity and environment	Environmental similarity often occurs
Cultural differences not always considered	Heredity is less well controlled than in twin studies	Twins raised separately are often raised by different branches of the same family
		Twins have often spent some years together before being separated

from 20 Western countries, each of which showed the **Flynn effect**: a rapid rise in mean IQ in most Western countries in recent decades. Flynn (1987) reported that there had been an increase of 2.9 points per decade on nonverbal IQ and of 3.7 points on verbal IQ. This large and rapid increase could not possibly be a result of genetic factors. Embarrassingly for psychologists, we don't know precisely *why* the Flynn effect does occur. However, several environmental factors probably contribute to the effect, and here are some likely contenders:

- Increases in the number of years of education.
- Greater access to information (e.g., internet; television).
- Increased cognitive complexity of the average job now compared to the past.
- A large increase in the percentage of middle-class families.

As a footnote, there is some evidence that the Flynn effect is coming to an end. For example, Sundet, Barlaug, and Torjussen (2004) found in Norway that there had been no general increase in IQ since the mid-1990s.

Key Study

Sameroff et al. (1987, 1993): The Rochester Longitudinal Study

Sameroff et al. (1987, 1993) carried out a longitudinal study in New York State to investigate the environmental factors that might be linked to intellectual delay in young children. They selected pregnant women to be part of their study and followed 215 children, testing their IQs at ages 4 and 13. The families represented a range of socioeconomic backgrounds, maternal age groups, and number of other siblings.

Sameroff et al. (1993) identified 10 family risk factors related to lower IQ:

- Mother has a history of mental illness.
- Mother did not go to high school.
- Mother has severe anxiety.
- Mother has rigid attitudes and values concerning her child's development.
- Few positive interactions between mother and child during infancy.
- Head of household has a semi-skilled job.
- Father does not live with the family.
- Child belongs to a minority group.
- Family suffered 20 or more stressful events during the child's first 4 years of life.

There was a clear negative association between the number of risk factors associated with a child and his/her IQ (see the figure on the following page). At age 4, this correlation was −.58, and it was −.61 at age 13. Thus, there was a moderately strong association between risk factors and IQ. At the age of 4, high-risk children were 24 times more likely than low-risk children to have IQs below 85. On average, each risk factor reduced the child's IQ by 4 points.

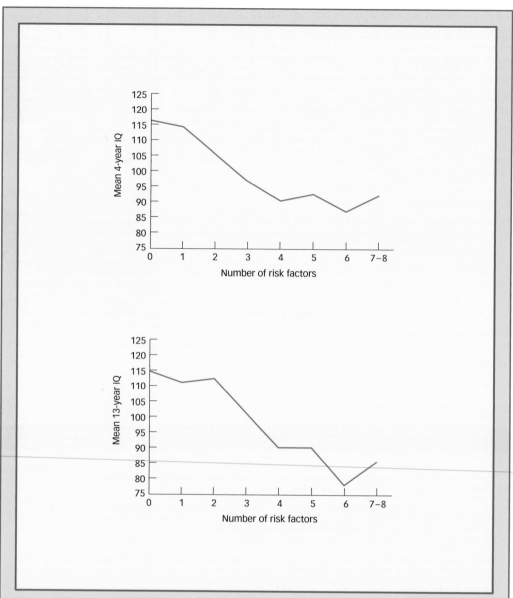

These graphs show the negative association between IQ and number of environmental risk factors. The top graph presents data for mean 4-year IQ scores, and the bottom graph presents data for mean 13-year IQ scores.

Discussion points
1. Select one of the risk factors and suggest how it might affect intellectual development.
2. What are the political implications of this study?

KEY STUDY EVALUATION
It is difficult to interpret the above findings. For example, Sameroff et al. (1993) reported that the mother not going to high school and the head of the household having a semi-skilled job were associated with low IQ in the children. It is entirely possible that genetic factors played a part in producing these environmental factors and in leading to low IQ in children. Thus, we can't be confident that the environmental factors themselves actually produced a negative effect on the children's IQ.

SIZE DOES MATTER!

There is a popular view that people with big heads (and so presumably large brains) are more intelligent than those with small heads. However, when psychologists first studied the link between brain size and intelligence, they found practically no relationship. However, these early studies were very limited because the findings were based on imprecise estimates of brain size. One technique was based on skull size, but that provides a very inaccurate estimate. Another equally flawed technique was to measure the sizes of the shrunken brains of people who had recently died. Nowadays we can obtain good measures of brain size in living people by using brain-imaging techniques such as magnetic resonance imaging (MRI). Since male brains are slightly larger than female brains on average, what is often done is to use MRI to correlate brain size with intelligence in each sex separately.

McDaniel (2005) reported a meta-analysis based on 37 different samples. The average correlation between brain size or volume and intelligence was +.33. This indicates that people with larger brains do tend to be more intelligent. McDaniel also considered each sex separately. The average correlation between brain volume and intelligence was +.40 for females and +.34 for males. All of these correlations are impressive in view of the fact that brain volume is a crude measure.

It is not clear exactly *why* brain size is associated with intelligence. However, there is evidence from studies on children that nutritionally enhanced diets produce increases in IQ (Benton, 2001). As Peters (1995) pointed out, the relationship between brain size and IQ may be influenced by nutritional factors—good nutrition benefits brain-size development and intelligence.

Males vs. females

We have seen that females have smaller brains than males and that brain size is positively associated with intelligence. The possible inference that men are more intelligent than women does *not* follow—in fact, the two sexes have essentially the same mean IQ—(Mackintosh, 1998). However, the pattern of abilities differs somewhat between the sexes. Females tend to have greater verbal (language-based) abilities than males, and males have greater spatial abilities (e.g., solving jigsaw puzzles; reading maps) (Anderson, 2004). Halpern (2004) discussed interesting findings obtained from numerous Western cultures. Reading literacy was higher in girls than boys in all 25 cultures for which information was available. However, boys outperformed girls in 31 out of 32 cultures in science achievement and in 27 out of 32 cultures in mathematics achievement.

There is recent evidence that there may be important sex differences in brain structures underlying intelligence. For example, Haier et al. (2005) considered two kinds of nerve tissue in the brain: gray matter and white matter. Women had more white matter and fewer gray matter brain areas related to intelligence than did men. We don't know why this difference exists. However, it indicates the value of moving beyond simply measuring brain size towards a focus on the detailed make-up of individual brains.

In sum, the fact that even primitive measures such as brain volume predict individual differences in intelligence moderately well indicates that we can enhance our understanding of intelligence by focusing on the brain. It is probable that future research will indicate the value of focusing on the precise make-up of brain volume (e.g., percentage gray matter; percentage white matter) rather than crude measures such as brain volume.

Chapter Summary

Introduction
- Social considerations are more important in definitions of intelligence in collectivistic cultures than in individualistic ones.
- Most self-report questionnaire measures of emotional intelligence mainly assess established personality dimensions such as extraversion and neuroticism.

- Ability-based measures of emotional intelligence are promising. For example, high scorers on the MSCEIT are rated more positively for personal qualities, interpersonal sensitivity, sociability, and potential for leadership than low scorers.
- Intelligence is a good predictor of job performance, especially with complex jobs. The main reason is that more intelligent people learn job-related knowledge faster than less intelligent ones.
- Individual differences in intelligence predict health and longevity. This is in part a result of the fact that more intelligent people on average have more money and better living conditions. However, it is also relevant that more intelligent individuals have superior health literacy to less intelligent ones.

Intelligence testing
- Intelligence tests have a mean of 100 and a standard deviation of about 16.
- Useful intelligence tests are standardized and have high reliability and validity.

Theories of intelligence
- Factor theorists use factor analysis to decide on the number and nature of the factors underlying intelligence.
- Spearman proposed a two-factor theory based on a general factor and numerous test-specific factors.
- Thurstone identified seven primary mental abilities and didn't include a general factor.
- The consensual view is that the structure of intelligence is hierarchical, with the general factor at the top, fairly general factors resembling primary mental abilities at the intermediate level, and specific factors at the lowest level.
- Gardner originally proposed seven intelligences (subsequently increased to ten). These intelligences were claimed to be independent of each other, but are probably correlated to some extent.

Heredity and environment
- The effects of heredity and environment on intelligence are interdependent.
- Three types of interdependence are active covariation, passive covariation, and reactive covariation.
- On average, identical twins brought up together resemble each other in IQ more than do fraternal twins. In addition, identical twins brought up apart resemble each other nearly as much as those brought up together. These findings suggest that individual differences in intelligence depend in part on genetic factors.
- The heritability of intelligence increases with age. Adolescents and adults select their own environment to a greater extent than children, and so the impact of shared environment on intelligence decreases.
- The Flynn effect shows a strong impact of environmental factors on intelligence in many Western countries. This effect may now be decreasing.
- Children who are exposed to various risk factors in early childhood can show reductions in IQ as a consequence.

Size does matter!
- When brain size is estimated from skull size, there is generally no association with intelligence.
- When brain size is measured accurately using MRI, there is a moderate positive correlation between brain size and intelligence.
- On average males have larger brains than females, but there is no gender difference in IQ. Of potential importance, women have more white matter and fewer gray matter areas related to intelligence than men.

Further Reading

- Gottfredson, L.S. (1997). Why g matters: The complexity of everyday life. *Intelligence*, *24*, 79–132. This article discusses evidence showing that individual differences in intelligence influence many aspects of everyday life.
- Mackintosh, N.J. (1998). *IQ and human intelligence*. Oxford, UK: Oxford University Press. This is an excellent book by a leading British psychologist. It stands out for providing a balanced and insightful account of human intelligence.
- Matthews, G., Zeidner, M., & Roberts, R.D. (Eds.) (2007). *The science of emotional intelligence: Knowns and unknowns. Series in affective science.* New York: Oxford University Press. This edited book provides an up-to-date account of the strengths and weaknesses of research on emotional intelligence by leading experts.
- Miele, F. (2002). *Intelligence, race, and genetics: Conversations with Arthur R. Jensen*. Boulder, CO: Westview Press. The importance of genetic factors is explored in a very readable way through discussions between Jensen (a major supporter of the hereditarian position) and the journalist Frank Miele.
- Salovey, P., & Grewal, D. (2005). The science of emotional intelligence. *Current Directions in Psychological Science*, *14*, 281–285. This short article gives a good overview of development in research on emotional intelligence.
- Sternberg, R.J., & Pretz, J.E. (Eds.) (2004). *Cognition and intelligence: Identifying the mechanisms of the mind*. Cambridge, UK: Cambridge University Press. Individual differences in intelligence are considered from the perspective of cognitive psychology in this edited book with contributions by leading experts.

Chapter 12

Contents

What does personality look like?

INTRODUCTION

One of the things that gives life much of its interest and excitement (and sometimes misery and grief!) is the fact that people differ from each other in almost endless ways. Some are nearly always cheerful and friendly, others are unfriendly and depressed, and still others are aggressive and hostile. Much of this variety reflects individual differences in personality. What do we mean by "personality"? According to Child (1968, p. 83), personality consists of "the more or less stable, internal factors that make one person's behavior consistent from one time to another, and different from the behavior other people would manifest in comparable situations." There are *four* key words in that definition:

1. *Stable*: Personality remains fairly constant and unchanging over time.
2. *Internal*: Personality lies within us, but how we behave is determined in part by our personality.
3. *Consistent*: If personality remains constant over time, and if personality determines behavior, then we would expect people to behave reasonably consistently.
4. *Different*: When we talk of personality, we assume there are considerable individual differences leading different people to behave differently in similar situations.

How can we describe human personality? It is generally assumed that personality consists of various **traits**, which are "broad, enduring, relatively stable characteristics used to assess and explain behavior" (Hirschberg, 1978, p. 45). For example, suppose you notice that someone is talkative, smiles a lot, participates fully in social events, and has many friends. One way of explaining their behavior would be to assume they possess a high level of the trait of sociability.

Imagine you are a psychologist, and you have been given the task of designing a questionnaire to assess human personality. How many different personality traits would you put into your questionnaire? You might find yourself thinking how very different the people are from each other. This might lead you to assume there must be upwards of 20 or 30 personality traits that should be included in your questionnaire. We will be discussing this issue shortly. You will probably be surprised to discover that personality researchers' most popular answer to the question of how many personality traits humans possess is . . . *five*!

Why do individual differences in personality traits exist? Perhaps the most obvious answer (favored by many theorists including Freud and Bandura) is that they depend in large measure on each individual's experiences in life. For example, someone growing up in a very secure and supportive family environment will have a less anxious personality than someone growing up in a family characterized by conflicts. In fact, family

Key Term

Traits:
stable aspects of a person that influence his/her personality.

environment seems to have surprisingly little impact on adult personality. We can use data from twin studies to distinguish between shared environment (environmental factors having a similar effect on twins or siblings) and nonshared environment (environmental factors unique to a given individual). Nonshared environment accounts for about 60% of individual differences in personality, but shared environment contributes practically nothing (Plomin et al., 1997). As we will see, genetic factors (which are easily overlooked) turn out to have a fairly strong impact on individual differences in personality.

There is one final point before we embark on a discussion of theories of personality. In many countries (including the UK and the US), there are relatively few researchers who specialize in the area of personality. This helps to explain why there is a greater historical emphasis in this chapter than in most of the other chapters in this book.

THEORY OF PSYCHOSEXUAL DEVELOPMENT

According to Sigmund Freud (1856–1939), the experiences children have during the first 5 years of life are very important. Their personalities develop during that period, and adult personality depends very much on the experiences of early childhood. Freud assumed that there are several personality types arising from childhood experiences (see the figure below). According to his theory of psychosexual development, children pass through five stages:

1. *Oral stage*: This lasts up to the age of 18 months. Infants in this stage enjoy various activities involving their mouth, lips, and tongue. Children may experience problems at this stage of development (e.g., because of rapid weaning). These problems can produce adults with an oral receptive character (very dependent on other people) or an oral aggressive character (hostile and domineering).
2. *Anal stage*: This lasts between 18 and 36 months, and involves the anal area as the main source of satisfaction. This is the stage at which toilet training occurs. Children experiencing problems at this stage may become adults with an anal retentive character (mean, stubborn, and orderly) or they may become very generous and giving (anal receptive character).
3. *Phallic stage*: This stage lasts between the ages of 3 and 6. During this stage, the penis or clitoris becomes the main source of satisfaction. At about the age of 5, boys acquire the **Oedipus complex**, in which they have sexual desires for their mother and consequent fear of their father. This complex is resolved by identification with the father. A similar process in girls is based on the Electra complex (not a term used by

Key Term

Oedipus complex:
the Freudian notion that boys at the age of 5 desire their mother and so become frightened of their father.

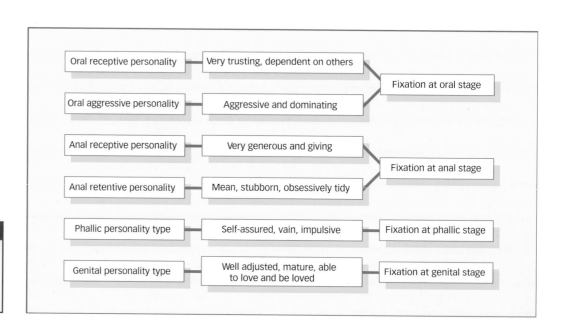

Freud), in which they desire their father. Those experiencing problems at this stage develop a phallic character. Men with a phallic character are vain and self-assured, whereas women with a phallic character fight hard for superiority over men.

4. *Latency stage*: This lasts from the age of 6 until puberty. During this stage, boys and girls experience relatively few sexual feelings and ignore each other.

5. *Genital stage*: This lasts from puberty onwards. In this stage, the main source of sexual pleasure is in the genitals. The key difference from the phallic stage is that the focus in the genital stage is on sexual pleasure with another person. Children avoiding problems during the earlier stages develop a genital character in adulthood. People with this character are mature, and can love and be loved.

Freud's stages of psychosexual development

Stage	Approximate age	Summary
Oral	0–18 months	Satisfaction from eating, sucking, etc.
Anal	18–36 months	Interest in and satisfaction from anal region
Phallic	3–6 years	Genitals become source of satisfaction
Latency	6 years old–puberty	Boys and girls spend little time together
Genital	From onset of puberty	Genitals main source of sexual pleasure

According to Freud, there can be serious consequences if a child is frustrated by receiving insufficient gratification at any psychosexual stage. There can also be serious consequences if a child receives excessive gratification at a given stage. What consequences are likely to follow? Freud argued that frustration or excessive gratification leads to **fixation**, in which basic sexual energy remains attached to that stage during adulthood. When an adult experiences major problems, he/she will show **regression**, with their behavior resembling how they behaved when they were children. Adults typically regress to the psychosexual stage at which they fixated as children. An important implication of this part of the theory is that adult mental disorders typically have their origins in childhood problems and difficulties (see Chapter 21). An account of Freud's overall theoretical approach is given in Chapter 2.

Useful mnemonic

To help you remember Freud's stages of psychosexual development, the following mnemonic is made from the initial letter of each stage: Old Age Pensioners Love Greens!

FINDINGS

There is reasonable support for the *general* approach taken by Freud, in that childhood experiences clearly influence the development of human personality (see Westen, 1998, for a review). However, this is *not* the same as arguing that there is support for Freud's specific theoretical assumptions. Mickelson, Kessler, and Shaver (1997) considered a random sample of more than 5000 adults. Parental loss or separation in childhood was associated with low attachment security and high ratings of insecure attachment in adulthood. Those adults who had experienced serious traumas in childhood (e.g., sexual abuse; severe neglect) were more likely than other adults to have anxious attachments to other people.

Franz et al. (1996) also reported evidence suggesting that childhood experiences have a long-term impact. Adult levels of depression at the age of 41 were predicted well by parental coldness when they were only 5 years old. In addition, an overall measure of difficult childhood experiences (e.g., divorce; frequent moves; loss) predicted depression in middle age.

There is a real problem with interpreting most findings showing a relationship between childhood experiences and adult problems. What we have is only correlational evidence of an association, and correlations can't be used to prove causes. For example, suppose an adult with serious emotional problems had parents who made her childhood miserable. It is possible that the unhappy childhood experiences helped to create the

Key Terms

Fixation:
in Freudian theory, spending a long time at a given stage of psychosexual development.

Regression:
in Freudian theory, returning to an earlier stage of psychosexual development when someone is highly stressed.

Case Study: *Little Hans*

When Hans was 3 years old, he began to exhibit a lot of interest in his penis, which caused his mother to threaten to cut it off. When he was about 5, he saw a horse-drawn van tip over on its side. This caused him to develop a fear of horses, and to refer to "black things around horses' mouths and the things in front of their eyes." As a result of his fear of horses, Hans was unwilling to leave the safety of his own home.

Freud's diagnosis was that Little Hans suffered from an Oedipus complex. According to Freud, he was sexually attracted to his mother, but was very frightened his father would punish him for this. The fear that Hans had for his father turned into a fear of horses, with Freud arguing that horses' black muzzles and blinkers resembled the mustache and glasses of Hans' father. The fact that Hans' fear of horses caused him to remain at home had the significant advantage that he could spend more time with his mother, to whom allegedly he was sexually attracted.

emotional problems in adulthood. However, it is also possible that genetic factors common to the parents and to their child are responsible. Kendler et al. (1992) carried out a twin study, and tried to remove statistically the influence of genetic factors from their findings. They still found that parental loss through separation (e.g., divorce) was associated with depression in adult life, whereas parental loss through death was not. In a similar twin study, Kendler, Neale, et al. (1996) found that childhood parental loss through separation was associated with a tendency to alcoholism. This association was still present when the impact of genetic factors was removed.

There is support for some of the personality types identified by Freud. For example, Kline and Storey (1977) discovered that the three main characteristics of the anal retentive character (stubbornness, meanness, orderliness) are often found together in the same person. There is also evidence that some people possess all the features of the oral aggressive character (Kline, 1981). However, evidence for the existence of some of the personality types suggested by Freud does *not* show the theory is correct. Freud assumed that these personality types depend on specific childhood experiences, but there is practically no convincing evidence that that is the case.

The evidence that Freud himself reported to support his own theoretical approach was very flimsy. It consisted mainly of about a dozen case studies, most of which are not at all convincing. For example, consider the famous case of Little Hans (see the Case Study above), which was claimed to illustrate the development of the Oedipus complex.

Most people (including the author) are totally unconvinced by Freud's account of Little Hans. Indeed, it seems to say more about Freud than about Little Hans! There is very little evidence that Hans desired sexual contact with his mother or that he was very frightened of his father. In addition, the idea that Hans' great sexual excitement somehow turned into a state of high anxiety is fanciful.

Evaluation

+ Freud put forward the first systematic theory of personality.

+ Adult personality depends in part on the experiences of early childhood.

+ At least some of the personality types suggested by Freud do seem to exist.

+ The notion that individuals with certain types of personality are more vulnerable than others to the development of mental disorders is both powerful and convincing (see Chapter 21).

+ It is very hard to test the hypothesis that early childhood experiences have actually determined adult personality many years later.

− Adult personality depends more on heredity and on the experiences of adolescence and adulthood than assumed by Freud (discussed later in the chapter).

− Freud's stage-based theory implies that personality development occurs in a more orderly way than is actually the case.

− "Psychoanalysts seriously shot themselves in the foot by never evolving from case study methods [based on individual patients] as their primary mode of knowledge generation and hypothesis testing" (Westen & Gabbard, 1999).

PERSONALITY ASSESSMENT

How can we assess personality? Four major kinds of personality tests have been developed:

1. self-report questionnaires
2. ratings
3. objective tests
4. projective tests.

We will shortly consider all four kinds of personality tests. As with intelligence tests (see Chapter 11), useful personality tests possess three characteristics:

1. *Reliability*: This means that the test produces consistent results. A test's reliability can be assessed by giving it on two occasions to the same individuals.
2. *Validity*: This means that the test measures what it is supposed to be measuring. The most important type of validity is **concurrent validity**, in which test scores are correlated with a relevant external criterion or measure of the underlying construct the test is supposed to be measuring. For example, suppose we have devised a measure of trait anxiety, a personality characteristic relating to the experience of anxiety. The scores of patients with anxiety disorders could be used as an external criterion—such patients should score much higher than most healthy individuals on the test. If we adopt the same approach, but assess the criterion at some point in time *after* the assessment of personality, this is known as **predictive validity**.
3. *Standardization*: This involves giving the test to large, representative samples of people so the significance of an individual's score on the test can be evaluated. For example, a score of 19 on a test of extraversion is meaningless on its own. However, it becomes meaningful if we know that only 10% of the population have such a high score.

QUESTIONNAIRES

Almost everyone in our society has filled in several personality questionnaires. What happens is that you have to decide whether various statements about your thoughts, feelings, and behavior are true. Here are some sample items: Do you tend to be moody? Do you have many friends? Do you like to be involved in numerous social activities?

The questionnaire-based approach is the most popular way of assessing personality. One of its advantages is that it is easy to use. Another advantage is that an individual knows more about himself/herself than do other people.

The most obvious problem with questionnaires is that individuals may fake their responses. Such faking typically takes the form of **social desirability bias.** This is the tendency to respond to questionnaire items in the socially desirable (but inaccurate) way. This bias is especially likely to be present in personnel selection. As Cook (1993, p. 144) pointed out, "No one applying for a sales job is likely to say true to 'I don't much like talking to strangers,' nor is someone trying to join the police force likely to agree that he/she has pretty undesirable acquaintances."

How can we deal with social desirability bias? The most common method is to use a Lie scale consisting of items where the socially desirable answer is very unlikely to be the honest answer (e.g., "Do you ever gossip?"; "Do you always keep your promises?"). If someone answers most of the questions on the Lie scale in the socially desirable direction, it is assumed they are faking their responses. Of course, this is unfair on the small minority of genuinely saintly people in the population!

> **Key Terms**
>
> **Concurrent validity:** assessing **validity** by correlating scores on a test with some currently available relevant criterion.
>
> **Predictive validity:** assessing **validity** by correlating scores on a test with some future criterion.
>
> **Social desirability bias:** the tendency to provide socially desirable rather than honest answers on questionnaires and in interviews.

The social desirability bias is the desire to give false answers in order to be deemed socially desirable. This could have ramifications in terms of the accuracy of a job application, for example!

In spite of the possibility of social desirability bias, most well-known personality questionnaires possess high reliability and low to moderate validity. Why is validity typically much lower than reliability? Remember that validity is typically assessed by correlating questionnaire scores with some external criterion (e.g., extraversion with number of friends). The problem in a nutshell is that there is no such thing as a perfect external criterion. For example, most people would agree that extraverts tend to have more friends than introverts. However, no one seriously believes that an individual's level of extraversion is the *only* factor determining how many friends he/she has. The imperfections of all external criteria serve to reduce the validity of personality questionnaires, as do inadequacies within the questionnaires themselves.

What is the best way of assessing validity? The answer is consensual validity. **Consensual validity** involves comparing two kinds of information:

1. Self-report questionnaire scores obtained from participants.
2. Ratings of those participants by those who know them well (e.g., friends; relatives) for the same aspect(s) of personality.

McCrae and Costa (1990) obtained promising findings based on the assessment of consensual validity. Self-report questionnaire data on five major personality factors were obtained, and ratings on the same five factors were collected from spouses and peers. The average correlation between self-report scores and spouse rating scores was +.56, and it was +.50 between self-report scores and peer rating scores. These correlations are reasonably high and indicate fairly good consensual validity.

RATINGS

As we have just discussed, ratings involve observers providing information about other people's behavior. There are various ways this can be done. For example, raters can simply be given a personality questionnaire and asked to complete it as they think a friend of theirs would have done. Alternatively, they can be given a list of different kinds of behavior (e.g., "initiates conversation"), rating their ratees (those being rated) on those aspects of behavior.

Ratings have some advantages over self-report questionnaires. In particular, the problem that people filling in a questionnaire may distort their responses to present a favorable impression (social desirability bias) doesn't apply to observers' ratings. However, the rating approach poses problems of its own. First, the items of behavior to be rated may be interpreted somewhat differently by different raters. For example, an item such as, "behaves in a friendly way towards others," might be interpreted to mean much more interaction with other people by a very sociable rater than by an unsociable one. Second, most raters have observed other people in only some of the situations in which they find themselves in everyday life. Someone who appears distant and aloof at work may relax and be very friendly outside the work environment. The partial view a rater has of his/her ratees may lead to inaccurate assessment of the ratees' personalities.

In spite of the limitations of using ratings, they typically possess high reliability. What about validity? That has been addressed by means of consensual validity, in which rating data are correlated with self-report data. As we saw earlier, consensual validity is moderately high (McCrae & Costa, 1990).

OBJECTIVE TESTS

Once upon a time, there was much interest in objective tests. **Objective tests** involve measuring behavior under laboratory conditions with the participants not knowing what the experimenter is looking for. For example, asking people to blow up a balloon until it bursts is a measure of timidity, and the extent to which people sway when standing on tiptoe is a measure of anxiety.

There was enthusiasm for objective tests several decades ago because they appeared free from the problems of deliberate distortion that can influence the responses on self-report questionnaires. The reason is that the participants aren't aware that their personality is being assessed, and so have no particular motivation to respond one way rather than another. However, it is often difficult to know what any given objective test is actually measuring, and the results are often much influenced by apparently minor changes in procedure. Most objective tests have low reliability and validity, and so are of very limited value (Cooper, 2002).

PROJECTIVE TESTS

The final form of personality assessment is by **projective tests**. People are given an unstructured task to perform (e.g., devising a story to fit a picture; describing what can be seen in an inkblot). The underlying notion is that people confronted by such ambiguous stimuli and unstructured tasks will reveal their innermost selves. Most users of projective tests favor the psychodynamic approach pioneered by Sigmund Freud, and such tests are used mainly for clinical purposes.

An example of a Rorschach inkblot.

One of the best-known projective tests is the Rorschach Inkblot Test introduced by the Swiss psychologist Hermann Rorschach in 1921. The standard form of the Rorschach test involves presenting 10 inkblots. Participants suggest what each inkblot might represent, and indicate which part of the inkblot formed the basis of their response. Another well-known projective test is the Thematic Apperception Test developed by Henry Murray (Morgan & Murray, 1935). People are presented with various pictures. For each picture, they have to say what is happening, what led up to the situation depicted, and what will happen next. The stories produced are interpreted in the attempt to identify the individual's underlying motivational conflicts.

Projective tests are generally low in both reliability and validity (Eysenck, 1994). There are two main reasons for this state of affairs. First, the unstructured nature of the tests means the participants' responses are determined by their current moods or concerns rather than by deep-rooted characteristics. Second, the very subjective nature of the interpretation of responses on projective tests means that much depends on the expertise of the person carrying out the interpretation. Nonexpert interpretation reduces the validity of the tests, and the subjectivity of interpretation reduces their reliability.

We will consider the Rorschach Inkblot Test in more detail to see some of its limitations. Three aspects of a participant's responses are used to interpret their meaning: content; location; and determinants. Content refers to the nature of what is seen by the participant, location refers to the part of the inkblot used to produce the response, and, finally, the determinants are the inkblot's characteristics (e.g., color; form) influencing the choice of response. Most Rorschach experts argue that location and determinants are more informative than content. Alas, the evidence suggests that content possesses more validity than location or determinants (Eysenck, 1994)!

TRAIT APPROACH TO PERSONALITY

For many years, there was a major controversy between two groups of personality researchers. In one group (associated especially with Cattell), it was assumed that many personality traits resemble each other, because there is no reason to assume that personality is tidily organized into unrelated traits. According to members of this group, personality traits often resemble other traits, and we need to identify numerous personality traits to provide a comprehensive account of personality. In the other group (associated especially with H.J. Eysenck), it was assumed that major personality traits are unrelated or independent of each other. In more technical terms, traits should *not* correlate or be associated with each other. For good statistical reasons, those making these latter assumptions identify far fewer traits than those belonging to the former group. For example, Cattell claimed that there were 16 personality traits whereas H.J. Eysenck argued that there were only three! Ask yourself which group your money is on before reading further . . .

CATTELL'S APPROACH

Perhaps the greatest problem faced by trait theorists trying to devise a personality questionnaire is to try to ensure they include *all* of the important personality traits. How can this goal be achieved? Raymond Cattell came up with the ingenious answer of using the **fundamental lexical hypothesis**, according to which each language contains words describing all of the main personality traits.

Cattell's use of the fundamental lexical hypothesis led him to the work of Allport and Odbert (1936), who had identified 4500 words used to describe personality. These 4500 words were reduced to 160 trait words, in part by eliminating words having the same meaning and by removing unfamiliar words. Cattell (1946) then added 11 traits from the personality literature in psychology, producing a total of 171 trait names, which were claimed to cover almost everything of importance in the area of personality.

Cattell still found himself with an unwieldy number of personality traits. As a result, he used findings from several previous rating studies to identify traits that resembled each other. This allowed him to eliminate some more traits, leaving him with 35 traits. He called them **surface traits**, because they were easily observable. Cattell carried out rating studies in which raters assessed people they knew well. These studies suggested that there are about 16 **source traits**, which are basic traits underlying the surface traits.

Cattell argued correctly that any given method of assessing personality has limitations. Since different methods have different limitations, we can in principle best work out the main personality traits by combining information from various methods. Accordingly, Cattell made extensive use of three methods of assessing personality:

1. *Life (L) data*: Observers' ratings of other people's behavior.
2. *Questionnaire (Q) data*: Self-report questionnaires.
3. *Objective test (T) data*: Careful assessment of personality under controlled conditions (e.g., measuring anxiety by seeing how much people sway when standing on tiptoe).

Cattell found that there was reasonable similarity in the personality traits identified using the questionnaire and life or rating methods. However, the findings with the objective test method were very different. This method has largely been abandoned because it produces very inconsistent findings. For example, you would probably sway much more when standing on tiptoe shortly after a visit to the pub than when completely sober!

16PF

Cattell's work suggesting that there are 16 source traits led him to develop the Sixteen Personality Factor Questionnaire, generally known as the 16PF. As the name indicates, it was intended to assess 16 personality factors, some relating to intelligence and social attitudes rather than to personality in a narrow sense. The construction of the 16PF was based on Cattell's assumption that personality traits are often associated or correlated with each other, so many of his 16 factors are fairly closely related to each other (see the box on the left).

In spite of the 16PF's massive popularity, it provides an inadequate assessment of personality. All systematic factor analyses of this test have shown that it doesn't measure anything like 16 different personality traits. For example, Barrett and Kline (1982) gave the 16PF to almost 500 people. They then carried out five different factor analyses on their data, some precisely in line with Cattell's recommendations. Barrett and Kline obtained between seven and nine factors in each factor analysis, and these factors generally didn't relate closely to those proposed by Cattell.

What is going on here? A key problem is that several of Cattell's factors are very similar to each other. For example, the following factors assessing anxiety all correlate very highly with each other: placid–apprehensive; relaxed–tense; affected by feelings–emotionally stable. Any thorough factor analysis reveals that these three factors are simply too similar to each other to be distinguished.

Key Terms

Fundamental lexical hypothesis:
the assumption that dictionaries contain words describing all of the main personality traits.

Surface traits:
personality traits that are readily observable and are related to underlying source traits.

Source traits:
personality traits underlying the more superficial surface traits.

The factors of Cattell's 16PF

Remember that each pair represents a continuum.

Reserved . . . . .Outgoing
Less intelligent . . . . .More intelligent
Affected by feelings . . . . .More emotionally stable
Humble .Assertive
Sober . . . . .Happy-go-lucky
Expedient . . . . .Conscientious
Shy . . . . .Venturesome
Tough-minded . . . . .Tender-minded
Trusting .Suspicious
Practical .Imaginative
Forthright . . . . .Shrewd
Placid . . . . .Apprehensive
Conservative . . . . .Experimenting
Group-dependent . . . . .Self-sufficient
Casual . . . . .Controlled
Relaxed . . . . .Tense

Evaluation

+ Cattell's notion of using the fundamental lexical hypothesis to assist in uncovering all the main personality traits is a valuable one.

+ Cattell's attempt to combine information from several methods (questionnaires, ratings, objective tests) was thorough and systematic.

− There are only about eight different personality traits in the 16PF, and so Cattell's main questionnaire is badly flawed.

− Cattell's approach was not very theoretical or explanatory. As Cattell (1957, p. 50) admitted, "I have always felt justifiably suspicious of theory built much ahead of data."

H.J. EYSENCK'S APPROACH

H.J. Eysenck's approach was very different to that of Cattell. He argued that the best strategy is to focus on a small number of *independent* personality traits or factors, all of which are entirely separate from each other. More specifically, he identified three major traits or "superfactors" (see the figure below), all of which are assessed by the Eysenck Personality Questionnaire (EPQ):

- **Extraversion:** Those scoring high on extraversion (extraverts) are more sociable and impulsive than those scoring low (introverts).
- **Neuroticism:** Those scoring high on neuroticism are more anxious and depressed than those scoring low.
- **Psychoticism:** Those scoring high on psychoticism are aggressive, hostile, and uncaring.

You may well feel that there must be more to personality than these three factors (and you're probably right!). However, many aspects of personality can be understood as consisting of combinations of two (or even all three) of these factors. For example, there is no trait of "optimism," but individuals high in extraversion and low in neuroticism are typically optimistic.

Where do individual differences in extraversion, neuroticism, and psychoticism come from? According to H.J. Eysenck (1982, p. 28), "genetic factors contribute something like two-thirds of the variance in major personality dimensions."

How do genetic factors produce individual differences in personality? According to H.J. Eysenck (e.g., 1967), heredity influences the responsiveness of parts of the

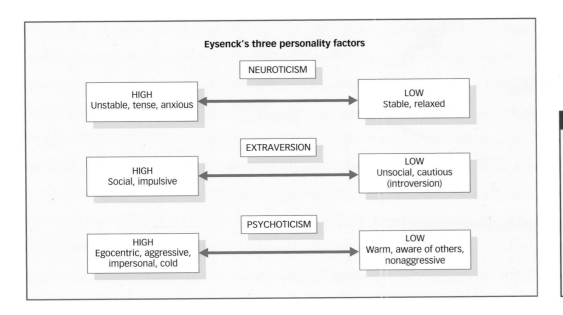

Eysenck's three personality factors

NEUROTICISM

| HIGH Unstable, tense, anxious | ⟷ | LOW Stable, relaxed |

EXTRAVERSION

| HIGH Social, impulsive | ⟷ | LOW Unsocial, cautious (introversion) |

PSYCHOTICISM

| HIGH Egocentric, aggressive, impersonal, cold | ⟷ | LOW Warm, aware of others, nonaggressive |

Key Terms

Extraversion:
a personality factor based on sociability and impulsiveness.

Neuroticism:
a personality factor based on negative emotional experiences (e.g., anxiety and depression).

Psychoticism:
a personality factor based on aggression, hostility, and a lack of caring.

Jack Nicholson in *The Shining*—perhaps this character would score highly on Eysenck's psychoticism personality factor—he is aggressive, impulsive, impersonal, cold, and lacking in empathy and concern for others.

Personality dimensions

Personality dimensions such as extraversion are at one end of a continuum, with their opposite at the other end. Personality testing does not simply determine that a person is either extraverted or introverted, but places them at the relevant point on the continuum, showing their degree of extraversion/introversion, as in the diagram below. This person is slightly more extraverted than introverted.

| 1 | 2 | 3 | 4 | 5 | 6 | 7 | 8 | 9 | 10 |

EXTRAVERSION...................●..........................INTROVERSION
(Social, outgoing, active)   (Unsocial, quiet, passive)

In order to determine whether individual differences in personality are due to genetic factors or environment, a number of studies using twins have been carried out. Resulting evidence suggests that 40% of individual differences in personality are due to genetic factors.

Key Term

Visceral brain:
a brain system including the hippocampus, septum, and hypothalamus claimed by H.J. Eysenck to be most responsive in individuals high in neuroticism.

physiological system. Introverts were assumed to have a higher level of cortical arousal (activity in the brain) than extraverts. As a result, they are in danger of becoming over-aroused, and so tend to prefer reading books to going to exciting parties. In contrast, extraverts generally have a low level of brain activity, and so seek stimulating situations to prevent themselves being bored. Those high in neuroticism are supposed to have greater activity than those low in neuroticism in the **visceral brain**, which consists of several parts of the brain (hippocampus, amygdala, cingulum, septum, and hypothalamus). The physiological differences between individuals high and low in psychoticism remain shrouded in mystery.

Findings

We will consider each of H.J. Eysenck's main assumptions in turn. The notion that extraversion, neuroticism, and psychoticism are all major personality traits has been investigated numerous times (see H.J. Eysenck & M.W. Eysenck, 1985, for a review). The evidence indicates strongly that extraversion and neuroticism are very important but not psychoticism. For example, Saville and Blinkhorn (1981) studied Cattell's 16PF questionnaire to find out which independent factors it contained. They found that the 16PF largely measures extraversion and neuroticism (but *not* psychoticism). These are very important findings, because they suggest that the approach based on associated or correlated factors works less well than one based on independent or uncorrelated factors.

H.J. Eysenck's assumption that genetic factors account for 67% of individual differences in personality is an exaggeration. The best approach to this issue involves studying identical twins (known technically as monozygotic twins) and fraternal twins (dizygotic twins). Identical twins share 100% of their genes, whereas fraternal twins share only 50% of their genes. If genetic factors are important, then identical twins should be more similar in personality than fraternal twins. More precise conclusions can be drawn if we consider twin pairs brought up apart as well as twin pairs brought up together. As you can imagine, it is not exactly easy to find many pairs of identical twins brought up apart!

The most thorough attempt to study the influence of genetic factors on extraversion and neuroticism was reported by Pedersen, Plomin, McClearn, and Friberg (1988). Amazingly, they studied 95 identical twin pairs brought up apart, 220 pairs of fraternal twins brought up apart, as well as numerous identical and fraternal twin pairs brought up together. They found that 31% of individual differences in neuroticism and 41% of individual differences in extraversion were a result of genetic factors. So far as psychoticism is concerned, Zuckerman (1989) reviewed four twin studies, and concluded that 40% of individual differences in psychoticism come from heredity.

We turn now to evidence concerning the physiological bases of the personality factors. The only one for which there is much support is extraversion, for which it will be remembered that H.J. Eysenck claimed that introverts are generally more cortically aroused than extraverts. One way of testing this hypothesis is by using electroencephalography (EEG), which provides a measure of brain-wave activity. Gale (1983) considered 33 EEG studies reporting a total of 38 experimental comparisons. Extraverts were significantly less cortically aroused than introverts in 22 comparisons, whereas introverts were significantly less aroused than extraverts in 5 comparisons. Introverts and extraverts didn't differ in the remaining 11 cases. Thus, introverts tend to be more cortically aroused than extraverts, but this is often not the case.

H.J. Eysenck (1967) argued that individual differences in neuroticism depend on the level of activity within the "visceral brain." This hypothesis has been tested by taking various indirect measures (e.g., heart rate; skin conductance) from individuals high and low in neuroticism (or the closely related personality factor of trait anxiety) in stressful and nonstressful conditions. There is very little support for the hypothesis. Fahrenberg (1992, pp. 212–213) concluded his review of the literature as follows: "Over many decades research has failed to substantiate the physiological correlates that are assumed for emotionality [neuroticism] and trait anxiety. There is virtually no distinct finding that has been reliably replicated across studies and laboratories."

A young woman (background) undergoing an EEG examination. The EEG test records the electrical activity of the brain via small electrodes attached to the scalp. Gale (1983) reviewed studies using this technique to test the hypothesis that introverts are more cortically aroused than extraverts.

Evaluation

- It has proved more useful to identify a small number of unrelated or uncorrelated personality traits than a larger number of correlated ones (more evidence is discussed below).

- Extraversion and neuroticism are major personality traits or factors.

- H.J. Eysenck made a thorough attempt to explain the mechanisms underlying individual differences in his three personality factors.

- The role of genetic factors in determining individual differences in personality is much less than was claimed by H.J. Eysenck.

- There is little support for the physiological bases of personality proposed by H.J. Eysenck.

- Psychoticism is not a major personality trait or factor. It is also poorly named, being more closely related to psychopathy or antisocial personality than to psychosis (Eysenck, 1994).

BIG FIVE

For the past 20 years, the most popular view concerning the structure of human personality is that there are five major personality traits commonly referred to as the Big Five. It is assumed that these five factors are independent or uncorrelated. Theorists differ somewhat in terms of the exact traits or factors identified, but there is a fairly high level of consensus. The most influential version of the Big Five approach is that of McCrae and Costa (1985), who identified the following five factors (the first letters of which conveniently form the word OCEAN):

Openness (curious, imaginative, creative)
Conscientiousness (hard-working, ambitious, persistent)
Extraversion (sociable, optimistic, talkative)
Agreeableness (good-natured, cooperative, helpful)
Neuroticism (anxious, insecure, emotional).

Costa and McCrae (1992) produced the NEO-PI Five-Factor Inventory to measure the above five factors. What causes individual differences in these personality factors? It is assumed that genetic factors play a significant role in determining individual differences in all five factors (e.g., McCrae & Costa, 1999), although environmental factors are also assumed to be important.

Findings

Five traits or factors closely resembling those put forward by McCrae and Costa (1985, 1990) have been found numerous times. For example, Goldberg (1990) collected more than 1000 words describing personality. Students produced self-descriptions based on these terms, and the data were factor analyzed in 10 different ways. The consistent finding was that five factors were extracted: emotional stability (opposite of neuroticism); agreeableness; conscientiousness; surgency (very similar to extraversion); and intellect (resembling openness).

Goldberg (1990) carried out a second study based on 479 common trait terms in which he obtained self-report and rating data. He found strong evidence for the same five factors in both kinds of data, and came to the following conclusion: "Analyses of any reasonably large sample of English trait adjectives in either self- or peer-descriptions [ratings] will elicit a variant of the Big-Five factor structure" (Goldberg, 1990, p. 1223).

There is reasonable evidence that questionnaires of the Big Five factors are valid. For example, McCrae and Costa (1990) compared self-report measures on each of the five factors with ratings by their marriage partners. All the correlations between self-report and rating data were moderately high, ranging from +.53 for neuroticism to +.59 for openness.

If the Big Five factors are important, then scores on these factors should correlate significantly with various external criteria. Paunonen (2003) found precisely that, and his findings based on averaging across four samples of students are shown in the figure below.

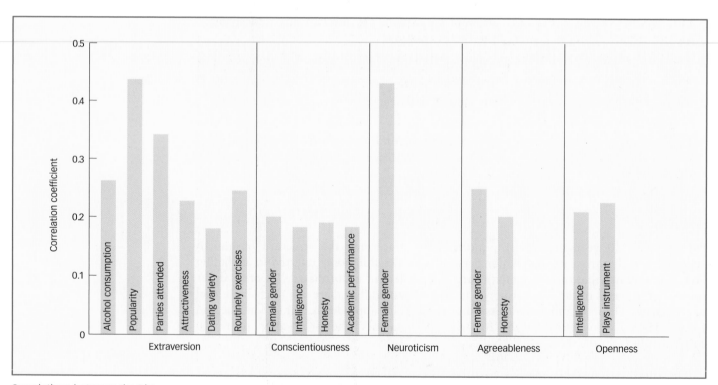

Correlations between the Big Five factors and several external criteria. Based on data in Paunonen (2003).

The assumption that the Big Five are all independent of each other and so are uncorrelated has been tested. The evidence indicates that this assumption is incorrect. For example, Costa and McCrae (1992) reported that the factors of neuroticism and conscientiousness correlated −.53 with each other, and that extraversion and openness correlated +.40. Thus, some factors are not nearly as separate from each other as they should be.

Key Study

Loehlin, McCrae, Costa, and John (1998): Big Five and genetic factors

The early research of Costa, McCrae, and other researchers showed that we can describe the structure of human personality reasonably well in terms of the five factors of openness, conscientiousness, extraversion, agreeableness, and neuroticism. That is a considerable achievement. However, it is important to move from *description* to *explanation*. For example, it is important to explain why there are individual differences with respect to all five personality factors. Paul Costa and Robert McCrae have consistently assumed that genetic factors help to account for individual differences in the Big Five personality factors, and Loehlin et al. (1998) carried out a thorough study to test this assumption.

As discussed earlier in the chapter, twin studies have been used to assess the role of genetic factors in determining individual differences in the Big Five factors. Since monozygotic or identical twins share 100% of their genes but dizygotic or fraternal twins share only 50% of their genes, then identical twins should resemble each other more in personality than fraternal twins if genetic factors are important. There are two kinds of environmental influences: (1) shared environment refers to the common influences within a family making children resemble each other; and (2) nonshared environment refers to all those influences unique to any given child. Loehlin et al. decided to estimate the importance of each kind of influence in producing individual differences in personality.

Loehlin et al. (1998) administered various self-report questionnaires and other measures to 807 pairs of twins, 490 of whom were identical and 317 were fraternal. What they found was as follows: "51% to 58% of individual difference variation along the Big Five dimensions is genetic in origin, 42% to 49% is due to experience unique to the individual, to temporary situational factors, and to gene–environment interaction, and none is due to effects of environment shared by the twins" (Loehlin et al., 1998, p. 447). The detailed findings are shown in the table below, with all figures indicating the percentage of individual differences in each personality factor attributable to a genetic or specific environmental source:

Factor	Genetic variance	Shared environmental variance	Nonshared environmental variance
Extraversion	57%	0%	44%
Agreeableness	51%	0%	49%
Conscientiousness	52%	0%	48%
Neuroticism	58%	0%	42%
Openness	56%	0%	44%

Discussion points

1. In what ways do you think the environments of identical twins would be more similar than the environments of fraternal twins?
2. How would you account for the differences in personality between identical twins?

KEY STUDY EVALUATION

The findings provide strong support for the assumption that genetic factors have a substantial influence on individual differences in personality. It is impressive that this is the case for all Big Five factors. The findings also indicate that similarities in personality between twins do not depend at all on shared environmental influences (e.g., within the family).

The study can be criticized in various ways. First, it is possible that the environments experienced by identical twins were on average more similar than those experienced by fraternal twins. If so, this may mean that the influence of genetic factors is exaggerated in the figures. Second, the kinds of environmental factors influencing personality were not identified. However, Torgersen and Janson (2002) found that differences in personality in identical twins depended in part on differences in their reactions to childhood and adolescent stressors. Third, the fact that twins differ from nontwins in having a sibling of the same age may mean that we cannot safely generalize from twins to nontwins.

Evaluation

+ The Big Five personality traits have been obtained repeatedly in self-report and rating data, making the Big Five approach the dominant one in personality research.

+ Genetic factors are of importance in determining individual differences in all of the Big Five factors.

+ Each of the Big Five factors predicts important real-world behavior (Paunonen, 2003; see Ozer and Benet-Martinez, 2006, for a review).

– Some of the Big Five factors correlate with each other, and thus are not independent.

– There is a suspicion that some of the Big Five factors (e.g., openness; conscientiousness) may be less important than others.

– The Big Five approach is mostly descriptive, and fails to provide an adequate explanation of the processes underlying the various factors. As McCrae and Costa (1999, p. 147) admitted, "Shouldn't a five-factor theory explain why there are five factors and not six? And why these factors and not others?"

CROSS-CULTURAL PERSPECTIVES

The "old" approach to studying personality across different cultures simply involved giving questionnaires developed in Western cultures to individuals in various non-Western cultures. For example, Steel and Ones (2002) discussed findings from the Eysenck Personality Questionnaire obtained from 40 different countries (see the box on the opposite page). The fact that we can use Western questionnaires all around the world doesn't prove that the structure of personality is the same everywhere. However, detailed analyses of scores on the Eysenck Personality Questionnaire in 34 countries suggested that the same three personality factors were clearly present in all of them (Barrett, Petrides, Eysenck, & Eysenck, 1998).

McCrae, Terracciano, et al. (2005) collected *rating* data for the Big Five personality factors in 50 cultures. The same five factors within the same overall structure were found in nearly all of the cultures studied, with the major exceptions of Botswana and Nigeria. Thus, the structure of personality is similar in the great majority of cultures regardless of whether self-report (Barrett et al., 1998) or rating data (McCrae et al., 2005) are used.

The "new" cross-cultural approach involves using indigenous personality measures (those developed in the culture being studied) as well as standard Western measures. When that is done, it often turns out that some aspects of personality are culture specific. For example, Cheung and Leung (1998) administered the Chinese Personality Assessment Inventory and the Big Five items in China and Hong Kong. There was evidence for four of the Big Five factors but not for openness. In addition, they found a Chinese tradition factor having no relationship with the Big Five.

There are more profound differences among cultures than has been suggested so far. It has often been claimed that we should distinguish between individualistic and collectivistic cultures (see Chapter 1). The former emphasize personal responsibility and the latter focus on group obligations. The notion of semi-permanent personality traits determining behavior seems less applicable in collectivistic cultures, in which individuals are supposed to fit in flexibly with group expectations. Norenzayan, Choi, and Nisbett

Mean scores for psychoticism, extraversion, neuroticism, and lie scales for 40 countries or regions

Country or region	Psychoticism	Extraversion	Neuroticism	Lie	Sample size
Australia	6.96	19.31	15.48	7.58	654
Bangladesh	4.24	19.05	12.29	19.15	1075
Brazil	3.99	17.63	14.20	17.93	1396
Bulgaria	4.17	18.60	14.96	15.12	1038
Canada	4.28	18.05	12.77	13.92	1257
China	6.79	13.75	14.50	20.41	1000
Czechoslovakia	9.14	19.52	14.09	11.47	1912
Egypt	4.40	18.57	17.36	21.37	1330
Finland	4.90	16.26	14.60	11.57	949
France	5.49	17.75	15.09	14.59	811
Germany FR	6.23	18.40	13.68	10.96	1336
Greece	5.49	20.40	18.32	16.61	1301
Hong Kong	7.05	16.73	14.61	14.37	732
Hungary	3.86	16.57	14.58	15.63	962
Iceland	3.52	19.19	13.90	10.53	1144
India	8.17	22.80	16.26	18.38	981
Iran	4.52	17.69	16.05	17.13	624
Israel	3.60	22.62	8.51	17.39	1050
Italy	4.43	18.37	16.66	16.89	802
Japan	4.80	16.50	16.78	9.62	1318
Korea	4.97	16.49	18.71	15.74	1200
Lebanon	2.30	19.26	14.17	20.30	1239
Lithuania	5.01	16.45	15.10	17.50	1404
Mexico	4.49	20.63	14.15	15.41	988
Netherlands	2.88	17.36	11.52	16.09	876
Nigeria	3.58	24.50	9.43	17.76	430
Norway	2.22	18.65	10.33	11.68	802
Portugal	2.49	18.94	15.27	14.12	1163
Puerto Rico	4.43	21.01	14.15	17.01	1094
Romania	3.51	18.45	13.31	17.14	1014
Russia	3.41	16.55	18.04	14.18	1067
Sicily	5.89	17.36	17.16	16.42	785
Singapore	4.36	17.42	13.02	16.32	994
Spain	2.97	17.11	16.24	15.81	1030
Sri Lanka	4.27	18.67	12.09	20.86	1027
Uganda	6.06	19.44	15.78	13.56	1476
United Kingdom	3.84	18.03	14.97	12.11	1198
United States	3.32	21.53	15.20	9.46	879
Yugoslavia	7.46	17.32	14.37	17.94	971
Zimbabwe	6.50	19.75	14.65	15.20	838

Data supplied by Steel and Ones (2002).

(1999) found that people in Western cultures regard personality traits as stable, whereas East Asians regard traits as much more flexible and changeable. In line with this analysis, personality traits don't predict behavior as well in collectivistic cultures as in individualistic ones (Church & Katigbak, 2000).

EVALUATION OF THE TRAIT APPROACH

Trait-based approaches to personality seem to assume that individuals will behave consistently across different situations. In other words, individuals' personality (which doesn't change from situation to situation) has a strong influence on their behavior in all situations. This is known as strong **cross-situational consistency**. According to Mischel (1968), there is actually much less cross-situational consistency than predicted by trait theories. His literature review indicated that personality measures rarely correlate more

Key Term

Cross-situational consistency:
the extent to which any given individual responds in the same way to different situations.

Novel, formal, and public situations

Familiar, informal, and private situations

than about +.30 with behavior in any given situation. This means that personality accounts for no more than 9% of individual differences in behavior. Mischel concluded that personality predicts behavior poorly, and that behavior is overwhelmingly determined by the situation in which the individual finds himself/herself.

There are two major problems with Mischel's analysis. First, he assumed that situational factors were much more important than personality in determining behavior. However, he didn't actually test to see whether this was true! Sarason, Smith, and Diener (1975) worked out the percentage of the variance (differences in behavior among individuals) accounted for by personality and by the situation across 138 experiments. On average, the situation accounted for 10.3% of the variance, whereas personality accounted for 8.7% of the variance. Thus, it is simply incorrect that behavior is determined substantially more by the situation than by personality.

Second, Mischel (1968) only considered the effects of personality on behavior in *specific* situations. Individual differences in personality might be much more important if we considered behavior over extended periods of time. Precisely this was done by Fleeson (2001). Participants carried personal data assistants with them for a few weeks. Several times a day, they indicated how much their behavior exhibited each of five major personality traits: extraversion; agreeableness; conscientiousness; emotional stability [opposite of neuroticism]; and intellect [resembles openness].

What did Fleeson (2001) find? He confirmed Mischel's findings indicating that any given individual's behavior fluctuates considerably from one situation or time to another. However, the findings were very different when he compared individuals' average levels of each personality trait in the first week against those in the second week. Here there was very high consistency with an average correlation of about +.9. Fleeson (2004, p. 86) drew the following conclusions from these findings:

> Everyone routinely acts in a wide range of ways on a given dimension of behavior, yet different people's ranges of behaviors are centered on different portions of the dimension, and each individual's center remains very stable across large periods of time.

SOCIAL COGNITIVE THEORY

Albert Bandura, an American psychologist born in 1925, has spent many years developing his social cognitive approach. Bandura (1999) argued that we need to consider personal factors, environmental factors, and the individual's own behavior to obtain a full picture of what is happening. All three factors are assumed to influence each other in complex ways. Thus, the environment influences our behavior, but our personality and behavior also help to determine our environment. For example, extraverts actively seek out social situations more often than introverts (Furnham, 1981). This approach is known as the **triadic reciprocal model** (see the figure on the following page).

Bandura's theoretical approach is much more complex than that of traditional trait theories of personality. Trait theorists emphasize the notion that personality influences

Key Term

Triadic reciprocal model: Bandura's view that an individual's personality, the environment, and his/her own behavior all influence each other.

behavior, which corresponds to only one out of the six arrows in the triadic reciprocal model (the one running from personality to behavior). They also argue that the environment influences behavior (a second arrow in the triadic reciprocal model). However, few trait theorists focus on the other four arrows in that model. This is a real limitation. People's personalities influence the situations in which they find themselves as well as how they behave in those situations.

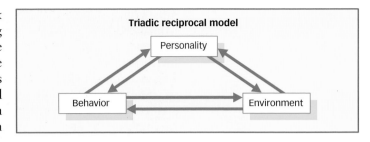

There are two other important differences between Bandura's social cognitive theory and trait theories. Bandura (e.g., 1999) argues strongly that we must take full account of the particular situation or context in which individuals find themselves if we are to predict their behavior. In contrast, most trait theorists claim that an individual's personality will influence their behavior in similar ways in most situations. Second, Bandura argued that individual differences in cognitive processes and strategies play an important role in determining differences in behavior. In contrast, trait theorists have generally had little or nothing to say about such processes.

SELF-EFFICACY

The notion of self-efficacy is of central importance within Bandura's social cognitive theory. **Self-efficacy** refers to the beliefs individuals have concerning their ability to cope with a particular task or situation and to achieve the desired outcome. In the words of Bandura (1977, p. 391), self-efficacy judgments are concerned, "not with the skills one has but with judgments of what one can do with the skills one possesses." It is assumed that high self-efficacy has beneficial effects on performance because it leads to increased task motivation. Self-efficacy is claimed to predict several aspects of behavior:

> Given appropriate skills and adequate incentives... efficacy expectations are a major determinant of people's choice of activities, how much effort they will expend, and how long they will sustain effort in dealing with stressful situations (Bandura, 1977, p. 194).

Previous success in a situation may make an individual more likely to believe they will succeed again, whereas previous failure may lead to reluctance to put much effort in or show much interest.

Four factors determine an individual's sense of self-efficacy in any given situation:

1. *Previous experiences* of success and/or failure the individual has had in that situation.
2. *Relevant vicarious [second-hand] experiences*: For example, if you see someone else cope successfully with a situation, this may increase your self-efficacy beliefs.
3. *Verbal (or social) persuasion*: Your feelings of self-efficacy may increase if someone argues persuasively that you have the skills to succeed in that situation.
4. *Emotional arousal*: High levels of arousal are often associated with anxiety and failure, and can reduce feelings of self-efficacy.

Findings

The key assumption is that self-efficacy beliefs should predict behavior. There is considerable support for this prediction. For example, Dzewaltowski (1989) assessed the ability of various factors to predict the amount of exercise students would take over a 7-week period. Self-efficacy beliefs concerning their ability to take part in an exercise program when faced with competing demands emerged as the best single predictor. Convincing evidence that self-efficacy predicts work-related performance was reviewed by Stajkovic and Luthans (1998). The average correlation between self-efficacy and work performance across 114 studies was +.38. Thus, self-efficacy was a moderately strong

Key Term

Self-efficacy:
an individual's beliefs concerning his or her ability to cope successfully with a particular task or situation.

predictor, producing a 28% increase in performance. Stajkovic and Luthans (p. 252) concluded as follows: "This 28% increase in performance due to self-efficacy represents a greater gain than, for example, those obtained in meta-analyses examining the effect on performance of goal setting (10.39% . . .), feedback interventions (13.6% . . .), or organizational behavior modification (17% . . .).

Stajkovic and Luthans (1998) discovered that self-efficacy was more strongly associated with high task performance on easy than on complex tasks. In addition, the strength of the association was consistently higher in laboratory settings than in more naturalistic field settings. Why did these differences occur? We would expect the relationship between self-efficacy and performance to be greater when participants possess detailed information about task demands, the best task strategy to adopt, and so on. Participants performing difficult tasks in field settings will often lack sufficient information to make accurate judgments of self-efficacy.

How does self-efficacy compare to standard personality factors in its ability to predict behavior? Caprara, Barbaranelli, and Pastorelli (1998) obtained measures of self-efficacy and of the Big Five factors in a study on academic achievement and peer preference. The Big Five factors nearly all failed to have any predictive power, except that openness predicted academic achievement. In contrast, self-efficacy predicted academic achievement and peer preference.

Evaluation

- Strong associations have often been found between self-efficacy and performance (e.g., Stajkovic & Luthans, 1998). These associations are generally larger than those of other variables with performance.

- The emphasis on self-efficacy shows the value of focusing on cognitive processes of relevance to motivation.

- Self-efficacy predicts performance less well when the task is difficult and/or is performed under naturalistic conditions.

- There are tricky issues about causality. The theoretical assumption is that self-efficacy influences performance. However, past performance influences self-efficacy judgments, so the association between self-efficacy and performance is difficult to interpret.

SELF-REGULATION

Bandura (1986) argued that our behavior is also influenced by self-regulation. **Self-regulation** involves using your cognitive processes to regulate and control your own behavior. For example, you may reward yourself if you achieve a given standard of performance. In broad terms, our behavior is often controlled by *internal* factors rather than the *external* ones (e.g., reward or reinforcement) emphasized by the behaviorists. Bandura (1977, pp. 128–129) provided vivid examples to support this position: "Anyone who attempted to change a pacifist into an aggressor or a devout religionist into an atheist would quickly come to appreciate the existence of personal sources of behavioral control."

Bandura (1986) identified three processes of central importance to self-regulation:

1. *Self-observation*: Individuals observe their own behavior (e.g., the quality of their work; their productivity).
2. *Judgmental processes*: Individuals take account of their personal standards, of standard norms (i.e., other people's performance), and of the role of personal and external factors in influencing their performance.
3. *Self-reaction*: Individuals experience positive self-reactions (e.g., pride; self-satisfaction) when their behavior reaches or exceeds their personal standards. They experience self-criticism or dissatisfaction when their behavior falls short of those standards.

Key Term

Self-regulation:
using one's own cognitive processes to control and regulate one's own behavior and goals.

According to the behaviorists, the way we behave is strongly influenced by external rewards.

There are some links between self-regulation and self-efficacy. According to Bandura (1999, p. 176), "After people attain the standard they have been pursuing, those who have a strong sense of efficacy generally set a higher standard for themselves."

Findings

The prediction that people using self-regulation strategies should outperform those making little use of such strategies has been supported several times. Kitsantas (2000) reported positive evidence in a study on three groups of college students: overweight students who had failed to lose weight; previously overweight students who had successfully lost weight; and students with no weight problems. All participants completed a questionnaire indicating the self-regulation strategies they used, and their self-efficacy beliefs concerning their ability to use these strategies successfully. The self-regulation strategies considered included the following: goal setting and/or planning (e.g., desired weight); self-monitoring to keep track of progress in losing weight; self-evaluation of progress in weight control; and attempts to seek help in efforts to lose weight.

What did Kitsantas (2000) find? First, overweight students who didn't lose weight used fewer self-regulation strategies than did the other two groups (see the top figure on the right). This was especially the case for self-evaluation of progress, a strategy used far less by overweight students than by students in the other groups. Second, overweight students who didn't lose weight had lower levels of self-efficacy than students in the other groups (see the bottom figure on the right). Third, the use of several self-regulation strategies was only effective when combined with high self-efficacy. Thus, there is little point in using good strategies if you use them half-heartedly—you have to believe they are going to be effective.

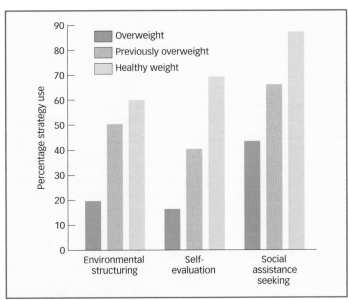

Use of various self-regulation strategies by overweight, previously overweight, and healthy weight participants. Data from Kitsantas (2000).

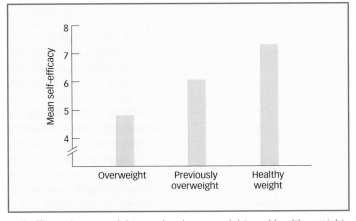

Self-efficacy in overweight, previously overweight, and healthy weight groups. Data from Kitsantas (2000).

Evaluation

⊕ Much human behavior is motivated by self-reinforcement rather than directly by external rewards (e.g., money).

⊕ Most previous theories de-emphasized the role of internal factors (e.g., self-observation; self-reaction) in influencing motivation and behavior.

⊖ Several factors influence self-regulation. As a result, an apparent failure to support the theory can be explained away with reference to factors not explicitly included in the study.

⊖ "Sometimes a behavior is maintained with no obvious external reinforcer. In such a case, the [social cognitive] theorists assert that the behavior is being supported by self-reinforcement . . . if self-reinforcement accounts for behavior sometimes, why isn't it adequate all the time? Why is external reinforcement ever necessary? How do you decide when it's needed and when it isn't?" (Carver & Scheier, 2000, p. 372).

Overall Evaluation

⊕ Self-efficacy and self-regulation both influence how any given individual will behave in a given situation.

⊕ Bandura's approach has deservedly been very influential within health psychology. The extent to which people adopt healthy forms of behavior (e.g., giving up smoking; losing weight; taking exercise) depends to an important extent on self-efficacy and self-regulation.

⊖ Social cognitive theory focuses on cognitive factors and de-emphasizes emotional ones. However, much human motivation and behavior is influenced by our emotions rather than by cool calculation.

⊖ Bandura has paid little attention to the impact of genetic factors on individual differences in personality and behavior.

⊖ Bandura has focused on predicting and understanding people's behavior in *specific* situations. It is unclear whether his theory could account for individual differences in *broad* areas of life.

Chapter Summary

Theory of psychosexual development
- According to Freud, children pass through five stages of psychosexual development: oral; anal; phallic; latency; and genital. Various personality types are associated with problems at a given psychosexual stage.
- Excessive (or insufficient) gratification at any stage can lead to fixation. Adults experiencing severe problems often regress to the stage at which they fixated.
- Childhood experiences clearly influence the development of adult personality in some ways.
- There is evidence for at least some of the personality types identified by Freud.
- Freud's general approach is supported by the evidence. However, his more specific assumptions (e.g., the Oedipus complex; regression to earlier stages of development) are mostly incorrect.

Personality assessment
- Personality can be assessed by self-report questionnaires, ratings, objective tests, and projective tests. Useful tests need to be standardized with good reliability and validity.

- Questionnaires are affected by social desirability bias, which can be detected by the use of lie scales. In spite of such bias, most well-known personality questionnaires have high reliability and low to moderate validity.
- Ratings suffer from the limitation that most raters have only partial information about the people they are rating. However, the reliability and validity of ratings (especially reliability) are generally reasonably good.
- Most objective and projective tests possess low reliability and validity and so are of rather limited usefulness.

Trait approach to personality

- Cattell made use of the fundamental lexical hypothesis, according to which each language contains words describing all of the main personality traits.
- Cattell assessed personality by using questionnaires, life or rating data, and objective tests. The personality traits identified by questionnaire and rating data were similar to each other.
- Cattell's 16PF questionnaire was designed to assess 16 personality factors, but actually measures only about half that number.
- H.J. Eysenck identified three superfactors: extraversion; neuroticism; and psychoticism. The evidence confirms the importance of the first two, but psychoticism is less important.
- Individual differences in all three superfactors depend in part on genetic factors.
- There is general agreement that there are five main personality traits (the Big Five), often identified as openness, conscientiousness, extraversion, agreeableness, and neuroticism. These factors are claimed to be independent of each other, but are not actually so.
- Individual differences in each of the Big Five factors depend in part on genetic factors.
- Most trait approaches have ignored the existence of culture-specific traits. In addition, the notion of stable and relatively unchanging personality traits is more applicable in individualistic than in collectivistic cultures.

Social cognitive theory

- According to Bandura's triadic reciprocal model, personal factors, environmental factors, and the individual's own behavior all influence each other in complex ways.
- Self-efficacy is an important determinant of behavior. The level of self-efficacy in any given situation depends on previous experiences of success in that situation, relevant vicarious experiences, verbal or social persuasion, and emotional arousal.
- Behavior is also influenced by self-regulation. Three processes of central importance to self-regulation are self-observation, judgmental processes, and self-reaction.
- There is empirical support for the predicted positive effects of self-efficacy and self-regulation on performance.
- Bandura's approach focuses on cognitive factors and behavior in fairly specific situations. It de-emphasizes emotional factors and general patterns of behavior.

Further Reading

- Carver, C.S., & Scheier, M.F. (2004). *Perspectives on personality: International edition* (5th ed.). New York: Allyn & Bacon. This textbook provides good basic coverage of approaches to personality.
- Mathews, G., Deary, I.K., & Whiteman, M.C. (2003). *Personality traits* (2nd ed.). Cambridge, UK. Cambridge University Press. Major trait approaches to personality are discussed in an authoritative way by the authors of this book.
- Ozer, D.J., & Benet-Martinez, V. (2006). Personality and the prediction of consequential outcomes. *Annual Review of Psychology, 57*, 401–421. The authors show how each of the Big Five personality factors helps us to predict individuals' physical and psychological well-being, quality of relationships, and so on.
- Pervin, L.A., Cervone, D., & John, O.P. (2005). *Personality theory and research* (9th ed.). Chichester, UK: Wiley. Provides a thorough introduction to the field of personality.
- Triandis, H.C., & Suh, E.M. (2002). Cultural influences on personality. *Annual Review of Psychology, 53*, 133–160. The authors of this chapter provide a good overview of theory and research on cross-cultural research in personality.

INTRODUCTION TO Developmental Psychology

T he four chapters in this section of the book (Chapters 13–16) deal with developmental psychology. Developmental psychology is mainly concerned with the psychological changes occurring during the time between birth and adulthood. However, some developmental psychologists are interested in changes throughout the lifespan. Our primary focus is on infancy and childhood, because that is the period of life in which the most dramatic changes in development occur.

Developmental psychology (as Sigmund Freud was one of the first psychologists to acknowledge) is of crucial importance to an understanding of adult behavior. What we are now as adults depends to a large extent on the experiences we had during the years of childhood. In the words of the poet William Wordsworth in his poem, *The Rainbow*, "The Child is father of the Man." The fact that the childhood years are vitally important means that society has a responsibility to ensure that all children are provided with the opportunities and support they need to develop into well-adjusted and successful adults.

It is also worth pointing out that the study of children is intrinsically fascinating, especially to parents. As a parent myself, I still remember very clearly being put in my place by my daughter Fleur, who was 2¼ at the time. We were on a cross-channel ferry, and I said to her, "Look, Fleur, there's a boat." I instantly felt deflated when she replied, "It's not a boat, Daddy, it's a yacht!" At the age of 4, Juliet (my other daughter) also managed to deflate me when she said earnestly, "A professor should know at least everything."

Much research in developmental psychology involves laboratory studies. The potential danger with laboratory studies is that the findings obtained may be of limited relevance to everyday life. However, researchers are well aware of the dangers, and increasing numbers of studies are being carried out in naturalistic surroundings (e.g., school playgrounds). The main advantage of naturalistic studies is that they are more likely to provide findings of relevance to children's everyday lives and behavior. However, such studies tend to suffer from the disadvantage that they are less well controlled than laboratory studies. The best way of dealing with these issues is to carry out both laboratory and naturalistic studies. If broadly similar findings are obtained from both kinds of studies, we can have some confidence that the findings are genuine and applicable to everyday life.

Most research on children used to involve obtaining relatively simple response measures (e.g., reaction times). However, there has been a substantial increase in studies in which much more complex types of behavior have been assessed. There are two key reasons for this change. First, the ready availability of video-recording equipment means that children's behavior can be replayed over and over again to extract its full richness. Second, computer-based software packages for analyzing complex sets of data are now in wide use, and greatly simplify data analyses.

What we become as adults is largely dependent on the experiences we had in childhood.

ECOLOGY OF DEVELOPMENT

Bronfenbrenner (1979) proposed an approach to developmental psychology that has proved influential. According to his ecological model, children should be studied in terms of the ecology or the social and cultural environment in which they grow up. He argued that development occurs within various environmental structures arranged "like a set of Russian dolls" (p. 3). There are four basic structures or systems:

- *Microsystem.* A microsystem consists of a child's direct experiences in a given setting. Children typically encounter various microsystems in their everyday lives (e.g., school microsystem; home microsystem). Most developmental research focuses on children's behavior within a single microsystem.
- *Mesosystem.* This consists of the inter-relationships among the child's various microsystems. For example, the child's ability to form friendships at school may depend in part on how securely attached he/she is to his/her parents at home.
- *Exosystem.* This consists of factors (e.g., parents' workplaces; mass media) that are not experienced directly by the child, but which nevertheless have an indirect impact on him/her.
- *Macrosystem.* This consists of the general beliefs and ideology of the culture, which can have various indirect influences on children. For example, if a child's parents have occupations highly valued by society, this may influence his/her behavior at home.

Bronfenbrenner's (1979) ecological approach is attractive for two reasons. First, it helps to integrate the closely related areas of developmental and social psychology. Second, it is much broader in scope than most developmental theories, in which the emphasis is often mainly at the level of specific microsystems. However, a limitation of Bronfenbrenner's approach is that it does not generate many precise and testable predictions.

It follows from Bronfenbrenner's approach that developmental psychologists should carry out cross-cultural studies. Such studies would help to clarify the role played by the macrosystem in influencing children's development. There is an increasing amount of cross-cultural developmental research, some of which is discussed in the following chapters. For example, evidence that children in collectivistic cultures exhibit more altruistic behavior than those in individualistic cultures (e.g., Whiting & Whiting, 1975) is discussed in Chapter 15, and cross-cultural differences in attachment behavior (e.g., Sagi, van IJzendoorn, & Koren-Karie, 1991) are dealt with in Chapter 16. Evidence of cross-cultural differences even in preschool was reported by Tobin, Wu, and Davidson (1989). American children in preschool differed considerably from each other in their behavior, and sometimes fought each other for attractive toys. In contrast, Chinese children behaved in a highly regulated way—they all went to the toilet at the same time, and they were expected to play in a cooperative and helpful way with each other.

There are major cross-cultural differences in the duration of childhood and adolescence, both of which last for many more years in affluent cultures where life expectancy is high. Indeed, it is sometimes argued that adolescence only exists in Western cultures! Consider the !Kung San people living in the Kalahari desert. When children in this culture reach puberty, they have already acquired good hunting and gathering skills that allow them to be self-sufficient and economically independent (Cole & Cole, 1993).

ORGANIZATION OF CHAPTERS 13–16

Developmental psychology deals largely with cognitive and social development, and the four chapters in this section reflect that distinction. Chapters 13 and 14 are concerned with cognitive development, and Chapters 15 and 16 with social development.

Chapter 13 focuses on the development of various important abilities including perception, memory, language, and theory of mind. In Chapter 14, the emphasis shifts to general theories of cognitive development including the very influential approaches proposed by Jean Piaget and Lev Vygotsky. Chapter 15 deals with the development of several aspects of social development (e.g., moral development; development of prosocial and antisocial behavior; gender development). Finally, in Chapter 16, we consider the most general and important aspects of social development. These include the child's attachment to its parents, the consequences of parental deprivation and divorce, friendships, and relationships with children of the same age.

It is important not to infer from the organization of these chapters that cognitive and social development are completely separate. In fact, cognitive development is influenced by social development, and social development depends in part on cognitive development. The links between these two major forms of development are emphasized at several points in the four chapters.

Chapter 13

Contents

Cognitive development: Specific abilities

13

This chapter and the next are concerned with children's cognitive development. You only have to compare infants a few months old with children aged 12 or 13 to see that dramatic improvements in cognitive skills and abilities occur over a period of a few years. The task of developmental psychologists is twofold. First, they need to describe *what* changes during the course of cognitive development. That is the easy part. Second, and much more challenging, they have to work out *how* and *why* these changes occur.

In this chapter, we consider the development of major cognitive abilities. We start with perceptual development, which is of fundamental importance to the young child as he/she comes to grips (literally) with the environment. After that, we consider memory development, finding that children's memories improve considerably during childhood. We then turn to the crucial issues of language development. The central puzzle here is that language acquisition is a very complex accomplishment, but the overwhelming majority of young children seem to learn their native language with amazing speed. Psychologists are still struggling to understand precisely how this is done. Finally, we focus on another key aspect of cognitive development. Young children at about the age of 4 start to develop an understanding that other people often have different beliefs and intentions to their own. This is known as developing a theory of mind, and it has substantial effects on children's interactions with others.

PERCEPTUAL DEVELOPMENT

How much can the newborn baby (or neonate) see and hear? It used to be assumed that the answer was "very little." Towards the end of the nineteenth century, William James described the world of the newborn baby as a "buzzing, blooming confusion, where the infant is seized by eyes, ears, nose and entrails all at once." This suggests that the infant is bombarded by information in every sensory modality, and can't attach meaning to this information. In fact, that view underestimates the capabilities of infants. Many basic perceptual mechanisms are working at a very early age, and infants are *not* merely helpless observers of their world.

There is increasing evidence that even fetuses are capable of perceptual learning. For example, Kisilevsky et al. (2003) exposed 38-week-old fetuses to a tape recording of their mother or a female stranger reading a poem. Fetal heart rate increased when the poem was read by the mother but decreased when read by the stranger. Thus, fetuses can discriminate between different voices prior to birth.

BASIC ASPECTS OF VISION

Newborns are at a great disadvantage to adults with respect to several basic aspects of vision. First, "The visual field of the newborn human infant . . . consists of a narrow tunnel around the line of vision, and the ability to resolve visual details is roughly 40 times poorer than that of adult humans" (Sireteanu, 1999, p. 59). Second, color vision is either nonexistent or nearly so during the first weeks of life. According to Teller (1997, p. 2197), "By two months, rudimentary color vision has arrived. Most infants can probably discriminate red, blue, and green from each other, but not yet yellows and yellow-greens." Third, the eyes of newborns have a fixed focal length for the first 3 months of life. In contrast, older children and adults show accommodation, in which the curvature of the eye's lens alters to bring objects at different distances into focus. Newborns don't show accommodation, and so only objects 8 inches in front of them can be seen clearly. Fourth, binocular disparity (in which there is a difference or disparity between the images projected on to the retinas of the two eyes) assists depth perception. Infants below the age of 3 months lack binocular disparity (Teller, 1997).

Newborns are able to relate visual and auditory information, for example, the sight and sound of a musical mobile.

On the positive side, newborns' eye movements are fairly systematic rather than random. Of particular importance, newborns generally seem to search for the edges of objects. When an edge is detected, a newborn's next few eye movements tend to be small so as to keep the visual focus close to it (Haith, 1980). In addition, newborns show some evidence of **size constancy**, which involves a given object being perceived as having the same size regardless of its distance from us. Slater, Mattock, and Brown (1990) familiarized newborns with either a small or a large cube over several trials. After that, the two cubes were presented successively. The larger cube was presented at a greater distance from the newborns than the smaller cube, with the size of the retinal image being the same in both cases (see the figure below). All the newborns could distinguish between the cubes, because they spent longer looking at the new cube than the old one. The fact the newborns could tell the difference between two cubes having the same-sized retinal image indicates they possessed at least some elements of size constancy. Sai (2005) found that newborns can combine visual and auditory information. Newborns only showed a preference for the mother's face when they had been exposed previously to her face and voice at the same time.

Two cubes of different sizes may project retinal images of the same size, depending on their distance from the viewer.

The visual abilities that are deficient in newborns and infants develop rapidly during the early months of life. Improvements in most aspects of visual perception depend on naturally occurring developmental changes. For example, Maurer, Lewis, Brent, and Levin (1999) studied human infants who had been treated for cataracts in one or both eyes. Initially, their visual acuity was at the level of newborn infants. Strikingly, however, they showed substantial improvement in visual acuity after only a 1-hour exposure to the visual world. This shows the great plasticity of the visual system. It also shows that prolonged visual experience is not necessary for the development of visual acuity.

The position with respect to binocular disparity is more complicated. Banks, Aslin, and Letson (1975) studied adults who had had a problem with binocular vision because of having a squint in childhood that was subsequently corrected. Adults who had a squint at birth and received surgery by 30 months of age had good binocular disparity. Those who had a squint diagnosed between 2 and 7 years of age and surgery within 3 years of diagnosis had reasonably good binocular disparity. However, adults who had a squint at birth and surgery between the ages of 4 and 20 had little or no binocular disparity.

The above complex findings suggest that there is a critical or sensitive period for the development of binocularity during the early years of life. If children don't develop binocularity during the early years of life because of an uncorrected squint, then it is very difficult to develop it later. It has also proved difficult to treat **amblyopia** (impaired vision resulting from disuse of an eye) in older children and adults, thus providing more evidence of a critical period. However, visual acuity in adults with amblyopia can be improved if they receive prolonged practice on a difficult visual task (Levi, 2005).

FACE PERCEPTION

Faces (especially its mother's face) form a very important part of the newborn infant's visual environment. This has led some theorists to argue that natural selection has equipped humans with an innate bias favoring facial stimuli. For example, Morton and Johnson (1991) argued that human infants are born with a mechanism containing information about the structure of human faces. This mechanism is known as CONSPEC, because the information about faces it contains relates to conspecifics (members of the same species).

The key prediction from this theoretical approach is that newborn infants should exhibit a clear preference for facial stimuli over other stimuli. There is much evidence supporting this prediction. For example, Johnson, Dziurawiec, Ellis, and Morton (1991) found that newborns in the first hour after birth showed more visual tracking of realistic faces than of scrambled but symmetrical faces. This suggests that some aspects of face perception don't depend on learning.

In spite of the plausibility of the notion that there is an innate bias for faces, there is increasing evidence that it is probably wrong. An alternative view has been developed by Turati and colleagues (e.g., Turati, 2004). According to this view, there is nothing special about faces. Instead, newborns simply have a preference for stimuli having more patterning in their upper than in their lower part. This is found with faces, but is also found with numerous other stimuli.

Support for the above view was reported by Simion et al. (2002) and by Turati, Simion, Milani, and Umiltà (2002). Simion et al. found that newborns preferred visual stimuli having more elements in the top half than in the bottom half. Importantly, this was the case even when the stimuli didn't look anything like faces. Turati et al. (2002) found (as predicted) that newborns aged between 1 and 3 days did *not* prefer face-like stimuli to nonface-like stimuli when the number of elements in the upper part was held constant. The key finding was that newborns preferred a stimulus of only a nonface-like arrangement in the upper part to a stimulus consisting only of a face-like arrangement in the lower part (see the figure below). These findings suggest that, "Newborns direct their gaze toward faces because they belong to a broader stimulus category that is characterized by a greater number of high-contrast areas in the upper portion of the pattern" (Turati et al., 2002).

Simion, Turati, Valenza, and Leo (2006) replicated the finding that newborns prefer scrambled faces with more elements in the top area to natural faces. However, 3-month-olds preferred facial stimuli to scrambled faces. This suggests that cognitive mechanisms specialized for faces develop over the first few weeks or months of life.

Key Term

Amblyopia:
a condition involving impaired vision as a result of disuse of one eye in the absence of any obvious damage to it.

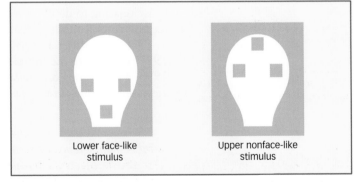

Lower face-like stimulus   Upper nonface-like stimulus

Newborns preferred an upper nonface-like stimulus (shown on the right) to the lower face-like stimulus (shown on the left). From Turati et al. (2002). Copyright © American Psychological Association. Reprinted with permission.

DEPTH PERCEPTION

Gibson and Walk (1960) studied depth perception by designing a "visual cliff" involving a glass-top table

A drawing of Gibson and Walk's "visual cliff." Babies between 6.5 and 12 months of age were reluctant to crawl over the "cliff" edge, even when called by their mothers, suggesting that they perceived the drop created by the check pattern.

(see figure on the left). A check pattern was positioned close to the glass under one half of the table (the "shallow" side) and far below the glass under the other half (the "deep" side). Infants between the ages of 6.5 and 12 months were placed on the shallow side of the table, and encouraged to crawl over the edge of the visual cliff on to the deep side. Most failed to do so. This finding suggests they possessed some elements of depth perception. It may be relevant that binocular vision (which is helpful in depth perception) has typically developed by the age of 6 months (Teller, 1997).

Adolph (2000) argued that the development of depth perception is more complex than assumed by Gibson and Walk (1960). According to Gibson and Walk, infants acquire *general* knowledge (e.g., an association between depth information and falling) that stops them from crossing the visual cliff. In contrast, Adolph's sway model assumes that infants' knowledge is highly *specific*. According to this model, infants learn how to avoid risky gaps when sitting, but subsequently have to learn how to avoid such gaps when crawling.

Adolph (2000) obtained support for her sway model by studying 9-month-old infants more familiar with sitting than with crawling. The key findings were that, "The babies avoided reaching over risky gaps in the sitting posture but fell into risky gaps while attempting to reach in the crawling posture" (Adolph, 2000, p. 290). The implication is that learning with the visual cliff is specific to a given posture (e.g., sitting) and new learning is needed when infants become more mobile. However, slightly older infants show general rather than specific learning. Witherington et al. (2005) found that newly walking infants consistently avoided the deep side of the visual cliff. These infants had learned to avoid risky gaps while crawling, and this learning simply transferred over to walking. The take-home message is that learning to avoid gaps is specific to a given posture in younger infants but becomes more general in older ones.

THEORETICAL APPROACHES

Perceptual development is complex, with different perceptual abilities developing at different ages and in various ways. Some aspects of visual perception (e.g., relating visual and auditory information; aspects of face perception; aspects of size constancy) are present at birth or very shortly thereafter. These aspects reflect either innate visual capacities or very rapid learning. Other aspects of visual perception (e.g., visual acuity; color vision) develop several weeks after birth, and probably depend on maturational factors. There are still other aspects of perception (e.g., binocular disparity) for which there may be a critical or sensitive period of their development. Finally, some aspects (e.g., those relating to depth perception) develop only after several months of life and probably require certain kinds of learning.

Theorists differ in terms of how they interpret all this evidence. Some (e.g., Teller, 1997) emphasize the limitations of infants' visual perception whereas others (e.g., Slater, 1990, 1998) focus on the strengths of their perception. Here are Teller's (1997, p. 2196) views on the situation in which newborn infants find themselves:

Their acuity and contrast sensitivity are very poor but are measurable. Their . . . eye movements reveal the capacity to analyze the direction of motion of large, high-contrast objects . . . However, they should reveal no appreciation of stereo depth, no capacity to respond to low contrasts or to fine spatial details, and probably no color vision. Their visual worlds are probably marked less by blooming and buzzing than by the haziness of low-contrast-sensitivity, the blurriness of spatial filtering, and the blandness of monochrome [black-and-white].

In contrast, Slater (1990, p. 262) is more upbeat in his assessment of infants' perceptual skills:

> No modality [none of the senses] operates at adult-like levels at birth, but such levels are achieved surprisingly early in infancy, leading to recent conceptualizations of the "competent infant" . . . early perceptual competence is matched by cognitive incompetence, and much of the re-organization of perceptual representation is dependent upon the development and construction of cognitive structures that give access to a world of objects, people, language, and events.

Evidence that visual perception in newborns is influenced by cognitive incompetence was provided by Slater et al. (1990). They presented newborns with a visual display in which a rod was seen moving from side to side behind a box. The newborns never saw the entire rod. Instead, they could see the top and bottom of the rod above and below the box. Adults and infants aged 3 or 4 months assume there is a single rod of which they can see only the ends (Kellman & Spelke, 1983). However, the newborn infants seemed to perceive the rod behind the box as a broken one.

In sum, newborns immediately possess some of the main aspects of visual perception. After that, there are rapid and substantial improvements in visual perceptual abilities during the early months of life. Teller (1997) emphasizes the role of maturational changes in producing these improvements. In contrast, Slater (1990, 1998) focuses on the development of the cognitive system and the infant's growing store of knowledge as the engines of improvements in visual perception.

MEMORY DEVELOPMENT

Children's ability to learn and remember information becomes better and better during development. Why does this happen? According to Siegler (1998), there are four possible explanations:

1. *Basic processes and capacity*: For example, the capacity of short-term or working memory may increase.
2. *Strategies*: Children possess more memory strategies as they develop, and may use these strategies more efficiently.
3. *Metamemory*: **Metamemory** is "knowledge about memory. The development of metamemory is the development of the ability to monitor and regulate one's own memory behavior" (Goswami, 1998, p. 206).
4. *Content knowledge*: Older children possess more knowledge than younger ones, and this may make it easier to learn and remember new information.

All four explanations are discussed below. As we will see, the evidence suggests that *all* of them possess some validity, and jointly they account for the dramatic improvement shown by children in the course of development. However, most research on memory development suffers from important limitations. We know older children possess memory skills and strategies not possessed by younger ones. However, we lack a clear sense of the processes involved in the development of these skills and strategies.

BASIC PROCESSES AND CAPACITY

One of the most important parts of the human memory system is working memory (see Chapter 8). In essence, working memory allows us to process and store information at the same time. An example of a task requiring the use of working memory is as follows (Swanson, 1999). The participants are given a sentence such as, "Now suppose somebody wanted to have you take them to the supermarket at 8651 Elm Street." The task was to recall the name of the street and then to recall the number. Swanson found with children aged from 6 upwards that working memory improved continuously throughout childhood. Swanson also found that age differences in working memory predicted reasonably well children's performance in reading and arithmetic. This suggests that working memory capacity is an important factor in cognitive development.

Key Term
Metamemory: knowledge about one's memory and about how it works.

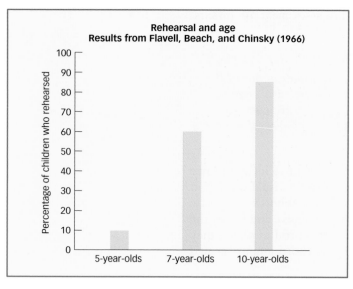

Baddeley (1986) argued that working memory consists of a central executive (resembling an attentional system), a phonological loop (used for verbal rehearsal), and a visuospatial sketchpad that stores visual and spatial information (see Chapter 8). Gathercole et al. (2004) found that the capacity of all three components of working memory increased progressively from the age of 4 through to early adolescence.

MEMORY STRATEGIES

Adults use several memory strategies (e.g., verbal rehearsal; mnemonics) to assist them in learning and remembering. As we would expect, there are developmental changes in the use of strategies. For example, Flavell, Beach, and Chinsky (1966) found on a picture-learning task that far more 10-year-olds than 7- or 5-year-olds rehearsed the learning material (see figure on the left).

Consider a task such as remembering a list of four words belonging to each of six categories, with the words presented in a random order. Adults would typically use an organizational strategy in which they rehearsed (and recalled) the words category by category. This organizational strategy leads to improved recall of the list compared to strategies in which the list isn't organized category by category.

What do children do when learning similar lists? Schneider, Knopf, and Stefanek (2002) presented children of various ages with pictures belonging to familiar categories (e.g., animals; food). The children sorted the pictures and then they recalled them in any order (free recall). Of central interest was the extent to which the children organized the stimuli into categories at learning (sorting task) and at recall. As expected, free recall increased steadily between the ages of 8 and 17. This increase was accompanied by progressive increases in use of an organizational strategy at learning and recall (see the figure below).

Schlagmüller and Schneider (2002) studied the rate of acquisition of an organizational strategy during sorting in children aged between 8 and 12. The findings were very clear-cut: "The transition from non-strategic to strategic occurred rapidly, indicating that children 'jumped' from random behavior to nearly perfect sorting scores" (Schlagmüller & Schneider, 2002, p. 313).

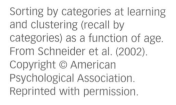

Sorting by categories at learning and clustering (recall by categories) as a function of age. From Schneider et al. (2002). Copyright © American Psychological Association. Reprinted with permission.

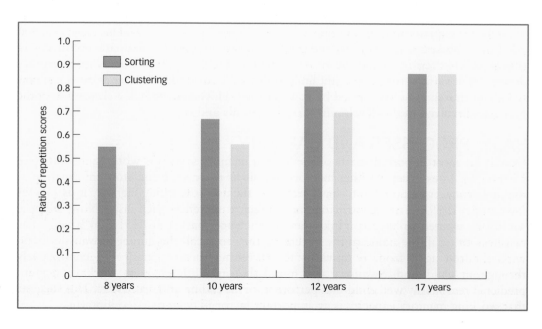

METAMEMORY

As children grow older, they show increased metamemory or knowledge about their own memory and how it works (see Schneider, 1999, for a review). For example, Yussen and Levy (1975) found that preschoolers' memory span was five items less than they had predicted, whereas 9-year-olds only overestimated their memory span by one item.

Does metamemory knowledge generally predict memory performance? Schneider and Pressley (1989) found in a meta-analysis of 60 studies that the correlation between metamemory and memory performance was +.41, indicating a moderate relationship. Why isn't the relationship stronger? Children may not be motivated to use effective memory strategies they possess, they may feel a good memory strategy isn't needed when a word list is short, and so on.

CONTENT KNOWLEDGE

If the amount of relevant knowledge is of major significance in determining memory performance, then a well-informed child might remember some things better than an ill-informed adult. This prediction was tested by Chi (1978), who studied digit recall and reproduction of chess positions in 10-year-olds skilled at chess and adults knowing little about chess. The adults performed better than the children on digit recall. However, the children's recall of chess positions was more than 50% better than that of the adults (see figure on the right).

Schneider, Gruber, Gold, and Opwis (1993) compared children and adults having similar chess expertise. Both groups remembered chess positions comparably well and much better than nonexpert children and adults. Thus, memory for chess positions depends largely on expertise and hardly at all on age.

Content knowledge also influences memory in other ways. For example, there is evidence that the memory performance of even very young children is influenced by scripts, which are knowledge structures indicating the typical sequence for common events. Bauer and Thal (1990) studied script knowledge in children aged 21 or 22 months. The children were presented with a sequence of actions (e.g., giving teddy a bath involved putting the bear in the tub, washing it with the sponge, and then drying it with the towel). In one condition, sequences of actions were presented in the wrong or an unnatural order. The children tended to recall the sequences in the correct order even when they had been presented in the wrong order. Presumably this occurred because the children possessed (and made use of) the relevant scripts. Bauer, Hertsgard, Dropik, and Daly (1998) found that even 16-month-olds could recall events presented in a logical sequence (e.g., starting the engine before driving a car) after a 2-week retention interval. This presumably occurred because they could create organized representations of such events.

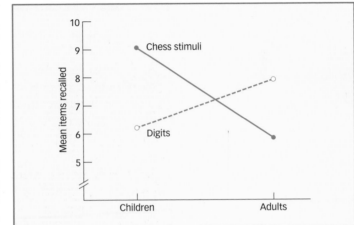

Immediate recall of chess positions and digits in children (mean age = 10 years 6 months) with expert knowledge of chess and in adults with limited knowledge of chess. Adapted from Chi (1978).

IMPLICIT MEMORY

Virtually all the research discussed so far has involved explicit memory (based on conscious recollection of information). This can be contrasted with implicit memory, a form of memory *not* dependent on conscious recollection. There are important differences between explicit and implicit memory (see Chapter 8). As we have seen, there are generally large improvements in explicit memory performance during development. This is in marked contrast to the findings from studies of implicit

Earliest memories

Lamont (2001) has demonstrated musical memories from before birth in research that is part of the UK's BBC *Child of Our Time* project. She compared babies from 11 families where in the last 3 months of pregnancy daily half-hour sessions of particular music had been played with babies from another 11 families who had had no such experience. The research is ongoing, but results indicate strongly that the experimental babies do have a musical long-term memory.

memory. According to Murphy, McKone, and Slee (2003, p. 125), "The usual finding of implicit memory studies to date is of no age-related increase . . . Of 18 published studies, 15 have concluded that implicit memory is stable across a wide age range (3 years to adulthood)."

A typical study of implicit memory was carried out by Russo, Nichelli, Gibertoni, and Cornia (1995). Children identified degraded pictures of objects, some of which had been seen before in intact form. Implicit memory was measured by the extent to which performance was better with objects previously seen. Very similar levels of implicit memory were observed in 4-year-olds, 6-year-olds, and young adults. In contrast, explicit memory for the pictures was highest in the adult group and lowest in the 4-year-olds.

Key Study

Murphy et al. (2003): Age and implicit memory

As we have seen, there is much evidence suggesting that age doesn't affect implicit memory even though it has large effects on explicit memory. Why are there such small (or nonexistent) effects of age on implicit memory? One possibility is that implicit memory doesn't involve metamemory or strategic processes, because participants don't know their memory is being tested. This is probably part of the answer. However, Murphy et al. explored another possibility. They pointed out that explicit memory is strongly influenced by the amount of relevant knowledge that a child possesses (e.g., Chi, 1978), and wondered whether the same was true of implicit memory. Previous research didn't provide an answer because most of the implicit memory tests used involved identification of common objects presented in degraded form. As a result, even young children possessed good knowledge about the stimuli used.

Accordingly, Murphy et al. used an implicit memory condition in which older children would possess much more knowledge than younger ones. They presented a word list with one word belonging to each of 20 categories. The category members were selected to be atypical but known to even the younger children (e.g., kite as a toy; mushroom as a vegetable). At test, the participants were simply asked to say the first five members of each category that came to mind. In this condition, adults showed 2½ times as much implicit memory as 5- to 7-year-old children and 1½ times as much implicit memory as 10- to 13-year-old children. Murphy et al. also used a very similar condition involving explicit memory and found the usual superiority in recall of adults over young children.

It could be argued that Murphy et al. hadn't really demonstrated changes in implicit memory with age because there was a possibility that explicit processes were involved despite the instructions they used. However, no participants in the implicit memory condition reported explicitly trying to recall information from the study list. Murphy et al. (2003) pursued this issue. Children aged 4 or 5 and adults performed the same implicit memory task as before under conditions involving full attention (only study list) or divided attention (detect sequences of odd or even numbers as well as study list). The assumption was that it would be very difficult to use explicit memory under divided attention conditions. Implicit memory increased with age even when the opportunity to use explicit processes was much reduced (see figure on the following page).

Discussion points
1. What are some of the practical implications of this research?
2. What are the main differences between implicit and explicit memory?

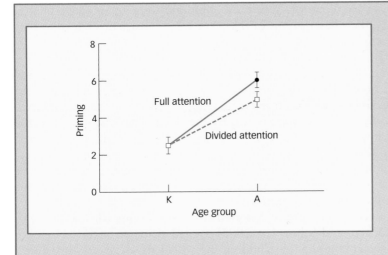

Implicit memory (priming) in kindergarten (K) and adult (A) groups in full-attention and divided-attention conditions. From Murphy et al. (2003). Copyright © 2003 Elsevier. Reproduced with permission.

KEY STUDY EVALUATION
The study by Murphy et al. (2003) is important because it shows that there can be large age effects in implicit memory. It also identified increases in children's knowledge base over time as the probable factor determining whether increasing age is accompanied by improved implicit memory. However, the study is limited in that it doesn't conclusively eliminate the possibility that explicit memory was involved in the allegedly implicit memory condition. In addition, it remains unclear precisely how increased knowledge helps to produce enhanced implicit memory performance.

In sum, implicit memory is more basic than explicit memory, and makes much less use of metamemory and strategic processes. This helps to explain why there are generally few or no developmental changes in implicit memory. However, implicit memory may differ less dramatically from explicit memory than is sometimes supposed, in that both forms of memory are influenced by the amount of relevant knowledge possessed by participants.

EYEWITNESS TESTIMONY

There has been a substantial increase in the number of children testifying in court in sexual abuse cases. This raises important issues about the accuracy of the information they provide, and has led to much research (see Bruck & Ceci, 1999, for a review). It is worrying that many children seem to be suggestible, which can lead to systematic errors in their recall of events. In general, suggestibility is greater during the early years of childhood than the later ones (Bruck & Ceci, 1999).

In a representative study, Thompson, Clarke-Stewart, and Lepore (1997) studied the effects of interviewer bias on children's memories. Five- and 6-year-olds witnessed one of two events. In the innocent event, a janitor called Chester cleaned some dolls and other toys in a playroom. In the abusive event, Chester handled the dolls roughly and in a mildly abusive way. Some children were then questioned by an accusatory interviewer who suggested the janitor had been abusive. Other children were questioned by an exculpatory [free from blame] interviewer who suggested the janitor was innocent. The remaining children were questioned by a neutral interviewer who avoided making any suggestions. The children were asked by their parents to describe what the janitor had done immediately after the interview and 2 weeks later.

Thompson et al. (1997) found that children's eyewitness memories were generally accurate when questioned by the neutral interviewer. However, when questioned by the accusatory or exculpatory interviewer, the children's accounts typically conformed to the interviewer's suggestions. Thus, the janitor was reported by the children as having behaved abusively when the interviewer was accusatory but as having behaved innocently when the interviewer was exculpatory. When the children were then asked neutral questions by their parents, their descriptions of the event were consistent with what they had said to the interviewer.

It is perhaps unsurprising that young children were influenced by blatant interviewer bias in the Thompson et al. (1997) study. However, children are fairly suggestible in many situations. For example, Bruck, Ceci, and Hembrooke (1997) asked preschool children on five separate occasions to describe two true events (e.g., a recent punishment) and two false events (e.g., witnessing a thief stealing food). By the third interview, nearly all the children accepted that both the false events had actually happened. The children continued to argue that the false events were true when questioned later by a new interviewer adopting a nonsuggestive approach. The descriptions of the true and false events were similar. For example, they contained similar numbers of spontaneous statements and details (e.g., about conversations).

Why do children produce systematically distorted reports of events when exposed to suggestive influences? Roebers and Schneider (2005) argued that two main factors are involved. First, there is social compliance. Children may yield to social pressure and a lack of social support even when their own recollection is accurate. Second, there is cognitive incompetence. Children may come to believe their own distorted memory reports because of limitations in processing, attention, or language.

The evidence suggests that both factors play a part. The notion that social compliance is important is supported by the work of Poole and Lindsay (1996). Children produced false memories after being repeatedly questioned by a suggestive interviewer. However, many of these false memories faded when the children weren't re-interviewed for a reasonably long period of time. The notion that children's memories may sometimes actually be altered is supported by several studies in which children continued to produce false memories after being warned that the interviewer may have been mistaken in his/her suggestions (see Bruck & Melnyk, 2004, for a review).

What can be done to increase the accuracy of children's eyewitness reports? Several answers are discussed by Baddeley, Eysenck, and Anderson (2009), but we will focus on one of the simplest and effective strategies. Gross and Hayne (1999) argued that much of the information about an event stored away by young children is likely to be in non-verbal form. If so, recall might be improved by asking children to draw what they could remember about an event before asking them to describe what they had seen. In their study, Gross and Hayne asked 5- and 6-year-old children to remember a visit to a Cadbury's chocolate factory 1 day, 6 months, and 1 year later. At the two shorter intervals, children in the drawing condition recalled 30% more information than those who only provided verbal reports. After 1 year, children in the drawing condition recalled almost twice as much information as those in the verbal-report-only condition.

LANGUAGE DEVELOPMENT

Young children seem to acquire language with breathtaking speed. From the age of about 16 months onwards, children often acquire upwards of 10 new words every day. By the age of 5, children have mastered most of the grammatical rules of their native language. However, very few parents are consciously aware of the rules of grammar. Thus, young children simply "pick up" the complex rules of grammar without much formal teaching.

STAGES OF LANGUAGE DEVELOPMENT

We need to distinguish between *receptive language* (language comprehension) and *productive language* (language expression or speaking). Children (and adults) have better receptive than productive language. For example, some young children produce only a few words but nevertheless have a comprehension vocabulary in excess of 150 words (Bates, Bretherton, & Synder, 1988).

Children need to learn four kinds of knowledge about language:

1. *Phonology:* The sound system of a language.
2. *Semantics:* The meaning conveyed by words and sentences.

3. *Syntax*: The set of grammatical rules indicating how words may be combined to make sentences.
4. *Pragmatics*: The principles determining how language is modified to fit the context (e.g., we speak more simply to a child than to an adult).

Children generally acquire the above kinds of knowledge in the order listed. They initially learn to make sounds, followed by developing an understanding of what those sounds mean. After that, they learn grammatical rules, and how to alter what they say to fit the situation. Evidence that some aspects of phonological development occur remarkably early in life was reported by Mehler et al. (1994). Four-day-old French infants could discriminate between the French and Russian languages, showing a clear preference for French.

Early vocalizations

The babbling of infants up to 6 months of age is similar in all parts of the world. By about 8 months of age, however, infants show signs of the language they have heard in their vocalizations. Indeed, adults can sometimes guess accurately from their babbling whether infants have been exposed to French, Chinese, Arabic, or English (De Boysson-Bardies, Sagart, & Durand, 1984).

Up until the age of 18 months, young children are limited to single-word utterances (although they may be trying to convey much more meaning than their short utterances would suggest). Almost two-thirds of the words used by young children in Europe and the United States are nouns referring to objects or to people. Children naturally refer to things of interest to them (e.g., the people and objects surrounding them). Gentner (1982) found the same emphasis on nouns in children learning Japanese and Kaluli. Words are sometimes used to cover more objects than they should (over-extension), such as when my younger daughter referred to every man as "Daddy." Words are also sometimes used too narrowly (under-extension). For example, a child may think the word "cereal" refers only to the brand of cereal he/she eats for breakfast.

Overextension occurs when a child hears a word in the presence of an object, and then goes on to label all similar things with that same word. Hence, all furry creatures with four legs may be called a "cat."

Telegraphic period

The second stage of language development starts at about 18 months. This is the **telegraphic period**, during which children's speech is abbreviated like a telegram costing so much per word. Content words such as nouns and verbs are included, but function words (e.g., "a"; "the"; "and"), pronouns, and prepositions are omitted.

Even though young children are mostly limited to two-word utterances, they can still communicate numerous meanings. For example, "Daddy chair" may mean "I want to sit in Daddy's chair," "Daddy is sitting in his chair," or "Daddy, sit in your chair!"

Brown (1973) argued that young children possess a basic order rule: a sentence consists of agent + object + location (e.g., "Daddy eats lunch at home"). Their two-word utterances follow the basic order rule. For example, an utterance containing an agent and an action will be in the order agent–action (e.g., "Daddy walk") rather than the reverse "walk Daddy"). Similarly, action and object will be spoken in the order action–object (e.g., "drink Coke").

Subsequent developments

Children's language develops considerably between 2 and 5 years of age. For example, the maximum sentence measured in terms of morphemes (meaningful units) increases from four morphemes at 24 months to eight morphemes at 30 months (Fenson et al., 1994). Children gradually acquire various **grammatical morphemes**, which are modifiers that alter meaning. Examples include prepositions, prefixes, and suffixes (e.g., "in"; "on"; plural –s; "a"; and "the"). Nearly all children learn the various grammatical morphemes

This is a wug

Now there is another one.
There are two of them.
There are two _____.

in the same order, starting with simple ones (e.g., including "in" and "on" in sentences) and moving on to more complex ones (e.g., reducing "they are" to "they're").

Do children simply imitate adults' speech rather than learning rules? Evidence that they don't comes from children's grammatical errors. For example, a child will say, "The dog runned away," which adults are unlikely to do. Presumably the child makes that mistake because he/she is applying the rule that the past tense of a verb is usually formed by adding –ed to the present tense. Using a grammatical rule in situations in which it doesn't apply is known as **over-regularization**. Evidence that over-regularization doesn't occur simply because children are imitating other children was reported by Berko (1958). Children were shown two pictures of an imaginary animal or bird. They were told, "This is a wug. This is another wug. Now there are two . . ." (see figure on the left). Even young children produced the regular plural form "wugs" despite not having heard the word before.

At one time, it was thought that the development of vocabulary and of grammar occurred independently. In fact, the two forms of development are actually closely related. For example, Dionne, Dale, Boivin, and Plomin (2003) assessed vocabulary and grammar in children at the ages of 2 and 3. Vocabulary at age 2 predicted grammar at age 3, and grammar at age 2 predicted vocabulary at age 3. Such findings suggest (but don't prove) that the processes underlying vocabulary and grammar development are similar. Conboy and Thal (2006) studied children between the ages of 20 and 30 months who were bilingual in English and Spanish. Their key finding was that grammatical development (e.g., complexity of utterances) in each language was associated mainly with vocabulary development in the same language. Thus, grammatical development within a given language depends more on the child's vocabulary in that language than on its more general maturational or conceptual development.

THEORIES OF LANGUAGE DEVELOPMENT

Numerous theories have been put forward to explain children's language acquisition. Most can be categorized as inside-out theories or outside-in theories (Hirsch-Pasek & Golinkoff, 1996). Inside-out theorists (e.g., Chomsky; Pinker) argue that language acquisition depends heavily on innate factors and only modestly on the child's own experiences. In contrast, outside-in theorists (e.g., Bruner; Tomasello) argue that experience is of central importance in children's language acquisition.

There are other differences between inside-out and outside-in theorists (Harris & Butterworth, 2002). Most inside-out theorists claim that language development occurs in relative isolation from other forms of cognitive and social development. However, outside-in theorists argue that general cognitive and social mechanisms (e.g., those involved in perception or thinking) are involved in language development. These two theoretical positions are discussed below. Note that it is entirely possible that there is an element of truth in both positions, with innate factors *and* experience both being of vital importance in language development.

Key Term

Over-regularization: extending a grammatical rule to situations in which it does not apply.

Early language acquisition				
Age	**0–6 months**	**6 months–1 year**	**1–2½ years**	**2–5 years**
Babbling	✓			
Some phonemes learned	✓	✓		
First spoken word		✓		
Beginning of grammatical rules			✓	
Basic rules of grammar acquired				✓

Inside-out theories

Inside-out or nativist theorists are very impressed by the speed with which most young children acquire language. They claim that language acquisition is simply too fast for it to depend entirely on learning by experience. Accordingly, they argue that infants are born with knowledge of the structure of human languages. For example, Chomsky (1965) argued that humans possess a **language acquisition device** consisting of innate knowledge of grammatical structure. Children require some exposure to (and experience with) the language environment provided by their parents and other people to develop language. Such experience determines which specific language any given child will learn.

Chomsky (1986) later replaced the notion of a language acquisition device with the idea of a universal grammar, which forms part of our innate knowledge of language.

According to his Principles and Parameters Theory, there are **linguistic universals,** which are features common to nearly every language. There are substantive and formal universals. Substantive universals concern categories common to all languages (e.g., noun and verb categories). Formal universals are concerned with the general form of syntactic or grammatical rules.

Pinker (1984, 1989) is broadly sympathetic to Chomsky's approach. However, he argued that exposure to language is more important than admitted by Chomsky. According to Pinker, children use "semantic bootstrapping" to allocate words to their appropriate word class. Suppose a young child hears the sentence, "William is throwing a stone," while watching a boy carrying out that action. The child will realize from his/her observations that "William" refers to the actor, "stone" to the object acted on, and "is throwing" to an action. The child then uses his/her innate knowledge of word categories to work out that "William" is the subject of the sentence, "stone" is the object, and "throwing" is the verb.

Lenneberg (1967) put forward the critical period hypothesis. According to this hypothesis, language learning depends on biological maturation, and so is easier prior to puberty. This might help to explain why most people report that it was easier to learn their own language than to learn a second language when they were teenagers.

Findings

Chomsky argued that word order was a linguistic universal. We can test this by considering the preferred word order for the subject, verb, and object in sentences in numerous languages. In principle, there are six possible orderings, two of which (object–verb–subject; object–subject–verb) are not found among the world's languages (Greenberg, 1963). The most popular word order is subject–object–verb (44% of languages), followed by the subject–verb–object word order found in English (35% of languages). The subject precedes the object in 98% of languages, presumably because it makes sense to consider the subject (typically the actor) of a sentence before the object.

Bickerton (1984) put forward the language bioprogram hypothesis, according to which children will create a grammar even if not exposed to a proper language during their early years. Support was obtained by considering laborers from China, Japan, Korea, Puerto Rico, Portugal, and the Philippines taken to the sugar plantations of Hawaii 100 years ago. These laborers developed a pidgin language which was very simple and lacked most grammatical structures. Here is an example: "Me cape buy, me check make." The meaning is, "He bought my coffee; he made me out a check" (Pinker, 1984). The offspring of these laborers developed a language known as Hawaiian Creole. This is a proper language and is fully grammatical. Here is an example of this language: "Da firs japani came ran away from japan come." This means, "The first Japanese who arrived ran away from Japan to here."

We don't know the extent to which the development of Hawaiian Creole depended on the laborers' prior exposure to language. Clearer evidence that a language can develop in groups almost completely lacking in exposure to a developed language was reported by Senghas, Kita, and Özyürek (2003). They studied deaf Nicaraguan children at special schools. Attempts (mostly unsuccessful) were made to teach them Spanish. However, these deaf children began to develop a new system of gestures that expanded into a basic sign language passed on to successive groups of children who joined the school. Since

Key Terms

Language acquisition device: an innate knowledge of the grammatical structure of language.

Linguistic universals: features that are found in all (or virtually all) languages.

Case Study: *Genie*

Genie spent most of her time up to the age of 13 in an isolated room (Curtiss, 1977). She had practically no contact with other people, and was punished if she made any sounds. After Genie was rescued in 1970, she learned some aspects of language, especially vocabulary. However, she showed very poor learning of grammatical rules. There are problems in interpreting the evidence from Genie. She was exposed to great social as well as linguistic deprivation, and her father's "justification" for keeping her in isolation was that he thought she was very retarded. Thus, there are various possible reasons for Genie's limited ability to learn language.

Ethical issues: Deprivation studies are useful examples from which we can draw some inferences, but they rarely provide data that can be regarded as scientific. What are some of the ethical issues that arise from looking at the effects of deprivation? Should the psychologist be concerned with compensation for the deprivation experienced, e.g., linguistic support for individuals like Genie?

Do the ethical problems concerning work like this outweigh any practical advancement of our understanding as psychologists?

Nicaraguan Sign Language bore very little relation to Spanish or to the gestures made by hearing children, it appears that it is a genuinely new language owing remarkably little to other languages.

There is mixed evidence relating to the critical period hypothesis. Support for the hypothesis was reported by Johnson and Newport (1989), who studied Chinese and Korean immigrants to the United States. Those who had arrived in the United States at an early age performed much better than those who had arrived later when asked to decide whether sentences were grammatically correct. That suggests that there may be a critical period for the learning of syntax.

In principle, the best way to test the critical period hypothesis would be to consider children having little chance to learn language during their early years. For example, Genie spent most of her time up to the age of 13 in an isolated room (Curtiss, 1977). She had practically no contact with other people, and was punished if she made any sounds. After being rescued, she managed to learn the meanings of numerous words, but her learning of grammatical rules was very poor. These findings seem consistent with the critical period hypothesis. However, there are various possible reasons for Genie's poor learning of language. She was exposed to great social as well as linguistic deprivation, and her father claimed that he thought she was very retarded.

Evaluation

+ Nativist theories potentially explain why nearly all children master their native language very rapidly.

+ Chomsky's theory is supported by the way in which pidgin languages develop into creole languages and by the development of Nicaraguan Sign Language.

+ Chomsky's theory makes sense of the fact that language is rule-based even though few speakers of a language can express these rules clearly.

+ There is support for a weakened version of the critical period hypothesis, according to which some aspects of language are more difficult to acquire outside the critical period (Harley, 2001).

− Chomsky's theory is difficult to test. For example, he assumed that very young children have access to a considerable amount of grammatical knowledge. However, if their language performance doesn't reflect this assumed knowledge, this can be explained away by arguing that the children were not motivated, had problems with attention or memory, and so on.

− Chomsky argued that the language children hear doesn't contain enough information to allow them to work out grammatical rules from scratch. This argument is not persuasive. As discussed later, mothers and other adults typically talk to young children in simple, short sentences so as to facilitate their language acquisition.

− The entire idea of an innate grammar seems implausible. According to Bishop (1997, p. 123), "What makes an innate grammar a particularly peculiar idea is the fact that innate knowledge must be general enough to account for acquisition of Italian, Japanese, Turkish, Malay, as well as sign language acquisition by congenitally deaf children." Tomasello (2005) described the problem of relating a universal innate grammar to any given language as the "linking problem."

Outside-in theories

Outside-in theories (e.g., Tomasello's constructivist theory) emphasize the central role of experience in allowing young children to acquire language. In essence, outside-in theorists argue that the language input to which young children are exposed is adequate for language acquisition, whereas inside-out theorists are skeptical. We start with a discussion of research on child-directed speech, which is very relevant to this disagreement.

When mothers (and fathers) talk to their young children, they use very short, simple sentences; this is known as **child-directed speech**. Other features of child-directed speech are that it involves a slow rate of speaking, use of a restricted vocabulary, and extra stress on key words (Dockrell & Messer, 1999). Mothers, fathers, and other adults also try to help children's language development by expansions. **Expansions** consist of fuller and more grammatical versions of what the child has just said. For example, a child might say, "Dog out," with its mother responding, "The dog wants to go out."

Child-directed speech helps young children to acquire language by using very short, simple sentences, often with target words receiving extra stress "What a pretty DAISY!"

Saxton (1997) argued that many expansions provide children with an immediate contrast between their own incorrect speech and the correct version. For example, a child may say, "He shooted fish," to which the adult might reply, "He shot the fish!" Children seem to process expansions fairly thoroughly, because they are more likely to repeat adult expansions than other adult utterances (Farrar, 1992).

Child-directed speech helps children to learn vocabulary. For example, Weizman and Snow (2001) considered factors influencing children's vocabulary at the age of 7. Children with the largest vocabularies had mothers who included many sophisticated words when speaking to them. In addition, their mothers tended to introduce these sophisticated words in helpful ways (e.g., providing explicit information about the meaning of each word).

From what has been discussed so far, it may seem as if we know for sure that language acquisition relies heavily on child-directed speech. In fact, however, finding that children having the most exposure to child-directed speech acquire language the fastest doesn't prove that the child-directed speech was responsible. Another possibility is that adults use more child-directed speech with children who find it easiest to acquire language.

Cross-cultural research suggests that child-directed speech may *not* be essential for language acquisition. Schieffelin (1990) studied the Kaluli of New Guinea. Kaluli adults talk to children as if they were adults, but Kaluli children develop language at about the normal rate. However, cultures in which child-directed speech is little used may provide different kinds of assistance to children learning language. For example, Ochs and Schieffelin (1995) argued that children in such cultures become involved in social and communal activities, which assists shared understanding and language development.

In an important study, Haggan (2002) discovered many Kuwaiti mothers who claimed they did not use child-directed speech with their children. However, observations of their actual behavior indicated some evidence that all of them did actually make use of child-directed speech.

Cognitive and constructivist approaches

Piaget (see Chapter 14) argued that children acquire language only after developing relevant cognitive abilities. More specifically, he claimed that children form schemas consisting of organized knowledge about the world and events they have experienced. Children need to have

Key Terms

Child-directed speech:
the simplified sentences spoken by mothers and other adults when talking to young children.

Expansions:
fuller and more detailed versions of what a child has just said provided by an adult or an older child.

developed various cognitive processes and structures (e.g., schemas) before they can develop language. This is the cognition hypothesis.

It follows from Piaget's cognition hypothesis that children having slow cognitive development should also have slow linguistic development. This is often (but by no means always) the case. For example, consider children with **Williams syndrome**. This is a rare genetic disorder involving unusual facial characteristics ("elfin face") and typically an IQ in the 50–65 range. They have slow cognitive development. However, their language abilities are relatively good and they often have surprisingly large vocabularies (Tager-Flusberg, 1999). Such findings seem at odds with the cognition hypothesis. However, the onset of language in children with Williams syndrome is later than in healthy children, and their language comprehension is poor (Karmiloff-Smith, Grant, Berthoud, Davies, Howlin, & Udwin, 1997).

Tomasello has developed a constructivist theory based in part on Piaget's views. The essence of his theory is as follows:

> Children acquire linguistic competence in the particular language they are learning only gradually, beginning with more concrete linguistic structures based on particular words and morphemes [small units of meaning], and then building up to more abstract and productive structures based on various types of linguistic categories, schemas, and constructions (Tomasello & Brooks, 1999, p. 161).

According to Tomasello's theory, children's language development is based on their cognitive understanding of the scenes or events they experience in their everyday lives. They generally find it easiest to learn nouns, because nouns refer to concrete objects or people within scenes. It is more difficult to learn verbs, because their meaning is typically more abstract. Tomasello (1992) put forward the Verb Island hypothesis, according to which children initially treat each verb independently as if it had its own island of organization.

We can relate the central assumptions of constructivist and nativist theories to the issue of language productivity or creativity. According to Tomasello's constructivist theory, young children should initially show very limited productivity. According to nativist theories, young children should rapidly show high levels of productivity or creativity in their language utterances.

Findings

A central assumption of the constructivist approach is that initial language learning (especially of verbs) should be slow. Supporting evidence was reported by Tomasello (1992) based on observations of his 1-year-old daughter. She used some verbs in only one kind of sentence frame (e.g., "Cut ____"), which indicates limited learning. Other verbs were used in several kinds of sentence frames (e.g., "Draw ____"; "Draw ____ on ____"; "Draw ____ for ____"). Such differences among verbs are consistent with the Verb Island hypothesis discussed above.

Tomasello, Akhtar, Dodson, and Rekau (1997) taught children aged between 18 and 23 months two new nouns and two new verbs. The children produced 10 times more combinations of words using the novel nouns than the novel verbs. This relative lack of productivity with novel verbs is more consistent with the constructivist approach than with the nativist one.

According to Tomasello's theory, most language processes develop over time as a result of increased exposure to language. Thus, the learning of specific language skills should be gradual. In contrast, nativist theories tend to assume that specific language skills should emerge suddenly. Matthews, Lieven, Theakston, and Tomasello (2005) tested these predictions in a study using two groups of children, one with a mean age of 2 years 9 months and the other with a mean age of 3 years 9 months. The children were presented with short sentences containing low-, medium-, and high-frequency verbs in an ungrammatical subject–object–verb order (e.g., "Bear elephant tugged").

Key Term

Williams syndrome: a genetic disorder involving low IQ but reasonable language development.

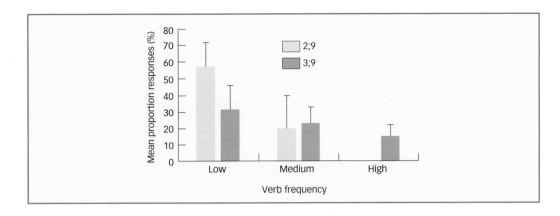

Mean proportion of responses copying the ungrammatical word order heard in younger children (mean age 2 years 9 months) and older children (mean age 3 years 9 months). From Matthews et al. (2005). Copyright © 2005 Elsevier. Reproduced with permission.

Did the children in their own speech copy the ungrammatical order they had heard or did they use the grammatically correct order? Both groups of children (especially the younger group) were more likely to copy the ungrammatical order with low-frequency verbs than with high-frequency ones (see the figure above). Thus, using the correct grammatical order in spite of having heard an incorrect grammatical order is a gradual process that is found initially mainly with very familiar verbs.

Evaluation

+ The notion that language acquisition depends on various cognitive processes and is facilitated by child-directed speech is plausible.

+ The finding that children gradually learn to use the appropriate word order (e.g., Matthews et al., 2005) is more in line with the constructivist approach than with the nativist one.

+ Children show relatively little productivity early in language acquisition (especially with verbs), as predicted by the constructivist approach.

+ Children acquiring English find verb learning more difficult than noun learning, as predicted by Tomasello's theory.

− More thorough longitudinal research is needed to show how cognitive processes influence language acquisition.

− We need more detail on the processes children use in proceeding from initial concrete linguistic structures to more general abstract schemas.

THEORY OF MIND

One of the crucial differences between most 5-year-olds and most 2- or 3-year-olds is that the former understand that other people's beliefs about the world may differ from their own. This is really important, because social communication is limited if a child assumes that everyone else has the same beliefs that he/she has. Research in this area revolves around the notion of **theory of mind**, which "conveys the idea of understanding social interaction by attributing beliefs, desires, intentions, and emotions to people" (Astington & Jenkins, 1999, p. 1311).

Theory of mind has been assessed by using various false-belief tasks. For example, Wimmer and Perner (1983) used models to present children with the following story. A boy called Maxi puts some chocolates in a blue cupboard. While he is out of the

Key Term

Theory of mind:
the understanding that other people may have different beliefs, emotions, and intentions than one's own.

Theory of mind

According to Premack (2007), *"When an infant sees an individual in distress, for example, a child who cries when her teddy bear breaks, the infant consoles her, pats her, speaks softly to her, and may even try to fix the teddy bear."* This illustrates theory of mind, i.e., being able to understand other people's feelings and beliefs. It is thought that this attribute is crucial for good social cognition, and research suggests that some other animals may have a degree of theory of mind. Obviously this would be advantageous to social animals, such as chimpanzees. Premack describes a laboratory experiment where young chimpanzees chose between two containers. Only one of the containers held a food reward. The apes could not see the reward being placed but they could see that a human was sometimes able to observe this. When allowed to seek help from the human three out of four chimps pointed to the person who had been able to observe the food being placed. This suggests that they did have the understanding that the human's perception was different from their own, that they do have a theory of mind.

Goodall's view is even stronger. In a 2004 UK BBC *Horizon* television program she said *"There's absolutely no question that chimpanzees understand the needs and the emotions of other chimpanzees and respond correctly. They can even understand the needs of another human being, so clearly they do have theory of mind."* Her view is supported by experiments at the Max Plank Institute involving subordinate and dominant chimpanzees. Normally a subordinate will not take food if a dominant is present. But if a subordinate chimp saw a banana being hidden out of the dominant chimp's view then the former would snatch it. This clearly implies that the subordinate chimp understood that the other chimp's perception and knowledge was different from its own.

---

room, his mother moves the chocolate to a green cupboard. The children indicated where Maxi would look for the chocolate when he returned to the room. Most 4-year-olds argued mistakenly that Maxi would look in the green cupboard. This indicates an absence of theory of mind, because these children simply assumed that Maxi's beliefs were the same as their own. In contrast, most 5-year-olds produced the right answer.

Similar findings have been reported in numerous other studies. Wellman, Cross, and Watson (2001) reported a meta-analysis based on 178 false-belief studies. In general, most 3-year-olds performed poorly on false-belief tasks, whereas a substantial majority of 5-year-olds were correct. The findings were similar in seven different countries (United States, United Kingdom, Korea, Australia, Canada, Austria, and Japan), except that a theory of mind developed slowest in Austria and Japan. Thus, evidence from several countries suggests that a theory of mind develops at about the age of 4.

Flynn (2006) studied the development of theory of mind in detail over a period of several months. She found that young children, most of whom were 3 years old at the start of the experiment, showed a gradual development in the understanding of false beliefs on theory-of-mind tests. For some time before the children were able to explain other people's behavior with reference to their false beliefs they were in a state of confusion in which they failed to provide any explanation.

How can we explain children's development of theory of mind? Various answers have been suggested, of which we will focus on two. Astington and Jenkins (1999) argued that language development is central to children's development of theory of mind. In contrast, Riggs, Peterson, Robinson, and Mitchell (1998) argued that what is crucial is the development of reasoning ability. For example, children given the Maxi problem have to imagine a state of affairs (i.e., chocolate in the blue cupboard) that would exist if his mother hadn't moved the chocolate to the green cupboard). This is known as counterfactual reasoning, and was assumed by Riggs et al. to be the key to theory of mind.

FINDINGS

While it is generally assumed that theory of mind typically develops around the age of 4, some aspects of theory of mind may develop earlier. For example, O'Neill (1996) carried out a study in which 2-year-old children watched an attractive toy being placed on a high shelf in the presence or absence of their parent. The children subsequently asked their parent to let them have the toy. Those children whose parent had been absent previously were much more likely to name the toy and to gesture towards it than were those whose parent had been present. Thus, even 2-year-olds may have some awareness of the knowledge possessed by others.

The role of language ability in theory of mind was examined by Lohmann, Carpenter, and Call (2005) on two false-belief tasks with 3- and 4-year-old children. Their key finding was that performance on both tasks was better among children with higher vocabulary and grammar scores. Astington and Jenkins (1999) carried out a longitudinal study on 3-year-olds to test the assumption that language development underlies improvement on false-belief tasks with age. The children were given various theory-of-mind tasks (e.g., false-belief tasks) and measures of language competence three times over a 7-month period. Language development at one point in time predicted later theory-of-mind performance. Similar findings were reported by Slade and Ruffman (2005) over a 6-month period. These findings suggest that language ability may play a causal role in the development of theory of mind.

According to Riggs et al. (1998), the ability to engage in counterfactual reasoning underlies successful performance on false-belief tasks. They tested their theory by presenting a story to 3- and 4-year-old children. In this story, Maxi and his mother put chocolate in a cupboard. While Maxi is out at school, his mother uses some of the chocolate to make a cake, putting the rest of it in the fridge. After that, Maxi comes home. The children were asked a standard false-belief question: "Where does Maxi think the chocolate is?" They were also asked a second question: "If mum had not made a cake, where would the chocolate be?" Answering this question correctly required counterfactual reasoning but not an understanding of false beliefs.

What did Riggs et al. (1998) discover? Children who were correct on the false-belief question were nearly always correct on the reasoning problem, and those incorrect on the false-belief question nearly always failed the reasoning problem. Thus, they concluded that deficient counterfactual reasoning is the main reason for failure on false-belief tasks. However, matters may be more complicated than that. Perner, Sprung, and Steinkogler (2004) found that 3½-year-olds achieved 75% correct performance in simple counterfactual reasoning but only achieved that level on false-belief questions 1½ years later. Thus, the ability to engage in counterfactual reasoning is clearly not sufficient to guarantee success on false-belief tasks.

Not everyone thinks that theory of mind depends on *general* abilities such as language or counterfactual reasoning. For example, Saxe, Carey, and Kanwisher (2004) carried out a meta-analysis of brain-imaging studies on false-belief tasks performed by adults. Theory-of-mind processing was associated with activation in parts of the medial prefrontal cortex and the temporo-parietal junction toward the back of the brain. These areas are *not* associated with general processes relating to language or attention. Theory-of-mind tasks may involve relatively *specific* processes (whose nature is poorly understood).

O'Neill's (1996) study, in which 2-year-olds gestured towards and named the toy that was placed in the room while their parents were absent, demonstrates a possession of at least some aspects of theory of mind in young children.

AUTISM

Autism is a serious condition characterized by very poor social interaction, impaired communication (e.g., reluctance to maintain a conversation), and repetitive patterns of behavior. According to various theorists (e.g., Baron-Cohen, Leslie, & Frith, 1985; Leslie, 1987), the central problem of autistic children is that they lack a theory of mind. More specifically, they don't understand that other people have different ideas and knowledge to their own, and they don't appreciate that behavior is influenced by beliefs and thoughts. As a result, autistic children can't make sense of the social world, and this prevents them from communicating effectively with other people.

> **Key Term**
>
> **Autism:**
> a severe disorder involving very poor communication skills, deficient social and language development, and repetitive behavior.

Baron-Cohen et al. (1985) studied healthy 4-year-old children as well as autistic and Down's syndrome children with a mental age of at least 4. All these children were given the following story (see the figure below):

Sally puts her marble in the basket. Then she goes out. Anne takes Sally's marble, and puts it into her box. Then Sally comes back from her walk. Where will she look for her marble?

The Sally–Anne test. C denotes the child observer, and E is the experimenter.

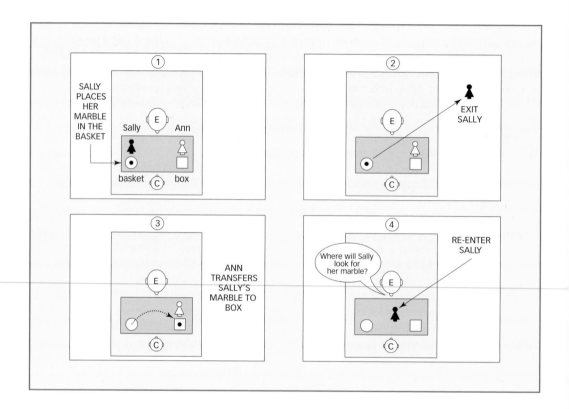

More than 80% of the healthy and Down's syndrome children correctly pointed to the basket, compared to only 20% of the autistic children. Thus, the autistic children didn't understand that other children may have a different perspective to their own.

Autistic children's poor performance on false-belief tasks may well reflect fairly *general* cognitive deficits. Performance on false-belief tasks depends on executive functions (e.g., Müller, Zelazo, & Imrisek, 2005). Executive functions include planning, shifting set, and inhibition of dominant responses, and there is evidence that autistic children are impaired with respect to these executive functions (see Hill and Frith, 2003, for a review). For example, Hughes and Russell (1993) used a task in which participants had to turn a knob or flick a switch to obtain a marble in a box, but could not obtain it by reaching into the box. Autistic children found it much harder than children with learning difficulties to inhibit the response of reaching immediately for the marble. Planning in autistic children has been studied by observing their performance on the Tower of Hanoi, in which disks have to be moved according to various rules to attain a specified goal state. It has been found consistently that autistic children show very poor planning on this task (Hill & Frith, 2003).

Case Study: *Autistic Talents*

Not all aspects of autism are as negative as might be imagined. Some autistic children have startling artistic abilities and can produce drawings in full detail and perspective much earlier than other children.

An autistic girl named Nadia was studied by Selfe (1983). When she was only 5 years old, Nadia could draw realistic pictures of horses, cockerels, and cavalrymen from memory, although she did not speak and had various severe motor problems.

Other talents shown by autistic children and adults include feats of mental arithmetic, for example being able to calculate the day of the week for any given date in the previous 500 years. There have also been gifted autistic musicians who learn to play musical instruments by ear, with no formal training.

These talents may all be linked in some way to the autistic child's narrow focus on the world, through which they can become preoccupied with certain objects or processes in great detail.

Kanner (1943) called gifts like these "islets of ability," which suggests that other aspects of autistic children's intelligence are hidden beneath the surface of a sea of difficulties.

Drawings by 5-year-old Nadia, who is autistic (left), and an average 6½-year-old child (right).

Overall Evaluation

+ The development of a theory of mind is of real importance in allowing children to communicate well with other people.

+ Some aspects of cognitive development (e.g., counterfactual reasoning; language) associated with the development of a theory of mind have been identified.

+ Autistic children's difficulties with false-belief tasks reflect at least in part problems with general executive functions.

− Deficiencies in executive functions are found in several clinical conditions (e.g., attention-deficit/hyperactivity disorder), and so autism must involve deficiencies over and above those in executive functions.

− False-belief tasks are complex and there is no consensus concerning the balance of general and specific processes underlying performing on such tasks when carried out by healthy individuals (Apperly, Samson, & Humphreys, 2005).

− There is probably no *single* theory of mind. What is more likely is that children acquire a progressively deeper understanding of others' beliefs over time.

− The theory-of-mind approach fails to account for all of the problems faced by autistic children. As Smith, Cowie, and Blades (2003, p. 481) pointed out, "It is not obvious how specific language problems . . . obsessive behaviors, or 'islets of ability' [in autistic children] could be linked to a lack of understanding minds."

Chapter Summary

Perceptual development

- Newborns have poor visual acuity, no color vision, and lack binocular disparity.
- Newborns make systematic eye movements, show elements of size constancy, and can relate visual and auditory information.
- It has been claimed that newborns have an innate bias for faces. However, it is more likely that they have a preference for stimuli with more patterning in their upper part.
- Infants of 6 months show some elements of depth perception by avoiding going over the edge of a "visual cliff." There is some evidence that learning with the visual cliff is specific to a given posture (e.g., sitting), and so new learning is needed when the infant starts crawling.
- Some theorists talk of the "competent infant" who possesses early perceptual competence accompanied by cognitive incompetence.

Memory development

- The capacity of the working memory system increases during childhood.
- Children make increased use of memory strategies (e.g., rehearsal; organization) as they grow older.
- Children gradually acquire metamemory or knowledge about their own memory.
- Children's memory performance improves as they acquire relevant content knowledge.
- Children's explicit memory (involving conscious recollection) improves much more than their implicit memory (not involving conscious recollection), because implicit memory depends much less on strategic processes and metamemory.
- Children's eyewitness testimony can be distorted by suggestibility. The main factors responsible are social compliance and cognitive incompetence.

Language development

- Children typically acquire knowledge of language in the following order: phonology; semantics; syntax; and pragmatics.
- Children start with single-word utterances and then move into the telegraphic period at 18 months.
- Inside-out theorists (e.g., Chomsky) argue that language acquisition depends heavily on innate factors (e.g., a language acquisition device).
- Inside-out theorists argue that linguistic universals are found in nearly every language, and that there is a critical period during which language learning is easiest.
- There is some evidence that children can create a grammar even if not exposed to a proper language during their early years as predicted by inside-out theories.
- The entire idea of an innate grammar is implausible and difficult to test.
- Outside-in theorists (e.g., Tomasello) emphasize the central role of exposure to language (especially child-directed speech) in allowing young children to acquire language.
- As predicted by outside-in theories, most language learning is gradual.
- As yet, little is known of the precise cognitive processes involved in language acquisition.

Theory of mind

- Most 5-year-olds have developed a theory of mind, meaning that they understand that other people may have beliefs, knowledge, and emotions different from their own.
- Factors underlying the development of theory of mind include language development and the development of reasoning ability (especially counterfactual reasoning).
- Autistic children lack a theory of mind and so can't make sense of the social world. Impaired executive functioning is one reason for their deficiencies in developing a theory of mind.
- Some of the problems of autistic children (e.g., specific language difficulties; obsessive behavior) aren't caused by a lack of theory of mind.

Further Reading

- Baddeley, A.D., Eysenck, M.W., & Anderson, M.C. (2009). *Memory.* Hove, UK: Psychology Press. The development of memory during childhood is discussed in this introductory textbook.
- Goswami, U. (Ed.). (2006). *Cognitive development: Critical concepts in psychology.* Hove, UK: Psychology Press. This edited book contains chapters by leading experts on the major areas within cognitive development.
- Harris, M., & Butterworth, G. (2002). *Developmental psychology: A student's handbook.* Hove, UK: Psychology Press. The development of language in the early years of life is covered in an accessible way in Chapters 7 and 8 of this textbook.
- Slater, A.M., & Bremner, J.G. (Eds.). (2003). *An introduction to developmental psychology.* Oxford, UK: Blackwell. Issues relating to cognitive development are discussed in separate sections on infancy, childhood, and adolescence in this edited book.
- Smith, P.K., Cowie, H., & Blades, M. (2003). *Understanding children's development* (4th ed.). Oxford: Blackwell. Several chapters in this textbook (e.g., Chapters 10 and 11) provide detailed coverage of important aspects of cognitive development.

Chapter 14

Contents

Theories of cognitive development

14

In the last chapter, we considered the dramatic changes in perception, memory, and language that occur during childhood. In this chapter, our focus shifts to more general theoretical approaches to cognitive development. The question of central importance in this area of research is the following: How can we describe (and explain) the enormous advances in thinking, reasoning, and problem solving shown by nearly all children during the years of childhood?

The first general systematic theory of cognitive development was proposed by Jean Piaget (1896–1980), and has been the most influential developmental theory of all time. Another important theoretical approach to cognitive development was put forward by the Russian psychologist, Lev Vygotsky (1896–1934). He was one of untold millions who suffered under Stalin, with his various writings being suppressed in Russia. As a consequence, few people knew of his work during his life, which ended prematurely because of tuberculosis. Vygotsky's work began to be translated into other languages in the 1960s and 1970s, and was then recognized as of major importance.

The pioneering approaches of Piaget and Vygotsky are discussed in this chapter. After that, we switch our attention to more contemporary approaches. It is generally accepted that the best way of understanding cognitive development is to identify the *learning* processes used by children. This approach has been followed in several theories in which the emphasis is on the processes and structures associated with information processing and learning. In this chapter, we focus on Robert Siegler's (1998, 2005) influential theory.

A key reason why it is important to study cognitive development is because of its potential relevance to education. If we can understand the processes involved in learning and cognitive development, we will be well placed to improve the educational system. The educational implications of the theories discussed in this chapter are considered in the final section.

PIAGET'S THEORY

Piaget's central focus was on cognitive development. More specifically, he was interested in how children learn and adapt to the world. In order for adaptation to occur, there must be constant interactions between the child and the world. According to Piaget, two processes are of key importance:

- **Accommodation:** The individual's cognitive organization is altered by the need to deal with the environment. Thus, the individual adjusts to the outside world.
- **Assimilation:** The individual deals with new environmental situations on the basis of his/her existing cognitive organization. Thus, the individual child's interpretation of the outside world is adjusted to fit him/her.

Key Terms

Accommodation:
in Piaget's theory, changes in an individual's cognitive organization to deal with the environment.

Assimilation:
in Piaget's theory, dealing with new environmental situations by using existing cognitive organizations.

The Swiss psychologist Jean Piaget, 1896–1980.

The clearest example of the dominance of assimilation over accommodation is play. In play, reality is interpreted according to the individual's whim (e.g., a stick becomes a gun). In contrast, dominance of accommodation is seen in imitation. In imitation, the child simply copies the actions of someone else.

There are two other key Piagetian concepts: schema and equilibration. **Schema** refers to organized knowledge used to guide action. The first schema infants develop is the body schema, when they realize there is an important distinction between "me" and "not me." This body schema helps the infant in its attempts to explore and make sense of the world.

Equilibration is based on the notion that the individual needs to keep a stable internal state (equilibrium) in a changing environment. When a child tries unsuccessfully to understand its experiences in terms of existing schemas, there is an unpleasant state of *disequilibrium* or lack of balance. The child then uses assimilation and accommodation to restore a state of equilibrium or balance. Thus, disequilibrium motivates the child to learn new skills and knowledge to return to the desired state of equilibrium.

We can identify two extreme positions with respect to the changes occurring during cognitive development. At one extreme, the amount of knowledge available to children increases considerably, but there are no dramatic changes in *how* they think. At the other extreme, the ways of thinking found in adolescence differ profoundly from those of early childhood. Piaget identified himself with the latter position, believing that there are fundamental differences in cognition among children of different ages.

Of key importance, Piaget argued that all children pass through several stages. We will briefly mention three of the main assumptions of his stage theory: First, there are large enough changes in the course of cognitive development to permit the identification of separate processing stages. Second, all children pass through the same *sequence* of stages in the same order (although at different rates). Third, the cognitive operations and structures defining each stage form an integrated whole.

What stages of cognitive development did Piaget identify? He argued that there are four major stages (see figure on the following page):

1. *The sensori-motor stage (birth to 2 years)*: This stage is basically intelligence in action, with the child's main focus on the impact of his/her behavior on the environment.
2. *The pre-operational stage (2–7 years)*: Thinking in this stage is dominated by perception.
3. *The concrete operations stage (7–11 years)*: Logical reasoning is only applied to objects that are real or can be seen.
4. *The formal operations stage (11 upwards)*: Logical reasoning is applied to potential events and abstract ideas as well as concrete objects.

An example of the dominance in play of assimilation over accommodation—pretending hairbrushes are microphones.

How did Piaget test his stage theory? He was rather skeptical about the value of the typical experimental approach based on strict use of the experimental method. Instead, Piaget preferred a less structured and formal approach. He used the **clinical method**, in which children are questioned informally to reveal the nature of their understanding of problems.

There is one other crucial point. Piaget focused very much on describing the strengths and limitations of

Key Terms

Schema:
in Piaget's theory, organized knowledge used to guide action.

Equilibration:
using the processes of accommodation and assimilation to produce a state of equilibrium or balance.

Clinical method:
an informal question-based approach used by Piaget to assess children's understanding of problems.

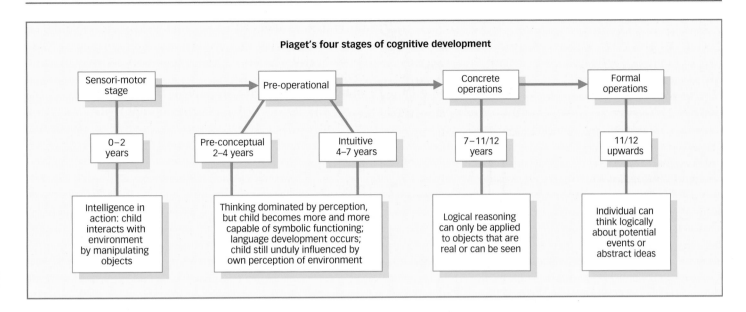

Piaget's four stages of cognitive development

Sensori-motor stage	Pre-operational		Concrete operations	Formal operations
0–2 years	Pre-conceptual 2–4 years	Intuitive 4–7 years	7–11/12 years	11/12 upwards
Intelligence in action: child interacts with environment by manipulating objects	Thinking dominated by perception, but child becomes more and more capable of symbolic functioning; language development occurs; child still unduly influenced by own perception of environment		Logical reasoning can only be applied to objects that are real or can be seen	Individual can think logically about potential events or abstract ideas

children's thinking at different developmental stages. However, he failed to explain precisely *why* and *how* children's thinking develops, and he attached remarkably little importance to the role of learning. Piaget's approach can be defended by arguing that we need to know *what* needs to be explained before trying to provide an adequate explanation.

FINDINGS

According to Piaget, the key achievement of the sensori-motor stage is **object permanence**. This involves the child being aware that objects continue to exist when no longer in view. Initially, the infant has no awareness at all of object permanence; it is literally a case of "out of sight, out of mind." Towards the end of the first year, however, the infant seems to show partial object permanence. What happens is that the experimenter hides an object at location A, which the infant then finds. After that, the same object is hidden at location B, but the infant mistakenly searches at location A. This finding (**perseverative search**) allegedly occurs because the infant doesn't regard objects as existing independently of his/her own behavior.

Piaget's assumption that infants show perseverative search because they don't remember where the object has been hidden is rejected by some researchers. In one study (Baillargeon & Graber, 1988), 8-month-old infants saw a toy being hidden behind one of two screens. Fifteen seconds later they saw a hand lift the toy out either from the place in which it had been hidden or from behind the other screen. The infants were only surprised when the toy was lifted from behind the "wrong" screen. This indicates that they *did* remember where it had been put (see figure on the following page).

Another major achievement of the sensori-motor stage is imitation, which allows the infant to add considerably to its range of actions. Towards the end of the sensori-motor stage, the infant shows evidence of **deferred imitation**, which is the ability to imitate behavior seen before. In a study by Hayne, Boniface, and Barr (2000), the experimenter demonstrated a

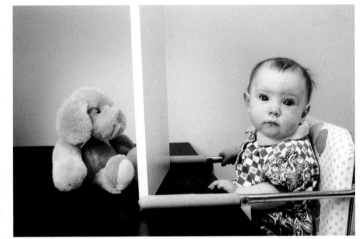

Object permanence is the term used to describe the awareness that objects continue to exist even when they are no longer visible.

Key Terms
Object permanence: an awareness that objects continue to exist when they can no longer be seen.
Perseverative search: mistakenly searching for an object in the place in which it was previously found rather than the place in which it is currently hidden.
Deferred imitation: in Piaget's theory, the ability to imitate behavior observed at an earlier time.

Baillargeon and Graber found that 8-month-old infants were surprised when a cup they had seen being put behind the left-hand screen was then retrieved from behind the right-hand screen.

novel action using an unfamiliar object, and infants then tried to reproduce that action after an interval of time. Infants aged 6, 12, and 18 months all showed deferred imitation when the same stimulus object was used for the demonstration and the subsequent test.

We turn now to the pre-operational stage. According to Piaget, pre-operational children are unduly influenced by their immediate perception of the environment. They pay attention to only one aspect of the total situation (this is called **centration** by Piaget), which can make them prone to error. For example, they don't show **conservation**, which is the understanding that certain aspects of a visual display don't vary in spite of changes in perceptual aspects.

The thinking of pre-operational children is also characterized by egocentrism. **Egocentrism** is the tendency

Key Study

Piaget: Conservation

In his classic studies on conservation of quantity, Piaget presented children with two glasses of the same size and shape containing the same quantity of liquid. When the child agrees there is the same quantity of liquid in both glasses, the liquid from one of them is poured into a glass that is taller and thinner. The child is then asked if the two glasses (the original one and the new one) contain the same amount to drink, or if one contains more. Pre-operational children fail to show conservation. They argue mistakenly either that there is more liquid in the new container ("because it's higher") or that there is more liquid in the original container ("because it's wider"). In either case, the child centers or focuses on only *one* dimension (height or width).

Piaget claimed that pre-operational children fail on conservation tasks partly because of centration. However, they also fail because they lack the cognitive operation of reversibility. **Reversibility** involves the ability to undo (or reverse mentally) some operation. Thus, reversibility allows the realization that the effect of pouring liquid from one container into another could be negated by simply pouring it back into its original container.

Discussion points
1. In what real-life situations might the ability to conserve be important?
2. What are the limitations of Piaget's research?

Key Terms

Centration:
attending to only one aspect of a situation.

Conservation:
the principle that quantities remain constant under various changes to their appearance.

Egocentrism:
the assumption that one's way of thinking is the only possibility.

Reversibility:
the ability to undo, or reverse mentally, an action or operation.

to assume that one's way of thinking about things is the only possible way. It often involves a lack of differentiation between the self and the world, so the child can't distinguish clearly between psychological and physical events. This produces:

- *Realism*: The tendency to regard psychological events as having a physical existence.
- *Animism*: The tendency to endow physical objects and events with psychological qualities.
- *Artificialism*: The tendency to consider that physical objects and events were created by people.

An example of artificialism concerns my elder daughter Fleur at the age of 3. We were on Wimbledon Common in London, and I told her the sun would come out when I had counted to 10. When it did so, she was very confident that Daddy could control the sun, and often begged me to make the sun appear on overcast days!

Children in the pre-operational stage often fail to show conservation. However, they possess more knowledge of conservation than seemed to be the case in Piaget's studies. For example, Wheldall and Poborca (1980) argued that children often fail on conservation tasks because they don't understand the question. Accordingly, they devised a nonverbal version of the liquid conservation task. Only 28% of their 6- and 7-year-old children showed conservation with the standard verbal version compared to 50% with the nonverbal version.

McGarrigle and Donaldson (1974) argued that children presented with a conservation task typically assume that the experimenter deliberately *intends* to change the amount of liquid or other substance. This assumption biases them against showing conservation. It follows that children would show more evidence of conservation if the change made on a conservation task appeared to be accidental. This prediction was supported by McGarrigle and Donaldson—see the Key Study below.

Key Study

McGarrigle and Donaldson (1974): The "naughty teddy"

McGarrigle and Donaldson showed that changing the way in which a conservation task is presented can make a large difference. They presented 6-year-old children with two rows of counters. All the children agreed there were equal numbers of counters in each row. In one condition, the experimenter deliberately messed up one of the rows. Number conservation was shown on 40% of the trials. This finding suggests that most of the children lacked the underlying competence necessary to show number conservation. However, the findings were rather different in a second condition, in which a "naughty teddy bear" messed up one of the rows in what looked like an accidental way. In this condition, number conservation was obtained on 70% of the trials.

Why did McGarrigle and Donaldson (1974) find such a large difference between the two conditions? The high level of performance in the "naughty teddy" conditions presumably occurred because most of the children had some understanding of number conservation. In the other condition, the fact that the experimenter deliberately altered the situation may have led the children to assume that the experimenter *intended* to change the number of counters in one of the rows. Whether or not that is correct, the fact remains that performance in that condition failed to reflect the underlying level of competence. However, it should be noted that Eames, Shorrocks, and Tomlinson (1990) failed to replicate McGarrigle and Donaldson's findings.

Discussion points

1. Why do you think that McGarrigle and Donaldson found such a large difference between their two conditions?
2. What problems for Piaget's theory arose from his failure to distinguish carefully between performance and competence (i.e., the child's potential)?

KEY STUDY EVALUATION

Recent research suggests that McGarrigle and Donaldson may have been mistaken. It is possible that the children were so absorbed in the "naughty teddy" routine that they didn't actually notice the transformation and that is why, with naughty teddy, they said the display hadn't changed. To test this possibility, Moore and Frye (1986) arranged for naughty teddy to actually add a counter (or take one away). Children said no change had taken place, which suggests that they were simply not attending to the display.

However, other evidence provides support for McGarrigle and Donaldson's (1974) findings. Light, Buckingham, and Robbins (1979) also found that the existence of number conservation in children depended very much on whether or not the changes introduced by the experimenter seemed deliberate. It is likely that the percentage of children showing conservation is influenced by a number of factors (e.g., whether the experimenter changes the situation deliberately; whether the children attend to the changes).

A drawing of the model used in Piaget's three mountains task. Children were shown the model from one angle, then shown photographs of the model from other viewpoints, and asked to choose which view someone standing at one of the other labeled points would see. Pre-operational children usually selected the view from the point at which they themselves had seen the model.

Piaget studied egocentrism in pre-operational children by using the three mountains task (see figure on the left). Children aged between 3½ and 5 looked at a model of mountains, and decided which out of various pictures showed the view that would be seen by someone looking at the display from a different angle. Children younger than 8 nearly always selected the photograph of the scene as they themselves saw it. According to Piaget, this error occurred because young children can't escape from an egocentric perspective.

Hughes (1975) argued that children performed poorly on the three mountains task because it doesn't relate to their experience. He tested this argument by using a piece of apparatus in which two walls intersected at right angles to form what looked like a plus sign. A boy doll and a policeman doll were put into the apparatus, and the child was asked whether the policeman doll could see the boy doll. After that, the child was told to hide the boy so the policeman couldn't see him. Nearly all the children could do this, and any errors were corrected. Finally, a second policeman was used, and the children were told to hide the boy doll so that neither of the policemen could see him. According to Piaget, the children should have hidden the boy doll so they themselves couldn't see it, and so should have failed the task.

What happened in Hughes' (1975) experiment? Ninety percent of the children performed the task successfully, which is a much higher figure than reported by Piaget with the three mountains task. The main reason for the difference is probably that the task used by Hughes was much more meaningful and interesting. However, the task was also simpler than the one used by Piaget.

When children move from the pre-operational to the concrete operational stage they show an increasing independence of thought from perception. Part of this change involves an understanding of conservation and of reversibility. It also involves the development of various cognitive operations of a logical or mathematical nature, including the actions implied by mathematical symbols (e.g., $+$, $-$, $\div$, $\times$, $>$, $<$, and $=$). These cognitive operations are usually combined or organized into a system or structure. For example, the operation "greater than" can't really be considered independently of the operation "less than." You have only grasped the full meaning of "A is greater than B" if you realize that statement means that "B is less than A." Piaget used the term **grouping** to refer to a set of logically related operations.

One of the tasks used to test conservation of number. Children are asked if there are the same number of beads in the two rows before and after they are rearranged.

We will consider two of the achievements that Piaget claimed were associated with the concrete operational stage. First, there is **transitivity**, which allows three or more elements to be placed in the correct order. For example, if Mark is taller than Peter, and Peter is taller than Robert, then it follows from the notion of transitivity that Mark must be taller than Robert. Piaget found that children in the concrete operational stage could solve such problems. However, Pears and Bryant (1990) found evidence of transitivity in 4-year-olds. The children were shown several small towers, each consisting of two colored bricks (e.g., a red brick on a yellow brick; a yellow brick on a green brick; and a green brick on a blue brick). They were told to construct a large tower in which the order of the bricks corresponded to that in the small towers. Thus, the large tower would have red at the top, followed in sequence by yellow, green, and blue. Before building the large tower, the children showed a reasonable ability to work out the correct order of the bricks, thus making transitive inferences several years earlier than assumed by Piaget.

Second, children in the concrete operational stage achieve various forms of conservation. As predicted by Piaget, more complex forms of conservation (e.g., conservation of volume) are achieved some years after easier forms of conservation (e.g., conservation of number; see the figure above right) (Tomlinson-Keasey et al., 1979). Why is conservation of volume only achieved at about the age of 11 or 12? According to Piaget, it involves taking account of the operations involved in the conservation of liquids *and* of mass. We can see this by considering how it is assessed. For example, two identical balls of clay are placed in two identical transparent containers filled to the same level (see figure on the right). One ball of clay is then molded into a new shape, with conservation being shown if the child realizes that this will not change the amount of water it displaces.

This apparatus tests conservation of volume. Children are asked if the liquids will be at the same level again when the new shape of clay is put back into the glass. Conservation of volume is not usually attained until about the age of 11 or 12.

Piaget de-emphasized the role of specific learning experiences and cultural factors in determining performance on conservation tasks. For example, Price-Williams, Gordon, and Ramirez (1969) found that the children of Mexican potters had slow development of conservation of volume using beakers, but fast development when a ball of clay was stretched into an oblong shape.

According to Piaget, children and adults in the formal operations stage have the ability to think in terms of many possible states of the world. This allows us to

Key Terms

Grouping:
in Piaget's theory, a set of logically related operations.

Transitivity:
this involves the ability to place at least three entities in the correct order.

Children were asked to work out what would affect the frequency of the swings of the pendulum. They were asked to consider changing the weights on the pendulum, the length of the string, how hard they pushed it, and which direction it was pushed in.

think in abstract terms and so escape from concrete reality. Piaget studied formal operational thought by presenting children with a set of weights and a string that could be lengthened or shortened. The task was to work out what determines the frequency of the swings of a pendulum formed by suspending a weight on a string from a pole (see figure on the left). *Only* the length of the string is important, but younger children often claim mistakenly that the strength of the push given to the pendulum is the main factor.

Piaget greatly overestimated the intellectual prowess of most adolescents. Bradmetz (1999) assessed formal operational thinking in 62 15-year-olds using various Piagetian tasks. Only *one* participant showed substantial evidence of formal operational thought. Bradmetz also found that overall performance on the tests of formal thought correlated +.61 with general intelligence. Thus, the cognitive abilities associated with formal thought resemble those assessed by traditional intelligence tests.

Evaluation

- Piaget's theory was a very ambitious attempt to describe children's cognitive development from being irrational and illogical to being rational and logical.

- The notions that children learn certain basic operations (e.g., reversibility), and that these operations then allow them to solve numerous problems, are valuable ones.

- Stage theories such as Piaget's *exaggerate* the differences between stages and *minimize* the differences within stages. For example, children in the concrete operations stage show conservation of quantity for familiar materials before they show it for unfamiliar materials (Durkin, 1995). Thus, successful performance depends on *specific* learning experiences as well as on *general* cognitive operations emphasized by Piaget.

- Piaget *underestimated* the cognitive abilities of young children, but *overestimated* those of adolescents and adults. However, as Lourenço and Machado (1996) pointed out, Piaget was interested in children's deep understanding of problems, and simply producing correct answers to problems at a young age doesn't necessarily require deep understanding.

- Piaget provided a detailed description of the major changes in cognitive development but didn't adequately explain the processes involved. In the words of Siegler and Munakata (1993), there appears to be a "miraculous transition" from one developmental stage to the next.

- Piaget de-emphasized the role of social factors in cognitive development. For example, children's cognitive development benefits from social interactions with adults and other children.

- Piaget virtually ignored individual differences. He admitted, "I'm not really interested in the individual. I'm interested in what is general in the development of intelligence and knowledge" (Bringuier, 1980, p. 86).

VYGOTSKY'S THEORY

Textbook writers typically argue that Vygotsky's approach to cognitive development was radically different from that of Piaget, and there are some major differences. However, we should not exaggerate the scale of these differences. Smith (1996) assembled 10 quotations from Vygotsky and 10 from Piaget, and asked various experts to decide who had written each one. On average, these experts performed at little better than chance level!

In some ways, the approaches of Piaget and Vygotsky complement each other. As Shayer (2003) pointed out, Piaget was mainly concerned with determining children's thinking abilities at different stages of cognitive development. In contrast, Vygotsky was more interested in the *dynamics* of change, namely, the factors responsible for cognitive development.

One of the difficulties in discussing Vygotsky's ideas is that he kept changing them. However, a constant feature of his approach (and a real difference from Piaget) was his emphasis on the importance of social factors in influencing cognitive development. According to Vygotsky (1930/1981, p. 163), "Social relations or relations among people genetically [developmentally] underlie all higher functions and their relationships." More specifically, Vygotsky (p. 163) argued as follows: "Any function in the child's cultural development appears twice, or on two planes. First, it appears on the social plane, and then on the psychological plane." Within this approach, the child is an apprentice who learns directly from social interaction and from communication with older children having knowledge he/she lacks (Durkin, 1995).

We can contrast Vygotsky's approach with that of Piaget, who argued that children acquire knowledge through self-discovery. However, there are some important similarities. Vygotsky and Piaget both agreed that activity forms the basis for learning and for the development of thinking. In addition, they both argued that learning is most effective when the information presented to children is closely related to their current knowledge and abilities.

Vygotsky argued that there are four stages in children's formation of concepts. He identified these four stages on the basis of a study (one of the very few he carried out) in which children were presented with wood blocks having labels consisting of nonsense syllables. Each nonsense syllable consistently referred to blocks having certain characteristics (e.g., circular and thin blocks). The children had the concept-formation task of working out the meaning of each nonsense syllable. Vygotsky's four stages were as follows:

1. *Vague syncretic stage*: Children fail to use systematic strategies and show little understanding of the concepts.
2. *Complex stage*: Nonrandom strategies are used, but are not successful in finding the main features of each concept.
3. *Potential concept stage*: Systematic strategies are used, but are limited to focusing on one feature at a time (e.g., shape).
4. *Mature concept stage*: Systematic strategies relating to more than one feature at a time are used, and lead to successful concept formation.

It is interesting that Vygotsky's findings resembled those of Piaget with very different tasks. Vygotsky found that children had problems with concept formation because they focused on only one salient or obvious feature of stimuli. This is very similar to Piaget's discovery that pre-operational children fail on conservation tasks because they attend to only one aspect of the situation.

ZONE OF PROXIMAL DEVELOPMENT

Vygotsky emphasized the notion of the **zone of proximal development**. This was defined by Vygotsky (1978, p. 86) as "the distance between the actual developmental level as determined by independent problem solving and the level of potential development as determined through problem solving under adult guidance or in collaboration with more capable peers." In other words, the zone of proximal development involves "problem solving that is beyond one's unassisted efforts but which can be achieved with assistance" (Granott, 2005, p. 141).

Two aspects of the zone of proximal development are of particular importance. First, children apparently lacking certain skills when tested on their own may perform more effectively in the social context provided by someone having the necessary knowledge. Second, when a given child's level of understanding is moderately challenged, he/she is most likely to acquire new knowledge rapidly and without a sense of failure. Vygotsky assumed that children differ in the size of the zone of proximal development. Those with

The Russian psychologist Lev Semeonovich Vygotsky, 1896–1934.

| Key Term

Zone of proximal development: in Vygotsky's theory, the gap between the child's current problem-solving ability and his/her potential ability.

Left to his own devices, could this boy make his sister a birthday cake? His mother uses scaffolding to create a situation within which he can begin to move into a zone of proximal development.

Case Study: *Weaving*

Evidence that the zone of proximal development and scaffolding are used effectively in cultures other than typical Western ones was reported by Greenfield and Lave (1982) in a study on the Zinacanteco Mexicans. Young girls who wanted to learn weaving skills started by spending almost half their time simply watching expert women weavers. After that, the girls were closely supervised by the skilled weavers as they acquired the necessary skills. The skilled weavers were generally successful at structuring the assistance they provided so that the girls remained within the zone of proximal development. Finally, the girls developed sufficient skills so that they could take responsibility for their own weaving.

larger zones of proximal development derive more benefit from instructions than those with smaller zones.

Wood, Bruner, and Ross (1976) extended the notion of a zone of proximal development. They introduced the concept of **scaffolding**. This refers to the context provided by knowledgeable people such as adults to help children to develop their cognitive skills. Effective scaffolding means the child doesn't need to climb too far at any point. Another important aspect of scaffolding is that there is a gradual withdrawal of support as the child's knowledge and confidence increase. Scaffolding and the zone of proximal development are closely related, but scaffolding focuses more on the strategies used by the adult and less on changes in the child.

Granott (2005) identified four major components of efficient scaffolding:

1. It is temporary and is dismantled when the child makes sufficient cognitive progress.
2. The person providing scaffolding increases his/her input if the child reduces its input, and decreases his/her input if the child increases its input.
3. The input of the person providing scaffolding is at a higher level than that of the child; this supports and stimulates the child.
4. Both partners should find their interactions on the task pleasant and rewarding.

LANGUAGE

Vygotsky attached great importance to the development of language through three stages. Language and thought are unrelated during the first stage of development. During the second stage, language and thought develop in parallel and continue to have very little impact on each other. During the third stage, children use the speech of others and talking to themselves to assist in their thinking and problem solving. By the age of 7, egocentric speech (i.e., speaking without heeding anyone else present) gives way to inner speech.

According to Vygotsky, language becomes increasingly central to cognitive development over the years. Berk (1994, p. 62) described some of the processes that Vygotsky had in mind: "When a child discusses a challenging task with a mentor [person providing guidance], that individual offers spoken directions and strategies. The child incorporates the language of those dialogs into his or her private speech and then uses it to guide independent efforts."

Vygotsky's views on the role of language in cognitive development were very different from those of Piaget. At the risk of oversimplification, Vygotsky argued that cognitive development depends crucially on language development and use. In contrast, Piaget argued that cognitive development typically precedes (and is little affected by) language development.

Findings

Moss (1992) reviewed studies on the scaffolding provided by mothers during the preschool period. There were three main aspects to the mothers' scaffolding strategies. First, the mother instructed her child in new skills the child couldn't use on its own. Second, the mother encouraged her child to maintain useful problem-solving tactics it had shown spontaneously. Third, the mother persuaded the child to discard immature and inappropriate forms of behavior. In general, scaffolding emerged as an effective technique for promoting learning in preschool children.

Conner, Knight, and Cross (1997) studied the effects of scaffolding on 2-year-olds performing various problem-solving and language tasks. Most previous studies had focused only on mothers' scaffolding, but Conner et al. also considered fathers'

Key Term

Scaffolding:
the context provided by an adult or other knowledgeable person helping children to develop their cognitive skills.

scaffolding. Mothers and fathers were equally good at scaffolding, and the quality of scaffolding predicted the children's performance on various tasks during the teaching sessions. The beneficial effects of good scaffolding were still evident at a follow-up session. Children who had originally received better scaffolding continued to perform better than those who had received poor scaffolding.

Vygotsky's notion that inner speech is of value in thinking has received support. Behrend, Harris, and Cartwright (1992) used whispering and observable lip movements as measures of inner speech. Children using the most inner speech performed difficult tasks better than children making little use of inner speech. Berk (1994) found that 6-year-olds spent 60% of the time talking to themselves while solving problems in mathematics. Those whose speech contained numerous comments about what needed to be done on the current problem did better at mathematics over the following year. This confirmed Vygotsky's view that self-guiding speech makes it easier for children to direct their actions.

Vygotsky argued that private speech becomes more internal as children's level of performance improves. Berk (1994) discussed a study in which 4- and 5-year-old children made Lego models in each of three sessions. As predicted by Vygotsky, the children's speech became increasingly internalized from session to session as their model-making performance improved. Thus, as Vygotsky assumed, private speech is of most value to children confronted by novel tasks they don't fully understand.

Vygotsky assumed that children do not produce egocentric or private audible speech after the age of 7. However, Girbau (2002) found evidence against that assumption in a study in which children of 8 and 10 played in pairs with a Lego construction set. Egocentric speech was found in both age groups, and was somewhat more frequent in the older group.

Evaluation

- Piaget underestimated the importance of the social environment in cognitive development, and Vygotsky deserves credit for recognizing its key role.

- Vygotsky's ideas have led to the introduction of several useful teaching techniques (e.g., scaffolding; see later in chapter).

- As Vygotsky predicted, inner speech helps the problem-solving activities of young children.

- Many of Vygotsky's ideas were rather speculative, and he carried out very little research.

- Vygotsky exaggerated the importance of the social environment. Children's rate of cognitive development is determined more by internal factors (e.g., level of motivation; interest in learning) than he believed.

- Vygotsky didn't specify clearly what kinds of social interaction are most beneficial for learning (e.g., general encouragement vs. specific instructions).

- Social interactions are not always beneficial to learning. As parents discover, interactions with their children can lead to confrontations and stubbornness rather than to enlightenment.

CONTEMPORARY APPROACHES

Piaget and Vygotsky discussed in detail the changes in thinking and behavior shown by children during development. However, there were serious limitations in their approaches. Piaget was surprisingly uninterested in the role played by learning in cognitive development, and devoted little effort to understanding how children move from stage to stage. Vygotsky was interested in the processes responsible for children's cognitive development, but carried out practically no research. These gaps in our knowledge have recently been addressed by several theorists, and we will shortly consider the contributions of one of them (Robert Siegler).

Before discussing Siegler's theory, we will consider the complex issue of how to study children's learning processes. Piaget and his followers tested children of different ages at a given point in time, an approach that didn't allow them to observe cognitive changes as they occurred. The obvious alternative is to use a longitudinal approach in which a given group of children is studied over a relatively long period of time. This is superior to Piaget's cross-sectional approach. However, it is hampered by the fact that major changes in children's development often take place over years rather than over weeks or months.

The **microgenetic method** has proved an especially valuable longitudinal approach. Use of this method involves carrying out short-term longitudinal studies in which intensive training is provided to accelerate changes in thinking (Miller & Coyle, 1999). The other key feature of the microgenetic method is that a substantial amount of data is obtained from each child in order to maximize the chances of understanding the learning process. The microgenetic method has a potential limitation: "Although [it] reveals how behavior *can* change, it is less clear whether behavior typically *does* change in this way in the natural environment" (Miller & Coyle, 1999, p. 212). This issue will be discussed in the context of Siegler's research, much of which involves use of the microgenetic method.

OVERLAPPING WAVES THEORY

Siegler (e.g., 1998, 2004, 2005) proposed an influential approach to cognitive development known as overlapping waves theory. According to this theory, children tackle most problems by using strategies that are goal-directed approaches varying from trial to trial. The key assumption is that children at any given time typically have various strategies or ways of thinking about a problem, and they exhibit considerable *variability* in strategy use (see the figure below). Common sense might suggest that any given child will adopt a particular strategy to solve problems of a given type. In contrast, it is assumed within overlapping waves theory that children often change their strategy from problem to problem.

How do children decide which strategy to use on a given problem? According to the theory, children choose adaptively among strategies, taking account of the speed and accuracy of problem solving with each strategy. Over time, there are several reasons why strategies change. First, children make increasingly adaptive choices among strategies based in part on the feedback they receive. Second, they execute each strategy more efficiently. Third, they make increasing use of the more advanced strategies among those at their disposal. Fourth, they acquire new strategies, sometimes by combining elements of pre-existing ones.

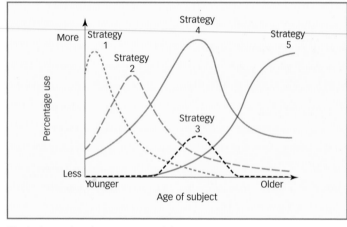

Siegler's overlapping waves model.

FINDINGS

Children are remarkably variable in their strategy use across a wide range of problems (see Siegler, 2004, for a review). This is so even when children are presented with the same problem on two occasions close in time. For example, Siegler and Shrager (1984) with preschoolers and Siegler and McGilly (1989) with older children found that about one-third changed strategies in such circumstances. Most of these changes in strategy were *not* a result of learning, because almost half of them involved a shift from a more advanced to a less advanced strategy.

One reason for children's variability of strategy use is that they often fail to use the optimal strategy after having discovered it. For example, Siegler and Stern (1998) gave 7-year-olds problems of the form $A + B - B = ?$ (e.g., $18 + 24 - 24 = ?$). The best strategy with such problems is simply to say the first number. The children took an average of only seven trials to discover this strategy, but they didn't use it consistently even 100 trials later. Part of the reason for this was that almost 90% of the children used the best strategy on one or more trials before being able to report verbally that they were using it.

It could be argued that variable strategy use is of relatively little interest because it merely reflects a lack of intellectual ability in children who often change strategies. That is *not* the case. Children who initially use several strategies with a given type of problem learn *faster* than those who initially use only one or two (see Siegler, 2005, for a review). Why is this? According to Siegler and Araya (2005), new strategies are often constructed from components of two existing strategies. This construction process is most likely to occur when both existing strategies have been used recently.

Detailed information about the processes involved in the adoption of a new strategy was reported by Siegler and Jenkins (1989). Children aged 4 and 5 were given addition problems (e.g., 3 +8). One of the most effective strategies used by young children with such problems is the count-on strategy. This involves starting with the larger number and counting on from that point. Thus, in our example, children would start with 8, and count 9, 10, 11.

Siegler and Jenkins (1989) gave children 30 sessions devoted to solving addition problems. None of the children used the count-on strategy initially, but nearly all of them discovered it during the course of the study. Most of the children took much longer than usual on the problem immediately before their first use of the strategy. This suggests they were thinking carefully about the best strategy to use.

As predicted by overlapping waves theory, the children often used other strategies after discovering the count-on strategy. However, they showed a much more consistent use of the count-on strategy after being presented with some challenging problems in the eighth week of the study. These problems (e.g., 26 +2 = ?) were easy to solve using the count-on strategy but very difficult to solve with other strategies (e.g., counting all the way from 1).

There was a final interesting finding from the study by Siegler and Jenkins (1989). Several children who used the count-on strategy had little conscious understanding of it. Indeed, some of them denied using the strategy at all in spite of very clear videotape evidence! Thus, implicit knowledge (knowledge without conscious awareness) can guide children's choice of strategy.

We return now to the issue of whether the rapid strategy changes found with use of the microgenetic method are basically similar to those shown by children in the natural environment. Relevant evidence was reported by Siegler and Svetina (2002). Children were given matrix problems in which they selected an object to complete a matrix or visual display. Changes in performance occurring naturally were assessed by giving matrix problems to children aged 6 and 7 and looking for differences between them. Other 6-year-olds were given systematic training in solving matrix problems using the microgenetic method. There were striking similarities between the patterns of change produced by the microgenetic method and by the natural environment. More specifically, there was matching on 10 out of 11 measures of change when the two conditions were compared.

Evaluation

+ It is very useful to study changes in children's strategies using short-term longitudinal studies involving intensive training.

+ The microgenetic method produces changes in cognitive strategies faster than happens in more naturalistic conditions, but the changes in both cases are similar (Siegler & Svetina, 2002).

+ Children often have several strategies available to them, and cognitive development depends in part on competition among these strategies.

− It remains relatively unclear how children discover new strategies.

− "The theory seems most applicable to domains in which children use clearly-defined strategies; its applicability to areas in which strategies are less well defined remains to be demonstrated" (Siegler, 1998, p. 97).

EDUCATIONAL IMPLICATIONS

The theoretical views of Piaget and Vygotsky have been very influential in education. We start by considering how their influence has been felt. After that, we discuss the Cognitive Acceleration through Science Education (CASE) program. This program represents an ambitious attempt to combine the insights of Piaget and Vygotsky to promote more effective teaching of science.

PIAGET'S APPROACH

Piaget himself didn't focus very much on the usefulness of his theory for educational practice. However, many of his ideas are of clear relevance to education, and many educationalists have applied them to teaching. According to Piaget, children learn best when engaged in a process of **self-discovery** involving initiative and an active approach. Teachers can foster self-discovery in their students by creating a state of disequilibrium in which the child's existing schemas or cognitive structures are shown to be inadequate. Disequilibrium can be produced by asking children difficult questions and encouraging them to ask questions.

Piaget's preferred approach can be contrasted with the traditional approach in which the teacher provides relatively passive children with knowledge. Piaget argued that this approach (**tutorial training**) is much less effective than self-discovery. In his own words, "Every time we teach a child something, we prevent him from discovering it on his own."

Brainerd (2003) reviewed the literature on self-discovery, and found it was generally less effective than tutorial training. He discussed five studies in which self-discovery of conservation concepts was compared to guided discovery, in which teachers directed students' attention to relevant features of the conservation task. Guided discovery was clearly more effective than self-discovery in all five studies.

Piaget argued that cognitive development depends very much on children acquiring a range of schemas or cognitive structures mostly based on mathematical or logical principles. It follows that it should be useful for children to study mathematics and logic as well as science subjects that provide illustrations of those principles at work. Of crucial importance is the notion that the learning material shouldn't be too complex or too far removed from the child's existing schemas.

The major weakness of Piaget's position is that the cognitive structures he emphasized are of limited relevance for many kinds of learning. For example, concrete and formal operations are of little assistance in the learning of foreign languages or history. Thus, Piaget's approach applies only to a small number of school subjects.

VYGOTSKY'S APPROACH

According to Vygotsky (1986, p. 188), "The only good kind of instruction is that which marches ahead of development and leads it; it must be aimed not so much at the ripe as the ripening functions." This can best be achieved when children's learning efforts are guided and encouraged by someone more knowledgeable. Thus, children can be regarded as apprentices who are taught the necessary skills by those already possessing them. This is known as scaffolding. As we saw earlier in the chapter, it can enhance children's learning. Effective teachers reduce their control over the learning process when children are performing successfully, and increase their control when children start making errors.

According to Vygotsky, those involved in teaching children should focus on the child's zone of proximal development. They should concentrate on knowledge only slightly beyond the child's current competence. It can be argued that the ideal tutors are children slightly older and more advanced than those being taught. Such tutors have useful knowledge to communicate but they still remember the limitations in their own knowledge and understanding when they were 1 or 2 years younger.

The approach described above is known as **peer tutoring**, and it is generally effective. For example, Ellis and Gauvain (1992) compared 7-year-old Navaho and Euro-American children performing a maze game. They were tutored by either one or two 9-year-old tutors working together. The children from both cultures benefited more from the paired tutors than from the individual tutors, and the benefit was the same in both cultures. Van Keer (2004) studied the effects of peer tutoring on the reading comprehension ability of

11-year-olds. Peer tutoring was effective when the tutor was a child who was older than the learner but not when the tutor was the same age as the learner. In the latter case, the knowledge of the peer tutor was insufficient to promote the learner's reading performance.

In spite of many examples of enhanced learning produced by scaffolding (including peer tutoring), these techniques have four main limitations. First, the learner may become uninvolved in the learning process if the tutor has too much status. Second, scaffolding seems better suited to some kinds of tasks (e.g., construction tasks) than to others. For example, Howe, Tolmie, and Rodgers (1992) found that peer tutoring was of very little benefit on a task concerned with understanding motion down an incline. Third, the main focus of scaffolding is on the contribution made by the tutor to the child's understanding. In fact, however, the success (or otherwise) of scaffolding often depends crucially on the responsiveness of the tutor to the child's thoughts and actions. Fourth, scaffolding can be hard to control and to analyze because it involves complex interactions between tutor and child (Granott, 2005).

Peer tutoring: two brothers teach their younger sister to read.

CASE PROGRAM

At a superficial level, it may appear that the approach to education based on Vygotsky's ideas is radically different from that of Piaget. As DeVries (2000) pointed out, Vygotsky seemed to emphasize factors *external* to the child (e.g., tutors; teachers) in promoting learning. In contrast, Piaget emphasized *internal* factors (e.g., adaptation), with the child in charge of the learning process. In fact, however, Vygotsky and Piaget were both fully aware of the importance of both external and internal factors. For example, Vygotsky's notion that tutors should teach within the zone of proximal development is a clear recognition of the importance of internal factors within the child.

Some of Piaget's and Vygotsky's ideas have been incorporated into the Cognitive Acceleration through Science Education (CASE) program (see Shayer, 1999, for a review). This program was originally used about 25 years ago in secondary schools in the UK and has since been developed and extended. The CASE program has five main features, and a typical lesson involves working through them in the order listed:

1. *Concrete preparation*: This involves the teacher setting the scene for what is to come. He/she ensures that the students understand the scientific terms that will be used and know how to use any equipment that will be needed.
2. *Cognitive conflict*: This is created by exposing students to unexpected ideas or findings that don't fit their preconceptions and that can't easily be understood on the basis of their current ways of thinking.
3. *Construction*: This involves resolving the cognitive conflicts that have been created by means of discussions involving either small groups or the entire class.
4. *Metacognition*: This involves asking students open-ended questions requiring them to explain their thinking and focus on tricky issues. One student argued that this motivated students to have something worth saying, "Otherwise you'd feel a right prat" (Shayer, 2003, p. 482).
5. *Bridging*: This involves relating students' new understanding to other aspects of science and their everyday experience. For this to be successful, teachers must have identified good examples to produce the required bridging.

How does the CASE approach use Piaget's and Vygotsky's ideas? First, the teacher's use of his/her greater knowledge than the students to provide information during the concrete preparation and bridging phases is in line with Vygotsky's thinking. Second, the use of cognitive conflict resembles Piaget's emphasis on the importance of disequilibrium. Third, the phase of metacognition requires students to engage in a process resembling

Piaget's self-discovery. Fourth, the construction phase resembles in some ways the peer tutoring approach based on Vygotsky's ideas.

How successful has the CASE program been? In general, the findings have been very impressive (Shayer, 1999). Students from numerous schools who have taken part in the CASE program have performed much better than other students on the nationwide General Certificate of Secondary Education (GCSE) examinations taken by 16-year-olds in the UK. This is true for students of very varying levels of ability. It is also true across science, mathematics, and English. For example, consider the 1997 GCSE results. On the basis of past performance, the percentages of CASE students predicted to obtain C grades or better were as follows: 19% in science, 18% in mathematics, and 26% in English. The actual percentages were 48% (science), 44% (mathematics), and 49% (English).

Evaluation

+ The CASE program represents an important combination of some of the main ideas of Piaget and Vygotsky to provide an approach taking full account of external (teacher-related) and internal (child-related) factors.

+ The CASE program has proved successful across a wide range of ability and has led to substantial increases in academic performance. It has even led to increases in general intelligence (Shayer, 1999). Its success has led to the development of other programs such as Cognitive Acceleration through Mathematics (CAME) and Cognitive Acceleration through Technology Education (CATE).

− The CASE program incorporates five main features, and it is hard to assess the relative contributions of each feature to its overall success.

− The complexity of the CASE program means that teachers require fairly lengthy and detailed training to use it successfully.

Chapter Summary

Piaget's theory
- According to Piaget, children proceed in turn through the sensori-motor, pre-operational, concrete operations, and formal operations stages.
- Two of the main achievements of the sensori-motor stage are object permanence and deferred imitation.
- Pre-operational children fail to exhibit conservation because they focus on only one aspect of a situation at a time and they lack the cognitive operation of reversibility. Their thinking is characterized by egocentrism.
- Children in the concrete operations stage show an increasing independence of thought from perception. They acquire various cognitive operations of a logical or mathematical nature, and show evidence of conservation and transitivity.
- Children in the formal operations stage can think in abstract terms and can contemplate hypothetical states of affairs.
- Piaget underestimated the cognitive abilities of young children but overestimated those of adolescents and adults. His approach is descriptive rather than explanatory.

Vygotsky's theory
- According to Vygotsky, the child is like an apprentice who learns directly from social interaction with those who are more knowledgeable.
- Vygotsky argued that children have a zone of proximal development extending beyond their current level of achievement.
- According to Vygotsky, language and thought are independent of each other in young children but language (e.g., inner speech) becomes increasingly central to cognitive development over the years.

- Studies on scaffolding show the importance of the zone of proximal development.
- It has been found that inner speech is of value in effective thinking in children.
- Vygotsky exaggerated the importance of the child's social environment in cognitive development.

Contemporary approaches
- Advances in cognitive development can be studied effectively by the microgenetic method in which intensive training is provided over a relatively short period of time.
- According to Siegler's overlapping waves theory, children typically exhibit considerable variability in the strategies they use to tackle any given type of problem.
- Using several different strategies facilitates the construction of new strategies based on combining elements of existing strategies.
- The rapid strategy changes produced by use of the microgenetic method closely resemble those occurring in a natural environment.
- Overlapping waves theory is mainly applicable to tasks on which most children use well-defined strategies.

Educational implications
- According to Piaget, children learn best from self-discovery that can be fostered by creating disequilibrium. It is also important for children to acquire a range of schemas or cognitive structures.
- Many of the cognitive structures emphasized by Piaget are based on mathematical or logical principles and are of little relevance to several school subjects.
- Vygotsky's emphasis on the child as an apprentice led to the development of scaffolding (e.g., peer tutoring). Scaffolding has proved effective, but its success depends very much on the relationship between tutor and child.
- The CASE program combines some of Piaget's and Vygotsky's best ideas to provide a very successful approach to teaching consisting of five main features. The complexity of the CASE program makes it difficult to identify the relative contribution of each of its features to its success.

Further Reading

- Feldman, D.H. (2004). Piaget's stages: The unfinished symphony of cognitive development. *New Ideas in Psychology*, *22*, 175–231. Feldman updates Piaget's views in light of our current understanding of cognitive development.
- Granott, N. (2005). Scaffolding dynamically toward change: Previous and new perspectives. *New Ideas in Psychology*, *23*, 140–151. Nira Granott provides a thorough analysis of scaffolding and discusses its relevance to Vygotsky's theories.
- Harris, M., & Butterworth, G. (2002). *Developmental psychology: A student's handbook*. Hove, UK: Psychology Press. This book provides good coverage of Piaget's and Vygotsky's theoretical approaches to cognitive development.
- Shayer, M. (1999). Cognitive acceleration through science education II: Its effects and scope. *International Journal of Science Education*, *21*, 883–902. The nature of the CASE program and its effects on academic achievement are discussed in this article by a central figure in that program.
- Shayer, M. (2003). Not just Piaget; not just Vygotsky, and certainly not Vygotsky as *alternative* to Piaget. *Learning and Instruction*, *13*, 465–485. This article contains an interesting comparison of the views of Piaget and Vygotsky.
- Siegler, R.S. (2005). Children's learning. *American Psychologist*, *60*, 769–778. Siegler gives a useful overview of his theory and of the research relevant to it.
- Smith, P.K., Cowie, H., & Blades, M. (2003). *Understanding children's development* (4th ed.). *Oxford*, UK: Blackwell. Chapters 12, 13, and 15 provide detailed introductory coverage of the main theories of cognitive development.

Chapter 15

Contents

Social development in everyday life

15

As children grow up, they have a large increase in their social involvement with other children, and a clearer sense of their place in society. Several kinds of learning underlie children's development of social behavior. For example, they acquire knowledge about themselves and about society's expectations concerning the appropriate behavior of boys and girls. The first part of the chapter deals with the issue of gender development. The second part is concerned with how children learn to control their own behavior so they can function successfully in social situations. For example, children learn to engage in prosocial or helping behavior, and they also discover that antisocial or aggressive behavior is generally counterproductive. Finally, there is moral development. If children are to fit into society, they have to learn to distinguish between right and wrong.

GENDER DEVELOPMENT

When a baby is born, everyone immediately asks, "Is it a boy or a girl?" As the baby develops, its treatment by its parents and other people is much influenced by its sex. In addition, the growing child's thoughts about itself and its place in the world increasingly depend on whether it is male or female. Most children by the age of 2 identify themselves and others accurately as male or female, and infants of 9–12 months respond differently to photographs of male and female strangers (Brooks-Gunn & Lewis, 1981). From the age of 3 or 4, children have fixed stereotypes about the activities (e.g., mowing the lawn; housekeeping) and jobs (e.g., doctor; nurse) appropriate for males and females. These are known as **sex-role stereotypes**.

The literature on sex-role developments contains a bewildering variety of terms. In general, "sex" refers to biological and anatomical differences, whereas "gender" refers to socially determined aspects of thinking and behavior. In practice, however, this sharp distinction is often blurred. Other terms in common use are gender identity and sex-role behavior. **Gender identity** refers to a child's or adult's awareness of being male or female. **Sex-typed behavior** is behavior consistent with the prevailing sex-role stereotypes.

Egan and Perry (2001) pointed out that there is more to gender identity than simply being aware one is male or female. It also involves feeling one is a typical member of one's sex, feeling content with one's own biologically determined sex, and experiencing pressure from parents and peers to conform to sex-role stereotypes. Egan and Perry assessed these various aspects of gender identity in boys and girls between the ages of 10 and 14. Boys on average had much higher scores than girls on feeling oneself to be typical of one's sex, on feeling content with one's biological sex, and on experiencing pressure from others to conform with sex-role stereotypes. Thus, it is regarded as more important by individual children and by society at large (at least in Western cultures) for boys to conform to stereotypical views of male behavior than for girls to conform to stereotypical views of female behavior.

355

Studying and gender

A UK government survey has found that in 2005 boys were falling further behind girls in terms of exam achievement. For example, in English schools, at Key Stage 2 level 4+ was achieved by 67% of boys and 71% of girls. By Key Stage 3 the gap widened and level 5+ was reached by 58% of boys and 64% of girls. High school GCSE exam results showed an even wider gap, with 52.2% of boys and 62.1% of girls gaining five or more GCSEs at grades A*–C. The gap varies depending on the subject, but was greatest for English with a 16% difference between boys and girls reaching grade C or above.

A specific example is Merseyside in North West England, where at GCSE in 2007 8% more girls than boys achieved five or more grades A*–C.

http://findoutmore.dfes.gov.uk/2006/07/gender_and_achi.html

OBSERVED SEX DIFFERENCES

Some ideas about sex-typed behavior are (thankfully!) in steep decline. Few people accept that men should go out to work and have little to do with looking after the home and the children, whereas women should stay at home and look after the children. However, many stereotypes still exist, and it is important to consider the actual behavior of boys and girls.

Most observed sex differences in behavior are fairly small. However, Golombok and Hines (2002) identified a few sex differences present in the first 2 years of life. Girl infants stay closer to adults than do boy infants, but boys are more upset by situations outside their control than are girls. In addition, girls on average learn to talk at an earlier age than boys. Shaffer (1993) pointed out that girls show more emotional sensitivity than boys. For example, girls from the age of 5 are more interested than boys in babies, and respond more attentively to them. Girls also have less developmental vulnerability than boys, with more boys showing mental retardation, language disorders, and hyperactivity.

In the United Kingdom, girls are outperforming boys in nearly all school subjects. Consider, for example, performance in the 2005 GCSE examinations (typically taken by UK students at the age of 16). The top grade of A* was achieved by girls on 13.1% of their courses compared to only 7.1% by boys. The comparable figures for the next grade (A) were 21.2% (girls) and 15.5% (boys). The precise reasons for this difference are unknown. However, more boys than girls regard studying as "uncool."

Berk (2006) provided a list of gender differences in mental abilities and personality including some of the differences discussed already. Boys have slightly better spatial and mathematical abilities, they have a higher activity level, and they experience more developmental problems. Girls have slightly higher verbal abilities and school achievement. They also exhibit more emotional sensitivity (e.g., kindness; considerateness), more fear and anxiety, tend to be more compliant, and suffer more from depression. Note, however, that nearly all these gender differences are small.

Else-Quest et al. (2006) carried out a meta-analysis to assess gender differences in children's temperament. Girls scored higher than boys on the factor of effortful control, especially its dimensions of perceptual sensitivity and inhibitory control. Boys scored higher than girls on surgency (similar to extraversion), especially its dimensions of activity and high-intensity pleasure.

There are fewer (and smaller) differences between the sexes than is generally assumed. Why is there this gap between appearance and reality? One reason is that we sometimes misinterpret the evidence of our senses to fit our stereotypes. Condry and Condry (1976) asked college students to watch a videotape of an infant. How the infant's behavior was interpreted depended on whether it was called David or Dana. The infant was perceived as being "angry" in its reaction to a jack-in-the-box if it had been called David but "anxious" if it had been called Dana. Stern and Karraker (1989) reviewed 23 studies resembling the one by Condry and Condry. Overall, knowledge of an infant's gender reliably influenced young children's behavior, but adults' behavior was much less consistently affected by such knowledge.

SOCIAL LEARNING THEORY

According to social learning theory (Bandura, 1977; see Chapter 7), gender development occurs as a result of the child's experiences. Children learn to behave in ways that are rewarded and to avoid behaving in ways that are punished. Since society has expectations about the ways in which boys and girls should behave, the operation of socially delivered rewards and punishments produces sex-typed behavior. For example, parents encourage girls rather than boys to play with dolls, with the opposite being the case when it comes to playing with guns.

Bandura (1977) also argued that children learn sex-typed behavior by observing the actions of various models of the same sex (e.g., parents; other children; teachers). This is observational learning (discussed more fully in Chapter 7), and it leads children to copy or imitate others' behavior. Much observational learning occurs when children watch television or films. Signorielli (2001) found fewer gender stereotypes on television over the years. For example, female characters are now more likely to have careers than was the case 20 years ago. However, women on television are still typically portrayed as emotional and caring, whereas men are dominant and powerful. Children are also exposed to gender stereotypes in other ways. For example, gender stereotypes are very strong in most video games (Calvert et al., 2003).

Bussey and Bandura (1999) expanded social learning theory in their social cognitive theory. They identified three forms of learning promoting gender development:

Fathers may play a major role in the development of sex-typed behavior in their sons.

1. Observational learning or modeling, in which the child chooses to imitate those aspects of others' behavior that he/she believes will increase feelings of mastery.
2. Direct tuition, in which other people teach the child about gender identity and sex-typed behavior.
3. Enactive experience, in which the child learns about sex-typed behavior by discovering the outcomes (positive or negative) resulting from their actions.

Findings
Observational learning was studied by Perry and Bussey (1979). Children of 8 or 9 watched male and female adult models choose between sex-neutral activities (e.g., selecting an apple or a pear). Afterwards, the children generally made the same choices as the same-sex model. This finding suggests that observational learning may play an important role in gender development. However, Barkley et al. (1977) reviewed the literature, and found children showed a bias in favor of the same-sex model in only 18 out of 81 studies.

Many studies have considered the effects of direct tuition on gender development. Fagot and Leinbach (1989) found that parents encouraged sex-typed behavior and discouraged sex-inappropriate behavior in their children before the age of 2. For example, girls were rewarded for playing with dolls and discouraged from climbing trees. Those parents making most use of direct tuition had children who behaved in the most sex-typed way. However, Golombok and Hines (2002) found in a review that there is only a modest tendency for parents to encourage sex-appropriate activities and discourage sex-inappropriate ones. This tendency may occur because parents want to encourage certain forms of behavior and discourage others. However, another possibility is that parents are responding to different pre-existing preferences in boys and girls. The review found that boys and girls receive equal parental warmth, encouragement of achievement, discipline, and amount of interaction.

Evaluation

+ The social learning approach emphasizes the social context in which the development of gender takes place.

+ As social learning theorists claim, some sex-typed behavior occurs because it has been rewarded. In addition, sex-inappropriate behavior is avoided because it is discouraged or punished.

+ Observational learning probably plays a part in the development of sex-role behavior.

Parents may try to discourage what they see as sex-inappropriate behavior. This little girl is helped out of the tree, while her brother is permitted to continue climbing.

Social learning theorists assume that learning processes are very similar at all ages. However, this assumption is wrong. For example, consider young children and adolescents watching a film in which a man and a woman are eating a meal together. Young children's observational learning might involve focusing on the eating behavior of the same-sexed person, whereas adolescents might focus on his/her social behavior.

 Social learning theorists focus mainly on children's learning of *specific* forms of behavior. However, children also engage in *general* learning (e.g., acquiring organized beliefs about differences between the sexes).

GENDER SCHEMA THEORY

Martin and Halverson (e.g., 1987) put forward a cognitive approach to gender development known as gender schema theory. According to this theory, children as young as 2 or 3 who have acquired basic gender identity form **gender schemas**. These schemas consist of organized beliefs about each gender, and they influence what children attend to. These schemas also play a part in how children interpret the world. According to Shaffer (1993, p. 513), "Gender schemas 'structure' experience by providing an organization for processing social information."

The first schema formed is an ingroup/outgroup schema. It consists of organized information about which toys and activities are suitable for boys and which are suitable for girls. Another early schema is an own-sex schema. This contains information about how to behave in gender-typed ways (e.g., how to dress dolls for a girl).

Martin, Wood, and Little (1990) argued that the development of gender schemas goes through three stages:

> **Key Term**
>
> **Gender schemas:**
> organized beliefs about
> suitable activities and
> behavior for each gender.

1. Children learn specific things associated with each gender (e.g., boys play with guns; girls play with dolls).

2. Children from about the age of 4 or 5 start to link together the different kinds of information they possess about their own gender (e.g., children who like to play with dolls also wear dresses) to form more complex gender schemas. This is only done with respect to their own gender.

3. Children from the age of 8 form complex gender schemas of the opposite sex as well as their own.

Findings

According to the theory, gender schemas are used by children to organize and make sense of their experiences. If they are exposed to information not fitting one of their schemas (e.g., a boy combing the hair of a doll), then the information should often be distorted to fit the schema. Martin and Halverson (1983) tested this prediction. They showed 5- and 6-year-old children pictures of schema-consistent activities (e.g., a girl playing with a doll) and of schema-inconsistent activities (e.g., a girl playing with a toy gun). Schema-inconsistent activities were often misremembered 1 week later as schema-consistent (e.g., a boy playing with a toy gun).

Bradbard et al. (1986) presented boys and girls between the ages of 4 and 9 with gender-neutral objects such as burglar alarms and pizza cutters. Some objects were described as "boy" objects whereas others were described as "girl" objects. There were two key findings. First, children spent much more time playing with objects they

Schema-consistent activities

Schema-inconsistent activities

had been told were appropriate to their gender. Second, even a week later the children remembered whether any given object was a "boy" or a "girl" object. Martin, Eisenbud, and Rose (1995) also found that children prefer toys that are labeled for their own gender. In addition, the children predicted that same-sex peers would also prefer the same toys. Finally, initially very attractive toys were the ones most likely to lose their appeal when labeled as appropriate for the other gender.

Martin et al. (1990) provided evidence that children's gender schemas develop through the three stages they identified (discussed earlier). They described someone of unspecified sex who had a given sex-linked characteristic (e.g., worked as a nurse), and asked the children to predict other characteristics that person was likely to possess. Younger children found this task difficult because they hadn't reached stage 2 in the development of gender schemas. Older children performed better when the gender-linked characteristic was appropriate to their own gender because they were more likely to have reached stage 3.

According to the theory, gender schemas influence children's behavior. Thus, the amount of sex-typed behavior displayed by a child at a given time should depend on the gender-related knowledge he/she has acquired previously. This prediction was tested by Campbell, Shirley, and Candy (2004) in a longitudinal study in which children were tested at 24 and 36 months. Knowledge and gender schemas and sex-typed behavior both increased over the 12-month period, but there was no evidence that the extent of sex-typed behavior depended on the amount of previously acquired gender-related knowledge. These findings mean that it is unclear whether gender knowledge *causes* subsequent sex-typed behavior.

Evaluation

- Gender schemas exist and influence children's behavior.
- The assumption that children are actively involved in making sense of the world in light of their schema-based knowledge is plausible.
- The theory de-emphasizes the role of social factors in gender development.
- The association between possession of a gender schema and behavior is not very strong. As Bussey and Bandura (1999, p. 679) pointed out, "Children do not categorize themselves as 'I am a girl' or 'I am a boy' and act in accordance with that schema across situations and activity domains." Campbell et al.'s (2004) findings cast some doubt on the notion that gender schemas causally influence subsequent sex-typed behavior.
- The theory doesn't really explain *why* gender schemas develop and take the form they do.

PROSOCIAL BEHAVIOR

Some children and adults are very helpful and cooperative, whereas others are aggressive and unpleasant. The terms "prosocial behavior" and "antisocial behavior" are used to describe these very different ways of treating people. Prosocial behavior can be defined as "any voluntary, intentional action that produces a positive or beneficial outcome for the recipient regardless of whether that action is costly to the donor, neutral in its impact, or beneficial" (Grusec, Davidov, & Lundell, 2002, p. 2). Prosocial behavior is more general than altruism, which is voluntary helping behavior that benefits someone else but provides no obvious self-gain to the person who behaves altruistically. It is often assumed that altruism depends on empathy, which is the ability to share the emotions of another person in order to understand his/her needs. In contrast, antisocial behavior (discussed in the next section) is behavior that harms or injures someone else. There is a full discussion of prosocial behavior in adults in Chapter 18.

Even quite small children can show concern when they see others are unhappy.

How common is prosocial behavior in children? Eisenberg-Berg and Hand (1979) studied 4- and 5-year-olds in preschool classes, recording evidence of prosocial behavior (e.g., sharing; comforting). On average, each child exhibited such behavior five or six times per hour.

GENDER DIFFERENCES

It is assumed in most Western cultures that girls are more empathic and show more prosocial behavior than boys. There is some support for that assumption. Olweus and Endresen (1998) asked adolescent boys and girls to read a description of a distressed fellow student. Older adolescent girls showed greater empathic concern than younger adolescent girls regardless of whether the distressed student was male or female. Boys showed the same developmental pattern as girls when the description referred to a girl. However, older adolescent boys showed *less* empathic concern for a distressed boy than did younger adolescent boys. This is presumably because being concerned about another boy was perceived as being in conflict with their masculine identity.

Grusec et al. (2002) reviewed the evidence on gender differences in prosocial behavior. Girls typically show more prosocial behavior than boys. However, gender differences in prosocial behavior are generally smaller when such behavior is assessed by direct observation than when assessed by self-report measures. In addition, gender differences in prosocial behavior are smaller when the behavior involves sharing or helping than when it involves showing consideration or kindness.

We would expect children to exhibit more prosocial behavior in collectivistic cultures in which the emphasis is on group wellbeing than in Western individualistic cultures in which the emphasis is on individuals' own welfare (see Chapter 1). Evidence consistent with that expectation was reported by Whiting and Whiting (1975). They studied the behavior of young children between the ages of 3 and 10 in six cultures (United States, India, Okinawa – an island in South West Japan, Philippines, Mexico, and Kenya). There were substantial differences in altruistic behavior across these cultures (see figure below). The least altruistic behavior was shown in the United States, which is a very individualistic culture.

Findings such as those of Whiting and Whiting (1975) have led many experts to conclude that members of non-industrialized and collectivistic cultures are more altruistic than those of industrialized and individualistic cultures. However, this may well not be altogether correct. Fijneman, Willemsen, and Poortinga (1996) found that people living in collectivistic cultures expect more help from others than do those living in individualistic cultures. Thus, their motives in helping may be based on what they expect in return rather than on being altruistic. Collectivistic and individualistic cultures are similar in that individuals expect to give only a little more help than they receive in return. Thus, there is a norm of reciprocity or mutual exchange in both types of cultures, and they may differ little in their level of altruism.

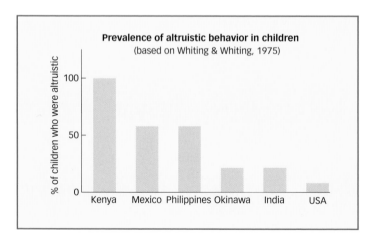

Prevalence of altruistic behavior in children
(based on Whiting & Whiting, 1975)

EMPATHY

According to Hoffman (1987), there are four main stages in the development of empathy:

- *Stage 1: Global empathy.* This stage starts during the first year of life, before the infant can distinguish between self and other. The infant will sometimes start crying when another infant cries, but this is an involuntary reaction rather than genuine empathy.
- *Stage 2: "Egocentric" empathy.* This stage starts in the second year of life. The developing sense of self allows the child to realize it is someone else rather than the

child itself who is in distress. However, the child still can't distinguish clearly between someone else's emotional state and its own.

- *Stage 3: Empathy for another's feelings.* This stage starts at about 2 or 3. It involves genuine empathy based on a clear awareness of (and empathy for) the various emotions others experience.
- *Stage 4: Empathy for another's life condition.* This stage starts in late childhood. Children in this stage are aware that other people have separate identities and life experiences. This permits them to understand how others are likely to be feeling even when it is not clear from their behavior.

Findings

Zahn-Waxler, Robinson, and Emde (1992) obtained evidence of empathic concern in children of between 13 and 20 months on 10% of occasions on which someone else's distress wasn't caused by the child. This empathic concern took several forms including sad or upset facial expressions and expressing concern (e.g., "I'm sorry"). The level of empathic concern more than doubled among children aged between 23 and 25 months.

Zahn-Waxler et al. (1992) also obtained evidence about altruistic behavior in response to another person's distress. The kinds of altruistic behavior shown by the children included sharing food, hugging, and giving a bottle to a crying baby. There was a marked increase with age in altruistic behavior in response to distress not caused by the children (see the figure on the right).

Empathy generally increases over the early school years. One reason for this is because children begin to understand an increasingly wide range of emotions. In addition, they use more cues when working out what others are feeling (Ricard & Kamberkkilicci, 1995).

There are substantial differences in prosocial behavior among children of any given age. Why is this? Part of the answer seems to involve genetic factors. Zahn-Waxler et al. (1992) carried out a study on identical and fraternal twins aged between 14 and 20 months. Their mothers *reported* on various types of prosocial behavior (e.g., attempts to help). There was more similarity in the amount of prosocial behavior shown by identical than by fraternal twins, suggesting that genetic factors are important. However, Zahn-Waxler et al. obtained different findings when *observing* the twins' reactions to simulated distress. There was no clear evidence that the prosocial behavior of the identical twins was more similar than that of the fraternal twins. In subsequent research, Zahn-Waxler et al. (2001) found in a twin study that individual differences in empathy depended moderately on genetic factors.

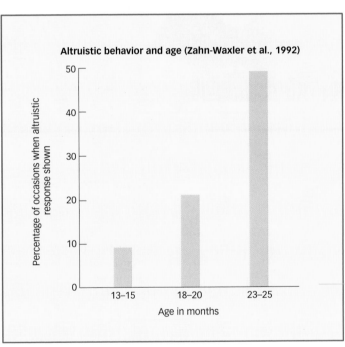

Altruistic behavior and age (Zahn-Waxler et al., 1992)

Evaluation

+ As predicted by the theory, there is evidence of genuine empathy at a surprisingly early age.

+ There is general (but not detailed) support for the four stages of empathy development proposed by Hoffman (1987).

− The role of genetic factors in determining individual differences in empathy may be de-emphasized in the theory.

− The theory says little about how parental behavior influences the development of empathy (see later).

PARENTAL INFLUENCE

Parental behavior is a major determinant of how much prosocial behavior their children will display. Schaffer (1996) argued that *five* types of parental behavior are of particular value in teaching children to be altruistic:

1. *Provisions of clear and explicit guidelines* (e.g., "You mustn't hit other people, because you will hurt and upset them").
2. *Emotional conviction.* Guidelines to children should be given in a fairly emotional way.
3. *Attributing altruistic or prosocial characteristics to the child* (e.g., "You are a really helpful girl").
4. *Parental modeling.* The parent should behave altruistically.
5. *Empathic and warm parenting.*

If the mother of an aggressive child emphasizes how much the other child is being hurt, the aggressive child is more likely to feel empathy and stop the undesirable behavior.

Findings

There is support for the factors identified by Schaffer (1996) as promoting altruistic behavior. So far as factor 1 (clear and explicit guidelines) is concerned, Krevans and Gibbs (1996) found that children were more likely to show empathy for other people and to exhibit prosocial behavior when their mothers repeatedly asked them to consider the likely effects of their behavior on others.

Evidence that children are more likely to show altruistic behavior if their parents have emotional conviction (factor 2) was reported by Zahn-Waxler, Radke-Yarrow, and King (1979). They observed the reactions of children between the ages of 18 and 30 months towards the victims of distress. The average percentage of occasions on which children showed altruistic behavior was twice as high (42% vs. 21%) when the mother made extensive use of emotional explanations than when she did not.

What about factor 3 (attributing prosocial characteristics to the child)? It is also important that children learn to associate their prosocial behavior to internal factors (e.g., "I'm a helpful person") rather than external ones (e.g., "I'm being helpful in order to be praised"). Fabes et al. (1989) found that external rewards aren't an effective way of producing prosocial behavior. They promised toys to some children if they sorted colored paper squares for children who were sick in hospital. Other children weren't offered any reward for carrying out the same task. After a while, all the children were told they could continue to sort the colored squares, but they wouldn't receive any reward for doing so. The children who had been rewarded were less likely to continue to be helpful than those who had not been rewarded.

Evidence relevant to factor 4 (parental modeling) was reported by Grusec, Saas-Kortsaak, and Simutis (1978). Children aged between 8 and 10 played a game to win marbles, some or all of which could be donated to help poor children. The participants observed an adult playing the game before them. The adult either gave away half or none of her marbles, and she either exhorted or didn't exhort the children to give away half of their marbles. Most children who saw the adult give marbles did so themselves, whereas exhortations to give marbles had only a small effect. Thus, the children were more influenced by the model's behavior than by her exhortations. However, only a few children donated any marbles when they played the marble game again 3 weeks later.

Burleson and Kunkel (2002) studied the emotional support skills of children aged 6 and 8. They found that the mothers' comforting skills predicted their children's emotional support skills. The comforting skills of the children's peers also predicted their emotional support skills.

We turn now to factor 5 (empathic and warm parenting). Zahn-Waxler et al. (1979) and Robinson, Zahn-Waxler, and Emde (1994) found that children having a warm and loving relationship with their parents are the ones most likely to show high levels of prosocial behavior. Waters, Wippman, and Sroufe (1979) found that children who had formed secure attachments in infancy showed more empathy later in childhood.

It can reasonably be argued that many studies on altruism or prosocial behavior are rather artificial. Zarbatany, Hartmann, and Gelfand (1985) argued that it is important to distinguish between "true" altruism and conformity to adult expectations. They found that older children seemed more generous than younger ones, but this was mainly because older children were more responsive to adult expectations. The finding by Grusec et al. (1978) that there were no long-term effects of observational learning on prosocial behavior is what might be expected if the children were simply conforming to what they perceived to be the model's expectations.

MEDIA INFLUENCES

Can prosocial behavior be increased by watching suitable television programs? Evidence that it can has been reported in several studies discussed shortly. If prosocial television programs are to be effective, then it is essential that children understand the prosocial message. Calvert and Kotler (2003) asked children aged between about 7 and 11 to indicate what they had learned from their favorite prosocial television programs. Encouragingly, the children could name many such programs and could also describe accurately the lessons conveyed by those programs.

Sprafkin, Liebert, and Poulos (1975) studied the effects of television programs on 6-year-olds. Some watched an episode of *Lassie* in which a boy was seen to risk his life to rescue a puppy from a mine shaft. Other groups of children saw a different episode of *Lassie* in which no helping was involved, or they saw an episode of a situation comedy called *The Brady Bunch*. After watching the program, all the boys had the chance to help some distressed puppies. However, to do so they had to stop playing a game in which they might win a big prize. The children who had watched the rescue from the mine shaft spent an average of over 90 seconds helping the puppies compared to under 50 seconds by those watching the other program.

Sprafkin et al.'s (1975) study monitored the effects of an episode of *Lassie* in terms of its potential to influence prosocial behavior in 6-year-olds.

Hearold (1986) reviewed more than 100 studies on the effects of prosocial television programs on children's behavior. She concluded that such programs do generally make children behave in more helpful ways. Indeed, the beneficial effects of prosocial programs on prosocial behavior were almost twice as great as the adverse effects of television violence on aggressive behavior. However, helping behavior was usually assessed shortly after watching a prosocial television program. There is evidence that the long-term effects are often rather weak or even nonexistent (e.g., Sagotsky, Wood-Schneider, & Konop, 1981).

Mares and Woodard (2005) carried out a meta-analysis of 34 studies concerned with the effects of watching prosocial television content on children's behavior. There were consistently moderate positive effects. The beneficial effects were especially great when children viewed altruistic behavior that could easily be imitated.

ANTISOCIAL BEHAVIOR

There are various forms of antisocial behavior, including shoplifting and vandalism as well as behavior that is aggressive and violent. However, aggression is of particular importance, and will be our central focus (see Chapter 18 for a discussion of aggression in adults). Aggression involves hurting other people on purpose. It is "any form of behavior directed towards the goal of harming or injuring another living being who is motivated to avoid such treatment" (Baron & Richardson, 1993). There can be problems in deciding whether a given piece of behavior is aggressive. Aggression involves the *intent* to harm someone, and it is sometimes difficult to know whether a child intended to cause harm.

There are large changes during the course of development in both the amount of aggression and the types of aggression displayed. The amount of aggression decreases during the first few years of life, but may then increase again. Holmberg (1980) found

Studies have shown boys to be more physically aggressive than girls. However, Bjorkqvist et al. (1992) found that girls show more indirect aggression than boys.

in children of 12 months that 50% of all behavior directed at another child was aggressive. However, this dropped dramatically to 17% at 42 months. Cairns (1986) found that boys (but not girls) showed an increase in aggression between the ages of 9 and 14.

How does the type of aggression change during development? According to Schaffer (1996, p. 279), "As children get older there is a tendency for aggression to become increasingly expressed in verbal rather than physical form. The 2-year-old has little choice but to express anger through direct bodily action; by the age of 10 shaming, humiliation, sarcasm, and teasing have all been added to the repertoire of responses for hurting others."

There are differences between males and females in aggression. Bjorkqvist, Lagerspetz, and Kaukiainen (1992) studied physical aggression, verbal aggression, and indirect aggression (e.g., gossiping; writing unkind notes) in adolescent boys and girls. The boys displayed much more physical aggression than the girls, but the girls showed more indirect aggression than the boys. Tallandini (2004) studied aggressive behavior in boys and girls aged between 4 and 8. She wondered whether there would be gender differences in the types of aggressive behavior in make-believe play situations lacking any immediate social interaction. Boys and girls did not differ in overall levels of aggression. However, boys displayed more physical aggression than girls, and girls tended to show more indirect and verbal aggression than boys.

Most children show reasonable stability in their level of aggression throughout childhood. Eron (1987) found that children who were aggressive at the age of 8 tended to be aggressive at the age of 18. Indeed, those aggressive at the age of 8 were *three* times more likely than other children to have a police record at the age of 18. These same children were also more likely to have been involved in criminal activities and to have behaved violently towards their spouse by the age of 30.

MEDIA INFLUENCES

The average 16-year old in Western society has seen 13,000 violent murders on television, and this presumably has some influence on his/her behavior. There is, indeed, a positive relationship between the amount of television violence children have seen and the aggressiveness of their behavior. Unfortunately, it is hard to interpret this finding. Watching violent programs may cause aggressive behavior. On the other hand, it may be that naturally aggressive children choose to watch more violent programs than nonaggressive children.

Case Study: *St. Helena*

A study was carried out on the island of St. Helena in the south Atlantic, which is best known for the fact that Napoleon spent the last few years of his life there. Its inhabitants received television for the first time in 1995, but there is no evidence of any adverse effects on the children. According to Charlton (1998):

The argument that watching violent television turns youngsters to violence is not borne out, and this study on St. Helena is the clearest proof yet. The children

have watched the same amounts of violence, and in many cases the same programs as British children. But they have not gone out and copied what they have seen on TV.

What are the factors preventing television violence from influencing the children of St. Helena? According to Charlton (1998), "The main ones are that children are in stable home, school and community situations. This is why the children on St. Helena appear to be immune to what they are watching."

Why might aggression be increased by watching violent television programs? One possibility is that children learn ways of behaving aggressively from observing people behaving violently, and this behavior may be imitated subsequently. This is what Bandura (1973) referred to as observational learning or modeling. Another possibility is that children gradually become less responsive to (and emotionally concerned by) acts of violence as they see more and more of them on television and in films. This reduced responsiveness may produce an increased acceptance of violent behavior.

Findings

Eron (1987) carried out a major longitudinal study in which over 600 8-year-olds were studied for 22 years. The amount of television watched at the age of 8 predicted well the level of aggression and of criminality at the age of 18. However, the 8-year-olds watching the most television violence were already more aggressive than other 8-year-olds. Thus, it may be that watching violent programs causes aggressive behavior *and* that being aggressive leads to increased watching of violent programs.

Leyens, Camino, Parke, and Berkowitz (1975) studied juvenile delinquents at a school in Belgium. They lived in four dormitories, two of which had high levels of aggressive behavior and two of which had low levels. During a special Movie Week, the boys in two of the dormitories (one high in aggression and the other low) watched only violent movies, whereas the boys in the other two dormitories watched only nonviolent movies. There was an increased level of physical aggression only among the boys watching the violent movies. This effect was much stronger shortly after watching the violent movies than later on. However, the study is limited in that the researchers didn't distinguish clearly between real and pretend aggression.

Comstock and Paik (1991) reviewed more than 1000 findings on the effects of media violence. They found that the short-term effects were stronger than the long-term ones. Five factors increased the effects of media violence on aggressive behavior:

1. Violent behavior is presented as being an efficient way of getting what you want.
2. The person behaving violently is portrayed as similar to the viewer.
3. Violent behavior is presented realistically rather than, for example, in cartoon form.
4. The victim's suffering isn't shown.
5. The viewer is emotionally excited while watching the violence.

More recent research has largely confirmed these findings. Anderson et al. (2003) carried out a meta-analysis on studies of media violence and aggression. Media violence increased the likelihood of aggressive and violent behavior both immediately afterwards and in the long term. There were greater effects of media violence on less severe than on more severe forms of aggression, but they were clearly present at all levels of aggression. In spite of clear evidence that media violence causes aggressive behavior, "Additional laboratory and field studies are needed for a better understanding of underlying psychological processes" (Anderson et al., 2003, p. 81).

There has been a dramatic increase in recent years in the amount of time children spend playing video games, many of which involve violence. What are the effects of playing such video games? Griffiths (2000) reviewed the evidence. Very young children often behave more aggressively after playing a violent video game, but the effects are much smaller in older children.

Is it that aggressive children choose to play aggressive video games, or do the games make children aggressive?

A child attacks a Bobo doll.

SOCIAL LEARNING THEORY

According to Bandura (1973), "The specific forms that aggressive behavior takes, the frequency with which it is displayed, and the specific targets selected for attack are largely determined by social learning factors." More specifically, observational learning or modeling is of great importance in producing aggressive behavior. Observational learning involves imitating or copying the behavior of others. Aggressive behavior can also be acquired when the child's aggressive behavior is rewarded or reinforced by getting his/her own way or by gaining attention.

Bandura tested his theoretical ideas in a famous series of experiments involving a Bobo doll (see Chapter 7). This doll is inflatable and has a weighted base causing it to bounce back when punched. Bandura, Ross, and Ross (1963) showed young children one of two films. One film showed a female adult model behaving aggressively towards the Bobo doll. The other film showed the adult model behaving nonaggressively towards the doll. As predicted, those children who saw the model behave aggressively were much more likely to attack the Bobo doll. Bandura (1965) extended the findings. He found that children were much more likely to copy the adult model's aggressive behavior when it was rewarded than when it was punished.

Observational learning

Of the hundreds of studies Bandura was responsible for, one group stands out above the others—the Bobo doll studies. He made a film of one of his students, a young woman, essentially beating up a Bobo doll. In case you don't know, a Bobo doll is an inflatable, egg-shape balloon creature with a weight in the bottom that makes it bob back up when you knock it down. Nowadays, it might have Darth Vader painted on it, but back then it was simply "Bobo" the clown.

The woman punched the clown, shouting "sockeroo!" She kicked it, sat on it, hit it with a little hammer, and so on, shouting various aggressive phrases. Bandura showed his film to groups of kindergartners who, as you might predict, liked it a lot. They then were let out to play. In the playroom, of course, were several observers with pens and clipboards in hand, a brand new Bobo doll, and a few little hammers.

And you might predict as well what the observers recorded: a lot of little kids beating the daylights out of the Bobo doll. They punched it and shouted "sockeroo," kicked it, sat on it, hit it with the little hammers, and so on. In other words, they imitated the young lady in the film, and quite precisely at that.

This might seem like a real nothing of an experiment at first, but consider: these children changed their behavior without first being rewarded for approximations to that behavior! And while that may not seem extraordinary to the average parent, teacher, or casual observer of children, it didn't fit so well with standard behavioristic learning theory. Bandura called the phenomenon observational learning or modeling, and his theory is usually called social learning theory.

From http://www.ship.edu/~cgboeree/bandura.html

The Bobo doll studies are famous, but they are limited in various ways. First, Bandura didn't distinguish clearly between real aggression and playfighting. Much of the aggressive behavior he observed was only playfighting (Durkin, 1995). Second, while children readily imitate aggressive behavior towards a doll, they are much less likely to imitate aggressive behavior towards another child. Third, children respond to the Bobo doll because of its novelty value. Children who have played with the doll before are only 20% as likely to imitate aggressive behavior against it as children who haven't seen it before (Cumberbatch, 1990).

BIOLOGICAL APPROACH

Bandura emphasized *external* or environmental factors causing aggression. However, we mustn't ignore *internal* factors such as the child's heredity or personality. Rhee and

Waldman (2002) carried out a meta-analysis of twin and adoption studies concerned with antisocial behavior (e.g., aggressive behavior; delinquency). They found that 41% of individual differences in antisocial behavior were a result of genetic factors (see figure on the right). In addition, 43% of individual differences were a result of nonshared environmental influences (those differing among the children within a family), and the remaining 16% were a result of shared environmental influences. The figures were very similar for males and females, and indicate that antisocial behavior is fairly strongly influenced by genetic factors in both sexes.

Eley, Lichtenstein, and Stevenson (1999) argued that we need to distinguish between aggressive antisocial behavior (e.g., fighting; bullying) and nonaggressive antisocial behavior (e.g., theft; truancy). They found with British and Swedish identical and fraternal twins that aggressive antisocial behavior is influenced far more by genetic factors than is nonaggressive antisocial behavior.

There are important interactions between genetic and environmental factors. This can be seen in a study by Yates, Cadoret, and Troughton (1999) on adopted infants whose

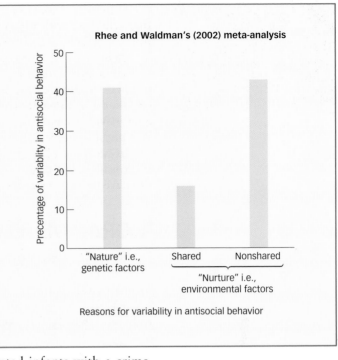

biological mothers had been put in prison. When these adopted infants with a crime-linked genetic background were brought up in dysfunctional families, they showed substantial antisocial behavior in adolescence. However, when the adopted infants were brought up in favorable homes, they showed no more antisocial behavior than adopted infants without a crime-linked genetic background. Thus, a good family environment can counteract adverse genetic influences

In sum, there is clear evidence that genetic and environmental factors play a role in determining aggressive behavior. However, what is of most importance is the way in which genetic factors *interact* with social and other environmental factors to produce various forms of antisocial behavior.

FAMILY PROCESSES

Patterson (1982) argued that how aggressive any given child is depends very much on family processes. He claimed that what is important is the functioning of the family as a whole rather than simply the behavior of the child or its parents. There is typical mutual provocation in families with a highly aggressive child, with the behavior of the parents and of the child having a coercive quality about it. That means it leads directly to increased aggression by other members of the family.

Findings

Patterson (1982) and Patterson, DeBaryshe, and Ramsey (1989) observed the interaction patterns of families in their homes. There was a typical pattern of escalating aggression in the families of aggressive children. First, the child behaved aggressively (e.g., refusing to do what his mother requested). Second, the mother responded aggressively (e.g., shouting angrily at her son). Third, the child reacted in a more aggressive and hostile way (e.g., shouting back loudly at his mother). Fourth, the mother responded more aggressively than before (e.g., hitting her son). Patterson (1982) called this pattern of behavior a **coercive cycle**: a small increase in aggression by the parent or child is matched or exceeded by the other person's aggressive behavior.

According to Patterson et al. (1989), most aggressive behavior displayed by parents and their children in aggressive families is an attempt to stop the other person being aggressive to them. In fact, however, these attempts often serve to provoke further aggression. Children with this type of aggressive approach are often rejected by their peers, and thus suffer severe problems in social adjustment.

Key Term
Coercive cycle: a pattern of behavior in which aggression by one family member produces an aggressive response, and so on.

Patterson et al. (1989) also found that parents in aggressive families rarely provided their children with affection or even with encouragement. This lack of attention leads boys to behave aggressively to attract attention from their parents.

Pagani et al. (2004) found evidence of a coercive cycle in a study of 15- and 16-year-old sons and daughters who displayed verbal and physical aggression towards their mothers. In most cases, there had been aggression within the family dating back to early childhood, with parents and children both involved in behaving aggressively. In addition, aggressive parental punishment within the previous 6 months was associated with verbal and physical aggression towards mothers.

In sum, there is convincing evidence that children's aggressive behavior can usefully be considered in terms of family dynamics. As yet, however, the factors responsible for the development of coercive cycles in the first place remain unclear.

MORAL DEVELOPMENT

In this section, we discuss changes in moral development during childhood. According to Shaffer (1993), morality implies "a set of principles or ideals that help the individual to distinguish right from wrong and to act on this distinction." Morality is important because society can't function effectively unless there is reasonable agreement on what is right and wrong. Of course, there are some moral and ethical issues (e.g., animal experimentation) on which members of most societies have very different views. However, if there were controversy on all major moral issues, society would become chaotic.

Human morality has three major components (see figure on the left).

1. *Cognitive*: How we think about moral issues and decide what is right and wrong.
2. *Emotional*: The feelings (e.g., guilt; pride) associated with moral thoughts and behavior.
3. *Behavioral*: The extent to which we behave honorably or lie, steal, and cheat.

It might be thought that any given individual would show consistency among these three components. For example, someone who has high moral standards with the cognitive component would also have high moral standards with the emotional and behavioral components. In fact, however, there are often large discrepancies between components. For example, someone may know at the cognitive level that it is wrong to cheat, but may still cheat at the behavioral level.

KOHLBERG'S THEORY

Lawrence Kohlberg (1927–1987) put forward a cognitive–developmental theory of children's morality, based on the assumption that we should focus on children's cognitive structures. Kohlberg argued that all children follow the same sequence of stages in their moral development. What leads them to develop their moral reasoning? According to Kohlberg, disequilibrium or inconsistency among an individual's views provides the motivation for him/her to change and develop his/her moral reasoning.

Kohlberg's theory consists of three levels of moral development with two stages at each level (see the figure on the following page).

- *Level 1*: **Pre-conventional morality.** What is regarded as right or wrong is determined by the rewards or punishments likely to follow rather than by thinking about moral issues. Stage 1 of this level is based on a punishment-and-obedience orientation. Stealing is wrong because it involves disobeying authority and leads to punishment.

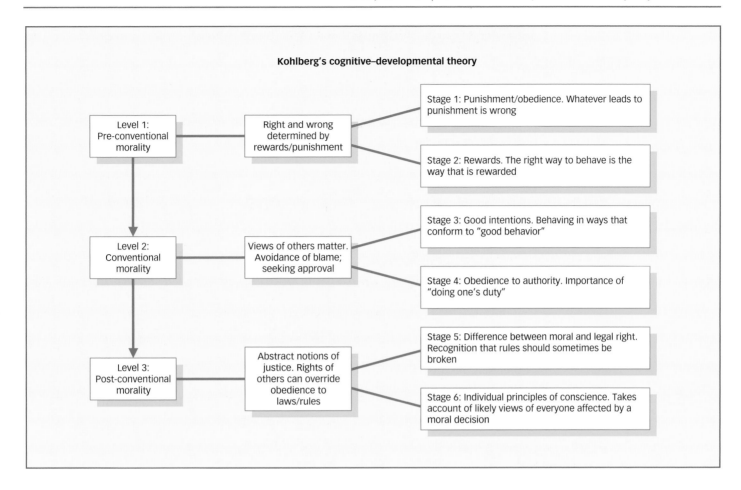

Stage 2 is based on the notion that the right way to behave is the one that is rewarded. There is more attention to the needs of other people than in Stage 1, but mainly on the basis that if you help other people they will help you.

- *Level 2*: **Conventional morality.** The views and needs of others are much more important at Level 2 than at Level 1. At Level 2, children are very concerned to have the approval of others for their actions and to avoid being blamed for behaving wrongly. At Stage 3, the emphasis is on having good intentions and on conforming to most people's views of good behavior. At Stage 4, children believe it is important to do one's duty and to obey the laws or rules of those in authority.
- *Level 3*: **Post-conventional morality.** At Level 3, people recognize that the laws or rules of authority figures should sometimes be broken. Abstract notions about justice and the need to treat other people with respect can override the need to obey rules and laws. At Stage 5, there is a growing recognition that what is morally right may differ from what is legally right. Finally, at Stage 6, the individual takes into account the likely views of everyone who will be affected by a moral decision. In practice, it is rare for anyone to operate most of the time at Stage 6.

Findings

Most of Kohlberg's research involved presenting children with hypothetical moral dilemmas—see Key Study on the following page.

According to Kohlberg, all children follow the same sequence of moral stages. This assumption can be tested by carrying out a longitudinal (long-term) study to see how children's moral reasoning changes over time. Colby, Kohlberg, Gibbs, and Lieberman (1983) conducted a 20-year study of 58 American males. There was a large decrease in Stage 1 and Stage 2 moral reasoning between

Key Terms

Conventional morality:
this is the second level in Kohlberg's theory; at this level, moral reasoning focuses on having others' approval.

Post-conventional morality:
the third level in Kohlberg's theory; at this level, moral reasoning focuses on justice and the need to respect others.

Key Study

Kohlberg (1963): Moral dilemmas

The main experimental approach used by Kohlberg involved presenting his participants with a series of moral dilemmas. Each dilemma required them to decide whether it is preferable to uphold some law or other moral principle or to reject that moral principle in favor of some basic human need. Here is one of the moral dilemmas Kohlberg used:

> In Europe, a woman was dying from cancer. One drug might save her, a form of radium that a druggist in the same town had recently discovered. The druggist was charging 2000 dollars, ten times what the drug cost him to make. The sick woman's husband, Heinz, went to everyone he knew to borrow the money, but he could only get together about half of what it cost. He told the druggist that his wife was dying and asked him to sell it cheaper or let him pay later. But the druggist said "No." The husband got desperate and broke into the man's store to steal the drug for his wife.

The moral principle in this dilemma is that stealing is wrong. However, it was the good motive of wanting to help his sick wife that led Heinz to steal the drug. It is precisely because there are powerful arguments for and against stealing the drug that there is a moral dilemma.

   Findings obtained from such moral dilemmas led Kohlberg to identify the three levels and six stages of moral reasoning described earlier.

Discussion points
1. How adequate do you find Kohlberg's use of moral dilemmas to study moral development?
2. What do you think of Kohlberg's stage-based approach to moral development?

KEY STUDY EVALUATION

Kohlberg's theory addresses some of the problems of Piaget's approach, in that it is more flexible and less tied to specific age-based stages of development. Meta-analyses have shown that the six stages of Kohlberg's theoretical framework apply across most cultures, and it is almost universally the case that individuals work through the various stages in the same order. However, individual differences in experience or cultural differences may affect the speed with which a person moves through the stages. For example, in some cultures children can work, be married, or be regarded as full members of adult society at much younger ages than Western children. It is possible that these individuals move through Kohlberg's stages much earlier than Western children do. In addition, some Western children's lives do not conform to the stereotypical well-balanced family background with a strong moral sense of right and wrong that seems to lie behind some of Kohlberg's stages. This may also have a profound effect on a child's moral development.

the ages of 10 and 16, with a compensatory increase in Stage 3 and Stage 4 moral reasoning (see the figure on the following page). Most impressively for Kohlberg's theory, all the participants progressed through the moral stages in exactly the predicted sequence. More worryingly for the theory, only about 10% of individuals in their thirties showed Stage 5 moral reasoning, and there was practically no evidence of Stage 6 reasoning.

   Dawson (2002) discussed four longitudinal studies on moral development. The findings largely replicated those of Colby et al. (1983), in that there was a clear progression through Kohlberg's various stages. However, there was some evidence that there is an additional stage of moral development occurring between Kohlberg's Stages 3 and 4. Evidence that shifts in moral development can be from a higher to a lower stage was reported by Patenaude, Niyonsenga, and Fafard (2003). They found that 13% of medical students showed a decline in moral development during their first 3 years at medical school. Patendaude et al. speculated that this might be a result of the structure of medical education.

Snarey (1985) reviewed 44 studies from 27 cultures. People in nearly all cultures went through the first four stages of moral development in the same order and at about the same time. There was little evidence of people omitting any stage of moral development or returning to an earlier stage. However, there was more evidence of Stage 5 reasoning in Western cultures than in most rural or village cultures. Snarey argued that this does *not* mean that the moral reasoning of those living in Western cultures is superior. Rather, it reflects the individualistic emphasis of most Western cultures (e.g., the greater value attached to human life).

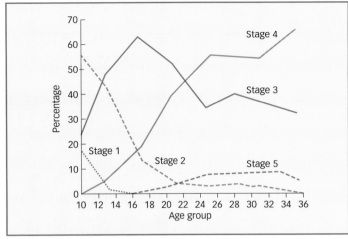

Percentage of individuals aged between 10 and 36 at each of Kohlberg's moral stages of development. Data from Colby et al. (1983).

Walker, Gustafson, and Hennig (2001) tested Kohlberg's hypothesis that disequilibrium or inconsistency in thinking about moral issues motivates children to advance their moral reasoning. They assumed that children whose stage of moral reasoning differed considerably from one moral dilemma to another were in a state of disequilibrium. As predicted, children in a state of disequilibrium were most likely to show a rapid advance to the next stage of moral reasoning.

Does an individual's level of moral reasoning predict his/her behavior? Kohlberg (1975) compared cheating behavior among college students at different levels of moral reasoning. About 70% of students at the pre-conventional level cheated compared to 55% at the conventional level and only 15% at the post-conventional level (see the figure below). Stams et al. (2006) carried out a meta-analysis of 50 studies on moral reasoning in juvenile delinquents. On average, juvenile delinquents were at a much lower stage of moral reasoning than controls, and this was especially the case for delinquents with psychopathic disorder. However, juvenile delinquency was also associated with socioeconomic status, gender, and intelligence.

Finally, cross-cultural studies indicate that there is more diversity in moral reasoning than suggested by Kohlberg. For example, Shweder (1990) compared Hindus in India with Americans living in Chicago. After the death of a relative, Hindus regard eating

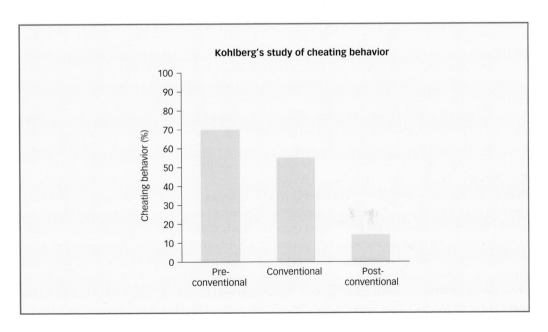

Cheating behavior as a function of college students' moral stage. Data from Kohlberg (1975).

chicken or fish, or cutting one's hair, as serious transgressions because they reduce the chances of salvation. None of these acts was regarded as immoral by Americans. In contrast, many children living in Chicago regard sexual inequality as an important moral issue, much more so than children living in India.

Evaluation

+ Kohlberg has provided a detailed and accurate description of the development of moral reasoning.

+ Disequilibrium or inconsistency seems to motivate children to advance their moral reasoning (e.g., Walker et al., 2001).

− Most people don't develop beyond Stage 4, so Stages 5 and 6 are of limited applicability.

− Kohlberg focused on moral judgments made in response to artificial dilemmas, and these judgments sometimes fail to predict behavior accurately. In addition, people's level of moral reasoning is often higher when confronted by hypothetical problems than when experiencing real-life problems (Walker et al., 1995). The reason is because, "It's a lot easier to be moral when you have nothing to lose" (Walker et al., 1995, pp. 381–382).

− Kohlberg paid insufficient attention to differences in moral reasoning from one culture to another.

− Kohlberg de-emphasized the emotional and behavioral components of morality.

GILLIGAN'S THEORY

Carol Gilligan (1977, 1982) disliked what she regarded as the sexist bias of Kohlberg's approach. Kohlberg initially based his theory on interviews with male participants, so bias may have been introduced. Kohlberg reported that most women were at Stage 3 of moral development whereas men were at Stage 4.

Gilligan (1982) argued that boys develop the morality of justice, in which they focus on the use of laws and moral principles. In contrast, girls develop the morality of care, in which their main focus is on human wellbeing and compassion for others. According to Gilligan, Kohlberg showed sexist bias by regarding the morality of justice as superior to the morality of care. However, note that Kohlberg's theory did include the morality of care. More generally, Gilligan argued that theories of moral reasoning should accord equal importance to the care orientation and the justice orientation.

According to Gilligan and Wiggins (1987), the above gender differences have their origins in early childhood. Women are the main caregivers in most societies, and girls learn the morality of care through their strong attachment to their mother. In contrast, boys are less attached to their mother. They tend to identify with their father, who is often perceived as an authority figure. This identification process leads boys to develop the morality of justice.

Findings

Benenson, Morash, and Petrakos (1998) tested Gilligan's views on the origins of moral orientation. They studied mothers playing with their 4- or 5-year-old children. The girls seemed more attached to their mothers than the boys. For example, girls remained closer to their mothers, had more mutual eye contact with their mothers, and derived more enjoyment from the play session. However, these findings do not necessarily mean that girls identify more strongly than boys with their mothers.

Jaffee and Hyde (2000) carried out a thorough meta-analysis of 113 studies of moral reasoning. Overall, there was a very small tendency for males to show more justice reasoning than females. There was also a slightly larger tendency for females to show more care reasoning than males. According to Jaffee and Hyde (p. 719):

> *The small magnitude of these effects [the ones just described], combined with the finding that 73% of the studies that measured justice reasoning and 72% of the studies that measured care reasoning failed to find significant gender differences, leads us to conclude that, although distinct moral orientations may exist, these orientations are not strongly associated with gender.*

Schwartz and Rubel (2005) explored related issues in a very large cross-cultural study involving 127 samples in 70 different countries. The importance of 10 basic values to men and women in these countries was assessed. The value of most relevance to care orientation was benevolence, which is concerned with the preservation and enhancement of other people's welfare. As predicted by Gilligan's theory, women regarded benevolence as slightly more important than men. Across the 127 samples, women rated benevolence as a more important value than did men in 114 of them. The findings were less clear with respect to justice orientation. The two values most relevant to justice orientation were self-direction (independent thought and choice of action) and universalism (understanding, tolerance, and protection for the welfare of everyone). Men generally regarded self-direction as slightly more important than women, which is consistent with Gilligan's approach. However, men regarded universalism as slightly less important than women, which seems inconsistent with prediction from Gilligan's theory.

In spite of Schwartz and Rubel's (2005) findings, there is some evidence of interesting differences from one culture to another. Skoe (1998) found as predicted by Gilligan that Canadian and American women between the ages of 17 and 26 showed more complex care-based understanding than men. However, there was no gender difference in care-based understanding in Norway, in which the culture emphasizes gender equality in the workplace and in society generally.

Evaluation

- There is some justification for arguing that Kohlberg exaggerated the importance of the morality of justice and minimized that of the morality of care.

- Several studies have shown that boys have a more advanced morality of justice than girls and that girls have a more advanced morality of care.

- Some gender differences in basic values of relevance to morality that have been found in numerous cultures are consistent with Gilligan's theory.

- Gender differences in type of morality are typically very small.

- Gilligan emphasized the cognitive component in morality at the expense of the behavioral and emotional components.

Chapter Summary

Gender development
- Most gender differences are small. However, girls have less developmental vulnerability than boys and outperform boys in nearly all school subjects in the United Kingdom.
- According to social learning theory, gender development occurs as a result of the child's experiences (especially those involving reward or punishment). Observational learning is also important.

- As predicted by social learning theory, some sex-typed behavior occurs because it has previously been rewarded. However, the theory de-emphasizes the importance of more general learning (e.g., organized beliefs).
- According to gender schema theory, young children develop gender schemas that influence what children attend to and how they interpret the world.
- Gender schema theory de-emphasizes the role of social factors in gender development. Another limitation is that the association between gender schemas and behavior is not very strong.

Prosocial behavior

- Girls show more altruistic behavior than boys across numerous cultures. However, this gender difference is typically smaller when assessed by direct observations rather than by self-report.
- Children and adults in collectivistic cultures exhibit more altruistic behavior than those in individualistic ones, but more altruistic behavior is expected in return in the former cultures.
- According to Hoffman (1987), there are four stages in the development of empathy: global empathy; "egocentric" empathy; empathy for another's feelings; and empathy for another life's condition.
- The amount of prosocial behavior shown by children depends in part on parental behavior (e.g., provision of explicit guidelines; emotional conviction; and attributing prosocial characteristics to the child).
- Watching prosocial television programs can enhance children's prosocial behavior, but the effects are typically rather short-term.

Antisocial behavior

- Boys are more physically aggressive than girls, but girls display more indirect (e.g., verbal) aggression than boys.
- Observing media violence can produce aggressive behavior in children. The short-term effects are generally greater than the long-term ones. They are also greater when violent behavior is presented as being an efficient way of getting what you want, and when the person behaving violently is similar to the observer.
- One of the ways in which children develop aggressive behavior is through observational learning of models.
- Individual differences in aggressive behavior depend in part on genetic factors, especially on interactions between genetic and environmental factors.
- The family dynamics in families with an aggressive child often lead to a pattern of escalating aggression and violence.

Moral development

- Human morality has three components (cognitive; emotional; and behavioral). There are often large discrepancies among these components within an individual.
- According to Kohlberg, there are three levels of moral development: pre-conventional morality; conventional morality; and post-conventional morality. There are two stages at each level.
- Children in nearly all cultures proceed through the first four stages of moral development in the same order and at about the same ages. However, most cultures have some idiosyncratic moral beliefs.
- Gilligan criticized Kohlberg for showing sexist bias by regarding the morality of justice as superior to the morality of care. According to her theory, boys develop the former morality to a greater extent than girls but the opposite is the case with the morality of care.
- There is some support for Gilligan's theory, but the predicted gender differences tend to be very small.

Further Reading

- Berk, L.E. (2006). *Child development* (7th ed.). New York: Pearson. There are up-to-date accounts of the topics discussed in this chapter in this textbook.
- Cole, M., & Cole, S.R. (2004). *The development of children* (5th ed.). New York: Worth. This book provides an introduction to key topics in social development.
- Penner, L.A., Dovidio, J.F., Piliavin, J.A., & Schroeder, D.A. (2005). Prosocial behavior: Multilevel perspectives. *Annual Review of Psychology, 56,* 365–392. This thorough review includes a discussion of the origins of prosocial behavior.
- Shaffer, D.R. (2004). *Social and personality development* (5th ed.). Belmont, CA: Wadsworth. There is detailed material on topics such as moral development and sex-role identity in this textbook.
- Smith, P.K., Cowie, H., & Blades, M. (2003). *Understanding children's development* (4th ed.). Oxford: Blackwell. Several chapters in this textbook (especially 6 and 8) contain good introductory accounts of the topics discussed in this chapter.

Chapter 16

Contents

Attachments and friendships

16

Human beings are social creatures. As a result, it is not surprising that much of the early learning of infants is in the area of social development. What is of central importance to social development are the warm, positive, and deep relationships infants and children form with other people. This chapter focuses on relationships of all kinds, ranging from weak and short-lived ones to very strong and long-lasting ones. It is probably true that nothing in human development is more important than the formation of such relationships.

Of special importance to infants is the **attachment** (a strong and long-lasting emotional tie) they typically form to their mother or other significant caregiver. The nature and strength of the attachments formed by infants have long-term consequences for their future psychological wellbeing. Some children either never form strong attachments with other adults, or their attachments are disrupted. There has been concern that deprivation (especially maternal deprivation) may have severe long-term effects on children, socially and intellectually.

Children's social and emotional development depends in part on their parents' child-rearing practices. Styles of child rearing vary considerably across cultures. Child-rearing practices reflect the dominant values of the culture—this is one way in which parents pass on those values to the next generation.

The success or otherwise of young children's attachment to their parents or other significant adults forms only part of their social development. Children must also develop social skills and competence so they can interact successfully with other children. Children with friends are happier and more successful than those without.

ATTACHMENT

According to Shaffer (1993), an attachment is "a close emotional relationship between two persons, characterized by mutual affection and a desire to maintain proximity [closeness]." Virtually all developmental psychologists agree it is crucially important for infants and children to form strong attachments.

The main attachment of the infant is typically to its mother, but strong attachments can also be formed to other people with whom the infant has regular contact. Weston and Main (1981) studied 44 infants. Twelve were securely attached to both parents, 11 were securely attached only to their mother, 10 were securely attached only to their father, and 11 were insecurely attached to both parents. The first attachment that infants form in early childhood is very important because it is the starting point for their lifelong social and emotional involvement with other people.

Bowlby (1969, 1988) argued that the development of attachment goes through five phases:

1. The infant responds in a similar way to everyone.
2. At around 5 months, the infant starts to *discriminate* among other people (e.g., smiling mainly at his/her mother). This phase witnesses the start of attachment.
3. At around 7 months, the infant remains close to his/her mother or caregiver. He/she shows "separation protest" by becoming upset when his/her mother leaves.

Key Term
Attachment: strong and long-lasting emotional ties to another person.

4. From the age of 3 years, the child–caregiver attachment becomes a goal-corrected partnership. This means the child takes account of the caregiver's needs.
5. From the age of 5 years, the child has an internal working model of the child–caregiver relationship. As a result, the attachment remains strong even when the child doesn't see the caregiver for some time.

STRANGE SITUATION TEST

The most-used way of assessing infants' attachment behavior is by the Strange Situation procedure (Ainsworth & Bell, 1970). The infant (usually about 12 months old) is observed during a sequence of eight short episodes (see the box below). Some of the time the infant is with its mother. At other times, it is with its mother and a stranger, just with a stranger, or on its own. The child's reactions to the stranger, to separation from its mother, and to being reunited with its mother are all recorded. These reactions allow the child's attachment to its mother to be assigned to one of three categories:

1. *Secure attachment*: The infant is distressed by the mother's absence. However, it becomes contented after her return, and there are clear differences between the infant's

The eight stages of the Strange Situation experiment

Stage	People in the room	Procedure
1 (30 seconds)	Mother or caregiver and infant plus researcher	Researcher brings the others into the room and quickly leaves
2 (3 minutes)	Mother or caregiver and infant	Mother or caregiver sits; infant is free to explore
3 (3 minutes)	Stranger plus mother or caregiver and infant	Stranger comes in and after a while talks to mother or caregiver and then to the infant. Mother or caregiver leaves the room
4 (3 minutes)	Stranger and infant	Stranger keeps trying to talk and play with the infant
5 (3 minutes)	Mother or caregiver and infant	Stranger leaves as mother or caregiver returns to the infant. At the end of this stage the mother or caregiver leaves
6 (3 minutes)	Infant	Infant is alone in the room
7 (3 minutes)	Stranger and infant	Stranger returns and tries to interact with the infant
8 (3 minutes)	Mother or caregiver and infant	Mother or caregiver returns and interacts with the infant, and the stranger leaves

reaction to the mother and the stranger. About 70% of American infants show secure attachment.

2. *Resistant attachment*: The infant is insecure in the mother's presence and becomes very distressed when she leaves. It resists contact with the mother when she returns and is wary of the stranger. About 10% of American infants are resistant.
3. *Avoidant attachment*: The infant doesn't seek contact with the mother, and shows little distress when separated from her. The infant avoids contact with the mother when she returns. The stranger is treated similarly to the mother. About 20% of American infants are avoidant.

Main, Kaplan, and Cassidy (1985) identified a fourth type of attachment behavior in the Strange Situation: disorganized and disoriented attachment. Infants with this type of attachment lacked any coherent strategy for coping with the Strange Situation, and their behavior was a confusing mixture of approach and avoidance.

Fraley and Spieker (2003) argued that it is an oversimplification to assign all children's attachment patterns to three (or four) categories. For example, two children might both be classified as showing avoidant attachment, but one might display much more avoidant behavior. We can take account of such individual differences by using *dimensions* (going from very low to very high) instead of *categories*. Fraley and Spieker identified two attachment dimensions:

1. *Avoidant/withdrawal vs. proximity-seeking strategies:* This is concerned with the extent to which the child tries to maintain physical closeness to his/her mother.
2. *Angry and resistant strategies vs. emotional confidence:* This is concerned with the child's emotional reactions to the attachment figure's behavior.

As can be seen in the figure on the right, secure, resistant, and avoidant attachment all fit neatly into this two-dimensional framework. The dimensional approach is preferable to the categorical one because it takes much more account of small differences in attachment behavior.

Infant attachment is very important for subsequent development. For example, Wartner, Grossman, Fremmer-Bombik, and Suess (1994) found that attachment classifications at 6 years were very similar to those at 12 months. Stams, Juffer, and Van IJzendoorn (2002) found that children who were securely attached to their mother at 12 months had superior social and cognitive development at the age of 7.

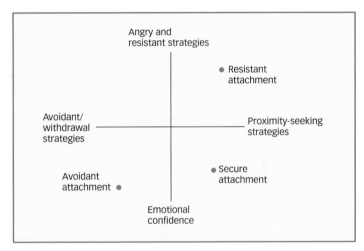

The locations of secure, resistant, and avoidant attachments within a two-dimensional framework (proximity seeking vs. avoidance/withdrawal, angry and resistant vs. emotional confidence). Based on Fraley and Spieker (2003).

Cross-cultural differences

Sagi et al. (1991) used the Strange Situation test to study attachment behavior in infants in the United States, Israel, Japan, and Germany. Their findings are shown in the figure on the following page. The Israeli infants were less likely than American infants to show avoidant attachment with their mother even though they lived on a kibbutz or collective farm and didn't see much of her. Japanese infants showed a complete absence of avoidant attachment. It is not surprising that none of them treated a stranger similarly to their mother given that historically most Japanese mothers practically never leave their infants alone with a stranger. Durrett, Otaki, and Richards (1984) studied Japanese families in which the mothers were pursuing careers and so had to leave their children in the care of others. Their children showed a similar pattern of attachment styles to that found in the United States.

German infants showed a different pattern of attachment to those from the other three countries. They were less likely to be securely attached and more likely to be avoidantly attached. Why is this? Part of the answer is that German parents regard some

Children from different countries vary in their attachment types. The graph summarizes research from Sagi et al. (1991) and Ainsworth and Bell (1970).

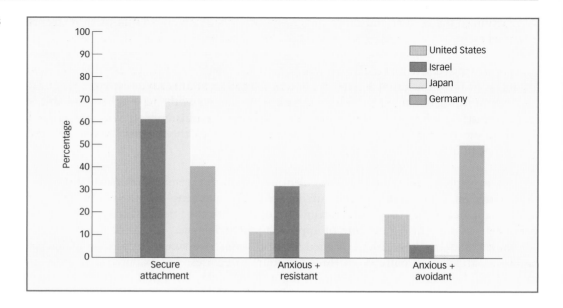

aspects of securely attached behavior as indicating that the infants are spoiled (Sagi & Lewkowicz, 1987). In addition, German parents prefer infants to be independent, non-clinging, and obedient (Grossman et al., 1985).

It is important not to exaggerate cultural differences in attachment. Van IJzendoorn and Kroonenberg (1988) carried out a meta-analysis of studies using the Strange Situation. The variation in attachment style *within* cultures was 1.5 times greater than the variation *between* cultures. That means that the notion there is a *single* British or American culture is an oversimplification. In fact, there are several sub-cultures within most large countries.

Theories of attachment

Why do some infants have a secure attachment with their mother, whereas others don't? Ainsworth, Blehar, Waters, and Wall (1978, p. 152) provided an influential answer with their maternal sensitivity hypothesis: "The most important aspect of maternal behavior commonly associated with the security–anxiety dimension of infant attachment is . . . sensitive responsiveness to infant signals and communications." This hypothesis has received much support. De Wolff and van IJzendoorn (1997) carried out a meta-analysis and reported a correlation of +.24 between maternal sensitivity and security of infant attachment. This indicates a positive (but fairly weak) association. De Wolff and van IJzendoorn also found that aspects of mothers' behavior having only partial resemblance to sensitivity were also important. These aspects included stimulation (any action of the mother directed at her baby) and attitude (mother's expression of positive emotion to her baby).

Most research on the maternal sensitivity hypothesis is correlational and so doesn't prove that differences in maternal sensitivity *cause* differences in security of attachment. Clearer evidence can be obtained by looking at the effects on infant attachment of interventions designed to increase maternal sensitivity. A meta-analysis of relevant studies indicated that such interventions made infants more securely attached (Bakermans-Kranenburg, van IJzendoorn, & Juffer, 2003).

The maternal sensitivity hypothesis exaggerates the role of the mother. Van IJzendoorn and de Wolff (1997) carried out a meta-analysis of studies in which *paternal* sensitivity had been assessed. There was a correlation of +.13 between the father's sensitivity and infant–father attachment. Thus, paternal sensitivity is modestly associated with the infant's security of attachment to the father. However, the association is smaller than that between maternal sensitivity and security of infant–mother attachment.

Another limitation with the maternal sensitivity hypothesis is that it ignores the role played by the infant himself/herself. We can assess that role by studying pairs of identical twins (sharing 100% of their genes) and fraternal twins (sharing 50% of their genes). If the infant's characteristics influence his/her attachment style, then identical twins should show more agreement than fraternal twins with respect to attachment style. O'Connor and Croft (2001) found modest support for this hypothesis, suggesting that genetic factors probably influence young children's attachment type to a small extent.

We mustn't exaggerate the role played by the infant's genetic make-up and personality in determining its attachment style. There is only a modest tendency for infants' attachment type with their father to be the same as their attachment type with their mother (De Wolff & van IJzendoorn, 1997). This suggests that an infant's attachment to his/her mother and father depends mainly on the characteristics of his/her parents.

Overall Evaluation

- There is convincing evidence of the usefulness of the Strange Situation test and of the three attachment types identified by Ainsworth and Bell (1970).

- Maternal sensitivity has been shown to have a significant effect on infants' attachment behavior.

- Attachment type in infants predicts their subsequent social and cognitive development to some extent.

- The Strange Situation procedure is laboratory-based and rather artificial. Infants' attachment behaviors are stronger in the laboratory than at home (Bronfenbrenner, 1979).

- It has not been clearly established that attachment type in infancy *directly* influences later social and cognitive development.

- Ainsworth and Bell (1970) identified categories of attachment, but a dimensional approach (e.g., Fraley & Spieker, 2003) is more sensitive and thus preferable.

DEPRIVATION EFFECTS

So far we have focused on the attachment that a young child forms with its mother or other caregiver. In the real world, of course, a child's attachments can be disrupted by divorce or the death of a parent, or even prevented from being formed in the first place. In this section, we will discuss the effects on young children of being separated from one or more of the most important people in their lives.

MATERNAL DEPRIVATION HYPOTHESIS

John Bowlby (1907–1990) focused on the relationship between mother and child. According to Bowlby (1951), "An infant and young child should experience a warm, intimate and continuous relationship with his [sic!] mother (or permanent mother-figure) in which both find satisfaction and enjoyment." No one in their senses would disagree with that. However, Bowlby went much further in his controversial maternal deprivation hypothesis. According to this hypothesis, breaking the bond between mother and child during the early years of life often has serious effects on the child's intellectual, social, and emotional development. Bowlby also claimed that many of the negative effects of maternal deprivation are permanent and irreversible. Contrary to popular belief, Bowlby argued that about 25% (rather than 100%) of children suffer

Bowlby endorsed the concept of monotropy, whereby an infant has an innate tendency to become attached to one particular individual.

long-term damage from maternal deprivation (Di Dwyer, personal communication). Finally, Bowlby endorsed **monotropy**, the notion that human infants have an innate tendency to form strong bonds with one particular individual (typically the mother).

Findings

Bowlby based his maternal deprivation hypothesis in part on the work of Spitz (1945) and Goldfarb (1947). Spitz visited several very poor orphanages and other institutions in South America. Most children in these orphanages were apathetic because they received very little warmth or attention from the staff. Many of these children suffered from **anaclitic depression**, a state involving resigned helplessness and loss of appetite.

Goldfarb (1947) compared two groups of infants from a poor and inadequately staffed orphanage (see the figure below). One group spent 3 years at the orphanage before fostering, whereas the other group spent only the first few months of their lives there before being fostered. Those children who had spent 3 years at the orphanage did less well than the others on intelligence tests over a period of several years after leaving the orphanage. They were also less socially mature and were more likely to be aggressive.

The findings of Spitz (1945) and Goldfarb (1947) provide less support for the maternal deprivation hypothesis than Bowlby assumed. The institutions they studied were deficient in several ways, with the children suffering from a general lack of stimulation and attention as well as maternal deprivation. Thus, we can't be sure whether the problems experienced by the children in these studies were a result of the absence of the mother, the presence of poor institutional conditions, or a combination of both factors.

Bowlby (1946) compared juvenile delinquents who had committed crimes with other emotionally disturbed adolescents who hadn't committed any crimes. Thirty-two percent of the juvenile delinquents (but none of the emotionally disturbed adolescents) showed

Key Terms

Monotropy:
the notion that infants have an innate tendency to form strong bonds with one particular individual (typically the mother).

Anaclitic depression:
a condition involving loss of appetite and feelings of helplessness.

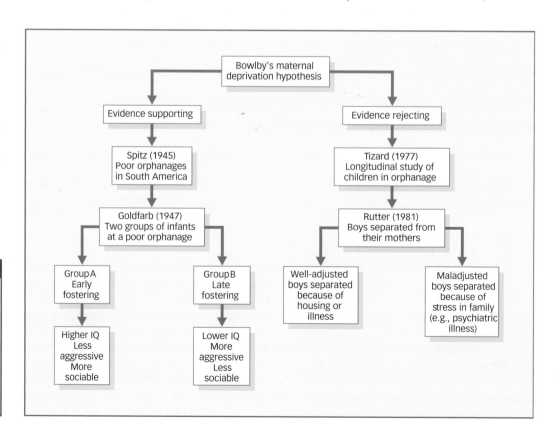

affectionless psychopathy, a condition involving a lack of guilt and remorse. Bowlby found that 64% of the juvenile delinquents with affectionless psychopathy had experienced deprivation in early childhood. In contrast, only 10% of the juvenile delinquents *without* affectionless psychopathy had been maternally deprived. These findings suggested that maternal deprivation can lead to affectionless psychopathy. However, subsequent studies failed to replicate the findings.

According to Bowlby's monotropy hypothesis, infants form only one strong attachment (typically to the mother). This hypothesis is simply wrong. Schaffer and Emerson (1964) found that 59% of infants had formed more than one attachment by 10 months (see figure on the right). The figure rose to 87% by 18 months. At the older age, only about half the infants were mainly attached to their mother, with 30% being mainly attached to their father. Thus, relatively few children only have a strong attachment to their mother as assumed by Bowlby.

DEPRIVATION AND PRIVATION

Rutter (1981) argued that Bowlby's (1946) findings on affectionless psychopathy should be re-interpreted based on an important distinction between deprivation and privation. **Deprivation** occurs when a child has formed an important attachment but is then separated from the major attachment figure. In contrast, **privation** occurs when a child has never formed a close relationship with anyone. Many of Bowlby's juvenile delinquents had experienced several changes of home and of principal caretaker during their early childhood. This suggested to Rutter that their later problems were a result of privation rather than of deprivation as Bowlby had claimed.

According to Rutter (1981), the effects of privation are much more severe and long-lasting than those of deprivation. He concluded that privation often leads to "an initial phase of clinging, dependent behavior, followed by attention-seeking, uninhibited, indiscriminate friendliness and finally a personality characterized by lack of guilt, an inability to keep rules and an inability to form lasting relationships."

There were other disagreements between Bowlby and Rutter. According to Bowlby, deprivation in and of itself often causes long-term difficulties. According to Rutter, the effects of deprivation depend on the precise reasons for the separation. Rutter (1981) studied boys aged 9–12 who had been maternally deprived when younger. Most of the well-adjusted boys had been separated from their mothers because of factors such as housing problems or physical illness. In contrast, most of the maladjusted boys had been separated because of problems with social relationships within the family (e.g., psychiatric illness). Thus, family discord rather than separation as such causes difficulties for children.

Bowlby argued that most of the negative effects of maternal deprivation couldn't be reversed or undone, but Rutter and other experts disagreed. Most of the evidence doesn't support Bowlby's position: for example, Tizard (1977, 1986) and Tizard and Hodges (1978)—see the Key Study below.

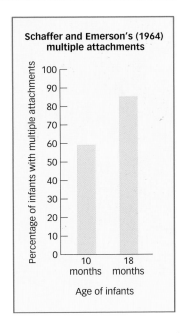

Schaffer and Emerson's (1964) multiple attachments

Key Study

Hodges and Tizard: Long-term effects of privation

Tizard (1977, 1986) and Tizard and Hodges (1978) studied children who had spent up to the first 7 years of their lives in an institution. Each child had been looked after on average by 24 different caregivers by the age of 2, and so they didn't have the opportunity to form a strong continuous relationship with any one adult. Some of these children returned to their own families, whereas others were adopted.

The children's progress was assessed at the ages of 8 and 16. Most of the adopted children had formed close relationships with their adoptive parents. This was less true of the children who had returned to their own families, because their parents were often unsure they wanted their children back. Both groups of children

Key Terms

Affectionless psychopathy: a disorder found among juvenile delinquents involving a lack of guilt and remorse.

Deprivation: the state of a child who has formed a close relationship to someone but is later separated from that person.

Privation: the state of a child who has never formed a close attachment with anyone.

experienced difficulties at school and in forming good relationships with other children.

At the age of 16, the family relationships of the adopted children were as good as those of families in which none of the children had been removed from the family home. However, children who had returned to their families showed little affection for their parents, and their parents were not very affectionate towards them. Both groups of adolescents were less likely than adolescents in ordinary families to have a special friend or to regard other adolescents as sources of emotional support. Overall, however, the adopted children were better adjusted than would have been predicted by Bowlby.

Discussion points

1. How has the research of Hodges and Tizard added to our knowledge of the effects of privation?
2. How might we account for the different patterns of behavior shown by adopted children and children who returned to their families?

KEY STUDY EVALUATION

One of the criticisms of this study is that some of the children "dropped out" before the end of the study. This left a biased sample because children who could not be traced or were not willing to take part may well have been different from those left in the study. In fact Hodges and Tizard reported that those adopted children who remained in the study had earlier shown somewhat more adjustment problems than the restored children who dropped out. This left a "better" sample of adopted children and might explain why they did better.

It is also important to note that there were considerable individual differences within each group: some of the restored children actually had good family relations and some of the adopted children didn't.

As this was a natural experiment, cause and effect cannot be assumed, so it cannot be said that privation causes long-term negative social effects; it can only be inferred.

A few researchers have considered the effects of extreme privation and isolation on children. The resilience of most of these children is surprising. For example, Koluchová (1976) studied identical twin boys (Andrei and Vanya) who had spent most of the first 7 years of their lives locked in a cellar. They had been treated very badly and were often beaten. They could barely talk and relied mainly on gestures. The twins were adopted by extremely dedicated women at about the age of 9. By the time they were 14, their behavior was essentially normal. By the age of 20, they were of above-average intelligence and had excellent relationships with the members of their foster family. They took further education and both married and had children.

Similar findings have been reported in studies on Romanian children exposed to very severe deprivation and neglect in Romania before being adopted by caring British families. O'Connor, Rutter, et al. (2000) compared Romanian children adopted between 24 and 42 months (late-placed adoptees) and those adopted between 6 and 24 months (earlier-placed adoptees). Both groups showed significant recovery from their ordeal in Romania. However, the late-placed adoptees had greater difficulty in achieving good cognitive and social development than earlier-placed adoptees.

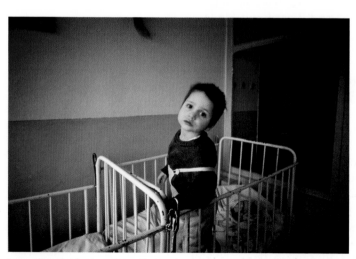

Late-placed adoptees from Romania were less able to recover from the severe deprivation they had experienced and go on to develop good cognitive and social skills than those children who had been adopted earlier in life.

Case Study: *The Riley Family*

Jean Riley (54) and her husband Peter (58) adopted two children from Romania who are now aged 17 and 9. Cezarina, when they first saw her, was cross-eyed, filthy, and about 4 years behind in her physical development. First Cezarina's physical problems had to be sorted out, but from then on she made good progress. However, Cezarina is "laid back" about things that seem important to Jean and Peter. Jean understands this attitude, though, because clearly examinations seem less important when a child has had to struggle to survive.

According to Jean, Cezarina is bright, but needs to have information reinforced over and over again. She has also struggled to understand jokes and sarcasm, although this may be due to difficulties with learning the language. Jean sees Cezarina as naive and emotionally immature. Cezarina says herself that initially she was frustrated because she couldn't communicate. She does see herself as being different from other girls, although she likes the same things, such as fashion and pop music. Jean runs The Parent Network for the Institutionalized Child, a group for people who have adopted such children. Cezarina has partly recovered from her poor early experiences. (Account based on an article in *Woman*, September 21, 1998.)

An important study was carried out by Rutter et al. (1998) on 111 Romanian children adopted in the UK before the age of 2. The children arrived with severe developmental impairment, but in 2 years their progress was described as dramatic.

These findings provide further support for the notion that most children are able to recover even from very difficult and distressing childhoods.

Evaluation

- Maternal deprivation often has adverse short- and long-term effects on children.

- As Rutter argued, the negative effects of privation are typically greater than those of deprivation.

- The assumption of the monotropy hypothesis that infants form only one strong attachment is wrong.

- The finding that family discord is more important than maternal deprivation in producing negative effects on children goes against Bowlby's theory.

- Many (or even most) of the adverse effects of maternal deprivation and privation are reversible, especially when the deprivation or privation is relatively short-lived. There is more reversibility of effects than predicted by Bowlby.

DIVORCE AND DAY CARE

Some of the major sources of disruption to children's attachments in Western societies (and in many other cultures) have become much more common in recent decades. For example, fewer than 5% of marriages in the United Kingdom ended in divorce 50 years ago. Nowadays the figure is 40%, and is even higher in the United States. Another major change in most Western societies has been the substantial increase in the number of mothers going out to work. In several countries, very large numbers of young children are put into day care for several days a week while their mothers are at work. In the United States, 80% of children under the age of 6 spend an average of 40 hours in non-parent care every week (National Research Council and Institute of Medicine, 2003). Until the 1960s, this happened only rarely.

We consider possible negative effects on children of these large increases in divorce and in day care. Common sense would suggest that the adverse effects of divorce are much greater than those of day care. Divorce produces a major and permanent change in the situation of the children affected by it. In contrast, children in day care typically experience many hours of loving attention from both parents. However, according to Bowlby's (1969) attachment theory, any disruption of the bond between mother and child during the first few years of life can impair his/her social and emotional development.

DIVORCE

Children who experience the divorce of their parents typically go through a series of transitions extending over a long period of time. First, there are marital conflicts that are distressing to children. Second, there is the actual separation followed by divorce. Third, various adjustments need to be made by the parents and their children. These often include moving house and having less money available, and the children may have to react to a new relationship as the parents find new partners and perhaps remarry.

Over half of children whose parents divorce lose contact with the parent who isn't looking after them (nearly always the father) within 2 years. The effects are generally more serious than losing one's father through death. Children of divorced parents usually feel their parents chose to divorce even though they were opposed to it (Hetherington, 1989). This creates anger rarely found when the father dies. In addition, children of divorced parents often experience guilt and a sense that they are partially responsible for the divorce.

Findings

Hetherington, Cox, and Cox (1982) studied the effects of divorce on 4-year-old middle-class children over a 2-year period. The first year after divorce was the *crisis phase*. During that time, mothers became stricter than before and were less affectionate. In return, the children (especially boys) behaved more aggressively. During the crisis phase, fathers became less strict and often gave treats to their children.

The *adjustment phase* was usually reached about 2 years after divorce. There was more routine and order about the children's everyday lives. In addition, the mothers had gone back to treating their children in a more patient and understanding way. Overall, there was less emotional distress than in the crisis phase. However, the boys of divorced parents had worse relations and showed more disobedient behavior than boys whose parents hadn't divorced.

Hetherington (1988) found 6 years after divorce that 70% of the mothers had remarried. The children of divorced parents were more independent and had more impact on decision making than those in intact families. Sons still tended to be disobedient with their mothers, who found it difficult to exercise control.

Joint custody vs. sole custody

Bauserman (2002) conducted a meta-analysis of 33 studies between 1982 and 1999 which examined 1846 sole-custody and 814 joint-custody children. The study showed that following parental divorce children in joint-custody arrangements had fewer behavioral and emotional problems, higher self-esteem, better family relations, and better school performance than children in sole-custody arrangements. These children were as well-adjusted as intact-family children on the same measures, possibly because joint custody gives the child an opportunity to maintain continuing contact with both parents.

The findings actually indicate that joint *physical* custody is not the most important factor at all, in fact just spending substantial time with both parents, especially with their fathers, leads to better adjustment. Also, less conflict is reported by joint-custody couples, possibly because both parents could participate in their children's lives equally, as opposed to spending time arguing about childcare decisions. These findings challenge the perception that joint custody exposes children to ongoing parental conflict and therefore is more harmful. The studies in this review showed that higher levels of conflict were reported by sole-custody parents.

This does not mean that joint custody should be given in all situations. Sole custody with one parent would clearly be preferable when the other parent is abusive or neglectful, or has a serious mental or physical health problem. Informed decisions of what environment is best for a child in a custody situation depend on the judges, lawyers, social workers, psychologists, and other professionals involved in divorce counseling and litigation being aware of these findings.

Even 10 years after a divorce, the children involved regarded it as the most stressful event of their lives (Wallerstein, 1987). They felt they had been seriously deprived by not growing up in a family with both parents. Many of the girls feared rejection and betrayal by men.

The effects of parental divorce are very variable. On the one hand, some children of divorced parents suffer long-term adverse effects. O'Connor, Thorpe, Dunn, and Golding (1999) found that women who had experienced divorce in childhood were more likely to be severely depressed than those whose parents hadn't divorced (17% vs. 12%, respectively). On the other hand, some children of divorced parents become very competent and caring adults from coping with the consequences of experiencing divorce (Hetherington & Stanley-Hagan, 1999). Only 2 years after parental divorce, about 80% of children cope and function well (Hetherington, 2002).

It may not just be a stressful home environment that determines the adverse effects of divorce on a child; the child's genes may also be an influencing factor.

Parents who divorce don't only provide their children with a difficult and stressful home environment. They also provide their children's genes. It is thus possible that some of the adverse effects of divorce on children may be a result of their genes rather than of the experience of divorce itself. We can shed some light on this issue by comparing the effects of divorce on children in biological and adoptive families. Children in adoptive families don't share genes with their adoptive parents, and so adverse effects of divorce in such families are a result of environmental factors. In contrast, adverse effects of divorce in biological families could be a result of genetic factors, environmental factors, or both.

O'Connor, Caspi, Defries, and Plomin (2000) studied the effects of divorce on children in biological families. Mental disorder in children of divorced parents seemed to be due entirely to the effects of the divorce itself. In contrast, genetic factors were partially responsible for adverse effects on self-esteem, social competence, and academic competence in children of divorced parents in biological families.

Similar finding were reported by O'Connor et al. (2003) in a study on the effects of genetic risk (measured by parents' self-reports of negative emotionality) on children's adjustment to parental separation. Children at genetic risk had comparable social adjustment to those not at risk, provided that their parents had not separated. However, genetic risk strongly predicted poor adjustment in children whose parents had separated. These findings suggest that the negative effects of parental separation are significantly greater on children at genetic risk, indicating that genetic factors interact with environmental ones to determine children's adjustment.

DAY CARE

Do infants who spend several days a week in day care suffer as a result? The answer depends on the kinds of caregiving provided while the mother is working and on the nature of the family to which the child belongs. However, it is difficult to interpret the evidence from day-care studies. Children who receive day care may well differ in several ways from those who do not, and so it is generally not clear whether differences between the two groups of children are a result of the day care or the pre-existing differences (see Shpancer, 2006, for a review).

Findings

Evidence that there can be negative effects of day care was reported in a review by Clarke-Stewart (1989). On average, 36% of infants whose mothers worked full time were insecurely attached compared to 29% of infants whose mothers didn't work or worked only part time. As Clarke-Stewart (1989, p. 270) pointed out, the reason for the difference may not be "that 40 hours of day care is hard on infants but that 40 hours of work is hard on mothers." Harrison and Ungerer (2002) considered the mother's position in families in which she had returned to paid employment during the first year of her infant's life. Infants were less likely to be securely attached to their mother if she wasn't committed to work and had anxieties about making use of child care.

The National Institute of Child Health and Development (NICHD) considered attachment security in more detail. Children in day care were most likely to show insecure attachment if there was a lack of maternal sensitivity and day care was of poor quality (NICHD, 1997).

Finding an association between day-care quality and children's development is *not* sufficient to show that it has a causal effect on children's development. The reason is that children experiencing high-quality day care tend to have parents who are better educated and more responsive than those experiencing low-quality care (Marshall, 2004). Thus, it is difficult to determine whether it is the parenting or the day care that is responsible for the association between day-care quality and children's development.

The above issue was addressed in a large NICHD study in which over 1000 children were studied from birth to 4½ years. When the effects of family environment were controlled, the influence of day-care quality was surprisingly modest (NICHD, 2003). More specifically, day-care quality didn't seem to influence children's social development (e.g., social competence; behavior problems), but had small effects on memory and language quality.

Erel, Oberman, and Yirmiya (2000) carried out several meta-analyses on studies of the effects of day care. They related day care to seven measures of child development:

1. *Secure vs. insecure attachment to the mother.*
2. *Attachment behaviors*: Avoidance and resistance (reflecting insecure attachment), and exploration (reflecting secure attachment).
3. *Mother–child interaction*: Responsiveness to mother, smiling at mother, obeying mother, and so on.
4. *Adjustment*: Self-esteem, lack of behavior problems, and so on.
5. *Social interaction with peers.*
6. *Social interaction with nonparental peers.*
7. *Cognitive development*: School performance, IQ, and so on.

Erel et al. (2000) found that day care had nonsignificant effects on all seven measures described above. This was the case regardless of the amount of day care per week, the number of months the child had had in day care, and the child's gender.

In sum, day care generally has no negative effects on young children. However, some reports suggest extensive day care for infants in the first year of life can have adverse effects on security of attachment (Belsky, 1988) and cognitive development (Baydar & Brooks-Gunn, 1991). Even here the effects are rather small. Thus, the great majority of infants and children don't suffer in any way (socially, emotionally, or cognitively) from spending many hours a week in day care.

PEER RELATIONSHIPS

Children of all ages spend significant amounts of time with their peers (individuals of about the same age) and are interested in social interaction. Tremblay-Leveau and Nadel (1996) used a situation in which an infant was included or excluded from an interaction between the experimenter and another child. Children of 11 months were five times more likely to interact with the other child (e.g., smiling; putting their body between the experimenter and the other child) when excluded than when not excluded.

There is a marked increase in the preference for associating with same-sex peers during the course of development. Maccoby (1998) has reviewed evidence showing that this occurs in numerous cultures around the world. From about the age of 3, children prefer to play with same-sex rather than opposite-sex peers. When they start going to school, the percentage of children associating with same-sex children in the playground increases steadily between the ages of 4 and 12. This same-sex preference is also found with respect to friendship. A child's best friend between middle childhood and adolescence is typically someone of the same sex.

Rose and Rudolph (2006) considered in detail the differences in same-sex peer friendships in boys and girls, nearly all of which increase during the years of childhood. Girls tend to gain more than boys from such friendships at the emotional level, including greater closeness, affection, trust, and enhancement of worth. However, girls also experience more stress from same-sex friendships (e.g., having a friend tell their secrets; having someone stop being their friend; having a friend stop talking to them). Girls also rely more than boys on same-sex friends for social support when they are stressed. In contrast, boys have a greater tendency than girls to interact in groups with a well-defined dominance hierarchy and to engage in competitive play. This can lead to aggressive behavior. According to Rose and Rudolph, the gender differences in same-sex friendships mean that girls are more vulnerable to developing emotional problems (e.g., low self-esteem; depression). In contrast, boys are more vulnerable to developing behavioral problems (e.g., aggression; antisocial behavior).

A child's best friend between middle childhood and adolescence is usually of the same sex.

Peer relations and romantic relationships

A continuing longitudinal study (Simpson, Collins, Tran, & Haydon, 2007) at the University of Minnesota has tracked 78 individuals through infancy, early childhood, adolescence, and adulthood, monitoring them at 12 months, 6–8 years, 16 years, and early adulthood. The research focus was on attachment, interaction with peers, and close friendships during childhood. The young adults' interactions with romantic partners and their expressions of emotions were also monitored. As well as supporting previous studies on attachment, for example that securely attached infants had higher social competence with their peers in childhood, the study has found that these positive peer relationships seem in their teens to have led to closer and more secure peer friendships. As young adults these people were more expressive and emotionally attached to their romantic peers.

Professor Collins, leader of the research team, says that the current findings highlight one developmental pathway through which significant peer relationship experiences during the early years of life relate to the daily experiences in romantic relationships during early adulthood.

SOCIAL COMPETENCE

There are various ways of assessing how well children relate to their peers. Researchers can use observational techniques to measure social behavior (e.g., smiling; aggressive actions). Another method is to use peer ratings, in which all the children in a group rate each other on one or more social dimensions (e.g., likeability).

Coie, Dodge, and Coppotelli (1982) asked children aged 8, 11, and 14 to identify three classmates they liked most and three they liked least. They used this information to assign the children to five categories:

1. *Popular* (often liked most; seldom liked least)
2. *Controversial* (often liked most; often liked least)
3. *Average* (sometimes liked most; sometimes liked least)
4. *Neglected* (seldom liked most; seldom liked least)
5. *Rejected* (seldom liked most; often liked least).

What factors were associated with being liked most and being liked least? The main factors associated with being liked most were being supportive, cooperating with peers, leading peers, and being physically attractive. The main factors associated with being liked least were disrupting the group, getting into trouble with the teacher, starting fights, and being snobbish.

It would be tempting (but wrong!) to assume that all children assigned to the same category have similar behavior. Cillessen, van IJzendoorn, van Lieshout, and Hartup (1992) found that about half of rejected children were aggressive, and also tended to be uncooperative and dishonest. About one-eighth of the rejected children were submissive and shy, and the remaining rejected children exhibited few extreme forms of behavior. As might be expected, children rejected because they were aggressive were much more likely than the other rejected children to continue to be in the rejected group 1 year later (58% vs. 34%, respectively).

Children neglected or rejected by their peers often experience emotional and/or behavioral problems subsequently. For example, Keiley, Bates, Dodge, and Pettit (2000) discovered that children rejected by their peers in kindergarten had an increased probability of behavioral problems in middle childhood. Miller-Johnson et al. (1999) found an association between childhood rejection by peers and extreme forms of delinquency in adolescence. It is difficult to show that behavioral problems and delinquency are caused by children's difficulties with their peers. Rejected and neglected children tend to live in poverty and to experience harsh parenting (see Deater-Deckard, 2001, for a review), and these factors are also likely to play a part.

What are the key differences between children low and high in social competence? As Lemerise and Arsenio (2000) pointed out, there are two main differences. First, there are cognitive differences, with socially competent children being more skilled at social information processing (Crick & Dodge, 1994). Second, there are emotional differences, with socially incompetent children experiencing many negative emotions and having poor emotional regulation or control (Eisenberg & Fabes, 1992).

Social information processing

Crick and Dodge (1994) put forward a model emphasizing the importance of social information processing (see the figure below). There are six steps in their model, and every step needs to be completed successfully to show social competence:

1. Attend to (and encode) the social cues in a situation (e.g., another child's nonverbal behavior).
2. Interpret or make sense of those social cues (e.g. deciding why someone else has behaved in a certain way).

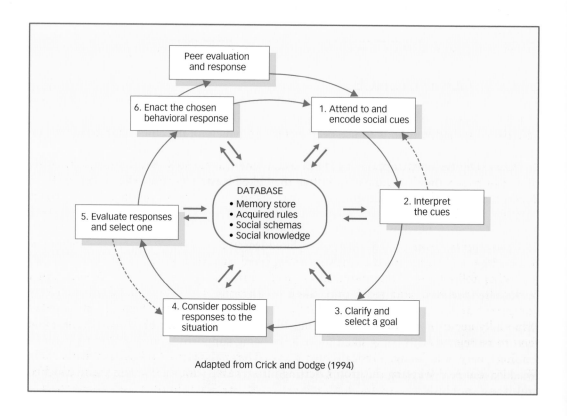

Adapted from Crick and Dodge (1994)

3. Select a goal or desired outcome for the situation (e.g., making a new friend).
4. Consider possible responses to the situation (e.g., offer help to the other person).
5. Select the response offering the greatest prospect of achieving the desired goal or outcome.
6. Produce the chosen response.

These six steps generally (but not invariably) occur one after the other in the order given above.

How does the model explain higher levels of social competence over time? First, children's database of social knowledge increases with age. As a result, they have more responses from which to choose, and they learn to predict more accurately the likely consequences of producing any given response. Second, children over time show increases in capacity and/or speed of processing, and these increases allow them to process social information more efficiently.

Strassberg and Dodge (1987) showed the importance of Step 2 in the model. Rejected and nonrejected children watched videotapes of other children at play, and interpreted what they saw. Rejected children were more likely than nonrejected children to provide aggressive interpretations of the social interactions in the videotapes. Crick and Ladd (1990) assessed Step 5 in the model. Children were presented with a situation and evaluated what would happen if they responded in a given way. Children rejected by their peers predicted that verbal aggression would produce positive outcomes. In addition, neglected children predicted that behaving assertively would lead to more negative outcomes than did nonneglected children.

Evaluation

+ The model provides a detailed account of children's processing of social information.

+ Individual differences in processing of social information predict social competence.

− The relationship between social information processing and social competence is fairly weak. Thus, other factors must also be involved.

− Powerful emotions are sometimes involved in social information processing, but Crick and Dodge's (1994) model has little to say about emotional processes.

EMOTIONAL REGULATION

Eisenberg and Fabes (1992) identified two factors influencing social competence:

1. *Emotionality*: This relates to "stable individual differences in the typical intensity with which individuals experience their emotions" (Eisenberg & Fabes, 1992, p. 122).
2. *Emotion regulation*: This involves the ability to control, modify, and manage emotional reactions and behavior.

Children can be assigned to four categories on the basis of whether their emotionality is low or high and whether their emotion regulation is low or high.

What follows from the above theoretical approach? Children low in emotionality (especially negative emotions) and high in emotion regulation should be socially competent and popular with other children. In contrast, children high in emotionality (especially negative emotions) and low in emotion regulation lack social competence and tend to be rejected by their peers.

Eisenberg and Fabes's (1992) theory has been supported by findings from studies in Western and non-Western cultures. Eisenberg et al. (1997) found that American children who had low emotionality and high regulation at one point in time were more socially competent than other children subsequently. Eisenberg et al. (1996) found that children with high emotionality and low regulation subsequently had poorer social functioning than other children. Eisenberg, Pidada, and Liew (2001) studied children in Java, Indonesia, a collectivistic culture in which emotion regulation is valued very highly. The findings were very similar to those previously obtained in the United States. Eisenberg, Liew, and Pidada (2004) also studied children in Indonesia. The children were 9 years old at the start of the study and 12 at the end. For boys, high regulation and low emotionality at the age of 9 predicted social skills, adjustment, and peer liking 3 years later. The effects were much weaker for girls, in part because most of them were fairly well regulated and socially competent.

Evaluation

+ Emotional factors are important to an understanding of individual differences in social competence.

+ Emotionality (especially negative emotionality) combined with poor emotion regulation is associated with lack of social competence and rejection.

− The theory doesn't consider the cognitive processes involved in peer interactions.

− The direction of causality is often unclear. For example, high negative emotionality and poor regulation may cause children to be rejected, but rejection may cause increased negative emotionality and impaired regulation.

− The processes responsible for the development of emotion regulation aren't discussed in detail.

FRIENDSHIP PATTERNS

Children with friends are generally better adjusted and happier than those without. However, we must distinguish between the quantity (number) and quality (closeness) of friends. Berndt (1989) obtained some evidence that friendship quality is more important than friendship quantity in a study on 11- and 12-year-old children moving school. Friendship quality was positively related to the friendship support the children received during this period of transition. However, the number of friends was *negatively* related to friendship support.

What are the main characteristics of friendship? Bukowski, Hoza, and Boivin (1994) devised a Friendship Qualities Scale with five sub-scales assessing companionship, closeness, help, security, and conflict. Children aged between 10 and 12 rated friends and other peers on all five sub-scales. Friends received higher scores on four of the sub-scales (companionship, closeness, help, and security). In addition, friends who were still friends 6 months later received higher scores than friends who ceased to be friends. Finally, friends received lower scores than nonfriends on the conflict sub-scale.

Newcomb and Bagwell (1995) obtained similar findings in a meta-analysis to identify factors characterizing friendship relationships more than nonfriendship ones. Not surprisingly, friendships showed more evidence of positive engagement (social contact, talking, cooperation, and positive affect). Friendships were also associated with various relationship properties such as closeness, loyalty, mutual liking, equality, and similarity. Two further factors associated with friendship were conflict management and task activity. Conflict management involved more effective negotiation when conflicts arose, and task activity involved effective focusing on the task in hand.

As might be imagined, children tend to choose as friends those who are similar to them. However, friends are more similar with respect to some attributes than others. Of key importance is reputational salience, which is the importance of any given attribute in determining a child's status. Friends are more similar on attributes having high reputational salience than on those having low reputational salience. Challman (1932) found that friends were generally similar in terms of social cooperation, an attribute having high reputational salience. However, they weren't very similar with respect to intelligence, an attribute having low reputational salience. Haselager, Hartup, van Lieshout, and Riksen-Walraven (1995) found with 11-year-olds that friends were more similar for antisocial behavior (an attribute of high reputational salience) than for prosocial (helpful) behavior or social withdrawal.

Changes with age

It seems likely that the nature of friendship changes in various ways during the course of childhood. This issue was addressed by Newcomb and Bagwell (1995) They found there was a large increase in positive engagement with friends between preschool (up to 5 years) and childhood years (between 6 and 9 years), and a further increase between the childhood years and early adolescence (10–13 years). However, there was also a similar increase in positive engagement with nonfriends.

Newcomb and Bagwell (1995) found more convincing evidence of age-related changes specific to friendship when they considered closeness and loyalty. These relationship properties increased systematically throughout the period from preschool up to early adolescence. Newcomb and Bagwell (1995, p. 340) concluded, "It has been hypothesized that adolescent friendships are characterized by greater intimacy than are the friendships of young children . . . The current meta-analytic findings provide strong empirical support for this age-related difference."

Hartup and Stevens (1997) argued that friendships possess a deep structure and a surface structure. According to them, "We use *deep structure* to refer to the social meaning (essence) of relationships and *surface structure* to refer to the social exchanges that characterize them at any given moment" (Hartup & Stevens, 1997, p. 356). They made two predictions:

1. The deep structure of friendships doesn't change during the course of development;
2. The surface structure of friendships changes systematically during development.

According to Hartup and Stevens (1997), reciprocity or mutuality is of central importance in friendship deep structure. Thus, friendship at all ages is based on a fair balance between giving and taking. However, *what* is given and taken (the surface structure) varies during development. Goodnow and Burns (1985) found that young children's expectations of friendship revolved around concrete reciprocities and common interests (e.g., "And I give them food, so they give me food back," p. 120). Among school children, reciprocity takes the form of shared interests (e.g., "A good friend is someone who likes you and spends time with you and forgives you and doesn't actually bash you up," p. 120).

In adolescence, the types of reciprocity between friends are rather different. When adolescents described their ideal friend, they indicated that he/she was someone who was supportive in the sense of being understanding and trustworthy. Thus, reciprocity or mutuality focuses on common activities in young children, on shared interests during the main schools years, and on emotional reciprocity among adolescents.

Adolescents tend to value support, empathy, and emotional reciprocity in friends.

> ## Evaluation
>
> ⊕ It is clearly established that children's friendships possess some similarities (e.g., reciprocity; positive engagement) throughout childhood and adolescence.
>
> ⊕ Changes in the nature of children's friendships during development have been shown; these include increases in closeness and complexity.
>
> ⊖ Relatively few studies on children's friendships are designed to test clear theoretical predictions.
>
> ⊖ Most research has only studied children's friendships at a given point in time. As a result, little is known about reasons for changes over time within friendships. For example, we lack detailed understanding of the processes causing friendships to become stronger or weaker.

PARENTS, PEERS, OR GENES?

The evidence discussed in this chapter (and in the previous one) suggests that children's development is strongly influenced by the way they are treated by their parents. However, matters may not be so simple. Consider, for example, the association between high levels of parental negativity and antisocial behavior in their adolescent children. It may seem natural to assume it is the parents' behavior that causes poor adjustment in the children. However, there are other possibilities. For example, antisocial behavior by children may cause their parents to react in a hostile way. In this section of the chapter we focus on attempts to clarify the meaning of such findings.

BEHAVIORAL GENETICS

Behavioral genetics is an important approach to understanding some causal factors responsible for children's social development. In essence, this approach involves studying the interaction between genetic factors and environmental ones in determining behavior. O'Connor et al. (1998) used the perspective of behavioral genetics to explain the fact that negative parental behavior is associated with antisocial behavior in their children. They studied adopted children, some of whose biological mothers had a history of antisocial behavior prior to the birth of their child. It was assumed that adopted children whose mother had such a history would be genetically at risk for antisocial behavior. The tendency of the adoptive parents to use negative control in the form of hostility, guilt induction, and withdrawal from the relationship was assessed.

O'Connor et al.'s (1998) key finding was as follows: "Children at genetic risk received more negative control from their adoptive parents than children not at genetic risk from middle childhood to early adolescence." Thus, children at genetic risk for antisocial behavior elicit negative behavior from their adoptive parents. Thus, genetic factors in the children influence the association between negative parental behavior and antisocial behavior in children. However, note that O'Connor et al. did *not* find that negative parental behavior is due entirely to genetic factors in their adopted children. Parental behavior depends on numerous factors including financial problems, the quality of the marital relationship, and the parent's own experiences as a child (Hetherington, 1993).

Do parents matter?

David Bell, the Chief Inspector of Schools in England, certainly seems to think so. His statement (2003) that today's rising 5-year-olds are "less prepared to start school than ever" is based on his opinion that social, behavioral, and verbal skills in this group are at an all-time low. He describes these children as unable to listen, settle down, and be quiet. He also says that some are unable to speak properly or use a knife and fork. Bell cites lack of parental discipline and poor stimulation as causes. Others have identified use of television and videos as "child minders" rather than real humans to interact with these children.

What factors determine how similar or dissimilar children within the same family are to each other (e.g., in personality)? Behavioral geneticists identify three relevant factors:

1. Genetic influences.
2. Shared environmental influences, which children of the same family have in common.
3. Nonshared environmental influences, consisting of those influences unique to each child.

Loehlin (1985) studied personality in monozygotic or identical twins, dizygotic or fraternal twins, and in unrelated children brought up in the same household. Identical twins were fairly similar in personality, as was indicated by an average correlation of +.50 across various personality traits. Fraternal twins resembled each other less in personality, with the average correlation being +.30. Of most relevance to the present discussion, unrelated children brought up in the same household had an average correlation of +.07. This means that unrelated children brought up together scarcely resembled each other at all. Thus, in opposition to what might have been expected, shared environment has very little impact on children's personality development. These findings were confirmed in a review by Plomin, Asbury, and Dunn (2001). They concluded that, "Most environmental variance affecting the development of psychological dimensions . . . is not shared by children growing up in the same family" (Plomin et al., 2001, p. 225).

In sum, the evidence suggests that genetic factors account for about 40% of individual differences in personality, and we have seen that shared environment is relatively unimportant. It follows that nonshared environment is of great importance. We turn next to an influential attempt to identify the main nonshared environmental factors influencing children's personality.

GROUP SOCIALIZATION THEORY

Harris (1995) argued that there are two main ways of explaining *why* shared environment has little influence on personality development. First, it is possible that, "parental behaviors have no effect on the psychological characteristics their children will have as adults" (p. 458). Second, children growing up in the same family may have different experiences within the home (e.g., because they are treated very differently by their parents). When I became a parent, I resolved to treat all my children (two girls and a boy) in the same way. However, it rapidly became clear that this wasn't a good strategy, because they all had such different personalities and interests.

Harris (1995, 2000) argued in her provocative and controversial group socialization theory that parents have essentially no long-term effects on their children's personality development. She accepted that children learn much about social behavior within the family environment. However, Harris (1995, p. 462) argued that such learning doesn't generalize to other situations: "Children learn separately how to behave at home (or in the presence of their parents) and how to behave when they are not at home . . . In the home, they may be reprimanded for mistakes and praised when they behave appropriately; out of the home they may be ridiculed for mistakes and ignored when they behave appropriately."

What environmental factors are important in Harris's theory? According to Harris (1995, p. 481), "Experiences in childhood and adolescent peer groups . . . account for environmental influences on personality development." We can relate this assumption to our earlier discussion in which we saw that nonshared environmental factors are much more important than shared ones in determining personality development. According to group socialization theory, experiences in peer groups are the central nonshared environmental factors.

Before turning to the relevant evidence, it is important to clarify the meaning of the term "nonshared environment," which is broader in meaning than is sometimes realized.

As Westen (1998, p. 349) pointed out, "It [nonshared environment] includes shared events to which different children respond differently . . . Thus, early separation from a parent may have a substantially different effect on a child who is temperamentally higher in negative affect than one with an easier temperament, even though the environmental event is identical and hence shared."

Findings

We discussed evidence indicating the importance of relationships with peers earlier in the chapter. For example, Miller-Johnson et al. (1999) found that delinquency in adolescence often followed on from childhood rejection by peers. Deater-Deckard (2001) reviewed evidence showing that peer rejection and avoidance of peer interaction in childhood are both associated with subsequent emotional and behavioral problems (e.g., antisocial behavior). As discussed earlier, Rose and Rudolph (2006) found that girls' same-sex friendships focus on emotional closeness whereas those of boys focus on competition and achievement. These differences plausibly play some role in the development of sex-typed differences in adult life.

A key prediction from the theory is that parental and family influences on children's social development should be very small. Some of the evidence discussed earlier is consistent with that prediction. For example, O'Connor et al. (1998) found that some of the apparent effects of parental behavior on children's behavior were caused by genetic factors in the children. Such evidence suggests that many theorists may have exaggerated the importance of parental factors in determining children's development.

According to Harris (1995, 2000), the effects of parental behavior on their children should be limited to the home environment. Forgatch and DeGarmo (1999) observed the effects of an intervention program designed to improve parental child-rearing style. The intervention produced significant improvement in the children's behavior at home, but had no effect on teachers' ratings of the children when at school.

Harris de-emphasized the importance of environmental influences operating within the family. Evidence apparently inconsistent with that notion was reported by Paulhus, Trapnell, and Chen (1999), who studied children differing in birth order within the same family. First-borns tended to be most achieving and conscientious, whereas later-borns were most likely to be liberal, rebellious, and agreeable.

The finding that nonshared environmental factors are often much more important than shared ones in accounting for individual differences in socialization is consistent with the notion that parents have little influence on their children. However, there are other possibilities. For example, suppose parents treat their children differently, and that this differential treatment influences their development. Such parental influences would be classified as nonshared environmental influences. Alternatively, suppose children respond differently to their parents' behavior. Any effects of such parental behavior on children's development would also be classified as nonshared environmental influences.

Evidence relevant to the issues raised in the previous paragraph was reported by Bergeman et al. (1988). They found that in identical twins brought up apart, high family conflict was associated with increased impulsivity only in children predisposed to impulsivity. Frequent family activities were associated with reduced neuroticism (tendency to experience negative emotions; see Chapter 12) among children predisposed to neuroticism. However, frequent family activities were associated with *increased* neuroticism among children not predisposed to neuroticism. Thus, some nonshared environmental influences reflect the different effects of parental behavior on the children within a family.

One of the most general problems with group socialization theory is the assumption that parental and peer influences are very different from each other. In fact, parents and peers generally share some of the values and beliefs within any given community. Indeed, many parents try through choice of school and other ways to ensure that most of the peers their child spends a lot of time with have cultural values similar to their own. In addition, it is not simply the case that any given child passively absorbs the values of the peers he/she encounters. Many children will communicate their own values to their peers, and these values will often reflect those of their own parents.

Evaluation

+ Group socialization theory is a comprehensive attempt to explain why nonshared environmental factors have much more impact than shared ones on the development of socialization in children.

+ Many theorists (including Freud) exaggerated the importance of shared experiences within the family in influencing children's social development.

+ Children's experiences in peer groups do seem to have lasting effects on their social development.

− There are various possible explanations of the finding that individual differences in socialization depend heavily on nonshared environmental factors. It is not necessarily the case that parental influences are weak or nonexistent.

− The notion that what children experience in one context (e.g., home) has no impact on their behavior in another context (e.g., at school) is too extreme.

− It is improbable that parents, teachers, and siblings have the very small effects on children's socialization assumed by Harris (1995, 2000).

Chapter Summary

Attachment
- According to Bowlby, young children's development of attachment goes through five phases, during the last of which the child has an internal working model of the child–caretaker relationship.
- Ainsworth's research with the Strange Situation test led her to identify three types of attachment: secure; resistant; and avoidant. It is preferable to focus on two attachment dimensions: avoidant/withdrawal vs. proximity-seeking; and resistant vs. emotional confidence.
- Cross-cultural studies using the Strange Situation test indicate that German infants are less likely to be securely attached and more likely to be avoidantly attached than those from most other countries. More generally, however, the variation in attachment style within cultures is greater than the variation between cultures.
- Any given child's attachment style is determined in part by maternal sensitivity. It is also determined (but to a lesser extent) by paternal sensitivity. In addition, the child's genetic make-up helps to determine its attachment style.

Deprivation effects
- According to Bowlby's maternal deprivation hypothesis, breaking the bond between mother and child during the early years of life often has serious long-term consequences, some of which are permanent and irreversible. For example, Bowlby argued that deprivation in early childhood is common in adolescents with affectionless psychopathy, but this finding has not been replicated.

- Rutter argued with supporting evidence that privation has much more severe effects than deprivation.
- There is convincing evidence that most of the effects of even extreme privation are reversible. This is especially the case when deprivation or privation is relatively short-lived.

Divorce and day care

- Children whose parents divorce typically take years to cope with the consequences. There is an initial crisis phase lasting about 1 year followed by an adjustment phase. Even 10 years after a divorce, the children involved regard it as the most stressful event of their lives.
- Mental disorder in children of divorced parents is a result of the effects of the divorce itself. In contrast, genetic factors play a role in accounting for adverse effects on self-esteem and academic competence in children of divorced parents.
- The quality of day care doesn't influence children's social development but has small effects on memory and language quality.
- When children put into day care are compared with those not put into day care, the differences in terms of social and cognitive development are typically small or nonexistent.

Peer relationships

- There is a marked increase in the preference for associating with same-sex peers rather than opposite-sex peers during the course of development up to the age of about 12.
- Coie et al. proposed five categories of social acceptance: popular; controversial; average; neglected; and rejected. Children neglected or rejected by their peers often develop emotional or behavioral problems subsequently.
- Socially competent children are skilled at social information processing, they have good emotional regulation, and they are low in emotionality.
- Friendship quality is more important than friendship quantity in making children well-adjusted and happy.
- Friendship relationships are associated with positive engagement, closeness, loyalty, mutual liking, and equality.
- Friends tend to be similar with respect to attributes having high reputational relevance.
- The nature of children's friendships changes during development. For example, friendships later in childhood tend to be closer and more complex than those early in childhood.

Parents, peers, or genes?

- The approach known as behavioral genetics has been applied to the finding that negative parental behavior is associated with antisocial behavior in their children. Part of the explanation is that children genetically at risk for antisocial behavior elicit negative parental behavior.
- Behavioral genetics has shown that children's personality is determined much more by nonshared than by shared environmental factors.
- According to Harris's group socialization theory, experiences in peer groups play a major role in children's personality development, whereas parental behavior has only a small impact limited to the home.
- There is some evidence that parental behavior influences children's behavior more at home than at school.
- Group socialization theory de-emphasizes the possibility that parental behavior may contribute to nonshared environmental influences because its effects vary from child to child within the family.

Further Reading

- Berk, L.E. (2006). *Child development* (7th ed.). New York: Pearson. Research on children's attachments and friends is discussed in detail in this textbook.
- Cole, M., & Cole, S.R. (2004). *The development of children* (5th ed.). New York: Worth. The topics dealt with in this chapter are covered at greater length in this American textbook.
- Harris, M., & Butterworth, G. (2002). *Developmental psychology: A student's handbook*. Hove, UK: Psychology Press. Several chapters in this British textbook (e.g., 6 and 14) address the topics discussed in this chapter.
- Shaffer, D.R. (2004). *Social and personality development* (5th ed.). Belmont, CA: Wadsworth. There is a reasonably comprehensive discussion of topics such as attachment and the development of friendships in this book.
- Smith, P.K., Cowie, H., & Blades, M. (2003). *Understanding children's development* (4th ed.). Oxford, UK: Blackwell. Several chapters in this textbook (especially 4 and 5) contain good introductory accounts.

PART V

INTRODUCTION TO
Social
Psychology

The next four chapters are all concerned with social psychology. According to Hogg and Vaughan (2005, p. 655), social psychology is, "The scientific investigation of how the thoughts, feelings and behavior of individuals are influenced by the actual, imagined or implied presence of others." Other areas of psychology (e.g., cognitive psychology; psychology of emotion) are also concerned with individuals' thoughts and feelings. However, social psychology is different because it focuses on the impact of other people on individuals, even when those other people are not actually present. For example, most people wouldn't drop litter in the street even if no one was observing them (Hogg & Vaughan, 2005), because most people within our society disapprove of such behavior.

In my opinion, social psychology is both the most fascinating *and* the most frustrating area of research in psychology. It is fascinating because most of us enjoy trying to understand our own social behavior and that of our friends and acquaintances. It is frustrating because it has proved very hard to come to grips with the complexities of social behavior. Almost any aspect of social behavior is influenced by so many factors that it is fairly difficult to find a factor having no influence whatsoever!

RESEARCH METHODS IN SOCIAL PSYCHOLOGY

The most important research method in social psychology is experimentation based on use of the experimental method (see Chapter 1). Such experimentation often takes place in the laboratory, but social psychologists also carry out field experiments under naturalistic conditions in the real world. Most experiments in social psychology involve the manipulation of some aspect of the situation (the independent variable) to observe its effects on behavior (the dependent variable). Suppose we want to study the effects of social disapproval (e.g., "Please stop doing that!") on someone's behavior. We will probably find that such effects depend heavily on the current social context. For example, your behavior is more likely to be influenced if the disapproving person is an authority figure (e.g., your boss) and the situation is a formal one than if the disapproving person is a stranger and the situation is an informal one (e.g., a pub).

Social psychologists also have access to several nonexperimental methods. First, there are surveys, in which questionnaires and/or interviews are used to obtain detailed information. One of the advantages of such research is that a considerable amount of information can be obtained from a large number of individuals in a relatively short space of time. Second, there are field studies, in which the researcher simply observes the social behavior of groups (e.g., children in a playground; adolescent gangs). Field studies are rich sources of information, but it is often hard to interpret. Third, there are case studies, in which an individual or a group is studied in great detail. Case studies are especially

401

Social psychology looks at how the feelings and behavior of individuals are influenced by others—even when they are not there.

valuable in the investigation of rare phenomena (e.g., coping with natural disasters; weird cults). A limitation of most case studies is that the researcher's theoretical convictions may influence his/her interpretation of the evidence.

LEVELS OF EXPLANATION

Social psychology has connections to several other disciplines and areas of psychology. Disciplines such as social anthropology, sociology, and sociolinguistics are all relevant to social psychology, as are areas of psychology such as cognitive psychology and the study of individual differences. It follows that social psychologists use several levels of explanation. Doise (1986) identified four levels of explanation in social psychology:

1. *Intrapersonal level.* This is concerned with each individual's psychological processes (e.g., interpretation of social situations).
2. *Interpersonal and situational level.* This focuses only on the interactions among individuals within a given situation at a given time.
3. *Positional level.* This resembles the previous level, but some account is taken of role or social position (e.g., status, identity) outside of the immediate situation.
4. *Ideological level.* This level is concerned with the impact of general social beliefs and social identity on social behavior.

Social psychology in Europe differs substantially from that in the United States. Most European social psychologists accept that social psychology should encompass all four levels identified by Doise (1986). In contrast, many American social psychologists are mainly interested in the intrapersonal level, especially the ways in which individuals make sense of their social environment.

ORGANIZATION OF CHAPTERS 17–20

We start our coverage of social psychology with Chapter 17. This chapter deals with social cognition, which consists of "cognitive processes and structures that influence and are influenced by social behavior" (Hogg & Vaughan, 2005, p. 655). Most research in this area is at the intrapersonal level–the focus is on the ways in which individuals think about and make sense of their social behavior and that of others. Of all the socially relevant information we have stored in memory, information about ourselves is regarded as being of particular importance. Accordingly, the self-concept is discussed in Chapter 17.

Chapter 18 focuses on our dealings with other people as individuals with an emphasis on the emotional level. For example, if we feel positively about someone else, we are likely to behave in a helpful way towards them. In contrast, we may behave aggressively if we feel negatively about another person. At a more intimate level, close emotional relationships may lead to marriage. Such interpersonal relationships are discussed in Chapter 18.

Chapter 19 deals with various group processes. There are important phenomena associated with groups, including pressures to conform, the emergence of a leader, and the development of group cohesiveness. Explanations for such phenomena are discussed, and there is also an analysis of the behavior of very large groups or crowds.

Chapter 20 addresses various intergroup processes, especially those in which groups are in conflict. The main topics in this chapter are prejudice and discrimination, and what can be done to reduce them. There is also a consideration of stereotypes, because we need to know why and how people form stereotypes of other groups in society in order to understand prejudice fully.

In sum, there is a natural progression as we move through the chapters, with the focus expanding from the individual through groups and on to relationships between groups. Chapter 17 focuses on individual thoughts and cognitive structures, Chapter 18 deals mainly with our treatment of other individuals, Chapter 19 analyzes group phenomena, and Chapter 20 provides explanations of intergroup conflict. As you can see, the scope of social psychology is very broad!

Chapter 17

Contents

Social cognition 17

INTRODUCTION

This chapter deals with cognitive approaches to social psychology. Such approaches have become of increasing interest and importance in recent decades. They involve an emphasis on **social cognition**, "the cognitive processes and structures that influence and are influenced by social behavior" (Hogg & Vaughan, 2005, p. 655). Most research in this area is at the intrapersonal level, meaning that the focus is on the ways in which individuals think about and make sense of their own social behavior and that of others.

We begin our discussion of social cognition with attitudes, which involve beliefs and feelings about other people, groups, or objects. This is followed by a consideration of the factors that produce attitude change. In everyday life, we try to understand *why* we or other people are behaving in certain ways. Various attribution theories have addressed that issue directly, and form the basis for the next topic in the chapter. Finally, we turn to the self-concept. Of all the socially relevant information we have stored in long-term memory, information about ourselves and our self-concept is especially important.

ATTITUDES

What factors influence our behavior in social situations? Numerous factors are at work, including our personalities, our previous experiences in similar situations, the expectations of others, and our relationships with them. One important way of understanding social behavior is by studying the ways in which individuals think about themselves, about the groups to which they belong, and about other groups in society.

Much early research in social cognition was concerned with attitudes. According to Hogg and Vaughan (2005, p. 645), an attitude is "[a] a relatively enduring organization of beliefs, feelings and behavioral tendencies towards socially significant objects, groups, events or symbols; (b) a general feeling or evaluation—positive or negative—about some person, object or issue." If you want to find out about stereotypes (a type of attitude), read the relevant section in Chapter 20.

MEASUREMENT ISSUES

We cannot observe attitudes directly, but we can measure them indirectly using self-report questionnaires. Participants are presented with statements (e.g., "American movies are generally better than British movies"; "Most American movies are very superficial"). For each statement, they indicate their agreement or disagreement on a five-point (sometimes seven-point) scale (e.g., strongly agree; agree; neither agree nor disagree; disagree; strongly disagree). What I have just described is known as a **Likert scale**.

The greatest problem with this approach is that people may not be honest. They may show **social desirability bias**, deliberately distorting their responses to make them more socially desirable than is actually the case. This is especially likely to occur when their actual attitudes are disapproved of within society (e.g., negative views of minority groups).

There have been various attempts to minimize these problems. First, there is the **bogus pipeline**. Participants are connected to an impressive-looking machine and told the machine will detect any lies they tell. Participants are much more likely to reveal socially undesirable attitudes (e.g., racial and other kinds of prejudice) when attached to the bogus pipeline than when completing attitude scales under standard conditions (see Jones & Sigall, 1971). Tourangeau, Smith, and Rasinski (1997) found that use of the bogus pipeline led people to admit to cocaine use, frequent oral sex, and excessive drinking. In spite of its effectiveness in reducing social desirability bias, the bogus pipeline raises ethical issues (e.g., use of deception; invasion of privacy).

Second, we can assess **implicit attitudes**, which are outside conscious awareness and control. For example, Cunningham, Preacher, and Banaji (2001) asked participants to decide rapidly whether words had a positive or negative meaning by pressing one key for good words and another key for bad words. Immediately before each word was presented, a white or a black face was presented briefly. Participants' performance was scored by dividing the trials into two sets: (1) the white face followed by a positive word and the black face followed by a negative word; and (2) the white face followed by a negative word and the black face followed by a positive word. Fewer errors were made on trials belonging to the first set. The implication is that the participants had negative implicit attitudes toward blacks. Of interest, a standard self-report questionnaire of explicit attitudes (the Modern Racism Scale) did *not* reveal prejudiced attitudes.

WHY DO WE HAVE ATTITUDES?

Nearly everyone possesses thousands of attitudes, so presumably they must have some value for us. Shavitt (1989) argued that attitudes fulfill four major functions:

1. *Knowledge function*: Attitudes toward objects provide an efficient and relatively effort-free way of responding to them.
2. *Utilitarian function*: Attitudes assist us in behaving in ways likely to produce rewards and avoid punishments. In general, our attitudes toward any given object are favorable or unfavorable on the basis of our relevant past experience.
3. *Self-esteem maintenance*: Attitudes can lead us to align ourselves with liked objects (e.g., a successful football team), and this can maintain our self-esteem.
4. *Social identity function*: Attitudes provide a way of expressing our personal values and identifying with social groups perceived as endorsing the same attitudes.

ATTITUDES AND BEHAVIOR

What is the relationship between attitudes and behavior? It seems reasonable to assume that our attitudes are important in determining our behavior toward the objects of those attitudes. This plausible assumption has received surprisingly modest empirical support. LaPiere (1934) showed how great a difference there can be between attitudes and behavior. He was a white man who traveled around the United States with a young Chinese couple. LaPiere found that only one out of 66 hotels turned them away, and they were served at all 184 restaurants at which they stopped. Afterwards, LaPiere sent a letter to all the establishments asking whether they would accept Chinese guests. In all, 128 of the establishment owners replied, and more than 90% of them said they would not!

The above findings are not unusual. Wicker (1969) summarized the findings from 32 studies in which the relationship between attitudes and behavior was examined. The correlation between attitude and behavior rarely exceeded +.3, and the mean correlation was only +.15.

There is not always a large discrepancy between attitudes and behavior. For example, there is a fairly strong relationship between people's attitudes toward major political parties and their actual voting behavior (see Franzoi, 1996). What factors determine the strength of the association between attitudes and behavior? First, it matters whether attitudes and behavior are measured at the same *level of specificity*. *General* measures of attitudes usually fail to predict very *specific* types of behavior. For example, in the LaPiere (1934) study, the behavior of the establishment owners was to a specific, well-dressed, well-spoken Chinese couple, In contrast, the attitude questionnaire the owners completed referred to Chinese guests in general.

Second, there is the time interval. The relationship between attitudes and behavior is weaker when there is a long interval of time between the assessments of attitudes and behavior (6 months in the LaPiere, 1934, study). For example, opinion polls 1 week

Key Term

Implicit attitudes:
attitudes that are outside conscious awareness and control.

before an election predict voting behavior better than polls 1 month beforehand (Fishbein & Coombs, 1974).

Third, there is *direct* experience. Attitudes formed through direct experience predict behavior much better than do attitudes formed without such experience (Fazio & Zanna, 1981).

THEORIES OF REASONED ACTION AND PLANNED BEHAVIOR

We can often predict behavior from attitudes fairly well provided the research is carried out carefully. However, people's behavior is often strongly influenced by social factors (e.g., Asch, 1951, found strong evidence for conformity pressures; see Chapter 18). Thus, we need theories assuming that behavior depends on attitudes *and* social factors. Fishbein and Ajzen (1975) did this in their theory of reasoned action, subsequently extended into the theory of planned behavior (Ajzen, 1985, 1991; see figure on the right).

The key assumptions of the theory of reasoned action are as follows:

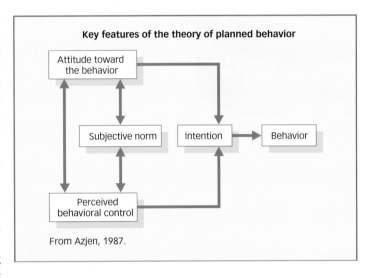

Key features of the theory of planned behavior

From Ajzen, 1987.

- Measures of attitudes should be compatible [consistent] with measures of behavior in terms of action, object, context, and time.
- Behavior depends in part on a subjective norm reflecting the perceived social pressures to carry out (or avoid) the behavior in question.
- An individual's behavior is determined by his/her behavioral intention (i.e., how he/she intends to behave). This behavioral intention is determined by attitudes towards the behavior and by the subjective norm.
- Attitude towards the behavior depends on behavioral beliefs (beliefs about the likely consequences) and on outcome evaluations (the person's evaluation of each consequence).
- Subjective norms depend on normative beliefs (the extent to which the individual believes other people expect him/her to behave in a certain way) and on motivation to comply (the extent to which the individual wants to conform to those expectations).

Ajzen (1985, 1991) argued that the theory of reasoned action focused only on behavior under the individual's control. Accordingly, he extended the theory by adding perceived behavioral control as another factor, thereby producing the theory of planned behavior. It was assumed that people are more likely to form the intention to perform a particular action if they perceive themselves to have a high level of behavioral control with respect to that action.

The theory of planned behavior is better equipped to handle situations involving a low level of perceived behavioral control. Consider a smoker with very positive attitudes about quitting smoking, where the subjective norm also favors the intention to stop smoking. According to the theory of reasoned action, the smoker would stop smoking. In practice, however, many smokers feel that smoking is an addiction. Such smokers will have low perceived behavioral control, and this leads to the accurate prediction that they will typically be unable to stop smoking.

FINDINGS

Smetana and Adler (1980) obtained questionnaire data from 136 women waiting to learn the results of a pregnancy test. The correlation between intention to have (or not to have) an abortion correlated +.96 with the behavior of those women who were pregnant. Van den Putte (1993) carried out a meta-analysis based on 150 tests of the theory of reasoned action. There were two main findings. First, the overall correlation between attitude plus subjective norm and behavioral intention was +.68. Second, the overall correlation

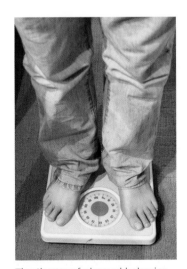

The theory of planned behavior perhaps accounts better for a dieter's failure to lose weight than the theory of reasoned action. Low perceived behavioral control prevents success.

New Year resolutions, such as attending a gym, do not always last. Despite the intentions (planned behavior) it is past behavior that often determines our actions.

between behavioral intention and behavior was +.62. Thus, the theory provides reasonably accurate predictions of behavior.

Most of the studies considered by van den Putte (1993) were *correlational*, with measures of attitudes, intentions, and behavior being obtained at the same time. Such evidence cannot show that behavior is *caused* by attitudes and intentions. Kraus (1995) carried out a meta-analysis on 88 studies in which attitudes were assessed some time *prior* to behavior. There was an overall correlation of +.38 between attitudes and behavior, suggesting (but not proving) that attitudes can determine behavior.

In spite of the successes of the theory of reasoned action, the theory of planned behavior is preferable. Armitage and Conner (2001) carried out a meta-analysis. They found that perceived behavioral control (only included in the theory of planned behavior) contributed significantly to the prediction of behavior. Overall, the theory of planned behavior accounted for 39% of the variance in intention and 27% of the variance in behavior. The theory was more effective at predicting behavior when behavior measures were self-report rather than objective or observed (accounting for 31% vs. 21% of the variance in behavior, respectively).

Behavior is often predicted better by *past behavior* than by the cognitions or beliefs included in the theories under discussion. Relevant evidence from seven studies was discussed by Conner and Armitage (1998, p. 1438): "Past behavior explained a mean 13.0% of variance in behavior after taking account of intentions and PBC [perceived behavioral control]." For example, Norman and Smith (1995) found that amount of physical exercise was predicted better by the amount of exercise participants had taken in the past than by their cognitions (e.g., intentions).

Ouellette and Wood (1998) argued there are two main ways in which current behavior is influenced by past behavior. First, well-practiced types of behavior typically occurring in a given situation (e.g., using a seatbelt in your car) become habitual and involve automatic processes. Second, poorly learned types of behavior that have been used in several situations are under the control of conscious processes. With these types of behavior, past behavior influences current behavior *indirectly* by altering intentions. Thus, some of the influence of past behavior on current behavior (via altered intentions) can be accounted for by the theory of planned behavior, but some (based on automatic processes) cannot.

Evaluation

+ The two theories provide a general framework for understanding the relationship between attitudes and behavior.

+ Those factors emphasized by the theories typically influence behavioral intentions and actual behavior.

+ The theory of planned behavior is an advance on the theory of reasoned action.

− The theoretical assumption that we make rational decisions about how to behave is limited because our behavior is often influenced by emotional factors.

− The theories explain behavior resulting from a conscious consideration of possibilities. However, people often behave in habitual ways based on automatic or implicit processes. This may explain why very few New Year's resolutions produce lasting changes in behavior.

− The whole approach is based on a limited view of attitudes. According to Böhner (2001, p. 280), these theories "have used a narrow definition of *attitudes towards behavior* (beliefs about the likelihood and value of behavioral consequences) and have relegated the attitude concept to the background as one among many predictors of behavior."

ATTITUDE CHANGE AND PERSUASION

Why is it important to understand the factors involved in persuasion and attitude change? An important reason relates to the growing field of preventive medicine, in which the emphasis is on preventing diseases from happening. People need to adopt healthier lifestyles for preventive medicine to work, and techniques of persuasion are very important in making this happen.

Despite prominent public health campaigns to encourage safer sexual practices, a study in the USA found that only 17% of heterosexuals use condoms regularly.

About 1.5 million Americans are infected with the human immunodeficiency virus (HIV) that causes AIDS. HIV is also common throughout Western Europe and many other parts of the world among both heterosexuals and homosexuals. Thus, it is very important for everyone to minimize the risks of contracting HIV and AIDS. The most effective approach is to use condoms (apart from avoiding all sexual contact!). Persuasive messages have emphasized the importance of using condoms (so-called safer sex), and have emphasized the life-threatening risks of not doing so. However, these messages are generally disregarded. For example, an American study found that only 17% of heterosexuals use condoms regularly (Miller, Turner, & Moses, 1990). Why is this? Kimble, Robinson, and Moon (1992) found that American college students believed (wrongly) that the risks of unprotected sex were very small within a caring relationship.

FIVE FACTORS

How can we persuade someone to change his/her attitudes? According to McGuire (1969), five kinds of factors are involved in persuasion:

1. *Source*: Sources differ greatly in attractiveness, power, credibility, and so on. Communicators who are trustworthy, attractive, who have expertise and credibility, and who are similar to the receiver of the message usually produce more attitude change than communicators lacking these characteristics (Petty & Cacioppo, 1981). Two biases may lead us to disregard the source's message (Deaux & Wrightsman, 1988): (1) **reporting bias**, when we think the source is unwilling to tell the truth (e.g., most politicians); and (2) **knowledge bias**, when we think the source's knowledge is likely to be inaccurate.

2. *Message*: The information presented may appeal to reason or emotion, it may or may not contain many facts, and so on. Are emotional messages more effective than nonemotional ones? Rogers (1983) addressed this issue in his protection motivation theory. According to this theory, threatening messages initiate two processes:

   (i) Threat appraisal: This involves assessing the severity of the danger and of the individual's vulnerability to the possible consequences.

   (ii) Coping appraisal: This involves the recipient assessing his/her ability to perform the required coping behavior to avoid the negative consequences.

   It follows from this theory that increasing threat leads to stronger intentions to adopt the recommended behavior when coping appraisal is high, but to weaker intentions when coping appraisal is low. Sturges and Rogers (1996) found support for these predictions (see figure on the right). Young adults listened to messages

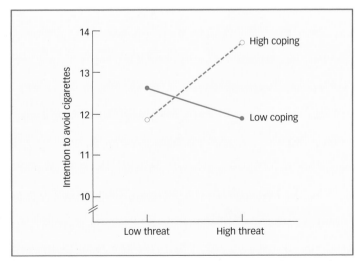

Strength of intention to avoid cigarettes as a function of degree of threat (low vs. high) and ease of coping (low vs. high). Based on data in Sturges and Rogers (1996).

It is easier to persuade people to perform small actions than large ones.

arguing that the dangers of tobacco were modest or great, and that it was easy or difficult to keep away from tobacco.

3. *Channel*: The message may be presented visually or aurally, or both (e.g., television adverts). Chaiken and Eagly (1983) compared attitude change for a message presented in audio, video, or written form. With simple messages, videotape was the most effective and the written form was the least effective. With complex messages, however, the written form was the most effective and audiotape was the least effective. The written form has the advantage with complex messages because it can be processed as slowly as necessary for the recipient to understand it.

4. *Recipient*: The effectiveness of a persuasive message depends in part on the recipient's interest in it, his/her personality, and his/her pre-existing attitudes. Eagly and Carli (1981) found that women are influenced more than men by messages on topics with which men are more familiar. However, the opposite is the case with messages on topics with which women are more familiar. Thus, familiarity and knowledge make us less susceptible to attitude change.

   Duck, Hogg, and Terry (1999) studied the **third-person effect**, the belief that we are personally less influenced than other people by persuasive messages. As predicted, most students said they were less influenced by AIDS adverts than other people.

5. *Target behavior*: People can be persuaded to perform small actions (e.g., voting for a given political party) more easily than large ones (e.g., spending weeks canvassing for that party).

DUAL-PROCESS MODELS

We turn now to models of attitude change. There are two major dual-process models: the elaboration likelihood model (e.g., Petty & Wegener, 1998) and the heuristic-systematic model (e.g., Chaiken, Giner-Sorolla, & Chen, 1996). According to both models, people are generally motivated to hold correct attitudes. However, they may be unable (or unwilling) to process persuasive messages thoroughly.

The elaboration likelihood model assumes that recipients of messages can be persuaded via two distinct routes:

1. *Central route*: This involves detailed consideration and elaboration of the persuasive message.
2. *Peripheral route*: This involves being influenced more by noncontent aspects of the message (e.g., number of arguments) and by the context (e.g., communicator's

Key Term
Third-person effect: the belief that one is personally less influenced by persuasive messages than most other people.

attractiveness or credibility) than by the message content. Individuals using this route pay little attention to the persuasive message.

What determines which processing route will be used? People often use the peripheral route because they have limited time and resources to devote to most messages. However, they will use the central route if their motivation and ability are high. Thus, individuals interested in the topic of the message who possess relevant background knowledge are especially likely to use central processing.

According to the elaboration likelihood model, central processing leads to stronger attitudes than peripheral processing. Central processing produces attitude structures in which the elements are more closely associated and integrated with previous knowledge.

The heuristic-systematic model resembles the elaboration likelihood model in assuming that two kinds of processes can be applied to persuasive messages. Systematic processing closely resembles the central route since it involves thoughtful consideration of message content. It is most likely to be used when messages have personal relevance, and when the recipient already possesses strong attitudes on the message topic. Heuristic processing resembles the peripheral route in requiring little effort and attention. Individuals not very interested in (or knowledgeable about) a persuasive message use simple heuristics or rules of thumb (e.g., "Statistics don't lie"; "Agree with the expert").

When a message is ambiguous, recipients may initially engage in heuristic processing. This heuristic processing may then bias subsequent systematic processing, producing attitudes consistent with the implications of the initial heuristic processing.

What are the main differences between the two models? As Böhner (2001, p. 263) pointed out, "The ELM [elaboration likelihood model] provides the more comprehensive framework, incorporating effortful processing as well as a variety of low-effort processes." However, the heuristic-systematic model provides more specific assumptions about the ways its two processes interact.

Findings

Petty, Cacioppo, and Goldman (1981) tested the elaboration likelihood model and obtained good evidence that there are two separate routes to persuasion (see Key Study below).

Key Study

Petty et al. (1981): Two routes to persuasion

Petty, Cacioppo, and Goldman (1981) tested the elaboration likelihood model. Students read a message strongly supporting the notion that a new large-scale exam should be introduced, with all students having to pass this exam to graduate. Some participants were told this exam might be introduced the following year to provide them with strong motivation to use the central route. The other participants were told there would be no change for 10 years, and so they would not be affected personally. This was designed to produce low motivation to process the essay thoroughly, so they would use the peripheral route. The message was either attributed to a source high in expertise (the Carnegie Commission on Higher Education), or to a source low in expertise (a local high school class). The arguments presented were either strong and based on statistics, or weak and based on personal opinions.

What did Petty et al. (1981) find? For students expected to use the central route, the quality of the arguments was the key factor determining how persuaded they were. For those students expected to use the peripheral route, the source of the message was the key factor influencing its persuasiveness. Thus, there are two separate routes to persuasion.

Discussion points
1. Do persuasive messages influence you via the central or the peripheral route?
2. What kinds of motivational factors might lead someone to pay close attention to a persuasive message?

KEY STUDY EVALUATION
A possible problem with Petty et al.'s study could be that the groups of participants were not balanced; factors relating to all levels of cognitive processing could be so different between the two groups that their responses could not reasonably be compared. The manipulation of the key variables, that is, quality and source of message, does demonstrate the significance of these factors in determining the response to the message received, but the possibility of intervening variables such as low attention levels and/or low recall levels in the case of the second, peripheral-route group would suggest that direct comparison between the groups would be questionable. The feelings of the participants toward assessments would need to be measured before the study so that later comparison could be made. Students who perform badly in exams in general may respond negatively toward the message, irrespective of its content or context or whether it will affect them directly.

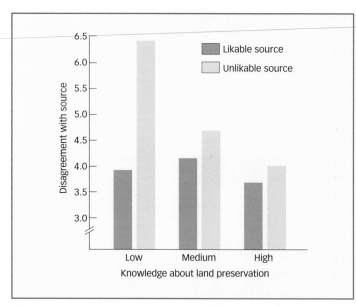

Disagreement with source as a function of knowledge about land preservation (low, medium, or high) and source likability (likable vs. unlikable). Data from Wood and Kallgren (1988).

According to the two models we are considering, central or systematic and peripheral or heuristic processing can be used in parallel (at the same time). Supporting evidence was reported by Wood and Kallgren (1988) in a study in which participants read an account of an interview in which a student described as an expert or a nonexpert, and as likable or unlikable, argued against land preservation. Participants with most knowledge about land preservation made extensive use of central or systematic processing, as shown by their good recall of the message. In addition, they were influenced by the student's expertise, and so used the heuristic or rule of thumb, "Agree with the expert." Thus, these participants used central/systematic *and* peripheral/heuristic processing (see figure on the left)

Chaiken (1987) reported more direct evidence that heuristics influence attitude change. Some participants memorized eight phrases relevant to the heuristic that length implies strength (e.g., "the more the merrier"). The participants then received a message in which the speaker claimed to have two or ten reasons supporting compulsory exams. These participants showed more attitude change when the speaker claimed to have ten reasons rather than two, presumably because they used the heuristics contained in the phrases.

Chaiken and Maheswaran (1994) found that heuristic processing could bias subsequent systematic processing when a message was ambiguous. Their participants received a message about a new answerphone, the XT 100, from a low- or high-credibility source. Source credibility (which affects heuristic processing) *only* influenced systematic processing and attitudes towards the new answerphone when the message was ambiguous.

Evaluation

+ The two dual-process models provide more adequate accounts of attitude change than previous theories.

+ Attitude change typically depends on contextual information (e.g., likability or expertise of the communicator) as well as on message content.

+ Several factors determining whether processing is mainly central/systematic or peripheral/heuristic have been identified.

− The notion that there are only two forms of processing of persuasive messages is oversimplified. In fact, there are numerous forms of processing varying in the amount of effortful message evaluation involved (Petty, 1995).

− It is assumed within the elaboration likelihood model that central and peripheral processes can occur together. However, it is unclear how these processes interact.

− According to the heuristic-systematic model, information not processed systematically influences attitudes via the retrieval of heuristics from memory. However, this assumption has rarely been tested.

COGNITIVE DISSONANCE THEORY

Festinger (1957) proposed an important theory of attitude change. He argued that someone holding two inconsistent cognitions or thoughts experiences **cognitive dissonance** (an uncomfortable state produced by the discrepancy between the cognitions). This motivates the person to reduce the dissonance. This can be done by changing one or both of the cognitions or by introducing a new cognition. Festinger also argued that people will often resolve a discrepancy between their attitudes and behavior by altering their attitudes. Most people have claimed that attitudes determine behavior, but Festinger argued that behavior sometimes determines attitudes.

A common example of cognitive dissonance is found in smokers. They have the cognition or thought that smoking can cause several diseases and they also have the cognition that they often engage in smoking behavior. How can they reduce dissonance? One way is to stop smoking, but another way is to persuade themselves that smoking is less dangerous than generally assumed. Gibbons, Eggleston, and Benthin (1997) found that smokers about to quit smoking regarded it as very dangerous, and this was a factor in them deciding to quit. However, when these same individuals started to smoke again, they perceived smoking to be much *less* dangerous than they had before! This change of attitude helped to justify their decision to resume smoking.

Findings

One approach to testing Festinger's theory is by means of **induced compliance**, in which people are persuaded to behave in ways inconsistent with their attitudes. Festinger and Carlsmith (1959) used induced compliance in a study in which participants spent 1 hour performing very boring tasks (e.g., emptying and refilling a tray with spools). The experimenter then asked each participant to tell the next participant that the experiment had been very enjoyable. The participants were offered either $1 or $20 to lie in this way. Finally, all participants provided their honest opinion of how much they liked the tasks they had performed.

Which group do you think expressed more positive views about the experiment? Advocates of operant conditioning (see Chapter 7) might well argue that the experiment was more rewarding for participants receiving $20, and so they should have viewed the experiment more positively. In fact, those receiving only $1 had much more favorable opinions than those receiving $20 (see figure on the following page). According to Festinger and Carlsmith, those receiving $20 could argue that the money was sufficient justification for lying, and so there was little cognitive dissonance. In contrast, those

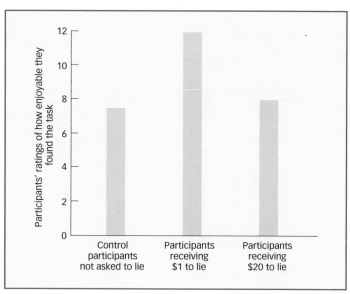

Data from Festinger and Carlsmith (1959).

receiving $1 had considerable cognitive dissonance. They said the experiment was very enjoyable when they knew it wasn't, and the small amount of money couldn't really justify lying. They couldn't change the lie, so the only way to reduce dissonance was by making their attitude towards the experiment more positive.

Another approach to testing the theory is **effort justification**, in which people exert much effort to achieve some fairly trivial goal. Axsom and Cooper (1985) used this approach. Some female dieters were allocated to a high-effort program, spending a considerable amount of time doing effortful (but irrelevant) tasks such as reading out tongue twisters. Other dieters were allocated to a low-effort program, performing tasks that were irrelevant but much less time-consuming. Women in the high-effort program were much more likely than those in the low-effort program to lose weight (94% vs. 39%, respectively). Women in the high-effort program could only justify the substantial effort they had put into the program by working hard to lose weight. Those in the low-effort program had much less need to justify the time and effort expended.

Festinger (1957) argued that people will only change their attitudes when they attribute their unpleasant internal state to cognitive dissonance. Zanna and Cooper (1974) gave some participants a placebo (inactive) pill, which they were mistakenly told would cause them to feel aroused. When these participants were put into an unpleasant state of cognitive dissonance, they attributed this state to the pill rather than to cognitive dissonance. As a result, they failed to show attitude change.

Evaluation

+ Cognitive dissonance theory has been applied successfully to numerous situations.

+ There is much support for the prediction that the weaker the reasons for behaving inconsistently with one's attitudes, the stronger the pressure to change those attitudes (Festinger & Carlsmith, 1959).

− The induced-compliance effect wasn't replicated by Choi, Choi, and Cha (1992) with Korean participants. The need for cognitive consistency is probably less strong in collectivistic societies than in individualistic ones (see Chapter 1). Kashima, Siegal, Tanaka, and Kashima (1992) found that Australians believed that consistency between attitudes and behavior was more important than did the Japanese. People in collectivist societies focus on behaving in socially acceptable ways even when their behavior conflicts with their beliefs.

− The theory ignores important individual differences. For example, those high in self-monitoring (using cues from other people to control one's own behavior) experience much less cognitive dissonance than those low in self-monitoring (see Franzoi, 1996).

ATTRIBUTION THEORIES

In our everyday lives, it is important to work out *why* other people are behaving in certain ways. For example, suppose someone you have only just met is very friendly. They may genuinely like you, or they may want something from you. It is obviously very useful to understand the reasons for their apparent friendliness.

According to Heider (1958), people are naive scientists who relate observable behavior to unobservable causes. We produce attributions, which are beliefs about the reasons why other people behave as they do. Heider distinguished between *internal* attributions (based on something within the individual being observed) and *external* attributions (based on something outside the individual) (see figure on the right). Internal attributions are called **dispositional attributions** and external attributions are called **situational attributions**. A dispositional attribution is made when we decide someone's behavior is a result of their personality or other characteristics. In contrast, a situational attribution is made when someone's behavior is attributed to the current situation.

The above distinction can be exemplified by considering a male office worker who works very slowly and inefficiently. A dispositional attribution would be that he is lazy or incompetent. A situational attribution would be that he has been asked to do work inappropriate to his skills or that the company for which he works has failed to monitor sufficiently what he does.

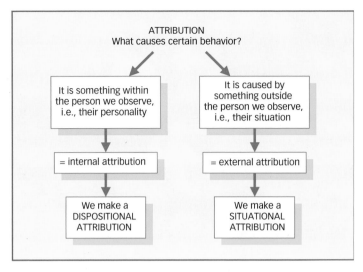

KELLEY'S ATTRIBUTION THEORY

Kelley (1967, 1973) extended attribution theory, arguing that the ways people make causal attributions depend on the information available. When you have much relevant information from several sources, you can detect the *covariation* of observed behavior and its possible causes. For example, if a man is generally unpleasant to you, it may be because he is an unpleasant person or (heaven forbid!) that you are not very likable. If you know how he treats other people, and you know how other people treat you, you can work out why he is unpleasant to you.

In everyday life, however, we often only have information from a *single* observation to guide us in making a causal attribution. For example, you see a car knock down and kill a dog. In such cases, you use whatever information is available. If there was ice on the road or it was a foggy day, this increases the chances you will make a situational attribution of the driver's behavior. In contrast, if it was a clear, sunny day and there was no other traffic on the road, you will probably make a dispositional attribution of the driver's behavior (e.g., he is a poor or inconsiderate driver).

Covariation

According to Kelley (1967), people making causal attributions use the covariation principle. This is defined as follows: "An effect is attributed to a condition that is present

Key Terms

Dispositional attributions: deciding that someone's behavior is caused by their internal dispositions or characteristics.

Situational attributions: deciding that someone's behavior is caused by the situation in which they find themselves.

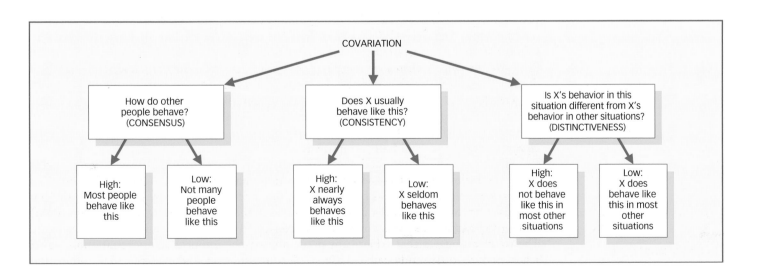

Are we more likely to assume that this man is sleeping rough because of situational factors (he's been taken ill, forgotten his house keys) or dispositional factors (he can't keep a job, he's drunk and rowdy in accommodation, for example)?

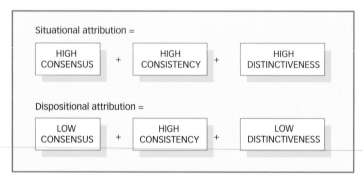

when the effect is present, and absent when the effect is absent" (Fincham & Hewstone, 2001, p. 200). This principle is used when the individual has information from multiple observations. We use three types of information when interpreting someone's behavior (see the figure below):

- *Consensus*: The extent to which others in the same situation behave in the same way.
- *Consistency*: The extent to which the person usually behaves in the way he/she is currently behaving.
- *Distinctiveness*: The extent to which the person's behavior in the present situation differs from his/her behavior in the presence of others.

Information about consensus, consistency, and distinctiveness is used when deciding whether to make a dispositional or situational attribution (see figure on the left). If someone's behavior has high consensus, high consistency, and high distinctiveness, we typically make a situational attribution. Here is an example: everyone is rude to Bella; Mary has always been rude to Bella in the past; Mary has not been rude to anyone else. With this information, Mary's behavior is attributed to Bella's unpleasantness rather than her own unpleasantness.

In contrast, we make a dispositional attribution if someone's behavior has low consensus, high consistency, and low distinctiveness. Here is an example: only Mary is rude to Susan; Mary has always been rude to Susan in the past; Mary is rude to everyone else. In this case, Mary's behavior is attributed to Mary's unpleasant personality.

Findings

McArthur (1972) tested Kelley's attribution theory. He presented American participants with the eight possible patterns of information based on the three factors identified by Kelley: high vs. low on consensus, consistency, and distinctiveness. The participants attributed causality for the events described. For example, consider the sentence, "Neil fell asleep during Professor Brown's lecture." The fact that Neil fell asleep might be attributed to the person (i.e., Neil), to the circumstances (e.g., hot lecture theatre), or to the entity (e.g., Professor Brown's lectures are mind-numbingly dull).

What findings would be expected? Suppose Neil has fallen asleep during Professor Brown's lectures in the past, that other students don't, and that Neil also falls asleep in other people's lectures. The fact that Neil fell asleep during one of Professor Brown's lectures should be attributed to Neil (the person). Suppose Neil has fallen asleep during Professor Brown's lectures in the past, that other students do the same, and that Neil doesn't fall asleep in other people's lectures. Neil falling asleep during one of Professor Brown's lectures should be attributed to Professor Brown. Finally, suppose that Neil hasn't slept in the Professor Brown's lectures in the past. This should lead participants to attribute the fact that Neil fell asleep during one of Professor Brown's lectures to the circumstances (e.g., Neil had too much to drink last night).

McArthur (1972) obtained some support for Kelley's theory. However, participants made much less use of consensus information than predicted. Thus, people's causal attributions of an individual's behavior were influenced very little by the information that "almost everyone" or "hardly anyone" behaves in the same way. High consensus suggests that situational factors are strong and low consensus suggests that such factors are weak. The findings suggest that Americans de-emphasize the importance of situational factors when making attributions of behavior. In contrast, Cha and Nam (1985) found that

Korean participants made effective use of consensus information, and thus took account of situational factors. Reasons for cultural differences in attributions are discussed later.

Subsequent research in Western cultures has provided support for the prediction that low consensus, high consistency, and low distinctiveness should be associated with situational attributions. There is also support for the prediction that high consensus, high consistency, and high distinctiveness should be associated with entity attributions (Forsterling, 1989). However, no pattern of the three factors is reliably predictive of circumstance attributions (Fincham & Hewstone, 2001).

Evaluation

- The notion that causal attributions of others' behavior depend on the pattern of information available is very influential.

- There is some support for the covariation principle, and for the importance of consistency, distinctiveness, and consensus.

- In practice, we typically know little about the details of people's actual information processing.

- Experiments testing the theory are mostly very artificial. They provide participants with all the covariation information needed to make causal attributions. In real life, people typically make causal attributions on the basis of much more limited information.

- Even when information about consistency, consensus, and distinctiveness is available in everyday life, it is unlikely that such information typically influences our thinking (Pennington, personal communication).

Fundamental attribution error

One of the best-known errors or biases in social cognition is the **fundamental attribution error**. It involves exaggerating the influence of dispositions [personality] as causes of behavior while minimizing the role of situational factors. For example, suppose you meet someone for the first time and find them rather irritable and rude. You may well conclude they have an unpleasant personality, ignoring the possibility they have a headache or are troubled by problems.

Why do we possess the fundamental attribution error? Most of us like to think that life is fair. An emphasis on dispositional factors is consistent with the notion that, "We get what we work for, get what we ask for, and get what we deserve" (Gilbert, 1995, p. 108). The fundamental attribution error also makes our lives seem predictable. If the behavior of others is determined by their personalities, this makes their future behavior more predictable than if it varies considerably from situation to situation. We can also consider the fundamental attribution error (and other biases) in the context of evolutionary psychology (see Chapter 1). According to terror management theory (Haselton & Nettle, 2006), it makes good evolutionary sense for humans to be biased in ways that avoid costly errors. For example, suppose we assume that someone who is aggressive in one situation is likely to be aggressive in other situations because of his/her personality. This may be incorrect, but it ensures that we are on our guard when we next meet that person.

We might expect the fundamental attribution error to be common in individualistic cultures in which the emphasis is on individual responsibility and independence (see Chapter 1). However, many cultures are collectivistic (e.g., Asian cultures) and have an emphasis on group cohesiveness rather than on individual needs. Such cultures focus on situational explanations of people's behavior because their members have to be responsive to the wishes of others. Accordingly, there should be little evidence of the fundamental attribution error in collectivistic cultures.

Key Term

Fundamental attribution error:
exaggerating the importance of personality and minimizing the role of the situation in determining another person's behavior.

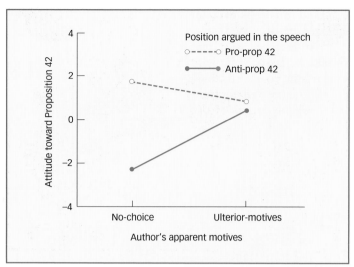

Participants' assessment of Rob's true attitudes towards Proposition 42 (making students not fulfilling certain academic requirements ineligible for athletic scholarships) as a function of condition (no-choice = Rob assigned a point of view; ulterior-motives = Rob might want to please his professor) and position argued for in the speech. From Fein et al. (1990). Copyright © American Psychological Association. Reprinted with permission.

Findings

Choi and Nisbett (1998) asked American and Korean participants to read an essay supporting or opposing capital punishment. They were informed the essay writer had been told which side of the issue to support. The American participants showed a much stronger fundamental attribution error (i.e., arguing that the essay writer was expressing his/her true attitudes) than the Korean ones.

Most studies in Western cultures have obtained evidence of the fundamental attribution error (e.g., Jones & Harris, 1967). However, Fein, Hilton, and Miller (1990) argued that American students would be less likely to underestimate situational factors if the other person had strong reasons for suppressing his/her true attitudes. Participants read an essay by "Rob Taylor." Some participants were told Rob had been assigned to write in favor of (or against) a particular point of view. Other participants were told the professor who would be evaluating Rob had very strong views on the topic, and that Rob's essay expressed the same views as those of his professor.

Participants who thought Rob had been assigned a point of view made the fundamental attribution error, deciding Rob's true attitudes were those expressed in the essay (see the figure above). In contrast, participants believing Rob had a good reason for hiding his true attitudes (i.e., pleasing his professor) decided the essay didn't reflect his true attitudes. Thus, we don't make the fundamental attribution error when people have a hidden motive for their behavior. For example, we expect politicians to express agreement with the views of their party purely for situational reasons (e.g., to gain advancement).

Evaluation

+ People (especially in Western cultures) often exaggerate the importance of dispositions and minimize that of situations as causes of behavior.

− The fundamental attribution error is much weaker in collectivistic cultures than in individualistic ones.

− The fundamental attribution error is less important in everyday life than in the laboratory. In everyday life, we realize that many people (e.g., politicians; car salespeople) have hidden motives influencing their behavior.

Actor–observer effect

Suppose a mother is discussing with her son why he has done poorly in an examination. The son may argue that the questions were unusually hard, that the marking was unfair, and so on. However, his mother may focus on the child's laziness and lack of motivation. Thus, the son sees his own behavior as being determined by external or situational factors, whereas his mother focuses on her son's internal or dispositional factors.

Jones and Nisbett (1972) argued that the processes involved in the above example operate in numerous situations. According to them, "There is a pervasive tendency for actors to attribute their actions to situational requirements, whereas observers tend to attribute the same actions to stable personal dispositions" (Jones & Nisbett, 1972, p. 80).

Findings

Choi and Nisbett (1998) studied cultural differences in the actor–observer effect. American and Korean participants read an essay having been told the writer had been exposed to situational pressure to argue for the position expressed in the essay. Participants then carried out two tasks: (1) they rated the extent to which the essay writer expressed his/her genuine attitudes; and (2) they wrote an essay under the same conditions as the essay writer and then rated the extent to which they themselves had expressed their genuine attitudes. American participants showed the actor–observer effect, arguing that the essay writer expressed his/her true attitudes more than they had themselves. In contrast, the Korean participants argued that the essay writer was no more likely than themselves to be expressing his/her true attitudes.

Storms (1973) argued that we exaggerate the situation's importance in determining our own behavior because we can see the situation (e.g., other people) but not ourselves. Conversations were videoed from the actor's point of view and from the observer's point of view. When actors viewed the video taken from the observer's point of view (so they could see themselves), they generally attributed their own behavior to dispositional rather than situational factors. Thus, our attributions are unduly influenced by information that is the focus of attention.

Robins, Spranca, and Mendelsohn (1996) argued that the actor–observer effect is expressed too vaguely. Various internal and external factors might influence attributions, and we need to identify the *specific* factors involved. Pairs of students interacted, and then rated the importance of two internal factors (personality; mood) and two external factors (partner; situation) in influencing their behavior and that of their partner.

There was support for the actor–observer effect for one internal factor (personality) and for one external factor (partner) (see the figure below). However, there was *no* support for this effect for the other internal factor (mood), and the findings were opposite to prediction for the other external factor (situation). Why were actors' attributions strongly influenced by one external factor (partner) but not by another (situation)? Presumably the actors' focus of attention was more on their partner than on more general aspects of the situation.

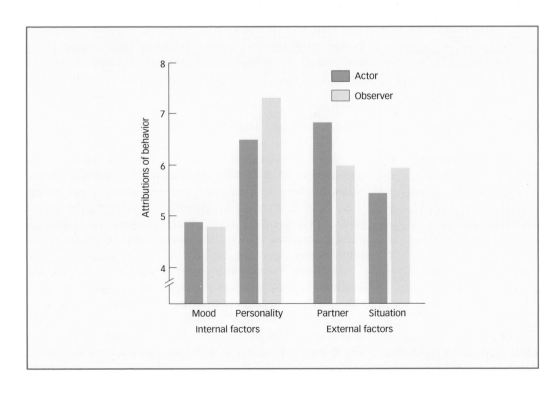

Data from Robins, Spranca, and Mendelsohn (1996).

INTEGRATION MODEL

Various attempts have been made to develop theoretical models specifying the mechanisms underlying attributions of other people's behavior. In this section, we focus on the integration model put forward by Trope and Gaunt (2000). It assumes there are two successive stages:

1. *Behavior identification*: The observer uses a mixture of dispositional and situational information to provide a description of the actor's behavior (e.g., "Fred behaved anxiously"). This description is influenced most by salient or conspicuous information.
2. *Diagnostic evaluation*: The observer uses the identified behavior from stage 1 to consider whether to favor the dispositional hypothesis or the situational hypothesis (e.g., "Fred was placed in a very stressful situation"). Thus, the observer integrates the available information to decide the causes of the actor's behavior.

According to this model, the first stage is carried out relatively automatically, whereas the second stage is more effortful and demanding. Observers under cognitive load (i.e., busy doing something else) will make little use of the second stage. As a result, whatever explanation of the actor's behavior (dispositional or situational) is salient or dominant at stage 1 will be favored.

Findings

Gilbert, Pelham, and Krull (1988) asked participants to watch a video of a woman behaving anxiously. They couldn't hear what she was saying, but the topics she was supposed to be discussing were included as subtitles in the video. In one condition, the topics were anxiety-provoking (e.g., hidden secrets). In the other condition, the topics were fairly neutral (e.g., world travel). In fact, all participants saw exactly the same video apart from the subtitles (see figure on the left).

Half the participants memorized the list of topics (cognitive load), whereas the other half only watched the video. Afterwards participants indicated the extent to which the woman's anxiety was a result of her disposition. The information that was most salient was the woman's anxious behavior. It follows from the model that participants under cognitive load should have

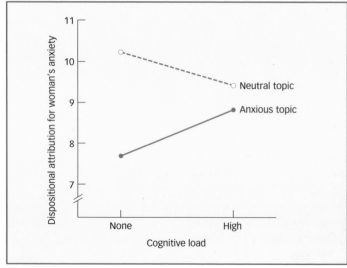

Strength of attribution of a woman's anxious behavior to personality or disposition as a function of the topic she discussed (neutral vs. anxious) and the participant's cognitive load (none vs. high). Data from Gilbert et al. (1988).

focused mainly on her behavior and so provided dispositional attributions regardless of the topics discussed. That is what was found. Participants not under cognitive load were able to process information about the topics discussed and so gave stronger dispositional attributions when the woman talked about neutral topics.

According to the integration model, situational attributions should be given when two factors are present: (1) situational information is salient or conspicuous; and (2) participants experience cognitive load and so don't use stage 2. This prediction was confirmed by Trope and Gaunt (2000). Participants read an essay allegedly written by someone instructed to favor the legalization of marijuana. The situational pressure was made salient by presenting the instructions for the essay in an audio recording. As predicted, participants under cognitive load (holding digits in memory) took considerable account of situational factors when deciding whether the essay writer was expressing his/her genuine attitudes.

Evaluation

+ Our attributions of others' behavior are influenced by automatic and by effortful processes.

+ Attributions of others' behavior are often different when we engage in effortful cognitive processing than when we don't.

− The distinction between automatic and effortful processes is oversimplified because processes vary in how effortful they are.

− More research is needed to identify more precisely the processes underlying our explanations of others' behavior.

− Individual differences are generally ignored. For example, relatively well-off people tend to attribute poverty in others to laziness, whereas poorer people attribute poverty in others to problems within society (Furnham, 1982).

THE SELF

Baumeister (1998) argued that one of the key characteristics of the self is its unity or oneness (i.e., we perceive ourselves as having a single self). He identified three other key aspects of the self-concept:

1. We have reflexive consciousness, meaning that we are consciously aware of having a self.
2. The self exists almost entirely within a social context, and is used when relating to others.
3. The self seems to make decisions and to cause us to behave in certain ways.

Cross and Madson (1997, p. 5) argued that there are important gender differences in the self-concept: "Men in the United States are thought to construct and maintain an independent self-construal, whereas women are thought to construct and maintain an interdependent self-construal." There is much evidence to support this viewpoint. Clancy and Dollinger (1993) asked men and women to put together sets of pictures that described themselves. Most of the pictures chosen by women showed them with others (e.g., family members). In contrast, most of the pictures chosen by men showed them on their own. In other studies reviewed by Cross and Madson, men were found to evaluate themselves more positively with respect to independence (e.g., power; self-sufficiency) than interdependence (e.g., sociability; likability). The opposite pattern has been found with women.

SOCIAL IDENTITY THEORY

Social identity theory (e.g., Turner et al., 1987; see Chapter 20) is an important approach to the self-concept. Of crucial importance within the theory is the distinction between personal identity and social identity, both of which help to define our sense of self. **Personal identity** is based on our personal relationships and characteristics, and includes ways in which we differ from other people (e.g., in personality). In contrast, **social identity** is based on our membership of various groups (e.g., student; woman; European). Most theoretical approaches to the self have focused almost exclusively on personal identity, and have ignored the notion that the self is strongly influenced by various social identities.

We possess numerous personal and social identities. According to Hogg and Vaughan (2005, p. 127), "We have as many social identities as there are groups that we feel we belong to, and as many personal identities as there are interpersonal relationships we are involved in and clusters of idiosyncratic attributes that we believe we possess." The identity dominant at any given time often depends on the match between the current situation and our various personal and social identities. For example, if I attend a psychology conference, my identity as a psychologist is likely to be dominant.

Turner (1999) discussed two other factors influencing the identity we adopt. First, there are our past experiences. For example, if it has made me happy to identify myself as a psychologist in the past, then that increases the likelihood that I will do so across a range of situations. Second, there are present expectations. If I expect the people I am interacting with will be more positively disposed toward a writer than a psychologist, then I may be tempted to adopt the identity of a writer rather than a psychologist!

What is the relationship between personal and social identity? When we find ourselves in a situation emphasizing our shared social identity with others, we tend to adopt a social identity rather than a personal one. For example, women who go out in a group may adopt the social identity of a woman. If so, they focus on ways in which they are similar to other women and de-emphasize the ways they differ from most other women. Thus, increased social identity is often accompanied by a decrease in personal identity.

Findings

Since most of the research discussed later in the chapter is on personal identity, we focus here on social identity. If someone's commitment to a group (and relevant social identity) is sufficiently strong, they are likely to accept very negative consequences from continued group involvement. For example, Baltesen (2000) discussed the employees of Baan, an IT company in the Netherlands. They all belonged to a very religious community, and so there was a strong sense of social identity among them. As a result, they remained in the company even when it encountered severe financial problems. Their reaction to these problems was to introduce daily prayers in the hope the company might survive.

A central assumption of social identity theory is that group members like their group to be distinct from other groups in positive ways (e.g., more successful; more dynamic). However, it is sometimes difficult for a group to be both distinctive *and* perceived positively. In such cases, we might expect that the need for a distinctive social identity based on group membership would be

---

Case Study: *Football Supporters*

At the 1998 soccer world cup finals in France many English supporters became involved in major antisocial incidents, while Scottish supporters were mainly nonviolent. The media focused on "hooligans" as the source of the disruption, and the absence of "hooligans" as the cause of nonviolence. However, an ethnographic study (Stott, Hutchison, & Drury, 2001) of these supporters showed these two supporter crowds had their own social identities. The England crowd redefined their identity so that even normally nonviolent members came to believe that violence toward their rivals, the outgroup, was legitimate, a belief reinforced by the difference this made between themselves, the ingroup, and the nonviolent outgroup. Similarly, the Scotland supporters, a nonviolent crowd, used the same social identity model in establishing their own nonviolent identity as the ingroup, being clearly different from their outgroup who were using violence. In this way social identity theory can explain both the presence and the absence of antisocial crowd behavior, a view which challenges the simplistic "hooligan" approach.

even more important than the group being perceived positively. For example, Poland has been invaded several times in its history, and so Polish people should have a strong sense of national identity. As predicted, Polish students accepted they possessed various negative characteristics (e.g., excessive drinking; quarrelsome; vulgar) associated with being Polish to maintain their national social identity (Mlicki & Ellemers, 1996).

What causes a *change* in social identity? Drury and Reicher (2000) argued that a key factor is a discrepancy between ingroup and outgroup views of one's group. For example, many of those involved in a long-running campaign in the UK against the building of the M11 motorway link road in north-east London regarded themselves initially as citizens having a neutral relationship with the police. However, the discovery that the police regarded them as irresponsible caused many of them to change their social identify and become more radical. As one female campaigner expressed it, "I've got very determined just lately, determined to get on with things, and I don't ever think that I'm going to lead an ordinary life again" (Drury & Reicher, 2000, p. 594)

Evaluation

+ Our sense of self is *flexible*, with the identity dominant at any given time being determined in part by the current situation.

+ The distinction between personal identity and social identity is important.

+ Previous theories mostly ignored social identity, which is of great importance to the sense of self.

- It is difficult to assess precisely which personal and social identities are possessed by any given individual

- We often cannot predict which identity will be dominant in any given situation because so many factors are involved.

- "It is [not] clear how we should conceive of the social self, which can be as varied as the groups to which we belong" (Ellemers, Spears, & Doosje, 2002, p. 164).

Self-esteem

An important part of the self-concept is **self-esteem**. This is the evaluative aspect of the self-concept, and concerns how worthwhile and confident an individual feels about himself/herself. Several theorists (e.g., Baumeister, 1995; Tesser, 1988) have argued that most people are highly motivated to maintain or enhance their self-esteem, and that much social behavior serves the goal of maximizing self-esteem. However, other

A reservoir of self-esteem?

It has been suggested that self-esteem can act as a defense mechanism. For example, when an individual is in a situation where they are unsure of their identity, their self-esteem, based on previous successful experiences, protects the self while the uncertainty is being resolved. But in doing so the self-esteem is used up. Self-esteem can be replenished in more successful social situations where self-verification is not an issue. This suggests that persistent low self-esteem could be the result of the person being in several situations where self-verification is difficult or not possible (Cast & Burke, 2002).

Key Term

Self-esteem:
the evaluative part of the **self-concept** concerned with feelings of confidence and being worthwhile.

It has been found that whereas American students overestimate their own academic performance but not that of their close friends, Japanese students overestimate their own performance but they overestimate the performance of their friends even more, suggesting that collectivistic students are motivated to enhance others more than themselves.

theorists (e.g., Swann, 1987) have argued that people are motivated more to maintain *consistent beliefs* about themselves. According to this self-consistency theory, people like to feel they understand themselves. If they allow positive information about themselves to boost their self-esteem, they would have the disturbing task of changing their self-concept. As a result, people maintain consistent beliefs about themselves, even when some of those beliefs are negative.

Findings

If people are motivated to enhance their self-esteem, they should take credit for success by attributing it to internal or dispositional factors (e.g., "I worked very hard"; "I have a lot of ability"). In contrast, they should deny responsibility for failure by attributing it to external or situational factors (e.g., "The task was very hard"; "I didn't have enough time"). Tendencies to take credit for success but to accept no blame for failure define the **self-serving bias**.

Several studies have reported evidence of the self-serving bias. Bernstein, Stephan, and Davis (1979) considered students who had obtained a good or a poor grade on an exam. Those with good grades typically attributed it to their intelligence, their hard work, or both. In contrast, those receiving poor grades attributed it to bad luck or an unreasonable lecturer. Campbell and Sedikides (1999) carried out a meta-analysis of studies on self-serving bias. In line with the bias, success was consistently attributed to internal factors. However, failure was sometimes attributed to internal factors and sometimes to external factors.

Why are attributions for failure so inconsistent? Duval and Silvia (2002) persuaded self-focused participants that failure could or could not be followed by improvement. Failure was attributed internally when subsequent improvement was likely, but it was attributed externally when subsequent improvement was improbable.

The self-serving bias is stronger in individualistic cultures than in collectivistic ones (see Smith & Bond, 1998, for a review). For example, Kashima and Triandis (1986) asked American and Japanese students to remember detailed information about landscapes shown on slides. Both groups tended to explain their success in terms of situational factors (e.g., luck) and their failures in terms of task difficulty. However, the Americans were more inclined to explain their successes in terms of high ability than their failures in terms of low ability, whereas the Japanese showed the opposite pattern.

The emphasis on enhancing self-esteem can also be seen in the **false uniqueness bias**, which is the tendency to regard oneself as better than most other people. This bias has been found consistently in North Americans (e.g., Campbell, 1986). However, Japanese people don't show the false uniqueness bias, even when rating themselves on attributes regarded as central to success in Japanese culture (see Heine, Lehman, Markus, & Kitayama, 1999).

Is high self-esteem important? It may seem obvious that high self-esteem is desirable, and individuals with high self-esteem experience more pleasant mood states than those with low self-esteem (Campbell, Chew, & Scratchley,

> ### Key Terms
>
> **Self-serving bias:**
> the tendency to take credit for success but to refuse to accept blame for failure.
>
> **False uniqueness bias:**
> the mistaken tendency to think of oneself as being better than most other people.

1991). However, high self-esteem can have negative consequences. Colvin, Block, and Funder (1995) identified individuals whose opinions about themselves were significantly more favorable than those of their friends. When studied in the laboratory, these individuals interrupted other people, they expressed hostility, they were socially awkward, and they made others feel irritable. In other words, individuals with inflated self-esteem are arrogant and self-centered.

Heine et al. (1999) argued that striving for high self-esteem (or the closely related high self-confidence) is much less common in collectivistic cultures than in individualistic ones. They argued that in Japanese culture, "To say that an individual is self-confident gets in the way of interdependence, or it reveals one's failure to recognize higher standards of excellence and thus to continue to self-improve, or both" (Heine et al., 1999, p. 785). In support of their theory, Heine et al. discussed unpublished research in which European Canadian and Japanese students ranked 20 traits in terms of how much they would ideally like to possess them. European Canadians rated self-confidence as the trait they would *most* like to possess, whereas the Japanese rated it as the trait they would *least* like to possess.

In sum, there are major cultural differences in the importance attached to high self-esteem. As Heine et al. (1999, p. 785) concluded:

> *Conventional theories of self-esteem are based on a North American individualized view of self that is motivated to achieve high self-esteem. In contrast, the most characteristic view of self in Japan (and elsewhere) is different from its North American counterpart . . . It is maintaining a self-critical outlook that is crucial to developing a worthy and culturally appropriate self in Japan.*

Evaluation

+ Important biases (e.g., the self-serving and false uniqueness biases) used in Western cultures to enhance self-esteem have been identified.

+ Clear cross-cultural differences in the existence of biases designed to bolster self-esteem and in the importance attached to high self-esteem have been found.

− There is controversy concerning the desirability of high self-esteem within Western cultures.

− Most studies on self-esteem rely on self-report measures that may be distorted and that only take account of information of which the individual has conscious awareness.

Chapter Summary

Attitudes
- Assessing attitudes by self-report questionnaires can be problematical because of social desirability bias. Two ways of minimizing this problem are to use the bogus pipeline or to assess implicit attitudes.
- Attitudes fulfill knowledge, utilitarian, and social identity functions, and help to maintain self-esteem.
- Attitudes often predict behavior only weakly. According to the theory of planned behavior an individual's behavior is also determined by subjective norms, his/her behavior intention, behavioral beliefs, outcome evaluations, and perceived behavioral control.

- Some of the influence of past behavior on current behavior can't be accounted for by the theory of planned behavior. The theory focuses on very specific attitudes, namely attitudes towards behavior.

Attitude change and persuasion

- Persuasion depends on five factors: source; message; channel; recipient; and target behavior.
- According to the elaboration likelihood model, attitude change depends on either a central route involving much attention or a peripheral route requiring minimal use of resources. In similar fashion, the heuristic-systematic model distinguishes between systematic and heuristic processing of messages.
- Many of the findings on attitude change can be accounted for by the notion that messages can be processed by two systems varying in their attentional demands. However, it is more realistic to assume that there are several forms of processing varying in the amount of effortful message evaluation involved.
- According to Festinger, cognitive dissonance motivates people to reduce dissonance by changing one or both of their inconsistent cognitions. He also argued that behavior sometimes influences attitudes. The need for cognitive consistency is weaker in collectivistic cultures than in individualistic ones.

Attribution theories

- According to Heider, we explain other people's behavior in terms of internal (dispositional) or external (situational) attributions.
- According to Kelley, we use information about consensus, consistency, and distinctiveness when making attributions. It is not clear that this is what happens in real life.
- The fundamental attribution error is much stronger in individualistic cultures than in collectivistic ones. It is not found when we suspect the other person has a hidden motive influencing his/her behavior.
- The actor–observer effect is also much stronger in individualistic cultures. The actual effects observed even in individualistic cultures are more complex than would be expected by advocates of the actor–observer effect.
- According to Trope and Gaunt's integration model, there are successive stages of behavior identification and diagnostic evaluation when making attributions. The second stage requires much more effort than the first one and is omitted if necessary.

The self

- Men in Western cultures tend to regard themselves as independent rather than as interdependent, whereas women show the opposite pattern.
- According to social identity theory, we possess several personal and social identities.
- According to social identity theory, we want any group to which we belong to be distinctive and to be perceived positively. Changes in social identity occur when there is a discrepancy between ingroup and outgroup views of one's group.
- Most people in individualistic Western cultures are motivated to enhance their self-esteem. Evidence for this can be seen in the self-serving and false uniqueness biases.
- In collectivist cultures, there is much less striving for high self-esteem than in individualistic ones. There is also much less evidence for the self-serving and false uniqueness biases.

Further Reading

- Augoustinos, M., Walker, I., & Donaghue, N. (2006). *Social cognition: An integrated introduction* (2nd ed.). London: Sage. This textbook provides detailed and up-to-date coverage of the entire field of social cognition.
- Hewstone, M., & Stroebe, W. (2001). *Introduction to social psychology* (3rd ed.). Chapters 5, 7, and 8 provide informative accounts of several of the main topics in social cognition.
- Hogg, M.A., & Vaughan, G.M. (2005). *Social psychology* (4th ed.). Harlow, UK: Prentice Hall. Chapters 2 through 4 of this excellent textbook provide detailed and informative coverage of the topics discussed in this chapter.

Contents

Social behavior and relationships

18

In this chapter we focus on the main ways we respond to (and interact with) other people. One important example is prosocial behavior. This involves behaving positively towards others, doing our best to help them even at some cost to ourselves. Aggressive or antisocial behavior is much more negative—it involves deliberately trying to hurt someone else.

It might seem as if prosocial and antisocial or aggressive behavior are simply opposite extremes of a single dimension, but this is *not* the case. In fact, prosocial and antisocial or aggressive behavior are largely independent of each other (Krueger, Hicks, & McGue, 2001). Thus, there is no general tendency for individuals high in prosocial behavior to be low in aggressive behavior, or vice versa.

This chapter is also concerned with interpersonal relationships, which are a vital part of all our lives. We consider the factors determining whether we are initially attracted to another person, the factors maintaining a friendship or other relationship, and the factors leading to its break-up. As we will see, some aspects of interpersonal relationships (especially marriage) differ considerably from one culture to another.

PROSOCIAL BEHAVIOR

This section of the chapter is concerned with prosocial behavior, which is discussed from the developmental perspective in Chapter 15. **Prosocial behavior** resembles helping behavior, but they are not the same: "The definition of 'prosocial behavior' is narrower [than that of helping behavior] in that the action is intended to improve the situation of the help-recipient, the actor is not motivated by the fulfillment of professional obligations, and the recipient is a person and not an organization" (Bierhoff, 2001, p. 286).

Many clear examples of prosocial behavior involve altruism. **Altruism** is voluntary helping behavior that is costly to the individual who is altruistic, and typically involves empathy. According to Hogg and Vaughan (2005, p. 649), empathy is "the ability to feel another person's experiences; identifying with and experiencing another person's emotions, thoughts, and attitudes."

WHAT EXPLAINS ALTRUISM?

We can obtain some understanding of why altruism exists from the perspective of evolutionary psychology. Advocates of evolutionary psychology (an approach based on the assumption that much human behavior can be explained in evolutionary terms; see Chapter 2) claim that individuals are highly motivated to ensure their genes survive. How does this explain altruism? As Gross (1996, p. 413) pointed out, "If a mother dies in the course of saving her three offspring from a predator, she will have saved a $\frac{1}{2}$ times her own genes (since each offspring inherits one half of its mother's genes). So, in terms of genes, an act of apparent altruism can turn out to be extremely selfish."

Key Terms
Prosocial behavior: cooperative, affectionate, or helpful behavior designed to benefit another person.
Altruism: a form of **prosocial behavior** that is costly to the individual and is motivated by the desire to help the other person.

Parents invest a lot of time and resources in their children, which may be explained by biological theories of relationships—the parents' chances of passing on their genes are improved if they can help their children to survive and succeed.

Evolutionary psychology helps to explain why people often behave altruistically toward members of their own family. However, most people also behave altruistically toward nonrelatives. Evolutionary psychologists (e.g., Trivers, 1971) have explained this in terms of reciprocal altruism. **Reciprocal altruism** is summed up in the expression, "I'll scratch your back if you scratch mine." Thus, altruistic behavior may occur because the individual behaving altruistically toward someone else expects that person to return the favor. According to Trivers, reciprocal altruism is most likely to be found under certain conditions:

1. The costs of helping are fairly low and the benefits are high.
2. We can identify those who cheat by receiving help but not helping in return.

Fehr and Fischbacher (2003, p. 785) pointed out that reciprocal altruism and cooperation are much more common in humans than in other species: "Most animal species exhibit little division of labor and cooperation is limited to small groups. Even in other primate societies, cooperation [and reciprocal altruism] is orders of magnitude less developed than it is among humans." It is not altogether obvious from the perspective of evolutionary psychology why there should be this substantial difference between the human and other species.

Findings

Burnstein, Crandall, and Kitayama (1994) asked participants to choose between helping various individuals differing in genetic relatedness or kinship. Choices were strongly influenced by kinship, especially for life-and-death situations. Fellner and Marshall (1981) found that 86% of people were willing to be a kidney donor for their children, 67% would do the same for their parents, and 50% would be a kidney donor for their siblings (see the figure on the left).

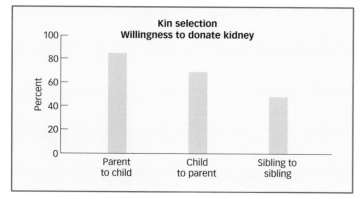

Korchmaros and Kenny (2001) argued that we should distinguish between genetic relatedness and emotional closeness. College students chose which family member they would be most likely to provide with life-saving assistance. Altruistic behavior was determined partly by genetic relatedness (predicted by evolutionary psychology) and partly by emotional closeness (not predicted by evolutionary psychology).

Fijneman, Willemsen, and Pooringa (1996) found that individuals in collectivistic cultures (with an emphasis on group membership) gave more help to other people than was the case with individuals in individualistic cultures (with an emphasis on individual responsibility). On the face of it, these cultural differences seem to indicate that reciprocal altruism doesn't apply in individualistic cultures. However, those living in individualistic cultures expected less help from others than did those living in collectivistic cultures. As a result, there was reciprocal altruism in most cultures, with individuals typically giving as much help as they expected to receive in return.

Reciprocal altruism is only an effective strategy when we can identify those who cheat by receiving help without offering any help themselves. It is easier to do this in small communities than in large ones. Steblay (1987) carried out a meta-analysis. He concluded that individuals living in large cities are less willing to pass on a telephone message, less helpful to a lost child, less willing to do small favors, and less likely to post letters that have gone astray.

Key Term

Reciprocal altruism: the notion that individuals will behave altruistically towards someone else if they anticipate that person will respond altruistically.

Why do many individuals behave altruistically even when those they help are very unlikely to reciprocate? According to Fehr and Fischbacher (2003), the answer is that it allows those individuals to gain a reputation for behaving altruistically that will increase the likelihood that they will be assisted by others in the future. They discussed a study in which participants decided whether to help another person who was not in a position to reciprocate that help. The crucial manipulation was whether participants' behavior would allow them to gain a reputation for altruism. Of those who could gain a reputation, 74% provided help, compared to only 37% of those who could not. Thus, many people are willing to behave altruistically in order to gain a general reputation for altruism.

Reluctance to show reciprocal altruism when it isn't possible to detect cheaters in advance was found in a series called *Shafted* seen briefly on British television. At the end of each show, both contestants indicated privately whether they wanted to share the money that had accumulated during the show or have it all for themselves. If they both voted to share the money, they received 50% each. If one person decided they wanted all the money and the other voted to share it, the former person received all the money. Finally, if they both voted to have all the money, no one received anything. In the final show, the money at stake was £220,000 (about $440, 000). Both players voted to have all the money because they couldn't trust the other player to be altruistic. It was cruel to observe the looks on their faces when they realised that neither of them would receive anything. Indeed, it was so cruel that the series ended prematurely after that show.

Evaluation

+ Evolutionary psychologists have put forward persuasive reasons for the existence of altruistic behavior toward relatives and nonrelatives.

+ The evolutionary approach explains why altruistic behavior is much more likely to be shown to close relatives than to nonrelatives.

+ Evolutionary psychologists focus more than other psychologists on the important issue of *why* altruism is so important to the human species.

− Evolutionary psychology provides only a partial explanation of altruistic behavior towards strangers.

− The evolutionary approach ignores several factors (e.g., emotional closeness; the individual's personality) that help to determine the precise circumstances in which altruistic behavior is found.

BYSTANDER INTERVENTION

A haunting image of our time is of someone being attacked violently in the middle of a city with no one coming to their assistance. This reluctance to help was shown in the case of Kitty Genovese, who was stabbed to death in New York as she returned home at 3 o'clock in the morning on March 13, 1964. According to the *New York Times*, 38 witnesses watched Kitty Genovese being attacked three times over a 30-minute period. No one intervened and only one person called the police. This suggests a truly horrifying reluctance of people to help victims in desperate need of assistance.

Many textbook writers (including me, alas!) have assumed that the details of what happened to Kitty Genovese reported by the *New York Times* were accurate. In fact, the newspaper greatly exaggerated what had happened. For example, it is highly probable that only three people saw either of the stabbings (there were two not three). Even those three eyewitnesses would have seen Kitty being attacked for only a few seconds.

Case Study: *The Kitty Genovese Murder* (as misleadingly reported by the *New York Times*)

At approximately 3.20 in the morning on March 13, 1964, 28-year-old Kitty Genovese was returning to her home in a middle-class area of Queens, New York, from her job as a bar manager. She parked her car and started to walk to her second-floor apartment some 30 meters away. She got as far as a streetlight, when a man who was later identified as Winston Mosely grabbed her. She screamed. Lights went on in the nearby apartment building. Kitty yelled, "Oh my God, he stabbed me! Please help me!" A window opened in the apartment building and a man's voice shouted, "Let that girl alone!" Mosely looked up, shrugged, and walked off down the street. As Kitty Genovese struggled to get to her feet, the lights went off in the apartments. The attacker came back some minutes later and renewed the assault by stabbing her again. She again cried out, "I'm dying! I'm dying!" Once again the lights came on and windows opened in many of the nearby apartments. The assailant again left, got into his car and drove away. Kitty staggered to her feet as a city bus drove by. It was now 3.35 a.m. Mosely returned and found his victim in a doorway at the foot of the stairs. He then raped her and stabbed her for a third time—this time fatally. It was 3.50 when the police received the first call. They responded quickly and were at the scene within 2 minutes, but Kitty Genovese was already dead.

The only person to call the police, a neighbor of Ms. Genovese, revealed that he had phoned only after much thought and after making a call to a friend to ask advice. He said, "I didn't want to get involved." Later it emerged that there were 38 other witnesses to the events over the half-hour period. Many of Kitty's neighbors heard her screams and watched from the windows, but no one came to her aid. The story shocked America and made front-page news across the country. The question people asked was why no one had offered any help, or even called the police earlier when it might have helped. Urban and moral decay, apathy, and indifference were some of the many explanations offered. Two social psychologists, Bibb Latané and John Darley, were unsatisfied with these explanations and began a series of research studies to identify the situational factors that influence whether or not people come to the aid of others. They concluded that an individual is less likely to provide assistance the greater the number of other bystanders present.

Two psychologists (John Darley and Bibb Latané) read the article in the *New York Times*. They wondered why Kitty Genovese wasn't helped by any of the (allegedly) numerous eyewitnesses who saw her being attacked. They argued that a victim might be better placed when there was just one bystander rather than many. In such a situation, responsibility for helping the victim falls firmly on one person rather than being spread among many people. Thus, the witness or bystander has a sense of personal responsibility. If there are many observers of a crime, there is a **diffusion of responsibility**, with each person bearing only a small portion of the blame for not helping. Thus, there is less feeling of personal responsibility.

We also need to consider culturally determined expectations of behavior (known as social norms). According to the norm of social responsibility, we should help those who need help. Darley and Latané (1968) argued that this norm is more strongly activated when only one person observes a victim's fate than when there are several bystanders.

Bystander apathy in the internet age

Researchers in Israel (Barron & Yechiam, 2002) hypothesized that people would respond to a query much better if they thought they were being targeted as an individual, rather than as a set of people. They created an imaginary person, Sarah, on Yahoo who was enquiring about possible courses at a technical institute. Some of Sarah's emails were sent to individuals, and some to groups of five people.

The results showed that 50% of the sample did not reply at all if there were four others on the address list, but only 36% of the single recipients failed to reply. And almost 33% of single recipients sent back a very helpful response—with additional useful information—compared to 16% of the group sample.

This suggests that automatic emails to groups of people are not as successful in outcome as individual ones. This should hold true whether one is asking for a volunteer to help with an office birthday cake or a commercial advertiser trying to increase hits on a website. So the implication is that to be truly effective people need to be contacted singly. If they see they are part of a group they may feel that someone else will respond as required so they need not do anything. They will become virtual bystanders!

Key Term

Diffusion of responsibility: the reduction in a sense of responsibility as the number of observers of an incident increases.

Findings

In their classic study, Darley and Latané (1968) put participants in separate rooms, and told them to put on headphones. They were instructed to discuss their personal problems, speaking into a microphone, and hearing others' contributions over their headphones. They were led to believe there were up six people involved in the discussion, but all of the apparent contributions by other participants were only tape recordings.

Each participant was told that one of the other participants was prone to seizures. After a while they heard him say:

> *I—er—I—uh—I've got one of these-er-seizure—er-er—things coming on and— and—and I could really—er—use some help so if somebody would—er—er—help— er—er—help—er—uh—uh—uh [choking sounds] . . . I'm gonna die—er—er— I'm . . . gonna die—er-help—er—er—seizure—er . . . [choking sounds, silence].*

Of those who thought they were the only person to know that someone was having an epileptic fit, 100% left the room and reported the emergency. However, only 62% of participants responded if they thought there were five other bystanders. Of those participants believing they were the only bystander, 50% responded within 45 seconds of the onset of the fit versus 0% of those thinking there were five other bystanders.

There were two other interesting findings. First, participants who thought there were five other bystanders denied this had influenced their behavior. Second, participants not reporting the emergency were not indifferent. Most of them had trembling hands and sweating palms, and they seemed more emotionally aroused than those reporting the emergency.

The chances of bystanders helping a victim depend in part on what the bystanders were doing beforehand. Batson et al. (1978) sent participants from one building to another to perform a task. On the way, they went past a male student slumped on the stairs coughing and groaning. Only 10% of those told their task was important stopped to assist the student compared to 80% told the task was trivial.

What situations produce most helping behavior? The chances of a bystander lending assistance to a victim are much greater if the situation is interpreted as a genuine emergency. Brickman et al. (1982) carried out a study in which participants heard a bookcase falling on another participant followed by a scream. When someone else interpreted the situation as an emergency, participants offered help more rapidly than when the other person said there was nothing to worry about.

The perceived relationship between those directly involved in an incident often has a major influence on bystanders' behavior. Shotland and Straw (1976) staged a fight between a man and a woman. The woman either screamed, "I don't know you" or "I don't know why I ever married you." Far more bystanders intervened when they thought the fight involved strangers rather than a married couple (65% vs. 19%, respectively). Thus, bystanders are reluctant to become involved in the personal lives of strangers.

Who is most likely to offer assistance to a victim? Huston, Ruggiero, Conner, and Geis (1981) argued that bystanders with relevant skills or expertise will be especially likely to provide assistance. They found that those helping in dangerous emergencies generally had relevant skills (e.g., life-saving; first aid; self-defense). Men are more likely than women to help when the situation involves danger or there is an audience (Eagly & Crowley, 1986). Men are more likely to help women than other men, especially when the women are attractive. In contrast, women are equally likely to help men and women. Bystanders are generally more likely to help a victim similar to themselves (Hogg & Vaughan, 2005). Levine (2002) used a situation in which a victim was exposed to physical

Bystanders who have some relevant skill to offer are more likely to get involved than those who don't know what to do.

Late Samaritans

Darley and Batson's (1973) study assessed helping behavior in students from a theological college—where they were studying to be ministers or priests.

The students had to give a presentation at a nearby building—half had to talk about the Bible parable the Good Samaritan; the other half had to talk about the jobs the students enjoyed most. The students were also split up into three groups and were told one of the following:

- You are ahead of schedule and have plenty of time.
- You are right on schedule.
- You are late.

On their way to the talk, they passed a "victim," actually a stooge, who was collapsed in a doorway, coughing and groaning. The students were observed to see whether or not they stopped to help.

Darley and Batson found that the topic of the student's talk did not seem to influence helping. However, the perceived time pressure did. The results were as follows:

Group condition	% helping
Ahead of schedule	63
Right on schedule	45
Late	10

Bizarrely, several "late" condition students who were going to give a talk on the Good Samaritan actually stepped over the victim to get past.

---

violence. Victims were more likely to be helped when described as belonging to the bystanders' ingroup (a group with which they identified) rather than an outgroup (a group with which they didn't identify).

What characteristics of victims influence whether they receive assistance? Piliavin, Rodin, and Piliavin (1969) staged incidents in the New York subway, with a male victim staggering and collapsing on the floor. He either carried a cane and seemed sober, or he smelled of alcohol and carried a bottle of alcohol. Bystanders were much less likely to help when the victim was "drunk" than when he was "ill." Drunks are regarded as responsible for their own plight and it could be unpleasant to help a smelly drunk who might vomit or become abusive. More generally, we are much inclined to help "deserving" victims than "undeserving" ones.

AROUSAL/COST–REWARD MODEL

Piliavin, Dovidio, Gaertner, and Clark (1981) put forward the arousal/cost–reward model to account for the various findings from bystander intervention studies. According to this model, bystanders go through five steps before deciding whether to assist a victim:

1. Becoming aware of someone's need for help; this depends on attention.
2. Experience of arousal.
3. Interpreting cues and labeling their arousal state.
4. Working out the rewards and costs associated with different actions.
5. Making a decision and acting on it.

The fourth step is the most important. Some of the major rewards and costs involved in helping and not helping are as follows (relevant studies are in brackets):

- *Costs of helping*: Physical harm, delay in carrying out other activities (Piliavin et al., 1969).
- *Costs of not helping*: Ignoring personal responsibility, guilt, criticism from others, ignoring perceived similarity (Darley & Latané, 1969; Levine, 2002).
- *Rewards of helping*: Praise from victim, satisfaction from having been useful if relevant skills are possessed (Huston et al., 1981).
- *Rewards of not helping*: Able to continue with other activities as normal (Batson et al., 1978; Darley & Batson, 1973).

Evaluation

+ The model provides a comprehensive account of the factors determining bystanders' behavior.

+ Potential rewards and costs associated with helping or not helping influence bystanders' behavior.

− The model implies that bystanders deliberately consider all the elements in the situation. In fact, bystanders often respond impulsively and without deliberation.

− Bystanders don't always need to be aroused before helping a victim. For example, someone with much relevant experience (e.g., a doctor responding to someone having a heart attack) may provide efficient help without becoming very aroused.

AGGRESSION

This section of the chapter focuses on aggression, which is also covered from the developmental perspective in Chapter 15. **Aggression** is:

any behavior directed toward another individual that is carried out with the proximate [immediate] intent to cause harm. In addition, the perpetrator must believe that the behavior will harm the target and that the target is motivated to avoid the behavior. (Bushman & Anderson, 2001, p. 274).

Note that the harm has to be *deliberate*. Someone who slips on the ice and crashes into someone by accident may cause harm, but isn't behaving aggressively. Note also that the victim must want to avoid harm. Whipping a masochist who derives sexual pleasure from the activity doesn't constitute aggressive behavior.

Members of the human race often behave aggressively and violently. There have been about 15,000 wars in the last 5600 years, which works out at almost 2.7 wars per year. However, there are cultural differences in the size of the problems posed by aggression and violence. For example, Brehm, Kassin, and Fein (2005) discussed the murder rate in numerous countries in 1994. The murder rate was almost 80 per 100,000 people in Colombia, it was over 20 in Russia, and it was 9 in the United States. In contrast, it was only about 1 or 2 per 100,000 in the United Kingdom, Egypt, and China.

Bonta (1997) discussed 25 societies in which violent aggression scarcely exists. For example, consider the Chewong people living in the mountains of the Malay Peninsula. Their language doesn't have any words for concepts such as fighting, aggression, or warfare. Bonta found that 23 of the 25 peaceful societies he studied strongly believed in the advantages of cooperation and the disadvantages of competition. Cultural expectations (known as social norms) are important. For example, social norms in many Western societies encourage people to be competitive and go-getting, and this may help to explain the high levels of aggression in those societies.

The potentially serious costs of aggressive behavior mean that nearly everyone is opposed to it. However, it is commonly believed that aggressive behavior can sometimes have beneficial effects. Suppose you are really angry with your boss or teacher and you release this anger by aggressively punching a pillow or kicking the furniture. According to Freud, this produces **catharsis**, in which the aggressive behavior releases the anger and frustration and reduces the likelihood of subsequent aggression.

Do you believe in catharsis? In fact, the evidence suggests that releasing aggression *increases* rather than *decreases* subsequent aggression! Bushman, Baumeister, and Stack (1999) asked students to write an essay. The essays were returned with extremely negative comments written on them to produce anger in the students. After that, some students spent 2 minutes punching a punching bag (catharsis condition) whereas others did not (control condition). Finally, the students performed a task against a competitor. When

Key Terms

Aggression:
behavior intended to harm or injure another person.

Catharsis:
the notion that behaving aggressively can cause a release of negative emotions such as anger and frustration.

Freud proposed that some aggressive behavior is cathartic, in that it releases anger and tension thereby reducing subsequent aggression. Would you feel better after a pillow fight?

they performed better than the competitor, they had to decide the intensity of shock the competitor should receive. Students in the catharsis condition (punching the punch bag) behaved more aggressively than those in the control condition when choosing the shock intensity.

FACTORS CAUSING AGGRESSION

Aggression is caused by more factors than you can shake a stick at. Accordingly, we will focus on only a few of the most important ones. These factors include aspects of the situation, the personality of the individual, physiological processes, and cognitive processes.

Situational factors

Aggression is much more likely in some situations than in others. Think of occasions when you have behaved aggressively. Many probably involved frustrating situations. Dollard et al. (1939) argued in their frustration–aggression hypothesis that there are close links between frustration and aggression. Pastore (1952) argued that we should distinguish between *justified* and *unjustified* frustration. For example, suppose you are waiting for a bus but the bus driver goes by without stopping. That would be unjustified frustration. However, if it is clear that the bus is out of service, that would be justified frustration. Pastore presented participants with various scenarios, and found that unjustified frustration led to much higher levels of anger than did justified frustration.

Berkowitz (1974) argued that frustration is most likely to lead to aggressive behavior when the situation contains aggressive cues (e.g., a gun or other weapon). Support for his views comes from the **weapons effect**, an increase in aggression caused by the mere sight of a weapon (e.g., a gun). Berkowitz and LePage (1976) used a situation in which male university students received electric shocks from another student. They were then given the chance to give electric shocks to that student. In one condition, a revolver and a shotgun were close to the shock machine. In another condition, nothing was placed nearby. More shocks were given in the presence of the guns. According to Berkowitz (1968, p. 22), "Guns not only permit violence, they can stimulate it as well. The finger pulls the trigger, but the trigger may also be pulling the finger."

Carlson, Marcus-Newhall, and Miller (1990) carried out a meta-analysis on 56 studies concerned with the effects of aggression-related cues on aggressive behavior. Such cues generally led to increased aggressive behavior in negatively aroused individuals. Aggression-related cues also produced aggression-related thoughts even in individuals who hadn't been frustrated, indicating the power of such cues.

Personality

What kinds of people are the most aggressive? Common sense suggests that individuals with low self-esteem have negative thoughts and emotions about themselves and the world, and this causes them to be aggressive. In fact, aggression and violence generally occur more frequently in individuals having *high* self-esteem than in those with low self-esteem (Baumeister, Smart, & Boden, 1996).

Subsequent research has shown that it is only certain individuals with high self-esteem who are at risk of becoming aggressive. More specifically, those most at risk are narcissistic individuals. As well as having high self-esteem, they are arrogant and regard themselves as special and superior to other people. Bushman and Baumeister (1998) provoked their participants by criticizing harshly an essay they had written. Narcissistic individuals were the ones most likely to behave aggressively towards the person who had criticized them. Their self-esteem is rather fragile, and they become aggressive when their unrealistically positive self-image is threatened.

We might expect individuals who focus on the immediate (but not long-term) consequences of their behavior to be more aggressive than most people. Support for this expectation was reported by Joireman, Anderson, and Strathman (2003). Individuals who were high in impulsivity and sensation seeking were more aggressive on several measures than were those low in impulsivity and sensation seeking.

> **Key Term**
>
> **Weapons effect:**
> an increase in aggression produced by the sight of a weapon.

Physiological arousal

Think back to occasions on which you have felt angry and behaved aggressively. You probably felt very aroused at the time, suggesting that heightened arousal is one factor associated with aggression. According to Zillmann's excitation-transfer theory, what is important is how the arousal is *interpreted*. If we interpret our aroused state as a consequence of being provoked, then we become angry and aggressive. If we interpret our aroused state as being due to some nonprovoking factor, we shouldn't become aggressive.

Support for excitation-transfer theory was reported by Zillman, Johnson, and Day (1974)—see the Key Study below.

Key Study

Zillmann et al. (1974): Excitation-transfer theory

Support for excitation-transfer theory was reported by Zillman, Johnson, and Day (1974). Male participants were provoked by a confederate of the experimenter. Half the participants rested for 6 minutes and then pedaled on a cycling machine for 90 seconds, whereas the other half pedaled first and then rested. Immediately afterwards, all participants chose the shock intensity to be given to the person who had provoked them. Both groups were moderately aroused at that time, because the effects of pedaling on arousal last for several minutes.

What do you think happened? Zillman et al. (1974) predicted that participants who had just finished cycling would attribute their level of arousal to the cycling and so wouldn't behave aggressively. In contrast, those who had just rested for 6 minutes would attribute their arousal to the provocation, and so would administer a strong electric shock. The results were as predicted.

Discussion points
1. Do you think that excitation transfer happens often in everyday life?
2. Consider ways in which people's attributions of the cause of their arousal could be manipulated.

KEY STUDY EVALUATION
Like many social psychology experiments, Zillmann et al.'s study raises some ethical issues. If participants do not know the true nature of the study, can they give informed consent to take part? Would it be possible to run the experiment if the participants knew of its true intention beforehand? Would those who behaved more aggressively and were prepared to give strong "shocks" have problems later dealing with this probably unwelcome self-knowledge?

Biological factors

Human aggression depends in part on biological factors. Rhee and Waldman (2002) carried out a meta-analysis of twin and adoption studies on antisocial behavior (including aggressive behavior). Identical twins (sharing 100% of their genes) were more similar in antisocial behavior than fraternal twins (sharing 50% of their genes). That means that genetic factors influence aggressive behavior. More specifically, Rhee and Waldman (2002) found that 41% of the variability in antisocial behavior was a result of genetic influences.

Sex hormones (especially male sex hormones) influence aggressive behavior. Supporting evidence was reported by van Goozen, Frijda, and van de Poll (1995). Transsexuals (individuals who change sex) were studied before and after 3 months of sex hormone treatment. Female-to-male transsexuals showed increased proneness to aggression after receiving male sex hormones. In contrast, male-to-female transsexuals deprived of male sex hormones had decreased proneness to anger and aggression.

GENERAL AGGRESSION MODEL

We have seen that several factors are involved in aggression. Anderson, Anderson, and Deuser (1996) and Anderson and Bushman (2002) proposed a general aggression model based on these factors (see the figure below). This model consists of four stages:

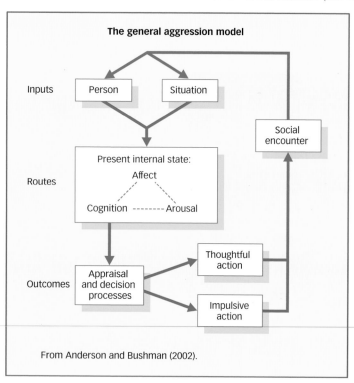

The general aggression model

From Anderson and Bushman (2002).

- *Stage 1*: At this stage, the key variables are situational cues (e.g., weapons present) and individual differences (e.g., aggressive personality). For example, Krueger et al. (2001) found that negative affectivity (a personality dimension relating to several negative emotions) correlated +.28 with antisocial or aggressive behavior.
- *Stage 2*: What happens at stage 1 can cause various effects at stage 2, including affect (e.g., hostile feelings), arousal (e.g., activation of the autonomic nervous system), and cognition (e.g., hostile thoughts). All of these effects are connected to each other.
- *Stage 3*: What happens at stage 2 leads to appraisal processes (e.g., interpretation of the situation; possible coping strategies; consequences of behaving aggressively).
- *Stage 4*: Depending on the outcome of the appraisal processes at stage 3, the individual decides whether or not to behave aggressively.

Findings

The general aggression model combines elements of several previous theories. As a result, many of the findings discussed already (e.g., weapons effect) are consistent with the model's predictions. Bartholow, Anderson, Carnagey, and Benjamin (2005) studied the weapons effect using hunting guns (e.g., shotguns; long-range rifles) and assault guns (e.g., handguns; machine guns) as stimuli. They found that hunters associated aggressive concepts more with assault guns than with hunting guns, whereas the opposite was the case for nonhunters. It was predicted from the model that photographs of assault guns would produce more aggressive behavior than photographs of hunting guns in hunters, but the opposite in nonhunters. Aggressive behavior was measured by the intensity of noise that participants were willing to administer to an opponent on a task. The findings were as predicted (see the figure below).

Dill, Anderson, and Deuser (1997) studied the role of appraisal processes. Participants watched a videotape of pairs of people arguing with each other. Those participants having an aggressive personality perceived more aggression and hostility in this interaction than did those with a non-aggressive personality. Individual differences in aggressive behavior may well depend in part on differences in perception and interpretation of any given situation.

Anderson and Bushman (2001) carried out a meta-analysis of studies on violent video games. They considered the effects on aggressive behavior, aggressive thoughts or cognitions, aggressive affect or emotion, and physiological arousal. The situational cues provided by violent video games were associated with aggressive behavior. The overall effect was of moderate size, and its magnitude was similar in males and females, and in children and adults.

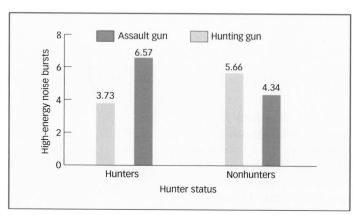

Mean aggressive behavior (number of high-energy noise blasts) as a function of hunter status (hunter vs. nonhunter) and type of gun shown photographically (assault vs. hunting). From Bartholow et al. (2005). Copyright © 2005 Elsevier. Reproduced with permission.

According to the general aggression model, aggressive cognitions or thoughts play a central role in the development of the aggressive personality. As predicted, Anderson and Bushman (2001) found that exposure to violent video games increased aggressive cognitions. Exposure to violence also increased aggressive affect or emotion and increased physiological arousal as predicted by the model. As Anderson and Bushman (2001, p. 358) concluded, "Every theoretical prediction derived from prior research and from GAM [general aggression model] was supported by the meta-analysis of currently available research on violent video games."

Evaluation

+ The model is more comprehensive in scope than previous theories of aggression.

+ Priming effects (e.g., weapons effect) and appraisal processes are of major importance in determining whether someone will behave aggressively.

+ There is evidence for an aggressive or antisocial personality (e.g., Krueger et al., 2001) and those high in impulsivity and sensation seeking also tend to be aggressive (Joireman et al., 2003).

− Negative affect, arousal, and negative cognitions all have complex effects on behavior, and it is often difficult to predict whether someone will behave aggressively.

− We probably lack conscious awareness of some of our appraisal processes, but most of the measures used (mainly self-report questionnaires) only assess appraisal processes of which we have conscious awareness.

− The general aggression model provides more of a general framework than a detailed theoretical account.

AGGRESSION IN RELATIONSHIPS

In the real world, most aggression occurs within close relationships and families. For example, Straus, Gelles, and Steinmetz (1980) found in American families that physical assault designed to injure the other person had occurred in 28% of married couples. Why is there so much aggression within close relationships? Gelles (1997) argued that aggressive behavior occurs when the rewards of aggression are perceived to be greater than the likely costs. The perceived costs of behaving aggressively or violently can be relatively low in some close relationships for the following reasons:

1. There are few external social controls because outsiders are reluctant to become involved.
2. There are power inequalities between men and women, with men having more power and physical strength.
3. Some men regard aggression positively as forming part of their image of being a man.

Are men responsible for most of the physical aggression within heterosexual relationships? In fact, the differences in aggression between men and women are surprisingly small in Western cultures. Archer (1982) carried out a meta-analysis of 82 studies and concluded as follows:

> When measures were based on specific acts, women were significantly more likely than men to have used physical aggression toward their partners and to have used it more frequently, although the effect size was very small . . . When measures were based on the physical consequences of aggression (visible injuries or injuries requiring medical treatment), men were more likely than women to have injured their partners, but again, effect sizes were relatively small (p. 664).

Thus, women are slightly more likely than men to behave aggressively in a relationship, but men are more likely to inflict physical injury. It might be thought that most female aggression in relationships occurs as self-defense against physical aggression from the male partner. However, this is not supported by the evidence. Straus (1993) found that women admitted they had initiated the aggression in 53% of cases of physical aggression within marriages.

The great majority of studies have been carried out in Western cultures. Men are much more likely to be physically aggressive to their female partners than vice versa in many non-Western cultures (see Archer, 2000, for a review). Why are there these cultural differences? First, in most Western cultures both sexes share the social norm that physical aggression is worse when the aggressor is a man. Second, the belief that men have the right to control their wives' behavior is much less prevalent in Western cultures than in some other, male-dominated cultures.

FORMATION OF INTERPERSONAL RELATIONSHIPS

Numerous factors are involved in the formation of interpersonal relationships, and there are several types of interpersonal relationships. However, we focus mostly on six key factors determining our choice of friends and romantic partners: physical attractiveness; proximity; familiarity; attitude similarity; demographic similarity [similarity in background characteristics]; and similarity in personality. Why are various kinds of similarity so important? Rubin (1973) suggested various answers. First, communication is easier with people who are similar to us. Second, similar others may (with a bit of luck!) confirm the rightness of our attitudes and beliefs. Third, if we like ourselves, then we will probably like others who resemble us. Fourth, those who are similar to us are likely to enjoy the same activities.

PHYSICAL ATTRACTIVENESS

When meeting a stranger, we notice their physical appearance. This includes how they are dressed, whether they are clean or dirty, and often includes an assessment of their physical attractiveness. People tend to agree about whether someone is physically attractive. Women whose faces resemble those of young children are often perceived as attractive. Thus, photographs of females with relatively large and widely separated eyes, a small nose, and a small chin are regarded as attractive. However, wide cheekbones and narrow cheeks are also seen as attractive (Cunningham, 1986), and these features are uncommon in young children.

Cunningham (1986) also studied physical attractiveness in males. Men having features such as a square jaw, small eyes, and thin lips were regarded as attractive by women. These features can be regarded as indicating maturity, as they are rarely found in children.

Average faces are regarded as attractive. Langlois, Roggman, and Musselman (1994) found that male and female computer-generated composites or "averaged" faces were perceived as more attractive than the individual faces forming the composite. Why was this? Langlois discovered that averaged faces were regarded as more familiar than the individual faces. They argued that this sense of familiarity made the averaged faces seem attractive. Averaged faces are also more symmetrical than individual faces, and symmetry is associated with attractiveness (Grammer & Thornhill, 1994).

According to evolutionary psychologists, men should prefer women whose physical features indicate high fertility. Zaadrstra et al. (1993) discussed two such features. First, the body mass index (BMI), based on the

David Beckham fits Cunningham's "attractive male" characteristics— square jaw, small eyes, and thin lips.

relationship between height and weight, is between 20 and 30 in the most fertile women. Second, the waist-to-hip ratio is approximately .70 in the most fertile women.

The evidence suggests that waist-to-hip ratio is important in physical attraction. Singh (1993) found that women with a waist-to-hip ratio of .70 were judged to be the most attractive. The evidence on BMI is less supportive of evolutionary psychology. Rubinstein and Caballero (2000) found that there was a steady decrease in BMI for the winners of the Miss America Pageant between 1923 and 1999. In addition, the emphasis on thinness in women within most Western cultures is by no means universal. Anderson, Crawford, Nadeau, and Lindberg (1992) considered 52 different cultures, and found that women with a heavy body were preferred in cultures in which the food supply was very unreliable. It was mainly in Western cultures in which the food supply is very reliable that women with a slender body were preferred (see the table below).

The above findings may be somewhat suspect. Fan, Liu, Wu, and Dai (2004) pointed out that most studies on BMI and waist-to-hip ratio used only two-dimensional images. They used three-dimensional images, and found that the most important determinant of physical attractiveness was the volume–height index (VHI), defined as the body volume divided by the square of the height. VHI is highly correlated with BMI but predicts ratings of female physical attractiveness better.

Dion, Berscheid, and Walster (1972) found that physically attractive people are thought to have more positive traits and characteristics than less attractive ones. They interpreted their findings as supporting the "beauty-is-good" stereotype. However, these findings were equally consistent with the "unattractiveness-is-bad" stereotype. Griffin and Langlois (2006) found that it was actually more the case that being unattractive is a disadvantage rather than that being attractive is a positive advantage.

Matching hypothesis

Walster, Aronson, Abrahams, and Rottman (1966) put forward the matching hypothesis. According to this hypothesis, people are attracted to those of about the same level of physical attractiveness as themselves. We are initially attracted to those who are beautiful or handsome, but realize that we are unlikely to be found attractive by someone much more physically attractive. As a result, we become attracted to those about as physically attractive as we are (perhaps with some reluctance!).

The evidence obtained by Walster et al. (1966) and by Walster and Walster (1969) supported the matching hypothesis—see the Key Study below.

Anderson et al. (1992): Results

Preference	Food supply			
	Very unreliable	Moderately unreliable	Moderately reliable	Very reliable
Heavy body	71%	50%	39%	40%
Moderate body	29%	33%	39%	20%
Slender body	0%	17%	22%	40%

Key Study

Walster et al.: The matching hypothesis

Walster et al. (1966) organized a dance at which students were randomly allocated partners of the opposite sex. Halfway through the dance, the students filled in a questionnaire giving their views on their partner. These views were compared with judges' ratings of the students' physical attractiveness. The more physically attractive students were liked most by their partners. However, Walster et al. found 6 months later that partners were more likely to have dated if they were similar in physical attractiveness.

Walster and Walster (1969) also organized a dance. This time, however, the students had met each other beforehand. This may have led them to think realistically about the qualities they were looking for in a partner. As predicted, students expressed the most liking for those at the same level of physical attractiveness.

Discussion points
1. Does the matching hypothesis seem correct in your experience?
2. Why does physical attractiveness play such an important part in dating behavior and in relationships?

KEY STUDY EVALUATION
Walster et al.'s matching hypothesis suggests that people are attracted to those of about the same level of physical attractiveness as themselves. This may indeed be the case in many situations, but it does not take account of many social factors that can also influence who we find attractive. Relationships often occur between people who have different levels of attractiveness but have got to know each other through working together or living nearby. Here mechanisms other than pure physical attractiveness are operating. In other situations, people who are generally considered very attractive may find that others think they are unapproachable. Some people may believe that a less attractive partner will be less likely to stray than a very attractive partner, and so have more confidence in the relationship.

Feingold (1988) carried out a meta-analysis of studies in which the physical attractiveness of relationship partners was assessed. The average correlation was +.49 between physical attractiveness levels of the partners in romantic couples. This indicates that couples are generally fairly similar in physical attractiveness, and supports the matching hypothesis.

PROXIMITY

Proximity or nearness influences our choice of friends and those with whom we develop a relationship. Festinger, Schachter, and Back (1950) studied married graduate students assigned randomly to apartments in 17 different two-story buildings. About two-thirds of their closest friends lived in the same building. Close friends living in the same building were twice as likely to be living on the same floor as on the other floor.

The importance of proximity extends to romantic relationships leading to marriage. Bossard (1932) looked at 5000 marriage licenses in Philadelphia. Those getting married tended to live close to each other. That is less true nowadays because people are much more mobile. It is also less true because of the dramatic increase in the use of the internet as a way of forming a relationship. McKenna, Green, and Gleason (2002) found that individuals who expressed their true selves best on the internet were most likely to form a lasting and close relationship. Of interest, they also found that undergraduate students had greater liking for each other after an internet meeting than after a face-to-face meeting.

Friendships arise and are maintained between people who live close to each other, and who enjoy similar leisure pursuits.

IMPRESSION FORMATION

What happens when we form an initial impression of someone else? According to Asch (1946), we use an implicit personality theory, assuming that a person who has one particular personality trait will have various other, related traits. For example, suppose you know that a fellow student is a generally anxious person. You might expect him/her to be fairly disorganized in his/her studying and to lack confidence in his/her abilities.

Asch (1946) claimed that key aspects of personality (central traits) influence the impression we form of others more than do other aspects of personality (peripheral traits). He also argued that our very first impressions are of crucial importance in determining our overall view of someone else. Information about another person that is presented first will have more influence than information presented later—this is known as the **primacy effect**, and there is much evidence for its existence (e.g., Asch, 1946; Belmore, 1987). What causes the primacy effect? Belmore (1987) found that people reading statements about another person spent less and less time on each successive statement.

In one of his studies, Asch (1946) gave participants a list of seven adjectives, which were said to describe an imaginary person called X. All the participants were given the following six adjectives: intelligent, skilful, industrious, determined, practical, and cautious. The seventh adjective was warm, cold, polite, or blunt. Then the participants had to select other adjectives that best described X.

The findings were clear-cut. The adjectives "warm" and "cold" were central traits, having marked effects on how all the other information about X was interpreted. For example, when X was warm, 91% of the participants thought he was generous, and 94% thought he was good-natured. In contrast, when X was cold, only 8% of the participants thought he was generous, and 17% thought he was good-natured. Thus, people believe that those who are warm have several other desirable characteristics, whereas those who are cold possess mostly undesirable characteristics.

Asch's (1946) study was very artificial. Kelley (1950) carried out a less artificial study in which students rated a guest lecturer described beforehand as being rather cold or very warm. The lecturer was rated much more positively on several dimensions (e.g., sociability; popularity; humor) when he was described as warm. The warm–cold manipulation also influenced the students' behavior. They interacted more with him and asked more questions when he had been described as warm.

There are other central traits in addition to the warm–cold dimension. For example, Rosenberg, Nelson, and Vivekananthan (1968) claimed that two dimensions are of crucial importance in impression formation:

1. *Social evaluation*: The good end of this dimension has adjectives such as sociable, popular, and warm, and the bad end includes unsociable, cold, and irritable.
2. *Intellectual evaluation*: This dimension ranges from skilful and persistent (good end) to stupid and foolish (bad end).

In contrast, Vonk (1993) found that three dimensions were of central importance: evaluation (good–bad), potency (strong–weak), and social orientation (sociable–independent). Asch's warm–cold dimension formed an important part of the evaluation dimension, and there was no evidence supporting the notion of a separate intellectual dimension.

> ## Key Term
>
> **Primacy effect:**
> in social psychology, the notion that our impressions of other people are heavily influenced by the first information about them we encounter.

SIMILARITY

As was mentioned earlier, there are several ways in which two people can be similar or dissimilar. These include similarity in personality, attitude similarity, and demographic similarity. We will make a start by considering similarity in personality.

The saying, "Opposites attract," implies that we are most likely to become friends or to have a relationship with those who are very different from us. However, there is another saying, "Birds of a feather flock together," implying that we are attracted to similar people. Nearly all the evidence supports this latter view. For example, Burgess and Wallin (1953) obtained information about 42 personality characteristics from 1000 engaged couples. There was no evidence at all for the notion that opposites attract. The couples showed a significant amount of similarity for 14 personality characteristics (e.g., feelings easily hurt; leader of social events).

Byrne (1971) found that strangers holding similar attitudes to participants were rated as more attractive than those holding dissimilar attitudes. Is this difference more a result of our liking of those with similar attitudes or of our dislike for those having dissimilar attitudes? Rosenbaum (1986) addressed that issue, finding that dissimilarity of attitudes increased disliking more than similarity of attitudes increased liking. This may happen because we feel threatened and fear disagreements when we discover that the other person has attitudes very different to our own.

Sprecher (1998) studied the importance of similarity in romantic relationships, opposite-sex friendships, and same-sex friendships. Similarity of interests and leisure activities was more important than similarity of attitudes and values in same- and opposite-sex friendships. However, the opposite was the case for romantic relationships. Demographic similarity or similarity of background characteristics was relatively unimportant in all three kinds of relationship.

There is a final (and unexpected) way in which similarity influences those to whom we are attracted. Jones, Pelham, Carvallo, and Mirenberg (2004) downloaded birth records from a Texas state government website. By chance alone, only 6.27% of the married couples should have had surnames starting with the same letter. In fact, they found that 10.37% of the couples had the same surname initial, which is 65% more than expected by chance. However, it might be unwise to marry someone on the basis of having the same surname initial!

There are two exceptions to the hypothesis that we are more attracted to those who are similar to us. First, there are cross-cultural differences. Heine and Renshaw (2002) found that Americans liked those who were perceived to be similar to them, but this was not true of Japanese participants. Japanese participants tended to like individuals who were familiar to them. Second, Amodio and Showers (2005) found that the importance of similarity in liking for a romantic partner depended on the level of commitment. Perceived similarity was positively related to liking in high-commitment relationships, but was actually *negatively* related to liking in low-commitment relationships. The latter finding may have occurred because being with someone dissimilar provides opportunities for personal growth for the participants (who were young college students).

RULES IN INTERPERSONAL RELATIONSHIPS

Most interpersonal relationships are governed by unspoken rules. The rules applied to interpersonal relationships vary depending on the nature of the relationship. However, Argyle, Henderson, and Furnham (1985) found some general rules when their participants rated the importance of several rules in each of 22 relationships. The six most important rules (in descending order of importance) were as follows:

1. Respect the other person's privacy.
2. Don't discuss with someone else things said in confidence.
3. Look the other person in the eye during conversation.
4. Don't criticize the other person publicly.
5. Don't indulge in sexual activity with the other person (except in romantic relationships, of course!).
6. Seek to repay all debts, favors, or compliments.

How do we know these rules are actually important? Argyle et al. (1985) studied broken friendships. As predicted, "the lapse of friendship was attributed in many cases to the breaking of certain rules, especially rules of rewardingness and rules about relations with third parties, e.g., not being jealous, and keeping confidences" (Argyle, 1988, pp. 233–234).

There are several rules governing interpersonal relationships. If any of these rules are broken, e.g., don't discuss with someone else things said in confidence, this will likely jeopardize the friendship.

There are interesting cultural differences in the importance attached to certain rules. For example, people in Hong Kong and Japan were more likely than those in Britain or Italy to support rules such as obeying superiors, preserving group harmony, and avoiding loss of face (Argyle et al., 1986).

What functions are served by rules within interpersonal relationships? According to Argyle and Henderson (1984), some rules (regulatory rules) reduce conflict within relationships, because they indicate what is acceptable. There are also reward rules, which ensure that the rewards provided by each person are appropriate.

SEX DIFFERENCES

Friendships between men are generally less intimate than those between women. Why is this so? Reis, Senchak, and Solomon (1985) considered various explanations. First, men may define intimacy differently to women. This explanation was rejected, because men and women didn't differ in their intimacy ratings of video fragments of people interacting.

Second, there may be no differences in friendship intimacy, but men are less inclined to label their own behavior as intimate. However, Reis et al. (1985) asked participants to indicate the level of intimacy revealed in actual conversation narratives, carefully edited so that it was totally unclear whether they came from a man or a woman. Male and female participants both perceived the narrative to be more intimate when it came from a woman.

Third, men may lack the social skills needed for same-sex intimacy. Reis et al. (1985) asked men and women to have an intimate conversation with their best friend. Men performed this task as well as women, indicating that they have the necessary skills for intimate friendship. After rejecting all of the above explanations, Reis et al. concluded that women's role in society (e.g., caring for children) motivates them to develop intimate and nurturing relationships.

MATE SELECTION

One of the key findings in the area of mate selection is that like mates with like. We tend to mate with those reasonably similar to us in physical attractiveness, attitudes, and personality. However, men tend to prefer younger women and women tend to prefer older men. Buss (1989) found in 37 cultures around the world that men in every culture preferred women younger than themselves, and women preferred men older than themselves in all cultures except Spain. Buss found that the personal qualities of kindness and intelligence were regarded as important by both sexes in virtually every culture.

According to evolutionary psychologists, what men and women find attractive in the opposite sex are features maximizing the probability of producing offspring who will survive and prosper. The reason is that we want our genes to carry over into the next generation. Younger women are preferred to older ones because older women are less

In Buss's (1989) study, women preferred older men, as they were deemed more able to provide adequately for potential offspring. However, in modern Western society, where many women no longer rely economically on their partner, the opposite is also often seen.

likely to be able to have children. Women prefer older men because they are more likely to provide adequately for the needs of their offspring.

The approach offered by evolutionary psychologists is inadequate (see also discussion in Chapter 3). Evolutionary psychologists don't explain why men and women in nearly all cultures regard kindness and intelligence as being more important than age. More generally, culture accounted for 14% of the variation in mate preferences in Buss's (1989) data, whereas gender accounted for only 2.4% of the variation. Evolutionary psychologists consistently underestimate the importance of cultural factors when explaining social behavior.

Buss (1989) found in his cross-cultural study that men in nearly all cultures claimed to be more influenced by physical attractiveness than did women. Feingold (1990) carried out various meta-analyses, also finding that physical attractiveness is rated as more important for romantic attraction by men. However, this gender difference was greater when based on self-report rather than on behavioral data. This suggests that females may not be fully aware of the importance they actually attach to male physical attractiveness. For example, Sprecher (1989) found that women attributed the attraction they experienced toward a man to his earning potential and expressiveness rather than his physical attractiveness. In fact, however, men and women were equally influenced by physical attractiveness when choosing a partner.

Feingold (1992) carried out meta-analyses of studies (mostly American) that had focused on self-reports of the attributes that men and women desired in a potential mate. The largest gender differences were found with respect to status and ambition, with women rating these attributes as more important than men.

DEVELOPMENT OF CLOSE RELATIONSHIPS

What is a "close relationship"? According to Berscheid and Reis (1998, p. 199), we

would require the interaction pattern to reveal that the partners frequently influence each other's behavior . . . that each person's influence on the other is diverse . . . that the influence is strong, and, moreover, that all these properties have characterized the partners' interaction for a considerable duration of time.

It is difficult to assess the development of close relationships scientifically. For example, we can't easily study the process of falling in love under laboratory conditions! What is typically done is to use questionnaires to assess the processes involved in relationships, the level of satisfaction with relationships, and so on. There are two main potential problems with such questionnaire data. First, people may deliberately distort their answers (e.g., exaggerating how in love they are). Second, people often lack a detailed *conscious* understanding of the processes involved in a close relationship.

LOVE

Our feelings for those with whom we develop close or romantic relationships typically include love. As would be expected, love is important within marriage. Huston et al. (2001) assessed how much newlyweds loved each other. Those who subsequently divorced within 2 years of marriage were less in love shortly after marriage than were those who remained married.

What exactly do we mean by "love"? Some people argue that we should leave it to poets to answer that question. However, many psychologists have shed light on the mystery of love. For example, Lamm and Wiesmann (1997) distinguished among "liking," "loving," and "being in love." According to them, "liking" means wanting to interact with the other person, "loving" means trusting and feeling psychologically close to the other person, and "being in love" includes feeling psychologically close but also means being aroused by the other person.

Bartels and Zeki (2000) considered love from the perspective of brain imaging. Male and female participants who were "truly, deeply, and madly in love" had their brain activity recorded while looking at pictures of their partner and of friends. Love produced a pattern of activation and deactivation that overlapped with patterns previously found with other emotions. However, the evidence indicated that "a unique network of areas is responsible for evoking this affective state [i.e., love]." The areas activated by love (e.g., anterior cingulate; insula; and caudate nucleus) are also activated by other emotions. One brain

On average, women disclose more personal and sensitive information about themselves to same-sex friends than men do.

area deactivated by love was the right prefrontal cortex, which is activated by sadness and depression. Another brain area deactivated by love was the amygdala, an area activated by fear and aggression.

Psychological closeness or intimacy forms a very important part of love. Central to intimacy is **self-disclosure** (revealing personal or intimate information about oneself). For example, Sprecher and Hendrick (2004) studied intimate relationships. The amount of self-disclosure was positively associated with the quality of the relationship in terms of satisfaction, love, and commitment.

It is often claimed that women have higher levels of self-disclosure in their various relationships than do men. Dindia and Allen (1992) reviewed over 200 studies. They found that women self-disclose more than men with their romantic partners of the opposite sex and with their same-sex friends. However, these gender differences were fairly small. Lin (1992) found that relationship intimacy depended much more on the amount of emotional self-disclosure than of self-disclosure of factual information.

Early attachments

Freud argued that the behavior exhibited by adults is strongly influenced by their childhood experiences. Thus, for example, children who had an intense and secure attachment to their mother or other caregiver generally become adults capable of emotional intimacy. In contrast, children who had an insecure attachment to their mother find it more difficult to enjoy loving relationships in adulthood. Hazan and Shaver (1987) obtained some support for this position. Adults who had had secure attachments as children described their love experiences as happy, friendly, and trusting. Adults who had had anxious and ambivalent [with mixed emotions] attachments reported love as involving obsession and extreme sexual attraction and jealousy. Finally, adults who had had insecure, avoidant attachments in childhood feared intimacy and jealousy, and weren't convinced they needed love to be happy. These types of childhood attachment are discussed more fully in Chapter 16.

Klohnen and Bera (1998) studied 21-year-old women who were avoidantly attached (e.g., distrustful, self-reliant) or securely attached (e.g., trusting, emotionally open). The differences between these two groups had their origins in childhood. The avoidantly attached women were more likely to have suffered the loss of a parent and to have experienced open conflict during childhood. By the age of 43, 95% of the securely attached women had been married and only 24% had divorced. Only 72% of the avoidantly attached women had been married, and 50% of them had divorced.

Meyers and Landsberger (2002) considered the effects of attachment style on marital satisfaction. There were the expected positive effects of secure attachment style on marital satisfaction and negative effects of avoidant attachment style. More

Key Term
Self-disclosure: revealing personal or intimate information about oneself to someone else.

specifically, secure attachment style reduced psychological distress, which in turn enhanced marital satisfaction. Avoidant attachment style increased psychological distress and reduced social support, and these effects in turn reduced marital satisfaction. Thus, the effects of attachment style on marital satisfaction tend to be *indirect* rather than *direct*.

Sternberg's theory

Sternberg (1986) developed a triangular theory of love. Within this theory, love consists of three components: intimacy; passion; and decision/commitment. Sternberg (1986, p. 120) defined these components as follows:

> *The intimacy component refers to feelings of closeness, connectedness, and bondedness in loving relationships . . . The passionate component refers to the drives that lead to romance, physical attraction, sexual consummation, and related phenomena . . . The decision–commitment component refers to, in the short term, the decision that one loves someone else, and in the long term, the commitment to maintain that love.*

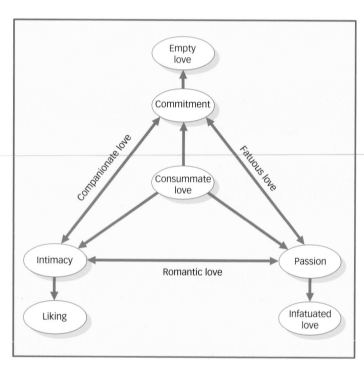

Sternberg (1998) developed these ideas. He argued that the three components differ in several ways from each other. Intimacy and commitment are usually fairly stable in close relationships, whereas passion is relatively unstable and can fluctuate considerably. We have some control over our level of commitment, whereas intimacy is difficult to control and passion is even harder to control deliberately.

Sternberg (1986) argued that there are several kinds of love based on different combinations of the three components (see figure on the left).

- *Liking or friendship*: Intimacy but not passion or commitment.
- *Romantic love*: Intimacy and passion but not commitment.
- *Companionate love*: Intimacy and commitment but not passion.
- *Empty love*: Commitment but not passion or intimacy.
- *Fatuous love*: Commitment and passion but not intimacy.
- *Infatuated love*: Passion but not intimacy or commitment.
- *Consummate love*: Commitment, passion, and intimacy.

Findings

Who do we love and like the most? Sternberg and Grajek (1984) found that men love and like their lover better than their mother, father, sibling closest in age, or their best friend. Women also loved and liked their lover and best friend more than their mother, father, or sibling closest in age. However, they loved their lover and their best friend of the same sex equally, but liked their best friend more than their lover.

There is much additional evidence indicating that strong love doesn't have to involve sexual desire and arousal. For example, Hatfield et al. (1988) asked young people between the ages of 4 and 18 to assess their feelings for an opposite-sexed boyfriend or girlfriend. The intensity of love feelings was similar at all ages.

Aron and Westbay (1996) asked participants to indicate the centrality of 68 words and phrases to the concept of love. Data analysis produced three factors similar to those of Sternberg. The passion factor was closely associated with euphoria, butterflies in the stomach, heart rate increases, gazing at the other, wonderful feelings and sexual passion. Intimacy was closely associated with openness, feeling free to talk about anything, supportiveness, honesty, and understanding. Commitment was closely associated with devotion, putting the other first, protectiveness, and loyalty.

Aron and Westbay (1996) asked participants to complete a questionnaire based on the three love components with respect to their current or most recent love relationship. For both men and women, intimacy was the most important component in love, followed by commitment, with passion the least important.

Evaluation

+ Sternberg has identified probably the three key factors associated with love.

+ Most love relationships can be easily categorized (e.g., as romantic love; fatuous love) on the basis of the pattern across the three components.

− The three components are fairly closely associated or correlated with each other, and so are not entirely separate.

− There has been a heavy reliance on self-report questionnaires, which only assess those aspects of love that can be expressed in words.

ATTRIBUTIONS

Those involved in a close relationship often try to understand the other person's behavior. This involves attributing their behavior to various causes (see Chapter 17). According to Fincham (e.g., Fincham & Hewstone, 2001), attributions for negative events or behavior are especially important to the wellbeing of a relationship. He distinguished between distress-maintaining and relationship-enhancing attributions. Distress-maintaining attributions are those in which the partner's negative behavior is attributed to his/her personality and so is very likely to occur again. In contrast, relationship-enhancing attributions involve blaming the situation rather than the partner for his/her negative behavior (e.g., "His/her work is very stressful and demanding").

Two main predictions follow from this theoretical approach. First, distress-maintaining attributions should decrease satisfaction with the relationship. Second, the couple's attributions should predict their behavior towards each other. These predictions have been tested mostly with married couples.

Findings

Bradbury and Fincham (1990) found couples were much more likely to attribute their spouse's negative behavior to personal, unchanging characteristics in poor marriages than in good ones. In poor marriages, positive behavior by the spouse was dismissed as being a result of the situation and thus unlikely to last.

The key issue is deciding what causes what. Do negative attributions play a role in causing marital dissatisfaction (as predicted by the theory), or does marital dissatisfaction lead to negative attributions? Fincham and Bradbury (1993) carried out a 12-month study to answer this question. Initial attributions predicted subsequent marital satisfaction, whereas level of marital satisfaction didn't predict subsequent attributions. Thus, attributions influence marital satisfaction rather than the other way around.

Bradbury and Fincham (1992) found that attributions made by married couples influence their behavior towards each other. Wives who made distress-maintaining attributions were more likely than those making relationship-enhancing attributions to behave negatively in response to their husband's negative behavior. This pattern was observed in marriages low and high in marital satisfaction.

Evaluation

+ Spouses' attributions about each other's behavior are associated with their level of marital satisfaction and with their behavior towards each other.

+ Distress-maintaining attributions cause reduced marital satisfaction rather than vice versa.

− Marriage partners typically explain their spouse's behavior on the basis of very detailed, specific knowledge about him/her, but this is not emphasized within the attribution theory approach.

− Focusing on relationship-enhancing attributions has positive effects in the short term, but is not always positive in the long term. For example, suppose the husband has been unemployed for several months because he is extremely lazy. Attributing his inability to find work to a lack of jobs may encourage him to make little effort to find work and may lead to future problems within the marriage.

INVESTMENT MODEL

What determines an individual's commitment to his/her current relationship? The obvious answer is the degree of attraction or love he/she has towards his/her partner. No one disputes that. However, Rusbult (e.g., 1983) argued in his investment model that other factors are also important. More specifically, three factors jointly determine an individual's commitment to a relationship:

• *Satisfaction*: This is based on the rewards and costs of the relationship coupled with an evaluation of those rewards and costs relative to those the individual feels he/she deserves.
• *Perceived quality of alternatives*: Individuals are more committed to their current relationship if there are no preferable options (e.g., an attractive alternative partner).
• *Investment size*: Commitment is greater the more time, effort, money, and personal sacrifices have been invested in a relationship.

Findings

Rusbult (1983) tested the investment model in a longitudinal (long-term) study of heterosexual couples. Changes in any of the three factors (satisfaction; quality of alternatives; investment) produced the predicted changes in commitment. The only finding that failed to support the model was that increased costs failed to reduce either satisfaction or commitment.

According to the investment model, individuals compare their current relationship with alternatives. Rusbult et al. (2000) found that most people compare their relationship against those of others. There was strong evidence of perceived superiority (regarding one's own relationship as better than those of other people). Couples with high levels of commitment had greater perceived superiority. The level of perceived superiority within married couples predicted their level of adjustment 20 months later and also predicted whether the marriage would end in divorce.

Why do many women who have repeatedly been physically abused keep returning to the man responsible? It wasn't possible to predict which women would return from a women's shelter to their partner based on their feelings for him (Rusbult & Martz, 1995). As predicted by the model, what mattered was the woman's level of investment in the relationship (e.g., joint children) coupled with poor alternatives (e.g., insufficient money to survive on her own).

Le and Agnew (2003) carried out a meta-analysis of 52 studies on the investment model. The model was supported by three main findings. First, about 65% of the variance (variability) in commitment was accounted for by the three variables of satisfaction, quality of alternatives, and size of investment. Second, the level of commitment predicted the likelihood of relationship break-up. Third, the strength of support for the model did not vary as a function of ethnicity or duration of the relationship.

Evaluation

⊕ Commitment to a relationship depends on the attractiveness of alternatives and level of investment in the relationship as well as on the satisfaction it provides.

⊕ Commitment leads to perceived superiority, and this helps to maintain relationships.

⊖ The investment model largely ignores individual differences. For example, individuals distrustful of others because of childhood experiences are less likely than other people to commit themselves fully to a relationship (Shaver, Hazan, & Bradshaw, 1988).

⊖ It is assumed theoretically that satisfaction, perceived quality of alternatives, and investment size all have *separate* influences on commitment. However, reality is often more complex. For example, someone with low commitment to a current relationship may actively seek an attractive alternative and may refuse to invest in the relationship (e.g., by having a child).

Chapter Summary

Prosocial behavior

- According to evolutionary psychology, people often behave altruistically toward members of their family to ensure the survival of their own genes. Their helping behavior with nonrelations involves reciprocal altruism, which is much greater in the human species than in others.
- According to Darley and Latané, bystanders are often reluctant to assist a victim because there is a diffusion of responsibility. In addition, the norm of social responsibility is only weakly activated when there are several bystanders.
- According to the arousal/cost–reward model, bystanders who are aroused by an incident decide whether to assist a victim by working out the rewards and costs involved. In fact, however, bystanders often respond impulsively and without deliberation.

Aggression

- Aggression is especially prevalent in many Western societies in part because social norms encourage people to be competitive and go-getting.

- Aggressive behavior is most likely when the situation contains aggressive cues, the individual concerned is impulsive or sensation seeking, and he/she interprets his/her aroused state as being a result of provocation.
- According to the general aggressive model, people decide whether to behave aggressively after appraising or interpreting the situation, considering possible coping strategies, and working out the likely consequences of behaving aggressively.
- In Western cultures, men and women are about equally likely to behave aggressively in close relationships. Aggressive behavior in such relationships occurs because there are few external social controls and because of power inequities between men and women

Formation of interpersonal relationships

- Women whose faces resemble those of young children are perceived as attractive, as are men whose facial features indicate maturity. Physical attractiveness in women also depends on factors such as waist-to-hip ratio, body mass index, and volume–height index.
- There is support for the matching hypothesis, according to which we are attracted to those of about the same physical attractiveness as ourselves.
- There is a primacy effect when we form an initial impression of someone else. Our impressions are influenced most by a few central traits (e.g., warm–cold) rather than by more peripheral traits.
- We are attracted to other people who are similar to us in personality and attitudes, partly because they are easier to relate to.
- The maintenance of interpersonal relationships involves adhering to various unspoken rules (e.g., respect the other person's privacy).
- Friendships between women tend to be more intimate than those between men. This may be the case because women's role in society (e.g., caring for children) encourages them to develop intimate relationships.
- Men prefer women younger than themselves and women prefer men older than themselves. This has been explained in evolutionary terms. However, the evolutionary approach cannot readily explain why men and women both attach more importance to kindness and intelligence in a mate than to age.

Development of close relationships

- Self-disclosure (especially emotional disclosure) is important within close relationships. Women self-disclose more than men with their romantic partners of the opposite sex.
- As Freud predicted, adults who had a secure attachment to their mother in childhood are more likely to have rewarding and lasting romantic relationships than those who had an insecure attachment to their mother.
- According to Sternberg, love consists of intimacy, passion, and decision/commitment. There are several kinds of love based on different combinations of these components, but intimacy is the most important component.
- Attributing one's partner's negative behavior to his/her personality leads to decreased marital satisfaction. Wives making such attributions are more likely than those making more positive attributions to behave negatively in response to their husband's negative behavior.
- According to the investment model, an individual's commitment to a relationship depends on satisfaction, perceived quality of alternatives, and investment size.
- Couples with high levels of commitment regard their own relationship as better than those of other people to a greater extent than other couples, and are less likely to divorce.
- Women who have been physically abused by their husband but who keep returning to him do so because of high investment and a lack of attractive alternatives.

Further Reading

- Anderson, C.A., & Bushman, B.J. (2002). Human aggression. *Annual Review of Psychology*, *53*, 27–51. This chapter by two leading experts provides a useful framework for considering human aggression.
- Brehm, S.S., Kassin, S.M., & Fein, S. (2005). *Social psychology* (6th ed.). Boston, MA: Houghton Mifflin. All of the main topics discussed in this chapter are considered in this introductory textbook.
- Hewstone, M., & Stroebe, W. (2001). *Introduction to social psychology* (3rd ed.). Oxford, UK: Blackwell. There is good coverage of prosocial behavior, aggressive behavior, friendship, and close relationships in Chapters 9, 10, and 12 of this edited book.
- Hogg, M.A., & Vaughan, G.M. (2005). *Social psychology* (4th ed.). Harlow, UK: Prentice Hall. Chapters 12, 13, and 14 of this textbook cover in detail the topics discussed in this chapter.
- Myers, D.G. (2005). *Social psychology* (8th ed.). New York: McGraw-Hill. Several chapters in this well-established textbook are concerned with social behavior and relationships.
- Rusbult, C.E., & Van Lange, P.A.M. (2003). Interdependence, interaction and relationships. *Annual Review of Psychology*, *54*, 351–375. The authors discuss the ways in which relationships are affected by several different factors.

Chapter 19

Contents

Group processes

What we say (and how we behave) is heavily influenced by other people. They possess useful knowledge about the world, and it is often sensible to pay attention to what they say. In addition, we want to be liked by other people, and to fit into society. As a result, we sometimes hide what we really think, and behave in ways that will earn the approval of others. All these issues relate to **social influence**, "the process whereby attitudes and behavior are influenced by the real or implied presence of other people" (Hogg & Vaughan, 2005, p. 655).

Social influence is observed when the behavior of individuals is determined by the instructions given by those in a position of authority (e.g., police; doctors). We start this chapter by considering obedience to authority. However, most social influence occurs within groups. The rest of this chapter is concerned with groups and with their influences on the beliefs and behavior of group members. What do we mean by a group? According to Brown (2000, p. 3), "A group exists when two or more people define themselves as members of it and when its existence is recognized by at least one other [person or group]."

There are many kinds of group processes. These include conformity pressures, group cohesiveness, and group norms. The performance of groups often differs from that of individuals. Within groups, we need to consider the role of the leader (the person most influencing group members). Finally, social or group influence affects the behavior of individuals in crowds.

As you read this chapter, think about individuals and groups you encounter every day. Which individuals and groups have most influence over your behavior? Why is this the case? As we will see, a key finding in this area is that our behavior is often influenced much more by other people than we like to think.

OBEDIENCE TO AUTHORITY

In nearly all societies, some people are given power and authority over others. In our society, for example, parents, teachers, and managers have varying degrees of authority. This generally doesn't cause problems. If the doctor tells us to take some tablets three times a day, most of us accept he/she is the expert and do as requested. Suppose, however, you are asked by a person in authority to do something wrong. For example, Adolf Eichmann was found guilty of ordering the deaths of millions of Jews during the Second World War. He denied any moral responsibility, claiming he had simply been carrying out other people's orders. The best-known research on obedience to authority was carried out by Stanley Milgram, and is discussed in the Key Study on the following page.

Key Term

Social influence:
a process in which an individual's attitudes and/or behavior are influenced by another person or by a group.

Key Study

Milgram: Obedience to authority

Milgram (1963, 1974) reported the findings from several studies carried out at Yale University. Pairs of participants were given the roles of teacher and learner for a simple learning test. In fact, the "learner" was always a confederate employed by Milgram to behave in certain ways. The "teacher" was told to give electric shocks to the "learner" every time the wrong answer was given and to increase the shock intensity each time even though the learner had a heart condition. The apparatus was actually arranged so that the learner received no electric shocks, but the teacher didn't know that. At 180 volts, the learner yelled, "I can't stand the pain," and by 270 volts the response had become an agonized scream. The maximum shock intensity was 450 volts, which was potentially fatal. If the teacher was unwilling to give the shocks, the experimenter urged him/her to continue.

Milgram's (1974) "obedience" experiment. Top left: the "shock box"; top right: the experimenter demonstrating the shock box to the "teacher"; bottom left: wiring the "learner" up to the apparatus; bottom right: one of the "teachers" refusing to continue with the experiment.

Would you have been willing to give the maximum (and potentially deadly) 450-volt shock? Milgram found that everyone he asked denied they personally would do any such thing. He also found that 110 experts on human behavior (e.g., psychiatrists) predicted that no one would go on to the 450-volt stage. In fact, about 65% of Milgram's participants (there was no gender difference) gave the maximum shock using his standard procedure—this is *hugely* different from expert predictions!

Milgram (e.g., 1974) discovered two ways in which obedience to authority could be reduced (see the figure on the following page):

1. Increasing the obviousness of the learner's plight.
2. Reducing the experimenter's authority or influence.

The impact of the first factor was studied by comparing obedience in four situations differing in the extent to which the learner was made aware of the suffering he/she was inflicting (the percentage of totally obedient participants is

Reducing obedience to authority was achieved by:	
Increasing the obviousness of the learner's plight …	**Reducing the authority or influence of the experimenter …**
victim not seen or heard 66%	at Yale University 65%
victim not seen but heard 62%	at a run-down office 48%
victim one meter away 40%	with experimenter sitting next to the participant 65%
victim's hand placed on shock plate 30%	with experimenter giving orders via telephone 20.5%
	with confederates of experimenter refusing to give shocks 10%

shown in brackets):

- *Touch-proximity*: The participant had to force the learner's hand onto the shock plate (36%).
- *Proximity*: The learner was 1 meter away from the participant (40%).
- *Voice feedback*: The victim could be heard but not seen (62%).
- *Remote feedback*: The victim couldn't be heard or seen (66%).

Milgram (1974) reduced the experimenter's authority by staging an experiment in a run-down office building rather than in Yale University. The percentage of totally obedient participants decreased from 65% at Yale University to 48% in the run-down office building. The experimenter's influence was also reduced by having him give orders by telephone rather than sitting close to the teacher. This reduced obedience from 65% to 20.5%. Finally, the authority of the experimenter was reduced by having him being apparently an ordinary member of the public rather than a white-coated scientist. This reduced obedience to 20%.

In a further study, Milgram (1974) used three teachers, two of whom were confederates working for the experimenter. In one condition, the two confederates were rebellious and refused to give severe shocks. Only 10% of the participants were fully obedient in this condition.

Discussion points
1. Do most people simply obey authority in a rather mindless way?
2. What are the main factors determining whether or not there is obedience to authority?

KEY STUDY EVALUATION
Milgram's work on obedience to authority has always been regarded as rather controversial. His most surprising finding was that approximately two-thirds of the participants proceeded to the maximum 450-volt electric shock, whereas experts expected that no one would do so. However, it needs to be emphasized that most of those who used the maximum electric shock did so very reluctantly, and showed clear signs of stress and internal conflict. It is possible that this was due in part to the fact that Milgram's studies took place in the 1970s, after attitudes to rebellion and individualism had been changed by the social and political movements of the previous decade. Parallels have been drawn between Milgram's findings and the behavior of people such as Nazi concentration camp guards, who protested that they were only following orders (discussed further shortly). However, other studies have shown that levels of obedience can be reduced in real-life situations when groups of people challenge authority. Permission to run studies such as Milgram's original one would probably not be granted today on ethical grounds, but at least his work showed that conformity and obedience depend on many factors and are more prevalent than might be imagined.

Modigliani and Rochat (1995) re-analyzed Milgram's own data based on audio recordings of conversations between the experimenter and the teacher. Of participants who protested verbally at an early stage, not one administered the maximum shock, and only 17% delivered more than 150 volts. There was considerably less disobedience among participants who only began to protest later in the experiment. Thus, it was important for participants to "break the ice" by voicing their concerns very early in the experiment if they were to refuse to obey the experimenter's instructions.

Milgram's studies were carried out in the United States during the 1960s and 1970s, and it is important to know whether his findings generalize to other cultures at other times. Bond and Smith (1996) considered the relevant cross-cultural evidence. The percentage of totally obedient participants was very high in several countries. It was 80% or higher in Italy, Spain, Germany, Austria, and Holland, in many cases several years after Milgram's studies.

Milgram's research was laboratory-based, and it would be valuable to use more naturalistic situations. Hofling et al. (1966) carried out a real-life study in which 22 nurses were telephoned by someone claiming to be "Dr. Smith." The nurses were asked to check that a drug called Astroten was available. When the nurses did this, they saw on the bottle that the maximum dosage was 10 mg. When they reported back to Dr. Smith, he told them to give 20 mg of the drug to a patient.

There were two good reasons why the nurses should have refused to obey. First, the dose was double the maximum safe dose. Second, the nurses didn't know Dr. Smith, and they were supposed to take instructions only from doctors they knew. However, the nurses' training had led them to obey instructions from doctors. There is a clear power structure in medical settings, with doctors in a more powerful position than nurses. The nurses were more influenced by the power structure than by the hospital regulations: all but one did as Dr. Smith instructed.

Similar findings were reported by Lesar, Briceland, and Stein (1997) in a study on medication errors in American hospitals. Nurses typically carried out doctors' orders even when they had good reasons for doubting the wisdom of those orders. However, Rank and Jacobsen (1997) found that only 11% of nurses obeyed a doctor's instructions to give too high a dose to patients when they talked to other nurses beforehand.

Theoretical accounts

Why is there so much obedience to authority? Milgram (1974) argued there are three main reasons:

1. Experience has taught us that authorities are generally trustworthy and legitimate, and so obedience to authority is often appropriate. For example, it would be disastrous if those involved in carrying out an emergency operation refused to obey the surgeon's orders!
2. The orders given by the experimenter moved gradually from the reasonable to the unreasonable. This made it difficult for participants to notice when they began to be asked to behave unreasonably.
3. The participants were put into an "agentic" state, in which they became the instruments of an authority figure and so ceased to act according to their conscience. Someone in the agentic state thinks, "I am not responsible, because I was ordered to do it!" According to Milgram (1974), this tendency to adopt the agentic state, "is the fatal flaw nature has designed into us."

Milgram was too pessimistic. Most obedient participants experienced a strong conflict between the experimenter's demands and their own conscience. They seemed very tense and nervous, they perspired, they bit their lips, and they clenched and unclenched their fists. Such behavior does *not* suggest they were in an agentic state.

Some researchers (e.g., Blass & Schmitt, 2001) have drawn a distinction between social power based on harsh *external* influences (e.g., hierarchy-based legitimate power) and social power based on soft influences *within* the authority figure (e.g., expertise; credibility). Milgram emphasized the importance of harsh influences, but soft influences are also important. Blass and Schmitt presented participants with a 12-minute edited version of Milgram's documentary film, *Obedience*. They had to choose the best explanation for the strong obedience to authority shown in the film from the following choices based on various sources of power:

- *Legitimate*: Experimenter's role as authority figure.
- *Expert*: Experimenter's superior expertise and knowledge.
- *Coercive*: The power to punish the participant for noncompliance.
- *Informational*: The information conveyed to the participant was sufficient to produce obedience.
- *Reward*: The power to reward the participant for compliance.
- *Referent*: The power occurring because the participant would like to emulate the authority figure.

The sources of power most often chosen were legitimate power (a harsh influence) and expertise (a soft influence) (see figure on the right). These findings are important in two ways. First, they show that Milgram was only partially correct when explaining obedience to authority in terms of legitimate power. Second, they indicate that obedience to authority in the Milgram situation depends on at least two different sources of power.

Milgram argued there are links between his findings and the horrors of Nazi Germany. However, we mustn't exaggerate the similarities. First, the values underlying Milgram's studies were the positive ones of understanding more about human learning and memory, in contrast to the vile ideas prevalent in Nazi Germany. Second, most participants in Milgram's studies had to be watched closely to ensure their obedience, which wasn't necessary in Nazi Germany. Third, most of Milgram's participants experienced great conflict and agitation, whereas those who carried out atrocities in Nazi Germany often seemed unconcerned about moral issues.

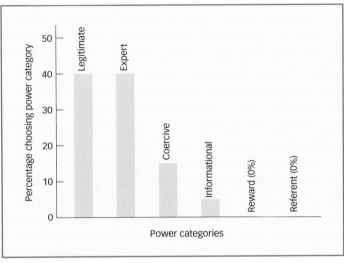

Percentages choosing each power category as the best explanation for obedient participants' behavior in Milgram's research. Based on data in Blass and Schmitt (2001).

Why was the actual behavior of Milgram's participants so different from what most people would have expected? The **fundamental attribution error** (the tendency to over-estimate the importance of other people's personality in determining their behavior) is involved (see Chapter 17). When we decide how many people would show total obedience in Milgram's situation, we think as follows: "Only a psychopath would give massive electric shocks to another person. There are very few psychopaths about, and so practically no one would be totally obedient." This line of reasoning focuses only on the role of personality. In fact, Milgram's participants were strongly influenced by situational factors such as the

Key Term

Fundamental attribution error:
exaggerating the importance of personality and minimizing the role of the situation in determining another person's behavior.

Unquestioning obedience to authority may have catastrophic consequences. The pictures show row upon row of SS members marching down a road during the 1933 Nuremberg rally, and (right) survivors of the Auschwitz concentration camp at the end of the war in 1945, following a decade of persecution, imprisonment, and genocide.

Case Study: *The My Lai Massacre*

The My Lai massacre has become known as one of the most controversial incidents in the Vietnam War. On December 14, 1969 almost 400 Vietnamese villagers were killed in under 4 hours. The following transcript is from a CBS News interview with a soldier who took part in the massacre.

Q. How many people did you round up?
A. Well, there was about forty, fifty people that we gathered in the center of the village. And we placed them in there, and it was like a little island, right there in the center of the village, I'd say…And…
Q. What kind of people—men, women, children?
A. Men, women, children.
Q. Babies?
A. Babies. And we huddled them up. We made them squat down and Lieutenant Calley came over and said, "You know what to do with them, don't you?" And I said yes. So I took it for granted that he just wanted us to watch them. And he left, and came back about ten or fifteen minutes later and said, "How come you ain't killed them yet?" And I told him that I didn't think you wanted us to to kill them, that you just wanted us to guard them. He

said, "No. I want them dead." So—
Q. He told this to all of you, or to you particularly?
A. Well, I was facing him. So, but the other three, four guys heard it and so he stepped back about ten, fifteen feet, and he started shooting them. And he told me to start shooting. So I started shooting, I poured about four clips into the group.
Q. You fired four clips from your …
A. M-16.
Q. And that's about how many clips—I mean, how many—
A. I carried seventeen rounds to each clip.
Q. So you fired something like sixty-seven shots?
A. Right.
Q. And you killed how many? At that time?
A. Well, I fired them automatic, so you can't—You just spray the area on them and so you can't know how many you killed 'cause they were going fast. So I might have killed ten or fifteen of them.
Q. Men, women and children?
A. Men, women and children.
Q. And babies?
A. And babies.

experimenter's insistence that the participant continue to give shocks, the scientific expertise of the experimenter, and so on. Of particular importance, the experimenter repeatedly told concerned participants that he took full responsibility for what happened. Tilker (1970) found that there was a substantial reduction in obedience when participants were told that they (rather than the experimenter) were responsible for their actions.

Evaluation

+ A high level of obedience to authority has been found in many cultures over several decades.

+ Milgram's findings seem to be among the most unexpected and surprising in the history of psychology.

+ Milgram's findings are directly relevant to many everyday situations (e.g., doctor and nurse interactions; teacher and student interactions).

− There are limitations with Milgram's notion of an agentic state and with his emphasis on the legitimacy of the authority figure as the major influence on participants' behavior.

− The findings are less dramatic than commonly assumed. As Jones (1998, p. 32) argued, "The degree of compliance [in the Milgram studies] could be readily understood once the extremely active role of the experimenter was fully detailed, something that was not at all clear in the earlier experimenter reports."

− There are serious ethical problems with Milgram's research (see Chapter 2). First, participants didn't give their informed consent. Second, they weren't free to leave the experiment if they wanted to do so—the experimenter urged them to continue if they wanted to stop. Third, participants were subjected to considerable conflict and distress. However, 84% of Milgram's participants reported they were glad to have taken part in his research (Milgram, 1974).

CONFORMITY

Conformity "refers to the act of changing one's behavior to match the responses of others" (Cialdini & Goldstein, 2004, p. 606). It involves yielding to group pressures in the absence of an explicit order or request, something nearly everyone does sometimes. Suppose you go to a movie with friends. You really didn't like it, but all your friends thought it was absolutely brilliant. Admit it—you would be tempted to conform by pretending that you also found the movie brilliant.

The figure below shows some differences between obedience and conformity. Research on conformity differs in three ways from research on obedience. First, the participant decides what to do rather than being told how to behave. Second, the participant is typically of equal status to the group members trying to influence him/her, whereas he/she is usually of lower status than the person issuing the orders in studies on obedience. Third, participants' behavior in conformity studies is mainly influenced by the need for acceptance, whereas obedience is determined by social power.

Conformity is often considered undesirable. However, that is only true sometimes. For example, suppose all your friends studying psychology have the same view on a given topic in psychology, but it differs from yours. If they know more about the topic, it is probably sensible to conform to their views rather than sticking rigidly to your own!

ASCH'S RESEARCH

Will individuals conform to group pressure when the correct answer is obvious but every other member of the group produces the same incorrect answer? Solomon Asch (1951, 1956) carried out very important research and came up with an answer to that question that may well differ from your expectation!—see the Key Study below.

Even the most independent of individuals can feel the need to conform under social pressure from peers.

Differences between obedience and conformity	
OBEDIENCE	**CONFORMITY**
Occurs within a hierarchy. Actor feels the person above has the right to prescribe behavior. Links one status to another. Emphasis is on power.	Regulates the behavior among those of equal status. Emphasis is on acceptance.
Behavior adopted differs from behavior of authority figure.	Behavior adopted is similar to that of peers.
Prescription for action is explicit.	Requirement of going along with the group is often implicit.
Participants embrace obedience as an explanation for their behavior	Participants often deny conformity as an explanation for their behavior.

Key Study

Asch: Conformity and group pressure

Asch devised a situation in which approximately seven people sat looking at a display. They had to say out loud which one of three lines (A, B, or C) was the same length as a given stimulus line, with the experimenter working his/her way around the group members in turn. All but one were confederates of the experimenter, instructed to give the same wrong answer on some trials. The one genuine participant was the last (or the last but one) to offer his/her opinion on each trial. The performance of participants exposed to such group pressure was compared to performance in a control condition with no confederates.

Asch's (1951) findings were dramatic. On the crucial trials on which the confederates all gave the same wrong answer, the genuine participants also gave the wrong answer on between 33% and 37% of these trials in different studies. Compare these figures against an error rate of under 1% in the control condition.

Key Term

Conformity:
yielding to group pressures in the absence of a direct request or order.

Asch showed lines like this to his participants. Which line do you think is the closest in height to line X? A, B, or C? Why do you think over 30% of participants answered A?

Thus, even though the correct answers were obvious, there was substantial conformity to the incorrect answers given by the other group members.

Asch (1956) manipulated various aspects of the situation to understand more fully the factors underlying conformity behavior. The conformity effect increased as the number of confederates increased from one to three, but there was no increase thereafter. However, a small increase in conformity has sometimes been found as the number of confederates goes up above three (see van Avermaet, 2001).

Another important factor is whether the genuine participant has a supporter in the form of a confederate giving the correct answer on all trials. Asch (1956) found that the presence of a supporter meant that conformity was observed on only 5% of trials. More surprisingly, a confederate whose answers were even more incorrect than those of the other confederates also produced a substantial reduction in conformity.

Asch's research raises ethical issues. His participants didn't provide fully informed consent, because they were misled about key aspects of the experimental procedures (e.g., presence of confederates). In addition, they were put in a difficult and embarrassing position.

Discussion points
1. Do Asch's findings apply outside the artificial situation he used in his studies?
2. Asch carried out his research in the United States. Why might the findings be different in other cultures?

KEY STUDY EVALUATION
Asch is renowned for his work on conformity. In a situation where the correct answer was obvious people would agree with an incorrect answer on about 35% of trials. Only 25% of Asch's participants gave the correct answer on all the trials despite the incorrect answers of their fellow participants. The remaining 75% showed at least some tendency to conform to the confederates' views. Thus, a clear majority of participants were somewhat influenced by the confederates. However, the study took place in America in the 1950s before "doing your own thing" came to be regarded as socially acceptable. Also, Asch's participants were put in a difficult and embarrassing position, which may have led to greater levels of conformity because of the particular culture prevailing at the time. When participants had a supporter present, who gave the correct answer before the participant responded, conformity to the incorrect response dropped dramatically. This suggests that social pressure and the feeling of being in a conflict situation may have been a major factor in the unexpectedly high level of conformity in the original study.

Asch's research on conformity is among the most famous in the whole of social psychology. Oddly, however, there was nothing very social about his research because he used groups of strangers! Suppose we introduced more social factors into the situation by having the participants identify other group members as belonging to one of their ingroups or to an outgroup. This was done by Abrams et al. (1990) using first-year students of introductory psychology as participants. The confederates were introduced as first-year students of psychology from a nearby university (ingroup) or as students of ancient history from the same university (outgroup). You would probably guess that participants would show more conformity in the presence of an ingroup. However, the size of the effect was dramatic. There was conformity on 58% of trials in the presence of an ingroup compared to only 8% with an outgroup. Thus, conformity depends to a large extent on the individual's perception of other group members as an ingroup or an outgroup.

Theoretical implications

Deutsch and Gerard (1955) argued that people might conform in Asch-type studies for two reasons. First, there is **normative influence**, which occurs when someone conforms because he/she wants to be liked or respected by group members. Second, there is **informational influence**, which occurs when someone conforms because of the superior knowledge or judgment of others (see the figure above). Bond (2005) presented a meta-analysis of 125 Asch-type conformity studies. Normative influence was stronger when participants made public responses and were face-to-face with the majority (as in Asch's research). In contrast, informational influence was stronger when participants made private responses and communicated only indirectly with the majority.

Erb et al. (2002) explored factors determining which type of influence was dominant. The majority had mainly a normative influence when an individual's previously formed opinions were strongly opposed to those of the majority. In contrast, the influence was mostly informational when an individual's opinions differed only moderately from those of the majority.

Cross-cultural studies

Asch's research was carried out in the United States in the 1940s and 1950s. Americans may be more conformist than other people, and perhaps people were more conformist before it became fashionable to "do your own thing." In fact, the effects observed by Asch are reasonably robust. There have been numerous cross-cultural studies of conformity using Asch's experimental design (see the figure below). The participants gave the wrong answer on average on 31.2% of trials across these studies (Bond & Smith, 1996), only slightly lower than what Asch found.

We would expect conformity to be greater in collectivistic cultures than in individualistic ones. Collectivistic cultures (e.g., China) emphasize group needs over those of individuals, and emphasize a sense of group identity. In contrast, individualistic cultures (e.g., the UK; the United States) emphasize the desirability of individuals having a personal sense of responsibility. Thus, nonconformity is seen as deviance in collectivistic cultures but as uniqueness in individualistic ones (Kim & Markus, 1999). Bond and Smith (1996) analyzed numerous Asch-type studies in several countries. Conformity was greater in collectivistic cultures in Asia, Africa, and elsewhere (37.1% of trials) than in individualistic cultures in North America and Europe (25.3%).

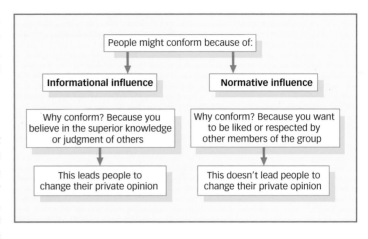

Key Terms

Normative influence: this occurs when an individual conforms so that others in the group will like or respect him/her.

Informational influence: this occurs when an individual conforms because others in the group are believed to possess more knowledge.

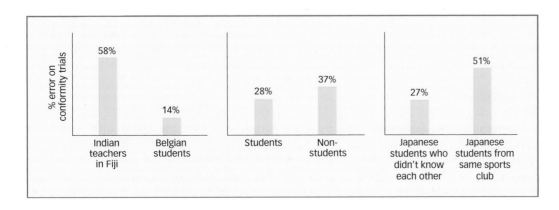

When Asch's study was replicated cross-cultural differences emerged.

⊕ Asch's findings have been very influential, because he found much conformity even in an unambiguous situation in which the correct answer was obvious.

⊕ Asch identified key factors (e.g., number of confederates; presence vs. absence of a supporter) determining the level of conformity.

⊕ Asch's findings have been replicated in many countries over a period of several decades.

⊖ Asch only studied conformity in a trivial situation in which the participants' deeply held beliefs were not called into question.

⊖ Asch's situation was limited in that he only assessed conformity among strangers. In fact, conformity effects are much greater when the group members all belong to the same ingroup (Abrams et al., 1990).

⊖ Asch did not explain in detail *why* there are conformity effects, because he did not identify the underlying psychological processes.

MINORITY INFLUENCES ON MAJORITIES

Asch was concerned with the influence of the majority on a minority (typically of one) within a group. However, social influences operate in both directions: majorities influence minorities, but minorities also exert influence on majorities. The most developed theory in this area is that of Moscovici (1976, 1980), and so we will consider his research.

What happens when a minority influences a majority? According to Moscovici's dual-process theory, disagreements from a minority of group members can cause the members of the majority to engage in a validation process. This validation process involves focusing on the information contained in the arguments put forward by the minority (i.e., informational influence). This can lead to **conversion**, in which there is more effect on private beliefs than public behavior. It is difficult for a minority to influence the majority, and Moscovici (1980) argued that this happens most often when the minority puts forward a clear and consistent position.

What happens when a majority influences a minority? Moscovici (1980) argued that members of the minority are subject to a comparison process, in which they focus on the differences between their views and those of the majority. This triggers the need for consensus, which often leads to **compliance**, involving public rather than private influence (i.e., normative influence). Thus, there is a greater effect on public behavior than on private beliefs. Compliance often occurs rapidly and without much thought. In contrast, conversion is more time-consuming and occurs only after cognitive conflict and much thought. The take-home message is that a minority can have more profound effects on the majority than the majority has on the minority.

An important real-life example of a minority influencing a majority was the suffragette movement in the early years of the 20th century. A relatively small group of suffragettes argued strongly for the initially unpopular view that women should be allowed to vote. The hard work of the suffragettes, combined with the justice of their case, finally led the majority to accept their point of view.

Key Terms

Conversion:
the influence of a minority on a majority based on convincing the majority that its views are correct; see **compliance**.

Compliance:
the influence of a majority on a minority based on the power of the majority; see **conversion**.

Findings

Moscovici, Lage, and Naffrenchoux (1969) found that minorities have to be consistent to influence majority judgments. Groups of six participants were presented with blue slides varying in intensity, and each member of the group said a simple color. Two confederates of the experimenter said "Green" on every trial or on two-thirds of the trials. The percentage of "Green" responses given by the majority was 8% when the minority responded consistently, but only 1% when the minority responded inconsistently.

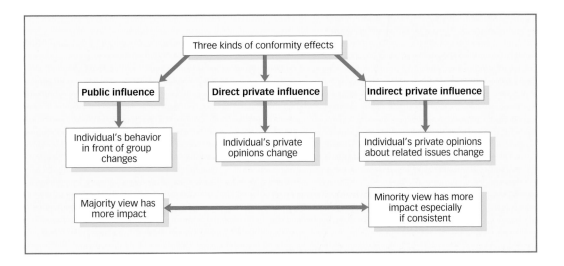

Maass and Clark (1983) carried out a study on attitudes to gay rights. In one condition, the majority favored gay rights and the minority did not, and in another condition the majority opposed gay rights and the minority favored gay rights. Publicly expressed attitudes generally conformed to the majority view. However, privately expressed attitudes tended to agree with those of the minority.

Nemeth, Mayseless, Sherman, and Brown (1990) found that minorities can make group members engage in more thorough processing than majorities, as predicted by Moscovici's dual-process theory. Participants listened to word lists. A majority or a minority consistently drew attention to words belonging to certain categories. There was then a recall test for the words presented. The words to which attention had been drawn were much better recalled when a minority had drawn attention to them, presumably because they had been processed more thoroughly.

Wood et al. (1994) identified three conformity effects predicted by Moscovici (see the figure above):

1. *Public influence*, in which the individual's behavior in front of the group is influenced by the views of others. This should occur mostly when majorities influence minorities.
2. *Direct private influence*, in which there is a change in the individual's private opinions about the issue discussed by the group. This should be found mainly when minorities influence majorities.
3. *Indirect private influence*, in which the individual's private opinions about related issues change. This should also be found mostly when majorities are influenced by minorities.

Wood et al. carried out various meta-analyses to test for the existence of these three effects. As predicted, majorities in most studies had more public influence than minorities. Also as predicted, minorities had more indirect private influence than majorities, especially when their opinions were consistent. However, majorities had more direct private influence than minorities, which is opposed to the prediction from Moscovici's theory.

David and Turner (1999) argued that minority influences will *only* be found when the minority is perceived as part of the ingroup. The participants were moderate feminists exposed to the minority views of extreme feminists. The participants were influenced by the minority when they believed their fellow participants were mostly anti-feminists, but not when they were said to be moderate feminists. Why was this? The extreme feminists were more likely to be perceived as part of the ingroup (feminists vs. nonfeminists) by individual moderate feminists when most of the other participants were identified as anti-feminists. In contrast, the extreme feminists were relegated to an outgroup when most of the participants were identified (correctly) as moderate feminists.

Evaluation

- (+) Minorities often influence majorities.

- (+) The influence of minorities on majorities is mainly in the form of private rather than public agreement, with the opposite pattern being found when majorities influence minorities.

- (−) The common finding that minorities are less influential than majorities on direct private measures (e.g., Erb et al., 2002; Wood et al., 1994) is not readily explained by Moscovici's dual-process theory.

- (−) Majorities generally differ from minorities in several ways (e.g., power; status). Differences in the social influence exerted by majorities and minorities may depend on power or status rather than on their majority or minority position within the group.

- (−) Moscovici exaggerated the differences between the ways in which majorities and minorities exert influence. As Smith and Mackie (2000, p. 371) concluded, "Minorities are influential when their dissent offers a consensus, avoids contamination [i.e., obvious bias], and triggers private acceptance—the same processes by which all groups achieve influence."

BASIC GROUP CHARACTERISTICS

Groups come in all shapes and sizes, and their goals can vary enormously (e.g., build a bridge; climb mountains; have fun). However, virtually all groups share certain key features. Every group has a level of cohesiveness varying between very low and very high, with its level of cohesiveness having consequences for its functioning. Every group also has norms indicating the behavior regarded as acceptable or desirable. Individuals need to abide by most of these norms to be fully accepted by the other group members.

Finally, there are systematic changes in the relationship between individuals and the group. For example, the individual's commitment to the group increases as he/she moves toward full membership of the group, but then decreases again as he/she experiences growing dissatisfaction with the group.

GROUP COHESIVENESS

What is **group cohesiveness**? According to Brown (2000, p. 46), it can be defined in terms of "group members' attraction to the idea of the group, its consensual prototypical [ideal example] image and how that is reflected in typical member characteristics and behavior."

Key Term
Group cohesiveness: the extent to which group members are attracted to the idea of the group.

It is often assumed that group cohesiveness leads to improved group performance. Mullen and Copper (1994) found in a meta-analysis that the average correlation between group cohesiveness and group performance was only +.25. This suggests that group cohesiveness is not of great importance in determining performance. However, the association between cohesiveness and performance was greater in some types of groups (e.g., sports teams) than in others (e.g., laboratory groups). Cohesiveness based on interpersonal attraction was more weakly related to group performance than cohesiveness based on commitment to the group's task.

The correlational evidence discussed above doesn't allow us to decide whether cohesiveness helps to determine performance or whether performance helps to determine cohesiveness. In general, the evidence indicates there are stronger effects of performance on cohesiveness than of cohesiveness on performance (Mullen & Copper, 1994). However, that was not the case in a study by Slater and

Conforming to group norms is a part of group membership. At a soccer game, supporters are conforming to prescribed norms such as wearing certain clothes and singing certain songs.

Sewell (1994). They assessed cohesiveness and performance in university hockey teams at two points during the season. There were effects of cohesiveness on performance and of performance on cohesiveness, but those of cohesiveness on performance were greater.

The effects of group cohesiveness are greater on job satisfaction than on group performance. One reason may be because more social support is available in cohesive groups. This could help to explain why members of cohesive groups cope better with stress than members of noncohesive groups (Bowers, Weaver, & Morgan, 1996).

SOCIAL NORMS

What are social norms? According to Fehr and Fischbacher (2004, p. 185), **social norms** "are standards of behavior that are based on widely shared beliefs how individual group members ought to behave in a given situation." Social norms fulfill several purposes. First, they provide guidance as to appropriate behavior (especially in ambiguous situations), and play a part in explaining conformity behavior and groupthink (discussed shortly). Second, most group norms are related to the goals of the group, and so facilitate achievement of those goals (see section on collective behavior later in the chapter). Third, norms help to maintain group identity. Fourth, "The human capacity to establish and enforce social norms is perhaps the most decisive reason for the uniqueness of human cooperation in the animal word" (Fehr & Fischbacher, 2004, p. 189).

Newcomb (1961) carried out a classic study on norm formation at Bennington College, a small private institution in the United States. There was a great contrast between its predominantly liberal political ethos and the extremely conservative, upper-middle-class families from which most of the students came. There was a presidential election shortly after the first-year students arrived at Bennington College, with most of them preferring the conservative Republican candidate to the more liberal Democratic candidate, Roosevelt (62% vs. 29%, respectively). Very few favored Socialist or Communist candidates (9%). In contrast, 54% of third- and fourth-year students favored Roosevelt and 28% chose Socialist or Communist candidates, with only 18% favoring the Republican candidate. Thus, over time the liberal norms of Bennington College became more important to the students than their parents' conservative norms. Newcomb, Koenig, Flacks, and Warwick (1967) found that, 25 years after leaving Bennington College, the ex-students remained liberal in their political views.

The impact of norms on behavior was studied by Neighbors, Larimer, and Lewis (2004). Heavy-drinking students at the University of Washington estimated how much the average student drank (perceived drinking norm) and were then shown the true figure (actual drinking norm). Not surprisingly, the perceived drinking norm was typically much higher than the actual drinking norm. Over the following 6 months, these students showed a highly significant reduction in drinking behavior, and reductions in perceived drinking norms were responsible for much of this reduction. Thus, the students' behavior was much influenced by their perception of social norms for students' drinking.

Key Term

Social norms: agreed standards of behavior within a group (e.g., family; organization).

Fehr and Fischbacher (2004) argued that human cooperation is based mainly on a social norm of conditional cooperation: all group members should cooperate unless others defect (i.e., refuse to cooperate). This argument was tested by Fehr and Fischbacher (2004) in a study in which there were two players together, each of whom had to decide at the same time whether to be cooperative (i.e., contribute money to a group project) or to defect (i.e., contribute nothing). The experimenter then multiplied the total amount allocated and divided it equally between the two players. A third participant decided whether to punish one or both players by reducing the money they received. This participant was far more likely to punish defectors than cooperators, and especially defectors paired with a cooperator (see figure on the right). This provides strong evidence for the social norm of conditional cooperation, because those who broke that norm were far and away the ones most likely to be punished.

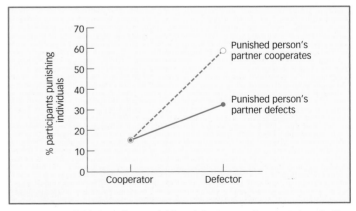

Percentage of third parties punishing defectors and cooperators in the Prisoners' Dilemma as a function of whether the partners of the defector/cooperator defected or cooperated. Based on data in Fehr and Fischbacher (2004).

There are cross-cultural differences with respect to many norms. Shweder, Mahapatra, and Miller (1990) asked Indian and American children and adults to assess the perceived seriousness of 39 norm-breaking actions. There was little agreement between inhabitants of the two countries. For example, Indian children regarded the following as very serious norm-breaking actions: "The day after his father's death, the eldest son had a haircut and ate chicken"; "A widow in your community eats fish two or three times a week."

DYNAMIC CHANGES

Most groups undergo dynamic changes as some people join the group and others leave it. Moreland and Levine (1982) put forward an influential theoretical approach to understanding group changes over time. They emphasized group socialization, which is concerned with the relationships between a group and its members. There are three key features of the theory (see the figure below). First, individuals' level of commitment to the group varies over time. Second, there are role transitions, in which the relationship between the individual and the group changes. Third, and related to role transitions, there are five phases of group socialization:

1. *Investigation phase*: Prospective group members assess whether they would like to join the group, and the group decides whether to accept them. After acceptance, there is the role transition of entry into the group.
2. *Socialization phase*: The group teaches new members about its norms and goals, and new members try to change the group to suit themselves. If this phase is completed successfully, it leads to the role transition of group acceptance.
3. *Maintenance phase*. Members engage in role negotiation. Members unhappy with their role in the group may produce a partial split from the group (this is known as divergence).
4. *Resocialization phase*. Divergence is sometimes followed by attempts to bring the member back fully into the group. If such attempts fail, then exit becomes the next role transition.
5. *Remembrance phase*. After the member has left the group, there may be occasions on which happy memories of group membership are recalled.

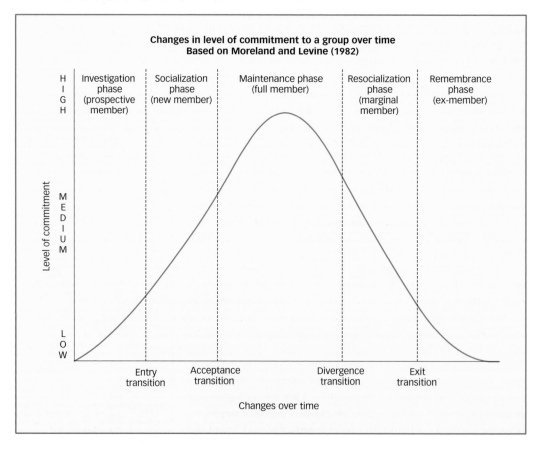

Moreland (1985) carried out a study in which five-person groups met once a week for 3 weeks to discuss topical issues. All of the members were actually new to the group but two members of each group (experimental participants) were told incorrectly that the other three group members (control participants) had already met together on two previous occasions.

Several of Moreland's (1985) findings were consistent with predictions from Moreland and Levine's (1982) theory. First, the experimental participants became more committed to the group over time. Second, the experimental participants gradually came to regard everyone as a full member of the group. Third, the tendency for experimental participants to behave more favorably to the other experimental participant than to the control participants diminished over time.

According to the theory, group members become increasingly committed to the group during the initial stages of group membership. It follows that relatively new group members should claim to be more influenced by group norms than those who have been members for longer. Jetten, Hornsey, and Adarves-Yorno (2006) confirmed this prediction in several experiments when group members were addressing an ingroup audience. However, there was no difference between new and more established group members in reported conformity to group norms when addressing an outgroup. New group members probably claimed to be conformist because it strengthened their position in the group rather than because that is what they really believed.

The theory fully acknowledges the fact that group members and groups systematically influence each other, but is limited in its applicability. As Levine, Moreland, and Ryan (1998, p. 285) admitted, the theory "is meant to apply primarily to small, autonomous [independent], voluntary groups, whose members interact on a regular basis, have affective ties with one another, share a common frame of reference, and are behaviorally interdependent."

GROUP DECISION MAKING

How do you think decision making differs between individuals and groups? Many people think groups are more cautious, basing their decisions on a consensus of the views of all (or most) group members. In fact, what often happens is **group polarization**, which "occurs when the group's initial average position becomes more extreme following group interaction" (Smith & Mackie, 2000, p. 346). Smith and Bond (1998) reported that group polarization had been found in seven countries including the United States. However, it had not been found in studies carried out in Liberia, Taiwan, Uganda, or Germany.

Most research in this area is limited. The great majority of studies have used groups without appointed leaders consisting of college or university students who don't know each other beforehand. In addition, the decisions that were made rarely had any genuine consequences for the groups concerned. Thus, the extent to which group polarization is a phenomenon applying to real groups making real decisions is not entirely clear.

What factors influence group polarization? One important factor is social comparison (Sanders & Baron, 1977). Individuals want to be positively evaluated by other group members. If they see other group members endorsing positions closer to some socially valued goal than their own, they will change their position toward that goal. Isenberg (1986) carried out a meta-analysis of 33 studies on group polarization. Social comparison had a reasonably strong effect on group polarization, especially when value- or emotion-laden issues were discussed rather than factual issues.

Another important factor is persuasive arguments. Suppose that most members of a group initially favor a given type of decision. During the discussion, individuals are likely to hear new arguments supporting their own position (Larson, Foster-Fishman, & Keys, 1994). As a result, their views are likely to become more extreme. Isenberg (1986) found in a meta-analysis that persuasive arguments had a powerful overall effect on group polarization. However, the effects were much stronger when the groups discussed factual rather than emotional or value-laden issues.

Self-categorization theory

According to social identity theory (discussed in Chapters 17 and 20), our identity is determined in large part by the groups to which we belong (known as ingroups). This

Key Term
Group polarization: the tendency for groups to produce fairly extreme decisions.

theoretical approach has been developed into self-categorization theory (e.g., Turner, 1987), according to which members of an ingroup often want to distinguish their group from other groups. They can do this by *differentiating* themselves from the views of an outgroup by adopting relatively extreme views themselves. This is achieved by finding the viewpoint that best represents the combination of what the ingroup members have in common *and* what most clearly distinguishes the ingroup from an outgroup.

Mackie and Cooper (1984) found evidence for the roles played by ingroups and outgroups. Student participants listened to a tape on which the members of another group argued either that standardized tests for university entry should be retained or that such tests should be abandoned. The group on the tape was identified as an ingroup or an outgroup. As expected, an ingroup had much stronger effects than an outgroup in altering the views of the group listening to the tape, and so produced far more group polarization. Changes in views among those listening to the tape produced by the outgroup tended to be in the *opposite* direction to the one advocated by that group. That is as predicted by self-categorization theory.

Several studies have provided more detailed support for the theory. Hogg, Turner, and Davidson (1990) found that groups became more cautious after confrontation with a riskier outgroup. In contrast, they became riskier after confrontation with a more cautious outgroup.

Evaluation

+ Group polarization is an important phenomenon that has been found in several countries.

+ Several factors (e.g., persuasive arguments; social comparison; self-categorization) influencing group polarization have been identified.

− Most studies are artificial and limited, being concerned with groups of strangers making decisions having no real consequences.

− As yet, we lack a comprehensive theory specifying the roles of persuasive arguments, social comparison, and self-categorization in producing group polarization.

Groupthink

The processes within groups leading to group polarization can sometimes have very damaging consequences. This is especially so when groups succumb to an extreme form of group polarization known as groupthink. **Groupthink** (a term introduced by Janis, 1972, 1982) is "a mode of thinking in which the desire to reach unanimous agreement overrides the motivation to adopt proper rational decision-making procedures" (Hogg & Vaughan, 2005, p. 339).

The tragedy of the space shuttle *Challenger* is an example of groupthink. Several engineers had warned it could be dangerous to launch this space shuttle in cold temperatures. The reason was that the cold might cause the O-ring seals in the rocket boosters to fail, thus causing a catastrophic explosion. On the morning of January 28, 1986, the temperature was below freezing. However, there was much public interest in the launch of *Challenger*—it was the first time an ordinary member of the public (a teacher called Christa McAuliffe) had travelled in space. NASA proceeded with the launch, and the *Challenger* exploded 73 seconds after liftoff, killing all seven people on board. The explosion was probably caused by failure of the O-ring seals.

What causes groupthink? According to Janis (1982), five features are typically present:

Key Term

Groupthink:
an excess focus on consensus that typically produces poor group decisions.

1. The group is very cohesive.
2. The group considers only a few options.
3. The group is insulated from information coming from outside the group.
4. There is much stress because of great time pressure.
5. The group is dominated by a very directive leader.

The above five factors can produce an illusion of group invulnerability, in which the group members are very confident of their decision-making ability.

Tetlock et al. (1992) considered in detail eight of the cases used by Janis (1982) to support his groupthink theory. They agreed with Janis that groups showing groupthink typically had a strong leader and a high level of conformity. However, contrary to Janis's theory, groups showing groupthink were generally less (rather than more) cohesive than other groups. In addition, the evidence didn't indicate that exposure to stressful circumstances contributed to the development of groupthink.

Kramer (1998) argued that many well-known faulty decisions were influenced at least as much by political considerations as by deficient group processes. For example, the *Challenger* disaster owed much to the fact that NASA was very keen to attract positive publicity to maintain its government funding. If NASA had decided not to proceed with the launch, there might have been accusations of incompetence.

There is another major limitation with many alleged cases of groupthink. Much of the information about what actually happened (e.g., the launch of the *Challenger*) is based on the recollections of those involved. Many of them may have had deliberately distorted recollections, claiming for example to have been much more opposed to the decision than they were.

Janis (1972, 1982) argued in favor of vigilant decision making, in which there is critical appraisal and open discussion of the options. Supporting evidence was reported by Peterson, Owens, Tetlock, Fan, and Martorana (1998). They studied top management teams during a time when the team was successful and a time when it was unsuccessful. Symptoms of vigilant decision making were generally present during the successful time and symptoms of groupthink during the unsuccessful time. However, as Peterson et al. (1998, p. 272) concluded, "Successful groups showed some indicators of groupthink, whereas unsuccessful groups showed signs of vigilance."

Case Study: *Groupthink*

Conformity to group opinion has many important applications, such as in juries and in the management committees of large organizations. The way individuals behave in these groups is likely to matter a lot. Janis (1972) coined the term "groupthink" to describe how the thinking of people in these situations is often disastrously affected by conformity. Janis was describing the "Bay of Pigs" disaster to his teenage daughter and she challenged him, as a psychologist, to be able to explain why such experts could make such poor decisions. (The Bay of Pigs invasion took place in 1961. President Kennedy and a group of government advisors made a series of bad decisions that resulted in this extremely unsuccessful invasion of the Bay of Pigs in Cuba—disastrous because 1000 men from the invasion force were only released after a ransom payment of 53 million dollars' worth of food and medicine, and also because ultimately the invasion resulted in the Cuban missile crisis and a threat of nuclear war.) Janis suggested that there are a number of group factors that tend to increase conformity and result in bad decision making.

- *Group factors.* People in groups want to be liked and therefore tend to do things to be accepted as one of the group.
- *Decisional stress.* A group feels under pressure to reach a decision. To reduce this sense of pressure they try to reach the decision quickly and with little argument.
- *Isolation.* Groups often work in isolation, which means there are no challenges to the way they are thinking.
- *Institutional factors.* Often people who are appointed to higher positions are those who tend to conform, following the principle that a good soldier makes a good commander.
- *Leadership.* The group is led by a strong leader who has clear ideas about what he/she wants the group to do.

Evaluation

+ Groupthink has been demonstrated in several contexts and countries.

+ As Janis predicted, factors such as a strong leader and pressures toward conformity increase the likelihood of groupthink.

− Janis was wrong to assume that a high level of cohesiveness is needed for groupthink. Exposure to threatening circumstances is also less important than he claimed.

− There are few laboratory studies in which all of the factors allegedly involved in producing groupthink have been manipulated.

− Janis minimized the importance of political factors in producing groupthink.

LEADERSHIP

What is leadership? How can we tell who is the leader of a group? According to Brown (2000, p. 91), "What really characterizes leaders is that they can influence others in the group more than they themselves are influenced."

LEADERS' CHARACTERISTICS

It is often assumed that leaders differ from followers in intelligence and personality. For example, leaders may tend to be cleverer, more extraverted, and more dominant individuals than followers. This theory sounds plausible, but has attracted much criticism. For example, leaders seem to differ enormously in personality. It is difficult to find much similarity among George Bush in the US, Gordon Brown in the UK, and Nelson Mandela in South Africa. Most of the evidence only weakly supports the theory. Mann (1959) reviewed numerous studies. More than 70% of them showed a positive relationship between perceived leadership status and intelligence, adjustment, extraversion, dominance, masculinity, and conservatism. However, the relationships were weak: "In no case is the median correlation between an aspect of personality . . . and performance higher than 0.25, and most of the median correlations are closer to 0.15."

The great person theory is often dismissed out of hand, but its deficiencies have been exaggerated. Lord, de Vader, and Alliger (1986) pointed out that correlations between personality measures and leadership may be low because of unreliability of measurement. They carried out a meta-analysis of the studies discussed by Mann (1959), correcting for unreliability of measurement. The correlation between intelligence and leadership perception increased from +.25 to +.52 and that between masculinity–femininity and leadership perception went up from +.15 to +.34.

So far we have focused on the personality characteristics of those *perceived* to have leadership status. A separate issue is to identify the personality characteristics of *effective* leaders in terms of group performance. Heslin (1964) reviewed the literature and found that the intelligence and adjustment of the leader correlated strongly with group performance.

There has been much controversy as to whether men or women make better leaders. Eagly, Karau, and Makhijani (1995) carried out a meta-analysis and found there were practically no overall gender differences in effectiveness. However, men performed slightly better than women in masculine leader roles (e.g., the military), whereas women performed slightly better than men in feminine leader roles (e.g., in educational or government organizations).

The great person theory doesn't acknowledge that the qualities needed for effective leadership depend on the *situation*. For example, a more aggressive approach is needed

Do leaders share any common characteristics?

to lead an adolescent gang than a group discussing flower arranging. Hains, Hogg, and Duck (1997) studied groups of college students meeting to discuss a social issue. In each group, a member was selected at random as leader. When the members identified strongly with the group, leaders with views close to the average in the group were rated as more effective leaders than those with views differing from group members. Thus, effective leaders need to embody the group norms to be effective, which implies that the characteristics of effective leadership are much more *flexible* and situation-specific than implied by the great person theory.

FIEDLER'S CONTINGENCY MODEL

It is important to study both the leader's personality *and* the situations in which leadership is exercised, because the effectiveness of any given leadership style is contingent on [depends on] the conditions in which the group finds itself. The most influential contingency model is the one proposed by Fiedler (1967, 1978; see the figure below).

There are four basic components in Fiedler's contingency model. One refers to the leader's personality and the others refer to features of the situation in which the leader must lead. The leader's personality is assessed on the basis of his/her liking for the least preferred co-worker. The least preferred co-worker (LPC) scale requires leaders to rate the most difficult person with whom they work. High scorers (high LPC) evaluate their least preferred co-worker relatively favorably, and are said to adopt a relationship-oriented leadership style. In contrast, low scorers (low LPC) are task-oriented.

Three situational factors jointly determine the favorableness of the situation for the leader:

1. *Leader–member relations*: The relations between the leader and the other group members can vary from very good to very poor.
2. *Task structure*: The amount of structure in the task performed by the group can vary from high structure and goal clarity to low structure and goal clarity.

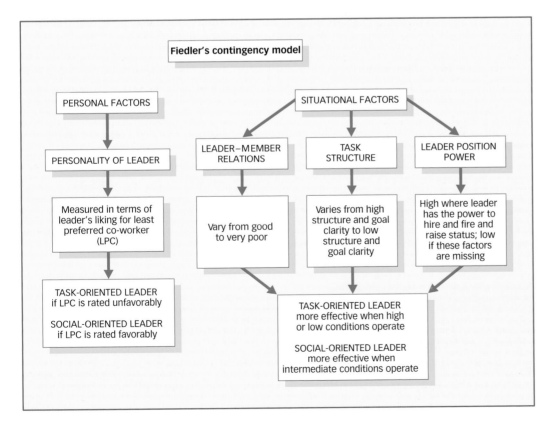

The personal and situational factors determining leaders' effectiveness according to Fiedler's contingency model.

3. *Position power*: The power and authority of the leadership position are high if the leader can hire and fire, raise pay or status, and has support from the organization, but are low if these factors are missing.

Any given leadership situation can be categorized as high or low on each situational factor, giving eight possible combinations or levels of situation favorableness. The most favorable situation for a leader involves good leader–member relations, high task structure, and high position power. The least favorable situation involves poor leader–member relations, a lack of task structure, and low position power for the leader. According to Fiedler, the most important situational factor is leader–member relations and the least important is position power.

We turn now to the key predictions of the model. Task-oriented leaders (low LPC) will be more effective than relationship-oriented leaders (high LPC) when the situation is very favorable or very unfavorable, but less effective when the situation is of intermediate favorableness. Why did Fiedler make these predictions? When the situation is very favorable, the leader doesn't need to be unduly concerned about relationship issues because group morale is very high. When the situation is very unfavorable, feelings within the group probably can't be improved much, and so it is best for the leader to focus on the task in hand. When the situation is of intermediate favorableness, a relationship-oriented leader can improve group morale.

Findings

Fiedler and Potter (1983) summarized the findings from over 100 studies on leadership effectiveness based on group performance. Task-oriented (low LPC) leaders were generally more successful than relationship-oriented (high LPC) leaders when the situational favorableness was low or high. However, the opposite was the case when the level of situational favorableness was moderate.

Schriesheim, Tepper, and Tetrault (1994) carried out a meta-analysis based on data from 1282 groups. Their findings were in broad agreement with those of Fiedler and Potter (1983). However, small differences in the favorableness of the situation sometimes produced large differences in the effectiveness of task-oriented or relationship-oriented leaders, which is contrary to the theory.

Fiedler argued that the most important situational factor was leader–member relations and the least important was position power. Singh, Bohra, and Dalal (1979) asked people to rate several situations for their favorableness to the leader. The relative importance of the three situational factors varied across situations, indicating that Fiedler's approach is too rigid. Contrary to the theory, position power was important in each of four studies, and it was the most influential situational factor in two of them.

Miller, Butler, and Cosentino (2004) extended Fiedler's model by relating *followers'* personality and situational favorability to their performance. The participants were junior personnel serving with the US Army in Europe. As might be expected on Fiedler's approach, relationship-oriented followers performed better than task-oriented ones in moderately favorable situations, whereas the opposite was the case with highly unfavorable situations. However, the additional finding that relationship-oriented followers performed better than task-oriented ones in very favorable situations is inconsistent with Fiedler's general approach.

Evaluation

⊕ The effectiveness of leaders depends on the relationship between their personal characteristics and the particular situation in which they find themselves.

⊕ Task-oriented leaders are most effective when the situation is very favorable or unfavorable, whereas relationship-oriented leaders are most effective when the situation is of intermediate favourableness. Similar finding have been obtained when relationship-oriented followers are compared against task-oriented followers.

- It is oversimplified to argue that leaders are either task- or relationship-oriented. Those elected by their groups as leaders are often task- *and* relationship-oriented (Sorrentino & Field, 1986).

- Fiedler's notion that an individual's leadership style is invariant across situations is too static given that many individuals change their style to fit changing situations (Hogg & Vaughan, 2005).

- According to the contingency model, leader–member relations are solely a function of the situation. However, characteristics of the leader (e.g., warmth; agreeableness) also influence his/her relations with others within the group.

- The model tells us little about the dynamic processes occurring over time. For example, what factors determine the rise and fall of leaders?

TRANSACTIONAL VS. TRANSFORMATIONAL LEADERSHIP

Several theorists have argued that the most effective leaders are those variously described as charismatic, inspirational, or transformational. For example, Bass (1985) distinguished between transactional and transformational leadership. **Transactional leadership** involves various exchanges or bargains between leaders and followers. In contrast, **transformational leadership** involves providing one's followers with inspiration, and persuading them to rise above their own self-interests to achieve the leader's vision. Bass assumed that transactional leadership can be effective, but that transformational leaders are generally even more effective, especially when the situation is difficult and rapid changes are required. According to Bass (1985, p. 154), "Transformational leadership is more likely to reflect social values and to emerge in times of distress and change while transactional leadership is more likely to be observed in a well-ordered society."

Avolio, Bass, and Jung (1999) clarified what is involved in transactional and transformational leadership. They reported findings based on 3786 participants who described their leader using the Multifactor Leadership Questionnaire. Six factors were identified:

1. *Charismatic/inspirational*: Leader provides followers with a clear sense of purpose, and persuades them to identify with him/her.
2. *Intellectual stimulation*: Leader encourages followers to question conventional ways of solving problems.
3. *Individualized consideration*: Leader tries to understand the needs of his/her followers, and to get them to develop their potential.
4. *Contingent reward*: Leader makes it clear what he/she expects from followers, and how they will be rewarded if successful.
5. *Active management-by-exception*: Leader monitors the performance of followers, and helps to correct problems.
6. *Passive-avoidant leadership*: Leader becomes involved only when problems become serious.

An additional factor analysis of the data produced two correlated factors of transformational and transactional leadership. The factor of transformational leadership was based mainly on the charismatic/inspirational and

Key Terms
Transactional leadership: a form of leadership involving exchanges or bargains between the leader and his/her followers.
Transformational leadership: a form of leadership based on inspiration or charisma.

intellectual stimulation factors, whereas the transactional factor was based on individualized consideration and contingent reward.

Findings

Most studies have found that transactional and transformational leadership styles are effective. Howell and Hall-Merenda (1999, p. 681) discussed several studies on transactional leadership: "The majority of research findings suggest that contingent reward leadership [an important aspect of transactional leadership] has a positive effect on individual follower performance." Yammarino, Spangler, and Bass (1993) carried out a longitudinal study of 193 graduates from the US Naval Academy. Measures of transformational leadership obtained at the start of the study predicted later performance appraisal.

Lowe, Kroeck, and Sivasubramiam (1996) carried out a meta-analysis. Transformational leadership was generally superior to transactional leadership in producing effective performance in work groups. This superiority of transformational leadership was obtained with groups as diverse as student leaders in laboratory studies, nursing supervisors, and German bank managers.

Kirkpatrick and Locke (1996) pointed out that most studies are correlational. Transformational leadership may correlate with follower performance because of the impact of the leader on his/her followers. However, followers may use their knowledge of the leader's success when deciding whether he/she is transformational. Kirkpatrick and Locke distinguished between these possibilities in a study in which trained actors pretended to be transformational or nontransformational leaders. Group performance on a simulated production task was higher when the leader communicated a vision (e.g., instilling confidence in the followers; raising expectations for high performance) and when he/she provided suggestions for implementing the vision. Thus, aspects of transformational leadership can have a direct influence on group performance. However, leaders adopting a charismatic communication style (e.g., sounding dynamic and confident; making direct eye contact; animated facial expression) were no more effective than those adopting a neutral or noncharismatic communication style.

Bass (1985) argued that transformational leadership is especially likely to be effective when the situation is stressful and uncertain. This prediction has rarely been tested because most studies have focused on relatively stable conditions. However, it was tested by Bass, Avolio, Jung, and Berson (2003), who studied US Army platoons performing combat simulation exercises. In fact, platoon performance was predicted equally well by platoon leaders' ratings on transformational leadership and on transactional leadership, which is inconsistent with the original prediction. The beneficial effects of both types of leadership on performance depended in part on increased cohesion within the platoon.

Eagly, Johannsen-Schmidt, and van Ergen (2003) carried out a meta-analysis of 45 studies comparing the leadership styles of men and women. The gender differences were small. However, female leaders tended to be more transformational than male ones, and also made more use of the contingent reward component of transactional leadership. Male leaders were more likely than female ones to use the active management-by-exception and passive-avoidant components of transactional leadership. These findings suggest the value of female leadership: "All of the aspects of leadership style on which women exceeded men relate positively to leaders' effectiveness whereas all of the aspects on which men exceeded women have negative or null relations to effectiveness" (Eagly et al., 2003, p. 569).

Some transformational leaders have misused their skills to produce tragic consequences. For example, Marshall Applewhite was a transformational leader who claimed that his Heaven's Gate group had reached a new stage of evolution in which they had no further need for their bodies. After discarding their bodies, they would go off in a spaceship traveling with the Hale-Bopp comet. On the basis of these claims, Marshall Applewhite persuaded nearly 40 members of his group to commit mass suicide in March 1997.

Case Study: *The Heaven's Gate Mass Suicide*

The daily papers from March 27, 1997 were full of news that 39 people had committed suicide in a hilltop mansion in Rancho Santa Fe, California. As the story broke, it became apparent that the victims were members of a cult that called itself "Heaven's Gate." The Heaven's Gate cult emerged in the 1970s and was led by Marshall Applewhite and Bonnie Nettles. They were self-described "space age shepherds" who intended to lead a flock of humans to a higher level of existence.

Through the teachings of their charismatic leaders, who claimed to be extraterrestrial representatives of the "Kingdom Level Above Human," the cult members believed their bodies were mere vessels. By renouncing sex, drugs, alcohol, their birth names, and all relationships with family and friends, disciples prepared to ascend to space, shedding their "containers," or bodies, and entering God's Kingdom. The cult members were led to believe that the appearance of comet Hale Bopp was a sign to move on to a more pure existence in outer space.

Investigations revealed that the mass suicide appeared to be a carefully orchestrated event. It took place over 3 days and involved three groups, proceeding in a calm, ritualistic fashion. Some members apparently assisted others and then went on to take their own dose of a fatal mixture. Lying on cots or mattresses with their arms at their sides, the victims each carried identification. Each of the members of the organization gave a brief videotaped statement prior to their death. The essence of the statements was that they believed they were going to a better place.

Three things seem to be essential to the concept of a cult. Members think in terms of "us" and "them," with a total alienation from anyone perceived as "them." Intense, though often subtle, indoctrination techniques are used to recruit and hold members. The third ingredient is the presence of a charismatic cult leader who makes people want to follow his or her beliefs. Cultism usually involves some sort of belief that everything outside the cult is evil and threatening; inside the cult is the safe and special path to salvation through the cult leader and his or her teachings.

The cult leader must be extremely attractive to those who convert. He or she must satisfy the fundamental need to have someone to trust, depend on, and believe in totally. Charismatic leaders like Applewhite and Nettles gave purpose and meaning to the lives of their followers. Unquestioning devotion caused 38 Heaven's Gate cult members to voluntarily commit suicide. Marshall Applewhite was the 39th person to die in the mass suicide.

Evaluation

- Transactional and transformational leadership are both effective, with transformational leadership generally being more effective.

- Theories of transformational or charismatic leadership have focused on factors (e.g., vision for the future; instilling confidence in followers) ignored in other theories of leadership.

- The theoretical approach assumes that leadership is a dynamic process that changes over time, which is an advance on Fiedler's approach.

- Some theoretical approaches focusing on transformational or charismatic leadership exaggerate the impact of the leader on the followers and minimize the impact of the followers on the leader.

- Too much transformational leadership "may be dysfunctional, because it imbues the leader with excessive power and fragments the group through continual change. The limits of transformational leadership are not specified" (Hogg & Vaughan, 2005, p. 330).

- Transformational leaders can be dangerous if the achievement of their goals involves the destruction of group members or some other group.

COLLECTIVE BEHAVIOR

Individuals often behave differently when in a crowd than when on their own or with a few friends. For example, lynch mobs in the southern parts of the United States murdered about 2000 people (mostly blacks) during the first half of the twentieth century. Those involved in those atrocities would not have behaved in that way if they hadn't been part of a highly emotional crowd.

Le Bon (1895) was a French journalist who put forward a famous theory of crowd behavior. According to him, a man forming part of a crowd:

> *descends several rungs in the ladder of civilization, he is . . . a creature acting by instinct . . . [He can be] induced to commit acts contrary to his most obvious interest and best known habits. An individual in a crowd is a grain of sand amid other grains of sand.*

Le Bon referred to the "law of mental unity" driving a crowd to behave like a mob. He also used the term *social contagion* to describe how irrational and violent feelings and behavior can spread rapidly through a crowd.

Do you think Le Bon was basically correct? If you do, part of the reason is that the media focuses on crowds behaving badly and provides little coverage of well-behaved, dignified crowds. As we will see, Le Bon grossly exaggerated the mindlessness of crowds, and crowd behavior is much more diverse than he imagined.

CROWD BEHAVIOR

Reicher (1984) studied a civil disturbance in the St. Pauls area of Bristol in England involving the police and the mainly black community. There was considerable violence, with many people being seriously injured and several police cars being destroyed. However, the crowd's behavior was much more controlled than might have been thought. The crowd displayed violence toward the police and symbols of the state (e.g., banks), but didn't attack or destroy local shops and houses. Moreover, the crowd's actions were confined to a small area lying at the heart of the community. If the crowd members had simply wanted to behave violently, then the violence would have spread into the surrounding areas. Finally, those involved denied they had lost their identities during the riots. The opposite was closer to the truth, because they experienced an increased sense of pride in their community.

How can we explain these unexpected findings? According to Reicher (1984), individuals in a crowd attend less than usual to themselves, focusing instead on the situation and the other crowd members to provide them with cues as to how to behave. This makes them responsive to group norms or standards. These group norms sometimes endorse taking aggressive action, but very often endorse responsible behavior. This theory was subsequently developed into the social identity model of deindividuation effects by Reicher, Spears, and Postmes (1995) (discussed later).

Marsh, Rosser, and Harré (1978) also found that crowds share a social purpose. They analyzed the behavior of soccer fans, discovering they had long-lasting social structures and patterns of behavior (e.g., ritualized aggression). Those fans showing the most ability to follow the rules and norms were very highly regarded and influential members of their groups.

The stereotype of soccer fans is that they form themselves into highly aggressive groups. Marsh et al. (1978) found that unrestrained fighting between rival fans happened very rarely. For example, soccer fans supporting the home team regarded it as their right to chase fans of the away team from the ground after the match, but the rival sets of fans usually kept their distance. Soccer fans often use violent language and make threatening gestures, but these activities rarely turn into actual fighting.

Waddington, Jones, and Critcher (1987) argued that most crowd violence depends on the *context* in which the crowd finds itself rather than on the characteristics of the individuals within the crowd. They compared two public rallies held during the coal miners' strike in Britain in 1984, only one of which led to violence. In contrast to the peaceful rally, the violent one was controlled by the police rather than by the rally organizers. The violent rally hadn't been

Hundreds of thousands of fans attend soccer matches each week but only a tiny percentage show hooligan behavior.

planned carefully with the police, and insufficient thought had been given to preventing large numbers of people being forced into a small area.

DEINDIVIDUATION

Le Bon (1895) argued that the anonymity of individuals in a crowd or mob can remove normal social constraints and so lead to violence. In similar fashion, Zimbardo (1970) and Diener (1980) argued for the importance of **deindividuation**, which is the loss of a sense of personal identity occurring in crowds. It is most likely to occur in conditions of high arousal, anonymity, and diffused responsibility (i.e., responsibility for what happens is spread among the members of the crowd).

According to Diener (1980), deindividuation is produced through decreased self-awareness and has the following effects:

- Poor monitoring of one's own behavior.
- Reduced concern to have social approval of one's behavior.
- Reduced capacity to think rationally.

> **Key Term**
>
> **Deindividuation:**
> the loss of a sense of personal identity that occurs when individuals find themselves in a crowd.

Left: Uniforms, such as those worn by nurses, increase an individual's sense of anonymity and make it more likely that they will conform to the role associated with the uniform. Right: Johnson and Downing (1979) pointed out the similarity between the clothes of Zimbardo's deindividuated participants and those of the Ku Klux Klan.

Zimbardo (1970) reported a study on deindividuation. Female participants were told to give electric shocks to other women in a Milgram-type study (see earlier in chapter). Deindividuation was produced in half the participants by having them wear laboratory coats and hoods covering their faces. In addition, the experimenter addressed them as a group rather than as individuals. The intensity of shocks given by the deindividuated participants was *twice* as great as that of participants who wore their own clothes and were treated as individuals.

Johnson and Downing (1979) pointed out that the clothing worn by the deindividuated participants in Zimbardo's (1970) study resembled that worn by the Ku Klux Klan (a secret organization that carried out many violent acts against American blacks). Deindividuated individuals dressed as nurses actually gave *fewer* electric shocks than those wearing their own clothes. Thus, deindividuation can have desirable rather than undesirable effects on behavior (see figure on the right).

Mann (1981) analyzed newspaper accounts of crowds watching someone threatening to commit suicide by

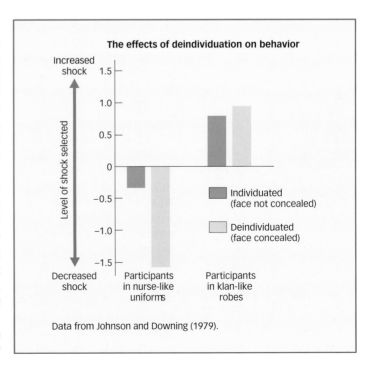

The effects of deindividuation on behavior

Data from Johnson and Downing (1979).

jumping from a bridge or building. Crowds often encouraged the potential suicide to jump. This aggressive crowd behavior was much more likely when those in the crowd were fairly anonymous (and thus deindividuated) because the crowd was large or the incident took place after dark. Similar findings were reported by Silke (2003), who studied 500 violent attacks carried out in Northern Ireland, 206 of them by offenders wearing disguises to mask their identities. Disguised offenders (who can be regarded as deindividuated) inflicted more serious physical injuries on their victims, attacked more people, and were more likely to threaten victims after their initial attack.

> ## Evaluation
>
> + Deindividuation can contribute toward groups and crowds behaving in an anti-social or aggressive way.
>
> + Anonymity (a key part of deindividuation) often leads groups to behave badly because it reduces the chances that individuals will be punished for behaving anti-socially or illegally.
>
> − Deindividuation doesn't always lead groups and crowds to behave badly; indeed, it can have the opposite effect (e.g., Johnson & Downing, 1979).
>
> − Other theoretical approaches (see below) provide superior explanations of group behavior.

EMERGENT-NORM THEORY

According to Turner and Killian's (1972) emergent-norm theory, two factors must be present for individuals in crowds to behave aggressively:

1. The crowd should develop a group norm or standard endorsing the use of aggression.
2. Individuals in the crowd should be identifiable, because this increases the social pressures on them not to deviate from the group norm.

When both factors are present, crowd members should conform to the new or emergent norm.

We can see what is involved by considering a confrontation between a group of demonstrators and the police. A new norm that people should defend themselves against the police may emerge, which may lead to stone throwing. Individuals in the crowd who can be identified by others feel strong pressures to conform to the stone-throwing behavior.

Mann, Newton, and Innes (1982) compared the deindividuation and emergent-norm approaches. Participants observed two people having a discussion, and they could react by pressing buttons to provide crowd noise. The participants were anonymous or identifiable, and they were given fake information indicating the group norm was aggressive (loud noise) or nonaggressive (soft noise). According to deindividuation theory, anonymous individuals should have behaved more aggressively than identifiable ones, which is what Mann et al. found. However, there was some support for emergent-norm theory, because participants were more aggressive when told there was an aggressive group norm. However, that theory's prediction that the level of aggression should be greatest among identifiable participants exposed to the aggressive group norm was *not* supported. Overall the findings supported deindividuation theory more than emergent-norm theory. A problem for emergent-norm theory is that it is unclear *how* group norms are supposed to emerge.

SOCIAL IDENTITY MODEL OF DEINDIVIDUATION EFFECTS

Reicher et al. (1995) and Postmes and Spears (1998) put forward a social identity model of deindividuation effects. According to deindividuation theory, deindividuated individuals become uninhibited and freed from social constraints. According to Reicher et al.'s model, precisely the *opposite* is the case—when individuals in a group become deindividuated, their behavior is strongly influenced by the prevailing group norms.

Postmes and Spears (1998) emphasized three main assumptions of the social identity model:

1. Deindividuation leads *not* to a loss of self but only to a decreased focus on personal identity.
2. Deindividuation increases responsiveness to (or conformity with) *specific* situational group norms (i.e., what most people would regard as appropriate behavior in any given situation). This can produce very restrained behavior or aggressive behavior.
3. Deindividuation is neutral with respect to *general* social norms (standards of behavior not taking account of the particular context).

A key prediction from this theory is that deindividuation may or may not lead to anti-social behavior by group members, depending on the prevailing situational group norms. For example, consider the death of Princess Diana on August 31, 1997. This tragic event led large crowds of tearful people to show their sadness and sense of loss (in line with situational group norms) but did *not* lead to any breaking of general social norms.

Postmes and Spears (1998) carried out a meta-analysis of 60 studies on group and crowd behavior, and found only modest support for deindividuation theory. Manipulations designed to produce deinividuation (e.g., anonymity; large groups) were associated with antinormative behavior (behavior breaking general social norms). However, the average correlation or association between deindividuation manipulations and antinormative behavior was only +.09, so there was only a slight tendency for deindividuation to lead to behavior opposed to general social norms.

What norms appeared as the public waited to pay their respects to Diana, Princess of Wales?

Other analyses by Postmes and Spears (1998) undermined deindividuation theory even further. It is assumed within that theory that manipulations of anonymity lead to antisocial behavior because they reduce the individual's self-awareness. However, the evidence provided no support for this viewpoint. Second, manipulations designed to produce deindividuation *increased* adherence to situational group norms, whereas deindividuation theory predicts a *decrease*.

The above findings can readily be explained by the social identity model of deindividuation effects. According to that model, individuals in crowds typically adopt the social identity of the crowd and their behavior is determined by situational group norms. That is precisely what was reported by Postmes and Spears (1998, p. 253):

The most striking result was that the deindividuation conditions of anonymity, larger groups, and reductions in self-awareness fostered adherence to situational norms. Thus, the factors that social psychologists have identified as playing a crucial role in the formation of collective behavior appeared to lead to a specific form of social regulation rather than its breakdown.

According to the social identity model, anonymity of individuals to the outgroup should *increase* adherence to group norms. In contrast, anonymity of individuals to the ingroup should often *reduce* adherence to group norms. The first prediction has been supported in several studies (e.g., Reicher et al., 1995). The second prediction was tested by Reicher, Levine, and Gordijn (1998). First-year psychology students responded to questionnaire statements about lying (e.g., "It is fine to give false excuses if one didn't prepare for a seminar") having been told they would discuss the various issues with a member of the academic staff afterwards. Some students were visible to the other students, whereas others sat in individual booths. As predicted, students anonymous to their fellow ingroup members were less likely to agree that lying was acceptable than those visible to other students. Visibility increased the students' perception of the power of their ingroup, and made them more willing to endorse statements contrary to the beliefs of the outgroup (academic staff).

Evaluation

⊕ Deindividuation is important in increasing conformity behavior by crowds, and its effects can be positive (e.g., after the death of Princess Diana) as well as negative.

⊕ The social identity model accounts for most findings, including the controlled aggression found by Reicher (1984).

⊕ The theoretical assumption that deindividuation increases adherence to group norms has received much support.

⊖ The effects of anonymity on behavior depend on how anonymity influences power relations between groups.

⊖ Members of a large group may experience exhilaration or great excitement, but the model has little to say about such emotional states.

⊖ It is difficult to measure key concepts such as personal identity and social identity.

Chapter Summary

Obedience to authority

- Milgram found that about 65% of people were prepared to administer potentially lethal electric shocks when an authority figure (the experimenter) ordered them to do so.
- Milgram discovered that obedience to authority was less when the obviousness of the other person's plight was increased or the authority and influence of the experimenter were reduced.
- Similar findings to those of Milgram in the United States have been found in many other countries, and obedience to authority has been shown in real-life situations.
- Milgram argued that participants were put into an "agentic" state in which they became the passive instruments of the authority figure. This seems unlikely, because most of the obedient participants experienced a strong conflict between the experimenter's demands and their own conscience.

Conformity

- Asch found that pressures to conform led many people to give the same wrong answers as other group members even though the correct answer was obvious; this is mainly a result of normative influence.
- Conformity in the Asch situation is much less when one other person in the group gives the correct answer or the other group members belong to an outgroup.
- Conformity is significantly greater in collectivistic cultures than in individualistic ones.
- According to Moscovici, minorities influence the majority through conversion (more private than public influence), whereas majorities influence minorities through compliance (more public than private influence).
- Minority influences are found mainly when the minority is perceived as part of the ingroup rather than the outgroup.
- Moscovici exaggerated the differences between the ways in which majorities and minorities exert influence.

Basic group characteristics

- The association between group cohesiveness and performance is fairly weak. There are generally stronger effects of performance on cohesiveness than of cohesiveness on performance.
- Social norms provide guidance concerning what behavior by group members is appropriate. They also help to maintain group identity, make it easier for the group to attain its goals, and promote cooperation.
- Groups (and their members) go through five phases: investigation; socialization; maintenance; resocialization; and remembrance.

- Group polarization occurs frequently in groups. It depends on persuasive arguments, social comparison, and self-categorization.
- Groupthink is most likely to occur when a group has a strong leader and there are pressures toward conformity. Political pressures help to explain many well-known examples of groupthink.

Leadership
- According to the great person theory, leaders are cleverer, more extraverted, and more dominant than their followers. There is some support for this theory, but it ignores important situational factors.
- According to Fiedler's contingency model, task-oriented leaders are more effective than relationship-oriented leaders when the situation is very favorable or unfavorable but less effective when the situation is of intermediate favorableness.
- The contingency model assumes mistakenly that all leaders are either task- or relationship-oriented but not both.
- According to Bass, transformational leadership is generally more effective than transactional leadership.
- Theories focusing on transformational or charismatic leadership minimize the impact of followers on the leader.

Collective behavior
- According to Le Bon, crowds behave in irrational and violent ways as a result of social contagion. Much of the evidence fails to support this viewpoint.
- Several theorists have argued that deindividuation is partly responsible for crowds behaving in antisocial ways. However, it doesn't always have that effect.
- According to emergent-norm theory, a crowd will behave violently when there is a group norm endorsing the use of aggression and individuals in the group are identifiable. There is mixed evidence on this theory.
- According to the social identity model, deindividuation increases conformity with situational group norms (which may endorse violent or restrained behavior). This approach has proved successful, but doesn't fully explain the strong emotional states often found in crowd members.

Further Reading

- Baron, R.S., & Kerr, N. (2003). *Group process, group decision, group action* (2nd ed.). Buckingham, UK: Open University Press. Several of the topics discussed in this chapter are dealt with at greater length in this textbook.
- Blass, T. (2000). *Obedience to authority—Current perspectives on the Milgram paradigm*. Mahwah, NJ: Lawrence Erlbaum Associates, Inc. This interesting edited book is devoted to assessing the relevance of Milgram's ideas and research to real-world events in which enormous suffering was caused by excessive obedience to authority.
- Cialdini, R.B., & Goldstein, N.J. (2004). Social influence: Compliance and conformity. *Annual Review of Psychology, 55*, 591–621. This paper provides a good overview of current theory and research in areas such as conformity and obedience to authority.
- Goethals, G.R., & Sorenson, G. (Eds.). (2004). *Encyclopedia of leadership*. Thousand Oaks, CA: Sage. There are numerous interesting short contributions on psychological approaches to leadership.
- Hogg, M.A., & Vaughan, G.M. (2005). *Social psychology* (4th ed.). Harlow, UK: Prentice Hall. Several chapters in this textbook (especially 7, 8, and 9) contain comprehensive coverage of the topics discussed in this chapter.
- Kruglanski, A.W., & Higgins, E.T. (2003). *Social psychology: A general reader*. Hove, UK: Psychology Press. This book contains important articles on most of the topics discussed in this chapter.

Chapter 20

Contents

Intergroup processes

Everyday life is full of examples of interactions between groups. Some of these interactions are of major political or historical importance, as is the case with the numerous wars fought between different groups or countries. Other interactions are on a more minor scale (e.g., competitive team sports; work discussions between different groups). If we define "group" broadly, then we encounter members of other groups (and those we perceive to be members of our own group) nearly every day of our lives. Thus, the study of intergroup processes and behavior is of great importance.

What exactly do we mean by intergroup behavior? According to Hogg and Vaughan (2005, p. 392), "Any perception, cognition or behavior that is influenced by people's recognition that they and others are members of distinct social groups is intergroup behavior." Social psychologists have devoted considerable attention to the problems that can develop between groups. This is reflected in our coverage of intergroup processes, which includes sections on stereotypes and on prejudice and discrimination. Finally, we consider how prejudice and discrimination can be reduced or even eliminated.

SOCIAL IDENTITY

Suppose someone asked you to describe your best friend in detail. Your description would certainly refer to their personal qualities (e.g., their personality). However, it would probably also include some indication of the groups to which they belong (e.g., student at college; member of the hockey team). According to social identity theory (Tajfel, 1978, 1981), the groups to which we belong form an important part of our self-concept. The term **social identity** is used to refer to an individual's sense of himself/herself based on group membership. More specifically, "We have as many social identities as there are groups that we feel we belong to" (Hogg & Vaughan, 2005, p. 127).

Why is it important for us to possess social identities? According to social identity theory, having a positive social identity makes us feel good about ourselves and enhances our self-esteem. One way we can achieve a positive social identity is to draw favorable comparisons between a group to which we belong (the ingroup) and some relevant outgroup (**ingroup bias** or favoritism). Drawing favorable comparisons between our ingroup and outgroups is important to our social identities. As Tajfel (1979, p. 188) expressed it, "We are what we are because *they* are not what we are."

The good news about social identity is that it increases our self-esteem and gives us a sense of belonging. However, there is also bad news. If we boost our self-esteem by comparing our ingroup favorably to various outgroups, this may lead us to display prejudice and discrimination toward members of those outgroups. The downside of social identity is discussed later in the chapter.

Findings

There is much evidence of ingroup bias or favoritism toward the ingroup at the expense of the outgroup. For example, Tajfel, Flament, Billlig, and Bundy (1971) assigned 14- and 15-year-old boys to two groups. They asked individuals within the groups to assign points (which could be exchanged for money) to other participants. Nearly all the boys showed ingroup bias by awarding more points to members of their own group than the other group.

According to social identity theory, ingroup bias occurs as a *direct* result of individuals identifying themselves with the ingroup, and so should always be found. However, there is an alternative explanation based on self-interest. Perhaps individuals reward ingroup members more than outgroup members because they expect to be benefited in return by other ingroup members. Support for the notion that self-interest is involved in ingroup bias was reported by Gaertner and Insko (2000). Some participants were told they wouldn't receive any bonus money in contrast to the other ingroup members and most of the outgroup members. These participants didn't show any ingroup bias because other ingroup members couldn't benefit them in return.

Most laboratory studies on ingroup bias have involved the allocation of positive outcomes (e.g., points; money). According to social identity theory, individuals should also show ingroup bias or favoritism when allocating *negative* outcomes (e.g., punishments). Support for this prediction was reported by Verkuyten, Drabbles, and van den Nieuwenhuijzen (1999). Dutch participants indicated how strongly they identified themselves with the Dutch majority ingroup in the Netherlands. Individuals who identified themselves most strongly with the Dutch ingroup revealed the greatest negative emotions toward ethnic minorities. In similar fashion, Germans during the Second World War who identified most strongly with being German were more strongly opposed to the Jews than were Germans with less national ingroup identification (Goldhagen, 1996).

According to social identity theory, ingroup bias leads to increased self-esteem for its members. Rubin and Hewstone (1998) reviewed the literature, and found that 9 out of 12 studies reported supporting evidence. For example, Lemyre and Smith (1985) allowed some participants to give rewards to members of either an ingroup or an outgroup, and thus to show ingroup bias. The other participants had to give rewards either to one or two ingroups or to one or two outgroups, and so could not show ingroup bias. Those participants who could show ingroup bias had higher self-esteem than those unable to do so.

As we have seen, an important reason for ingroup bias is that it enhances an individual's self-esteem. Individuals who initially have low self-esteem should exhibit more ingroup bias than those with high self-esteem, because they have a stronger motive to enhance their self-esteem. This prediction has received very little support. Rubin and Hewstone (1998) found that only 3 out of 19 studies reported the predicted findings.

Strong negative emotions need to be created in order to make an ingroup justify its harmful behavior toward an outgroup.

Evaluation

+ Our self-concept depends importantly on the groups with which we identify.

+ Social identity theory has been applied successfully to several phenomena within social psychology, including ingroup bias, stereotyping, prejudice, and prejudice reduction (see later in the chapter).

− The prediction that individuals low in self-esteem should exhibit more ingroup bias than those high in self-esteem has not been supported.

− According to social identity theory, people very readily adopt social identities. However, there are (unknown) limits to this process. As Augoustinos and Walker (1995, p. 131) pointed out, "People do not accept any social identity thrust upon them, they actively seek, avoid, resist, dispute, and negotiate social identities."

− Social identity theory focuses on the cognitive processes underlying group identification, and has little to say about emotional and motivational factors.

Members of the Star Wars Fan Club convention—a social identity?

STEREOTYPES

When we think about some group in society (e.g., Catholics; Italians), we often make use of stereotypes. A **stereotype** is, "a cognitive representation or impression of a social group that people form by associating particular characteristics and emotions with the group" (Smith & Mackie, 2000). Stereotypes are schemas or organized packets of knowledge relating to specific groups or individuals. For example, many people have a stereotype of the English as intelligent, tolerant, and reserved, even though they know many English people who are completely different from this stereotype! Note that this example is not typical, because most stereotypes are negative and related to prejudice.

It is often assumed that stereotypes are very inaccurate. However, there is often a grain of truth in stereotypes. For example, McCauley and Stitt (1978) asked various groups of Americans to guess the percentages of adult Americans and of black Americans who hadn't completed high school, were born illegitimate, had been the victims of violent crime, and so on. There were differences in the guesses for most questions, thus showing the existence of stereotypes. Surprisingly, however, the participants *underestimated* the actual differences between the two groups, so their stereotypes had some basis in fact. In contrast, Terracciano et al. (2005) carried out a large-scale study on national character across 49 cultures. They found no relationship between national stereotypes (based on personality) and mean personality trait levels across those cultures, suggesting that there is no validity to stereotypes about national character.

ASSESSING STEREOTYPES

Traditionally, stereotypes were nearly always assessed by means of questionnaires. For example, McCauley and Stitt (1978) asked participants questions such as, "What percentage of people in the world generally are efficient?" and "What percentage of Germans are efficient?" The average answer to the former question was 50%, whereas it was 63% to the latter one. The stereotype of Germans was assessed by using several such pairs of questions focusing on large differences in responses depending on whether the questions referred to Germans or to people in general.

There are two major problems with most questionnaire measures. First, there is social desirability bias. Individuals having very negative stereotypes of other groups may feel it is socially desirable to pretend their stereotypes are less negative than is actually the case. Second, some aspects of an individual's stereotypes may not be accessible to conscious

Key Term

Stereotype:
a simplified cognitive generalization or categorization (typically negative) about a group. It is often based on easily identifiable characteristics (e.g., sex; ethnicity).

awareness. Thus, individuals may lack the ability to report accurately on their stereotypes when completing a questionnaire.

Traditional questionnaire methods provide an assessment of *explicit* attitudes and stereotypes that is, those of which the individual is consciously aware. Some of the limitations with questionnaires can be overcome by assessing *implicit* attitudes and stereotypes, that is, those of which the individual is not consciously aware. The Implicit Association Test (IAT) was devised by Greenwald, McGhee, and Schwartz (1998) to assess unconscious stereotypes. We will consider the version of this test used by Cunningham, Preacher, and Banaji (2001) with white participants. On some trials, participants were presented with faces, and pressed one key for white faces and a second key for black faces. On other trials, they were presented with good (e.g., love, happy) and bad (e.g., poison, terrible) words, and pressed the same two keys to indicate whether each word was good or bad. In condition 1, white faces and good words were classified using one key and black faces and bad words were classified using the second key. In condition 2, white faces and bad words involved one key and black faces and good words the second key. Reaction times were much faster in condition 1 than in condition 2, suggesting the existence of implicit pro-white and anti-black stereotypes.

How different are explicit and implicit stereotypes? Cunningham et al. (2001) found that three different measures of implicit racial stereotypes all correlated positively with scores on a measure of explicit racial stereotypes (the Modern Racism Scale). The mean correlation was +.35, revealing a modest tendency for individuals having implicit racial stereotypes to have explicit ones as well. More strikingly, participants showed more evidence of prejudice on the implicit measures, indicating that the implicit measures assess prejudice *not* revealed by questionnaires.

Akrami and Ekehammar (2005) considered further the relationship between explicit and implicit stereotypes. In their first analysis, there was no relationship between explicit and implicit racial prejudice or stereotypes. However, they argued that the explicit scores of some participants were misleadingly low because they had a strong motivation to control their prejudiced reactions. When they "corrected" the explicit scores by taking account of their motivation to control prejudice, Akrami and Ekehammar found that the measures of explicit and implicit stereotypes correlated significantly with each other.

In sum, explicit and implicit measures of stereotypes typically overlap to some extent. However, implicit measures seem to assess important aspects of stereotypes that cannot be measured by explicit measures.

What characteristics do you think each of these people might possess?

WHY DO WE HAVE STEROTYPES?

Nearly everyone possesses numerous stereotypes. This suggests that stereotypes probably fulfill one or more important functions. It has often been argued (e.g., Macrae & Bodenhausen, 2000) that stereotypes provide a simple and economical way of perceiving the world. Thus, for example, we can readily categorize someone we meet for the first time on the basis of their sex, age, clothing, and so on. However, stereotypes don't only minimize the amount of information processing we need to carry out. They also fulfill important social and motivational functions. They help us to achieve a sense of social identity by allowing us to distinguish ourselves clearly from the members of other groups (Oakes, Haslam, & Turner, 1994). These two approaches are considered in turn below.

Stereotypes can help us achieve a sense of social identity.

Cognitive approach

The cognitive approach is based on the assumption that stereotypes reduce the amount of processing needed when we meet or think about other people. This could happen because relevant stereotypical information is activated automatically and effortlessly whenever we encounter a member of a given group. However, matters aren't as simple as that. Most people we meet can be categorized in several different ways (e.g., female; young; French; student), and so several stereotypes should be activated. How do we decide which stereotype to focus on? According to Macrae and Bodenhausen (2000), we initially activate all relevant stereotypes in any given situation. There is then a competition for mental dominance, in which the non-dominant stereotypes are actively inhibited.

Findings

Macrae, Milne, and Bodenhausen (1994) tested the notion that stereotypes reduce cognitive processing. Participants performed two tasks at the same time. One task involved forming impressions of various imaginary people when given their names and personality traits, and the other was a comprehension task. Half the participants were told the job held by each of the imaginary people on the impression-formation task, and so could make use of stereotypical information. For example, participants told that someone was a doctor could activate stereotypical information about the kind of person having that job (e.g., intelligent; hard-working; caring).

What would we predict? If the use of stereotypes reduces the amount of processing required, participants able to use stereotypes should have performed better on both tasks than those who couldn't use stereotypes. That was exactly what Macrae et al. (1994) found.

Sinclair and Kunda (1999) focused on the issue of the factors determining which stereotype is dominant in any given situation. They argued that we activate positive stereotypes and inhibit negative ones when motivated to think well of another person. In contrast, we activate negative stereotypes and inhibit positive ones when motivated to think badly about someone else. They had a black doctor provide positive or negative feedback concerning the participant's performance on a test of

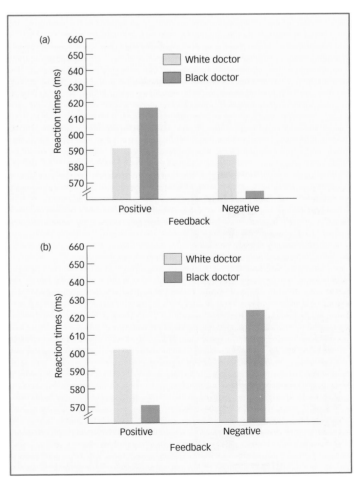

Speed of responding to black words (a) and to doctor words (b) as a function of feedback (positive or negative) received from a white doctor or a black doctor. From Sinclair and Kunda (1999). Copyright © by the American Psychological Association. Reprinted with permission.

interpersonal skills. It was assumed that participants receiving positive feedback from the black doctor would activate the doctor stereotype and inhibit the black stereotype. In contrast, those receiving negative feedback would activate the black stereotype and inhibit the doctor stereotype. The findings were precisely as predicted (see figure on the previous page). As Sinclair and Kunda (1999, p. 903) concluded, "The same individuals may be viewed through the lenses of different stereotypes by perceivers with different goals; the same Black doctor may be categorized and viewed as a doctor after delivering praise but as a Black person after delivering criticism." There was very little evidence of changes in stereotypes when the feedback was provided by a white doctor.

Evaluation

+ Stereotypes reduce the amount of cognitive processing required.

+ Stereotypical information irrelevant in a given context is inhibited.

− As we will see shortly, stereotypes are much more *flexible* than implied by the cognitive approach.

− The nature of any given stereotype varies as a function of the particular social context in which it is used (see below).

Social approach

According to the cognitive approach, most stereotypes are relatively permanent and rigid, with the same stereotypical information being activated in different situations. A very different perspective is offered by social identity theory (discussed earlier in the chapter). According to that theory, there is considerable *variability* in the specific stereotypical information activated across situations. For example, positive stereotypical information about the French may be activated when eating in a French restaurant or visiting Paris. In contrast, negative stereotypical information about the French may be activated when listening to an arrogant French politician on television or thinking about extreme right-wing French groups.

It is often assumed that stereotypes represent irrational and invalid prejudices, and so are generally undesirable. In contrast, social identity theory claims that it is inevitable (and even desirable) that individuals categorize themselves and others on the basis of their social identities as members of groups. Thus, part of our sense of who we are stems from identifying with certain groups and not identifying with other groups.

Findings

There is much evidence that the stereotypical information we focus on depends on the prevailing social context. For example, Cinnirella (1998) assigned British students to one of three tasks:

1. Provide stereotype ratings of the British only.
2. Provide stereotype ratings of the Italians only.
3. Provide stereotype ratings of the British and of the Italians.

The key assumption was that participants in condition 3 would be motivated to differentiate clearly between the British and Italian stereotypes. As a result, the positive features of the British stereotype and the negative ones of the Italian stereotype should be most evident in that condition.

What did Cinnirella (1998) find? As predicted, some components of the British stereotype (industrious, reserved) were more pronounced in condition 3 than in condition 1. In addition, the Italian stereotype was more negative in condition 3 than in condition 2. The Italians were rated as less industrious, intelligent, and progressive when compared against the British than when considered on their own.

Many people have a stereotype of the English as intelligent, tolerant, and reserved.

After you. No, after you.

Haslam et al. (1992) also found that stereotypes are flexible and influenced by social context. They assessed the stereotypes of Americans possessed by Australian students at the start and end of the Gulf War in 1991. The students did this either using Australia and Britain as the frame of reference (restricted range) or with Australia, Britain, Iraq, and the Soviet Union as the frame of reference (extended range). The favorability of the American stereotype changed as a function of the time of testing (start vs. end of conflict) and the frame of reference (see figure on the right). When the frame of reference included only Australia and Britain, the students (most of whom were anti-war) showed a reduction in stereotype favorableness over time. However, when the frame of reference included Iraq (a country with whom Australia was in conflict), the favorability of the American stereotype *increased* over time. This occurred because America was regarded as an ingroup when compared against Iraq. These findings show that stereotypes can vary considerably as a function of the specific context in which they are elicited.

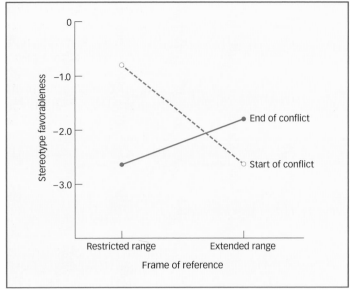

Stereotype favorableness for Americans held by Australian students as a function of time (start vs. end of 1991 Gulf War) and frame of reference (restricted range vs. extended range). Data from Haslam et al. (1992).

Evaluation

➕ Stereotypes are influenced by the immediate social context. Thus, they are flexible, and not unchanging as implied by the cognitive approach.

➕ Perceiving oneself and others in terms of social identities and stereotypes is natural and inevitable.

➖ In spite of much variability in stereotypes across situations, it is still likely that most stereotypes possess a fairly unchanging central core of meaning as suggested by cognitive theorists.

➖ We often can't predict the precise nature of an individual's stereotypes in any given situation. As Turner (1999, p. 26) pointed out, "Like all perception, they [stereotypes] vary with the expectations, needs, values, and purposes of the perceiver."

HOW ARE STEREOTYPES MAINTAINED?

Various factors help to maintain stereotypes after formation. In general, information consistent with our stereotypes is attended to and stored away in memory. In contrast, information inconsistent with our stereotypes is often ignored and/or forgotten. Bodenhausen (1988) studied the negative stereotypes many Americans have about people of Spanish origin. In his first study, American participants pretended they were jurors at a trial. The defendant was described to some as Carlos Ramirez, a Spanish-sounding name. To others, he was described as Robert Johnson. The participants then read the evidence, and decided how likely it was the defendant was guilty. Those who knew him as Carlos Ramirez rated him as more guilty than those who knew him as Robert Johnson. Thus, stereotypes lead to biased processing of information.

In his second study, Bodenhausen (1988) found out more about the processes involved. He argued that stereotypes might lead people to *attend* only to information fitting their stereotype, or it might lead them to *distort* the information to make it support their stereotype. In order to prevent participants from attending selectively to stereotype-fitting information, Bodenhausen asked them to rate each item of evidence immediately in terms of whether it favored or did not favor the defendant. Carlos Ramirez was no longer rated as more guilty than Robert Johnson. Thus, stereotypes make us attend to information fitting the stereotype and cause us to disregard other items of information.

It might be imagined that most people would remember information congruent or in line with their stereotypical views and forget incongruent information. In fact, matters are actually more complicated than that. Stangor and McMillan (1992) carried out meta-analyses to establish which kind of information is better remembered. Among individuals having weak or moderate stereotypes, information *incongruent* with the stereotype was generally remembered better than congruent information. However, congruent information was better remembered than incongruent information among individuals having strong stereotypes. Thus, memory processes serve to maintain stereotypes only for those already possessing strong stereotypes.

WHY IS IT HARD TO CHANGE STEREOTYPES?

It is generally remarkably difficult to produce long-lasting changes in someone's stereotypes. Why is this? Sherman, Stroessner, Conrey, and Azam (2005) argued that it is important to consider our attributions about other people's behavior. As we saw in Chapter 17, other people's behavior can be attributed to dispositional or internal causes (e.g., personality) or it can be attributed to situational causes. Sherman et al. presented participants with a range of behaviors exhibited by a gay man from Chicago called Robert. Participants prejudiced against homosexuality gave *internal* attributions to Robert's stereotype-consistent behaviour but *external* attributions to his stereotype-inconsistent behavior (see figure on the left). When someone's behavior is attributed to internal or dispositional causes, we expect that behavior to continue in the future. However, we don't expect behavior attributed to external causes to continue. Thus, even though the participants found that some of Robert's behavior was not consistent with the stereotype of gays, they nevertheless expected that in future he would mainly behave in a stereotype-consistent way.

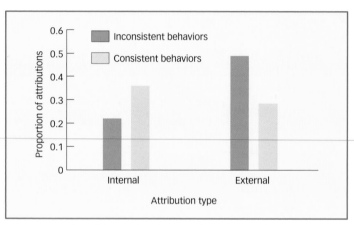

Mean proportion of internal and external attributions for stereotype-consistent and stereotype-inconsistent behaviors for participants high in prejudice. (There were no significant effects for participants low in prejudice.) From Sherman et al. (2005). Copyright © by the American Psychological Association. Reprinted with permission.

Another popular explanation of the persistence of stereotypes is based on the subtyping model (e.g., Brewer, Dull, & Lui, 1981). According to this model, individuals violating the stereotype of their group are simply assigned to a separate subtype, and so are regarded as unrepresentative of the group. For example, suppose we have a stereotype that Germans are efficient, but we meet an inefficient German professor (they do exist!). This may lead us to conclude that members of the subtype German professors are inefficient, but all other Germans are efficient (Weber & Crocker, 1983).

Kunda and Oleson (1995) predicted that people will use almost any information about deviant (stereotype-breaking) individuals to justify subtyping them and thus regarding them as unrepresentative. Participants read a copy of an interview with an introverted lawyer called Steve. He was a deviant, because the stereotype of lawyers in the United States is that they are extraverted. In order to provide the participants with some (flimsy) grounds for subtyping Steve, some were told that he worked for a small firm or for a large firm. Other participants were given no information about the size of firm for which Steve worked, and control participants didn't read the interview. All groups provided ratings of how introverted or extraverted lawyers are at the end of the experiment.

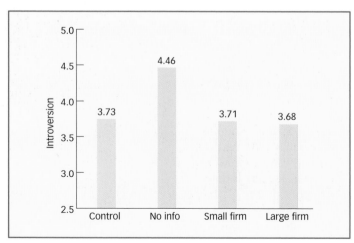

Beliefs about lawyers' introversion without specific information (control condition) or after reading about a specific lawyer called Steve (other conditions). From Kunda and Oleson (1995). Copyright © by the American Psychological Association. Reprinted with permission.

The findings are shown in the figure on the previous page. The ratings of the control group represent the standard stereotypical view that lawyers are not introverted. Those participants given the irrelevant information that Steve worked for a small or a large firm maintained their stereotypical view that lawyers are extraverted, using that information to avoid generalizing from Steve to lawyers in general. In contrast, the no-information participants who had no grounds for regarding Steve as unrepresentative of lawyers changed their stereotypical view of lawyers in the direction of perceiving them as more introverted.

PREJUDICE AND DISCRIMINATION

Many people regard prejudice and discrimination as meaning the same thing. In fact, prejudice is an attitude or belief, whereas discrimination refers to behavior or action. According to Smith and Mackie (2000, p. 156), **prejudice** is "the positive or negative evaluation of a social group and its members." It differs from stereotyping in that the emphasis with prejudice is more on emotional factors and less on cognitive ones. **Discrimination** involves negative actions (e.g., aggression; exclusion from society) directed at the members of some group.

It seems reasonable to assume that prejudice and discrimination would be closely related. Thus, the more negative your attitudes toward another group (prejudice) the more negative your behavior toward that group is likely to be (discrimination). In fact, Dovidio, Brigham, Johnson, and Gaertner (1996) carried out a meta-analysis. They found that prejudice correlated only +.32 with discrimination, indicating there is only a modest association between them. There are generally greater social pressures to avoid discrimination (which is readily observable by others) than to avoid prejudice (which is less obvious to other people).

Discrimination can take many forms. Allport (1954) argued that there are five stages of discrimination. In some situations (e.g., Nazi Germany), the level of discrimination increases rapidly from the early stages to the later ones. Here are Allport's five stages:

1. *Anti-locution*: Verbal attacks are directed against some other group.
2. *Avoidance*: The other group is systematically avoided. This can involve steps to identify group members (e.g., the Star of David worn by Jews in Nazi Germany).
3. *Discrimination*: The other group is deliberately treated less well than other groups in civil rights, job opportunities, membership of clubs, and so on.
4. *Physical attack*: Members of the other group are attacked and their property is destroyed.
5. *Extermination*: There are deliberate attempts to kill all members of the other group (e.g., the gas chambers built by the Nazis to murder the Jews).

> ## Key Terms
>
> **Prejudice:**
> an attitude or belief (usually negative) toward the members of some group on the basis of their membership of that group.
>
> **Discrimination:**
> negative actions or behavior directed against the members of some group.
>
> **Racism:**
> prejudice and/or discrimination against another group because of their race or ethnicity.

Many groups have been on the receiving end of prejudice and discrimination. However, the most vulnerable groups are those that are easily identifiable. This helps to explain why race, gender, and age are the "top three" categories used for purposes of stereotyping, prejudice, and discrimination (S. T. Fiske, 1998). We focus mainly on racism (probably the most intensively studied form of prejudice), but also consider sexism briefly.

RACISM

Racism can be defined as prejudice and discrimination against others because of their race or ethnicity. The evils of racism can be seen in the mass slaughter during the twentieth century in several countries including Germany, the former Yugoslavia, Rwanda, and South Africa. There is superficial evidence that racism is in decline in countries such as Britain and the United States. For example, S. T. Fiske (2002) argued

Discrimination against specific groups is sometimes aided by distinguishing visual characteristics (skin color, or style of dress, for example). Sometimes, however, minority group members are not clearly distinguishable from the majority and are forced to identify themselves. This was the case in Nazi Germany where Jews had to wear a Star of David on their clothing, making them a focus for racial hatred.

In a study by Allport and Postman (1947) participants were shown this picture. Later they were more likely to recall that the black man was holding the razor.

that only 10% of individuals in Western societies have overt and obvious racial biases. However, as many as 80% of people possess various subtle racial biases, which lead to "awkward social interactions, embarrassing slips of the tongue, unchecked assumptions, stereotypic judgments, and spontaneous neglect" (S. T. Fiske, 2002, p. 124).

Dovidio and Gaertner (1991) argued that large numbers of people exhibit aversive racism. **Aversive racism** can be defined as "attitudes toward members of a racial group that incorporate both egalitarian [belief in equality] social values and negative emotions, causing one to avoid interaction with members of the group" (Franzoi, 1996, p. 405). The notion of ambivalent racism (McConahay, 1986) is similar. Individuals with ambivalent racism experience much conflict between their beliefs in equality and sympathy for those who are oppressed and their beliefs that individuals are responsible for what happens to them. As a result, many white Americans are willing to praise successful black Americans, but have poor opinions of black Americans who appear unwilling to work hard.

Swim, Aikin, Hall, and Hunter (1995) argued there are three main ways in which modern racism (very similar to aversive racism) manifests itself. First, modern racists deny there is prejudice and discrimination against minority groups. Second, they show annoyance and impatience at the fact that minority groups demand equal treatment with the majority group. Third, they have feelings of resentment at the prospect of minority groups receiving positive action to assist them.

We can study racism by seeing whether a given ambiguous situation is interpreted differently depending on whether the central figure is, say, white or black. This was done by Duncan (1976), who asked white American students to watch a conversation between a black man and a white man. When the white person gently shoved the black person, the action was interpreted as violent by only 13% of the participants. In contrast, 73% of the participants interpreted the same action as violent when the black man did the shoving.

Racial bias influences even basic perceptual processes. Payne (2001) presented a photograph of a male face (white or black) briefly. The photograph of an object was then presented, and participants decided rapidly whether it was a handgun or a handtool. White participants were more likely to identify a tool mistakenly as a gun when preceded by a black face than when preceded by a white face, and this seems to have happened automatically. Individuals high in explicit prejudice showed more racial bias on this task than those low in explicit prejudice. Allport (1954) discussed his famous study in the United States in which white Americans saw the drawing top left. They were asked afterwards to indicate who had the knife in his hand. Many participants misremembered (and perhaps misperceived), claiming that it was the black man.

SEXISM

Sexism involves prejudice against individuals purely on the basis of their sex. Probably the commonest sexist assumptions are that women are more caring than men, but men are more assertive and competent. These assumptions have been found in many parts of the world, including Australia, Europe, North America, and South America (Deaux, 1985).

Sexism is apparent in what is known as the "glass ceiling": women in most Western societies are as well qualified as men, but occupy under 10% of top positions (e.g., CEO). Eagly and Karau (2002) explained this in their role congruity theory. According to this theory, women are thwarted in their attempts to achieve top positions because of two forms of prejudice:

1. Men typically evaluate women's potential for leadership less highly than that of men. This is because there are large discrepancies between the perceived qualities needed for

leadership (e.g., decisive; action-oriented; courageous) and perceptions of the female gender role (e.g., helpful; sympathetic; nurturant).

2. Leadership behavior that is decisive and action-oriented and thus conforms to expectation is regarded more favorably when shown by a man than by a woman.

Davison and Burke (2000) reviewed several studies in which half the participants received a résumé (CV) with a male name attached to it and the other half received the same résumé with a female name attached. Men were preferred to women for jobs rated as male sex-typed (i.e., involving skills typically associated with men). The relevance of this finding is that most leadership positions are male sex-typed.

Additional support for role congruity theory comes from Eagly, Makhijani, and Konsky (1992) in a review of studies in which leadership behavior was described and ascribed to a man or a woman. In their meta-analysis of 61 studies, this behavior was rated less highly when performed by a woman. Of most importance, the tendency to devalue women's leadership behavior was much greater when the behavior was stereotypically masculine (e.g., directive or autocratic).

In sum, there is much support for role congruity theory. However, the prejudicial effects obtained in most of the studies and meta-analyses accounted for only 1–5% of the variability in the data. Thus, it is not clear whether such effects can account fully for the "glass ceiling."

AUTHORITARIAN PERSONALITY

Adorno, Frenkel-Brunswik, Levinson, and Sanford (1950) argued that people with an authoritarian personality are most likely to be prejudiced. The **authoritarian personality** includes the following characteristics:

- Rigid beliefs in conventional values.
- General hostility toward other groups.
- Intolerance of ambiguity.
- Submissive attitude toward authority figures.

How does the authoritarian personality develop? According to Adorno et al. (1950), it has its roots in childhood experiences. Children receiving a harsh upbringing with little affection and much punishment from their parents are most likely to develop an authoritarian personality. This treatment causes the child to have much hostility toward his/her parents. However, this hostility remains unconscious because the child is unwilling to admit to it. This hostility is displaced on to nonthreatening minority groups, and appears in the form of prejudice. Thus, the hostility that harshly treated children can't express toward their parents is later redirected onto innocent groups.

> ### Key Term
>
> **Authoritarian personality:** a type of personality characterized by rigid beliefs, hostility toward other groups, and submissive attitudes toward those in authority.

Adorno et al. (1950) devised various questionnaires. One was the F (Facism)-Scale, designed to measure the attitudes of the authoritarian personality. Here is a sample item: "Most of our social problems would be solved if we could somehow get rid of the immoral, crooked, and feeble-minded people."

Adorno et al. (1950) found that high scorers on the F-Scale were more prejudiced than low scorers. Pettigrew and Meertens (1995) reported that authoritarian individuals in France, the Netherlands, Britain, and Germany were prejudiced against a wide range of outgroups. Adorno et al. also found (as predicted by their theory) that high scorers on the F-Scale reported being treated more harshly than nonauthoritarian individuals during childhood. However, the finding of an association between certain childhood experiences and an authoritarian personality doesn't prove that the childhood experiences *caused* the authoritarian personality.

Children who receive a harsh upbringing with little parental affection are most likely to develop an authoritarian personality. The child's anger toward his/her parents is repressed only to emerge in later life in the form of prejudice.

The nine personality traits of the authoritarian personality, from Adorno et al.'s F-Scale

Traits	Description
Conventionalism	Very conventional, great dislike of change
Authoritarian–Submissive	Deferential to authority
Authoritarian–Aggressive	Very hostile to people who challenge authority
Anti-inception	Very intolerant of behavior that is "Wrong" in any way
Superstition & stereotype	Believes in fate
Power & "toughness"	Has a dominating and bullying manner
Destructiveness & cynicism	Very hostile toward anyone with whom they disagree
Projectivity	Projects own unconscious impulses onto other people
Sex	Has an exaggerated interest in sexual behavior that is not regarded as "normal"

Adorno et al.'s approach has several limitations. First, Altemeyer (1988) obtained evidence suggesting that the roots of authoritarianism lie in adolescence rather than early childhood. Adolescents whose parents are authoritarian imitate their parents' behavior, and are often rewarded for doing so.

Second, measures of the authoritarian personality assess social attitudes rather than personality. Personality changes little over time but it is easy to produce changes in authoritarianism scores. For example, Altemeyer (1988) found that showing people scenarios concerning threatening social changes produced substantial increases in authoritarianism scores.

Third, and most important, prejudice depends more on cultural norms than on individual personality. For example, Pettigrew (1958) found that the levels of authoritarianism were the same in South Africa and in the United States. However, there was much more prejudice in South Africa than the United States because of political and cultural factors.

REALISTIC GROUP CONFLICT

Sherif (1966) argued that prejudice often results from intergroup conflict (see Jackson, 1993, for a review). Each group has its own interests and goals. When two groups compete for the same goal this creates realistic conflict, which can cause the members of each group to become prejudiced against the members of the other group. That is the central assumption of realistic conflict theory. Sometimes two groups have the same interests and are pursuing the same goal. When that happens, the two groups will often cooperate with each other and there will be an absence of prejudice.

Findings

In a famous study by Sherif et al. (1961), prejudice was created between two groups of ordinary boys at a summer camp—see the Key Study on the following page.

Sherif et al.'s (1961) key findings have been replicated in various cultures. However, competition doesn't always lead to prejudice and intergroup conflict. Tyerman and Spencer (1983) argued that competition mainly has dramatic effects when those involved are initially strangers, as in the Sherif et al. study. Tyerman and Spencer observed scouts who already knew each other well as they competed in groups against each other in their annual camp. Competition didn't produce the negative effects obtained by Sherif et al.

People who feel strongly about a particular cause are sometimes likely to experience violent clashes with people who do not share the same values. Here, the Argentinean Piqueteros movement, supporters of President Cristina Fernandez's government, clash in Buenos Aires with demonstrators from the opposition (farmers protesting against President Fernandez's tax hike on grain exports).

Key Study

Sherif et al. (1961): The Robber's Cave study

In this study 22 boys who didn't initially know each other spent 2 weeks at a summer camp in the United States. There were two groups (the Eagles and the Rattlers), who were told that the group performing better in various competitions would receive a trophy, knives, and medals. This competition led to a fight breaking out between the members of the two groups, and the Rattlers' flag was burned.

There was much prejudice. Each group regarded its own members as friendly and courageous whereas the members of the other group were smart-alecks and liars. When the boys identified their friends, 93% of them were members of the same group and only 7% came from the other group.

Various attempts were made to reduce the conflict between the Eagles and the Rattlers. For example, the camp's drinking water was turned off, and the two groups had to combine forces to restore the supply. Other tasks requiring co-operation between the groups were rescuing a truck that had got stuck and pitching tents. A consequence of pursuing these common goals was that the groups became much friendlier toward each other. When asked again to identify their friends at the camp, 30% of their choices after these cooperative activities were members of the other group.

Discussion points
1. Why has the study by Sherif et al. been so influential?
2. How important is group conflict as a cause of prejudice?

KEY STUDY EVALUATION
Sherif et al.'s study has been regarded as very important because it showed ordinary boys acting in different ways toward each other depending on the situation. Competition resulted in dislike and hostility; a common goal led to friendship and good feelings. It might be interesting to speculate about whether the results would have been different if all the participants had been girls. It has been argued that while they are growing up girls are rewarded for cooperation, whereas boys are rewarded for competitiveness. It could also be argued that the participants were not a representative group, in that they were not randomly selected.

Ember (1981) studied 26 small societies. As predicted by realistic group conflict theory, intergroup violence was much more frequent when societies had to compete for resources because of population pressures or severe food shortages.

Zárate, Garcia, Garza, and Hitlan (2004) studied prejudice against Mexican immigrants at the University of Texas at El Paso, which is on the border between the United States and Mexico. They predicted from realistic group conflict theory that prejudice against Mexican immigrants would be increased if participants focused on similarities between the two groups in work-related traits. The findings supported this prediction (see figure on the following page), presumably because this manipulation threatened participants' sense of job security. There was also evidence for the importance of cultural threat. When differences between Mexican immigrants and native Americans on interpersonal traits were emphasized, this led to increased prejudice.

Mean evaluation of an outgroup (Mexican immigrants) as a function of participants having previously rated how similar or different the outgroup was to their ingroup with respect to work-related traits or interpersonal traits (the self condition is a control condition). High evaluation scores indicate more prejudice than low scores. From Zarate et al. (2004). Copyright © 2004 Elsevier. Reproduced with permission.

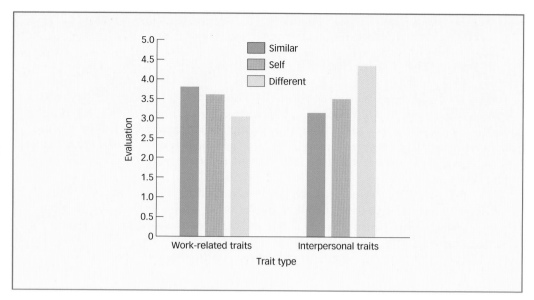

Evaluation

⊕ Competition between two groups for the same goal can lead to prejudice.

⊕ Realistic conflict theory helps to explain the large increases in prejudice found when countries are at war with each other.

⊖ According to the theory, conflicts arise when group interests are threatened. However, group interests are defined very vaguely: "A real or imagined threat to the safety of the group, an economic interest, a political advantage, a military consideration, prestige, or a number of others" (Sherif, 1966, p. 15).

⊖ Realistic conflict is not always sufficient to produce prejudice (e.g., Tyerman & Spencer, 1983). It is also not necessary, because millions of people have prejudiced attitudes toward people in other cultures with whom they are not in competition. Additional factors such as cultural threat also need to be considered (e.g., Zárate et al., 2004).

SOCIAL IDENTITY THEORY

According to social identity theory (discussed earlier), individuals seek to distinguish their ingroup as clearly as possible from outgroups. They typically regard their ingroup favorably in comparison with outgroups to boost their self-esteem. As a result, members of outgroups may be exposed to prejudice and discrimination.

Doosje, Branscombe, Spears, and Manstead (1998) considered the attitudes of Dutch people toward Indonesia (previously a Dutch colony). Some participants had a high level of national identification with being Dutch, whereas others had only a low level. As predicted by social identity theory, those having the greatest ingroup bias (i.e., high level of national identification) felt less guilty about Dutch treatment of the Indonesians. They were also less willing to compensate the Indonesians than were those having little ingroup bias (i.e., low level of national identification).

Verkuyten, Drabbles, and van den Nieuwenhuijzen (1999) tested predictions of social identity theory in Dutch participants aged between 16 and 18. These participants indicated how strongly they identified themselves with the majority ingroup in Holland. Their level of prejudice was assessed by asking them to indicate their emotional reactions to descriptions of situations involving ethnic minorities (e.g., "More and more Islamic people who have different views and habits have come to live in the Netherlands. Because of this there is an increasing danger that the Dutch norms and values are threatened"). Individuals identifying themselves most strongly as Dutch revealed the greatest negative emotions toward ethnic minorities. Thus, group identification was related to prejudice as predicted by social identity theory.

In sum, social identity theory helps to account for individual differences in prejudice. However, it provides a limited view, because it ignores important factors such as intergroup competition and conflict. Another limitation is that the theory indicates why prejudice and social conflict exist, but doesn't make it clear in detail *how* they develop.

REDUCING PREJUDICE AND DISCRIMINATION

What can be done to reduce (and ideally eliminate) prejudice and discrimination? Psychologists have provided several answers to that question, and some of the main ones are discussed here.

INTERGROUP CONTACT HYPOTHESIS

Allport (1954) argued in his intergroup contact hypothesis that the most effective way of reducing prejudice is by intergroup contact. Four conditions need to be met if such contact is to prove successful:

1. The two groups have equal status within the situation in which the contact takes place.
2. The two groups work toward common goals. Efforts to achieve these common goals are based on intergroup cooperation.
3. Intergroup contact must occur often (and long) enough to permit the development of meaningful relationships between the members of the different groups.
4. There should be social and institutional support for intergroup acceptance.

Wright, McLaughlin-Volpe, and Ropp (1997) developed some of Allport's ideas. They found evidence for the **extended contact effect**: prejudice is reduced when a member of your ingroup is very friendly with a member of the other group.

Having children work in groups helps reduce racial barriers.

Findings

Aronson and Osherow (1980) obtained support for the intergroup contact hypothesis. Schools in Austin, Texas had recently been desegregated, and there were concerns about racial conflict. One class of black and white children was divided into small groups for a learning task (e.g., the life of Abraham Lincoln). Within each group, every child learned a different part of the information. Each group member then taught what he/she had learned to the others. After that, the children received a mark based on their overall topic knowledge. This approach was called the **jigsaw classroom**, because all the children contributed just as all the pieces of jigsaw are needed to complete it.

The findings from the jigsaw classroom were promising. The children showed higher self-esteem, better

> **Key Terms**
>
> **Extended contact effect:**
> knowledge that a member of your ingroup has formed a close relationship with a member of another group can reduce prejudice against that other group.
>
> **Jigsaw classroom:**
> an approach to teaching designed to reduce prejudice in which the teacher ensures that all children in the class contribute to the achievement.

Case Study: *New Era Schools Trust*

The New Era Schools Trust (or NEST) runs three boarding schools in South Africa, in Durban, Johannesburg, and Cape Town. The unique aim of all the NEST schools is not only to produce well-educated and personable young people, but also to eliminate any trace of racial prejudice in their students. To achieve this, all races are mixed together from the very first day at school, living and studying alongside each other in a way that is rare even in post-apartheid South Africa. The teachers are similarly multiracial, and there is an equal mix of boys and girls.

Not only are the different races regarded as equal in NEST schools, their cultures are also given equal value. Schools in South Africa have generally taken the view that African culture is irrelevant, and have taught exclusively from a white perspective. At NEST schools the pupils study Xhosa poets as well as Keats, and the lives of Zulu warriors as well as Napoleon. This sense of total equality permeates everything—there are no prefects or top-down discipline, no uniforms or corporal punishment, and everyone takes a hand in doing the chores.

NEST has found that more black parents than white parents wish their children to attend a NEST school. White children tend to have better access to well-equipped schools where they are not required to help clean the dormitories, whereas many black parents are keen for their children to leave the deprivation of the townships to receive their education. This imbalance is lessening, however, as white parents realize what good academic success the NEST schools are achieving. In 1992 their pass rate was 100%, when private white schools and white church schools averaged 90%.

(Based on an article by Prue Leith, *The Times*, May 1993.)

school performance, more liking for their classmates, and reduced prejudice. However, these effects were small, probably because the jigsaw classroom was only used for 12 hours spread over 6 weeks.

Rosenfield, Stephan, and Lucker (1981) identified problems with the jigsaw classroom. Minority group members low in competence were blamed for slowing down the learning of the more competent students. This confirmed existing prejudiced attitudes rather than reducing them.

A thorough test of the intergroup contact hypothesis was carried out at Wexler Middle School in Waterford in the United States (see Brown, 1986). The number of black and white students was similar so that it wouldn't be regarded as a black or a white school. Much was done to make all the students feel equal, with very little streaming on the basis of ability. Cooperation was encouraged by having the students work together to buy special equipment for everyone.

The results over the first 3 years were moderately encouraging. There were many black–white friendships, but they rarely extended to visiting each other's homes. There was a steady reduction in discrimination, with the behavior of the black and white students toward each other being friendly. However, some stereotyped beliefs remained. Black and white students agreed that black students are tougher and more assertive than white students, and that white students are cleverer and work harder.

Tropp and Pettigrew (2005) pointed out that most studies on intergroup contact have focused only on the effects of such contact on the majority group. Tripp and Pettigrew found by carrying out meta-analyses that the beneficial effects of intergroup contact are greater for majority than for minority groups. The correlation between amount of intergroup contact and prejudice was −.23 for majority groups compared to only −.18 for minority groups. Tropp and Pettigrew found that the beneficial effects of intergroup contact on majority groups were especially large when the conditions under which that contact occurred were those regarded as optimal by Allport (1954). However, this was *not* the case for minority groups. Members of minority groups may be so aware of their lower status that it reduces any positive effects of intergroup contact.

Evaluation

➕ The intergroup contact hypothesis identified several factors influencing whether intergroup contact will reduce prejudice.

➕ Much evidence provides general support for the hypothesis in majority groups. However, while it is fairly easy to reduce prejudice to individual members of another group, it is much more difficult to ensure this *generalizes* to all members of the other group.

➖ It is difficult to interpret the finding that high levels of intergroup contact are associated with low levels of prejudice within the majority group. One possibility is that prejudiced individuals do their best to avoid intergroup contact.

➖ The intergroup contact hypothesis has little to say about *how* or *why* contact reduces prejudice, and it doesn't indicate how positive contact with individual members of an outgroup might generalize to include other members of that outgroup.

➖ Intergroup contact typically has little effect on prejudice within minority groups (Tropp & Pettigrew, 2005).

SALIENT CATEGORIZATION AND RECATEGORIZATION

Suppose someone prejudiced against an outgroup has positive social interactions with a member of that outgroup. Such interactions may well lead to liking for that individual. However, this often doesn't lead to reduced prejudice toward the outgroup as a whole. We will now consider two theoretical approaches designed to solve this problem (and other issues relating to prejudice).

Salient categorization

Why do positive experiences with one member of an outgroup often fail to generalize to other members of that outgroup? According to Hewstone and Brown (1986), the group member is generally regarded as "an exception to the rule." What is needed is to make the outgroup member's group membership salient or obvious so that he/she is perceived as typical or representative of his/her group. Thus, salient categorization may provide the key. Salient categorization is an important ingredient in the multicultural approach, according to which group differences should be acknowledged and celebrated.

According to social identity theorists (see earlier in the chapter) emphasizing group differences has to be handled sensitively if it is to reduce prejudice. For example, individuals typically distinguish between an ingroup and an outgroup, and show ingroup bias or favoritism that can easily turn into prejudice. There is a danger that salient categorization may simply serve to *increase* prejudice against other groups.

Van Oudenhouven, Groenewoud, and Hewstone (1996) tested the notion that it is important for the group membership of an outgroup member to be salient or obvious if prejudice is to be reduced. Dutch participants spent 2 hours interacting with a Turkish confederate in one of three conditions:

1. The experimenter never mentioned the confederate's ethnicity (low salience).
2. The experimenter only mentioned the confederate's ethnicity at the end of the 2-hour period (moderate salience).
3. The confederate's ethnicity was emphasized throughout the session (high salience).

Attitudes toward Turks in general were more favorable in the moderate and high salience conditions than in the low salience condition.

Brown, Vivian, and Hewstone (1999) carried out a study in which British participants worked with a German confederate to obtain a substantial reward. The German confederate either seemed to correspond fairly closely to the typical German stereotype or was clearly atypical. In addition, participants were given false information about how similar or dissimilar German people are with respect to several characteristics. It was assumed that it would be easiest to generalize from the German confederate to all Germans when the confederate was regarded as typical and when the Germans were thought to be similar to each other. As predicted, participants in that condition had the most favorable attitudes toward the Germans.

Voci and Hewstone (2003) studied prejudice toward immigrants shown by Italian hospital workers. They found that the effects of intergroup contact on prejudice depended very much on group salience. As predicted, reduced prejudice occurred most frequently when hospital workers had positive contact with immigrants, and the group to which immigrants belonged was salient. Positive contact plus group salience reduced anxiety about immigrants, which then led to reduced prejudice.

Evaluation

+ Salient categorization has been shown experimentally to reduce prejudice to entire outgroups rather than simply to specific individuals.

+ Much nonexperimental research in education has found that multiculturalism (which resembles salient categorization) improves intergroup relations more than the alternative color-blind or recategorization approach (see Richeson & Nussbaum, 2004, and next section).

− When people already possess a clear stereotype of another group, it may be very difficult to persuade them that a given individual is actually a typical member of that group.

− "If the cooperative interaction goes wrong . . . then structuring the interaction at the intergroup level could make matters worse . . . there is a risk of reinforcing negative stereotypes of the outgroup precisely because those people are seen as typical of it" (Brown, 2000, p. 353).

Recategorization

As we saw earlier, there is evidence of ingroup bias in which individuals regard their own group as superior to other groups. This phenomenon suggests a way of dealing with prejudice. Prejudice could be eliminated by a process of **recategorization** in which the ingroup and outgroup are recategorized to form a single ingroup. Precisely this was proposed by Gaertner et al. (1993). Recategorization is of central importance with the

Television and the reduction of prejudice

The Children's Television Workshop (CTW) does more than make the *Sesame Street* series. In a research project with Israel Educational Television and Al-Quds University's Institute for Modern Media, in east Jerusalem they made a similar set of television programs for preschoolers aimed at Israeli and Palestinian children (*Rechov Sumsum/Shara'a Simsim* Research Symposium, 1999). Prejudiced attitudes toward the other culture had been found in children as young as 4 years old. The agenda of the programs was to emphasize similarities between children in the two cultures. The series *Rechov Sumsum/Shara'a Simsim* (Hebrew and Arabic translation, respectively) was broadcast to viewers in Israel and the West Bank in 1998. A follow-up study in 1999 showed a small but real reduction in the prejudiced attitudes of child viewers.

color-blind perspective, according to which category memberships should be reduced or eliminated.

Gaertner et al. (1994) studied recategorization in a multi-ethnic high school in the United States. They carried out a survey, part of which consisted of items focusing on the notion that there was a single ingroup within the school. Those students who thought the school consisted of one large ingroup had the most positive attitudes toward other ethnic groups in the school.

Dovidio, Gaertner, and Validzic (1998) had two groups working together on a task. These groups were equal or unequal in status, and their area of expertise was either the same or different. There was most recategorization of the two groups as a single ingroup when the two groups were equal in status and their expertise differed. As predicted, this was the *only* condition in which outgroup prejudice was eliminated. Dovidio et al. speculated that intergroup contact reduces prejudice mainly when it serves to produce recategorization.

Individuals often exhibit much more prejudice than was shown in the study by Dovidio et al. (1998). A test of the importance of recategorization under more realistic conditions was conducted by Dovidio et al. (2004). White participants watched a videotape showing examples of racial discrimination, followed by assessment of their level of prejudice. Those who had previously been exposed to a recategorization manipulation (told that a terrorist threat was directed at black and white Americans) showed reduced prejudice compared to another group told that a terrorist threat was directed only at white Americans.

Recategorization can involve some loss of social identity as an individual's ingroup is combined into a larger group, and this may have negative consequences. Evidence that this is a danger was reported by Crisp, Stone, and Hall (2006), who divided their participants into those with low and those with high ingroup identification. Participants who identified with their ingroup showed evidence of *increased* prejudice following recategorization.

Evaluation

+ Recategorization has been shown to produce beneficial effects including prejudice reduction whether the initial prejudice was high (e.g., Dovidio et al., 2004) or low (e.g., Dovidio et al., 1998).

− It is difficult to change perceptions of an outgroup in the face of pre-existing strong and habitual prejudice, as is often the case in the real world.

− Individuals may perceive that any potential gains from recategorization are outweighed by the loss of their social identity stemming from their current ingroup membership (e.g., Crisp et al., 2006).

OVERALL SUMMARY

Intergroup contact often reduces prejudice within majority groups under the appropriate conditions (e.g., the two groups are of equal status within the situation; meaningful relationships are developed). Two mechanisms that can enhance the beneficial effects of intergroup contact are salient categorization and recategorization, both of which stem from the social identity approach. However, there are limitations and dangers associated with use of both mechanisms, and salient categorization can increase ingroup bias and thus prejudice. It is important for future research to discover *why* intergroup contact generally fails to reduce prejudice within minority groups, and to use that knowledge to devise ways of remedying the situation.

Chapter Summary

Social identity

- According to social identity theory, social identities make us feel good about ourselves and enhance our self-esteem.
- Ingroup bias or favoritism has been found with the allocation of both positive and negative outcomes.
- Ingroup bias increases the self-esteem of members of the ingroup. However, there is no tendency for individuals who initially have low self-esteem to exhibit more ingroup bias than those with high self-esteem.
- Social identity theory focuses on the cognitive processes underlying group identification and de-emphasizes emotional and motivational factors.

Stereotypes

- Contrary to what is often believed to be the case, there is a grain of truth in most stereotypes.
- Problems with questionnaire assessment of stereotypes (e.g., social desirability bias) can be overcome by assessing implicit stereotypes or attitudes.
- According to the cognitive approach, stereotypes reduce the amount of processing needed when we meet or think about other people. However, stereotypes are used much more flexibly than is assumed within this approach.
- According to the social approach, the stereotypical information we focus on depends on the prevailing social context. However, most stereotypes have an unchanging central core of meaning.
- It is difficult to change stereotypes because individuals violating the stereotype of their group are regarded as unrepresentative and are assigned to a separate subtype.

Prejudice and discrimination

- There is only a modest association between prejudice and discrimination, because there are greater social pressures to avoid discrimination.
- Millions of people in Western societies exhibit aversive or ambivalent racism, which involves a conflict between egalitarian values and negative emotions.
- According to role congruity theory, women occupy few top positions for two reasons. First, they are regarded as not possessing the qualities needed for leadership. Second, decisive leadership is regarded less favorably when shown by a woman than by a man.
- According to Adorno et al. (1950), individuals with an authoritarian personality are prejudiced because they displace hostility toward their parents onto minority groups. In fact, however, prejudice depends more on cultural norms than on personality.
- According to realistic group conflict theory, prejudice results from intergroup conflict. There is support for this theory, but intergroup conflict is neither necessary nor sufficient to produce prejudice.
- According to social identity theory, individuals showing the greatest ingroup bias should be most prejudiced against outgroups. There is support for this prediction, but the theory ignores other determinants of prejudice (e.g., intergroup conflict).

Reducing prejudice and discrimination

- According to Allport's intergroup contact hypothesis, intergroup contact between two groups of equal status working toward common goals produces reduced prejudice.
- There is reasonable support for the intergroup contact hypothesis. However, support is stronger for majority groups than for minority ones, and it may mainly be people who are already unprejudiced who seek intergroup contact.
- Producing a reduction in prejudice is often easier when an outgroup member's group membership is made salient or obvious.
- Prejudice can be reduced by recategorization, in which the ingroup and the outgroup are recategorized to form a single ingroup. However, there can be problems if group members have a sense of loss of their social identity.

Further Reading

- Brewer, M.B. (2003). *Intergroup relations* (2nd ed.). Philadelphia: Open University Press. This is a wide-ranging book that includes much coverage of prejudice and prejudice reduction.
- Hewstone, M., Rubin, M., & Willis, H. (2002). Intergroup bias. *Annual Review of Psychology*, *53*, 575–604. This paper contains a good account of various theoretical accounts of intergroup bias and conflict.
- Hogg, M.A., & Vaughan, G.M. (2005). *Social psychology* (4th. ed.). Harlow, UK: Prentice Hall. Chapters 10 and 11 of this excellent textbook provide clear discussions of intergroup phenomena including prejudice.
- Wright, S.C., & Taylor, D.M. (2003). The social psychology of cultural diversity: Social stereotyping, prejudice, and discrimination. In M.A. Hogg & J. Cooper (Eds.), *The Sage handbook of social psychology*. London: Sage. All of the main topics dealt with in this chapter are discussed thoroughly by Wright and Taylor in this book.

INTRODUCTION TO
Abnormal Psychology

We live in an era in which huge numbers of people struggle to cope with various serious psychological problems. In the United States, as Comer (2001, p. 7) pointed out:

Up to 10 of every hundred adults have a significant anxiety disorder, 10 suffer from profound depression, 5 display a personality disorder . . . 1 has schizophrenia . . . and 11 abuse alcohol or other drugs. Add to these figures as many as 600,000 suicide attempts, 500,000 rapes, and 3 million cases of child abuse each year, and it becomes apparent abnormal psychological functioning is a pervasive problem.

Twenge (2000) assessed trait anxiety (tendency to experience much anxiety) among American children and college students. The mean score for both groups was much higher than used to be the case. This led Twenge (2000, p. 1007) to conclude that, "The average American child in the 1980s reported more anxiety than child psychiatric patients in the 1950s." This suggests that we live in a world that is becoming ever more stressed. I am not so sure. It is probably truer to say that the nature of life's stressors has changed somewhat over the past century or so. As little as 100 years ago, for example, life expectancy in the Western world was 30 years less than now. As a result, young and middle-aged people in those days were probably much more worried and stressed about their physical health than is the case today. We may worry about how to find the money for a good holiday somewhere in the sun. However, 100 years ago most people couldn't afford to have any holidays at all, and it was often a struggle to put food on the table.

The focus of this chapter is on abnormal psychology. The achievements of psychologists in this area can be seen very clearly by considering history. For many centuries, the treatment applied to those suffering from mental disorders was positively barbaric. It was believed that mental disorders were caused by demons or other supernatural forces. Popular "cures" for mental illness involved making things as unpleasant as possible for the demons. The techniques used included immersing the patient in boiling hot water, flogging, starvation, and torture. It was thought these "cures" would persuade the demons to leave the patient's body and so remove his/her disorder.

As is well-known, Sigmund Freud (at the end of the nineteenth century) was the first psychologist to argue strongly that psychological approaches to treatment were needed (see Chapter 2). He was also the first psychologist to provide a detailed and systematic therapeutic approach by developing psychoanalysis (discussed in detail later). As a result of these contributions (and numerous others in many areas of psychology), he is deservedly the most famous psychologist of all time.

THE DOCTOR THINKS THAT "NO WELL-REGULATED INSTITUTION SHOULD BE UNPROVIDED WITH THE CIRCULATING SWING." 1818.

An illustration of an early nineteenth century swing used to treat depression. The "circulating swing" was supposed to bring the depressive "back to sound reasoning."

If we go back before the time of Sigmund Freud, it is worth mentioning the Austrian mystic and physician Franz Mesmer (1734–1815). He treated patients suffering from various complaints by sitting them around a tub containing magnetized iron filings with protruding iron rods. It was claimed that cures were produced by the "animal magnetism" generated by this bizarre arrangement. Subsequently, however, it became clear that the sleep-like or hypnotic state involved in the exercise (rather than any animal magnetism!) was responsible for the cures that were achieved. The importance of Mesmer's work is that he showed (although he didn't realize it at the time!) that mental disorders could be cured by psychological techniques.

Chapters 21 and 22 are devoted to the key issues relating to mental disorders. These key issues can be expressed in the form of five questions. First, how can we best describe and categorize mental disorders? Second, what are the major psychological approaches that have been applied to mental disorders in recent decades? Third, what are the factors responsible for the development of the various mental disorders? Fourth, what are the main forms of psychological therapy that have been used to treat individuals with mental disorders? Fifth, how can we assess the effectiveness of different forms of psychological therapy in producing beneficial changes in individuals suffering from mental disorders?

We can illustrate the above issues by considering a hypothetical individual, Matthew. Matthew is extremely shy, and dislikes most social occasions. Indeed, he is so frightened of possible humiliation when involved in a social situation that he will often make what sound to other people like feeble excuses to avoid them. He goes to see a clinical psychologist, because he is so concerned about his condition.

The successful treatment of Matthew's conditions involves several steps. First, we need to decide the precise nature of the problem. Thus, diagnosing his condition is important. Second, it may be useful to consider Matthew's condition within the context of the main models or theoretical approaches to abnormal psychology. Third, we need to combine our diagnosis of his condition with an appropriate model to appreciate the factors responsible for his problem. Fourth, we need to treat Matthew to eliminate his symptoms and prevent them from recurring. Fifth, we need to use various measures (e.g., assessing his mood state, ability to function in everyday life, and his general behavior) to reassure ourselves that the treatment has been effective.

Chapter 21 deals with the various psychological problems and disorders that individuals can experience. This area is also known as **psychopathology**, which is "the field concerned with the nature and development of mental disorders" (Davison & Neale, 1998, p. G-19). More than 200 mental disorders have been identified, and most (but not all) of these disorders are found in virtually every country in the world. More specifically, Chapter 21 provides answers to the first three questions posed above. In other words, it is concerned with issues such as the diagnosis of mental disorders, identifying the main theoretical approaches to abnormality, and developing an understanding of the factors responsible for the main mental disorders.

The emphasis in Chapter 22 is very different from the one adopted in Chapter 21: it is concerned with *practical* issues relating to the forms of therapy provided by clinical psychologists, psychiatrists, and others. It is over 100 years since Freud first proposed a systematic form of treatment for mental disorders, since when numerous other forms of treatment have been devised. Chapter 22 answers the fourth and fifth questions posed earlier. That is to say, there is a detailed discussion of the major forms of therapy associated with each of the main approaches to abnormality. After this has been

Key Term

Psychopathology: the study of the nature and development of mental disorders; an abnormal pattern of functioning.

accomplished there is an attempt to evaluate the effectiveness of these forms of treatment. As we will see, it is surprisingly difficult to come to definitive conclusions concerning the relative effectiveness of different forms of therapy. However, the good news is that all of the main types of treatment have been shown beyond any doubt to be at least moderately effective in the treatment of a wide range of mental disorders. There is also some evidence that certain forms of treatment are especially successful and effective when applied to specific mental disorders.

Chapter 21

Contents

Approaches to abnormality

21

WHAT IS ABNORMALITY?

It is more difficult than you might imagine to decide whether a given individual is abnormal or suffers from a mental disorder. Why is that? The central problem is that concepts such as "abnormality" and "mental disorder" are vague. As Lilienfeld and Marino (1999) pointed out, the concept of "mental disorder" has fuzzy boundaries, so that "there is no . . . set of criteria in nature that can be used to definitively distinguish all cases of disorder from all cases of nondisorder" (p. 400).

One reason we cannot be precise about these issues is because they depend in part on the prevailing social norms and values. For example, consider changing views about homosexuality as reflected in a major classificatory system known as the Diagnostic and Statistical Manual of Mental Disorders (DSM). In DSM-II, published in 1968, homosexuality was classified as a mental disorder involving sexual deviation. By 1987, with the publication of DSM-III-R (the revised third edition), only homosexuals having "persistent and marked distress about their sexual orientation" were regarded as having a disorder.

FOUR Ds

In spite of the vagueness of the concept of "abnormality" or "mental disorder," we can identify features often (but not invariably) associated with it. Comer (2001) argued there are four central features (known as the four Ds):

- *Deviance*: This involves thinking and behaving in ways not regarded as acceptable within a given society. According to Comer (2001, p. 3), "Behavior, thoughts, and emotions are deemed abnormal when they violate a society's ideas about proper functioning. Each society establishes norms—explicit and implicit rules for proper conduct . . . Behavior, thoughts, and emotions that violate norms of psychological functioning are called abnormal."
- *Distress*: It is not sufficient for behavior to be deviant for it to be regarded as abnormal. For example, Comer (2001) pointed out that there are people in Michigan called the Ice Breakers, who go swimming in extremely cold lakes every weekend between November and February. This behavior violates society's norms. However, it wouldn't generally be regarded as abnormal, in part because the Ice Breakers experience no distress. Thus, deviant thoughts and behavior need to cause distress to the individual and/or others to be considered abnormal.
- *Dysfunction*: According to Comer (2001, p. 4), "Abnormal behavior tends to be dysfunctional; that is, it interferes with daily functioning. It so upsets, distracts, or confuses people that they cannot care for themselves properly, participate in ordinary social interactions, or work productively." Most people exhibit dysfunctional behavior in this sense when bereaved, but the duration of such behavior is less than in most cases of abnormality.

Abnormal behavior...?

...Not when rescuing a cat!

- *Danger*: Individuals whose behavior poses a threat or danger to themselves or to others are generally regarded as abnormal. However, most individuals having a mental disorder do *not* pose a danger to anyone, and some dangerous individuals (e.g., armed criminals) don't suffer from a mental disorder.

Comer (2001, p. 5) concluded that the four-D approach is an imprecise way of defining or identifying abnormality: "While we may agree to define psychological abnormalities as patterns of functioning that are deviant, distressful, dysfunctional, and sometimes dangerous . . . these criteria are often vague and subjective. When is a pattern of behavior deviant, distressful, dysfunctional, and dangerous enough to be considered abnormal? The question may be impossible to answer."

CLASSIFICATION SYSTEMS

Several classification systems are used to diagnose mental disorders. For example, we have already mentioned the Diagnostic and Statistical Manual of Mental Disorders (DSM), which contains over 200 mental disorders. Another prominent system is the International Classification of Diseases (ICD). This is produced by the World Health Organization, and is much used throughout Europe and other parts of the world. The two classificatory systems are broadly similar, and so we will focus on only one of them (DSM).

The current version of DSM is DSM-IV, published in 1994 (a slightly revised version known as DSM-IV-TR (text revision) was published in 2000). It consists of five axes. The first three are always used, whereas the last two are optional:

Axis 1: *Clinical disorders*. This axis permits the patient's disorder to be diagnosed on the basis of symptom patterns.
Axis 2: *Personality disorders and mental retardation*. This axis identifies long-term patterns of impaired functioning stemming from personality disorders or mental retardation.
Axis 3: *General medical conditions*. This axis concerns any physical illness that might influence the patient's emotional state or ability to function effectively.
Axis 4: *Psychosocial and environmental problems*. This axis is concerned with any significant stressful events occurring within 12 months of the onset of the mental disorder.
Axis 5: *Global assessment of functioning*. This axis provides an overall measure of the patient's functioning at work and at leisure on a 100-point scale.

It has been argued that DSM suffers from two major problems. First, it is an American-based system, and it fails to take proper account of cultural factors. Second, a persistent criticism of DSM is that it is flawed by sex bias. More specifically, it is claimed that male-biased assumptions about what should be regarded as abnormal have influenced the diagnostic categories used in DSM. We consider these issues in turn.

CULTURAL DIFFERENCES

DSM-IV contains a modest attempt to take account of cultural factors. It refers to **culture-bound syndromes**, which are "locality-specific patterns of aberrant [deviant] behavior and troubling experience that may or may not be linked to a particular DSM-IV diagnostic category." Here are three examples of the culture-bound syndromes identified by DSM-IV in an appendix (other examples are shown in the box opposite):

- *Ghost sickness*. The main symptom is an excessive focus on death and on those who have died (common in Native American tribes).
- *Koro*. This disorder involves extreme anxiety that the penis or nipples will recede into the body, and possibly cause death (south and east Asia).
- *Amok*. This disorder involves brooding followed by a violent outburst; it is found mainly in men (originally identified in Malaysia).

Key Term

Culture-bound syndromes: patterns of disordered behavior typically found in only certain cultures.

Some examples of culture-bound syndromes

Country	Syndrome	Key features
Caribbean	Blacking out	Sudden fainting + hysterical blindness
China	Pa-feng	Fear of wind
Greece	Nevra	Emotional distress, stomach complaints, dizziness, and so on
Japan	Taijin kyofusho	Extreme fear that one's body or body parts are offensive to other people
Latin America	Mal de ojo	The "evil eye," responsible for behavioral problems and poor health
South Africa	Amafufunyana	Violent behavior caused by spirit possession
West Africa	Brain fag	Problems in concentrating and thinking produced by excessive study (!)

Case Study: *A Culture-Bound Syndrome?—Hikikomori*

A condition attracting considerable concern in Japan over recent years is *Hikikomori*. There has been no official calculation of the number of cases, but some specialists have estimated that it may be affecting up to a million people. The condition affects mostly middle-class males in their late teens or early twenties who are otherwise healthy.

Sufferers withdraw completely from society, typically by locking themselves in their rooms, sometimes for up to 20 years. There have been some high-profile cases reported in the Japanese media where young men have left their homes and committed violent crimes, including murder. However, most of the sufferers are not violent and tend more towards depression and lethargy. Other symptoms can include insomnia, regressive behavior, paranoia and aspects of agoraphobia and obsessive-compulsive disorder.

The Japanese government is of the opinion that *Hikikomori* is a social disorder rather than a mental disorder, and that it reflects the current economic downturn in the country. (In a similar way, *Karoshi*—death from overwork—was a symptom of Japan's huge economic success in the 1990s.)

Kleinman and Cohen (1997, p. 76) dismissed the appendix of DSM-IV as "little more than a sop thrown to cultural psychiatrists and psychiatric anthropologists." This is fair comment when we consider the range of culture-bound syndromes around the world.

SEX BIAS

Is there sex bias in DSM? Many argue that there is focus on various personality disorders. For example, it is claimed that histrionic personality disorder (characterized by excessive emotionality) represents distortions of stereotypical feminine traits. In contrast, antisocial personality disorder (characterized by aggression and hostility) represents distortions of stereotypical masculine traits. Evidence suggesting the existence of sex bias was reported by Ford and Widiger (1989). Therapists were presented with written case studies of patients with each of those personality disorders. Histrionic personality disorder was correctly diagnosed much more often when the patient was described as female than when described as male (80% vs. just over 30%). Antisocial personality disorder was correctly diagnosed over 40% of the time when the patient was male but under 20% of the time when the patient was female.

As Funtowicz and Widiger (1999) pointed out, the findings of Ford and Widiger (1989) may reflect sex bias in the DSM criteria or they may be a result of biases in the therapists making the diagnoses. Funtowicz and Widiger argued that sex bias would be shown if the criteria for diagnosing personality disorders occurring more often in females are lower than those for personality disorders occurring more often in males. They asked clinical psychologists to indicate the extent to which the criteria for DSM-IV personality disorders involve social dysfunction, occupational dysfunction, or subjective distress. The diagnostic criteria were as stringent for "female" personality disorders as for "male" ones, thus providing no evidence of sex bias.

FACTORS CAUSING MENTAL DISORDERS

It is important to establish the causes of mental disorders, in part because the knowledge gained could be used to reduce the incidence of such disorders in future. In this section, we consider etiology, which is the range of factors causally involved in the development of mental disorders.

It is a complex matter to find out *why* some people suffer from any given mental disorder. However, we can start by distinguishing between one-dimensional and multi-dimensional causal models (Durand & Barlow, 2006). According to one-dimensional models, the origins of a mental disorder can be traced to a *single* underlying cause. For example, severe depression might be caused by a major loss (e.g., death of a loved one) or schizophrenia by genetic factors. In practice, one-dimensional models have consistently failed to account for the evidence. Accordingly, they have been replaced by multidimensional models assuming that any given mental disorder is typically caused by *several* factors in interaction.

Probably the most popular multidimensional approach is the **diathesis–stress model**. In this model, the occurrence of mental disorders depends on two types of factors:

1. *Diathesis*. This is a vulnerability or predisposition to disorder within the individual. Diathesis used to be thought of simply as a genetic vulnerability, but has broadened to include any personal vulnerabilities.

2. *Stress*. This is some severe or disturbing environmental event (e.g., divorce; death of a spouse).

The main types of factors identified as contributing to the development of mental disorders are as follows:

- *Genetic factors*. Twin studies, family studies, and adoption studies may indicate that some people are genetically more vulnerable than others to developing a disorder.
- *Brain chemicals*. Individuals with unusually low or high levels of certain brain chemicals may be vulnerable to various mental disorders.
- *Cultural factors*. Cultural values and expectations may be important in causing some disorders. For example, most Western cultures emphasize the desirability of thinness in women, and this may help to trigger eating disorders.

> **Key Term**
>
> **Diathesis–stress model:** the notion that mental disorders are caused jointly by a diathesis or vulnerability within the individual *and* a distressing event.

Death of a loved one rates as one of the most stressful life events we experience, and may have long-term psychological repercussions, such as depression.

- *Social factors.* Individuals experiencing severe life events (e.g., divorce; unemployment) may be at risk for various psychological disorders, as may those lacking social support or belonging to poorly functioning families.
- *Psychological factors.* Individuals having certain kinds of beliefs, or who have learned particular inappropriate ways of behaving, may be vulnerable to mental disorders. For example, someone who exaggerates the threat of most situations may develop an anxiety disorder.

The factors above interact with each other. For example, someone may have a very high or low level of a given brain chemical because of genetic factors or because he/she has recently experienced a severe life event. Another example concerns the impact of cultural expectations on eating disorders. This is not the *only* factor causing eating disorders, because the overwhelming majority of women in Western societies don't suffer from eating disorders. Eating disorders occur in individuals exposed to cultural expectations of thinness *and* who are vulnerable (e.g., because of genetic factors).

In what follows, we will consider the factors responsible for various mental disorders. First, we consider major depressive disorder, which is by far the most common of the mood disorders. Next we consider some of the main anxiety disorders, which are also found in millions of individuals. Finally, we consider schizophrenia, one of the most serious mental disorders.

MOOD DISORDERS: DEPRESSION

Various mood disorders are identified in DSM-IV. Of particular importance is major depressive disorder, which affects literally millions of people around the world. Less common but more severe is a mood disorder known as bipolar disorder (see figure on the right). This is a condition involving depressive and manic (elated) episodes. Over 90% of those suffering from clinical depression have major depressive disorder rather than bipolar disorder, and so we focus on that condition. The diagnosis of **major depressive disorder** requires that five of the following symptoms occur nearly every day for 2 weeks: sad, depressed mood; loss of interest and pleasure in usual activities; difficulties in sleeping; changes in activity level; weight loss or gain; loss of energy and tiredness; negative self-concept, self-blame, and self-reproach; problems with concentration; recurring thoughts of suicide or death. About 10% of men and 20% of women become clinically depressed at some time in their lives.

Factors involved

We start by considering the role of genetic factors in depression as assessed by twin studies. The key measure is the **concordance rate**: this is the likelihood that, if one twin has the disorder, the other twin also has it. If genetic factors are important, the concordance rate should be higher in identical than in fraternal twins. That is what

Case Study: *Major Depressive Disorder*

Chrissie seemed a successful young woman, with a good job and social life, but when a new boss started at work with a blame culture approach she rapidly felt unable to cope, worthless, apathetic, and full of self-doubts. She became exhausted, and her GP diagnosed her as having major depressive disorder and she was off work for 6 months.

As a child, Chrissie had been criticized all the time by her parents and felt she could never do anything right, not even hold her knife and fork acceptably nor eat neatly. It seems that the heavy, negative manner of her new boss had caused the memories from childhood of helplessness and failure to resurface, and the associated emotions had led to the persistent very low mood.

Treatment from a sympathetic GP and a psychotherapist who used CBT (cognitive-behavior therapy) reinforced with clinical hypnotherapy helped her recover.

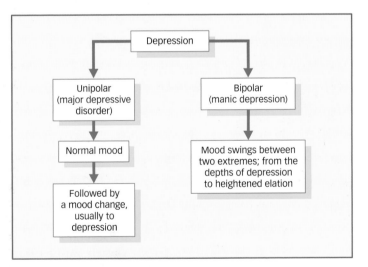

Key Terms

Major depressive disorder:
a disorder characterized by symptoms such as sad, depressed mood, tiredness, and loss of interest in various activities.

Concordance rate:
as applied to twins, the probability that one twin has a given disorder given that the co-twin has it.

has been found. Allen (1976) reviewed several twin studies, and reported that the concordance rate was 40% for identical twins compared to only 11% for fraternal twins. McGuffin, Katz, Watkins, and Rutherford (1996) found that the concordance rate for major depressive disorder was 46% for identical twins and 20% for fraternal twins.

Additional evidence that genetic factors are important comes from adoption studies. Wender et al. (1986) considered adopted children who later developed major depression. The biological parents of these individuals were *eight* times as likely to have suffered from clinical depression as their adoptive parents.

Depressed patients may have abnormal levels of various neurotransmitters or other substances. Some evidence suggests that patients with major depressive disorder often have low levels of norepinephrine and serotonin (see Comer, 2007). However, Thase et al. (2002) found that depressed patients (especially those with severe depression) had *increased* levels of norepinephrine. The reality is complex. Rampello, Nicoletti, and Nicoletti (2000) reported that patients with major depressive disorder have an *imbalance* in the activity of several neurotransmitters including norepinephrine, serotonin, dopamine, and acetycholine. In addition, patients with major depressive disorder often have high levels of the hormone cortisol, which is present in large amounts when individuals are stressed (Thase et al., 2002).

Evidence that life events and cognitive factors can both be involved in the development of major depressive disorder was reported by Lewinsohn, Joiner, and Rohde (2001). They measured dysfunctional attitudes (e.g., "My life is wasted unless I am a success"; "I should be happy all the time") in adolescents not having a major depressive disorder at the outset of the study. One year later, Lewinsohn et al. assessed the negative life events experienced by the participants over the 12-month period. Those who experienced many negative life events had an increased likelihood of developing a major depressive disorder only if they were initially high in dysfunctional attitudes (see the figure on the left).

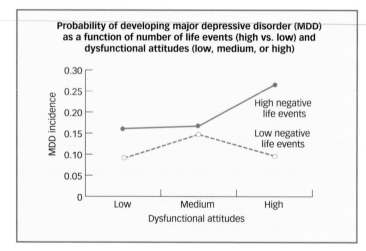

Probability of developing major depressive disorder (MDD) as a function of number of life events (high vs. low) and dysfunctional attitudes (low, medium, or high)

Life events often play a role in triggering depression. For example, Brown (1989) reviewed the findings from several studies. On average, about 55% of depressed patients had at least one severe life event in the months before onset, compared to only about 17% of controls. However, Brown and Harris (1978) found that the impact of life events was greatly influenced by whether the individual had an intimate friend. They focused on women who had experienced at least one very stressful life event in the 8 months before interview. Of those women who didn't have an intimate friend, 37% became depressed. In contrast, only 10% of women having a very close friend became depressed.

ANXIETY

There are several anxiety disorders, and we focus on four of them. Note that anxious patients often suffer from two or more different anxiety disorders; this is known as **comorbidity**. For example, Barlow, Di Nardo, Vermilyea, and Blanchard (1986) found comorbidity in 66% of anxious patients presenting at their clinic. Hettema et al. (2005) identified a major reason for comorbity based on a twin study focusing on the underlying genetic risk factors for the anxiety disorders. Similar genetic influences were present for generalized anxiety disorder (persistent worry and anxiety in several areas of life), panic disorder (described below), and agoraphobia (described below).

Panic disorder is an anxiety disorder in which the individual experiences repeated panic attacks. According to DSM-IV, a panic attack involves intense fear or discomfort, with four or more bodily symptoms suddenly appearing (e.g., palpitations, shortness of breath, accelerated heart rate, feeling of choking, sweating, chest pain, feeling dizzy, and fear of dying). Many patients with panic disorder also suffer from agoraphobia. **Agoraphobia** is a condition in which the individual is frightened to leave the house, because he/she is very concerned about having a panic attack in a public place. In DSM-IV, the term "panic disorder with agoraphobia" describes such individuals.

Posttraumatic stress disorder is triggered by a specific distressing event such as rape, war, or natural disaster. According to DSM-IV, this condition is associated with three main symptoms:

1. *Re-experiencing the event*: The event is often recalled and nightmares about it are common. Stimuli triggering memories of the traumatic event cause intense emotional upset.
2. *Avoidance of stimuli associated with the event or reduced responsiveness to such stimuli*: The individual tries to avoid trauma-related stimuli or thoughts. There is fluctuation between re-experiencing the traumatic event and a numbing of response to stimuli associated with the event.
3. *Increased arousal*: There are problems with sleep, difficulties with concentration, and an increased startle response.

Case Study: *Sarah—A Case of Agoraphobia*

Sarah, a woman in her mid-thirties, was shopping for bargains in a crowded department store during the January sales. Without warning and without knowing why, she suddenly felt anxious and dizzy. She worried that she was about to faint or have a heart attack. She dropped her shopping and rushed straight home. As she neared home, she noticed that her feelings of panic lessened.

A few days later she decided to go shopping again. On entering the store, she felt herself becoming increasingly anxious. After a few minutes she had become so anxious that a shop keeper asked her if she was OK and took her to a first aid room. Once there her feelings of panic became worse and she became particularly embarrassed at all the attention she was attracting.

After this she avoided going to the large store again. She even started to worry when going into smaller shops because she thought she might have another panic attack, and this worry turned into intense anxiety. Eventually she stopped shopping altogether, asking her husband to do it for her.

Over the next few months, Sarah found that she had panic attacks in more and more places. The typical pattern was that she became progressively more anxious the further away from her house she got. She tried to avoid the places where she might have a panic attack, but as the months passed, she found that this restricted her activities. Some days she found it impossible to leave the house at all. She felt that her marriage was becoming strained and that her husband resented her dependence on him.

Key Terms

Agoraphobia:
a disorder in which there is fear of public places from which it might be difficult to escape in the event of a panic attack.

Posttraumatic stress disorder:
a disorder triggered by a very distressing event and involving re-experiencing of the event, avoidance of stimuli associated with the event, and increased arousal.

Clearly Sarah's behavior was abnormal, in many of the ways described in the text. It was statistically infrequent and socially deviant. It interfered with her ability to function adequately, both from her own point of view and of her husband. She did not have many of the signs of mental healthiness.

Adapted from Stirling and Hellewell (1999).

Social phobia involves extreme concern about one's own behavior and the reactions of others. About 70% of sufferers are female and it is mostly found among young people in their late teens and twenties. The main criteria for social phobia in DSM-IV include the following:

- Marked and persistent fear of situations in which the individual will be exposed to unfamiliar people or to scrutiny.
- Exposure to the feared social situation nearly always produces considerable anxiety.
- The individual recognizes that the fear experienced is excessive.
- The feared situations are avoided or responded to with great anxiety.
- The phobic reactions interfere significantly with the individual's working or social life, or there is marked distress.

Case Study: *A Social Phobic*

Jim had always been shy. He had married a schoolfriend who was lively and outgoing, and she had managed their social contacts and social life for them both. Jim had coped with working in a small music store, but when this was taken over by a large chain he had to make phone calls to customers and speak to the public and this had caused such anxiety that social phobia was diagnosed. He had become too anxious to be able to do his job and felt exhausted and defeated and a failure. He lost any sense of self-efficacy and was virtually housebound by the time he sought help.

Cognitive-behavioral therapy helped Jim to confront his phobia, see that his fears were groundless, and construct and practice strategies for managing his natural anxiety successfully.

Richards, T.A. (2008). A case study: Jim. http://www.anxietynetwork.com/spcase.html

Specific phobia involves strong and irrational fear of some specific object or situation. Specific phobias include fear of snakes and spiders, but can extend to fear of the number 13, fear of knees, and fear of being infested with worms.

Factors involved

What factors trigger panic disorder? Genetic factors play a role. Kendler et al. (1993) found that the concordance rate was 24% for identical twins compared to 11% for fraternal twins. Both figures are much higher than the 2% found in the population as a whole. According to the cognitive approach (e.g., Clark, 1986), patients with panic disorder greatly exaggerate the threateningness of internal stimuli (e.g., fast heart rate). This may sometimes happen because patients previously had a respiratory disease leading them to be especially sensitive about their internal state. Verburg, Griez, Meijer, and Pols (1995) found that 43% of their panic disorder patients had suffered from at least one respiratory disease during their lives compared to only 16% among patients with other anxiety disorders. Finally, life events can help to trigger panic disorder. Barrett (1979) found that panic patients reported significantly more undesirable life events in the 6 months

Key Terms

Social phobia:
a disorder in which the individual has excessive fear of many social situations and will often avoid them.

Specific phobia:
a strong and irrational fear of a given object (e.g., spider; snake) or situation (e.g., enclosed space).

before the onset of their disorder than did controls over the same time period.

Posttraumatic stress disorder (PTSD) is always triggered by some distressing event, and is especially likely to occur if the event is life threatening. However, when many people are exposed to the same traumatic event (e.g., a sinking ship), only some of them develop posttraumatic stress disorder. Thus, factors in addition to the traumatic event itself need to be taken into account. Skre et al. (1993) found that the concordance rate for posttraumatic stress disorder was greater in identical twins than in fraternal ones. Foy, Resnick, Sipprelle, and Carroll (1987) found that genetic factors interacted with the severity of the traumatic event in soldiers. A low level of combat exposure was much more likely to lead to posttraumatic stress disorder in men having family members with other disorders. However, a high level of combat exposure led to posttraumatic stress disorder in two-thirds of soldiers regardless of whether family members had other disorders.

PTSD can be triggered by a life-threatening event. Here, an Indian woman weeps near the debris of her damaged house hit by the 2004 Asian tsunami, the final death toll of which exceeded 225,000.

Social phobia has a genetic component. Kendler, Karkowski, and Prescott (1999) carried out a study on a large sample of female identical and fraternal twins. The concordance rate was significantly higher for identical twins than for fraternal twins. Personality (individual differences in which depend on genetic factors) seems to be involved in the development of social phobia. Stemberger, Turner, and Beidel (1995) found that most social phobics are very introverted. Very introverted people tend to avoid social situations, and so introversion may be a risk factor for social phobia. Social factors are also involved. Arrindell et al. (1989) found that social phobics recalled their parents being rejecting, lacking in emotional warmth, or overprotective. Bruch and Heimberg (1994) found that adult social phobics said their parents overemphasized the opinions of others, failed to stress the importance of family sociability, and isolated their family from others.

SCHIZOPHRENIA

Schizophrenia is a very serious condition. About 1% of the population of the UK suffer from schizophrenia during their lives, and the figure is similar in most other countries. The symptoms of schizophrenia vary somewhat, but typically include problems with attention, thinking, social relationships, motivation, and emotion.

Case Study: *A Schizophrenic Disorder*

A young man of 19 (WG) was admitted to the psychiatric services on the grounds of a dramatic change in character. His parents described him as always being extremely shy with no close friends, but in the last few months he had gone from being an average-performing student to failing his studies and leaving college. Having excelled in nonteam sports such as swimming and athletics, he was now taking no exercise at all. WG had seldom mentioned health matters, but now complained of problems with his head and chest. After being admitted, WG spent most of his time staring out of the window, and uncharacteristically not taking care over his appearance. Staff found it difficult to converse with him and he offered no information about himself, making an ordinary diagnostic interview impossible. WG would usually answer direct questions, but in a flat emotionless tone. Sometimes his answers were not even connected to the question, and staff would find themselves wondering what the conversation had been about. There were also occasions when there was a complete mismatch between WG's emotional expression and the words he spoke. For example, he giggled continuously when speaking about a serious illness that had left his mother bedridden. On one occasion, WG became very agitated and spoke of "electrical sensations" in his brain. At other times he spoke of being influenced by a force outside himself, which took the form of a voice urging him to commit acts of violence against his parents. He claimed that the voice repeated the command "You'll have to do it."

Adapted from Hofling, 1974.

According to DSM-IV, the criteria for schizophrenia include:

1. Two or more of the following symptoms: delusions, hallucinations, disorganized speech, grossly disorganized or catatonic (rigid) behavior, and negative symptoms (lack of emotion, lack of motivation, speaking very little or uninformatively).
2. Continuous signs of disturbance for at least 6 months.
3. Social and/or occupational dysfunction or poor functioning.

Factors involved

Genetic factors play a major role in the development of schizophrenia. Gottesman (1991) summarized the findings from about 40 twin studies. The concordance rate was 48% for identical or monozygotic twins compared to only 17% for fraternal or dizygotic twins. However, genetic factors are not all-important. The finding that 50% of identical twins whose co-twin develops schizophrenia do *not* develop the disorder themselves indicates that environmental factors also play a key role in the causation of schizophrenia.

There is dispute as to whether genetic factors are as important in the development of schizophrenia as suggested by Gottesman (1991). For example, Joseph (2003) considered the nine most recent studies on schizophrenia. The concordance rate was 22.4% for identical twins and 4.6% for fraternal twins. These figures are much lower than those reported by Gottesman (1991). However, bear in mind that the lifetime risk of schizophrenia in the general population is only 1%. That means that you have a substantially increased chance of schizophrenia if you have a twin (especially identical) with the condition.

Wahlberg et al. (1997) showed how genetic factors interact with environmental ones. They studied adopted children whose biological mothers had schizophrenia. These children showed high levels of thought disorder if raised by families who communicated in unclear and confusing ways. In contrast, children with schizophrenic mothers had very good psychological health if raised by families who communicated clearly.

Schizophrenia is generally diagnosed when someone is in their late teens or early twenties. However, the early signs of schizophrenia can be detected in early childhood—perhaps because of the impact of genetic factors. For example, Walker et al. (1994) studied family home movies taken during the early childhood of children who did or didn't develop schizophrenia subsequently. At a very early age (sometimes as early as 2), the children who subsequently developed schizophrenia had more motor abnormalities, more negative emotional expressions, and more odd hand movements.

Social factors are emphasized by the social causation hypothesis, which was designed to explain why schizophrenics tend to belong to the lower social classes. According to this hypothesis, members of the lower social classes have more stressful lives than middle-class people, and this makes them more vulnerable to schizophrenia. The key issue here is whether belonging to the lower social classes makes individuals likely to develop schizophrenia, or whether developing schizophrenia leads to reduced social status. Turner and Wagonfeld (1967) reported some support for the social causation hypothesis in their finding that the fathers of schizophrenics tend to belong to the lower social classes.

Stressful life events sometimes help to trigger the onset of schizophrenia. Day et al. (1987) found in several countries that schizophrenics tended to have experienced a high number of stressful life events in the few weeks before the onset of schizophrenia.

Finally, Frith (1992) argued that cognitive factors may be involved in the development of schizophrenia. He claimed that positive symptoms of schizophrenia (e.g., delusions of control; auditory hallucinations) may occur

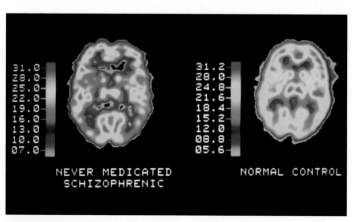

PET scans of schizophrenic (left) and normal brains (right). The darkest areas show low levels of activity.

because schizophrenics have problems with self-monitoring. Patients fail to keep track of their own intentions, as a consequence of which they mistakenly experience their own thoughts as alien. McGuire et al. (1996) reported support for this theory. They found that schizophrenics suffering from hallucinations had reduced activity in those parts of the brain involved in monitoring inner speech.

Chapter Summary

What is abnormality?
- Decisions about what is abnormal depend in part on the prevailing social norms and values.
- Four features typically associated with abnormality are deviance, distress, dysfunction, and danger. However, these criteria are vague and often difficult to apply in practice.

Classification systems
- The two main classification systems are DSM and ICD.
- DSM consists of five axes. It refers to culture-bound syndromes but de-emphasizes cross-cultural differences.
- Most classification systems make use of categories. However, dimensional systems that avoid rigid categorization are more realistic.

Factors causing mental disorder
- According to the diathesis–stress model, the occurrence of mental disorder depends on individual vulnerability and stressful events.
- Factors involved in the development of major depressive disorder include genetic influences, life events, and dysfunctional attitudes.
- Genetic factors play a role in triggering the main anxiety disorders. Previous history of respiratory disease is associated with panic disorder, severity of the traumatic event with posttraumatic stress disorder, and an introverted personality and rejecting or overprotective parents with social phobia.
- Genetic factors play a major role in the development of schizophrenia. Social factors, stressful life events, and problems with self-monitoring are also involved.

Further Reading

- Bennett, P. (2003). *Abnormal and clinical psychology: An introductory textbook* (2nd ed.). Maidenhead, UK: Open University Press. There is accessible coverage of the main issues within abnormal psychology in this readable book.
- Comer, R.J. (2007). *Abnormal psychology* (6th ed.). New York: Worth. Most of the important issues are discussed in a thorough and accessible way in this up-to-date textbook.
- Davison, G.C., Neale, J.M., & Kring, A.M. (2004). *Abnormal psychology* (9th ed.). New York: Worth. This well-established textbook has readable accounts of the whole of abnormal psychology.
- Durand, V.M., & Barlow, D.H. (2006). *Essentials of abnormal psychology* (4th ed.). New York: Thomson/Wadsworth. As the title implies, this textbook by leading clinical psychologists focuses on central issues within abnormal psychology.

Chapter 22

Contents

Therapeutic approaches

22

Individuals with mental disorders exhibit a wide range of symptoms. There may be problems associated with thinking and the mind (e.g., the hallucinations of the schizophrenic), with behavior (e.g., the avoidance behavior of the phobic), or with physiological and bodily processes (e.g., the highly activated physiological system of someone with posttraumatic stress disorder). However, note that thinking, behavior, and physiological processes are all highly *interdependent*, meaning that they all affect each other.

Therapeutic approaches could focus on producing changes in thinking, in behavior, or in physiological functioning. That is precisely what has happened. The psychodynamic approach was designed to change thinking, and the same is true of cognitive therapy. Behavior therapy emphasizes the importance of changing behavior. Drug therapy and other biologically based forms of therapy focus on physiological and biochemical changes. Finally, cognitive-behavior therapy falls somewhere between behavior therapy and psychodynamic therapy, in that it attempts to produce changes in clients' thought processes *and* in their behavior. In spite of the differing emphases across therapies, most therapists assume that their preferred form of therapy will have beneficial effects in thinking, behavior, and physiological functioning.

When considering various forms of therapy, we must avoid making the treatment etiology fallacy (MacLeod, 1998). This is the mistaken notion that the success of a given form of treatment reveals the cause of the disorder. For example, aspirin is an effective cure for headache. However, that doesn't mean that a lack of aspirin causes headaches!

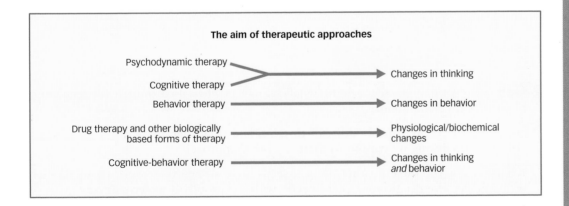

DRUG THERAPY

We will consider drug therapy for depression, anxiety, and schizophrenia in turn. As we saw earlier, patients with major depressive disorder often have low levels of the neurotransmitters serotonin and norepinephrine. Tricyclic antidepressant drugs appear to increase the activity of those neurotransmitters, and generally reduce the symptoms of depression (Elkin, 1994). However, there can be a high relapse rate

523

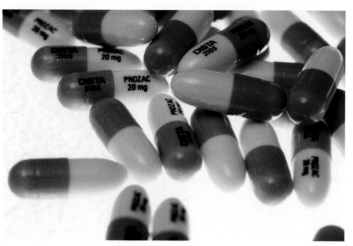

Prozac is an antidepressant drug which inhibits the uptake of serotonin, a neurotransmitter produced in the brain.

unless drug therapy is continued over a long period of time. The most common drugs used to treat depression are the selective serotonin reuptake inhibitors (SSRIs), of which Prozac is the best-known. They increase serotonin activity and are as effective as the tricylics (Hirschfeld, 1999). They have the advantage over the tricyclics that it is harder to overdose on SSRIs.

The benzodiazepines (e.g., Librium and Valium) are often used to treat anxiety disorders. In 2003, over 13 million prescriptions for benzodiazepines were written in the UK (Garfield, 2003). The benzodiazepines are reasonably effective in the treatment of generalized anxiety disorder (Rickels, DeMartinis, & Aufdrembrinke, 2000), and have also been used to treat social phobia. Mitte (2005) found in a meta-analysis of 65 studies that drug-based approaches to the treatment of generalized anxiety disorder are mostly effective, and are comparably effective to cognitive-behavior therapy. In spite of these successes, there are several unwanted effects of benzodiazepines:

1. Anxious symptoms often return when patients stop taking the drugs.
2. There are various side effects (e.g., lack of coordination; poor concentration; memory loss).
3. There can be physical dependence, with patients finding it difficult to manage without drugs.

Tricyclic drugs (generally used to treat major depression) have been used successfully to treat panic disorder. Barlow, Gorman, Shear, and Woods (2000) found that tricyclic drugs were as effective as cognitive-behavior therapy in reducing the symptoms of panic disorder, but were less effective at 6-month follow-up.

Schizophrenia is increasingly treated with atypical antipsychotic drugs (e.g., Clozaril; Risperdal; Zyprexa). These drugs have fewer side effects than the previous neuroleptic drugs used to treat schizophrenia. However, patients taking Clozaril have a 1–2% risk of developing a life-threatening condition involving a substantial reduction in white blood cells. The good news is that atypical drugs benefit 85% of schizophrenic patients compared to 65% given neuroleptic drugs (Awad & Voruganti, 1999).

Evaluation

⊕ Drug therapy often produces rapid beneficial effects when used to treat depression, anxiety, and schizophrenia.

⊕ Schizophrenia is notoriously difficult to treat, and drug therapy is probably more effective at reducing its symptoms than any other approach.

⊖ Relapse is more common after drug therapy than after other types of therapy, probably because drugs don't deal directly with the problems underlying any given mental disorder.

⊖ It is often difficult to know precisely *why* any given drug is effective in the treatment of a particular disorder because of our limited understanding of the underlying biochemical factors.

⊖ The drop-out rate is often rather high when drug therapy is used.

⊖ Nearly all drugs have unwanted side effects.

PSYCHODYNAMIC THERAPY

The first form of psychodynamic therapy was psychoanalysis, developed by Sigmund Freud early in the twentieth century. According to Freud, neuroses such as the anxiety disorders occur because of conflicts among the three parts of the mind: the ego (rational mind), the id (sexual and other instincts), and the superego (conscience). These conflicts cause the ego to use various defense mechanisms to defend itself. The key defense mechanism is repression. **Repression** involves forcing painful, threatening, or unacceptable thoughts and memories out of consciousness into the unconscious mind. Repressed memories mostly refer to childhood and to the conflicts between the instinctive (e.g., sexual) motives of the child and the restraints imposed by his/her parents. Evidence for repression is discussed in Chapter 8.

Freud asked his patients to lie on a couch during psychoanalysis. This is a photograph of his couch in his London house, which is now the Freud Museum.

According to Freud, adults experiencing great personal problems tend to show regression. **Regression** involves going backwards through the stages of psychosexual development they went through in childhood (see Chapter 12). Children often fixate or spend an unusually long time at a given stage of psychosexual development if it was associated with conflicts or with excessive gratification. Regression typically occurs back to a stage at which the person had previously fixated.

Freud argued that the way to cure neurosis was to allow the client to gain access to his/her repressed ideas and conflicts and to face up to whatever emerged from the unconscious. He insisted that the client should focus on the feelings associated with the repressed ideas, and shouldn't simply regard them unemotionally in order to gain insight. Insight "involves a conscious awareness of some of the wishes, defenses, and compromises . . . that have interacted to produce emotional conflict or deficits in psychological development" (Kivlighan, Multon, & Patton, 2000, p. 50).

How can we uncover repressed memories and allow the client to gain insight? One method used by Freud was **free association**, in which the client said the first thing coming into his/her mind. Free association is ineffective if the client shows resistance and is reluctant to say what he/she is thinking. Nevertheless, the presence of resistance (revealed by long pauses) suggests that the client is getting close to an important repressed idea, and that further probing by the therapist is needed.

Another method is the analysis of dreams, which Freud described as "the via regia [royal road] to the unconscious." Freud argued that the mind has a censor that keeps repressed material out of conscious awareness. This censor is less vigilant (it nods off?) during sleep, and so repressed ideas from the unconscious are more likely to appear in dreams than in waking thought. However, these repressed ideas usually emerge in disguised form because of their unacceptable nature. As a result, the therapist has to work with the client to decide on the true meaning of each dream (see Chapter 5 for more on Freud's theory of dreaming).

Progress in therapy depends partly on **transference**. This involves the client transferring onto the therapist the powerful emotional reactions previously directed at his/her own parents or other highly significant individuals.

FINDINGS

There is support for the notion that at least some adult mental disorders have their origins in childhood. For example, Kendler, Pedersen, Farahmand, and Persson (1996) studied adult female twins who had experienced parental loss through separation in childhood. These twins tended to suffer from depression and alcoholism in adult

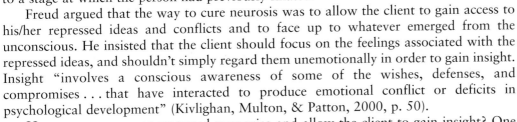

Key Terms
Repression: motivated forgetting of traumatic or other very threatening events.
Regression: in Freudian theory, returning to an earlier stage of psychosexual development when someone is highly stressed.
Free association: a technique used in psychoanalysis in which the client says whatever comes immediately to mind.
Transference: in Freudian theory, the transfer of the patient's strong feelings for one person (e.g., a parent) onto the therapist.

Case Study: *Anna O*

Freud's theory was largely based on the observations he made during consultations with patients. He suggested that his work was similar to that of an archaeologist, who digs away layers of earth before uncovering what he or she was seeking. In a similar way, the psychoanalyst seeks to dig down to the unconscious and discover the key to the individual's personality dynamic.

Anna O was a girl of twenty-one, of a high degree of intelligence. Her illness first appeared while she was caring for her father whom she tenderly loved, during the severe illness which led to his death. The patient had a severe paralysis of both right extremities, disturbance of eye-movements, and intense nausea when she attempted to take nourishment, and at "one time for several weeks a loss of the power to drink, in spite of tormenting thirst." She occasionally became confused or delirious and mumbled several words to herself. If these same words were later repeated to her, when she was in a hypnotic stage, she engaged in deeply sad, often poetically beautiful, day dreams, we might call them, which commonly took as their starting point the situation of a girl beside the sick-bed of her father. The patient jokingly called this treatment "chimney sweeping."

Dr Breuer [Freud's colleague] soon hit upon the fact that through such cleansing of the soul more could be accomplished than a temporary removal of the constantly recurring mental "clouds."

During one session, the patient recalled an occasion when she was with her governess, and how "that lady's little dog, that she abhorred, had drunk out of a glass. Out of respect for the conventions the patient had remained silent, but now under hypnosis she gave energetic expression to her restrained anger," and then drank a large quantity of water without trouble, and woke from hypnosis with the glass at her lips. "The symptom thereupon vanished permanently."

"Permit me to dwell for a moment on this experience. No one had ever cured an hysterical symptom by such means before, or had come so near [to] understanding its cause. This would be a pregnant discovery if the expectation could be confirmed that still other, perhaps the majority of symptoms, originated in this way and could be removed by the same method."

Such was indeed the case, almost all the symptoms originated in exactly this way, as we were to discover. The patient's illness originated at the time when she was caring for her sick father, "and her symptoms could only be regarded as memory symbols of his sickness and death."

"While she was seated at her father's sick bed, she was careful to betray nothing of her anxiety and her painful depression to the patient. When, later, she reproduced the same scene before the physician, the emotion which she had suppressed on the occurrence of the scene burst out with especial strength, as though it had been pent up all along."

"In her normal state she was entirely ignorant of the pathogenic scenes and of their connection with her symptoms. She had forgotten those scenes. . . . When the patient was hypnotized, it was possible, after considerable difficulty, to recall those scenes to her memory, and by this means of recall the symptoms were removed."

Adapted from Freud (1910).

---

life. Caspi, Moffitt, Newman, and Silva (1996) found that children who were inhibited at the age of 3 tended to be depressed at the age of 21.

It is difficult to test Freud's notion that insight is of crucial importance, because the concept is rather vague. For example, Hoglend et al. (1994) found that psychiatrists showed poor agreement among themselves concerning the insight levels shown by anxious and depressed patients in therapy. However, impressive findings using the Insight Rating Scale (in which expert judges evaluate clients' reports of the counseling session just finished) were reported by Kivlighan et al. (2000). They studied 12 clients who received 20 sessions in psychoanalytic counseling. There were steady decreases in symptoms across sessions and steady increases in insight. Of key importance, clients showing an increase in insight had reduced symptoms over the following week. This suggests that (as predicted by Freud) insight plays a role in causing symptom reduction.

Eysenck (1952) reviewed several studies, and claimed that the recovery rate was 72% for clients receiving no systematic treatment against only 44% for those receiving psychoanalysis. These findings suggest that psychoanalysis is actually bad for you! However, Eysenck regarded partially recovered clients as not having recovered at all, which doesn't make much sense. When the same data were re-analyzed using more reasonable criteria to define recovery, the success rate for psychoanalysis was 83% compared to 30% for those not treated (Bergin, 1971).

There is a lack of well-controlled studies on the effectiveness of psychodynamic therapy, especially with respect to the anxiety disorders (Fonagy, Roth, & Higgitt, 2005). However, such therapy has proved useful in the treatment of major depressive disorder and schizophrenia (Jarvis, 2004).

Evaluation

- Psychoanalysis was the first systematic form of psychological treatment for mental disorders, and has proved moderately effective (see Lambert & Bergin, 1994).
- Psychoanalysis strongly influenced the development of later forms of psychodynamic therapy and also cognitive therapy with its emphasis on the individual's mistaken interpretations of himself/herself.
- "The concepts on which it [the psychodynamic model] are based are difficult to define and to research . . . Because processes such as id drives, ego defenses, and fixation are abstract and supposedly operate at an unconscious level, there is no way of knowing for certain if they are occurring" (Comer, 2001, p. 59).
- Freud argued that insight is needed to produce recovery, and some evidence supports that view (e.g., Kivlighan et al., 2000). However, it is generally unclear whether insight causes recovery or whether recovery is needed to produce insight.
- Much of what the client says may be influenced by suggestions implanted previously by the therapist and so may not reflect his/her genuine views.

BEHAVIOR THERAPY

Behavior therapy developed during the 1950s and 1960s, but its origins go back several decades before that. The underlying notions are that most mental disorders are caused by maladaptive learning, and that the best treatment consists of appropriate new learning. Behavior therapists believe that abnormal behavior develops through conditioning (see Chapter 7). There are two main forms of conditioning: (1) classical conditioning involving learning by association; and (2) operant conditioning involving learning by reinforcement or reward. Behavior therapists argue that classical and operant conditioning can change unwanted behavior into a more desirable pattern of behavior. Some experts limit the term "behavior therapy" to treatment using classical conditioning, and use the term "behavior modification" to refer to treatment based on operant conditioning.

Behavior therapy has an emphasis on *current* problems and behavior, and on removing any symptoms the client finds troublesome. This contrasts with psychoanalysis, where the focus is on uncovering unresolved conflicts from childhood. In principle, behavior therapy has the advantage that it is based on scientific evidence acquired from laboratory studies of conditioning.

Here are three forms of behavior therapy:

1. *Exposure therapy.* **Exposure therapy** involves putting the client in feared situations (e.g., social situations for social phobics), with the feared situation becoming gradually more intense over time. It is used extensively in the treatment of phobias or extreme fears. Exposure therapy has proved successful in the treatment of most anxiety disorders (see Eysenck, 1997). It is often

regarded as the "gold standard" against which other forms of therapy should be compared. It is assumed that phobic fears are acquired by classical conditioning, with the conditioned or phobic stimulus (e.g., a snake) being associated with a painful or aversive stimulus creating fear. The repeated presentation of the conditioned stimulus in exposure therapy leads to extinction or habituation of the fear response.

2. *Aversion therapy.* In classical aversive conditioning, a neutral or positive stimulus is paired with an unpleasant or aversive stimulus (e.g., electric shock). This causes an aversive reaction (e.g., anxiety) to the neutral or positive stimulus. **Aversion therapy** is based on aversive conditioning. For example, an alcoholic is given aversive stimuli (e.g., electric shocks) while starting to drink alcohol. The intention is that alcohol will produce feelings of anxiety and so inhibit drinking. Alcoholism has also been treated by using drugs causing vomiting or impeding breathing (e.g., Antabuse). There are promising signs that drugs based on tryptophan metabolites may prove useful in treating alcoholism. They make patients feel ill if they have even a small amount of alcohol. In addition, they increase serotonin levels and so enhance patients' sense of wellbeing if they don't drink (see Martin & Bonner, 2005). Aversion therapy can be fairly effective in the short term, but generally not in the long term (Comer, 2007; Roth & Fonagy, 2005).

3. *Token economy.* The **token economy** involves selective positive reinforcement or reward. It is used with institutionalized patients who are given tokens (e.g., colored counters) for behaving appropriately. These tokens can be used to obtain various privileges (e.g., obtaining cigarettes). Ayllon and Azrin (1968) carried out a classic study. Female schizophrenic patients who had been hospitalized for an average of 16 years were given plastic tokens for actions such as making their beds or combing their hair. The tokens were exchanged for pleasant activities (e.g., seeing a movie). Use of a token economy increase eight-fold the number of chores the patients performed every day. Dickerson, Tenhula, and Green-Paden (2005) reviewed 13 studies of the token economy being used with schizophrenics. Beneficial effects were reported in 11 of these studies. The token economy is not used much nowadays in the treatment of schizophrenics, who are now mostly treated in the community. One reason for reduced use of the token economy is that it is very hard to exert the required level of environmental control within the community.

Key Terms

Aversion therapy:
a form of treatment in which an aversive stimulus is paired with a positive one (e.g., sight of alcohol) to inhibit the response to the positive stimulus (e.g., drinking).

Token economy:
use of **operant conditioning** to change the behavior of mental patients by selective positive reinforcement or reward.

Evaluation

(+) Behavior therapy has proved effective in treating several mental disorders, especially those with easily identifiable behavioral symptoms (e.g., avoidance responses of phobic individuals). For example, exposure therapy has many successes to its credit.

(+) Behavior therapy has a scientific basis and conditioning experiences are sometimes involved in the development of mental disorders.

(−) The role of environmental factors in causing mental disorders is exaggerated, and that of genetic and other biological factors minimized.

(−) Some forms of behavior therapy are not very effective. As Roth and Fonagy (1996, p. 226) pointed out, "There is little support for techniques using chemical or electrical aversion. Its use in service settings is made even more difficult to recommend given that there is (unsurprisingly) a high rate of attrition [dropping out from therapy]." Aversion therapy also poses ethical issues because of the high levels of discomfort and stress involved.

(−) Token economies sometimes produce token (i.e., minimal) learning. They work because the environment is carefully structured so that only good behavior is consistently rewarded. Patients find it hard to transfer what they have learned to the much less structured environment provided by the real world.

COGNITIVE AND COGNITIVE-BEHAVIOR THERAPY

The cognitive approach to therapy was developed mainly by Albert Ellis (1962) and Aaron Beck (1967). This approach is based in part on the psychodynamic model. This is especially so with its emphasis on the important role played by mental processes in the development and maintenance of mental disorder. However, as we will see, there are many major differences between the two approaches.

The central notion in the cognitive approach is that individuals suffering from mental disorders have distorted and irrational thoughts and beliefs. In practice, this approach has mainly been applied to major depressive disorder and to the anxiety disorders. Warren and Zgourides (1991) discussed the kinds of distorted beliefs much more common among individuals with anxiety disorders than among healthy individuals. Examples include, "I *must* perform well and/or win the approval of others, or else it's awful," and "My life conditions *must* give me the things I want easily and with little frustration . . . or else life is unbearable."

Beck (1976) argued that many of the cognitive distortions of depressed patients center around the **cognitive triad** (see the figure on the right). This consists of negative thoughts that depressed individuals have about themselves, about the world, and about the future. Depressed patients typically regard themselves as helpless, worthless, and inadequate. They interpret events in the world in an unrealistically negative and defeatist way. The final part of the cognitive triad involves depressed individuals seeing the future as totally hopeless, because their worthlessness will prevent any improvement occurring in their situation.

According to Beck, two maladaptive forms of thinking in depressed patients are negative automatic thoughts and overgeneralization. Negative automatic thoughts (e.g., "I always make a mess of things") are triggered effortlessly when depressed individuals experience failure. Overgeneralization involves drawing very general negative conclusions from specific evidence. For example, failing to obtain one particular job is interpreted as meaning that the depressed person will never find a job again.

What about the anxiety disorders? It is assumed that anxious clients overestimate the threateningness of certain external or internal stimuli. For example, spider phobics exaggerate the threat posed by spiders, and patients with panic disorder exaggerate the threateningness of an aroused bodily state. According to Beck, Emery, and Greenberg (1985), the level of anxiety that an individual will experience when facing a threatening event can be estimated from the following equation:

$$\frac{\text{Perceived probability of threat} \times \text{perceived cost of event}}{\text{Perceived ability to cope} \times \text{perceived "rescue factors"}}$$

Individuals with anxiety disorders exaggerate the probability of a threatening event happening and the psychological cost of that event happening. In addition, they minimize their ability to cope with such an event and doubt whether rescue factors (e.g., help from others) will be forthcoming.

Why do anxious patients maintain distorted and irrational thoughts and beliefs year after year in the face of contrary evidence from the world around them? The short answer is **safety-seeking behaviors**. These are forms of behavior designed to prevent feared events from happening and thus reduce anxiety. For example, social phobics believe mistakenly that safety-seeking behaviors such as avoiding eye contact, talking very little, and not

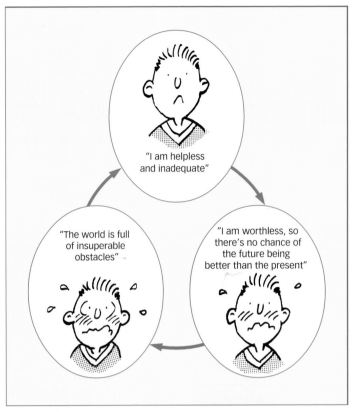

"I am helpless and inadequate"

"The world is full of insuperable obstacles"

"I am worthless, so there's no chance of the future being better than the present"

This girl is happy to handle this snake, but a snake phobic, according to Beck, would overestimate the danger the snake posed.

Key Terms

Cognitive triad: the depressed person's negative views of the self, the world, and the future.

Safety-seeking behaviors: actions taken by anxious patients to prevent feared consequences and to reduce their anxiety level.

talking about themselves prevent social catastrophe (Clark & Wells, 1995). In similar fashion, some patients with panic disorder believe that sitting quietly and controlling their breathing reduces the severity of panic attacks and wards off heart attacks.

There is convincing evidence that anxious and depressed patients have irrational beliefs. For example, Newmark, Frerking, Cook, and Newmark (1973) found that 65% of anxious patients (but only 2% of healthy controls) agreed with the statement, "It is essential that one be loved or approved of by virtually everyone in his community." However, the crucial issue is whether these beliefs help to produce clinical anxiety and depression (as assumed by cognitive therapists) or whether these irrational beliefs are a by-product of becoming clinically anxious or depressed. Some evidence that irrational beliefs can be involved in triggering clinical depression was discussed in Chapter 21. Lewinsohn, Joiner, and Rohde (2001) found that severe life events were followed by major depressive disorder mainly in those individuals who were previously found to have irrational beliefs.

What is involved in cognitive therapy? According to Beck and Weishaar (1989, p. 308), "Cognitive therapy consists of highly specific learning experiences designed to teach patients (1) to monitor their negative, automatic thoughts (cognitions); (2) to recognize the connections between cognitions, affect [emotion], and behavior; (3) to examine the evidence for and against distorted automatic thoughts; (4) to substitute more reality-oriented interpretations for their biased cognitions; and (5) to learn to identify and alter the beliefs that predispose them to distort their experiences."

Cognitive therapy differs from psychodynamic therapy in that the focus is on the patient's current concerns and beliefs rather than those of childhood. It also differs in that "The concept of unconscious processes is largely irrelevant to cognitive therapy" (Sacco & Beck, 1985, p. 5).

Consider as an example cognitive therapy for social phobia, in which there is extreme fear of social situations. Social phobics' belief that their social behavior is very inadequate

Case Study: *Social Phobia*

Dinesh is a 25-year-old software engineer. He was an award-winning student at engineering college. After graduating he got a job and within a short span of time impressed his superiors with his quality of work.

In spite of his achievements, Dinesh faced social problems. In social situations he felt that everybody was watching him and that he might do something embarrassing. At official meetings, he was tense and did not express his views. The most difficult task was attending parties. He was extremely tense, at times trembling, giddy with fear that others might ridicule him. Then he began to stay away.

Dinesh was suffering from social phobia, the irrational fear of social situations. Sufferers are scared and anxious in social situations. The anxiety is because they feel that something awful will happen to them, for example, they may behave in an embarrassing way and others will ridicule them. This results in sweating, trembling, palpitations, and feeling giddy. Even though the individual is aware that such behavior is silly, they are not able to overcome it. They start avoiding social situations and this results in difficulties in carrying out their work and personal activities. This deteriorated interaction with others and personal distress results in a lower level of functioning and low self-esteem.

For those afflicted with the disorder, both medical and nonmedical treatments are available. In terms of medication, drugs like fluoxetine and recent arrivals like moclobemide are useful. But drugs take effect only after a few weeks, and do not provide a permanent cure.

Psychological treatment in the form of cognitive-behavior therapy is useful. This aims at uncovering a person's automatic negative thoughts and cognitive schema, and helps them to understand and overcome these negative thoughts, in a gradual and systematic way. Relaxation therapy is also useful in helping an individual overcome basic anxiety.

Coming back to Dinesh, he was on medication and underwent cognitive-behavior therapy. Gradually, he overcame his phobia. He is now attending parties and meetings, is able to travel, and feels good about himself.

Adapted from Anandaram (2001).

can be challenged by presenting them with video recordings of their actual social behavior (Harvey, Clark, Ehlers, & Rapee, et al., 2000). Their belief that avoiding eye contact and other safety-seeking behaviors serves to prevent social catastrophe can be challenged by instructing them not to use any of these behaviors in social situations. This has proved effective in therapy (e.g., Morgan & Raffle, 1999).

Cognitive therapists discovered that restructuring a client's thoughts and beliefs didn't always produce full recovery. For example, a social phobic might accept that there is much less to fear in social situations than they had previously believed. However, he/she might still be reluctant to put himself/herself in difficult situations. This led to the development of cognitive-behavior therapy. The basic notion is that the client needs to change his/her dysfunctional thoughts *and* his/her inappropriate behavior. Kendall and Hammen (1998) argued that four basic assumptions underlie cognitive-behavior therapy:

1. Patients typically respond on the basis of their *interpretations* of themselves and the world around them rather than what is *actually* the case.
2. Thoughts, behaviors, and feelings are all interrelated, and all influence each other. Thus, no single factor is more important than the others.
3. In order for therapeutic interventions to be successful, they must clarify and change how people think about themselves and the world around them.
4. It is important to change both the client's cognitive processes and his/her behavior. The reason is that the benefits of therapy are likely to be greater than when only cognitive processes or behavior change.

Clark (1996) provided an example of cognitive-behavior therapy involving a 40-year-old man with panic disorder. The patient tried to protect himself against having a heart attack during panic attacks by taking paracetamol and by taking deep breaths. This hypothesis was tested by the therapist and the patient alternately sprinting and jogging around a football pitch. In addition, the patient was given the homework of taking strenuous daily exercise without trying to control his breathing. The patient rapidly accepted that his problem centered on his own mistaken beliefs.

Butler et al. (2005) considered the findings from 16 meta-analyses concerned with the therapeutic value of cognitive-behavior therapy. This form of therapy was notably successful with major depressive disorder, generalized anxiety disorder, panic disorder with or without agoraphobia, social phobia, and posttraumatic stress disorder. In addition, cognitive-behavior therapy was more effective than antidepressants in the treatment of major depressive disorder, and had beneficial effects when used with schizophrenic patients.

Evaluation

+ Cognitive therapy is effective in the treatment of anxiety disorders and depression, and cognitive-behavior therapy is even more effective (Butler et al., 2005).

+ The effectiveness of exposure therapy (used in behavior therapy) is increased when patients avoid safety-seeking behaviors as predicted by cognitive-behavior therapists (e.g., Salkovskis et al., 1999).

− Cognitive-behavior therapy is less effective in treating schizophrenia than depression or anxiety.

− There is a danger of exaggerating the importance of cognitive processes. Many clients develop more rational and less distorted ways of thinking about important issues with no beneficial changes in their maladaptive behavior.

Case Study: *Acrophobia: Fear of Heights*

Acrophobics have an overpowering fear of heights, a phobic fear that produces intense anxiety, panic attacks, and sends heart rate and blood pressure sky high. Traditionally, therapy has been based on the usual approaches—psychodynamic, behavioral, cognitive, bio-medical, and so on. However, a novel and highly successful new technique, virtual reality (VR), has been developed in California by Lamson (2004).

Sixty participants were recruited from advertisements and were assigned randomly to either the experimental (VR) or the control (drugs) group. Each participant set themselves a target to be reached after a week's therapy, and over 90% of the VR group achieved theirs.

The VR group wore headsets that took them into a cafe with an open terrace. During the 50-minute therapy session the participant had to "walk" across the terrace and over a plank that led to a bridge set in a hilly scene. Lamson monitored participants' blood pressure and heart rate, and found that the fear response did subside during the 50-minute session. This therapy is a development of exposure therapy, but avoids the extreme anxiety of confronting the phobic stimulus in reality. It also avoids the risks, such as side effects, of even successful drug therapy. Perhaps one of the strengths of VR therapy is that it gives the clients confidence; they have been successful in the virtual world so this encourages them to be optimistic about success in the real world. As Lamson says, "within 3 months the woman who could barely start up a step ladder was on the roof cleaning the gutters."

Lamson, R. (2004). http://www.newscientist.com/channel/ health/mental-health/mg14219290.700.html

EFFECTIVENESS OF THERAPY

On the face of it, it seems easy to assess the effectiveness of therapy, and to decide whether one form of therapy is more or less effective than another. We could carry out a study including three groups of clients having the same diagnosis:

- One group receives therapy A.
- One group receives therapy B.
- One group remains on a waiting list.

We could then compare the percentages of clients recovering in the three groups, which would reveal the relative effectiveness of therapies A and B. However, there are several problems in assessing therapeutic effectiveness, some of which are discussed below.

First, there are several ways of assessing recovery, and therapists differ in what they regard as suitable outcome measures. For example, a major goal of therapy for psychodynamic therapists is to resolve inner conflicts, whereas for behavior therapists it is to produce desirable changes in overt behavior. Strupp (1996) pointed out that the effectiveness of any therapy can be considered from three perspectives:

1. *Society's perspective*: The individual's ability to function in society; the individual's adherence to social norms.
2. *Client's own perspective*: His/her overall subjective wellbeing; his/her ability to function effectively socially and at work.
3. *Therapist's perspective*: The client's thinking and behavior are related to the theoretical framework underlying the therapy used by the therapist.

Not surprisingly, the extent to which a client has recovered may vary considerably depending on which perspective we adopt.

Second, there is a conflict at the heart of much research on therapeutic effectiveness. This conflict involves deciding whether to adopt a scientific approach involving a high level of control over what happens, or to adopt a more realistic approach rooted in clinical practice. This conflict is a very real one because it is seldom possible to be scientific *and* realistic at the same time. Seligman (1995) focused on this conflict in his distinction between efficacy studies and effectiveness studies. **Efficacy studies** are scientific, well-controlled clinical trials (e.g., holding constant the number of therapy sessions) focusing on the elimination of well-defined problems. In contrast, **effectiveness studies** deal with actual clinical practice with all of its scientific shortcomings, and the focus is on subjective outcome measures (e.g., quality of life).

Key Terms

Efficacy studies: assessments of therapeutic effectiveness based on well-controlled investigations of well-defined clinical problems.

Effectiveness studies: assessments of therapeutic effectiveness based on typical clinical practice; see **efficacy studies**.

Should researchers carry out efficacy studies or effectiveness studies? Both kinds of studies are worthwhile. Efficacy studies (often regarded as the "gold standard" or best approach) allow us to identify factors responsible for benefit to clients and thus to interpret the findings with confidence. However, it is difficult to *generalize* the findings from such controlled studies to typical clinical practice. The strengths and weaknesses of effectiveness studies are exactly the opposite. They are informative about the typical outcomes in clinical practice. However, the uncontrolled nature of such studies makes it hard to be sure about the findings reported or about the interpretations of those findings. Our confidence in any given form of therapy would clearly be greatest if it produced good outcomes in efficacy *and* effectiveness studies. The limited evidence available suggests that beneficial effects of therapy tend to be greater in efficacy studies than in effectiveness ones (Weisz et al., 1995), in part because there is more focus on adherence to detailed treatment plans in the former studies.

Third, most waiting-list clients are actively seeking advice from other people while awaiting treatment (Cross, Sheehan, & Khan, 1980). Surprisingly, clients receiving treatment seek outside help even more than waiting-list controls. Changes in treated and untreated client groups over time depend to an unknown extent on these nontherapist sources of assistance.

HOW EFFECTIVE ARE DIFFERENT FORMS OF THERAPY?

In spite of the above issues, we can work out approximately the effectiveness of any form of therapy. Increasingly, researchers make use of meta-analysis, in which the findings from numerous studies are combined to provide an overall estimate of therapeutic effectiveness. For example, Shadish, Matt, Navarro, and Phillips (2000) conducted a meta-analysis of studies in which therapy was carried out under typical clinical conditions. All major forms of therapy were effective, and there were only small differences in effectiveness among them.

The finding that all forms of therapy are of comparable effectiveness has by no means always been reported—see the Key Study below.

Key Study

Matt and Navarro (1997): A review of the effects of therapy

Matt and Navarro (1997) considered 63 meta-analyses in which different types of therapy had been compared. Altogether, these meta-analyses were based on over 3800 studies involving tens of thousands of patients. On average, 75% of patients receiving treatment improved more than the average untreated control patient. Moderate beneficial effects were found with all forms of therapy: "The general class of interventions referred to as psychotherapy . . . appear to have universally positive effects compared to no-treatment controls across a wide range of different classes of interventions, patient populations, settings, outcomes, and research designs . . . Not a single meta-analysis concluded that psychotherapeutic interventions were ineffective" (Matt & Navarro, 1997, p. 5).

In about one-third of these meta-analyses, differences were reported in the effectiveness of different therapies. In general, behavior therapy and cognitive therapy tended to be more effective than psychodynamic or client-centered therapy. However, Matt and Navarro argued that those differences were more apparent than real. Clients treated by behavior or cognitive therapy often had less serious symptoms than those treated by psychodynamic or client-centered therapy. Nevertheless, it is striking that there are remarkably few studies in which psychodynamic therapy has been shown to be significantly more effective than alternative forms of therapy (Fonagy et al., 2005).

Matt and Navarro (1997) accepted that the information obtained from meta-analyses is generally limited in some ways. For example, it seems likely that the effectiveness of any given form of psychotherapy depends on several factors such as the nature of the disorder, the seriousness of the disorder, patient characteristics, and the precise outcomes that are assessed. However, the 63 meta-analyses considered by Matt and Navarro did not permit clear conclusions about the influence that such factors might have on therapeutic effectiveness.

Discussion points

1. What are the strengths and weaknesses of meta-analyses as a way of discovering the effectiveness of therapy?
2. How impressed are you by the apparent effectiveness of most forms of therapy revealed by Matt and Navarro?

KEY STUDY EVALUATION

A major criticism of Matt and Navarro's research concerns its lack of standardization. The specific conditions of individual cases are vital in determining the effectiveness of therapy. Linked to this is the timescale used. Regression or relapse would indicate failure of therapy, but this is impossible to discover from Matt and Navarro's study. A much lengthier approach, capable of handling disparate sets of data, with a methodology using detailed case notes and follow-up research would be needed to address this problem.

Accuracy is difficult to determine in meta-analyses, and it would be of value to consider making more use of the case-study-centered approach. However, the inevitable cost and time implications militate against this more focused type of study.

Effective treatments for various mental disorders (based on information in Roth & Fonagy, 2005)

Disorder	Clearly effective	Limited support for efficacy
Major depressive disorder	Cognitive-behavior therapy Interpersonal psychotherapy	Short-term psychodynamic therapy
Social phobia	Exposure therapy Exposure therapy + cognitive therapy	
Generalized anxiety disorder	Cognitive-behavior therapy Applied relaxation	
Panic disorder (+with agoraphobia)	Exposure therapy Cognitive-behavior therapy Panic control therapy	
Posttraumatic stress disorder	Cognitive-behavior therapy Eye movement desensitization	Structured psychodynamic therapy
Specific phobia	Exposure therapy	
Schizophrenia	Family intervention programs	Cognitive therapy for delusions Psychoeducation + psychological intervention

Roth and Fonagy (2005) analyzed exhaustively the effectiveness of different forms of therapy. For each disorder, they identified those forms of treatment that have been shown to be clearly effective, and those that currently have limited support (see the box above). Family intervention programs were identified as clearly effective in the treatment of schizophrenia. These programs involve schizophrenics and their families devising appropriate strategies and working together to achieve certain objectives. These programs have proved effective, but recent research suggests that the benefits are often greatly reduced over a 5-year period after treatment (Montero et al., 2006).

Roth and Fonagy erred on the side of caution, since there is reasonable evidence for the effectiveness of forms of therapy not emphasized by them. For example, psychodynamic therapy has proved effective in the treatment of schizophrenic patients having an initially high level of global functioning (Hauff et al., 2002). In addition, recent research indicates drug therapy is as effective as cognitive-behavior therapy in the treatment of generalized anxiety disorder (Mitte, 2005) and in the treatment of depression and several anxiety disorders (Otto et al., 2006).

WHY IS THERAPY EFFECTIVE?

There are two main reasons why any given therapy might be effective. First, there are **specific factors**, which are aspects of therapy specific or unique to that form of therapy. For example, Freud may have been correct in assuming that recovery will follow when patients gain insight into the nature of their problems. Second, there are **common factors**, which are aspects (e.g., therapist warmth; therapist empathy; therapeutic alliance between therapist and client) common to most forms of therapy.

Matt and Navarro (1997) considered 10 meta-analyses in which three types of group were compared:

1. Specific therapy groups, for whom any benefits may depend on specific effects or common effects.
2. Placebo control groups (involving general encouragement but no specific therapy), for whom any benefits are likely to depend on common effects.
3. Waiting-list control groups, for whom no benefits are expected.

The evidence indicated that 57% of placebo control patients did better than the average waiting-list control patient, indicating that common or placebo effects exist. However, 75% of the patients receiving specific therapy did better than the average placebo control patient, indicating that specific effects are much more powerful than common ones.

Stevens, Hynan, and Allen et al. (2000) reported similar findings in an analysis of 80 outcome studies in which specific therapy groups, common factor or placebo groups, and waiting-list control groups were compared. They also carried out a further analysis taking account of the severity of the mental disorder. With the less severe disorders, the impact of specific and common factors was comparable. With the more severe disorders, in contrast, *only* specific factors influenced the outcome. These findings make sense—a therapist *only* needs to be friendly and sympathetic to assist patients with minor disorders, but this is not enough to help patients with severe problems.

What characteristics should therapists possess (other than being friendly) to maximize their effectiveness? Lafferty, Beutler, and Crago (1989) found that effective therapists had greater empathy with or emotional understanding of their clients. In addition, effective therapists provided greater directiveness and support during therapy.

Najavits and Strupp (1994) considered the behavior of effective and ineffective therapists during treatment. They distinguished between positive behaviors (e.g., warmth, understanding, helping) and negative behaviors (e.g., ignoring, rejecting, and attacking). The effective therapists showed more positive behaviors and fewer negative behaviors than did the ineffective ones.

...warmth, acceptance and empathy on the part of the therapist.

Key Terms

Specific factors:
features unique to a given form of therapy that help the patient to recover; see **common factors**.

Common factors:
general factors found in most forms of therapy (e.g., therapist's personal qualities) that help the client to recover; see **specific factors**.

THE FUTURE?

If the truth be told, the picture I have painted so far is oversimplified. The notion that most therapists rigidly stick to a single therapeutic approach is increasingly incorrect. In reality, therapists typically practice **eclecticism**, using techniques drawn from various types of therapy rather than just one approach. As Kopta, Lueger, Saunders, and Howard (1999, p. 455) pointed out, "An increasingly popular view is that the long-term dominance of the major psychotherapies has ended and that integrationism and eclecticism is now the direction for technical advances in treatment."

Several years ago, Prochaska and Norcross (1994) found that 38% of American therapists identified their approach as eclectic. This can be compared with 33% using only a psychodynamic approach, 5% using only cognitive therapy, and 5% using only behavior therapy. Unfortunately, relatively few studies have considered the effectiveness of eclectic approaches to treatment. A potential warning was sounded by Otto, Smits, and Reese (2006), who considered research in which anxiety disorders were treated by combined drug therapy and cognitive-behavior therapy. They concluded as follows: "In the anxiety disorders, there are some benefits [to combined therapy] in the short-term, but combined treatment may limit the maintenance of treatment gains offered by CBT [cognitive-behavior therapy] alone" (Otto et al., 2006, p. 72).

Key Term
Eclecticism: the use of a range of different forms of treatment by a therapist rather than favoring a single therapeutic approach.

Chapter Summary

Drug therapy

- Drug therapy is used to treat mental disorders. Selective serotonin reuptake inhibitors (SSRIs) are commonly used to treat depression, the benzodiazepines are used for anxiety, and atypical antipsychotic drugs are used with schizophrenics. Relapse rates can be high because the drugs don't deal directly with the underlying problems.

Psychodynamic therapy

- According to Freud, successful therapy involves the client gaining insight into his/her repressed ideas and conflicts from childhood via free association and dream analysis. The psychodynamic approach triggered by Freud's psychoanalytic approach is moderately successful. However, it is unclear whether it works for the reasons proposed by Freud.

Behavior therapy

- Behavior therapists argue that classical and operant conditioning produce undesirable behavior and that conditioning can be used to produce desirable behavioral changes. Behavior therapy includes exposure therapy (which has proved very successful). It also includes aversion therapy and the token economy, both of which often fail to work in the long-term.

Cognitive and cognitive-behavior therapy

- According to the cognitive approach, patients suffering from mental disorders have distorted beliefs. In depressed patients, such thoughts center on the cognitive triad. In anxious patients, such thoughts center on exaggerating the threateningness of external and/or internal stimuli.
- Anxious patients' distorted beliefs are maintained because patients use safety-seeking behaviors that are mistakenly thought to prevent catastrophe.
- According to cognitive therapists, therapy should focus on eliminating patients' false beliefs. According to cognitive-behavior therapists, therapy should focus on changing behavior as well as eliminating false beliefs.
- Cognitive and cognitive-behavior therapy seem to be more effective in the treatment of anxiety and depression than more severe disorders such as schizophrenia.

Effectiveness of therapy

- Problems in assessing the effectiveness of therapy include selection of outcome measures, differences between efficacy and effectiveness studies, and the occurrence of nontherapist sources of assistance.
- Meta-analyses typically indicate that all major forms of therapy are moderately effective and differ only slightly in terms of effectiveness. However, there is increasing evidence that cognitive-behavior therapy is especially effective in treating depression and several anxiety disorders.
- Therapeutic effectiveness depends on specific and common factors. Both kinds of factors are important with less severe disorders, but specific factors are much more important than common ones with severe disorders.
- Effective therapists have high levels of empathy and provide more directiveness and support during therapy than less effective ones.
- Therapists increasingly use an eclectic approach, using techniques drawn from several different therapeutic approaches. Relatively little is known of the value of this approach.

Further Reading

- Butler, A.C., Chapman, J.E., Forman, E.M., & Beck, A.T. (2005). The empirical status of cognitive-behavioral therapy: A review of meta-analyses. *Clinical Psychology Review*, *26*, 17–31. Convincing evidence that cognitive-behavior therapy is effective in the treatment of many disorders is presented in this review article.
- Comer, R.J. (2007). *Abnormal psychology* (6th ed.). New York: Worth. Most of the important issues are discussed in a thorough and accessible way in this up-to-date textbook.
- Durand, V.M., & Barlow, D.H. (2006). *Essentials of abnormal psychology* (4th ed.). New York: Thomson/Wadsworth. As the title implies, this textbook by leading clinical psychologists focuses on central issues within abnormal psychology.
- Jarvis, M. (2004). *Psychodynamic psychology: Classical theory and contemporary research*. London: Thomson. Matt Jarvis provides an entertaining and balanced view of the entire psychodynamic approach.
- Roth, A., & Fonagy, P. (with contributions from G. Parry, M. Target, & R. Woods) (2005). *What works for whom? A critical review of psychotherapy research* (2nd ed.). New York: Guilford Press. The authors of this valuable book provide comprehensive coverage of the factors determining the effectiveness of different forms of therapy.

INTRODUCTION TO
Research Methods

P sychology is basically (and increasingly) a scientific subject. It is thus extremely important for experiments and other studies in psychology to be carried out in as scientific a fashion as possible. Thus, an understanding of research methods is crucial for students of psychology.

ORGANIZATION OF CHAPTERS 23–25

Chapter 23 is concerned with some of the main research methods used by psychologists. You may be surprised to discover how many types of study there are. The "gold standard" involves use of the experimental method. However, there are also correlational studies, naturalistic observations, in-depth case studies, interview-based studies, and discourse analysis. Examples of all of these are provided and discussed.

Chapter 24 is concerned with a consideration of how to carry out experiments and other studies effectively. Relevant issues include deciding on the hypotheses to be tested, selecting participants, designing the experiment so as to avoid unwanted variables and errors, and deciding on the experimental design. Good experimental research involves avoiding various problems that can invalidate it. For example, the experimenter may unwittingly influence the participants' behavior. This and other problems are discussed. There is also a section on issues relating to the design of various kinds of non-experimental studies including interviews, surveys, and case studies.

Chapter 25 focuses on data analysis. After we have collected data from an experimental or nonexperimental study, it is necessary to interpret those data and decide what conclusions are warranted. There are many ways in which data can be analyzed in order to provide a basis for interpreting them. There is a major distinction between *quantitative* analyses and *qualitative* analyses. Quantitative analyses use numerical data (e.g., reaction times; percentage correct responses), whereas qualitative analyses use non-numerical data (e.g., transcripts of interviews; information obtained from a case study).

An important goal of data analysis is to communicate findings to other people, and the use of charts and graphs for that purpose is discussed in Chapter 25. Other key issues are deciding *which* statistical test to use when quantitative analysis is called for, and then knowing *how* to perform the necessary calculations. Much experimental research is carried out under laboratory conditions, and an important issue is whether laboratory findings will generalize to everyday life (whether they possess ecological validity).

In sum, the main issues involved in carrying out psychological studies successfully are dealt with in this section. After reading all three chapters, you should be well equipped to carry out your own studies in psychology! I hope you find the process of carrying out and analyzing your own studies as fascinating as I have with my own research.

Contents

Psychological inquiry

In common with other sciences, psychology is concerned with theories and with data. A **theory** provides a general explanation or account of certain findings or data. It also generates a number of **experimental hypotheses**, which are predictions or expectations about behavior based on the theory. For example, someone might propose a theory in which it is argued that some people are more hostile than others. This theory could be used to produce various hypotheses or predictions, such as the following: Hostile people will express anger more often than nonhostile ones; hostile people will react more strongly than nonhostile ones to frustrating situations; hostile people will be more sarcastic than nonhostile people.

Psychologists spend a lot of their time collecting data in the form of measures of behavior. Data are collected in order to test various hypotheses. Most people assume that this data collection involves proper or true experiments carried out under laboratory conditions, and it is true that literally millions of laboratory experiments have been carried out in psychology. However, psychologists make use of several methods of investigation, each of which has provided useful information about human behavior.

As you read through the various methods of investigation, it is natural to wonder which methods are the best and which are the worst. In some ways, it may be more useful to compare the methods used by psychologists to the clubs used by the golf professional. The driver is not a better or worse club than the putter, it is simply used for a different purpose. In similar fashion, each method of investigation used by psychologists is very useful for testing some hypotheses, but is of little or no use for testing other hypotheses. However, as we will see, the experimental method provides the best way of being able to make inferences about cause and effect.

EXPERIMENTAL METHOD

The method of investigation used most often by psychologists is the experimental method. In order to understand what is involved in the experimental method, we will consider a concrete example.

DEPENDENT AND INDEPENDENT VARIABLES

Suppose that a psychologist wants to test the experimental hypothesis that loud noise will have a disruptive effect on the performance of a task. As with most hypotheses, this one refers to a **dependent variable**, which is some aspect of behavior that is going to be measured. In this case, the dependent variable is some measure of task performance.

Most experimental hypotheses state that the dependent variable will be affected systematically by some specified factor, which is known as the **independent variable**. In the case we are considering, the independent variable is the intensity of noise. More generally, the independent variable is some aspect of the experimental situation that is manipulated by the experimenter.

We come now to the most important principle involved in the use of the experimental method: the independent variable of interest is manipulated, but all other variables are *controlled*. It is assumed that, with all other variables controlled, the one and only

Key Terms

Theory:
a general explanation of a set of findings; it is used to produce experimental hypotheses.

Experimental hypotheses:
the testable predictions generated by a theory; these usually specify independent and dependent variables.

Dependent variable:
some aspect of the participant's behavior that is measured in a study.

Independent variable:
some aspect of the experimental situation that is manipulated by the experimenter.

The experimental process can be summarized thus:

- Experimenter acts on independent variable
- Changes in independent variable lead to changes in dependent variable
- Changes in dependent variable measured by experimenter

variable that is being manipulated is the cause of any subsequent change in the dependent variable. In terms of our example, we might expose one group of participants to very intense noise, and a second group to mild noise. What would we need to do to ensure that any difference in the performance of the two groups was a result of the noise rather than any other factor? We would control all other aspects of the situation by, for example, always using the same room for the experiment, keeping the temperature the same, and having the same lighting.

CONFOUNDING VARIABLES

Another way of expressing the essence of the experimental method is that it is of fundamental importance to avoid any **confounding variables**. These are variables that are manipulated or allowed to vary systematically along with the independent variable. The presence of any confounding variables has grave consequences, because it prevents us from being able to interpret our findings. For example, suppose that the participants exposed to intense noise performed the task in poor lighting conditions so that they could hardly see what they were doing, whereas those exposed to mild noise enjoyed good lighting conditions. If the former group performed much worse than the latter group, we would not know whether this was because of the intense noise, the poor lighting, or some combination of the two.

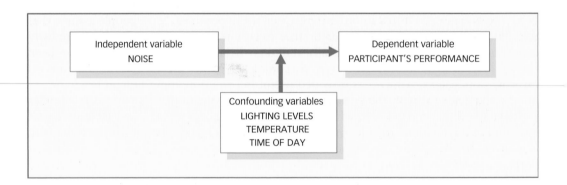

You might think that it would be easy to ensure that there were no confounding variables in an experiment. However, there are many well-known published experiments containing confounding variables. Consider, for example, a study by Jenkins and Dallenbach (1924). They gave a learning task to a group of participants in the morning, and then tested their memory for the material later in the day. The same learning task was given to a second group of participants in the evening, and their memory was tested the following morning after a night's sleep.

What did Jenkins and Dallenbach find? Memory performance was much higher for the second group than for the first. They argued that this was because there is less interference with memory when people are asleep than when they are awake. Can you see the flaw in this argument? The two groups learned the material at different times of day, and so time of day was a confounding variable. Hockey, Davies, and Gray (1972) discovered many years later that the time of day at which learning occurs is probably more important than whether or not the participants sleep between learning and the memory test.

PARTICIPANTS AND SETTINGS

Proper use of the experimental method requires careful consideration of the ways in which the participants are allocated to the various conditions. A detailed account is given in Chapter 24, so we will focus here only on experiments in which there are different participants in each condition. Suppose that the participants exposed to intense noise were on average much less intelligent than those exposed to mild noise. We would then be unable to tell whether poorer performance by the former participants was a result of the intense noise or their low intelligence. The main way of guarding against this possibility is by means of **randomization**, in which the participants are allocated at random to the two conditions.

Numerous studies are carried out using students as participants. This raises the issue of whether students are representative of society as a whole. For example, it is possible that students would be less distracted than other people by intense noise because they are used to studying over long periods of time in conditions that can be noisy, such as halls of residence.

The experimental method is used mainly in laboratory experiments. However, it is also used in **field experiments**, which are experiments carried out in natural settings such as in the street, in a school, or at work. Some of the advantages of the experimental method are common to

Ideally, psychological experiments should select a random sample of the population, although true randomness can be hard to achieve.

both laboratory and field experiments, whereas other advantages and limitations are specific to one type of experiment. We will consider the common advantages next, with more specific advantages and limitations being discussed after that.

In many studies, use is made of pre-existing groups of people. For example, we might compare the performance of males and females, or that of young and middle-aged individuals. Do such studies qualify as genuine experiments? The answer is "No." Use of the experimental method requires that the independent variable is *manipulated* by the experimenter, but clearly the experimenter cannot decide whether a given person is going to be male or female for the purposes of the study!

COMMON ADVANTAGES
Causal relationships
What is generally regarded as the greatest advantage of the experimental method is that it allows us to establish cause and effect relationships. In the terms we have been using, the independent variable in an experiment is often regarded as a cause, and the dependent variable is the effect. Philosophers of science have argued about whether or not causality can be established by experimentation. However, the general opinion is that causality can only be inferred. If y (e.g. poor performance) follows x (e.g. intense noise), then it is reasonable to infer that x caused y.

We can see why findings from studies based on the experimental method do not necessarily establish causality from the following imaginary example. An experiment on malaria is carried out in a hot country. Half of the participants sleep in bedrooms with the windows open, and the other half sleep in bedrooms with the windows closed. Those sleeping in bedrooms with the windows open are found to be more likely to catch malaria. It would obviously be wrong to argue that having the window open caused malaria. Having the window open or closed is relevant to catching the disease, but it tells us nothing directly about the major causal factor in malaria (infected mosquitoes).

Replication
The other major advantage of the experimental method concerns what is known as **replication**. If an experiment has been conducted in a carefully controlled way, it should be possible for other researchers to repeat or replicate the findings obtained from that experiment. There have been numerous failures to replicate using the experimental method, but the essential point is that the chances of replication are greater when the experimental method is used than when it is not.

LABORATORY VS. FIELD EXPERIMENTS
Laboratory and field experiments both involve use of the experimental method, but they differ in that field experiments are carried out in more natural settings. As an example of a field experiment, let us consider a study by Shotland and Straw (1976; see p. 433).

Key Terms
Randomization: the allocation of participants to conditions on a random basis.
Field experiment: a study in which the experimental method is used in a naturalistic situation.
Replication: the ability to repeat the findings obtained from an experiment.

When bystanders saw a staged fight in an experiment by Shotland and Straw (1976) they were more likely to help when they thought two strangers were involved than if they thought the couple were married.

They arranged for a man and a woman to stage an argument and a fight fairly close to a number of bystanders. In one condition, the woman screamed, "I don't know you." In a second condition, she screamed, "I don't know why I ever married you!" When the bystanders thought the fight involved strangers, 65% of them intervened, against only 19% when they thought it involved a married couple. Thus, people were less likely to lend a helping hand when it was a "lovers' quarrel" than when it was not. The bystanders were convinced that the fight was genuine, as was shown by the fact that 30% of the women were so alarmed that they shut the doors of their rooms, turned off the lights, and locked their doors.

The greatest advantage of laboratory experiments over field experiments is that it is generally easier to eliminate confounding variables in the laboratory than in the field. The experimenter is unlikely to be able to control every aspect of a natural situation.

Another clear advantage of laboratory experiments over field experiments is that it is much easier to obtain large amounts of very detailed information from participants in the laboratory. For example, it is hard to see how information about participants' physiological activity or speed of performing a range of complex cognitive tasks could be obtained in a field experiment carried out in a natural setting. There are two main reasons why field experiments are limited in this way. First, it is not generally possible to introduce bulky equipment into a natural setting. Second, the participants in a field experiment are likely to realize they are taking part in an experiment if attempts are made to obtain a lot of information from them.

One of the advantages of field experiments over laboratory experiments is that the behavior of the participants is often more *typical* of their normal behavior. However, the greatest advantage of field experiments over laboratory experiments is that they are less artificial. The artificiality of laboratory experimentation was emphasized by Heather (1976, pp. 31–33):

> *Psychologists have attempted to squeeze the study of human life into a laboratory situation where it becomes unrecognizably different from its naturally occurring form . . . Experiments in psychology . . . are social situations involving strangers, and it might be suggested that the main kind of knowledge gleaned from years of experimentation with human subjects is information about how strangers interact in the highly artificial and unusual setting of the psychological experiment.*

The effects of being observed

An important reason why laboratory experiments are more artificial than field experiments is because the participants in laboratory experiments are aware that their behavior is being observed. As Silverman (1977) pointed out, "Virtually the only condition in which a subject [participant] in a psychological study will not behave as a subject [participant] is if he does not know he is in one." One consequence of being observed is that the participants try to work out the experimenter's hypothesis, and then act accordingly. In this connection, Orne (1962) emphasized the importance of **demand characteristics**, which are "the totality of cues which convey an experimental hypothesis to the subjects." Orne found that the participants in one of his studies were willing to spend several hours adding numbers on random number sheets and then tearing up each completed sheet. Presumably the participants interpreted the experiment as a test of endurance, and this motivated them to keep going.

Another consequence of the participants in laboratory experiments knowing they are being observed is **evaluation apprehension**. Rosenberg (1965) defined this as "an active anxiety-toned concern that he [the participant] win a positive evaluation from the experimenter or at least that he provide no grounds for a negative one."

Key Terms

Demand characteristics: cues used by participants to try to guess the nature of the study or to work out what the experiment is about.

Evaluation apprehension: anxiety-toned concern felt by participants to perform well and please the experimenter.

Sigall, Aronson, and Van Hoose (1970) contrasted the effects of demand characteristics and evaluation apprehension on the task of copying telephone numbers. The experimenter told participants doing the task for the second time that he expected them to perform it at a rate that was actually slower than their previous performance. Adherence to the demand characteristics would have led to slow performance, whereas evaluation apprehension and the need to be capable would have produced fast times. The participants actually performed more quickly than they had done before, indicating the greater importance of evaluation apprehension.

This conclusion was strengthened by the findings from a second condition, in which the experimenter not only said that he expected the participants to perform at a slower rate, but also told them that those who rush are probably obsessive-compulsive. The participants in this condition performed the task slowly, because they wanted to be evaluated positively.

Participants in psychological experiments usually try to perform the task set by the experimenter as well as they can, in order to gain his or her approval.

Another way in which laboratory experiments tend to be more artificial than field experiments was identified by Wachtel (1973). He used the term **implacable experimenter** to describe the typical laboratory situation, in which the experimenter's behavior (e.g., instructions) affects the participant's behavior but the participant's behavior does not influence the experimenter's behavior. There are two problems with experiments using an implacable or unyielding experimenter. First, because the situation (including the experimenter) is allowed to influence the participant but the participant isn't allowed to affect the situation, it is likely that the effects of situations on our behavior are over-estimated. Second, because much of the richness of the dynamic interactions between individual and situation has been omitted, there is a real danger that seriously over-simplified accounts of human behavior will emerge.

Artificiality

How much does it matter that laboratory experiments are artificial? As Coolican (1998) pointed out, "In scientific investigation, it is often *necessary* to create artificial circumstances in order to *isolate* a hypothesized effect." If we are interested in studying basic cognitive processes such as those involved in perception or attention, then the artificiality of the laboratory is unlikely to affect the results. On the other hand, if we are interested in studying social behavior, then the issue of artificiality does matter. For example, Zegoib, Arnold, and Forehand (1975) found that mothers behaved in a warmer and more patient way with their children when they knew they were being observed than when they did not.

Carlsmith, Ellsworth, and Aronson (1976) drew a distinction between **mundane realism** and **experimental realism**. Mundane realism refers to experiments in which the situation is set up to resemble situations often found in everyday life. In contrast, experimental realism refers to experiments in which the situation may be rather artificial, but is sufficiently interesting to produce full involvement from the participants. Milgram's (1974) research on obedience to authority is a good example of experimental realism (see Chapter 19). The key point is that experimental realism may be more important than mundane realism in producing findings that generalize to real-life situations.

Laboratory experiments

Advantages

- Establishes cause-and-effect relationships
- Allows for replication
- Good control of confounding variables

Limitations

- Artificial
- Participants know they are being observed (demand characteristics and evaluation apprehension)
- Low in external validity
- Ethical concerns, such as the right to withdraw

Key Terms

Implacable experimenter:
the typical laboratory situation in which the experimenter's behavior is uninfluenced by the participant's behavior.

Mundane realism:
the use of an artificial situation that closely resembles a natural situation.

Experimental realism:
the use of an artificial situation in which the participants become fully involved.

Field experiments

Advantages

- Establishes cause and effect relationships
- Allows for replication
- Behavior of participants more typical than in a laboratory experiment: high external validity

Limitations

- Ethical issues, such as a lack of voluntary informed consent
- Low in internal validity: poor control

Ethical issues

What we will do here is discuss a few ethical issues that are of special relevance to laboratory or field experiments. So far as laboratory experiments are concerned, there is a danger that the participants will be willing to behave in a laboratory in ways they would not behave elsewhere. For example, Milgram (1974) found in his work on obedience (see Chapter 19) that 65% of his participants were prepared to give very intense electric shocks to someone else when the experiment took place in a laboratory at Yale University. In contrast, the figure was only 48% when the same study was carried out in a run-down office building. Thus, participants are often willing to do what they would not normally do in the setting of a prestigious laboratory.

Another ethical issue that applies especially to laboratory experiments concerns the participant's right to withdraw from the experiment at any time. It is general practice to inform participants of this right at the start of the experiment. However, participants may feel reluctant to exercise this right if they think it will cause serious disruption to the experimenter's research.

So far as field experiments are concerned, the main ethical issue relates to the principle of voluntary informed consent, which is regarded as central to ethical human research. By their very nature, most field experiments do not lend themselves to obtaining informed consent from the participants. For example, the study by Shotland and Straw (1976) would have been rendered almost meaningless if the participants had been asked beforehand to give their consent to witnessing a staged quarrel! The participants in that study could reasonably have complained about being exposed to a violent quarrel.

Another ethical issue with field experiments is that it is not possible in most field experiments to tell the participants that they have the right to withdraw at any time without offering a reason.

Summary

The respective strengths and weaknesses of laboratory experiments and field experiments can be summed up with reference to two different kinds of validity: internal validity and external validity. Internal validity refers to the validity of an experiment within the confines of the context in which it is carried out, whereas external validity refers to the validity of an experiment outside the research situation itself. Laboratory experiments tend to be high in internal validity but low in external validity, whereas field experiments are high in external validity but low in internal validity.

QUASI-EXPERIMENTS

"True" experiments based on the experimental method provide the best way of being able to draw causal inferences with confidence. However, it is often the case that there are practical or ethical reasons why it is simply not possible to carry out a true experiment. In such circumstances, investigators often carry out what is known as a **quasi-experiment**. Quasi-experimental designs "resemble experiments but are weak on some of the characteristics" (Raulin & Graziano, 1994). There are two main ways in which quasi-experiments tend to fall short of being true experiments. First, the manipulation of the independent variable is often not under the control of the experimenter. Second, it is usually not possible to allocate the participants randomly to groups.

There are numerous hypotheses in psychology that can only be studied by means of quasi-experiments rather than true experiments. For example, suppose that we are interested in studying the effects of divorce on young children. We could do this by comparing children whose parents had divorced with those whose parents were still married. There would, of course, be no possibility of allocating children at random to the

Key Term

Quasi-experiment:
a type of experiment resembling a "true" experiment, but with some aspects of the experimental method omitted.

divorced or non-divorced parent groups! Studies in which pre-existing groups are compared often qualify as quasi-experiments. Examples of such quasi-experiments would be comparing the learning performance of males and females, or comparing the social behavior of introverted and extraverted individuals.

NATURAL EXPERIMENTS

The **natural experiment** is a type of quasi-experiment in which a researcher makes use of some naturally occurring event for research purposes. An example of a natural experiment is a study by Williams (1986) on the effects of television on aggressive behavior in Canadian children aged between 6 and 11 years. Three communities were compared: one in which television had just been introduced, one in which there was only one television channel, and one in which there were several channels. The children in the first community showed a significant increase in verbal and physical aggression during the first 2

Adams and Adams (1984) designed a natural experiment around the eruption of the Mount St. Helens volcano in which they assessed the effects of stress on the population of a small town threatened by the eruption.

years after television was introduced, whereas those in the other two communities did not. This was not a true experiment, because the children were not allocated randomly to the three conditions or communities.

Adams and Adams (1984) carried out a natural experiment following the eruption of the Mount St. Helens volcano in 1980. As the volcanic eruption had been predicted, they were able to assess the inhabitants of the small town of Othello before and after it happened. There was a 50% increase in mental health appointments, a 198% increase in stress-aggravated illness, and a 235% increase in diagnoses of mental illness.

Advantages and limitations

What are the advantages of natural experiments? The main one is that the participants in natural experiments are often not aware that they are taking part in an experiment, even though they are likely to know that their behavior is being observed. Another advantage of natural experiments is that they allow us to study the effects on behavior of independent variables that it would be unethical for the experimenter to manipulate. For example, Adams and Adams (1984) were interested in observing the effects of a major stressor on physical and mental illness. No ethical committee would have allowed them to expose their participants deliberately to stressors that might cause mental illness, but they were able to take advantage of a natural disaster to conduct a natural experiment.

What are the limitations of natural experiments? The greatest limitation occurs because the participants have not been assigned at random to conditions. As a result, observed differences in behavior between groups may be a result of differences in the types of participants in the groups rather than the effects of the independent variable. Consider, for example, the study by Williams (1986) on television and aggression. The children in the community that had just been exposed to television might have been naturally more aggressive than the children in the other two communities. However, the children in the three communities did not differ in their level of aggression at the start of the study.

It is usually possible to check whether the participants in the various conditions are comparable. For example, they can be compared with respect to variables such as age, sex, socioeconomic status, and so on. If the groups do differ significantly in some respects irrelevant to the independent variable, then this greatly complicates the task of interpreting the findings of a natural experiment.

The other major limitation of natural experiments involves the independent variable. In some natural experiments, it is hard to know exactly what aspects of the independent variable have caused any effects on behavior. For example, there is no doubt that the eruption of Mount St. Helens was a major stressor. It caused stress in part because of the

Key Term
Natural experiment: a type of quasi-experiment in which use is made of some naturally occurring event.

possibility that it might erupt again and produce more physical devastation. However, social factors were also probably involved. If people in Othello observed that one of their neighbors was highly anxious because of the eruption, this may have heightened their level of anxiety.

Ethical issues

It can be argued that there are fewer ethical issues with natural experiments than with many other kinds of research. The reason is that the experimenter is not responsible for the fact that the participants have been exposed to the independent variable. However, natural experiments can raise various ethical issues. First, there can be the issue of informed voluntary consent, in view of the fact that the participants are often not aware that they are taking part in an experiment. Second, experimenters carrying out natural experiments need to be sensitive to the situation in which the participants find themselves. People who have been exposed to a natural disaster such as a volcanic eruption may resent it if experimenters start asking them detailed questions about their mental health or psychological wellbeing.

CORRELATIONAL STUDIES

Suppose that we were interested in the hypothesis that watching violence on television leads to aggressive behavior. One way of testing this hypothesis would be to obtain two kinds of information from a large number of people: (1) the amount of violent television they watched; and (2) the extent to which they behaved aggressively in various situations. If the hypothesis is correct, then we would expect that those who have seen the most violence on television would tend to be the most aggressive. In technical terms, this study would be looking for a **correlation**, or association, between watching violent programs and being aggressive. Thus, the closer the link between them, the greater would be the correlation or association.

One of the best-known uses of the correlational approach is in the study of the role of nature and nurture in intelligence. Similarity in intelligence within pairs is worked out by means of a correlation. Identical twins are more alike genetically than fraternal twins. As a result, their levels of intelligence should be more similar than those of fraternal twins if heredity plays an important role in determining intelligence. As predicted, the correlation indicating the degree of similarity in intelligence is nearly always higher for identical twins than for fraternal twins. However, it has proved hard to provide a detailed interpretation of the findings.

ADVANTAGES AND LIMITATIONS

Correlational designs are generally regarded as inferior to experimental designs, because it is hard (or impossible) to establish cause and effect. In our example, the existence of an association between the amount of television violence watched and aggressive behavior would certainly be consistent with the hypothesis that watching violent programs can cause aggressive behavior. However, there are other possible interpretations of the data. The causality may actually operate in the opposite direction. In other words, aggressive individuals may choose to watch more violent programs than those who are less aggressive. There may be a third variable that accounts for the association between the variables of interest, that is, watching violent programs and aggressive behavior. For example, people in disadvantaged families may watch more television programs of all kinds than those in nondisadvantaged families, and their deprived circumstances may also cause them to behave aggressively. If that were the case, then the number of violent television programs watched might have no direct effect at all on aggressive behavior.

In spite of the interpretive problems posed by the findings of correlational studies, there are several reasons why psychologists continue to use this method.

Key Term

Correlation:
an association that is found between two variables.

First, many hypotheses cannot be examined directly by means of experimental designs. For example, the hypothesis that smoking causes a number of physical diseases cannot be tested by forcing some people to smoke and forcing others not to smoke! All that can be done is to examine correlations or associations between the number of cigarettes smoked and the probability of suffering from various diseases.

Second, it is often possible to obtain large amounts of data on a number of variables in a correlational study much more rapidly and efficiently than would be possible using experimental designs. Use of a questionnaire, for example, would permit a researcher to investigate the associations between aggressive behavior and a wide range of activities (such as watching violent movies in the cinema; reading violent books; being frustrated at work or at home).

Third, interpretive problems are much reduced if there is no association between two variables. For example, if it were found that there was no association at all between the amount of violent television watched and aggressive behavior, this would provide fairly strong evidence that aggressive behavior is not caused by watching violent programs on television.

Fourth, the interpretive problems with associations or correlations between two variables are often not as great as in the example of violent programs and aggression. Suppose, for example, we discover a correlation between age and happiness, in which older people are generally less happy than younger people. Although it would not be possible to offer a definitive interpretation of this finding, we could be entirely confident that unhappiness does not cause old age!

> **Correlational studies**
>
> *Advantages*
> - Allows study of hypotheses that cannot be examined directly
> - More data on more variables can be collected more quickly than in an experimental set-up
> - Problems of interpretation are reduced when no association is found
> - Even when strong correlations are found it may be obvious that no causal relationship exists
>
> *Limitations*
> - Interpretation of results is difficult
> - Cause and effect cannot be established
> - Direction of causality is uncertain
> - Variables other than the one of interest may be operating

ETHICAL ISSUES

Correlational analyses are used very widely. As a result, it is not possible to identify any particular ethical issues that apply to most studies in which such analyses are carried out. However, correlational analyses are often used in socially sensitive research, which raises political and/or social issues. For example, consider the correlational evidence suggesting that individual differences in intelligence depend in part on genetic factors. Some people have argued mistakenly that this implies that race differences in intelligence also depend on genetic factors. The key ethical issue here (and in many other correlational studies) is for the researcher to be fully aware of the social sensitivity of the findings that he or she has obtained.

Another ethical issue is raised by the real possibility that the public at large will misinterpret the findings from correlational studies. For example, the finding that there was a correlation between the amount of television violence watched by children and their level of aggression led many influential people to argue that television violence was having a damaging effect. In other words, they mistakenly supposed that correlational evidence can demonstrate a causal relation. Television companies may have suffered from such overinterpretation of findings.

NATURALISTIC OBSERVATION

Naturalistic observation involves methods designed to examine behavior without the experimenter interfering with it in any way. This approach was originally developed by the ethologists Lorenz and Tinbergen. They studied animals in their natural habitat rather than in the laboratory, and discovered much about their behavior. An example of the use of naturalistic observation in human

The issue of whether or not there is a correlation between violence on television and aggressive behavior is frequently debated in the media.

research is the work of Brown, Fraser, and Bellugi (1964). They studied the language development of three children (Adam, Eve, and Sarah) by visiting them at home about 35 times a year.

One of the key requirements of the method of naturalistic observation is to avoid *intrusion*. Dane (1994, p. 1149) defined this as "anything that lessens the participants' perception of an event as natural." There are various ways in which intrusion can occur. For example, there will be intrusion if observations are made in an environment that the participants regard as a research setting. There will also be intrusion if the participants are aware that they are being observed. In many studies, the experimenter is in the same room as the participants, and so they are almost certain to realize they are being observed. When this is the case, the experimenter may try to become a familiar and predictable part of the situation before any observations are recorded.

The participants in naturalistic observation often display a wide range of verbal and nonverbal behavior. How can observers avoid being overloaded in their attempts to record this behavior? One approach is to focus only on actions or events that are of particular interest to the researcher; this is known as event sampling. Another approach is known as time sampling, in which observations are only made during specified time periods (e.g., the first 10 minutes of each hour). A third approach is point sampling, in which one individual is observed in order to categorize their current behavior, after which a second individual is observed.

In considering the data obtained from naturalistic observation, it is important to distinguish between recording and interpretation or coding. For example, an observer may record that the participant has moved forward, and interpret that movement as an aggressive action. In practice, however, observers typically only focus on interpreting or coding the participants' behavior. For example, Bales (1950) developed the interaction process analysis, which allows observers to record inferred meanings for the forms of behavior shown by members of a group (e.g., "offers suggestion").

There have been various attempts to develop ways of categorizing people's behavior in naturalistic observation without interpreting it. For example, McGrew (1972) devised a detailed and comprehensive recording system to place the social interactions of children at nursery school into 110 categories.

ADVANTAGES AND LIMITATIONS

What are the advantages of naturalistic observation? First, if the participants are unaware that they are being observed, then it provides a way of observing people behaving naturally. When this happens, there are no problems from demand characteristics, evaluation apprehension, the implacable experimenter, and so on. Second, many studies based on naturalistic observation provide richer and fuller information than typical laboratory experiments. For example, participants' behavior may be observed in a range of different social contexts rather than on their own in the laboratory. Third, it is sometimes possible to use naturalistic observation when other methods cannot be used. For example, the participants may be unwilling to be interviewed or to complete a questionnaire. In the case of participants being observed at work, it may be impossible to obtain permission to disrupt their work in order to carry out an experiment.

What are the limitations of naturalistic observation? These are some of the major ones:

- The experimenter has essentially no control over the situation; this can make it very hard or impossible to decide what caused the participants to behave as they did.
- The participants are often aware that they are being observed, with the result that their behavior is not natural.
- There can be problems of reliability with the observational measures taken, because of bias on the part of the observer or because the categories into which behavior is coded are imprecise. Attempts to produce good reliability often involve the use of very precise but narrow categories, leading to much of the participants' behavior simply being ignored. Reliability can be assessed by correlating the observational records of two

different observers. This produces a measure of inter-rater reliability.

- The fact that observations are typically interpreted or coded prior to analysis can cause problems with the validity of measurement. For example, it may be assumed invalidly that all instances of one child striking another child represent aggressive acts, when in fact many of them are only playful gestures. Thus, great care needs to be taken in **operationalization**, which is a procedure in which a variable (e.g., aggressive act) is defined by the operations taken to measure it.
- There are often problems of replication with studies of naturalistic observation. For example, the observed behavior of children in a school may depend in part on the fact that most of the teachers are very lenient and fail to impose discipline. The findings might be very different at another school in which the teachers are strict.

> **Naturalistic observation**
>
> *Advantages*
> - People tend to behave naturally
> - Information that is gathered is rich and full
> - Can be used where other methods are not possible
>
> *Limitations*
> - Experimenter has no control over the situation
> - Participants can be aware of being watched and this can affect behavior
> - Problems of reliability as a result of bias or imprecise categorization of behavior
> - Problems of validity resulting from observers' or coders' assumptions
> - Replication is not usually possible

ETHICAL ISSUES

Naturalistic observation poses ethical problems if the participants do not realize that their behavior is being observed. In those circumstances, they obviously cannot give their voluntary informed consent to be involved in the study. There can also be problems about confidentiality. Suppose, for example, that naturalistic observation takes place in a particular school, and the published results indicate that many of the children are badly behaved. Even if the name of the school is not mentioned in the report, many people reading it will probably be able to identify the school because they know that the researchers made detailed observations there.

CASE STUDIES

The great majority of studies in psychology have involved the use of experimental or correlational methods on groups of participants. These approaches permit the use of statistical techniques providing information about the extent to which the results obtained from a given sample can be generalized to some larger population.

There are often good reasons why it is not feasible to use numerous participants in a study. For example, a brain-damaged patient may have a very unusual pattern of impaired performance, and there may not be other patients having the same pattern. Another example might be a therapist who has a patient with a rare mental disorder, but there is no possibility of him or her collecting data from other patients with the same disorder. In such circumstances, it can be very useful to carry out a **case study**, in which one individual is investigated thoroughly and over a period of time.

Some researchers have argued that the study of individual cases can be more fruitful than the study of groups of participants. One of the most convincing statements of that argument was put forward by Gordon Allport (1962):

> *Why should we not start with individual behavior as a source of hunches . . . and then seek our generalizations but finally come back to the individual not for the mechanical application of laws but for a fuller and more accurate assessment than we are now able to give? . . . We stop with our wobbly laws of generality and seldom confront them with the concrete person.*

Some of those who have favored single-case studies have been of an anti-scientific persuasion. However, a prominent experimentalist who advocated the use of single-case studies was the behaviorist B.F. Skinner. In a discussion of research on operant conditioning, Skinner (1966) argued, "instead of studying a thousand rats for one hour each, or a hundred rats for ten hours each, the investigator is likely to study one rat for a thousand hours."

Key Terms

Operationalization:
a procedure in which variables of interest are defined by the operations taken to measure them.

Case study:
detailed investigation of a single individual.

Can psychologists learn as much from the detailed study of the behavior of a single rat as they can from a more superficial study of a large number of rats?

There are several types of case studies, and they are carried out for various reasons, some of which will be considered here. One reason is to test a current theory. For example, Atkinson and Shiffrin (1968) argued that information only enters the long-term memory store via the short-term memory store (see Chapter 8). As a result, a brain-damaged individual with impaired short-term memory should also have impaired long-term memory. Evidence that seemed to be inconsistent with this theory was reported in a case study on KF, who was involved in a motorcycle accident (Shallice & Warrington, 1970). He had very poor short-term memory for words and digits, but his long-term learning and recall were unaffected.

Case studies can also be used to refine theories. Baddeley and Hitch (1974) argued that people possess a phonological loop that is used in the rehearsal of verbal information (see Chapter 8). It used to be assumed that rehearsal within the phonological loop requires use of the speech muscles. However, Baddeley and Wilson (1985) carried out a case study on a student, GB. He suffered from anarthria, which meant that he could not use his speech muscles and was unable to speak. In spite of this disorder, GB was able to make use of the articulatory loop.

Key Study

Freud: Developing new theories

Case studies are also of value in the development of new theories. For example, Sigmund Freud carried out a case study on Dr. Schreber, a lawyer who suffered from paranoia (a mental disorder involving delusions). Freud was puzzled by the fact that Dr. Schreber and other paranoid patients had a number of apparently unrelated delusions. These included a jealous feeling that their spouses or lovers had been unfaithful to them, the belief that others were plotting against them, the belief that several members of the opposite sex were in love with them, and delusions of grandeur.

Freud's discussions with Dr. Schreber led him to an analysis of paranoia. According to Freud, homosexual desires underlie paranoia. However, because homosexuality was viewed with disfavor by society at that time, Freud felt that these desires remain unconscious and become distorted in various ways. One such distortion is for a male paranoiac to think his wife or lover loves another man, which produces jealousy. Delusions of grandeur were accounted for by assuming that the male paranoid individual's thought "I love a man," turns into "I love no one," and then into "I love no one but myself." This analysis led Freud to develop a new (but implausible) theory of paranoia.

Discussion points
1. Can you spot any problems with the case study on Dr. Schreber?
2. Is there any way in which we could test Freud's proposed interpretation of the case study?

Actress Joanne Woodward portrayed the different "personalities" of Chris Sizemore in the film *The Three Faces of Eve*.

Some case studies are based on very unusual individuals. For example, there was Chris Sizemore, who was the central character in the film *The Three Faces of Eve*. Some of the time she was Eve White, a well-behaved and inhibited woman. At other times, she was Eve Black, who was promiscuous and impulsive. At still other times, she was Jane, who was more stable than either of the other two personalities. The existence of individuals with multiple personalities raises issues about our usual assumption that everyone has one personality and one self.

ADVANTAGES AND LIMITATIONS

What are the advantages of case studies? First, as we have seen, a single-case study can provide good evidence that a particular theory is in error. Of course, it is then desirable to find and test other individuals to check the findings from the first case study. Second, a case study can help to refine our theoretical understanding. Third, case studies can provide rich information that is used by the researcher or therapist to develop new theoretical ideas. An example of this is the case of Dr. Schreber, which was discussed in the Key Study earlier. Fourth, case studies can provide information about exceptional types of behavior or performance that had been thought to be impossible.

What are the limitations of case studies? The greatest limitation is their typically low reliability. The findings that are obtained from one unusual or exceptional individual are unlikely to be repeated in detail from another individual. Thus, it is often very hard to generalize from a single-case study. Second, many case studies involve the use of lengthy, fairly unstructured, interviews. Such case studies share the limitations that are identified for interviews in the next section. Third, researchers generally only report some of the data they obtained from their interviews with the participant. They may be unduly selective in terms of what they choose to report or to omit.

ETHICAL ISSUES

Case studies with clinical patients can pose important issues about confidentiality. A therapist such as Sigmund Freud may want to publish details of his case studies because they seem to support his theoretical position. However, the patient may be very unwilling for personal information about him or her to be published. Case studies with brain-damaged patients can pose ethical issues about voluntary informed consent. For example, patients with severe language impairments may find it hard to understand what will be involved in a case study, and so they cannot give proper informed consent.

INTERVIEWS

As Coolican (1994) pointed out, there are various kinds of interview, which vary enormously in terms of the amount of structure they contain. In what follows, we make use of his categorization of different types of interview.

NONDIRECTIVE INTERVIEWS

Nondirective interviews possess the least structure, with the person being interviewed (the interviewee) being free to discuss almost anything he or she wants. The role of the interviewer in nondirective interviews is to guide the discussion and to encourage the interviewee to be more forthcoming. This type of interview is used very often in psychotherapy, but has little relevance to research.

INFORMAL INTERVIEWS

Informal interviews resemble nondirective interviews, in that the interviewer listens patiently and focuses mainly on encouraging the interviewee to discuss issues in more depth or detail. However, informal interviews differ in that there are certain general topics that the interviewer wishes to explore. One of the best-known examples involving informal interviews was a large-scale study of workers at the Hawthorne works of Western Electric. The aim of this study was to explore industrial relations via a series of interviews. What emerged from informal interviews was that the relatively minor issues initially raised by the workers generally reflected deeper and more serious worries (Roethlisberger & Dickson, 1939; see p. 579).

GUIDED INTERVIEWS

Informal but guided interviews possess a little more structure than informal interviews. The interviewer identifies beforehand the issues to be addressed, but how and when to

---

Why use case studies?

- To test current theories
- To refine existing theories
- To develop new theories
- To test usual assumptions

There are various types of interviews used for psychological experimentation, from nondirective interviews to fully structured designs that have a standard set of questions with restricted-choice answers.

raise those issues is decided during the course of the interview. Structured but open-ended interviews use a formal procedure in which all interviewees are asked precisely the same questions in the same order. Such a procedure prevents the interviewee from side-tracking the interview and taking control of it away from the interviewer. The interviews are open-ended, in the sense that the questions that are asked allow plenty of scope for various kinds of answers (e.g. "How do you see your career developing?").

CLINICAL INTERVIEWS

The clinical interview or clinical method resembles the structured but open-ended interview. In essence, all of the interviewees or participants are asked the same questions, but the choice of follow-up questions depends on the answers that are given. Piaget made much use of the clinical method in his research on cognitive development in children (see Chapter 14). Piaget understood that children might perform poorly on a task because they did not understand fully what the experimenter wanted them to do. One way of trying to avoid this problem was by giving the experimenter the flexibility to ask questions in various ways. In spite of this, critics of Piaget have argued that the children he studied often failed to solve problems because of the complex language used by the experimenter.

FULLY STRUCTURED INTERVIEWS

Finally, there is the fully structured interview. In this type of interview, a standard set of questions is asked in the same fixed order to all of the interviewees, and they are only allowed to choose their answers from a restricted set of possibilities (e.g. "Yes"; "No"; "Don't know"). As Coolican (1994, pp. 121–122) pointed out, "this approach is hardly an interview worth the name at all. It is a face-to-face data-gathering technique, but could be conducted by telephone or by post."

ADVANTAGES AND LIMITATIONS

What are the advantages of the interview method? As might be expected, the precise advantages depend on the type of interview. Relatively unstructured interviews have the advantage that they are responsive to the personality, interests, and motivations of the interviewee. In principle, they can perhaps reveal more about the interviewee than is likely to be the case with more structured interviews. One of the advantages of fairly structured interviews is that it is easy to compare the responses of different interviewees, all of whom have been asked the same questions. Another advantage is good reliability, in that two different interviewers are likely to obtain similar responses from an interviewee when they ask exactly the same questions in the same order. A further advantage is that there is a reasonable probability of being able to replicate or repeat the findings from a study using structured interviews. Finally, structured interviews have the advantage that it is usually fairly easy to analyze the data obtained from them.

What are the limitations of the interview method? So far as unstructured interviews are concerned, there is the problem that the kinds of information obtained from different interviewees vary in an unsystematic way. As a result, the data from unstructured interviews tend to be hard to analyze. A further limitation with unstructured interviews is that what the interviewee says is determined in a complex way by the interaction between him or her and the interviewer. In other words, the personality and other characteristics of the interviewer typically influence the course of the interview, and make it hard to work out which of the interviewee's contributions are and are not affected by the interviewer. Finally, the fact that the information obtained from interviewees in unstructured interviews is influenced by the interviewer means that the data obtained can be viewed as unreliable.

One of the main limitations with structured interviews is that what the interviewee says may be somewhat constrained and artificial because of the high level of structure built into the interview. Another limitation is that there is little or none of the flexibility associated with unstructured interviews.

Finally, we need to consider three limitations that are common to all types of interview. First, there is the issue of social desirability bias. Most people want to present a favorable impression of themselves to other people, and this may lead them to distort their answers to personal questions. For example, people are much more willing to admit that they are unhappy when filling in a questionnaire anonymously than when being interviewed (Eysenck, 1990). Second, interviews can only extract information of which the

People are more willing to answer embarrassing or personal questions on an anonymous written questionnaire than in a face-to-face interview.

interviewee is consciously aware. This is a significant limitation, because people are often unaware of the reasons why they behave in certain ways (Nisbett & Wilson, 1977). Third, there is the limitation that many interviewers lack some of the skills necessary to conduct interviews successfully. Good interviewers are able to make an interview seem natural, they are sensitive to nonverbal cues, and they have well-developed listening skills (Coolican, 1994).

ETHICAL ISSUES

Interviews (especially clinical interviews) are often concerned with personal issues about which the interviewee is sensitive. This clearly raises the issue of confidentiality. There are various ways in which confidentiality can be broken. For example, Coolican (1994) discussed a study by Vidich and Bensman (1958) in which direct quotations from interviewees in Springdale in the United States were published. Made-up names were used, but the people of Springdale were able to identify the actual individuals on the basis of what they said.

Confidentiality can also be broken if a detailed written account or video recording of an interview falls into the wrong hands. Finally, of course, the interviewer himself or herself may disclose sensitive personal information about the interviewee to other people.

There is another ethical issue that is of particular importance with structured interviews. Interviewees may be aware that several other interviewees are being asked the same questions, and that their answers will be compared. As a result, some interviewees may feel that they must answer embarrassing questions in order not to spoil the experiment.

DISCOURSE ANALYSIS

According to Potter and Wetherell (1987), **discourse analysis** is concerned with "all forms of spoken interaction, formal and informal, and written texts of all kinds." The basic underlying assumption is that the ways in which we use language are greatly affected by the social context. Thus, for example, when politicians give speeches, it would be naive to assume that what they say simply reflects their genuine beliefs and views. It is generally accepted that what they say is designed to have certain effects on their audience, on other politicians, and on the public.

There is much evidence to indicate that people do adjust what they say or write to fit the circumstances. For example, consider studies using the bogus pipeline. The participants are wired up to an impressive-looking machine (the bogus pipeline), and informed that it can detect any lies they produce. Most white participants express more

Key Term
Discourse analysis: a qualitative form of analysis applied to language productions in spoken or written form.

negative attitudes towards black people when wired up to the bogus pipeline than under standard conditions (see Chapter 20). The implication is that the attitudes that people express normally are constructed so as to be socially acceptable to other people.

Gilbert and Mulkay (1984) carried out a discourse analysis based on interviews with 34 scientists. The importance of social factors in discourse was revealed by comparing what these scientists said during the interviews with their academic publications. The general pattern was for scientists to be much more confident about the meaning of their findings when interviewed than they were in their writings.

As Curtis (1997, p. 24) pointed out, "The idea that there is one way to perform discourse analysis is both naive and illusory." Nevertheless, he identified seven features that are often found in discourse analysis:

1. Select some written or spoken material that is relevant to the issues you want to study.
2. Read or listen to the discourse several times, trying to decide how it has been constructed. Account needs to be taken of the social context in which it was produced.
3. Develop a qualitative coding system focusing on the functions or purposes that seem to be served by the discourse.
4. Produce some tentative hypotheses about the purposes served by the discourse, but be willing to modify these hypotheses if subsequent analysis indicates that they are inadequate.
5. How has the person producing the discourse tried to legitimize or make persuasive his or her version of events?
6. Examine the discourse for evidence of extreme case formulations. People often use extreme terms (e.g., always; never) to make their preferred interpretation seem more persuasive.
7. Examine the discourse carefully to see whether the purposes or functions it serves vary from one part to another.

People adjust what they say to fit the circumstances.

ADVANTAGES AND LIMITATIONS

One of the advantages of discourse analysis is that it is based on the correct assumption that our use of language is often much influenced by the social context. This is true of how we remember events in our lives as well as our expressed attitudes and beliefs. As Coolican (1994, p.178) pointed out:

When we remember and attribute in real life, as opposed to the psychology experiment, our accounts attend to blame, defense, accountability, explanation and so on. What we often do is to present rememberings as facts when they are really constructions.

For example, the way you describe events in your life is likely to vary depending on whether you are talking to your parents, to your best friend, or to an acquaintance.

Another advantage is that discourse analysis focuses on the ways in which language is used in real-life settings. As such, it avoids much of the artificiality of most experiments. In addition, the claims of those who favor discourse analysis that language is the primary mode of communication among human beings are correct.

There are several limitations of discourse analysis, many of which were discussed by Burman and Parker (1993). A major limitation is that the validity of discourse analysis is open to considerable doubt, and that procedures for assessing validity are lacking. For example, if two researchers interpret a given piece of discourse in very different ways, we cannot be sure which of them has produced the more valid interpretation.

A further limitation is that we often have little information about the reliability or consistency with which the discourse analysis has been carried out. When such information is available, it frequently indicates that reliability is low (Coolican, 1994).

Another limitation is that what emerges from discourse analysis may be unduly influenced by the views and beliefs of the researcher. As Human (1992) expressed it, discourse analysis is sometimes simply "a researcher's ideas with examples." A key reason why this can happen is because there are so few constraints on the researcher as he or she tries to make sense of any given written or spoken discourse.

A final limitation is that discourse analysis is based solely on the analysis of language in its various forms. However, language is by no means the only means of communication open to people. Account needs to be taken of nonverbal communication of various kinds (e.g., body language).

ETHICAL ISSUES

It is often important for the researcher to make sure that anyone whose discourse is to be analyzed has given their permission for it to be used for that purpose. However, that ethical issue may not arise if the discourse is in the public domain (e.g., a speech or television interview given by a politician).

There can also be ethical issues if the researcher's proposed interpretation is likely to offend those who provided the discourse. For example, Wetherell and Potter (1988) carried out discourse analysis on interviews with white New Zealanders. They concluded that those interviewed had racist attitudes towards the Maoris, although they did not directly say so in the interviews. In such circumstances, it is important for the researcher to discuss his or her proposed interpretation with the participants before the results of the study are published or made generally available.

A final ethical issue stems from the fact that discourse analysis often involves detailed analysis of an individual's discourse. As a result, it is sometimes impossible to adhere to the ethical principles that the information provided by participants should be confidential and that individuals should not be identifiable.

Chapter Summary

Experimental method

- The key principle of the experimental method is that the independent variable is manipulated (with all other variables controlled) in order to observe its effect on some dependent variable. In other words, it is important to avoid confounding variables. The experimental method is used in laboratory and field experiments. Use of the experimental method allows us to infer causality, and it often permits replication. Laboratory experiments have various advantages over field experiments: it is usually easier to eliminate confounding variables, and to obtain detailed behavioral and physiological information. The greatest advantage of field experiments over laboratory experiments is that they are less artificial, and suffer less from factors such as demand characteristics, evaluation apprehension, and the implacable experimenter.

Quasi-experiments

- Quasi-experiments fall short of true experiments either because the experimenter has not manipulated the independent variable or because the participants are not allocated at random to conditions. Natural experiments are quasi-experiments involving some naturally occurring event. Advantages of natural experiments include the possibility that the participants will not be aware they are taking part in an experiment and the opportunity to study the effects of very stressful events. Limitations include problems of interpreting the findings because of a lack of randomization or because of the use of complex independent variables.

Correlational studies

- Correlational designs are inferior to experimental designs because they do not permit inferences about causality. However, many issues can only be studied by assessing correlations or associations between variables. It is often possible to obtain large amounts of data very rapidly in correlational studies. The problems of interpretation are much reduced if there is no correlation or association between two variables.

Naturalistic observation

- Naturalistic observation involves the use of methods designed to assess behavior without the experimenter interfering in any way. Methods of data collection include event sampling, time sampling, and point sampling. We should distinguish between data recording and interpretation or coding. Naturalistic observation can provide rich and full information from people who are unaware that they are being observed. However, the experimenter has essentially no control over the situation, the participants are often aware they are being observed, and there can be problems with the reliability and validity of measurement.

Case studies

- A single individual is investigated thoroughly in a case study. Case studies can be carried out to test a current theory, to refine a theory, to permit the development of new theoretical ideas, and to reveal the exceptional characteristics of certain individuals. Case studies generally have very low reliability, and this makes it hard to generalize from a single-case study. Case studies based on interviews often suffer from the limitation that what the participant says is determined in part by the interviewer or researcher, who may then be too selective in what he or she reports of the interview.

Interviews

- There are several types of interview ranging from the unstructured to the totally structured. Unstructured interviews are responsive to the personality, interests, and motivations of the interviewee, but the data obtained tend to be unreliable. In contrast, structured interviews permit comparisons among interviewees, and they tend to be fairly reliable, but what the interviewee says can be constrained and artificial. All types of interviews can produce problems as a result of social desirability bias, and interviewees can only provide information of which they are consciously aware.

Discourse analysis

- Discourse analysis is based on the assumption that our use of language is much affected by the social context. It involves a careful analysis to identify the underlying purposes of the person who produced the discourse, using a qualitative coding system. Limitations of discourse analysis include low validity and reliability, and the danger that the views of the researcher will influence the findings too much. Ethical issues arise unless the permission of anyone providing discourse for analysis is obtained, and it can be hard to maintain confidentiality of the data.

Further Reading

- Coolican, H. (2004). *Research methods and statistics in psychology* (4th ed.). London: Hodder & Stoughton.
- Dyer, C. (1995). *Beginning research in psychology*. Oxford: Blackwell. This book provides good coverage of several nonexperimental research methods.
- Foster J.J., & Parker, J. (1995). *Carrying out investigations in psychology: Methods and statistics*. Leicester, UK: BPS Books. This is another useful textbook.

Chapter 24

Contents

Design of investigations

24

In order to carry out a study successfully, care and attention must be devoted to each stage in its design and implementation. This chapter is concerned with these issues mostly with respect to experimental designs. However, there is also full consideration of the factors involved in producing good nonexperimental designs.

As we will see, several decisions need to be made when designing an experimental study:

1. The investigator must decide what he or she hopes to achieve by carrying out the study. This involves generating appropriate aims and hypotheses.
2. The investigator has to work out how the variables specified in the hypotheses are to be manipulated and/or measured.
3. Appropriate procedures need to be used when selecting participants for the study.
4. Attention needs to be paid in the experimental design to ensuring that the effects of any situational variables on the participants' behavior are minimized.
5. If the investigator is using an experimental design, then he or she has to select an appropriate one. This includes a decision as to whether each participant will be included in only one condition or in both conditions.
6. Care has to be paid to the relationship between the participants and the investigator in order to prevent systematic biases in the data obtained.

The success or otherwise of the investigator's study can be evaluated in terms of various criteria. If the design and its implementation are appropriate, then the reliability of the findings and their replicability will tend to be high. In addition, use of an appropriate design maximizes the validity of the findings.

AIMS AND HYPOTHESES

The first step that needs to be taken when designing an experimental or nonexperimental study is to decide on the aims and hypotheses of the study. The aims are usually more general than the hypotheses, and they help to explain the reasons for the investigator deciding to test some specific hypothesis or hypotheses. In other words, the aims tell us *why* a given study is being carried out, whereas the hypotheses tell us *what* the study is designed to test.

EXPERIMENTAL STUDIES

The distinction between aims and hypotheses can be seen more clearly if we consider an example. Suppose that we decide to test the levels-of-processing theory put forward by Craik and Lockhart (1972), which states that information that has been processed for meaning will be remembered better than information that has not. In order to do this, we might present all of our participants with the same list of nouns and then ask them to provide free recall 30 minutes later. Half of them might be asked to think of adjectives to go with the nouns (processing of meaning or semantic processing), whereas the other half

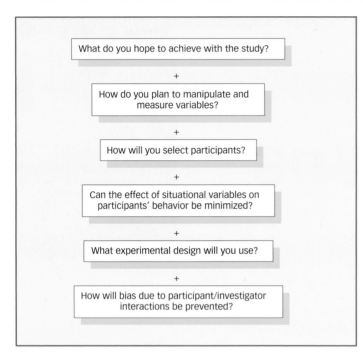

What do you hope to achieve with the study?

+

How do you plan to manipulate and measure variables?

+

How will you select participants?

+

Can the effect of situational variables on participants' behavior be minimized?

+

What experimental design will you use?

+

How will bias due to participant/investigator interactions be prevented?

are asked to think of rhyming words (nonsemantic processing). In such a study, the main aim is to investigate levels-of-processing theory. In more general terms, the aim is to see whether long-term memory is influenced by the kind of processing that occurs at the time of learning. The experimental hypothesis is more specific: Free recall from long-term memory is higher when there is semantic processing at the time of learning than when there is non-semantic processing.

NONEXPERIMENTAL STUDIES

The situation with regard to the aims and hypotheses is somewhat different in qualitative research, in which the data are *not* in numerical form. Qualitative research is often based on interviews, observations, or case studies. Qualitative researchers frequently have no specific hypotheses at the outset of the study; rather, the hypotheses to be tested emerge from a detailed consideration of the data. The aims of qualitative research tend to be more general and wide-ranging than those of traditional research.

An example of qualitative research is the work of Marsh, Rosser, and Harré (1978) with soccer fans. Marsh's original aim was to try to understand the aggressive behavior that they often display, but he had few if any preconceptions or hypotheses in mind at the outset of the study. During the course of the study, Marsh et al. (1978) began to realize that there were complex rules or social norms that were shared by football fans, and which played an important role in determining their behavior (see Chapter 19).

HYPOTHESES

Most experimental research starts with someone thinking of an **experimental hypothesis** (also known as the alternative hypothesis). This is simply a prediction or expectation of what will happen in a given situation. For example, you might think of the experimental hypothesis that loud noise will have an effect on people's ability to carry out a task, such as learning the information in a chapter of an introductory psychology textbook.

Variables

As with most experimental hypotheses, the one just mentioned predicts that some aspect of the situation (in this case, the presence of loud noise) will have an effect on the participants' behavior (in this case, their learning of the information in the chapter). In more technical language, the experimental hypothesis refers to an **independent variable**, which is usually some aspect of the experimental situation that is manipulated by the experimenter. In our example, the presence versus absence of loud noise is the independent variable. The hypothesis also refers to a **dependent variable**, which is some aspect of the participants' behavior. In our example, some measure of learning would be used to assess the dependent variable. In a nutshell, most experimental hypotheses predict that a given independent variable will have some specified effect on a given dependent variable.

One-tailed or two-tailed?

It should be noted at this point that there are two types of experimental hypothesis: directional or one-tailed hypotheses, and nondirectional or two-tailed hypotheses. A *directional* or *one-tailed hypothesis* predicts the *nature* of the effect of the independent variable on the dependent variable. In terms of our example, a directional hypothesis might be as follows: Loud noise will reduce people's ability to learn the information contained in the chapter of a textbook. A *nondirectional* or *two-tailed hypothesis* predicts that the independent variable will have an effect on the dependent variable, but the *direction* of the effect is not specified. In terms of our example, a nondirectional hypothesis would be as follows: Loud noise will have an effect on people's ability to learn the information contained in the chapter of a textbook. This hypothesis allows for the possibility that loud noise might actually improve learning.

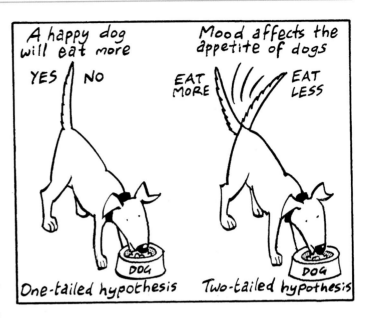

Null hypothesis

The experimental hypothesis consists of the predicted effect of the independent variable on the dependent variable. This can be contrasted with the null hypothesis. The **null hypothesis** simply states that the independent variable will have no effect on the dependent variable. In terms of our example, a suitable null hypothesis would be as follows: Loud noise will have no effect on people's ability to learn the information contained in the chapter of the textbook. In a sense, the purpose of most studies using the experimental method is to decide between the merits of the experimental hypothesis and those of the null hypothesis.

Why do we need a null hypothesis when what we are interested in is the experimental hypothesis? The key reasons are because the null hypothesis is much more precise than the experimental hypothesis, and we need precise hypotheses in order to use statistical tests properly. For example, the null hypothesis that loud noise will have no effect on people's learning ability is precise because it leads to the prediction that the single most likely outcome is that performance will be equal in the loud noise and no noise conditions. Failing that, there will probably only be a small difference between the two conditions, with the difference being equally likely to go in either direction. In contrast, consider the experimental hypothesis that loud noise will reduce people's learning ability. This hypothesis is very imprecise, because it does not indicate how much learning ability will be impaired. This lack of precision makes it impossible to decide the *exact* extent to which the findings support or fail to support the experimental hypothesis.

Manipulating the independent variable

It might seem easy to do a study to test the experimental hypothesis that loud noise disrupts learning. However, there are various pitfalls that need to be avoided. The first issue that needs to be considered is how to manipulate the independent variable. In our example, we want to compare loud noise with no noise, so we have to decide exactly how loud we want the noise to be. If it is very loud, then it might damage the hearing of our participants, and so would be totally unacceptable. If it is fairly soft, then it is unlikely to have any effect on the learning ability of our participants. It is also likely to make a difference whether the noise is meaningful (e.g., music or speech) or meaningless (e.g., the noise of a road drill).

Measuring the dependent variable

The second issue is how to measure the dependent variable or aspect of the participants' behavior. We could ask the participants various questions to measure their understanding of the material in the textbook chapter. However, selecting the questions so that they are not too easy or too hard requires careful thought.

SELECTING PARTICIPANTS

Studies in psychology rarely involve more than about 100 participants. However, researchers generally want their findings to apply to a much larger group of people than those acting as participants. In technical terms, the participants selected for a study form

> **Key Term**
>
> **Null hypothesis:** prediction that the **independent variable** will have no effect on the **dependent variable**.

a *sample*. This sample is taken from some larger *population*, which consists of all the members of the group from which the sample has been drawn. For example, we might select a sample of 20 children aged 5 for a study, in which case the population might consist of all the 5-year-olds living in one US state.

When we carry out a study, we want the findings obtained from our sample to be true of the population from which they were drawn. In order to achieve this, we must use a *representative sample*, that is, participants who are representative or typical of the population in question. However, numerous studies have been carried out with non-representative samples; the term *sampling bias* is used to refer to this state of affairs. Coolican (1994, p. 36) was pessimistic about the chances of selecting a representative sample:

> *The simple truth is that a truly representative sample is an abstract ideal unachievable in practice. The practical goal we can set ourselves is to remove as much sampling bias as possible.*

RANDOM SAMPLES

To return to our earlier example, we might study the effects of loud noise on learning in students preparing for a psychology exam. The best way of obtaining a representative sample from that population would be to make use of **random sampling**. We could obtain lists of names of all the students due to sit the psychology exam in a given year. After that we could use some random method to select our sample. This could be done by picking names out of a hat, or by sticking a pin repeatedly into the lists.

Another approach is to assign a number to everyone in the population from which the sample is to be selected. After that, a computer can be used to generate a series of random numbers that can be used to select the sample. Alternatively, random number tables can be used in a similar way to produce the sample.

If we wanted to have a representative sample of the entire adult population, then we could apply one of the methods of random selection just described to the electoral roll. However, even that would be an imperfect procedure. Several groups of people, including the homeless, illegal immigrants, and prisoners, are not included in the electoral roll.

As Cardwell, Clark, and Meldrum (1996) pointed out, there is a modified version of random sampling that is easier to use. This is **systematic sampling**. It involves selecting the participants by a quasi-random procedure. For example, if we have a list of all the members of the population, we could select every hundredth name from that list as participants. This procedure is not as effective as random sampling because it cannot be claimed that every member of the population is equally likely to be selected.

> Systematic sampling is not as effective as random sampling, but it does help to overcome the biases of the researcher. If we select every hundredth name on the list, we avoid missing out names that we cannot pronounce, or do not like the look of.

Random sampling typically fails to produce a truly representative sample, because it is actually very hard for an experimenter to obtain a random sample. There are various reasons for this. First, it may not be possible to identify all of the members of the larger population from which the sample is to be selected. Second, it may not be possible to contact all those who have been selected randomly to appear in the sample.

Third, some of those who are selected to be in the sample are likely to refuse to take part in the study. This might not matter if those who agreed to take part in research were very similar in every way to those who did not. However, there is considerable evidence that volunteers differ in various ways from nonvolunteers. Manstead and Semin (1996, p. 93) discussed some of the evidence, and concluded, "there *are* systematic personality differences between volunteers and nonvolunteers." Volunteers tend to be more sensitive to the demand characteristics (cues used by participants to work out what a study is about), and they are also more likely to comply with those demand characteristics.

Key Terms

Random sampling:
selecting participants on some random basis (e.g., coin tossing).

Systematic sampling:
a modified version of **random sampling** in which the participants are selected in a quasi-random way (e.g., every hundredth name from a population list).

In sum, it is worth bearing in mind what Coolican (1998, p. 720) had to say about random samples: "Many students write that their sample was 'randomly selected.' In fact, research samples are very rarely selected at random."

STRATIFIED AND QUOTA SAMPLES

Another way of obtaining a representative sample is by using what is known as **stratified sampling**. The first step is to decide which characteristics of the population might be relevant for the study we want to carry out. These characteristics might include gender and the part of the country in which they live. This allows us to think in terms of sub-groups. After that, we select participants at random from within each of the sub-groups.

Suppose that we want to carry out a study on A-level psychology students in high schools in England. We know that 75% of A-level psychology students are female, and that 40% of all A-level psychology students live in the north of England. We could then ensure that the participants used in our experiment were selected in a random way so that 75% of them were female, and 40% of them lived in the north of England. If we make use of enough criteria, then stratified sampling can be an effective way of finding a representative sample.

There is a modified version of stratified sampling that is known as **quota sampling**. It resembles stratified sampling in that participants are selected in proportion to their representation in the population. However, it differs in that the researcher decides who to include in each sub-group, rather than the decision being made at random. Quota sampling is often used in market research. It tends to be faster than stratified sampling. However, it has the disadvantage that people who are readily available (e.g., the unemployed) are more likely to be included than those who are not.

The problem with stratified and quota sampling is that it is often hard to know which sub-groups to identify. It is a waste of time and effort if we use characteristics (e.g., gender) that are of no relevance to the study. What is more troublesome is if we fail to identify sub-groups on the basis of some characteristic (e.g., GCSE exam performance in England) that is actually highly relevant.

> Stratified sampling is time-consuming and difficult to carry out effectively. Pressures on time and tight budgets may make this sampling technique impossible.

OPPORTUNITY SAMPLING

Random sampling, stratified sampling, and quota sampling are often expensive and time-consuming. As a result, many researchers use **opportunity sampling**. This involves selecting participants on the basis of their availability rather than by any other method. Opportunity sampling is often used by students carrying out experiments, and it is also very common in natural experiments (see Chapter 23). Opportunity sampling is the easiest way to proceed. However, it has the severe disadvantage that the participants may be nothing like a representative sample. For example, students who are friends of the student carrying out a study may be more willing to take part than students who are not.

SAMPLE SIZE

One of the issues that anyone carrying out a piece of research has to consider is the total number of participants to be included. What is the ideal number of participants in each condition? There is no definite answer to that question, but here are some of the relevant factors:

- It is generally expensive and time-consuming to make use of large samples running into hundreds of participants.
- If it requires very large samples to obtain a statistically significant effect of some independent variable on some dependent variable, then this suggests that the effect is small and of little practical importance.
- If we use very small samples (fewer than 10 participants in each condition), then this reduces the chances of obtaining a significant effect.
- In general terms, sampling bias is likely to be greater with small samples than with large ones.

Key Terms

Stratified sampling: a modified version of **quota sampling**, in which the selection of participants according to certain characteristics is decided by the researcher, rather than in a random way.

Quota sampling: selecting participants at random from a population so that they are similar to it in certain respects (e.g., proportion of females; proportion of teenagers).

Opportunity sampling: selecting participants only on the basis of their availability.

Consider the total number of participants to be included...

If there is a golden rule that applies to deciding on sample size, it is the following:

The smaller the likely effect being studied, the larger the sample size needed to demonstrate it.

For most purposes, however, having about 15 participants in each condition is a reasonable number.

GOOD PRACTICE IN EXPERIMENTATION

In order for an experiment to be designed and carried out successfully, there are several considerations that the researcher needs to bear in mind. Some of the main considerations are discussed in detail in this section.

STANDARDIZED PROCEDURES

In order to carry out an experiment successfully, it is very important that every participant in a given condition is treated in the same way. In other words, it is necessary to use standardized procedures. For example, consider the instructions that are given to the participants. In order to ensure that all of the participants get precisely the same instructions, the experimenter should write them down. He or she should then either read them to the participants, or ask the participants to read them to themselves.

In similar fashion, standardized procedures should be used for the collection of data. Suppose we want to assess the effects of loud noise on learning from a book chapter. We might ask the participants to write down everything they could remember about the chapter. However, it would be very hard to compare the recalls of different participants with any precision. A standardized procedure would be to ask all of the participants the same set of, say, 20 questions relating to the chapter. Each participant then obtains a score between 0 and 20 as a measure of what he or she has learned.

Is it easy to make sure that standardized procedures are being used? No, it is not. Most experiments can be thought of as social encounters between the experimenter and the participant, and it is customary to behave in different ways towards different people. Robert Rosenthal (1966) studied some of the ways in which experimenters fall short of standardized procedures. He found, for example, that male experimenters were more pleasant, friendly, honest, encouraging, and relaxed when their participants were female than when they were male. This led him to conclude as follows: "Male and female subjects [participants] may, psychologically, simply not be in the same experiment at all."

> ### Key Term
>
> **Confounding variables:** variables that are mistakenly manipulated or allowed to vary along with the independent variable.

CONFOUNDING VARIABLES

Another issue to consider is whether or not our experiment contains any **confounding variables**. These are variables that are mistakenly manipulated along with the independent variable. Suppose there is a study in which one group of participants receives no noise and reads a chapter at midday, whereas the other group of participants receives loud noise and reads the same chapter at midnight. If we find that the latter group learns less well than the former group, we would not know whether this was because of the loud noise or because they did their learning late at night when they were very tired. In this example, time of day is a confounding variable.

Confounding variables are especially likely to be found in nonexperimental investigations in which the researcher has no control over the independent variable. One of the

The type of experimenter could act as a confounding variable. Some participants may feel more comfortable than others in the study situation...

classic examples concerns the work on maternal deprivation that was carried out on institutionalized children (see Chapter 16). Bowlby (1951) argued that these children had poorer social and intellectual development than other children because of the absence of the mother. However, these children also had to cope with the unstimulating environment of the institutions of those days, and this was a confounding variable that Bowlby tended to ignore.

Confounding variables are a form of constant error. **Constant error** is present when the effects of any unwanted variable on the dependent variable differ between conditions. There are numerous types of constant error. The participants in one condition may be more tired than those in another condition, or they may be more intelligent, or they may be more motivated.

Any study of the effects of maternal deprivation on these orphans would have to consider the confounding variable of the unstimulating environment of the orphanage itself.

CONTROLLED VARIABLES

How do we avoid having any confounding variables? One useful approach is to turn them into **controlled variables**, which are variables that are held constant or controlled. Suppose that we want to study the effects of noise on learning, and we are concerned that the time of day may have an effect. We could make time of day into a controlled variable by testing all of our participants at a given time of day, such as late morning or early evening. If we did this, we would know that time of day could not distort our findings.

RANDOM ERROR

Random error occurs when variables that are totally irrelevant to the experiment influence the behavior of the participants. The key difference between random error and constant error is that random error generally affects both conditions equally and so has *unsystematic effects*, whereas constant error has *systematic effects* on one condition but not on the other. Constant error is more serious than random error, because it can lead us to misinterpret our findings. However, random error is also of concern, because it introduces unwanted variation in the dependent variable.

There are almost limitless types of random error. For example, suppose we are interested in comparing learning performance under noise and no-noise conditions. Participants in either condition may learn poorly because they have a splitting headache, because they have just argued with a close friend, because a relationship broke up last week, because the weather is bad, or because they are worried about an important examination they have to take next week. The experimenter cannot control most forms of random error, but should try to control those that can be controlled. For example, he or she should ensure that the lighting conditions, the heating conditions, the experimenter's tone of voice, and so on remain constant for all participants.

OPERATIONALIZATION

Psychologists carry out studies to test experimental hypotheses, such as "anxiety impairs performance" or "maternal deprivation leads to maladjustment." There is an immediate problem with designing a study to test such hypotheses: there is little or no agreement on the best way to measure psychological concepts or variables such as "anxiety," "performance," "maternal deprivation," or "maladjustment." The most common approach to this problem is to make use of **operationalization**. This involves defining each variable of interest in terms of the operations taken to measure it. Such a definition is referred to as an operational definition. For example, anxiety might be defined as the score on the trait anxiety scale of Spielberger's State–Trait Anxiety Inventory, and performance might be defined as the number of five-letter anagrams that can be solved in 5 minutes.

Key Terms

Constant error: any unwanted variable that has a systematically different effect on the dependent variable in different conditions.

Controlled variables: variables, not of interest to the experimenter, that are held constant or controlled.

Random error: unsystematic and unwanted "nuisance variables" that influence the **dependent variable**.

Operationalization: a procedure in which variables of interest are defined by the operations taken to measure them.

Operationalization has the great advantage that it generally provides a clear and objective definition of even complex variables. However, there are various limitations associated with the use of operational definitions. First, operational definitions are entirely circular. As Stretch (1994, p. 1076) pointed out:

> *A psychological construct is defined in terms of the operations necessary to measure it, and the measurements are defined to be measures of the psychological construct.*

Second, an operational definition typically only covers part of the meaning of the variable or concept. For example, defining anxiety in terms of the score on a self-report questionnaire largely ignores physiological and behavioral aspects of anxiety, and no one believes that performance can *only* be assessed in terms of rate of anagram solution.

In spite of these important limitations with operational definitions, it is hard to carry out research without using them. Stretch (1994, p. 1076) argued that operational definitions should be used in a careful fashion:

> *A useful rule of thumb is to consider many different ways of measuring the psychological construct of interest and determine the extent to which each method could yield different experimental results. If you find that the measurement techniques radically affect the results that emerge, this should indicate that more work is needed on developing the underlying psychological and measurement models to explain these effects.*

EXPERIMENTAL DESIGNS

If we wish to compare two groups with respect to a given independent variable, it is essential to make sure that the two groups do not differ in any other important way. This general rule is important when it comes to selecting participants to take part in an experiment. Suppose all the least able participants received the loud noise, and all the most able participants received no noise. We would not know whether it was the loud noise or the low ability level of the participants causing poor learning performance.

How should we select our participants so as to avoid this problem? There are three main types of experimental design:

- *Independent design*: Each participant is selected for only one group.
- *Matched participants design*: Each participant is selected for only one group, but the participants in the two groups are matched for some relevant factor or factors (e.g., ability; sex; age).
- *Repeated measures design*: Each participant appears in both groups, so that there are exactly the same participants in each group.

INDEPENDENT DESIGN

With the independent design, the most common way of deciding which participants go into which group is by means of randomization. In our example, this could involve using a random process such as coin tossing to decide whether each participant is exposed to loud noise or to no noise. It is possible with randomization for all the most able participants to be selected for the same group. However, what happens in the great majority of cases is that the participants in the two groups are similar in ability, age, and so on.

MATCHED PARTICIPANTS DESIGN

With the matched participants design, we make use of information about the participants to decide which group each participant should join. In our example, we might have information about the participants' ability levels. We could then use this information to make sure that the two groups were matched in terms of range of ability.

REPEATED MEASURES DESIGN

With the repeated measures design, every participant is in both groups. In our example, that would mean that each participant learns the chapter in loud noise and that they also learn the chapter in no noise. The great advantage of the repeated measures design is that we do not need to worry about the participants in one group being cleverer than those in the other group: As the same participants appear in both groups, the ability level (and all other individual characteristics) must be identical in the two groups!

The main problem with the repeated measures design is that there may well be order effects. Their experiences during the experiment may change the participants in various ways. They may perform better when they appear in the second group because they have gained useful information about the experiment or about the task. On the other hand, they may perform less well on the second occasion because of tiredness or boredom. It would be hard to use a repeated measures design in our example: Participants are almost certain to show better learning of the chapter the second time they read it, regardless of whether they are exposed to loud noise.

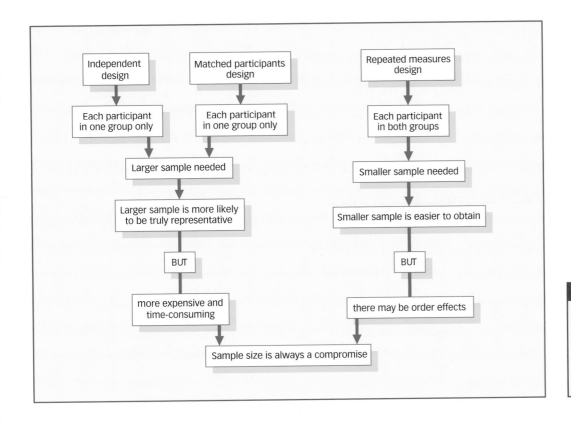

Key Term

Counterbalancing:
this is used with the repeated measures design, and involves ensuring that each condition is equally likely to be used first and second by the participants.

Counterbalancing

Suppose we used a repeated measures design in which all of the participants first learned the chapter in loud noise and then learned it in no noise. We would expect the participants to show better learning in no noise simply because of order effects. A better procedure would be to have half the participants learn the chapter first in loud noise and then in no noise, while the other half learn the chapter first in no noise and then in loud noise. In that way, any order effects would be balanced out. This approach is known as **counterbalancing**. It is the best way of preventing order effects from disrupting the findings from an experiment.

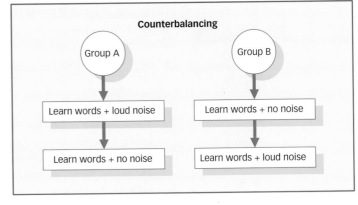

GOOD PRACTICE IN NONEXPERIMENTAL DESIGNS

There are several kinds of nonexperimental studies (see Chapter 23). They include naturalistic observation, participant observation, studies based on correlational analysis, interviews and surveys, and case studies. Case studies involve the collection of detailed information from individuals rather than from groups of participants. We begin by considering some general points that need to be taken into account when designing and implementing a nonexperimental study.

GENERAL CONSIDERATIONS

One of the key issues in many nonexperimental studies is to decide whether the participants should be made aware of the fact that they are taking part in research. The main argument for making the participants aware of what is happening is an ethical one. Voluntary informed consent is regarded as of central importance in ensuring that research is ethically acceptable, and it is impossible to obtain that consent from people who do not know they are taking part in a study. However, participants who are made aware may fail to behave in a natural way. Their behavior may be affected by **evaluation apprehension** (desire to impress the experimenter) or by their guesses about the experimental hypothesis being tested (**demand characteristics**).

Some of the issues to be considered are the same as those that apply to experimental studies. For example, if the participants are intended to form a representative sample from a larger population, then it is desirable to use a suitable form of sampling (e.g., random sampling or systematic sampling). The issue of sampling is perhaps especially important with respect to case studies, which involve intensive investigation of individuals. However, there are many nonexperimental studies in which the investigator has little or no control over the selection of participants.

OBSERVATIONAL STUDIES

Observational studies differ from each other in various ways. First, we can distinguish between participant observation research, in which the investigator is involved in the study as an active participant, and nonparticipant observation research, in which the investigator only observes the behavior of the participants.

Second, there is a distinction between unstructured observation and structured observation. According to Dyer (1995, p. 153), unstructured observation is research "where the aim is simply to ensure that everything which appears to be of relevance to the research at a given moment is recorded." In contrast, an investigator using structured observation makes prior decisions about what to observe, and this "renders the research process relatively inflexible and incapable of responding to unpredictable situations" (1995, p. 154).

Participant observation

The key factor in participant observation is that the researcher has to do his or her best to become accepted by the social group being studied. The goal is to develop a good understanding of what it is like to be a member of that group, and this can only be done when its members accept and trust the researcher. It follows that participant observation research is very time-consuming, because it can take weeks or months for the researcher to gain the confidence of group members.

Dyer (1995) discussed three stages that are involved in carrying out a participant observation study:

1. *Entering the field*: An important early step is to be accepted by the "gatekeeper" who controls access to the group to be studied; in a school, it is likely to be the Principal. It is usually desirable to let the fact that you are doing research emerge gradually over time. However, there are major ethical issues to be considered, and it is important to have the informed consent of those responsible for the running of the school or other organization.

2. *Being in the field*: For the duration of the study, you have the hard task of trying to fit in as a member of the group and of remaining detached as an observer. You should take field notes, which are an extensive record of what members say and do. These field notes should be condensed into a field diary that is written up every day, and should identify key themes. Finally, the field diary is used as the basis for the research report. The initial field notes might include information in the following categories suggested by Lovland (1976): Acts (short actions); activities (actions taking up at least several days); meanings (participants' explanations for their actions); participation (the various roles participants play); relationships among the group members; and settings (the situations in which the group members find themselves).

Try to fit in as a member of the group and remain detached as an observer.

3. *Leaving the field*: There are major ethical issues in participant observation research, because it tends to deal with personal and sensitive issues. It is thus very important to make sure that the group members have the chance to read and comment on your research, and that you take their comments seriously.

Nonparticipant observation

Most nonparticipant observation research starts with the researcher thinking of an experimental hypothesis. If structured observations are to be made, it is then necessary to devise the behavioral categories that are going to be used by the observers. The categories should possess the following features:

1. They should be defined in a reasonably precise and objective way so there is as little ambiguity as possible about which forms of behavior by the participants qualify for each category.
2. The system of categories needs to be comprehensive, in the sense that all aspects of behavior that are relevant to the experimental hypothesis should be included.
3. The categories should be usable in the context of the study. For example, a researcher studying the reactions of drivers stuck in traffic hold-ups might include various categories of facial expression. This is only sensible provided that the observer is going to be able to see drivers' facial expressions clearly from his or her viewing position.

Another key decision concerns the way in which the participants' behavior is to be sampled. Dyer (1995) identified four possible sampling procedures:

1. *Continuous observation*: The observer records behavior falling into the various categories nonstop over a fairly lengthy period of time (e.g., 60 minutes).
2. *Time-interval sampling*: The sampling period is divided into a series of short time intervals (e.g., 60 seconds), and the observer decides whether any given participant produces each category of behavior during each period. Any behavior is simply recorded as absent or present, so that no distinction is drawn between a given behavior exhibited once versus more than once during a single time interval.
3. *Time-point sampling*: The sampling period is divided into a series of short time intervals, and the observer decides whether the various categories of behavior are present at the end of each sampling period.
4. *Random sampling*: This is like time-point sampling, except that the points in time at which behavior is sampled are selected at random.

SURVEY STUDIES

The survey method involves collecting information from a large group of individuals. This information is often gathered using questionnaires, but can include interviews or phone contacts. It is important in any survey study to ensure that the sample selected is as representative as possible (see earlier). A problem that applies to nearly all sampling methods is that of nonresponding. Some individuals who are selected to form part of the sample are likely to refuse to participate. Others agree to participate, but then fail to provide all of the information requested. Persuasion and persistence should be used to minimize the problem of nonresponding, but it is very rare for the response rate to be 100% in a survey study.

Survey designs

According to Dyer (1995), there are four main types of survey: one-shot survey; before–after design; two-groups controlled comparison design; and two-groups before–after design.

One-shot surveys. The one-shot survey is the simplest, but also generally the least informative type of survey. Information is obtained from a single sample at a given point in time. The reason why it is fairly uninformative is that we cannot compare the findings from our sample against those of other groups. As a result, we can only describe what we have found to be the case in the sample we tested.

Before–after surveys. The before–after design is an advance on the one-shot survey, in that data are collected from a single sample on two occasions. The design is most likely to produce interesting findings if some major event or experience intervenes between the first and second data collections. For example, attitudes in the UK towards the Labour party could have been obtained shortly before and after the general election of 1997. Suppose (as seems to have been the case) that attitudes were more positive after the election than before. This might have been due to the election victory, but there are other possibilities. Attitudes to the Labour party might have become more positive even if there had not been an election, or it may be that people tend to respond differently on the second occasion that an attitude questionnaire is completed than on the first. In general, it is hard to interpret the findings based on the before–after design.

Two-groups controlled comparison surveys. The two-groups controlled comparison design is potentially more informative than the designs discussed so far. In essence, there are two similar groups of participants, one of which is exposed to some treatment before data collection, whereas the other is not. For example, attitudes towards the opposite sex could be assessed in those who have (or have not) recently experienced the breakdown of a heterosexual relationship. If the former group was more negative in their attitudes, it could be argued that this was due to the breakdown of the relationship. However, this requires the assumption that the two groups had the same attitudes before the breakdown occurred, and we cannot be sure that that assumption is justified.

Two-groups before–after surveys. The two-groups before–after design is an advance on the two-groups controlled comparison design. Two samples or groups are tested for the first time, then one group is exposed to some treatment, and finally both groups are tested for a second time. Dyer (1995) gave as an imaginary example a study in which the participants are allocated at random to two groups. The attitudes of all of them towards Third World issues are assessed. One group is then exposed to several presentations of a television commercial focusing on the need to provide economic aid to Third World countries. Finally, the attitudes of both groups towards Third World countries are assessed. This survey method is the most complicated one to use, but the findings are easier to interpret than those from other survey methods.

Questionnaire construction

In order to address the specific issues that interest them, researchers using the survey method often construct their own questionnaire. The first step is to generate as many ideas as possible that might be relevant to the questionnaire. Then those ideas that seem of little relevance are discarded, working on the basis (Dyer, 1995, p. 114) that:

It is better to ask carefully designed and quite detailed questions about a few precisely defined issues than the same number on a very wide range of topics.

Do events such as a general election victory affect attitudes towards a political standpoint, or vice versa?

Closed and open questions. There is an important distinction between closed and open questions. Closed questions invite the respondent to select from various possible answers (e.g., yes or no; yes, unsure, or no; putting different answers in rank order), whereas open questions allow respondents to answer in whatever way they prefer. Most questionnaires use closed questions, because the answers are easy to score and to analyze. Open questions have the disadvantage of being much harder to analyze, but they can be more informative than closed questions.

Ambiguity and bias. Questions that are ambiguous or are likely to be interpreted in various ways should be avoided. Questions that are very long or complicated should also be avoided, because they are likely to be misunderstood. Finally, questions that are biased should be avoided. Here is an example of a biased question: "In view of the superiority of Britain, why should we consider further political integration with the rest of Europe?"

Reliability and validity. Good questionnaires need to have high reliability or consistency of measurement. They also need reasonable validity, meaning that they should measure what they claim to measure. Reliability can be assessed by means of the test–retest method, in which the questionnaire is given to the same individuals on two different occasions. The scores can then be correlated by means of a test such as Spearman's rho (see Chapter 25). If the correlation is fairly high (about $+0.7$ or $+0.8$), then the questionnaire can be regarded as reliable.

There are several ways of assessing the validity of a test. For example, there is empirical validity, in which the scores on a questionnaire are compared against some external criterion. For example, suppose that someone devised a questionnaire to measure conscientiousness. It seems reasonable to assume that conscientious people will perform better on examinations, and so we could use examination performance as the external criterion. Conscientiousness scores on the questionnaire could be correlated with examination performance using Spearman's rho, with the assumption being that there would be a significant positive correlation.

Question styles: A survey on chocolate

Closed question: Do you like chocolate? (tick one)

YES   NO   NOT SURE

Open question: Why do you like or dislike chocolate?
Ambiguous question: Is chocolate likely to do you more harm than a diet that consists mainly of junk food?
Biased question: Plain chocolate is a more sophisticated taste than milk chocolate. Which type do you prefer?

Attitude scale construction

Many of the points made about questionnaire construction also apply to the construction of attitude scales. However, there are some differences.

Likert scales. One of the most common ways to construct an attitude scale is to use the Likert procedure. Initially various statements are collected together, and the participants' task is to indicate their level of agreement on a five-point scale running from "strongly disagree" at one end to "strongly agree" at the other end. For positive statements (e.g., "Most Hollywood stars are outstanding actors"), strongly disagree is scored as 1 and strongly agree as 5, with intermediate points being scored 2, 3, or 4. For negative statements (e.g., "Most Hollywood stars are not outstanding actors"), the scoring is reversed so that strongly disagree is scored as 5 and strongly agree as 1.

Most attitude scales based on the Likert method contain some unsatisfactory items. One way of finding out which items are unsuitable is by correlating each item separately with the total score on the scale. Only items that correlate positively at a moderate level with the total score ($+0.3$ and above) are retained for the scale.

Reliability and validity. The reliability of an attitude scale can be assessed by the test–retest method. Its validity can generally be assessed by some measure of empirical validity. For example, we could obtain evidence about the validity of a scale concerned with attitudes towards religion by correlating the scores with a measure such as regularity of attendance at church, by using Spearman's rho. However, it is important to note that the correlation may be low either because an attitude scale lacks validity or because there is often a large difference between people's attitudes and their behavior (see Chapter 19).

CORRELATIONAL STUDIES

Correlational studies typically involve obtaining two different measures from a group of participants, and then assessing the degree of association between the measures by using a test of correlation such as Spearman's rho. For example, participants' level of extraversion could be correlated with their number of friends, based on the prediction that extraverts are likely to have more friends than introverts.

Correlational studies are easy to carry out. For example, there are thousands of questionnaires for measuring personality or attitudes, and it is possible to take any two at random and administer them to a large group of people. After that, the scores on the two questionnaires can be correlated. However, the fact that correlational studies are easy to perform does *not* mean that good correlational studies are easily carried out. What features characterize good correlational studies?

Correlation or causation?

An underlying theory

First, the study should be based on some underlying theory. The two variables that are measured in the study should both be of clear relevance to the theory. In addition, the predicted direction of the correlation (positive or negative) should follow from the theory. For example, there is the matching hypothesis, according to which we are attracted to those who are about as physically attractive as we are. This was tested in a correlational study by Murstein (1972). The physical attractiveness of couples was judged from photographs. There was a strong positive correlation, with the most physically attractive individuals tending to have someone very attractive as their partner, whereas those who were physically unattractive had unattractive partners.

In many correlational studies, one of the variables can be regarded as the predictor variable with the other one as the outcome variable. The predictor variable can be seen as occurring before the outcome variable in some sense. It is called the predictor variable because it forms the basis for predicting the value of the outcome variable. For example, there is a positive correlation between the Type A behavior pattern (hostility, impatience, tension) and coronary heart disease (Miller et al., 1991). Here the Type A behavior pattern is the predictor variable and coronary heart disease is the outcome variable. This approach may suggest the existence of a causal relationship. However, it is very important to remember that "correlations cannot prove causes." There could be a third factor (e.g., genetic vulnerability) that leads to the Type A behavior pattern and to susceptibility to heart disease.

Careful measurement

Another feature of good correlational studies is that the variables are carefully measured. Let us consider an example. Martin, Kulper, and Westra (1989) argued that Type A individuals are much more highly motivated than Type B individuals, who are relaxed, patient, and calm. This suggests that Type A individuals might have better job performance than Type Bs; thus, there should be a positive correlation between Type A and job performance. How can job performance be measured? In the case of managers whose jobs involve forward planning, motivating their staff, monitoring the performance of their staff, and so on, it may be very hard to assess their work performance in a single measure. It would be preferable to study a group such as insurance salespeople. Their main work goal is to sell as much insurance as possible, and so the amount of insurance sold over a given period of time (e.g., 3 months) would provide a reasonable measure of job performance.

Wide range

A final feature of good correlational studies is that the scores on both variables vary considerably from individual to individual. For example, IQ is supposed to reflect general intellectual ability, and so one might predict that there would be a positive correlation between IQ and job performance. This has been found numerous times (Eysenck, 1994). Suppose, however, that we correlated IQ and job performance among chartered accountants. The great majority of chartered accountants have high IQs, and so we have what is known as restriction of range. This restriction of range would reduce the strength of the association between IQ and job performance, and so it should be avoided.

PROBLEMS WITH EXPERIMENTAL RESEARCH

In most experimental research (and some nonexperimental research), the experimenter and the participants interact with each other. This can produce various kinds of problems. The ways in which experimenters behave and talk may influence the behavior of the participants in ways that have nothing to do with the independent variable or variables being manipulated. In addition, the participants may form mistaken ideas of what the experiment is about, and these mistaken ideas may affect their behavior. Some of the main problems stemming from the relationship between the researcher and the participants are discussed in this section.

The way in which experimenters behave and talk may influence the behavior of the participant.

EXPERIMENTER EFFECTS

The ideal experimenter is someone who behaves in exactly the same mildly positive way with every participant, and who does not allow his or her expectations and experimental hypotheses to influence the conduct of a study. In reality, the experimenter's expectations, personal characteristics, and so on often have an effect on the participants' behavior; these are known as **experimenter effects**.

> **Key Term**
>
> **Experimenter effects:**
> the various ways in which the experimenters' expectancies, personal characteristics, misrecordings of data, and so on can influence the findings of a study.

Experimenter expectancy

One of the most important experimenter effects is experimenter expectancy, in which the experimenter's expectations have a systematic effect on the performance of the participants. Perhaps the first systematic demonstration of experimenter expectancy involved a horse known as Clever Hans. The horse was apparently able to count, tapping its hoof the right number of times when asked a simple mathematical question (e.g., 8 + 6). Pfungst (1911) studied Clever Hans. He found that Clever Hans could not produce the correct answer when the horse was blindfolded. What happened normally was that the experimenter made slight movements when the horse had tapped out the correct number, and Clever Hans was simply using these movements as the cue to stop tapping.

Clever Hans, the "counting" horse.

Key Study

Rosenthal (1966): Experimenter effects

One of the best-known studies on experimenter effects was reported by Rosenthal (1966). He asked student experimenters to count the number of head turns and body contractions made by flatworms. Before the experiment started, the students were told that they should expect a lot of activity from half of the worms, but very little activity from the others. In fact, worms were assigned at random to the two groups, so there was no reason for assuming that they would actually differ in activity level.

What do you think Rosenthal found? Somewhat surprisingly, the experimenters reported *twice* as many head turns and *three* times as many body contractions in the worms that were allegedly "highly active" as in the "inactive" ones! Rosenthal argued that this was an experimenter expectancy effect, but it is more likely that it was a result of the experimenters failing to follow the proper procedures and/or misrecording of the data. As Coolican (1994) pointed out, there was no evidence of expectancy effect in at least 40 experiments specifically designed to find it. There is evidence that the behavior of human participants, especially those high in need for approval, can be influenced by the experimenter's behavior. However, it seems less likely that flatworms would respond to a smile or a frown from the experimenter!

Discussion points

1. Are you surprised that it has proved hard to replicate Rosenthal's findings on flatworms?
2. In what circumstances would you expect to find experimenter effects (see later)?

KEY STUDY EVALUATION

Psychological experiments like Rosenthal's are carried out by humans on humans. As such they are unique social situations in which social interactions play an important part. Inevitably, problems can arise in the form of experimenter effects. According to Rosenthal, the participants could be influenced to expect certain results to occur within the experiment. However, it is possible that the experimenter could have given clues as to how the participants were expected to behave, either verbal or nonverbal in nature. Rosenthal suggested that the perceived competence and authority of the research could also produce experimenter effects. This would be influenced by the participant's own personal characteristics such as a need for approval.

Other effects

Barber (1976) argued that there are numerous ways in which the experimenter can influence the findings obtained. In addition to experimenter expectancy, he identified several other kinds of experimenter effects (summarized in Coolican, 1994). These effects are listed here. In this list, a distinction is drawn between the investigator (the person *directing* the research) and the experimenter (the person actually *carrying out* the experiment). For example, an academic psychologist will often be the investigator, whereas an undergraduate or postgraduate student is the experimenter. So far as the studies carried out by undergraduate studies are concerned, the investigator and the experimenter will typically be the same person.

1. *Investigator paradigm effect*: The entire approach adopted by the investigator can make it harder or easier to obtain certain findings.
2. *Investigator experimental design effect*: For example, if an investigator wanted to show that a learning program for disadvantaged children was not effective, he or she

could arrange for the program to last for a very short period of time to reduce the chances that there would be any noticeable effects.

3. *Investigator loose procedure effect*: If the instructions and other aspects of the procedure are not clearly specified, there is more scope for the results to be influenced by the investigator.

4. *Investigator data analysis effect*: The investigator can decide to carry out several unplanned analyses of the data *after* seeing what patterns seem to be present.

5. *Investigator fudging effect*: There is evidence that Burt, who believed strongly that intelligence depends on heredity, fudged some of his twin data.

6. *Experimenter personal attributes effect*: For example, an experimenter who liked women but not men might treat male and female participants differently, and so produce a spurious gender effect in the data.

7. *Experimenter failure to follow the procedure effect*: If this happens, then the independent variable may not be manipulated as it should be, which makes it hard to interpret the findings.

8. *Experimenter misrecording effect*: Experimenters are most likely to misrecord data if the information provided by participants is ambiguous (e.g., did the participant give a little smile?).

9. *Experimenter fudging effect*: The experimenter may fudge the data to please the investigator or to obtain good marks for his or her study.

Reducing experimenter effects

What steps can be taken to minimize experimenter effects? One approach is to use a **double blind** procedure, in which neither the experimenter working with the participants nor the participants knows the experimental hypothesis (or hypotheses) being tested. The double blind procedure reduces the possibility of experimenter bias, but it is often too expensive and impractical to use. However, the incidence of experimenter effects is probably less than it used to be, for the simple reason that more and more experiments involve participants interacting with computers rather than with human experimenters. In addition, data are increasingly stored directly in computers, making it harder to misrecord the information obtained from participants.

DEMAND CHARACTERISTICS

A common criticism of laboratory research is that the situation is so artificial that participants behave very differently from the way they do normally. Guy Claxton (1980) discussed an amusing example of this. He considered a laboratory task, in which participants have to decide as rapidly as possible whether sentences such as "Can canaries fly?" are true or false. Under laboratory conditions, people perform this task uncomplainingly. However, as Claxton pointed out, "If someone asks me 'Can canaries fly?' in the pub, I will suspect either that he is an idiot or that he is about to tell me a joke."

Why do people behave in unusual ways under laboratory conditions? The American psychologist Orne (1962) emphasized the importance of what he termed *demand characteristics*, which are "the totality of cues which convey an experimental hypothesis to the subjects [participants]." Demand characteristics include "the rumors or campus scuttlebutt about the research, the information conveyed during the original situation, the person of the experimenter, and the setting of the laboratory, as well as all explicit and implicit communications during the experiment proper." (In case you are wondering, the word "scuttlebutt" means gossip.) Orne's basic idea is that most participants do their best to comply with what they perceive to be the demands of the experimental situation, but their perception will often be inaccurate.

As Orne showed, the demand characteristics in an experiment are so powerful that the participants can often be persuaded to do some very strange things. He discussed one study in which the participants spent several hours adding numbers on random number sheets, then tearing up each completed sheet into at least 32 pieces. Many of the participants treated the situation as a test of endurance, and this motivated them to keep going.

> ### Key Term
>
> **Double blind:**
> a procedure in which neither the experimenter nor the participants knows the precise aims of the study; where possible, they do not know the condition in which each participant has been placed.

There is another problem with demand characteristics, which applies to participants who have previously taken part in an experiment in which they were deceived about the experimental purpose. As a result of being deceived, some participants tend thereafter to respond in the opposite direction to the one suggested by an experiment's demand characteristics. Why should this be so? Silverman, Shulman, and Wiesenthal (1970) explained this effect in the following way:

> *Deceived subjects [participants] may have become so alerted to possible further deceptions that they tend to respond counter to any cues regarding the experimenter's hypothesis. An element of gamesmanship may enter the experimental situation in that subjects [participants] become wary of "tricks" underlying the obvious, and do not want to be caught in them.*

Reducing demand characteristics

Information about the demand characteristics in any given experimental setting can be obtained by asking the participants afterwards to describe in detail what they felt the experiment was about. Armed with this information, the experimenter can take steps to make sure that the results of future experiments are not adversely affected by demand characteristics.

Some (but not all) of the problems of demand characteristics can be reduced by the double blind procedure described earlier. Another possibility in some studies is the **single blind** procedure, in which the participants are not informed of the condition in which they have been placed. However, this raises ethical issues, because full informed consent cannot be obtained in such circumstances.

EVALUATION APPREHENSION

Demand characteristics are not the only reason why we might expect participants in experiments to behave in ways that differ from their typical everyday behavior. As we saw in Chapter 23, Rosenberg (1965) argued that it is important to take account of what he called *evaluation apprehension*. What this means is that most participants in experiments are concerned to be evaluated positively by the experimenter or, failing that, to avoid being evaluated negatively. It could be argued that the main reason why participants comply with the demand characteristics of experimental situations is because of their evaluation apprehension. However, that would be overstating matters. As discussed in Chapter 23, Sigall, Aronson, and Van Hoose (1970) set up a situation in which evaluation apprehension would lead participants to perform a task rapidly but demand characteristics would led them to perform it slowly. What they found was that the participants' performance was determined more by evaluation apprehension than by demand characteristics.

GENERAL ISSUES IN INVESTIGATIONS

So far in this chapter, we have considered several specific issues that are important to ensure that the design of a study is appropriate. In this section, we address some important general criteria that can (and should) be used to evaluate how successfully a study has been designed and carried out. The criteria to be discussed are participant reactivity; validity; generalizability; and reliability.

PARTICIPANT REACTIVITY

A weakness that is found in many studies is what is known as **participant reactivity**. This refers to a situation in which an independent variable has an effect on behavior simply because the participants know that they are being observed or studied. Any measure of the participants' behavior that could suffer from this effect is called a reactive measure, and reactivity is the term used to refer to the changes in behavior produced in this way.

Key Terms

Single blind:
a procedure in which the participants are not informed of the condition in which they have been placed.

Participant reactivity:
the situation in which an independent variable has an effect on behavior merely because the participants are aware they are being observed.

Key Study

Roethlisberger and Dickson (1939): The Hawthorne effect

In order to clarify the meaning of participant reactivity, we will consider a series of studies carried out at the Hawthorne Western Electric plant in Chicago (Roethlisberger & Dickson, 1939). They found that the workers became more productive when the amount of lighting was increased, suggesting that work rate increases when the working conditions become easier. However, they also found that *decreasing* the amount of lighting led to increased productivity! In general, it was found that productivity increased when *any* changes were made to the working conditions, whether these changes were to wages, length of the working day, or to rest. Productivity even improved when there was a return to the original working conditions. Presumably what was happening was that the workers responded to the interest being shown in them, rather than to the specific changes in their working environment.

The term "Hawthorne effect" came to be used to refer to changes produced because people know they are being studied, although the same phenomenon is now generally referred to as participant reactivity. There are several published findings that may have been influenced by participant reactivity. For example, Klaus and Kennell (1976) reported that mothers who were allowed to interact for several hours a day with their newborn babies developed a closer relationship with them than did mothers who spent less time with their babies (see Chapter 16). The extra-contact mothers were mostly unmarried teenagers, and it has been argued that this effect was a result of the interest shown in them by the hospital workers rather than to the extra contact itself. This interpretation is supported by the fact that this finding has generally not been replicated in studies of mothers who are less likely to be flattered at being the center of attention (Durkin, 1995).

Participant reactivity or the Hawthorne effect is a serious problem, because it can lead us to misinterpret our findings. How can we decide whether some effect is a result of participant reactivity? In essence, we need to make sure that participant reactivity is the same in both conditions, by making it equally clear to both groups that they are being studied and that their behavior is of interest. If the effect is still found, then it cannot have been caused by participant reactivity. For example, if extra contact of mothers and babies was still associated with a closer relationship even when equal interest was shown in the mothers given only routine contact, then it would be reasonable to conclude that it was the contact itself that produced the effect.

Discussion points
1. How much of a problem is participant reactivity in research?
2. When would you *not* expect to find evidence of participant reactivity?

KEY STUDY EVALUATION

Examining human relations in the workplace grew out of Roethlisberger and Dickson's (1939) study, which aimed to consider the relationship between working conditions and productivity. The initial emphasis was on the extrinsic rewards the worker received, and it was found that there was no relationship between extrinsic rewards and productivity. What became apparent was that intrinsic rewards had a greater effect. These intrinsic rewards derived from the workers' own attitudes towards their work both individually and as part of an informal group. The human need to be part of a social group and to be accepted within it determines attitudes to work and the motivation needed to perform successfully far more than financial rewards. From the Hawthorne study new research was stimulated, which examined the range of needs experienced by the workforce. To increase productivity it was found that social needs had to be met, such as friendship, group support, acceptance, approval, recognition, status, and the need for "self-actualization," which involves the development of an individual's talents, creativity, and personality to the full.

VALIDITY AND GENERALIZABILITY

One of the key requirements of a study or experiment is that any findings obtained are valid, in the sense that they are genuine and provide us with useful information about the phenomenon being studied. Campbell and Stanley (1966) drew a distinction between internal validity and external validity, which is of most relevance to experiments and quasi-experiments. **Internal validity** refers to the issue of whether the effects observed are genuine and are caused by the independent variable. In contrast, **external validity** refers to the extent to which the findings of a study can be generalized to situations and samples other than those used in the study. This distinction between two kinds of validity is an important one: many experiments possess internal validity while lacking external validity (see Chapter 23).

Internal validity

We will shortly consider some of the reasons why an experiment may lack external validity, but what are some of the main threats to the internal validity of an experiment? Coolican (1994) pointed out that there are many such threats, most of which were discussed earlier in the chapter. For example, the existence of any confounding factors threatens internal validity, as does the use of unreliable or inconsistent measures. Problems with internal validity can also arise if an experiment is designed without careful attention being paid to issues such as standardization, counterbalancing, and randomization. Other threats to internal validity include experimenter effects, demand characteristics, participant reactivity, and the use of inappropriate statistical tests. In a nutshell, virtually all of the principles of experimental design are intended to enhance internal validity, and failures to apply these principles threaten internal validity. If internal validity is high, then there are good prospects for being able to replicate the findings. If it is low, then replication is likely to be difficult or impossible.

External validity and generalizability

What about external validity? There are close links between external validity and **generalizability**, because both are concerned with the issue of whether the findings of an experiment or study are applicable to other situations. More specifically, Coolican (1994) argued that there are four main aspects to external validity or generalizability, which we consider in turn:

- *Populations*: Do the findings obtained from a given sample of individuals generalize to a larger population from which the sample was selected?
- *Locations*: Do the findings of the study generalize to other settings or situations? If the findings generalize to various real-life settings, then the study is said to possess ecological validity. Silverman (1977, p. 108) was skeptical about the ecological validity of laboratory experiments: "the conclusions we draw from our laboratory studies pertain to the behavior of organisms in conditions of their own confinement and control and are probably generalizable only to similar situations (institutions, perhaps, such as schools or prisons or hospitals)."
- *Measures or constructs*: Do the findings of the experiment or study generalize to other measures of the variables used? For example, suppose we find that people who are high on the personality dimension of trait anxiety as assessed by Spielberger's State–Trait Anxiety Inventory have worse long-term memory measured by recall than those low in trait anxiety. Would we obtain the same findings if trait anxiety were assessed by a different questionnaire or if we used a recognition test of long-term memory?
- *Times*: Do the findings generalize to the past and to the future? For example, it could be argued that the sweeping changes in many cultures in recent decades have affected conformity behavior as studied by Asch, and obedience to authority as studied by Milgram (see Chapter 19).

What can we do to maximize the external validity of an experiment? Unfortunately, there is no easy answer to that question. What usually happens is that the external validity of an experiment only becomes clear when other researchers try to generalize the findings to other samples or populations, locations, measures, and times. It might be thought that the findings of field experiments are more likely than those of laboratory experiments to generalize to other real-life locations or settings, but that is not necessarily so.

Surveys of women's daily activities and attitudes towards domestic work carried out even a few decades ago bear little relevance to conditions and attitudes current today.

Meta-analyses. One way of trying to determine whether certain findings generalize is to carry out what is known as a **meta-analysis**. What is done in a meta-analysis is to combine all of the findings from many studies designed to test a given hypothesis into a single analysis. If the meta-analysis indicates that some finding has been obtained consistently, this suggests that it generalizes across populations, locations, measures, and times. For example, Smith, Glass, and Miller (1980) discussed a meta-analysis on over 400 studies concerned with the effectiveness of psychotherapy. They concluded that psychotherapy was reasonably effective, because patients receiving psychotherapy improved more than did 75% of the patients not receiving any therapy.

The greatest limitation of meta-analyses is that differences in the quality of individual studies are often ignored. This can lead to the situation in which a finding is accepted as genuine when it has been obtained in several poorly designed studies but not in a smaller number of well-designed studies. Another problem is that it is often hard to know which studies to include and which to exclude. For example, Smith et al. considered all forms of nonbehavioral therapy together. However, some forms of nonbehavioral therapy were more effective than others (Barlow & Durand, 1995), so it was perhaps undesirable to put them together into a single meta-analysis.

RELIABILITY

One of the main goals of experimental research is to design and carry out studies in such a way that *replication* or repetition of its findings is possible. In order to achieve that goal, it is important that the measures we use should possess good *reliability* or consistency. As Coolican (1994, p. 50) pointed out:

> *Any measure we use in life should be reliable, otherwise it's useless. You wouldn't want your car speedometer or a thermometer to give you different readings for the same values on different occasions. This applies to psychological measures as much as any other.*

Problems relating to reliability are likely to arise when the experimenter is trying to code the complex behavior of participants using a manageable number of categories. For example, it is common in studies of naturalistic observation to record certain events (e.g., performing an aggressive act). However, it may be hard to define those events with enough precision to produce reliable results. One way of assessing this is by asking two (or more) judges to provide ratings in the observational situation. The ratings can then be compared to provide a measure of interjudge reliability.

Key Term

meta-analysis:
an analysis in which all of the findings from many studies relating to a given hypothesis are combined for statistical testing to obtain an overall picture.

Reliability

Internal reliability = consistency within the method of measurement. For instance, a ruler should be measuring the same distance between 0 and 5 centimeters as between 5 and 10 centimeters.

External reliability = consistency between uses of the method of measurement. For instance, the ruler should measure the same on a Monday as it does on a Friday.

- Reliability = consistent and stable
- Validity = measuring what is intended
- Standardization = comparisons can be made between studies and samples

Chapter Summary

Aims and hypotheses

- The first stage in designing a study is to decide on its aims and hypotheses. There will generally be an experimental or alternative hypothesis and a null hypothesis. The experimental hypothesis may be directional or one-tailed, or it may be nondirectional and two-tailed.

Selecting participants

- The participants selected for a study represent a sample from some population. They should form a representative sample; in other words, sampling bias should be avoided. The best approach is random sampling, but other reasonable methods are systematic sampling, stratified sampling, and quota sampling. Opportunity sampling is the easiest but least satisfactory method. The sample size depends on the likely size of the effect being studied.

Good practice in experimentation

- It is important to use standardized procedures. It is also important to avoid confounding variables and other forms of constant error, and to keep random error to a minimum. Operationalization is useful, but operational definitions typically cover only part of the meaning of the independent or dependent variable in question.

Experimental designs

- There are three main types of experimental design: independent design; matched participants design; and repeated measures design. With an independent design, randomization is generally used to allocate the participants to groups. Counterbalancing is often used with the repeated measures design in order to balance out any order effects and prevent them from disrupting the findings.

Good practice in nonexperimental designs

- We can distinguish between participant observation and nonparticipant observation research. Participant research involves the three stages of entering the field, being in the field, and leaving the field. Nonparticipant observation research involves devising precise, comprehensive, and usable behavioral categories. The sampling of behavior can be continuous, based on time intervals, based on time points, or random. Survey studies can use various designs: one-shot; before–after; two-groups controlled comparison; two groups before–after. When questionnaires or attitude scales are constructed, the items need to be short, unambiguous, and unbiased, and the tests need to be reliable and valid. Correlational studies should be based on an underlying theory, the variables should be carefully measured, and the scores on both variables should vary considerably from individual to individual.

Problems with experimental research

- Most research involves interactions between the experimenter and the participants. This can introduce various systematic biases, which can be divided into experimenter effects and demand characteristics. Experimenter effects include experimenter expectancy, experimenter misrecording, and experimenter fudging. Demand characteristics involve the participants responding on the basis of their beliefs about the experimental hypothesis or hypotheses. In addition, the behavior of participants is sometimes influenced by evaluation apprehension.

General issues in investigations

- In some studies, the independent variable has an effect on behavior simply because the participants know they are being observed. This is known as participant reactivity or the Hawthorne effect. It is a serious problem, because it can lead us to misinterpret our findings. It is important for a study to have internal validity, meaning that the findings are genuine and caused by the independent variable. External validity, which refers to the extent to which the findings of a study can be generalized, is also important. Issues of generalizability apply to populations, locations, measures, and times. Information about the generalizability of any particular findings can be obtained by means of a meta-analysis. The measures used in a study should possess good reliability or consistency. If they do not, then they are inadequate measures of the variables in question, and it will be hard to replicate or repeat any findings obtained.

Further Reading

- Coolican, H. (2004). *Research methods and statistics in psychology* (4th ed). London: Hodder & Stoughton. Most of the topics discussed in this chapter are dealt with in a clear fashion in this textbook.
- Dyer, C. (1995). *Beginning research in psychology*. Oxford, UK: Blackwell. The various forms of nonexperimental study are discussed in a very accessible way by this author.

Contents

Data analysis

25

The data obtained from a study may or may not be in numerical or quantitative form, that is, in the form of numbers. If they are not in numerical form, then we can still carry out qualitative analyses based on the experiences of the individual participants. If they are in numerical form, then we typically start by working out some descriptive statistics to summarize the pattern of findings. These descriptive statistics include measures of central tendency within a sample (e.g., mean) and measures of the spread of scores within a sample (e.g., range). Another useful way of summarizing the findings is by means of graphs and figures. Several such ways of summarizing the data are discussed later on in this chapter.

In any study, two things might be true: (1) there is a difference (the experimental hypothesis), or (2) there is no difference (the null hypothesis). Various statistical tests have been devised to permit a decision between the experimental and null hypotheses on the basis of the data. Decision making based on a statistical test is open to error, in that we can never be sure whether we have made the correct decision. However, certain standard procedures are generally followed, and these are discussed in this chapter.

Finally, there are important issues relating to the validity of the findings obtained from a study. One reason why the validity of the findings may be limited is that the study itself was not carried out in a properly controlled and scientific fashion. Another reason why the findings may be partially lacking in validity is that they cannot readily be applied to everyday life, a state of affairs that occurs most often with laboratory studies. Issues relating to these two kinds of validity are discussed towards the end of the chapter.

QUALITATIVE ANALYSIS OF DATA

There is an important distinction between quantitative research and qualitative research. In quantitative research, the information obtained from the participants is expressed in numerical form. Studies in which we record the number of items recalled, reaction times, or the number of aggressive acts are all examples of quantitative research. In qualitative research, on the other hand, the information obtained from participants is *not* expressed in numerical form. The emphasis is on the stated experiences of the participants and on the stated meanings they attach to themselves, to other people, and to their environment. Those carrying out qualitative research sometimes make use of direct quotations from their participants, arguing that such quotations are often very revealing.

There has been rapid growth in the use of qualitative methods since the mid-1980s. This is due in part to increased dissatisfaction with the quantitative or scientific approach that has dominated psychology for the past 100 years. Coolican (1994) discussed a quotation from Reason and Rowan (1981), which expresses that dissatisfaction very clearly:

> There is too much measurement going on. Some things which are numerically precise are not true; and some things which are not numerical are true. Orthodox research produces results which are statistically significant but humanly insignificant; in human inquiry it is much better to be deeply interesting than accurately boring.

Many experimental psychologists would regard this statement as being clearly an exaggeration. "Orthodox research" with its use of the experimental method has

Why do people behave in this way when on vacation? What motivates them to risk their health in the sun?

transformed our understanding of attention, perception, learning, memory, reasoning, and so on. However, qualitative research is of clear usefulness within some areas of social psychology, and it can shed much light on the motivations and values of individuals. As a result, investigators using interviews, case studies, or observations often make use of qualitative data, although they do not always do so.

Investigators who collect qualitative data use several different kinds of analysis, and so only general indications of what can be done with such data will be presented here. However, there would be general agreement among such investigators with the following statement by Patton (1980; cited in Coolican, 1994):

> *The cardinal principle of qualitative analysis is that causal relationships and theoretical statements be clearly emergent from and grounded in the phenomena studied. The theory emerges from the data; it is not imposed on the data.*

How do investigators use this principle? One important way is by considering fully the categories spontaneously used by the participants *before* the investigators develop their own categories. An investigator first of all gathers together all the information obtained from the participants. This stage is not always entirely straightforward. For example, if we simply transcribe tape recordings of what our participants have said, we may be losing valuable information. Details about which words are emphasized, where the speaker pauses, and when the speaker speeds up or slows down should also be recorded, so that we can understand fully what he or she is trying to communicate.

The investigator then arranges the items of information (e.g., statements) into various groups in a preliminary way. If a given item seems of relevance to several groups, then it is included in all of them. Frequently, the next step is to take account of the categories or groupings suggested by the participants themselves. The final step is for the investigator to form a set of categories based on the information obtained from the previous steps. However, the investigator is likely to change some of the categories if additional information comes to light.

Qualitative investigators are not only interested in the number of items or statements falling into each category. Their major concern is usually in the variety of meanings, attitudes, and interpretations found within each category. For example, an investigator might study attitudes towards studying psychology by carrying out interviews with psychology students. One of the categories into which their statements were then placed might be "negative attitudes towards statistics." A consideration of the various statements in this category might reveal numerous reasons why psychology students dislike statistics!

When qualitative researchers report their findings, they will often include some raw data (e.g., direct quotations from participants) as well as analyses of the data based on categories. In addition, they often indicate how their hypotheses changed during the course of the investigation.

EVALUATION

Qualitative analysis is often less influenced than is quantitative analysis by the biases and theoretical assumptions of the investigator. In addition, it offers the prospect of understanding the participants in a study as rounded individuals in a social context. This contrasts with quantitative analysis, in which the focus is often on rather narrow aspects of behavior.

The greatest limitation of the qualitative approach is that the findings that are reported tend to be unreliable and hard to replicate. Why is this so? The qualitative approach is subjective and impressionistic, and so the ways in which the information is categorized and then interpreted often differ considerably from one investigator to another.

There are various ways in which qualitative researchers try to show that their findings are reliable (Coolican, 1994). Probably the most satisfactory approach is to see whether the findings obtained from a qualitative analysis can be replicated. This can be done by comparing the findings from an interview study with those from an observational study.

Alternatively, two different qualitative researchers can conduct independent analyses of the same qualitative data, and then compare their findings.

Qualitative researchers argue that the fact that they typically go through the "research cycle" more than once helps to increase reliability. Thus, for example, the initial assumptions and categories of the researcher are checked against the data, and may then be changed. After that, the new assumptions and categories are checked against the data. Repeating the research cycle is of value in some ways, but it does not ensure that the findings will have high reliability.

INTERPRETATION OF INTERVIEWS, CASE STUDIES, AND OBSERVATIONS

Qualitative analyses as discussed in the previous section are carried out in several different kinds of studies. They are especially common in interviews, case studies, and observational studies, although quantitative analyses have often been used in all three types of studies. Some of the advantages and limitations of these types of studies are discussed in Chapter 23. What we do in this section is consider the interpretation of interviews, case studies, and observations.

INTERVIEWS

As discussed in Chapter 23, interviews vary considerably in terms of their degree of structure. In general terms, unstructured interviews (e.g., nondirective or informal) lend themselves to qualitative analyses, whereas structured interviews lend themselves to quantitative analysis. As Coolican (1994) pointed out, there are various skills that interviewers need in order to obtain valuable data. These skills involve establishing a good understanding with the person being interviewed, adopting a nonjudgmental approach, and developing effective listening skills.

Cardwell, Clark, and Meldrum (1996) illustrated the value of the interview approach by discussing the work of Reicher and Potter (1985) on a riot in the St. Paul's area of Bristol in the UK in April 1980. Many of the media reports on the riot were based on the assumption that those involved in the riot were behaving in a primitive and excessively emotional way. Unstructured interviews with many of those involved indicated that in fact they had good reasons for their actions. They argued that they were defending their area against the police, and they experienced strong feelings of solidarity and community spirit. This interpretation was supported by the fact that very little of the damage affected private homes in the area.

Reicher and Potter argued that the St. Paul's crowd saw themselves as a legitimate presence and the police as an illegitimate presence. Each group attached a different meaning to their actions. Does that make interpretation of discourse problematic?

Evaluation

There are various problems involved in interpreting interview information.

First, there is the problem of **social desirability bias**. Most people want to present themselves in the best possible light, so they may provide socially desirable rather than honest answers to personal questions. This problem can be handled by the interviewer asking additional questions to establish the truth.

Second, the data obtained from an interviewer may reveal more about the social interaction processes between the interviewer and the person being interviewed (the interviewee) than about the interviewee's thought processes and attitudes.

Third, account needs to be taken of the **self-fulfilling prophecy**. This is the tendency for someone's expectations about another person to lead to the fulfillment of those expectations. For example, suppose that a therapist expects his or her patient to behave very anxiously. This expectation may cause the therapist to treat the patient in such a way that the patient starts to behave in the expected fashion.

Key Terms
Social desirability bias: the tendency to provide socially desirable rather than honest answers on questionnaires and in interviews.
Self-fulfilling prophecy: the tendency for someone's expectations about another person to lead to the fulfillment of those expectations.

CASE STUDIES

Case studies (intensive investigations of individuals) come in all shapes and sizes. Probably the best-known case studies are those of Freud and others in the field of clinical psychology. However, detailed case studies have also been carried out in personality research and in studies of cognitive functioning in brain-damaged patients.

One way in which case studies have been used to study personality involves an approach known as **psychobiography**. This was defined by McAdams (1988, p. 2) as "the systematic use of psychological (especially personality) theory to transform a life into a coherent and illuminating story." A key feature of psychobiography is identification of the most important events in an individual's account of his or her own life story. How can this be done? According to McAdams (1988, pp. 12–13), we should look for

clues about primacy (what comes first in a story), uniqueness (what stands out in the story), omission (what seems to be missing from the story), distortion and isolation (what doesn't follow logically in the story), and incompletion (when the story fails to end in a satisfying way).

Weiskrantz (1986) reported a very different kind of case study. He studied DB, who had had an operation designed to reduce the number of severe migraines from which he suffered. As a result of this operation, DB exhibited what is known as "blindsight." He was able to tell whether a visual stimulus had been presented, and he could point at it, even though he had no conscious awareness of having seen it. These findings are important, because they suggest that many perceptual processes can occur in the absence of conscious awareness.

Case Study: *The Effects of Extreme Deprivation*

Freud and Dann (1951) studied six preschool children who had lost their parents during the Second World War. It is not known how long each child had spent with their parents before being taken to Nazi concentration camp nurseries. The children remained together, despite moving camp several times, and appeared to have received only the most basic forms of care and attention. In the absence of a caring adult, they had formed close and loving bonds with each other. These strong bonds provided a protective and stable influence in their lives.

The children were rescued at the end of the war and brought to England for medical and psychological treatment. Their mental and physical development had been restricted, so that they had very poor speech skills. They feared adults and clung to each other for reassurance. Gradually they began to form bonds with the adults who cared for them, and their social and language skills improved.

Despite all the problems they had experienced, the children did not show the levels of extreme disturbance that were once expected when there is a complete lack of "mothering" (Bowlby, 1951). Freud and Dann's study highlights the fundamental importance of having someone to bond with, even if it is not the mother, as well as the reversibility of the effects of extreme deprivation.

Case studies are often seen as rather unscientific and unreliable. The sample is not representative of the wider population, the study cannot be repeated, and interpretation of the findings is very subjective. However, case studies can be of great interest because they highlight unique and unexpected behavior, and can stimulate research that may contradict established theories such as Bowlby's. Freud and Dann's work offers insights into human experience that would otherwise be impossible to gain: ethical considerations prevent the deliberate separation of children and parents in order to study the effects of deprivation.

Evaluation

We need to be very careful when interpreting the evidence from a case study. The greatest danger is that very general conclusions may be drawn on the basis of a single atypical individual. For this reason, it is important to have supporting evidence from other sources before drawing such conclusions.

It is often hard to interpret the evidence from case studies. For example, Freud claimed that the various case studies he reported served to show the validity of his theoretical ideas. However, such evidence is suspect, because there was a real chance of

Key Term

Psychobiography: the study of individual personality by applying psychological theory to the key events in a person's life.

contamination in the data Freud obtained from his patients. What any patient said to Freud may have been influenced by what Freud had said to him or her previously, and Freud may have used his theoretical views to interpret what the patient said in ways that distorted it.

How, then, should the findings from a case study be interpreted? Probably the greatest value of a case study is that it can suggest hypotheses that can then be tested under more controlled conditions with larger numbers of participants. In other words, case studies usually provide suggestive rather than definitive evidence. In addition, case studies can indicate that there are limitations in current theories. The discovery of blindsight in DB suggested that visual perception depends much less on conscious awareness than was thought to be the case by most theorists.

OBSERVATIONS

As discussed in Chapter 23, there are numerous kinds of observational studies, and the data obtained may be either quantitative or qualitative. We consider issues relating to interpreting the data from observational studies by focusing on a concrete example. Jourard (1966) watched pairs of people talking in cafes, and noted down the number of times one person touched another at one table during 1 hour. In San Juan, the capital of Puerto Rico, the total number of touches was 180. In contrast, the total in Paris was 110, and in London it was 0. One problem with interpreting these data is that the kinds of people who go to cafes in San Juan, Paris, and London may be quite different. It is also entirely possible that those who spend much of their time in cafes are not representative of the general population. These issues of representativeness apply to many observational studies.

Evaluation

Jourard's (1966) findings do not really tell us why there is (or was, in 1966) much more touching in San Juan than in London. It is possible that Londoners are simply less friendly and open, but there are several other possibilities (e.g., Londoners are more likely to go to cafes with business colleagues). The general issue here is that it is often very hard to interpret or make sense of the data obtained from observational studies, because we can only speculate on the reasons why the participants are behaving in the ways that we observe.

Another issue was raised by Coolican (1994) in his discussion of the work of Whyte (1943). Whyte joined an Italian street gang in Chicago, and became a participant observer. The problem he encountered in interpreting his observations was that his presence in the gang influenced their behavior. A member of the gang expressed this point as follows: "You've slowed me down plenty since you've been down here. Now, when I do something, I have to think what Bill Whyte would want me to know about it and how I can explain it."

CONTENT ANALYSIS

Content analysis is used when originally qualitative information is reduced to numerical terms. **Content analysis** started off as a method for analyzing messages in the media, including articles published in newspapers, speeches made by politicians on radio and television, various forms of propaganda, and health records. More recently, the method of content analysis has been applied more widely to almost any form of communication. As Coolican (1994, p. 108) pointed out:

The communications concerned were originally those already published, but some researchers conduct content analysis on materials which they ask people to produce, such as essays, answers to interview questions, diaries, and verbal protocols [detailed records].

One of the types of communication that has often been studied by content analysis is television advertising. For example, McArthur and Resko (1975) carried out a content

> **Key Term**
>
> **Content analysis:**
> a method involving the detailed study of, for example, the output of the media, speeches, and literature.

Content analysis of advertising can tell us a great deal about society's attitudes to men and women.

analysis of American television commercials. They found that 70% of the men in these commercials were shown as experts who knew a lot about the products being sold. In contrast, 86% of the women in the commercials were shown only as product users. There was another interesting gender difference: Men who used the products were typically promised improved social and career prospects, whereas women were promised that their family would like them more.

More recent studies of American television commercials (e.g., Brett & Cantor, 1988) indicate that the differences in the ways in which men and women are presented have been reduced. However, it remains the case that the men are far more likely than women to be presented as the product expert.

The first stage in content analysis is that of sampling, or deciding what to select from what may be an enormous amount of material. For example, when Cumberbatch (1990) carried out a study on over 500 advertisements shown on British television, there were two television channels showing advertisements. Between them, these two channels were broadcasting for about 15,000 hours a year, and showing over 250,000 advertisements. Accordingly, Cumberbatch decided to select only a sample of advertisements taken from prime-time television over a 2-week period.

The issue of sampling is an important one. For example, television advertisers target their advertisements at particular sections of the population, and so arrange for the advertisements to be shown when the relevant groups are most likely to be watching television. As a result, advertisements for beer are more likely to be shown during a soccer match than during a program about fashion. By focusing on prime-time television, Cumberbatch (1990) tried to ensure that he was studying advertisements designed to have general appeal.

The other key ingredient in content analysis is the construction of the **coding units** into which the information is to be categorized. In order to form appropriate coding units, the researcher needs to have considerable knowledge of the kinds of material to be used in the content analysis. He or she also needs to have one or more clear hypotheses, because the selection of coding units must be such as to permit these hypotheses to be tested effectively.

The coding can take many forms. The categories used can be very specific (e.g., use of a given word) or general (e.g., theme of the communication). Instead of using categories, the coders may be asked to provide *ratings*. For example, the apparent expertise of those appearing in television advertisements might be rated on a 7-point scale. Another form of coding involves *ranking* items, or putting them in order. For example, the statements of politicians could be ranked in terms of the extent to which they agreed with the facts.

EVALUATION

One of the greatest strengths of content analysis is that it provides a way of extracting information from a wealth of real-world settings. The media influence the ways we think and feel about issues, and so it is important to analyze media communications in detail. Content analysis can reveal issues of concern. For example, Cumberbatch (1990) found in his study of advertisements on British television that only about 25% of the women appearing in these advertisements seemed to be over 30 years old, compared to about 75% of the men. On the face of it, this would seem to reflect a sexist bias.

The greatest limitation of content analysis is that it is often very hard to interpret the findings. Consider, for example, the difference in the ages of men and women appearing in advertisements found by Cumberbatch (1990). One interpretation is that this difference occurred because most television viewers prefer to see older men and younger women in advertisements. However, it is also possible that those making the advertisements thought mistakenly that this is what the viewers wanted to see.

> **| Key Term**
>
> **Coding units:**
> the categories into which observations are placed prior to analysis.

> **Gender and advertising**
>
> Cumberbatch (1990) found that men outnumbered women in advertisements by 2 : 1. In addition, 75% of the men in ads were aged over 30, whereas 75% of women in ads were aged under 30. Male voices were used where the information in the soundtrack concerned technical expertise, whereas women's voices were used in sexy and sensuous ways. What does this say about the way we view men and women in society? Comparing the results of studies such as Cumberbatch's with earlier ones (e.g., McArthur & Resko, 1975) can begin to provide answers to questions such as this.

Food Diary – Week 1

Time	What eaten	B	V	L	Antecedents & Consequences
8.00	All-bran				A: Still full from yesterday. C: Must make an effort not to binge today
12.00	1 apple				A: Hungry. C: Still hungry, mustn't eat more in case it starts me off on a binge.
3.00	1 lb grapes, 2 choc. bars		!		A: Had phone call from John, he will be home late. C: Disgusted with myself. I am the most hopeless person in the world.
6.00	peanuts + choc, picked from shopping	!!			A: No food in flat. Had to go shopping. Couldn't stop myself putting loads of sweets in the trolley. Ate loads of stuff in the car. Had to go on eating once at home.
7.00	2 portions of curry, 3 choc. bars	!!	!!		C: Very angry with myself. I feel so lonely. Totally exhausted, went to bed early.

B = Binge, V = Vomited, L = Laxatives

Food Diary – Week 4

Time	What eaten	B	V	L	Antecedents & Consequences
8.00	Cottage cheese, 2 sl. toast with honey				Enjoyed this.
11.00	apple				
12.30	baked potato, tuna fish				Eaten in the canteen at work. Tina said "You haven't been here for ages". Could have run away, felt everybody was looking at me.
3.00	yoghurt, crunch bar				
6.00	1 sl. toast				
7.00	fish + vegetables, 1 portion ice cream				Had not planned dessert. John suggested ice cream. My initial response was to say no, but I knew I would then finish the packet off whilst washing up. So I had a portion and enjoyed it sitting with John. John put it away and made coffee, which we drank relaxing on the sofa. Washing up left.

Diary studies are often used in clinical psychology, such as in this example from the diary of a bulimia sufferer. Diaries may be used to record actions, thoughts, and feelings, but may not be totally accurate, particularly if the diarist is embarrassed to reveal the truth about himself or herself. Food diaries reproduced from Schmidt and Treasure (1993), with permission. Copyright © 1993 Psychology Press.

There are other possible interpretations, but the available data do not allow us to discriminate among them.

There are also problems of interpretation with other communications such as personal diaries or essays. Diaries or essays may contain accurate accounts of what an individual does, thinks, and feels. On the other hand, individuals may provide deliberately distorted accounts in order to protect their self-esteem, to make it appear that their lives are more exciting than is actually the case, and so on.

Another problem is that the selection and scoring of coding units can be rather subjective. The coding categories that are used need to accurately reflect the content of the communication, and each of the categories must be defined as precisely as possible.

QUANTITATIVE ANALYSIS: DESCRIPTIVE STATISTICS

Suppose that we have carried out an experiment on the effects of noise on learning with three groups of nine participants each. One group was exposed to very loud noise, another group to moderately loud noise, and the third group was not exposed to noise at all. What they had learned from a book chapter was assessed by giving them a set of questions, producing a score between 0 and 20.

What is to be done with the raw scores? There are two key types of measures that can be taken whenever we have a set of scores from participants in a given condition. First, there are measures of central tendency, which provide some indication of the size of average or typical scores. Second, there are measures of dispersion, which indicate the extent to which the scores cluster around the average or are spread out. Various measures of central tendency and of dispersion are considered next.

MEASURES OF CENTRAL TENDENCY

Measures of central tendency describe how the data cluster together around a central point. There are three main measures of central tendency: the mean; the median; and the mode.

Mean

The **mean** in each group or condition is calculated by adding up all the scores in a given condition, and then dividing by the number of participants in that condition. Suppose that the scores of the nine participants in the no-noise condition are as follows: 1, 2, 4, 5, 7, 9, 9, 9, 17. The mean is given by the total, which is 63, divided by the number of participants, which is 9. Thus, the mean is 7.

The main advantage of the mean is the fact that it takes all the scores into account. This generally makes it a sensitive measure of central tendency, especially if the scores resemble the **normal distribution**, which is a bell-shaped distribution in which most scores cluster fairly close to the mean. However, the mean can be very misleading if the distribution differs markedly from the normal and there are one or two extreme scores in one direction. Suppose that eight people complete one lap of a track in go-karts. For seven of them, the times taken (in seconds) are as follows: 25, 28, 29, 29, 34, 36, and 42. The eighth person's go-kart breaks down, and so the driver has to push it around the track. This person takes 288 seconds to complete the lap. This produces an overall mean of 64 seconds. This is clearly misleading, because no one else took even close to 64 seconds to complete one lap.

Mean		
Scores	Number	
1	1	
2	2	
4	3	
5	4	
7	5	
9	6	
9	7	
9	8	
17	9	
63	9	Total
63 ÷ 9	= 7	

Median

Another way of describing the general level of performance in each condition is known as the **median**. If there is an odd number of scores, then the median is simply the middle score, having an equal number of scores higher and lower than it. In the example with nine scores in the no-noise condition (1, 2, 4, 5, 7, 9, 9, 9, 17), the median is 7. Matters are slightly more complex if there is an even number of scores. In that case, we work out the mean of the two central values. For example, suppose that we have the following scores in size order: 2, 5, 5, 7, 8, 9. The two central values are 5 and 7, and so the median is

Scores
1
2
4
5
7 = Median
9
9
9
17

$$\frac{5+7}{2} = 6$$

The main advantage of the median is that it is unaffected by a few extreme scores, because it focuses only on scores in the middle of the distribution. It also has the advantage that it tends to be easier than the mean to work out. The main limitation of the median is that it ignores most of the scores, and so it is often less sensitive than the mean. In addition, it is not always representative of the scores obtained, especially if there are only a few scores.

Scores
1
2
4
5
7
9
9 = Mode
9
17

Mode

The final measure of central tendency is the **mode**. This is simply the most frequently occurring score. In the example of the nine scores in the no-noise condition, this is 9. The main advantages of the mode are that it is unaffected by one or two extreme scores, and that it is the easiest measure of central tendency to work out. In addition, it can still be worked out even when some of the extreme scores are not known. However, its limitations generally outweigh these advantages. The greatest limitation is that the mode tends to be unreliable. For example, suppose we have the following scores: 4, 4, 6, 7, 8, 8, 12, 12, 12. The mode of these scores is 12. If just one score changed (a 12 becoming a 4), the mode would change to 4! Another limitation is that information about the exact values of the scores obtained is ignored in working out the mode. This makes it a less sensitive measure than the mean. A final limitation is that it is possible for there to be more than one mode.

Levels of measurement

From what has been said so far, we have seen that the mean is the most generally useful measure of central tendency, whereas the mode is the least useful. However, we need to

Key Terms

Mean:
an average worked out by dividing the total of all participants' scores by the number of participants.

Normal distribution:
a bell-shaped distribution in which most scores cluster fairly close to the mean.

Median:
the middle score out of all participants' scores in a given condition.

Mode:
the most frequently occurring score among the participants in a given condition.

The mode is useful where other measures of central tendency are meaningless, for example when calculating the number of children in the average family. It would be unusual to have 0.4 or 0.6 of a child!

take account of the level of measurement when deciding which measure of central tendency to use (the various levels are discussed further on pp. 598–599 of this chapter). At the interval and ratio levels of measurement, each added unit represents an equal increase. For example, someone who hits a target four times out of ten has done twice as well as someone who hits it twice out of ten. Below this is the ordinal level of measurement, in which we can only order, or rank, the scores from highest to lowest. At the lowest level, there is the nominal level, in which the scores consist of the numbers of participants falling into various categories. The mean should only be used when the scores are at the interval level of measurement. The median can be used when the data are at the interval or ordinal level. The mode can be used when the data are at any of the three levels. It is the only one of the three measures of central tendency that can be used with nominal data.

MEASURES OF DISPERSION

The mean, median, and mode are all measures of central tendency. It is also useful to work out what are known as measures of dispersion, such as the range, interquartile range, variation ratio, and standard deviation. These measures indicate whether the scores in a given condition are similar to each other or whether they are spread out.

Range

The simplest of these measures is the **range**, which can be defined as the difference between the highest and the lowest score in any condition. In the case of the no-noise group (1, 2, 4, 5, 7, 9, 9, 9, 17), the range is $17 - 1 = 16$.

In fact, it is preferable to calculate the range in a slightly different way (Coolican, 1994). The revised formula (when we are dealing with whole numbers) is as follows: (highest score – lowest score) $+1$. Thus, in our example, the range is $(17 - 1) + 1 = 17$. This formula is preferable because it takes account of the fact that the scores we recorded were rounded to whole numbers. In our sample data, a score of 17 stands for all values between 16.5 and 17.5, and a score of 1 represents a value between 0.5 and 1.5. If we take the range as the interval between the highest possible value (17.5) and the lowest possible value (0.5), this gives us a range of 17, which is precisely the figure produced by the formula.

Range								9								
								9								
Scores:	1	2		4	5		7	9								17
Range:	1	2	3	4	5	6	7	8	9	10	11	12	13	14	15	16	17

Key Term

Range:
the difference between the highest and lowest score in any condition.

What has been said so far about the range applies only to whole numbers. Suppose that we measure the time taken to perform a task to the nearest one-tenth of a second, with the fastest time being 21.3 seconds and the slowest time being 36.8 seconds. The figure of 21.3 represents a value between 21.25 and 21.35, and 36.8 represents a value between 36.75 and 36.85. As a result, the range is 36.85 – 21.25, which is 15.6 seconds.

The main advantages of the range as a measure of dispersion are that it is easy to calculate and that it takes full account of extreme values. The main weakness of the range is that it can be greatly influenced by one score that is very different from all of the others. In the example, the inclusion of the participant scoring 17 increases the range from 9 to 17. The other important weakness of the range is that it ignores all but two of the scores, and so is likely to provide an inadequate measure of the general spread or dispersion of the scores around the mean or median.

Range

Suppose that the scores obtained in a study were as follows:

Group A: 5, 10, 15, 20, 25, 30, 35, 40, 45, 50   total = 275
Mean = 27.5
Median = 27.5

Group B: 15, 20, 20, 25, 25, 30, 35, 35, 35, 35   total = 275
Mean = 27.5
Median = 27.5

Although the means and medians are the same for both sets of scores, the spread of scores is quite different. This becomes highly relevant if we are assessing something like the range of abilities in children in a class.

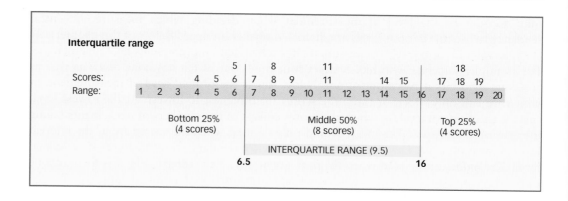

Interquartile range

The **interquartile range** is defined as the spread of the middle 50% of scores. For example, suppose that we have the following set of scores: 4, 5, 6, 6, 7, 8, 8, 9, 11, 11, 14, 15, 17, 18, 18, 19. There are 16 scores, which can be divided into the bottom 25% (4), the middle 50% (8), and the top 25% (4). The middle 50% of scores start with 7 and run through to 15. The upper boundary of the interquartile range lies between 15 and 17, and is given by the mean of these two values, i.e., 16. The lower boundary of the interquartile range lies between 6 and 7, and is their mean; i.e., 6.5. The interquartile range is the difference between the upper and lower boundaries, i.e., 16 – 6.5 = 9.5.

The interquartile range has the advantage over the range that it is not influenced by a single extreme score. As a result, it is more likely to provide an accurate reflection of the spread or dispersion of the scores. It has the disadvantage that it ignores information from the top and the bottom 25% of scores. For example, we could have two sets of scores with the same interquartile range, but with more extreme scores in one set than in the other. The difference in spread or dispersion between the two sets of scores would not be detected by the interquartile range.

Standard deviation

The most generally useful measure of dispersion is the **standard deviation**. It is harder to calculate than the range but generally provides a more accurate measure of the spread of scores. However, you will be pleased to learn that many calculators allow the standard deviation to be worked out rapidly and effortlessly, as in the worked example.

The first step is to work out the mean of the sample. This is given by the total of all of the participants' scores (ΣX = 130; the symbol Σ means the sum of) divided by the number of participants (N = 13). Thus, the mean is 10.

The second step is to subtract the mean in turn from each score (X – M). The calculations are shown in the fourth column. The third step is to square each of the scores in the fourth column, $(X - M)^2$. The fourth step is to work out the total of all the squared scores, $\Sigma(X - M)^2$. This comes to 136. The fifth step is to divide the result of the fourth step by one less than the number of participants, N – 1 = 12. This gives us 136 divided by 12, which equals 11.33. This is known as the **variance**, which is in squared units.

Finally, we use a calculator to take the square root of the variance. This produces a figure of 3.37; this is the standard deviation.

The method for calculating the standard deviation that has just been described is used when we want to estimate the standard deviation of the population. If we want merely to describe the spread of scores in our sample, then the fifth step involves dividing the result of the fourth step by N.

What is the meaning of this figure for the standard deviation? We expect about two-thirds of the scores in a sample to lie within one standard deviation of the mean. In

Key Terms
Interquartile range: the spread of the middle 50% of an ordered or ranked set of scores. **Standard deviation:** a measure of the spread of scores in a bell-shaped or normal distribution. It is the square root of the variance, takes account of every score, and is a sensitive dispersion measure. **Variance:** a measure of dispersion that is the square of the standard deviation.

Standard deviation: A worked example

Participant	Score X	Mean M	Score − Mean X − M	(Score − Mean)² (X − M)²
1	13	10	3	9
2	6	10	−4	16
3	10	10	0	0
4	15	10	5	25
5	10	10	0	0
6	15	10	5	25
7	5	10	−5	25
8	9	10	−1	1
9	10	10	0	0
10	13	10	3	9
11	6	10	−4	16
12	11	10	1	1
13	7	10	−3	9
13	130	10		136

Total of scores = ΣX = 130

Number of participants = N = 13

$$\text{Mean} = \frac{\Sigma X}{N} = \frac{130}{13} = 10$$

$$\text{Variance} = \frac{136}{13 - 1} = 11.33$$

Standard deviation = $\sqrt{11.3}$ = 3.37

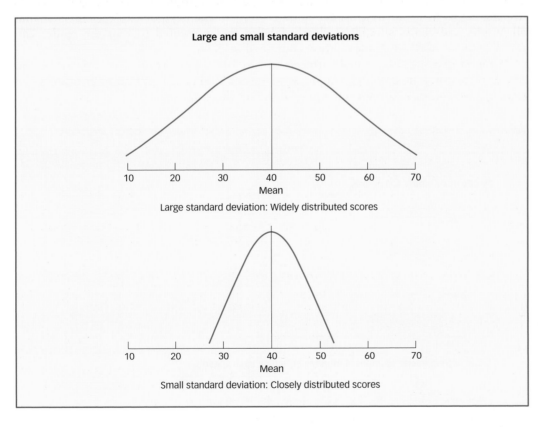

Large and small standard deviations

Large standard deviation: Widely distributed scores

Small standard deviation: Closely distributed scores

our example, the mean is 10.0, one standard deviation above the mean is 13.366, and one standard deviation below the mean is 6.634. In fact, 61.5% of the scores lie between those two limits, which is only slightly below the expected percentage.

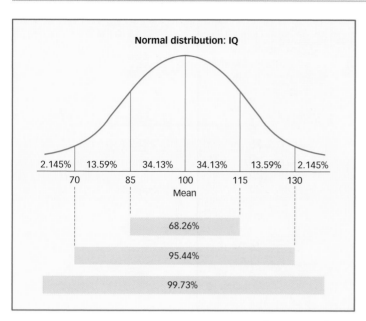

Normal distribution: IQ

The standard deviation has special relevance in relation to the so-called normal distribution. As was mentioned earlier, the normal distribution is a bell-shaped curve in which there are as many scores above the mean as below it. Intelligence (or IQ) scores in the general population provide an example of a normal distribution. Other characteristics such as height and weight also form roughly a normal distribution. Most of the scores in a normal distribution cluster fairly close to the mean, and there are fewer and fewer scores as you move away from the mean in either direction. In a normal distribution, 68.26% of the scores fall within one standard deviation of the mean, 95.44% fall within two standard deviations, and 99.73% fall within three standard deviations.

The standard deviation takes account of all of the scores and provides a sensitive measure of dispersion. As we have seen, it also has the advantage that it describes the spread of scores in a normal distribution with great precision. The most obvious disadvantage of the standard deviation is that it is much harder to work out than the other measures of dispersion.

DATA PRESENTATION

Information about the scores in a sample can be presented in several ways. If it is presented in a graph or chart, this may make it easier for people to understand what has been found, compared to simply presenting information about the central tendency and dispersion. We will shortly consider some examples. The key point to remember is that all graphs and charts should be clearly labeled and presented so that the reader can rapidly make sense of the information contained in them.

Suppose that we ask 25 male athletes to run 400 meters as rapidly as possible, and record their times (in seconds). Having worked out a table of frequencies (see the boxed example below), there are several ways to present these data.

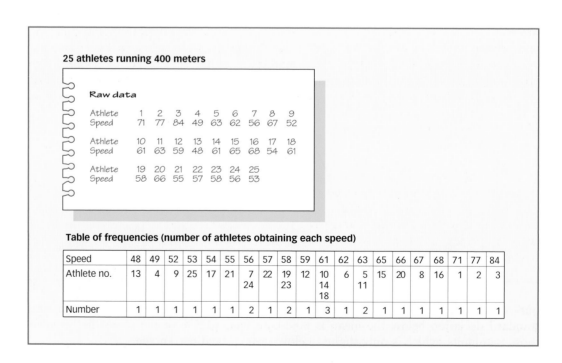

25 athletes running 400 meters

Raw data

Athlete	1	2	3	4	5	6	7	8	9
Speed	71	77	84	49	63	62	56	67	52

Athlete	10	11	12	13	14	15	16	17	18
Speed	61	63	59	48	61	65	68	54	61

Athlete	19	20	21	22	23	24	25
Speed	58	66	55	57	58	56	53

Table of frequencies (number of athletes obtaining each speed)

Speed	48	49	52	53	54	55	56	57	58	59	61	62	63	65	66	67	68	71	77	84
Athlete no.	13	4	9	25	17	21	7 24	22	19 23	12	10 14 18	6	5 11	15	20	8	16	1	2	3
Number	1	1	1	1	1	1	2	1	2	1	3	1	2	1	1	1	1	1	1	1

FREQUENCY POLYGON

One way of summarizing these data is in the form of a **frequency polygon**. This is a simple form of chart in which the scores from low to high are indicated on the x or horizontal axis and the frequencies of the various scores (in terms of the numbers of individuals obtaining each score) are indicated on the y or vertical axis. The points on a frequency polygon should only be joined up when the scores can be ordered from low to high. In order for a frequency polygon to be most useful, it should be constructed so that most of the frequencies are neither very high nor very low. The frequencies will be very high if the width of each class interval (the categories used to summarize frequencies) on the x axis is too broad (e.g., covering 20 seconds), and the frequencies will be very low if each class interval is too narrow (e.g., covering only 1 or 2 seconds).

Each point in a frequency polygon should be placed in the middle of its class interval. There is a technical point that needs to be made here (Coolican, 1994). Suppose that we include all times between 53 and 57 seconds in the same class interval. As we have only measured running times to the nearest second, this class interval will cover actual times between 52.5 and 57.5 seconds. In this case, the mid-point of the class interval (55 seconds) is the same whether we take account of the actual measurement interval (52.5–57.5 seconds) or adopt the simpler approach of focusing on the lowest and highest recorded times in the class interval (53–57 seconds, respectively). When the two differ, it is important to use the actual measurement interval.

How should we interpret the findings shown in the frequency polygon? It is clear that most of the participants were able to run 400 meters in between about 53 and 67 seconds. Only a few of the athletes were able to better a time of 53 seconds, and there was a small number who took longer than 67 seconds.

HISTOGRAM

A similar way of describing these data is by means of a **histogram**. In a histogram, the scores are indicated on the horizontal axis and the frequencies are shown on the vertical axis. In contrast to a frequency polygon, however, the frequencies are indicated by rectangular columns. These columns are all the same width but vary in height in accordance with the corresponding frequencies. As with frequency polygons, it is important to make sure that the class intervals are not too broad or too narrow. All class intervals are represented, even if there are no scores in some of them. Class intervals are indicated by their mid-point at the center of the columns.

Histograms are clearly rather similar to frequency polygons. However, frequency polygons are sometimes preferable when you want to compare two different frequency distributions. The information contained in a histogram is interpreted in the same way as the information in a frequency polygon. In the present example, the histogram indicates that most of the athletes ran 400 meters fairly quickly. Only a few had extreme times.

BAR CHART

Frequency polygons and histograms are suitable when the scores obtained by the participants can be ordered from

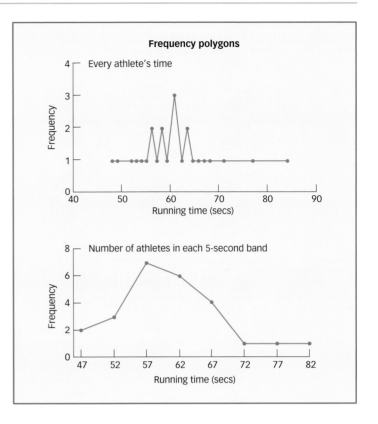

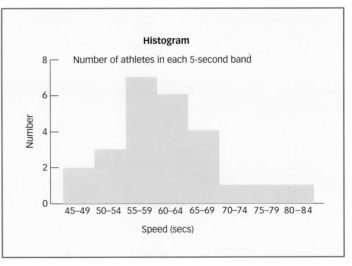

Key Terms

Frequency polygon: a graph showing the frequencies with which different scores are obtained by the participants in a study.

Histogram: a graph in which the frequencies with which different scores are obtained by the participants in a study are shown by rectangles of different heights.

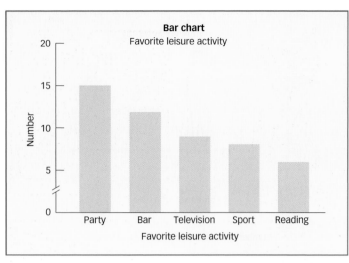

Bar chart
Favorite leisure activity

low to high. In more technical terms, the data should be either interval or ratio (see next section). However, there are many studies in which the scores are in the form of categories rather than ordered scores; in other words, the data are nominal. For example, 50 people might be asked to indicate their favorite leisure activity. Suppose that 15 said going to a party, 12 said going to a bar, 9 said watching television, 8 said playing sport, and 6 said reading a good book.

These data can be displayed in the form of a **bar chart**. In a bar chart, the categories are shown along the horizontal axis, and the frequencies are indicated on the vertical axis. In contrast to the data contained in histograms, the categories in bar charts cannot be ordered numerically in a meaningful way. However, they can be arranged in ascending (or descending) order of popularity. Another difference from histograms is that the rectangles in a bar chart do not usually touch each other.

The scale on the vertical axis of a bar chart normally starts at zero. However, it is sometimes convenient for presentational purposes to have it start at some higher value. If that is done, then it should be made clear in the bar chart that the lower part of the vertical scale is missing. The columns in a bar chart often represent frequencies. However, they can also represent means or percentages for different groups (Coolican, 1994).

How should we interpret the information in a bar chart? In the present example, a bar chart makes it easy to compare the popularity of different leisure activities. We can see at a glance that going to a party was the most popular leisure activity, whereas reading a good book was the least popular.

STATISTICAL TESTS

The various ways in which the data from a study can be presented are all useful in that they give us convenient and easily understood summaries of what we have found. However, to have a clearer idea of what our findings mean, it is generally necessary to carry out one or more statistical tests. The first step in choosing an appropriate statistical test is to decide whether your data were obtained from an experiment in which some aspect of the situation (the independent variable) was manipulated in order to observe its effects on the dependent variables (i.e., the scores). If so, you need a test of difference (see pp. 600–605 of this chapter). On the other hand, if you simply have two observations from each of your participants in a nonexperimental design, then you need a test of association or correlation (see pp. 605–610 of this chapter).

In using a statistical test, you need to take account of the experimental hypothesis. If you predicted the direction of any effects (e.g., loud noise will disrupt learning and memory), then you have a directional hypothesis, which should be evaluated by a one-tailed test. If you did not predict the direction of any effects (e.g., loud noise will affect learning and memory), then you have a nondirectional hypothesis, which should be evaluated by a two-tailed test (see Chapter 24).

Another factor to consider when deciding which statistical test to use is the type of data you have obtained. There are four types of data of increasing levels of precision:

- **Nominal:** The data consist of the numbers of participants falling into various categories (e.g., fat, thin; men, women).
- **Ordinal:** The data can be ordered from lowest to highest (e.g., the finishing positions of athletes in a race).
- **Interval:** The data differ from ordinal data, because the units of measurement are fixed throughout the range; for

---

Key Terms

Bar chart:
a graph showing the frequencies with which the participants in a study fall into different categories.

Nominal data:
data consisting of the numbers of participants falling into qualitatively different categories.

Ordinal data:
data that can be ordered from smallest to largest.

Interval data:
data in which the units of measurement have an invariant or unchanging value.

example, there is the same "distance" between a height of 1.82 meters and 1.70 meters as between a height of 1.70 meters and one of 1.58 meters.

- **Ratio:** The data have the same characteristics as interval data, with the exception that they have a meaningful zero point; for example, time measurements provide ratio data because the notion of zero time is meaningful, and 10 seconds is twice as long as 5 seconds. The similarities between interval and ratio data are so great that they are sometimes combined and referred to as interval/ratio data.

Interval

Nominal

Ratio

Ordinal

Statistical tests can be divided into **parametric tests** and **nonparametric tests**. Parametric tests should only be used when the data obtained from a study satisfy various requirements. More specifically, there should be interval or ratio data, the data should be normally distributed, and the variances in the two conditions should be reasonably similar. In contrast, nonparametric tests can nearly always continue to be used, even when the requirements of parametric tests are satisfied. In this chapter, we confine ourselves to a discussion of some of the most useful nonparametric tests.

STATISTICAL SIGNIFICANCE

So far we have discussed some of the issues that influence the choice of statistical test. What happens after we have chosen a statistical test, and analyzed our data, and want to interpret our findings? We use the results of the test to choose between the following:

- Experimental hypothesis (e.g., loud noise disrupts learning).
- Null hypothesis, which asserts that there is no difference between conditions (e.g., loud noise has no effect on learning).

If the statistical test indicates that there is only a small probability of the difference between conditions (e.g., loud noise vs. no noise) having occurred if the null hypothesis were true, then we reject the null hypothesis in favor of the experimental hypothesis.

Why do we focus initially on the null hypothesis rather than the experimental hypothesis? The reason is that the experimental hypothesis is rather imprecise. It may state that loud noise will disrupt learning, but it does not indicate the *extent* of the disruption. This imprecision makes it hard to evaluate an experimental hypothesis directly. In contrast, a null hypothesis such as loud noise has no effect on learning *is* precise, and this precision allows us to use statistical tests to decide the probability that it is correct.

Psychologists generally use the 5% (.05) level of **statistical significance**. What this means is that the null hypothesis is rejected (and the experimental hypothesis is accepted) if the probability that the results were due to chance alone is 5% or less. This is often expressed as $p = .05$, where p = the probability of the result if the null hypothesis is true. If the statistical test indicates that the findings do not reach the 5% (or $p = .05$) level of statistical significance, then we retain the null hypothesis and reject the experimental hypothesis. The key decision is whether or not to reject the null hypothesis and that is why the .05 level

Key Terms

Ratio data:
as **interval data**, but with a meaningful zero point.

Parametric tests:
statistical tests that require interval or ratio data, normally distributed data, and similar variances in both conditions.

Nonparametric tests:
statistical tests that do not involve the requirements of parametric tests.

Statistical significance:
the level at which the decision is made to reject the **null hypothesis** in favor of the **experimental hypothesis**.

From percentage to decimal

10% = .10
5% = .05
1% = .01
2.5% = ?

To go from decimal to percentage, multiply by 100: move the decimal point two places to the right.
   To go from percentage to decimal, divide by 100: move the decimal point two places to the left.

of statistical significance is so important. However, our data sometimes indicate that the null hypothesis can be rejected with greater confidence, say, at the 1% (.01) level. If the null hypothesis can be rejected at the 1% level, it is customary to state that the findings are highly significant. In general terms, you should state the precise level of statistical significance of your findings, whether it is the 5% level, the 1% level, or whatever.

These procedures may seem easy. In fact, there are two errors that may occur when reaching a conclusion on the basis of the results of a statistical test:

- **Type I error**: We may reject the null hypothesis in favor of the experimental hypothesis even though the findings are actually due to chance; the probability of this happening is given by the level of statistical significance that is selected.
- **Type II error**: We may retain the null hypothesis even though the experimental hypothesis is actually correct.

It would be possible to reduce the likelihood of a Type I error by using a more stringent level of significance. For example, if we used the 1% ($p = .01$) level of significance, this would greatly reduce the probability of a Type I error. However, use of a more stringent level of significance increases the probability of a Type II error. We could reduce the probability of a Type II error by using a less stringent level of significance, such as the 10% ($p = .10$) level. However, this would increase the probability of a Type I error. These considerations help to make it clear why most psychologists favor the 5% (or $p = .05$) level of significance: it allows the probabilities of both Type I and Type II errors to remain reasonably low.

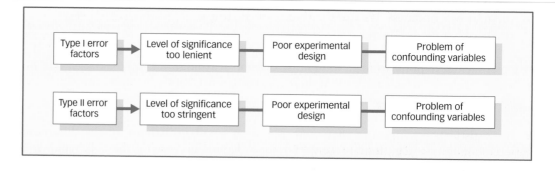

Psychologists generally use the 5% level of significance. However, they would use the 1% or even the 0.1% level of significance if it were very important to avoid making a Type I error. For example, clinical psychologists might require very strong evidence that a new form of therapy was more effective than existing forms of therapy before starting to use it on a regular basis. The 1% or 0.1% ($p = .001$) level of statistical significance is also used when the experimental hypothesis seems improbable. For example, very few people would accept that telepathy had been proved to exist on the basis of a single study in which the results were only just significant at the 5% level!

TESTS OF DIFFERENCE

In this section, we consider those statistical tests that are applicable when we are interested in deciding whether the differences between two conditions or groups are significant. As discussed in Chapter 24, there are three kinds of design that can be used when we want to compare two conditions. First, there is the independent design, in which each participant is allocated at random to one and only one condition. Second, there is the repeated measures design, in which the same participants are used in both conditions. Third, there is the matched participants design, in which the participants in the two

Key Terms

Type I error:
mistakenly rejecting the null hypothesis in favor of the experimental hypothesis when the results are actually a result of chance.

Type II error:
mistakenly retaining the null hypothesis when the experimental hypothesis is actually correct.

conditions are matched in terms of some variable or variables that might be relevant (e.g., intelligence; age).

When deciding which statistical test to use, it is very important to take account of the particular kind of experimental design that was used. If the independent design has been used, then the Mann-Whitney U test is likely to be an appropriate test to use. If the repeated measures or matched participants design has been used, then the sign test or the Wilcoxon matched pairs signed ranks test is likely to be appropriate. Each of these tests is discussed in turn next.

Mann-Whitney U test

The Mann-Whitney U test can be used when an independent design has been used, and the data are either ordinal or interval. The worked example in the box shows how this test is calculated.

Suppose that we have two conditions. In both conditions, the participants have to fire arrows at a board, and the score obtained is recorded. There are 10 participants in Condition A, in which no training is provided before their performance is assessed. There

---

Mann-Whitney U test: A worked example

Experimental hypothesis: Extensive training improves performance
Null hypothesis: Training has no effect on performance

Participant	Condition A	Rank	Participant	Condition B	Rank
1	4	2	1	21	15
2	10	9	2	26	18
3	12	11	3	20	14
4	28	20	4	22	16
5	7	5	5	32	22
6	13	13	6	5	3
7	12	11	7	12	11
8	2	1	8	6	4
9	9	7.5	9	8	6
10	27	19	10	24	17
			11	29	21
			12	9	7.5

Smaller sample = condition A

Sum of ranks in smaller sample (T) = 98.5

Number of participants in smaller sample (N_A) = 10

Number of participants in larger sample (N_B) = 12

Formula: $U = N_A N_B + \left(\dfrac{N_A(N_A + 1)}{2} \right) - T$

Example: $U = (10 \times 12) + \left(\dfrac{10(10 + 1)}{2} \right) - 98.5 = 76.5$

Formula for calculating U': $U' = N_A N_B = U$

Example: $U' = (10 \times 12) - 76.5 = 43.5$

Comparing U and U', U' is the smaller value. The calculated value of U' (43.5) is checked against the tabled value for a one-tailed test at 5%.

Table values

	$N_A = 10$
$N_B = 12$	34

Conclusion: As 43.5 is greater than 34, the null hypothesis should be retained—i.e., training has no effect on performance in this task.

are 12 participants in Condition B, and they receive extensive training before their performance is assessed. The experimental hypothesis was that extensive training would improve performance; in other words, the scores in Condition B should be significantly higher than those in Condition A.

The first step is to rank all of the scores from both groups together, with a rank of 1 being given to the smallest score, a rank of 2 to the second smallest score, and so on. If there are tied scores, then the mean of the ranks involved is given to each of the tied participants. For example, two participants were tied for the 7th and 8th ranks, and so they both received a rank of 7.5.

The second step is to work out the sum of the ranks in the smaller sample, which is Condition A in our example. This value is known as T, and it is 98.5 in the example.

The third step is to calculate U from the formula in which N_A is the number of participants in the smaller sample and N_B is the number in the larger sample.

$$U = N_A N_B + \left(\frac{N_A(N_A + 1)}{2} \right) - T$$

The fourth step is to calculate U′ from the formula $U' = N_A N_B - U$.

The fifth step is to compare U and U′, selecting whichever is the smaller value provided that the results are in the correct direction. The smaller value (i.e., 43.5) is then looked up in Appendix 1. The observed value must be equal to, or smaller than, the tabled value in order to be significant. In this case, we have a one-tailed test, because the experimental hypothesis stated that extensive training would improve performance and the statistical significance is the standard 5% (.05). With 10 participants in our first condition and 12 in our second condition, the tabled value for significance is 34 (value obtained from the table at the bottom of p. 621 of the Appendices). As our value of 43.5 is greater than 34, the conclusion is that we retain the null hypothesis. It should be noted that the presence of ties reduces the accuracy of the tables, but the effect is small unless there are several ties.

Sign test

The sign test can be used when a repeated measures or matched participants design has been used, and the data are ordinal. If the data are interval or ratio, then it would be more appropriate to use the Wilcoxon matched pairs signed ranks test. The worked example in the box opposite illustrates the way in which the sign test is calculated.

Suppose that there were 12 participants in an experiment. In Condition A these participants were presented with 20 words to learn in a situation with no noise; learning was followed 5 minutes later by a test of free recall in which they wrote down as many words as they could remember in any order. Condition B involved presenting 20 different words to learn in a situation of loud noise, again followed by a test of free recall. The experimenter predicted that free recall would be higher in the no-noise condition. Thus, there was a directional hypothesis.

In order to calculate the sign test it is necessary first of all to draw up a table like the one in the example, in which each participant's scores in Condition A and in Condition B are recorded. Each participant whose score in Condition A is greater than his or her score in Condition B is given a plus sign (+) in the sign column, and each participant whose score in Condition B is greater than his or her score in Condition A is given a minus sign (−) in the sign column. Each participant whose scores in both conditions are the same receives a 0 sign in the sign column, and are ignored

The sign test is ideal to use if the data are ordinal as it analyzes at a very basic level, e.g., in a race it can tell you that "John beat Peter." It can also be used with interval or ratio data, but as it only gives a crude analysis, these data would be better applied to the Wilcoxon test, which can give a more sophisticated analysis, e.g., "John beat Peter by 2 seconds."

Sign test: A worked example

Experimental hypothesis: Free recall is better when learning takes place in the absence of noise than in its presence

Null hypothesis: Free recall is not affected by whether or not noise is present during learning

Participant	Condition A (no noise)	Condition B (loud noise)	Sign
1	12	8	+
2	10	10	0
3	7	8	−
4	12	11	+
5	8	3	+
6	10	10	0
7	13	7	+
8	8	9	−
9	14	10	+
10	11	9	+
11	15	12	+
12	11	10	+

Number of + signs = 8
Number of − signs = 2
Number of 0 signs = 2

Number of participants with differing scores (N) = 8 + 2 = 10
Number of participants with less-frequent sign (S) = 2

Question: Is the value of S in this example the same as or lower than the tabled value for S?

Table values

	5%
N = 10	S = 1

Conclusion: In this experiment the value of S is higher than the tabled value when N = 10. The null hypothesis (that noise has no effect on learning and memory) cannot be rejected.

in the subsequent calculations—they do not contribute to N (the number of paired scores), as they provide no evidence about effect direction.

In the example, there are eight plus signs, two minus signs, and two participants had the same scores in both conditions. If we ignore the two participants with the same scores in both conditions, this gives us N = 10. Now all we need to do is to work out the number of these 10 participants having the less frequently occurring sign; this value is known as S. In terms of our example, S = 2. We can refer to the relevant table (Appendix 2) with N = 10 and S = 2 and the statistical significance is the standard 5%. The obtained value for S must be the same as or lower than the value for S given in the table. The tabled value for a one-tailed test is 1. Thus, our obtained S value of 2 is not significant at the 5% level on a one-tailed test. We therefore conclude that we cannot reject the null hypothesis that noise has no effect on learning and memory.

Wilcoxon matched pairs signed ranks test

The Wilcoxon matched pairs signed ranks test can be used when a repeated measures or matched participants design has been used and the data are at least ordinal. This test or the sign test can be used if the data are ordinal, interval, or ratio. However, the Wilcoxon matched pairs signed ranks test uses more of the information obtained from a study, and so is usually a more sensitive and useful test than the sign test.

Wilcoxon matched pairs signed ranks test: A worked example

Experimental hypothesis: Free recall is better when learning takes place in the absence of noise than in its presence

Null hypothesis: Free recall is not affected by whether or not noise is present during learning

Participant	Condition A (no noise)	Condition B (loud noise)	Difference (d) (A – B)	Rank
1	12	8	4	7.5
2	10	10	0	–
3	7	8	−1	2.5
4	12	11	1	2.5
5	8	3	5	9
6	10	10	0	–
7	13	7	6	10
8	8	9	−1	2.5
9	14	10	4	7.5
10	11	9	2	5
11	15	12	3	6
12	11	10	1	2.5

Sum of positive ranks (7.5 + 2.5 + 9 + 10 + 7.5 + 5 + 6 + 2.5) = 50

Sum of negative ranks (2.5 + 2.5) = 5

Smaller value (5) + T

Number of participants who scored differently in condition A and B (N) = 10

Question: For the results to be significant, the value of T must be the same as, or less than, the tabled value.

Table values

	5%	1%
N = 10	S = 1	5

Conclusion: In this experiment T is less than the tabled value at the 5% level and the same as the tabled value at the 1% level of significance, so the null hypothesis is rejected in favor of the experimental hypothesis.

The worked example uses the data from the sign test. The first step is to place all the data in a table in which each participant's two scores are in the same row. The second step is to subtract the Condition B score from the Condition A score for each participant to give the difference (d). The third step is to omit all the participants whose two scores are the same, i.e., d = 0. The fourth step is to rank all the difference scores obtained in the second step from 1 for the smallest difference, 2 for the second smallest difference, and so on. For this purpose, ignore the + and − signs, thus taking the absolute size of the difference. The fifth step is to add up the sum of the positive ranks (50 in the example) and separately to add up the sum of the negative ranks (5 in the example). The smaller of these values is T, which in this case is 5. The sixth step is to work out the number of participants whose two scores are not the same, i.e. d ≠ 0. In the example, N = 10.

The obtained value of T must be the same as, or less than, the tabled value (see Appendix 3) in order for the results to be significant. The tabled value for a one-tailed test and N = 10 is 11 at the 5% level of statistical significance, and it is 5 at the 1% level. Thus, the findings are significant at the 1% level on a one-tailed test. The null hypothesis is rejected in favor of the experimental hypothesis that free recall is better when learning takes place in the absence of noise than in its presence (p = .01). The presence of ties means that the tables are not completely accurate, but this does not matter provided that there are only a few ties.

You may be wondering how it is possible for the same data to produce a significant finding on a Wilcoxon matched pairs signed ranks test but not on a sign test. Does this indicate that statistics are useless? Not at all. The sign test is insensitive (or lacking in power) because it takes no account of the *size* of each individual's difference in free recall in the two conditions. It is because this information is made use of in the Wilcoxon matched pairs signed ranks test that a significant result was obtained using that test. Thus, the Wilcoxon matched pairs signed ranks test has more power than the sign test to detect differences between two conditions.

CORRELATIONAL STUDIES

In the case of correlational studies, the data are in the form of two measures of behavior from each member of a single group of participants. What is often done is to present the data in the form of a **scattergraph** (also known as a scattergram). It is given this name because it shows the ways in which the scores of individuals are scattered.

Scattergraphs

Suppose that we have carried out a study on the relationship between the amount of television violence seen and the amount of aggressive behavior displayed. We could have a scale of the amount of television violence seen on the horizontal axis, and a scale of the amount of aggressive behavior on the vertical axis. We could then put a dot for each participant indicating where he or she falls on these two dimensions. For example,

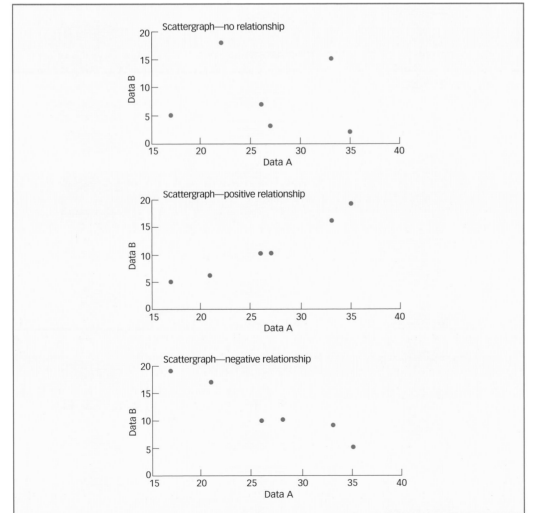

A positive correlation: The taller the player, the higher the score.

A negative correlation: The more time spent playing computer games, the less time spent studying.

No correlation: Where there is no relationship, variables are uncorrelated.

Key Term
Scattergraph: a two-dimensional representation of all the participants' scores in a correlational study; also known as a scattergram.

suppose that one individual watched 17 hours of television and obtained a score of 8 for aggressive behavior. We would put a cross at the point where the invisible vertical line from the 17 meets the invisible horizontal line from the 8.

How do we interpret the information contained in a scattergraph? If there is a positive relationship between watching violence and aggression, then the dots should tend to form a pattern going from the bottom left of the scattergraph to the top right. If there is no relationship between the two variables, then the dots should be distributed in a fairly random way within the scattergraph. If there is a negative relationship between the two variables, then the dots will form a pattern going from the top left to the bottom right. In the present example, this would mean that watching a lot of television violence was associated with a *low* level of aggression.

As we will see shortly, the strength of a correlation between two variables can be assessed statistically by Spearman's rho. What, then, is the value of a scattergraph? Spearman's rho is limited in that it sometimes indicates that there is no relationship between two variables even when there is. For example, Spearman's rho would not reveal the existence of a strong curvilinear (bow-shaped) relationship between two variables, but this would be immediately obvious in a scattergraph.

Spearman's rho

Suppose that we have scores on two variables from each of our participants, and we want to see whether there is an association or correlation between the two sets of scores. This can be done by using a test known as Spearman's rho, provided that the data are at least ordinal. Spearman's rho or r_s indicates the strength of the association. If r_s is +1.0, then there is a perfect positive correlation between the two variables. If r_s is −1.0, then there is a perfect negative correlation between the two variables. If r_s is 0.0, then there is generally no relationship between the two variables. The working of this test is shown in the example opposite.

An experimenter collects information about the amount of television violence seen in the past month and about the amount of aggressive behavior exhibited in the past month from 12 participants. She predicts that there will be a positive association between these two variables, that is, those participants who have seen the most television violence (variable A) will tend to be the most aggressive (variable B). In other words, there is a directional hypothesis.

The first step is to draw up a table in which each participant's scores for the two variables are placed in the same row.

The second step is to rank all the scores for variable A. A rank of 1 is assigned to the smallest score, a rank of 2 to the second smallest score, and so on up to 12. What do we do if there are tied scores? In the example, participants 9 and 12 had the same score for variable A. The ranks that they are competing for are ranks 5 and 6. What is done is to take the average or mean of the ranks at issue: $(5 + 6)/2 = 5.5$.

The third step is to rank all the scores for variable B, with a rank of 1 being assigned to the smallest score. Participants 6, 7, 9, and 11 are all tied, with the ranks at issue being ranks 4, 5, 6, and 7. The mean rank at issue is $(4 + 5 + 6 + 7)/4 = 5.5$.

The fourth step is to calculate the difference between the two ranks obtained by each individual, with the rank for variable B being subtracted from the rank for variable A. This produces 12 difference (d) scores.

The fifth step is to square all of the d scores obtained in the fourth step. This produces 12 squared difference (d^2) scores.

The sixth step is to add up all of the d^2 scores in order to obtain the sum of the squared difference scores. This is known as Σd^2, and comes to 30 in the example.

The seventh step is to work out the number of participants. In the example, the number of participants (N) is 12.

The eighth step is to calculate rho from the following formula:

$$rho = 1 - \frac{(\Sigma d^2 \times 6)}{N(N^2 - 1)}$$

In the example, this becomes

$$1 - \frac{(30 \times 6)}{12(143)} = 1 - 0.105 = +0.895$$

The ninth and final step is to work out the significance of the value of rho by referring the result to the table (see Appendix 4). The obtained value must be as great as, or greater than, the tabled value. The tabled value for a one-tailed test with N = 12 is +0.503 at the .05 level, it is +0.671 at the .01 level, and it is +0.727 at the .005 level. Thus, it can be concluded that the null hypothesis should be rejected in favor of the experimental hypothesis that there is a positive correlation between the amount of television violence watched and aggressive behavior ($p = .005$).

An important point about Spearman's rho is that the statistical significance of the obtained value of rho depends very heavily on the number of participants. For example, the tabled value for significance at the .05 level on a one-tailed test is +0.564 if there are 10 participants. However, it is only +0.306 if there are 30 participants. In practical terms,

---

A worked example of a test for correlation between two variables using Spearman's rho

Experimental hypothesis: There is a positive association between amount of television violence watched and aggressive behavior

Null hypothesis: There is no association between amount of television violence watched and aggressive behavior

Participants	TV violence seen (hours)	Aggressive behavior (out of 10)	Rank A	Rank B	Difference d	d²
1	17	8	7.5	9	−1.50	2.25
2	6	3	2	2	0.00	0.00
3	23	9	10	10.5	−0.50	0.25
4	17	7	7.5	8	−0.50	0.25
5	2	2	1	1	0.00	0.00
6	20	6	9	5.5	+3.50	12.25
7	12	6	4	5.5	0.00	2.25
8	31	10	12	12	0.00	0.00
9	14	6	5.5	5.5	+0.50	0.00
10	26	9	10.5	10.5	+0.50	0.25
11	9	6	5.5	5.5	−2.50	6.52
12	14	4	3	3	+2.50	6.25

Sum of squared difference scores (Σd^2) = 30
Number of participants (N) = 12

Formula: rho $= 1 - \dfrac{(\Sigma d^2 \times 6)}{N(N^2 - 1)}$

Example: $1 - \dfrac{(30 \times 6)}{12(143)} = 1 - 0.105 = +0.895$

Is the value of rho (+0.895) as great as or greater than the tabled value?

Table values

	.05 level	.01 level	.005 level
N = 12	+0.503	+0.671	+0.727

Conclusion: Null hypothesis rejected in favor of experimental hypothesis, i.e., there is a positive correlation between the amount of television violence watched and aggressive behavior ($p = .005$).

this means that it is very hard to obtain a significant correlation with Spearman's rho if the number of participants is low.

TEST OF ASSOCIATION

The **chi-squared test** is a test of association. It is used when we have nominal data in the form of frequencies, and when each and every observation is independent of all the other observations. For example, suppose that we are interested in the association between eating patterns and cholesterol level. We could divide people into those having a healthy diet with relatively little fat and those having an unhealthy diet. We could also divide them into those having a fairly high level of cholesterol and those having a low level of cholesterol. In essence, the chi-squared test tells us whether membership of a given category on one dimension (e.g., unhealthy diet) is associated with membership of a given category on the other dimension (e.g., high cholesterol level).

In the worked example opposite, we will assume that we have data from 186 individuals with an unhealthy diet, and from 128 individuals with a healthy diet. Of those with an unhealthy diet, 116 have a high cholesterol level and 70 have a low cholesterol level. Of those with a healthy diet, 41 have a high cholesterol level and 87 have a low cholesterol level. Our experimental hypothesis is that there is an association between healthiness of diet and low cholesterol level.

The first step is to arrange the frequency data in a 2 ×2 "contingency table" as in the worked example, with the row and column totals included. The second step is to work out what the four frequencies would be if there were no association at all between diet and cholesterol levels. The expected frequency (by chance alone) in each case is given by the following formula:

$$\text{expected frequency} = \frac{\text{row total} \times \text{column total}}{\text{overall total}}$$

For example, the expected frequency for the number of participants having a healthy diet and high cholesterol is 157 × 128 divided by 314, which comes to 64. The four expected frequencies (those expected by chance alone) are also shown in the table.

The third step is to apply the following formula to the observed (O) and expected (E) frequencies in each of the four categories:

$$\frac{\left(|O - E| - \frac{1}{2}\right)^2}{E}$$

In the formula, $|O - E|$ means that the difference between the observed and the expected frequency should be taken, and it should then have a + sign put in front of it regardless of the direction of the difference. The correction factor (i.e., $-\frac{1}{2}$) is only used when there are two rows and two columns.

The fourth step is to add together the four values obtained in the third step in order to provide the chi-squared statistic or χ^2. This is 7.91 + 5.44 + 7.91 + 5.44 = 26.70.

The fifth step is to calculate the number of "degrees of freedom" (df). This is given by (the number of rows − 1) × (the number of columns − 1). For this we need to refer back to the contingency table. In the example, this is 1 × 1 = 1. Why is there 1 degree of freedom? Once we know the row and column totals, then only one of the four observed values is free to vary. Thus, for example, knowing that the row totals are 157 and 157, the column totals are 128 and 186, and the number of participants having a healthy diet and high cholesterol is 41, we can complete the entire table. In other words, the number of degrees of freedom corresponds to the number of values that are free to vary.

The sixth step is to compare the tabled values in Appendix 5 with chi-squared = 26.70 and one degree of freedom. The observed value needs to be the same as, or greater than, the tabled value for a two-tailed test in order for the results to be significant.

The tabled value for a two-tailed test with df = 1 is 3.84 at the .05 level, 5.41 at the .02 level, and 10.83 at the .001 level. Thus, we can reject the null hypothesis, and conclude that there is an association between healthiness of diet and cholesterol level (p = .001).

Key Term
Chi-squared test: a test of association that is used with nominal data in the form of frequencies.

Test of association: Chi-squared test, a worked example

Experimental hypothesis: There is an association between healthiness of diet and low cholesterol level

Null hypothesis: There is no association between healthiness of diet and low cholesterol level

Contingency table:

	Healthy diet	Unhealthy diet	Row total
High cholesterol	41	116	157
Low cholesterol	87	70	157
Column total	128	186	314

Expected frequency if there were no association:

Formula: $\dfrac{\text{row total} \times \text{column total}}{\text{expected frequency}} = \text{overall total}$

	Healthy diet	Unhealthy diet	Row total
High cholesterol	64	93	157
Low cholesterol	64	93	157
Column total	128	186	314

Calculating chi-squared statistic (χ^2):

Formula: $\chi^2 = \Sigma \dfrac{\left(|O - E| - \frac{1}{2}\right)^2}{E} = 26.7$

Note: Correction factor $\left(-\frac{1}{2}\right)$ is only used where there are two rows and two columns

Category	Observed	Expected	$\lvert O - E \rvert$	$\dfrac{\left(\lvert O - E \rvert - \frac{1}{2}\right)^2}{E}$
Healthy, high cholesterol	41	64	23	7.91
Unhealthy, high cholesterol	116	93	23	5.44
Healthy, low cholesterol	87	64	23	7.91
Unhealthy, low cholesterol	70	93	23	5.44
				26.70

Calculating degrees of freedom:

Formula: (no. of rows − 1) × (no. of columns − 1) = degrees of freedom (2 − 1) × (2 − 1) = 1

Compare chi-squared statistic with tabled values:

Table values

	.05 level	.01 level	.001 level
df = 1	3.84	6.64	10.83

Question: Is the observed chi-squared value of 26.70 and one degree of freedom the same as or greater than the tabled value?

Conclusion: The chi-squared value is greater than the tabled value, so the null hypothesis can be rejected, and the experimental hypothesis, that there is an association between healthiness of diet and cholesterol level, accepted.

It is easy to use the chi-squared test wrongly. According to Robson (1994), "There are probably more inappropriate and incorrect uses of the chi-square test than of all the other statistical tests put together." In order to avoid using the chi-squared test wrongly, it is important to make use of the following rules:

- Ensure that every observation is independent of every other observation; in other words, each individual should be counted once and in only *one* category.

- Make sure that each observation is included in the appropriate category; it is not permitted to omit some of the observations (e.g., those from individuals with intermediate levels of cholesterol).
- The total sample should exceed 20; otherwise, the chi-squared test as described here is not applicable. More precisely, the minimum expected frequency should be at least 5 in every category.
- The significance level of a chi-squared test is nearly always assessed by consulting the two-tailed values in the Appendix table regardless of whether the hypothesis is directional or nondirectional. The one exception is if you have one variable divided into two categories and a directional hypothesis. Why is the chi-squared so unusual in typically requiring you to use two-tailed values? The reason is that *any* differences between expected and observed values (whether predicted or not) increase the obtained value.
- Remember that showing there is an association is not the same as showing that there is a causal effect; for example, the association between a healthy diet and low cholesterol does not demonstrate that a healthy diet *causes* low cholesterol.

ISSUES OF EXPERIMENTAL AND ECOLOGICAL VALIDITY

Assume that you have carried out a study, and then analyzed it using a statistical test. The results were statistically significant, so you are able to reject the null hypothesis in favor of the experimental hypothesis. When deciding how to interpret your findings, you need to take account of issues relating to experimental and ecological validity. **Experimental validity** is based on the extent to which a given finding is genuine, and is a result of the independent variable that was manipulated. In other words, it is essentially the same as internal validity, which is discussed in Chapter 24. In contrast, **ecological validity** refers to the extent to which research findings can be generalized to a range of real-world settings. It is clearly desirable for a study to possess both of these forms of validity.

EXPERIMENTAL VALIDITY

How can we assess the experimental or internal validity of the findings from a study? The key point is made in Chapter 24: We can only have confidence that the independent variable produced the observed effects on behavior or the dependent variable provided that all of the principles of experimental design were followed. These principles include the standardization of instructions and procedures; counterbalancing; randomization; and the avoidance of confounding variables, experimenter effects, demand characteristics, and participant reactivity.

We can check these by asking various questions about a study, including the following:

- Were there any variables (other than the independent variable) that varied systematically between conditions?
- Did all the participants receive the same standardized instructions?
- Were the participants allocated at random to the conditions?
- Did the experimenter influence the performance of the participants by his or her expectations or biases?
- Were the participants influenced by any demand characteristics of the situation?
- If the participants knew they were being observed, did this influence their behavior?

Probably the most convincing evidence that a study possesses good experimental validity is if its findings can be repeated or replicated in other studies. Why is that so? Suppose, for example, that we obtain significant findings in one study because we failed to allocate our participants at random to conditions. Anyone else carrying out the same study, but allocating the participants at random, would be very unlikely to repeat the findings of our study.

ECOLOGICAL VALIDITY

As Coolican (1994) pointed out, the term ecological validity has been used in various ways. It is sometimes used to refer to the extent to which a given study was carried out

Case Study: *Criticism of Intelligence Testing*

Gould's (1982) study included criticism of intelligence testing based on the methodological and theoretical problems experienced when these tests are used. Gould suggested that many IQ tests contain errors of validity. They have design flaws in relation to the wording used, which is often based on cultural definitions of meaning. Lack of access to the relevant cultural interpretations would disadvantage certain groups and individuals. For example, the Yerkes Tests of Intelligence were based on American culture and cultural knowledge, so that immigrants' performance was almost always poorer than that of the native groups. Gould also emphasized the fact that the procedures used were flawed, especially during the testing of black participants.

Interpretation of findings from the use of Yerkes tests ignored the role of experience and education in IQ, and focused on the role of heredity. The research evidence was used to support racist social policy, which restricted work opportunities for ethnic groups within society and denied many the right to seek political refuge in America.

in a naturalistic or real-world setting rather than in an artificial one. However, as was mentioned earlier, it is probably more useful to regard ecological validity as referring to the extent to which a study generalizes to various real-world settings. Bracht and Glass (1968) put forward a definition of ecological validity along those lines. According to them, the findings of ecologically valid studies generalize to other locations or places, to other times, and to other measures. Thus, the notion of ecological validity closely resembles that of external validity (see Chapter 24), except that external validity also includes generalization to other populations.

How do we know whether the findings of a study possess ecological validity? The only conclusive way of answering that question is by carrying out a series of studies in different locations, at different times, and using different measures. Following that approach is generally very costly in terms of time and effort.

It is often possible to obtain some idea of the ecological validity of a study by asking yourself whether there are important differences between the way in which a study has been conducted and what happens in the real world. For example, consider research on eyewitness testimony (see Chapter 8). The participants in most laboratory studies of eyewitness testimony have been asked to pay close attention to a series of slides or a video depicting some incident, after which they are asked various questions. The ecological validity of such studies is put in danger for a number of reasons. The participants have their attention directed to the incident, whereas eyewitnesses to a crime or other incident may fail to pay much attention to it. In addition, eyewitnesses are often very frightened and concerned about their own safety, whereas the participants in a laboratory study are not.

It may seem reasonable to argue that we could ensure ecological validity by taking research out of the laboratory and into the real world. However, powerful arguments against doing that with memory research were put forward by Banaji and Crowder (1989):

Imagine astronomy being conducted with only the naked eye, biology without tissue cultures ... or chemistry without test tubes! The everyday world is full of principles from these sciences in action, but do we really think their data bases should have been those of everyday applications? Of course not. Should the psychology of memory be any different? We think not.

In sum, investigators should consider the issue of ecological validity seriously when interpreting their findings. They should try to identify the main ways in which the situation or situations in which their participants were placed differ

Ecological validity

The term ecological validity refers to the extent to which any study's findings can be generalized to other settings. Although many laboratory studies may lack ecological validity, so do some of those conducted in natural settings.

Consider Skinner's work on pigeons pecking at a disk to receive food pellets. Could the results of his study be generalized to explain how dog handlers train their dogs to seek out illegal drugs and explosives? Do the procedures for operant conditioning remain the same, i.e., the use of reinforcement to shape behavior?

Imagine you are an observer watching birds in their natural environment, collecting data on how the parents are caring for their offspring. You disturb the parent birds by making too much noise, and they abandon their nesting site. Would your research have ecological validity because it was carried out in the natural environment? Could you generalize your findings to other settings?

from those of everyday life. They should also take account of the desirability of measuring behavior that is representative of behaviors that occur naturally. At the very least, they should interpret their findings cautiously if there are several major differences. Finally, they should discuss relevant published research that indicates the likely impact of these differences on participants' behavior.

WRITING UP A PRACTICAL

Practicals in psychology are written up in a standard way. Thus, your write-ups need to be organized in a certain fashion. Initially, this may seem difficult. However, it has the great advantage that this organization makes it easy for someone reading your write-ups to know where to look to find information about the type of participants used, the statistical analyses, and so on. The details of how to produce a write-up differ slightly depending on whether it is based on an experimental or a nonexperimental design. However, the general approach is exactly the same, and the essence of that approach is given later. The sections are arranged in the order they should appear in your write-ups. It is essential to refer to coursework assessment criteria issued by the relevant examination board.

Finally, be sure to write in a formal way. For example, write "It was decided to study the effects of attention on learning" rather than, "I decided to study the effects of attention on learning."

Title

This should give a short indication of the nature of your study. In the case of an experimental study, it might well refer to the independent and dependent variables. A non-experimental study would include reference to the qualitative nature of the investigation.

Abstract

This should provide a brief account of the purpose of the study, the key aspects of the design, the use of statistics, and the key findings and their interpretation.

Introduction

This should start with an account of the main concepts and background literature relevant to your study. It should then move on to a consideration of previous work that is of *direct* relevance to your study. Avoid describing several studies that are only loosely related to your study.

Aims and hypotheses

The aims refer to the general context of the research and indicate why you selected the hypotheses to be tested. This should be followed by specifying the hypotheses. If it is an experimental study, the hypotheses should refer to the relevant independent and dependent variables.

Method

Design. Here you should indicate the number of groups, the use of an independent samples or repeated measures design (if applicable), the nature of the independent and dependent variables (if any), the experimental hypothesis, and the null hypothesis. You should also indicate any attempts made to control the situation effectively so as to produce an effective design.

Participants. The number of participants should be given together with relevant information about them (e.g., age, gender, educational background). You should indicate how they were selected for your study and, in the case of an experiment, refer to the way in which they were allocated to conditions.

Apparatus and materials. There should be a brief description of any apparatus used in the study, together with an account of any stimuli presented to the participants (e.g., 20 common 5-letter nouns). The stimuli should be referred to in a numbered section in an appendix where they can be examined in detail.

Procedure. The sequence of events experienced by the participants, including any instructions given to them, should be indicated here. Standardized instructions may be given in detail in an appendix.

Results

It is generally useful to restate the aims of the study and to indicate the independent and dependent variables in the case of an experiment.

Also, it is desirable to provide a summary table of the performance of participants. Tables of central tendency and standard deviation are usually informative ways of getting an overall "picture" of results. A bar chart or some other suitable figure may provide ready visual access to a large body of information.

- Make sure that tables and figures are clearly labeled.
- Make sure that raw data appear in a numbered section of the appendix.

Statistical test and level of significance. Start by indicating which hypothesis has been tested by any given statistical test. The test that has been applied to the data should be indicated, together with the justification for the selection of the test. Also there should be reference to the level of statistical significance that was achieved with respect to the test statistic chosen. Make sure you indicate whether a one-tailed or a two-tailed test was used, and relate your findings to the experimental and null hypotheses.

Discussion

The discussion should start by considering your findings, especially with respect to the results of the statistical test or tests. Be as precise as possible in terms of what your findings show (and do not show!). You may wish to comment on individual results that were inconsistent with the rest of the participants' data.

The next part of this section should consist of how your findings relate to previous findings referred to in the introduction. Ask yourself if they support or refute existing theories or approaches and how you might account for the behavior of the participants.

Next, identify any weaknesses in your study, and indicate how they could be eliminated in a subsequent study. For example, there may have been ethical issues that arose during the investigation which only became apparent after you had started.

Finally, consider whether there are interesting ways in which your study could be extended to provide more information about the phenomenon you have been investigating. This is a very satisfactory section to deal with because your imagination can take over, producing ideal studies unencumbered by the necessity to go and find participants! Always remember, though, that possible extension studies should be relevant and the likely outcome to them should be mentioned.

References

Full information about any references you have referred to in the write-up should be provided here. Textbooks (including this one) typically have a reference section set out in conventional style and you should refer to it.

Chapter Summary

Qualitative analysis of data
- Qualitative research is concerned with the experiences of the participants, and with the meanings they attach to themselves and their lives. Investigators using interviews, case studies, or observations often (but not always) make use of qualitative data. A key principle of qualitative analysis is that theoretical understanding emerges from the data, and is not imposed by the researcher. Qualitative researchers typically categorize the data after taking account of all of the data and of the participants' own categories. Findings based on qualitative data tend to be unreliable and hard to replicate.

Interpretation of interviews, case studies, and observations

• It can be hard to interpret the information obtained from interviews because of social desirability bias, complex interactional processes, and the self-fulfilling prophecy. The greatest danger with case studies is drawing very general conclusions from a single atypical individual. Case studies can suggest hypotheses, which can then be tested with larger groups. The findings of observational studies are often difficult to interpret, because it is not clear *why* the participants are behaving as they are. In addition, the participants in observational studies may not be representative.

Content analysis

• Content analysis has been used as a method for analyzing messages in the media as well as communications that participants have been asked to produce, such as diaries. The first step is the construction of coding units into which the selected information can be categorized. Coders may be asked to provide ratings or rankings as well as to categorize.

Quantitative analysis: Descriptive statistics

• When we have obtained scores from a group of participants, we can summarize our data by working out a measure of central tendency and a measure of dispersion or spread of scores around the central tendency. The mean is the most generally useful measure of central tendency, but other measures include the median and mode. The standard deviation is the most useful measure of dispersion. Other measures include the range and the variation ratio.

Data presentation

• Summary data from a study can be presented in the form of a figure, so that it is easy to observe general trends. Among the possible ways of presenting the data in a figure are the following: frequency polygon; histogram; and bar chart. Frequency polygons and histograms are used when the scores can be ordered from low to high, whereas bar charts are used when the scores are in the form of categories.

Statistical tests

• If the experimental hypothesis predicts the direction of effects, then a one-tailed test should be used. Otherwise, a two-tailed test should be used. There are four types of data of increasing levels of precision as follows: nominal; ordinal; interval; and ratio. Psychologists generally use the 5% level of statistical significance. This produces fairly small probabilities of incorrectly rejecting the null hypothesis in favor of the experimental hypothesis (Type I error) or of incorrectly retaining the null hypothesis (Type II error). A test of difference is used when data are obtained from a study in which an independent variable was manipulated to observe its effects. The Mann-Whitney U test is the appropriate test of difference if an independent design was used. The sign test can be used when a repeated measures or matched participants design was used and the data are nominal or ordinal. The same is true of the Wilcoxon matched pairs signed ranks test, except that the data must be at least ordinal.

• The data from correlational studies are in the form of scores on two response variables from every participant. These data can be presented in the form of a scattergraph or scattergram. The correlation between two sets of scores can be calculated by means of Spearman's rho test, provided that the data are at least ordinal.

• The chi-squared test is a test of association. It is used when we have nominal data in the form of frequencies, and when each and every observation is independent of all the other observations. The test is nearly always two-tailed. All the expected frequencies should be 5 or more. Finding an association is not the same as showing the existence of a causal effect.

Issues of experimental and ecological validity

• Experimental validity is based on the extent to which a given finding is genuine, and is a result of the independent variable that was manipulated. A study is most likely to be high in experimental validity when all the principles of experimental design (e.g., randomization; standardization) have been followed. Replication provides some assurance that experimental validity is high. Ecological validity refers to the extent to which the findings of a study generalize to other locations, times, and measures. The ecological validity of a study is best assessed by carrying out a range of further studies using different locations, times, and measures.

Further Reading

- Banister, P., Burman, E., Parker, I., Taylor, M., & Tindall, C. (1994). *Qualitative methods in psychology: A research guide*. This gives extensive coverage of the main types of qualitative analysis.
- Coolican, H. (1999). *Research methods and statistics in psychology* (3rd ed.). London: Hodder & Stoughton. This textbook gives detailed but user-friendly coverage of the topics discussed in this chapter.
- Coolican, H. (2004). *Research methods and statistics in psychology* (4th ed.). London: Hodder & Stoughton. This book gives an excellent account of statistics as well as of research methods.

Appendices

Contents

Research Methods: Appendices

In order to use the statistical tables on the following pages, you first need to decide whether:

1. Your data are in numerical form, in which case they are suitable for quantitative analysis; otherwise, use qualitative analysis.
2. You have obtained nominal, ordinal, interval, or ratio data.
3. Your data show a difference between the two conditions (the experimental hypothesis) or not (the null hypothesis).
4. You can use parametric tests (i.e., if data are interval or ratio, normally distributed, and the variances in the two conditions are similar); otherwise nonparametric tests can be used. Nonparametric tests can be used in nearly all cases, and it is the most useful of these that are described in this book.

Once you have obtained your results, you can construct a table of frequencies, and decide which type of chart or graph you wish to use in order to present your data graphically in the clearest way possible.

The next step to take is to analyze your data, as follows:

1. Calculate measures of central tendency: mean, median, and mode.
2. Calculate measures of dispersion: range, interquartile range, variation ratio, and standard deviation.

You will then need to apply further statistical analysis using the statistical tests described in Chapter 25. Please refer to the worked examples for each of these and follow the step-by-step instructions in the main text.

HOW TO DECIDE WHICH TEST TO USE

The main purpose of these tests is to decide the probability of the null hypothesis being correct, and to evaluate its significance. Each test involves calculating your observed value from your results, and then looking up the critical value in a table of values, to see whether your value is greater than, equal to, or less than the critical value. Use the appropriate column or table, depending on (a) whether you used a one- or two-tailed test and (b) which level of significance or probability (p) you wish to check. If p is less than or equal to .05 or 5%, which is the standard probability of significance used by psychologists, the null hypothesis is rejected in favor of the experimental hypothesis. To see whether the findings are highly significant, look at whether the null hypothesis still holds true at $p = .01$, or 1%, or even $p = .001$, or .1%.

If your experimental hypothesis is directional (i.e., you predicted the direction of any effects), you need to use a one-tailed test; otherwise you have a nondirectional hypothesis, in which case you need to use a two-tailed test.

If the design of your test of difference is independent, as long as the data are ordinal or interval, the Mann-Whitney U test can be used. If you have used a repeated measures or matched participants design, the sign test can be used, as long as the data are ordinal; or if the data are interval or ratio, the Wilcoxon matched pairs signed ranks test can be used. The latter is more sensitive than the sign test. The sign test provides us with a crude analysis, which is sufficient when data are ordinal, but when actual values are obtained (interval or ratio data) the Wilcoxon test will provide a more sophisticated analysis. Therefore, although it is possible to use the sign test for interval or ratio data, it would be best to limit its use to analysis of ordinal data.

If you manipulated the independent variable (some aspect of the situation), you need to use a test of difference (such as the Mann-Whitney U test, the sign test or the Wilcoxon matched pairs signed ranks test); otherwise, you need to use a test of correlation (such as Spearman's rho test, as long as the data are ordinal, interval, or ratio) or a test of association (such as the chi-squared test, as long as the data are nominal).

HOW TO USE THE TABLES

Mann-Whitney U test
Appendix 1, pages 620–621

In the Mann-Whitney U test, use the smaller value of U and U' to look up the critical value of U for a one- or two-tailed test, as appropriate, at .05, initially (bottom table, page 621). If the tabled value is equal to or less than your value at that level, the null hypothesis is retained; if it is greater than your value, it is rejected and your experimental hypothesis is proved.

Sign test
Appendix 2, page 622

In the sign test, look up the critical value of S for a one- or two-tailed test, as appropriate, for N, the number of participants with differing scores, at .05, initially. If the tabled value is equal to or less than your value at that level, the null hypothesis is retained; if it is greater than your value, it is rejected and your experimental hypothesis is proved.

Wilcoxon test
Appendix 3, page 623

In the Wilcoxon test, look up the critical value of T for a one- or two-tailed test, as appropriate, for N, the number of participants with differing scores, at .05, initially. If the tabled value is equal to or less than your value at that level, the null hypothesis is retained; if it is greater than your value, it is rejected and your experimental hypothesis is proved.

Spearman's rho test
Appendix 4, page 624

In Spearman's rho test, look up the critical value of r_s for a one- or two-tailed test, as appropriate, for N, the number of participants, at .05, initially. If the tabled value is greater than or equal to your value at that level, the null hypothesis is retained; if it is less than your value, it is rejected and your experimental hypothesis is proved.

Chi-squared test
Appendix 5, page 625

In the chi-squared test, look up the critical value of chi-squared (also shown as χ^2) for a two-tailed test for df, the degrees of freedom, at .05 initially. If the tabled value is greater than or equal to your value at that level, the null hypothesis is retained; if it is less than your value, it is rejected and your experimental hypothesis is proved.

TIPS

Remember that decisions based on statistical tests are open to error, but if you follow the standard procedures outlined in Chapter 25 the potential for errors can be minimized. Try to be as unbiased as possible, and try not to assume too much about the results in advance.

Ensure that you have not made errors of either Type I, which can be reduced by using a greater level of significance (e.g., $p = .01$, or 1%, or even $p = .001$, or .1%), or Type II, which can be reduced by using a lesser level of significance (e.g., $p = .10$, or 10%).

In the Mann-Whitney U test, remember that ties are possible—this reduces the accuracy, but has only a small effect unless there are several ties.

In the chi-squared test, do follow the rules on pages 609–610 of Chapter 25 to avoid incorrect use of this test.

The tests described in Chapter 25 provide different levels of analysis, and they require a particular type of data. The following chart outlines the tests that can be used for different data types and experimental designs. Please note that this chart deals only with the statistical tests described in Chapter 25.

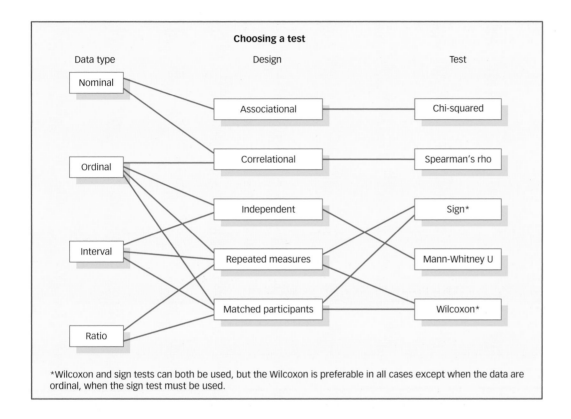

*Wilcoxon and sign tests can both be used, but the Wilcoxon is preferable in all cases except when the data are ordinal, when the sign test must be used.

APPENDIX 1: MANN-WHITNEY U TEST

Critical values of U for a one-tailed test at .005; two-tailed test at .01*

										N_A										
N_B	1	2	3	4	5	6	7	8	9	10	11	12	13	14	15	16	17	18	19	20
1	—	—	—	—	—	—	—	—	—	—	—	—	—	—	—	—	—	—	—	—
2	—	—	—	—	—	—	—	—	—	—	—	—	—	—	—	—	—	—	0	0
3	—	—	—	—	—	—	—	—	0	0	0	1	1	1	2	2	2	2	3	3
4	—	—	—	—	—	0	0	1	1	2	2	3	3	4	5	5	6	6	7	8
5	—	—	—	—	0	1	1	2	3	4	5	6	7	7	8	9	10	11	12	13
6	—	—	—	0	1	2	3	4	5	6	7	9	10	11	12	13	15	16	17	18
7	—	—	—	0	1	3	4	6	7	9	10	12	13	15	16	18	19	21	22	24
8	—	—	—	1	2	4	6	7	9	11	13	15	17	18	20	22	24	26	28	30
9	—	—	0	1	3	5	7	9	11	13	16	18	20	22	24	27	29	31	33	36
10	—	—	0	2	4	6	9	11	13	16	18	21	24	26	29	31	34	37	39	42
11	—	—	0	2	5	7	10	13	16	18	21	24	27	30	33	36	39	42	45	48
12	—	—	1	3	6	9	12	15	18	21	24	27	31	34	37	41	44	47	51	54
13	—	—	1	3	7	10	13	17	20	24	27	31	34	38	42	45	49	53	56	60
14	—	—	1	4	7	11	15	18	22	26	30	34	38	42	46	50	54	58	63	67
15	—	—	2	5	8	12	16	20	24	29	33	37	42	46	51	55	60	64	69	73
16	—	—	2	5	9	13	18	22	27	31	36	41	45	50	55	60	65	70	74	79
17	—	—	2	6	10	15	19	24	29	34	39	44	49	54	60	65	70	75	81	86
18	—	—	2	6	11	16	21	26	31	37	42	47	53	58	64	70	75	81	87	92
19	—	0	3	7	12	17	22	28	33	39	45	51	56	63	69	74	81	87	93	99
20	—	0	3	8	13	18	24	30	36	42	48	54	60	67	73	79	86	92	99	105

*Dashes in the body of the table indicate that no decision is possible at the stated level of significance.
For any N_A and N_B the observed value of U is significant at a given level of significance if it is *equal* to or *less* than the critical values shown.

Source: R. Runyon and A. Haber (1976). *Fundamentals of behavioural statistics* (3rd ed.). Reading, MA: McGraw Hill, Inc. With the kind permission of the publisher. Copyright © The McGraw-Hill Companies Inc.

Critical values of U for a one-tailed test at .01; two-tailed test at .02*

										N_A										
N_B	1	2	3	4	5	6	7	8	9	10	11	12	13	14	15	16	17	18	19	20
1	—	—	—	—	—	—	—	—	—	—	—	—	—	—	—	—	—	—	—	—
2	—	—	—	—	—	—	—	—	—	—	—	0	0	0	0	0	0	0	1	1
3	—	—	—	—	—	—	0	0	1	1	1	2	2	2	3	3	4	4	4	5
4	—	—	—	—	0	1	1	2	3	3	4	5	5	6	7	7	8	9	9	10
5	—	—	—	0	1	2	3	4	5	6	7	8	9	10	11	12	13	14	15	16
6	—	—	—	1	2	3	4	6	7	8	9	11	12	13	15	16	18	19	20	22
7	—	—	0	1	3	4	6	7	9	11	12	14	16	17	19	21	23	24	26	28
8	—	—	0	2	4	6	7	9	11	13	15	17	20	22	24	26	28	30	32	34
9	—	—	1	3	5	7	9	11	14	16	18	21	23	26	28	31	33	36	38	40
10	—	—	1	3	6	8	11	13	16	19	22	24	27	30	33	36	38	41	44	47
11	—	—	1	4	7	9	12	15	18	22	25	28	31	34	37	41	44	47	50	53
12	—	—	2	5	8	11	14	17	21	24	28	31	35	38	42	46	49	53	56	60
13	—	0	2	5	9	12	16	20	23	27	31	35	39	43	47	51	55	59	63	67
14	—	0	2	6	10	13	17	22	26	30	34	38	43	47	51	56	60	65	69	73
15	—	0	3	7	11	15	19	24	28	33	37	42	47	51	56	61	66	70	75	80
16	—	0	3	7	12	16	21	26	31	36	41	46	51	56	61	66	71	76	82	87
17	—	0	4	8	13	18	23	28	33	38	44	49	55	60	66	71	77	82	88	93
18	—	0	4	9	14	19	24	30	36	41	47	53	59	65	70	76	82	88	94	100
19	—	1	4	9	15	20	26	32	38	44	50	56	63	69	75	82	88	94	101	107
20	—	1	5	10	16	22	28	34	40	47	53	60	67	73	80	87	93	100	107	114

*Dashes in the body of the table indicate that no decision is possible at the stated level of significance.
For any N_A and N_B the observed value of U is significant at a given level of significance if it is *equal* to or *less* than the critical values shown.

Source: R. Runyon and A. Haber (1976). *Fundamentals of behavioural statistics* (3rd ed.). Reading, MA: McGraw Hill, Inc. With the kind permission of the publisher. Copyright © The McGraw-Hill Companies Inc.

Critical values of U for a one-tailed test at .025; two-tailed test at .05*

N_B	N_A 1	2	3	4	5	6	7	8	9	10	11	12	13	14	15	16	17	18	19	20
1	—	—	—	—	—	—	—	—	—	—	—	—	—	—	—	—	—	—	—	—
2	—	—	—	—	—	—	—	0	0	0	0	1	1	1	1	1	2	2	2	2
3	—	—	—	—	0	1	1	2	2	3	3	4	4	5	5	6	6	7	7	8
4	—	—	—	0	1	2	3	4	4	5	6	7	8	9	10	11	11	12	13	13
5	—	—	0	1	2	3	5	6	7	8	9	11	12	13	14	15	17	18	19	20
6	—	—	1	2	3	5	6	8	10	11	13	14	16	17	19	21	22	24	25	27
7	—	—	1	3	5	6	8	10	12	14	16	18	20	22	24	26	28	30	32	34
8	—	0	2	4	6	8	10	13	15	17	19	22	24	26	29	31	34	36	38	41
9	—	0	2	4	7	10	12	15	17	20	23	26	28	31	34	37	39	42	45	48
10	—	0	3	5	8	11	14	17	20	23	26	29	33	36	39	42	45	48	52	55
11	—	0	3	6	9	13	16	19	23	26	30	33	37	40	44	47	51	55	58	62
12	—	1	4	7	11	14	18	22	26	29	33	37	41	45	49	53	57	61	65	69
13	—	1	4	8	12	16	20	24	28	33	37	41	45	50	54	59	63	67	72	76
14	—	1	5	9	13	17	22	26	31	36	40	45	50	55	59	64	67	74	78	83
15	—	1	5	10	14	19	24	29	34	39	44	49	54	59	64	70	75	80	85	90
16	—	1	6	11	15	21	26	31	37	42	47	53	59	64	70	75	81	86	92	98
17	—	2	6	11	17	22	28	34	39	45	51	57	63	67	75	81	87	93	99	105
18	—	2	7	12	18	24	30	36	42	48	55	61	67	74	80	86	93	99	106	112
19	—	2	7	13	19	25	32	38	45	52	58	65	72	78	85	92	99	106	113	119
20	—	2	8	13	20	27	34	41	48	55	62	69	76	83	90	98	105	112	119	127

*Dashes in the body of the table indicate that no decision is possible at the stated level of significance.
For any N_A and N_B the observed value of U is significant at a given level of significance if it is *equal* to or *less* than the critical values shown.

Source: R. Runyon and A. Haber (1976). *Fundamentals of behavioural statistics* (3rd ed.). Reading, MA: McGraw Hill, Inc. With the kind permission of the publisher. Copyright © The McGraw-Hill Companies Inc.

Critical values of U for a one-tailed test at .05; two-tailed test at .10*

N_B	N_A 1	2	3	4	5	6	7	8	9	10	11	12	13	14	15	16	17	18	19	20
1	—	—	—	—	—	—	—	—	—	—	—	—	—	—	—	—	—	—	0	0
2	—	—	—	—	0	0	0	1	1	1	1	2	2	2	3	3	3	4	4	4
3	—	—	0	0	1	2	2	3	3	4	5	5	6	7	7	8	9	9	10	11
4	—	—	0	1	2	3	4	5	6	7	8	9	10	11	12	14	15	16	17	18
5	—	0	1	2	4	5	6	8	9	11	12	13	15	16	18	19	20	22	23	25
6	—	0	2	3	5	7	8	10	12	14	16	17	19	21	23	25	26	28	30	32
7	—	0	2	4	6	8	11	13	15	17	19	21	24	26	28	30	33	35	37	39
8	—	1	3	5	8	10	13	15	18	20	23	26	28	31	33	36	39	41	44	47
9	—	1	3	6	9	12	15	18	21	24	27	30	33	36	39	42	45	48	51	54
10	—	1	4	7	11	14	17	20	24	27	31	34	37	41	44	48	51	55	58	62
11	—	1	5	8	12	16	19	23	27	31	34	38	42	46	50	54	57	61	65	69
12	—	2	5	9	13	17	21	26	30	34	38	42	47	51	55	60	64	68	72	77
13	—	2	6	10	15	19	24	28	33	37	42	47	51	56	61	65	70	75	80	84
14	—	2	7	11	16	21	26	31	36	41	46	51	56	61	66	71	77	82	87	92
15	—	3	7	12	18	23	28	33	39	44	50	55	61	66	72	77	83	88	94	100
16	—	3	8	14	19	25	30	36	42	48	54	60	65	71	77	83	89	95	101	107
17	—	3	9	15	20	26	33	39	45	51	57	64	70	77	83	89	96	102	109	115
18	—	4	9	16	22	28	35	41	48	55	61	68	75	82	88	95	102	109	116	123
19	0	4	10	17	23	30	37	44	51	58	65	72	80	87	94	101	109	116	123	130
20	0	4	11	18	25	32	39	47	54	62	69	77	84	92	100	107	115	123	130	138

*Dashes in the body of the table indicate that no decision is possible at the stated level of significance.
For any N_A and N_B the observed value of U is significant at a given level of significance if it is *equal* to or *less* than the critical values shown.

Source: R. Runyon and A. Haber (1976). *Fundamentals of behavioural statistics* (3rd ed.). Reading, MA: McGraw Hill, Inc. With the kind permission of the publisher. Copyright © The McGraw-Hill Companies Inc.

APPENDIX 2: SIGN TEST

	Level of significance for one-tailed test				
	.05	.025	.01	.005	.0005
	Level of significance for two-tailed test				
N	.10	.05	.02	.01	.001
5	0	—	—	—	—
6	0	0	—	—	—
7	0	0	0	—	—
8	1	0	0	0	—
9	1	1	0	0	—
10	1	1	0	0	—
11	2	1	1	0	0
12	2	2	1	1	0
13	3	2	1	1	0
14	3	2	2	1	0
15	3	3	2	2	1
16	4	3	2	2	1
17	4	4	3	2	1
18	5	4	3	3	1
19	5	4	4	3	2
20	5	5	4	3	2
25	7	7	6	5	4
30	10	9	8	7	5
35	12	11	10	9	7

Calculated S must be *equal* to or *less* than the tabled (critical) value for significance at the level shown.

Source: F. Clegg (1983). *Simple statistics*. Cambridge, UK: Cambridge University Press. Reproduced by permission of Cambridge University Press.

APPENDIX 3: WILCOXON SIGNED RANKS TEST

	Levels of significance			
	One-tailed test			
	.05	.025	.01	.001
	Two-tailed test			
Sample size	.1	.05	.02	.002
N = 5	T ≤ 0			
6	2	0		
7	3	2	0	
8	5	3	1	
9	8	5	3	
10	11	8	5	0
11	13	10	7	1
12	17	13	9	2
13	21	17	12	4
14	25	21	15	6
15	30	25	19	8
16	35	29	23	11
17	41	34	27	14
18	47	40	32	18
19	53	46	37	21
20	60	52	43	26
21	67	58	49	30
22	75	65	55	35
23	83	73	62	40
24	91	81	69	45
25	100	89	76	51
26	110	98	84	58
27	119	107	92	64
28	130	116	101	71
29	141	125	111	78
30	151	137	120	86
31	163	147	130	94
32	175	159	140	103
33	187	170	151	112

Calculated T must be *equal* to or *less* than the tabled (critical) value for significance at the level shown.

Source: From R. Meddis (1975). *Statistical handbook for non-statisticians*. London: McGraw-Hill.

APPENDIX 4: SPEARMAN'S RHO TEST

	Level of significance for two-tailed test			
	.10	.05	.02	.01
	Level of significance for one-tailed test			
	.05	.025	.01	.005
N = 4	1.000			
5	0.900	1.000	1.000	
6	0.829	0.886	0.943	1.000
7	0.714	0.786	0.893	0.929
8	0.643	0.738	0.833	0.881
9	0.600	0.700	0.783	0.833
10	0.564	0.648	0.745	0.794
11	0.536	0.618	0.709	0.755
12	0.503	0.587	0.671	0.727
13	0.484	0.560	0.648	0.703
14	0.464	0.538	0.566	0.675
15	0.443	0.521	0.604	0.654
16	0.429	0.503	0.582	0.635
17	0.414	0.485	0.566	0.615
18	0.401	0.472	0.550	0.600
19	0.391	0.460	0.535	0.584
20	0.380	0.447	0.520	0.570
21	0.370	0.435	0.508	0.556
22	0.361	0.425	0.496	0.544
23	0.353	0.415	0.486	0.532
24	0.344	0.406	0.476	0.521
25	0.337	0.398	0.466	0.511
26	0.331	0.390	0.457	0.501
27	0.324	0.382	0.448	0.491
28	0.317	0.375	0.440	0.483
29	0.312	0.368	0.433	0.475
30	0.306	0.362	0.425	0.467

For $n > 30$, the significance of r_s can be tested by using the formula:

$$t = r_s \sqrt{\frac{n-2}{1-r_s^2}} \quad df = n - 2$$

and checking the value of t.

Calculated r_s must *equal* or *exceed* the tabled (critical) value for significance at the level shown.

Source: J.H. Zhar (1972). Significance testing of the Spearman rank correlation coefficient. *Journal of the American Statistical Association*, *67*, 578–80. Reprinted with permission. Copyright © 1972 by the American Statistical Association. All rights reserved.

APPENDIX 5: CHI-SQUARED TEST

df	Level of significance for one-tailed test					
	.10	.05	.025	.01	.005	.0005
	Level of significance for two-tailed test					
	.20	.10	.05	.02	.01	.001
1	1.64	2.71	3.84	5.41	6.64	10.83
2	3.22	4.60	5.99	7.82	9.21	13.82
3	4.64	6.25	7.82	9.84	11.34	16.27
4	5.99	7.78	9.49	11.67	13.28	18.46
5	7.29	9.24	11.07	13.39	15.09	20.52
6	8.56	10.64	12.59	15.03	16.81	22.46
7	9.80	12.02	14.07	16.62	18.48	24.32
8	11.03	13.36	15.51	18.17	20.09	26.12
9	12.24	14.68	16.92	19.68	21.67	27.88
10	13.44	15.99	18.31	21.16	23.21	29.59
11	14.63	17.28	19.68	22.62	24.72	31.26
12	15.81	18.55	21.03	24.05	26.22	32.91
13	16.98	19.81	22.36	25.47	27.69	34.53
14	18.15	21.06	23.68	26.87	29.14	36.12
15	19.31	22.31	25.00	28.26	30.58	37.70
16	20.46	23.54	26.30	29.63	32.00	39.29
17	21.62	24.77	27.59	31.00	33.41	40.75
18	22.76	25.99	28.87	32.35	34.80	42.31
19	23.90	27.20	30.14	33.69	36.19	43.82
20	25.04	28.41	31.41	35.02	37.57	45.32
21	26.17	29.62	32.67	36.34	38.93	46.80
22	27.30	30.81	33.92	37.66	40.29	48.27
23	28.43	32.01	35.17	38.97	41.64	49.73
24	29.55	33.20	36.42	40.27	42.98	51.18
25	30.68	34.38	37.65	41.57	44.31	52.62
26	31.80	35.56	38.88	42.86	45.64	54.05
27	32.91	36.74	40.11	44.14	46.96	55.48
28	34.03	37.92	41.34	45.42	48.28	56.89
29	35.14	39.09	42.69	46.69	49.59	58.30
30	36.25	40.26	43.77	43.49	50.89	59.70
32	38.47	42.59	46.19	50.49	53.49	62.49
34	40.68	44.90	48.60	53.00	56.06	65.25
36	42.88	47.21	51.00	55.49	58.62	67.99
38	45.08	49.51	53.38	57.97	61.16	70.70
40	47.27	51.81	55.76	60.44	63.69	73.40
44	51.64	56.37	60.48	65.34	68.71	78.75
48	55.99	60.91	65.17	70.20	73.68	84.04
52	60.33	65.42	69.83	75.02	78.62	89.27
56	64.66	69.92	74.47	79.82	83.51	94.46
60	68.97	74.40	79.08	84.58	88.38	99.61

Calculated value of χ^2 must *equal* or *exceed* the tabled (critical) value for significance at the level shown.

Abridged from R.A. Fisher and F. Yates (1974). *Statistical tables for biological, agricultural and medical research* (6th ed.). Harlow, UK: Addison Wesley Longman.

Glossary

accommodation: in Piaget's theory, changes in an individual's cognitive organization to deal with the environment.

adaptive expertise: using acquired knowledge to solve familiar problems efficiently; see routine expertise.

adipocytes: body cells that store fat; several overweight individuals often have many more of these cells than those of normal weight.

adipose tissue: tissue consisting of fat cells.

affectionless psychopathy: a disorder found among juvenile delinquents involving a lack of guilt and remorse.

aggression: behavior intended to harm or injure another person.

agoraphobia: a disorder in which there is fear of public places from which it might be difficult to escape in the event of a panic attack.

agrammatism: a condition in brain-damaged patients in which speech lacks grammatical structure and many function words and word endings are omitted.

algorithms: computational procedures providing a specified set of steps to a solution.

alpha bias: the tendency to exaggerate differences between the sexes.

altruism: a form of prosocial behavior that is costly to the individual and is motivated by the desire to help the other person.

amblyopia: a condition involving impaired vision as a result of disuse of one eye in the absence of any obvious damage to it.

amnesia: a condition caused by brain damage in which there is substantial impairment of long-term memory; the condition includes both anterograde amnesia and retrograde amnesia.

anaclitic depression: a condition involving loss of appetite and feelings of helplessness.

androgens: sex hormones found in greater amounts in males than in females.

anterograde amnesia: a reduced ability to remember information acquired *after* the onset of amnesia.

antibodies: protein molecules that attach themselves to invaders, marking them out for subsequent destruction.

antigens: foreign bodies such as viruses.

apparent motion: the illusion of movement created by the rapid presentation of still images.

assimilation: in Piaget's theory, dealing with new environmental situations by using existing cognitive organizations.

attachment: strong and long-lasting emotional ties to another person.

attitudes: beliefs about some person, group, or object, with these beliefs having an evaluative component (good vs. bad).

attributions: beliefs about the causes of behavior.

auditory phonological agnosia: a condition in which there is poor auditory perception of unfamiliar words and non-words but not of familiar words.

authoritarian personality: a type of personality characterized by rigid beliefs, hostility towards other groups, and submissive attitudes towards those in authority.

autism: a severe disorder involving very poor communication skills, deficient social and language development, and repetitive behavior.

aversion therapy: a form of treatment in which an aversive stimulus is paired with a positive one (e.g., sight of alcohol) to inhibit the response to the positive stimulus (e.g., drinking).

aversive racism: a combination of beliefs in equality for all and negative emotions towards members of other races.

avoidance learning: a form of operant conditioning in which an appropriate avoidance response prevents presentation of an unpleasant or aversive stimulus.

bar chart: a graph showing the frequencies with which the participants in a study fall into different categories.

behaviorism: an American school of psychology with an emphasis on measuring and predicting observable behavior.

beta bias: the tendency to minimize differences between the sexes.

binocular rivalry: this occurs when an observer perceives only one visual stimulus when two are presented, one to each eye.

blindsight: the ability of some brain-damaged patients to respond appropriately to visual stimuli in the absence of conscious visual perception.

blocking: the failure of a conditioned stimulus to produce a conditioned response because another conditioned stimulus already predicts the presentation of the unconditioned stimulus.

body mass index (BMI): an individual's weight in kilos dived by his/her height in meters squared; the normal range is between 20 and 25.

bogus pipeline: a set-up in which participants are attached to a machine they have been told can detect lies.

bounded rationality: the notion that people are as rational as their processing limitations permit.

case study: detailed investigation of a single individual.

category-specific deficits: disorders caused by brain damage in which patients have problems with some semantic categories but not with others.

catharsis: the notion that behaving aggressively can cause a release of negative emotions such as anger and frustration.

centration: attending to only one aspect of a situation.

change blindness: failure to detect changes in the visual environment.

change blindness blindness: people's mistaken belief that they would notice visual changes that are in fact very rarely detected.

chi-squared test: a test of association that is used with nominal data in the form of frequencies.

child-directed speech: the simplified sentences spoken by mothers and other adults when talking to young children.

chunks: stored units formed from integrating smaller pieces of information.

circadian rhythm: any biological rhythm repeating every 24 hours or so.

classical conditioning: a basic form of learning in which simple responses (e.g., salivation) are associated with a new or conditioned stimulus.

clause: part of a sentence that contains a subject and a verb.

clinical method: an informal question-based approach used by Piaget to assess children's understanding of problems.

co-articulation: the finding that the production of a phoneme in one speech segment is influenced (and distorted) by the production of the previous sound and preparations for the next sound.

coding units: the categories into which observations are placed prior to analysis.

coercive cycle: a pattern of behavior in which aggression by one family member produces an aggressive response, and so on.

cognitive appraisal: assessment of a situation to decide whether it is stressful and whether the individual has the resources to cope with it.

cognitive dissonance: an unpleasant psychological state occurring when someone has two discrepant cognitions or thoughts.

cognitive neuroscience: an approach within cognitive psychology that involves combining brain-imaging data with behavioral measures to understand human cognition.

cognitive triad: the depressed person's negative views of the self, the world, and the future.

collectivism: characteristic of cultures emphasizing interdependence, sharing of responsibility, and group membership.

common factors: general factors found in most forms of therapy (e.g., therapist's personal qualities) that help the client to recover; see **specific factors**.

comorbidity: presence in the same individual of two or more mental disorders at the same time.

compliance: the influence of a majority on a minority based on the power of the majority; see **conversion**.

concordance rate: as applied to twins, the probability that one twin has a given disorder given that the co-twin has it.

concurrent validity: assessing **validity** by correlating scores on a test with some currently available relevant criterion.

conditioned reflex: the new association between a stimulus and response formed in **classical conditioning**.

conditioned response: a response which is produced by the conditioned stimulus after a learning process in which the conditioned stimulus has been paired several times with the **unconditioned stimulus**.

conditioned stimulus: a stimulus that becomes associated through learning with the **unconditioned stimulus**.

conformity: yielding to group pressures in the absence of a direct request or order.

confounding variables: variables that are mistakenly manipulated or allowed to vary along with the independent variable.

connectionist networks: they consist of elementary units or nodes that are strongly interconnected; each network has various layers.

consensual validity: the extent to which scores on a self-report questionnaire correlate with scores obtained from ratings provided by other people.

conservation: the principle that quantities remain constant under various changes to their appearance.

consolidation: a process mostly completed within several hours, but which can last for years, which fixes information in **long-term memory**.

constant error: any unwanted variable that has a systematically different effect on the dependent variable in different conditions.

content analysis: a method involving the detailed study of, for example, the output of the media, speeches, and literature.

controlled variables: variables, not of interest to the experimenter, that are held constant or controlled.

conventional morality: this is the second level in Kohlberg's theory; at this level, moral reasoning focuses on having others' approval.

conversion: the influence of a minority on a majority based on convincing the majority that its views are correct; see **compliance**.

coping: efforts to deal with demanding situations to master the situation or reduce the demands.

core self-evaluations: a personality dimension including self-esteem, emotional stability (low **neuroticism**), internal locus of control, and generalized self-efficacy.

correlation: an association that is found between two variables.

counterbalancing: this is used with the repeated measures design, and involves ensuring that each condition is equally likely to be used first and second by the participants.

cross-cultural psychology: an approach to psychology focusing on the similarities and differences across cultures.

cross-situational consistency: the extent to which any given individual responds in the same way to different situations.

culture-bound syndromes: patterns of disordered behavior typically found in only certain cultures.

declarative memory: a form of long-term memory concerned with knowing that something is the case; it includes **episodic memory** and **semantic memory**.

deferred imitation: in Piaget's theory, the ability to imitate behavior observed at an earlier time.

deindividuation: the loss of a sense of personal identity that occurs when individuals find themselves in a crowd.

deliberate practice: systematic practice in which the learner is given informative feedback about his/her performance and has the opportunity to correct his/her errors.

demand characteristics: cues used by participants to try to guess the nature of the study or to work out what the experiment is about.

dependent variable: some aspect of the participant's behavior that is measured in a study.

deprivation: the state of a child who has formed a close relationship to someone but is later separated from that person.

derived etic: this involves researchers in various cultures developing techniques that are appropriate within their culture and then comparing the findings; see **imposed etic**.

diathesis–stress model: the notion that mental disorders are caused jointly by a diathesis or vulnerability within the individual *and* a distressing event.

dichotic listening task: a task in which pairs of items are presented one to each ear, followed by recall of all items.

differential parental investment: the notion that females have greater parental investment than males, as a result of which they are more selective in their choice of mates.

diffusion of responsibility: the reduction in a sense of responsibility as the number of observers of an incident increases.

digit span: the number of random digits that can be repeated back correctly in order after hearing them once; it is used as a measure of short-term memory capacity.

discourse analysis: a qualitative form of analysis applied to language productions in spoken or written form.

discrimination: [in intergroup processes] negative actions or behavior directed against the members of some group.

discrimination: [in conditioning and learning] the strength of the **conditioned response** to one **conditioned stimulus** is strengthened at the same time as that to a second conditioned stimulus is weakened.

dispositional attributions: deciding that someone's behavior is caused by their internal dispositions or characteristics.

dizygotic twins: fraternal twins derived from two fertilized ova and sharing 50% of their genes.

double blind: a procedure in which neither the experimenter nor the participants know the precise aims of the study; where possible, they do not know the condition in which each participant has been placed.

double dissociation: the finding that some individuals (often brain-damaged) do well on task A and poorly on task B, whereas others show the opposite pattern.

eclecticism: the use of a range of different forms of treatment by a therapist rather than favoring a single therapeutic approach.

ecological validity: the extent to which the findings of laboratory studies are applicable to everyday settings and generalize to other locations, times, and measures.

effectiveness studies: assessments of therapeutic effectiveness based on typical clinical practice; see **efficacy studies**.

efficacy studies: assessments of therapeutic effectiveness based on well-controlled investigations of well-defined clinical problems.

effort justification: creating a conflict between attitudes and behavior when people make great efforts to achieve a modest goal.

egocentrism: the assumption that one's way of thinking is the only possibility.

elaborative inferences: inferences that add details to a text that is being read but that are not essential to understanding.

emic constructs: these are constructs that are meaningful within any given culture but vary considerably across cultures.

emotional intelligence: the ability to understand one's own emotions as well as those of others.

empathy: the ability to understand another person's point of view and to share their emotions.

encoding specificity principle: the notion that retrieval depends on the overlap between the information available at retrieval and the information within the memory trace.

endogenous mechanisms: mechanisms that are internal and biological and are relatively uninfluenced by external factors.

episodic memory: a form of long-term memory concerned with personal experiences or episodes that happened in a given place at a specific time; see **semantic memory**.

equilibration: using the processes of accommodation and assimilation to produce a state of equilibrium or balance.

equipotentiality: the notion in **operant conditioning** that any response can be conditioned in any stimulus situation.

estrogens: sex hormones found in greater amounts in females than in males.

etic constructs: these are constructs that are meaningful within most or all cultures.

evaluation apprehension: anxiety-toned concern felt by participants in a study to perform well and to be evaluated positively by the experimenter.

evolutionary psychology: an approach based on the notion that much human behavior can be understood on the basis of Darwin's theory of evolution.

expansions: fuller and more detailed versions of what a child has just said provided by an adult or an older child.

experimental hypotheses: the testable predictions generated by a theory; these usually specify independent and dependent variables.

experimental method: an approach to research involving manipulation of some aspect of the environment (independent variable) to observe its effects on the participants' behavior (dependent variable).

experimental realism: the use of an artificial situation in which the participants become fully involved.

experimental validity: the extent to which a finding is genuine, and is a result of the **independent variable** being manipulated.

experimenter effects: the various ways in which the experimenters' expectancies,

personal characteristics, misrecordings of data, and so on can influence the findings of a study.

expertise: the specific knowledge an expert has about a given domain (e.g., that an engineer may have about bridges).

explicit learning: learning that involves conscious awareness of what has been learned; see **implicit learning**.

exposure therapy: a form of treatment in which clients are repeatedly exposed to stimuli or situations they greatly fear.

extended contact effect: knowledge that a member of your ingroup has formed a close relationship with a member of another group can reduce prejudice against that other group.

external validity: the validity of an experiment outside the research situation itself; the extent to which its findings are applicable to everyday life and generalize across populations, locations, measures, and times, see **internal validity**.

extinction: [in conditioning and learning] the elimination of a response when it is not followed by reward (**operant conditioning**) or by the unconditioned stimulus (**classical conditioning**).

extinction: [in visual perception and attention] a disorder of visual attention in which a stimulus presented to the side opposite the brain damage is not detected when another stimulus is presented at the same time.

extraversion: a personality factor based on sociability and impulsiveness.

factor analysis: a statistical technique applied to intelligence tests to find out the number and nature of the aspects of intelligence they are measuring.

false uniqueness bias: the mistaken tendency to think of oneself as being better than most other people.

falsifiability: the notion that all scientific theories can in principle be disproved by certain findings.

fatal familial insomnia: an inherited disorder in which the ability to sleep disappears in middle age and is followed by death several months later.

field experiment: a study in which the experimental method is used in a naturalistic situation.

figure–ground segregation: the perceptual organization of the visual field into a figure (object of central interest) and a ground (less important background).

fixation: in Freudian theory, spending a long time at a given stage of psychosexual development.

fixed interval schedule: a situation in which every the first response produced after a given interval of time is rewarded or reinforced.

fixed ratio schedule: a situation in which every nth response is rewarded.

flashbulb memories: vivid and detailed memories of dramatic events (e.g., September 11).

Flynn effect: the rapid rise in average IQ in several Western countries in recent decades.

framing effect: the influence of irrelevant aspects of a situation (e.g., wording of the problem) on decision making.

free association: a technique used in psychoanalysis in which the client says whatever comes immediately to mind.

frequency polygon: a graph showing the frequencies with which different scores are obtained by the participants in a study.

Freudian slip: an error in speech or action that is motivated by unconscious desires.

functional fixedness: the inflexible use of the usual function(s) of an object in problem solving.

functional magnetic resonance imaging (fMRI): a technique providing information about brain activity based on the detection of magnetic changes; it has reasonable temporal and spatial resolution.

fundamental attribution error: exaggerating the importance of personality and minimizing the role of the situation in determining another person's behavior.

fundamental lexical hypothesis: the assumption that dictionaries contain words describing all of the main personality traits.

gametes: sexual reproductive cells consisting of sperm in males and of eggs in females.

gender identity: a boy's or a girl's awareness of being male or female, respectively.

gender schemas: organized beliefs about suitable activities and behavior for each gender.

generalizability: the extent to which the findings of a study apply to other settings, populations, times, and measures.

generalization: the tendency of a **conditioned response** to occur (but in a weaker form) to stimuli similar to the **conditioned stimulus**.

genotype: an individual's potential in the form of genes.

glycogen: a carbohydrate produced by combining glucose molecules to create an energy store.

grammatical morphemes: modifiers (e.g., prefixes; suffixes) that alter the meaning of words and phrases.

group cohesiveness: the extent to which group members are attracted to the idea of the group.

group norms: rules and standards generally accepted by group members.

group polarization: the tendency for groups to produce fairly extreme decisions.

group socialization: dynamic processes in which group members and groups influence each other.

grouping: in Piaget's theory, a set of logically related operations.

groupthink: an excess focus on consensus that typically produces poor group decisions.

hard determinism: the notion that all of our actions are totally determined by a combination of causes; see **soft determinism**.

hassles: the irritating challenges of everyday life that can increase stress levels.

health literacy: the ability to understand health-related issues (e.g., taking medications appropriately).

heritability: the ratio of genetically caused variation to total variation (a combination of genetic and environmental variation) within a given population.

heuristics: rules of thumb that often (but not invariably) solve any given problem.

hill climbing: a **heuristic** that involves changing the present state of a problem into one apparently closer to the goal.

histogram: a graph in which the frequencies with which different scores are obtained by the participants in a study are shown by rectangles of different heights.

idiot savants: individuals who have limited outstanding expertise in spite of being mentally retarded.

ill-defined problems: problems in which the definition of the problem statement is imprecisely specified; the initial state, goal state, and methods to be used to solve the problem may be unclear; see **well-defined problems**.

immune system: a system of cells in the body involved in fighting disease.

implacable experimenter: the typical laboratory situation in which the experimenter's behavior is uninfluenced by the participant's behavior.

implementation intentions: intentions specifying in detail how an individual is going to achieve some goal.

implicit attitudes: attitudes that are outside conscious awareness and control.

implicit learning: learning information without conscious awareness of having learned; see **explicit learning**.

imposed etic: this involves applying techniques and/or theories based on one culture to other cultures without considering differences among cultures; see **derived etic**.

inattentional blindness: failure to detect an unexpected object appearing in a visual display; see **change blindness**.

inclusive fitness: the notion that natural selection favors individuals who maximize replication of their genes either directly via reproduction or indirectly by helping others who are genetically related to them.

incubation: the finding that a problem is solved more easily when it is put aside for some time; sometimes claimed to depend on unconscious processes.

independent variable: some aspect of the experimental situation that is manipulated by the experimenter.

individualism: characteristic of cultures emphasizing independence, personal responsibility, and personal uniqueness.

induced compliance: creating **cognitive dissonance** by persuading people to behave in ways opposed to their attitudes.

infantile amnesia: the inability of adults to recall autobiographical memories from early childhood.

informational influence: this occurs when an individual conforms because others in the group are believed to possess more knowledge.

ingroup bias: the tendency to favor one's ingroup over one or more outgroups.

insight: the experience of suddenly realizing how to solve a problem.

insight: a Freudian term meaning conscious understanding of traumatic thoughts and feelings that have been subject to **repression**.

integrative agnosia: a condition in which the patient experiences great difficulty in integrating features of an object when engaged in object recognition.

intelligence quotient: a measure of general intellectual ability; the mean IQ is 100.

internal validity: the validity of an experiment in terms of the context in which it is carried out, including the extent to which its findings can be replicated; also the extent to which research findings are genuine and can be regarded as being caused by the **independent variable**; see **external validity**.

interquartile range: the spread of the middle 50% of an ordered or ranked set of scores.

interval data: data in which the units of measurement have an invariant or unchanging value.

jargon aphasia: a brain-damaged condition in which speech is reasonably correct grammatically, but there are great problems in finding the right words.

jigsaw classroom: an approach to teaching designed to reduce prejudice in which the teacher ensures that all children in the class contribute to the achievement.

kin selection: the notion that natural selection favors individuals assisting those genetically related to them.

knowledge bias: the tendency to disregard a message if the source seems to lack accurate knowledge.

language acquisition device: an innate knowledge of the grammatical structure of language.

latent content: in Freud's theory, the underlying meaning of a dream that is difficult to recollect consciously; see **manifest content**.

law of effect: the probability of a response being produced is increased if it is followed by reward but is decreased if it is followed by punishment.

leptin: a protein secreted by fat cells that decreases feeding behavior.

life events: predominantly negative occurrences (and often of major consequence) that typically produce increased stress levels.

Likert scale: an approach to attitude measurement in which respondents indicate the strength of their agreement or disagreement with various statements.

linguistic universals: features that are found in all (or virtually all) languages.

long-term working memory: this is used by experts to store relevant information in long-term memory and to access it through retrieval cues in **working memory**.

loss aversion: the notion that individuals are more sensitive to potential losses than they are to potential gains.

major depressive disorder: a disorder characterized by symptoms such as sad, depressed mood, tiredness, and loss of interest in various activities.

manifest content: in Freud's theory, the remembered, "cleaned up" meaning of a dream; see **latent content**.

McGurk effect: the **phoneme** perceived in speech is influenced by visual and acoustic information when the two are in conflict.

mean: an average worked out by dividing the total of all participants' scores by the number of participants.

means–end relationship: the knowledge that responding in a particular way in a given situation will produce a certain outcome.

means–ends analysis: a **heuristic** for solving problems based on noting the difference between a current and a goal state, and creating a sub-goal to overcome this difference.

median: the middle score out of all participants' scores in a given condition.

melatonin: a hormone playing a key role in the onset of sleep.

meta-analysis: an analysis in which all of the findings from many studies relating to a given hypothesis are combined for statistical testing to obtain an overall picture.

metacognition: an individual's beliefs and knowledge about his/her own cognitive processes and strategies.

metamemory: knowledge about one's memory and about how it works.

microgenetic method: an approach to studying children's changes in cognitive strategies by means of short-term longitudinal studies.

misdirection: the various techniques used by magicians to make spectators focus on some irrelevant aspect of the situation while they perform the crucial part of a trick.

mixed error effect: speech errors that are semantically and phonologically related to the intended word.

mode: the most frequently occurring score among the participants in a given condition.

monotropy: the notion that infants have an innate tendency to form strong bonds with one particular individual (typically the mother).

monozygotic twins: identical twins derived from a single fertilized ovum and sharing 100% of their genes.

mood-state-dependent memory: the finding that memory is better when the mood state at retrieval is the same as that at learning than it is when the two mood states differ.

morphemes: the smallest units of meaning within words.

multitasking: performing two or more tasks at the same time by switching rapidly between them.

mundane realism: the use of an artificial situation that closely resembles a natural situation.

natural experiment: a type of quasi-experiment in which use is made of some naturally occurring event.

negative affectivity: a personality dimension involving a tendency to experience negative emotional states such as anxiety and depression.

negative contrast effect: a marked reduction in response rate in operant conditioning when there is a decrease in the size of the reinforcer.

negative punishment: a form of operant conditioning in which the probability of a response being produced is reduced by following it with the removal of a positive reinforcer or reward.

negative transfer: past experience in solving problems disrupts the ability to solve a current problem.

neglect: a disorder of visual attention in which stimuli (or parts of stimuli) presented to the side opposite the brain damage are not detected; the condition resembles extinction but is more severe.

neologisms: made-up words that are often found in the speech of patients with jargon aphasia.

neoteny: an extended period or duration of childhood resulting from evolution.

neuropeptide Y: a neurotransmitter that increases feeding behavior.

neuroticism: a personality factor based on negative emotional experiences (e.g., anxiety and depression).

nominal data: data consisting of the numbers of participants falling into qualitatively different categories.

nonparametric tests: statistical tests that do not involve the requirements of parametric tests.

nonshared environment: environmental influences that are unique to a given individual.

normal distribution: a bell-shaped distribution in which most scores cluster fairly close to the mean.

normative influence: this occurs when an individual conforms so that others in the group will like or respect him/her.

normative theories: as applied to decision making, theories focusing on how people should make decisions.

null hypothesis: prediction that the independent variable will have no effect on the dependent variable.

obesity: the condition of being substantially overweight, defined as having a body mass index exceeding 30.

object permanence: an awareness that objects continue to exist when they can no longer be seen.

objective tests: a method of assessing personality under laboratory conditions in an unobtrusive way.

observational learning: learning occurring as a consequence of watching the behavior of another person (often called a model).

Oedipus complex: the Freudian notion that boys at the age of 5 desire their mother and so become frightened of their father.

operant conditioning: a form of learning in which behavior is controlled by its consequences (i.e., rewards or positive reinforcers and unpleasant or aversive stimuli).

operationalization: a procedure in which variables of interest are defined by the operations taken to measure them.

opportunity sampling: selecting participants only on the basis of their availability.

optic ataxia: a condition involving brain damage in which the patient has difficulty in making visually guided movements in spite of having reasonably intact visual perception.

ordinal data: data that can be ordered from smallest to largest.

over-regularization: extending a grammatical rule to situations in which it does not apply.

oxytocin: a hormone produced in response to stress that reduces anxiety and increases sociability.

panic disorder: a disorder in which an individual suffers from panic attacks and is very concerned about having further attacks.

paradigm: according to Popper, a general theoretical orientation commanding wide support.

parametric tests: statistical tests that require interval or ratio data, normally distributed data, and similar variances in both conditions.

parsing: an analysis of the syntactical or grammatical structure of sentences.

partial penetrance: a characteristic of certain genes, in which they influence behavior only under certain conditions.

participant reactivity: the situation in which an independent variable has an effect on behavior merely because the participants are aware they are being observed.

peak experiences: heightened experiences associated with feelings of joy and wonder.

peer tutoring: teaching of one child by another, with the child doing the teaching generally being slightly older than the one being taught.

perseverative search: mistakenly searching for an object in the place in which it was previously found rather than the place in which it is currently hidden.

personal identity: those aspects of the self-concept that depend on our personal relationships and characteristics.

phenomenology: an approach in which the focus is on the individual's direct reports of experience.

phenotype: an individual's observable characteristics based on his/her genotype plus life experiences.

phonemes: basic speech sounds that distinguish one word from another and so convey meaning.

phonemic restoration effect: the finding that listeners are unaware that a phoneme has been deleted from an auditorily presented sentence.

phonological dyslexia: a condition in which familiar words can be read but there is impaired ability to read unfamiliar words and non-words.

phonological similarity effect: the finding that immediate recall of word lists in the correct order is impaired when the words sound similar to each other.

phonology: information about the sounds of words and parts of words.

phrase: a group of words expressing a single idea; it is shorter than a clause.

positive punishment: a form of operant conditioning in which the probability of a response is reduced by following it with an unpleasant or aversive stimulus; sometimes known simply as punishment.

positive transfer: past experiencing of solving problems makes it easier to solve a current problem.

post-conventional morality: the third level in Kohlberg's theory; at this level, moral reasoning focuses on justice and the need to respect others.

posttraumatic stress disorder: a disorder triggered by a very distressing event and involving re-experiencing of the event, avoidance of stimuli associated with the event, and increased arousal.

pre-conventional morality: the first level in Kohlberg's theory; at this level, moral reasoning focuses on rewards for good actions and punishments for bad actions.

predictive validity: assessing validity by correlating scores on a test with some future criterion.

preformulation: this is used in speech production to reduce processing costs by using phrases often used previously.

prejudice: an attitude or belief (usually negative) towards the members of some group on the basis of their membership of that group.

preparedness: the notion that each species finds some forms of learning more "natural" and easier than others.

primacy effect: in social psychology, the notion that our impressions of other people are heavily influenced by the first information about them we encounter.

primary reinforcers: rewarding stimuli that are needed to live (e.g., food; water).

privation: the state of a child who has never formed a close attachment with anyone.

proactive interference: disruption of memory by previous learning, often of similar material; see **retroactive interference**.

problem representation: the way in which the problem solver represents a problem based on what seem to be its crucial features.

problem space: an abstract description of all the possible states of affairs that can occur in a problem situation.

progress monitoring: this is a **heuristic** used in problem solving in which insufficiently rapid progress towards solution produces criterion failure and the adoption of a different strategy.

projective tests: a method of assessing personality in which people are given an unstructured test to perform (e.g., describing inkblots).

proposition: a statement that makes an assertion or denial and which can be true or false.

prosocial behavior: cooperative, affectionate, or helpful behavior designed to benefit another person.

psychobiography: the study of individual personality by applying psychological theory to the key events in a person's life.

psychological refractory period (PRP) effect: the slowing of response to the second of two stimuli when presented close together in time.

psychopathology: the study of the nature and development of mental disorders; an abnormal pattern of functioning.

psychoticism: a personality factor based on aggression, hostility, and a lack of caring.

quasi-experiment: a type of experiment resembling a "true" experiment, but with some aspects of the experimental method omitted.

quota sampling: selecting participants at random from a population so that they are similar to it in certain respects (e.g., proportion of females; proportion of teenagers).

racism: prejudice and/or discrimination against another group because of their race or ethnicity.

random error: unsystematic and unwanted "nuisance variables" that influence the **dependent variable**.

random sampling: selecting participants on some random basis (e.g., coin tossing).

randomization: the allocation of participants to conditions on a random basis.

range: the difference between the highest and lowest score in any condition.

ratio data: as **interval data**, but with a meaningful zero point.

rationalization: in Bartlett's theory, the tendency to recall stories in distorted ways influenced by the reader's cultural expectations and **schemas**.

recategorization: the process of producing a new categorization in which the ingroup and the outgroup are combined into a single ingroup.

reciprocal altruism: the notion that individuals will behave altruistically towards someone else if they anticipate that person will respond altruistically.

reductionism: the notion that psychology can ultimately be reduced to more basic sciences such as physiology or biochemistry.

regression: in Freudian theory, returning to an earlier stage of psychosexual development when someone is highly stressed.

reliability: the extent to which a test gives consistent findings on separate occasions.

REM sleep: a stage of sleep involving rapid eye movements and associated with dreaming.

reminiscence bump: the tendency of older people to recall a disproportionate number of autobiographical memories from the years of adolescence and early adulthood.

replicability: the ability to repeat or replicate findings obtained from an experiment.

replication: the ability to repeat the findings obtained from an experiment.

reporting bias: the tendency to disregard a message if the source seems untrustworthy.

repression: motivated forgetting of traumatic or other very threatening events.

retroactive interference: disruption of memory by learning of other material during the retention interval; see **proactive interference**.

retrograde amnesia: impaired memory for events occurring before the onset of **amnesia**.

reversibility: the ability to undo, or reverse mentally, an action or operation.

routine expertise: using acquired knowledge to develop strategies for dealing with novel problems; see **adaptive expertise**.

saccades: fast eye movements or jumps that cannot be altered after being initiated.

safety-seeking behaviors: actions taken by anxious patients to prevent feared consequences and to reduce their anxiety level.

satisficing: selection of the first choice that meets certain minimum requirements; the word is formed from the two words satisfactory and sufficing.

scaffolding: the context provided by an adult or other knowledgeable person helping children to develop their cognitive skills.

scattergraph: a two-dimensional representation of all the participants'

scores in a correlational study; also known as a scattergram.

schema: in Piaget's theory, organized knowledge used to guide action.

schemas: in Bartlett's theory, organized information about the world, events, or people stored in long-term memory.

scripts: organized information or schemas representing typical events.

secondary reinforcers: stimuli that are rewarding because they have been associated with **primary reinforcers**; money and praise are examples.

segmentation problem: the listener's problem of dividing the almost continuous sounds of speech into separate **phonemes** and words.

selective placement: placing adopted children in homes with similar educational and social backgrounds to those of their biological parents.

self-actualization: the need to discover and fulfill one's own potential.

self-concept: the organized body of information an individual possesses about himself/herself.

self-disclosure: revealing personal or intimate information about oneself to someone else.

self-discovery: an active approach to learning in which the child is encouraged to use his/her initiative.

self-efficacy: an individual's beliefs concerning his or her ability to cope successfully with a particular task or situation.

self-esteem: the evaluative part of the **self-concept** concerned with feelings of confidence and being worthwhile.

self-fulfilling prophecy: the tendency for someone's expectations about another person to lead to the fulfillment of those expectations.

self-regulation: using one's own cognitive processes to control and regulate one's own behavior and goals.

self-serving bias: the tendency to take credit for success but to refuse to accept blame for failure.

semantic memory: a form of long-term memory consisting of general knowledge about the world, language, and so on; see **episodic memory**.

sensory buffer: a mechanism that maintains information for a short period of time before it is processed.

sensory-specific satiety: reduced pleasantness of any taste (or food smell) to which an individual has been repeatedly exposed.

sex-role stereotypes: culturally determined beliefs about appropriate male and female behavior.

sex-typed behavior: behavior consistent with **sex-role stereotypes**.

shadowing task: a task in which there are two auditory messages, one of which has to be repeated back aloud or shadowed.

shaping: a form of operant conditioning in which behavior is changed slowly in the desired direction by requiring responses to become more and more like the wanted response for reward to be given.

shared environment: environmental influences common to the children within a given family.

single blind: a procedure in which the participants are not informed of the condition in which they have been placed.

situational attributions: deciding that someone's behavior is caused by the situation in which they find themselves.

size constancy: objects are perceived to have a given size regardless of the size of the retinal image.

social cognition: the cognitive processes involved in making sense of social situations and behavior.

social desirability bias: the tendency to provide socially desirable rather than honest answers on questionnaires and in interviews.

social identity: the part of the **self-concept** depending on the various groups to which we belong.

social influence: a process in which an individual's attitudes and/or behavior are influenced by another person or by a group.

social norms: agreed standards of behavior within a group (e.g., family; organization).

social phobia: a disorder in which the individual has excessive fear of many social situations and will often avoid them.

soft determinism: the notion that all behavior has a cause, but some forms of behavior are more constrained by the current situation than are others.

source traits: personality traits underlying the more superficial surface traits.

specific factors: features unique to a given form of therapy that help the patient to recover; see **common factors**.

specific phobia: a strong and irrational fear of a given object (e.g., spider; snake) or situation (e.g., enclosed space).

spillover effect: any given word is fixated longer during reading when it is preceded by a rare or unpredictable word rather than a common or predictable word.

split attention: allocation of attention to two nonadjacent regions of visual space.

split-brain patients: individuals in whom the corpus callosum connecting the two halves of the brain has been severed.

spontaneous recovery: the re-emergence of responses over time in **classical conditioning** following experimental extinction.

spreading activation: the notion that activation or energy spreads from an activated node (e.g., word) to other related nodes.

standard deviation: a measure of the spread of scores in a bell-shaped or normal distribution. It is the square root of the variance, takes account of every score, and is a sensitive measure of dispersion or variation.

standardized test: a test given to large representative samples so that an individual's scores can be compared to those of the population.

statistical significance: the level at which the decision is made to reject the **null hypothesis** in favor of the **experimental hypothesis**.

stereotype: a simplified cognitive generalization or categorization (typically negative) about a group. It is often based on easily identifiable characteristics (e.g., sex; ethnicity).

stratified sampling: a modified version of **quota sampling**, in which the selection of participants according to certain characteristics is decided by the researcher, rather than in a random way.

subliminal stimuli: these are stimuli presented below the level of conscious awareness.

sunk-cost effect: expending additional resources to justify some previous commitment (i.e., throwing good money after bad).

surface dyslexia: a condition in which brain-damaged patients cannot read irregular words but can read regular ones.

surface traits: personality traits that are readily observable and are related to underlying source traits.

syllable: a rhythmic unit of speech; words consist of one or more syllables.

systematic sampling: a modified version of **random sampling** in which the participants are selected in a quasi-random way (e.g., every hundredth name from a population list).

telegraphic period: a stage of language development in which children use short but informative utterances, as in a telegram.

template: as applied to chess, an abstract, schematic structure consisting of a mixture of fixed and variable information about chess pieces.

theory: a general explanation of a set of findings; it is used to produce experimental hypotheses.

theory of mind: the understanding that other people may have different beliefs, emotions, and intentions than one's own.

third-person effect: the belief that one is personally less influenced by persuasive messages than most other people.

tip-of-the-tongue phenomenon: the experience of having a specific concept in mind but being unable to access the correct word to describe it.

token economy: use of **operant conditioning** to change the behavior of mental patients by selective positive reinforcement or reward.

traits: stable aspects of a person that influence his/her personality.

transactional leadership: a form of leadership involving exchanges or bargains between the leader and his/her followers.

transference: in Freudian theory, the transfer of the patient's strong feelings for one person (e.g., a parent) onto the therapist.

transformational leadership: a form of leadership based on inspiration or charisma.

transitivity: this involves the ability to place at least three entities in the correct order.

triadic reciprocal model: Bandura's view that an individual's personality, the environment, and his/her own behavior all influence each other.

tutorial training: a traditional approach in which the teacher imparts knowledge to fairly passive students.

Type A personality: a personality type characterized by impatience, competitiveness, time pressure, and hostility.

Type D personality: a personality type characterized by high **negative affectivity** and social inhibition.

Type I error: mistakenly rejecting the null hypothesis in favor of the experimental hypothesis when the results are actually a result of chance.

Type II error: mistakenly retaining the null hypothesis when the experimental hypothesis is actually correct.

unconditioned reflex: the new association between a stimulus and response formed in classical conditioning.

unconditioned response: an unlearned response to an unconditioned stimulus.

unconditioned stimulus: a stimulus that produces an unconditioned response in the absence of learning.

unconscious perception: perception occurring below the level of conscious awareness.

underspecification: a strategy used to reduce processing costs in speech production by producing simplified expressions.

utility: the subjective desirability of a given outcome in decision making.

validity: the extent to which a test measures what it claims to be measuring.

variable interval schedule: a situation in which the first response produced after a given interval of time is rewarded but with some variation around that time interval.

variable ratio schedule: on average every nth response is rewarded, but there is some variation around that figure.

variance: a measure of dispersion that is the square of the standard deviation.

viewpoint-dependent theories: theories of object recognition based on the assumption that objects can be recognized more easily from some angles than from others; see **viewpoint-invariant theories.**

viewpoint-invariant theories: theories of object recognition based on the assumption that objects can be recognized equally easily from all angles; see **viewpoint-dependent theories.**

visceral brain: a brain system including the hippocampus, septum, and hypothalamus claimed by H.J. Eysenck to be most responsive in individuals high in neuroticism.

visual agnosia: a condition in which there are great problems in recognizing objects presented visually even though visual information reaches the visual cortex.

weapon focus: the finding that eyewitnesses pay so much attention to a weapon that they tend to ignore other details.

weapons effect: an increase in aggression produced by the sight of a weapon.

well-defined problems: problems in which the initial state, goal, and methods available for solving them are clearly laid out; see **ill-defined problems.**

Williams syndrome: a genetic disorder involving low IQ but reasonable language development.

word meaning deafness: a condition in which there is selective impairment of the ability to understand spoken (but not written) words.

working memory: a system having the functions of cognitive processing and the temporary storage of information.

zeitgeber: external events (e.g., light) that partially determine biological rhythms.

zone of proximal development: in Vygotsky's theory, the gap between the child's current problem-solving ability and his/her potential ability.

References

Abrams, D., Wetherell, M., Cochrane, S., Hogg, M.A., & Turner, J.C. (1990). Knowing what to think by knowing who you are: Self-categorization and the nature of norm formation, conformity and group polarization. *British Journal of Social Psychology*, 29, 97–119.

Adams, P.R., & Adams, G.R. (1984). Mount Saint Helen's ashfall: Evidence for a disaster stress reaction. *American Psychologist*, 39, 252–260.

Adolph, K.E. (2000). Specificity of learning: Why infants fall over a veritable cliff. *Psychological Science*, 11, 290–295.

Adorno, T.W., Frenkel-Brunswik, E., Levinson, D., & Sanford, R. (1950). *The authoritarian personality*. New York: Harper.

Aglioti, S., Goodale, M.A., & DeSouza, J.F.X. (1995). Size-contrast illusions deceive the eye but not the hand. *Current Biology*, 5, 679–685.

Ahlskog, J.E., Randall, P.K., & Hoebel, B.G. (1975). Hypothalamic hyperphagia: Dissociation from hyperphagia following destruction of noradrenergic neurons. *Science*, 190, 399–401.

Ainsworth, M.D.S., & Bell, S.M. (1970). Attachment, exploration and separation: Illustrated by the behaviour of one-year-olds in a strange situation. *Child Development*, 41, 49–67.

Ainsworth, M.D.S., Blehar, M.C., Waters, E., & Wall, S. (1978). *Patterns of attachment: A psychological study of the strange situation*. Hillsdale, NJ: Lawrence Erlbaum Associates, Inc.

Aizenstein, H.J., Stenger, V.A., Cochran, J., Clark, K., Johnson, M., Nebes, R.D., et al. (2004). Regional brain activation during concurrent implicit and explicit sequence learning. *Cerebral Cortex*, 14, 199–208.

Ajzen, I. (1985). From intentions to actions: A theory of planned behavior. In J. Kuhl & J. Beckmann (Eds.), *Action-control: From cognition to behavior*. Heidelberg, Germany: Springer-Verlag.

Ajzen, I. (1987). Attitudes, traits, and actions: Dispositional prediction of behavior in personality and social psychology. *Advances in Experimental Social Psychology*, 20, 1–63.

Ajzen, I. (1991). The theory of planned behavior. *Organizational Behavior and Human Decision Processes*, 50, 179–211.

Akrami, N., & Ekehammar, B. (2005). The association between implicit and explicit prejudice: The moderating role of motivation to control prejudiced reactions. *Scandinavian Journal of Psychology*, 46, 361–366.

Al-Rashid, R.A. (1971). Hypothalamic syndrome in acute childhood leukemia. *Clinical Pediatrics*, 10, 53–54.

Alderfer, C.P. (1969). An empirical test of a new theory of human needs. *Organizational Behavior and Human Performance*, 4, 142–175.

Allen, M.G. (1976). Twin studies of affective illness. *Archives of General Psychiatry*, 33, 1476–1478.

Allison, T., & Cicchetti, D.V. (1976). Sleep in mammals: Ecological and constitutional correlates. *Science*, 194, 732–734.

Allopenna, P.D., Magnuson, J.S., & Tanenhaus, M.K. (1998). Tracking the time course of spoken word recognition using eye movements: Evidence for continuous mapping models. *Journal of Memory and Language*, 38, 419–439.

Allport, G.W. (1954). *The nature of prejudice*. Reading, MA: Addison-Wesley.

Allport, G.W. (1962). The general and the unique in psychological science. *Journal of Personality*, 30, 405–422.

Allport, G.W., & Odbert, H.S. (1936). Trait-names: A psycho-lexical study. *Psychological Monographs*, 47, No. 211.

Allport, G.W., & Postman, L. (1947). *The psychology of rumor*. New York: Holt, Rinehart, & Winston.

Almeida, D.M. (2005). Resilience and vulnerability to daily stressors assessed via diary methods. *Current Directions in Psychological Science*, 14, 64–68.

Almer, G., Hainfellner, J.A., Brücke, T., Jellinger, K., Kleinert, R., Bayer, G., et al. (1999). Fatal familial insomnia: A new Austrian family. *Brain*, 122, 5–16.

Altemeyer, B. (1988). *Enemies of freedom: Understanding right-wing authoritarianism*. San Francisco: Jossey-Bass.

Altenberg, B. (1990). Speech as linear compositon. In G. Caie, K. Haastrup, A.L. Jakobsen, J.E. Nielsen, J. Sevaldsen, H. Sprecht et al. (Eds.), *Proceedings from the fourth Nordic conference for English studies*. Copenhagen, Denmark: Copenhagen University Press.

American Psychiatric Association. (1994). *Diagnostic and statistical manual of mental disorders* (4th ed.). Washington, DC: Author.

American Psychological Association. (1982). *Ethical principles in the conduct of research with human participants*. Washington, DC: American Psychological Association.

Amodio, D.M., & Showers, C.J. (2005). "Similarity breeds liking" revisited: The moderating role of commitment. *Journal of Social and Personal Relationships*, 22, 817–836.

Anand, B.K., & Brobeck, J.R. (1951). Hypothalamic control of food intakes in rats and cats. *Yale Journal of Biological Medicine*, 24, 123–140.

Anandaram, T.S.J. (2001). Face your phobia. *The Hindu*, September 2. www.hinduonnet.com/thehindu/

Andersen, B.L., Cyranowski, J.M., & Espindle, D. (1999). Men's sexual self-schema. *Journal of Personality and Social Psychology*, 76, 645–661.

Anderson, C.A., Anderson, K.B., & Deuser, W.E. (1996). A general framework for the study of affective aggression: Effects of weapons and extreme temperatures on accessibility of aggressive thoughts, affect, and attitudes. *Personality and Social Psychology Bulletin*, 22, 366–376.

Anderson, C.A., Berkowitz, L., Donnerstein, E., Huesmann, L.R., Johnson, J.D., Linz, D., et al. (2003). The influence of media violence on youth. *Psychological Science in the Public Interest*, 4, 81–110.

Anderson, C.A., & Bushman, B.J. (2001). Effects of violent video games on aggressive behavior, aggressive cognition, aggressive affect, physiological arousal, and prosocial behavior: A meta-analytic review of the scientific literature. *Psychological Science*, 12, 353–359.

Anderson, C.A., & Bushman, B.J. (2002). Human aggression. *Annual Review of Psychology*, 53, 27–51.

Anderson, J.L., Crawford, C.B., Nadeau, J., & Lindberg, T. (1992). Was the Duchess of Windsor right? A cross-cultural review of the socioecology of ideals of female body shape. *Ethology and Sociobiology, 13*, 197–227.

Anderson, M. (2004). Sex differences in intelligence. In R.L. Gregory (Ed.), *The Oxford companion to the mind* (2nd ed.). Oxford, UK: Oxford University Press.

Anderson, R.C., & Pichert, J.W. (1978). Recall of previously unrecallable information following a shift in perspective. *Journal of Verbal Learning and Verbal Behavior, 17*, 1–12.

Andlin-Sobocki, P., Jönsson, B., Wittchen, H.-U., & Olesen, J. (2005). Costs of disorders of the brain in Europe. *European Journal of Neurology, 12*(Suppl. 1), 1–90.

Andlin-Sobocki, P., Olesen, J., Wittchen, H.-U., & Jonsson, B. (2005). Cost of disorders of the brain in Europe. *European Journal of Neurology, 12*, 1–27.

Andlin-Sobocki, P., & Wittchen, H.U. (2005). Cost of affective disorders in Europe. *European Journal of Neurology, 12*, 34–38.

Andrews, B., Brewin, C.R., Ochera, J., Morton, J., Bekerian, D.A., Davies, G.M., et al. (1999). Characteristics, context and consequences of memory recovery among adults in therapy. *British Journal of Psychiatry, 175*, 141–146.

Annett, M. (1999). Handedness and lexical skills in undergraduates. *Cortex, 35*, 357–372.

Apperly, I.A., Samson, D., & Humphreys, G.W. (2005). Domain-specificity and theory of mind: Evaluating neuropsychological evidence. *Trends in Cognitive Sciences, 9*, 572–577.

Archer, S. (1982). The lower age boundaries of identity development. *Child Development, 53*, 1551–1556.

Archer, J. (2000). Sex differences in aggression between heterosexual partners: A meta-analytic review. *Psychological Bulletin, 126*, 651–680.

Argyle, M. (1988). Social relationships. In M. Hewstone, W. Stroebe, J.-P. Codol, & G.M. Stephenson (Eds.), *Introduction to social psychology*. Oxford, UK: Blackwell.

Argyle, M., & Henderson, M. (1984). The rules of friendship. *Journal of Social and Personal Relationships, 1*, 211–237.

Argyle, M., Henderson, M., Bond, M., Iizuka, Y., & Contarello, A. (1986). Cross-cultural variations in relationship rules. *International Journal of Psychology, 21*, 287–315.

Argyle, M., Henderson, M., & Furnham, A. (1985). The rules of social relationships. *British Journal of Social Psychology, 24*, 125–139.

Armitage, C.J. (2004). Evidence that implementation intentions reduce dietary fat intake: A randomised trial. *Health Psychology, 23*, 319–323.

Armitage, C.J., & Conner, M. (2001). Efficacy of the theory of planned behaviour: A meta-analytic review. *British Journal of Social Psychology, 40*, 471–499.

Aron, A., & Westbay, L. (1996). Dimensions of the prototype of love. *Journal of Personality and Social Psychology, 70*, 535–551.

Aronoff, J. (1967). *Psychological needs and cultural systems: A case study*. Princeton, NJ: Van Nostrand.

Aronson, E., & Osherow, N. (1980). Cooperation, prosocial behavior, and academic performance: Experiments in the desegregated classroom. In L. Bickerman (Ed.), *Applied social psychology annual*. Beverly Hills, CA: Sage.

Arrindell, W.A., Kwee, M.G., Methorst, G.J., van der Ende, J., Pol, E., & Moritz, B.J. (1989). Perceived parental rearing styles of agoraphobic and socially phobic in-patients. *British Journal of Psychiatry, 155*, 526–535.

Asch, S.E. (1946). Forming impressions of personality. *Journal of Abnormal and Social Psychology, 41*, 258–290.

Asch, S.E. (1951). Effects of group pressure on the modification and distortion of judgments. In H. Guetzkow (Ed.), *Groups, leadership and men*. Pittsburgh, PA: Carnegie.

Asch, S.E. (1956). Studies of independence and conformity: A minority of one against a unanimous majority. *Psychological Monographs, 70* (Whole No. 416).

Aspinwall, L.G., & Taylor, S.E. (1997). A stitch in time: Self-regulation and proactive coping. *Psychological Bulletin, 121*, 417–436.

Association for the Study of Dreams. (2001, July 15). Right-wingers have the scariest dreams. *Sunday Times*, p. 9.

Astington, J.W., & Jenkins, J.M. (1999). A longitudinal study of the relation between language and theory-of-mind development. *Developmental Psychology, 35*, 1311–1320.

Atkinson, R.C., & Shiffrin, R.M. (1968). Human memory: A proposed system and its control processes. In K.W. Spence & J.T. Spence (Eds.), *The psychology of learning and motivation* (Vol. 2). London: Academic Press.

Atkinson, R.L., Atkinson, R.C., Smith, E.E., & Bem, D.J. (1993). *Introduction to psychology* (11th ed.). New York: Harcourt Brace College Publishers.

Atkinson, R.L, Atkinson, R.C., Smith, E.E., Bem, D.J., & Nolen-Hoeksema, S. (1996). *Hilgard's introduction to psychology* (12th ed.). New York: Harcourt Brace.

Augoustinos, M., & Walker, I. (1995). *Social cognition: An integrated introduction*. London: Sage.

Avolio, B.J., Bass, B.M., & Jung, D.I. (1999). Re-examining the components of transformational and transactional leadership using the Multifactor Leadership Questionnaire. *Journal of Occupational and Organizational Psychology, 72*, 441–462.

Awad, A.G., & Voruganti, L.N.P. (1999). Quality of life and new antipsychotics in schizophrenia: Are patients better off? *International Journal of Social Psychiatry, 45*, 268–275.

Awh, E., & Pashler, H. (2000). Evidence for split attentional foci. *Journal of Experimental Psychology: Human Perception and Performance, 26*, 834–846.

Axsom, D., & Cooper, J. (1985). Cognitive dissonance and psychotherapy: The role of effort justification in inducing weight loss. *Journal of Experimental Psychology, 53*, 30–40.

Ayllon, T., & Azrin, N.H. (1968). *The token economy: A motivational system for therapy and rehabilitation*. New York: Appleton-Century-Crofts.

Baars, B.J. (1997). Consciousness versus attention, perception, and working memory. *Consciousness and Cognition, 5*, 363–371.

Baars, B.J. (2002). The conscious access hypothesis: Origins and recent evidence. *Trends in Cognitive Sciences, 6*, 47–52.

Baars, B.J., & Franklin, S. (2003). How conscious experience and working memory interact. *Trends in Cognitive Sciences, 7*, 166–172.

Bachen, E., Cohen, S., & Marsland, A.L. (1997). Psychoimmunology. In A. Baum, S. Newman, J. Weinman, R. West, & C. McManus (Eds.), *Cambridge handbook of psychology, health, and medicine*. Cambridge, UK: Cambridge University Press.

Baddeley, A.D. (1986). *Working memory*. Oxford, UK: Oxford University Press.

Baddeley, A.D. (1990). *Human memory: Theory and practice*. Hove, UK: Psychology Press.

Baddeley, A.D. (2001). Is working memory still working? *American Psychologist, 56*, 851–864.

Baddeley, A.D., Eysenck, M.W., & Anderson, M.C. (2009). *Memory*. Hove, UK: Psychology Press.

Baddeley, A.D., Gathercole, S., & Papagno, C. (1998). The phonological loop as a language learning device. *Psychological Review, 105*, 158–173.

Baddeley, A.D., & Hitch, G.J. (1974). Working memory. In G.H. Bower (Ed.), *The psychology of learning and motivation* (Vol. 8). London: Academic Press.

Baddeley, A.D, & Logie, R.H. (1999). Working memory: The multiple component model. In A. Miyake & P. Shah (Eds.), *Models of working memory*. New York: Cambridge University Press.

Baddeley, A.D., & Wilson, B. (1985). Phonological coding and short-term memory in patients without speech. *Journal of Memory and Language, 24*, 490–502.

Baillargeon, R., & Graber, M. (1988). Evidence of location memory in 8-month-old infants in a nonsearch AB task. *Developmental Psychology, 24,* 502–511.

Bakermans-Kranenburg, M.J., van IJzendoorn, M.H., & Juffer, F. (2003). Less is more: Meta-analyses of sensitivity and attachment interventions in early childhood. *Psychological Bulletin, 129,* 195–215.

Balaz, M.A., Gutsin, P., Cacheiro, H., & Miller, R.R. (1982). Blocking as a retrieval failure: Reactivation of associations to a blocked stimulus. *Quarterly Journal of Experimental Psychology, 34B,* 99–113.

Bales, R.F. (1950). *Interaction process analysis: A method for the study of small groups.* Reading, MA: Addison-Wesley.

Baltesen, R. (2000). Maar het Baan-gevoel blijft. *FEM/DeWeek, 21,* 22–24.

Banaji, M.R., & Crowder, R.G. (1989). The bankruptcy of everyday memory. *American Psychologist, 44,* 1185–1193.

Bancroft, J. (2005). The endocrinology of sexual arousal. *Journal of Endocrinology, 186,* 411–427.

Bandura, A. (1965). Influences of models' reinforcement contingencies on the acquisition of initiative responses. *Journal of Personality and Social Psychology, 1,* 589–593.

Bandura, A. (1973). *Aggression: A social learning analysis.* Englewood Cliffs, NJ: Prentice Hall.

Bandura, A. (1977). *Social learning theory.* Englewood Cliffs, NJ: Prentice Hall.

Bandura, A. (1986). *Social foundations of thought and action: A social cognitive theory.* Englewood Cliffs, NJ: Prentice Hall.

Bandura, A. (1999). Social cognitive theory of personality. In L.A. Pervin & O.P. John (Eds.), *Handbook of personality: Theory and research* (2nd ed.). New York: Guilford Press.

Bandura, A., Ross, D., & Ross, S.A. (1963). Transmission of aggression through imitation of aggressive models. *Journal of Abnormal and Social Psychology, 66,* 3–11.

Banich, M.T. (1997). *Neuropsychology: The neural bases of mental function.* New York: Houghton Mifflin.

Banks, M.S., Aslin, R.N., & Letson, R.D. (1975). Sensitive periods for the development of human binocular vision. *Science, 190,* 675–677.

Banyard, P. (1999). *Controversies in psychology.* London: Routledge.

Bar-On, R. (1997). Bar-On Emotional Quotient Inventory: Technical manual. Toronto: Multi-Health Systems.

Barber, T.X. (1976). *Pitfalls in human research.* Oxford, UK: Pergamon.

Barkley, R.A., Ullman, D.G., Otto, L., & Brecht, J.M. (1977). The effects of sex typing and sex appropriateness of modelled behaviour on children's imitation. *Child Development, 48,* 721–725.

Barlow, D.H., Di Nardo, P.A., Vermilyea, J.A., & Blanchard, E.B. (1986). Comborbidity and depression among the anxiety disorders: Issues in diagnosis and classification. *Journal of Nervous and Mental Disease, 174,* 63–72.

Barlow, D.H., & Durand, V.M. (1995). *Abnormal psychology: An integrative approach.* New York: Brooks/Cole.

Barlow, D.H., Gorman, J.M., Shear, M.K., & Woods, S.W. (2000). Cognitive-behavioral therapy, imipramine, or their combination for panic disorder: A randomized controlled trial. *Journal of the American Medical Association, 283,* 2529–2536.

Baron, R.A. (1977). *Human aggression.* New York: Plenum.

Baron, R.A., & Richardson, D.R. (1993). *Human aggression* (2nd ed.). New York: Plenum.

Baron-Cohen, S., Leslie, A.M., & Frith, U. (1985). Does the autistic child have a "theory of mind"? *Cognition, 21,* 37–46.

Barrett, J.E. (1979). The relationship of life events to the onset of neurotic disorders. In J.E. Barrett (Ed.), *Stress and mental disorder.* New York: Raven Press.

Barrett, L., & Russell, J.A. (1998). Independence and bipolarity in the structure of affect. *Journal of Personality and Social Psychology, 74,* 967–984.

Barrett, L.F., Tugade, M.M., & Engle, R.W. (2004). Individual differences in working memory capacity and dual-process theories of the mind. *Psychological Bulletin, 130,* 553–573.

Barrett, P.T., & Kline, P. (1982). An item and radial parcel analysis of the 16PF Questionnaire. *Personality and Individual Differences, 3,* 259–270.

Barrett, P.T., Petrides, K.V., Eysenck, S.B.G., & Eysenck, H.J. (1998). The Eysenck Personality Questionnaire: An examination of the factorial similarity of P, E, N, and L across 34 countries. *Personality and Individual Differences, 25,* 805–819.

Barrick, M.R., & Mount, M.K. (1993). Autonomy as a moderator of the relationships between the Big 5 personality dimensions and job performance. *Journal of Applied Psychology, 78,* 111–118.

Barron, G., & Yechiam, E. (2002). Private e-mail requests and the diffusion of responsibility. *Computers in Human Behaviour, 18,* 507–520; and *New Scientist* July 20, 2002, p. 9.

Barry, H., & Schlegel, A. (1984). Measurements of adolescent sexual behaviour in the standard sample of societies. *Ethnology, 23,* 315–329.

Bartels, A., & Zeki, S. (2000). The neural basis of romantic love. *NeuroReport, 11,* 3829–3834.

Bartholow, B.D., Anderson, C.A., Carnagey, N.L., & Benjamin, A.J. (2005). Interactive effects of life experience and situational cues on aggression: The weapons priming effect in hunters and non-hunters. *Journal of Experimental Social Psychology, 41,* 48–60.

Bartlett, F.C. (1932). *Remembering.* Cambridge, UK: Cambridge University Press.

Bartolomeo, P., & Chokron, S. (2002). Orienting of attention in left unilateral neglect. *Neuroscience and Biobehavioral Reviews, 26,* 217–234.

Bass, B.M. (1985). *Leadership and performance beyond expectations.* New York: Free Press.

Bass, B.M., Avolio, B.J., Jung, D.I., & Berson, Y. (2003). Predicting unit performance by assessing transformational and transactional leadership. *Journal of Applied Psychology, 88,* 207–218.

Bates, E., Bretherton, I., & Snyder, L. (1988). *From first words to grammar: Individual differences and dissociable mechanisms.* Cambridge, UK: Cambridge University Press.

Batson, C.D., Cochrane, P.J., Biederman, M.F., Blosser, J.L., Ryan, M.J., & Vogt, B. (1978). Failure to help when in a hurry: Callousness or conflict? *Personality and Social Psychology Bulletin, 4,* 97–101.

Bauer, P.J., Hertsgard, L.A., Dropik, P., & Daly B.P. (1998). When even arbitrary order becomes important: Developments in reliable temporal sequencing of arbitrarily ordered events. *Memory, 6,* 165–198.

Bauer, P.J., & Thal, D.J. (1990). Scripts or scraps: Reconsidering the development of sequential understanding. *Journal of Experimental Child Psychology, 50,* 287–304.

Baumeister, R.F. (1995). Self and identity: An introduction. In A. Tesser (Ed.), *Advances in social psychology.* New York: McGraw-Hill.

Baumeister, R.F. (1998). The self. In D.T. Gilbert, S.T. Fiske, & G. Lindzey (Eds.), *Handbook of social psychology* (Vol. 1, 4th ed.). Boston: McGraw-Hill.

Baumeister, R.F. (2000). Gender differences in erotic plasticity: The female sex drive as socially flexible and responsive. *Psychological Bulletin, 126,* 347–374.

Baumeister, R.F., Smart, L., & Boden, J.M. (1996). Relation of threatened egotism to violence and aggression: The dark side of high self-esteem. *Psychological Review, 103,* 5–33.

Bauserman, R. (2002). Child adjustment in joint-custody versus sole-custody arrangements: A meta-analytic review. *Journal of Family Psychology, 16*(1), 91–102.

Baydar, N., & Brooks-Gunn, J. (1991). Effects of maternal employment and child-care arrangments on pre-schoolers' cognitive and behavioral outcomes. *Developmental Psychology, 27*, 932–945.

Baynes, K., & Gazzaniga, M. (2000). Consciousness, introspection, and the split-brain: The two minds/one body problem. In M.S. Gazzaniga (Ed.), *The new cognitive neurosciences*. Cambridge, MA: MIT Press.

Beauvois, M.-F., & Dérouesné, J. (1979). Phonological alexia: Three dissociations. *Journal of Neurology, Neurosurgery and Psychiatry, 42*, 1115–1124.

Beck, A.T. (1967). *Depression: Clinical, experimental and theoretical aspects*. New York: Hoeber Medical Division, Harper & Row.

Beck, A.T. (1976). *Cognitive therapy of the emotional disorders*. New York: New American Library.

Beck, A.T., Emery, G., & Greenberg, R. (1985). *Anxiety disorders and phobias*: A cognitive perspective. New York: Basic Books.

Beck, A.T., & Weishaar, M.E. (1989). Cognitive therapy. In R.J. Corsini & D. Wedding (Eds.), *Current psychotherapies*. Itacca, IL: Peacock.

Behrend, D.A., Harris, L.L., & Cartwright, K.B. (1992). Morphological cues to verb meaning: Verb inflections and the initial mapping of verb meanings. *Journal of Child Language, 22*, 89–106.

Belloc, N.B., & Breslow, L. (1972). Relationship between physical health status and health practices. *Preventive Medicine, 1*, 409–421.

Belmore, S.M. (1987). Determinants of attention during impression formation. *Journal of Experimental Psychology: Learning, Memory, and Cognition, 13*, 480–489.

Belsky, J. (1988). Infant day care and socio-emotional development: The United States. *Journal of Child Psychology and Psychiatry, 29*, 397–406.

Bem, S.L. (1993). *The lenses of gender*. New Haven: Yale University Press.

Benenson, J.F., Morash, D., & Petrakos, H. (1998). Gender differences in emotional closeness between preschool children and their mothers. *Sex Roles, 38*, 975–985.

Bentley, E. (2000). *Awareness: Biorhythms, sleep and dreaming*. London: Routledge.

Benton, D. (2001). Micro-nutrient supplementation and the intelligence of children. *Neuroscience and Biobehavioral Reviews, 25*, 297–309.

Bergeman, C.S., Plomin, R., McClearn, G.E., Pedersen, N.L., & Friberg, L.T. (1988). Genotype–environment interaction in personality development: Identical twins reared apart. *Psychology and Aging, 3*, 399–406.

Berger, R.J., & Phillips, N.H. (1995). Energy conservation and sleep. *Behavioural Brain Research, 69*, 65–73.

Bergin, A.E. (1971). The evaluation of therapeutic outcomes. In A.E. Bergin & S.L. Garfield (Eds.), *Handbook of psychotherapy and behavior change*. New York: Wiley.

Berk, L.E. (1994, November). Why children talk to themselves. *Scientific American*, pp. 60–65.

Berk, L.E. (2006). *Child development* (7th ed.). New York: Pearson.

Berko, J. (1958). The child's learning of English morphology. *Word, 14*, 150–177.

Berkowitz, L. (1968, September). Impulse, aggression and the gun. *Psychology Today*, pp. 18–22.

Berkowitz, L. (1974). Some determinants of impulsive aggression: The role of mediated associations with reinforcements of aggression. *Psychological Review, 81*, 165–176.

Berkowitz, L., & LePage, A. (1967). Weapons as aggression-eliciting stimuli. *Journal of Personality and Social Psychology, 7*, 202–207.

Bermond, B., Nieuwenhuyse, B., Fasotti, L., & Schwerman, J. (1991). Spinal cord lesions, peripheral feedback, and intensities of emotional feelings. *Cognition and Emotion, 5*, 201–220.

Berndt, R.S., Mitchum, C.C., & Haendiges, A.N. (1996). Comprehension of reversible sentences in "agrammatism": A meta-analysis. *Cognition, 58*, 289–308.

Berndt, T.J. (1989). Obtaining support from friends during childhood and adolescence. In D. Belle (Ed.), *Children's social networks and social supports*. New York: Wiley.

Bernstein, W.M., Stephan, W.G., & Davis, M.H. (1979). Explaining attributions for achievement: A path analytic approach. *Journal of Personality and Social Psychology, 37*, 1810–1821.

Berry, J.W. (1969). On cross-cultural comparability. *International Journal of Psychology, 4*, 119–128.

Berscheid, E., & Reis, H.T. (1998). Attraction and close relationships. In D.T. Gilbert, S.T. Fiske, & G. Lindzey (Eds.), *The handbook of social psychology* (Vol. 2, 4th ed.). New York: McGraw-Hill.

Bickerton, D. (1984). The language bioprogram hypothesis. *Behavioural and Brain Sciences, 7*, 173–221.

Biederman, I. (1987). Recognition-by-components: A theory of human image understanding. *Psychological Review, 94*, 115–147.

Biederman, I., & Gerhardstein, P.C. (1993). Recognising depth-rotated objects: Evidence for 3-D viewpoint invariance. *Journal of Experimental Psychology: Human Perception and Performance, 19*, 1162–1182.

Bierhoff, H.-W. (2001). Prosocial behaviour. In M. Hewstone & W. Stroebe (Eds.), *Introduction to social psychology* (3rd ed.). Oxford, UK: Blackwell.

Bishop, D.V.M. (1997). *Uncommon understanding: Development and disorders of language comprehension in children*. Hove, UK: Psychology Press.

Bjorkqvist, K., Lagerspetz, K.M.J., & Kaukianen, A. (1992). Do girls manipulate and boys fight? Developmental trends regarding direct and indirect aggression. *Aggressive Behavior, 18*, 157–166.

Blandin, Y., & Proteau, L. (2000). On the cognitive basis of observational learning: Development of mechanisms for the detection and correction of errors. *Quarterly Journal of Experimental Psychology, 53A*, 846–867.

Blass, T., & Schmitt, C. (2001). The nature of perceived authority in the Milgram paradigm: Two replications. *Current Psychology: Developmental, Learning, Personality, Social, 20*, 115–121.

Bodenhausen, G.V. (1988). Stereotype biases in social decision making: Testing process models of stereotype use. *Journal of Personality and Social Psychology, 55*, 726–737.

Böhner, G. (2001). Attitudes. In M. Hewstone & W. Stroebe (Eds.), *Introduction to social psychology* (3rd ed.). Oxford, UK: Blackwell.

Boland, J.E., & Blodgett, A. (2001). Understanding the constraints on syntactic generation: Lexical bias and discourse congruency effects on eye movements. *Journal of Memory and Language, 45*, 391–411.

Bolger, N., Foster, M., Vinokur, A.D., & Ng, R. (1996). Close relationships and adjustment to a life crisis: The case of breast cancer. *Journal of Personality and Social Psychology, 70*, 283–294.

Bolles, R.C. (1990). A functionalist approach to feeding. In E. Capaldi & T.L. Powley (Eds.), *Taste, experience and feeding*. Washington, DC: American Psychological Association.

Bond, R. (2005). Group size and conformity. *Group Processes and Intergroup Relations, 8*, 331–354.

Bond, R., & Smith, P.B. (1996). Culture and conformity: A meta-analysis of studies using Asch's line judgment task. Psychological Bulletin, 119, 111–137.

Bonta, B.D. (1997). Co-operation and competition in peaceful societies. *Psychological Bulletin, 121*, 299–320.

Booth-Kewley, S., & Friedman, H.S. (1987). Psychological predictors of heart disease: A quantitative review. *Psychological Bulletin, 101*, 343–362.

Bosma, H., Stansfield, S.A., & Marmot, M.G. (1998). Job control, personal characteristics, and heart disease. *Journal of Occupational Health Psychology, 3,* 402–409.

Bossard, J. (1932). Residential propinquity as a factor in marriage selection. *American Journal of Sociology, 38,* 219–224.

Bouchard, T.J., Lykken, D.T., McGue, M., Segal, N.L., & Tellegen, A. (1990). Sources of human psychological differences: The Minnesota study of twins reared apart. *Science, 250,* 223–228.

Bouchard, T.J., & McGue, M. (1981). Familial studies of intelligence: A review. *Science, 212,* 1055–1059.

Bourke, P.A., Duncan, J., & Nimmo-Smith, I. (1996). A general factor involved in dual-task performance decrement. *Quarterly Journal of Experimental Psychology, 49A,* 525–545.

Bowden, E.M., Jung-Beeman, M., Fleck, J., & Kounios, J. (2005). New approaches to demystifying insight. *Trends in Cognitive Sciences, 9,* 322–328.

Bowers, C.A., Weaver, J.L., & Morgan, B.B. (1996). Moderating the performance effects of stressors. In J.E. Driskell & E. Salas (Eds.), *Stress and human performance.* Mahwah, NJ: Lawrence Erlbaum Associates, Inc.

Bowlby, J. (1946). *Forty-four juvenile thieves.* London: Bailliere, Tindall & Cox.

Bowlby, J. (1951). *Maternal care and mental health.* Geneva: World Health Organization.

Bowlby, J. (1969). *Attachment and love: Vol. 1. Attachment.* London: Hogarth.

Bowlby, J. (1988). *A secure base: Clinical applications of attachment theory.* London: Routledge.

Brace, C.L. (1996). Review of *The Bell Curve. Current Anthropology, 37,* 5157–5161.

Bracht, G.H., & Glass, G.V. (1968). The external validity of experiments. *American Educational Research Research Journal, 5,* 437–474.

Brackett, M., Mayer, J.D., & Warner, R.M. (2004). Emotional intelligence and the prediction of behaviour. *Personality and Individual Differences, 36,* 1387–1402.

Bradbard, M.R., Martin, C.L., Endsley, R.C., & Halverson, C.F. (1986). Influence of sex stereotypes on children's exploration and memory: A competence versus performance distinction. *Developmental Psychology, 22,* 481–486.

Bradbury, T.N., & Fincham, F.D. (1990). Attributions in marriage: Review and critique. *Psychological Bulletin, 107,* 3–33.

Bradbury, T.N., & Fincham, F.D. (1992). Attributions and behavior in marital interaction. *Journal of Personality and Social Psychology, 63,* 613–628.

Bradmetz, J. (1999). Precursors of formal thought: A longitudinal study. *British Journal of Developmental Psychology, 17,* 61–81.

Brainerd, C.J. (2003). Jean Piaget, learning research, and American education. In B.J. Zimmerman & D.H. Schuunk (Eds.), *Educational psychology: A century of contributions.* Mahwah, NJ: Lawrence Erlbaum Associates, Inc.

Bransford, J.D., & Johnson, M.K. (1972). Contextual prerequisites for understanding: Some investigations of comprehension and recall. *Journal of Verbal Learning and Verbal Behavior, 11,* 717–726.

Braun, R., Balkin, T.J., Wesensten, N.J., Carson, R.E., Varga, M., Baldwin, P., et al. (1997). Regional blood flow throughout the sleep–wake cycle: An $H_2^{15}O$ PET study. *Brain, 120,* 1173–1197.

Brehm, S.S., Kassin, S.M., & Fein, S. (2005). *Social psychology* (6th ed.). Boston, MA: Houghton Mifflin.

Breland, K., & Breland, M. (1961). The misbehaviour of organisms. *American Psychologist, 61,* 681–684.

Breslow, L., & Enstrom, J.E. (1980). Persistence of health habits and their relationship to mortality. *Preventive Medicine, 9,* 469–483.

Brett, D.J., & Cantor, J. (1988). The portrayal of men and women in US television commercials: A recent content analysis and trends over 15 years. *Sex Roles, 18,* 595–609.

Brewer, M.B., Dull, V., & Lui, L. (1981). Perceptions of the elderly: Stereotypes as prototypes. *Journal of Personality and Social Psychology, 41,* 656–670.

Brickman, P., Rabinowitz, V.C., Karuza, J., Coates, D., Cohn, E., & Kidder, L. (1982). Models of helping and coping. *American Psychologist, 37,* 368–384.

Bringuier, J.C. (1980). *Conversations with Jean Piaget.* Chicago: University of Chicago Press.

Broadbent, D.E. (1958). *Perception and communication.* Oxford, UK: Pergamon.

Bronfenbrenner, U. (1979). *The ecology of human development: Experiments by nature and design.* Cambridge, MA: Harvard University Press.

Brooks-Gunn, J., Klebanov, P.K., & Duncan, G.J. (1996). Ethnic differences in children's intelligence test scores: Role of economic deprivation, home environment, and maternal characteristics. *Child Development, 67,* 396–408.

Brooks-Gunn, J., & Lewis, M. (1981). Infant social perception: Responses to pictures of parents and strangers. *Developmental Psychology, 17,* 647–649.

Brown, A.S., Bracken, E., Zoccoli, S., & Douglas, K. (2004). Generating and remembering passwords. *Applied Cognitive Psychology, 18,* 641–651.

Brown, G.W. (1989). Depression. In G.W. Brown & T.O. Harris (Eds.), *Life events and illness.* New York: Guilford Press.

Brown, G.W., & Harris, T. (1978). *Social origins of depression.* London: Tavistock.

Brown, R. (1973). *A first language: The early stages.* London: George Allen & Unwin.

Brown, R. (1986). *Social psychology* (2nd ed.). New York: The Free Press.

Brown, R., Fraser, C., & Bellugi, U. (1964). The acquisition of language. *Monographs of the Society for Research in Child Development, 29,* 92.

Brown, R., & Kulik, J. (1977). Flashbulb memories. *Cognition, 5,* 73–99.

Brown, R., & McNeill, D. (1966). The "tip of the tongue" phenomenon. *Journal of Verbal Learning and Verbal Behavior, 5,* 325–327.

Brown, R.J. (2000). *Group processes: Dynamics within and between groups* (2nd ed.). Oxford, UK: Blackwell.

Brown, R.J., Vivian, J., & Hewstone, M. (1999). Changing attitudes through intergroup contact: The effects of group membership salience. *European Journal of Social Psychology, 29,* 741–764.

Bruch, M.A., & Heimberg, R.G. (1994). Differences in perceptions of parental and personal between generalized and nongeneralized social phobics. *Journal of Anxiety Disorders, 8,* 155–168.

Bruck, M., & Ceci, S.J. (1999). The suggestibility of children's memory. *Annual Review of Psychology, 50,* 419–439.

Bruck, M., Ceci, S.J., & Hembrooke, H. (1997). Children's reports of pleasant and unpleasant events. In D. Read & S. Lindsay (Eds.), *Recollections of trauma: Scientific research and clinical practice.* New York: Plenum.

Bruck, M., & Melnyk, L. (2004). Individual differences in children's suggestibility: A review and synthesis. *Applied Cognitive Psychology, 18,* 947–996.

Brugha, T.S., Bebbington, P.E., Stretch, D.D., MacCarthy, B., & Wykes, T. (1997). Predicting the short-term outcome of first episodes and recurrences of clinical depression: A prospective study of life events, difficulties, and social support networks. *Journal of Clinical Psychiatry, 58,* 298–306.

Bukowski, W.M., Hoza, B., & Boivin, M. (1994). Measuring friendship quality during pre- and early adolescence: The development and psychometric properties of the Friendship Qualities Scale. Journal of Social and Personal Relationships, 11, 471–484.

Bulik, C.M, Sullivan, P.F., & Kendler, K.S. (2003). Genetic and environmental contributions to obesity and binge eating. *International Journal of Eating Disorders, 33*, 293–298.

Burger, J.M. (1993). *Personality* (3rd ed.). Pacific Grove, CA: Brooks/Cole.

Burgess, R.L., & Wallin, P. (1953). Marital happiness of parents and their children's attitudes to them. *American Sociological Review, 18*, 424–431.

Burleseon, B.R., & Kunkel, A. (2002). Parental and peer contributions to the emotional support skills of the child: From whom do children learn to express support? *Journal of Family Communication, 2*, 81–97.

Burman, E., & Parker, I. (1993). *Discourse analytic research: Repertoires and readings of texts in action*. London: Routledge.

Burns, B.D. (2004). The effects of speed on skilled chess performance. *Psychological Science, 15*, 442–447.

Burnstein, E., Crandall, C., & Kitayama, S. (1994). Some neo-Darwinian roles for altruism: Weighing cues for inclusive fitness as a function of the biological importance of the decision. *Journal of Personality and Social Psychology, 67*, 773–789.

Bushman, B.J., & Anderson, C.A. (2001). Is it time to pull the plug on the hostile versus instrumental aggression dichotomy? *Psychological Review, 108*, 273–279.

Bushman, B.J., & Baumeister, R.F. (1998). Threatened egotism, narcissism, self-esteem, and direct and displaced aggression: Does self-love or self-hate lead to violence? *Journal of Personality and Social Psychology, 75*, 219–229.

Bushman, B.J., Baumeister, R.F., & Stack, A.D. (1999). Catharsis, aggression, and persuasive influence: Self-fulfilling or self-defeating prophecies? *Journal of Personality & Social Psychology, 76(3)*, 367–376.

Buss, D.M. (1989). Sex differences in human mate preferences: Evolutionary hypotheses tested in 37 cultures. *Behavioral and Brain Sciences, 12*, 1–49.

Buss, D.M. (1999). *Evolutionary psychology: The new science of the mind*. Boston: Allyn & Bacon.

Bussey, K., & Bandura, A. (1999). Social cognitive theory of gender development and differentiation. *Psychological Review, 106*, 676–713.

Butler, A.C., Chapman, J.E., Forman, E.M., & Beck, A.T. (2005). The empirical status of cognitive-behavioural therapy: A review of meta-analyses. *Clinical Psychology Review, 26*, 17–31.

Buunk, B.P., Angleitner, A., Oubaid, V., & Buss, D.M. (1996). Sex differences in jealousy in evolutionary and cultural perspective. *Psychological Science, 7*, 359–363.

Byrne, D. (1971). *The attraction paradigm*. New York: Academic Press.

Cabanac, M., & Rabe, E.F. (1976). Influence of a monotonous food on body weight regulation in humans. *Physiology and Behavior, 17*, 675–678.

Cahn, B.R., & Polich, J. (2006). Meditation states and traits: EEG, ERP, and neuroimaging studies. *Psychological Bulletin, 132*, 180–211.

Cairns, R. (1986). Predicting aggression in girls and boys. *Social Science, 71*, 16–21.

Calvert, S.L., & Kotler, J.A. (2003). Lessons from children's television: The impact of the children's Television Act on children's learning. *Journal of Applied Developmental Psychology, 24*, 275–335.

Camerer, C., Babcock, L., Loewenstein, G., & Thaler, R. (1997). Labor supply of New York City cabdrivers: One day at a time? *Quarterly Journal of Economics, CXII*, 407–441.

Cameron, C.M., & Gatewood, J.B. (2003). Seeking numinous experiences in the unremembered past (1). (Survey suggests Americans visit heritage sites for spiritual reasons) *Ethnology, 42*, 55–72.

Campbell, A., Shirley, L., & Candy, J. (2004). A longitudinal study of gender-related cognition and behaviour. *Developmental Science, 7*, 1–9.

Campbell, D.T., & Stanley, J.C. (1966). *Experimental and quasi-experimental designs for research*. Chicago: Rand McNally.

Campbell, J.D. (1986). Similarity and uniqueness: The effects of attribute type, relevance, and individual differences in self-esteem and depression. *Journal of Personality and Social Psychology, 50*, 281–294.

Campbell, J.D., Chew, B., & Scratchley, L.S. (1991). Cognitive and emotional reactions to daily events: The effects of self-esteem and self-complexity. *Journal of Personality, 59*, 473–505.

Campbell, W.K., & Sedikides, C. (1999). Self-threat magnifies the self-serving bias: A meta-analytic integration. *Review of General Psychology, 3*, 23–43.

Campfield, L.A., Smith, F.J., Guisez, Y., Devos, R., & Burn, P. (1995). Recombinant mouse OB protein: Evidence for a peripheral signal linking adiposity and central neural networks. *Science, 269*, 546–549.

Caprara, G.V., Barbaranelli, C., & Pastorelli, C. (1998). *Comparative test of longitudinal predictiveness of personal self-efficacy and big five factors*. Paper presented at the European conference on Personality, University of Surrey, UK.

Capron, C., & Duyne, M. (1989). Assessment of effects of socio-economic status on IQ in a full cross-fostering study. *Nature, 340*, 552–554.

Cardwell, M., Clark, L., & Meldrum, C. (1996). *Psychology for A level*. London: Collins Educational.

Carey, M.P., Kalra, D.L., Carey, K.B., Halperin, S., & Richard, C.S. (1993). Stress and unaided smoking cessation: A prospective investigation. *Journal of Consulting and Clinical Psychology, 61*, 831–838.

Carlsmith, H., Ellsworth, P., & Aronson, E. (1976). *Methods of research in social psychology*. Reading, MA: Addison-Wesley.

Carlson, K.A., & Russo, J.E. (2001). Biased interpretation of evidence by mock jurors. *Journal of Experimental Psychology: Applied, 7*, 91–103.

Carlson, M., Marcus-Newhall, A., & Miller, N. (1990). Effects of situational aggression cues: A quantitative review. *Journal of Personality and Social Psychology, 58*, 622–633.

Carroll, J.B. (1986). Factor analytic investigations of cognitive abilities. In S.E. Newstead, S.H. Irvine, & P.L. Dann (Eds.), *Human assessment: Cognition and motivation*. Dordrecht, The Netherlands: Nyhoff.

Carroll, J.B. (1993). *Human cognitive abilities: A survey of factor analytic studies*. New York: Cambridge University Press.

Cartwright, D.S. (1979). *Theories and models of personality*. Dubuque, IO: Brown Company.

Cartwright, S., & Cooper, C.L. (1997). *Managing workplace stress*. Thousand Oaks, CA: Sage.

Carver, C.S., Pozo, C., Harris, S.D., Noriega, V., Scheier, M., Robinson, D., et al. (1993). How coping mediates the effect of optimism on distress: A study of women with early stage breast cancer. *Journal of Personality and Social Psychology, 65*, 375–390.

Carver, C.S., & Scheier, M.F. (2000). *Perspectives on personality* (4th ed.). Boston: Allyn & Bacon.

Caspi, A., Moffitt, T.E., Newman, D.L., & Silva, P.A. (1996). Behavioral observations at age 3 years predict adult psychiatric disorders: Longitudinal evidence from a birth cohort. *Archives of General Psychiatry, 53*, 1033–1039.

Cast, A.D., & Burke, P. (2002). A theory of self-esteem. *Social Forces, 80(3)*, 1041–1068.

Cattell, R.B. (1946). *Description and measurement of personality*. Dubuque, IA: Brown Company Publishers.

Cattell, R.B. (1957). *Personality and motivation structure and measurement*. New York: World Book Company.

Ceci, S.J., & Liker, J.K. (1986). A day at the races: A study of IQ, expertise, and cognitive complexity. *Journal of Experimental Psychology: General, 115*, 255–266.

Central Statistical Office (1996). *Social trends*. London: Central Statistical Office.

Cha, J.-H., & Nam, K.D. (1985). A test of Kelley's cube theory of attribution: A cross-cultural replication of McArthur's study. *Korean Social Science Journal, 12*, 151–180.

Chaiken, S. (1987). The heuristic model of persuasion. In M.P. Zanna, J.M. Olson, & C.P. Herman (Eds.), *Social influence: The Ontario symposium* (Vol. 5). Hillsdale, NJ: Lawrence Erlbaum Associates, Inc.

Chaiken, S., & Eagly, A.H., (1983). Communication modality as a determinant of persuasion: The role of communicator salience. *Journal of Personality and Social Psychology, 45*, 241–256.

Chaiken, S., Giner-Sorolla, R., & Chen, S. (1996). Beyond accuracy: Defense and impression motives in heuristic and systematic information processing. In P.M. Gollwitzer & J.A. Bargh (Eds.), *The psychology of action: Linking cognition and motivation to behavior*. New York: Guilford Press.

Chaiken, S., & Maheswaran, D. (1994). Heuristic processing can bias systematic processing: Effects of source credibility, argument ambiguity, and task importance on attitude judgment. *Journal of Personality and Social Psychology, 66*, 460–473.

Challman, R.C. (1932). Factors influencing friendships among pre-school children. *Child Development, 3*, 146–158.

Chan, A.S., Ho, Y.-C., & Cheung, M.-C. (1998). Music training improves verbal memory. *Nature, 396*(6707), 128.

Channon, S., Shanks, D., Johnstone, T., Vakili, K., Chin, J., & Sinclair, E. (2002). Is implicit learning spared in amnesia? Rule abstraction and item familiarity in artificial grammar learning. *Neuropsychologica, 40*, 2185–2197.

Charlton, A. (1998, January 12). TV violence has little impact on children, study finds. *The Times*, p. 5.

Charness, N. (1981). Search in chess: Age and skill differences. *Journal of Experimental Psychology: Human Perception and Performance, 7*, 467–476.

Chase, W.G., & Simon, H.A. (1973). Perception in chess. *Cognitive Psychology, 4*, 55–81.

Chen, Z., & Klahr, D. (1999). All other things being equal: Children's acquisition of the control of variable strategy. *Child Development, 709*, 1098–1120.

Cherry, E.C. (1953). Some experiments on the recognition of speech with one and two ears. *Journal of the Acoustical Society of America, 25*, 975–979.

Cheung, F.M., & Leung, K. (1998). Indigenous personality measures: Chinese examples. *Journal of Cross-Cultural Psychology, 29*, 233–248.

Chi, M.T. (1978). Knowledge, structure and memory development. In R.S. Siegler (Ed.), *Children's thinking: What develops?* Hillsdale, NJ: Lawrence Erlbaum Associates, Inc.

Child, I.L. (1968). Personality in culture. In E.F. Borgatta & W.W. Lambert (Eds.), *Handbook of personality theory and research*. Chicago: Rand McNally.

Choi, I., Choi, K.W., & Cha, J.-H. (1992). *A cross-cultural replication of Festinger and Carlsmith (1959)*. Unpublished manuscript, Seoul National University, Korea.

Choi, I., & Nisbett, R.E. (1998). Situational salience and cultural differences in the correspondence bias and actor–observer bias. *Personality and Social Psychology Bulletin, 24*, 949–960.

Chomsky, N. (1965). *Aspects of the theory of syntax*. Cambridge, MA: MIT Press.

Chomsky, N. (1986). *Knowledge of language: Its nature, origin, and use*. New York: Praeger.

Church, A.T., & Katigbak, M.S. (2000). Trait psychology in the Philippines. *American Behavioral Science, 44*, 73–94.

Churchland, P.S., & Sejnowski, T.J. (1991). Perspectives on cognitive neuroscience. In R.G. Lister & H.J. Weingartner (Eds.), *Perspectives on cognitive neuroscience*. Oxford, UK: Oxford University Press.

Cialdini, R.B., & Goldstein, N.J. (2004). Social influence: Compliance and conformity. *Annual Review of Psychology, 55*, 591–621

Cillessen, A.H.N., Van IJzendoorn, H.W., van Lieshout, C.F.M., & Hartup, W.W. (1992). Heterogeneity among peer-rejected boys: Subtypes and stabilities. *Child Development, 63*, 893–905.

Cinnirella, M. (1998). Manipulating stereotype ratings tasks: Understanding questionnaire context effects on measures of attitudes, social identity and stereotypes. *Journal of Community and Applied Social Psychology, 8*, 345–362.

Clancy, S.A., Schacter, D.L., McNally, R.J., & Pitman, R.K. (2000). False recognition in women reporting recovered memories of sexual abuse. *Psychological Science, 11*, 26–31.

Clancy, S.M., & Dollinger, S.J. (1993). Photographic depictions of the self: Gender and age differences in social connectedness. *Sex Roles, 29*, 477–495.

Claparède, E. (1911). Recognition et moitié. *Archives de Psychologie, 11*, 75–90.

Clark, D.M. (1986). A cognitive approach to panic. *Behaviour Research and Therapy, 24*, 461–470.

Clark, D.M. (1996). Panic disorder: From theory to therapy. In P. Salkovskis (Ed.), *Frontiers of cognitive therapy*. New York: Guilford Press.

Clark, D.M., & Wells, A. (1995). A cognitive model of social phobia. In R.R.G. Heimberg, M. Liebowitz, D.A. Hope, & S. Scheier (Eds.), *Social phobia: Diagnosis, assessment and treatment*. New York: Guilford.

Clark, R.D., & Hatfield, E. (1989). Gender differences in receptivity to sexual offers. *Journal of Psychology and Human Sexuality, 2*, 39–55.

Clarke-Stewart, A. (1989). Infant day care: Maligned or malignant? *American Psychologist, 44*, 266–273.

Claxton, G. (1980). Cognitive psychology: A suitable case for what sort of treatment? In G. Claxton (Ed.), *Cognitive psychology: New directions*. London: Routledge & Kegan Paul.

Cleeremans, A., & Jiménez, L. (2002). Implicit learning and consciousness: A graded, dynamic perspective. In R.M. French & A. Cleeremans (Eds.), *Implicit learning and consciousness: An empirical, philosophical and computational consensus in the making*. Hove, UK: Psychology Press.

Cobos, P., Sánchez, M., Pérez, N., & Vila, J. (2004). Effects of spinal cord injuries on the subjective component of emotions. *Cognition and Emotion, 18*, 281–287.

Coch, D., Sanders, L.D., & Neville, H.J. (2005). An event-related potential study of selective auditory attention in children and adults. *Journal of Cognitive Neuroscience, 17*, 605–622.

Coenen, A. (2000). The divorce of REM sleep and dreaming. *Behavioral and Brain Sciences, 23*, 922–924.

Cohen, F., & Lazarus, R.S. (1973). Active coping processes, coping dispositions, and recovery from surgery. *Psychosomatic Medicine, 35*, 375–389.

Cohen, S., & Williamson, G.M. (1991). Stress and infectious disease in humans. *Psychological Bulletin, 109*, 5–24.

Coie, J.D., Dodge, K.A., & Coppotelli, H. (1982). Dimensions and types of social status: A cross-age perspective. *Developmental Psychology, 18*, 557–570.

Colby, A., Kohlberg, L., Gibbs, J., & Lieberman, M. (1983). A longitudinal study of moral judgement. *Monographs of the Society for Research in Child Development, 48*(Nos. 1–2, Serial No. 200).

Cole, M., & Cole, S.R. (1993). *The development of children* (2nd ed.). New York: Scientific American Books.

Cole, M., Gay, J., Glick, J., & Sharp, D.W. (1971). *The cultural context of learning and thinking*. New York: Basic Books.

Collette, F., & Van der Linden, M. (2002). Brain imaging of the central executive component of working memory. *Neuroscience & Biobehavioral Reviews, 26,* 105–125.

Collins, D.L., Baum, A., & Singer, J.E. (1983). Coping with chronic stress at Three Mile Island: Psychological and biochemical evidence. *Health Psychology, 2,* 149–166.

Colman, A.M. (2001). *Oxford dictionary of psychology.* Oxford, UK: Oxford University Press.

Coltheart, M. (2001). Assumptions and methods in cognitive neuropsychology. In A. Rapp (Ed.). *Handbook of cognitive neuropsychology.* Philadelphia: Psychology Press.

Coltheart, M., Rastle, K., Perry, C., Langdon, R., & Ziegler, J. (2001). The DRC model: A model of visual word recognition and reading aloud. *Psychological Review, 108,* 204–258.

Colvin, C.R., Block. J., & Funder, D.C. (1995). Overly positive self-evaluation and personality: Negative implications for mental health. *Journal of Personality and Social Psychology, 6,* 1152–1162.

Comer, R.J. (2001). *Abnormal psychology* (4th ed.). New York: Worth.

Comer, R.J. (2007). *Abnormal psychology* (6th ed.). New York: Worth.

Comstock, G., & Paik, H. (1991). *Television and the American child.* San Diego, CA: Academic Press.

Conboy, B.T., & Thal, D.J. (2006). Ties between the lexicon and grammar: Cross-sectional and longitudinal studies of bilingual toddlers. *Child Development, 77,* 712–735.

Condry, J., & Condry, S. (1976). Sex differences: A study in the eye of the beholder. *Child Development, 47,* 812–819.

Conner, D.B., Knight, D.K., & Cross, D.R. (1997). Mothers' and fathers' scaffolding of their 2-year-olds during problem-solving and literary interactions. *British Journal of Developmental Psychology, 15,* 323–338.

Conner, M., & Armitage, C.J. (1998). Extending the theory of planned behaviour: A review and avenues for further research. *Journal of Applied Social Psychology, 28,* 1429–1464.

Considine, R.V., Sinha, M.K., Heiman, M.L., Kriauciunas, A., Stephens, T.W., Nyce, M.R. et al. (1996). Serum immunoreactive-leptin concentrations in normal-weight and obese humans. *New England Journal of Medicine, 334,* 292.

Conway, A.R.A., Cowan, N., & Bunting, M.F. (2001). The cocktail party phenomenon revisited: The importance of working memory capacity. *Psychonomic Bulletin & Review, 8,* 331–335.

Conway, M.A., & Holmes, A. (2004). Psychosocial stages and the accessibility of autobiographical memories across the life cycle. *Journal of Personality, 72,* 461–480.

Conway, M.A., & Pleydell-Pearce, C.W. (2000). The construction of autobiographical memories in the self-memory system. *Psychological Review, 107,* 261–288.

Conway, M.A., & Rubin, D.C. (1993). The structure of autobiographical memory. In A.F. Collins, S.E. Gathercole, M.A. Conway, & P.E. Morris (Eds.). *Theories of memory.* Hove, UK: Psychology Press.

Cook, A.E., & Myers, J.L. (2004). Processing discourse roles in scripted narratives: The influences of context and world knowledge. *Journal of Memory and Language, 50,* 268–288.

Cook, M. (1993). *Personnel selection and productivity* (Rev. ed.). New York: Wiley.

Coolican, H. (1994). *Research methods and statistics in psychology* (2nd ed.). London: Hodder & Stoughton.

Coolican, H. (1998). Research methods. In M.W. Eysenck (Ed.), *Psychology: An integrated approach.* London: Addison-Wesley-Longman.

Cooney, J.W., & Gazzaniga, M.S. (2003). Neurological disorders and the structure of human consciousness. *Trends in Cognitive Sciences, 7,* 161–165.

Cooper, C. (2002). *Individual differences* (2nd ed.). London: Arnold.

Corbetta, M., & Shulman, G.L. (2002). Control of goal-directed and stimulus-driven attention in the brain. *Nature Reviews Neuroscience, 3,* 201–215.

Cosentino, S., Chute, D., Libon, D., Moore, P., & Grossman, M. (2006). How does the brain support script comprehension? A study of executive processes and semantic knowledge in dementia. *Neuropsychology, 20,* 307–318.

Costa, P.T., & McCrae, R.R. (1992). *NEO–PI–R, Professional manual.* Odessa, FL: Psychological Assessment Resources.

Cowan, N. (2000). The magical number 4 in short-term memory: A reconsideration of mental storage capacity. *Behavioral and Brain Sciences, 24,* 87–185.

Craik, F.I.M., & Lockhart, R.S. (1972). Levels of processing: A framework for memory research. *Journal of Verbal Learning and Verbal Behavior, 11,* 671–684.

Crick, N.R., & Dodge, K.A. (1994). A review and reformulation of social information-processing mechanisms in children's social adjustment. *Psychological Bulletin, 115,* 74–101.

Crick, N.R., & Ladd, G.W. (1990). Children's perceptions of the outcomes of aggressive strategies: Do the ends justify being mean? *Developmental Psychology, 26,* 612–620.

Crisp, R.J., Stone, C.H., & Hall, N.R. (2006). Recategorisation and subgroup identification: Predicting and preventing threats from common ingroups. *Personality and Social Psychology Bulletin, 32,* 230–243.

Cronbach, L.J. (1957). The two disciplines of scientific psychology. *American Psychologist, 12,* 671–684.

Cross, D.G., Sheehan, P.W., & Khan, J.A. (1980). Alternative advice and counsel in psychotherapy. *Journal of Consulting and Clinical Psychology, 48,* 615–625.

Cross, S.E., & Madson, L. (1997). Models of the self: Self-construals and gender. *Psychological Bulletin, 122,* 5–37.

Crystal, D. (1997). *A dictionary of linguistics and phonetics* (4th ed). Cambridge, MA: Blackwell.

Cumberbatch, G. (1990). *Television advertising and sex role stereotyping: A content analysis* (Working paper IV for the Broadcasting Standards Council). Communications Research Group, Aston University, Birmingham, UK.

Cunningham, M.R. (1986). Measuring the physical in physical attractiveness: Quasi experiments on the sociobiology of female facial beauty. *Journal of Personality and Social Psychology, 50,* 925–935.

Cunningham, W.A., Preacher, K.J., & Banaji, M.R. (2001). Implicit attitude measures: Consistency, stability, and convergent validity. *Psychological Science, 12,* 163–170.

Curtis, A. (1997). Discourse analysis—The search for meanings. *Psychology Review, 4,* 23–25.

Curtis, A. (2000). *Psychology and health.* London: Routledge.

Curtiss, S. (1977). *Genie: A psycholinguistic study of a modern-day "wild child."* London: Academic Press.

Cutler, A., & Butterfield, S. (1992). Rhythmic cues to speech segmentation: Evidence from juncture misperception. *Journal of Memory and Language, 31,* 218–236.

Czeisler, C.A., Duffy, J.F., Shanahan, T.L., Brown, E.N., Mitchell, J.F., Rimmer, D.W., et al. (1999). Stability, precision, and near-24-hour period of the human circadian pacemaker. *Science, 284,* 2177–2181.

Dalgleish, T. (1998). Emotion. In M.W. Eysenck (Ed.), *Psychology: An integrated approach.* Harlow, UK: Longman.

Damasio, H., Grabowski, T., Frank, R., Galaburda, A.M., & Damasio, A.R. (1994). The return of Phineas Gage: The skull of a famous patient yields clues about the brain. *Science, 264,* 1102–1105.

Dane, F.C. (1994). Survey methods, naturalistic observations, and case-studies. In A.M. Colman (Ed.), *Companion encyclopaedia of psychology* (Vol. 2). London: Routledge.

Daneman, M., & Carpenter, P.A. (1980). Individual differences in working memory and reading. *Journal of Verbal Learning and Verbal Behavior, 19,* 450–466.

Darley, J.M., & Batson, C.D. (1973). From Jerusalem to Jericho: A study of situational and dispositional variables in helping behaviour. *Journal of Personality and Social Psychology, 27,* 100–108.

Darley, J.M., & Latané, B. (1968). Bystander intervention in emergencies: Diffusion of responsibility. *Journal of Personality and Social Psychology, 8,* 377–383.

Darwin, C. (1859). *The origin of species.* London: Macmillan.

David, B., & Turner, J.C. (1999). Studies in self-categorization and minority conversion: The in-group minority in intragroup and intergroup contexts. *British Journal of Social Psychology, 38,* 115–134.

David, D.H., & Lyons-Ruth, K. (2005). Differential attachment responses of male and female infants to frightening maternal behaviour: Tend or befriend versus fight or flight? *Infant Mental Health Journal, 26,* 1–18.

Davies, M., Stankov, L., & Roberts, R.D. (1998). Emotional intelligence: In search of an elusive construct. *Journal of Personality and Social Psychology, 75,* 989–1015.

Davis, M. (2001). Tonight's the night. *New Scientist, 170*(2296), 12.

Davison, G.C., & Neale, J.M. (1998). *Abnormal psychology* (7th ed.). New York: Wiley.

Davison, H.K., & Burke, M.J. (2000). Sex discrimination in simulated employment contexts: A meta-analytic investigation. *Journal of Vocational* Behavior, 56, 225–248.

Dawson, M.E., & Schell, A.M. (1983). Electrodermal responses to attended and non-attended significant stimuli during dichotic listening. *Journal of Experimental Psychology: Human Perception and Performance, 8,* 315–324.

Dawson, T.L. (2002). New tools, new insights: Kohlberg's moral judgment stages revisited. *International Journal of Behavioral Development, 26,* 154–166.

Day, R., Nielsen, J.A., Korten, A., Ernberg, G., et al. (1987). Stressful life events preceding the acute onset of schizophrenia: A cross-national study from the World Health Organization. *Culture, Medicine and Psychiatry, 11,* 123–205.

De Boysson-Bardies, B., Sagart, L., & Durand, C. (1984). Discernible differences in the babbling of infants according to target language. *Journal of Child Language, 11,* 1–16.

De Castro, J.M., & de Castro, E.S. (1989). Spontaneous meal patterns of humans: Influence of the presence of other people. *American Journal of Clinical Nutrition, 50,* 237–247.

De Corte, E. (2003). Transfer as the productive use of acquired knowledge, skills, and motivation. *Current Directions in Psychological Science, 12,* 142–146.

De Groot, A.D. (1965). *Thought and choice in chess.* The Hague, The Netherlands: Mouton.

De Knuif, P. (1945). *The male hormone.* New York: Harcourt Brace & Co.

De Wolff, M.S., & van IJzendoorn, M.H. (1997). Sensitivity and attachment: A meta-analysis on parental antecedents of infant attachment. *Child Development, 68,* 571–591.

Deater-Deckard, K. (2001). Annotation: Recent research examining the role of peer relationships in the development of psychopathology. *Journal of Child Psychology and Psychiatry, 42,* 565–579.

Deaux, K. (1985). Sex and gender. *Annual Review of Psychology, 36,* 49–81.

Deaux, K., & Wrightsman, L.S. (1988). *Social psychology* (5th ed.). Pacific Grove, CA: Brooks/Cole.

Debner, J.A., & Jacoby, L.L. (1994). Unconscious perception: Attention, awareness and control. *Journal of Experimental Psychology: Learning, Memory, and Cognition, 20,* 304–317.

Defeyter, M.A., & German, T.P. (2003). Acquiring an understanding of design: Evidence from children's insight problem solving. *Cognition, 89,* 133–155.

Dehaene, S., & Naccache, L. (2001). Towards a cognitive neuroscience of consciousness: Basic evidence and workspace framework. *Cognition, 79,* 1–37.

Dehaene, S., Naccache, L., Cohen, L., Le Bihan, D., Mangin, J., Poline, J., et al. (2001). Cerebral mechanisms of word masking and unconscious repetition priming, *Nature Neuroscience, 4,* 752–758.

Dehaene, S., Naccache, L., Le Cle'H, G., Koechlin, E., Mueller, M., Dehaene-Lambertz, G., et al. (1998). Imaging unconscious semantic priming. *Nature, 395,* 597–600.

Delahanty, D.L., Dougall, A.L., Hawken, L., Trakowski, J.H., Schmitz, J.B., Jenkins, F.J., et al. (1996). Time course of natural killer cell activity and lymphocyte proliferation in healthy men. *Health Psychology, 15,* 48–55.

Delaney, P.F., Ericsson, K.A., & Knowles, M.E. (2004). Immediate and sustained effects of planning in a problem-solving task. *Journal of Experimental Psychology: Learning, Memory, and Cognition, 30,* 1219–1234.

Dell, G.S. (1986). A spreading-activation theory of retrieval in sentence production. *Psychological Review, 93,* 283–321.

Dell, G.S., & O'Seaghdha, P.G. (1991). Mediated and convergent lexical priming in language production: A comment on Levelt et al. (1991). *Psychological Review, 98,* 604–614.

DeLucia, P.R., & Hochberg, J. (1991). Geometrical illusions in solid objects under ordinary viewing conditions. *Perception and Psychophysics, 50,* 547–554.

Denollet, J. (2005). DS14: Standard assessment of negative affectivity, social inhibition, and Type D personality. *Psychosomatic Medicine, 67,* 89–97.

Denollet, J., Sys, S.U., Stroobant, N., Rombouts, H., Gillebert, T.C., & Brutsaert, D.L. (1996). Personality as independent predictor of long-term mortality in patients with coronary heart disease. *Lancet, 347,* 417–421.

Deutsch, J.A., & Deutsch, D. (1963). Attention: Some theoretical considerations. *Psychological Review, 70,* 80–90.

Deutsch, M., & Gerard, H.B. (1955). A study of normative and informational influence upon individual judgement. *Journal of Abnormal and Social Psychology, 51,* 629–636.

DeVries, R. (2000). Vygotsky, Piaget, and education: A reciprocal assimilation of theories and educational practices. *New Ideas in Psychology, 18,* 187–213.

Dickens, W.T., & Flynn, J.R. (2001). Heritability estimates versus large environmental effects: The IQ paradox resolved. *Psychological Review, 108,* 346–369.

Dickerson, F.B., Tenhula, W.N., & Green-Paden, L.D. (2005). The token economy for schizophrenia: Review of the literature and recommendations for future research. *Schizophrenia Research, 75,* 405–416.

Dickerson, S.S., & Kemeny, M.E. (2004). Acute stressors and cortisol responses: A theoretical integration and synthesis of laboratory research. *Psychological Bulletin, 130,* 355–391.

Dickinson, A., & Dawson, G.R. (1987). Pavlovian processes in the motivational control of instrumental performance. *Quarterly Journal of Experimental Psychology B, 39,* 201–213.

Diener, E. (1980). Deindividuation: The absence of self-awareness and self-regulation in group members. In P.B. Paulus (Ed.), *Psychology of group influence.* Hillsdale, NJ: Lawrence Erlbaum Associates, Inc.

Dietrich, A. (2003). Functional neuroanatomy of altered states of awareness: The transient hypofrontality hypothesis. *Consciousness and Cognition, 12,* 231–256.

Dijkerman, H.C., Milner, A.D., & Carey, D.F. (1998). Grasping spatial relationships: Failure to demonstrate allocentric visual coding in a patient with visual form agnosia. *Consciousness and Cognition, 7,* 424–437.

Dijksterhuis, A. (2004). Think different: The merits of unconscious thought in preference development and decision making. *Journal of Personality and Social Psychology, 87,* 586–598.

Dijksterhuis, A., Bos, M.W., Nordgren, L.F., & van Baaren, R.B. (2006). On making the right choice: The deliberation-without-attention effect. *Science, 311,* 1005.

Dijksterhuis, A., & Nordgren, L.F. (2006). A theory of unconscious thought. *Perspectives on Psychological Science, 1,* 95–109.

Dill, K.E., Anderson, C.A., & Deuser, W.E. (1997). Effects of aggressive personality on social expectations and social perception. *Journal of Research in Personality, 31,* 272–292.

Dindia, K., & Allen, M. (1992). Sex differences in self-disclosure: A meta-analysis. *Psychological Bulletin, 112,* 106–124.

Dion, K.K, Berscheid, E., & Walster, E. (1972). What is beautiful is good. *Journal of Personality and Social Psychology, 24,* 285–290.

Dionne, G., Dale, P.S., Boivin, M., & Plomin, R. (2003). Genetic evidence for bidirectional effects of early lexical and grammatical development. *Child Development, 74,* 394–412.

Dockrell, J., & Messer, D.J. (1999). *Children's language and communication difficulties: Understanding, identification, and intervention.* London: Cassell.

Dodds, R.A., Ward, T.B., & Smith, S.M. (2004). A review of the experimental literature on incubation in problem solving and creativity. In M.A. Runco (Ed.), *Creativity research handbook* (Vol. 3). Cresskill, NJ: Hampton Press.

Doise, W. (1986). *Levels of explanation in social psychology.* Cambridge, UK: Cambridge University Press.

Dollard, J., Doob, L.W., Miller, N.E., Mowrer, O.H., & Sears, R.R. (1939). *Frustration and aggression.* New Haven, CT: Yale University Press.

Domhoff, G.W. (2001). Why did empirical dream researchers reject Freud? A critique of historical claims by Mark Solms. *Dreaming, 14,* 3–17.

Doosje, B., Branscombe, N.R., Spears, R., & Manstead, A.S.R. (1998). Guilty by association: When one's group has a negative history. *Journal of Personality and Social Psychology, 75,* 872–886.

Dovidio, J.F., Brigham, J.C., Johnson, B.T., & Gaertner, S. (1996). Stereotyping, prejudice, and discrimination: Another look. In C.N. Macrae, C. Stangor, & M. Hewstone (Eds.), *Stereotypes and stereotyping.* Guilford Press: New York.

Dovidio, J.F., & Gaertner, S.L. (1991). Changes in the expression and assessment of racial prejudice. In H.J. Knopke, R.J. Norrell, & R.W. Rogers (Eds.), *Opening doors: Perspectives on race relations in contemporary America.* Tuscaloosa, AL: University of Alabama Press.

Dovidio, J.F., Gaertner, S.L., & Validzic, A. (1998). Intergroup bias: Status, differentiation, and a common in-group identity. *Journal of Personality and Social Psychology, 75,* 109–120.

Dovidio, J.F., ten Vergert, M., Stewart, T.L., Gaertner, S.L., Johnson, J.D., Esses, V.M., et al. (2004). Perspective and prejudice: Antecedents and mediating mechanisms. *Personality and Social Psychology Bulletin, 30,* 1537–1549.

Driver, J., & Vuilleumier, P. (2001). Perceptual awareness and its loss in unilateral neglect and extinction. *Cognition, 79,* 39–88.

Drummond, S.P., Brown, G.G., Gillin, J.C., Stricker, J.L., Wong, E.C., & Buxton, R.B. (2000). Altered brain response to verbal learning following sleep deprivation. *Nature, 403,* 655–657.

Drury, J., & Reicher, S. (2000). Collective action and psychological change: The emergence of new social identities. *British Journal of Social Psychology, 39,* 579–604.

Duck, J.M., Hogg, M.A., & Terry, D.J. (1999). Social identity and perceptions of media persuasion: Are we always less influenced than others? *Journal of Applied Social Psychology, 29,* 1879–1899.

Duncan, J., Bundesen, C., Olson, A., Humphreys, G., Chavda, S., & Shibuya, H. (1999). Systematic analysis of deficits in visual attention. *Journal of Experimental Psychology: General, 128,* 450–478.

Duncan, S.L. (1976). Differential social perception and attribution of intergroup violence: Testing the lower limits of stereotyping of blacks. *Journal of Personality and Social Psychology, 34,* 590–598.

Duncker, K. (1945). On problem solving. *Psychological Monographs, 58* (Whole No. 270).

Dunne, M.P., Martin, N.G., Statham, D.J., Slutske, W.S., Dinwiddie, S.H., Bucholz, K.K., et al. (1997). Genetic and environmental contributions to variance in age at first sexual intercourse. *Psychological Science, 8,* 211–216.

Durand, V.M., & Barlow, D.H. (2006). *Essentials of abnormal psychology* (4th ed.). New York: Thompson/Wadsworth.

Durkin, K. (1995). *Developmental social psychology: From infancy to old age.* Oxford, UK: Blackwell.

Durrett, M.E., Otaki, M., & Richards, P. (1984). Attachment and the mother's perception of support for the father. *International Journal of Behavioral Development, 7,* 167–176.

Duval, T.S., & Silvia, P.J. (2002). Self-awareness, probability of improvement, and the self-serving bias. *Journal of Personality and Social Psychology, 82,* 49–61.

Dyer, C. (1995). *Beginning research in psychology.* Oxford, UK: Blackwell.

Dzewaltowski, D.A. (1989). Toward a model of exercise motivation. *Journal of Sport and Exercise Psychology, 32,* 11–28.

Eagly, A.H., & Carli, L. (1981). Sex of researchers and sex-typed communications as determinants of sex differences in influenceability: A meta-analysis of social influence studies. *Psychological Bulletin, 90,* 1–20.

Eagly, A.H., & Crowley, M. (1986). Gender and helping behaviour: A meta-analytic review of the social psychological literature. *Psychological Bulletin, 100,* 283–308.

Eagly, A.H., Johannsen-Schmidt, M.C., & van Ergen, M.L. (2003). *Psychological Bulletin, 129,* 569–591.

Eagly, A.H., & Karau, S.J. (2002). Role congruity theory of prejudice toward female leaders. *Psychological Review, 109,* 573–598.

Eagly, A.H., Karau, S.J., & Makhijani, M.G. (1995). Gender and the effectiveness of leaders: A meta-analysis. *Psychological Bulletin, 117,* 125–145.

Eagly, A.H., Makhijani, M.G., & Konsky, B.G. (1992). Gender and the evaluation of leaders: A meta-analysis. *Psychological Bulletin, 111,* 3–22.

Eagly, A.H., & Steffen, V.J. (1986). Gender and aggressive behaviour: A meta-analytic review of the social psychological literature. *Psychological Bulletin, 90,* 1–20.

Eames, D., Shorrocks, D., & Tomlinson, P. (1990). Naughty animals or naughty experimenters? Conservation accidents revisited with video-simulated commentary. *British Journal of Developmental Psychology, 8,* 25–37.

Ebbinghaus, H. (1913). *Memory* (H. Ruyer & C.E. Bussenius, Trans.). New York: Teachers College, Columbia University. (Original work published 1885)

Egan, S.K., & Perry, D.G. (2001). Gender identity: A multidimensional analysis with implications for psychosocial adjustment. *Developmental Psychology, 37,* 451–463.

Eisenberg, N., & Fabes, R.A. (1992). Emotion regulation and the development of social competence. In M.S. Clark (Ed.), *Emotion and social behavior: Vol. 14. Review of personality and social psychology.* Newbury Park, CA: Sage.

Eisenberg, N., Fabes, R.A., Guthrie, I.K., Murphy, B.C., Maszk, P., Holmgren, R., et al. (1996). The relations of regulation and emotionality to problem behavior in elementary school children. *Development and Psychopathology, 8,* 141–162.

Eisenberg, N., Fabes, R.A., Shepard, S.A., Murphy, B.C., Guthrie, I.K., Jones, S., et al. (1997). Contemporaneous and longitudinal prediction of children's social functioning from regulation and emotionality. *Child Development, 68,* 642–664.

Eisenberg, N., Liew, J., & Pidada, S.U. (2004). The longitudinal relations of regulation and emotionality to quality of Indonesian children's socio-emotional functioning. *Developmental Psychology, 40,* 790–804.

Eisenberg, N., Pidada, S., & Liew, J. (2001). The relations of regulation and negative emotionality to Indonesian children's social functioning. *Child Development, 72,* 1747–1763.

Eisenberg-Berg, N., & Hand, M. (1979). The relationship of preschoolers' reasoning about prosocial moral conflicts to prosocial behaviour. *Child Development, 50*, 356–363.

Ekman, P., Friesen, W.V., & Ellsworth, P. (1972). *Emotion in the human face: Guidelines for research and an integration of findings*. New York: Pergamon.

Ekman, P., Friesen, W.V., O'Sullivan, M., Chan, A., Diacoyanni-Tarlatzis, I., Heider, K., et al. (1987). Universals and cultural differences in the judgments of facial expressions of emotion. *Journal of Personality and Social Psychology, 53*, 712–717.

Elder, J.H., & Goldberg, R.M. (2002). Ecological statistics of Gestalt laws for the perceptual organisation of contours. *Journal of Vision, 2*, 324–353.

Eley, T.C., Lichtenstein, P., & Stevenson, J. (1999). Sex differences in the aetiology of aggressive and non-aggressive antisocial behaviour: Results from two twin studies. *Child Development, 70*, 155–168.

Elkin, I. (1994). The NIMH Treatment of Depression Collaborative Research Program: Where we began and where we are. In S. Garfield & A. Bergin (Eds.), *Handbook of psychotherapy and behavior change* (4th ed.). New York: John Wiley.

Ellemers, N., Spears, R., & Doosje, B. (2002). Self and social identity. *Annual Review of Psychology, 53*, 161–186.

Ellis, A. (1962). *Reason and emotion in psychotherapy*. Secaucus, NJ: Prentice Hall.

Ellis, A.W., Miller, D., & Sin, G. (1983). Wernicke's aphasia and normal language processing: A case study in cognitive neuropsychology. *Cognition, 15*, 111–144.

Ellis, A.W., & Young, A.W. (1988). *Human cognitive neuropsychology*. Hove, UK: Psychology Press.

Ellis, S., & Gauvain, M. (1992). Social and cultural influences on children's collaborative interactions. In L.T. Winegar & J. Valsiner (Eds.), *Children's development within social context: Vol. 2. Research and methodology*. Hillsdale, NJ: Lawrence Erlbaum Associates, Inc.

Else-Quest, N.M., Hyde, J.S., Goldsmith, H.H., & Van Hulle, C.A. (2006). Gender differences in temperament: A meta-analysis. *Psychological Bulletin, 132*, 33–72.

Elstein, A.S., Christensen, C., Cottrell, J.J., Polson, A., & Ng, M. (1999). Effects of prognosis, perceived benefit, and decision style on decision making in critical care. *Critical Care Medicine, 27*, 58–65.

Ember, M. (1981). *Statistical evidence for an ecological explanation of warfare*. Paper presented at the 10th annual meeting of the Society for Cross-Cultural Research. Syracuse, NY.

Empson, J.A.C. (1989). *Sleep and dreaming*. London: Faber & Faber.

Endler, N.S., & Parker, J.D.A. (1990). Multidimensional assessment of coping: A critical evaluation. *Journal of Personality and Social Psychology, 58*, 844–854.

Engle, R.W., Tuholski, S.W., Laughlin, J.E., & Conway, A.R.A. (1999). Working memory, short-term memory, and general fluid intelligence: A latent-variable approach. *Journal of Experimental Psychology: General, 128*, 309–331.

Epping-Jordan, J.E., Compas, B.E., & Howell, D.C. (1994). Predictors of cancer progression in young adult men and women: Avoidance, intrusive thoughts, and psychological symptoms. *Health Psychology, 13*, 539–547.

Erb, H-P., Bohner, G., Rank, S., & Einwiller, S. (2002). Processing minority and majority communications: The role of conflict with prior attitudes. *Personality and Social Psychology Bulletin, 28*, 1172–1182.

Erel, O., Oberman, Y., & Yirmiya, N. (2000). Maternal versus nonmaternal care and seven domains of children's development. *Psychological Bulletin, 126*, 727–747.

Erez, A., & Judge, T. A. (2001). Relationship of core self-evaluations to goal setting, motivation, and performance. *Journal of Applied Psychology, 86*, 1270–1279.

Erickson, T.A., & Mattson, M.E. (1981). From words to meaning: A semantic illusion. *Journal of Verbal Learning and Verbal Behavior, 20*, 540–552.

Ericsson, K.A., & Kintsch, W. (1995). Long-term working memory. *Psychological Review, 102*, 211–245.

Ericsson, K.A., Krampe, R.T., & Tesch-Römer, C. (1993). The role of deliberate practice in the acquisition of expert performance. *Psychological Review, 100*, 363–406.

Ericsson, K.A., & Lehmann, A.C. (1996). Expert and exceptional performance: Evidence of maximal adaptation to task constraints. *Annual Review of Psychology, 47*, 273–305.

Eriksen, C.W., & St. James, J.D. (1986). Visual attention within and around the field of focal attention: A zoom lens model. *Perception and Psychophysics, 40*, 225–240.

Erikson, E.H. (1968). *Identity: Youth and crisis*. New York: W.W. Norton.

Eron, L.D. (1987). The development of aggressive behavior from the perspective of a developing behaviorism. *American Psychologist, 42*, 435–442.

Essock-Vitale, S.M., & McGuire, M.T. (1985). Women's lives viewed from an evolutionary perspective: II. Patterns of helping. *Ethology and Sociobiology, 6*, 155–173.

Evans, P. (1998). Stress and coping. In M. Pitts & K. Phillips (Eds.), *The psychology of health* (2nd ed.). London: Routledge.

Evans, P., Clow, A., & Hucklebridge, F. (1997). Stress and the immune system. *The Psychologist, 10*, 303–307.

Eysenck, H.J. (1952). The effects of psychotherapy: An evaluation. *Journal of Consulting Psychology, 16*, 319–324.

Eysenck, H.J. (1967). *The biological basis of personality*. Springfield, IL: C.C. Thomas.

Eysenck H.J. (1981). *The intelligence controversy: H.J. Eysenck vs. Leon Kamin*. New York: Wiley.

Eysenck, H.J. (1982). *Personality, genetics and behavior*. New York: Praeger.

Eysenck, H.J., & Eysenck, M.W. (1985). *Personality and individual differences*. New York: Plenum.

Eysenck, M.W. (1990). *Happiness: Facts and myths*. Hove, UK: Psychology Press.

Eysenck, M.W. (1992). *Anxiety: The cognitive perspective*. Hove, UK: Lawrence Erlbaum Associates Ltd.

Eysenck, M.W. (1994). *Individual differences: Normal and abnormal*. Hove, UK: Psychology Press.

Eysenck, M.W. (1997). *Anxiety and cognition: A unified theory*. Hove, UK: Psychology Press.

Eysenck, M.W. (2006). *Fundamentals of cognition*. Hove, UK: Psychology Press.

Eysenck, M.W., & Keane, M.T. (2005). *Cognitive psychology: A student's handbook*. Hove, UK: Psychology Press.

Fabes, R.A., Fultz, J., Eisenberg, N., May-Plumlee, T., & Christopher, F.S. (1989). Effects of rewards on children's pro-social motivation: A socialization study. *Developmental Psychology, 25*, 509–515.

Fagot, B.I., & Leinbach, M.D. (1989). The young child's gender schema: Environmental input, internal organisation. *Child Development, 60*, 663–672.

Fahrenberg, J. (1992). Psychophysiology of neuroticism and anxiety. In A.Gale & M.W. Eysenck (Eds.), *Handbook of individual differences: Biological perspectives*. Chichester, UK: Wiley.

Fan, J., Liu, F., Wu. J., & Dai, W. (2004). Visual perception of female attractiveness. *Proceedings of the Royal Society of London Series B: Biological Sciences, 271*, 347–352.

Farah, M.J. (2001). Consciousness. In B. Rapp (Ed.), *The handbook of cognitive neuropsychology*. Hove, UK: Psychology Press.

Farooqi, S., Matarese, G., Lord, G., Keogh, J., Lawrence, E., Agwu, C., et al. (2002). Beneficial effects of leptin on obesity, T cell hyporesponsiveness, and neuroendocrine/metabolic dysfunction of human congenital leptin deficiency. *Journal of Clinical Investigations, 110*, 1093–1103.

Farrar, M.J. (1992). Negative evidence and grammatical morpheme acquisition. *Developmental Psychology, 28,* 90–98.

Fazio, R.H., & Zanna, M.P. (1981). Direct experience and attitude–behaviour consistency. In L. Berkowitz (Ed.), *Advances in experimental social psychology* (Vol. 14). New York: Academic Press.

Febbraro, A.R. (2003). Alpha bias and beta bias in research on labour and love: The case of enhancement versus scarcity. *Feminism & Psychology, 13,* 201–223.

Fehr, E., & Fischbacher, U. (2003). The nature of human altruism. *Nature, 425,* 785–791.

Fehr, E., & Fischbacher, U. (2004). Third-party punishment and social norms. *Evolution and Human Behavior, 25,* 63–87.

Fein, S., Hilton, J.L., & Miller, D.T. (1990). Suspicion of ulterior motivation and the correspondence bias. *Journal of Personality and Social Psychology, 58,* 753–764.

Feingold, A. (1988). Matching for attractiveness in romantic partners and same-sex friends: A meta-analysis and theoretical critique. *Psychological Bulletin, 104,* 226–235.

Feingold, A. (1990). Gender differences in effects of physical attractiveness on romantic attraction: A comparison across five research paradigms. *Journal of Personality and Social Psychology, 59,* 981–993.

Feingold, A. (1992). Good-looking people are not what we think. *Psychological Bulletin, 111,* 304–341.

Fellner, C.H., & Marshall, J.R. (1981). Kidney donors revisited. In J.P. Rushton & R.M. Sorrentino (Eds.), *Altruism and helping behaviour.* Hillsdale, NJ: Lawrence Erlbaum Associates, Inc.

Fenson, L., Dale, P.S., Reznick, J.S., Bates, E., Thal, D.J., & Pethick, S.J. (1994). Variability in early communicative development. *Monographs of the Society for Research in Child Development, 59,* 173.

Fenstermacher, S.K., & Saudino, K.J. (2006). Multivariate heritability for imitation, cognitive ability and task orientation at age two. *Behavior Genetics, 36,* 963–964.

Ferreira, F. (2003). The misinterpretation of noncanonical sentences. *Cognitive Psychology, 47,* 164–203.

Ferreira, F., & Clifton, C. (1986). The independence of syntactic processing. *Journal of Memory and Language, 25,* 348–368.

Ferreira, F., & Swets, B. (2002). How incremental is language production? Evidence from the production of utterances requiring the computation of arithmetic sums. *Journal of Memory and Language, 46,* 57–84.

Fery, P., & Morais, J. (2003). A case study of visual agnosia without perceptual processing or structural descriptions' impairment. *Cognitive Neuropsychology, 20,* 595–618.

Festinger, L. (1957). *A theory of cognitive dissonance.* Stanford, CA: Stanford University Press.

Festinger, L., & Carlsmith, J.M. (1959). Cognitive consequences of forced compliance. *Journal of Abnormal and Social Psychology, 47,* 382–389.

Festinger, L., Schachter, S., & Back, K. (1950). *Social pressures in informal groups: A study of a housing community.* New York: Harper.

Fiedler, F.E. (1967). *A theory of leader effectiveness.* New York: McGraw-Hill.

Fiedler, F.E. (1978). The contingency model and the dynamics of the leadership process. In L. Berkowitz (Ed.), *Advances in experimental social psychology* (Vol. 12). New York: Academic Press.

Fiedler, F.E., & Potter, E.H. (1983). Dynamics of leadership effectiveness. In H.H. Blumberg, A.P. Hare, V. Kent, & M. Davies (Eds.), *Small groups and social interaction* (Vol. 1). Chichester, UK: Wiley.

Fijneman, Y.A., Willemsen, M.E., & Poortinga, Y.H. (1996). Individualism–collectivism: An empirical study of a conceptual issue. *Journal of Cross-Cultural Psychology, 27,* 381–402.

Fincham, F.D., & Bradbury, T.N. (1993). Marital satisfaction, depression, and attributions: A longitudinal analysis. *Journal of Personality and Social Psychology, 64,* 442–452.

Fincham, F.D., & Hewstone, M. (2001). Attribution theory and research: From basic to applied. In M. Hewstone & W. Stroebe (Eds.), *Introduction to social psychology* (3rd ed.). Oxford, UK: Blackwell.

Finlay-Jones, R.A., & Brown, G.W. (1981). Types of stressful life events and the onset of anxiety and depressive disorders. *Psychological Medicine, 11,* 803–815.

Fishbein, M., & Ajzen, I. (1975). *Belief, attitude, intention and behavior: An introduction to theory and research.* Reading, MA: Addison-Wesley.

Fishbein, M., & Coombs, F.S. (1974). Basis for decision: An attitudinal analysis of voting behavior. *Journal of Applied Social Psychology, 4,* 95–124.

Fiske, A.P. (2002). Using individualism and collectivism to compare cultures—A critique of the validity and measurement of the constructs: Comment on Oyserman et al. (2002). *Psychological Bulletin, 128,* 78–88.

Fiske, S.T. (1998). Stereotyping, prejudice, and discrimination. In D.T. Gilbert, S.T. Fiske, & G. Lindzey (Eds.), *The handbook of social psychology* (Vol. 2, 4th ed.). New York: McGraw-Hill.

Fiske, S.T. (2002). What we know now about bias and intergroup conflict, the problem of the century. *Current Directions in Psychological Science, 11,* 123–128.

Fivush, R., & Nelson, K. (2004). Culture and language in the emergence of autobiographical memory. *Psychological Science, 15,* 573–577.

Flavell, J.H., Beach, D.R., & Chinsky, J.M. (1966). Spontaneous verbal rehearsal in a memory task as a function of age. *Child Development, 37,* 283–299.

Fleeson, W. (2001). Toward a structure- and process-integrated view of personality: Traits as density distributions of states. *Journal of Personality and Social Psychology, 80,* 1011–1027.

Fleeson, W. (2004). Moving personality beyond the person-situation debate. *Current Directions in Psychological Science, 13,* 83–87.

Flynn, E. (2006). A microgenetic investigation of stability and continuity in theory of mind development. *British Journal of Developmental Psychology, 24,* 631–654.

Flynn, J.R. (1987). Massive IQ gains in 14 nations: What IQ tests really measure. *Psychological Bulletin, 101,* 271–291.

Flynn, J.R. (1994). IQ gains over time. In R.J. Sternberg (Ed.), *Encyclopedia of human intelligence.* New York: Macmillan.

Folkman, S., & Lazarus, R.S. (1985). If it changes it must be a process: Study of emotion and coping during three stages of a college examination. *Journal of Personality and Social Psychology, 48,* 150–170.

Folkman, S., Lazarus, R.S., Dunkel-Schetter, C., DeLongis, A., & Gruen, R.J. (1986). Dynamics of a stressful encounter: Cognitive appraisal, coping, and encounter outcomes. *Journal of Personality and Social Psychology, 50,* 992–1003.

Folkman, S., & Moskowitz, J.T. (2004). Coping: Pitfalls and promise. *Annual Review of Psychology, 55,* 745–774.

Fonagy, P., Roth, A., & Higgitt, A. (2005). The outcome of psychodynamic psychotherapy for psychological disorders. *Clinical Neuroscience Research, 4,* 367–377.

Ford, M.R., & Widiger, T.A. (1989). Sex bias in the diagnosis of histrionic and antisocial personality disorders. *Journal of Consulting and Clinical Psychology, 57,* 301–305.

Forgatch, M.S., & DeGarmo, D.S. (1999). Parenting through change: An effective prevention program for single mothers. *Journal of Consulting and Clinical Psychology, 67,* 711–724.

Forsterling, F. (1989). Models of covariation and causal attribution: How do they relate to the analysis of variance? *Journal of Personality and Social Psychology, 57,* 615–625.

Foster, D.H., & Gilson, S.J. (2002). Recognizing novel three-dimensional objects by summing signals from parts and views. *Proceedings of the Royal Society London B, 269,* 1939–1947.

Foulkes, D., & Vogel, G. (1965). Mental activity at sleep onset. *Journal of Abnormal Psychology, 70,* 231–243.

Fouts, G.T., & Click, M. (1979). Effects of live and TV models on observational learning in introverted and extraverted children. *Perceptual and Motor Skills, 48,* 863–867.

Foy, D.W., Resnick, H.S., Sipprelle, R.C., & Carroll, E.M. (1987). Premilitary, military, and postmilitary factors in the development of combat-related post-traumatic stress disorder. *The Behavior Therapist, 10,* 3–9.

Fraley, R.C., & Spieker, S.J. (2003). Are infant attachment patterns continuously or categorically distributed? A taxometric analysis of Strange Situation behaviour. *Developmental Psychology, 39,* 387–404.

France, L. (2005). The death of yesterday. *The Observer Magazine,* 23 January 2005.

Frankenhaeuser, M. (1975). Sympathetic-adreno medullary activity behavior and the psychosocial environment. In P.H. Venables & M.J. Christie (Eds.), *Research in psychophysiology.* New York: Wiley.

Franklin, S., Turner, J., Ralph, M.A.L., Morris, J., & Bailey, P.J. (1996). A distinctive case of word meaning deafness? *Cognitive Neuropsychology, 13,* 1139–1162.

Franz, C., Weinberger, J., Kremen, W., & Jacobs, R. (1996). *Childhood antecedents of dysphoria in adults: A 36-year longitudinal study.* Unpublished manuscript, Williams College.

Franzoi, S.L. (1996). *Social psychology.* Madison, WI: Brown & Benchmark.

Frazier, L., & Rayner, K. (1982). Making and correcting errors in the analysis of structurally ambiguous sentences. *Cognitive* Psychology, *14,* 179–210.

French, R.M., & Cleeremans, A. (2002). *Implicit learning and consciousness: An empirical, philosophical and computational consensus in the making.* Hove, UK: Psychology Press.

Freud, A., & Dann, S. (1951). An experiment in group upbringing. *Psychoanalytic Study of the Child, 6,* 127–168.

Freud, S. (1900). *The interpretation of dreams* (J. Crick, Trans.). London: Oxford University Press.

Freud, S. (1910). The origin and development of psychoanalysis. *American Journal of Psychology, 21,* 181–218.

Freud, S. (1917). Introductory lectures on psychoanalysis. In J. Strachey (Ed.), *The complete psychological works* (Vol. 16). New York: Norton.

Freud, S. (1955). Beyond the pleasure principle, group psychology, and other works. In J. Strachey (Ed. & Trans.), *The standard edition of the complete psychological works of Sigmund Freud* (Vol. 18). London: Hogarth Press. (Original work published 1920–1922)

Freud, S. (1957). Repression. In J. Strachey (Ed. & Trans.), *The standard edition of the complete psychological works of Sigmund Freud* (Vol. 14, pp. 146–158). London: Hogarth. (Original work published 1915)

Friedman, M., & Rosenman, R.H. (1959). Association of specific overt behavior pattern with blood and cardiovascular findings. *Journal of the American Medical Association, 96,* 1286–1296.

Friedman, N.P., & Miyake, A. (2004). The relations among inhibition and interference control functions: A latent-variable analysis. *Journal of Experimental Psychology: General, 133,* 101–135.

Frith, C.D. (1992). *The cognitive neuropsychology of schizophrenia.* Hove, UK: Psychology Press.

Frost, R. (1998). Toward a strong phonological theory of visual word recognition: True issues and false trails. *Psychological Bulletin, 123,* 71–99.

Funnell, E. (1983) Phonological processes in reading: New evidence from acquired dyslexia. *British Journal of Psychology, 74,* 159–180.

Funtowicz, M.N., & Widiger, T.A. (1999). Sex bias in the diagnosis of personality disorders: An evaluation of the DSM-IV criteria. *Journal of Abnormal Psychology, 108,* 195–201.

Furnham, A. (1981). Personality and activity preference. *British Journal of Social and Clinical Psychology, 20,* 57–68.

Furnham, A. (1982). Why are the poor always with us? Explanations for poverty in Britain. *British Journal of Social Psychology, 21,* 311–322.

Furnham, A. (1988). *Lay theories: Everyday understanding of problems in the social sciences.* Oxford, UK: Pergamon.

Gaertner, L., & Insko, C.A. (2000). Intergroup discrimination in the minimal group paradigm: Categorisation, reciprocation, or fear? *Journal of Personality and Social Psychology, 79,* 77–94.

Gaertner, S.L., Dovidio, J.F., Anastasio, P.A., Bachman, B.A., & Rust, M.C. (1993). The common ingroup identity model: Recategorisation and the reduction of intergroup bias. In W. Stroebe & M. Hewstone (Eds.), *European review of social psychology* (Vol. 4). London: Wiley.

Gaertner, S.L., Rust, M.C., Dovidio, J.F., Bachman, B.A., & Anastasio, P.A. (1994). The contact hypothesis: The role of a common ingroup identity on reducing intergroup bias. *Small Group Research, 25,* 224–249.

Gaffan, E.A., Hansel, M., & Smith, L. (1983). Does reward depletion influence spatial memory performance? *Learning and Motivation, 14,* 58–74.

Gale, A. (1983). Electroencephalographic studies of extraversion–introversion: A case study in the psychophysiology of individual differences. *Personality and Individual Differences, 4,* 371–380.

Galton, F. (1869). *Hereditary genius: An inquiry into its laws and consequences.* London: Macmillan & Co.

Gamundi, A., Akaârir, M., Coenen, A.M.L., Esteban, S., Rial, R.V., & Nicolau, M.C. (2005). Mammalian sleep may have no adaptive advantage over simple activity–rest cycles. *Medical Hypotheses, 64,* 130–132.

Ganster, D.C., Fox, M.L., & Dwyer, D.J. (2001). Explaining employees' health care costs: A prospective examination of stressful job demands, personal control, and physiological reactivity. *Journal of Applied Psychology, 86,* 954–964.

Ganster, D.C., Schaubroeck, J., Sime, W.E., & Mayes, B.T. (1991). The nomological validity of the Type A personality among employed adults. *Journal of Applied Psychology, 76,* 143–168.

Garcia, J., & Koelling, R.A. (1966). Relation of cue to consequences in avoidance learning. *Psychonomic Science, 4,* 123–124.

Gardner, H. (1983). *Frames of mind: The theory of multiple intelligences.* New York: Basic Books.

Gardner, H. (1993). *Multiple intelligences: The theory in practice.* New York: Basic Books.

Gardner, H. (1998). Are there additional intelligences? The case for naturalist, spiritual, and existential intelligences. In J. Kane (Ed.), *Education, information, and transformation.* Englewood Cliffs, NJ: Prentice Hall.

Gardner, H., Kornhaber, M.L., & Wake, W.K. (1996). *Intelligence: Multiple perspectives.* Orlando, FL: Harcourt Brace.

Garfield, S. (2003, February 2). Unhappy anniversary. *The Observer.*

Garnham, A., Oakhill, J., & Johnson-Laird, P.N. (1982). Referential continuity and the coherence of discourse. *Cognition, 11,* 29–46.

Garrett, M.F. (1982). Production of speech: Observations from normal and pathological language use. In A.W. Ellis (Ed.), *Normality and pathology in cognitive functions.* London: Academic Press.

Gathercole, S.E., Pickering, S.J., Ambridge, B., & Wearing, H. (2004). The structure of working memory from 4 to 15 years of age. *Developmental Psychology, 40*, 177–190.

Gauld, A., & Stephenson, G.M. (1967). Some experiments relating to Bartlett's theory of remembering. *British Journal of Psychology, 58*, 39–50.

Gazzaniga, M.S. (1992). Brain modules and belief formation. In F.S. Kessel, P.M. Cole, & P.L. Johnson (Eds.), *Self and consciousness: Multiple perspectives*. Hillsdale, NJ: Lawrence Erlbaum Associates, Inc.

Gazzaniga, M.S., Ivry, R.B., & Mangun, G.R. (1998). *Cognitive neuroscience: The biology of the mind*. New York: W.W. Norton.

Gazzaniga, M.S., Ivry, R.B., & Mangun, G.R. (2002). *Cognitive neuroscience: The biology of the mind* (2nd ed.). New York: Norton.

Geher, G. (Ed.). (2004). *Measuring emotional intelligence: Common ground and controversy*. New York: Nova Science Publishing.

Gelfand, M.J., Triandis, H.C., & Chan, D.K.-S. (1996). Individualism versus collectivism or versus authoritarianism? *European Journal of Social Psychology, 26*, 397–410.

Gelles, R.J. (1997). *Intimate violence in families*. Thousand Oaks, CA: Sage.

Gentner, D. (1982). Why nouns are learned before verbs: Linguistic relativity vs. natural partitioning. In S.A. Kuczaj (Ed.), *Language development: Vol. 2. Language, thought, and culture*. Hillsdale, NJ: Lawrence Erlbaum Associates, Inc.

Gergely, G., Bekkering, H., & Kiraly, I. (2002). Rational imitation in preverbal infants. *Nature, 415*, 755.

Gershoff, E.T. (2002). Corporal punishment by parents and associated child behaviours and experiences: A meta-analytic and theoretical review. *Psychological Bulletin, 128*, 539–579.

Gibbons, F.X., Eggleston, T.J., & Benthin, A.C. (1997). Cognitive reactions to smoking relapse: The reciprocal relation between dissonance and self-esteem. *Journal of Personality and Social Psychology, 72*, 184–195.

Gibbs, W.W. (1996, August). Gaining on fat. *Scientific American*, pp. 70–76.

Gibson, E.J., & Walk, R.D. (1960, April). The "visual cliff." *Scientific American*, pp. 64–71.

Gick, M.L., & Holyoak, K.J. (1980). Analogical problem solving. *Cognitive Psychology, 12*, 306–355.

Giersch, A., Humphreys, G., Boucart, M., & Kovacs, I. (2000). The computation of contours in visual agnosia: Evidence for early computation prior to shape binding and figure–ground coding. *Cognitive Neuropsychology, 17*, 731–759.

Gilbert, D.T. (1995). Attribution and interpersonal perception. In A. Tesser (Ed.), *Advanced social psychology*. New York: McGraw-Hill.

Gilbert, D.T., Pelham, B.W., & Krull, D.S. (1988). On cognitive busyness: When person perceivers meet persons perceived. *Journal of Personality and Social Psychology, 54*, 733–740.

Gilbert, G.N., & Mulkay, M. (1984). *Opening Pandora's box: A sociological analysis of scientists' discourse*. Cambridge, UK: Cambridge University Press.

Gilligan, C. (1977). In a different voice: Women's conception of the self and morality. *Harvard Educational Review, 47*, 481–517.

Gilligan, C. (1982). *In a different voice: Psychological theory and women's development*. Cambridge, MA: Harvard University Press.

Gilligan, C., & Wiggins, G. (1987). The origins of morality in early childhood relationships. In J. Kagan & S. Lamb (Eds.), *The emergence of morality in young children*. Chicago: University of Chicago Press.

Girbau, D. (2002). A sequential analysis of private and social speech in children's dyadic communication. *The Spanish Journal of Psychology, 5*, 110–118.

Glaser, W.R. (1992). Picture naming. *Cognition, 42*, 61–105.

Glover, S. (2004). Separate visual representations in the planning and control of action. *Behavioral and Brain Sciences, 27*, 3–78.

Gobet, F., & Clarkson, G. (2004). Chunks in expert memory: Evidence for the magical number four . . . or is it two? *Memory, 12*, 732–747.

Gobet, F., Voogt, A. de, & Retschitzki, J. (2004). *Moves in mind: The psychology of board games*. Hove: Psychology Press.

Gobet, F., & Waters, A.J. (2003). The role of constraints in expert memory. *Journal of Experimental Psychology: Learning, Memory & Cognition, 29*, 1082–1094.

Goddard, H.H. (1913). *Feeble-mindedness: Its causes and consequences*. New York: Macmillan.

Godden, D., & Baddeley, A. (1975). Context dependent memory in two natural environments: In land and under water. *British Journal of Psychology, 79*, 99–104.

Godden, D., & Baddeley, A. (1980). When does context influence recognition memory? *British Journal of Psychology, 71*, 99–104

Goldberg, L.R. (1990). An alternative "description of personality": The big-five factor structure. *Journal of Personality and Social Psychology, 59*, 1216–1229.

Goldfarb, W. (1947). Variations in adolescent adjustment of institutionally reared children. *American Journal of Orthopsychiatry, 17*, 499–557.

Goldhagen, D.J. (1996). *Hitler's willing executioners: Ordinary Germans and the Holocaust*. New York: Knopf.

Goldstein, E.B. (1996). *Sensation and perception* (4th ed.). New York: Brooks/Cole.

Goleman, D. (1991, November 26). Doctors find comfort is a potent medicine. *The New York Times*.

Gollwitzer, P.M. (1999). Implementation intentions. *American Psychologist, 54*, 493–503.

Gollwitzer, P.M., & Brandstätter, V. (1997). Implementation intentions and effective goal pursuit. *Journal of Personality and Social Psychology, 73*, 186–199.

Golombok, S., & Hines, M. (2002). Sex differences in social behaviour. In P.K. Smith & C.H. Hart (Eds.), *Blackwell handbook of childhood social development*. Oxford, UK: Blackwell.

Goodall, J. (2004). *Horizon: The demonic ape*. http://www.bbc.co.uk/science/horizon/2004/demonicapetrans.shtml

Goodnow, J.J., & Burns, A. (1985). *Home and school: A child's eye view*. Sydney, Australia: Allen & Unwin.

Goswami, U. (1998). *Cognition in children*. Hove, UK: Psychology Press.

Gottesman, I.I. (1991). *Schizophrenia genesis: The origins of madness*. New York: W.H. Freeman.

Gottfredson, L.S. (1997). Why g matters: The complexity of everyday life. *Intelligence, 24*, 79–132.

Gottfredson, L.S., & Deary, I.J. (2004). Intelligence predicts health and longevity, but why? *Current Directions in Psychological Science, 13*, 1–4.

Gould, S.J. (1982, May 6). A nation of morons. *New Scientist*, pp. 349–352.

Graesser, A.C., Millis, K.K., & Zwaan, R.A. (1997). Discourse comprehension. *Annual Review of Psychology, 48*, 163–189.

Graesser, A.C., Singer, M., & Trabasso, T. (1994). Constructing inferences during narrative text comprehension. *Psychological Review, 101*, 371–395.

Graf, P., & Schachter, D.L. (1985). Implicit and explicit memory for new associations in normal and amnesic subjects. *Journal of Experimental Psychology: Learning, Memory, and Cognition, 11*, 501–518.

Grafton, S., Hazeltine, E., & Ivry, R. (1995). Functional mapping of sequence learning in normal humans. *Journal of Cognitive Neuroscience, 7*, 497–510.

Grammer, K., & Thornhill, R. (1994). Human (*Homo sapiens*) facial attractiveness and sexual selection: The role of symmetry and averageness. *Journal of Comparative Psychology, 108*, 233–242.

Granott, N. (2005). Scaffolding dynamically toward change: Previous and new perspectives. *New Ideas in Psychology, 23*, 140–151.

Green, M. (1995, October 14). In A. Coghlan, Dieting makes you forget. *New Scientist.*

Green, S. (1994). *Principles of biopsychology*, Hove, UK: Psychology Press.

Greenberg, J.H. (1963). Some universals of grammar with particular reference to the order of meaningful elements. In J.H. Greenberg (Ed.), *Universals of language.* Cambridge, MA: MIT Press.

Greenberg, L., Elliott, R., & Lietaer, G. (1994). Research on experiential psychotherapies. In A.E. Bergin & S.L. Garfield (Eds.), *Handbook of psychotherapy and behavior change* (4th ed., pp. 509–539). New York: Wiley.

Greenfield, P.M., & Lave, J. (1982). Cognitive aspects of informal education. In D.A. Wagner & H.W. Stevenson (Eds.), *Cultural perspectives on child development.* San Francisco: W.H. Freeman.

Greeno, J.G. (1974). Hobbits and orcs: Acquisition of a sequential concept. *Cognitive Psychology, 6*, 270–292.

Greenwald, A.G. (2003). On doing two things at once: III. Confirmation of perfect timesharing when simultaneous tasks are ideomotor compatible. *Journal of Experimental Psychology: Human Perception and Performance, 29*, 859–868.

Greenwald, A.G., McGhee, D.E., & Schwartz, J.L.K. (1998). Measuring individual differences in implicit cognition: The Implicit Association Test. *Journal of Personality and Social Psychology, 74*, 1464–1480.

Grier, J.W., & Burk, T. (1992). *Biology of animal behaviour* (2nd ed.). Oxford, UK: W.C. Brown.

Griffin, A.M., & Langlois, J.H. (2006). Stereotype directionality and attractiveness stereotyping: Is beauty good or is ugly bad? *Social Cognition, 24*, 187–206.

Griffiths, M.D. (2000). Cyberaffairs. *Psychology Review, 7*, 28–31.

Gross, R. (1996). *Psychology: The science of mind and behaviour* (3rd ed.). London: Hodder & Stoughton.

Gross, J., & Hayne, H. (1999). Drawing facilitates children's verbal reports after long delays. *Journal of Experimental Psychology: Applied, 5*, 265–283.

Grossman, K., Grossman, K.E., Spangler, S., Suess, G., & Uzner, L. (1985). Maternal sensitivity and newborn responses as related to quality of attachment in Northern Germany. In J. Bretherton & E. Waters (Eds.), Growing points of attachment theory. *Monographs of the Society for Research in Child Development, 50*, No. 209.

Grusec, J.E., Davidov, M., & Lundell, L. (2002). Prosocial and helping behavior. In P.K. Smith & C. Hart (Eds.), *Handbook of childhood social development.* Malden, MA: Blackwell.

Grusec, J.E., Saas-Kortsaak, P., & Simutis, Z.M. (1978). The role of example and moral exhortation in the training of altruism. *Child Development, 49*, 920–923.

Gruzelier, J. (2000). The relevance of neuro-psychophysiological evidence to cognitive, social and phenomenological theories of hypnosis. *International Journal of Psychophysiology, 35*, 40–40.

Guasti, M.T., & Luzzatti, C. (2002). Syntactic breakdown and recovery of clausal structure in agrammatism. *Brain and Cognition, 48*, 385–391.

Haart, E.G. O.-de, Carey, D.P., & Milne, A.B. (1999). More thoughts on perceiving and grasping the Müller–Lyer illusion. *Neuropsychologia, 37*, 1437–1444.

Haggan, M. (2002). Self-reports and self-delusion regarding the use of motherese: Implications from Kuwaiti adults. *Language Sciences, 24*, 17–28.

Haggbloom, S.J., Warnick, R., Warnick, J.E., Jones, V.K., Yarbrough, G.L., Russell T.M., et al. (2002). The 100 most eminent psychologists of the 20th century. *Review of General Psychology, 6*, 139–152.

Haier, R.J., Jung, R.E., Yeo, R.A., Head, K., & Alkire, M.T. (2005). The neuroanatomy of general intelligence: Sex matters. *Neuroimage, 25*, 320–327.

Haimov, I., & Lavie, P. (1996). Melatonin—a soporific hormone. *Current Directions in Psychological Science, 5*, 106–111.

Hains, S.C., Hogg, M.A., & Duck, J. M. (1997). Self-categorisation and leadership: Effects of group prototypicality and leader stereotypicality. *Personality and Social Psychology Bulletin, 23*, 1087–1100.

Haith, M.M. (1980). *Rules that babies look by: The organization of newborn visual activity.* Hillsdale, NJ: Lawrence Erlbaum Associates, Inc.

Hall, C., & van de Castle, R. (1966). *The content analysis of dreams.* New York: Appleton-Century-Crofts.

Hall, C.S. (1966). *The meaning of dreams.* New York: McGraw-Hill.

Halpern, D.F. (2004). A cognitive-process taxonomy for sex differences in cognitive abilities. *Current Directions in Psychological Science, 13*, 135–139.

Hanley, J.R., & McDonnell, V. (1997). Are reading and spelling phonologically mediated? Evidence from a patient with a speech production impairment. *Cognitive Neuropsychology, 14*, 3–33.

Hanley, S.J., & Abell, S.C. (2002). Maslow and relatedness: Creating an interpersonal model of self-actualisation. *Journal of Humanistic Psychology, 42*, 37–57.

Hardman, D., & Harries, C. (2002). How rational are we? *The Psychologist, 15*, 76–79.

Hare-Mustin, R.T., & Maracek, J. (1988). The meaning of difference: Gender theory, post-modernism and psychology. *American Psychologist, 43*, 455–464.

Harley, K., & Reese, E. (1999). Origins of autobiographical memory. *Developmental Psychology, 35*(5), 1338–1348.

Harley, T.A. (2001). *The psychology of language: From data to theory* (2nd ed.). Hove, UK: Psychology Press.

Harris, C.R. (2002). Sexual and romantic jealousy in heterosexual and homosexual adults. *Psychological Science, 13*, 7–12.

Harris, J.R. (1995). Where is the child's environment? A group socialisation theory of development. *Psychological Review, 102*, 458–489.

Harris, J.R. (2000). Socialisation, personality development, and the child's environments: Comment on Vandell (2000). *Developmental Psychology, 36*, 711–723.

Harris, M., & Butterworth, G. (2002). *Developmental psychology: A student's handbook.* Hove, UK: Psychology Press.

Harrison, L.J., & Ungerer, J.A. (2002). Maternal employment and infant–mother attachment security at 12 months postpartum. *Developmental Psychology, 38*, 758–773.

Harrison, Y., & Horne, J.A. (2000). The impact of sleep deprivation on decision making: A review. *Journal of Experimental Psychology: Applied, 6*, 236–249.

Hartup, W.W., & Stevens, N. (1997). Friendships and adaptation in the life course. *Psychological Bulletin, 121*, 355–370.

Harvey, A.G., Clark, D.M., Ehlers, A., & Rapee, R.M. (2000). Social anxiety and self-impression: Cognitive preparation enhances the beneficial effects of video feedback following a stressful social task. *Behaviour Research and Therapy, 38*, 1183–1192.

Haselager, G.J.T., Hartup, W.V., van Lieshout, C.F.M., & Riksen-Walraven, M. (1995). *Friendship similarity in middle childhood as a function of sex and sociometric status.*

Unpublished manuscript, University of Nijmegen, The Netherlands.

Haselton, M.G., & Nettle, D. (2006). The paranoid optimist: An integrative evolutionary model of cognitive biases. *Personality and Social Psychology Review, 10,* 47–66.

Haslam, S.A., Turner, J.C., Oakes, P.J., McGarty, C., & Hayes, B.K. (1992). Context-dependent variation in social stereotyping: 1. The effects of intergroup relations as mediated by social change and frame of reference. *European Journal of Social Psychology, 22,* 3–20.

Hatano, G., & Inagaki, K. (1986). Two courses of expertise. In H. Stevenson, H. Azuma, & K. Hatuka (Eds.), *Child development in Japan.* San Francisco: Freeman.

Hatfield, E., Sprecher, S., Traupmann Pillemer, J., Greenberg, D., & Wexler, P. (1988). Gender differences in what is desired in the sexual relationship. *Journal of Psychology and Human Sexuality, 1,* 39–52.

Hauff, E., Varvin, S., Laake, P., Melle, I., Vaglum, P., & Friis, S. (2002). Inpatient psychotherapy compared with usual care for patients who have schizophrenic psychoses. *Psychiatric Services, 53(4),* 471–473.

Hayne, H., Boniface, J., & Barr, R. (2000). The development of declarative memory in human infants: Age-related changes in deferred imitation. *Behavioral Neuroscience, 114,* 77–83.

Hazan, C., & Shaver, P.R. (1987). Romantic love conceptualised as an attachment process. *Journal of Personality and Social Psychology, 52,* 511–524.

Hearold, S. (1986). A synthesis of 1043 effects of television on social behaviour. In G. Comstock (Ed.), *Public communication and behaviour* (Vol. 1). Orlando, FL: Academic Press.

Heath, W.P., & Erickson, J.R. (1998). Memory for central and peripheral actions and props after varied post-event presentation. *Legal and Criminal Psychology, 3,* 321–346.

Heather, N. (1976). *Radical perspectives in psychology.* London: Methuen.

Heider, F. (1958). *The psychology of interpersonal relations.* New York: Wiley.

Heine, S.J., Lehman, D.R., Markus, H.R., & Kitayama, S. (1999). Is there a universal need for positive self-regard? *Psychological Review, 106,* 766–794.

Heine, S.J., & Renshaw, K. (2002). Interjudge agreement, self-enhancement, and liking: Cross-cultural divergences. *Personality and Social Psychology Bulletin, 28,* 578–587.

Henderson, J.M., & Hollingworth, A. (2003). Global transsaccadic change blindness during scene perception. *Psychological Science, 14,* 493–497.

Heslin, R. (1964). Predicting group task effectiveness from member characteristics. *Psychological Bulletin, 62,* 248–256.

Hetherington, A.W., & Ranson, S.W. (1940). Hypothalamic lesions and adiposity in the rat. *Anatomical Record, 78,* 149–72.

Hetherington, E.M. (1988). Parents, children, and siblings six years after divorce. In R.A. Hinde & J. Stevenson-Hinde (Eds.), *Relationships within families: Mutual influences.* Oxford, UK: Clarendon Press.

Hetherington, E.M. (1989). Coping with family transitions: Winners, losers, and survivors. *Child Development, 60,* 1–14.

Hetherington, E.M. (1993). An overview of the Virginia longitudinal study of divorce and remarriage with a focus on early adolescence. *Journal of Family Psychology, 7,* 39–56.

Hetherington, E.M. (2002, January 27). In B. Summerskill and E. Vulliany, For the sake of the children . . . Divorce. *The Observer.*

Hetherington, E.M., Cox, M., & Cox, R. (1982). Effects of divorce on parents and children. In M. Lamb (Ed.), *Non-traditional families.* Hillsdale, NJ: Lawrence Erlbaum Associates, Inc.

Hetherington, E.M., & Stanley-Hagan, M. (1999). The adjustment of children with divorced parents: A risk and resiliency perspective. *Journal of Child Psychology and Psychiatry, 40,* 129–140.

Hetherington, M.M., Anderson, A.S., Norton, G.N.M., & Newson, L. (2006). Situational effects on food intake: A comparison of eating alone and eating with others. *Physiology and Behavior, 88,* 498–505.

Hettema, J.M., Prescott, C.A., Myers, J.M., Neale, M.C., & Kendler, K.S. (2005). The structure of genetic and environmental risk factors for anxiety disorders in men and women. *Archives of General Psychiatry, 62,* 182–189.

Hewstone, M.R.C., & Brown, R.J. (1986). Contact is not enough: An intergroup perspective on the contact hypothesis. In M.R.C. Hewstone & R.J. Brown (Eds.), *Contact and conflict in intergroup encounters.* Oxford, UK: Blackwell.

Hilborn, R.C. (1999). *Chaos and nonlinear dynamics: An introduction for scientists and engineers.* Oxford: Oxford University Press.

Hill, E.L., & Frith, U. (2003). Understanding autism: Insights from mind and brain. *Philosophical Transactions of the Royal Society London B, 358,* 281–289.

Hill, J.O., & Peters, J.C. (1998). Environmental contributions to the obesity epidemic. *Science, 280,* 1371–1374.

Hirsch-Pasek, K., & Golinkoff, R.M. (1996). *The origins of grammar: Evidence from early language comprehension.* Cambridge, MA: MIT Press.

Hirschberg, N. (1978). A correct treatment of traits. In H. London (Ed.), *Personality: A new look at metatheories.* New York: Macmillan.

Hirschfeld, R.M. (1999). Efficacy of SSRIs and newer antidepressants in severe depression: Comparison with TCAs. *Journal of Clinical Psychiatry, 60,* 326–335.

Hobson, J.A. (1988). *The dreaming brain.* New York: Basic Books.

Hobson, J.A., & McCarley, R.W. (1977). The brain as a dream-state generator: An activation–synthesis hypothesis of the dream process. *American Journal of Psychiatry, 134,* 1335–1348.

Hobson, J.A., Pace-Schott, E.F., & Stickgold, R. (2000). Dreaming and the brain: Toward a cognitive neuroscience of conscious states. *Behavioral and Brain Sciences, 23,* 793–842.

Hockey, G.R.J., Davies, S., & Gray, M.M. (1972). Forgetting as a function of sleep at different times of day. *Quarterly Journal of Experimental Psychology, 24,* 386–393.

Hoebel, B.G., & Hernandez, L. (1993). Basic neural mechanisms of feeding and weight regulation. In A.J. Stunkard & T.A. Wadden (Eds.), *Obesity: Theory and therapy* (2nd ed.). New York: Raven Press.

Hoebel, B.G., & Teitelbaum, P. (1966). Weight regulation in normal and hypothalamic hyperphagic rats. *Journal of Comparative and Physiological Psychology, 61,* 189–193.

Hoffman, M.L. (1975). Altruistic behaviour and the parent–child relationship. *Journal of Personality and Social Psychology, 31,* 937–943.

Hoffman, M.L. (1987). The contribution of empathy to justice and moral judgement. *Cognitive Psychology, 2,* 400–410.

Hofling, C.K. (1974). *Textbook of psychiatry for medical practice.* Philadelphia: Lippincott.

Hofling, K.C., Brotzman, E., Dalrymple, S., Graves, N., & Pierce, C.M. (1966). An experimental study in nurse–physician relationship. *Journal of Nervous and Mental Disorders, 143,* 171–180.

Hofstede, G. (1980). *Culture's consequences: International differences in work-related values.* Beverly Hills, CA: Sage.

Hofstede, G. (1983). Dimensions of national cultures in fifty countries and three regions. In J. Derogowski, S. Dzuirawiece, & R. Annis. (Eds.), *Explorations in cross-cultural psychology.* Lisse, The Netherlands: Swets & Zeitlinger.

Hogg, M.A., Turner, J.C., & Davidson, B. (1990). Polarised norms and social frames of reference: A test of the self-categorisation theory of group polarisation. *Basic and Applied Social Psychology, 11,* 77–100.

Hogg, M.A., & Vaughan, G.M. (2005). *Social psychology* (4th ed.). Harlow, UK: Prentice Hall.

Hoglend, P., Engelstad, V., Sorbye, O., Heyerdahl, O., & Amlo, S. (1994). The role of insight in exploratory psychodynamic psychotherapy. *British Journal of Medical Psychology, 67,* 305–317.

Hollingworth, A. & Henderson, J.M. (2002). Accurate visual memory for previously attended objects in natural scenes. *Journal of Experimental Psychology: Human Perception and Performance, 28,* 113–136.

Hollis, K.L. (1997). Contemporary research on Pavlovian conditioning: A "new" functional analysis. *American Psychologist, 52,* 956–965.

Holmberg, M.C. (1980). The development of social interchange patterns from 12 to 42 months. *Child Development, 51,* 448–456.

Holmes, T.H., & Rahe, R.H. (1967). The social readjustment rating scale. *Journal of Psychosomatic Research, 11,* 213–218.

Holmes, V.M. (1988). Hesitations and sentence planning. *Language and Cognitive Processes, 3,* 323–361.

Hong, Y.-Y., Chiu, C.-Y., & Kung, T.M. (1997). Bringing culture out in front: Effects of cultural meaning system activation on social cognition. In K. Leung, Y. Kashinma, U. Kim, & S. Yamaguchi (Eds.), *Progress in Asian social psychology* (Vol. 1). Singapore: Wiley.

Hong, Y.Y., Morris, M.W., Chiu, C.Y., & Benet-Martinez, V. (2000). Multicultural minds: A dynamic constructivist approach to culture and cognition. *American Psychologist, 55,* 709–720.

Horgan, D.D., & Morgan, D. (1990). Chess expertise in children. *Applied Cognitive Psychology, 4,* 109–128.

Horne, J. (1988). *Why we sleep? The functions of sleep in humans and other mammals.* Oxford, UK: Oxford University Press.

Horne, J. (2001). State of the art: Sleep. *The Psychologist, 14,* 302–306.

Hotopf, W.H.N. (1980). Slips of the pen. In U. Frith (Ed.), *Cognitive processes in spelling.* London: Academic Press.

House, J.S., Landis, K.R., & Umberson, D. (1988). Social relationships and health. *Science, 241,* 540–545.

Howard, D. (2006). *Implicit learning: A new frontier in cognitive psychology.* http://college.georgetown.edu/research/mind/14849.html

Howe, C., Tolmie, A., & Rodgers, C. (1992). The acquisition of conceptual knowledge in science by primary school children: Group interaction and the understanding of motion down an incline. *British Journal of Developmental Psychology, 10,* 113–130.

Howe, C.D., Butt, J.L., & Timmons, M.C. (2004). *The tyranny of too much.* http://blackfriarsinc.com/totm.html

Howe, M.J.A. (1998). *Principles of abilities and human learning.* Hove, UK: Psychology Press.

Howe, M.L., & Courage, M.L. (1997). The emergence and early development of autobiographical memory. *Psychological Review, 104*(3), 499–523.

Howe, M.L., Courage, M.L., & Edison, S.C. (2003). When autobiographical memory begins. *Developmental Review, 23,* 471–494.

Howell, J.M., & Hall-Merenda, K. (1999). The ties that bind: The impact of leader–member exchange, transformational and transactional leadership, and distance on predicting follower performance. *Journal of Applied Psychology, 84,* 680–694.

Howitt, D., & Owusu-Bempah, P. (1990). Racism in a British journal? *The Psychologist, 3,* 396–400.

Hüber-Weidman, H. (1976). *Sleep, sleep disturbances and sleep deprivation.* Cologne, Germany: Kiepenheuser & Witsch.

Hughes, C., & Russell, J. (1993). Autistic children's difficulty with mental disengagement from an object: Its implications for executive dysfunction in autism. *Psychological Medicine, 27,* 209–220.

Hughes, M. (1975). *Egocentrism in preschool children.* Unpublished PhD thesis, University of Edinburgh, UK.

Hulin, C.L., Henry, R.A., & Noon, S.L. (1990). Adding a dimension: Time as a factor in the generalisability of predictive relationships. *Psychological Bulletin, 107,* 328–340.

Human, I.E. (1992). Multiple approaches to remembering. *The Psychologist, 5,* 450–451.

Humphrey, N. (1983). *Consciousness regained: Chapters in the development of mind.* Oxford, UK: Oxford University Press.

Humphrey, N. (2002*). The mind made flesh: Frontiers of psychology and evolution.* Oxford, UK: Oxford University Press.

Humphreys, G.W. (1999). Integrative agnosia. In G.W. Humphreys (Ed.), *Case studies in the neuropsychology of vision.* Hove, UK: Psychology Press.

Hunter, J.E. (1983). *Overview of validity generalization for the U.S. Employment Service.* (USES Test Report No. 43). Washington, DC: U.S. Department of Labor, Employment, and Training Administration.

Hunter, J.E. (1986). Cognitive ability, cognitive aptitudes, job knowledge, and job performance. *Journal of Vocational Behavior, 29,* 340–362.

Hunter, J.E., & Hunter, R.F. (1984). Validity and utility of alternative predictors of job performance. *Psychological Bulletin, 96,* 72–98.

Hunter, J.E., & Schmidt, F.L. (1996). Intelligence and job performance: Economic and social implications. *Psychology Public Policy and Law, 2,* 447–472.

Huston, T.L., Caughlin, J.P., Houts, R.M., Smith, S.E., & George, L.J. (2001). The connubial crucible: Newlywed years as predictors of marital delight, distress, and divorce. *Journal of Personality and Social Psychology, 80,* 237–252.

Huston, T.L., Ruggiero, M., Conner, R., & Geis, G. (1981). Bystander intervention into crime: A study based on naturally occurring episodes. *Social Psychology Quarterly, 44,* 14–23.

Ihlebaek, C., Love, T., Eilertsen, D.E., & Magnussen, S. (2003). Memory for a staged criminal event witnessed live and on video. *Memory, 11,* 319–327.

Isen, A.M., Johnson, M.M.S., Mertz, E., & Robinson, G.F. (1985). The influence of positive affect on the unusualness of word associations. *Journal of Personality and Social Psychology, 48,* 1413–1426.

Isenberg, D.J. (1986). Group polarization: A critical review and meta-analysis. *Journal of Personality and Social Psychology, 50,* 1141–1151.

Isurin, L., & McDonald, J.L. (2001). Retroactive interference from translation equivalents: Implications for first language forgetting. *Memory & Cognition, 29,* 312–319.

Iyengar, S.S., & Lepper, M.R. (2000). When choice is demotivating: Can one desire too much of a good thing? *Journal of Personality and Social Psychology, 79,* 995–1006.

Jackson, J.W. (1993). Realistic group conflict theory: A review and evaluation of the theoretical and empirical literature. *Psychological Record, 43,* 395–404.

Jacobsen, L.K., Picciotto, M.R., Heath, C.J., Frost, S.J., Tsou, K.A., Dwan, R.A., et al. (2007). Prenatal and adolescent exposure to tobacco smoke modulates the development of white matter microstructure. *Journal of Neuroscience, 27*(49), 13491–13498.

Jaffee, S., & Hyde, J.S. (2000). Gender differences in moral orientation: A meta-analysis. *Psychological Bulletin, 126,* 703–726.

Jakobsen, P. (2004). Quick beginners' guide to magic: Discover the secrets you need to know to become a successful magician. Retrieved from www.themagicschool.com.

Jakobson, L.S., Archibald, Y.M., Carey, D.P., & Goodale, M.A. (1991). A kinematic analysis of reaching and grasping movements in a patient recovering from optic ataxia. *Neuropsychologia, 29,* 803–809.

James, T.W., Culham, J., Humphrey, G.K., Milner, A.D., & Goodale, M.A. (2003). Ventral occipital lesions impair object recognition but not object-directed grasping: An fMRI study. *Brain*, 126, 2463–2475.

James, W. (1890). *Principles of psychology*. New York: Holt.

Janis, I. (1972). *Victims of groupthink: A psychological study of foreign-policy decisions and fiascos*. Boston, MA: Houghton-Mifflin.

Janis, I. (1982). *Groupthink* (2nd ed.). Boston, MA: Houghton Mifflin.

Janovics, J., & Christiansen, N.D. (2002). *Emotional intelligence in the workplace*. Paper presented at the 16th Annual Conference of the Society of Industrial and Organizational Psychology, San Diego, CA, May.

Jared, D., Levy, B.A., & Rayner, K. (1999). The role of phonology in the activation of word meanings during reading: Evidence from proof-reading and eye movements. *Journal of Experimental Psychology: General*, 128, 219–264.

Jarvis, M. (2004). *Psychodynamic psychology: Classical theory and contemporary research*. London: Thomson.

Jenkins, H.M., Barrera, F.J., Ireland, C., & Woodside, B. (1978). Signal-centred action patterns of dogs in appetitive classical conditioning. *Learning and Motivation*, 9, 272–296.

Jenkins, J.G., & Dallenbach, K.M. (1924). Obliviscence during sleeping and waking. *American Journal of Psychology*, 35, 605–612.

Jensen, A.R. (1969). How much can we boost IQ and scholastic achievement? *Harvard Educational Review*, 39, 1–123.

Jetten, J., Hornsey, M.J., & Adarves-Yorno, I. (2006). When group members admit to being conformist: The role of relative intragroup status in conformity self-reports. *Personality and Social Psychology Bulletin*, 32, 162–173.

Johnson, J.S., & Newport, E.L. (1989). Critical period effects in second language learning: The influence of maturational state on the acquisition of English as a second language. *Cognitive Psychology*, 21, 60–99.

Johnson, M.H., Dziurawiec, S., Ellis, H., & Morton, J. (1991). Newborns' preferential tracking of face-like stimuli and its subsequent decline. *Cognition*, 40, 1–19.

Johnson, R.D., & Downing, L.L. (1979). Deindividuation and valence of cues: Effects on prosocial and antisocial behavior. *Journal of Personality and Social Psychology*, 37, 1532–1538.

Joireman, J., Anderson, J., & Strathman, A. (2003). The aggression paradox: Understanding links among aggression, sensation seeking, and the consideration of future consequences. *Journal of Personality and Social Psychology*, 84, 1287–1302.

Jones, E.E. (1998). Major developments in five decades of social psychology. In D.T. Gilbert, S.T. Fiske, & G. Lindzey (Eds.), *Handbook of social psychology* (Vol. 1, 4th ed., pp. 3–57). New York: McGraw-Hill.

Jones, E.E., & Harris, V.A. (1967). The attribution of attitudes. *Journal of Experimental Social Psychology*, 3, 1–24.

Jones, E.E., & Nisbett, R.E. (1972). The actor and the observer: Divergent perceptions of the causes of behaviour. In E.E. Jones, D.E. Kanouse, H.H. Kelley, R.E. Nisbett, S. Vlins, & B. Weiner (Eds.), *Attribution: Perceiving the causes of behavior*. Morristown, NJ: General Learning Press.

Jones, E.E., & Sigall, H. (1971). The bogus pipeline: A new paradigm for measuring affect and attitude. *Psychological Bulletin*, 76, 349–364.

Jones, J.T., Pelham, B.W., Carvallo, M., & Mirenberg, M.C. (2004). How do I love thee? Let me count the Js: Implicit egotism and interpersonal attraction. *Journal of Personality and Social Psychology*, 87, 665–683.

Joseph, J. (2003). *The gene illusion: Genetic research in psychiatry and psychology under the microscope*. Ross-on-Wye: PCCS Books.

Josephs, R.A., Larrick, R.P., Steele, C.M., & Nisbett, R.E. (1992). Protecting the self from the negative consequences of risky decisions. *Journal of Personality & Social Psychology*, 62, 26–37.

Jourard, S.M. (1966). An exploratory study of body-accessibility. *British Journal of Social and Clinical Psychology*, 5, 221–231.

Judge, T.A., & Bono, J.E. (2001). Relationship of core self-evaluation traits—self-esteem, generalized self-efficacy, locus of control, and emotional stability—with job satisfaction and job performance: A meta-analysis. *Journal of Applied Psychology*, 86, 80–92.

Judge, T.A., Erez, A., Bono, J.E., & Thoresen, C.J. (2002). Are measures of self-esteem, neuroticism, locus of control, and generalized self-efficacy indicators of a common core construct? *Journal of Personality and Social Psychology*, 83, 693–710.

Judge, T.A., Erez, A., Bono, J.E., & Thoresen, C.J. (2003). The core self-evaluations scale: Development of a measure. *Personnel Psychology*, 56, 303–331.

Judge, T.A., Locke, E.A., & Durham, C.C. (1997). The dispositional causes of job satisfaction: A core evaluations approach. *Research in Organizational Behavior*, 19, 151–188.

Just, M.A., Carpenter, P.A., Keller, T.A., Emery, L., Zajac, H., & Thulborn, K.R. (2001). Interdependence of non-overlapping cortical systems in dual cognitive tasks. *NeuroImage*, 14, 417–426.

Kahn, D., & Hobson, J.A. (2005). State-dependent thinking: A comparison of waking and dreaming thought. *Consciousness and Cognition*, 14, 429–438.

Kahneman, D., & Tversky, A. (1984). Choices, values and frames. *American Psychologist*, 39, 341–350.

Kalat, J.W. (1998). *Biological psychology* (6th ed.). Pacific Grove, CA: Brooks/Cole Publishing Co.

Kallio, S., Revonsuo, A., Hamalainen, H., Markela, J., & Gruzelier, J. (2001). Anterior brain functions and hypnosis: A test of the frontal hypothesis. *International Journal of Clinical and Experimental Hypnosis*, 49, 95–108.

Kamin, L. (1981). *The intelligence controversy: H.J. Eysenck vs. Leon Kamin*. New York: Wiley.

Kamin, L.J. (1969). Predictability, surprise, attention and conditioning. In R. Campbell & R. Church (Eds.), *Punishment and aversive behaviour*. New York: Appleton-Century-Crofts.

Kane, M.J., & Engle, R.W. (2000). Working-memory capacity, proactive interference, divided attention: Limits on long-term memory retrieval. *Journal of Experimental Psychology: Learning, Memory, and Cognition*, 26, 336–358.

Kanner, L. (1943). Autistic disturbances of affective contact. *Nervous Child*, 2, 217–250.

Kaplan, G.A., & Simon, H.A. (1990). In search of insight. *Cognitive Psychology*, 22, 374–419.

Karasek, R.A. (1979). Job demands, job decision latitude, and mental strain: Implications for job redesign. *Administrative Science Quarterly*, 24, 285–308.

Karmiloff-Smith, A., Grant, J., Berthoud, I., Davies, M., Howlin, P., & Udwin, O. (1997). Language and Williams syndrome: How intact is "intact"? *Child Development*, 68, 246–262.

Karnath, H.O., Himmelbach, M., & Küker, W. (2003). The cortical substrate of visual extinction. *NeuroReport*, 14, 437–442.

Karney, B.R., & Frye, N.E. (2002). But we've been getting better lately: Comparing prospective and retrospective views of relationship development. *Journal of Personality and Social Psychology*, 82, 222–238.

Kashima, Y., Siegal, M., Tanaka, K., & Kashima, E.S. (1992). Do people believe behaviours are consistent with attitudes? Towards a cultural psychology of attribution processes. *British Journal of Social Psychology*, 31, 111–124.

Kashima, Y., & Triandis, H.C. (1986). The self-serving bias in attributions as a coping strategy: A cross-cultural study. *Journal of Cross-Cultural Psychology*, 17, 83–97.

Kassin, S.M., Tubb, V.A., Hosch, H.M., & Memon, A. (2001). On the "general acceptance" of eyewitness testimony research. *American Psychologist, 56,* 405–416.

Kaup, B., & Zwaan, R.A. (2003). Effects of negation and situational presence on the accessibility of text information. *Journal of Experimental Psychology: Learning, Memory, and Cognition, 29,* 439–446.

Kavanau, J.L. (2005). Evolutionary approaches to understanding sleep. *Sleep Medicine, 9,* 141–152.

Kavanau, J.L. (2006). Is sleep's "supreme mystery" unravelling? An evolutionary analysis of sleep encounters no mystery; nor does life's earliest sleep, recently discovered in jellyfish. *Medical Hypotheses, 66,* 3–9.

Keesey, R.E., & Boyle, P.C. (1973). Effects of quinine adulteration upon body weight of LH-lesioned and intact male rats. *Journal of Comparative and Physiological Psychology, 84,* 38–46.

Keiley, M.K., Bates, J.E., Dodge, K.A., & Pettit, G.S. (2000). A cross-domain growth analysis: Externalizing and internalizing behaviors during 8 years of childhood. *Journal of Abnormal Child Psychology, 28,* 161–179.

Kelley, H.H. (1950). The warm–cold variable in first impressions of people. *Journal of Personality, 18,* 431–439.

Kelley, H.H. (1967). Attribution theory in social psychology. In D. Levine (Ed.), *Nebraska symposium on motivation* (Vol. 15). Lincoln, NE: University of Nebraska Press.

Kelley, H.H. (1973). The processes of causal attribution. *American Psychologist, 28,* 107–128.

Kellman, P.J., & Spelke, E.S. (1983). Perception of partly occluded objects in infancy. *Cognitive Psychology, 15,* 483–524.

Keltner, D., & Gross, J.J. (1999). Functional accounts of emotions. *Cognition and Emotion, 13,* 467–480.

Kendall, P.C., & Hammen, C. (1998). *Abnormal psychology: Understanding human problems* (2nd ed.). New York: Houghton Mifflin.

Kendler, K.S., Karkowski, L.M., & Prescott, C.A. (1999). Fears and phobias: Reliability and heritability. *Psychological Medicine, 29,* 539–553.

Kendler, K.S., Neale, M.C., Kessler, R.C., Heath, A.C., & Eaves, L.J. (1992). A population-based twin study of major depression in women: The impact of varying definitions of illness. *Archives of General Psychiatry, 49,* 257–266.

Kendler, K.S., Neale, M.C., Kessler, R.C., Heath, A.C., & Eaves, L.J. (1993). Panic disorder in women: A population-based twin study. *Psychological Medicine, 23,* 397–406.

Kendler, K.S., Neale, M.C., Prescott, C.A., Kessler, R.C., Heath, A.C., Corey, L.A., & Eaves, L.J. (1996). Childhood parental loss and alcoholism in women: A causal analysis using a twin-family design. *Psychological Medicine, 26,* 79–95.

Kendler, K.S., Pedersen, N.L., Farahmand, B.Y., & Persson, P.G. (1996). The treated incidence of psychotic and affective illness in twins compared with population expectation: A study in the Swedish Twin and Psychiatric Registries. *Psychological Medicine, 26,* 1135–1144.

Kenealy, P.M. (1997). Mood-state-dependent retrieval: The effects of induced mood on memory reconsidered. *Quarterly Journal of Experimental Psychology, 50A,* 290–317.

Kenrick, D.T. (2001). Evolutionary psychology, cognitive science, and dynamical systems: Building an integrative paradigm. *Current Directions in Psychological Science, 10,* 13–17.

Kermer, D.A., Driver-Linn, E., Wilson, T.D., & Gilbert, D.T. (2006). Loss aversion is an affective forecasting error. *Psychological Science, 17,* 649–653.

Kiecolt-Glaser, J.K., Garner, W., Speicher, C.E., Penn, G.M., Holliday, J., & Glaser, R. (1984). Psychosocial modifiers of immunocompetence in medical students. *Psychosomatic Medicine, 46,* 7–14.

Kim, H., & Markus, H.R. (1999). Uniqueness or deviance, harmony or conformity: A cultural analysis. *Journal of Personality and Social Psychology, 77,* 785–800.

Kimble, D.P., Robinson, T.S., & Moon, S. (1992). *Biological psychology* (2nd ed.). Orlando, FL: Harcourt Brace Jovanovich.

Kimmel, A.J. (1996). *Ethical issues in behavioural research.* Oxford, UK: Blackwell.

King, B.M., Smith, R.L., & Frohman, L.A. (1984). Hyper-insulinemia in rats with ventromedial hypothalamic lesions: Role of hyperphagia. *Behavioral Neuroscience, 98,* 152–155.

Kintsch, W. (1988). The role of knowledge in discourse comprehension: A construction–integration model. *Psychological Review, 95*(2), 163–182.

Kintsch, W. (1992). A cognitive architecture for comprehension. In H.L. Pick, P. van den Broek, & D.C. Knill (Eds.), *Cognition: Conceptual and methodological issues.* Washington, DC: American Psychological Association.

Kintsch, W. (1994). The psychology of discourse processing. In M.A. Gernsbacher (Ed.), *Handbook of psycholinguistics.* London: Academic Press.

Kintsch, W. (1998). *Comprehension: A paradigm for cognition.* New York: Cambridge University Press.

Kintsch, W., Welsch, D., Schmalhofer, F., & Zimny, S. (1990). Sentence memory: A theoretical analysis. *Journal of Memory & Language, 29,* 133–159.

Kirkpatrick, S.A., & Locke, E.A. (1996). Direct and indirect effects of three core charismatic leadership components on performance and attitudes. *Journal of Applied Psychology, 81,* 36–51.

Kisilevsky, B.S., Hains, S.M.J., Lee, K., Xie, X., Huang, H., Ye, H.H., et al. (2003). Effects of experience on foetal voice recognition. *Psychological Science, 14,* 220–224.

Kitsantas, A. (2000). The role of self-regulation strategies and self-efficacy perceptions in successful weight loss maintenance. *Psychology and Health, 15,* 811–820.

Kivlighan, D.M., Multon, K.D., & Patton, M.J. (2000). Insight and symptom reduction in time-limited psychoanalytic counselling. *Journal of Counseling Psychology, 47,* 50–58.

Klauer, K.C., & Zhao, Z. (2004). Double dissociations in visual and spatial short-term memory. *Journal of Experimental Psychology: General, 133,* 355–381.

Klaus, M.H., & Kennell, J.H. (1976). *Parent–infant bonding.* St. Louis, MO: Mosby.

Klein, G. (2001). The fiction of optimization. In G. Gigerenzer & R. Selten (Eds.), *Bounded rationality: The adaptive toolbox.* Cambridge, MA: MIT Press.

Klein, H.J., Wesson, M.J., Hollenbeck, J.R., & Alge, B.J. (1999). Goal commitment and the goal-setting process: Conceptual clarification and empirical synthesis. *Journal of Applied Psychology, 84,* 885–896.

Kleinman, A., & Cohen, A. (1997, March). Psychiatry's global challenge. *Scientific American,* pp. 74–77.

Kline, P. (1981). *Fact and fantasy in Freudian theory.* London: Methuen.

Kline, P., & Storey, R. (1977). A factor analytic study of the oral character. *British Journal of Social and Clinical Psychology, 16,* 317–328.

Klohnen, E.C., & Bera, S. (1998). Behavioural and experiential patterns of avoidantly and securely attached women across adulthood: A 31-year longitudinal perspective. *Journal of Personality and Social Psychology, 74,* 211–223.

Kluver, H., & Bucy, P.C. (1937). "Psychic blindness" and other symptoms following bilateral temporal lobectomy. *American Journal of Physiology, 119,* 352–353.

Kluver, H., & Bucy, P. (1939). Preliminary analysis of functions of the temporal lobes in monkeys. *Archives of Neurology and Psychiatry, 42,* 979–1000.

Knoblich, G., Ohlsson, S., Haider, H., & Rhenius, D. (1999). Constraint relaxation and chunk decomposition in insight problem solving. *Journal of Experimental Psychology: Learning, Memory, and Cognition, 25,* 1534–1555.

Knowlton, B.J., Ramus, S.J., & Squire, L.R. (1992). Intact artificial grammar learning in amnesia: Dissociation of classification learning and explicit memory for specific instances. *Psychological Science, 3,* 172–179.

Koehler, D.J., & Harvey, N. (2004). *Blackwell handbook of judgement and decision making.* Oxford, UK: Blackwell.

Koffka, K. (1935). *Principles of Gestalt psychology.* New York: Harcourt Brace.

Kohlberg, L. (1963). Development of children's orientations toward a moral order. *Vita Humana, 6,* 11–36.

Kohlberg, L. (1975). The cognitive-developmental approach to moral education. *Phi Delta Kappan,* June, 670–677.

Koluchová, J. (1976). The further development of twins after severe and prolonged deprivation: A second report. *Journal of Child Psychology and Psychiatry, 17,* 181–188.

Kopta, S.M., Lueger, R.J., Saunders, S.M., & Howard, K.I. (1999). Individual psychotherapy outcome and process research: Challenges leading to greater turmoil or a positive transition? *Annual Review of Psychology, 50,* 441–469.

Korchmaros, J.D., & Kenny, D.A. (2001). Emotional closeness as a mediator of the effect of genetic relatedness on altruism. *Psychological Science, 12,* 262–265.

Kosslyn, S.M. (1994). *Image and brain: The resolution of the imagery debate.* Cambridge, MA: MIT Press.

Kosslyn, S.M., & Thompson, W.L. (2003). When is early visual cortex activated during visual mental imagery? *Psychological Bulletin, 129,* 723–746.

Kramer, R.M. (1998). Revisiting the Bay of Pigs and Vietnam decisions 25 years later: How well has the groupthink hypothesis stood the test of time? *Organizational Behavior and Human Decision Processes, 73,* 236–271.

Kraus, S.J. (1995). Attitudes and the prediction of behaviour: A meta-analysis of the empirical literature. *Personality and Social Psychology Bulletin, 21,* 58–75.

Krevans, J., & Gibbs, J.C. (1996). Parents' use of inductive discipline: Relations to children's empathy and prosocial behavior. *Child Development, 67,* 3263–3277.

Krueger, R.F., Hicks, B.M., & McGue, M. (2001). Altruism and anti-social behaviour: Independent tendencies, unique personality correlates, distinct aetiologies. *Psychological Science, 12,* 397–402.

Kuhn, T.S. (1962). *The structure of scientific revolutions.* Chicago: Chicago University Press.

Kuhn, T.S. (1977). *The essential tension: Selected studies in scientific tradition and change.* Chicago: Chicago University Press.

Kuiper, K. (1996). *Smooth talkers.* Mahwah, NJ: Lawrence Erlbaum Associates, Inc.

Kunda, Z., & Oleson, K.C. (1995). Maintaining stereotypes in the face of disconfirmation: Constructing grounds for subtyping deviants. *Journal of Personality and Social Psychology, 68,* 565–579.

Kuo-shu, Y., & Bond, M.H. (1990). Exploring implicit personality theories with indigenous or imported constructs: The Chinese case. *Journal of Personality and Social Psychology, 58,* 1087–1095.

Kuppens, P., van Mechelen, I., Smits, D.J.M., & de Boeck, P. (2003). The appraisal basis of anger: Specificity, necessity, and sufficiency of components. *Emotion, 3,* 254–269.

LaBerge, S., Greenleaf, W., & Kedzierski, B. (1983). Physiological responses to dreamed sexual activity during lucid REM sleep. *Psychophysiology, 20,* 454–455.

Lachter, J., Forster, K.I., & Ruthruff, E. (2004). Forty-five years after Broadbent: Still no identification without attention. *Psychological Review, 111,* 880–913.

Lafferty, P., Beutler, L.E., & Crago, M. (1989). Differences between more and less effective psychotherapists: A study of select therapist variables. *Journal of Consulting and Clinical Psychology, 57,* 76–80.

Lambert, M., & Bergin, A.E. (1994). The effectiveness of psychotherapy. In A.E. Bergin & S.L. Garfield (Eds.), *Handbook of psychotherapy and behavior change* (4th ed., pp. 143–189). New York: Wiley.

Lamm, H., & Wiesmann, U. (1997). Subjective attributes of attraction: How people characterise their liking, their love, and their being in love. *Personal Relationships, 4,* 271–284.

Lamont, A.M. (2001). Retrieved from www.le.ac.uk/pc/aml11/babies.html

Langlois, J.H., Roggman, L.A., & Musselman, L. (1994). What is average and what is not average about attractive faces. *Psychological Science, 5,* 214–220.

LaPiere, R.T. (1934). Attitudes vs. actions. *Social Forces, 13,* 230–237.

Larivee, S., Normandeau, S., & Parent, S. (2000). The French connection: Some contributions of French-language research in the post-Piagetian era. *Child Development, 71*(4), 823.

Larsen, J.D., Baddeley, A., & Andrade, J. (2000). Phonological similarity and the irrelevant speech effect: Implications for models of short-term memory. *Memory, 8,* 145–157.

Larson, J.R., Foster-Fishman, P.G., & Keys, C.B. (1994). Discussion of shared and unshared information in decision-making groups. *Journal of Personality and Social Psychology, 67,* 446–461.

Latham, G.P. (2003). Goal setting: A five-step approach to behaviour change. *Organizational Dynamics, 32,* 309–318.

Latham, G.P., & Brown, T.C. (2006). The effect of learning vs. outcome goals on self-efficacy and satisfaction in an MBA programme. *Applied Psychology: An International Review, 55,* 606–623.

Latham, G.P., & Saari, L.M. (1982). The importance of union acceptance for productivity improvement through goal setting. *Personnel Psychology, 35,* 781–787.

Latham, G.P., & Yukl, G.A. (1975). Assigned versus participative goal setting with educated and uneducated woods workers. *Journal of Applied Psychology, 60,* 299–302.

Lazarus, R.S. (1982). Thoughts on the relations between emotion and cognition. *American Psychologist, 37,* 1019–1024.

Lazarus, R.S. (1991). *Emotion and adaptation.* Oxford, UK: Oxford University Press.

Lazarus, R.S. (1993). Coping theory and research: Past, present, and future. *Psychosomatic Medicine, 55,* 234–247.

Le, B., & Agnew, C.R. (2003). Commitment and its theorised determinants: A meta-analysis of the Investment Model. *Personal Relationships, 10,* 37–57.

Le Bon, G. (1895). *The crowd.* London: Ernest Benn.

LeDoux, J.E. (1992). Brain mechanisms of emotion and emotional learning. *Current Opinions in Neurobiology, 2,* 191–198.

LeDoux, J.E. (1996). *The emotional brain: The mysterious underpinnings of emotional life.* New York: Simon & Schuster.

Lee, S.M. (1993). Racial classifications in the United States census: 1890–1990. *Ethnic and Racial Studies, 16,* 75–94.

Lee, W.E., Wadsworth, M.E.J., & Hotop, M. (2006). The protective role of trait anxiety: A longitudinal cohort study. *Psychological Medicine, 36,* 345–351.

Lehman, D.R., Chiu, C.Y., & Schaller, M. (2004). Psychology and culture. *Annual Review of Psychology, 55,* 689–714.

Leibowitz, S.F., Hammer, N.J., & Chang, K. (1981). Hypothalamic paraventricular nucleus lesions produce overeating and obesity in the rat. *Physiology and Behavior, 27,* 1031–1040.

Lemerise, E.A., & Arsenio, W.F. (2000). An integrated model of emotion processes and cognition in social information processing. *Child Development, 71,* 107–118.

Lemyre, L., & Smith, P.M. (1985). Intergroup discrimination and self-esteem in the minimal group paradigm. *Journal of Personality and Social Psychology, 49,* 660–670.

Lenneberg, E.H. (1967). *The biological foundations of language.* New York: Wiley.

Lesar, T.S., Briceland, L., & Stein, D.S. (1997). Factors related to errors in medication prescribing. *Journal of the American Medical Association, 277,* 312–317.

Leslie, A.M. (1987). Pretence and representation: The origins of "theory of mind." *Psychological Review, 94,* 412–426.

Levelt, W.J.M., Roelofs, A., & Meyer, A.S. (1999). A theory of lexical access in speech production. *Behavioral and Brain Sciences, 22,* 1–38.

Levenson, R.W. (1999). The intrapersonal functions of emotions. *Cognition and Emotion, 13,* 481–504.

Levenson, R.W., Ekman, P., & Friesen, W.V. (1990). Voluntary action generates emotion-specific autonomic nervous-system activity. *Psychophysiology, 27,* 363–384.

Levi, D.M. (2005). Perceptual learning in adults with amblyopia: A re-evaluation of critical periods in human vision. *Developmental Psychobiology, 46,* 222–232.

Levin, D.T., Drivdahl, S.B., Momen, N., & Beck, M.R. (2002). False predictions about the detectability of visual changes: The role of beliefs about attention, memory, and the continuity of attended objects in causing change blindness. *Consciousness and Cognition, 11,* 507–527.

Levin, D.T., & Simons, D.J. (1997). Failure to detect changes to attended objects in motion pictures. *Psychonomic Bulletin and Review, 4,* 501–506.

Levine, J., Warrenburg, S., Kerns, R., Schwartz, G., Delaney, R., Fontana, A., et al. (1987). The role of denial in recovery from coronary heart disease. *Psychosomatic Medicine, 49,* 109–117.

Levine, J.A., Eberhardt, N.L., & Jensen, M.D. (1999, January). Role of nonexercise activity thermogenesis in resistance to fat gain in humans. *Science, 8,* pp. 212–214.

Levine, J.M., Moreland, R.L., & Ryan, C.S. (1998). Group socialization and intergroup relations. In C. Sedikides, J. Schopler, & C.A. Insko (Eds.), *Intergroup cognition and intergroup behavior* (pp. 283–308). Mahwah, NJ: Lawrence Erlbaum Associates, Inc.

Levine, M. (2002). *Walk on by?* [Relational Justice Bulletin]. Cambridge, UK: Relationships Foundation.

Lewinsohn, P.M, Joiner, T.E., Jr., & Rohde, P. (2001). Evaluation of cognitive diathesis–stress models in predicting major depressive disorder in adolescents. *Journal of Abnormal Psychology, 110,* 203–215.

Leyens, J.-P., Camino, L., Parke, R.D., & Berkowitz, L. (1975). Effects of movie violence on aggression in a field setting as a function of group dominance and cohesion. *Journal of Personality and Social Psychology, 32,* 346–360.

Libet, B., Gleason, C.A., Wright, E.W., & Pearl, D.K. (1983). Time of conscious intention to act in relation to onset of cerebral activity (readiness potential: The unconscious initiation of a freely voluntary act. *Brain, 106,* 623–642.

Lief, H., & Fetkewicz, J. (1995). Retractors of false memories: The evolution of pseudo-memories. *Journal of Psychiatry & Law, 23,* 411–436.

Light, P., Buckingham, N., & Robbins, A.H. (1979). The conservation task as an interactional setting. *British Journal of Educational Psychology, 49,* 304–310.

Lilienfeld, S.O., & Marino, L. (1999). Essentialism revisited: Evolutionary theory and the concept of mental disorder. *Journal of Abnormal Psychology, 108,* 400–411.

Lin, Y.C. (1992). *The construction of the sense of intimacy from everyday interaction.* Unpublished Ph.D. thesis, University of Rochester, New York.

Locke, E.A. (1968). Toward a theory of task motivation and incentives. *Organizational Behavior and Human Performance, 3,* 157–189.

Locke, E.A., & Latham, G.P. (1990). *A theory of goal setting and task performance.* Englewood Cliffs, NJ: Prentice Hall.

Locke, E.A., & Latham, G.P. (2002). Building a practically useful theory of goal setting and task motivation: A 35-year odyssey. *American Psychologist, 57,* 705–717.

Locke, E.A., & Latham, G.P. (2006). New directions in goal-setting theory. *Current Directions in Psychological Science, 15,* 265–268.

Loehlin, J.C. (1985). Fitting heredity–environment models jointly to twin and adoption data from the California Psychological Inventory. *Behavior Genetics, 15,* 199–221.

Loehlin, J.C., McCrae, R.R., Costa, P.T., & John, O.P. (1998). Heritabilities of common and measure-specific components of the Big Five personality factors. *Journal of Research in Personality, 32,* 431–453.

Loehlin, J.C., & Nichols, R.C. (1976). *Heredity, environment and personality.* Austin, TX: University of Texas Press.

Loftus, E.F., Loftus, G.R., & Messo, J. (1987). Some facts about "weapons focus." *Law and Human Behavior, 11,* 55–62.

Loftus, E.F., & Palmer, J.C. (1974). Reconstruction of automobile destruction: An example of the interaction between language and memory. *Journal of Verbal Learning and Verbal Behavior, 13,* 585–589.

Logie, R.H. (1999). State of the art: Working memory. *The Psychologist, 12,* 174–178.

Logie, R.H., Baddeley, A.D., Mane, A., Donchin, E., & Sheptak, R. (1989). Working memory and the analysis of a complex skill by secondary task methodology. *Acta Psychologica, 71,* 53–87.

Lohmann, H., Carpenter, M., & Call, J. (2005). Guessing versus choosing—and seeing versus believing—in false belief tasks. *British Journal of Developmental Psychology, 23,* 451–469.

Lopes, P.N., Brackett, M.A., Nezlek, J.B., Schutz, A., Sellin, I., & Salovey, P. (2004). Emotional intelligence and social interaction. *Personality and Social Psychology Bulletin, 30,* 1018–1034.

Lord, R.G., de Vader, C.L., & Alliger, G.M. (1986). A meta-analysis of the relation between personality traits and leadership perception: An application of validity generalisation procedures. *Journal of Applied Psychology, 71,* 402–410.

Lourenço, O., & Machado, A. (1996). In defence of Piaget's theory: A reply to 10 common criticisms. *Psychological Review, 103,* 143–164.

Lovibond, P.F., & Shanks, D.R. (2002). The role of awareness in Pavlovian conditioning: Empirical evidence and theoretical implications. *Journal of Experimental Psychology: Animal Behavior Processes, 28,* 3–26.

Lovland, J. (1976). *Doing social life: The qualitative study of human interaction in natural settings.* New York: Wiley.

Lowe, K.B., Kroeck, K.G., & Sivasubramiam, N. (1996). Effectiveness correlates of tranformational and transactional leadership: A meta-analytic review of the MLQ literature. *Leadership Quarterly, 7,* 385–425.

Luchins, A.S. (1942). Mechanisation in problem solving. The effect of Einstellung. *Psychological Monographs, 54,* 248.

Luchins, A.S., & Luchins, E.H. (1959). *Rigidity of behavior.* Eugene, OR: University of Oregon Press.

Luckow, A., Reifman, A., & McIntosh, D.N. (1998). *Gender differences in caring: A meta-analysis.* Poster presented at 106th annual convention of the American Psychological Association, San Francisco.

Lugaressi, E., Medori, R., Montagna, P., Baruzzi, A., Cortelli, P., Lugaressi, A., et al. (1986). Fatal familial insomnia and dysautonomia in the selective degeneration of thalamic nuclei. *New England Journal of Medicine, 315,* 997–1003.

Lumer, E.D., Friston, K.J., & Rees, G. (1998). Neural correlates of perceptual rivalry in the human brain. *Science, 280,* 1930–1934.

Maass, A., Clark, R.D., III, (1983). Internalization versus compliance: Differential processes underlying minority influence and conformity. *European Journal of Social Psychology, 13,* 197–215.

Maccoby, E.E. (1998). *The two sexes: Growing up apart, coming together.* Cambridge, MA: Harvard University Press.

MacDonald, M.C., Pearlmutter, N.J., & Seidenberg, M.S. (1994). Lexical nature of syntactic ambiguity resolution. *Psychological Review, 101,* 676–703.

MacGregor, J.N., Ormerod, T.C., & Chronicle, E.P. (2001). Information processing and insight: A process model of performance on the nine-dot and related problems. *Journal of Experimental Psychology: Learning, Memory, and Cognition, 27,* 176–201.

Mackie, D.M., & Cooper, J. (1984). Group polarization: The effects of group membership. *Journal of Personality and Social Psychology, 46,* 575–585.

Mackintosh, N.J. (1986). The biology of intelligence? *British Journal of Psychology, 77,* 1–18.

Mackintosh, N.J. (1998). *IQ and human intelligence.* Oxford, UK: Oxford University Press.

MacLeod, A. (1998). Therapeutic interventions. In M.W. Eysenck (Ed.), *Psychology: An integrated approach.* Harlow, UK: Addison Wesley Longman.

Macrae, C.N., & Bodenhausen, G.V. (2000). Social cognition: Thinking categorically about others. *Annual Review of Psychology, 51,* 93–120.

Macrae, C.N., Milne, A.B., & Bodenhausen, G.V. (1994). Stereotypes as energy-saving devices: A peek inside the cognitive toolbox. *Journal of Personality and Social Psychology, 66,* 37–47.

Madison, P. (1956). Freud's repression concept: A survey and attempted clarification. *International Journal of Psychoanalysis, 37,* 75–81.

Maes, H.H.M., Neale, M.C., & Eaves, L.J. (1997). Genetic and environmental factors in relative body weight and human adiposity. *Behavior Genetics, 27,* 325–351.

Main, M., Kaplan, N., & Cassidy, J. (1985). Security in infancy, childhood, and adulthood: A move to the level of representation. In I. Bretherton & E. Waters (Eds.), Growing points of attachment theory and research. *Monographs of the Society for Research in Child Development, 50*(1–2).

Mann, L. (1981). The baiting crowd in episodes of threatened suicide. *Journal of Personality and Social Psychology, 41,* 703–709.

Mann, L., Newton, J.W., & Innes, J.M. (1982). A test between deindividuation and emergent norm theories of crowd aggression. *Journal of Personality and Social Psychology, 42,* 260–272.

Mann, R.D. (1959). A review of the relationships between personality and performance in small groups. *Psychological Bulletin, 56,* 241–270.

Manns, J.R., Hopkins, R.O., & Squire, L.R. (2003). Semantic memory and the human hippocampus. *Neuron, 38,* 127–133.

Manstead, A.S.R., & Semin, G.R. (1996). Methodology in social psychology: Putting ideas to the test. In M. Hewstone, W. Stroebe, & G.M. Stephenson (Eds.), *Introduction to social psychology* (2nd ed.). Oxford, UK: Blackwell.

Maquet, P. (2000). Functional neuroimaging of normal human sleep by positron emission tomography. *Journal of Sleep Research, 9,* 207–231.

Marañon, G. (1924). Contribution a l'étude de l'action emotive de l'adrenaline. *Révue Française d'Endocrinologie, 2,* 301–325.

Mares, M.L., & Woodard, E. (2005). Positive effects of television on children's social interactions: A meta-analysis. *Media Psychology, 7,* 301–322.

Marmot, M.G., Bosma, H., Hemingway, H., Brunner, E., & Stansfeld, S. (1997). Contribution of job control and other risk factors to social variations in coronary heart disease incidence. *Lancet, 350,* 235–239.

Marsh, P., Rosser, E., & Harré, R. (1978). *The rules of disorder.* London: Routledge & Kegan Paul.

Marshall, N.L. (2004). The quality of early child care and children's development. *Current Directions in Psychological Science, 13,* 165–168.

Marslen-Wilson, W.D. (1990). Activation, competition, and frequency in lexical access. In G.T.M. Altmann (Ed.), *Cognitive models of speech processing: Psycholinguistics and computational perspectives.* Cambridge, MA: MIT Press.

Marslen-Wilson, W.D., & Tyler, L.K. (1980). The temporal structure of spoken language understanding. *Cognition, 8,* 1–71.

Martin, A., & Caramazza, A. (2003). Neuropsychological and neuroimaging perspectives on conceptual knowledge: An introduction. *Cognitive Neuropsychology, 20,* 195–221.

Martin, C.L., Eisenbud, L., & Rose, H. (1995). Children's gender-based reasoning about toys. *Child Development, 66,* 1453–1471.

Martin, C.L., & Halverson, C.F. (1983). The effects of sex-typing schemas on young children's memory. *Child Development, 54,* 563–574.

Martin, C.L., & Halverson, C.F. (1987). The roles of cognition in sex role acquisition. In D.B. Carter (Ed.), *Current conceptions of sex roles and sex typing: Theory and research.* New York: Praeger.

Martin, C.L., Wood, C.H., & Little, J.K. (1990). The development of gender stereotype components. *Child Development, 61,* 1891–1904.

Martin, C.R., & Bonner, A.B. (2005). Towards an integrated clinical psychobiology of alcoholism. *Current Psychiatry Reviews, 1,* 303–312.

Martin, R.A. (1989). Techniques for data acquisition and analysis in field investigations of stress. In R.W.J. Neufeld (Ed.), *Advances in the investigation of psychological stress.* New York: Wiley.

Martin, R.A., Kulper, N.A., & Westra, H.A. (1989). Cognitive and affective components of the Type A behaviour pattern: Preliminary evidence for a self-worth contingency model. *Personality and Individual Differences, 10,* 771–784.

Martin, R.C., Miller, M., & Vu, H. (2004). Lexical-semantic retention and speech production: Further evidence from normal and brain-damaged participants for a phrasal scope of planning. *Cognitive Neuropsychology, 21,* 625–644.

Martinez, A., Anllo-Vento, L., Sereno, M.I., Frank. L.R., Buxton, R.B., Dubowitz, D.J., et al. (1999). Involvement of striate and extrastriate visual cortical areas in spatial attention. *Nature Neuroscience, 4,* 364–369.

Marzi, C.A., Girelli, M., Natale, E., & Miniussi, C. (2001). What exactly is extinguished in unilateral visual extinction? *Neuropsychologia, 39,* 1354–1366.

Maslow, A.H. (1954). *Motivation and personality.* New York: Harper.

Maslow, A.H. (1962). *Toward a psychology of being.* Princeton, NJ: Van Nostrand.

Maslow, A.H. (1968). *Toward a psychology of being* (2nd ed.). New York: Van Nostrand.

Maslow, A.H. (1970). *Toward a psychology of being* (3rd ed.). New York: Van Nostrand.

Massaro, D.W. (1994). Psychological aspects of speech perception: Implications for research and theory. In M.A. Gernsbacher (Ed.), *Handbook of psycholinguistics.* San Diego, CA: Academic Press.

Masters, W.H., & Johnson, V.E. (1966). *Human sexual response.* Boston: Little, Brown.

Mathes, E.W., Zevon, M.A., Roter, P.M., & Joerger, S.M. (1982). Peak experience tendencies: Scale development and theory testing. *Journal of Humanistic Psychology, 22,* 92–108.

Matt, G.E., & Navarro, A.M. (1997). What meta-analyses have and have not taught us about psychotherapy effects: A review and future directions. *Clinical Psychology Review, 17,* 1–32.

Matthews, D., Lieven, E., Theakston, A., & Tomasello, M. (2005). The role of frequency in the acquisition of English word order. *Cognitive Development, 20,* 121–136.

Matthews, G., Roberts, R.D., & Zeidner, M. (2004). Seven myths about emotional intelligence. *Psychological Inquiry, 15,* 179–196.

Matthews, K.A. (1988). Coronary heart disease and Type A behaviour: Update on and alternative to the Booth-Kewley and Friedman (1987) quantitative review. *Psychological Bulletin, 104,* 373–380.

Matthews, K.A., Glass, D.C., Rosenman, R.H., & Bortner, R.W. (1977). Competitive drive, Pattern A, and coronary heart disease: A further analysis of some data from the Western Collaborative Group. *Journal of Chronic Diseases, 30,* 489–498.

Mattys, S.L. (2004). Stress versus coarticulation: Toward an integrated approach to explicit speech segmentation. *Journal of Experimental Psychology: Human Perception and Performance, 30,* 397–408.

Maurer, D., Lewis, T.L., Brent, H.P., & Levin, A.V. (1999). Rapid improvement in the acuity of infants after visual input. *Science, 286,* 108–110.

Mayer, J.D., Caruso, D., & Salovey, P. (1999). Emotional intelligence meets traditional standards for an intelligence. *Intelligence, 27,* 267–298.

Mayer, J.D., Salovey, P., & Caruso, D.R. (2002). *Mayer–Salovey–Caruso Emotional Intelligence Test (MSCEIT) user's manual.* Toronto: Multi-Health Systems.

Mayer, J.D., Salovey, P., & Caruso, D.R. (2004). Emotional intelligence: Theory, findings, and implications. *Psychological Inquiry, 15,* 197–215.

Mayer, J.D., Salovey, P., Caruso, D.R., & Sitarenios, G. (2003). Measuring emotional intelligence with the MSCEIT V2.0. *Emotion, 3,* 97–105.

Mayer, R.E. (1990). Problem solving. In M.W. Eysenck (Ed.), *The Blackwell dictionary of cognitive psychology.* Oxford, UK: Blackwell.

McAdams, D.P. (1988). *Intimacy, power, and the life history.* New York: Guilford.

McArthur, L.A. (1972). The how and what of why: Some determinants and consequences of causal attributions. *Journal of Personality and Social Psychology, 22,* 171–193.

McArthur, L.Z., & Resko, B.G. (1975). The portrayal of men and women in American TV commercials. *Journal of Social Psychology, 97,* 209–220.

McCarthy, R., & Warrington, E.K. (1984). A two-route model of speech production. *Brain, 107,* 463–485.

McCarthy, R.A., & Warrington, E.K. (1986). Visual associative agnosia: A clinico-anatomical study of a single case. *Journal of Neurology, Neurosurgery and Psychiatry, 49,* 1233–1240.

McCartney, K., Harris, M.J., & Bernieri, F. (1990). Growing up and growing apart: A developmental meta-analysis of twin studies. *Psychological Bulletin, 107,* 226–237.

McCauley, C., & Stitt, C.L. (1978). An individual and quantitative measure of stereotypes. *Journal of Personality and Social Psychology, 36,* 929–940.

McClelland, J.L., & Elman, J.L. (1986). The TRACE model of speech perception. *Cognitive Psychology, 18,* 1–86.

McCloskey, M. (2001). The future of cognitive neuropsychology. In B. Rapp (Ed.), *The handbook of cognitive neuropsychology: What deficits reveal about the human mind.* Philadelphia: Psychology Press.

McConahay, J.B. (1986). Modern racism, ambivalence, and the Modern Racism Scale. In J.F. Dovidio & S.L. Gaertner (Eds.), *Prejudice, discrimination, and racism.* San Diego, CA: Academic Press.

McCosker, H., Barnard, A., & Gerber, R. (2001). Undertaking sensitive research: Issues and strategies for meeting the safety needs of all participants. *Forum: Qualitative Social Research, 2,* 1–11.

McCrae, R.R., & Costa, P.T. (1985). Updating Norman's "adequate taxonomy": Intelligence and personality dimensions in natural language and in questionnaires. *Journal of Personality and Social Psychology, 49,* 710–721.

McCrae, R.R., & Costa, P.T. (1990). *Personality in adulthood.* New York: Guilford Press.

McCrae, R.R., & Costa, P.T. (1999). A five-factor theory of personality. In L.A. Pervin & O.P. John (Eds.), *Handbook of personality: Theory and research.* New York: Guilford Press.

McCrae, R.R., Terracciano, A., and 78 members of the Personality Profiles of Cultures Project (2005). Universal features of personality traits from the observer's perspective: Data from 50 cultures. *Journal of Personality and Social Psychology, 88,* 547–561.

McDaniel, M.A. (2005). Big-brained people are smarter: A meta-analysis of the relationship between in vivo brain volume and intelligence. *Intelligence, 33,* 337–346.

McDonald, S.A., & Shillcock, R.C. (2003). Eye movements reveal the on-line computation of lexical probabilities during reading. *Psychological Science, 14,* 648–652.

McGarrigle, J., & Donaldson, M. (1974). Conservation accidents. *Cognition, 3,* 341–350.

McGrew, W.C. (1972). *An ethological study of children's behavior.* New York: Academic Press.

McGuffin, P., Katz, R., Watkins, S., & Rutherford, J. (1996). A hospital-based twin register of the heritability of DSM-IV unipolar depression. *Archives of General Psychiatry, 53,* 129–136.

McGuire, P.K., Silbersweig, D.A., Wright, I., Murray, R.M., Frackowiak, R.S.J., & Frith, C.D. (1996). The neural correlates of inner speech and auditory verbal imagery in schizophrenia: Relationship to auditory verbal hallucinations. *British Journal of Psychiatry, 169,* 148–159.

McGuire, W.J. (1969). The nature of attitudes and attitude change. In G. Lindzey & E. Aronson (Eds.), *Handbook of social psychology* (Vol. 3, 2nd ed.). Reading, MA: Addison-Wesley.

McGurk, H., & MacDonald, J. (1976). Hearing lips and seeing voices. *Nature, 264,* 746–748.

McKenna, K.Y.A., Green, A.S., & Gleason, M.E.J. (2002). Relationship formation on the internet: What's the big attraction? *Journal of Social Issues, 58,* 9–31.

McKoon, G., & Ratcliff, R. (1992). Inference during reading. *Psychological Review, 99,* 440–466.

Meddis, R. (1979). The evolution and function of sleep. In D.A. Oakley & H.C. Plotkin (Eds.), *Brain, behaviour and evolution.* London: Methuen.

Meddis, R., Pearson, A.J.D., & Langford, G. (1973). An extreme case of healthy insomnia. *Electroencephalography and Clinical Neurophysiology, 35,* 213–224.

Medori, R., Montagna, P., Tritschler, H.J., LeBlanc, A., Cortelli, P., Tinuper, P., et al. (1992). Fatal familial insomnia: A second kindred with mutation of prion protein gene at codon 178. *Neurology, 42,* 669–670.

Mehler, J., Jusczyk, P.W., Dehaene-Lambertz, G., Dupoux, E., & Nazzi, T. (1994). Coping with linguistic diversity: The infant's viewpoint. In J.L. Morgan & K. Demuth (Eds.), *Signal to syntax: Bootstrapping from speech to grammar in early acquisition.* Mahwah, NJ: Lawrence Erlbaum Associates, Inc.

Meijer, J.H., Watanabe, K., Schaap, J., Albus, H., & Détári, L. (1998). Light responsiveness of the suprachiasmatic nucleus:

Long-term multiunit and single-unit recordings in freely moving animals. *Journal of Neuroscience, 18,* 9078–9087.

Meltzoff, A.N. (1985). Immediate and deferred imitation in 14- and 24-month-old infants. *Child Development, 56,* 62–72.

Meltzoff, A.N. (1988). Infant imitation after a 1-week delay: Long-term memory for novel acts and multiple stimuli. *Developmental Psychology, 24,* 470–476.

Merikle, P.M., Smilek, D., & Eastwood, J.D. (2001). Perception without awareness: Perspectives from cognitive psychology. *Cognition, 79,* 115–134.

Meulemans, T., & Van der Linden, M. (2003). Implicit learning of complex information in amnesia. *Brain and Cognition, 52,* 250–257.

Meyers, S.A., & Landsberger, S.A. (2002). Direct and indirect pathways between adult attachment style and marital satisfaction. *Personal Relationships, 9,* 159–172.

Mezzacappa, E.S., Katkin, E.S., & Palmer, S.N. (1999). Epinephrine, arousal, and emotion: A new look at two-factor theory. *Cognition and Emotion, 13,* 181–199.

Mickelson, K., Kessler, R.C., & Shaver, P. (1997). Adult attachment in a nationally representative sample. *Journal of Personality and Social Psychology, 73,* 1092–1106.

Miele, F. (2002). *Intelligence, race, and genetics: Conversations with Arthur R. Jensen.* Boulder, CO: Westview.

Milgram, S. (1963). Behavioural study of obedience. *Journal of Abnormal and Social Psychology, 67,* 371–378.

Milgram, S. (1974). *Obedience to authority: An experimental view.* New York: Harper & Row.

Miller, G.A. (1956). The magic number seven, plus or minus two: Some limits on our capacity for processing information. *Psychological Review, 63,* 81–93.

Miller, H.G., Turner, C.F., & Moses, L.E. (1990). *AIDS: The second decade.* Washington, DC: National Academy.

Miller, M.A., & Rahe, R.H. (1997). Life changes: Scaling for the 1990s. *Journal of Psychosomatic Research, 43,* 279–292.

Miller, P.H., & Coyle, T.R. (1999). Developmental change: Lessons from microgenesis. In E.K. Scholnick, K. Nelson, S.A. Gelman, & P.H. Miller (Eds.), *Conceptual development: Piaget's legacy.* Mahwah, NJ: Lawrence Erlbaum Associates, Inc.

Miller, R.L., Butler, J., & Cosentino, C.J. (2004). Followership effectiveness: An extension of Fiedler's contingency model. *Leadership and Organization Development Journal, 25,* 362–368.

Miller, R.R., Barnet, R.C., & Grahame, N.J. (1995). Assessment of the Rescorla–Wagner model. *Psychological Bulletin, 117,* 363–386.

Miller, T.Q., Turner, C.W., Tindale, R.S., Posavac, E.J., & Dugoni, B.L. (1991). Reasons for the trend toward null findings in research on Type A behaviour. *Psychological Bulletin, 110,* 469–485.

Miller-Johnson, S., Coie, J.D., Maumary-Gremaud, A., Lochman, J., & Terry, R. (1999). Relationship between childhood peer rejection and aggression and adolescent delinquency severity and type among African American youth. *Journal of Emotional and Behavioral Disorders, 7,* 137–146.

Milner, A.D., & Goodale, M.A. (1995). *The visual brain in action* (Oxford Psychology series, No. 27). Oxford, UK: Oxford University Press.

Milner, A.D., & Goodale, M.A. (1998). The visual brain in action. *Psyche, 4,* 1–14.

Milner, A.D., Perrett, D.I., Johnston, R.S., Benson, P.J., Jordan, T.R., Heeley, D.W. et al. (1991). Perception and action in "visual form agnosia." *Brain, 114,* 405–428.

Mischel, W. (1968). *Personality and assessment.* London: Wiley.

Mitchell, T.R., & Daniels, D. (2003). Motivation. In W.C. Borman, R.J. Ilgen, & R.J. Klimoski (Eds.), *Handbook of psychology: Vol. 12. Industrial organizational psychology.* New York: Wiley.

Mitte, K. (2005). Meta-analysis of cognitive-behavioural treatments for generalised anxiety disorder: A comparison with pharmacotherapy. *Psychological Bulletin, 131,* 785–795.

Miyake, A., Friedman, N.P., Emerson, M.J., Witzki, A.H., & Howerter, A. (2000). The unity and diversity of executive functions and their contributions to complex "frontal lobe" tasks: A latent variable analysis. *Cognitive Psychology, 41,* 49–100.

Miyake, A., & Shah, P. (1999). *Models of working memory: Mechanisms of active maintenance and executive control.* New York: Cambridge University Press.

Mlicki, P.P., & Ellemers, N. (1996). Being different or being better? National stereotypes and identifications of Polish and Dutch students. *European Journal of Social Psychology, 26,* 97–114.

Modigliani, A., & Rochat, F. (1995). The role of interaction sequences and the timing of resistance in shaping obedience and defiance to authority. *Journal of Social Issues, 51,* 107–123.

Monk, T. (2001, December 1). *In space, no one gets to sleep.* Retrieved from www.newscientist.com

Montero, I., Masanet, M.J., Bellver, F., & Lacruz, M. (2006). The long-term outcome of 2 family intervention strategies in schizophrenia. *Comprehensive Psychiatry, 47,* 362–367.

Moore, B.R. (1973). The form of the auto-shaped response with food or water reinforcers. *Journal of the Experimental Analysis of Behavior, 20,* 163–181.

Moore, C., & Frye, D. (1986). The effect of the experimenter's intention on the child's understanding of conservation. *Cognition, 22,* 283–298.

Moray, N. (1959). Attention in dichotic listening: Affective cues and the influence of instructions. *Quarterly Journal of Experimental Psychology, 11,* 56–60.

Moreland, R.L. (1985). Social categorization and the assimilation of "new" group members. *Journal of Personality and Social Psychology, 48,* 1173–1190.

Moreland, R.L., & Levine, J.M. (1982). Socialization in small groups: Temporal changes in individual–group relations. In L. Berkowitz (Ed.), *Advances in experimental social psychology* (Vol. 15, pp. 137–192). New York: Academic Press.

Morgan, C.D., & Murray, H.A. (1935). A method of investigating fantasies: The thematic apperception test. *Archives of Neurological Psychiatry, 34,* 289–306.

Morgan, H., & Raffle, C. (1999). Does reducing safety behaviours improve treatment response in patients with social phobia? *Australian and New Zealand Journal of Psychiatry, 33,* 503–510.

Morin, S.F. (1977). Heterosexual bias in psychological research on lesbianism and male homosexuality. *American Psychologist, 32,* 629–637.

Morris, N.M., Udry, J.R., Khan-Dawood, F., & Dawood, M.Y. (1987). Marital sex frequency and midcycle female testosterone. *Archives of Sexual Behavior, 16,* 27–37.

Morsella, E., & Miozzo, M. (2002). Evidence for a cascade model of lexical access in speech production. *Journal of Experimental Psychology: Learning, Memory, and Cognition, 28,* 555–563.

Morton, J., & Johnson, M.H. (1991). CONSPEC and CONLEARN: A two-process theory of infant face recognition. *Psychological Review, 98,* 164–181.

Moscovici, S. (1976). *Social influence and social change.* London: Academic Press.

Moscovici, S. (1980). Toward a theory of conversion behavior. In L. Berkowitz (Ed.), *Advances in experimental social psychology* (Vol. 13). New York: Academic Press.

Moscovici, S., Lage, E., & Naffrenchoux, M. (1969). Influence of a consistent minority on the responses of a majority in a colour perception task. *Sociometry, 32,* 365–380.

Moss, E. (1992). The socioaffective context of joint cognitive activity. In L.T. Winegar & J. Valsiner (Eds.), *Children's development within social context: Vol. 2. Research and methodology.* Hillsdale, NJ: Lawrence Erlbaum Associates, Inc.

Motley, M.T., Baars, B.J., & Camden, C.T. (1983). Experimental verbal slip studies: A review and an editing model of language encoding. *Communication Monographs, 50,* 79–101.

Mowrer, O.H. (1947). On the dual nature of learning: A re-interpretation of "conditioning" and "problem-solving." *Harvard Educational Review, 17,* 102–148.

Mullen, B., & Copper, C. (1994). The relation between group cohesiveness and performance: An integration. *Psychological Bulletin, 115,* 210–227.

Müller, N.G., Bartelt, O.A., Donner, T.H., Villringer, A., & Brandt, S.A. (2003). A physiological correlate of the "zoom lens" of visual attention. *Journal of Neuroscience, 23,* 3561–3565.

Müller, U., Zelazo, P.D., & Imrisek, S. (2005). Executive function and children's understanding of false belief: How specific is the relation? *Cognitive Development, 20,* 173–189.

Mumme, R.L. (1992). Do helpers increase reproductive success: An experimental analysis in the Florida scrub jay. *Behavioural Ecology and Sociobiology, 31,* 319–328.

Murphy, G., & Kovach, J.K. (1972). *Historical introduction to modern psychology.* London: Routledge & Kegan Paul.

Murphy, K., McKone, E., & Slee, J. (2003). Dissociations between implicit and explicit memory in children: The role of strategic processing and the knowledge base. *Journal of Experimental Child Psychology, 84,* 124–165.

Murphy, S., & Zajonc, R. (1996). An unconscious subjective emotional response. In D. Concar (Ed.), Act now, think later: Emotions. *New Scientist* (Suppl.).

Murray, C. (1998). *Income inequality and IQ.* Washington, DC: American Enterprise Institute.

Murstein, B.I. (1972). Physical attractiveness and marital choice. *Journal of Personality and Social Psychology, 22,* 8–12.

Muter, P. (1978). Recognition failure of recallable words in semantic memory. *Memory & Cognition, 52,* 271–280.

Muzur, A., Pace-Schott, E.F., & Hobson, J.A. (2002). The prefrontal cortex in sleep. *Trends in Cognitive Sciences, 6,* 475–481.

Najavits, L.M., & Strupp, H.H. (1994). Differences in the effectiveness of psychodynamic therapists: A process–outcome study. *Psychotherapy, 31,* 114–123.

National Institute of Child Health and Human Development (NICHD) Early Child Care Research Network. (1997). The effects of infant child care on infant–mother attachment security: Results of the NICHD study of early child care. *Child Development, 68,* 860–879.

National Institute of Child Health and Human Development (NICHD) Early Child Care Research Network. (2003). Does quality of child care affect child outcomes at age 4½? *Developmental Psychology, 39,* 451–469.

National Research Council and Institute of Medicine (2003). *Working families and growing kids: Caring for children and adolescents* (E. Smolensky & J.A. Gootman Eds.). Washington, DC: The National Academies Press.

Neighbors, C., Larimer, M.E., & Lewis, M.A. (2004). Targeting misperceptions of descriptive drinking norms: Efficacy of a computer-delivered personalised normative feedback intervention. *Journal of Consulting and Clinical Psychology, 72,* 434–447.

Neisser, U. (1967). *Cognitive psychology.* New York: Appleton-Century-Crofts.

Neisser, U., & Becklen, P. (1975). Selective looking: Attending to visually superimposed events. *Cognitive Psychology, 7,* 480–494.

Nemeth, C., Mayseless, O., Sherman, J., & Brown, Y. (1990). Exposure to dissent and recall of information. *Journal of Personality and Social Psychology, 58,* 429–437.

Newcomb, A.F., & Bagwell, C.L. (1995). Children's friendship relations: A meta-analytic review. *Psychological Bulletin, 117,* 306–347.

Newcomb, T.M. (1961). *The acquaintance process.* New York: Holt, Rinehart, & Winston.

Newcomb, T.M., Koenig, K., Flacks, R., & Warwick, D. (1967). *Persistence and change: Bennington College and its students after 25 years.* New York: John Wiley & Sons.

Newell, A., & Simon, H.A. (1972). *Human problem solving.* Englewood Cliffs, NJ: Prentice Hall.

Newmark, C.S., Frerking, R.A., Cook, L., & Newmark, L. (1973). Endorsement of Ellis' irrational beliefs as a function of psychopathology. *Journal of Clinical Psychology, 29,* 300–302.

Nielsen, T.A. (1999). Mentation during sleep. The NREM/REM distinction. In R. Lydic & H.A. Baghdoyan (Eds.), *Handbook of behavioral state control: Cellular and molecular mechanisms.* Boca Raton, FL: CRC Press.

Nilsson, J.P., Söderström, M., Karlsson, A.U., Lekander, M., Åkerstedt, T., Lindroth, N.E., et al. (2005). Less effective executive functioning after one night's sleep deprivation. *Journal of Sleep Research, 14,* 1–6.

Nisbett, R.E., & Wilson, T.D. (1977). Telling more than we can know: Verbal reports on mental processes. *Psychological Review, 84,* 231–259.

Nissen, M.J., & Bullemer, P. (1987). Attentional requirements of learning: Evidence from performance measures. *Cognitive Psychology, 19,* 1–32.

Nissen, M.J., Willingham, D., & Hartman, M. (1989). Explicit and implicit remembering: When is learning preserved in amnesia? *Neuropsychologia, 27,* 341–352.

Nordby, H., Hugdahl, K., Jasiukaitis, P., & Spiegel, D. (1999). Effects of hypnotisability on performance of a Stroop task and event-related potentials. *Perceptual and Motor Skills, 88,* 819–830.

Norenzayan, A., Choi, I., & Nisbett, R.E. (1999). Eastern and Western perceptions of causality for social behaviour: Lay theories about personalities and situations. In D.A. Prentice & D.T. Miller (Eds.), *Cultural divides: Understanding and overcoming group conflict.* New York: Russell Sage Foundation.

Norman, D.A. (1980). Twelve issues for cognitive science. *Cognitive Science, 4,* 1–32.

Norman, P., & Smith, L. (1995). The theory of planned behaviour and exercise: An investigation into the role of prior behaviour: Behavioural intentions and attitude variability. *European Journal of Social Psychology, 25,* 403–415.

Norris, D., McQueen, J.M., Cutler, A., & Butterfield, S. (1997). The possible-word constraint in the segmentation of continuous speech. *Cognitive Psychology, 34,* 191–243.

Novick, L.R., & Sherman, S.J. (2003). On the nature of insight solutions: Evidence from skill differences in anagram solution. *Quarterly Journal of Experimental Psychology, 56A,* 351–382.

Oakes, P.J., Haslam, S.A., & Turner, J.C. (1994). *Stereotyping and social reality.* Malden, MA: Blackwell.

Oatley, K., & Johnson-Laird, P.N. (1987). Towards a cognitive theory of emotions. *Cognition and Emotion, 1,* 29–50.

Ochs, E., & Schieffelin, B. (1995). The impact of language socialisation on grammatical development. In P. Fletcher & B. Macwhinney (Eds.), *The handbook of child language.* Oxford, UK: Blackwell.

O'Connor, T.G., Caspi, A., DeFries, J.C., & Plomin, R. (2000). Are associations between parental divorce and children's adjustment genetically mediated? An adoption study. *Developmental Psychology, 36,* 429–437.

O'Connor, T.G., & Croft, C.M. (2001). A twin study of attachment in pre-school children. *Child Development, 72,* 1501–1511.

O'Connor, T.G., Deater-Deckard, K., Fulker, D., Rutter, M., & Plomin, R. (1998). Genotype–environment correlations in late childhood and early adolescence: Antisocial behavioural problems and coercive parenting. *Developmental Psychology, 34,* 970–981.

O'Connor, T.G., Marvin, R.S., Rutter, M., Olrick, J.T., & Britner, P.A. (2003). Child–parent attachment following early institutional deprivation. *Development and Psychopathology, 15,* 19–38.

O'Connor, T.G., Rutter, M., Beckett, C., Keaveney, L., Kreppner, J.M., and the English and Romanian Adoptees Study Team (2000). *Child Development, 71,* 376–390.

O'Connor, T.G., Thorpe, K., Dunn, J., & Golding, J. (1999). Parental divorce and adjustment in adulthood: Findings from a community sample. *Journal of Child Psychology and Psychiatry, 40,* 777–789.

O'Craven, K., Downing, P., & Kanwisher, N. (1999). fMRI evidence for objects as the units of attentional selection. *Nature, 401,* 584–587.

Ogden, J. (1996). *Health psychology: A textbook.* Buckingham, UK: Open University Press.

Ohlsson, S. (1992). Information processing explanations of insight and related phenomena. In M.T. Keane & K.J. Gilhooly (Eds.), *Advances in the psychology of thinking.* London: Harvester Wheatsheaf.

Ohman, A., & Soares, J.J.F. (1994). "Unconscious anxiety": Phobic responses to masked stimuli. *Journal of Abnormal Psychology, 103,* 231–240.

Oliver, M.B., & Hyde, J.S. (1993). Gender differences in sexuality: A meta-analysis. *Psychological Bulletin, 114,* 29–51.

Olweus, D., & Endresen, I.M. (1998). The importance of sex-of-stimulus object: Trends and sex differences in empathic responsiveness. *Social Development, 3,* 370–388.

O'Neill, D.K. (1996). Two-year-old children's sensitivity to parent's knowledge state when making requests. *Child Development, 67,* 659–677.

Orbell, S., Hodgkins, S., & Sheeran, P. (1997). Implementation intentions and the theory of planned behaviour. *Personality and Social Psychology Bulletin, 23,* 945–954.

Orlinsky, D.E., Grave, K., & Parks, B.K. (1994). Process and outcome in psychotherapy—Noch Einmal. In A.E. Bergin & S.L. Garfield (Eds.), *Handbook of psychotherapy and behavior change* (4th ed., pp. 270–376). New York: Wiley.

Orne, M.T. (1962). On the social psychology of the psychological experiment: With particular reference to demand characteristics and their implications. *American Psychologist, 17,* 776–783.

O'Rourke, T.B., & Holcomb, P.J. (2002). Electrophysiological evidence for the efficiency of spoken word processing. *Biological Psychology, 60,* 121–150.

Oswald, I. (1980). *Sleep* (4th ed.). Harmondsworth, UK: Penguin Books.

Otto, M.W., Smits, J.A.J., & Reese, H.E. (2006). Combined psychotherapy and pharmacotherapy for mood and anxiety disorders in adults: Review and analysis. *Clinical Psychology: Science and Practice, 12,* 72–86.

Ouellette, J.A., & Wood, W. (1998). Habit and intention in everyday life: The multiple processes by which past behaviour predicts future behaviour. *Psychological Review, 124,* 54–74.

Owusu-Bempah, P., & Howitt, D. (1994). Racism and the psychological textbook. *The Psychologist, 7,* 163–166.

Oxford Dictionary of Psychology. (2001). Oxford, UK: Oxford University Press.

Oyserman, D., Coon, H.M., & Kemmelmeier, M. (2002). Rethinking individualism and collectivism: Evaluation of theoretical assumptions and meta-analyses. *Psychological Bulletin, 128,* 3–72.

Ozer, D.J., & Benet-Martinez, V. (2006). Personality and the prediction of consequential outcomes. *Annual Review of Psychology, 57,* 401–421.

Padilla, A.M. (1994). Bicultural development: A theoretical and empirical examination. In R.G. Malgady & O. Rodriguez (Eds.), *Theoretical and conceptual issues in Hispanic mental health.* Malabar, FL: Krieger.

Pagani, L.S., Tremblay, R.E., Nagin, D., Zoccolillo, M., Vitaro, F., & McDuff, P. (2004). Risk factor models for adolescent verbal and physical aggression toward mothers. *Journal of Behavioral Development, 28,* 528–537.

Palmer, B.R., Gignac, G., Manocha, R., & Stough, C. (2005). A psychometric evaluation of the Mayer–Salovey–Caruso emotional intelligence test version 2.0. *Intelligence, 33,* 285–305.

Panksepp, J. (1985). Mood changes. In P. Vinken, G. Bruyn, & H. Klawans (Eds.), *Handbook of clinical neurology* (Vol. 45). Amsterdam: Elsevier.

Panksepp, J. (2000). Emotions as natural kinds within the mammalian brain. In M. Lewis & J.M. Howland-Jones (Eds.), *Handbook of emotions* (2nd ed.). New York: Guilford Press.

Papagno, C., Valentine, T., & Baddeley, A.D. (1991). Phonological short-term memory and foreign-language learning. *Journal of Memory and Language, 30,* 331–347.

Parkin, A.J. (1996). *Explorations in cognitive neuropsychology.* Oxford, UK: Blackwell.

Parkin, A.J. (2001). The structure and mechanisms of memory. In B. Rapp (Ed.), *The handbook of cognitive neuropsychology: What deficits reveal about the human mind.* Philadelphia, PA: Psychology Press.

Parkinson, B. (2001). Putting appraisal in context. In K.R. Scherer, A. Schorr, & T. Johnstone (Eds.), *Appraisal processes in emotion: Theory, methods, research.* Oxford, UK: Oxford University Press.

Pashler, H. (1993). Dual-task interference and elementary mental mechanisms. In D.E, Meyer & S. Kornblum (Eds.), *Attention and performance* (Vol. XIV). London: MIT Press.

Pashler, H., Johnston, J.C., & Ruthruff, E. (2001). Attention and performance. *Annual Review of Psychology, 52,* 629–651.

Pastore, N. (1952). The role of arbitrariness in the frustration–aggression hypothesis. *Journal of Abnormal and Social Psychology, 47,* 728–731.

Patenaude, J., Niyonsenga, T., & Fafard, D. (2003). Changes in students' moral development during medical school: A cohort study. *Canadian Medical Association Journal, 168,* 840–844.

Patterson, G.R. (1982). *Coercive family processes.* Eugene, OR: Castilia Press.

Patterson, G.R., DeBaryshe, B.D., & Ramsey, E. (1989). A developmental perspective on antisocial behaviour. *American Psychologist, 44,* 329–335.

Patton, M.Q. (1980). *Qualitative evaluation methods.* London: Sage.

Paulhus, D.L., Trapnell, P.D., & Chen, D. (1999). Birth order effects on personality and achievement within families. *Psychological Science, 10,* 482–488.

Paunonen, S.V. (2003). Big Five factors of personality and replicated predictions of behaviour. *Journal of Personality and Social Psychology, 84,* 411–424.

Payne, B.K. (2001). Prejudice and perception: The role of automatic and controlled processes in misperceiving a weapon. *Journal of Personality and Social Psychology, 81,* 181–192.

Payne, J. (1976). Task complexity and contingent processing in decision making: An information search and protocol analysis. *Organizational Behavior and Human Performance, 16,* 366–387.

Payne, J.W., Bettman, J.R., & Johnson, E.J. (1988). Adaptive strategy selection in decision making. *Journal of Experimental Psychology: Learning, Memory and Cognition, 14,* 534–552.

Pears, R., & Bryant, P. (1990). Transitive inferences by young children about spatial position. *British Journal of Psychology, 81,* 497–510.

Pecoraro, N., Timberlake, W., & Tinsley, M. (1999). Incentive downshifts evoke search behavior in rats (*Rattus norvegicus*).

Journal of Experimental Psychology: Animal Behavior Processes, 25, 153–167.

Pedersen, N.L., Plomin, R., McClearn, G.E., & Friberg, I. (1988). Neuroticism, extraversion, and related traits in adult twins reared apart and reared together. *Journal of Personality and Social Psychology, 55,* 950–957.

Penner, L.A., Dovidio, J.F., Piliavin, J.A., & Schroeder, D.A. (2005). Prosocial behaviour: Multilevel perspectives. *Annual Review of Psychology, 56,* 365–392.

Peplau, L.A. (2003). Human sexuality: How do men and women differ? *Current Directions in Psychological Science, 12,* 37–40.

Perenin, M.-T., & Vighetto, A. (1988). Optic ataxia: A specific disruption in visuomotor mechanisms. 1. Different aspects of the deficit in reaching for objects. *Brain, 111,* 643–674.

Perfect, T.J. & Hollins, T.S. (1996). Predictive feeling of knowing judgements and postdictive confidence judgements in eyewitness memory and general knowledge. *Applied Cognitive Psychology, 10,* 371–382.

Perner, J., Sprung, M., & Steinkogler, B. (2004). Counterfactual conditionals and false belief: A developmental dissociation. *Cognitive Development, 19,* 179–201.

Perry, D.G., & Bussey, K. (1979). The social learning theory of sex differences: Imitation is alive and well. *Journal of Personality and Social Psychology, 37,* 1699–1712.

Peters, M. (1995). Does brain size matter? A reply to Rushton and Ankney. *Canadian Journal of Experimental Psychology, 49,* 570–576.

Peterson, C., Seligman, M.E., & Vaillant, G.E. (1988). Pessimistic explanatory style is a risk factor for physical illness: A thirty-five year longitudinal study. *Journal of Personality and Social Psychology, 55,* 23–27.

Peterson, D.M., & Bowler, D.M. (2000). Counterfactual reasoning and false belief understanding in children with autism. *Autism, 4,* 391–405.

Peterson, L.R., & Peterson, M.J. (1959). Short-term retention of individual verbal items. *Journal of Experimental Psychology, 58,* 193–198.

Peterson, R.S., Owens, P.D., Tetlock, P.E., Fan, E.T., & Martorana, P. (1998). Group dynamics in top management teams: Groupthink, vigilance, and alternative models of organizational failure and success. *Organizational Behavior and Human Decision Processes, 73,* 272–305.

Pettigrew, T.F. (1958). Personality and sociocultural factors in intergroup attitudes: A cross-national comparison. *Journal of Conflict Resolution, 2,* 29–42.

Pettigrew, T.F., & Meertens, R.W. (1995). Subtle and blatant prejudice in Western Europe. *European Journal of Social Psychology, 25,* 57–75.

Petty, R.E. (1995). Attitude change. In A. Tesser (Ed.), *Advanced social psychology.* New York: McGraw-Hill.

Petty, R.E., & Cacioppo, J.T. (1981). *Attitudes and persuasion: Classic and contemporary approaches.* Dubuque, IA: W.C. Brown.

Petty, R.E., Cacioppo, J.T., & Goldman, R. (1981). Personal involvement as a determinant of argument-based persuasion. *Journal of Personality and Social Psychology, 41,* 847–855.

Petty, R.E., & Wegener, D.T. (1998). Attitude change: Multiple roles for persuasion variable. In D.T. Gilbert, S.T. Fiske, & G. Lindzey (Eds.), *The handbook of social psychology* (4th ed., pp. 323–390). Boston: McGraw-Hill.

Pezdek, K. (2003). Event memory and autobiographical memory for the events of September 11, 2001. *Applied Cognitive Psychology, 17,* 1033–1045.

Pfungst, O. (1911). *Clever Hans, the horse of Mr von Osten.* New York: Holt, Rinehart, & Winston.

Phelps, J.A., Davis, J.O., & Schwartz, K.M. (1997). Nature, nurture, and twin research strategies. *Current Directions in Psychological Science, 6,* 117–121.

Pickel, K.L. (1999). The influence of context on the "weapon focus" effect. *Law and Human Behavior, 23,* 299–311.

Pickering, M.J., & Garrod, S. (2004). Toward a mechanistic psychology of dialog. *Behavioral and Brain Sciences, 27,* 169–226.

Pilgrim, D. (2000). Psychiatric diagnosis: More questions than answers. *The Psychologist, 13,* 302–305.

Piliavin, I.M., Rodin, J., & Piliavin, J.A. (1969). Good samaritarianism: An underground phenomenon? *Journal of Personality and Social Psychology, 13,* 289–299.

Piliavin, J.A., Dovidio, J.F., Gaertner, S.L., & Clark, R.D. (1981). *Emergency intervention.* New York: Academic Press.

Pillemer, D.B., Goldsmith, L.R., Panter, A.T., & White, S.H. (1988). Very long-term memories of the first year in college. *Journal of Experimental Psychology: Learning, Memory, & Cognition, 14,* 709–715.

Pilleri, G. (1979). The blind Indus dolphin, *Platanista indi. Endeavour, 3,* 48–56.

Pillsworth, E.G., Haselton, M.G., & Buss, D.M. (2004). Ovulatory shifts in female sexual desire. *Journal of Sex Research, 41,* 55–65.

Pinel, J.P.J. (1997). *Biopsychology* (3rd ed.). Boston: Allyn & Bacon.

Pinel, J.P.J. (2006). *Biopsychology* (6th ed.). Boston: Allyn & Bacon.

Pinker, S. (1984). *Language learnability and language development.* Cambridge, MA: Harvard University Press.

Pinker, S. (1989). Learnability and cognition: *The acquisition of argument structure.* Cambridge, MA: MIT Press.

Pinker, S. (1997). *How the mind works.* New York: Norton.

Plant, E.A., Peruche, B.M., & Butz, D.A. (2005). Eliminating automatic racial bias: Making race non-diagnostic for responses to criminal suspects. *Journal of Experimental Social Psychology, 41,* 141–156.

Plomin, R. (1988). The nature and nurture of cognitive abilities. In R.J. Sternberg (Ed.), *Advances in the psychology of human intelligence* (Vol. 4). Hillsdale, NJ: Lawrence Erlbaum Associates, Inc.

Plomin, R. (1990). The role of inheritance in behaviour. *Science, 248,* 183–188.

Plomin, R., Asbury, K., & Dunn, J. (2001). Why are children in the same family so different? Nonshared environment a decade later. *Canadian Journal of Psychiatry, 46,* 225–233.

Plomin, R., DeFries, J.C., & McClearn, G.E. (1997). *Behavioural genetics: A primer* (3rd ed.). New York: Freeman.

Poole, D.A., & Lindsay, D.S. (1996). *Effects of parents' suggestions, interviewing techniques, and age on young children's event reports.* Paper presented at NATO Advanced Study Institute, Port de Bourgenay, France.

Popper, K.R. (1969). *Conjectures and refutations.* London: Routledge & Kegan Paul.

Popper, K.R. (1972). *Objective knowledge.* Oxford, UK: Oxford University Press.

Posner, M.I. (1980). Orienting of attention: The VIIth Sir Frederic Bartlett lecture. *Quarterly Journal of Experimental Psychology, 32A,* 3–25.

Postmes, T., & Spears, R. (1998). Deindividuation and anti-normative behaviour: A meta-analysis. *Psychological Bulletin, 123,* 238–259.

Potter, J., & Wetherell, M. (1987). *Discourse and social psychology: Beyond attitudes and behaviour.* London: Sage.

Power, M.J., & Dalgleish, T. (1997). *Cognition and emotion: From order to disorder.* Hove, UK: Psychology Press.

Premack, D. (2007). Human and animal cognition: Continuity and discontinuity. *Proceedings of the National Academy of Sciences of the United States of America, 104*(35), 13861–13867.

Price-Williams, D., Gordon, W., & Ramirez, M. (1969). Skill and conservation: A study of pottery-making children. *Developmental Psychology, 1,* 769.

Privette, G., Hwang, K.K., & Bundrick, C.M. (1997). Cross-cultural measurement of experience: Taiwanese and Americans' peak performance, peak experience, and average events. *Perceptual and Motor Skills, 84,* 1459–1482.

Prochaska, J.O., & Norcross, J.C. (1994). *Systems of psychotherapy: A transtheoretical analysis* (3rd ed.). Pacific Grove, CA: Brooks/Cole.

Pronin, E., Wegner, D.M., & McCarthy, K. (2006). Everyday magical powers: The role of apparent mental causation in the overestimation of personal influence. *Journal of Personality and Social Psychology, 91,* 218–231.

Quinlan, P.T., & Wilton, R.N. (1998). Grouping by proximity or similarity? Competition between the Gestalt principles in vision. *Perception, 27,* 417–430.

Rafal, R., Smith, J., Krantz, J., Cohen, A., & Brennan, C. (1990). Extrageniculate vision in hemianopic humans: Saccade inhibition by signals in the blind field. *Science, 250,* 118–121.

Rahe, R.H., Mahan, J., & Arthur, R. (1970). Prediction of near-future health-change from subjects' preceding life changes. *Journal of Psychosomatic Research, 14,* 401–406.

Ralph, M.R., Foster, R.G., Davis, F.C., & Menaker, M. (1990). Transplanted suprachiasmatic nucleus determines circadian period. *Science, 247,* 975–978.

Rampello, L., Nicoletti, F., & Nicoletti, F. (2000). Dopamine and depression: Therapeutic implications. *CNS Drugs, 13,* 35–45.

Rank, S.G., & Jacobsen, C.K. (1977). Hospital nurses' compliance with medication overdose orders: A failure to replicate. *Journal of Health and Social Psychology, 18,* 188–193.

Rapee, R.M., & Lim, L. (1992). Discrepancy between self- and observer ratings of performance in social phobics. *Journal of Abnormal Psychology, 101,* 728–731.

Raulin, M.L., & Graziano, A.M. (1994). Quasi-experiments and correlational studies. In A.M. Colman (Ed.), *Companion encyclopaedia of psychology* (Vol. 2). London: Routledge.

Reason, J.T., & Rowan, J. (Eds.). (1981). *Human enquiry: A sourcebook in new paradigm research.* Chichester, UK: Wiley.

Reber, A.S. (1967). Implicit learning of artificial grammars. *Journal of Verbal Learning and Verbal Behavior, 6,* 317–327.

Reber, A.S. (1993). *Implicit learning and tacit knowledge: An essay on the cognitive unconscious.* Oxford: Oxford University Press.

Rechov Sumsum/Shara'a Simsim Research Symposium. (1999). Israel Education Television, Al-Quds University Institute of Modern Media and Children's Television Workshop: New York.

Redelmeier, D.A., & Tibshirani, R.J. (1997). Association between cellular-telephone calls and motor vehicle collisions. *The New England Journal of Medicine, 336,* 453–458.

Ree, M.J., Earles, J.A., & Teachout, M.S. (1994). Predicting job performance: Not much more than g. *Journal of Applied Psychology, 79,* 518–524.

Rees, G., Wojciulik, E., Clarke, K., Husain, M., Frith, C., & Driver, J. (2000). Unconscious activation of visual cortex in the damaged right hemisphere of a parietal patient with extinction. *Brain, 123,* 82–92.

Reicher, S., Levine, R.M., & Gordijn, E. (1998). More on deindividuation, power relations between groups and the expression of social identity: Three studies on the effects of visibility to the in-group. *British Journal of Social Psychology, 37,* 15–40.

Reicher, S., Spears, R., & Postmes, T. (1995). A social identity model of deindividuation phenomena. In W. Stroebe & M. Hewstone (Eds.), *European review of social psychology* (Vol. 6). Chichester, UK: Wiley.

Reicher, S.D. (1984). The St. Pauls' riot: An explanation of the limits of crowd action in terms of a social identity model. *European Journal of Social Psychology, 14,* 1–21.

Reicher, S.D., & Potter, J. (1985). Psychological theory as intergroup perspective: A comparative analysis of "scientific" and "lay" accounts of crowd events. *Human Relations, 38,* 167–189.

Reichle, E.D., Pollatsek, A., Fisher, D.L., & Rayner, K. (1998). Toward a model of eye movement control in reading. *Psychological Review, 105,* 125–157.

Reichle, E.D., Rayner, K., & Pollatsek, A. (2003). The E-Z Reader model of eye-movement control in reading: Comparisons to other models. *Behavioral and Brain Sciences, 26,* 445–526.

Reis, H.T., Senchak, M., & Solomon, B. (1985). Sex differences in the intimacy of social interaction: Further examination of potential explanations. *Journal of Personality and Social Psychology, 48,* 1204–1217.

Reiss, S., & Havercamp, S.M. (2005). Motivation in developmental context: A new method for studying self-actualisation. *Journal of Humanistic Psychology, 45,* 41–53.

Rescorla, R.A., & Wagner, A.R. (1972). A theory of Pavlovian conditioning: Variations in the effectiveness of reinforcement and nonreinforcement. In A.H. Black & W.F. Prokasy (Eds.), *Classical conditioning: II. Current research and theory.* New York: Appleton-Century-Crofts.

Rhee, S.H., & Waldman, I.D. (2002). Genetic and environmental influences on antisocial behaviour: A meta-analysis of twin and adoption studies. *Psychological Bulletin, 128,* 490–529.

Ricard, M., & Kamberkkilicci, M. (1995). Children's empathic responses to emotional complexity. *International Journal of Behavioral Development, 18,* 211–225.

Richeson, J.A., & Nussbaum, R.J. (2004). The impact of multiculturalism versus colour-blindness on racial bias. *Journal of Experimental Social Psychology, 40,* 417–423.

Rickels, K., DeMartinis, N., & Aufdrembrinke, B. (2000). A double-blind, placebo-controlled trial of abecarnil and diazepam in the treatment of patients with generalised anxiety disorder. *Journal of Clinical Psychopharmacology, 20,* 12–18.

Riddoch, G. (1917). Dissociations of visual perceptions due to occipital injuries, with especial reference to appreciation of movement. *Brain, 40,* 15–57.

Riddoch, M.J., & Humphreys, G.W. (2001). Object recognition. In B. Rapp (Ed.), *The handbook of cognitive neuropsychology: What deficits reveal about the human mind.* Hove, UK: Psychology Press.

Riggs, K.J., Peterson, D.M., Robinson, E.J., & Mitchell, P. (1998). Are errors in false belief tasks symptomatic of a broader difficulty with counterfactuality? *Cognitive Development, 13,* 73–90.

Robbins, T.W., Anderson, E.J., Barker, D.R., Bradley, A.C., Fearnyhough, C., Henson, R., et al. (1996). Working memory in chess. *Memory and Cognition, 24,* 83–93.

Robertson, S.I. (2001). *Problem solving.* Hove, UK: Psychology Press.

Robins, R.W., Spranca, M.D., & Mendelsohn, G.A. (1996). The actor–observer effect revisited: Effects of individual differences and repeated social interactions on actor and observer attributions. *Journal of Personality and Social Psychology, 71,* 375–389.

Robinson, J.L., Zahn-Waxler, C., & Emde, R.N. (1994). Patterns of development in early empathic behaviour: Environmental and child constitutional influences. *Social Development, 3,* 125–145.

Robson, C. (1994). *Experimental design and statistics in psychology* (3rd ed.). Harmondsworth, UK: Penguin.

Robson, J., Pring, T., Marshall, J., & Chiat, S. (2003). Phoneme frequency effects in jargon aphasia: A phonological investigation of non-word errors. *Brain and Language, 85,* 109–124.

Rodriguez, E., George, N., Lachaux, J., Martinerie, J., Renault, B., & Varela, F.J. (1999). Perception's shadow: Long-distance synchronization of human brain activity. *Nature, 397,* 430–433.

Roebers, C.M., & Schneider, W. (2005). Individual differences in young children's suggestibility: Relations to event memory, language abilities, working memory, and executive functioning. *Cognitive Development, 20*, 427–447.

Roediger, H.L. (1980). Memory metaphors in cognitive psychology. *Memory & Cognition, 8*, 231–246.

Roethlisberger, F.J., & Dickson, W.J. (1939). *Management and the worker.* Cambridge, MA: Harvard University Press.

Rogers, C.R. (1951). *Client-centered therapy.* Boston, MA: Houghton Mifflin.

Rogers, C.R. (1967). *On becoming a person.* London: Constable.

Rogers, C.R. (1975). Client-centered psychotherapy. In A.M. Freedman, H.I. Kaplan, & B.J. Sadock (Eds.), *Comprehensive textbook of psychiatry* (Vol. II). Baltimore, MD: Williams & Wilkins.

Rogers, R.W. (1983). Cognitive and physiological processes in fear appeals and attitude change: A revised theory of protection motivation. In J.T. Cacioppo & R.E. Petty (Eds.), *Social psycho-physiology: A sourcebook.* New York: Guilford Press.

Rolls, B.J., Rowe, E.A., & Rolls, E.T. (1982). How flavour and appearance affect human feeding. *Proceedings of the Nutrition Society, 41*, 109–117.

Rolls, B.J., van Duijvenvoorde, P.M., & Rolls, E.T. (1984). Pleasantness changes and food intake in a varied four-course meal. *Appetite, 5*, 337–348.

Rolls, E.T. (1981). Central nervous mechanisms related to feeding and appetite. *British Medical Bulletin, 37*, 131–134.

Rolls, E.T., & Rolls, J.H. (1997). Olfactory sensory-specific satiety in humans. *Physiology and Behavior, 61*, 461–473.

Rortvedt, A.K., & Miltenberger, R.G. (1994). Analysis of a high-probability instructional sequence and time-out in the treatment of child noncompliance. *Journal of Applied Behavior Analysis, 27*, 327–330.

Rose, A.J., & Rudolph, K.D. (2006). A review of sex differences in peer relationship processes: Potential trade-offs for the emotional and behavioural development of girls and boys. *Psychological Bulletin, 132*, 98–131.

Rosenbaum, M.E. (1986). The repulsion hypothesis: On the non-development of relationships. *Journal of Personality and Social Psychology, 51*, 1156–1166.

Rosenberg, M.J. (1965). When dissonance fails: On eliminating evaluation apprehension from attitude measurement. *Journal of Personality and Social Psychology, 1*, 28–42.

Rosenberg, S., Nelson, C., & Vivekananthan, P.S. (1968). A multidimensional approach to the structure of personality impressions. *Journal of Personality and Social Psychology, 9*, 283–294.

Rosenfield, D., Stephan, W.G., & Lucker, G.W. (1981). Attraction to competent and incompetent members of cooperative and competitive groups. *Journal of Applied Social Psychology, 11*, 416–433.

Rosenman, R.H., Brand, R.J., Jenkins, C.D., Friedman, M., Straus, R., & Wurm, M. (1975). Coronary heart disease in the Western Collaborative Group Study: Final follow-up experience of $8\frac{1}{2}$ years. *Journal of the American Medical Association, 22*, 872–877.

Rosenthal, R. (1966). *Experimenter effects in behavioral research.* New York: Appleton-Century-Crofts.

Rosenzweig, M.R. (1992). Psychological science around the world. *American Psychologist, 47*, 718–722.

Rosenzweig, M.R., Breedlove, S.M., & Leiman, A.L. (2002). *Biological psychology: An introduction to behavioral, cognitive, and clinical neuroscience* (3rd ed.). Sunderland, MA: Sinauer Associates.

Rosenzweig, M.R., Leiman, A.L., & Breedlove, S.M. (1999). *Biological psychology: An introduction to behavioral, cognitive, and clinical neuroscience* (2nd ed.). Sunderland, MA: Sinauer Associates.

Roser, M., & Gazzaniga, M.S. (2004). Auto Interpretive minds. *Current Directions in Science, 13*, 56–59.

Roth, A., & Fonagy, P. (1996). *What works for whom? A review of psychotherapy research.* New York: Guilford Press.

Roth, A., & Fonagy, P. (with contributions from G. Parry, M. Target, & R. Woods) (2005). *What works for whom? A critical review of psychotherapy research* (2nd ed.). New York: Guilford Press.

Rottenstreich, Y., & Hsee, C.K. (2001). Money, kisses, and electric shocks: On the affective psychology of risk. *Psychological Science, 12*, 185–190.

Rottenstreich, Y., & Shu, S. (2004). The connections between affect and decision making: Nine resulting phenomena. In D.J. Koehler & N. Harvey (Eds.), *Blackwell handbook of judgement and decision making.* Oxford, UK: Blackwell.

Rubin, D.C., Rahhal, T.A., & Poon, L.W. (1998). Things learned in early childhood are remembered best. *Memory & Cognition, 26*, 3–19.

Rubin, M., & Hewstone, M. (1998). Social identity theory's self-esteem hypothesis: A review and some suggestions for clarification. *Review of Personality and Social Psychology, 2*, 40–62.

Rubin, Z. (1973). *Liking and loving: An invitation to social psychology.* New York: Holt, Rinehart & Winston.

Rubinstein, J., Meyer, D., & Evans, J. (2001). Executive control of cognitive processes in task switching. *Journal of Experimental Psychology: Human Perception and Performance, 27*, 763–797.

Rubinstein, S., & Caballero, B. (2000). Is Miss America an undernourished role model? *Journal of the American Medical Association, 283*, 1569–1569.

Ruchkin, D.S., Grafman, J., Cameron, K., & Berndt, R.S. (2003). Working memory retention systems: A state of activated long-term memory. *Behavioral and Brain Sciences, 26*, 709–777.

Rudolph, J., Langer, I., & Tausch, R. (1980). Demonstrations of the psychic results and conditions of person-centred individual psychotherapy. *Zeitschrift für Klinische Forschung und Praxis, 9*, 23–33.

Rumelhart, D.R., & Ortony, A. (1977). The representation of knowledge in memory. In R.C. Anderson, R.J. Spiro, & W.E. Montague (Eds.), *Schooling and the acquisition of knowledge.* Hillsdale, NJ: Lawrence Erlbaum Associates, Inc.

Rusbult, C. (1983). A longitudinal test of the investment model: The development (and deterioration) of satisfaction and commitment in heterosexual involvements. *Journal of Personality and Social Psychology, 45*, 101–117.

Rusbult, C.E., & Martz, J.M. (1995). Remaining in an abusive relationship: An investment model analysis of nonvoluntary dependence. *Personality and Social Psychology Bulletin, 21*, 558–571.

Rusbult, C.E., van Lange, P.A.M., Wildschut, T., Yovetich, N.A., & Verette, J. (2000). Perceived superiority in close relationships: Why it exists and persists. *Journal of Personality and Social Psychology, 79*, 521–545.

Rushton, J.P. (1990). Race differences and r/K theory. *Ethology and Sociobiology, 11*, 131–140.

Russell, J.A., & Barrett, F.L. (1999). Core affect, prototypical emotional episodes, and other things called *emotion*: Dissecting the elephant. *Journal of Personality and Social Psychology, 76*, 805–819.

Russo, R., Nichelli, P., Gibertoni, M., & Cornia, C. (1995). Developmental trends in implicit and explicit memory: A picture completion study. *Journal of Experimental Child Psychology, 59*, 566–578.

Rutter, M. (1981). *Maternal deprivation re-assessed* (2nd ed.). Harmondsworth, UK: Penguin.

References

Rutter, M., and the English and Romanian Adoptees (ERA) Team. (1998). Developmental catch-up and deficit following adoption after severe global early privation. *Journal of Child Psychology and Psychiatry, 39*, 465–476.

Sabini, J., & Silver, M. (2005). Ekman's basic emotions: Why not love and jealousy? *Cognition and Emotion, 19*, 693–712.

Sacco, W.P., & Beck, A.T. (1985). Cognitive therapy for depression. In E.E. Beckham & W.R. Leber (Eds.), *Handbook of depression: Treatment, assessment and research.* Homewood, IL: Dorsey Press.

Sacks, O. (1985). *The man who mistook his wife for a hat.* London: Picador.

Sagi, A., & Lewkowicz, K.S. (1987). A cross-cultural evaluation of attachment research. In L.W.C. Tavecchio & M.H. van IJzendoorn (Eds.), *Attachment in social networks: Contributions to the Bowlby–Ainsworth attachment theory.* Amsterdam: North-Holland.

Sagi, A., van IJzendoorn, M.H., & Koren-Karie, N. (1991). Primary appraisal of the Strange Situation: A cross-cultural analysis of the pre-separation episodes. *Developmental Psychology, 27*, 587–596.

Sagotsky, G., Wood-Schneider, M., & Konop, M. (1981). Learning to cooperate: Effects of modelling and direct instructions. *Child Development, 52*, 1037–1042.

Sai, F.Z. (2005). The role of the mother's voice in developing mother's face preference: Evidence for intermodal perception at birth. *Infant and Child Development, 14*, 29–50.

Salkovskis, P.M., Clark, D.M., Hackmann, A., Wells, A., & Gelder, M.G. (1999). An experimental investigation of the role of safety-seeking behaviours in the maintenance of panic disorder with agoraphobia. *Behaviour Research and Therapy, 37*, 559–574.

Salovey, P., & Mayer, J.D. (1990). Emotional intelligence. *Imagination, Cognition and Personality, 9*, 185–211.

Sameroff, A.J., Seifer, R., Baldwin, A., & Baldwin, C. (1993). Stability of intelligence from preschool to adolescence: The influence of social and family risk factors. *Child Development, 64*, 80–97.

Sameroff, A.J., Seifer, R., Barocas, R., Zax, M., & Greenspan, S. (1987). Intelligence quotient scores of 4-year-old children: Social-environmental risk factors. *Paediatrics, 79*, 343–350.

Samuel, A.G. (1981). Phonemic restoration: Insights from a new methodology. *Journal of Experimental Psychology: General, 110*, 474–494.

Samuel, A.G. (1987). The effects of lexical uniqueness on phonemic restoration. *Journal of Memory and Language, 26*, 36–56.

Samuel, A.G. (1997). Lexical activation produces potent phonemic percepts. *Cognitive Psychology, 32*, 97–127.

Sanders, G.S., & Baron, R.S. (1977). Is social comparison irrelevant for producing choice shifts? *Journal of Experimental Social Psychology, 13*, 303–314.

Sapolsky, R.M. (1992). Neuroendocrinology of the stress response. In J.B. Becker, S.M. Breedlove, & D. Crews (Eds.), *Behavioral endocrinology.* Cambridge, MA: MIT Press.

Sarason, I.G., Smith, R.E., & Diener, E. (1975). Personality research: Components of variance attributable to the person and the situation. *Journal of Personality and Social Psychology, 32*, 199–204.

Saville, P., & Blinkhorn, S. (1981). Reliability, homogeneity and the construct validity of Cattell's 16PF. *Personality and Individual Differences, 2*, 325–333.

Savin, H.B. (1973). Professors and psychological researchers: Conflicting values in conflicting roles. *Cognition, 2*, 147–149.

Savoy, R.L. (2001). History and future directions of human brain mapping and functional neuroimaging. *Acta Psychologica, 107*, 9–42.

Saxe, R., Carey, S., & Kanwisher, N. (2004). Understanding other minds: Linking developmental psychology and functional neuroimaging *Annual Review of Psychology, 55*, 87–124.

Saxton, M. (1997). The contrast theory of negative input. *Journal of Child Language, 24*, 139–161.

Schachter, S. (1959). *The psychology of affiliation: Experimental studies of the sources of gregariousness.* Stanford, CA: Stanford University Press.

Schachter, S., & Singer, J.E. (1962). Cognitive, social, and physiological determinants of an emotional state. *Psychological Review, 69*, 379–399.

Schachter, S., & Wheeler, L. (1962). Epinephrine, chlorpromazine and amusement. *Journal of Abnormal and Social* Psychology, 65, 121–128.

Schaefer, C., Coyne, J.C., & Lazarus, R.S. (1981). The health-related functions of social support. *Journal of Behavioral Medicine, 4*, 381–406.

Schaffer, H.R. (1996). *Social development.* Oxford, UK: Blackwell.

Schaffer, H.R., & Emerson, P.E. (1964). The development of social attachments in infancy. *Monographs of the Society for Research on Child Development, 29.*

Scheerer, M. (1963). Problem-solving. *Scientific American, 208*(4), 118–128.

Schendan, H.E., Searl, M.M., Melrose, R.J., & Stern, C.E. (2003). An fMRI study of the role of the medial temporal lobe in implicit and explicit sequence learning. *Neuron, 37*, 1013–1025.

Schieffelin, B.B. (1990). *The give and take of everyday life: Language socialisation of Kaluli children.* Cambridge, UK: Cambridge University Press.

Schlagmüller, M., & Schneider, W. (2002). The development of organisational strategies in children: Evidence from a microgenetic longitudinal study. *Journal of Experimental Child Psychology, 81*, 298–319.

Schliefer, S.J., Keller, S.E., Camerino, M., Thornton, J.C., & Stein, M. (1983). Suppression of lymphocyte stimulation following bereavement. *Journal of the American Medical Association, 250*, 374–377.

Schmidt, U., & Treasure, J. (1993). *Getting better bit(e) by bit(e): A survival kit for sufferers of bulimia nervosa and binge eating disorders.* Hove, UK: Psychology Press.

Schmitt, D.P. (2005). Sociosexuality from Argentina to Zimbabwe: A 48-nation study of sex, culture, and strategies of human mating. *Behavioral and Brain Sciences, 28*, 247–311.

Schneider, W. (1999). The development of metamemory in children. *Attention and performance* (Vol. 17, pp. 487–514). Cambridge, MA: MIT Press.

Schneider, W., Gruber, H., Gold, A., & Opwis, K. (1993). Chess expertise and memory for chess positions in children and adults. *Journal of Experimental Child Psychology, 56*, 328–349.

Schneider, W., Knopf, M., & Stefanek, J. (2002). The development of verbal memory in childhood and adolescence: Findings from the Munich longitudinal study. *Journal of Educational Psychology, 94*, 751–761.

Schneider, W., & Pressley, M. (1989). *Memory development between two and twenty.* New York: Springer.

Schneider, W., & Shiffrin, R.M. (1977). Controlled and automatic human information processing: 1. Detection, search, and attention. *Psychological Review, 84*, 1–66.

Schochat, T., Luboshitzky, R., & Lavie, P. (1997). Noctural melatonin onset is phase locked to the primary sleep gate. *American Journal of Physiology, 273*, R364–R370.

Schoenborn, D.A. (1993). The Alameda Study? 25 years on. In S. Maes, H. Leventhal, & M. Johnston (Eds.), *International review of health psychology.* Chichester: Wiley.

Schriesheim, C.A., Tepper, B.J., & Tetrault, L.A. (1994). Least preferred co-worker score, situational control, and leadership effectiveness: A meta-analysis of contingency model performance predictions. *Journal of Applied Psychology, 79*, 561–573.

Schumacher, E.H., Seymour, T.L., Glass, J.M., Fencsik, D.E., Lauber, E.J., Kieras, D.E., & Meyer, D.E. (2001). Virtually perfect time sharing in dual-task performance: Uncorking the central cognitive bottleneck. *Psychological Science, 12,* 101–108.

Schwartz, B., Ward, A., Monterosso, J., Lyubomirsky, S., White, K., & Lehman, D.R. (2002). Maximizing versus satisficing: Happiness is a matter of choice. *Journal of Personality and Social Psychology, 83,* 1178–1197.

Schwartz, J.A., Chapman, G.B., Brewer, N.T., & Bergus, G.B. (2004). The effects of accountability on bias in physician decision making: Going from bad to worse. *Psychonomic Bulletin & Review, 11,* 173–178.

Schwartz, S.H., & Rubel, T. (2005). Sex differences in value priorities: Cross-cultural and multimethod studies. *Journal of Personality and Social Psychology, 89,* 1010–1028.

Schwier, C., van Maanen, C., Carpenter, M., & Tomasello, M. (2006). Rational imitation in 12-month-old infants. *Infancy, 10,* 303–311.

Sclafini, A., Springer, D., & Kluge, L. (1976). Effects of quinine adulteration on the food intake and body weight of obese and non-obese hypothalamic hyperphagic rats. *Physiology and Behavior, 16,* 631–640.

Segal, H. (1964). *Introduction to the work of Melanie Klein.* New York: Basic Books.

Segerstrom, S.C., & Miller, G.E. (2004). Psychological stress and the human immune system: A meta-analytic study of 30 years of inquiry. *Psychological Bulletin, 130,* 601–630.

Segraves, R., & Woodard, T. (2006). Female hypoactive sexual desire disorder: History and current status. *Journal of Sexual Medicine, 3,* 408–418.

Seidenberg, M.S., Waters, G.S., Barnes, M.A., & Tanenhaus, M. (1984). When does irregular spelling or pronunciation influence word recognition? *Journal of Verbal Learning & Verbal Behavior, 23,* 383–404.

Selfe, L. (1983). *Normal and anomalous representational drawing ability in children.* London: Academic Press.

Seligman, M.E.P. (1995). The effectiveness of psychotherapy: The Consumer Reports study. *American Psychologist, 50,* 965–974.

Senghas, A., Kita, S., & Özyürek, A. (2004). Children creating core properties of language: Evidence from an emerging sign language in Nicaragua. *Science, 305,* 1779–1782.

Shadish, W.R., Matt, G.E., Navarro, A.M., & Phillips, G. (2000). The effects of psychological therapies under clinically representative conditions: A meta-analysis. *Psychological Bulletin, 126,* 512–529.

Shaffer, D.R. (1993). *Developmental psychology: Childhood and adolescence* (3rd ed.). Pacific Grove, CA: Brooks/Cole.

Shallice, T., & Warrington, E.K. (1970). Independent functioning of verbal memory stores: A neuropsychological study. *Quarterly Journal of Experimental Psychology, 22,* 261–273.

Shallice, T., & Warrington, E.K. (1974). The dissociation between long-term retention of meaningful sounds and verbal material. *Neuropsychologia, 12,* 553–555.

Shanks, D.R., & St. John, M.F. (1994). Characteristics of dissociable human learning systems. *Behavioral and Brain Sciences, 17,* 367–394.

Shapiro, C.M., Bortz, R., Mitchell, D., Bartel, P., & Jooste, P. (1981). Slow-wave sleep: A recovery period after exercise. *Science, 214,* 1253–1254.

Sharpe, D. (1997). Of apples and oranges, file drawers and garbage: Why validity issues in meta-analysis will not go away. *Clinical Psychology Review, 17,* 881–901.

Shaver, P., Hazan, C., & Bradshaw, D. (1988). Love as attachment: The integration of three behavioral systems. In R.J. Sternberg & M. Barnes (Eds.), *The psychology of love.* New Haven, CT: Yale University Press.

Shavitt, S. (1989). Operationizing functional theories of attitude. In A.R. Pratkanis, S.J. Breckler, & A.G. Greenwald (Eds.), *Attitude structure and function.* Hillsdale, NJ: Lawrence Erlbaum Associates, Inc.

Shayer, M. (1999). Cognitive acceleration through science education II: Its effects and scope. *International Journal of Science Education, 21,* 883–902.

Shayer, M. (2003). Not just Piaget; not just Vygotsky, and certainly not Vygotsky as *alternative* to Piaget. *Learning and Instruction, 13,* 465–485.

Shekelle, R.B., Raynor, W.J., Jr., Ostfeld, A.M., Garron, D.C., Bieliauskas, L.A., Liu, S.C., et al. (1981). Psychological depression and 17-year risk of death from cancer. *Psychosomatic Medicine, 43,* 117–125.

Sherif, M. (1966). *Group conflict and co-operation: Their social psychology.* London: Routledge & Kegan Paul.

Sherif, M., Harvey, O.J., White, B.J., Hood, W.R., & Sherif, C.W. (1961). *Intergroup conflict and cooperation: The robber's cave experiment.* Norman, OK: University of Oklahoma.

Sherman, J.W., Stroessner, S.J., Conrey, F.R., & Azam, O.A. (2005). Prejudice and stereotype maintenance processes: Attention, attribution, and individuation. *Journal of Personality and Social Psychology, 89,* 607–622.

Sherwin, B.B. (1991). The impact of different doses of estrogen and progestin on mood and sexual behavior in postmenopausal women. *Journal of Clinical Endocrinology and Metabolism, 72,* 336–343.

Shiffrin, R.M., & Schneider, W. (1977). Controlled and automatic human information processing: 2. Perceptual learning, automatic attending, and a general theory. *Psychological Review, 84,* 127–190.

Shifren, J.L., Braunstein, G.D., Simon, J.A., Casson, P.R., Buster, J.E., Redmond, G.P., et al. (2000). Transdermal testosterone treatment in women with impaired sexual function after oophorectomy. *New England Journal of Medicine, 343,* 682–688.

Shotland, R.L., & Straw, M.K. (1976). Bystander response to an assault: When a man attacks a woman. *Journal of Personality and Social Psychology, 34,* 990–999.

Shpancer, N. (2006). The effects of daycare: Persistent questions, elusive answers. *Early Childhood Research Quarterly, 21,* 227–237.

Shweder, R.A. (1990). Cultural psychology: What is it? In J.W. Stigler, R.A. Shweder, & G. Gerdt (Eds.), *Cultural psychology* (pp. 1–5). Cambridge. UK: Cambridge University Press.

Shweder, R.A., Mahapatra, M., & Miller, J.G. (1990). Culture and moral development. In J. Stigler, R.A. Shweder, & G. Herdt (Eds.), *Cultural psychology: Essays in comparative human development* (pp. 130–204). New York: Cambridge University Press.

Sieber, J.E., & Stanley, B. (1988). Ethical and professional dimensions of socially sensitive research. *American Psychologist, 43,* 49–55.

Siegel, J.M. (2005). Clues to the functions of mammalian sleep. *Nature, 437,* 1264–1271.

Siegler, R.S. (1998). *Children's thinking* (3rd ed.). Upper Saddle River, NJ: Prentice Hall.

Siegler, R.S. (2004). Learning about learning. *Merrill-Palmer Quarterly, 50,* 353–368.

Siegler, R.S. (2005). Children's learning. *American Psychologist, 60,* 769–778.

Siegler, R.S., & Araya, R. (2005). A computational model of unconscious and conscious strategy discovery. In R. Kail (Ed.), *Advances in child development* (pp. 1–42). Oxford, UK: Elsevier.

Siegler, R.S., & Jenkins, E.A. (1989). *How children discover new strategies.* Hillsdale, NJ: Lawrence Erlbaum Associates, Inc.

Siegler, R.S., & McGilly, K. (1989). Strategy choices in children's time-telling. In I. Levin & D. Zakay (Eds.), *Time and human cognition: A life span perspective.* Amsterdam: Elsevier Science.

Siegler, R.S., & Munakata, Y. (1993). Beyond the immaculate transition: Advances in the understanding of change. *Society for Research in Child Development Newsletter, 36*, 10–13.

Siegler, R.S., & Shrager, J. (1984). Strategy choices in addition and subtraction: How do children know what to do? In C. Sophian (Ed.), *Origins of cognitive skills*. Hillsdale, NJ: Lawrence Erlbaum Associates, Inc.

Siegler, R.S., & Stern, E. (1998). A microgenetic analysis of conscious and unconscious strategy discoveries. *Journal of Experimental Psychology: General, 127*, 377–397.

Siegler, R.S., & Svetina, M. (2002). A microgenetic/cross-sectional study of matrix completions: Comparing short-term and long-term change. *Child Development, 73*, 793–809.

Sigall, H., Aronson, E., & Van Hoose, T. (1970). The co-operative subject: Myth or reality? *Journal of Experimental Social Psychology, 6*, 1–10.

Signorielli, N. (2001). Aging on television: the picture in the nineties. *Generations: Journal of the American Society on Aging, 25*, 34–38.

Silke, A. (2003). Deindividuation, anonymity, and violence: Findings from Northern Ireland. *Journal of Social Psychology, 143*, 493–499.

Silverman, I. (1977). *The human subject in the psychological laboratory*. Oxford, UK: Pergamon.

Silverman, I., Shulman, A.D., & Wiesenthal, D. (1970). Effects of deceiving and debriefing psychological subjects on performance in later experiments. *Journal of Personality and Social Psychology, 21*, 219–227.

Simcock, G., & Hayne, H. (2002). Breaking the barrier? Children fail to translate their preverbal memories into language. *Psychological Science, 13*, 225–231.

Simion, F., Turati, C., Valenza, E., & Leo, I. (2006). The emergence of cognitive specialisation in infancy: The case of face preference. *Attention and peformance, XX1*, 189–208.

Simion, F., Valenza, E., Macchi Cassia, V., Turati, C., & Umiltà, C. (2002). Newborns' preference for up–down asymmetrical configurations. *Developmental Science, 5*, 427–434.

Simon, H.A. (1957). *Models of man: Social and rational*. New York: Wiley.

Simon, H.A. (1966). Scientific discovery and the psychology of problem solving. In H.A. Simon (Ed.), *Mind and cosmos: Essays in contemporary science and philosophy*. Pittsburgh, PA: University of Pittsburgh.

Simon, H.A. (1974). How big is a chunk? *Science, 183*, 482–488.

Simon, H.A. (1978). Rationality as process and product of thought. *American Economic Association, 68*, 1–16.

Simon, H.A. (1990). Invariants of human behaviour. *Annual Review of Psychology, 41*, 1–19.

Simon, H.A., & Reed, S.K. (1976). Modelling strategy shifts on a problem solving task, *Cognitive Psychology, 8*, 86–97.

Simons, D., Krawczyk, D.C., & Holyoak, K.J. (2004). Construction of preferences by constraint satisfaction. *Psychological Science, 15*, 331–336.

Simons, D.J., & Chabris, F. (1999). Gorillas in our midst: Sustained inattentional blindness for dynamic events. *Perception, 28*, 1059–1074.

Simons, D.J., & Rensink, R.A. (2005). Change blindness: Past, present, and future. *Trends in Cognitive Sciences, 9*, 16–20.

Simonson, I., & Staw, B.M. (1992). De-escalation strategies: A comparison of techniques for reducing commitment to losing courses of action. *Journal of Applied Psychology, 77*, 419–426.

Simpson, J.P, Collins, W.A., Tran, S., & Haydon, K.C. (2007). Attachment and the experience and expression of emotions in adult romantic relationships: A developmental perspective. *Journal of Personality and Social Psychology, 92*(2), 355–367.

Sinclair, L., & Kunda, Z. (1999). Reactions to a black professional: Motivated inhibition and activation of conflicting stereotypes. *Journal of Personality and Social Psychology, 77*, 885–904.

Singer, M. (1994). Discourse inference processes. In M.A. Gernsbacher (Ed.), *Handbook of psycholinguistics*. San Diego, CA: Academic Press.

Singh, D. (1993). Body shape and women's attractiveness: The critical role of waist-to-hip ratio. *Human Nature: An Interdisciplinary Biosocial Perspective, 4*, 297–321.

Singh, R., Bohra, K.A., & Dalal, A.K. (1979). Favourableness of leadership situations studies with information integration theory. *European Journal of Social Psychology, 9*, 253–264.

Sireteanu, R. (1999). Switching on the infant brain. *Science, 286*, 59–61.

Skinner, B.F. (1938). *The behavior of organisms*. New York: Appleton-Century-Crofts.

Skinner, B.F. (1957). *Verbal behavior*. New York: Appleton-Century-Crofts.

Skinner, B.F. (1966). Operant behavior. In W.K. Honig (Ed.), *Operant behavior: Areas of research and application*. New York: Appleton-Century-Crofts.

Skinner, B.F. (1971). *Beyond freedom and dignity*. New York: Knopf.

Skinner, B.F. (1980). *The shaping of a behaviourist*. Oxford, UK: Holdan Books.

Skinner, E.A., Edge, K., Altman, J., & Sherwood, H. (2003). Searching for the structure of coping: A review and critique of category systems for classifying ways of coping. *Psychological Bulletin, 129*, 216–269.

Skoe, E.E.A. (1998). The ethic of care: Issues in moral development. In E.A.A. Skoe & A.L. von der Lippe (Eds.), *Personality development in adolescence: A cross-national and life span perspective*. London: Routledge.

Skre, I., Onstad, S., Torgersen, S., Lygren, S., & Kringlen, E. (1993). A twin study of DSM-III-R anxiety disorders. *Acta Psychiatrica Scandinavica, 88*, 85–92.

Slade, L., & Ruffman, T. (2005). How language does (and does not) relate to theory of mind: A longitudinal study of syntax, semantics, working memory and false belief. *British Journal of Developmental Psychology, 23*, 117–141.

Slater, A. (1990). Perceptual development. In M.W. Eysenck (Ed.), *The Blackwell dictionary of cognitive psychology*. Oxford, UK: Blackwell.

Slater, A. (1998). The competent infant: Innate organisation and early learning in infant visual perception. In A. Slater (Ed.), *Perceptual development: Visual, auditory and speech perception in infancy*. Hove, UK: Psychology Press.

Slater, A., Mattock, A., & Brown, E. (1990). Newborn infants' responses to retinal and real size. *Journal of Experimental Child Psychology, 49*, 314–322.

Slater, M.R., & Sewell, D.F. (1994). An examination of the cohesion–performance relationship in university hockey teams. *Journal of Sports Science, 12*, 423–431.

Sloboda, J.A., Davidson, J.W., Howe, M.J.A., & Moore, D.G. (1996). The role of practice in the development of performing musicians. *British Journal of Psychology, 87*, 287–309.

Sloman, A. (1997). *What sorts of machine can love? Architectural requirements for human-like agents both natural and artificial*. Retrieved from http://www.sbs.org.uk/literature.htm

Smania, N., Martini, M.C., Gambina, G., Tomelleri, G., Palamara, A., Natale, E., et al. (1998). The spatial distribution of spatial attention in hemineglect and extinction patients. *Brain, 121*, 1759–1770.

Smetana, J.G., & Adler, N.E. (1980). Fishbein's value X expectancy model: An examination of some assumptions. *Personality and Social Psychology Bulletin, 6*, 89–96.

Smith, C.A., & Kirby, L.D. (2001). Toward delivering on the promise of appraisal theory. In K.R. Scherer, A. Schorr, &

T. Johnstone (Eds.), *Appraisal processes in emotion: Theory, methods, research*. Oxford, UK: Oxford University Press.

Smith, C.A., & Lazarus, R.S. (1993). Appraisal components, core relational themes, and the emotions. *Cognition and Emotion, 7*, 233–269.

Smith, E.R., & Mackie, D.M. (2000). *Social psychology* (2nd ed.). Philadelphia: Psychology Press.

Smith, L. (1996). The social construction of rational understanding. In A. Tryphon & J. Voneche (Eds.), *Piaget–Vygotsky: The social genesis of thought*. Hove, UK: Psychology Press.

Smith, M. (2000). Conceptual structures in language production. In L. Wheeldon (Ed.), *Aspects of language production*. Hove, UK: Psychology Press.

Smith, M.L., & Glass, G.V. (1977). Meta-analysis of psychotherapy outcome measures. *American Psychologist, 32*, 752–760.

Smith, M.L., Glass, G.V., & Miller, T.I. (1980). *The benefits of psychotherapy*. Baltimore, MD: John Hopkins Press.

Smith, P.B., & Bond, M.H. (1998). *Social psychology across cultures* (2nd ed.). New York: Harvester Wheatsheaf.

Smith, P.K., Cowie, H., & Blades, M. (2003). *Understanding children's development* (4th ed.). Oxford, UK: Blackwell.

Smith, S., & Blankenship, S. (1991). Incubation and the persistence of fixation in problem solving. *American Journal of Psychology, 104*, 61–87.

Snarey, J.R. (1985). Cross-cultural universality of social-moral development: A critical review of Kohlbergian research. *Psychological Bulletin, 97*, 202–232.

Snodgrass, M., Bernat, E., & Shevrin, H. (2004). Unconscious perception at the objective detection threshold exists. *Perception and Psychophysics, 66*, 888–895.

Solms, M. (1997). *The neuropsychology of dreams*. Mahwah, NJ: Lawrence Erlbaum Associates, Inc.

Solms, M. (2000a). Dreaming and REM sleep are controlled by different brain mechanisms. *Behavioral and Brain Sciences, 23*, 843–850.

Solms, M. (2000b). Freudian dream theory today. *The Psychologist, 13*, 618–619.

Solms, M., & Turnbull, O. (2002). *The brain and the inner world. An introduction to the neuroscience of subjective experience*. Cambridge and New York: Cambridge University Press.

Solomon, R.L., & Wynne, L.C. (1953). Traumatic avoidance learning: Acquisition in normal dogs. *Psychological Monographs, 67*, 1–19.

Sorrentino, R.M., & Field, N. (1986). Emergent leadership over time: The functional value of positive motivation. *Journal of Personality and Social Psychology, 50*, 1091–1099.

Spearman, C. (1923). *The nature of intelligence and the principles of cognition*. London: Macmillan.

Spector, P.E., Dwyer, D.J., & Jex, S.M. (1988). The relationship of job stressors to affective, health, and performance outcomes: A comparison of multiple data sources. *Journal of Applied Psychology, 73*, 11–19.

Spelke, E.S., Hirst, W.C., & Neisser, U. (1976). Skills of divided attention. *Cognition, 4*, 215–230.

Sperling, G. (1960). The information available in brief visual presentations. *Psychological Monographs, 74* (Whole No. 498), 1–29.

Sperry, R.W. (1968). Hemisphere deconnection and unity in conscious awareness. *American Psychologist, 23*, 723–733.

Spiers, H.J., Maguire, E.A., & Burgess, N. (2001). Hippocampal amnesia. *Neurocase, 7*, 357–382.

Spitz, R.A. (1945). Hospitalism: An inquiry into the genesis of psychiatric conditions in early childhood. *Psychoanalytic Study of the Child, 1*, 113–117.

Sporer, S.L., Penrod, S., Read, D., & Cutler, B. (1995). Choosing, confidence and accuracy: A meta-analysis of the confidence–accuracy relation in eyewitness identification studies. *Psychological Bulletin, 118*, 315–327.

Sprafkin, J.N., Liebert, R.M., & Poulos, R.W. (1975). Effects of a pro-social televised example on children's helping. *Journal of Experimental Child Psychology, 20*, 119–126.

Sprecher, S. (1989). The importance to males and females of physical attractiveness, earning potential and expressiveness in initial attraction. *Sex Roles, 21*, 591–607.

Sprecher, S. (1998). Insider's perspectives on reasons for attraction to a close other. *Social Psychology Quarterly, 61*, 287–300.

Sprecher, S., & Hendrick, S.S. (2004). Self-disclosure in intimate relationships: Associations with individual and relationship characteristics over time. *Journal of Social and Clinical Psychology, 23*, 857–877.

Stajkovic, A.D., & Luthans, F. (1998). Self-efficacy and work-related performance: A meta-analysis. *Psychological Bulletin, 124*, 240–261.

Stams, G.J., Brugman, D., Dekovic, M., van Rosmalen, L., van der Laan, P., & Gibbs, J.C. (2006). The moral judgement of juvenile delinquents: A meta-analysis. *Journal of Abnormal Child Psychology, 34*, 692–708.

Stams, G.-J.J.M., Juffer, F., & van IJzendoorn, M.H. (2002). Maternal sensitivity, infant attachment, and temperament in early childhood predict adjustment in middle childhood: The case of adopted children and their biologically unrelated parents. *Developmental Psychology, 38*, 806–821.

Stangor, C., & McMillan, D. (1992). Memory for expectancy-congruent and expectancy-incongruent information: A review of the social and social developmental literatures. *Psychological Bulletin, 111*, 42–61.

Stanislaw, H., & Rice, F.J. (1988). Correlation between sexual desire and menstrual cycle characteristics. *Archives of Sexual Behavior, 17*, 499–508.

Stanley, B.G., Kyrkouli, S.E., Lampert, S., & Leibowitz, S.F. (1986). Neuropeptide Y chronically injected into the hypothalamus: A powerful neurochemical inducer of hyperphagia and obesity. *Peptides, 7*, 1189–1192.

Steblay, N.M. (1987). Helping behavior in rural and urban environments: A meta-analysis. *Psychological Bulletin, 102*, 346–356.

Steblay, N.M. (1997). Social influence in eyewitness recall: A meta-analytic review of line-up instruction effects. *Law and Human Behavior, 21*, 283–298.

Steblay, N.M., Dysart, J., Fulero, S., & Lindsay, R.C.L. (2001). Eyewitness accuracy rates in sequential and simultaneous line-up presentations: A meta-analytic comparison. *Law and Human Behavior, 25*, 459–474.

Steel, P., & Ones, D.S. (2002). Personality and happiness: A national-level analysis. *Journal of Personality and Social Psychology, 83*, 767–781.

Stemberger, J.P. (1982). The nature of segments in the lexicon: Evidence from speech errors. *Lingua, 56*, 235–259.

Stemberger, R.T., Turner, S.M., & Beidel, D.C. (1995). Social phobia: An analysis of possible developmental factors. *Journal of Abnormal Psychology, 104*, 526–531.

Stern, M., & Karraker, K.H. (1989). Sex stereotyping of infants: A review of gender labelling studies. *Sex Roles, 20*, 501–522.

Sternberg, R.J. (1985). *Beyond IQ: A triarchic theory of human intelligence*. Cambridge, UK: Cambridge University Press.

Sternberg, R.J. (1986). A triangular theory of love. *Psychological Review, 93*, 119–135.

Sternberg, R.J. (1998). *Love is a story*. Oxford: Oxford University Press.

Sternberg, R.J. (2003). *Cognitive psychology* (3rd ed.). Belmont, CA: Wadsworth.

Sternberg, R.J. (2004). Intelligence. In R.L. Gregory (Ed.), *The Oxford companion to the mind*. Oxford, UK: Oxford University Press.

Sternberg, R.J., & Ben-Zeev, T. (2001). *Complex cognition: The psychology of human thought*. Oxford, UK: Oxford University Press.

Sternberg, R.J., & Grajek, S. (1984). The nature of love. *Journal of Personality and Social Psychology, 47*, 312–329.

Sternberg, R.J., & Kaufman, J.C. (1998). Human abilities. *Annual Review of Psychology, 49*, 479–502.

Stevens, S., Hynan, M.T., & Allen, M. (2000). A meta-analysis of common factor and specific treatment effects across the outcome domains of the phase model of psychotherapy. *Clinical Psychology: Science and Practice, 7*, 273–290.

Stirling, J.D., & Hellewell, J.S.E. (1999). *Psychopathology*. London: Routledge.

Stone, A.A., Reed, B.R., & Neale, J.M. (1987). Changes in daily life event frequency precede episodes of physical symptoms. *Journal of Human Stress, 13*, 70–74.

Storms, M.D. (1973). Videotape and the attribution process: Reversing actors' and observers' points of view. *Journal of Personality and Social Psychology, 27*, 165–175.

Stott, C., Hutchison, P & Drury, J. (2001). "Hooligans" abroad? Inter-group dynamics, social identity and participation in collective "disorder" at the 1998 world cup finals. *British Journal of Social Psychology, 40*, 359–384

Strassberg, Z., & Dodge, K.A. (1987). *Focus of social attention among children varying in peer status*. Paper presented at the annual meeting of the Association for the Advancement of Behavior Therapy, Boston.

Straus, M.A. (1993). Physical assault by wives: A major social problem. In R.J. Gelles & D.R. Loseke (Eds.), *Current controversies on family violence* (pp. 67–87). Newbury Park, CA: Sage.

Straus, M.A., Gelles, R.J., & Steinmetz, S.K. (1980). *Behind closed doors: Violence in the American family*. New York: Doubleday.

Strayer, D.L., Drews, F.A., & Johnston, W.A. (2003). Cell-phone induced failures of visual attention during simulated driving. *Journal of Experimental Psychology: Applied, 9*, 23–32.

Strayer, D.L., & Johnston, W.A. (2001). Driven to distraction: Dual-task studies of simulated driving and conversing on a cellular telephone. *Psychological Science, 12*, 462–466.

Stretch, D.D. (1994). Experimental design. In A.M. Colman (Ed.), *Companion encyclopaedia of psychology* (Vol. 2). London: Routledge.

Stroud, L.R., Salovey, P., & Epel, E.S. (2002). Sex differences in stress responses: Social rejection versus achievement stress. *Biological Psychiatry, 52*, 318–327.

Strupp, H.H. (1996). The tripartite model and the Consumer Reports study. *American Psychologist, 51*, 1017–1024.

Stunkard, A.J., Sorensen, T.I.A., Hanis, C., Teasdale, T.W., Chakraborty, R., Schull, W.J., et al. (1986). An adoption study of human obesity. *New England Journal of Medicine, 314*, 193–198.

Sturges, J.W., & Rogers, R.W. (1996). Preventive health psychology from a developmental perspective: An extension of protection motivation theory. *Health Psychology, 15*, 158–166.

Styles, E.A. (1997). *The psychology of attention*. Hove, UK: Psychology Press.

Suh, S., & Trabasso, T. (1993). Inferences during reading: Converging evidence from discourse analysis, talk-aloud protocols, and recognition priming. *Journal of Memory and Language, 32*, 279–300.

Sulin, R.A., & Dooling, D.J. (1974). Intrusion of a thematic idea in retention of prose. *Journal of Experimental Psychology, 103*, 255–262.

Sullivan, L. (1976). Selective attention and secondary message analysis: A reconsideration of Broadbent's filter model of selective attention. *Quarterly Journal of Experimental Psychology, 28*, 167–178.

Sumerlin, J.R., & Bundrick, C.M. (2000). Happiness and self-actualisation under conditions of strain: A sample of homeless men. *Perceptual and Motor Skills, 90*, 191–203.

Sumerlin, J.R., & Norman, R.L. (1992). Self-actualisation and homeless men: A known-groups examination of Maslow hierarchy of needs. *Journal of Social Behavior and Personality, 7*, 469–481.

Sun, R., Slusarz, P., & Terry, C. (2005). The interaction of the explicit and the implicit in skill learning: A dual-process approach. *Psychological Review, 112*, 159–192.

Sundet, J.M., Barlaug, D.G., & Torjussen, T.M. (2004). The end of the Flynn effect? A study of secular trends in mean intelligence test scores of Norwegian conscripts during half a century. *Intelligence, 32*, 349–362.

Swann, W.B. (1987). Identity negotiation: Where two roads meet. *Journal of Personality and Social Psychology, 53*, 1038–1051.

Swanson, H.L. (1999). What develops in working memory? A life span perspective. *Developmental Psychology, 35*, 986–1000.

Sweller, J., & Levine, M. (1982). Effects of goal specificity on means–ends analysis and learning. *Journal of Experimental Psychology: Learning, Memory, and Cognition, 8*, 463–474.

Swim, J.K., Aikin, K.J., Hall, W.S., & Hunter, B.A. (1995). Sexism and racism: Old-fashioned and modern prejudices. *Journal of Personality and Social Psychology, 68*, 199–214.

Tager-Flusberg, H. (1999). Language development in atypical children. In M. Barrett (Ed.), *The development of language*. Hove, UK: Psychology Press.

Tajfel, H. (1978). Intergroup behaviour: Vol. 1. Individualistic perspectives. In H. Tajfel & C. Fraser (Eds.), *Introducing social psychology*. Harmondsworth, UK: Penguin.

Tajfel, H. (1979). Individuals and groups in social psychology. *British Journal of Psychology, 18*, 187–190.

Tajfel, H. (1981). *Human groups and social categories: Studies in social psychology*. Cambridge, UK: Cambridge University Press.

Tajfel, H., Flament, C., Billig, M.G., & Bundy, R.P. (1971). Social categorisation and intergroup behaviour. *European Journal of Social Psychology, 1*, 149–178.

Takahashi, Y. (1979). Growth hormone secretion related to the sleep and waking rhythm. In R. Doncker-Colin, M. Shkurovich, & M.B. Sterman (Eds.), *The functions of sleep*. New York: Academic Press.

Talarico, J.M., & Rubin, D.C. (2003). Confidence, not consistency, characterises flashbulb memories. *Psychological Science, 14*, 455–461.

Tallandini, M.A. (2004). Aggressive behavior in children dolls' house play. *Aggressive Behavior, 30*, 504–519.

Tarr, M.J., & Bülthoff, H.H. (1995). Is human object recognition better described by geon structural descriptions or by multiple views? Comment on Biederman and Gerhardstein (1993). *Journal of Experimental Psychology: Human Perception and Performance, 21*, 1494–1505.

Tarr, M.J., & Bülthoff, H.H. (1998). Image-based object recognition in man, monkey and machine. *Cognition, 67*, 1–20.

Taylor, S.E., Klein, L.C., Greendale, G., & Seeman, T.E. (1999). Oxytocin and HPA response to acute stress in women with or without HRT. Cited in Taylor et al. (2000)—article in *Psychological Review*.

Taylor, S.E., Klein, L.C., Lewis, B.P., Gruenewald, T.L., Gurung, R.A.R., & Updegraff, J.A. (2000). Biobehavioural responses to stress in females: Tend-and-befriend, not fight-or-flight. *Psychological Review, 107*, 411–429.

Teitelbaum, P., & Stellar, E. (1954). Recovery from the failure to eat produced by hypothalamic lesions. *Science, 120*, 894–895.

Teller, D.Y. (1997). First glances: The vision of infants. The Friedenwald lecture. *Investigative Ophthalmology and Visual Science, 38*, 2183–2203.

Terracciano, A., et al. (2005, October 7). National character does not reflect mean personality trait levels in 49 cultures. *Science*, pp. 96–100.

Tesser, A. (1988). Toward a self-evaluation maintenance model of social behaviour. In L. Berkowitz (Ed.), *Advances in experimental social psychology* (Vol. 21). San Diego, CA: Academic Press.

Tetlock, P.E. (1991). An alternative metaphor in the study of judgment and choice: People as politicians. *Theory and Psychology*, 1, 451–475.

Tetlock, P.E. (2002). Social functionalist frameworks for judgment and choice: Intuitive politicians, theologians, and prosecutors. *Psychological Review*, 109, 451–471.

Tetlock, P.E., & Mellers, B.A. (2002). The great rationality debate. *Psychological Science*, 13, 94–99.

Tetlock, P.E., Peterson, R.S., McGuire, C., Chang, S., & Feld, P. (1992). Assessing political group dynamics: A test of the groupthink model. *Journal of Personality and Social Psychology*, 63, 403–425.

Thase, M.E., Rush, A.J., Howland, R.H., Kornstein, S.G., et al. (2002). Double-blind switch study of sertraline treatment of antidepressant-resistant chronic depression. *Archives of General Psychiatry*, 59, 233–239.

Thompson, W.C., Clarke-Stewart, K.A., & Lepore, S. (1997). What did the janitor do? Suggestive interviewing and the accuracy of children's accounts. *Law and Human Behavior*, 21, 405–426.

Thurstone, L.L. (1938). *Primary mental abilities*. Chicago: University of Chicago Press.

Tilker, H.A. (1970). Socially responsible behavior as a function of observer responsibility and victim feedback. *Journal of Personality and Social Psychology*, 49, 420–428.

Tizard, B. (1977). *Adoption: A second chance*. London: Open Books.

Tizard, B. (1986). *The care of young children*. London: Institute of Education.

Tizard, B., & Hodges, J. (1978). The effect of early institutional rearing on the development of eight-year-old children. *Journal of Child Psychology and Psychiatry*, 19, 99–118.

Tobin, J.J., Wu, D.Y.H., & Davidson, D.H. (1989). *Preschool in three cultures: Japan, China, and the United States*. New Haven, CT: Yale University Press.

Tolman, E.C. (1959). Principles of purposive behavior. In S. Koch (Ed.), *Psychology: A study of a science: Vol. 2. General systematic formulations, learning, and special processes*. New York: McGraw-Hill.

Tomasello, M. (1992). *First verbs: A case study of early grammatical development*. Cambridge, UK: Cambridge University Press.

Tomasello, M. (2005). Beyond formalities: The case of language acquisition. *Linguistic Review*, 22, 183–197.

Tomasello, M., Akhtar, N., Dodson, K., & Rekau, L. (1997). Differential productivity in young children's use of nouns and verbs. *Journal of Child Language*, 24, 373–387.

Tomasello, M., & Brooks, P.J. (1999). Early syntactic development: A construction grammar approach. In M. Barrett (Ed.), *The development of language*. Hove, UK: Psychology Press.

Tomlinson-Keasey, C., Eisert, D.C., Kahle, L.R., Hardy-Brown, K., & Keasey, B. (1979). The mediating role of cognitive development in moral judgement. *Child Development*, 45, 291–298.

Torgersen, A.M., & Janson, H. (2002). Why do identical twins differ in personality: Shared environment reconsidered. *Twin Research*, 5, 44–52.

Tourangeau, R., Smith, T.W., & Rasinski, K.A. (1997). Motivation to report sensitive behaviors on surveys: Evidence from a bogus pipeline experiment. *Journal of Applied Social Psychology*, 27, 209–222.

Trappery, C. (1996). A meta-analysis of consumer choice and subliminal advertising. *Psychology and Marketing*, 13, 517–530.

Treisman, A.M. (1964). Verbal cues, language, and meaning in selective attention. *American Journal of Psychology*, 77, 206–219.

Treisman, A.M., & Davies, A. (1973). Divided attention to ear and eye. In S. Kornblum (Ed.), *Attention and performance IV: Information processing*. London: Academic Press.

Treisman, A.M., & Riley, J.G.A. (1969). Is selective attention selective perception or selective response: A further test. *Journal of Experimental Psychology*, 79, 27–34.

Tremblay-Leveau, H., & Nadel, J. (1996). Exclusion in triads: Can it serve "metacommunicative" knowledge in 11 and 24 months children? *British Journal of Developmental Psychology*, 14, 145–158.

Trevarthen, C. (2004). Split-brain and the mind. In R. Gregory (Ed.), *The Oxford companion to the mind* (2nd ed.). Oxford, UK: Oxford University Press.

Trevena, J.A., & Miller, J. (2002). Cortical movement preparation before and after a conscious decision to move. *Consciousness and Cognition*, 11, 162–190.

Triandis, H.C., Carnevale, P., Gelfand, M., Robert, C., Wasti, A., et al. (2001). Culture, personality and deception in intercultural management negotiations. *International Journal of Cross-Cultural Management*, 1, 73–90.

Triandis, H.C., McCusker, C., Betancourt, H., Iwao, S., Leung, K., et al. (1993). An etic–emic analysis of individualism and collectivism. *Journal of Cross-Cultural Psychology*, 24, 366–384.

Triandis, H.C., & Suh, E.M. (2002). Cultural influences on personality. *Annual Review of Psychology*, 53, 133–160.

Trivers, R.L. (1971). The evolution of reciprocal altruism. *Quarterly Review of Biology*, 46, 35–57.

Trope, Y., & Gaunt, R. (2000). Processing alternative explanations of behaviour: Correction or integration? *Journal of Personality and Social Psychology*, 79, 344–354.

Tropp, L.R., & Pettigrew, T.F. (2005). Relationships between intergroup contact and prejudice among minority and majority status groups. *Psychological Science*, 16, 951–957.

Trueswell, J.C., Tanenhaus, M.K., & Garnsey, S.M (1994). Semantic influences on parsing: Use of thematic role information in syntactic disambiguation. *Journal of Memory and Language*, 33, 285–318.

Tsal, Y. (1983). Movement of attention across the visual field. *Journal of Experimental Psychology: Human Perception and Performance*, 9, 523–530.

Tulving, E. (1972). Episodic and semantic memory. In E. Tulving & W. Donaldson (Eds.), *Organization of memory*. Hillsdale, NJ: Lawrence Erlbaum Associates, Inc.

Tulving, E. (1979). Relation between encoding specificity and levels of processing. In L.S. Cermak & F.I.M. Craik (Eds.), *Levels of processing in human memory*. Hillsdale, NJ: Lawrence Erlbaum Associates, Inc.

Tulving, E. (2002). Episodic memory: From mind to brain. *Annual Review of Psychology*, 53, 1–25.

Turati, C. (2004). Why faces are not special to newborns: An alternative account of the face preference. *Current Directions in Psychological Science*, 13, 5–8.

Turati, C., Simion, F., Milani, I., & Umiltà, C. (2002). Newborns' preference for faces: What is crucial? *Developmental Psychology*, 38, 875–882.

Turnbull, O.H., & Solms, M. (2007). Awareness, desire, and false beliefs: Freud in the light of modern neuropsychology. *Cortex*, 43, 1083–1090.

Turner, J.C. (1987). *Rediscovering the social group: A self-categorisation theory*. Oxford, UK: Blackwell.

Turner, J.C. (1999). Some current issues in research on social identity and self-categorisation theories. In N. Ellemers, R.

Spears, & B. Doosje (Eds.), *Social identity*. Oxford, UK: Blackwell.

Turner, J.C., Hogg, M.A., Oakes, P.J., Reicher, S.D., & Wetherell, M.S. (1987). *Rediscovering the social group: A self-categorization theory*. Oxford, UK: Blackwell.

Turner, R.H., & Killian, L.M. (1972). *Collective behavior* (2nd ed.). Englewood Cliffs, NJ: Prentice Hall.

Turner, R.J., & Wagonfeld, M.O. (1967). Occupational mobility and schizophrenia. *American Sociological Review, 32*, 104–113.

Turton, S., & Campbell, C. (2005). Tend and befriend versus fight or flight: Gender differences in behavioral response to stress among university students. *Journal of Applied Biobehavioral Research, 10*, 209–232.

Tversky, A. (1972). Elimination by aspects: A theory of choice. *Psychological Review, 79*, 281–299.

Tversky, A., & Kahneman, D. (1987). Rational choice and the framing of decisions. In R. Hogarth & M. Reder (Eds.), *Rational choice: The contrast between economics and psychology*. Chicago: University of Chicago Press.

Tversky, A., & Shafir, E. (1992). The disjunction effect in choice under uncertainty. *Psychological Science, 3*, 305–309.

Twenge, J.M. (2000). The age of anxiety? Birth cohort change in anxiety and neuroticism, 1952–1993. *Journal of Personality and Social Psychology, 79*, 1007–1021.

Tyerman, A., & Spencer, C. (1983). A critical test of the Sherifs' Robbers' Cave experiment: Intergroup competition and cooperation between groups of well-acquainted individuals. *Small Group Behaviour, 14*, 515–531.

Tyrell, J.B., & Baxter, J.D. (1981). Glucocorticoid therapy. In P. Felig, J.D. Baxter, A.E. Broadus, & L.A. Frohman (Eds.), *Endocrinology and metabolism*. New York: McGraw-Hill.

Uchino, B.N., Cacioppo, J.T., & Kiecolt-Glaser, K.G. (1996). The relationships between social support and physiological processes: A review with emphasis on underlying mechanisms and implications for health. *Psychological Bulletin, 119*, 488–531.

Uddin, L.Q., Rayman, J., & Zaidel, E. (2005). Split-brain reveals separate but equal self-recognition in the two cerebral hemispheres. *Consciousness and Cognition, 14*, 633–640.

Ünal, B., Critchley, J.A., Fidan, D., & Capewell, S. (2005). Life years gained from modern cardiological treatments and population risk factor changes in England and Wales, 1981–2000. *American Journal of Public Health, 95*, 103–108.

Underwood, B.J., & Postman, L. (1960). Extra-experimental sources of interference in forgetting. *Psychological Review, 67*, 73–95.

Underwood, G. (1974). Moray vs. the rest: The effect of extended shadowing practice. *Quarterly Journal of Experimental Psychology, 26*, 368–372.

Uvnäs-Moberg, K. (1996). Neuroendocrinology of the mother–child interaction. *Trends in Endocrinology and Metabolism, 7*, 126–131.

Valentine, E.R. (1992). *Conceptual issues in psychology* (2nd ed.). London: Routledge.

Valentine, T., Pickering, A., & Darling, S. (2003). Characteristics of eyewitness identification that predict the outcome of real line-ups. *Applied Cognitive Psychology, 17*, 969–993.

Vallar, G., & Baddeley, A.D. (1984). Phonological short-term store, phonological processing and sentence comprehension: a neuropsychological case study. *Cognitive Neuropsychology, 1*, 121–141.

Vallar, G., Di Betta, A.M., & Silveri, M.S. (1997). The phonological short-term store rehearsal system: Patterns of impairment and neural correlates. *Neuropsyschologica, 35*, 795–812.

Vallar, G., & Perani, D. (1987). The anatomy of spatial neglect in humans. In M. Jeannerod (Ed.), *Neurophysiological and neuropsychological aspects of spatial neglect*. Amsterdam: Elsevier.

Van Avermaet, E. (2001). Social influence in small groups. In M. Hewstone & W. Stroebe (Eds.), *Introduction to social psychology* (3rd ed., pp. 403–443). Oxford, UK: Blackwell.

Van den Putte, B. (1993). *On the theory of reasoning action*. Unpublished doctoral dissertation, University of Amsterdam, The Netherlands.

Van Dongen, H.P., Maislin, G., Mullington, J.M., & Dinges, D.F. (2003). The cumulative cost of additional wakefulness: Dose–response effects on neurobehavioural functions and sleep physiology from chronic sleep restriction and total sleep deprivation. *Sleep, 26*, 117–126.

Van Goozen, S.H.-M., Cohen-Kettenis, P.T., Gooren, L.J.G., Frijda, N.H., & van de Poll, N.E. (1995a). Gender differences in behaviour: Activating effects of cross-sex hormones. *Psychoneuroendocrinology, 20*, 343–363.

Van IJzendoorn, M.H., & de Wolff, M.S. (1997). In search of the absent father—Meta-analyses of infant–father attachment: A rejoinder to our discussants. *Child* Development, 68, 604–609.

Van IJzendoorn, M.H., & Kroonenberg, P.M. (1988). Cross-cultural patterns of attachment: A meta-analysis of the Strange Situation. *Child Development, 59*, 147–156.

Van Keer, H. (2004). Fostering reading comprehension in fifth grade by explicit instruction in reading strategies and peer tutoring. *British Journal of Educational Psychology, 74*, 37–70.

Van Os, J., Park, S.B.G., & Jones, P.B. (2001). Neuroticism, life events and mental health: Evidence for person–environment correlation. *British Journal of Psychiatry, 178*, s72–s77.

Van Oudenhouven, J.P., Groenewoud, J.T., & Hewstone, M. (1996). Co-operation, ethnic salience and generalisation of inter-ethnic attitudes. *European Journal of Social Psychology, 26*, 649–662.

Van Petten, C., Coulson, S., Rubin, S., Plante, E., & Parks, M. (1999). Time course of word identification and semantic integration in spoken language. *Journal of Experimental Psychology: Learning, Memory, and Cognition, 25*, 394–417.

Van Selst, M.V., Ruthruff, E., & Johnston, J.C. (1999). Can practice eliminate the Psychological Refractory Period effect? *Journal of Experimental Psychology: Human Perception and Performance, 25*, 1268–1283.

Vance, E.B., & Wagner, N.D. (1976). Written descriptions of orgasm: A study of sex differences. *Archives of Sexual Behavior, 5*, 87–98.

Vandello, J.A., & Cohen, D. (1999). Patterns of individualism and collectivism across the United States. *Journal of Personality and Social Psychology, 77*, 279–292.

Vanrie, J., Béatse, E., Wagemans, J., Sunaert, S., & van Hecke, P. (2002). Mental rotation versus invariant features in object perception from different viewpoints: An fMRI study. *Neuropsychologia, 40*, 917–930.

Vargha-Khadem, F., Gadian, D.G., Watkins, K.E., Connelly, A., Van Paesschen, W., & Mishkin, M. (1997). Differential effects of early hippocampal pathology on episodic and semantic memory. *Science, 277*, 376–380.

Veniegas, R., & Conley, T. (2000). Biological research on women's sexual orientations: Evaluating the scientific evidence. *Journal of Social Issues, 56*, 267.

Venner, A.A., Lyon, M.E., & Doyle-Baker, P.K. (2006). Leptin: A potential biomarker for childhood obesity? *Clinical Biochemistry, 39*, 1047–1056.

Verburg, K., Griez, E., Meijer, J. & Pols, H. (1995). Respiratory disorders as a possible predisposing factor for panic disorder. *Journal of Affective Disorders, 33*, 129–134.

Verkuyten, M., Drabbles, M., & van den Nieuwenhuijzen, K. (1999). Self-categorisation and emotional reactions to ethnic minorities. *European Journal of Social Psychology, 29*, 605–619.

Vidich, A.J., & Bensman, J. (1958). *Small town in mass society*. Princeton, NJ: Princeton University Press.

Viswesvaran, C., & Schmidt, F.L. (1992). A meta-analytic comparison of the effectiveness of smoking cessation methods. *Journal of Applied Psychology, 77*, 554–561.

Voci, A., & Hewstone, M. (2003). Integroup conflict and prejudice toward immigrants in Italy: The mediational role of anxiety and the moderational role of group salience. *Group Processes and Intergroup Relations, 6*, 37–54.

Vogel, G.W. (2000). Critique of current dream theories. *Behavioral and Brain Sciences, 23*, 1014.

von Neumann, J., & Morgenstern, O. (1947). *Theory of games and economic behavior* (2nd rev. ed.). Princeton, NJ: Princeton University Press.

Von Wright, J.M., Anderson, K., & Stenman, U. (1975). Generalisation of conditioned GSRs in dichotic listening. In P.M.A. Rabbitt & S. Dorni (Eds.), *Attention and performance V: Information processing*. New York: Academic Press.

Vonk, R. (1993). Individual differences and universal dimensions in Implicit Personality Theory. *British Journal of Social Psychology, 32*, 209–226.

Vygotsky, L.S. (1978). *Mind in society: The development of higher psychological processes*. Cambridge, MA: MIT Press.

Vygotsky, L.S. (1981). The genesis of higher mental functions. In J.V. Wertsch (Ed.), *The concept of activity in Soviet psychology*. Armonk, NY: Sharpe, Inc. (Original work published 1930)

Vygotsky, L.S. (1986). The genetic roots of thought and speech. In A. Kozulin (Trans. & Ed.), *Thought and language*. Cambridge, MA: MIT Press

Wachtel, P.L. (1973). Psychodynamics, behaviour therapy and the implacable experimenter: An inquiry into the consistency of personality. *Journal of Abnormal Psychology, 82*, 324–334.

Waddington, D., Jones, K., & Critcher, C. (1987). Flashpoints of public disorder. In G. Gaskell & R. Benewick (Eds.), *The crowd in contemporary Britain*. London: Sage.

Wagner, U., Gais, S., Haider, H., Verleger, R., & Born, J. (2004). Sleep inspires insight. Nature, 427, 352–355.

Wahlberg, K.E., Lynne, L.C., Oja, H., Keskitalo, P., et al. (1997). Gene-environment interaction in vulnerability to schizophrenia: Findings from the Finnish adoptive family study of schizophrenia. *American Journal of Psychiatry, 154*, 355–262.

Walker, E.F., Savoie, T., & Davis, D. (1994). Neuromotor precursors of schizophrenia. *Schizophrenia Bulletin, 20*, 441–451.

Walker, L.J., Gustafson, P., & Hennig, K.H. (2001). The consolidation/transition model in moral reasoning development. *Developmental Psychology, 37*, 187–197.

Walker, L.J., Pitts, R.C., Hennig, K.H., & Matsuba, M.K. (1995). Reasoning about morality and real-life moral problems. In M. Killen & D. Hart (Eds.), *Morality in everyday life: Developmental perspectives*. Cambridge, UK: Cambridge University Press.

Wallen, K. (2001). Sex and context. Hormones and primate sexual motivation. *Hormones and Behavior, 40*, 339–357.

Wallerstein, J.S. (1987). Children of divorce: Report of a ten-year follow-up of early latency-age children. *American Journal of Orthopsychiatry, 57*, 199–211.

Walsh, V., & Rushworth, M. (1999). A primer of magnetic stimulation as a tool for neuropsychology. *Neuropsychologia, 37*, 125–135.

Walster, E., Aronson, V., Abrahams, D., & Rottman, L. (1966). The importance of physical attractiveness in dating behavior. *Journal of Personality and Social Psychology, 4*, 508–516.

Walster, E., & Walster, G.W. (1969). *A new look at love*. Reading, MA: Addison Wesley.

Wampold, B.E., Mondin, G.W., Moody, M., Stich, F., Benson, K., & Ahn, H. (1997). A meta-analysis of outcome studies comparing bona fide psychotherapies: Empirically, "All must have prizes." *Psychological Bulletin, 122*, 203–215.

Wang, X.T. (1996). Domain-specific rationality in human choices: Violations of utility axioms and social contexts. *Cognition, 60*, 31–63.

Wang, X.T., Simons, F., & Brédart, S. (2001). Social cues and verbal framing in risky choice. *Journal of Behavioral Decision Making, 14*, 1–15.

Warr, P. (1996). *Psychology at work* (3rd ed.). Harmondsworth, UK: Penguin.

Warren, R., & Zgourides, G.D. (1991). *Anxiety disorders: A rational-emotive perspective*. New York: Pergamon Press.

Warren, R.M., & Warren, R.P. (1970). Auditory illusions and confusions. *Scientific American, 223*, 30–36.

Warrington, E.K., & Taylor, A.M. (1978). Two categorical stages of object recognition. *Perception, 7*, 695–705.

Wartner, U.G., Grossmann, K., Fremmer-Bombik, E., & Suess, G. (1994). Attachment patterns at age 6 in south Germany: Predictability from infancy and implications for pre-school behaviour. *Child Development, 65*, 1014–1027.

Waters, E., Wippman, J., & Sroufe, L.A. (1979). Attachment, positive affect, and competence in the peer group: Two studies in construct validation. *Child Development, 50*, 821–829.

Watson, D., & Clark, L.A. (1984). Negative affectivity: The disposition to experience aversive emotional states. *Psychological Bulletin, 96*, 465–490.

Watson, D., & Clark, L.A. (1992) Affects separable and inseparable: On the hierarchical arrangement of the negative affects. *Journal of Personality and Social Psychology, 62*, 489–505.

Watson, D., & Clark, L.A. (1994). *The PANAS-X: Manual for the Positive and Negative Affect Schedule—expanded form*. Unpublished manuscript, University of Iowa, Iowa City.

Watson, D., & Pennebaker, J.W. (1989). Health complaints, stress, and distress: Exploring the central role of negative affectivity. *Psychological Review, 96*, 234–254.

Watson, D., & Tellegen, A. (1985). Toward a consensual structure of mood. *Psychological Bulletin, 98*, 219–235.

Watson, J.B. (1913). Psychology as the behaviourist views it. *Psychological Review, 20*, 158–177.

Watson, J.B. (1924). *Psychology from the standpoint of a behaviorist* (2nd ed.). Philadelphia: Lippincott.

Watson, P.J., & Andrews, P.W. (2002). Toward a revised evolutionary adaptationist analysis of depression: The social navigation hypothesis. *Journal of Affective Disorders, 72*, 1–14.

Weber, E.U., & Hsee, C.K. (2000). Culture and individual judgement and decision making. *Applied Psychology: An International Review, 49*, 32–61.

Weber, R., & Crocker, J. (1983). Cognitive processes in the revision of stereotypic beliefs. *Journal of Personality and Social Psychology, 45*, 961–977.

Wegner, D.M. (2002). *The illusion of conscious will*. Cambridge, MA: MIT Press.

Wegner, D.M. (2003). The mind's best trick: How we experience conscious will. *Trends in Cognitive Sciences, 7*, 65–69.

Wegner, D.M., & Wheatley, T. (1999). Apparent mental causation: Sources of the experience of the will. *American Psychologist, 54*, 480–492.

Weiskrantz, L. (1986). *Blindsight: A case study and its implications*. Oxford, UK: Oxford University Press.

Weiskrantz, L., Barbur, J.L., & Sahraie, A. (1995). Parameters affecting conscious versus unconscious visual discrimination with damage to the visual cortex V1. *Proceedings of the National Academy of Sciences, USA, 92*, 6122–6126.

Weisz, J.R., Chaiyasit, W., Weiss, B., Eastman, K., & Jackson, E. (1995). A multimethod study of problem behaviour among Thai and American children in school: Teacher reports versus direct observations. *Child Development, 66*, 402–41□

Weizman, Z.O., & Snow, C.E. (2001). Lexical input as related to children's vocabulary acquisition: Effects of sophisticated exposure and support for meaning. *Developmental Psychology, 37*, 265–279.

Wellman, H.M., Cross, D., & Watson, J. (2001). Meta-analysis of theory-of-mind development: The truth about false belief. *Child Development, 72*, 655–684.

Wender, P.H., Kety, S.S., Rosenthal, D., Schulsinger, F., Ortmann, J., & Lunde, I. (1986). Psychiatric disorders in the biological and adoptive families of adopted individuals with affective disorders. *Archives of General Psychiatry, 43*, 923–929.

Westcott, M. (1988). *The psychology of human freedom: A human science perspective and critique.* New York: Springer-Verlag.

Westen, D. (1996). *Psychology: Mind, brain, and culture.* New York: Wiley.

Westen, D. (1998). The scientific legacy of Sigmund Freud: Toward a psychodynamically informed psychological science. *Psychological Bulletin, 124*, 333–371.

Westen, D., & Gabbard, G.O. (1999). Psychoanalytic approaches to personality. In L.A. Pervin & O.P. John (Eds), *Handbook of personality: Theory and research.* New York: Guilford Press.

Weston, D.R., & Main, M. (1981). The quality of the toddler's relationship to mother and to father: Related to conflict behaviour and the readiness to establish new relationships. *Child Development, 52*, 932–940.

Wetherell, M., & Potter, J. (1988). Discourse analysis and the identification of interpretive repertoires. In C. Antaki (Ed.), *Analysing everyday explanation: A casebook of methods.* London: Sage.

Wever, R. (1979). *Circadian rhythms system of man: Results of experiments under temporal isolation.* New York: Springer.

Whalley, L.J., & Deary, I.J. (2001). Longitudinal cohort study of childhood IQ and survival up to age 76. *British Medical Journal, 322*, 1–5.

Wheldall, K., & Poborca, B. (1980). Conservation without conversation: An alternative, non-verbal paradigm for assessing conservation of liquid quantity. *British Journal of Psychology, 71*, 117–134.

White, L.E., & Hain, R.F. (1959). Anorexia in association with a destructive lesion of the hypothalamus. *Archives of Pathology, 43*, 443–471.

Whiting, B.B., & Whiting, J.W. (1975). *Children of six countries: A psychological analysis.* Cambridge, MA: Harvard University Press.

Whyte, W.F. (1943). *Street corner society: The social structure of an Italian slum.* Chicago: University of Chicago Press.

Wickelgren, I. (1998). Obesity: How big a problem? *Science, 280*, 1364–1367.

Wickens, A. (2000). *Foundations of biopsychology.* Harlow, UK: Prentice Hall.

Wickens, C.D. (1984). Processing resources in attention. In R. Parasuraman & D.R. Davies (Eds.), *Varieties of attention.* London: Academic Press.

Wicker, A.W. (1969). Attitudes versus actions: The relationship of verbal and overt behavioural responses to attitude objects. *Journal of Social Issues, 25*, 41–78.

Wilkinson, L., & Shanks, D.R. (2004). Intentional control and implicit sequence learning. *Journal of Experimental Psychology: Learning, Memory, and Cognition, 30*, 354–369.

Williams, J.H. (1987). *Psychology of women: Behaviour in a biosocial context* (3rd ed.). New York: W.W. Norton & Co.

Williams, M.V., Parker, R.M., Baker, D.W., Pirikh, N.S., Pitkin, K., Costes, W.C., et al. (1995). Inadequate functional health literacy among patients at two public hospitals. *Journal of the American Medical Association, 274*, 1677–1682.

Williams, T.M. (Ed.). (1986). *The impact of television: A national experiment in three communities.* New York: Academic Press.

Wills, T.A. (1985). Supportive function of interpersonal relationships. In S. Cohen & S.L. Syme (Eds.), *Social support and health.* Orlando, FL: Academic Press.

Wilson, A.E., & Ross, M. (2003). The identity function of autobiographical memory: Time is on our side. *Memory, 11*, 137–149.

Wilson, S.R., & Spencer, R.C. (1990). Intense personal experiences: Subjective interpretations, and after-effects. *Journal of Clinical Psychology, 46*, 565–573.

Wimmer, H., & Perner, J., (1983). Beliefs about beliefs: Representation and the constraining function of wrong beliefs in young children's understanding of deception. *Cognition, 13*, 103–128.

Winningham, R.G., Hyman, I.E., & Dinnel, D.L. (2000). Flashbulb memories? The effects of when the initial memory report was obtained. *Memory, 8*, 209–216.

Witherington, D.C., Campos, J.J., Anderson, D.I., Lejeune, L., & Seah, E. (2005). Avoidance of heights on the visual cliff in newly walking infants. *Infancy, 7*, 285–298.

Wittenbrink, B., Judd, C.M., & Park, B. (1997). Evidence for racial prejudice at the implicit level and its relationship with questionnaire measures. *Journal of Personality and Social Psychology, 72*, 262–274.

Wixted, J.T. (2004). The psychology and neuroscience of forgetting. *Annual Review of Psychology, 55*, 235–269.

Woike, B., Gershkovich, I., Piorkowski, R., & Polo, M. (1999). The role of motives in the content and structure of autobiographical memory. *Journal of Personality and Social Psychology, 76*, 600–612.

Wojciulik, E., Kanwisher, N., & Driver, J. (1998). Modulation of activity in the fusiform face area by covert attention: An fMRI study. *Journal of Neurophysiology, 79*, 1574–1579.

Wolford, G., Miller, M.B., & Gazzaniga, M. (2000). The left hemisphere's role in hypothesis formation. *Journal of Neuroscience, 20*, RC64.

Wood, D.J., Bruner, J.S., & Ross, G. (1976). The role of tutoring in problem solving. *Journal of Child Psychology and Psychiatry, 17*, 89–100.

Wood, P.B. (1962). *Dreaming and social isolation.* Unpublished PhD thesis, University of North Carolina at Chapel Hill.

Wood, W., & Kallgren, C.A. (1988). Communicator attributes and persuasion: Recipients' access to attitude-relevant information in memory. *Personality and Social Psychology Bulletin, 14*, 172–182.

Wood, W., Lundgren, S., Ouellette, J.A., Busceme, S., & Blackstone, T. (1994). Minority influence: A meta-analytic review of social influence processes. *Psychological Bulletin, 115*, 323–345.

Woods, K.A., Camacho-Hubner, C., Savage, M.O., & Clark, A.J.L. (1996). Intrauterine growth retardation and postnatal growth failure associated with deletion of the insulin-like growth factor I gene. *New England Journal of Medicine, 335*, 1363–1367.

Woods, S.C., Seeley, R.J., Porte, D., Jr., & Schwartz, M.W. (1998). Signals that regulate food intake and energy homeostasis. *Science, 280*, 1378–1383.

Wright, G. (1984). *Behavioral decision theory.* Harmondsworth, UK: Penguin.

Wright, S.C., Aron, A., McLaughlin-Volpe, T., & Ropp, S. A. (1997). The extended contact effect: Knowledge of cross-group friendships and prejudice. *Journal of Personality and Social Psychology, 73*, 73–90.

Wu, A., Folkman, S., McPhee, S., & Lo, B. (1993). Do house officers learn from their mistakes? *Journal of the American Medical Association, 265*, 2089–2094.

Yammarino, F.J., Spangler, W.D., & Bass, B.M. (1993). Transformational leadership and performance: A longitudinal investigation. *Leadership Quarterly, 4*, 81–102.

Yasuda, K., Watanabe, O., & Ono, Y. (1997). Dissociation between semantic and autobiographic memory: A case report. *Cortex, 33*, 623–638.

Yates, W.R., Cadoret, R.J., & Troughton, E.P. (1999). The Iowa adoption studies: Methods and results. In M.C. LaBuda & E.L. Grigorenko (Eds.), *On the way to individuality: Current methodological issues in behavioral genetics*. Commack, NY: Nova Science Publishers.

Yearta, S., Maitlis, S., Briner, R.B. (1995). An exploratory study of goal setting in theory and practice: A motivational technique that works? *Journal of Occupational and Organisational Psychology, 68*, 237–252.

Yerkes, R.M., & Morgulis, S. (1909). The method of Pavlov in animal psychology. *Psychological Bulletin, 6*, 257–273.

Yussen, S.R., & Levy, V.M. (1975). Developmental changes in predicting one's own span of short-term memory. *Journal of Experimental Child Psychology, 19*, 502–508.

Zaadstra, B.M., Seidell, J.C., Vannoord, P.A.H., Tevelde, E.R., Habbema, J.D.F., Vrieswijk, B., & Karbaat, J. (1993). Fat and female fecundity: Prospective study of effect of body-fat distribution on conception rates. *British Medical Journal, 306*, 484–487.

Zadra, A.L. (1996). Recurrent dreams: Their relation to life events. In D. Barrett (Ed.), *Trauma and dreams*. London: Harvard University Press.

Zahn-Waxler, C., Radke-Yarrow, M., & King, R.A. (1979). Child rearing and children's prosocial initiations toward victims of distress. *Child Development, 50*, 319–330.

Zahn-Waxler, C., Robinson, J., & Emde, R.N. (1992). The development of empathy in twins. *Developmental Psychology, 28*, 1038–1047.

Zahn-Waxler, C., Schiro, K., Robinson, J.L., Emde, R.N., & Schmitz, S. (2001). Empathy and prosocial patterns in young MZ and DZ twins: Development and genetic and environmental influences. In R. Emde & J. Hewitt (Eds.), *Infancy to early childhood: Genetic and environmental influences on developmental change*. Oxford: Oxford University Press.

Zaninotto, P., Wardle, H., Stamatakis, E., Mindell, J., & Head, J. (2006). *Forecasting obesity to 2010*. London: National Centre for Social Research, Royal Free and University College Medical School.

Zanna, M.P., & Cooper, J. (1974). Dissonance and the pill: An attribution approach to studying the arousal properties of dissonance. *Journal of Personality and Social Psychology, 29*, 703–709.

Zárate, M.A., Garcia, B., Garza, A.A., & Hitlan, R.T. (2004). Cultural threat and perceived realistic group conflict as dual predictors of prejudice. *Journal of Experimental Social Psychology, 40*, 99–105.

Zarbatany, L., Hartmann, D.P., & Gelfand, D.M. (1985). Why does children's generosity increase with age: Susceptibility to experimenter influence or altruism? *Child Development, 56*, 746–756.

Zegoib, L.E., Arnold, S., & Forehand, R. (1975). An examination of observer effects in parent–child interactions. *Child Development, 46*, 509–512.

Zeidner, M., Matthews, G., & Roberts, R.D. (2004). Emotional intelligence in the workplace: A critical review. *Applied Psychology: An International Review, 53*, 371–399.

Zeier, H., Brauchli, P., & Joller-Jemelka, H.I. (1996). Effects of work demands on immunoglobin A and cortisol in air-traffic controllers. *Biological Psychology, 42*, 413–423.

Zillmann, D., Johnson, R.C., & Day, K.D. (1974). Attribution of apparent arousal and proficiency of recovery from sympathetic activation affecting excitation transfer to aggressive behaviour. *Journal of Experimental Social Psychology, 10*, 503–515.

Zimbardo, P. (1970). The human choice: Individuation, reason, and order versus deindividuation, impulse, and chaos. In W.J. Arnold & D. Levine (Eds.), *Nebraska Symposium on Motivation, 17* (pp. 237–307). Lincoln, NE: University of Nebraska Press.

Zimbardo, P.G. (1973). On the ethics of intervention in human psychological research: With special reference to the Stanford prison experiment. *Cognition, 2*, 243–256.

Zuckerman, M. (1989). Personality in the third dimension: A psychobiological approach. *Personality and Individual Differences, 10*, 391–418.

Zwaan, R.A., & van Oostendorp, H. (1993). Do readers construct spatial representations in naturalistic story comprehension? *Discourse Processes, 16*, 125–143.

Author index

Else-Quest, N.M. 356
Elstein, A.S. 225
Ember, M. 497
Emde, R.N. 361, 362
Emerson, M.J. 198
Emerson, P.E. 383
Emery, G. 529
Emery, L. 162, 163
Empson, J.A.C. 120, 121, 122
Endler, N.S. 98, 99
Endresen, I.M. 360
Endsley, R.C. 358
Engelstad, V. 526
Engle, R.W. 154, 155, 204
The English and Romanian Adoptees
     (ERA) Study Team 384, 385
Enstrom, J.E. 94
Epel, E.S. 89
Epping-Jordan, J.E. 99
Erb, H.-P. 463, 466
Erel, O. 388
Erez, A. 72, 73
Erickson, J.R. 211, 213
Erickson, T.A. 247
Ericsson, K.A. 188, 189, 224
Eriksen, C.W. 147
Erikson, E. 22
Erikson, E.H. 208
Ernberg, G. 520
Eron, L.D. 364, 365
Espindle, D. 68
Esses, V.M. 503
Essock-Vitale, S.M. 30
Esteban, S. 119
Evans, J. 155, 226
Evans, P. 90, 95
Eysenck, H.J. 37, 159, 267, 293, 295,
     296, 297, 300, 526
Eysenck, M.W. 27, 28, 44, 80, 129,
     208, 249, 293, 296, 297, 322, 527,
     555, 575
Eysenck, S.B.G. 300

Fabes, R.A. 362, 390, 391, 392
Fafard, D. 371
Fagot, B.I. 357
Fahrenberg, J. 297
Fan, E.T. 471
Fan, J. 441
Farah, M.J. 144
Farahmand, B.Y. 525
Farooqi, S. 59
Farrar, M.J. 327
Fasotti, L. 81
Fazio, R.H. 407
Fearnyhough, C. 196, 197
Febbraro, A.R. 34
Fehr, E. 430, 431, 467
Fein, S. 418, 435
Feingold, A. 442, 446
Feld, P. 471
Fellner, C.H. 430
Fensik, D.E. 157, 159
Fenson, L. 323
Fenstermacher, S.K. 179, 180
Ferkewicz, J. 203
Ferreira, F. 242, 247, 255
Fery, P. 138
Festinger, L. 413, 414, 442

Fidan, D. 17
Fiedler, F.E. 473, 474
Field, N. 475
Fijneman, Y.A. 360, 430
Fincham, F.D. 416, 417, 449, 450
Finlay-Jones, R.A. 92
Fischbacher, U. 430, 431, 467
Fishbein, M. 407
Fisher, D.L. 238
Fisher, R.A 625
Fiske, A.P. 11, 13
Fiske, S.T. 493
Fivush, R. 207
Flacks, R. 467
Flament, C. 486
Flavell, J.H. 318
Fleck, J. 221
Fleeson, W. 302
Flynn, E. 330
Flynn, J.R. 276, 280, 281
Folkman, S. 96, 98, 99
Fonagy, P. 527, 528, 533, 534
Fontana, A. 99
Ford, M.R. 35, 513
Forehand, R. 545
Forgatch, M.S. 396
Forman, E.M. 531
Forster, K.L. 153, 154, 155
Forsterling, F. 417
Foster, D.H. 136
Foster, M. 97
Foster, R.G. 112
Foster-Fishman, P.G. 469
Foulkes, D. 114
Fouts, G.T. 180
Fox, M.L. 90
Foy, D.W. 519
Frackowiak, R.S.J. 521
Fraley, R.C. 379, 381
France, L. 200
Frank, L.R. 149
Frank, R. 79
Frankenhaeuser, M. 90
Franklin, S. 109, 247
Franz, C. 289
Franzoi, S.L. 406, 414, 494
Fraser, C. 550
Frazier, L. 242
Fremmer-Bombik, E. 379
French, R.M. 180
Frenkel-Brunswik, E. 495
Frerking, R.A. 28, 530
Freud, A. 22, 23, 588
Freud, S. 6, 7, 22, 39, 40, 58, 121,
     122, 202, 207, 288, 290, 507,
     525, 526, 552
Friberg, I. 296
Friberg, L.T. 396
Friedman, H.S. 93
Friedman, M. 92
Friedman, N.P. 198
Friesen, W.V. 77, 78, 79, 83
Friis, S. 535
Frijda, N.H. 437
Friston, K.J. 110
Frith, C. 150
Frith, C.D. 520, 521
Frith, U. 331, 332
Frohman, L.A. 61

Frost, R. 238
Frost, S.J. 276
Frye, D. 342
Frye, N.E. 207
Fulero, S. 213
Fulker, D. 394, 396
Fultz, J. 362
Funder, D.C. 425
Funnell, E. 240
Funtowicz, M.N. 513
Furnham, A. 14, 302, 421, 444, 445

Gabbard, G.O. 290
Gadian, D.G. 201
Gaertner, L. 486
Gaertner, S.L. 434, 493, 494, 502, 503
Gaffan, E.A. 176
Gais, S. 222
Galaburda, A.M. 79
Gale, A. 297
Galton, F. 5
Gambina, G. 150
Gamundi, A. 119
Ganster, D.C. 90, 93
Garcia, B. 497, 498
Garcia, J. 170
Gardner, H. 273, 274, 275
Garfield, S. 524
Garner, W. 90
Garnham, A. 257
Garnsey, S.M. 242
Garrett, M.F. 255
Garrod, S. 255
Garron, D.C. 93
Garza, A.A. 497, 498
Gatewood, J.B. 57
Gathercole, S.E. 197, 318
Gauld, A. 249, 250
Gaunt, R. 420, 421
Gauvain, M. 350
Gay, J. 36
Gazzaniga, M.S. 107, 108, 129
Geher, G. 267
Geis, G. 433, 434
Gelder, M.G. 531
Gelfand, D.M. 363
Gelfand, M.J. 13
Gelles, R.J. 439
Gentner, D. 323
George, L.J. 446
George, N. 109
Gerard, H.B. 463
Gerber, R. 33
Gergely, G. 179, 189
Gerhardstein, P.C. 136
German, T.P. 219
Gershkovich, I. 208
Gershoff, E.T. 174
Gibbons, F.X. 413
Gibbs, J. 369, 370, 371
Gibbs, J.C. 362, 371
Gibbs, W.W. 63
Gibertoni, M. 320
Gibson, E.J. 315, 316
Gick, M.L. 219, 220
Giersch, A. 137
Gignac, G. 268
Gilbert, D.T. 227, 417, 420
Gilbert, G.N. 556

Subject index

Page numbers in **bold** indicate glossary definitions.